Marketing Across Cultures

WITHDRAWN

We work with leading authors to develop the strongest educational materials in marketing, bringing cutting-edge thinking and best learning practice to a global market.

Under a range of well-known imprints, including Financial Times Prentice Hall, we craft high quality print and electronic publications which help readers to understand and apply their content, whether studying or at work.

To find out more about the complete range of our publishing, please visit us on the World Wide Web at:
www.pearsoned.co.uk

Visit the *Marketing Across Cultures*, fourth edition Companion Website at **www.pearsoned.co.uk/usunier** to find valuable **student** learning material including:

- Links to relevant sites on the web
- Additional case study materials

4th edition

Marketing Across Cultures

Jean-Claude Usunier

Julie Anne Lee

Prentice Hall

FINANCIAL TIMES

An imprint of **Pearson Education**

Harlow, England • London • New York • Boston • San Francisco • Toronto
Sydney • Tokyo • Singapore • Hong Kong • Seoul • Taipei • New Delhi
Cape Town • Madrid • Mexico City • Amsterdam • Munich • Paris • Milan

Pearson Education Limited

Edinburgh Gate
Harlow
Essex CM20 2JE
England

and Associated Companies throughout the world

Visit us on the World Wide Web at:
www.pearsoned.co.uk

First published 1992
Second edition published 1996
Third edition published 2000
Fourth edition published 2005

ISBN 0 273 68529 5

British Library Cataloguing-in-Publication Data
A catalogue record for this book is available from the British Library

Library of Congress Cataloging-in-Publication Data
Usunier, Jean-Claude.
  Marketing across cultures / Jean-Claude Usunier, Julie Lee. – 4th ed.
    p. cm.
  Includes bibliographical references and index.
  ISBN 0-273-68529-5 (alk. paper)
    1. Export marketing – Social aspects.   2. International business enterprises –
Social aspects.   3. Intercultural communication.   I. Lee, Julie, 1948–   II. Title.

  HF1416.U85 2005
  658.8′4—dc22

                                        2004057632

10 9 8 7 6 5 4 3 2 1
08 07 06 05

Typeset in 10/12pt Minion by 35
Printed by Ashford Colour Press Ltd., Gosport

The publisher's policy is to use paper manufactured from sustainable forests.

Brief contents

Introduction: Marketing in the global villages xv
Acknowledgements xix

Part 1 The cultural variable in international marketing 1

Introduction to Part 1 2
1 The cultural process 4
2 Cultural dynamics 1: Time and space 21
3 Cultural dynamics 2: Interactions, mindsets and behaviours 50

Part 2 The integration of local consumption in a global marketing environment 83

Introduction to Part 2 84
4 Cross-cultural consumer behaviour 86
5 Local consumers and the globalization of consumption 118
6 The convergence of marketing environments worldwide 155
7 Cross-cultural market research 181

Part 3 Marketing decisions for the intercultural environment 215

Introduction to Part 3 216
8 Intercultural marketing strategy 218
9 Product policy 1: Physical, service and symbolic attributes 248
10 Product policy 2: Managing meaning 285
11 The critical role of price in relational exchange 316
12 International distribution and sales promotion 341

Part 4 Intercultural marketing communications 371

Introduction to Part 4 372
13 Language, culture and communication 374
14 Intercultural marketing communications 1: Advertising 409
15 Intercultural marketing communications 2: Personal selling, networking and public relations 457
16 Intercultural marketing negotiations 1: People, trust and tasks 494
17 Intercultural marketing negotiations 2: Some elements of national styles of business negotiation 534

Postscript 548
Author Index 550
Subject Index 567

Contents

Introduction: Marketing in the global villages   xv

Acknowledgements   xix

Part 1   The cultural variable in international marketing   1

Introduction to Part 1   2

1   The cultural process   4

1.1	Defining culture	4
1.2	Elements of culture	6
1.3	Culture and nationality	9
1.4	Culture and competence	13
1.5	Culture and social representations	15

Questions   16

Notes   17

References   17

Appendix 1: Teaching materials   19

A1.1	*Critical incident*: An old lady from Malaysia	19
A1.2	*Critical incident*: The parable	19
A1.3	*Reading*: Body rituals among the Naciremas	20

2   Cultural dynamics 1: Time and space   21

2.1	A model of action based on cultural assumptions	21
2.2	Time: Cross-cultural variability	23
2.3	Space	29
2.4	Cultural borrowing and change in societies	35
2.5	Cultural hostility	38

Questions   40

Notes   42

References   42

Appendix 2: Teaching materials   45

A2.1	*Cross-cultural scenario*: Inshallah	45
A2.2	*Cross-cultural interaction*: Engineering a decision	45
A2.3	*Cross-cultural interaction*: Opening a medical office in Saudi Arabia	46

A2.4   *Reading*: Language and time patterns: The Bantu case   47
A2.5   *Exercise*: World picture test   48

3   Cultural dynamics 2: Interactions, mindsets and behaviours   **50**

3.1   Concept of the self and others   50
3.2   Interaction models   56
3.3   Culture-based attitudes towards action   64
3.4   How to relate thinking to action   68
3.5   Dealing with desires and feelings   70
3.6   Coping with rules   72
3.7   Cultural assumptions and actual behaviour   75

Questions   77
Notes   78
References   78

Appendix 3: Teaching materials   81
A3.1   *Critical incident*: An American in Vietnam   81
A3.2   Rationales for A2.1 (cross-cultural scenario) and sections A2.2 and
        A2.3 (cross-cultural interactions)   81

Part 2   The integration of local consumption in a global marketing environment   **83**

Introduction to Part 2   84

4   Cross-cultural consumer behaviour   **86**

4.1   Culture and consumer behaviour   88
4.2   The influence of culture on selected aspects of consumer behaviour   93
4.3   Investigating the cross-cultural applicability of consumer behaviour
        concepts   96
4.4   Ethnic consumption   100
4.5   Marketing as an exchange of meanings   102
4.6   Conclusion   105

Questions   105
Notes   105
References   106

Appendix 4: Teaching materials   111
A4.1   *Exercise*: 'Ditcher's consumption motives'   111
A4.2   *Exercise*: Investigating the cross-cultural applicability of a consumer
        complaint scale   112
A4.3   *Case*: Mobile phones in the European Union   112
A4.4   *Exercise*: Cross-cultural consumer behaviour and the standardization/
        adaptation of service offers   115
A4.5   *Exercise*: Multidomestic versus Global   116

5 Local consumers and the globalization of consumption   118

5.1	Free trade doctrine and the denial of cultural variety in consumers' tastes	119
5.2	The global convergence of consumption patterns	121
5.3	The emergence of a global consumer culture	123
5.4	Local products and consumption experiences	126
5.5	Local consumer cultures and resistance to change	131
5.6	Emergent patterns of a mixed local/global consumer behaviour	135

Questions	138
Notes	139
References	140

Appendix 5: Teaching materials   145
A5.1	*Case*: Setting the stage – Disneyland Resort Paris	145
A5.2	*Case*: Papa Ingvar's worries	150

6 The convergence of marketing environments worldwide   155

6.1	Local marketing environments	155
6.2	Marketing: Borrowed concepts and practices	159
6.3	Regional convergence	162
6.4	A diverse marketing environment: The European Union	163
6.5	A changing marketing environment: Eastern Europe	168
6.6	A challenging marketing environment: East Asia	171
6.7	Limitations to the worldwide convergence of marketing environments	173

Questions	174
Note	174
References	174

Appendix 6: Teaching materials   177
A6.1	*Case*: Muslim Cola: Cola wars or cola crusades?	177
A6.2	*Case*: Odol	179

7 Cross-cultural market research   181

7.1	Equivalence in cross-cultural research	182
7.2	Translation equivalence	185
7.3	Measure equivalence	189
7.4	Comparability of samples	192
7.5	Data-collection equivalence	194
7.6	Researching internationally	198
7.7	Conclusion	202

Questions	203
Notes	203
References	205

Appendix 7: Teaching materials   209
A7.1	*Case*: Mobile phones in the European Union	209
A7.2	*Exercise*: Hair shampoo questionnaire	209

Part 3   Marketing decisions for the intercultural environment   215

Introduction to Part 3   216

8   Intercultural marketing strategy   218
8.1   Cost arguments and global strategies   218
8.2   The globalization of competition   225
8.3   Globalization of international marketing strategies   227
8.4   Market segments   231
8.5   Conclusion   236

Questions   236
References   236

Appendix 8: Teaching materials   241
A8.1   *Case*: Bollywood   241
A8.2   *Exercise*: *Dangerous Enchantment*   245

9   Product policy 1: Physical, service and symbolic attributes   248
9.1   Adaptation or standardization of product attributes   249
9.2   Physical attributes   250
9.3   Service attributes   255
9.4   Symbolic attributes   261

Questions   266
Notes   266
References   268

Appendix 9: Teaching materials   272
A9.1   *Case*: Movies worldwide   272
A9.2   *Case*: Fastfood: *Halal* or *Haram*?   277

10   Product policy 2: Managing meaning   285
10.1   National images diffused by the product's origin and by its brand name   286
10.2   Consumer product evaluation according to country of origin   288
10.3   National, international and global brands   294

Questions   304
Notes   305
References   307

Appendix 10: Teaching materials   312
A10.1   *Exercise*: Interpreting symbolic attributes   312
A10.2   *Case*: Soshi Sumsin Ltd   312
A10.3   *Case*: Derivados de Leche SA   314

11 The critical role of price in relational exchange   316

11.1	Price as a signal conveying meaning	316
11.2	Bargaining	317
11.3	Price and consumer evaluations	319
11.4	International price tactics	324
11.5	Market situations, competition and price agreements	330
11.6	Managing prices in highly regulated environments	332

Questions   334
References   335

Appendix 11: Teaching materials   337
A11.1 *Case*: Saito Importing Company   337
A11.2 *Case*: Riva International   338
A11.3 *Case*: Taman SA   340
A11.4 *Case*: AIDS – Global ethics and the pricing of AIDS drugs   340

12 International distribution and sales promotion   341

12.1	The cultural dimensions of distribution channels: The case of Japanese *Keiretsus*	341
12.2	Criteria for choosing foreign distribution channels	348
12.3	The role of distribution as a 'cultural filter'	350
12.4	Direct marketing worldwide	353
12.5	Sales promotion: Other customs, other manners	356

Questions   360
References   361

Appendix 12: Teaching materials   364
A12.1 *Case*: ComputerLand in Japan   364
A12.2 *Case*: The virtual beehive: The online marketing of US honey   365

Part 4 Intercultural marketing communications   371

Introduction to Part 4   372

13 Language, culture and communication   374

13.1	Verbal communication: The role of context	375
13.2	Non-verbal communication	380
13.3	Language shaping our world-views	383
13.4	Ethnocentrism, stereotypes and misunderstandings in intercultural communication	388
13.5	How to improve communication effectiveness in international business	392

Questions   395
Notes   396
References   398

Appendix 13: Teaching materials   400
A13.1 *Exercise*: Multicultural class   400
A13.2 *Exercise*: I 'love' cake   400
A13.3 *Case*: Longcloud – Languages in cyberspace   400
A13.4 *Case*: Supreme Canning   405
A13.5 *Critical incident*: Scandinavian Tools Company   406

14 Intercultural marketing communications 1: Advertising   409

14.1   Influence of culture on attitudes towards advertising   411
14.2   Culture and advertising strategy   413
14.3   Culture and advertising execution   416
14.4   Media worldwide: Technological advances and cultural convergence   425
14.5   The globalization of advertising   431
Questions   435
Notes   436
References   436
Appendix 14: Teaching materials   443
A14.1 *Case*: BrandUSA – Selling Uncle Sam like Uncle Ben's   443
A14.2 *Case*: Excel and the Italian advertising campaign   447
A14.3 *Exercise*: Borovets – a Bulgarian ski resort   449
A14.4 *Exercise*: Slogans and colloquial speech   450
A14.5 *Case*: AIDS (2) – Designing a communication campaign for Mexico   451

15 Intercultural marketing communications 2: Personal selling, networking and public relations   457

15.1   Intercultural commerce   457
15.2   Networks in business markets   463
15.3   Buyer–seller interactions   465
15.4   Sales force management in a cross-cultural perspective   467
15.5   Public relations across cultures   472
15.6   Bribery: Facts   474
15.7   Bribery: Ethical aspects   477
Questions   483
Notes   484
References   484
Appendix 15: Teaching materials   487
A15.1 *Case*: When international buyers and sellers disagree   487
A15.2 *Case*: Setco of Spain   488
A15.3 *Case*: Union Carbide at Bhopal   489
A15.4 *Case*: The *Brenzy nouveau* has arrived!   491

16 Intercultural marketing negotiations 1: People, trust and tasks   494

16.1   The dynamics of trust in relational marketing   495
16.2   The influence of culture on marketing negotiations   498
16.3   Behavioural predispositions of the parties   500

16.4   Underlying concepts of negotiation and negotiation strategies   504
16.5   Time-based misunderstandings in international marketing negotiations   510
16.6   Cultural misunderstandings during the negotiation process   513
16.7   Differences in outcome orientation: Oral versus written agreements as
       a basis for trust between the parties   517

Questions   522
Notes   522
References   523

Appendix 16: Teaching materials   527
A16.1   *Case*: McFarlane Instruments   527
A16.2   *Negotiation game*: Kumbele Power Plant   528
A16.3   *Case*: Doing business in China – A failure in getting paid   532

17   Intercultural marketing negotiations 2: Some elements of national styles of business negotiation

                                                                                      534

17.1   Orientals   534
17.2   Western styles   537
17.3   Negotiation styles in other areas of the world   539
17.4   Some basic rules for international marketing negotiations   542

Questions   542
References   543

Appendix 17: Teaching materials   545
A17.1   *Case*: Tremonti SpA   545

Postscript   548
Author Index   550
Subject Index   567

Supporting resources

Visit **www.pearsoned.co.uk/usunier** to find valuable online resources

Companion Website for students
- Links to relevant sites on the web
- Additional case study materials

For instructors
- Complete, downloadable Instructor's Manual
- PowerPoint slides that can be downloaded and used as OHTs

For more information please contact your local Pearson Education sales representative or visit **www.pearsoned.co.uk/usunier**

Introduction
Marketing in the global villages

Classical consumer marketing textbooks generally emphasize world markets and are often cross-border extensions of American marketing thought, blatantly ignoring people, languages and cultures and implicitly arguing in favour of uniformity. Whereas large multinational companies, such as Mars, Pepsi-Cola, L'Oréal or Nestlé, in fact do not follow traditional textbook recipes: their practice is always much more adaptive to and respectful of local contexts. This text offers a different approach to global marketing, based on the recognition of diversity in world markets and on local consumer knowledge and marketing practices. We invite the reader to undertake an exercise in de-centring. We try to break out of our 'Francocentric' and 'Aussie-centric' boxes, in much the same way as Gorn (1997) invites us to break out of 'North American boxes'. Understanding international diversity[1] in consumer behaviour, advertising, sales and marketing management becomes the central teaching objective for an international marketing textbook.

This text adopts a cultural approach to international marketing, which has two main dimensions:

1. A cross-cultural approach, which begins by *comparing* national marketing systems and local commercial customs in various countries. It aims to emphasize what is country specific and what is universal. Such an approach is essential for the preparation and implementation of marketing strategies in different national contexts.
2. An intercultural approach, which is centred on the study of *interaction* between business people, buyers and sellers (and their companies) who have different national/cultural backgrounds. This intercultural view also extends to the interaction between products (their physical and symbolic attributes, as well as the messages surrounding them) from a definite nation-culture and consumers from a different nation-culture. Thus, interaction is meant in a broad sense: not only between people, but also between people and messages, and people and products. In this book, commerce is emphasized as much as marketing. When the word *commerce* is used in this text, it refers to the complex dimensions of business relationships entwined with interpersonal relations.

The basic assumption behind this book is that culture penetrates our inner being subconsciously and at a deep level. World cultures share many common features. Nevertheless, when common elements are combined they all display a unique style, *vis-à-vis* kinship patterns, education systems, valuation of the individual and the group, emphasis on economic activities, friendship patterns, time-related organization patterns, the criteria for aesthetic appreciation, and so on. The examples that are used in this book are by their very nature eclectic. We have chosen examples that seem to be the most striking and pertinent.

This book does not try to describe cultures exhaustively, or from an insider's point of view. What we have attempted to provide for the reader is *a method for dealing with intercultural situations in international marketing*. The underlying postulate of this book is that international marketing relationships have to be built on solid foundations. Transaction costs in international trade are high: only a stable and firmly established link between business people can enable them to overcome disagreements and conflicts of interest. In international marketing it is advisable to be very methodical and long-term oriented, to select a limited number of partners and opportunities, and to develop them to their fullest extent.

Changes in the fourth edition

The book is now authored with a Euro-Australasian perspective that increases its global character and coverage. The fourth edition has been extensively rewritten in an effort to make the book as accessible as possible. We have also further taken into account the Internet revolution and its impact on international marketing, starting from an even broader perspective that takes into account people, local contexts and their idiosyncrasies as they can be observed from a large number of webpages. The book now comes with additional web references for each chapter and section of the book. References are made directly in the text to websites that allow in-depth and updated access to cultural and business information. Hundreds of additional web references are now accessible about each particular topic at: **www.hec.unil.ch/jusunier/ Marketing%20Across%20Cultures/Mkg_A_Cult_ index.htm**. We invite instructors and students to visit this page, to use it jointly with the book, and to give us feedback, suggestions, and information which they think might be relevant for increasing the site's relevance and exhaustiveness.

New cases have been added with web-based references. Some of them are now included in the end-of-chapter teaching materials sections. Such new cases as Muslim Cola (Chapter 6), Bollywood (Chapter 8), Movies Worldwide (Chapter 9), The Virtual Beehive (Chapter 12), Longcloud: Languages in Cyberspace (Chapter 13), BrandUSA: Selling Uncle Sam like Uncle Ben's? (Chapter 14), are all materials that tackle quite recent and sensitive issues in international marketing. Due to space constraints, some cases are only mentioned in the text with their assignment questions (such as 'Global ethics and the pricing of AIDS drugs' in Chapter 11). The text of these cases as well as many other cases can be found on the book website (with click-on references) at: **www.hec.unil.ch/jusunier/ teaching/International%20Marketing%20Cases/cases. htm**.

Target audience

This book is designed for instructors and students who consider global diversity as an asset and an opportunity, rather than a liability or a threat, and who find pleasure in discovering new ways of life and experiencing the challenge of cultural differences in world markets. *Marketing Across Cultures* is particularly useful and relevant in the case of multicultural, multilingual, and multinational classes, institutions and/or countries. This book is to be proposed as a primary textbook for those instructors who want to emphasize culture, sales, negotiations, and a cross-cultural approach to consumer behaviour and market research, and as a secondary text for other IM instructors who want to follow a more traditional approach to international marketing.

The fourth edition has been written for:

- senior undergraduate students who already have studied a marketing management course;
- postgraduate students (MBA in particular) for a cross-cultural/international marketing elective course;
- research students who have a in-depth interest in cultural and comparative aspects of International Business and Global Marketing; and
- senior executives for developing culturally-sensitive approaches to global marketing strategy.

For instructors

All cases mentioned in the book are freely accessible in their electronic version to instructors using the book. For accessing other cases on the *Marketing Across Culture*'s Site, contact **npjcu@hotmail.com** (please sign your mail with your institutional signature, indicate the URL of your personal webpage on your institution's site and attach your course outline).

Additional references per chapter and large bibliographies on some particular issues (country-of-origin, cross-cultural advertising, international business negotiations, and so on) are available to instructors on: **www.hec.unil.ch/jusunier/teaching/references/ index.htm**.

An instructor's manual with suggested answers for end-of-chapter questions, teaching notes for cases, slides, and additional learning resources is available at **www.pearsoned.co.uk/usunier**.

Outline

Part 1, comprising the first three chapters, is devoted to the cultural variable. These chapters try to define it, to delineate the components of culture, and finally to emphasize its dynamic nature. Part 2 deals with the globalization of markets, which is *the* central issue in international marketing; Chapters 4 and 5 examine consumer behaviour, taking both a local and a global perspective, while Chapter 6 deals with local and regional marketing environments and Chapter 7 with cross-cultural market research. Part 3 presents the general impact of globalization on international marketing strategies (Chapter 8), with special emphasis on a key issue for product policy, namely, the dilemma between adaptation and standardization (Chapter 9). Chapter 10 deals with the complex management of meanings related to brand names for international markets and to country of origin images. In Chapters 11 and 12, which concern price policies and the choice of distribution channels, emphasis has been deliberately placed on the culture-

based approaches to such decisions. That is why, for instance, we accentuate bargaining (with its cultural variations) in Chapter 11, and the Japanese *keiretsu* distribution system, in Chapter 12.

Part 4 presents marketing communications in an intercultural environment. It starts with a general overview (Chapter 13) of language, culture and communication issues, which are applied in the next two chapters to advertising issues, personal selling, public relations and bribery and ethical issues in international marketing. Chapters 16 and 17 are devoted to international marketing negotiations. Table I.1 presents a summary of the basic contents of Chapters 4 to 17, linking culture to marketing issues.

This book is written from both a European and an Australasian viewpoint with many examples relating to these two areas of the world. As with all international marketing texts, this one is not universal. It may be percieved as being less pragmatically written and less issue-oriented than most. Statements may sometimes be classed as value judgements, since they are not always supported by empirical evidence, as is

Table I.1 The impact of cultural differences on selected aspects of marketing

Area of marketing	Cultural differences influence . . .	Chapter
Consumer behaviour	Cross-cultural consumer attitudes and decision making	4
	Local consumers and global consumption	5
Local marketing environments	Local infrastructures and marketing knowledge	6
Market research	Equivalence and methods in cross-national market surveys	7
Overall marketing strategy	Global versus locally customized marketing strategies	8
Targeting market segments	Cross-border vs. country clustering	8
Product policy	Adaptation or standardization of product attributes	9
Brand image	Brand and country-of-origin evaluations by consumers	10
Price policy	Bargaining rituals/Price-quality evaluations/Price strategies towards consumers, competitors and suppliers	11
Distribution channels	Channel style and service, producer–distributor relationships	12
Communication	World-views (through language) and communication styles	13
Advertising	Tailoring messages to local audiences' cultural traits	14
Personal selling	Selling styles, sales force management, networking and public relations, bribery and ethical issues in an international context	15
Marketing negotiations	Negotiation strategies, processes and outcomes	16
National style of marketing negotiation:	Attitude, organization, scheduling, role of emotions and friendship, communication and interaction style	17

the case in American textbooks. Therefore this book may sometimes seem unusual to native English-speaking readers. We regard this approach as part of the message of the book: it is a more contextual, and therefore less explicit.

Each chapter concludes with questions and is followed by an appendix comprising some or all of the following: cases, exercises and critical incidents. In addition, many interesting links, cases and exercises have been included on the book's website (**www.hec.unil.ch/jusunier/teaching/index.htm**) and in the instructor's manual. Since different national versions of this book have been published (Dutch, English, French and German), it may be used in cross-cultural training settings.

Acknowledgements

We wish to acknowledge the help of the academic institutions that have provided us with the opportunity to teach and research international marketing over the last ten years. We are also indebted to many colleagues for their ideas and assistance and for encouraging us to put more and more emphasis on the cultural dimension of international marketing. We would also like to thank senior editor Thomas Sigel for his support and Peter Hooper, Aylene Rogers and Colin Reed at Pearson Education who have been instrumental in the production of this book, as well as Saskia Faulk for her great contribution in writing new cases. We accept responsibility for any errors and shortcomings.

Note

1. Here, diversity is not meant in its American sense with a strong anti-discrimination stance (reported for instance by Litvin, 1997), but rather in its simplest meaning of 'state or quality of being different or varied', with no value judgement about whether 'diversity' is good or bad. In fact it is neither good nor bad, as shown by Lian and Oneal (1997) through a cross-national study linking cultural diversity to economic development for 98 countries over the 1960–1985 period.

References

Gorn, Gerald J. (1997), 'Breaking out of the North American box', in Merrie Brucks and Debbie McInnis (eds), *Advances in Consumer Research*, vol. 24, Association for Consumer Research: Provo, UT, pp. 6–7.

Lian, Brad and John R. Oneal (1997), 'Cultural diversity and economic development: a cross-national study of 98 countries, 1960–1985', *Economic Development and Cultural Change*, vol. 46, no. 1, pp. 61–77.

Litvin, Deborah R. (1997), 'The discourse of diversity: from biology to management', *Organization*, vol. 4, no. 2, pp. 187–209.

Acknowledgements

We are grateful to the following for permission to reproduce copyright material:

University of North Carolina Press for extracts from *A Scientific Theory of Culture and Other Essays* by Bronislaw Malinowski © University of North Carolina Press 1944, renewed 1972; Charles E. Tuttle Co., Inc. of Boston, Massachusetts and Tokyo, Japan for an extract from *Read Japanese Today* by Leonard Walsh; Pearson Education Inc. for extracts from *Marketing in the International Environment* by Edward W. Cundiff & Marye Tharp © 1988 and *Cultural Dimension of International Business* by Gary P. Ferraro © 1998; Editions Economica for an extract from 'Gestation culturelle du temps: Le cas Bantu' by Usunier and Napoléon-Biguma published in *Management Interculturel: Modes et Modèles* by Gauthey & Xardel; HarperCollins Publishers for extracts from *Male and Female: A Study of the Sexes in a Changing World* by Margaret Mead © Margaret Mead 1949; Association Française du Marketing for extracts from the articles 'Une conception du comportement du consommateur chinois' by C-F. Yang published in *Recherche et Applications en Marketing* 1989 and 'Quelques facteurs de success pour la politique de produits de l'enterprise exportatrice' by O. Deher published in *Recherche et Applications en Marketing* 1986; IUMI for extracts from cases by Saskia Faulk and Jean-Claude Usunier; Thomson Learning for extracts from *International Marketing* by M.R. Czinkota and I.A. Ronkainen; Donald S. Tull for an extract from *Research for Marketing Decisions* by Green, Tull and Albaum; Advertising Age International for an extract from the article 'Marketing Director provides Smithkline reasons to smile' by Dagmar Mussey published in *Advertising Age International* © Crain Communications Inc. 1997; Harlequin Enterprises II BV for an extract from *Dangerous Enchantment* by Anne Mather © Anne Mather 1996; Penguin Group (USA) Inc. for extracts from *Going International* by L. Copeland and L. Griggs; The Economist Newspaper Limited for an extract from the article 'Leaders: Regulating the Internet' published in *The Economist* 10th June 2000 © The Economist Newspaper Limited, London 2000; AZCA Inc. for an extract from an article written by John T. Sakai; Harvard Business School Publishing for extracts from the article 'The silent language in overseas business' by Edward T. Hall published in *Harvard Business Review* May–June 1960; Emerald Group Publishing Limited for an extract from the article 'Advertising in Saudi Arabia regulation' by M. Luqmani, U. Yavas and Z. Quraeshi published in *International Marketing Review* Vol. 6 No. 1 1988; and The McGraw-Hill Companies for extracts from *International Marketing* by Philip R. Cateora 1983.

Page 1 © Getty Images/Photodisc; page 83 © 2002, Courtney Kealy, Getty Images; page 215 © 2003 Claro Cortes IV, Reuters/Corbis; page 371 © 2003 Pers-Anders Pettersson, Getty Images.

Table 1 reprinted with permission from Innovation (Summer 2002), the Quarterly of the Industrial Designers Society of America; pp: 703, 707, 6000; f: 703, 787, 8501; e: idsa@idsa.org; w: www.idsa.org; Table 2 from TNS Global E-Commerce Report, 2001, Author – Arno Hummerston; Table 3.1 reprinted from *Organizational Dynamics, Vol. 9, no. 1*. Hofstede, Geert, '*Motivation, Leadership and Organization: Do American theories apply abroad?*' pp. 42–63, Copyright 1980b, with permission from Elsevier; Table 3.2 Derr, C. Brooklyn & André Laurent, '*The internal and external career: A theoretical and cross-cultural perspective*', in Michael B. Arthur, Douglas T. Hall, Barbara S. Lawrence, *Handbook of Career Theory*, 1989, with permission from Cambridge University Press; Table 3.3 reprinted with permission from Hofstede, Geert, *Culture's Consequences*, 2nd Edition, 2001. © Geert Hofstede; Table A4.1 Solomon, Michael. R.,

Consumer Behaviour: Buying, Having And Being, 4th Edition, © 1999. Reprinted by permission of Pearson Education, Inc., Upper Saddle River. NJ; Table 7.1 *Consumer Behaviour*, 4th edn., Craig C. Samuel and Susan P. Douglas, 2001, © John Wiley & Sons Limited. Reprinted with permission; Table 7.3 © March 1978 by ESOMAR ® – The World Association of Research Professionals. This article first appeared in *European Research*, published by ESOMAR; Table 9.3 Lange, André and Newman-Baudais, Susan (2003), 'World Film Market Trends', Focus 2003, Marché du Film, European Audio-visual Observatory, May 2003, (www.obs.coe.int); Table A12.2 © National Honey Board, www.nhb.org; Table 13.2 from *Nielsen.NetRatings*, 2003, published by Nielsen/NetRatings Oxford, reproduced with permission; Table 14.1 from *Branding new and improved wars* in FAIR, Norman Solomon, October, 2002. Reprinted with permission; from '*The art of naming operations*', in *Parameters*, pp. 81–98. Seiminski, Gregory C. (1995). Reprinted with permission.

In some instances we have been unable to trace the owners of copyright material and we would appreciate any information that would enable us to do so.

Part 1 The cultural variable in international marketing

Introduction to Part 1

In an increasingly interdependent world where barriers to trade and to international exchanges constantly diminish, cultural differences remain the single most enduring feature that has to be taken into account for localizing marketing strategies. Part 1 of this book introduces key concepts in cultural studies that have great influence on the understanding of local markets and the design of international marketing strategies.

Chapter 1 starts by presenting the basic elements of culture and international marketing, providing both general definitions of culture and its main components such as language and social institutions. For the sake of simplicity, cultural boundaries are often equated with nationality: the limitations of such an assumption are presented. Finally, the chapter reviews how culture affects the development of skills and how certain forms of social representation tend to emerge as a result of meaning being shared in the cultural community. The objective of Chapter 1 is to enable readers to depart from their own cultural conditioning; the end-of-chapter teaching materials are designed for this.

Chapter 2 is an introduction to cultural dynamics, that is, how basic cultural assumptions influence behaviour, and it gives special emphasis to two key dimensions, time and space. These cultural assumptions have an impact on marketing-related issues such as material culture, sense of ownership, preference for durability, and so on. The chapter starts by presenting a model of action based on our cultural assumptions, which sees the final action as a complex outcome of individual decision making framed by deep-seated assumptions about a number of fundamental issues such as how humans relate to nature. It proceeds to examine cross-cultural variability in the way time is conceived and experienced as well as how people in different cultures manage their relationship to space. Since a great deal of contact and exchange between cultures has taken place over the centuries, the process by which foreign items and customs are borrowed and reinserted in the local scene by various societies is examined. Another important aspect of the intercultural encounter is hostility towards unknown people; the last section of this chapter discusses how and why cultural hostility develops in the form of prejudices and negative stereotypes.

Chapter 3 complements the preceding chapter and continues to explain how basic cultural assumptions influence human behaviour and interactions. It examines, first, how people in a particular culture build their concepts of who they are and who others are; a basic input to the interaction models found in any culture. A number of fundamental issues are then examined, such as: what kinds of attitudes towards action are developed? How do people relate thinking to action? How do people deal with desires and feelings? What is the range of cultural variation for coping with rules? This chapter ends with an examination of how cultural assumptions shape actual behaviour. It shows that the influence of culture on behaviour is most often indirect, profound, and moderated by a number of other influences.

The cultural process

International marketing automatically allocates a prominent place to the cultural variable, but not everything is culture based. It would be dangerous to equate the behaviour of individuals entirely with that of the cultural grouping to which they belong. Furthermore, the perception we have of other cultures often tends to be rather shallow or stereotyped, giving us only an imperfect picture of the operation of a cultural group. At this level, our interpretation can be defensive and our analysis overly simplistic.

In fact, the cultural variable is difficult to isolate and operationalize. One of the principal aims in international marketing is to identify, categorize, evaluate and finally select market segments. Country or nation-states are often a primary segmentation basis, due to the ease of implementation. While nation-states are an enduring reality, not all national territories hold homogeneous ethnic, linguistic and religious groups. The cultural variable is more complex, and the way in which it influences behaviour is difficult to analyze.

The objective of this chapter is to lay the foundation for arguments that will be developed later in the book. This involves the definition of culture and its major elements, and an examination of its relationship with nationality (i.e. national character) and individual psychology (i.e. personality/individual character). It is important to understand these concepts, in order to assess the impact of our own culture on our actions. Subconsciously, we use culture as a guide for communication and interaction with others in our own community. Perhaps more consciously, it is also used for interaction with people belonging to other cultural communities. Throughout this chapter we have borrowed from the fields of anthropology (particularly cultural anthropology), sociology, social psychology and cross-cultural psychology.

We strongly urge interested readers to use the notes and bibliographical references at the end of this and the following two chapters, and to refer to the original sources wherever possible. In addition, we use the notation *WS#* to refer to additional resources available on this book's website at at the specific location **www.pearsoned.co.uk/usunier**.

1.1

Defining culture

In French the word *culture* was defined by Emile Littré in his nineteenth-century dictionary, as 'cultivation, farming activity'. The abstract sense of the word probably originated in Germany where the word *Kultur* was used as early as the eighteenth century to refer to civilization. In the Anglo-Saxon world the abstract notion of culture came into widespread use at the beginning of the twentieth century.

Many definitions have been formulated for culture and because it is a vague, abstract notion, there are many candidates for the ultimate definition. Kroeber and Kluckhohn (1952) even devoted an article to a review of no fewer than 164 definitions of culture. This did not prevent them from adding their own. Most of these definitions are the work of anthropologists, who studied 'primitive' societies (American Indians, Pacific Islanders, African natives, and so on). Despite this, their definitions also take into account our 'civilized' societies and 'modern' cultures. Below, we cite several definitions, each one adding to the cultural jigsaw puzzle, to determine the main aspects of this abstract and elusive concept. Further definitions are available at *WS1.1*.

Particular solutions to universal problems

Kluckhohn and Strodtbeck (1961, p. 10) emphasize the following basic points:

1. '. . . there is a limited number of common human problems for which all peoples at all times must find some solution.'
2. 'While there is a variability in solutions of all the problems, it is neither limitless nor random but is definitely variable within a range of possible solutions.'
3. '. . . all alternatives of all solutions are present in all societies at all times, but are differentially preferred. Every society has, in addition to its dominant profile of value orientations, numerous variant or substitute profiles.'

How does culture link the individual to society?

Ralph Linton (1945, p. 21) emphasizes the link between culture and the individual with the following definition: 'A culture is the configuration of learned behaviour and results of behaviour whose component elements are shared and transmitted by the members of a particular society.' Linton also emphasizes the limits of cultural programming that society can impose on an individual (1945, pp. 14–15, emphasis added):

No matter how carefully the individual has been trained or how successful his conditioning has been, he remains a distinct organism with his own needs and with capacities for independent thought, feeling and action. Moreover *he retains a considerable degree of individuality.* . . . Actually, the role of the individual with respect to society is a double one. Under ordinary circumstances, the more perfect his conditioning and consequent integration into the social structure, *the more effective his contribution to the smooth functioning of the whole and the surer his rewards.* However, societies have to exist and function in an ever-changing world. The unparalleled ability of our species to adjust to changing conditions and to develop ever more effective responses to familiar ones rests upon the residue of

individuality which survives in every one of us after society and culture have done their utmost. As a simple unit in the social organism, the individual perpetuates the *status quo*. As an individual he helps to change the *status quo* when the need arises.

What use is culture to the individual?

According to Goodenough (1971), culture is a set of beliefs or standards, shared by a group of people, which help the individual decide what is, what can be, how to feel, what to do and how to go about doing it. On the basis of this definition there is no reason for culture to be equated with the whole of one particular society. It is, however, related to activities that are shared by a particular group of people. Thus individuals may share different cultures with several different groups and in a particular cultural situation they can 'switch into' the culture that is operational. The term 'operational' describes a culture that is shared by those who must cooperate on a task.

Goodenough's concept of 'operational culture' assumes that the individual can choose the culture in which to interact at any given moment or in any given situation. This is of course subject to the overriding condition that the culture has been correctly internalized from past experiences. Although the concept of operational culture is somewhat debatable, it does have the advantage of highlighting the multicultural nature of many individuals in today's societies, such as bi-nationals, multilinguals, and even people who have a particular national identity and an international professional or corporate culture. It also draws our attention to the important issue of the sources of an individual's acculturation.

How to define the 'borders' of a culture?

As Child and Kieser emphasize (1977, p. 2):

Cultures may be defined as patterns of thought and manners which are widely shared. The boundaries of the social collectivity within which this sharing takes place are problematic, so that it may make as much sense to refer to a class or regional culture as to a national culture.

In colloquial language, when we say 'Parisians', or 'Aussies', or 'Texans', or 'docs', or 'showbiz' we are referring to cultures as well as to the groups of people who share them. To determine their culture we must ask: to what extent do the characteristics of these groups, in terms of their patterns of thought, belief or behaviour, really differentiate them from other cultural groups?

Elements of culture

Culture is much more a process than a distinctive whole, entirely identifiable by the sum of its elements. Its elements are organically interrelated and work as a coherent set. Thus, it is not only a 'toolbox' but also provides people with some 'directions for use' in their daily life in the community. Tylor (1913) describes culture as a complex and interrelated set of elements, comprising knowledge, beliefs and values, arts, law, manners and morals and all other kinds of skills and habits acquired by a human being as a member of a particular society. These elements are acquired and also reinforced by our biological foundations, languages, social institutions and material and symbolic productions, as described in the next sections.

The biological foundations of culture

The anthropologist Bronislaw Malinowski (see *WS1.2* for information on his life and works) offers evidence for the relationship between the purely biological needs of people and the way in which people are organized and regulated within the framework of the cultural community. As Malinowski (1944, p. 75) states: 'We have to base our theory of culture on the fact that all human beings belong to an animal species. . . . No culture can continue if the group is not replenished continually and normally.' He develops the example of eating habits, which must be regarded as both biological *and* cultural:

Cultural determination is a familiar fact as regards hunger or appetite, in short the readiness to eat. Limitations of what is regarded as palatable, admissible, ethical; the magical religious, hygienic and social taboos on quality, raw materials, and preparation of food; the habitual routine establishing the time and the type of appetite – all these could be exemplified from our civilization, from the rules and principles of Judaism, or Islam, Brahmanism or Shintoism, as well as from every primitive culture.

Malinowski (1944, pp. 86–7) also evokes the cultural relativity of sexual behaviour:

The specific form in which the sexual impulse is allowed to occur is deeply modified by anatomical inroads (circumcision, infibulation, clitoridectomy, breast, foot and face lacerations); the attractiveness of a sex object is affected by economic status and rank; and the integration of the sex impulse involves the personal desirability of a mate as an individual and as a member of the group. It would be equally easy to show that fatigue, somnolence, thirst and restlessness are determined by such cultural factors as a call to duty, the urgency of a task, the established rhythm of activities.

The four essential elements of culture

The major significant elements of culture are:

- Language
- Institutions
- Material productions
- Symbolic productions

While each of these is discussed below, it is worth noting that there is nothing to prevent a particular cultural item from belonging to all four elements of culture simultaneously, which then appear as different layers. For instance, music is at once a language, an institution, an artistic production and also a symbolic element.

Language as an element of culture

Language has a prominent role as an element of culture. Linguist and anthropologist Benjamin Lee Whorf (Carroll, 1956, p. 65), a chemical engineer working for a fire insurance company, spent his spare time tracing the origins and grammar of American Indian languages. He is the author of a seminal, and quite controversial, hypothesis, often referred to as the Whorfian hypothesis or Whorf–Sapir hypothesis. Aspects of this theory have been incorporated, either explicitly or implicitly, at many points in this book, particularly those chapters in which language and linguistic issues figure strongly, including market research (Chapter 7), brands (Chapter 10), marketing communication – advertising (Chapters 14 and 15) and negotiation (Chapters 16 and 17). Whorf defines his basic tenet as follows:

The ethnologist engaged in studying a living primitive culture must often have wondered: 'What do these people think?

How do they think? Are their intellectual and rational processes akin to ours or radically different?' But thereupon he has probably dismissed the idea as a psychological enigma and has sharply turned his attention back to more readily observable matters. And yet the problem of thought and thinking in the native community is not purely and simply a psychological problem. It is quite largely cultural. It is moreover largely a matter of one especially cohesive aggregate of cultural phenomena that we call a language.

In short, Whorf defends the idea that the language we learn in the community where we are born and raised shapes and structures our world-view and our social behaviour. It influences the way in which we select issues, solve problems and finally, act. Although the Whorfian hypothesis has been harshly criticized by many linguists, it remains a *fundamental metaphor*, though not a fully validated scientific theory. We refer to it as a key issue when describing the pitfalls of intercultural communication (in Chapter 13). Language, especially through tenses and words, shapes time-related behaviour, which in turn has an influence on business attitudes (when negotiating or dealing with delivery times or appointments). For instance, the African Bantu people, unlike most Western cultures, do not have a specific word that clearly differentiates the 'here' and the 'now'. They have a common time–space localizer (see Appendix A2.4 'Reading'). (For further information on language and beliefs see *WS1.2* and Chapter 13.)

Institutions as an element of culture

Institutional elements are the 'spine' of the cultural process. They link the individual to the group. Institutions may include family as well as political institutions, or any kind of social organization within which the individual has to comply with rules in exchange for various rewards (e.g. being fed, loved, paid, and so on). These rules are not static and an individual may also sometimes act as a proactive agent of change.

Malinowski (1944) compiled a list of seven universal principles around which institutions are formed across cultures.

1. The principle of *reproduction* integrates people around blood relationships and marriage as an established contractual framework. It covers all kinds of kinship patterns where the family is the basic institution formed by parents and their children, as well as the extended family, including the clan organization and its nature (e.g. matrilineal, patrilineal), the regulation of interclan relationships, etc. The reproduction principle also incorporates the ways courtship and marriages are legally organized.

2. The principle of *territoriality* integrates people around common interests dictated by neighbourhood and vicinity. This type of institution may range from a horde of nomads to a village, a small town community, a region, a province or, at the largest level, the 'mega-tribe' composed of all the people sharing the same nationality. Cooperation may be enhanced by a commonly perceived threat of potential foes located outside the common territory. Initially territoriality is concrete, based on physical space and some kind of fencing or borders. In the modern world, it may be extended to abstract territories (associations, alumni and so on).

3. The principle of *physiology* integrates people around their sex, age, and physical traits or defects. This includes institutions such as the sexual division of labour, sex roles, the relationship patterns between age groups, and the way minority members of the community are treated (e.g. asylums for the mentally ill, or special homes for the disabled).

4. The principle of *spontaneous tendency to join together* integrates people around common goals. This includes various kinds of associations, such as primitive secret societies, clubs, artistic societies, etc.

5. The principle of *occupational and professional activities* integrates people around labour divisions and the kinds of expertise that have been developed. In modern societies, this includes industry organizations, trade unions, courts, the police, the army, educational institutions and religious bodies. In fact, it includes all those institutions that maintain the fabric of a society.

6. The principle of *hierarchy* integrates people around rank and status, including the nobility, the middle class and slaves, or more generally any kind of social class system or caste system. The social hierarchy may follow a variety of criteria, including ethnicity, education, wealth, etc.

7. The principle of *totality* integrates diverse elements into a reasonably coherent whole. The political process, whatever it may be (feudal, democratic, theocratic, dictatorial, etc.), expresses the need for totality. It deals with the collective decision process

at the highest level. The various strata of totality, such as the individual striving for identity and the community striving for coherence, may compete with each other. For example, a minority, willing to practise its religion and mores (e.g. polygamy), may be opposed to the state which tries to maintain the global coherence by limiting social customs to the dominant solution (e.g. monogamy). More generally, any sub-group of the 'mega-tribe', composed of all the nationals of a particular state, may feel that their particular interests are conflicting with those of the community as a whole. These conflicts will be stronger in nation-states where the nationals are less homogeneous from a cultural point of view, than when they share a common linguistic and cultural background.

Obviously, examining any one level of institution in isolation provides only a limited picture of how a culture operates. To gain a more complex picture, some researchers have begun to examine multilevel relationships between institutions and values at the individual level. One such database is the World Values Survey, which tracks the basic values and beliefs of various publics within and across countries (see *WS1.0*).

Material productions as an element of culture

Productions transmit, reproduce, update and continuously attempt to improve the knowledge and skills in the community.[1] These range from physical productions, as well as productions of intellect, artistry and service. Productions are diverse. They include tools, machines, factories, paper, books, instruments and media of communication, food, clothing, ornaments, etc. As a result, we often confuse an influential civilization (which corresponds to the German word *Kultur*) with a cultural community that successfully produces many goods and services. But material consumption or wealth orientation is not definitive proof of cultural sophistication. *There is no hierarchy, apart from the purely subjective, between world cultures.* As such, there are many different cultural attitudes to the material world, which, in community resource allocation, includes the priority given to productions and material achievements. For example, Kumar (2000) discusses the differing world-views in India and China. The Indian world-view based on Brahmanism has the goal of inner spirituality. It emphasizes ascription

over achievement and does not place a high value on wealth, acquisition or production. Conversely, the Chinese world-view is based on Confucian Pragmatism with the goal being harmonious social order. It emphasizes meritocracy and hard work, focusing on action in the material, rather than the spiritual world.

Symbolic productions as an element of culture

Symbolic and sacred elements are the basis for the description (and therefore management) of the relations between the physical and the metaphysical world. Cultures range from those where the existence of any kind of metaphysical world is completely denied, to those where symbolic representations of the metaphysical world are present in everyday life. A central preoccupation of cultural communities is to define, through religious and moral beliefs, whether there is life after death, and if so of what kind. The scientific movement, especially at the end of the nineteenth century, seemed close to eliminating these questions by pushing back the boundaries of the metaphysical world. Nowadays, most scientists recognize that the metaphysical question will never be resolved fully by scientific knowledge. What is in fact of interest to us is not the answers to these questions, but rather the consequences of moral and religious assumptions on individual and collective behaviours, which differ widely across cultures.

Productions of culture cannot be described only by their physical attributes, as they always contain a symbolic or sacred dimension. Mircea Eliade (1956, p. 79) describes how the arts of the blacksmith and the alchemist, the forerunners of modern metallurgy and chemistry, hold a powerful symbolic dimension:

The alchemist, like the smith, and like the potter before him, is a 'master of fire'. It is with fire that he controls the passage of matter from one state to another. The first potter who, with the aid of live embers, was successful in hardening those shapes which he had given to his clay, must have felt the intoxication of the demiurge: he had discovered a transmuting agent. That which natural heat – from the sun or the bowels of the earth – took so long to ripen, was transformed by fire at a speed hitherto undreamed of. This demiurgic enthusiasm springs from that obscure presentiment that the great secret lay in discovering how to 'perform' faster than Nature, in other words (since it is always necessary to talk in terms of the spiritual experience of the primitive man) how, without peril, to interfere in the processes of the cosmic forces. Fire turned out to be the means by which man could 'execute' faster, but it could also do something other than what already existed in Nature. It was therefore the manifestation of a magico-religious power which could modify the world and which, consequently, did not belong to this world. This is why the most primitive cultures look upon the specialist in the sacred – the shaman, the medicine-man, the magician – as a 'master of fire'.

Numerous illustrations of the strength of the symbolic dimension are given throughout the book. In the area of marketing communication, symbolic dimension is of the utmost importance. That is, products and their advertising communicate through the symbolism of colour, shape, label, brand name, and so on, but the interpretation of symbols is strongly culture bound.

Traditional societies have always been more consciously involved in symbolic thought and behaviour than modern societies. Since less is *explained*, more must be *related*. For example: Why does the sun shine every day? Should its disappearance be considered ominous? What should be done to satisfy it so that it goes on spreading its generous rays on the fields and rivers? The bloody ritual sacrifices in the pre-Columbian civilizations were heavily charged with symbolic content.[2] Human sacrifices were dedicated to the sun, as were the blood and the living heart, which was pulled out of the bodies of living people. The Spanish conquerors were utterly horrified by these sacrifices because they did not understand their meaning. The Spaniards were helped in their conquest by a myth. The Mayas and Aztecs were waiting for the return of Quetzalcoatl, a sort of man-god, who had been a benevolent ruler over his people and whose return was to herald a golden age. When the bearded Hernando Cortès landed in Mexico, accompanied by strange creatures (the Indians believed that horses and their riders were a single body), they saw him as Quetzalcoatl.

Of course, symbols are not only related to religious and metaphysical matters; they also extend into everyday life. It is a common mistake to believe that the symbolic dimension has largely disappeared in modern life. That it has been forgotten by modern people who have progressed along the road towards science and knowledge and pushed back the boundaries of the metaphysical world. The illusion of the pre-eminence of science, generated by technological breakthroughs in the nineteenth century, is now largely abandoned by today's top scientists. As Stephen Hawking points out (1988, p. 13):

ever since the dawn of civilization, people have not been content to see events as unconnected and inexplicable. They have craved an understanding of the underlying order in the world. Today we still yearn to know why we are here and where we came from.

Culture as a collective fingerprint: are some cultures superior?

Culture is identity: a sort of collective fingerprint. There are no 'good' or 'bad' elements of a particular cultural group. Cultural differences exist, but this is no reason for judging a particular culture as *globally* superior or inferior to others. Cultures may be evaluated and indeed ranked, but only on the basis of facts and evidence according to precise criteria and for very specific segments of culture-related activities. Some people may be said to make better warriors, others to hold finer aesthetic judgement, or to be more gifted in the composition of music and so on. But culture is a set of *coherent* elements. Straightforward comparison might allow us to indulge in the rather dangerous illusion that it is possible to select the best from each culture and make an 'ideal' combination. However, as we will see later on, it is not quite as easy as that.

A joke about Europeans illustrates this. It goes: 'Heaven is where the cooks are French, the mechanics are German, the policemen are English, the lovers are Italian and it is all organized by the Swiss. Hell is where the policemen are German, the mechanics are French, the cooks are British, the lovers are Swiss and it is all organized by the Italians.' Not only would it be difficult to take the best traits from a culture, while rejecting the worst, but also any attempt to combine the best of several cultures could eventually turn out to be a disaster. This is because *coherence* is needed at the highest level (corresponding to *identity* at the individual level).

1.3
Culture and nationality

Nationality is one way to divide individuals into larger groups – it is operational and obviously convenient. However, the direction of causality between the concepts of nationality and culture is not clear. It is likely that, historically, shared culture has been a fundamental building-block in the progressive construction of modern nation-states. But as soon as these states began to emerge, they struggled against local particularisms, patois and customs, and tried to homogenize institutions. Conflicts in large countries have often had a strong cultural base, including the War of Secession in the United States, the rivalry between the English and the Scots in the United Kingdom, and the progressive elimination of local powers in the highly centralized French state. They all have distinctive cultural elements at stake, including language, values, religion, concepts of freedom, etc.

Nevertheless, an attempt to equate culture directly with the nation-state, or country, would be misguided for a number of convergent reasons:

1. A country's culture can only be defined by reference to other countries' cultures. India is a country culture in comparison with Italy or Germany, but the Indian subcontinent is made up of highly diversified ethnic and religious groups including Muslims, Hindus, Sikhs, etc., and, with over 20 principal languages, is deeply multicultural.
2. Some nation-states are explicitly multicultural – Switzerland, for instance. One of the basic levels of organization is the canton (*Gau* in German), which defends local particularisms. Precise staffing levels have been established in public bodies, companies and banks, which prevent discrimination between linguistic communities whose numbers are unequal: the German-speaking Swiss make up almost three-quarters of the total population, the French-speakers a little more than 20 per cent, Italian-speakers 3–4 per cent and Romansch-speakers about 1 per cent. However, there is a common misconception that Switzerland administers its multiculturalism without encountering any difficulties.[3] The Swiss political system, which was established more than seven centuries ago, enables the people to manage successfully the complex trade-off between an exacerbated compliance with local peculiarities and a common attitude towards anything that is not Swiss.
3. Political decisions, especially during the last century, have imposed the formation of new states, particularly through the processes of colonization and decolonization. The borders of these new states, sometimes straight lines on a map, were

often fixed with little respect for cultural realities, and international negotiators obviously had very little in common with the people for whom they were making decisions. Many significant national cultures, such as that of the Kurds (split between the Iraqis, the Syrians, the Turks and the Iranians) have never been accorded the right to a territory or a state. Eritrea, in East Africa, became an independent country in 1993 after a 30-year struggle that culminated in a referendum vote for independence.

Sources of culture

The national element is not always the main source of culture when regarded from an 'operational culture' perspective (Goodenough, 1971). Figure 1.1 shows the basic sources of cultural background at the level of the individual. For instance, medical researchers or computer hardware specialists, whatever their nationality, share a common specialized education, common interests, and largely the same professional culture. This is developed through common training, working for the same companies, reading the same publications worldwide and contributing to research where international cross-cultural comparability of purely scientific methods and results is fundamental.

Likewise, the sense of belonging to an important ethnic group may override, and even nullify, the feeling of belonging to a particular nation-state. The Tamil population in Sri Lanka, which makes up about 20 per cent of the total Sri Lankan population and is mostly centred around Jaffna in the north of the island, is strongly linked with the large Tamil community in southern India (numbering 55 million), which supports them in their claim for autonomy. The Tamils are involved in a brutal struggle with the Singhalese community, which comprises the largest part of the population. The sense of belonging to a large ethnic group is, in this case, much stronger than the feeling of belonging to a national group.

National/cultural territories with specific, recognized borders are rarely fully homogeneous. The transition from one to another is often facilitated by 'cross-border' cultures. Examples of this are numerous. In the area around the border between France and Spain, for instance, two cultures, which are almost national cultures, exist side by side and offer continuity between the two countries: the Basque country to

Figure 1.1 Sources of culture

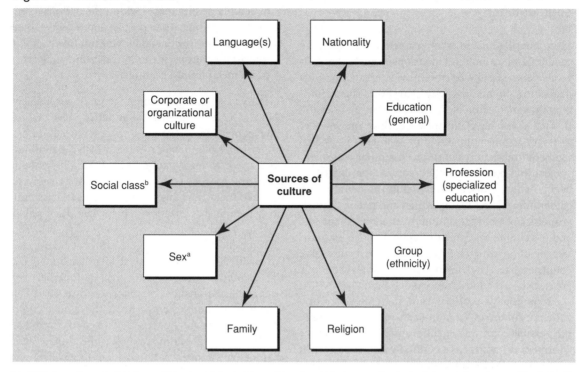

[a] In 1948 the anthropologist Margaret Mead published *Male and Female*, which draws on her in-depth knowledge of several South Pacific and Balinese cultures. It not only depicts their organization of relationships between men and women, the division of labour and roles in the community, but also explains how these patterns may be compared to those of contemporary American society. *Male and Female*, which has continued to be a best-seller, is an excellent and detailed introduction to sex cultures. Although rarely mentioned in this book, which is principally concerned with territory and national culture, the difference between masculine and feminine culture is in fact the most basic cultural distinction.

[b] Social class may be a distinctive source of culture, to a greater or lesser degree, depending on the country. For instance in France and England, where there are traditions of accepted birth inequalities and a strong historical orientation, social class is a very distinctive source of culture; the way one speaks immediately reveals one's social class. However, in the United States, Australia, Japan or the Scandinavian countries, this is not so marked. Social class like sex, but unlike most other sources, is not a territory-based source of culture.

the west and Catalonia to the east. The painter Salvador Dali, a Catalan born in Figueras, Spain, which is 20 km from the French border, was fascinated by the train station at Perpignan in France – the French part of Catalonia. In reality these two places, on either side of the border, belong to the same Catalan culture, which is sustained by the use of the Catalan language. Other examples show that some people have been able to reach a compromise: the Swedish-speaking minority on the west coast of Finland, for instance, or the Alsatians in France. Alsatians speak a mostly German-based patois, behave in the workplace like Germans and traditionally lean towards a sense of French nationality and the adoption of the French lifestyle outside the workplace. People who belong to these 'cross-border' cultures generally have a privileged position as 'exporters' from one country to another.

Physical and climatic conditions are also a fairly systematic source of differentiation, although subtle rather than fundamental. Almost every apparently unified country is made up of a 'North' and a 'South'. Even in a country that is homogeneous from a linguistic, ethnic, religious and institutional point of view, such as Sweden, has a fairly marked difference, at least for the Swedes, between the culture and lifestyle of a southern city and a northern town. This difference may not be as strongly perceived by foreigners, who initially appreciate only their own differences from Swedes and Sweden as a whole.

Cultural homogeneity and relevant segmentation

Most international market segments are based on geographical/geopolitical divisions, which are convenient and may also be efficient segmentation criteria depending on homogeneity. However, sociodemographic variables or lifestyles may also be relevant. In fact, firms have difficulty deciding on whether to target a transnational ethnic segment, a national segment or a cross-border regional segment. Lenartowicz and Roth (1999) suggest a process that begins with a review of the cultural literature to gather information that identifies and details cultural groupings before segmenting the market. Chapters 6 and 8 examine the issue of regional versus national segmentation, which is particularly important in large countries like the United States and in economic areas such as the European Union (EU).

Homogeneity clearly favours the emergence of a coherent culture in a nation-state, perhaps leading to the possible confusion of culture and country and the treatment of country as a culturally unified, coherent segment. A better understanding of the following sources of differentiation may lead to more cohesive sociodemographic microsegments:

1. Linguistic homogeneity.
2. Religious homogeneity.
3. Ethnic homogeneity.
4. Climatic homogeneity.
5. Geographical homogeneity.
6. Institutional and political homogeneity.
7. Social/income homogeneity.

The word 'homogeneity' implies one of the following:

1. The existence of a unique modality throughout the whole population (that is, only one religion, or one language) or a reduced standard deviation in comparison with the mean value of the characteristic across the whole population (e.g. in per capita income across all social strata).
2. An accepted diversity that is officially recognized and financed by the state. For instance, an agreement for maintaining several languages (as in Canada), more or less spoken and/or understood by everybody, or several different religions (as in Germany).

3. 'Perceived homogeneity', which is the perception of acceptable differences within the national community. For instance, people may observe huge differences in wealth and income but tolerate them for various reasons, including fatalism, indifference or on metaphysical grounds.

It is easy to see that global homogenization is unlikely. Hannerz (1991) offers an alternative view of how interactions and exchanges impact cultures. He discusses the *Creolization* of cultures, which is a continual process where information, meanings and symbolic forms are absorbed by a culture and then transformed to make them their own. The concept and assumptions behind globalization are further discussed in Chapter 4 and 5.

Logically, we might expect cultural homogeneity to directly impact national identity, but in fact the elements that tie subcultures together can strengthen nationality. For instance, Sweden is culturally more homogeneous than the United States and as such might be expected to hold a stronger national identity, but in reality it is the United States that has a stronger national identity (Keillor and Hult, 1999).

The concept of national culture

National culture reflects the culture of a nation and as such relies on the concept of within-country homogeneity and between-country differences. There are two major frameworks of national culture, which we will briefly introduce and then discuss in more detail in Chapter 3. First, Geert Hofstede (1980, 1991) empirically derived four dimensions of culture (individualism/collectivism, power distance, masculinity/femininity, and uncertainty avoidance) and later added a fifth dimension (long/short-term orientation). Hofstede's framework has been used extensively to investigate marketing issues. More recently, Schwartz (1994, 1997) and colleagues proposed an alternative framework with three dimensions at the country level: conservatism/autonomy, hierarchy/egalitarianism, and mastery/harmony. This framework has only received limited attention in marketing. The overlap between these frameworks is discussed in Chapter 3 (see Steenkamp, 2001).

The concept of national culture may seem dangerous in many respects, because it sums up a complex and multiform reality. In short, culture has many levels or layers, and national culture is at a level that is too general to avoid the traps of cliché and stereotype. To attain a better grasp of the concept, the following two questions need to be addressed:

1. Is the concept of national culture coherent and substantial enough to constitute an explanatory variable, not only in the scientific sense, but also from a pragmatic point of view?
2. How does national culture influence behaviour?

The answer to the first question is clear: the concept of national culture suffers a systematic lack of coherence. It is an 'intersection' of concepts, one being the result of the merging of culture (a mostly anthropology-based concept), and the other, being the more official nation-state. This is due to the fact that, in modern times, the most frequent mode of political organization of individuals within a particular society is that of the nation-state. As discussed earlier, cultures do not often correspond to nation-states but to linguistic, ethnic, religious or even organizational entities. The multiplicity of this concept probably explains why it has been systematically underestimated, especially in international trade theory. Theory-builders, who generally seek to construct formally convincing theoretical explanations, tend to remove such vague variables from their models even if they are explanatory. However, the fact that a construct is not easily measurable is no justification for ignoring it. Despite its limitations, the concept of national culture can still be an interesting Pandora's box. (For examples from the ex-Soviet Union see *WS1.3*.)

The second question merits consideration, but the two possible responses as to whether culture directly influences individual characteristics cannot be assessed on a scientific basis. On one hand, some people favour the idea that the cultural variable directly influences individual psychological characteristics, that is, culture has a distinct imprint on personality. Personality traits exist for which the average individual in one culture scores significantly higher (or lower) than individuals belonging to another culture. This corresponds to the idea of national character, or more precisely, the concept of modal personality, which has been developed in greater detail by Inkeles and Levinson (1969).[4] The modal personality approach largely grew out of enquiries as to why certain people are more violent, more aggressive, more domineering, and collectively more prone than others to declare war on foreign nations or to organize and implement genocide. These questions stemmed from the Second World War, especially the Nuremberg trials. Numerous empirical studies have been undertaken, particularly during the 1950s and 1960s, taking as a starting point the process of forming national character, which includes child-rearing practices, education systems, the socialization process of children, etc. Generally the results neither prove nor disprove the existence of national character.

On the other hand, some people favour the idea that individual psychology and therefore personality traits are largely free from the influence of culture. According to the anthropologist Ralph Linton (1945, pp. 14–15), the individual's 'integration into society and culture goes no deeper than his learned responses, and although in the adult the greater part of what we call the personality, there is still a good deal of the individual left over.' The question of whether personality is modal (culture-bound) or culture-free is not just academic. In Linton's view, individuals may have personalities quite separate from their cultural background. From a 'national character' perspective, one would expect to meet people with an average personality that reflects their culture. (For a biography of Linton see *WS1.3*.)

1.4
Culture and competence

Some environmental predispositions

Some peoples are considered to be more work oriented and more efficient when it comes to producing material goods. Climate has often been considered an environmental variable which has a strong influence on performance. Box 1.1 contains the beginning of Montesquieu's theory of climates (1748). While the physiological explanations are scarcely credible now, it is nevertheless a starting point for the north/south stereotype. The question is: do some countries/climates tend to harden (or soften) people, with the result that

Box 1.1

Of the difference of men in different climates

A cold air[a] constringes the extremities of the external fibres of the body; this increases their elasticity, and favors the return of the blood from the extreme parts to the heart. It contracts[b] those very fibres; consequently, it increases also their force and elasticity. People are therefore more vigorous in cold climates. Here the action of the heart and the reaction of the extremities of the fibres are better performed, the temperature of the humors is greater, the blood moves freer towards the heart, and reciprocally, the heart has more power. This superiority of strength must produce various effects; for instance, a greater boldness, that is, more courage; a greater sense of superiority, that is, more frankness, less suspicion, policy, and cunning. In short, this must be productive of very different tempers. Put a man into a close warm place, and, for the reasons above given, he will feel a great faintness. If, under this circumstance, you propose a bold enterprize to him, I believe you will find him very little disposed towards it: his present weakness will throw him into a despondency; he will be afraid of every thing, being in a state of total incapacity. The inhabitants of warm countries are, like old men, timorous; the people in cold countries are, like young men, brave. If we reflect on the late[c] wars, (which are more recent in our memory, and in which we can better distinguish some particular effects, that escape us at a greater distance of time), we shall find that the northern people, transplanted into southern regions[d], did not perform such exploits as their countrymen who, fighting in their own climate, possessed their full vigor and courage.

[a] This appears even in the countenance: in cold weather people look thinner.
[b] We know it shortens iron.
[c] Those for the succession to the Spanish monarchy.
[d] For instance in Spain.

(Source: Montesquieu, [1748], 1792, vol. 1, book XIV, ch. 11, pp. 224–5.)

they become more (or less) inclined towards activities of war, commerce or industry,[5] and more (or less) efficient in pursuing these activities? (See *WS1.4* for more information about Montesquieu.)

Climate may directly influence culture through heat, which physically discourages effort and action, or indirectly influence culture through the development of skills to adapt to climatic conditions. If the influence is purely direct, it may be controlled, as air conditioning will control heat, but this will be limited to specific contexts: battlefields remain at the mercy of the elements. If climate has both a direct and an indirect influence, via progressive genetic adaptation and/or cultural traits acquired through education and socialization, then air conditioning is still necessary but not enough. The indirect is likely to combine with the direct influence as climate has a long-term influence on the culture, which in turn influences skills and behaviour. Interestingly, climate has been found to have an indirect effect on a country's competitiveness. For instance, Van de Vliert (2003) found that temperate (less cold or hot) countries are more likely to overpay their workers, relative to the countries standing on the worldwide ladder of wealth.

National character and educational practices

Research into national character emphasizes the influence of educational practices on the development of adult personalities. Margaret Mead for instance, in her description of American character, notes that the United States is seen as an adolescent peer culture. In this setting, education favours diffuse, depersonalized authority where children face a demand for strong inner moral control. In many European countries, the cheerful, easy-going, informal Americans are often jokingly referred to as being big children.

One of the most efficient ways to study the formation process of national character is to observe education systems and child-rearing practices, particularly up to the age of 5 or 6. Some of the key elements of personality develop during this time, due to such factors as feeding and nourishing, weaning, personal hygiene and toilet training, the degree and modes of socialization into various parts of the community (with other children, with adults, with the opposite sex), the demands and prohibitions imposed on small children, and finally the reward/sanction systems that help to orientate their behaviour.[6]

Culture and skills

It seems that cultural background has an influence on perceptual and cognitive skills. Segall *et al.* (1990) clearly demonstrate the existence of differences in perception of visual illusions. They base their findings on the following simple theory: if people belonging to various human groups differ in their visual inference systems,[7] it is because the physical environment at which they are used to looking differs widely from group to group. Some people live in a constructed environment, based on straight lines and sharp angles (especially those of modern buildings and industrial objects), whereas other people live in a more rounded and curvilinear physical setting. The daily environment shapes people's visual inference. That is, the very same objects are seen differently. Thus, vision is considered to be a culturally built interpretation of specific retinal signals.

The variation in levels of competences and skills across cultural groups is another important issue. The first research on the intellectual abilities of non-European people was undertaken by researchers such as Levy-Bruhl, who classified the thought patterns of primitives as 'pre-logical'. Little by little this somewhat extreme attitude, that 'primitives' could never conceive of anything in the way that we do ('we' being the modern, Westernized people of European culture or origin), has given way to a more reasonable position. Franz Boas became interested in the idea of the psychic unity of mankind. That is, every human group studied presents common traits such as the ability to remember, to generalize, to form concepts and to think and reflect logically on abstract concepts. In fact it seems more likely that differences in ability in specific activities should be attributed to the cultural relativity of skills and competences developed by the individuals in the specific cultural grouping where they have been raised.

The scores on intelligence quotient (IQ) tests will always remain relative to the type of questions asked and the situations evoked in the verbal part of the test (reading, memorization and understanding of texts). Even that part of the test which is clearly quantitatively oriented (i.e. mathematics, geometry, statistics, logic), requires handling abstract and mathematical signs. One cannot claim that any test encompasses all the possible facets of human intelligence, or even that it offers total objectivity in the experimental and empirical methods used to evaluate them. It is therefore necessary to accept that definitions of intelligence are culturally contingent. This does not mean that all people are equally intelligent or that IQ tests are of no interest or have no practical benefits. It simply means that the results should be interpreted cautiously when tests are administered to people who do not originate from the culture where these tests were conceived and/or are not familiar with that culture.

1.5 Culture and social representations

The notion of social representation will be used throughout this book, even where there is no explicit reference to it. For instance, the acceptance (or prohibition in some countries) of comparative advertising is related to social representations of the necessity to inform consumers, to allow price competition and even to risk the denigration of one company by another through a comparative advertising campaign (see Chapter 14).

Moscovici (1961) considers social representation (SR) a 'forgotten concept'. He traces it back to Durkheim, for whom it was a class of psychic and social phenomena that relate the individual to the social aspect of collective life. Social representations are miniatures of behaviour, copies of reality and forms of operational knowledge used to reach and implement everyday decisions. For instance, people may use a combination of social representations in order to make their health-care decisions. Moscovici gives the following example that in the south-west of the United States Hispanic populations concurrently use four bases of knowledge for classifying and interpreting illnesses: the traditional popular medical knowledge, which relates mainly to pains and sufferance; the medical knowledge orally transmitted within Amerindian tribes; the modern (English) popular medical knowledge; and the medical scientific knowledge (established and recognized). According to the seriousness of the illness and the availability of money for paying for the cure, Hispanic populations let themselves be guided either by collective representations or by scientific information in order to choose which one of these four sources should be pursued in search of a cure.

Social representations are collective images that are progressively formulated within a particular society. As such, they can be surveyed by public opinion polls. Robert Farr (1988, p. 383) explains that social representations of health and sickness may have a strong influence on consumption patterns. For instance, villagers in many European countries tend to moan over the invasion of the countryside by urban development. The entire population compares the constraints of city life to the natural pace of country life. These social representations help to explain the development of natural and organic products, direct from the farm, with no additives or industrial processing, and the diffusion of ecological ideas in modern society.

Jodelet (1988, p. 360) posits that social representations are at the very intersection of the psychological/individual and social/collective levels. They serve as artificial reference images, or frameworks 'which enable us to interpret what happens to us, possibly even to give sense to the unexpected; categories which serve to classify circumstances, phenomena, individuals with whom we have to deal and theories which enable us to make a decision on these issues'.

The interpretation of our daily reality with this sort of preconceived reference framework could be considered pejoratively as merely reflecting our prejudices. However, this portrays a simplistic idea of the dynamic, collectively verified and validated nature of social representations, which are constantly updated through social situations, individual behaviour and social activities. The media, public opinion polls, news summaries, court decisions and legal penalties are all sources from which people derive their opinions and stimulate debate and social information processes, which in turn continuously update dynamic social representations.

Social representations do vary across societies. Therefore, they have a cultural value when we have to decide what is, what can be, how to feel, what to do, and how to go about doing it (operating culture). Social representations are less profound than basic cultural orientations, as they alter within shorter time spans (10 to 20 years versus centuries). Social representations are nonetheless important. They may oppose basic cultural orientations since their time-scale is short term and they are more suited to the urgent need for collective and individual adaptation to reality. (For more information on funerals, rites of passage, marriage, etc., see *WS1.5*.)

Questions

1. In light of the definitions of culture given in this chapter, is it possible for a culture to disappear? Why, or why not? Give an example.

2. A common problem, across cultures, is to attract/be attractive for potential partners. Discuss how, in Kluckhohn and Strodtbeck's terms, there is a range of possible solutions, and how they are differentially preferred across societies. Outline possible consequences for marketing.

3. Discuss the case of multi-language/multi-religion countries (e.g. India, Canada, Switzerland): how can people in these countries share a common culture? On which segments of culture?

4. Discuss the role of education (at home, at school and elsewhere) in the transmission of culture.

5. What is *national character*?

Notes

1. One may be wary of the ethnocentric (Western/modern) bias of the authors, i.e. an overemphasis on culture as striving only for the improvement of material productions; in some cultures, the dominant values may be extremely antagonistic towards material preoccupations.
2. The conquest of Mexico by Hernando Cortès is a fascinating example of the almost total destruction of a culture heavily loaded with symbolism (mostly that of the Aztecs and the Mayas), by only a very small group of Spanish invaders. When Cortès's army left the island of Cuba, sailing to Mexico, it numbered only 508 soldiers, 100 sailors and 10 horses. At that time Mexico City had half a million inhabitants.

   The Mayas, the Totonacs and the Mexicans were deeply religious people, totally subservient to the will of their gods and the sovereignty of their priest-kings. These people waged a ritualistic war on each other which was based on magic as much as military strategy and in which the desired outcome, decided in advance by the mysterious agreements of celestial powers, was not the conquest of land or the amassing of riches but the triumph of the gods, who received in sacrifice the heart and the blood of the vanquished. Disturbed by the mythical return of the ancestors and of the divine feathered serpent, Quetzalcoatl-Kukulcan, the Indians were blinded, unable to see the actual intentions of those whom they had termed the *Teules*, the Gods. And when the Indians understood that the Spaniards, whom they considered as demi-gods, were involved in a massive slaughter of Mexican Indians, from which none of them would emerge unscathed, it was too late. The Spaniards had taken advantage of their hesitation to penetrate deep into the Mexican empire, to provoke dissension, and to conquer lands and take slaves (Le Clézio, 1988, p. 19).

   See also *Historia Verdadera de la conquista de la Nueva España*, written by a member of the Cortès troop, Bernal Diaz del Castillo (1968), and *Historia General de las cosas de la Nueva Espana*, written by Bernadino de Sahagun a few years after the conquest (which took place around 1520) and the destruction of the Aztec and Maya cultures, with the objective of preserving as far as possible the traces of this civilization that had suffered such an abrupt disappearance. For a thorough analysis of culture collisions in colonial history see Urs Bitterli (1989).
3. A famous Swiss novelist, Charles Ferdinand Ramuz, has often set the relations between communities as a background to his novels. *La Séparation des races*, for instance, is the story of the kidnapping of a young girl from Bern by her Valaisan lover and the consequent mobilization of their respective communities.
4. The literature review carried out by Inkeles and Levinson (1969) is certainly the most exhaustive one (100 pages) available. It might appear somewhat dated, but since national character changes over decades and centuries, their review remains largely up to date.
5. War is assimilated here with commerce and industry because, from a historical perspective, war was a *normal* activity. The idea that war produces the vanquished and the victorious but that they are all losers, is rather a new one. When pursuing colonial wars, commerce and industry were legitimately included in the ultimate goals. The idea of bringing civilization to the barbarians included the extirpation of 'evil' beliefs, magic and sorcery, and their substitution by Christianity.
6. An important figure in these studies of childhood and society is Erik Erikson (1950), who has developed a theory of ego development stages (in the Freudian sense) on the basis of field observations of American Indians, Sioux and Yurok, US Americans, Germans and Russians. It is clearly beyond the reach of this book to sum up, even very briefly, the richness of the empirical and theoretical research on national differences that has been published by anthropologists, sociologists and psychologists. The references at the end of this chapter suggest two reviews of such cross-national research: Inkeles and Levinson (1969) and Segall *et al.* (1990).
7. By 'visual inference' is implied the mental system that enables people to transform retinal perceptions into a 'brain image' (Segall *et al.*, 1990, ch. 4).

References

Bitterli, Urs (1989), *Cultures in Conflict*, Polity Press: Oxford.

Carroll, John B. (1956), *Language, Thought and Reality: Selected writings of Benjamin Lee Whorf*, MIT: Cambridge, MA.

Child, J. and A. Kieser (1977), 'A contrast in British and West German management practices: Are recipes of success culture bound?', paper presented at the *Conference on Cross-Cultural Studies on Organizational Functioning*, Hawaii.

Diaz del Castillo, Bernal (1968), *Historia Verdadera de la Nueva España*, Espasa-Calpe: Madrid.

Eliade, Mircea (1956), *Forgerons et Alchimistes*, Flammarion: Paris. English translation (1962), *The Forge and the Crucible*, University of Chicago Press: Chicago.

Erikson, Erik (1950), *Childhood and Society*, Norton: New York.

Farr, Robert M. (1988), 'Les Représentations sociales', in Serge Moscovici (ed.), *Psychologie sociale*, PUF Fondamental: Paris.

Goodenough, Ward H. (1971), *Culture, Language and Society*, Modular Publications, 7, Addison-Wesley: Reading, MA.

Hannerz, Ulf (1991), Scenarios for Peripheral Cultures, King, A.D., *Culture, Globalization and the World System*, MacMillan: London, pp. 107–28.

Hawking, Stephen (1988), *A Brief History of Time*, Guild Publishing: London.

Hosftede, Geert (1980), *Culture's Consequences: International differences in work-related values*, Sage: Beverly Hills, CA.

Hosftede, Geert (1991), *Cultures and Organizations: Software of the mind*, McGraw-Hill: London.

Inkeles, Alex and Daniel J. Levinson (1969), 'National character: the study of modal personality and sociocultural systems', in Gardner Lindzey and Elliot Aronson (eds), *Handbook of Social Psychology*, vol. IV, Addison-Wesley: Reading, MA, pp. 418–506.

Jodelet, Denise (1988), 'Représentations sociales: phénomènes, concept et théorie', in Serge Moscovici (ed.), *Psychologie sociale*, PUF Fondamental: Paris.

Keillor, Bruce D. and G. Thomas M. Hult (1999), 'A five-country study of national identity: Implications for international marketing research and practice', *International Marketing Review*, vol. 16, no. 1, pp. 65–82.

Kluckhohn, Florence R. and Frederick L. Strodtbeck (1961), *Variations in Value Orientations*, Greenwood Press: Westport, CT.

Kroeber, Alfred L. and Clyde Kluckhohn (1952), *Culture: A critical review of concepts and definitions*, Anthropological Papers, no. 4, Peabody Museum.

Kumar, Rajesh (2000), 'Confucian pragmatism vs. brahmanical idealism understanding the divergent roots of Indian and Chinese economic performance', *Journal of Asian Business*, vol. 16, no. 2, pp. 49–69.

Le Clézio, J.M.G. (1988), *Le Rêve Mexicain ou la Pensée Interrompue*, Gallimard: Paris.

Lenartowicz, Tomasz and Kendall Roth (1999), 'A framework for culture assessment', *Journal of International Business Studies*, vol. 30, no. 4, pp. 781–98.

Linton, Ralph (1945), *The Cultural Background of Personality*, Appleton-Century: New York.

Malinowski, Bronislaw (1944), *A Scientific Theory of Culture and Other Essays*, University of North Carolina Press: Chapel Hill, NC.

Mead, Margaret (1948), *Male and Female*, William Morrow: New York.

Montesquieu, Charles de (1748), *The Spirit of Laws*, translated from the French by Thomas Nugent (1792), 6th edn, McKenzie and Moore: Dublin.

Moscovici, Serge (1961), *La Psychanalyse, son Public et son Image*, Presses Universitaires de France: Paris.

Schwartz, Shalom H. (1994), 'Beyond individualism/collectivism: new cultural dimensions of value', in Uichol Kim, Harry C. Triandis, Çigdem Kâgitçibasi, Sang-Chin Choi and Gene Yoon (eds), *Individualism and Collectivism: Theory, method and applications*, Sage: Thousand Oaks, CA, pp. 85–119.

Schwartz, Shalom H. (1997), 'Values and Culture', in Donald Munro, John F. Schumaker and Stuart C. Carr (eds), *Motivation and Culture*, Routledge: New York.

Segall, Marshall H., Pierre R. Dasen, John W. Berry and Ype H. Poortinga (1990), *Human Behavior in Global Perspective*, Pergamon: New York.

Steenkamp, Jan-Benedikt E.M. (2001), 'The role of national culture in international marketing research', *International Marketing Review*, vol. 18, no. 1, pp. 30–44.

Tylor, Edward (1913), *Primitive Culture*, John Murray: London.

Van de Vliert, Evert (2003), 'Thermoclimate, culture, and poverty as country-level roots of workers' wages', *Journal of International Business Studies*, vol. 34, no. 1, pp. 40–52.

Weeks, William H., Paul B. Pedersen and Richard W. Brislin (1987), *A Manual of Structured Experiences for Cross-cultural Learning*, Intercultural Press: Yarmouth, ME.

Teaching materials

A1.1 Critical incident

An old lady from Malaysia

The frail, old, almost totally blind lady appeared at every clinic session and sat on the dirt floor enjoying the activity. She was dirty and dishevelled, and obviously had very little, even by Malaysian kampong (local village) standards.

One day the visiting nurse happened upon this woman in her kampong. She lived by herself in a rundown shack about 10 by 10 feet [3 × 3 m]. When questioned how she obtained her food, she said she was often hungry, as she only received food when she worked for others – pounding rice, looking after the children, and the like.

The nurse sought to obtain help for the woman. It was finally resolved that she would receive a small pension from the Department of Welfare which would be ample for her needs.

At each weekly clinic, the woman continued to appear. She had become a centre of attention, laughed and joked freely, and obviously enjoyed her increased prestige. No change was noted in her physical status, however. She continued to wear the same dirty black dress and looked no better fed.

The nurse asked one of the rural health nurses to find out if the woman needed help in getting to a shop to buy the goods she seemed so sorely in need of.

In squatting near the woman, the rural health nurse noted a wad of bills in the woman's pocket. 'Wah,' she said, 'It is all here. You have spent nothing. Why is that?'

The woman laughed and then explained: 'I am saving it all for my funeral.'

(Source: Weeks *et al.*, 1987, pp. 24–5.)

A1.2 Critical incident

The parable

The leader tells the following parable to the group, illustrating with rough chalkboard drawings if desired:

Rosemary is a girl of about 21 years of age. For several months she has been engaged to a young man – let's call him Geoffrey. The problem she faces is that between her and her betrothed there lies a river. No ordinary river mind you, but a deep, wide river infested with hungry crocodiles.

Rosemary ponders how she can cross the river. She thinks of a man she knows who has a boat. We'll call him Sinbad. So she approaches Sinbad, asking him to take her across. He replies, 'Yes, I'll take you across if you'll spend the night with me.' Shocked at this offer, she turns to another acquaintance, a certain Frederick, and tells him her story. Frederick responds by saying, 'Yes, Rosemary, I understand your problem – but – it's your problem, not mine.' Rosemary decides to return to Sinbad, spends the night with him, and in the morning he takes her across the river.

Her reunion with Geoffrey is warm. But on the evening before they are to be married. Rosemary feels compelled to tell Geoffrey how she succeeded in getting across the river. Geoffrey responds by saying, 'I wouldn't marry you if you were the last woman on earth.'

Finally, at her wit's end, Rosemary turns to our last character, Dennis. Dennis listens to her story and says, 'Well, Rosemary, I don't love you . . . but I will marry you.' And that's all we know of the story.

(Source: Weeks *et al.*, 1987, pp. 25–6.)

Discussion guide

1. Before any discussion, participants should be asked to write down individually on a piece of paper the characters of whose behaviour they most approve, plus a sentence or two explaining their first choice.
2. Participants may be split into small groups of four or five, to share their views and raise relevant issues.
3. The discussion should centre around the cultural relativity of values and their relation to one's own cultural background.

 ## A1.3 Reading

Body rituals among the Naciremas

(See *WS1.A.*)

Cultural dynamics 1:
Time and space

The Swedish writer Selma Lagerlöf defines culture as 'what remains when that which has been learned is entirely forgotten'.[1] Thus depicted, culture may appear to be quite a nebulous or practically limited concept. Its main use would be as a 'synthesis variable': an explanation that serves as a last resort when all other concepts or more precise theories have been successfully validated. It would also serve as an explanatory variable for residuals, when other more interpretive explanations are unsuccessful.

However, Lagerlöf's definition does have the advantage of identifying two basic elements of cultural dynamics (at the level of the individual):

1. Culture is learned.
2. Culture is forgotten in the sense that we cease to be conscious of its existence as learned behaviour.

Yet culture remains present throughout our daily individual and collective activities, and is therefore entirely oriented towards our adaptation to reality (both as a constraint and as an opportunity). To this extent it is almost unthinkable that a culture could stand perfectly still, except in the case of primitive societies, which are located in remote places and subject to no exterior interference, thus offering a stable natural and social environment. At the periphery of a fixed set of basic cultural assumptions, other sources of culture intervene, and as a result new solutions are used for tackling existing issues or for solving entirely new problems.

This chapter begins with a model of action based on cultural assumptions (section 2.1), to provide a framework for the explanation of culture-related behaviour that extends throughout this chapter and the next.

Basic cultural assumptions explained in this chapter relate to time (section 2.2) and space (section 2.3). But these are not static, as cultures borrow from each other through time and space. Section 2.4 is dedicated to this and the corresponding changes in the importing society. The last section (2.5) is dedicated to cultural hostility. Territoriality is the organizing principle of cultures across space and hostility arises from prejudiced views of others and the fear of having to share with members of alien cultural groups.

2.1

A model of action based on cultural assumptions

Figure 2.1 presents how basic cultural assumptions in three major areas (time, space and the concept of the self and others) influence interaction models, which, in combination with basic assumptions, shape attitudes towards action. Fundamental assumptions about time, space and the concept of the self and others are explained in greater detail in this chapter and the first section of the next. Cultural assumptions are statements about the basic nature of reality. Some of them are based on the 'value orientations' of the anthropologists Florence Kluckhohn and Frederick Strodtbeck (1961) which are often cited – an indication of their analytical power, at least as far as it is perceived by the social scientists. (For more information about their research see *WS2.1*.) Cultural assumptions are basic responses, expressed in a rather dichotomous manner, to fundamental human problems. They

Figure 2.1 A model of cultural dynamics

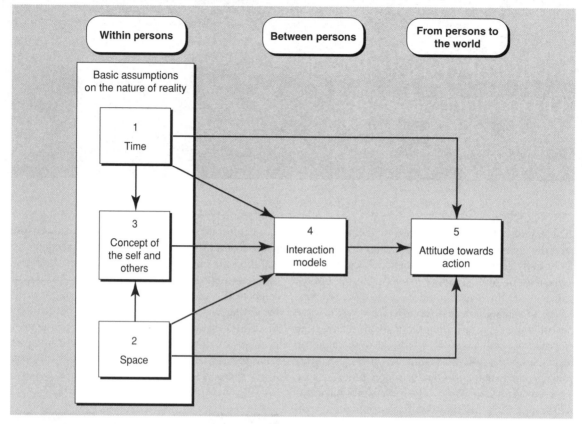

provide the members of a particular cultural community with a framework for the evaluation of solutions to these problems, combining a cognitive dimension (*people think it works that way*), an affective dimension (*people like it that way*) and a directive dimension (*people will do it that way*). Kluckhohn and Strodtbeck (1961, pp. 11, 12) have collated these common human problems under six main categories:

1. What is the character of innate human nature (human-nature orientation): good or evil, neutral, or a mix of good and evil? Is this state of human nature mutable or immutable?
2. What is the relation of humans to nature and supernature (nature orientation): subjugation to nature, harmony with nature or mastery over nature?
3. What is the temporal focus of human life (time orientation): past, present or future?
4. What is the modality of human activity (activity orientation): should people be (being), should

people do (doing) or should they do in order to be (being in becoming)?
5. What is the modality of the relationship between humans (relational orientation): linearity, collaterality or pure individuality?
6. What is the conception of space? Is it considered predominantly private, public or a mix of both?

Naturally these modalities are to be found in every society. People *are* and *do*, and there are always children and parents, in the sense that some kind of family nucleus exists everywhere. But different assumptions result in variations as to the kind of response that is dominant in a particular society. We have combined Kluckhohn and Strodtbeck's approach with those adopted by other authors (Hall, 1959, 1966, 1976, 1983; Hofstede, 1980; Triandis, 1983, 1994; Trompenaars, 1993) to depict differences in five tables: time related differences in Table 2.1, space related differences in Table 2.2, the concepts of self and others in Table 3.1, interaction models in Table 3.2, and attitudes towards action in Table 3.5.

Each of the five tables highlights common problems across cultures, depicts the most important solutions, and explains the dominant differences. This leads to a detailed inventory of basic differences in cultural assumptions and interaction models, which are mostly the result of learned behaviour. We have tried to give some country-specific illustrations, without too often citing 'typical' cultures, because to do so would be at the risk of stereotyping. Except for Hofstede's dimensions, which are considered mostly in the realm of 'interaction models', little empirical data is mentioned. For those interested in figures, rankings and scores, we have indicated where they can find such information, to the extent that it is available and significant. The objective is not to classify countries or cultures, but rather to provide readers with an understanding of how cultures differ, and to let them combine this with their own knowledge and experience in order to build their own view of how culture affects our relationships with others and our way of acting.

In doing this, we could not ignore the profound impact of technology on culture. There is the risk that many basic assumptions could be called 'modern' and their contrast would be naturally 'traditional'. The real world is fortunately more sophisticated: individualism is globally 'modern', but collectivism is not 'traditional' nor even 'conservative'. Many collectivist nations, especially in Asia, have been brilliant achievers in the past twenty years. 'Modern culture' is predominantly based on the Western values held by philosophers, scientists and politicians in Europe, during a time of industrial revolution and colonization, and later by the United States as the dominant political and cultural actor on the twentieth century world scene. The idea of a cultural assumption being 'modern' and therefore more legitimate is a misconception and sometimes taken to the extreme is considered as the only possible belief. Thus other assumptions tend to be repressed, leading to complex situations where people finally imitate behaviour that does not correspond to the assumptions really prevailing in their culture. As such, we try to refer to why and how a certain cultural assumption, interaction model or attitude towards action belongs to 'modern' culture. (For more information on cultural assumptions see *WS2.1*.)

At this point, some readers may be wondering about the relevance of culture to managerial issues

and international marketing, which represent the focus of this book. They will find an initial response in Table 3.5, point (c): we come from ideology-centred cultures where issues are most often addressed first at a very broad level. Later, attempts are made to link culture to action-related issues. We try to build convincing intellectual frameworks, occasionally at the expense of data. Some readers may consider a number of statements to be unsupported by data and evidence. We claim to be culturally relative. The next response is that, part of the cross-cultural learning experience resides in being confronted with a different mindset. Our belief is that developing cultural awareness is possible just from reading something written with a culturally alien mindset. Cultural assumptions are not completely in the realm of *unbewußtsein* (unconsciousness, deep-seated and inaccessible); in fact, they are rather in the realm of *unterbewußtsein*, that is located at a subconscious level, where interaction and self-questioning can reveal them.

In order to make the link to international marketing, we will refer as often as possible, to areas of international marketing on which these cultural differences have an impact. In subsequent chapters in the book they are also used as an explanatory framework for consumer behaviour (Chapter 4), market research (Chapter 7), marketing management (Chapters 8 to 12), advertising communication (Chapter 14), buyer–seller interactions and marketing negotiations (Chapters 15 to 17). The last four chapters build on Chapter 13, which is dedicated to language, culture and communication, and explains how language shapes our world-views. Point (e) in Table 3.2 (communication styles) is developed in Chapter 13.

Using Figure 2.1 as a guide, our exploration starts with the cultural variability in the concept of time.

2.2

Time: Cross-cultural variability

Many marketing concepts are time based: product life cycle, sales forecasting or the planning of new product launches to name but a few.[2] Normative time in marketing and management seems indisputable, and its very nature is rarely questioned. It is perceived as linear, continuous and economic. However, time, in a cross-cultural perspective, is probably the area where differences are both the largest and the most difficult to pinpoint, because (1) assumptions are very deep seated and (2) formally we adopt a common model of time.

People's relationship with time changes with respect to periods of history and levels of human development, the technology available for measuring time, the emphasis given to natural and social rhythms, and the prevailing metaphysical views. Each vision of time (*Zeitanschauung*) corresponds to a vision of the real world, its origins and destiny (*Weltanschauung*). Time appears predominantly through its social functions, in that it allows people to have a common framework of activities and helps to synchronize individual human behaviour. Encyclopaedic approaches to the concept of time (Attali, 1982) show that one time pattern has never eliminated a previous one. Each new time pattern superimposes itself on the one that previously prevailed. As a consequence, individual time perceptions may result from adding or mixing different basic patterns of time. Most of the literature in cultural anthropology considers time perceptions as cultural artefacts. As Gurevitch states (1976, p. 229): 'Time occupies a prominent place in the "model of the world" characterizing a given culture'. (For more on the concepts of time see *WS2.2*.)

Dimensions of time orientations

Table 2.1 shows time-related cultural assumptions, which correspond to four common problems:

1. To what extent should time be regarded as a tangible commodity (economicity of time)?
2. How should tasks and time be combined (monochronic versus polychronic use of time)?
3. Should lifetime(s) be seen as a single continuous line or as combining multiple cyclical episodes (linearity versus cyclicity of time)?
4. What are the appropriate temporal orientations: towards the past, the present and the future?

As you will see, there is some overlap between the prevailing solutions to these four questions. However, we have noted all four basic time assumptions because they need to be considered in a cultural model of time, which is exemplified at the end of this section by the Japanese *Makimono* time.

Economicity of time

Time may be seen as external to us, and as such to be treated like a tangible commodity. The concept of economic time is based on accurate time reckoning, dependent on precise dating and defined duration. It results in people using their time as 'wisely' as possible in scheduling or establishing timetables and deadlines. Measurement of parking meter time by units of 7.5 minutes or sport performance by the hundredths of a second is typical of precisely measured economic time with direct and explicit financial consequences. Many European countries as well as the United States and Australia are representative of the 'time-is-money' culture, where time is an economic good. Since time is a scarce resource, or at least perceived as such, people should try to achieve an optimal allocation between competing ways of using it. Norms tend to be very strict regarding time schedules, appointments and the precise setting of dates and durations. (For studies of time in cross-cultural psychology see *WS2.2*.)

Needless to say, attitudes towards money and the money value of time are inseparable from marketing (Jacoby *et al.*, 1976; Spears *et al.*, 2001). A strong economic time assumption has wide-reaching influences on consumer behaviour, because products may save time, as household appliances do, or services may be based on time values such as bank loans or life insurance policies. Economicity of time also has an impact on buyer–seller interaction, in the waiting process as well as the negotiation.

Monochronic versus polychronic use of time

Hall (1983) described two extreme behaviours of task scheduling which he calls monochronism (M-time) and polychronism (P-time). Individuals working under M-time do one thing at a time and tend to adhere to preset schedules. When confronted by a dilemma (e.g. a discussion with someone that lasts longer than planned), M-time people will politely stop the conversation, in order to keep to their schedule. In M-time societies, not only the start of a meeting but also its finish is often planned. P-time, on the other hand, stresses the involvement of people who do several things at the same time, easily modify preset schedules and seldom experience time as 'wasted'. P-time may seem quite hectic to M-time people: 'There is no recognized order as to who is to be served next, no queue or numbers indicating who has been

Table 2.1 Time-related cultural differences

Basic problem/Cultural orientations	Contrasts across cultures
Is time money?	
(a) Economicity of time	Time is regarded as a scarce resource or, conversely, as plentiful and indefinitely available.
How to schedule tasks	
(b) Monochronism versus polychronism	Only one task is undertaken at any (preset) time, following a schedule ('agenda society'), versus dealing simultaneously with different tasks, actions and/or communications (polychronism) for convenience, pleasure and efficiency.
Is time a continuous line?	
(c) Linearity (L) versus cyclicity (C) of time	Time is seen as linear-separable, cut in slices (L), versus an emphasis on the daily, yearly and seasonal cycles (C).
How should we emphasize past, present and future?	
(d) Temporal orientations	
(i) towards the past	People with high past orientation consider that the past is important, that resources must be spent on teaching history and building museums, referring to oral and written traditions and past works. Their basic assumption is that their roots are implanted in the past and no plant can survive without its roots. The converse is true for low past orientation.
(ii) towards the present	People with high present orientation consider that they basically live 'here and now'. Although not always enjoyable, the present must be accepted for what it is: the only *true* reality we live in.
(iii) towards the future	People easily and precisely envisage and plan their future. They are project oriented, prepare for the long term, appreciate the achievements of science, and so on. For them the future is inevitably 'bigger and better'. The converse is true for low future orientation.

waiting the longest' (Hall, 1983, p. 47). P-time people are more committed to persons than to schedules. When confronted with a conflict such as the one described above, they prefer to go on talking or working after preset hours interrupting their schedule, if they have one.

The PERT (programme evaluation and review technique) method is an example from a typical 'agenda culture', where M-time is the central assumption. PERT explicitly aims to reduce a universe of polychronic tasks (they really take place simultaneously, which is part of the problem) to a monochronic solution (the critical path). Management methods, originating in the US and Europe, favour pure monochronic organization. They clearly push aside polychronic attitudes, which tend to make plans and schedules rather hectic. When it comes to delays and being 'on time', precise monochronic systems give priority to meeting dates and commitments to schedules (Usunier, 1991, 2003).

To illustrate sources of tension between people who have internalized different time systems, Hall (1983, pp. 53–4) takes the example of a monochronic woman who has a polychronic hairdresser. The woman, who has a regular appointment at a specific time each week, feels frustrated and angry when she is kept waiting. At the same time, the hairdresser also feels frustrated. He inevitably feels compelled to 'squeeze people in', particularly his friends and acquaintances. The schedule is reserved for people he does not know personally and keeping to this schedule is not important to him. M- or P-time is important for business negotiations, buyer–seller interactions in general, or dealing with a foreign distributor (e.g. scheduling a promotional campaign).

Recent developments illustrate that M- and P-time represent simplistic assumptions of time-related behaviour. Recent studies about time and international business negotiations challenge the view held by Hall, that Americans are typical M-time people and Japanese or French people typical P-time persons (e.g. Kaufman *et al.*, 1991; Bluedorn *et al.*, 1999; Kaufman and Lindquist, 1999).

An enlightening discussion of the dimensions of P-time and M-time is offered by Palmer and Schoorman (1999) who distinguish three different dimensions in Hall's M- and P-time. These dimensions include:

1. *time use preference*: referring to narrowly defined polychronicity, that is the extent to which people prefer to engage in multiple tasks simultaneously;
2. *context*: M-time is associated with low context communication, conveying only explicit meaning in messages, and P-time with high context communication, where the information that surrounds an event as well as many indirectly meaningful cues are used to interpret a messages; and
3. *time tangibility*: referring to economic time, that is the extent to which time is viewed as a commodity that can be bought, sold, saved, spent or wasted.

Palmer and Schoorman (1999) suggest that these three dimensions interact to produce eight types of individual temporality. They surveyed 258 middle and senior executives, mostly American (78 per cent), from 25 nations. They found the majority to be Type A (44 per cent): polyphasic, time urgent and low context. The next highest proportion was M1 classic monochromic (32 per cent): monochromic, time urgent and low context. Thus, it is important to look at the interaction between time use and preference.

Linearity (L) versus cyclicity (C) of time

A strongly economic view of time, when it is combined with monochronism, emphasizes the linearity of time. Time is viewed as being a line with a point at the centre (the present). Each portion of the line can be cut into slices, which are supposed to have a certain value. Basic religious beliefs play a key role in supporting such a linear view of time. Christianity has a one-shot interpretation of worldly existence. Only on the final judgement day will Christians know if they are to be granted eternal life. However, the Asian religions, including Hinduism and Buddhism, assume that on the death of the body, the soul is born again in another body. The belief in regular reincarnation, until a pure soul is allowed to escape the cycle and go to *nirvana*, radically changes the nature of time in a specific life. This is not 'all the time I have got', it is simply one of my 'times' across several lives. For most Asians, cyclicity is central in their pattern of time. *Nirvana* is the final release from the cycle of reincarnation. It is attained by extinction of all desires and individual existence, culminating in absolute blessedness (in Buddhism), or in absorption into Brahman (in Hinduism). Naturally, patience is on the side of the people believing in cyclical reincarnation of the soul. For Christians, it is more urgent to achieve, because their souls are given only one worldly life. But, as the New Testament puts it clearly, those who do right, even in the very last moment, will be considered favourably. (For examples of time use in Indonesia and the USA see WS2.2.)

Another element that favours a cyclical view of time is the degree of emphasis put on the natural rhythms of years and seasons, the sun and the moon. It largely contrasts so-called 'modern' with 'traditional' societies, in as far as 'modern' means technology, mastering nature and, to a certain extent, the loss of nature-related reference points. The Japanese are known for having maintained a strong orientation to nature, even in a highly developed society. Their floral art of *Ikebana* and the emphasis on maintaining a contact with nature, even in highly urban environments, are testimonies to their attachment to the natural rhythms of nature. Even within a country, the relationship to nature influences the model of time adopted by urban as compared with rural people.

Elements of cyclicity are based mostly on metaphysical assumptions or on astronomical observations, but they also include some arbitrary divisions, which are more social than natural. The example of the duration of the week is a good example of the social origins of time cycles. Sorokin and Merton (1937) give the following illustrations of the variability of the week in terms of the number of days.

Our system of weekly division into quantitatively equal periods is a perfect type of conventionally determined time-reckoning. The Khasi week almost universally consists of eight days because the markets are usually held every eighth day. A reflection of the fact that the Khasi week had a social, rather than a 'natural', origin is found in the names of the days of the week which are not those of planets (a late and arbitrary development) but of places where the principal markets are held. In a similar fashion the Roman week was marked by *nundinae* which recurred every eighth day and upon which the agriculturists came into the city to sell their produce. The Muysca in Bogota had a three-day week; many East African tribes a four-day week; in Central America, the east Indian Archipelago, old Assyria (and now in Soviet Russia), there is found a five-day week . . . and the Incas had a ten-day week. The constant feature of virtually all these weeks of varying length is that they were always found to have been originally in association with the market.

Elements of cyclicity of time therefore have three main origins: (1) religious assumptions about reincarnation of the soul; (2) natural rhythms of years, seasons and days; and (3) the social division of time periods, which is more arbitrary, less natural and 'given', than we assume. Time is naturally both linear and cyclical. We do not argue that one vision of time is 'better' than the other. Generally cultures have definite time patterns that combine both views, as is shown later in this section by the example of Japanese *Makimono* time, and in reading A2.4, which presents the Bantu concept of time.

Temporal orientations: Past, present, future

The perception of time also tends to be related to temporal orientations *vis-à-vis* the arrow of time. As stated by Kluckhohn and Strodtbeck (1961, pp. 13–15):

The possible cultural interpretations of temporal focus of human life break easily into the three point range of past, present and future . . . Spanish-Americans, who have been described as taking the view that man is a victim of natural forces, are also a people who place the present time alternative in first position . . . Many modern European countries . . . have strong leanings to a past orientation . . . Americans, more strongly than most people of the world, place an emphasis upon the future – a future which is anticipated to be 'bigger and better'.

Being past oriented means that people emphasize the role of the past in explaining where we are now. Europeans are typical of this assumption, as are some Asian people. They will tend to restore old buildings, invest in museums, teach history at school, etc. It does not mean that temporal orientation to the past is only based on cultural assumptions. It also depends on individual psychological traits (Usunier and Valette-Florence, 1994). Furthermore, in societies undergoing a rapid process of economic change, past orientation is often temporarily underplayed.

Present orientation is the most logical assumption, in terms of quality of life at least. It means that people favour the 'here and now', believing that the past is over and the future is uncertain, theoretical and difficult to imagine. Religion may play an important role in pushing people towards a present orientation, if it emphasizes that only God decides the future. In terms of temporal orientations, the Arabic–Muslim character has been described as fatalistic and short-term oriented (Ferraro, 1990). As stated by Harris and Moran (1987, p. 474):

Who controls time? A Western belief is that one controls his own time. Arabs believe that their time is controlled, to a certain extent, by an outside force – namely Allah – therefore the Arabs become very fatalistic in their view of time . . . Most Arabs are not clockwatchers, nor are they planners of time.

In contrast, future orientation is naturally related to the view that people can master nature, and that the future can in some way be predicted or at least significantly influenced. In societies where future orientation is strong, it is backed by the educational system and by an 'imagination of the future' supported by reports on scientific breakthroughs and technological developments.

The dimensions of past, present and future time orientation were found to be important in the Chinese Value Survey (CVS), which was developed by Michael Bond in Hong Kong to measure values suggested by Chinese scholars (Chinese Culture Connection, 1987). The purpose was to introduce a deliberate Eastern bias into value surveys that had been historically developed by Western scholars. This new instrument was tested with students in 22 countries. It uncovered a dimension they termed Confucian Work Dynamism, which corresponds to a future-orientation on one hand and a post- and present-orientation on the other. East Asian countries scored highest, followed by Western countries and finally developing countries. Hofstede (2001) in his review of the CVS referred to this as Long Term Orientation (LTO) and Short Term Orientation (STO):

Long Term Orientation stands for the fostering of virtues oriented towards future rewards, in particular, perseverance and thrift. Its opposite pole, Short Term Orientation, stands for the fostering of virtues related to the past and present, in particular, respect for tradition preservation of 'face' and fulfilling social obligations.

The following summarizes some of the main connotations of LTO differences cited in Hofstede (2001). In LTO cultures delayed gratification is accepted and long-term virtues such as frugality, perseverance, savings, investing are emphasized. The most important events in life will occur in the future and persistence is an important personality trait. Conversely, in STO cultures, immediate gratification is expected, and short-term virtues such as social consumption and spending are emphasized. The most important events in life occurred in the past or present. Several studies have found interesting correlations with these dimensions. According to Hofstede (2001, p. 351) LTO scores are strongly correlated with national economic growth: 'Long-term orientation is thus identified as a major explanation of the explosive growth of the East Asian economies in the latter part of the 20th century'.

Combined cultural models of time: The Japanese *Makimono* time

Economic time usually goes with linear time, monochronism and future orientation. It is our 'modern' time, near to R.J. Graham's (1981, p. 335) concept of the 'European-American (Anglo) perception that allows time to have a past, present and future, and to be sliced into discrete units and then allocated for specific tasks.' This view holds that time can be saved, spent, wasted or even bought, just like money. Even among the cultures that share this pattern of time, there may be significant differences. Lane and Kaufman (1992, p. 15) contrast the prevailing patterns in Northern Europe with those in the US:

The closed stores on Saturday afternoons and Sundays and short weekday hours are extremely limited by United States standards. Such customs limit the actual clock hours that are available for shopping, reduce weekend employment, etc. The result is a system which encourages recreation and/ or social time in the evenings and on weekends, particularly on Sundays. In Europe it is very common to find people taking recreational walks, bike rides, visiting a park or sitting in the cafe. These are not completely foreign to the United States, but seem to exist in Europe on a much grander scale. The use of time in quiet visiting seems to be much greater.

Graham has tried to represent a synthesis of time perception dimensions, not only as a set of different perceptual dimensions, but also as complete temporal systems. He contrasts 'Anglo' time, which he describes as being 'linear-separable', with the 'circular-traditional' time of most Latin-American countries. This perception arises from traditional cultures where action and everyday life were not regulated by the clock, but rather by the natural cycles of the moon, sun and seasons. Graham proposes a third model, 'procedural-traditional', in which the amount of time spent on an activity is irrelevant, since activities are procedure-driven rather than time driven. This system is typical of the American Indians, and to a large extent it also typifies Bantu time (reading A2.4). Graham's 'procedural-traditional' time is hardly a 'time' in the Western sense.

But it is not as simple as it might appear: some people may share different cultures and move from one time model or another, depending on the other people involved and the particular situation, tapping into different 'operating cultures' (Goodenough, 1971). As Hall states (1983, p. 58): 'The Japanese are polychronic when looking and working inward, toward themselves. When dealing with the outside world . . . they shift to the monochronic mode . . . The French are monochronic intellectually, but polychronic in behaviour.'

A naive view of Japanese temporal orientations would lead one to assume that the Japanese are simply future oriented. In fact, a very knowledgeable observer of Japanese business, Robert Ballon, argues (in Hayashi, 1988) that the Japanese are neither future nor past oriented. For him the Japanese are present oriented and focused on the here and now. Hayashi explains the difficult attempt at finding cross-culturally equivalent terms by asserting that: 'Many kinds of Japanese behaviour are extratemporaneous' (p. 2), meaning that *they are not time based*. Hayashi explains further what he calls the *Makimono* time. In their model of time, the Japanese tend to posit the future as a natural extension of the present. The Japanese are basically people who work with a cyclical view of

Figure 2.2 Japanese *Makimono* time pattern

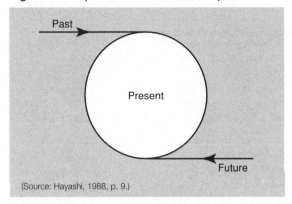

(Source: Hayashi, 1988, p. 9.)

time, based on their Buddhist background. They believe that souls of dead people transmigrate to newly born human beings, in an eternal cycle. As Hayashi states (1988, p. 10): 'In Japanese cultural time, the past flows continuously toward the present and also the present is firmly linked to the future. In philosophical terms, we might say the past and the future exist simultaneously in the present'.

Therefore, the linear-separable model of time, found in Western cultures, does not predominate in Japan. The notion of continuity is central in Japanese time, just as the notion of discontinuity is central in Western models of time. A Japanese definition would say 'the present is a temporal period that links the region of the past with the world of the future' (Hayashi, 1988, p. 18). The notion of continuity as well as the arrow of the future targeted to the present is central in the *Makimono* time pattern (Figure 2.2).

2.3

Space

The key words for space-related cultural assumptions are 'in' and 'out', member and non-member, belonging or not. Here space is meant in its most general sense: the three-dimensional expanse in which all material objects are located. Let us assume that it is mainly occupied by people, more precisely groups of people and their properties. Spaces can be physical, grouping people by a town, a county or a country. Space can also be abstract, grouping people by common characteristics including education, religion and professional associations. Space is the basis for the organizing principle of *territoriality*, which we mentioned in the previous chapter. People are by nature territorial. They must define who has ownership and control over certain spaces.

Table 2.2 contrasts space-related cultural assumptions, which correspond to four common problems and cultural orientations:

1. Whether people are insiders or outsiders (*personalization* versus *depersonalization*).
2. What the rights and obligations are for ingroup members (*ingroup orientation*).
3. Whether it is possible for outsiders to gain insider status, or a limited part of it (*concrete* versus *abstract territoriality*).
4. What the group membership conditions are for those willing to 'enter this space' (*group* versus *individualistic cultures*).

Personalization versus depersonalization

Whereas a *being* orientation results in 'personalization', a *doing* orientation results in 'depersonalization'. While we discuss each of these below, the words should be interpreted cautiously, as they will be discussed in more detail in Chapters 13 to 17 (dedicated to language and communication, advertising personal selling and international business negotiations).

'Personalization' means that assumptions about what a person can *do* (and what can be done with this person) depend fundamentally on who this person *is*. Therefore, it is of prime importance to obtain information on who this person is. Since not all is *prima facie* visible, it means that it will be necessary to spend time exploring who this person is. This is evident in cultures with a *being* orientation.

In the 'being' orientation emphasis is put on belonging, based on shared characteristics:

1. A set of people sharing family ties, a particular social class, a certain ethnic background, a religion, or a nationality.
2. Age (youngsters versus older people), sex (male versus female), marriage (married versus unmarried people).

What is specific in a strong *being* orientation is the underlying assumption that what people *are*, naturally, legitimately and forcefully, influences the roles,

Table 2.2 Space-related cultural differences

Basic problem/Cultural orientations	Contrasts across cultures
Is emphasis put on what people *do* (i.e. *doing*) or on what they *are* (i.e. *being*) based on belonging to family, age, sex, religious or social status groups?	
(a) Personalization versus depersonalization	Necessity of being personally acquainted with other people if one is to communicate and interact with them efficiently versus ability to communicate easily with unknown persons.
Who is a member of the group and what are the relevant ingroups?	
(b) Ingroup orientation	Belonging to the ingroup (or reference group: family, tribe, clan, club, professional society, nation, etc.) may be a *necessary condition* for being considered a reliable, *bona fide* partner.
How to gain membership?	
(c) Concrete versus abstract territoriality	What are the group membership conditions? For an individual who belongs to the outgroup, what are the prerequisites for assimilation (if any)?
How to deal with physical space?	
(d) Group cultures with close physical contact versus individualistic cultures desiring private space	Tendency to live near to one another, and to be undisturbed by such intimacy. Conversely, tendency to feel the need for private space around one's body, and to resent intrusion into this space (Hall, 1966).

power and capacities they have in the society. In the next chapter we will see that there is a strong link between a *being* orientation and the concept of the self and others, which mediates the *being* orientation and helps translate it into interaction models. A typical causal chain in the *being* style is: she is a woman, thus she belongs to the group of people in charge of reproduction and nurturing roles, thus she cannot work.

A strong *being* emphasis is manifested in what people call themselves and others. In many traditional societies, language designates people by a term meaning 'human being'. 'Bantu' for instance, means human being. This, more or less, assumes that others are not *real* human beings. Without going so far, the Japanese language gives a good example of a strict division between 'we' and 'they'. Japanese people call themselves *Nihon-jin* and foreigners *Gai-jin* (those from the outside). Similarly, Pakistanis in the UK call themselves *Apney* (our own people) and white English *Gorey* (Chapman and Jammal, 1997).

In contrast, 'depersonalization' means that it is not important to know who a person is, to decide what this person can *do* (and what can be done with him or her). Therefore, it is not necessary to spend a lot of time discovering who the person is (especially if time is strongly economic). 'Depersonalization' means that their belonging to certain space characteristics (class, ethnic, age groups, etc.) is considered rather unimportant compared with purely individual, non-space-related characteristics. This is evident in cultures with a *doing* orientation.

A *doing* orientation assumes that what people are *does not* naturally, nor legitimately, influence the roles, power and capacities individuals have in the society. Thus, what is important is what people can achieve, given their talents and abilities. In the purest version of the doing orientation, character and personality would be considered as unimportant in what individuals can achieve. Tasks are viewed as standard and people as interchangeable. Deeds are separated from emotions and *doing* belongs to a world of its own, radically separated from the *being*.

Ingroup orientation

Who is a member of the ingroup?
As explained by Triandis (1983, p. 144):

In every culture some people are defined as trustworthy, worthy of cooperation or even self-sacrifice for (ingroup), and other people are seen as 'outsiders' (outgroup). The basis of such distinction varies. In most cultures, tribe and family are crucial; in other cultures, nation, religion, language, or political ideology may be important; in still other cases, occupational group may be all-important. Thus the content of ingroups differs from culture to culture. Also, a person may belong to one, or to many, ingroups.

There is a natural relationship between the *being* orientation and the emphasis on group belonging, which has to do with natural law and the right of people to occupy a certain territory. The largest possible ingroups are nations. For many older countries, legitimacy is largely based on having ancestors in the place for a long time. Nationality, being legally based on *jus sanguinis* (law of the blood), may only be granted if at least one of their parents is a national. On the other hand, certain countries (e.g. the United States, Australia and France) base nationality on *jus soli* (law of the soil), that is, being born in the place is enough for a person to obtain citizenship.[3] Benefits related to nationality are strongly space-related: the right to live, work and enjoy citizenship on a definite territory. This strict opposition delineates two different ways of defining the content of the ingroup (in this case a national group): on the one hand, people emphasize blood and kin; on the other, they do not.

But ingroup orientation goes further. It is structured around kin-based loyalties and involves patterns of loyalty and obligation. The family is the most basic and smallest ingroup unit. Strong ingroup orientation is most often accompanied by a rhetoric based on family relationships, with a dominant father (outside oriented), a protective mother (inside oriented) and sisters and brothers, alternately considered as rivals within the ingroup (because they are competing for parents' love, affection and preference) and allies *vis-à-vis* the outgroup (because they share the same fundamental identity; they *are* of the same kin). The family space is that of the house and the surrounding ground: it is private but not closed to outsiders, who may enter under definite conditions.

Outgroup orientation, in contrast to ingroup orientation, is based on the assumption that there is a fundamental unity of mankind beyond the borders of ingroup spaces, including families, nations and cultures. If the two orientations are roughly opposed, it is not a complete opposition. In certain cultures they coexist, as in the Nordic European cultures, which combine a strong sense of national identity (ingroup) with a universal focus manifested in their strong commitment to peace, development of the poorest nations and international organizations (outgroup).

What does membership involve in terms of rights and obligations?
The ingroup bonds involve relationships of loyalty. This loyalty does not extend beyond the borders of the ingroup space. Loyalty is basically about showing allegiance, respecting the values of the ingroup and maintaining a sense of the honour of the group. Loyalty is fundamentally non-reciprocal: people do not expect other ingroup members' loyalty for being loyal themselves. Loyalty is not based on time, except for a sense of eternity: one may wait for 50 years to be rewarded for loyalty or one may never be rewarded; it just does not matter.

Loyalty can be based on kinship or patronage, which is often an extended form of kinship based on symbolic adoption, that is, taking another's child as one's own. The virtue manifested in loyalty is that of maintaining allegiance, even in the face of conflicts with other members of the ingroup or when experiencing unfair treatment from the most powerful members. Strong ingroup orientation increases an insider's loyalty, but simultaneously decreases the feeling of obligation towards outsiders. Morality is space related. It might, for instance, be considered as perfectly virtuous to lie to or steal from people to whom no loyalty is owed. The Mafia is a good illustration of an ingroup-oriented society. Morality is based on a set of values favouring strict loyalty, treason being punished by death sentence; the godfather who has ordered it goes to the burial ceremony because he still 'loves' the betrayer. Ingroup orientation partly explains behavioural relativity. Some national groups have a reputation for their compliant behaviour at home (where rules are strictly enforced) and for looser conduct when abroad. When they are away, they no longer feel the need to observe the rules that apply at home. They also consider that, when out of the ingroup space where bonds and loyalty are strong, they do not need to respect others' rules (even those that are similar to their ingroups) since outsiders do not deserve loyalty or even interest and respect.

Rights and obligations may be defined according to membership of particular ethnic groups, as in Africa, where only certain ingroups are allowed to be merchants. Mistrust of and disdain for retail activities explain why merchants are most often foreigners (Lebanese in West Africa, Indians in Zaire), particular local ethnic groups (Dioulas in Ivory Coast) or women (the 'mama Benz' in Benin).

Ingroup or outgroup orientation has a deep influence on the system of ethics and morality in a particular society. Impersonal rules applied by judges to people irrespective of the group to which they belong are typical of low ingroup orientation. A typical case where such orientations are important is when a family member has committed some crime, the family knows about it, but there is no evidence; what does the family do: denounce one of its members or keep silent?

Outgroup orientation values universal rules, applied to everybody. Human rights ethics are a typical feature of outgroup orientation. Objectivity and reciprocity are preferred over loyalty; or, to put it another way, loyalty is not to the group, not to people, but to the impersonal rules and values that govern the society as a whole, which is largely why the terms above are 'personalization' (people orientation) versus 'depersonalization' (rule orientation). However, people with an outgroup orientation, precisely because they have a more 'depersonalized' approach, are more sensitive to the problems of other human beings, far from their own space. Their tendency to behave in a more universal way, in no way means that they are less human.

These differences have a major impact on international business negotiations and personal selling, in particular in relation to how to make contacts. What information should be sought if one is to understand connections between the people one confronts? How are decisions made in a particular ingroup? These differences also impact consumer behaviour, especially where ingroup orientation exerts pressure on consumers' attitudes and buying decisions. Any society combines to various degrees, ingroup and outgroup

orientation and organizes them in particular ways. For example, 'affirmative action, equal opportunity' is a strong outgroup motto, typical of the US. However, the global rule is still that human beings cannot choose their favourite nationality. Yet if such a choice were available, it would be the purest form of outgroup orientation.

Pitfalls of excessive ingroup and outgroup orientations

Because extreme positions in space-related assumptions present drawbacks, there is always a combination of both, to varying degrees. On one hand, the pitfalls of ingroup orientation are: (1) tribalism – only people of an ingroup based on kin are considered worth interacting with and caring for; (2) localism – only people belonging to a small geographical unit are considered interesting people; and (3) provincialism – only values and behaviour that are in use in the community are considered appropriate. On the other hand, the pitfalls of excessive outgroup orientation are: (1) unrealistic universalism – the complete cancelling of borders will produce global welfare: a highly dubious assumption;[4] and (2) global village ethnocentrism – if we 'see' what happens everywhere on Earth at any moment a global consciousness will emerge; unfortunately although images are global, a common interpretation of them is not.

Concrete versus abstract territoriality

If people are very territorial, it is important to know how to gain access to them, even as an external partner, such as a business partner in a joint venture (bearing in mind that loyalty and morality are mostly values that are applicable to group members only). Group membership may be gained on the basis of either concrete or abstract territoriality. If we combine the ingroup/outgroup and the being/doing divides, a simple contrast is as follows:

1. When ingroup and being orientation are strong, membership is mostly gained on the basis of *concrete territoriality*.
2. When outgroup and doing orientation are strong, membership is based on *abstract territoriality*.

If membership is based on *concrete territoriality*, some necessary characteristics are innate or cannot be acquired by adult people, simply because the criteria are related to birth, socialization and education within the ingroup. In cases where it is impossible to gain membership, one must behave as a friendly and realistic outsider, who can target three possible positions in the long run:

1. A 'tolerated outsider' who is considered as different but useful for practical purposes. This status allows comfortable relationships and, in most cases, is a possible role for developing business. But two aspects have to be kept in mind: (a) such people should not imitate insider status or try to acquire it by too active an involvement in the community – 'proactive outsiders' will be reminded, at some stage, of their limited status as a full person; and (b) they should not play insider people off against each other to acquire power and influence: in general, they should not attempt to take advantage of conflict in the ingroup; ingroup conflicts are considered 'in-house business', not to be shown overtly, and never to be solved to an outsider's benefit.

2. A 'recognized outsider': this status is closer to membership, yet is still far from it. Generally a 'recognized outsider' will have been living in the culture for a long period of time, will speak the language fluently and will have established strong relational networks. At a conference some years ago, Robert J. Ballon, a Belgian Jesuit living in Japan for more than 30 years and knowledgeable about Japanese business (mentioned above in relation to Japanese time patterns), explained how he was always considered a pure foreigner, despite his profound knowledge of Japanese society and his very deep involvement with the country. 'Recognized outsiders' often serve the purpose of ambassadors, cultural translators or mediators from the outside world of foreign groups to the ingroup. They are recognized as useful and friendly people by the insiders, yet they would lose their usefulness if they were to become insiders.

3. 'Newly accepted insiders' have taken a further step, crossing the cultural group border. They often can do so because they crossed early enough to be considered as still educable persons, suitable for a profound transformation of their being, as in the case of foreigners who arrived as young adults, completed their education and married locally.

Such persons will, however, remain somewhat on the fringes, near to the external borders of the cultural community, often considered as adequate ambassadors or mediators from the ingroup to outgroups.

Membership based on *doing* and *abstract territoriality* corresponds largely to 'modern culture': outgroup orientation is highly valued and ingroup orientation is often, too quickly, equated with narrow-mindedness, provincialism, hostility towards foreigners and the like. What people have *done* up to now is evidenced by their curriculum vitae (CV). The interview guide for affirmative action compliance programmes considers as discriminatory such enquiries of applicants concerning age, citizenship, marital status, birthplace, education that is not job related, language, etc. – information that, in most countries outside the United States, is considered legitimate for ascertaining who the applicant *is*. In France, CVs include this information and are accompanied by a photograph and a handwritten letter, which is sometimes used for assessing the person's character by means of graphology.

Abstract territoriality is mostly based on professional achievements, evidenced by diplomas, membership of professional bodies, being an alumnus of an ivy-league university, and so on. The epitome of abstract territoriality is represented by the *golden boys*. For them *insider* trading is a fraud, showing that the use of their natural ingroup advantages is viewed as evil. The space of 'golden boys' is a mix of top MBA schools, market dealing rooms and a 'club of people constantly connected worldwide'. We can only imagine the profound differences between the 'golden boy' and the Bengali farmer.

Business school graduates (*Grandes écoles* in France), or those holding the title of doctor in Germany belong to these 'modern groups' that are based on doing and competence rather than being, age, sex and group membership. It is assumed that access to membership is organized on a non-discriminatory and objective basis and that it is in the best interest of society as a whole because the 'best people' are doing the 'appropriate job'. However, even in a *doing* framework, relational competence never disappears in favour of pure professional competence, simply because managing relationships is a dark side yet an important part of the *doing* competences. Paradoxically, when abstract territoriality is very strong, it largely re-creates primitive ingroup behaviour, but based on different criteria. The world of academia, for instance, is very 'out-groupist' for sex, nationality, religion or age, but it is very 'ingroupist' when it comes to doctoral degrees and the journals where people publish.

Group membership assumptions are important for marketing negotiations, when facing a national competitive environment as a foreign firm, for making public relations contacts, for the recruitment and promotion of salespeople, especially in Africa and the Middle East, and for any situation involving business ethics. The favouring of one party over another, on the ground of personal relationship, in either political or economic affairs, is viewed dimly – indeed it is often called corruption – by outgroup-oriented people, whereas it remains standard practice for ingroup-oriented people.

Group versus individualistic cultures

Territoriality refers also to possessiveness, control and authority over an area of physical space. Individuals need to refer to culture based rules concerning space because they have to defend their space against invasion or misuse by others. Chapman and Jamal (1997, p. 141) illustrate the impact of misinterpreted boundaries in their discussion of Pakistani immigrants in Bradford, UK:

the immigrants found the Bradford 'garden' incomprehensible. The immigrants perceived the frontier between the private domestic space and the public space to be the house-wall itself. The garden was treated as 'outside' the domestic space; the garden hedge, wall or fence, so carefully tended and guarded by the host community, was irrelevant; it was a classificatory boundary that was, in important senses, invisible. In consequence, the immigrants treated the 'garden' as a place to put things that were not desired in the house; this included household waste (food remains, general household rubbish), unwanted furniture, old mattresses, and so on.

The 'language of space' is culturally determined and provides the codes concerning social distance, such as how far should one stand from other people in order to respect their area of private space? A complete approach to relations with space was proposed by Edward T. Hall (1966) in *The Hidden Dimension*. In this book he developed the concept of 'proxemics'

– the term he coined for the interrelated observations and theories of man's use of space as a specialized elaboration of culture. According to Hall, in Western cultures, there are three primary zones of space: the intimate zone (0 to 18 inches; 0–45 cm), the personal zone (18 inches to 3 feet; 0.45–1 m), and the social zone (3 to 6 feet; 1–2 m). Touch can occur for westerners in the intimate and personal zones, but sensory involvement and communication is less intense in the social zone. (For more information on proxemics and US culture see *WS2.3.*)

In fact, what differs across cultures in terms of physical space assumptions is the following:

1. What are the sizes of the three zones? To what extent do they overlap?
2. Who is allowed to enter these zones of physical space?
3. What is considered adequate sensory exchange within definite interpersonal distances?

The last question is important in marketing terms. It relates to the senses (sight, sound, touch and smell), in as much as sensory perception is directly related to interpersonal distance. Americans, for instance, are famous for their suppression of personal odours in public spaces and this has created a mass market for room deodorizers, antiperspirants, mouthwashes and deodorants. Although smell suppression is globally 'modern', having also developed strongly outside the United States, it is not clear whether it will remain so in the future, with people striving for a more natural expression of themselves. Chapter 9, which deals with product policy, gives examples of how our sense of physical space mixes with sensory codes in a culturally significant way that enables consumers to attribute meaning to product characteristics.

The list of basic space-related cultural assumptions in Table 2.2 is not exhaustive. Some other aspects need to be mentioned. The availability of inhabitable physical space and the density of population vary greatly across countries, with profound impact on material culture. The high population density in Japan and in many Asian countries has made it essential to make things 'smaller' so that more can fit in. The assumption is that 'smaller is better'. This is one important reason why the Japanese have such a talent for miniaturizing objects. As shown in Chapter 12, Japanese space limitations at least partly explain the distribution system that prevails in that country. Conversely, the availability of space and other resources in North America is a reason for the largeness of objects, be they cars, restaurant servings, or advertising billboards. The prevalent assumption that 'bigger is better' is probably a significant background explanation for the failure of US car manufacturers to adapt to smaller car sizes after the oil crisis of the mid-1970s.

Contrasts in physical spaces should also be considered carefully in physically heterogeneous countries. A good example is Nepal, which has both the Himalaya mountains and subtropical plains in Tharuwan province near to India. Cultures adapt to their existing reality. The Nepali mountain people exhibit, on average, different values and behaviour from people in the lower areas. Their interpersonal solidarity and work orientation are stronger, because people would not survive otherwise.

A last area where significant space-related cultural differences are displayed can be found in urban planning. This includes how towns are organized and how urban and rural landscapes are integrated and interrelated.

2.4

Cultural borrowing and change in societies

It would be wrong to give the impression that cultures are truly different and exclusive in their assumptions. Through time and space, cultures intermingle. Negative events such as wars and colonization convey cultural exchange. It is fascinating to consider the naivety with which, in the process of cultural borrowing, successful cultural artefacts are borrowed from other cultures without the cultural assumptions underlying these artefacts being understood or even imagined. Yan (1991, pp. 51–2) for instance, quotes the reformer Liang Quichao, who wrote in 1897 on the subject of European countries, considered, unlike China, as innovative:

In innovative countries the sovereigns are wise, their mandarins faithful and courageous, their people intelligent and heroic, their politics successful, their business prosperous, their products excellent, etc. Travel in their country brings you such pleasure and joy that you forget to return home. Will you then pose further questions as to the prosperity of these countries?

Isolated cultures, united cultures

Cultures are rarely pure, except in a few areas where people have been almost untouched by foreign influences. An example of such cultural isolation might be Japan, which, during the era of the Tokugawa shoguns, withdrew from all contact with outside people and cultures. The Tokugawa period lasted for more than two centuries before the Meiji era, which began in 1868 and initiated a period of increased accessibility of foreign influences to Japan. Reischauer, a specialist in Japanese history, explains in his book *Japan: Past and present* (1946, 1990) that two centuries of complete peace were enforced with extreme vigour by the Tokugawa regime. The Tokugawa shoguns have left their mark on the behaviour of the Japanese people. In the sixteenth century the Japanese were keen, adventurous and somewhat bellicose. By the nineteenth century they had become docile and humble subjects, awaiting orders from their hierarchical superiors, which they implemented resignedly. Reischauer hypothesizes that the collective regimentation under the Tokugawa shoguns led to an inward-looking people who indulged in conformism, which served as consensus. He further notes that, at the beginning of the nineteenth century, antagonism in Japanese society was almost non-existent: the rules of propriety were strictly observed, and violence was extremely rare. Reischauer argues that when the Japanese were confronted with an unknown situation, they displayed very little ability to adapt, much less than other peoples.[5] The Tokugawa period appears good in many ways, especially as regards the general level of education and the development of the arts. However, it largely interrupted the natural evolution of economic and social change. The Tokugawa shoguns preserved an outdated political and social order. Only after the beginning of the Meiji era in 1868 did the Japanese begin to interact with Europeans, who had achieved enormous advances in scientific knowledge during the previous two centuries. The succession of these two periods, one of great isolation and one of openness towards foreign cultures, probably explains the paradoxical relationship of the Japanese with international trade and marketing. In one sense they are very ethnocentric, but simultaneously they are quite capable of overcoming their ethnocentrism to become, ultimately, highly successful international marketers.

In many other cases, cultures do mix. Contact may be bellicose, owing to the conflicting interests of countries and their cultures (religion, language, social and political systems) over borders. The perennial conflicts between the region south of the Mediterranean Sea (mostly Arab and Muslim) and the northern region (mostly Christian) are an example of this pattern of conflict and cooperation. That is, cultural encounters occur even in wartime. When besieged by the Turks in the fifteenth century, the Viennese were introduced by their opponents to a new, tasty and stimulating beverage known as coffee. It is through the Viennese as intermediaries that coffee was introduced into the West. Even during the Crusades (tenth to twelfth centuries), warriors on both sides had quiet moments during which they enjoyed each other's food. In *The Crusades through Arab Eyes* (1985, pp. 128–9), Amine Maalouf describes how the Templars grew accustomed to understanding and accepting the customs and beliefs of the Muslims. In the following extract, Templars, although themselves Christians, side with a Muslim visiting Jerusalem, the Damascene emir Usamah, in defending Islamic religious practices:

When I was visiting Jerusalem, I used to go to Al-Aqsa mosque, where my Templar friends were staying. Along one side of the building was a small oratory in which the *Franj* [an Arab word designating the French, or more generally European, Crusaders] had set up a church. The Templars placed this spot at my disposal so that I might say my prayer. One day I entered, said *Allahu Akbar*, and was about to begin my prayer, when a man, a *Franj*, threw himself upon me, and turned to the east, saying, 'Thus do we pray.' The Templars rushed forward and led him away. I then set myself to prayer once more, but this man, seizing upon a moment of inattention, threw himself upon me yet again, turned my face to the east, and repeated once more, 'Thus do we pray.' Once again the Templars intervened, led him away, and apologized to me, saying, 'He is a foreigner. He has just arrived from the land of the *Franj* and he has never seen anyone pray without turning his face to the east.' I answered that I had prayed enough and left, stunned by the behaviour of this demon who had been so enraged at seeing me pray while not facing the direction of Mecca.

Cultural borrowing is general . . . and disguised

The basic requirement for the introduction of a new cultural item (a product, a lifestyle, a word, a dance,

a song) is that it looks (and in fact is) coherent with the culture that adopts it. That is why cultural borrowing is often disguised, by a change of name or by means of 'reinvention', whereby a local inventor/discoverer is *found*. It is fascinating to see how many countries seek to claim credit for particular inventions (the Xerox machine, for instance) at the same time. (For examples of cultural borrowing see *WS2.4.*)

One may view culture as the accumulation of the best possible solutions to the common problems faced by the members of a particular society. This definition, very Anglo-Saxon in its problem-solving orientation, does have an advantage: it emphasizes the 'shopping' aspect of cultural dynamics. This concept is illustrated by Savishinsky (1998, p. 371) who describes the 'spiritual pilgrimage' of the Nacirema (to read more about their body rituals see A1.3): 'While the Nacirema generally took great pride in their culture, they were also uneasy and restless about it, and unsure whether people in other tribes might be enjoying some things that they didn't even know about . . . the Nacirema liked to leave the homeland they loved so much in order to search for clues to a better life.' Similarly, perhaps, young Australians often spend lengthy periods of time abroad, immersing themselves in foreign cultures and diverse lifestyles their own geographical isolation would otherwise not have allowed them to experience.

There have always been different kinds of travellers (explorers, warriors, merchants, colonials, etc.) who have brought back foreign innovations to their native country. Usually by accident, and sometimes by an almost systematic process, societies may find good imported solutions, as the Japanese have, because they are very conscious of their insularity and cultural isolation. For instance, Jeans, as informal trousers for casual wear, have made their way through all cultures. The fabric originally came from France (*de Nîmes* – denim) and the name from Italy – short for Jean Fustian from Genes (Genoa). Afterwards this 'American' invention made its way back to Italy and most other countries of the world.

Some words and concepts are easily borrowed in their original form despite being obviously related to some well-established stereotype of a particular country: *ersatz* (the high reputation of German chemistry), *leitmotiv* (German music), *showbiz* (US dominance), *élégance* (the French reputation for style), *kamikaze* or *hara-kiri* (the Japanese capacity for self-sacrifice), *mamma* (the Italian sense of the motherly role in the family). Sherry and Camargo (1987) show that the English language has had a profound influence on Japanese marketing: they report a heavy use of English loanwords in Japanese promotional texts and labels. *Mai* (English 'my'), for instance, is used extensively in compounds such as *mai homu* (my home), because the Japanese equivalent would sound too selfish and stress the private over the collective. Beyond the imported word, it is the foreign value, individualism that is also imported.

Although cultural opportunism is understandable, it is often hidden by the need to maintain cultural identity. Few societies are prepared to accept that a large part of their culture is really foreign: cultural borrowing is therefore somewhat hypocritical or at least disguised. Thus, cultural borrowings are disguised and they finally disappear. Numerous words, goods and even lifestyles (the 'weekend', for instance) have been largely borrowed. Such words as 'magazine' and 'assassin' have been directly imported from Arabic. During the Crusades, the Crusaders played endless games of dice, which Arabs call *az-zahar*: a word that the *Franj* adopted to designate not the game itself but *hazard*, the concept of chance (Maalouf, 1985). The example of the Japanese borrowing of Chinese writing more than fifteen centuries ago is a true example of imitation, but also of reinterpretation, which makes this appropriation a genuine element of Japanese culture (see Box 2.1).

The Japanese, when they first read ideograms (which they later called *kanji*) did not immediately recognize them as representing *ideas*, but experienced them more directly as *sounds*. Therefore the *kanji* system works as a pictogram system representing both ideas and sounds. It is further completed by two syllabaries, which represent only sounds: *hiragana* for native words and *katakana* for imported words. The *katakana* syllabary is typical of the Japanese attitude towards cultural imports: they do not object (as the

---

Box 2.1

The origins of Japanese writing

The Japanese write their language with ideograms they borrowed from China nearly two thousand years ago. Some two thousand years before that, the ancient Chinese had formed these ideograms, or characters, from pictures of things they knew. To them the sun had looked like this ☼, so this became their written word for **sun**. This form was gradually squared off and simplified to make it easier to write, changing its shape to 日. This is still the way the word sun is written in both China and Japan today.

The ancient Chinese first drew a tree like this ⚇. This was also gradually simplified and squared, to 木 which became the written word for **tree**. To form the word for **root** or **origin** the Chinese just drew in more roots at the bottom of the tree to emphasize this portion of the picture, 本, then squared and simplified the character to 本. This became the written word for **root** or **origin**. When the characters for **sun** 日 and **origin** 本 are put together in a compound they form the written word 日本, **Japan**, which means literally origin-of-the-sun. A picture of the sun in the east at sunrise coming up behind a tree 🌲 forms the written word for **east** 東. A picture of the stone lantern that guarded each ancient Chinese capital 髙 squared off and simplified to abstract form 京, forms the written word for **capital**. These two characters put together in a compound form the written word 東京, Eastern-capital, TÔKYÔ. The characters may look mysterious and impenetrable at first approach, but as these examples show, they are not difficult at all to understand. The characters are not just random strokes: each one is a picture, and has a meaning based on the content of the picture. The Japanese written language contains a number of these characters, but fortunately not as many as Westerners often assume. To graduate from grammar school a student must know 881 characters. At this point he is considered literate. A high school graduate must know 1,850. To read college textbooks, about three thousand characters are necessary. All these thousands of characters, however, are built up from less than 300 elements, or pictures, many of which are seldom used.

(Source: Len Walsh, 1969. Reproduced with permission.)

French do, for instance), but at the same time it is a necessity to signal clearly the foreign origin of some words and concepts by writing such words in *katakana*, which represent the same syllables as *hiragana* (an apparent waste of effort).

Other examples of cultural borrowing are numerous: music, clothes, architecture, building techniques, food, recipes, etc. Borrowing sometimes goes as far as pure and simple copying, and possibly product counterfeiting. The Japanese have been remarkably skilful at borrowing European music, becoming the most important producers of musical instruments worldwide. Even castañets – an ethnically Spanish product – are made in Japan for sale in Spain.

With the advent of the Internet and e-commerce, the potential for cultural borrowing has expanded exponentially (Borenstein and Saloner, 2001). For example, e-books may evolve to have built-in translators and culture-specific annotations, so that they adapt to different modes of thought and reading styles (Ohler, 2001). In this case, the reader would have no idea of its origin. Still, there appears to be resistance to this change, even within universities, where computer competencies are much higher than in the general population.

2.5
Cultural hostility

Limits to borrowing clearly appear when it is seen as a threat to cultural coherence. This is especially true of religious practices, social morals and even daily customs. For instance, it is not easy to import polygamy or clitoral excision for babies into cultures where monogamy and child protection are strongly established practices. As previously stated, there must be a minimum level of coherence and homogeneity in cultural assumptions and behaviour if people are to synchronize themselves and live peacefully together.

In fact, cultural similarity has been found to influence many factors, including the attractiveness of markets (Swift, 1999), relationship development (Anderson and Weitz, 1989), international co-operation (Van Oudenhoven and Van der Zee, 2002), trade relationships (Yu and Zietlow, 1995; Martinez-Zarzoso, 2003) and country image (Wong and Lamb, 1983). For example, Swift (1999) examined export

business managers perceptions of cultural closeness (using twenty cultural elements, including language, religion, food, drink, politics, etc.). They found that managers tended to like those overseas markets they perceived as more similar. In reality, this relationship is not as simple as it sounds. Cultural similarity has been viewed in terms of distance, but it is not an objective symmetrical distance (Shenkar, 2001). The extent of perceived similarity or distance can be influenced by many factors, including the tolerance of other cultures, the extent of interaction, cultural 'attractiveness', and the geographical proximity (Shenkar, 2001). In fact, some countries might be similar in many aspects of culture, but the proximity of their borders may increase their perceptions of cultural distance and their hostility.

Racism

Racism is often confused with cultural hostility, whereas in fact it precedes cultural hostility. But cultural hostility does not necessarily imply racism: one may be hostile to people of (some) other cultures, without being a racist. Behind racism there is a theory: that, because of their race (i.e. physiology), some human beings are inferior at various levels (intelligence, creative abilities, moral sense, etc.). The theories of Gobineau and Hitler's *Mein Kampf* are writings that clearly developed and propagated racist views (for information on *Mein Kampf* see WS1.4). The following passage on slavery, written by Montesquieu in 1748 (book XV, ch. 5, p. 242, my emphasis), exemplifies racism:

> Were I to vindicate our right to make slaves of the Negroes, these should be my arguments. The Europeans, having extirpated the Americans, were obliged to make slaves of the Africans, for clearing such vast tracts of land. Sugar would be too dear, if the plants which produce it were cultivated by any other than slaves. These creatures are all over black, and with such a flat nose, that they can scarcely be pitied. *It is hardly to be believed that God who is a wise being, should place a good soul, in such a black ugly body.*

Racist theses and opinions have been progressively abandoned (as scientific theories, at least) over the last two centuries. An issue that is still discussed is that of differing intellectual capacity among people of different races or ethnic groups. It is always measured by IQ tests, which are of Western/US origin. Although observed differences across ethnic groups are indisputable, their explanation is debated: some people argue about genetic differences being the explanatory variable, others attribute these differences to a series of non-genetic factors (Segall *et al.*, 1990). Environmental factors, for instance, such as the absence of a formal education system, on average tend to diminish IQ scores. Such detrimental factors are often found among groups with low and median IQ scores.

The IQ test itself is biased in as much as it penalizes, by its very construction, those who have been designated from the start as 'culturally inferior'. The IQ test does not take into account many skills and competences that were unknown to the authors of the test. Moreover, recent studies show that the *inter-individual* variability of genetic characteristics is much larger than the *inter-racial* groups' variability (Segall *et al.*, 1990, p. 102). In other words, genetic differences among Europeans, or genetic differences among South African Zulus, are *automatically* significantly higher than the genetic differences between the average European and the average Zulu – a strong anti-racist argument.[6] (For a free web-based IQ test see WS2.0.)

Cultural hostility

In contrast to racism, cultural hostility does not imply prior prejudices as to who is inferior or superior according to race or culture. Culture is part of one's own patrimony as a person. There is a strong affective dimension, when one feels that one's proper cultural values are threatened. This feeling may result from either of the following:

1. Simple interactions with people whose cultural values are quite different. One does not feel at ease, communication is experienced as burdensome and there is little empathy. A defensive response may then develop, frequently the case of unconscious (and minor) cultural hostility.
2. Collective reactions. Cases are so numerous worldwide that it would need many pages to quote them exhaustively: Transylvanian Hungarians and Romanians, people in ex-Yugoslavia, Armenians of High Karabakh and Azeris of the Azerbaijan enclave in Soviet Armenia; Walloons and Flemings in Belgium; Protestant and Catholic communities

in Ulster; etc. *Identity is a matter of culture rather than race.*

It is not only territorial conflicts but also economic competition that may cause cultural hostility. The Japanese are sometimes considered negatively in the United States, which has a large trade imbalance with Japan. In his controversial best-selling book, *The Japan that Can Say No*, Shintaro Ishihara (1991) argues that anti-Japanese racial prejudice is the main cause of 'Japan-bashing' in the United States. (For more information on Japan bashing, pamophjobis and other forms of cultural hostility see WS2.5.) Ishihara, a member of the Japanese diet, quotes what he said to politicians in Washington (p. 27):

I admit that Caucasians created modern civilization, but what bothers me is you seem to think that heritage makes you superior. In the thirteenth century, however, the Mongols under Genghis Khan and his successors overran Russia and Eastern Europe Caucasians adopted Mongol-style haircuts and shaved eyebrows . . . Just as Orientals of today are crazy about the clothing and hairstyle of the Beatles, Michael Jackson and Sting, Occidentals of Genghis Khan times copied Mongolian ways.

Cultural hostility, when directed at successful nations, is often a fairly ambiguous feeling, whereby admiration and envy for the other's achievements go along with contempt for many traits of the envied people and obvious unwillingness to understand the root causes of the other's success. This also results in naive copies of selected cultural artefacts as magical ways of becoming stronger – in *Robinson Crusoe* savages were about to eat Man Friday in order to gain his qualities. In the case of immigrants, Mauviel (1991, p. 73, our translation) comments on the frequent confusion between racism and cultural hostility:[7]

the dominant ideology has been so interiorized that a new, very subtle rhetoric enables us to avoid any direct, frank response to the problems concerning immigrants – the most important issue is not to be accused of 'racism'. And one places under this word the most dissimilar elements, which often have nothing to do with race in its biological acceptance . . . The media especially like the meaningless expression 'everyday racism'. As for the phrase 'ethnic group', which has replaced the word 'race', those who use the expression would have a hard time trying to define it.

There are differences across countries: Mauviel shows that the Italians are not so reluctant to speak openly on cultural hostility problems. The Italian press 'lets reality be seen, it does not cover it with an embarrassed veil, it allows the publication of the most diverse opinions'. He describes, for instance, the case of the Nigerian women at Chambave (near Torino), which 'as revealed by the press, demonstrates the irresponsibility of those who vow to have multiracial or multi-ethnic societies' (Box 2.2).

Part 4 further examines the mechanism of cultural hostility, which is sometimes increased by language and communication problems. Intercultural misunderstandings may stem from a lack of competency in the other's language, or from the natural tendency to adopt defensive stereotypes. It often results in a snowballing cultural hostility.

Box 2.2

Nigerian women of Chambave

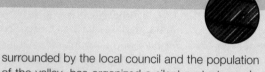

Hundreds, if not thousands, of Nigerian women – graduates in chemistry, law and other subjects, nurses, etc. – came to Italy in search of a better life. Most of them end up walking the streets, or are love traders on the *tangenziali*, the freeways round cities, and even on country roads. The most striking example to me, because of its symbolic meaning, is that of the 'train of sin', from Turin to Aosta, which brings thirty to forty Nigerian women every summer evening on the 9.15 p.m. bus to Chambave, which is located between Aosta and San Vincenzo; they are joining their 'shift' on highway 26. These *pendolari del amore* (commuters) have lost the dream that they previously held, namely that of being salespeople for Italian shoes. One should not be astonished that the mayor [of Chambave],

surrounded by the local council and the population of the valley, has organized a silent protest march. However, there is clearly a flourishing market, if one just looks at the evidence of the numerous cars with roaring engines that wait for the women. One may guess what the relations are between this village of nine hundred people and the African women, who are no longer prepared to accept being kept out of sight. In these matters, the most shocking hypocrisy is the rule; only conspicuous incidents that attract people's attention, like those at Chambave, help us to become aware of these new forms of shameful exploitation, a direct consequence of the under-development of the countries of the South.

(Source: Mauviel, 1991, pp. 81–2.)

Questions

1. Discuss cultural variation in the solutions that have been found across societies to the four common problems listed below:
   (a) How to secure oneself (to feel secure, subjectively, and to protect oneself, objectively) against unforeseeable negative events (a grave illness, an incident, etc.).
   (b) How to treat the eldest in the community, when they cannot work any more.
   (c) Who should have access to education, on what criteria, and how should its cost be financed, given that the resources available for education, private and public, are not infinite? To what extent should education be given to *all* members of a particular society, irrespective of their age, social class and personal capacities? On which bases should access to education be organized?
   (d) How should couples, the basic unit for the reproduction of the species, be formed? What role should love, common ethnic or social belonging, age or (even) sex play in such a process?

2. Discuss the marketing implications of differing cultural solutions to points (a) and (b) in question 1, in terms of the existence of certain products or services, provided by the market, the state or mutual bodies, organized within the family group or by a traditional community.

3. What is the influence of space availability (mostly determined by population density in a definite country or area) on material culture? Give examples.

4. Indicate how the following products and services are 'loaded' with time, in terms of time used in consumption, time-saving device, durability, waiting time, seasonality, time projections in the past and the future, etc. (as an example, Box 7.1 describes the time load in life insurance policies):
   (a) a dishwashing machine;
   (b) a haircut;
   (c) obtaining cash from your bank;
   (d) spending two-week vacations at *Club Méditerranée;*
   (e) fresh orange juice versus dried orange juice (i.e. concentrated powder).

5. How would you expect consumer behaviour to vary across cultures for the five products/services above? (Cite one example per case.)

6. You try to park your car. A sign indicates that parking in this area is limited to 15 minutes. Another sign reads: 'Long term parking, 300 metres'. What do these explicit signs suggest concerning temporal culture in this country?

7. Define what would be the most important criteria for recruitment in a being-oriented society as compared with a doing-oriented society.

8. In most countries, police and judiciary positions are subject to a condition of nationality (being a national is a requirement for entering the service) whereas in universities and research centres positions are open to applicants regardless of their nationality. Why?

9. Find examples of cultural borrowing (in everyday life, in the press, in people's behaviour, in work as well as leisure activities, the arts, etc.).

10. The scooter was invented just after the Second World War on a Californian airport, by putting a body on a motorcycle; this allowed quick movement on the tarmac. The invention was industrially developed by the Italians in the 1950s and 1960s. In the 1970s, the Japanese began to sell scooters worldwide. What does this suggest in terms of cultural borrowing?

11. Try to elaborate on the following assertion: 'The usual traffic in marketing and business texts is that this generally starts with the American text and this is then translated into other languages or sometimes used in the original version'. What are the problems likely to be encountered by non-US educators and practitioners when using such materials? On the other hand, what are the advantages of using them?

Notes

1. This aphorism (my translation) is attributed to the Swedish writer Selma Lagerlöf by Karl Petit (1960, p. 100). Selma Lagerlöf is the author of, among other works, *Gösta Berling* (1957), Editions Je sers: Paris, a unique account of the Swedish soul.
2. The concept of time, and therefore of time-related behaviour, has been studied in numerous fields (Jacoby *et al.*, 1976; Feldman and Hornik, 1981). Contributions are to be found in such diverse disciplines as psychology, economics, sociology, theology, linguistics, mathematics, physics, literature and anthropology.
3. In the real world nationality laws are much more complicated and, in many cases, combine the two bases, kin and soil, as relevant criteria for the award of nationality.
4. The rules of the GATT, the General Agreement on Tariffs and Trade, are partly based on such open-space assumptions.
5. Reischauer's book is now published under the title *Japan: The story of a nation*. The text has been updated since it was first published as *Japan, Past and present*, and the new version does not contain the ideas about the consequences of the Tokugawa period on Japanese behaviour, perhaps because they were resented by Japanese readers. Even distant historical events and periods may still be controversial today, when different interpretations are at stake.
6. See ch. 5 of Segall *et al.* (1990, pp. 93–112), which asks 'Are there racial differences in cognition?' and offers an in-depth review of the empirical studies of the difference in intellectual performance across ethnic groups.
7. Mauviel remarks that numerous studies have been dedicated to immigrant populations as such, but little research is concerned with the relations between the native lower-class population and the immigrant communities (this is true of France, and probably many other countries). This explains why we know little about cultural hostility, which has been more or less taboo as a research topic, probably because of the fear that unveiling somewhat negative attitudes could encourage their expression. This taboo is especially strong in countries with a significant colonial history (the United Kingdom, France, the Netherlands), which explains a certain feeling of guilt.
8. The rationales behind the alternative explanations for A2.1, A2.2 and A2.3 can be found in section A3.3.

References

Anderson, E. and B. Weitz (1989), 'Determinants of continuity in conventional industrial channel dyads', *Marketing Science*, vol. 8, pp. 310–23.

Attali, Jacques (1982), *Histoires du Temps*, Librairie Arthème Fayard: Paris.

Bluedorn, Allen C. (1998), 'An interview with anthropologist Edward T. Hall', *Journal of Management Inquiry*, vol. 7, no. 2, pp. 109–15.

Bluedorn, Allen C., Thamas J. Kalliath, Michal J. Strube and Gregg D. Martin (1999), 'Polychronicity and the Inventory of Polychronic Values (IPV): the development of an instrument to measure a fundamental dimension of organizational culture', *Journal of Managerial Psychology*, vol. 14, no. 314, pp. 205–18.

Borenstein, Severin and Garth Saloner (2001), 'Economics and electronic commerce', *Journal of Economic Perspectives*, vol. 15, no. 1, pp. 3–12.

Brislin, Richard W., Kenneth Kushner, Craig Cherrie and Mahealani Yong (1986), *Intercultural Interactions: A practical guide*, Sage: Newbury Park, CA.

Chapman, Malcom and Ahmad Jamal (1997), 'Acculturation: cross cultural consumer perceptions and the symbolism of domestic space', *Advances in Consumer Research*, vol. 24, pp. 138–43.

Chinese Culture Connection (1987), 'Chinese values and the search for culture-free dimensions of culture', *Journal of Cross-Cultural Psychology*, vol. 18, pp. 143–74.

Feldman, Lawrence P. and Jacob Hornik (1981), 'The use of time: an integrated conceptual model', *Journal of Consumer Research*, vol. 7, March, pp. 407–19.

Ferraro, Gary P. (1990), *The Cultural Dimension of International Business*, Prentice Hall: Englewood Cliffs, NJ.

Goodenough, Ward H. (1971), *Culture, Language and Society*, Modular Publications, no. 7, Addison-Wesley: Reading, MA.

Graham, Robert J. (1981), 'The role of perception of time in consumer research', *Journal of Consumer Research*, vol. 7, March, pp. 335–42.

Gurevitch, A.J. (1976), 'Time as a problem of cultural history', in L. Gardner *et al.* (eds), *Cultures and Time: At the crossroads of cultures*, Unesco Press: Paris.

Hall, Edward T. (1959), *The Silent Language*, Doubleday: New York.

Hall, Edward T. (1966), *The Hidden Dimension*, Doubleday: New York.

Hall, Edward T. (1976), *Beyond Culture*, Anchor Press/Doubleday: Garden City, NY.

Hall, Edward T. (1983), *The Dance of Life*, Anchor Press/Doubleday: New York.

Harris, Philip R. and Robert T. Moran (1987), *Managing Cultural Differences*, 2nd edn, Gulf Publishing Company: Houston, TX.

Hayashi, Shuji (1988), *Culture and Management in Japan*, Tokyo: University of Tokyo Press.

Hofstede, Geert (1980), *Culture's Consequences: International differences in work-related values*, Sage: Beverley Hills, CA.

Hofstede, Geert (2001), *Culture Consequences*, 2nd edn, Sage: Thousand Oaks, CA.

Ishihara, Shintaro (1991), *The Japan that Can Say No*, Simon & Schuster: New York.

Jacoby, Jacob., George J. Szybillo and Carol K. Berning (1976), 'Time and consumer behavior: an interdisciplinary overview', *Journal of Consumer Research*, vol. 2, pp. 320–39.

Kadima, K. and F. Lumwanu (1989), 'Aires linguistiques à l'intérieur du monde Bantu: Aspects généraux et innovations, dialectologie et classifications', in Théophile Obenga (ed.), *Les Peuples Bantu, migrations, expansion et identité culturelle*, Editions L'Harmattan: Paris, pp. 63–75.

Kagame, Alexis (1975), 'Aperception empirique du temps et conception de l'histoire dans la pensée Bantu', in *Les cultures et le temps*, Payot/Unesco: Paris, pp. 103–33.

Kaufman, Carol., Paul M. Lane and Jay D. Lundquist (1991), 'Exploring more than 24 hours a day: a preliminary investigation of polychromic time use', *Journal of Consumer Research*, vol. 18, December, pp. 392–401.

Kaufman-Scarborough, Carol and Jay D. Lundquist (1999), 'Time management and polychronicity: comparisons, contrasts, and insights for the workplace', *Journal of Managerial Psychology*, vol. 14, no. 3/4, p. 288.

Kluckhohn, Florence R. and Frederick L. Strodtbeck (1961), *Variations in Value Orientations*, Greenwood Press: Westport, CT.

Lane, Paul M. and Carol Felker Kaufman (1992), 'The United States chases time; Europeans pursue life: a cross-cultural comparison of perceived time', *Proceedings of the First Conference on the Cultural Dimension of International Marketing*, Odense, pp. 1–18.

Maalouf, Amine (1985), *The Crusades through Arab Eyes*, Schocken Books: New York.

Martinez-Zarzoso, I. (2003), 'Gravity model: An application to trade between regional blocs', *Atlantic Economic Journal*, vol. 31, no. 2, pp. 174–88.

Mauviel, Maurice (1991), 'La Grande Misère de l'antiracisme français', *Intercultures*, no. 12, January, pp. 69–82.

Montesquieu, Charles de (1748), *The Spirit of Laws*, translated from the French by Thomas Nugent (1792), 6th edn, McKenzie and Moore: Dublin.

Ohler, Jason (2001), 'Taming the technological beast', *The Futurist*, January–February, pp. 16–21.

Palmer, David K. and F. David Schoorman (1999), 'Unpacking the multiple aspects of time in polychronicity', *Journal of Managerial Psychology*, vol. 14, no. 3/4, p. 323.

Pearson, Emil (1977), *People of the Aurora*, Beta Books: San Diego.

Petit, Karl (1960), *Dictionnaire des Citations*, Marabout: Verviers.

Reischauer, Edwin O. (1946), *Japan: Past and present*, Alfred A. Knopf: New York.

Reischauer, Edwin O. (1990), *Japan: The story of a nation*, 4th edn, McGraw-Hill: New York.

Savishinsky, Joel (1998), 'The Nacirema and the Tsiruot', *International Journal of Intercultural Relations*, vol. 22, no. 3, pp. 369–74.

Segall, Marshall H., Pierre R. Dasen, John W. Berry and Ype H. Poortinga (1990), *Human Behaviour in Global Perspective*, Pergamon: New York.

Shenkar, Oded (2001), 'Cultural distance revisited: towards a more rigorous conceptualization and measurement of cultural differences', *Journal of International Business Studies*, vol. 32, no. 3, pp. 519–35.

Sherry, John F. Jr and Eduardo G. Camargo (1987), ' "May your life be marvellous:" English language labelling and the semiotics of Japanese promotion', *Journal of Consumer Research*, vol. 14, September, pp. 174–88.

Sorokin, Piritim and Robert Merton (1937) 'Social time: a methodological and functional analysis', *American Journal of Sociology*, vol. 42, pp. 615–29.

Spears, Nancy, Lin Xiaohua and John C. Mowen (2001), 'Time orientation in the United States, China, and Mexico: measurement and insights for promotional strategy', *Journal of International Consumer Marketing*, vol. 13, no. 1, pp. 57–75.

Swift, Jonathan B. (1999), 'Cultural closeness as a facet of cultural affinity', *International Marketing Review*, vol. 16, no. 3, pp. 182–201.

Triandis, Harry C. (1983), 'Dimensions of cultural variation as parameters of organizational theories', *International Studies of Management and Organization*, vol. XII, no. 4, pp. 139–69.

Triandis, Harry C. (1994), *Culture and Social Behavior*, McGraw-Hill: New York.

Trompenaars, Fons (1993), *Riding the Waves of Culture*, Nicholas Brealey: London.

Usunier, Jean-Claude (1991), 'Business time perceptions and national cultures: a comparative survey', *Management International Review*, vol. 31, no. 3, pp. 197–217.

Usunier, Jean-Claude (2003), 'The role of time in international business negotiations', in Pervez N. Ghauri and Jean-Claude Usunier (eds), *International Business Negotiations*, 2nd edn, Oxford: Elsevier, pp. 171–203.

Usunier, Jean-Claude and Constantin Napoléon-Biguma (1991), 'Gestion culturelle du temps: Le cas Bantou', in Franck Gauthey and Dominique Xardel (eds), *Management Interculturel: Modes et Modèles*, Economica: Paris, pp. 95–114.

Usunier, Jean-Claude and Pierre Valette-Florence (1994), 'Perceptual time patterns ("Time styles"): a psychometric scale', *Time and Society*, vol. 3, no. 2, pp. 219–41.

Van Oudenhoven, J.P. and K.I. Van der Zee (2002), 'Successful international cooperation: the influence of cultural similarity, strategic differences, and international experience', *Applied Psychology*, vol. 51, no. 4, p. 633.

Walsh, Len (1969), *Read Japanese Today*, Charles E. Tuttle: Rutland, VT, and Tokyo.

Weeks, William H., Paul B. Pedersen and Richard W. Brislin (1987), *A Manual of Structured Experiences for Cross-cultural Learning*, Intercultural Press: Yarmouth, ME.

Wong, C. and C. Lamb Jr. (1983), 'The impact of selected environmental forces upon consumers' willingness to buy foreign products', *Journal of the Academy of Marketing Science*, vol. 11, no. 2, pp. 71–84.

Yan, Chen (1991), 'L'Europe vue par l'empire du milieu', *Intercultures*, no. 12, January, pp. 45–56.

Yu, C.J. and D.S. Zietlow (1995), 'The determinants of bilateral trade among Asia-Pacific countries', *Asean Economic Bulletin*, vol. 11, no. 3, pp. 298–305.

Teaching materials

A2.1 Cross-cultural scenario

Inshallah

Stefan Phillips, a manager for a large US airline, was transferred to Dhahran, Saudi Arabia, to set up a new office. Although Stefan had had several other extended overseas assignments in Paris and Brussels, he was not well prepared for working in the Arab world. At the end of his first week Stefan came home in a state of near total frustration. As he sat at the dinner table that night he told his wife how exasperating it had been to work with the local employees, who, he claimed, seemed to take no responsibility for anything. Whenever something went wrong they would simply say '*Inshallah*' ('If God wills it'). Coming from a culture which sees no problem as insoluble, Stefan could not understand how the local employees could be so passive about job-related problems. 'If I hear one more *inshallah*,' he told his wife, 'I'll go crazy.'

Question

What might you tell Stefan to help him better understand the cultural realities of Saudi Arabia?[8]

(Source: Ferraro, 1990, p. 118. Reproduced with permission.)

A2.2 Cross-cultural interaction

Engineering a decision

Mr Legrand is a French engineer who works for a Japanese company in France. One day the general manager, Mr Tanaka, calls him into his office to discuss a new project in the Middle East. He tells Mr Legrand that the company is very pleased with his dedicated work and would like him to act as chief engineer for the project. It would mean two to three years away from home, but his family would be able to accompany him and there would be considerable personal financial benefits to the position – and, of course, he would be performing a valuable service to the company. Mr Legrand thanks Mr Tanaka for the confidence he has in him but says he will have to discuss it with his wife before deciding. Two days later he returns and tells Mr Tanaka that both he and his wife do not like the thought of leaving France and so he does not want to accept the position. Mr Tanaka says nothing but is somewhat dumbfounded by his decision.

Question

Why is Mr Tanaka so bewildered by Mr Legrand's decision?

1. He believes it is foolish for Mr Legrand to refuse all the financial benefits that go with the position.

2. He cannot accept that Mr Legrand should take any notice of his wife's opinion in the matter.

3. He believes Mr Legrand is possibly trying to bluff him into offering greater incentives to accept the offer.

4. He feels it is not appropriate for Mr Legrand to place his personal inclinations above those of his role as an employee of the company.

(Source: Brislin *et al.*, 1986, p. 158.)

 A2.3 Cross-cultural interaction

Opening a medical office in Saudi Arabia[8]

Dr Tom McDivern, a physician from New York City, was offered a two-year assignment to practice medicine in a growing urban centre in Saudi Arabia. Many of the residents in the area he was assigned to were recent immigrants from the much smaller outlying rural areas.

Because Western medicine was relatively unknown to many of these people, one of Dr McDivern's main responsibilities was to introduce himself and his services to those in the community. A meeting at a local school was organized for that specific purpose. Many people turned out. Tom's presentation went well. Some local residents also presented their experiences with Western medicine so others could hear the value of using his service. Some of Tom's office staff were also present to make appointments for those interested in seeing him when his doors opened one week later. The meeting was an obvious success. His opening day was booked solid.

When that day finally arrived, Tom was anxious to greet his first patients. Thirty minutes had passed, however, and neither of his first two patients had arrived. He was beginning to worry about the future of his practice while wondering where his patients were.

Question

What is the major cause of Tom's worries?

1. Although in Tom's mind and by his standards his presentation was a success, people actually only made appointments so as not to hurt his feelings. They really had no intention of using his services as modern medicine is so foreign to their past experiences.

2. Given the time lag between sign up and the actual day of the appointment, people had time to rethink their decision. They had just changed their minds.

3. Units of time differ between Arabs and Americans. Whereas to Tom his patients were very late, the Arab patient could still arrive and be on time.

4. Tom's patients were seeing their own traditional healers from their own culture; after that, they could go on to see this new doctor, Tom.

(Source: Brislin *et al.*, 1986, pp. 160–1.)

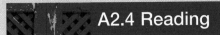

A2.4 Reading

Language and time patterns:
The Bantu case

Cultural and linguistic unity of the Bantu area

The Bantu area spreads along the southern side of a line that starts from Douala, Cameroon, by the Atlantic Ocean, and finishes at the mouth of the Tana river in the Indian Ocean. It divides northern and southern Africa. The Bantu area covers most of the southern cone of this continent.

These wide territories (several million square kilometres) are occupied by Bantu people, with the limited exception of some other small ethnic groups. The cultural unity of this people has been established on the basis of common linguistic features. As early as the middle of the nineteenth century, W. Bleek (quoted by Kadima and Lumwanu, 1989) had recognized that Bantu languages shared common lexical elements and many grammatical forms. In taking Bleek's work one stage further, anthropologists, historians and linguists have tried to identify the common social and cultural traits which allow a particular area to be classified as Bantu.

Alexis Kagame (1975), for instance, has studied Bantu linguistic systems, especially their underlying structures. He has collated what he terms 'compared Bantu philosophy'. The convergence of authors when describing the conception of time in Bantu cultures is quite marked.

The unification of time and space

At the heart of the Bantu's intuition of time lies the postulate of a very close relation between time and space. Within this postulate none of these basic dimensions of reality exist without the others. Alexis Kagame reveals this conceptual link.

Ontologically, Bantu culture puts whatever may be conceived or said into one of four categories:

1. The being – of intelligence (man).
2. The being – without intelligence (thing).
3. The being – as localizer (be it place or date).
4. The being – modal (incidentality, or modification of the being).

The major assumption made by Kagame is that translation of Bantu words in metaphysical categories is possible. He therefore translates *ha-ntu* by the being-localizer. This common word expresses the unity of space (place) and time (date). In the Bantu language this term means both the 'there' of locus and the 'now' of time. It is an indivisible localizer, both spatial and temporal.

The localizing prefix *ha-*, which forms *ha-ntu*, and its variants *pa-ntu* and *ka-ntu* are found in the eastern zone of the Bantu territory. Its equivalent in the western zone is *va*, whereas it is *go* in the south-eastern part of the Bantu area. The idea of unification between space and time in Bantu languages is shared by Emil Pearson, who has lived in the south-east of Angola since the 1920s. He writes in his book *People of the Aurora* (1977, p. 75):

In the Ngangela language there is no word, as far as I know, for 'time' as a continuous, flowing passage of events or the lack of same. Time is experiential or objective, that is, it is that which is meaningful to the person or thing which experiences it. *Time and space are cognate incidents of eternity.* The same word is used for both 'time' and 'space' (the latter in the sense of 'distance').

'Ntunda' can either express meaningful time or meaningful space. For example: 'Ntunda kua i li' – 'There is some distance'; and 'Ntunda i na hiti' – 'Time has passed'. The related verb 'Simbula', means 'delay', the thought being of awaiting 'meaningful time'. To the European the African may seem to be idling away useful time, whereas the latter, according to his philosophy, is awaiting experiential time, the time that is right for accomplishing his objective. 'Time' is locative, something that is virtually concrete, not something abstract. The locatives 'Ha', 'Ku' and 'Mu' are used for expressing 'time' as well as 'place'. Example: 'Ha Katete' – 'In the beginning' (as to either time or place); 'Ku lutue' can mean either 'in front' or 'in the future'. 'Mu nima' can mean 'behind' as to place, or 'after' as to time.

Bantu time experience

Two significant points sharply contrast the way Bantus experience time with the Western way of experiencing it within a technological environment. First, Bantus have no theoretical substantive to designate time as an entity *per se*, which can be quantified and measured. Second, for Bantus, the temporal dimension is intrinsic to the event itself. It is not an abstraction as in most Occidental developed cultures. To these cultures it appears as a content which flows regularly from the past to the future, through the present; a flow in which everything moves at the same speed, being 'in time'. For Bantu peoples time has no real value, no meaning, without the occurrence of an event which will serve as a 'marker'. The intuition of time only becomes effective when an action or an event happens: warriors' expedition, arrival of the train, rainfall, starvation on the increase. Time then becomes individualized. It is drawn out of anonymity. It is not anybody's time which would be abstractedly defined. It is concrete time concerning people I know. Instead of considering time as a straight railway track, where events may happen successively, it will only be spoken of as 'the time of this . . .' or 'the time of that . . .', or time which is favourable for this and that. That is why, on many occasions, there is no point in giving dates, that is to refer oneself to ideal time coordinates. History is not a series of dates, but a link between various events. Everything possesses its own internal time. Each event occurs at its own time.

(Source: Usunier and Napoléon-Biguma, 1991, pp. 95–114. Reproduced with the kind permission of the publisher and the co-author.)

 A2.5 Exercise

World picture test

Objective

To clarify participants' understanding of countries and cultures of the world through their knowledge of geography.

- *Participants*: Three or more persons. Facilitator.
- *Materials*: Paper and pens.
- *Setting*: No special requirements.
- *Time*: At least 30 minutes to one hour.

Procedure

1. Each participant is given a sheet of paper and a pen and asked to:
   (a) draw a map of the world as best they can within a five-minute time period;
   (b) name as many of the countries as they can;
   (c) mark any country they have visited for a week or longer;
   (d) exchange papers with other members of the group and discuss what differences are evidenced in what the other person put into their drawing and/or left out of the drawing.

2. Discuss the following points:
   (a) Does a person's awareness of the shape of a country reveal that person's awareness of the shape of the culture?
   (b) When a person leaves out a country, what does this mean?
   (c) When a person leaves out a continent, what does this mean?
   (d) What country did the person place in the centre of the map and what does that mean?
   (e) When a person draws a country out of place in relation to other countries, what does this mean?
   (f) Were they better acquainted with countries they had visited?
   (g) When the person objects violently to doing the drawing, what does that mean?
   (h) How well did persons draw home countries of other group members?
   (i) What do the persons plan to do as a result of what they learned in this exercise?

(Source: Weeks *et al.*, 1987, pp. 107–8.)

3

Cultural dynamics 2:
Interactions, mindsets and behaviours

There is a paragraph in Adam Smith's *Wealth of Nations*, where he comments about the 'Education of youth' ([1776], 1976, p. 286):

'If the teacher happens to be a man of sense, it must be an unpleasant thing to him to be conscious, while he is lecturing his students, that he is either speaking or reading nonsense, or what is very little better than nonsense. It must too be unpleasant to him to observe that the greater part of his students desert his lectures; or perhaps attend upon them with plain enough marks of neglect, contempt, and derision. If he is obliged, therefore, to give a certain number of lectures, these motives alone, without any other interest, might dispose him to take some pains to give tolerably good ones.

There are few domains in which cultural relativity is as strong as in education and teaching. This chapter will enable the reader to give some reasons, based on culture, why such a teacher as the one imagined by Adam Smith may survive perfectly well as a teacher, even if many students have left his class.

This chapter complements the previous one. Figure 2.1 illustrates that basic cultural assumptions are related to cultural models of time and space, and that both time and space influence our concept of the self and others. The first section in this chapter is dedicated to concepts of the self and others, which are central to the explanation of how people interact (section 3.2) and thus, their attitudes towards action (section 3.3 on why and how to act; 3.4 about relating thinking to action; 3.5 on wishes and feelings as they relate to action; and 3.6 on coping with rules). This material is all organized around common problems, explained in the three tables (3.1 to 3.3) that relate to Figure 2.1. The last section in the chapter (3.7)

discusses how basic cultural assumptions translate into everyday behaviour, especially in the work environment.

3.1

Concept of the self and others

The concept of the self and others does not relate directly to how a society is organized. It deals with how the organization of a society is internalized by people and is reflected in the view we have of ourselves in comparison with others. It is largely about people within a society responding positively and unconsciously to membership conditions, and thus being largely unaware of the conditions necessary for becoming an 'appropriate' member of the society. In fact, men and women, children and older people have to make assumptions about the why and how of their presence in this society, and these assumptions differ across societies.

The concept of the self is a kind of modal view of what people *are* in society and therefore what they are allowed to *do*. Our assumptions are related to the main sociodemographic categories (age, sex, social class), as well as to idealized conduct in particular roles (the perfect man, businessman, child, etc.). These ideal patterns are depicted in books, films, TV series, and any other kind of cultural artefact that conveys subliminal normative messages. For instance, we have an abundance of identification possibilities from films, such as *Harry Potter*, *Charlie's Angels*, and Aragorn in *The Lord of the Rings*. In viewing these, we constantly receive messages on how to behave. We find heroes to be desirable role models, even though we know that these characters are fictional.

The concept of the self has major implications in the area of consumer behaviour (Belk, 1988), many of which are discussed in Chapter 4. Briefly, our possessions are a major contributor to and reflector of our identities. As we ascribe meaning to what we buy and consume, our possessions become the means by which we strive to assert, complete, or attain our 'ideal' self (Wong and Ahuvia, 1995).

One of the most studied aspects of self-concept across cultures is the tendency toward an independent or interdependent self-construal. Markus and Kitayama (1991) identified these two relatively stable self-construals which emphasize the degree to which people see themselves as separate from or connected to others. They described the Western or individualist self as *independent*, 'containing significant dispositional attributes, and as detached from context', whereas the Eastern or collectivist self is *interdependent* 'with the surrounding context, [where] it is the "other" or the "self-in-relation-to-other" that is focal in individual experience' (p. 225). While each of us is able to draw on either aspect, the one that is salient determines which influence is most likely in a situation. Thus, in collectivist societies, the interdependent self is more likely to be salient, leading to norms, roles and values of the in-group becoming the 'obviously' correct way to behave (Triandis, 1990).

Table 3.1 presents major categories in the area of concepts of the self and others. From Table 3.1 there are four basic problems that we will address below: (1) Is human nature good or bad; (2) How do we

Table 3.1 Concepts of the self and others

Basic problem/Cultural orientations	Contrasts across cultures
How should we treat unknown people? (a) Is human nature basically good or bad?	Unknown people are considered favourably and shown confidence or, conversely, they are treated with suspicion when met for the first time.

Appraising others
 (b) When appraising others, emphasis placed on:
    (i) age
    (ii) sex
    (iii) social class
	Who are the persons to be considered trustworthy and reliable, with whom it is possible to do business?
	 (i) older (younger) people are seen more favourably.
	 (ii) trustworthiness is based on sex or not.
	 (iii) social class plays a significant role (or not) in concepts of the self and others.

Appraising oneself
 (c) Emphasis placed on the self-concept perceived as culturally appropriate:
    (i) self-esteem: low / high
    (ii) perceived potency: low / high
    (iii) level of activity: low / high
	To give the correct appearance one should behave:
	 (i) Shy and modest versus extrovert or even arrogant.
	 (ii) Power should be shown versus hidden.
	 (iii) Busy people or unoccupied/idle people are well regarded.

Relating the individual to the group (d) Individualism versus collectivism	The individual is seen as the basic resource and therefore individual-related values are strongly emphasized (personal freedom, human rights, equality between men and women); versus the group is seen as the basic resource and therefore group values are favoured (loyalty, sense of belonging, sense of personal sacrifice for the community, etc.).

assess or appraise others; (3) How do we appraise ourselves; and (4) How do we relate to the group?

Is human nature good or bad?

A basic assumption about *innate* human nature concerns whether it is good, evil or neutral. However we characterize it, human nature is subject to both positive and negative influences. This is complicated further by the view that this basic nature may or may not be changeable. Indicative of these hidden and largely unconscious assumptions, are attitudes on first contact. A friendly and open-minded attitude towards people one does not know is a good indicator of the assumption that innate human nature is good. When visiting the United States or Australia, Europeans are often amazed by how well they are received by people they have never been in contact with before. Although this cannot be explained solely by assumptions about human nature, it is clear that there is a strong positive belief towards new people. That is, they are viewed as basically good and able to improve themselves by education and perseverance (human nature is also seen as changeable). One may interpret this as having a functional side in relatively new countries. Generally, twentieth-century films of the 'Western' genre portrayed 'bad' Indians and 'good' European settlers. The assumptions of this human nature orientation are fairly straightforward: 'civilized' = good; 'uncivilized' (Indians, gamblers, desperadoes) = bad.

In contrast, the Latin Europeans and South Americans do not start from similar premises, which makes first contact with them more difficult. This can be seen in novels that reflect a view of basic human nature held by a particular people. For instance, the novels of the Colombian writer Gabriel Garcia Marques are typical of the view that human nature is basically bad (for more information on Gabriel Garcia Marques see *WS3.1*). In reality, the complete assumptions about human nature are of a dialectic nature. That is, the apparent contradiction between the two assumptions is resolved at a higher level of thinking. They would read more as:

- Human nature is basically good, but . . .
- Human nature is basically bad, but . . .
- Human nature lies somewhere between good and bad, and . . .

The two sides of each basic assumption coexist in most religions, which strive to improve individuals, especially through the social morals they develop. For ourselves, we still need to have reference points from which to evaluate others. These are largely culture based.

The dynamics of friendship necessarily relate to assumptions about human nature. If human nature is assumed to be good, then friendship develops quickly, but it is not necessarily very profound: since many people are supposed to be good, it is not as necessary to select a small group of 'true' friends. When it is assumed that human nature is generally bad, friendship develops more slowly because there is some initial distrust. Friendship will generally be more limited in terms of numbers, but more profound: a circle of friends may be a protective barrier against a society perceived as somewhat unfriendly, if not overtly hostile. Human nature orientation, although fundamental, is not directly related to action. It is indirectly related to marketing through collaboration, competition and the messages we create, which depict bad versus good characters, etc.

How do we appraise others?

Appraising others serves a multitude of purposes: making friends, choosing business partners, targeting potential customers, and so on. Apart from personality traits, which we judge by intuition, there are a number of clues, such as age, sex and behaviour, which we use to appraise others depending on our culture. Let us illustrate the basic clues and how culture-based interpretations may diverge.

Age may be associated with inexperience, doubtful character and lack of seriousness, or, by way of contrast, with open-mindedness, creativity, and the ability to change things and to undertake new ventures. Naturally, both sets of qualities are found in young people of all cultures. What is more interesting is how certain cultures, like Japan and Africa, place a higher value on older people, while others, like the United States, value younger people in society. This divergence of attitude probably occurs because the qualities typically found in the more highly valued age group are implicitly perceived as more congruent and favourable for the overall development of the society.

An emphasis on age is associated with other cultural orientations such as power distance, which is explained later in this chapter. It is also related to the dominant family models in a particular society. Where the family is nuclear and the structure is fairly weak, the authority image linked to parents' roles will also tend to fade, as will the positive view of older age groups as being in the 'adequate' age bracket. On the contrary, where an extended family is dominated by a patriarch, his role will favourably influence the image associated with the corresponding age bracket. On average, 'modern culture' values younger people because changes are extremely rapid (e.g. TV advertising revolves around young blonde women, shaggy-haired surfer boys or yuppie-like professionals), whereas in 'traditional culture' the elders are a source of wisdom and guidance for the community and as a consequence their age is valued.

Sex is probably the most important cultural difference, because of the definite roles and self-concepts imposed on boys and girls by culture. In *Male and Female*, Margaret Mead (see *WS3.1*) puts it in the following terms (1948, pp. 7–8):

The differences between the two sexes is one of the important conditions upon which we have built the many varieties of human culture that give human beings dignity and stature. In every known society, mankind has elaborated the biological division of labour into forms often very remotely related to the original biological differences that provided the original clues. Upon the contrast in bodily form, men have built analogies between sun and moon, night and day, goodness and evil, strength and tenderness, steadfastness and fickleness, endurance and vulnerability. Sometimes one quality has been assigned to one sex, sometimes to the other . . . Some people think of women as too weak to work out of doors, others regard women as the appropriate bearers of heavy burdens . . . some religions, including our European traditional religions, have assigned women an inferior role in the religious hierarchy, others have built their whole symbolic relationship with the supernatural world upon male imitations of the natural function of women. In some cultures women are regarded as sieves through whom the best guarded secrets will sift; in others it is the men who are the gossips.

The place of women in society has changed greatly over the last century. Some basic rights, such as voting, were long denied to women, and in many societies the place of women is still very different from that of men. Not all that long ago, the electoral status of women was still inferior to that of men even in advanced countries like Switzerland (in very traditional cantons

– Appenzell). For a variety of roles and capacities in the society, women are dependent on men, mostly on an economic basis. In some traditional Muslim countries, women are not allowed to work outside the home, and are often not permitted to go outside to shop or to manage the family budget. Worldwide differences in the self concept of women, and the concept of women held by men, are striking.

Gisela Frese-Weghöft, a teacher working for the German development agency in Gadima, North Yemen, explains the case of a young woman, aged 24, who is too old to be married and works at home with her sewing machine as a dressmaker. She earns money – which she does not need because she is cared for by the family.

From time to time she asks her brothers to buy some jewellery with the money. Sometimes she gives presents of jewellery to her sisters or gives the money to her brothers when she has too much. It is understood that a woman cannot manage money. The sewing supplies are purchased by the men of the family, since like most women in Gadima, she is strictly forbidden to go to the souk (market place). Some of the simplest women have invented a trick to bypass this prohibition. They disguise themselves with a dirty black sharshaff and old plastic sandals, and pretend to be one of the country women who sell their vegetables at the souk. In doing this, they should not speak much, so that nobody may recognize their voice or their pronunciation; women recognize each other, even when veiled. During these secret walks to the souk, they procure what their husbands never bring back or return what they have erroneously purchased. (Frese-Weghöft, 1989, p. 90, our translation.)

All societies place people in particular strata, such as *social classes and castes*. In economic-oriented societies they may divide people into the 'haves' and the 'have-nots', but other feasible criteria may be based on birth or education, even in the absence of obvious wealth or income criteria. Wong and Ahuvia (1995, p. 82) argue that 'Americans generally see one's social class as primarily reflecting one's personal income level which in turn is believed to reflect (at least in part) one's individual professional merit. But to the interdependent Chinese, class does not belong to oneself, but also to one's group, usually one's family, relatives, and kinship clan.' Like many other elements of the concept of the self and others, social class is important for consumer behaviour, as people express their class differences, real or fantasized, by consumption.

Social stratification is based on somewhat different criteria across cultures, even though social classes consistently appear across cultures. For instance, in India castes (a special order of social stratification) include four major hereditary classes into which the Hindu society is divided: the *Brahman, Kshatriya, Vaisya* and *Sudra* (see *WS3.1*). Thus, it is not the existence of social classes that differs, but the degree of emphasis placed on social stratification varies across societies. In countries where this emphasis is strong, people in higher classes see themselves as *being substantially different* from others in lower classes. This can extend to speaking the language differently (or even a different language), prohibiting inter-class marriages, and distinguishing oneself by specific tastes and lifestyles. Bista (1990, p. 79) describes the Hindu caste system in the following terms:

one has to engage in activities that are appropriate to one's caste. Those whose fate is to be workers continue to work, but this work does not necessarily lead to any form of result or reward. The caste principle admonishes that actions have to be without desire, i.e. without a goal. There is a purpose to action, but it is a purpose known only to a supernatural agency. Individual aspirations are inconsequential and behaviour is submissive to a controlling force that is unknown. Learned Hindus emphasize that the material world is *maya*, an illusion, and claim that this is not worth taking seriously.

How do we appraise ourselves?

People hold a certain view of themselves, and prefer spontaneously to choose the one that will be perceived as culturally appropriate by others in the ingroup. Triandis (1983) distinguishes three main areas of cultural contrasts: self-esteem, perceived potency and perceived activity. First, self-esteem can be low or high according to whether we think of ourselves as good or not good. Low self-esteem results in displaying a modest and self-effacing behaviour, whereas higher self-esteem results in demonstrating more assertiveness and self-assurance. Asians, on average, clearly display lower self-esteem than westerners. The reader must be cautious when interpreting these observations as it is a standard assumption about their culture; it does not mean that Asians deserve less esteem, but rather that they assume that they deserve less as an individual. (For more information

on the distinction between self-esteem and narcissism see *WS3.1*.) The second contrast is perceived potency, which means the extent to which people view themselves as powerful and able to accomplish almost any task, or exercise power. The French proverb '*Impossible n'est pas français*' is a typical high-perceived-potency saying. The third contrast is the level of personal activity. When the appropriate level of personal activity is seen as high, people will boast about their being 'workaholics', will work weekends, and generally be satisfied with overworking. When, by contrast, the appropriate image of the self is based on a low level of activity, as in the Hindu case quoted above, the standard attributes of a normal self-concept will be: few hours spent in the office, low involvement in work-related issues, and having time available for pure inactivity. These three dimensions interact, so that people who are low on self-esteem, perceived power and perceived activity feel powerless and often accept the world as it is. Conversely, people with high self-esteem, perceived power and perceived activity are more likely to be overconfident and take on difficult tasks, even to the extent of failure.

How do we relate the individual to the group?

The common problem, across all societies, is how to define the boundaries between people and the groups they belong to, in order to ensure the smooth and efficient functioning of society. Individualism and collectivism are mentioned in Table 3.1, in the box 'Concept of the self and others', because our belief is that they are deeply ingrained in the 'borders' of our self. People from individualist cultures have a more clear-cut view of where 'oneself' stops ('I, me, mine' as John Lennon's song says) and where 'others' start, whereas people from collectivist cultures have much fuzzier borders between their self and that of near others.

The 'rice argument' is frequently used to explain the differences between individualism and collectivism. Rice culture needs the coordinated flooding of rice fields, which promotes dependence among the group members and requires common action. Conversely, the basic staples in the West are 'individualist' cereals (wheat, barley, oats, etc.), where the farmer's achievements depend mostly on his or her own individual efforts.

Individualism is based on the principle of asserting your independence and individuality. All societies have individuals and groups, but *individualism* stresses the smallest unit as being that where the solution lies. Common individualist assumptions are as follows:

1. It is at the level of individuals that initiative, effort and achievements can best be developed, because people are separated and *different* (divisibility).
2. Individual achievements can be added to each other without loss (the sum equals the parts: the additive model).
3. Society has to maximize individual freedom, emphasize high individual achievers, and value individuals (the freedom orientation).

These assumptions are not necessarily 'true'. One may ascribe to them because of intellectual conviction, especially assumption 1, or to get personal leeway, as is the consequence of assumption 3. They are 'true' to the extent that they are largely a self-fulfilling prophecy. The obvious problems arise from assumption 2: collective action is, generally, not the direct result of simply adding individual deeds. The process is more complex, and this brings grist to the collectivist mill, which makes its own assumptions:

1. It is at group level, and not at the individual level, that initiative, effort and achievements can best be developed, because people are not really separate from each other; they belong to a *common* reality (the organic view).
2. Collective achievements are fundamentally different in nature from individual achievements, and the combination of parts (if such a computation is even possible) is much greater than the parts themselves (the multiplicative model).
3. Therefore, society has to maximize group coherence and social harmony, even at the expense of individual freedom, and if need be, by downsizing individual achievements (the concord orientation).

Collectivism is associated with 'traditional culture', whereas individualism is a strong component of 'modern culture', especially in the area of consumption, a splendid domain for enjoying individual freedom and expressing difference from others. Belk (1985), for instance, notes that, since the Middle Ages, the awareness of self has become less shared and more individualistic, which is evidenced by the growing popularity of self-oriented objects such as mirrors, self-portraits, chairs (rather than benches), etc.

Modern individualism has its roots in sixteenth- and seventeenth-century England. It is based on the ideas of English and Scottish philosophers (More, Bacon, Hume and Locke) and was effected by the Act of Habeas Corpus, the first legal edict forbidding the Sovereign from jailing somebody without lawful reason. This was furthered by the French *Déclaration des droits de l'homme et du citoyen*, in 1789. The French were only followers of the British, but they have been good exporters of the concept of human rights, even though neither the British nor the French practised them all the time, especially in their colonies. The United Nations Universal Declaration of Human Rights is in the same vein: it favours an individual-based view of what is a 'good' society. The individualist view of human rights is also typical of Amnesty International, which has heated debates with some Asian governments holding a different view of what human rights are.

The individualist/collectivist divide is a strong but not a simple difference. In individualist societies, people still belong to groups, live in communities and think of themselves as integrated into a larger whole. In collectivist societies, people still feel a need to express their personal identity, and strive often for individual success and self-actualization. Cooperation takes place in all societies, but the way people cooperate is likely to be driven by what is culturally appropriate. People from individualist societies are more likely to rely on individuality and rationality as motivations for co-operation, while those from collectivist societies are likely to be driven by collective rationality and social forces (Chen *et al.*, 1998). Similarly, conflicts need to be handled in all societies. People from collectivist societies are more likely to rely on formal rules and procedures to handle disagreements, which preserves ingroup harmony, while those from individualist societies rely more on their own experience and training to handle disagreements, which emphasizes self-sufficiency (Smith *et al.*, 1998). Notably, problems are likely to occur across cultures, as has been found with management teams.

The 'modern' aspect of individualist assumptions is now heavily challenged by the rise of collectivist nations in Asia and in South America, with their achievements in international trade and their high rate of economic growth. Robertson (2000) links the

Box 3.1

From Chanel chick to individualist

'Brand auntie', 'Chanel chick'

These curious turns of phrase reflect Japan's obsession with brands. From her Luis Vuitton bag to her Gucci shoes the '*Brand auntie*' thinks nothing of draping herself in luxury brands from head to toe.

The '*Chanel chick*' is a high-school girl with a bit of cash on her hands. She will do what it takes to get those hands on a Chanel or Hermes wristwatch (quite beyond her means at a cost of several hundreds of thousands of Yen), paying by monthly instalments if she has to. Her dinner, on the other hand, is a pre-packaged meal bought at the local convenience store.

Why do the Japanese, as represented by such chicks and aunties, cluster around these exorbitantly expensive luxury brand goods in a frenzy of consumption, where each buys exactly the same thing as everyone else?

The Japanese as a people have been dominated by conformity – the Me Too-ist obsession 'so-and-so has one, so for me not to is, well . . .'. The sharing of identical values was seen as the only way to create a comfortable society. This tradition saw the 'wa', or harmony, as most precious, and conforming with others was an unbreakable rule of communities at all levels of society. Doing something different from others, making a statement as an individual, meant 'murahachibu' – banishment from the group . . . Not straying from the herd continues to be seen as a prime virtue in Japan. This fundamental value of 'seeking to be like others' has created a 'desire to have the same things as others', which has further evolved into a sense that one 'must have the same things as others'. The result is a society where consensus on what is good or fashionable is easily reached, and the population quickly falls into step behind recognised innovators and opinion leaders.

Chanel chicks, Gucci grandmas, and Hermes honeys

In looking at which brands became the prime targets of this brand boom, we need to understand the Japanese obsession with Europe. Impressions of 'Western Prestige Brands' tend to lean heavily towards associations with Europe, seen generally as having an image of high quality, heritage, craftsmanship, elegance, and spirituality. Europe was seen as the model of modern civilisation by 19th Century Meiji-Era literati after the country opened its doors to the outside world after 200 years of isolation and the reverberations of this interaction with the colossus of European civilisation continue to echo in Japan to this day. The popularity of brands such as Luis Vuitton, Chanel, Gucci, and Hermes is without question intimately related to perceptions of the distinctive identities of each of these brands. But it is also extremely important to keep in mind that all these brands are at the same time wrapped inextricably with the generalised aspiration and obsession with European culture that has characterised Japan for the last 130 years.

(Source: Ohye, 2003.)

recent economic success in many Asian nations to traits associated with Confucian Dynamism or Long Term Orientation (LTO) as discussed in Chapter 2. This is the tendency toward a future-minded mentality (Hofstede and Bond, 1988). At the individual level, it manifests itself in scholarship, hard-work and perseverance, which have been instrumental in the success of many Asian nations. Thus, it is not individualism and collectivism that predict economic prosperity alone, but the interaction between many aspects of culture. The debate between individualism and collectivism is not yet finished; like water and oil they do not readily mix: even if they seem to blend when shaken vigorously, they separate when left to settle.

3.2

Interaction models

Individualism and collectivism refer to concepts of the self and others (as assumptions located *within* persons) as well as to a model of interaction *between* people. Table 3.2 lists a series of other aspects of what

Table 3.2 Interaction models

Cultural orientations	Contrasts across cultures
Equality or inequality in interpersonal interactions (a) Power Distance (PD)	Hierarchy is strong, power is centralized at the top (high PD); power is more equally distributed and superior and subordinates have a sense of equality as human beings (low PD).
Interacting *with* others or *for* others (b) Masculinity versus Femininity	Assertiveness and personal achievement are favoured (masc.) versus caring for others, adopting nurturing roles and emphasizing quality of life (fem.).
Dealing with uncertainty (c) Uncertainty avoidance (UA)	Tendency to avoid risks (high UA), to prefer stable situations, uncertainty-reducing rules and risk-free procedures, which are seen as a necessity for efficiency. Or, conversely, a risk-prone attitude (low UA) where people as individuals are seen as the engine of change, which is perceived as a requirement for efficiency.
Relying on oneself or on others (d) Self-reliance versus dependence	Do people rely on their own forces, find motivation and control within themselves (self-reliance) or do they need to find outside support, motivation and control from their environment (dependence)?
Developing appropriate communication with others (e) Communication styles	See Chapter 13 on Language, culture and communication.

are considered to be culturally appropriate interaction models in particular societies. Most of these factors are based on Hofstede (1980a, 1980b, 2001). Although Hofstede developed these concepts in relation to organizational issues and through collection of data at the corporate level, they are largely transferable to the society as a whole.

There are many publications devoted to the impact of cultural differences on management and organization (that is, *within* companies). The impact of these dimensions of national culture on various issues has been assessed such as structure, hierarchical relationships, management of expatriate personnel and variation in motivation patterns across cultures (e.g. see Hofstede, 2001; Adler, 2002). These issues are clearly outside the principal scope of this book, which is to consider the interaction of companies with their environment, that is, markets, customers, distribution channels or various influential groups (consumer movements, regulatory authorities, etc.). Nevertheless, a summary of the advances made in cultural differences is worth while, for three reasons at least. First, Hofstede's four dimensions of national cultures, although they have been measured for management and organization practices, also make sense for marketing and sales and, as such, have been studied extensively in international marketing. Second, replications show that the dimensions are fairly stable, at least in terms of the distance between cultures (Sondergaard, 1994; Hofstede, 2001; de Mooij and Hofstede, 2002). Third, although Hofstede's dimensions were developed at the national level, researchers have made progress in the measurement of some of these dimensions at the individual level. Measuring the dimensions at the individual level offers the opportunity to increase the validity of claims as well as the variance explained.

National cultures and the relativity of managerial practices

The cover picture of an issue of *Fortune* magazine accurately features the difficult question of the transposability of management styles: it shows an American with slanting eyes attempting to eat a hamburger using chopsticks. This metaphor illustrates how difficult it is to transpose elements of one culture onto another. Geert Hofstede was one of the first researchers to question the adaptability of US management theories and practices to other cultural contexts. Empirical studies for Hofstede's work were undertaken between 1967 and 1973 within a large multinational company, in 66 of its national subsidiaries. The database contains more than 116,000 questionnaires: all categories of personnel were interviewed, from ordinary workers to general managers. Out of 150 questions, 60 deal with the values and beliefs of the respondents on issues related to motivation, hierarchy, leadership, well-being in the organization, etc. The questionnaire was administered in two successive stages (1967–9 and 1971–3) so as to verify validity by replication. Versions of the questionnaire were drafted in 20 different languages. Not all subsidiaries were included in the final analysis; depending on the data under review, 40–55 countries were finally comparable. The results drawn from this data have been further validated by a systematic comparison with the results of 140 other sources of data (see Hofstede, 2001, appendix 6; for more information about Hofstede and his dimensions see *WS3.2*).

Interviewees all belonged to the same multinational corporation, IBM, which has a very strong corporate culture shared by its employees. Consequently there was no variance on this dimension across the sample. Each national sample allowed for a similar representation of age groups, sex and categories of personnel, thereby avoiding a potential source of variance across national subsidiaries' results. Finally, the only source of variance was the difference in national cultures and mentalities. Hofstede, by means of factor analysis of the respondents' scores, was able to derive four main conceptual dimensions on which national cultures exhibit significant differences. One of these four dimensions is *individualism/collectivism*, which, as we mentioned in the previous section, has been studied extensively. In collectivist countries there is a close-knit social structure, where people neatly distinguish between members of the ingroup and members of the outgroup (see Box 3.1): people expect their group to care for them in exchange for unwavering loyalty. In individualistic societies, social fabric is much looser: people are basically supposed to care for themselves and their immediate family. Exchange takes place on the base of reciprocity: if an individual gives something to another, some sort of return is expected within a reasonable time span. The three other dimensions are explained below. They correspond to the first three cells in Table 3.2.

Power distance

Power distance measures the extent to which a society and its individual members tolerate an unequal distribution of power in organizations and in society as a whole. It is shown as much by the behavioural values of superiors who display their power and exercise it, as by the behavioural values of subordinates who wait for their superiors to show their status and power, and are uncomfortable if they do not personally experience it. In low power distance societies, members of the organization tend to feel equal, and close to each other in their daily work relationships. They cope with situations of higher hierarchical distance by delegating power. In high power distance societies, superiors and subordinates feel separated from each other. It is not easy to meet and talk with higher ranking people, and the real power tends to be very much concentrated at the top. At society level, power distance translates as shown in Box 3.2 (for more information on power distance see *WS3.2*).

Masculinity/femininity

When responding to the common problem: 'do we interact *with* others or *for* others?' responses are made on the basis of dominant value systems, which roughly corresponds to male/assertive and the female/nurturing roles. A society is masculine when the dominant values favour assertiveness, earning money, showing off possessions and caring little for others. Conversely, feminine societies favour nurturing roles, interdependence between people and caring *for* others (who are seen as worth caring for, because they are temporarily weak). The masculinity/femininity dimension has been so called because, on average, men tended to score high on one extreme and women on the other, across societies.

In typically feminine societies, such as northern European countries, the welfare system is highly

Box 3.2

More equal than others

In a peaceful revolution – the last revolution in Swedish history – the nobles of Sweden in 1809 deposed King Gustav IV whom they considered incompetent, and surprisingly invited Jean Baptiste Bernadotte, a French general who served under their enemy Napoleon, to become King of Sweden. Bernadotte accepted and he became King Charles XIV; his descendants occupy the Swedish throne to this day. When the new King was installed he addressed the Swedish parliament in their language. His broken Swedish amused the Swedes and they roared with laughter. The Frenchman who had become King was so upset that he never tried to speak Swedish again. In this incident Bernadotte was a victim of culture shock: never in his French upbringing and military career had he experienced subordinates who laughed at the mistakes of their

superior. Historians tell us he had more problems adapting to the egalitarian Swedish and Norwegian mentality (he later became King of Norway as well) and to his subordinates' constitutional rights. He was a good learner, however (except for language), and he ruled the country as a highly respected constitutional monarch until 1844.

One of the aspects in which Sweden differs from France is the way its society handles *inequality*. There is inequality in any society. Even in the most simple hunter-gatherer band, some people are bigger, stronger or smarter than others. The next thing is that some people have more power than others: they are more able to determine the behaviour of others than vice-versa. Some people are given more status and respect than others.

(Source: Hofstede, 1991.)

developed, education is largely free and easily accessible, and there is openness to admit that people may have problems: patience and helpfulness are shown to those who are in trouble; both boys and girls learn to be modest and to have sympathy for the underdog. In typically masculine societies (whether individualist like the United States or collectivist like Japan) weaker people find, on average, less support from the society at large; people learn to admire the strong, like Rambo or Vin Diesel in the United States. The common problem behind the masculinity/femininity divide could perhaps be phrased differently: should we help people (at the risk of their being weakened by a lack of personal effort) or should we not (at the risk, for them, of being even worse)? Obviously, the response is not easy.

Uncertainty avoidance

A common problem faced by people in any society is how to deal with uncertainty. There are basically two ways: the first is based on the assumption that people have to deal with uncertainty, because it is in the very nature of the situations we face. The future is by definition unknown, but it can be evaluated, and people and institutions can deal with uncertainty. The other

extreme is marked by uncertainty aversion, which results in the assumption that uncertainty is bad and everything in society must aim to reduce uncertainty.

The dimension of uncertainty avoidance measures the extent to which people in a society tend to feel threatened by uncertain, ambiguous or undefined situations. Where uncertainty avoidance is high, organizations promote stable careers, produce rules and procedures, etc. 'Nevertheless societies in which uncertainty avoidance is strong are also characterized by a higher level of anxiety and aggressiveness that creates, among other things, a strong inner urge to work hard' (Hofstede, 1980a). Hofstede (1991, p. 116) points out that 'uncertainty avoidance should not be confused with risk avoidance . . . even more than reducing risk, uncertainty avoidance leads to a reduction of *ambiguity*'. Hofstede notes that risk is more specific than uncertainty and is often expressed as a probability that a specific outcome will occur, whereas uncertainty is a situation in which anything can happen. In fact, some people may engage in risky behaviour in order to reduce ambiguities, 'such as starting a fight with a potential opponent rather than sitting back and waiting' (Hofstede, 2001, p. 148). (See *WS3.2* for more information on uncertainty avoidance.)

The cultural relativity of management theories

Table 3.3 shows the value of the dimensions discussed above for 53 countries/regions. Figure 3.1 presents a diagrammatic map of countries when individualism and power distance are combined. Hofstede's main tenet concerns the *cultural relativity of management theories*. These management theories are rooted in the cultural context where they were developed, with the result that any simple direct transposition is difficult. For instance, Hofstede shows the link that exists between US-based motivation theories and US culture. Abraham Maslow's 'hierarchy of needs' and McClelland's theory of the achievement motive are directly related to two dimensions of US culture: its strong masculinity and individualism. People are seen as being motivated in an overtly conscious manner by the expectancy of some kind of results from their acts. They are basically motivated by extrinsic reasons and rewards. In contrast, Freudian theory, which has not been greatly applied by US management theorists, represents the individual as being driven by internal and largely unconscious forces, a complex interaction between the id, the superego and the ego. According to Hofstede, Austria, the birthplace of Sigmund Freud and his theories, scores significantly higher than the United States on uncertainty avoidance and lower on individualism. This may explain why motivation is more related to internalized social values. 'Freud's superego acts naturally as an inner uncertainty-absorbing device, an internalized boss' (Hofstede, 1980a).

Figure 3.1 Map of 53 countries ranked on power distance and individualism indices

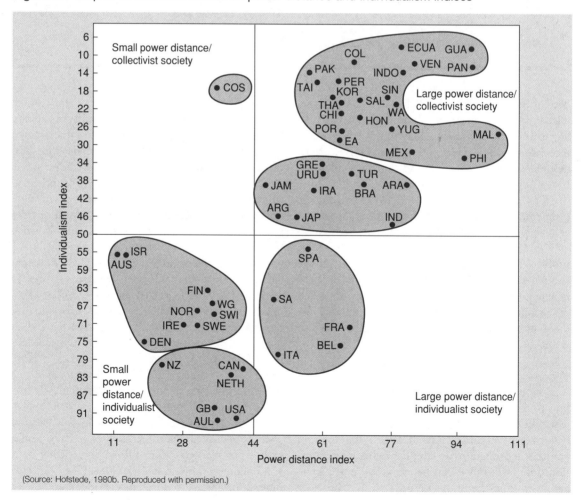

(Source: Hofstede, 1980b. Reproduced with permission.)

Table 3.3 Values of Hofstede's cultural dimensions for 53 countries or regions

Country/region	Dimensions				
	Power distance	Uncertainty avoidance	Individualism	Masculinity	Long-/Short-Term orientation
Arabic countries[a]	80	68	38	53	–
Argentina	49	86	46	56	–
Australia	36	51	90	61	31
Austria	11	70	55	79	31
Belgium	65	94	75	54	38
Brazil	69	76	38	49	65
Canada	39	48	80	52	23
Chile	63	86	23	28	–
Colombia	67	80	13	64	–
Costa Rica	35	86	15	21	–
Denmark	18	23	74	16	46
East African region[b]	64	52	27	41	25
Ecuador	78	67	8	63	–
Finland	33	59	63	26	41
France	68	86	71	43	39
Great Britain	35	35	89	66	25
Greece	60	112	35	57	–
Guatemala	96	101	6	37	–
Hong Kong	68	29	25	57	96
India	77	40	48	56	61
Indonesia	78	48	14	46	–
Iran	58	59	41	43	–
Ireland	28	35	70	68	43
Israel	13	81	54	47	–
Italy	50	75	76	70	34
Jamaica	45	13	39	68	–
Japan	54	92	46	95	80
Malaysia	104	36	26	50	–
Mexico	81	82	30	69	–
Netherlands	38	53	80	14	44
New Zealand	22	49	79	58	30
Norway	31	50	69	8	44
Pakistan	55	70	14	50	0
Panama	95	86	11	44	–
Peru	64	87	16	42	–
Philippines	94	44	32	64	19
Portugal	63	104	27	31	30
Salvador	66	94	19	40	–
Singapore	74	8	20	48	48
South Africa	49	49	65	63	–
South Korea	60	85	18	39	75
Spain	57	86	51	42	19
Sweden	31	29	71	5	33
Switzerland	34	58	68	70	40
Taiwan	58	69	17	45	87
Thailand	64	64	20	34	56
Turkey	66	85	37	45	–
United States	40	46	91	62	29
Uruguay	61	100	36	38	–

Table 3.3 *(continued)*

Country/region	Dimensions				
	Power distance	Uncertainty avoidance	Individualism	Masculinity	Long-/Short-Term orientation
Venezuela	81	76	12	73	–
West African region[c]	77	54	20	46	16
West Germany	35	65	67	66	31
Yugoslavia	76	88	27	21	–
Overall mean	57	65	43	49	39
Standard deviation	22	24	25	18	22

[a] Saudi Arabia, Egypt, United Arab Emirates, Iraq, Kuwait, Lebanon and Libya.
[b] Ethiopia, Kenya, Tanzania and Zambia.
[c] Ghana, Nigeria and Sierra Leone.

Note: For further information on individual countries, see the *CIA Factbook* at WS3.2.
(Source: Hofstede, 2001. Reproduced with permission.)

Interaction clashes

As will be shown in Chapter 15, the differences on dimensions illustrated above have to be taken into account when designing sales force stimulation systems across national subsidiaries with different cultural contexts. In masculine, individualistic countries, where there is also lower uncertainty avoidance, extrinsic rewards should be preferred (bonuses, gifts, holidays, monetary incentives). In societies that are more feminine, and/or more collectivist, and/or with higher uncertainty avoidance, intrinsic rewards should be chosen because they fit better with profound inner values. In addition, Oliver and Cravens (1999) found that the choice of employee benefits available also differed depending on the level of uncertainty avoidance and power distance. For instance, managers from countries with weak uncertainty avoidance and low power distance were more likely to offer cafeteria plans, where workers could choose how their benefit dollars were spent. This level of choice can create anxiety in people who are used to less uncertainty and are comfortable with the power being concentrated at the top.

Hofstede also examined the direct transposition of the American MBO (Management By Objectives) in France, where it became the DPPO (*Direction Participatifs Par Objectifs*). MBO stems from the United States where:

1. Subordinates are independent and feel sufficiently at ease with their bosses to negotiate meaningfully with them (low power distance).

2. Subordinates as well as superiors are willing to face ambiguity (low uncertainty avoidance).
3. The outcome is considered important by superiors and subordinates (high level of masculinity).

DPPO enjoyed brief success at the end of the 1960s but had become a flop by the mid-1970s. Indeed in the French cultural context DPPO created anxiety, in a country where hierarchy is traditionally strong (high power distance) and where that structure protects people against uncertainty. MBO assumes a depersonalized authority (role authority) whereas, according to Hofstede, from their childhood French people are used to high power distance and strongly personalized authority. Despite efforts to introduce Anglo-Saxon management methods, French bosses do not easily decentralize management and delegate authority.

In a study at Insead, reported by Hofstede, O.J. Stevens asked students of various nationalities to write their own diagnosis of and solution to a small case study about a conflict between the sales department and the product development department. The French saw the problem basically as one that the hierarchy should solve, a solution being sought from the chairperson. The Germans blamed the absence of formal rules and written procedures. The English saw the problem as resulting basically from a lack of interpersonal communication. Stevens concluded that 'the implicit model of the organization for most French was a pyramid (both centralized and formal); for German a well-oiled machine (formalized, but not centralized); and for most British a village market (neither formalized, nor centralized)' (Hofstede, 1980a, p. 60).

Organization types may be more adapted to some cultures than to others. In a matrix organization, for instance, there is a double hierarchical linkage (with a product division at the European level and a subsidiary general manager at the country level): this is not accepted very well by either the French or the Germans. For the French, it violates the principle of unity of command; for the Germans, it thwarts their need for organizational clarity and will not be deemed acceptable unless individual roles inside the organization are unambiguously defined.

Self-reliance versus dependence

Being self-reliant versus showing dependence has naturally to do with assumptions about the concept of the self. For example, valuing elders in the community will tend to decrease the legitimacy of self-reliance among younger age groups. Similarly traditional sex roles promote the dependence of women. Even social class may have an influence in as much as an implied family model reigns over cross-class relationships; people in higher social classes behave patronizingly towards those in lower classes. In industrial relations for instance, the 'paternalist' orientation of factory owners towards their workers typifies the role of the boss as a father and the employees as 'children'.

Self-reliant people rely on their own forces and find motivation and control within themselves, whereas dependence implies that they need to find outside support, motivation and control from their environment. As summarized in Table 3.4, low power distance and uncertainty avoidance, combined with

Table 3.4 Self-reliance versus dependence

Hofstede's dimension	Influence on self-reliance/dependence
Individualism	Increases self-reliance
Power distance	Promotes dependence
Masculinity	Increases self-reliance
Uncertainty avoidance	Promotes dependence
Long-term orientation	Promotes dependence

high individualism and masculinity will be related to more self-reliance (e.g. the United States and Australia; the best extreme contrast are Latin countries like Chile, Portugal or Brazil, see Table 3.3). The typical westerner is on average more self-reliant than the average easterner. And the typical northern European is more self-reliant than the typical Latin European.

Two assumptions are central in developing either self-reliance or dependence among individuals: (1) the locus of control – whether a person considers that events are contingent upon his or her own behaviour or are under the control of powerful, unpredictable and complex external forces; and (2) the implicit family role that underlies typical interaction patterns.

The first basic issue in relation to self-reliance versus dependence is whether people consider they have an external or an internal locus of control (Rotter, 1966). People with internal locus-of-control will show more self-reliance, because they believe in their ability to manage their own world and to control it by themselves. The locus-of-control concept was developed by Rotter at an individual level, but it applies fairly well as a contrasting dimension across cultures. (For more information on Rotter see *WS3.2*.)

The second issue in relation to dependence versus self-reliance is the kind of family role that a particular culture favours. In Latin societies, for instance, the parent/child relationship remains a very strong underlying model for interaction, and even in situations which are normally assumed as being between equals, some people may unconsciously and spontaneously develop parental attitudes. If conflict develops the superior will easily develop the attitude of a 'critical' parent (in the terms of Eric Berne's transactional analysis:[1] see *WS3.2*), leaving little option for their counterparts, but to behave in the manner of a 'compliant child' by obeying, or on the contrary, like a 'rebel child', or by leaving. Where parent/adult roles underlie models of interaction, many relationships will be in the realm of dependence: functional relationships will be based on filial dependence, whereas dysfunctional relationships will be played in the conflict mode.

For people who come from societies where self-reliance is standard behaviour, it is often extremely irritating not to be treated as an adult, equal in rights and obligations, but, symbolically, as a child. France is a good case in point: many aspects of the French culture favour dependence, with the major exception of a strong individualist orientation. This results in a pattern of varying dependence, where people constantly play a game of dispute and reconciliation in teamwork, where true self-reliance can only be fostered by creative activity and/or working independently.

Relationship with other frameworks

There are three major studies that have provided national level cultural scores, of which Hofstede's is by far the most influential. Of the other two Schwartz culture-level dimensions (Schwartz, 1994, 1999) is likely to be more relevant to marketing than Trompenaars (see Trompenaars and Hampden-Turner, 1998), although it is yet to be applied widely. Schwartz (1999) analyzed responses (from mostly teachers and students in 63 countries) to the Schwartz Values Scale at the country level to validate his culture-level framework. He found support for seven country-level value orientations, which are summarized as three dimensions: conservatism versus autonomy (intellectual and affective), hierarchy versus egalitarianism and mastery versus harmony. They are briefly defined below:

- Conservatism emphasizes maintenance of status quo, propriety and restraint of anything that might disrupt the group or the traditional order.
- Autonomy emphasizes intellectual autonomy (pursuing their own ideas and independent direction) and affective autonomy (pursuing affectively positive experiences).
- Hierarchy emphasizes unequal distribution of power, roles and resources.
- Egalitarianism emphasizes the welfare of others.
- Mastery emphasizes self assertion.
- Harmony emphasizes preserving the world as it is.

Schwartz dimensions are stronger in terms of the theoretical link between the constructs and items, but there has only been limited and mixed support for this framework in marketing (e.g. Watson et al., 2002). In addition, there is significant overlap with that of Hofstede. Schwartz correlated his culture-level value types with Hofstede dimensions finding significant overlap. That is, individualism is positively correlated with autonomy and egalitarian commitment and negatively with conservatism and hierarchy. Power distance is positively correlated with conservatism and negatively with autonomy. Uncertainty avoidance is

positively correlated with harmony. Mastery is positively correlated with masculinity. Steenkamp (2001) found similar overlap when he factor analyzed Hofstede's four dimensions and Schwartz's seven value types for the 24 countries that were in both data sets (Hofstede, 1991; Schwartz, 1994). He found a very similar pattern to that of Schwartz, except for his second factor, which included three of Schwartz value types; egalitarianism, hierarchy and harmony.

3.3

Culture-based attitudes towards action

Action is about changing the world, even in a minuscule way. Many actions do not involve problem solving: they are repetitive and programmed; they are daily or seasonal routines. Non-routine tasks require a more complex course of action, because they involve problematic features:

1. They must be based on a clear sense of purpose (why act?).
2. They involve a largely unpredictable future, and hence risk taking.
3. They need input from the past (taking lessons from previous experience).
4. They imply the need to articulate collective and individual interests.
5. They need to 'relate the hand to the brain, the heart and the mouth'.

Expressed metaphorically, this last feature means that action (hand), in a cross-cultural perspective, can hardly be separated from how people think (brain), how they relate their wishes and desires to actions (located somewhere between brain, heart and mouth), and how they mix feelings (located clearly in the heart, for most cultures) with deeds. Table 3.5 details the main contrasts across cultures in terms of attitudes towards action.

Most marketing and managerial action displays the problematic features given above. They are non-routine tasks, especially in an international context. Individuals and organizations naturally have a lot of leeway in making and implementing decisions, but most interpretive clues are from their own cultural background.

Table 3.5 Attitudes towards action

Basic problem/Cultural orientations	Contrasts across cultures
Why act?	
(a) Degree of fatalism: mastery of nature versus subjugation to nature; existence and degree of legitimacy of a Promethean (proactive) view of human life	People believe that it is possible to cope with any problem or any situation and that, to mankind, nothing is impossible; evil is when one does nothing ('master of destiny'); the converse is the belief that there are many situations where people cannot do anything; destiny binds us and we should not try to find alternatives (fatalistic orientation); evil is when one does not accept one's own destiny ('subjugation').
What is action?	
(b) 'Speech' versus 'deed' orientation	Contrast between cultures that value speech as action and those that separate them; contrast between a clear sequencing of action and a fuzzy view of action.
How to relate thinking to action (1)	
(c) Ideologism versus pragmatism	Ideologism: thinking patterns, communication (style of speech) and actions should always be set within the context of broad ideological principles (religious, political, social, legal, etc.); versus pragmatism: precise issues must be addressed; a practical attitude is favoured: orientation towards problem solving and concrete results.
How to relate thinking to action (2)	
(d) Intellectual styles	Differences in assigning a dominant role to theory, data, speech, modesty and virtue in assessing truthful propositions that need to be put into action.
How to relate wishes and desires to action	
(e) 'Wishful thinking' orientation (WT)	WT cultures tend to emphasize enthusiasm, imagination of the future and the capacity of desires to *shape* reality; non-WT cultures emphasize the principle of reality: desires and wishes have to be checked objectively against the constraints of the real world.
How to relate feelings to action	
(f) Affective (A) versus Neutral (N) cultures	People in N cultures separate feelings from actions, do not mix friendship with business; in A cultures, mixing both is seen as inevitable and positive.
How to deal with rules	
(g) Obeying practical rules versus coping with ideal rules	Rules can be made which are respected, discussed and implemented quite strictly or there may be a discrepancy between ideal rules and what people can actually do, leading them to undertake behaviour that involves exploring and bypassing rules.

Basic cultural assumptions, and combinations of these, have an influence on the way we cognitively evaluate real-world situations and the issues that face us. Some examples will demonstrate that we do know how to construct our reality but only within our native cultural community.

Why act?

Not everyone is preoccupied with doing, acting, being efficient and achieving tangible results that can be appraised by others. From an existential point of view this preoccupation with 'doing' is not really justified: in the long term we will all be dead, as Keynes said. Moreover, assuming that we all care about efficiency, there are many different ways of achieving it. Montesquieu ([1748], 1792, pp. 228–9) illustrates the spontaneous irritation of people who are 'doing' oriented towards those who are more 'being' oriented when, in *The Spirit of Laws*, he comments on what he calls *indolent nations*:

The Indians believe that repose and non-existence are the foundations of all things, and the end in which they terminate. Hence they consider entire inaction as the most perfect of all states, and the object of their desires. To the supreme Being they give the title of immoveable. The inhabitants of Siam (Thailand) believe that their utmost happiness consists in not being obliged to animate a machine or to give motion to a body.

Not only are the Indians and Siamese[2] (the Thai people) more 'being' oriented, they also have a quite different view of their relationship with nature from westerners (i.e. subjugation to nature rather than mastery over nature). As noted previously, their religions include belief in reincarnation: on the death of the body, the soul transmigrates or is born again in another body. Life therefore is not seen as 'one shot', but more as a cyclical phenomenon. This puts less pressure on people to be 'doing' oriented and means there is more inducement to *be* blameless and virtuous since it is these factors that will influence the status of further reincarnations; inaction is one of the surest ways to lead a blameless life. As Kumar (2000, p. 54) notes: 'Although brilliant in helping an individual cope with social reality, it is perhaps less attuned to dealing with the complexities of the larger social systems'.

The idea that we have a soul plays a substantial role in the sense of purpose that feeds our actions. It is only in the recent, 'modern' times that people have adopted the view that we are only made of material substances, whose molecules are recycled through flame or decay at the end, according to burial customs. As the Swiss psychologist, Carl G. Jung (see *WS3.3*), explains, it is a fairly new idea in world cultures:

Under the influence of scientific materialism became all that was not to be seen with eyes and touched with hands dubious, and even more, questionable, because suspected of metaphysics. Was only considered as 'scientific', and thus as altogether admissible, either what was recognized as material or what was derived from sensory perceptible causes. (Jung, [1931], 1990, p. 9, author's translation.)

Both ideas (having a soul or not) have their merits and it is obviously difficult to find supportive evidence for either one. Thus, it is more interesting to investigate the consequences for action of the assumption that we have a soul. When Kumar (2000) discusses the consequences of Brahmanism in India, he points out that the emphasis on 'thought' (being) over 'action' (doing) means that implementation receives less attention: there is 'an emphasis on developing grandiose schemes without concern for implementation at all' (p. 59).

The idea of a soul generally coexists with that of God. *Metempsychosis* (the migration of the soul from one body to another) is a very strong belief that arises as a response to an important common human problem: what is the relation between the physical world and the metaphysical world? Believers (people raised in the cultures where this belief is prevalent) are more patient, seemingly less 'doing' oriented, simply because achieving position in lives to come is more important than what is achieved in this life. Without discussing metempsychosis, let us look at some fundamental monotheist assumptions:

1. God as supernatural force, both protective and threatening.
2. God being almighty and therefore easy to offend.
3. God asking human beings to accept their destiny as it comes to them.
4. God also asking them to do as much as they can to act rightly and justly.

Fatalism is a belief that directly influences action, not necessarily in terms of acting less, but rather in terms of acting *differently*. It clearly posits the locus of control as being outside, in the metaphysical environment. It also provides convenient explanations for unpredictable events, which allow people to resume activity quickly after catastrophes (earthquakes, fires, car accidents). Fatalism makes mourning easier and facilitates the acceptance of strongly negative personal events, a bankruptcy for instance. (For more information on Fatalism see *WS3.3*.)

Where Christianity fundamentally differs from Islam is on assumption 3. The Christian creed more strictly separates the worldly from the heavenly sphere ('Render unto Caesar the things which are Caesar's; and unto God the things that are God's'). Furthermore, there is a less personal and direct relationship to God than in Islam, since, at least in Catholicism, it is largely mediated by the Church. This frees the tendencies towards mastery over nature, since God gives mankind leeway in relation to worldly enterprises. To a large extent, the punishment in the Promethean myth is forgotten about. In Christian religions, the way is cleared for proactive attitudes.

What is action?

Another important distinction to be made is whether a culture tends to classify words, speeches and, more generally, acts of communication, in the 'deeds' category. In many cultures there are popular sayings that effectively condemn speech on the basis that it is not real action ('do, not talk'). In the real world, life is more complicated: communications are a category of act, and their potential influence on others is beyond doubt. But whether communication (in what particular form?) is considered as being significantly related to action differs across cultures.

Let us take the example of poetry, which in Islam is highly esteemed. One can be fascinated by poetry, by the beauty of words and songs (and the fact of being fascinated can lead to the message of the poetry being acted on), as this commentary on the life of the Prophet illustrates:

Thus, Mohammed was sitting in the great courtyard of the Caaba, surrounded by the faithful, foreigners and Qureichits. The melodious music of the verses of the Koran was playing while the Prophet was gazing at the audience; the sparkle in His eyes and the beauty of the songs held the people spellbound. The people kept on repeating: 'If You

are a prophet, perform a miracle for us, so that we may believe in You.' And the messenger of God invariably answered: 'O Arab People, is not the miracle powerful enough, that your everyday language has been chosen for the Book, in which a single verse makes us forget about all your poems and all your songs?' It is said that, on hearing this response, non-believers committed themselves to convene all the poets of Arabia, so that they might create at least one verse, a few words, the beauty of which would match that of the Koran. The poets arrived at Caaba and began to perspire under the torrid sun. They toiled, they spared themselves no anguish in seeking to perform what had been requested of them. But as soon as they began to recite their works, even the fiercest opponents to the Prophet themselves were compelled to admit that none of their words could rival the verses of the Koran. Poetic spirit is so greatly esteemed among Arabs that many of those who were in the Caaba at that moment knelt down and were converted to Islam. The unrivalled beauty of the language had convinced them of its heavenly origin. (Mohammed Essad Bey, 1934, pp. 98–9, author's translation.)

The word 'poetry' comes from the Greek word *poio*, a verb meaning to 'make', to 'produce', to 'build'. Such an etymology, which is at first sight surprising, sheds some light on the opposing value judgements of the usefulness of poetry, which are made according to different basic cultural assumptions. On the one hand it may be seen as rather distanced from action in the real world, on the other as a direct source of inspiration for action. Indeed if a 'classical' model of action is assumed, i.e. one that is culturally European/ Western based, the following sequence occurs:

1. Analysis of the problem and the issues at stake.
2. Gathering of relevant information.
3. Listing and evaluating possible solutions.
4. Selecting the 'best' decision.
5. Implementation: that is, mainly articulating individual and collective action since the implementation process is generally scattered among numerous diverse agents, whereas the decision itself tends to be more individualized, or at least taken by a limited number of people.
6. Appraisal of the outcome, control of the difference between target and actual outcomes, and possibly feedback to a previous step in the sequence.

This sequence may be easily criticized for being culturally non-universal: Japanese people have no word for decision making (Lazer *et al.*, 1985), and action/ decision/control processes are viewed mainly as implementation issues. This is why they first insist on consulting each one of a large group of people at various levels in the organization, who will comment on how to do something (not necessarily on why). But even if we were to accept that this sequence is true, it would still involve a great deal of cultural relativity.

3.4

How to relate thinking to action

In relating thinking to action, the following categories are considered:

1. How should issues be addressed: broadly, with the premise that *the parts always represent the whole*, or narrowly, considering that *focus is the key to relevance* when acting?
2. What are the proofs that a certain course of action, based on previous reflection, is the right one: (a) data; (b) theory; (c) personal conviction; (d) virtue because it is morally correct to think and do so?

Ideologists versus pragmatists

If future partners do not share common 'mental schemes', it could be difficult for them to solve problems together. Buyers and sellers, for instance, should share some joint views of the world, especially on the following questions:

1. What is the relevant information for acting?
2. How should this information be sought, evaluated and fed into the decision-making process?

An important distinction in the field of cross-cultural psychology opposes ideologism to pragmatism (Glenn, 1981; Triandis, 1983). Ideologists will use a wide body of ideas that provide them with a formal and coherent description of the world: Marxism or liberalism, for instance. Every event is supposed to carry meaning when it is seen through this ideologist framework. On the other hand, the pragmatist attitude first considers the extreme diversity of real-world situations, and then derives its principles inductively. Reality will be seen as a series of rather independent and concrete problems to be solved ('issues'). These issues will make complete sense when related to practical, precise and even down-to-earth decisions.

Typically, ideologists will *take* decisions (*prendre des décisions*), that is, pick a solution from a range of possible decisions (which are located outside the person who decides). Conversely, pragmatists will *make* decisions, that is, they will both decide and implement them: decisions will be enacted, not selected. (For more information on pragmatism versus ideologism see *WS3.4*.)

Triandis (1983) hypothesizes that complex traditional societies will tend to be ideologist ones, whereas pluralistic societies or cultures experiencing rapid social change will tend to be pragmatist. This distinction may also be traced back to the difference between the legal systems of *common law* (e.g. UK and USA) and of *code law* (e.g. French and German). Whereas the first one favours legal precedents set by the courts and past rulings (cases) the latter favours laws and general texts. These are intended to build an all-inclusive system of written rules of law (code). Codes aim to formulate general principles that embody the entire set of particular cases. (See *WS3.4* for more information on code law versus common law.)

The ideologist orientation, which is to be found mostly in southern and eastern Europe, leads negotiators to try to set principles before any detailed discussion on specific clauses of the contract. They have a tendency to prefer and promote globalized negotiations in which all the issues are gathered in a 'package deal'. The pragmatist attitude, which is found mostly in northern Europe and the United States, leads negotiators to define problems of limited scope, then solve them one after the other. They tend to concentrate their thinking on factual aspects (deeds, not words; evidence, not opinions; figures, not value judgements) and are willing to reach real-world decisions, even if they have to be down-to-earth ones.

Thus, communication may be difficult when partners do not share the same mental scheme. The most unlikely situation for success is an ideologist-oriented contractor/supplier who tries to sell to a pragmatist-oriented owner/buyer. The ideologist will see the pragmatist as being overly interested in trivial details, too practical, too down-to-earth, and incapable of looking at issues from a higher standpoint. Pragmatists will resent ideologists for being too theoretical, lacking practical sense, concerned with issues that are too broad to lead to implementable decisions.

What information is relevant for action? How should it be used?

The dimensions of ideologism and pragmatism are not mutually exclusive. It would be a mistake to consider Americans as pure pragmatists with no leaning towards ideology. From a pragmatic view they identify problems clearly and precisely as 'issues' and collect evidence systematically. Their attitude is matter of fact. To be 'down to earth' is a positive expression in English, whereas its French equivalent is often pejorative (*être terre à terre*).[3] But it is also true that free-market/individual-oriented ideology has a strong presence in the United States, enshrined in the Constitution, in anti-trust legislation, in corporate law, and so on. However, ideology is rarely present on a daily basis, when information directly relevant to action is gathered or discussed. Ideology is generally accepted unquestioningly. It is therefore somewhat irrelevant to debate practical matters, as an ideologist would. Thus, they are more likely to be conscious of pragmatic considerations when ideology and ideas are the object of debate. In international business negotiations there is often a discussion of principles, but these may lead to a substantive outcome later on. The fundamental skill of diplomats (who are, in many respects, experts in matters of culture) is to obtain the acceptance and underwriting of basic principles by their counterparts, the effectiveness of which is only apparent at a later date.

Actual (empirical) reality versus potential reality: Which should be preferred?

It is a frequent mistake to believe that reality is simple, in the sense that it is directly related to our perceptions and the ways in which we act on it and try to change it. It is what we call 'common sense', that is, shared meaning which makes sense in the cultural community *simply because we share it*, even though it may appear nonsense to people belonging to other cultural communities. The English language is more realistic than the French language here, saying common sense (shared meaning) as opposed to the French *bon sens* (good sense), a value judgement that is sometimes wrong. Indeed our relation to the real world is heavily filtered by a series of convergent factors:

1. Our perceptual apparatus is partly culturally formed (see sections 1.4 and 9.4).
2. We implicitly choose to limit the search to certain categories of facts and represent them in a particular way.
3. We assess the truthfulness of these facts according to criteria that are determined in part by our cultural background. When and how they are established as true (meaning that there is a consensus about their being a part of the real world) is also culture-based.[4]
4. Even when these facts have been established as true, there still remain different interpretations of them, depending on culture-based values and social representations.[5]

We may favour either *actual/empirical* or *potential* reality. Actual empirical reality is the way in which we experience reality here and now (the way it is revealed by empirical science). Potential reality is the reality we imagine and dream about but which also motivates us to achieve. It is in a sense the *possible* future of actual reality. Our sense of potential reality relies much more on imagination than on actual perceptions. Since it is beyond the reach of our perceptions and we cannot experience it, we have to envisage potential reality. Potential reality is a rich ground for action, because it directly supports our Promethean desires to exert mastery over nature. It helps us to achieve objects and to undertake projects which can make us feel equal to gods ('space conquest' projects, for instance).

Galtung (1981) uses the distinction between actual reality and potential reality in order to contrast what he calls the 'intellectual styles' of four important cultural groups:[6] the Saxonic (prototype: the British and the Americans), the 'Teutonic' (prototype: the Germans), the 'Gallic' (prototype: the French), and the 'Nipponic' intellectual style (prototype: the Japanese). Saxons prefer to look for facts and evidence that result in factual accuracy and abundance. As Galtung states (1981, pp. 827–8) when he describes the intellectual style of Anglo-Americans:

data unite, theories divide. There are clear, relatively explicit canons for establishing what constitutes a valid fact and what does not; the corresponding canons in connection with theories are more vague . . . One might now complete the picture of the Saxonic intellectual style by emphasizing its weak point: not very strong on theory formation, and not on paradigm awareness.

Galtung contrasts the Saxonic style with the Teutonic and Gallic styles, which place theoretical arguments at the centre of their intellectual process. Data and facts are there to illustrate what is said rather than to demonstrate it:

Discrepancy between theory and data would be handled at the expense of data: they may either be seen as atypical or wholly erroneous, or more significantly as not really pertinent to the theory. And here the distinction between empirical and potential reality comes in: to the Teutonic and Gallic intellectual, potential reality may be not so much the reality to be even more avoided or even more pursued than the empirical one but rather a *more real reality*, free from the noise and impurities of empirical reality. (Galtung, 1981, p. 828.)

However, Teutonic and Gallic intellectual styles do differ in the role that is assigned to words and discourse. The Teutonic ideal is that of the ineluctability of true reasoning (*Gedankennotwendigkeit*),[7] that is, perfection of concepts and the indisputability of their mental articulation. The Gallic style is less preoccupied with deduction and intellectual construction. It is directed more towards the use of the persuasive strength of words and speeches in an aesthetically perfect way (*élégance*). Words have an inherent power to convince. They may create *potential reality*.

Finally the Nipponic intellectual style, imbued with Hindu, Buddhist and Taoist philosophies, favours a more modest, global and provisional approach. Thinking and knowledge are conceived of as being in a temporary state, open to alteration. The Japanese 'rarely pronounce absolute, categorical statements in daily discourse; they prefer vagueness even about trivial matters . . . because clear statements have a ring of immodesty, of being judgements of reality' (Galtung, 1981, p. 833). (For more information on Galtung see *WS3.4*.)

These distinctions are important for any situations where a certain course of action has to be based on favourable arguments, for instance, in assessing the quality of a marketing strategy and when doing market research. After the failure of a marketing campaign, people will tend to emphasize different issues: should they for instance (1) find supporting evidence of what went wrong, (2) convince salespeople to be more enthusiastic about the product, (3) re-think the theory behind the strategy, or (4) improve the quality of the troops in charge of implementation?

3.5

Dealing with desires and feelings

Management is based on the principle of reality, and not on the principle of pleasure (in Freudian terms), and therefore there is little interest in looking at people's desires and feelings, which are considered to be in the realm of the purely subjective, and deserving to be treated as almost non-existent. However, in a cross-cultural perspective, they are important, because people have different ways of relating their actions to their desires and feelings. In this section we are dealing with the two corresponding cells, (e) 'wishful thinking' orientation and (f) affective versus neutral cultures, in Table 3.5.

How to relate wishes and desires to action

As previously noted, words and deeds may either be classified in two separate categories or combined. They may be in opposition to each other in that words are empty or hollow, or complimentary in that words act on others: speech implies influencing and sometimes causes others to act. Most acts of authority are only words. To illustrate some culture-based misadventures in the relationship between words and deeds, Box 3.3 presents the role of wishful thinking (WT) in the international negotiation of a delivery date.

An important issue for cultural action styles is the problematical link between what one says and what one does. As previously discussed every culture mixes their use of actual/empirical and potential realities. But cultures differ in the ranking of these, and in the degree of distrust of potential reality. Obviously potential reality is more dangerous to deal with: it is easier to speak about it than to act on it. WT is related to any action that deals with the future and with potential reality: in bidding situations, the management of delivery delays, the announcement of prices, attitudes towards new projects, or in an advertising campaign where arguments unknowingly based on wishful thinking may 'explain why' the audience should be convinced by the message. (For more information about wishful thinking see *WS3.5*.)

Box 3.3

Wishful thinking

When selling industrial equipment or turnkey projects on world-wide markets, one or more delivery dates are usually stipulated. The effects of such an announcement may be severe: the buyer may cancel the order because the date is too late. However, this date rarely depends exclusively on the person who sets it.

Wishful thinking (WT) is a necessary input in this process: it explains why the initially announced delivery date (an actual reality) may be very different from the ultimate one (a potential reality). Wishful thinking is a true 'art of communication' which is preferred more in Latin cultures than in Anglo-Saxon cultures. There is no expression in French for *wishful thinking* (except perhaps *des voeux pieux*), so the English expression is used in French. The negative consequences of WT, such as deceitful behaviour, are much less emphasized in Latin than in Anglo-Saxon cultures. The fact that the phrase 'wishful thinking' is rather pejorative, shows that, normatively, in Anglo-Saxon cultures, it should be avoided, whereas in Latin cultures expressing desires appears more natural. Naturally, in addition to the cultural background there are also some personalities and psychological profiles which are more prone to wishful thinking.[8]

WT consists in first thinking, then saying, how one wants things to be, not how they are. Since nobody knows exactly how things will be in the future, a non-WT oriented person will try to say how he or she thinks quite realistically they will be, not as he or she wants them to be. WT is easier when a culture is present oriented, as people do not worry about periods which they do not clearly envisage: it is a convenient way to escape from the constraints of longer-term realities by focusing on the here and now. It dodges problems to be solved, and hides divergences and possible conflicts. But this is only in the short term. It is more inhibited if a culture clearly divides words from deeds (do what you say, say what you do). Conversely, if speech is considered an action, WT may possibly become a necessity (to galvanize people, while at the same time evoking an improbable future).

A seller with a strong WT communication has the tendency to tell a client spontaneously that the delivery date requested is entirely feasible. The seller also manoeuvres verbally around past realities which may not be wholly reassuring: a six-week delay in the last shipment, for instance. The buyer may also have a WT communication framework, and is in fact 'buying' friendly relations rather than hard data, preferring to be 'happy now'. On the other hand, if the buyer is not WT-prone, the seller is judged negatively and the order is not placed, unless there is some compelling rational argument such as a shortage of this type of supply, particularly high quality or exclusive technology.

(Source: Adapted from Usunier, 1989, pp. 89–90.)

Affective versus neutral cultures

The contrast between affective and neutral cultures is described by Trompenaars (1993, p. 63; see *WS3.5*): 'Members of cultures which are affectively neutral do not telegraph their feelings but keep them carefully controlled and subdued. Neutral cultures are not necessarily cold or unfeeling, nor are they emotionally constipated or repressed.' Countries were classified according to their response to a question asking if they would express their feelings openly if they felt upset about something at work. The highest score of neutrality was for the Japanese (83 per cent), followed by (the former West) Germany (75 per cent) and the United Kingdom (71 per cent). The Dutch are in the middle (55 per cent), whereas American people express their emotions more easily than the British, with only 40 per cent in favour of neutrality. Finally Italy and France are clearly more affective cultures, with only 29 per cent and 34 per cent respectively agreeing that they would not express their feelings openly.

The contrast between affective and neutral cultures is closely related to the being/doing divide in basic cultural assumptions and to dependence in the models of interaction. If people are strictly doing oriented they generally tend to disregard expressions of *being*. Feelings and affectivity are seen as *being* in the purely personal and private, individual, domain. Thus, Anglo-Saxon cultures tend to suppress these feelings and view their direct expression as inappropriate for effective interaction.

This practical problem which all cultures have to face is not an easy one. Over-suppression of emotions and feelings may result in flawed interaction and poor results in terms of action: people may discover quite late in a situation that personal antipathy is a major obstacle to further interaction. On the other hand, giving people a free hand to express all that they feel is somewhat dangerous, because feelings may be superficial or short-sighted and may needlessly offend the other party. The feelings/action issue is important for the choice of partners to improve communications in marketing negotiations, managing sales personnel, establishing relationships with foreign distribution channels, or preparing locally appropriate advertising materials.

Every culture has certain codes and rituals that allow for a compromise between the two extreme positions. What varies is the starting assumption:

1. Expressing emotions is legitimate and useful for action (affective cultures).
2. Expressing emotions needs to be separated from action (neutral cultures).

It needs, however, to be refined, by the addition of two further caveats. First, as emphasized by Trompenaars, people have no fewer emotions in neutral cultures than in affective cultures; perhaps the contrary is true. Since feelings and emotions are contained, they may pile up and result in hidden negative feelings. Second, much is based in personality traits and individual interaction; culture, in this area, should not be overestimated. Much is universal rather than culture-specific in the area of feelings and emotions. Chapter 13 on language, culture and communication explores the issue of affectivity versus neutrality in more detail.

3.6

Coping with rules

Rules and basic assumptions

A rule is an authoritative regulation or direction concerning method or procedure. Rules are formalized norms that generally comprise a scale of sanctions according to the gravity of the breach. Rules can be made which are respected, discussed and implemented quite explicitly, or there may be a discrepancy between ideal rules and what people can actually do, leading them to behaviour involving the exploring and bypassing of rules. Some typical indicators of rule-related behaviour deal with speed limits, traffic lights, queuing at banks or bus stations, how income statements are filled in, and so on. A naive interpretation of rules would be that they are made to be respected. The real function of rules is more complex. Written rules are fairly standard across cultures. But, the first precaution is to read rules in the light of basic assumptions and interaction models (see Tables 3.6 and 3.7):

1. A positive human nature orientation (HNO) leads to rules where sanctions are small and often positively reinforced with a reward for respecting the rule being preferred to a penalty. People are viewed as capable of being trusted to respect the rules and gain benefit from them (HNO good), whereas high sanctions and severe enforcement are the case in cultures with an HNO-bad assumption.
2. The level of power distance in a particular society has an influence on (a) the design of rules and (b) their implementation. Low power distance generally results in people being associated in some way with the design of rules, and in their being applied with a sense of fairness and equity to everybody, including those with larger power in the society (Hofstede points out that power is unequally distributed, even in low power distance societies). In contrast, high power distance results in people being subject to rules, in the design of which they were not involved. Furthermore, rules apply more strongly to those with less power, the most powerful being seen as somewhat beyond the reach of rules that apply only to 'ordinary people'.
3. As noted in the discussion in the previous chapter on space-related assumptions, strong ingroup

Table 3.6 Type of rules and behaviour according to HNO and power distance

		Power distance	
		Low	High
Human Nature Orientation	Good	Pragmatic rules (responsible compliance)	Challengeable rules (exploring behaviour)
	Bad	Mechanical rules (automatic compliance)	Oppressive rules (bypassing behaviour)

orientation often leads to the syndrome that rules are 'applicable only here' (that is, in the native community, not outside).

4. The inner drive to respect the rule: guilt (*inner feeling* of responsibility for committing an offence) versus shame (a painful *emotion, directed to the outside*, resulting from an awareness of having done something dishonourable as a group member).

Table 3.6 presents four ideal types of rule, and behaviour in relation to rules based on the type of HNO and the level of power distance. In this table, the HNO assumption must be understood in a somewhat comparative way between the ruler and the ruled: 'good' means that the ruled view themselves as 'better' than or equal to the ruler; 'bad' means that the ruled view themselves as 'as bad' as or 'even worse' than their rulers.

Types of rules and rule-related behaviour

Anglo-rules, including those of northern European countries, are basically 'pragmatic' rules: people generally comply with the rule out of a sense of responsibility built on positive motivation; rules are understood as helping society to work more smoothly and efficiently and everyone is supposed to benefit from their being respected. In this picture, people are universally at ease with their rules; even if they sometimes break them (nobody is perfect).

'Challengeable rules' correspond to those that exist in Italy or France where power distance is fairly high and ordinary people view themselves as having a better human nature than those at the top. It is not seen as wrong to investigate the extent to which rules can

be transgressed. Most often rules come directly from the top, without any 'instructions for use'. Rule exploring means looking for the margins of interpretation. The only way to explore a new rule is to breach it discreetly from the start in order to know whether it is intended to be applied seriously or whether it is one more empty text that nobody will respect.

'Mechanical rules' would be found in the German or Swiss case; they are made democratically because power distance is low, but there is distrust of people. Sanctions are explicit and implemented fairly literally: as in the well-oiled machine model of Stevens (the German model of organization as described by Hofstede; see section 3.2), respect for rules has a fairly mechanical and automatic side: they are applied literally.

The last stereotypical case is to be found in many developing and Third World countries with high power distance and negative assumptions as to the nature of human beings, powerful or not. Rules are often very strict, formal and somewhat unrealistic. Chapter 11 develops the example of foreign exchange control systems, which lead to the bypassing of the rule by over- or under-invoicing. Oppressive rules oblige people who have been subject to long-term rule to bypass the law and induce rulers into corrupt behaviour (they can implement unimplementable rules with some leniency in exchange for a bribe). Oppressive rules lead to a strange atmosphere, where there is a high discrepancy between what people say they will do and what they actually do, a sort of systematic social schizophrenia (for instance the policeman will change money in the forbidden parallel exchange market). The idea of possible discrepancies between ideal patterns and actual behaviour was expressed by Linton (1945, pp. 52–4):

All cultures include a certain number of what may be called ideal patterns . . . They represent the consensus of opinion on the part of the society's members as to how should people behave in particular situations . . . comparison of narratives usually reveals the presence of a real culture pattern with a recognizable mode of variation . . . it [the ideal pattern] represents a desideratum, a value, which has always been more honoured in the breach than in the observance.

Box 3.4 shows how rules can be more complicated than those officially displayed as a result of opportunistic behaviour and their being difficult to respect. In any country, an examination of the basic rules relating to the functioning of society (e.g. traffic, queuing, taxation) and how they are actually implemented, quickly provides a fairly good idea of local patterns in dealing with rules. (For more information on coping with rules see *WS3.6*.)

Universal versus local rules

Table 3.7 contrasts universal with local rules: universal rules are assumed to be applicable even beyond the borders of cultures and countries. An example lies in US laws being applicable extraterritorially, such as

Table 3.7 Universal versus local rules

Type of rule	Universal rules	Local rules
Ingroup orientation	Weak	Strong
Inner compliance dynamic	Guilt	Shame

anti-trust rules or the anti-corrupt legislation, FCPA, examined in Chapter 15. The legal concept of extraterritoriality is typical of outgroup orientation, and the US legal extraterritoriality is often resented by other sovereign states as an intrusion into their home affairs. On the other hand, strong ingroup orientation leads to the feeling that rules are only local, they apply to the people here, on their territory and not outside.

People who favour universal rules are characterized by an inner compliance dynamic based on guilt, that is, self-reproach caused by an inner feeling that one is responsible for a wrong or offence. The moral punishment is to a large extent interiorized within the psyche as in the Freudian concept of *schuld* (in

---

Box 3.4

Brazilian traffic lights

When I travel to Brazil, I stay in Rio de Janeiro with friends who work for the Brazilian census bureau (IBGE). There, I have learnt that the rules for traffic lights are not really the same as elsewhere. It is not as simple as 'red = stop', 'green = go'. Sometimes cars just do not stop when it is red for them. There seems to be no rule. Investigating more carefully, I gradually discovered that the rule is largely situation-specific. In the case of heavy traffic, it tends generally to be well respected, which shows a certain common sense on the part of Cariocas. In the case of lighter and smoother traffic, it depends mostly on the relative size of streets (not to mention the driver's personality and propensity to take risks). Those coming from a smaller street must take care before they benefit from their green light: people on the larger street may cross the red

lights after slowing down a little bit, but without stopping. Thus, out of rush-hours traffic lights are semi-optional for those driving on major avenues. The last case comes at night: one should never stop at red lights even when lawfully required to do so. One night as we were coming back from an IBGE party at Jacarepagua (a nice suburb of Rio), Roberto explained to me, as he drove across the town to Flamengo without apparently noticing traffic lights, that, a year ago, he had been assaulted by a man who had threatened to shoot him through the side window of his car. Naturally, he had given him all his money and was fortunate enough to get back home unhurt. The rule at night is therefore: never stop at a traffic light, it is better to slow down to catch the green and if necessary cross on the red.

German: debt, fault, culpability). Conversely, the inner compliance dynamic for ingroup-oriented people is based on shame and is more outer directed: it has to do with losing face, having one's honour threatened, that is, risking rejection by the other group members. Local rules are territory bound and concern breach of loyalty to the ingroup.

Adopting a more open view of how people attribute meaning to rules makes sense for a large array of international marketing issues. As far as consumer behaviour is concerned, rules on waiting, attitudes towards queuing, theft from stores by consumer or sales staff, the attention paid by consumers to instructions for use (of pharmaceuticals, food), the attitude towards filling in market research questionnaires, giving truthful information and, more generally, any ethical issue that involves social responsibility of manufacturers, service providers or consumers have to be examined with a view to their cross-cultural relativity.

3.7

Cultural assumptions and actual behaviour

As outlined in Chapter 1, all societies face common problems, and although there is a dominant solution, alternatives are always present, and they combine in a dialectic way. Let us take the example of how individual and collective actions are to be combined. Japanese people are often depicted as collectivist, in contrast to Americans who are deemed more individualistic. There is undoubtedly an element of truth in this distinction, but it is necessary to outline its limits. Who is more humane, more personal and more sensitive in interpersonal relations, more attentive and understanding than the average Japanese person? Who cares more about the community than the average American, whose objective is to 'socialize in the community'? In the United States the word 'community' is used extensively. Indeed Americans and Japanese share a common problem (as defined by Kluckhohn and Strodtbeck, 1961): that of combining individual actions and collective undertakings.

This problem may be solved only by a process which is essentially dialectic. In any society there exists a dominant cultural assumption about what the *first*

(but not the *sole*) priority should be: either the individual (as in the United States); or else the group is the basic survival unit to which the individual must be subordinated (as in Japan). Then comes the secondary cultural assumption, which dialectically complements the basic assumption: that the community is where people integrate to build a common society, and their reciprocal links should be strictly and explicitly codified (United States); or that the utmost level of sensitivity must be developed in interpersonal relations so that the working of the group is kept as smooth as possible (Japan).

The basic cultural assumptions described in the previous sections are in fact deep-rooted beliefs that generate basic values. Indirectly they guide our daily behaviour, but they may also clash with it. By their very nature they are subconscious, as is the process by which they shape our interaction with others and our conduct. There is some leeway for other sources of influence: for instance, we use social representations to make decisions. We are influenced by other values and other standards of demeanour, such as work rules, company codes of conduct, lifestyles or friendship patterns which work closer to the surface than basic cultural assumptions. These standards of demeanour help people to manage adjustments in the short term; they change over much shorter periods of time (ten or twenty years) than basic cultural assumptions (probably formed over centuries). This leads to two questions:

1. To what extent do less profound levels of culture, e.g. corporate culture or educational culture, influence people?
2. To what extent do people, more or less consciously, feel a contradiction between these different sources of prescriptive behaviour?

From Schein's (1981) culture model, Derr and Laurent (1989) present what they call the 'levels of culture triangle' (see Figure 3.2). Basic assumptions are at the bottom of the triangle. These influence the values and behavioural norms which derive from the society in its present state. At the top of the triangle are behavioural standards, which are prescribed in a much more direct and explicit way, which Derr and Laurent call 'artefacts': for instance, company procedures, business ethics codes and generally all those standards that unashamedly seek to shape employees' behaviour (inside the company). Whereas cultural

Figure 3.2 Basic cultural assumptions and actual behaviour

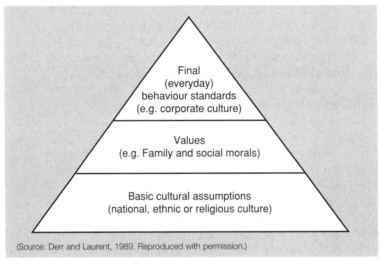

Final
(everyday)
behaviour standards
(e.g. corporate culture)

Values
(e.g. Family and social morals)

Basic cultural assumptions
(national, ethnic or religious culture)

(Source: Derr and Laurent, 1989. Reproduced with permission.)

assumptions are based on national culture, 'artefacts', values and norms are based on organizational culture.

Multinational companies (MNCs) offer their employees the most fruitful opportunities for intercultural exchange. One might believe that, despite differences in national culture, the values shared by executives in MNCs will converge, as they spend years working with different people. In order to grasp differences in cognitive styles, Laurent (1983) asked managers of different nationalities to indicate their agreement or disagreement with the following statement (item 24 of Laurent's questionnaire on management styles): 'It is important for a manager to have at hand precise answers to most of the questions that his subordinates may raise about their work.' (For more information on corporate and national culture see WS3.7.)

Figure 3.3 reproduces the percentage of respondents replying in the affirmative for various national groups. Obviously Swedes do not need omniscient managers (10 per cent). Among westerners, the Italians (66 per cent) and the French (53 per cent) believe that managers should have precise answers to most of their subordinates' questions. It seems that most Anglo-Saxon and northern European people tend to see managers as problem solvers, whereas Latin and Asian people see them more as *experts*.

These differences were observed in people working in their home country. In a later study, Laurent (1989) asked the same question of executives who had been working for a long time in MNCs where teams had been built up from a large number of different nationalities. One would expect to observe a decrease in the differences between national groups of managers. Surprisingly, the situation is exactly the opposite. Laurent observed an increase of differences across national groups. This suggests that, behind superficial agreements, people's basic cultural assumptions are reinforced. When a corporate culture tries to shape a manager's (or more generally an employee's) daily behaviour, it may succeed from the outside (because people are concerned about their job and career), but it only scratches the surface. It does not significantly affect the two bottom levels of Figure 3.2, values and basic cultural assumptions. Moreover, since this is forced upon them, not only do they fail to impinge on basic cultural assumptions, but they even reinforce them.

Does this mean that international experience has no effect on managers? It is more likely that international experience will influence our 'newer view' of the way the business world works than the basic cultural assumptions that guide our behaviour. For instance, Lee *et al.* (2000) in a study of Japanese and Korean manager's views on marketing tactics, including pricing, found that the importance of brand names and superior product design were more similar in firms that had a high level of internationalization, than those whose focus was domestic. Thus changes occur in the realm of organizational learning (see Kim, 1993), rather than in our fundamental cultural assumptions.

Figure 3.3 National differences in subordinates' expectations towards their superiors

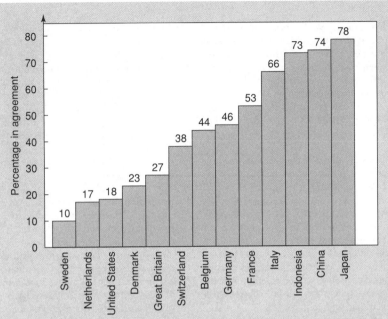

'It is important for a manager to have at hand precise answers to most of the questions that his subordinates may raise about their work.'

(Source: Laurent, 1983, and Adler *et al.*, 1989.)

Questions

1. What do you think the cultural roots to personal modesty might be?

2. Which examples would you suggest to exemplify American individualism?

3. In many countries, there is an institution called 'parliamentary democracy'. On which basic cultural values is it based, in your opinion? Is there a relationship between the development of marketing and parliamentary democracy?

4. Given country scores on Hofstede's four dimensions, what do you expect would be the problems encountered by a typical boss from country X in managing a typical employee from country Y (even at the risk of some stereotyping and sweeping generalization)?
   (a) An American boss managing Japanese subordinates.
   (b) A Japanese boss managing French subordinates.
   (c) A French boss managing Swedish subordinates.
   (d) A Swedish boss managing Japanese subordinates.

5. A conversation is in progress between a British manager and a French manager concerning a common (large) project. The project is at a very early stage (examining its feasibility, setting deadlines for construction, planning of steps in building process, etc.). The Frenchman is very enthusiastic and argues: 'Let's go, we can do it; *impossible n'est pas français!*' ['impossible is not a French word']. The Englishman feels somewhat uneasy about the turn of the conversation. Why?

6. Are there Japanese individualists? Why?

7. A sign indicates: 'Parking time limited to 10 minutes. Be fair.' Which views of time and rules does this reveal? Try to imagine signs with different information for people who have a different approach to rules.

Notes

1. Berne's theory (Berne, 1961, 1964) is based on a view of the self as composed of three stratas: the Parent, the Adult and the Child. Transactions between human beings can take place at the same level or across levels of the self, for instance when a person sends a message based on his Parent to the Child of another person. What we suggest here is simply that some cultures may favour Adult–Adult transactions in interpersonal relationships whereas others tend to promote Parent–Child transactions, especially in hierarchical situations.

2. Siam is the name originally given by the French to the present Thailand: Siamese are therefore Thai people.

3. This means implicitly: compared to Latins, such as myself. We are generally much less cautious in taking such steps, if indeed we ever stop to identify them clearly. Even the style of this book reveals that I come from an ideologist-oriented society (French). The expressions 'matter of fact' and 'down to earth', which are both positive in English, may be translated by *être terre à terre*. The French language also has two expressions, but one is pejorative and the other is positive – *avoir les pieds sur terre* (*Harrap's Concise French–English Dictionary*, 1984, Harrap: London, p. 369).

4. Those who wish to enlarge their world-view by freeing themselves, at least partially, from the mental programmes brought to them by culture, risk being misunderstood. This is in fact a legitimate reaction on the part of other members of the group. By trying to escape a single cultural programming, such people exhibit a definite lack of humility in setting themselves apart from the community. Furthermore, any homogeneous human group feels quite threatened when members of the group overstep the threshold of non-conformity. They may finally be understood (because the message is useful as an instrument of change that is needed in the society), or live alone, or be beheaded (e.g. Sir Thomas More).

5. Clifford Geertz in *Local Knowledge* (1983) quotes a long passage from a Danish traveller and trader, L.V. Helms, who when travelling in India accurately reports the ritual of the cremation of a dead man and his three (living) widows. Helms describes very carefully the background to the incident, which took place around 1850. He is horrified by the ritual, amazed by the absence of reaction of the crowd attending the event and stunned by the lack of fear of the three women who throw themselves alive into the flames.

Geertz emphasizes the relationship of culture to moral imagination: what is seen as shear barbarism by one culture is experienced as wholly normal by another. Another more recent example of cross-cultural differences in the interpretation of facts is given by the totally divergent views during the Gulf War about Saddam Hussein (whose actions are well known): bloodthirsty dictator to some, hero of the Arab world to others. When Saddam Hussein fired Scud missiles at Saudi Arabia and Israel, interpretations of this simple act were also totally divergent. For an interpretation of the Gulf War reportage as representing advertising for weapons, see Ottosen (1992).

6. The article by Johan Galtung that we quote deals with the intellectual style of academics. Since it describes 'intellectual styles' in general (not only the style of the intellectuals), this framework is used as depicting 'ideal types'. Johan Galtung, a Norwegian, is a renowned scholar in the field of peace research. His numerous articles and books are an important source of reflection on national culture and the conflicts between cultural communities.

7. The concept of *Gedankennotwendigkeit* is typical of German thinking patterns, where abstraction is taken to its limits. It is not by chance that German philosophers have a worldwide reach. The German language is probably the richest in the world in terms of abstract words. It favours pure conceptual thinking. The construction of *Gedankennotwendigkeit* is itself proof (sorry: an illustration) of this: *denken* means 'to think', *Gedanken* are 'thoughts'; *Not* means 'necessity', *wenden* is 'to turn', *-keit* is a suffix that abstracts the whole as 'the state of being . . .'. As a result of this rebus, *Gedankennotwendigkeit* is something like '*the state of being turned into necessary (unavoidable, pure) thoughts*' (*Langenscheidt German–English Dictionary*, 1970, Basic Books: New York, used for the translation of component words).

8. To use a (very elementary) Freudian distinction: the denial of WT employs the anal principle of tightening oneself up and controlling one's behaviour, when strongly integrating reality as a constraint; conversely, the use of WT denotes oral behaviour: favourable words (*paroles*), which describe reality in a much more pleasant way than it actually is, provide wishful thinkers (and above all, wishful *speakers*) with a mouth pleasure. This oral behaviour thwarts the frustrations of reality, like the little child that sucks its thumb when unhappy.

References

Adler, Nancy J. (2002), *International Dimensions of Organizational Behaviour*, 4th edn, South-Western Publishing: Cincinnati, OH.

Adler, Nancy J., Nigel Campbell and André Laurent (1989), 'In search of appropriate methodology: from outside the People's Republic of China looking in', *Journal of International Business Studies*, vol. XX, no. 1, p. 69.

Belk, Russel W. (1985), 'Cultural and historical differences in concepts of self and their effects on attitudes toward having and giving', *Proceedings of the 12th Annual Conference of the Association for Consumer Research*, ACR: Provo, UT, pp. 754–60.

Belk, Russel W. (1988), 'Possessions and the extended self', *Journal of Consumer Research*, vol. 5, pp. 139–68.

Berne, Eric (1961), *Transactional Analysis in Psychotherapy*, Grove Press: New York.

Berne, Eric (1964), *Games People Play*, Grove Press: New York.

Bista, Dor Bahadur (1990), *Fatalism and Development*, Orient Longman: Calcutta.

Brislin, Richard W., Kenneth Kushner, Craig Cherrie and Mahealani Yong (1986), *Intercultural Interactions: A practical guide*, Sage: Newbury Park, CA.

Chen, Chao C., Xiao-Ping Chen and James R. Meindl (1998), 'How can cooperation be fostered? The cultural effects of individualism-collectivism', *Academy of Management Review*, vol. 23, no. 2, pp. 285–304.

de Mooij, Marieke and Geert Hofstede (2002), 'Convergence and divergence in consumer behavior: Implications for international retailing', *Journal of Retailing*, vol. 78, no. 1, pp. 61–9.

Derr, C. Brooklyn and André Laurent (1989), 'The internal and external career: a theoretical and cross-cultural perspective', in M.B. Arthur, D.T. Hall and B.S. Lawrence (eds), *Handbook of Career Theory*, Cambridge University Press: Cambridge.

Essad Bey, Mohammed (1934), *Mahomet*, Payot: Paris.

Ferraro, Gary P. (1990), *The Cultural Dimension of International Business*, Prentice Hall: Englewood Cliffs, NJ.

Frese-Weghöft, Gisela (1989), *Ein Leben in der Unsicherbarkeit*, Rowohlt: Hamburg.

Galtung, Johan (1981), 'Structure, culture and intellectual style: an essay comparing Saxonic, Teutonic, Gallic and Nipponic approaches', *Social Science Information*, vol. 20, no. 6, pp. 817–56.

Geertz, Clifford (1983), *Local Knowledge*, Basic Books: New York.

Glenn, E. (1981), *Man and Mankind: Conflict and communication between cultures*, Ablex: Horwood, NJ.

Hofstede, Geert (1980a), *Culture's Consequences: International differences in work-related values*, Sage: Beverly Hills, CA.

Hofstede, Geert (1980b), 'Motivation, leadership and organization: do American theories apply abroad?', *Organizational Dynamics*, Summer, pp. 42–63.

Hofstede, Geert (1991), *Cultures and Organizations: Software of the mind*, McGraw-Hill: Maidenhead.

Hofstede, Geert (2001), *Culture Consequences*, 2nd edn, Sage Publications: Thousand Oaks, CA.

Hofstede, Geert and Michael Harris Bond (1988), 'The Confucius connection: from cultural roots to economic growth', *Organizational Dynamics*, vol. 16, no. 4, pp. 4–21.

Jung, Carl Gustav (1931), 'Das Grundproblem der gegenwärtigen Psychologie', in *Wirklichkeit der Seele*, DTV: Munich, 1990.

Kim, Daniel H. (1993), 'The link between individual and organizational learning', *Sloan Management Review*, vol. 36, no. 1, pp. 37–50.

Kluckhohn, Florence R. and Frederick L. Strodtbeck (1961), *Variations in Value Orientations*, Greenwood Press: Westport, CT.

Kumar, Rajesh (2000), 'Confucian pragmatism vs. brahmanical idealism understanding the divergent roots of Indian and Chinese economic performance', *Journal of Asian Business*, vol. 16, no. 2, pp. 49–69.

Laurent, André (1983), 'The cultural diversity of Western conceptions of management', *International Studies of Management and Organization*, vol. XII, nos. 1–2, pp. 75–96.

Laurent, André (1989), presentation to the European Foundation for Management Development Seminar 'Cultural shock', EFMD Annual Conference in March, Marseille.

Lazer, William, Shoji Murata and Hiroshi Kosaka (1985), 'Japanese marketing: towards a better understanding', *Journal of Marketing*, vol. 49, Spring, pp. 69–81.

Lee, Jangho, Thomas W. Roehl and Soonkyoo Choe (2000), 'What makes management style similar and distinct across borders? Growth, experience and culture in Korean and Japanese firms', *Journal of International Business Studies*, vol. 31, no. 4, pp. 631–52.

Linton, Ralph (1945), *The Cultural Background of Personality*, Appleton-Century: New York.

Markus, Hazel Rose and Shinobu Kitayama (1991), 'Culture and the self: implications for cognition, emotion and motivation', *Psychological Review*, vol. 98, no. 2, pp. 224–53.

Mead, Margaret (1948), *Male and Female*, William Morrow: New York.

Montesquieu, Charles de (1748), *The Spirit of Laws*, translated from the French by Thomas Nugent (1792), 6th edn, McKenzie and Moore: Dublin.

Ohye, Kazuko (2003), 'From Chanel chick to individualist', *The Issue*, Research International's client magazine, available at: www.research-int.com.

Oliver, Elizabeth Goad and Karen S. Cravens (1999), 'Cultural influences on managerial choice: an empirical study of employee benefit plans in the United States, *Journal of International Business Studies*, vol. 30, no. 4, pp. 745–62.

Ottosen, Rune (1992), 'The media and the Gulf War reporting: advertising for the arms industry?', *Bulletin of Peace Proposals*, vol. 23, no. 1, pp. 77–83.

Robertson, Christopher J. (2000), 'The global dispersion of Chinese values: a three-country study of confucian dynamism', *Management International Review*, vol. 40, no. 3, pp. 253–68.

Rotter, J.B. (1966), 'Generalized expectancies for internal versus external control of reinforcement', *Psychological Monographs*, vol. 80, no. 609.

Schein, Edgar H. (1981), 'Does Japanese management style have a message for American managers?', *Sloan Management Review*, Fall.

Schwartz, S.H. (1994), 'Are there Universal aspects in the content and structure of values?', *Journal of Social Issues*, vol. 50, pp. 19–45.

Schwartz, S.H. (1999), 'Cultural value differences: some implications for work', *Applied Psychology: International Review*, vol. 48, pp. 23–47.

Smith, Adam (1776), *The Wealth of Nations*, University of Chicago Press edition: Chicago, IL., 1976.

Smith, Peter B., Shaun Dugan, Mark F. Peterson and Kwok Leung (1998), 'Individualism: collectivism and the handling of disagreement. A 23 country study', *International Journal of Intercultural Relations*, vol. 22, no. 3, pp. 351–67.

Sondergaard, Michael (1994), 'Hofstede's Consequences: a study of reviews, citations and replications', *Organization Studies*, vol. 15, no. 3, pp. 447–56.

Steenkamp, Jan-Benedict (2001), 'The role of national culture in international marketing research', *International Marketing Review*, vol. 18, no. 1, pp. 30–44.

Triandis, Harry C. (1983), 'Dimensions of cultural variation as parameters of organizational theories', *International Studies of Management and Organization*, vol. XII, no. 4, pp. 139–69.

Triandis, Harry C. (1990), 'Cross-cultural studies of individualism and collectivism', in J. Berman (ed.), *Nebraska Symposium on Motivation, 1989*, University of Nebraska Press: Lincoln, Nebraska, pp. 41–133.

Trompenaars, Fons (1993), *Riding the Waves of Culture*, Nicholas Brealey: London.

Trompenaars, F. and C. Hampden-Turner (1998), *Riding the Waves of Culture: Understanding Cultural Diversity in Global Business*, 2nd edn, McGraw-Hill: New York.

Usunier, Jean-Claude (1989), 'Interculturel: la parole et l'action', *Harvard-L'Expansion*, no. 52, Spring, pp. 84–92.

Watson, John, Steven Lyonski, Tamara Gillan and Leslie Raymore (2002), 'Cultural values and important possessions: a cross-cultural analysis', *Journal of Business Research*, vol. 55, pp. 923–31.

Weeks, William H., Paul B. Pedersen and Richard W. Brislin (1987), *A Manual of Structured Experiences for Cross-cultural Learning*, Intercultural Press: Yarmouth, ME.

Wong, Nancy and Aaron Ahuvia (1995), 'From tofu to caviar: conspicuous consumption, materialism and self-concepts in east-Asian and Western cultures', *Proceedings of the Second Conference on the Cultural Dimension of International Marketing*, Odense, pp. 68–89.

Appendix 3

Teaching materials

A3.1 Critical incident

An American in Vietnam

An American in Vietnam recalls an illuminating story told him by a Vietnamese who complained about a lack of understanding between the two allies. They were discussing the fate of a province chief named Vong, once hailed by the Americans as the best province chief in Vietnam. Vong was accused of embezzling some 300,000 American dollars earmarked for an airstrip, and was tried and sentenced to be executed. It seemed a harsh sentence, considering the corruption prevalent at the time, and the American asked the Vietnamese if he agreed.

'No,' the Vietnamese said, 'Vong should be executed because he's a stupid man'.

'Stupid? Because he got caught?' the American asked.

The Vietnamese impatiently shook his head. 'No, no, not because he took the money,' he said. 'That is not important. But you know what this stupid man did? He pacified six more hamlets than his quota. This caused the general who gave him the quota to lose face, and that is stupid.'

The perplexed American said, 'In America, he'd get a medal for exceeding his quota.' The Vietnamese shook his head and said, 'You Americans will never understand the Vietnamese.'

Question

What aspects of the incident are significant in describing the difference in opinion between these two persons?

(Source: Weeks *et al.*, 1987, p. 22.)

A3.2

Rationales for section A2.1 (cross-cultural scenario) and sections A2.2 and A2.3 (cross-cultural interactions)

A2.1 Scenario: Inshallah

This scenario can best be understood by first appreciating the very different views in US culture and Saudi culture concerning 'locus of control'. In the US it is believed that ultimately people are responsible for their own destiny. If something goes wrong, it is believed, it is frequently possible for the individual to *do* something (that is, to change certain behaviour) to bring about the desired outcome. In Saudi Arabia, and indeed throughout the Arab world, people are taught from an early age that all things are subject to the direct will of Allah. All plans for the future (including, of course, business plans) are viewed with a sense of inevitability and will be realized only if God wills it. This is not to say that people in the Arab world would not work hard to help bring about the desired results. Rather, they believe that despite the effort, the desired ends will not happen unless God is willing. Perhaps Stefan would have been less frustrated if he had translated *inshallah* to mean 'if possible' or 'God willing' rather than as a knee-jerk response used to absolve oneself of all responsibility for one's actions.

(Source: Ferraro, 1990, p. 162. Reproduced with permission.)

A2.2 Interaction: Engineering a decision

1. There is little evidence for this in the story. While the financial benefits are relevant, to Mr Tanaka they are probably a minor consideration in the situation. Please choose another response.
2. It is quite probable that coming from a male-dominant Japanese society he does think it odd that Mr Legrand should mention his wife's opinion. However, the decision not to go to the Middle East also appears to be Mr Legrand's personal inclination so this does not fully account for Mr Tanaka's bewilderment. There is another explanation. Please choose again.
3. It is unlikely that Mr Tanaka would consider this. There are factors far removed from personal gain dominating his concern. Please choose again.
4. This is the most likely explanation. In Japanese and many other collectivist societies a person is defined much more as a collection of roles (parent, employee, servant, official) than by his or her individual identity. Therefore, fulfilling these roles to the best of one's ability is regarded as more important than one's personal inclinations. Thus Mr Tanaka would see that Mr Legrand's responsibility as a company employee would be to accept the position whether or not he is personally happy about the idea. Mr Legrand's refusal is thus bewildering and makes him think that his belief in Mr Legrand's dedication has been completely misplaced. Mr Legrand however comes from a culture where individual freedoms are highly valued and so exercises his right to refuse the offer with little compunction. The cultural conflict thus resides in different strengths of values applied to the roles occupied by a person in the culture.

(Source: Brislin *et al.*, 1986, pp. 177–8.)

A2.3 Interaction: Opening a medical office in Saudi Arabia

1. It is unlikely that people would sign up solely to satisfy a newcomer's feeling. There is a better explanation. Please select again.
2. If there is a considerable time lag between when a person makes a decision and the action upon it, it is possible that they may change their mind. However, there is no indication in the incident to support this. Please select another response.
3. Units of time reference differ markedly between Arab and American cultures. To an American, the major unit of time is five minutes. Fifteen minutes is a significant period of time. To an urban Arab, the unit of time that corresponds to our five-minute block is fifteen. Thus, when the Arab is 30 minutes late (by the clock), he is not even ten minutes late by his standards. This is the best answer. Tom's patients may still arrive.
4. While the patients may be seeing their own traditional healers, they would not necessarily do so in the strict sequence suggested by this alternative. There is a more precise explanation. Please choose again.

(Source: Brislin *et al.*, 1986, p. 179.)

Part 2 The integration of local consumption in a global marketing environment

ستاربكس
كافيه

STARBUCKS
COFFEE

Introduction to Part 2

Globalization has taken place at a rapid pace over the last half-century. The continuous expansion of cross-border marketing has been backed by the progressive elimination of barriers to trade, and the emergence of a global consumer culture. Although global convergence seems undeniable, some basic traits of local consumption experience tend to resist change. The general objective of this part is to show how global and local patterns coexist in both consumer behaviour and marketing environments. The cross-cultural approach to international marketing that is presented in Chapters 4 to 7 should enable future international marketers to understand local consumer behaviour in its full complexity. This approach allows adaptation of the design and implementation of market research across national markets when research instruments and data collection procedures are not similarly understood and do not produce equivalent findings cross-nationally.

Quite often basic concepts have been developed in a specific cultural environment, generally that of the United States, and it is necessary to investigate whether the consumer behaviour concepts and theories used cross the borders of cultures without losing part of their relevance and explanatory power. Consequently, Chapter 4 deals with the cross-cultural dimension of consumer behaviour theories. It starts by assessing how culture affects consumer behaviour and highlights its influence on selected concepts such as loyalty, involvement and dissatisfaction. The chapter also examines the topic of ethnic consumption. The last section in this chapter takes as its premise that marketing is based on exchanges of meanings between marketers and consumers. This perspective makes much sense in international marketing since meaning is directly based on language, and linguistic diversity remains quite high cross-nationally.

The encounters between local consumers and increasingly globalized consumption items are complex, contradictory and sometimes problematic. Chapter 5 first explains how the trend to globalization has been ideologically supported over the last two centuries by the free trade doctrine and how this doctrine tended to view products merely as commodities and to deny cross-national variety in consumers' tastes and consumption habits. Analysis of global trends in consumption patterns shows striking convergence at a broad, quantitative level: the utilitarian needs for reasonably priced, mass-produced products and services are strong drivers behind this fast-paced change. The emergence of a global consumer culture is based on increasing aspirations for a world-standard package of goods and services whose performance is highly predictable. However, the meaning attributed to products and consumption experiences remains to a large extent embedded in local contexts, that of shared habits within the cultural and linguistic groupings. Examples are given of how products whose consumption is becoming global, such as beer, are locally reinterpreted and vested with specific meanings, which must be taken into account when designing marketing strategy. In some cases, local consumer cultures can be strong enough to develop resistance to globalized consumption if it is perceived as detrimental to local cultural and economic interests. In most cases, however, the emergent pattern is that of a mix of local and global consumer behaviour based on kaleidoscopic ways of assembling diverse consumption experiences and making sense of them in everyday life.

Because of increased economic integration worldwide, marketing environments and practices converge at regional and global levels. Chapter 6 first shows how local marketing environments have borrowed and transformed concepts and practices coming mainly from the United States. Regional convergence is also taking place because of free trade areas and customs unions: three sections examine diversity and change in three major regional areas (the European Union, Eastern Europe and the CIS, and East Asia). The chapter concludes with a consideration of the limitations to the worldwide convergence of marketing environments, showing that some key distinguishing features, such as language, will remain deep obstacles to wholly standardized marketing strategies.

When market research takes place across borders, a number of survey instruments, such as questionnaires, scales, sampling techniques, interview techniques, etc., may not fit with the target contexts where data has to be collected. Chapter 7 exposes the technicalities of cross-cultural market research, that is, the problems posed by the possible inequivalence of instruments and methods across research contexts. The chapter reviews equivalence issues, such as conceptual, functional, translation and measure equivalence, which are examined in successive sections and illustrated by real-life examples. The issue of samples and sampling procedures is addressed because of the need of international marketing decision makers for findings that can be consistently compared across cultures and markets. Chapter 7 also examines how local respondents may react to survey instruments and which sort of data biases result from their unfamiliarity with the chosen data collection techniques. As a consequence, international research is often less technical than domestic research in terms of scientific survey instruments and needs more inputs of action research: this is illustrated in the last section with the example of the Japanese style of researching markets.

4

Cross-cultural consumer behaviour

'*Sehen Sie Mercedes mit anderen Augen. Die neue E-Klasse ist da*' says a 1995 Daimler-Benz poster for their new E-Class car ('Look at Mercedes with other eyes. The new E-Class arrives'). That is what this chapter is all about: looking with other eyes. It basically deals with the influence of culture on consumer behaviour. Looking with the 'same eyes' means that theories, underlying models, concepts and views of what consumers are, what their motives are, and how they behave are assumed to be universal. One may 'add glasses to the same eyes' so that what was previously invisible comes to light. But what Mercedes asks its potential consumers to do may be necessary: changing the eyes in order to have a different perspective. Table 4.1 sums up four perspectives, starting from the view that both consumers (the object) and underlying consumer behaviour theories (the eyes) can be either universal or specific. When reading Table 4.1, it is important to note that no cell corresponds to a better perspective than any other.

The first perspective, in its purest form, is now rarely found except in the text on globalization of markets by Levitt (1983) and more generally when consumers are viewed as truly global. It may make sense for particular classes of consumers, such as business people travelling worldwide, and their families ('the global nomads'). The *global perspective* has been widely used and in some cases has led to the design of successful marketing strategies. Kotler's *Marketing Management* is now in its eleventh edition (2003): it is a worldwide success that started at position 1 and has steadily shifted to position 2. It has been translated into many languages and is used in various national contexts. For instance, the adaptation of Kotler's book to the French context by Dubois is in its eleventh edition.

Hirschmann (1985) describes the ideological base of American consumer behaviour research as promoting conceptualizations and conjectures in a definite framework, where individuals actively seek information and make personal decisions that lead to pragmatic goals. She challenges these assumptions by looking at primitive aspects of consumption in definite US ethnic groups (Black, Italians, Jews, WASPS – White Anglo-Saxon Protestants). The view that underlying theories and concepts have to be

Table 4.1 Consumer behaviour in a cross-cultural perspective

		Consumer behaviour theories	
		Universal (etic)	Specific (emic)
Consumers	**Universal**	**(1)** Global perspective	**(3)** Ethnic consumption perspective
	Specific	**(2)** 'Imported' perspective	**(4)** Cultural meaning perspective

challenged is even more clearly relevant when one is looking at international markets.

In the *imported perspective*, the offerings are tailored to the local markets and marketing environments but the basic underlying theories are not changed. The imported perspective may sometimes enable one to discover significant differences in consumer behaviour (CB) that require adaptation, but it is not always sufficient. For instance, initially the behavioural intentions models were assumed to be universally applicable. Then, when looked at from the imported perspective researchers found different weightings between attitude and norms. That is, for consumers in individualist cultures attitudes were more influential on intentions than norms, while the reverse was true in collectivist cultures (Lee and Green 1991; Bagozzi *et al.*, 2000; Lee, 2000). Then, researchers began to look with new eyes finding that different models better suited different cultures (Malhotra and McCort, 2001; Bagozzi and Lee, 2002). In fact, as early as 1978, Van Raaij called for 'researchers in other cultures to study their own reality rather than to replicate American studies' (p. 699).

In this chapter we will progressively move to question the cross-cultural transposability of CB theories. This is not to say that similarities do not exist between cultures. The commonalities are demonstrated by the success of products and services designed in perspectives 1 and 2. But it is important to assess the cultural relativity of both consumers and the underlying models that are applied if we really want to understand their behaviour. For instance, Marieke de Mooij (2000, p. 104) investigated the convergence in CB, finding that: 'Although there is evidence of convergence of economic systems, there is no evidence of convergence of peoples' value systems. On the contrary, there is evidence that with converging incomes, people's habits diverge.'

It is important to know what one is looking for: similarities or differences (see *WS4.1*). Both exist; it is just a matter of being clear about which models one applies: those that let differences emerge or those that favour the discovery of similarities. This corresponds with the etic (universal) approach and the emic (specific) approaches. Luna and Gupta (2001) used this division in their integrative review of the cross-cultural consumer behaviour literature.

Section 4.1 discusses the influence of major cultural traits on consumer behaviour. We start with the question of whether the hierarchy of needs applies cross-culturally. Not only whether people locate their needs at different levels in the hierarchy, across cultures, but also, are the major assumptions in this model valid across cultures? This influences the motivations behind consumption. The next topic is the influence of individualism and collectivism on consumers' attitudes and buying behaviour. We also include a section on the individual level independent and interdependent self-concepts that are more or less likely to be salient in individualist and collectivist cultures. Finally, the influence of institutions, social conventions, and customs on consumer behaviour is discussed.

Section 4.2 examines the impact of culture on selected aspects of consumer behaviour. Since it is not feasible to deal with all aspects of consumer behaviour, Table 4.2 lists the types of cultural values and behaviours that have an impact on consumer attitudes, decision-making and buying behaviour. The table also suggests issues to be addressed in order to reach a better understanding of cultural differences in the area of consumer behaviour. The final sections review how consumers' loyalty, involvement, perceived risk, cognitive style, and the legal environment are affected by cultural variation.

Section 4.3 goes further, analyzing the difficulties of transferring certain consumer behaviour constructs across cultures, based on the example of consumer dissatisfaction. Marketers tend to apply consumer behaviour concepts in an ethnocentric manner, whereas they would learn more by focusing on a common problem: how do cultures solve a similar problem in a different way?

Section 4.4 examines the influences of ethnicity on consumption patterns. As we argued at the end of Chapter 2, cultural borrowing is intense, and immigrants bring with them their values and behaviour. Ethnic consumption is a major dimension of cross-cultural consumer behaviour in two respects: (1) ethnic consumption has introduced modified consumption patterns in those countries that have been opened to immigration for some time; and (2) some ethnic products have reached world-class status by being adopted in most countries of the world, through migration and international travel, such as Asian food.

Marketing is a process involving communication and exchange: consumers buy meanings as well as objects. Accordingly, section 4.5 focuses on the way in which cultural background influences communication and exchange. Two examples are used to illustrate this: the role of emotions in Japanese marketing and the role of symbolic linkage between objects and persons in the Italian style of marketing.

4.1

Culture and consumer behaviour

Although consumer behaviour has strong universal components, its cultural variations cannot be ignored. Without presenting an exhaustive list, there are some essential points of cultural influence on consumer behaviour that are worth considering in some detail:

1. Hierarchies of needs, which shape demand across product categories.
2. Culture-based values, especially individualist or collectivist orientations, which influence purchasing behaviour and buying decisions (individual versus family).
3. Institutions, which influence consumer behaviour, given that most consumption is rooted in social life, a large part of which is institutionalized.

Hierarchy of needs

Culture influences the 'hierarchy of needs' (Maslow, 1954) on at least two levels: first, one of the basic axioms of Maslow's theory is not true in every culture – namely, that needs at a definite level must be satisfied in order for higher-order needs to appear; and second, similar kinds of needs may be satisfied by very different products and consumption types. In Maslow's hierarchy of needs, physiological needs are at the lowest level because they are the most fundamental; safety needs (being sheltered and protected from dangers in the environment) emerge when physiological needs are satisfied; and then come what Maslow calls social needs, which include friendship and love relationships. The next level, esteem, is the desire for respect from others, which is strongly supported by status-improving goods. The last and final need, when all other levels have been satisfied, is the need for self-actualization, encompassing the development of one's own personality. (For more information on Maslow's hierarchy see WS4.2.)

Naturally, the level of economic development has some influence on the satisfaction of our needs: in a less developed economy, people usually focus on more basic survival needs. However, some cultures (e.g. Hindu) encourage the need for self-actualization, the highest level (the satisfaction of which does not necessarily imply material consumption). Thus, the basic need for safety (shelter, basic personal protection) is not satisfied according to the same criteria in different cultures. For instance, in certain developing countries, people may deprive themselves of food in order to afford a refrigerator, thereby satisfying the social status and self-esteem need before satisfying their physical need (Belk, 1988). The well-documented area of conspicuous consumption also contradicts the hierarchy of needs. As noted by Solomon (1994, p. 426), the term *conspicuous consumption* was coined by Veblen, who was initially inspired by anthropological studies of the Kwakiutl Indians.

These Indians had a ceremony called a *potlach* where the host showed off his wealth and gave extravagant presents to his guests. The more one gave away, the better one looked to the others. Sometimes, the host would use an even more radical strategy to flaunt his wealth. He would publicly destroy some of his property to demonstrate how much he had. This ritual was also used as a social weapon: Since guests were expected to reciprocate, a poorer rival could be humiliated by inviting him to a lavish potlach. The need to give away, even though he could not afford it, would essentially force the hapless guest into bankruptcy.[1]

The potlach example suggests that consumer motivations are rooted in the dynamics of social life. Thus one of the basic axioms of Maslow's theory – that needs must be satisfied at one level in order for the needs in the next level to appear – is not true from a cross-cultural point of view. Slightly caricatured, Maslow's picture of motivation describes an individual, starting from the belly and extending to the brain: although relevant, it cannot provide a universal view cross-culturally. After a review of the literature Mendenhall *et al.* (1995) illustrate the limited support for the cross-cultural applicability of Maslow's hierarchy of needs. That is, seven studies support it strongly, three give it partial support, and ten research studies refute it. In sum, the needs described by Maslow are themselves fairly consistent across cultures, but their rank ordering varies.

The degree of emphasis on specific needs and the link to satisfaction at different need levels is also culture bound. Rather than needs, which have a distinct rational and utilitarian connotation, consumer *desires* may be a more useful concept for cross-cultural consumer behaviour.[2]

Individualism and collectivism

Most of the available marketing literature depicts individual consumers who make their own decisions. While the individualistic conception remains very much at the heart of the mental picture of marketing, there has been recent recognition of shared or social intentions (Bagozzi, 2000). For instance, Bagozzi and Lee (2002, pp. 229–30) describe the concept of social intentions termed 'we-intentions to perform a group act . . . In this case a person plans to participate in a joint activity, but conceives of the activity less as individuals performing personal acts that contribute to a group performance than as a group action in which one is a member of the group'. While there is a great deal of support for attitudes and subjective norms explaining individual intentions, they suggested a greater influence of the group on we-intentions, including group norms and social identity. They found mixed support for their propositions when they examined American and Korean students' intentions for their group to eat lunch together. They did however find multiple group influences on we-intentions, including social identity for Koreans and group norms and subjective norms for Americans. In a similar study, Lee and Soutar (2004) also found that group norms strongly influence Singaporean's we-intentions to travel to Australia.

Two other areas of research have a history of examining group decisions: the industrial marketing literature in regard to organizational purchasing and buying centres; and the family decision making. The family is often seen as an interacting group of individuals, all influencing each other. While an *organic* conception of the family as a single decision-making unit is not easily grasped, some cross-cultural CB researchers have depicted the family group as an organic entity, as opposed to a casual collection of individuals who share information and some common interests and constraints, living together within the family cell. This is especially true in Asia.[3] Redding (1982, pp. 104, 112–13), for instance, emphasizes that:

In most Asian cultures there is a particular grouping to which a person belongs, which involves him in patterns of obligation and behaviour of a special kind . . . It would, for instance, be naive to suppose that the buying power of a teenage market in a Western country would be equivalent to one in, say, Hong Kong or Singapore. The discretion over the use of income is heavily influenced, in the case of the Chinese teenager, by the expected contribution to the family. The tradition of deference to parental wishes also affects buying patterns in clothing, leisure expenditure, etc., especially as it is normal to live at home until marriage.

The influence of collectivism on family decision making has been well reported in the literature especially in Asia. For instance, a Chinese individual must take into account members of the family when making a purchase decision, in contrast with the Western husband's or wife's interactive decision-making process regarding important household expenditures. This is supported by Chen *et al.* (1999) who found that both Taiwanese and Japanese families reported a high level of joint decision making. In addition, Rose (1999) found that Japanese mothers restrict their children's consumption, allowing less autonomy, while at the same time reporting a higher level of children's influence, than American mothers who encourage the development of independent consumption relatively early. Similarly, in a study of Thai and American families, Viswanathan *et al.* (2000) found stronger family ties, greater communication and a greater influence on consumption behaviour with Thai respondents as compared with Americans. Wimalasiri (2000) also found a stronger need for harmony in Fijian families where parents complied with a polite request from their children 28 per cent of the time but they only complied with a demand 9 per cent of the time, as compared to 30 per cent of American parents.

In the East, the extended family model has survived apparently Westernized ways of life (Laurent, 1982); it has a powerful influence on many purchase decisions. Even Chinese people, who may sometimes appear quite individualistically oriented when outside their national context, remain strongly bound by their family ties. Yang (1989) describes the influence of what she calls 'familism' on their behaviour as individuals, as family members and as consumers (Box 4.1).

Independent versus interdependent self

Consumers buy objects and services for the value they provide. In valuing things, consumers may attribute private and/or public meanings. Richins (1994, pp. 505–6) defines public meanings as the subjective

Box 4.1

The role of familism in Chinese consumer behaviour

The single most essential concept to characterize Chinese culture is undoubtedly familism (Ballah, 1970; Yang, 1972). Confucius himself defined five fundamental human relations, three of which relate to family relations: parent and child, husband and wife, and brother and sister. All five of them had roughly equal weight in terms of importance. Later, some of his influential disciples, however, made filial piety the most important among the five (Hsieh, 1967). In any event, a Chinese individual's relationship with family members is a permanent one, which is never grown out of. The Chinese definition of family is often very broad, including various lineages and generations. The single most influential group on an individual's behaviour is his family members, usually extended family members. The influences of family members on an individual's behaviour are extremely extensive; often they extend to areas definitely considered private by Western standards. In contrast to their relationships with their families, Chinese people's relationships with secondary groups beyond the family are usually ill-defined and sometimes non-existent.

The consequences of this emphasis on familism and filial piety are many. First, a Chinese individual's behaviour often cannot be considered as an act reflecting his own preferences or will. It is often the result of a consensus or compromise of himself and his family members, or a take-over by his family's,

most often his parents', preferences or wills. Second, social harmony is highly valued in a society whose basic social unit is the extended family (Chien, 1979). To maintain stable and peaceful coexistence is more important than anything else when there are a lot of people who are interdependent and interconnected with each other, constantly involved at any given time and place. Third, an individual's relationships with core family members are not only strong and spontaneous but also collective. The bonds are so natural that they are also very casual. They usually do not need deliberate cultivation by way of saying 'I love you' all the time or showering each other with gifts (Hsu, 1971). Finally an individual's relationship with other non-family members are usually formalized but peripheral. The affections of strangers are not deliberately sought after but can be naturally developed. Strangers are also likely to become a part of the 'extended' family and to be treated accordingly but not until trust has been established between them and a Chinese individual (Fei, 1948). In other words, the Chinese intergroup relationships are often limited to two types; i.e., family (inside) and non-family (outside). Other group memberships are not usually sought and therefore not easily established.

(Source: Yang, 1989.)

---

meanings assigned to an object by outside observers (non-owners) of that object, that is, by members of the society at large. Public meanings emerge through socialization and participation in shared activities and are reinforced in social interchanges. Private meanings are the sum of the subjective meanings that an object holds for a particular individual. Some of the private meanings may derive from socially shared interpretations, but some of them are unique to the consumer because they are associated with private and even intimate experiences.

Both Asians and westerners see the self as divided into an inner private self and an outer public self

based on social roles. It is important to go beyond the individualism/collectivism divide in order to understand how the concept of self distinguishes westerners and Orientals (and how this concept is articulated with the concept of others). The divide between individualism and collectivism may be considered as the other side of this reality, at the social rather than personal level.

At the personal level, Markus and Kitayama (1991) proposed two relatively stable dimensions of the self: as *independent* and *interdependent*. The *independent* self corresponds to the Western conception; it is based on assumption of individualism discussed in section 3.1, whereby people are seen as inherently separate and distinct. The inner self is the regulator of activity and personal consumption preferences are supposed to reflect a person's tastes, values and convictions. Self-expression is encouraged, especially in the area of consumption. The slogan is 'be yourself', that is, act in accordance with your private self (Wong and Ahuvia, 1995).

On the other hand, the *interdependent* self of most Asians is based on an assumption of collectivism. People are seen as not fully separable, that is, they are connected to each other by a multitude of overlaps and links: they share a common substance. So as a result, identity lies in familial and social relationships. People with interdependent selves tend to value the criteria of appropriate social conduct in their consumption behaviour.

These distinctive self-concepts are not mutually exclusive. All of us carry aspects of independence and interdependence; which one is used depends on the situation and reference group (Triandis, 1994). Consequently, people from collectivist cultures are more likely to rely on an interdependent self-concept and people from individualist cultures are more likely to rely on an independent self-concept in any given situation.

Research into the influence of an interdependent or independent self-concept is relatively recent for consumer behaviour. It has been made possible by the development of scales to measure these concepts.[4] These scales have been used to assess many aspects of consumer behaviour including reasons for purchase (Lee and Kacen, 1999), impulsive buying behaviour (Kacen and Lee, 2002), references for consumption symbols (Aaker and Schmitt, 2001), associations embedded in persuasion appeals (Aaker, 2000) and the persuasion of approach and avoidance appeals (Aaker and Lee, 2001) and emotional appeals (Aaker and Williams, 1998).

Chiou (1999) conducted an experiment with students in Taiwan and the United States, finding that consumers in individualist cultures used products to express their inner value, while consumers in collectivist cultures were more likely to use products to reinforce their social relationships. Similarly, Lee and Kacen (1999) examined the influence of the interdependent and independent self-concepts with students from Australia, the United States, Malaysia and Singapore, finding that the independent self-concept

was more strongly related to purchase reasons associated with uniqueness, while the interdependent self-concept was more strongly related to reasons associated with group affiliation.

Institutions, social conventions, habits and customs

Institutions, such as the state, the Church and trade unions also have an influence on the marketing environment. For example, the French Catholic hierarchy has generally been opposed to Sunday trading. In Germany, trade unions strongly oppose an extension of store opening hours. Stores generally close at 7 p.m. each working day, at 2 p.m. on Saturdays, and are closed on Sundays. These hours are legally mandated and contravening shops are heavily fined. The result is that many German consumers must shop quickly on Saturday mornings. Catalogue-based mail order and online shopping are good substitutes for consumers kept at their offices during shop opening hours. As a result, mail order sales are highly developed in Germany, with giant enterprises having developed in the industry, such as Neckermann, Bertelsmann and Quelle.

Other products are in a sense institution dependent, whatever their mode of distribution or consumption: examples include marriage-related goods such as a wedding dress or the products featured on wedding lists, or many kinds of traditional gift that are offered for specific occasions. One example is the initiative by a Parisian Catholic priest to take action against Halloween in favour of the next day, All Saints Day, traditionally an important holiday in France. In conjunction with the French Association of Bakers, a '*Gâteau de la Toussaint*' was developed to increase respect for the day of honouring the dead, thereby creating an institution-dependent product.

Of all the cultural conventions that structure daily life in the consumption domain, the most important is probably eating habits. (For information on Chinese eating habits, see *WS4.2*.) As emphasized by Wilk (1995, p. 372): 'Food is both substance and symbol; providing both physical nourishment and a key form of communication that carries many kinds of meanings.' Cultural variations, in addition to the social interpretation of eating habits, include the following:

Box 4.2

Café au lait and 'slow food'

In France, many people start the day with a simple *café au lait*, coffee with milk (a real poison according to doctors). In Germany, the UK and the US, people start with a larger breakfast, but eat less than the French at noon. American students in France are always astonished by the two-hour break for lunch: they tend to consider it as a 'loss of time', without seeing that this was part of the socializing process in and out of the family, depending on whether the meal is at home or outside. The regularity of meal hours is another difference that may have far-reaching consequences. Americans are more ready than other people to eat at 'non-standard' hours. For McDonald's and other fast-food restaurants this is a big opportunity in terms of peak scheduling because Americans do not rush to eat at very specific hours. In some European countries, it is quite difficult to maintain the 'fast' aspect of service, since staff must face high peak demand, especially at noon. As a result, the restaurants become 'slow food' restaurants, with customers waiting up to 20 minutes to be served. But European people do not mind that very much because what they want from McDonald's is not speed. On the contrary, they like to stay longer than the restaurant itself would like them to stay. In all likelihood what they seek is cheap and pleasant food, with a modern American image.

1. The number of meals consumed each day.
2. The standard duration of a meal, and the position of meals in the daily schedule.
3. The composition of each meal. The portions may differ in size, comprising various kinds of food (local ingredients or cooking style); the nutritional content may be composed so that the eater can cope with long or short time periods without further calorific input during the day.
4. Which beverages accompany the meal (water, coffee, tea, wine, beer, and so on) and what their 'status' is – refresher, energizer, coolant, relaxer, etc. (See Box 4.2.)
5. The social function, whether 'fuel' or daily 'social event'. The meal may be a communal event where people entertain themselves by eating and chatting together, or it may simply be a means of feeding oneself without any symbolic, personal or collective connotation.
6. Is the food ready-made or is it prepared from basic ingredients? Do servants help prepare the meal? What is the cultural meaning of the meal being prepared by the housewife or by her husband, for whom, in which particular situations?

The list of cultural variations in eating habits is endless, because nothing is more essential, more universally vital and at the same time more accurately defined by culture than eating habits. Eating habits should be considered as the whole process of purchasing food and beverages, cooking, tasting, and even commenting on them. For instance, Brunsø, *et al.* (1996) developed an instrument in western Europe to assess food-related lifestyles which included five areas: ways of shopping (e.g. information importance, joy of shopping); quality aspects (e.g. health, price-quality relation); cooking methods (e.g. involvement, convenience); consumption situations (e.g. snacks versus meals, social event); and purchase motives (e.g. self-fulfilment in food, social relationships). Askegaard and Brunsø (1999) tested the instrument in Singapore, by asking students to take the survey home and have the member of the household who does the most cooking and shopping for food fill it out. While 89 per cent of the respondents were female, 11 per cent were maids. They found that the 'cooking patterns in Singaporean families are definitely very different from the European ones. First of all, the presence of a maid and the regular habit of dining out makes the "woman's task" more diffuse to define in terms of responsibility for the family's health and nutrition. Furthermore, the issue of carrying out tasks (maid) versus controlling these tasks (wife or husband) may cause problems in terms of who is to respond to various sections on the survey' (p. 80).

In many countries, commercials advertising ready-made foods, such as canned or dried soups, faced resistance from the traditional role of the housewife, who was expected to prepare meals from natural ingredients for her family. As a result, advertisers were obliged to include a degree of preparation by the housewife in the advertising copy for such foods. (For more references on food and eating habits cross-nationally see *WS4.2.*)

4.2

The influence of culture on selected aspects of consumer behaviour

Table 4.2 presents selected aspects of consumer behaviour that can be influenced by cultural differences. This table is not designed to be an exhaustive list or review of the literature, since there has been a dramatic increase in the cross-cultural analysis of consumer behaviour. For more comprehensive reviews of the literature see Luna and Gupta (2001) and Sin *et al.* (1999). Some of the issues listed in Table 4.2 are developed at greater length later in this and other chapters, as indicated in the table.

Loyalty

Consumers can be loyal, that is, they repeat their purchases on a regular basis, buying the same brand or product, or buy at the same store or from the same catalogue or website. Loyal consumers prefer to be sure of what they buy. However, by doing this they reduce their opportunity to find other, and perhaps better, choices which would provide them with more value for their money. Disloyal consumers try new brands, shift from one brand to another when a new one is promoted, and take advantage of temporary price reductions. Disloyalty is the natural counterpart of loyalty (to a brand, a product, a store, etc.). What is culturally meaningful is to observe which one of these two opposite attitudes is considered as the legitimate, fundamental behaviour.

In the United States, *brand loyalty* is very carefully surveyed, and explanatory variables such as demographics, lifestyles or situational variables are researched. Standard behaviour is assumed to be disloyal, although there are large classes of loyal consumers. American consumers may switch brands because it is standard behaviour to test several competing products, thereby fostering price competition. In this culture, it is standard behaviour to respond spontaneously to advertising and sales promotion. Equally, it is assumed that consumers are not rewarded by buying the same brand (i.e. 'brand loyal') and/or shopping in the same store (i.e. 'store loyal'). The fact that consumers may enjoy the same stable environment, of which their favourite products would form a basic constituent, is somewhat underestimated.[5] Stated in a different way, it is assumed that American consumers enjoy change more than stability. Of course there are large groups of loyal consumers; habits and stability are a reality for many Americans. The number of these groups is, however, probably less than in other countries where brand loyalty is normal behaviour.

Loyalty is a key concept in collectivist cultures, which spreads from people to product, in as much as products are extensions of the self. There is an unusual level of single brand dominance in many Asian markets (Robinson, 1996) with one brand accounting for 40–50 per cent of market share over quite a long period of time. Chiou (1995) argues that consumers in collectivist (Asian) societies tend to be more loyal on average, for two reasons. First, they tend to rely more on information found in their reference group – often by word-of-mouth communication – rather than on information diffused by the media. Second, they tend to follow the group consensus until there is significant evidence that the new product is better. In one of the few studies examining loyalty outside Western cultures, Kim *et al.* (2002) found that consumers from China and South Korea tended to buy the same brands because these products fulfilled their experiential, social and function needs.

Steenkamp *et al.* (1999) assessed the influence of national culture on consumer innovativeness, which is defined as a predisposition to buy new and different products and brands, rather than remain with previous choices. In a sample of eleven western European countries, they found that consumer innovativeness was higher for people from more individualist cultures, from more masculine cultures and from cultures with less uncertainty avoidance. Similarly, Straughan and Albers-Miller (2001) studied cultural influences on loyalty in the United States, Australia, France and South Korea. They found that uncertainty avoidance and collectivism were both positively

Table 4.2 Possible impacts of cultural differences on selected aspects of consumer behaviour

Aspect of consumer behaviour	Impact of cultural differences: values involved/issues to be addressed	Section
Perception	Perception of shapes, colours and space varies across cultures.	2.3; 9.4
Motivation	Motivation to own, to buy, to spend, to consume, to show, to share, to give.	4.3
Learning and memory	Literacy levels. Memory as it is shaped by education. Familiarity with product classes shaped by education.	4.2; 4.3
Age	Do people know their exact age? Value of younger and older people in the society. Influence processes across age groups. How is purchasing power distributed across generations?	3.1
Self-concept		3.1; 4.1
Group influence	Individualism/collectivism. To what extent are individuals influenced in their attitudes and buying behaviour by their group? How does consumer behaviour reflect the need to self-actualize individual identity or to manifest group belonging?	3.1; 3.2 4.1
Social class	Are social classes locally important? Is social class belonging demonstrated through consumption? What type of products or services do social-status-minded consumers buy? Are there exclusive shops?	3.1; 4.1
Sex roles	The sexual division of labour; who makes the decisions? Shopping behaviour; who shops: he or she or both of them?	3.1; 3.2
Attitudes changes	Resistance to change in consumer behaviour (possibly related to high level of uncertainty avoidance, past orientation, fatalism), especially when change could clash with local values and behaviour (e.g. resistance to *fast-food* restaurants in France).	4.2
Decision making	Family models (nuclear versus extended family). Involvement. Compulsive buying.	4.0; 4.1 4.2
Purchase	Loyalty. Environmental factors, especially legal. Influence of salespersons on clients.	4.2 15.1 15.3
Post-purchase	Perceptions of product quality. Consumer complaining behaviour. Dissatisfaction/Consumerism.	4.3; 9.1 9.2; 9.3 10.2; 10.3; 11.3

related to loyalty, suggesting that companies entering markets with these characteristics will face more obstacles. Where consumers are more loyal, it may be necessary to build a loyal consumer base from scratch. Where consumers are less loyal, it may be more effective to persuade brand shifters to switch from other established brands, and then to try to turn the newly developed consumer base into a loyal one.

Thus, marketing strategies may need to differ where consumers are fundamentally more loyal, often less brand-conscious and less used to rational comparisons (such as price/quality cross-brand or cross-product comparisons), from those where consumers frequently shift from one brand to another.

Consumer involvement

The involvement of the consumer in product purchase or consumption varies across cultures. Yang (1989) depicts the Chinese consumer as being in a low-involvement situation when products are used for private consumption. In this case, Chinese consumers are likely to adopt a rather simple cognitive stance, favouring the physical functions of the product and being mostly concerned with price and quality. Conversely, there is a high level of purchase involvement when Chinese consumers buy products for their social symbolic value. These consumers greatly value social harmony and the smoothness of relationships within the extended family, therefore the social significance of a product is very important because it may express status, gratitude, approval or disapproval. While Kim et al. (2002) did not examine involvement; they did examine the relationship between needs and loyalty for women in their clothing purchase, which is likely to have a high level of involvement. In line with Yang's research, they found that Chinese female consumers bought the same brands to primarily satisfy experiential needs (fashion trends) and social status needs, and only to a much lesser extent for functional needs.

Perceived risk

Perceived risk is an important variable in consumer behaviour, and differs according to its breakdown into various components: physical risk, financial risk, social risk, and so on (Van Raaij, 1978). Whereas people in certain cultures may be more susceptible to physical risk (because the mortality rate is low, death is feared and avoided), others may be more sensitive to social risk (because a purchaser may risk the loss of face in other people's eyes). Let us take an example of perceived risk: when buying a car, in a country where road safety is not a high priority the perceived physical risk is low; where mileage is not relevant, because petrol is so cheap, there is a low perceived financial risk; but an engine breakdown may be seen as a disaster, because there is little or no available maintenance, therefore there is a high perceived reliability risk. These perceived risks are quite different from those experienced by the average purchaser of a car in a western European country. However, when purchase contexts are highly standardized worldwide, such as in the case of compact disks, there are only minor differences in risk-reducing behaviour across cultures (Mitchell et al., 1996).

Bao et al. (2003) studied risk aversion and face consciousness and their impact on decision-making styles with students from the United States and China. They found that the Chinese were more risk averse and face-conscious than the Americans. Further, risk aversion was positively associated with being confused by too many choices and negatively associated with fashion-consciousness and novelty, as well as the recreational and hedonistic characteristics of the shopping experience.

Consumer cognitive styles

The cognitive style assumed by the classical models of consumer behaviour (Howard and Sheth, 1969; Engel et al., 1986) is that of an individual reviewing opportunities, evaluating alternatives, rationally searching for information, relying on opinion leaders and word-of-mouth communication, and who is influenced by social environment and situational factors. The consumer is also swayed by marketing stimuli (particularly advertising and sales promotion), tries to choose the best alternative, progressively forms the intention to purchase, and finally (perhaps) actually buys the product.

Consumer behaviour models have a rather linear, analytical and abstract style. Many authors claim that Asian consumers tend to have a different cognitive style: the Chinese as well as the Japanese have a more synthetic, concrete and contextual orientation in their thought patterns (Lazer et al., 1985; Yau, 1988; Yang, 1989; Liefeld et al. 1999). For instance, Liefeld et al. (1999) found that information acquisition by attribute was not the dominant style of information processing employed by consumers, that processing by choice alternative or some combination of attribute and choice alternative strategy are equally common.

Legal marketing environment

To a large extent marketing regulations reflect the view that either consumers are predominantly considered to be self-reliant (consumers are informed and responsible people), or that they are dependent individuals who are disadvantaged in relation to the marketer. If considered self-reliant, they still need to be protected if they have not reached the age of self-reliance (children) or against what is considered as harmful to public morality. Even if assumed to be dependent, they need to be protected against abuses. The following examples reflect the divergence of moral perceptions, and differing attitudes to the status of consumers.

1. Many Latin countries consider that private interests cannot exploit the taste of the public for gambling, and, as a result, lotteries are state monopolies. Promotional campaigns that take the form of competitions are considered to be immoral, whereas they are permitted in Anglo-Saxon countries. Certain countries forbid promotional gifts or strictly limit their value, whereas other countries authorize them without any restriction. A possible reason for these diverging regulatory attitudes derives from the different responses to the following question: are people capable of a rational economic evaluation of the value of the gift and relating it to the full price they pay? Finally, are they considered capable of making a sound buying decision, even though they may have been unduly influenced? Section 12.5 examines the cultural relativity of regulatory approaches and consumer responses to sales promotion. (See also *WS12.5*.)

2. The moral content of certain practices often leads to public debate, which in turn influences the regulator introducing legislation. For example, there are different levels of acceptance of naked bodies in television or magazine advertising, which lead to moral controversies in the public domain when foreign advertisements, in imported magazines, satellite broadcasts or Internet sites, are perceived as shocking by the local audience. Another example is offered by the attitudes of regulators towards advertising targeted at children. Children are easy to influence, and it is sometimes argued that the excessive creation of desires, which parents cannot always satisfy, may destabilize family relationships.

The following topic is also often debated: how should children be hired and remunerated for taking part in a television commercial? Some European countries have such stringent regulations that many local commercials targeting children are produced in the United Kingdom, where regulation is more flexible.

3. There are many moral arguments about how women and stereotypically 'ideal' people are represented in commercials, which leads to a desire to identify oneself with those depictions. Chapter 14 presents the cultural relativity of attitudes towards advertising in general, advertising copy and the type of media used.

4.3

Investigating the cross-cultural applicability of consumer behaviour concepts

Any element of consumer behaviour is seen and filtered through cross-cultural lenses. For example, *word-of-mouth* communication seems a fairly universal concept: in any culture, people discuss and informally exchange information on their consumption experiences. Where little relevant information is available, as in the case of films for instance, or new products, or when consumers have a low level of familiarity with a complex product, people tend to seek information from acquaintances. However, it may be hypothesized that word-of-mouth communication will be stronger in collectivist and ingroup-oriented societies, where outside information provided by an impersonal marketer will be seen as less reliable than opinions from relatives and acquaintances.

The best solution for investigating cross-cultural applicability is always to start from the 'common problem' in Kluckhohn and Strodtbeck's (1961) terms. For instance: why and how can a consumer express dissatisfaction with a product or a service? The basic concept found in the consumer behaviour literature is not based on all solutions to the common problem, but on the dominant normative solution in a particular culture, generally Western and more specifically, American. Other alternatives must always be looked for, especially the alternative that the problem may not *have* a solution.

The example of consumer dissatisfaction

Reynolds and Simintiras (2000) suggest that we need to investigate the equivalence consumer satisfaction and dissatisfaction by assessing the comparability of (1) antecedent factors, (2) formation processes and (3) behavioural outcomes. First, are the antecedent factors including economic, temporal, cognitive and spatial resources comparable, in terms of the perceptions of the range and scarcity of resources as well as the criteria and processes used for allocation of resources? Are the categories and substitutability of resources comparable? Are the contextual or situational influences, such as spatial aspects, social surroundings, and tasks comparable? For instance, in Chapter 2 we looked at the variability of time and space. Where time is considered a resource, consumers are more likely to trade-off or substitute time for money. In this situation money may be less important and, thus, have a different meaning. Second, are the formation processes (including ideal, expected, deserved and minimum tolerable product performance) the same (Miller, 1977)? Do they perceive discrepancies in the same way? Third, will it influence action in the same way, such as repeat purchasing and switching behaviour? Some cultures have a higher social desirability bias and as such high reported satisfaction is unlikely to lead to the same level of repeat purchase as those from cultures with a lower social desirability bias (Reynolds and Simintiras, 2000).

Certainly attitudes towards consumerism vary across national contexts and the importance given to the consumer movement varies according to certain basic premises:

1. Is it legitimate that consumers should make their dissatisfaction known? This is not the case in societies where very long periods favourable to supply (such as locations where, for decades, the local supply has been systematically lower than the demand) have implanted the opposite idea. Shopping in eastern Europe illustrates the extent to which a customer complaint can seem an absurd step to take.
2. Is it legitimate for consumers to force a producer, whose product is of dubious quality, to close down? In other words, may consumers cause job losses and take away the livelihood of workers who are not ultimately responsible for the situation?
3. Will it make any difference for the individual or for the larger society?

These questions are posed not out of a desire to adopt any particular position but merely to demonstrate that it is not inherently obvious that the defence of the consumer has a wholly positive social value. Thus expressing dissatisfaction frankly and openly may be considered to be partially illegitimate. In an empirical examination of consumer complaint behaviour, Liu and McLure (2001) found confirmation that consumers in different cultures have different complaint behaviours and intentions. They found that the US respondents voiced their dissatisfaction more frequently than the South Korean respondents, including discussing the problem with the manager, asking for the firm to fix it and telling them so they can do better in the future. Conversely, the South Koreans responded privately more often, including avoiding the firm's product, buying from another firm or telling others about their bad experience.

Richins and Verhage (1985) studied the differences between US and Dutch consumers in their dissatisfaction and complaining behaviour. Their questionnaire was reviewed by a panel of Dutch experts and as a result they made some minor changes to the wording of the questions. They looked for conceptual equivalence of the dissatisfaction concept: does it have the same meaning, socially and individually, for the US and Dutch consumers to be 'dissatisfied with a product or a service'? They found 29 per cent of the variance to be attributable to national differences, the most salient ones being as follows:

Dutch consumers perceive more inconvenience and unpleasantness in making a complaint than do American consumers . . . Dutch consumers were less likely than Americans to feel a social responsibility to make complaints . . . Seemingly contradicting this finding, however, Dutch consumers are more likely than Americans to feel bothered if they don't make a complaint when they believe they should, a sort of guilt. Perhaps this seeming contradiction indicates that Dutch respondents tend to feel a personal rather than social obligation to make complaints. (1985, p. 203.)

The word *construct* relates to a concept that has several underlying dimensions, and may be measured quantitatively by identifying these various dimensions. The construct *consumer dissatisfaction and complaint behaviour* (Richins, 1983) identifies five domains of attitude towards complaining:

1. Beliefs about the effect experienced when one complains.
2. Perceptions of the objective cost or trouble involved in making a complaint.
3. Perception of retailer responsiveness to consumer complaints.
4. The extent to which consumer complaints are expected to benefit society at large.
5. The perceived social appropriateness of making consumer complaints.

Cross-cultural applicability may be investigated by enquiring whether each of these subdimensions makes sense in a particular national/cultural context. In the case of developing countries, Cavusgil and Kaynak (1984) proposed that micro-level sources (e.g. excessive prices, misleading advertising, lack of performance) and macro-level sources of consumer dissatisfaction (e.g. low income, inflation) may interact. They state: 'In general micro-level sources appear to lead, over time, to a diffuse, latent discontent with the state of the marketplace; that is to macro-level dissatisfaction. Unsatisfactory experiences with specific products and services seem to be reflected in a disillusionment with all institutions in the society' (p. 118). In addition, complaining behaviour does not have the same meaning at all if buyer and seller know each other personally, as either acquaintances or relatives: 'Personal relationships with vendors often prove advantageous. Usually food shoppers get to know how far they can trust a food retailer, and can negotiate prices and other terms' (Cavusgil and Kaynak, 1984, p. 122).[6]

Looking with other eyes: questioning consumer behaviour

'Looking with other eyes' implies decentring yourself. This is illustrated using a personal experience (Box 4.3).

If we apply the perspectives from Table 4.1, the universal or global approach provides few clues for understanding the case in Box 4.3. The other perspectives provide many more insights by focusing on consumer specifics. First, the driving licence requirements: people are allowed to learn and take the licence exam only with a manual car. Otherwise, as in the United Kingdom and Australia, one may take the test in an automatic and receive a licence that is restricted to automatics. The only exclusion is that handicapped persons are allowed to use automatic cars to obtain their licence. Thus, learning plays a key role in the resistance to change: having been educated on manual drive, they tend to stick to what they know. Second, many Europeans still believe that automatic gearbox cars are reputed to have high petrol consumption (or poor gas mileage in US terms). Nowadays this is not true, since technology has progressed to the point where the difference is almost nil, and in fact

---

Box 4.3

Differences between Europeans and North Americans in the use of automatic cars

Europeans overwhelmingly have manual gearboxes. This is in sharp contrast to the US where the opposite situation prevails. When in the US, I enjoyed the smoothness of automatic cars and long drives with less fatigue, because I saved hundred of movements. Back in France, I decided to buy a Ford with an automatic gearbox. It is not a standard feature of cars in Europe and I had to pay an extra $1,500 (manual cars are usually cheaper than automatic in the US) and wait a little longer to get the automatic car. After two years, I had to sell the car, because I was leaving the place for some time and I could not take it with me. Selling a car with an automatic gearbox in a European country turned out to be a difficult task. I had started with an attractive price, but I found no prospective buyer, although the car had not done many kilometres and was well maintained. Finally, after several weeks of inserting advertisements in local newspapers, I found a bus driver who was sick of changing gears and bought it for a little more than one-third of the price I had paid two years before. Europeans do not 'like' automatic cars.

favours automatic cars in urban traffic conditions. Third, automatic vehicles are associated with high social status. Large and expensive cars have automatic drive more often than do medium or small cars. Fourth and probably the strongest insight is symbolic: '*c'est une voiture d'infirme*': Most people saw automatic cars, in the middle range of the market, as being specifically for handicapped persons, rather than for those who are not disabled.

If we sum up on the basis of the perspectives presented in Table 4.1:

1. The *global perspective* assumes both universal theories and universal consumers. This perspective may miss the specific consumer insights from the market.
2. The *imported perspective* assesses specific consumer insight assuming universal theory. This perspective may allow the discovery of the social status and resistance to change arguments.
3. The *ethnic consumption* perspective applies specific theories but assumes consumers are universal. This perspective may allow the researcher to identify a small 'ethnic' target, that of North American expatriates (although many of them love manual gearboxes, which to them look more sporty).
4. The *cultural meaning perspective* applies specific theories to specific consumers. It is the only perspective that reveals the symbolic argument (automatic being associated with handicap), which is the major obstacle to selling the automatic car in Europe, even though they are much more comfortable to drive, as speedy and as fuel efficient as other cars.

Radical questioning

The application of different eyes requires radical questioning. Coming back to the differences in 'motivation' presented in Table 4.2, let us attempt to assess the extent that motivations may be radically different. One way to question consumer behaviour cross-nationally is simply to examine motivation in each of these basic actions: own, spend, save, buy, consume, display, share and give. The *motivation to own*, for instance, is based on the notion of ownership.[7] The English verb 'to own' has no equivalent in Swahili, the dominant language in East Africa. Possession,

that is, the rights of individuals over objects, is much more limited in scope. *Motivation to spend* may also be radically altered by negative views of money. *Motivation to save* may be altered by a lack of future orientation, and the feeling that one should not bet on one's future (see Box 7.1). *Motivation to buy* may be low when objects and material culture are discarded, independent of purchasing power, as in Hindu culture. *Motivation to consume* may be largely hindered by a strong ecological stance, as in Denmark or Germany where sensitivity to environmental problems has practically eliminated plastic bottling in favour of reusable glass. *Motivation to display* is naturally related to the self-concept and the prevailing pattern of property.

Motivation to give also varies across cultures: it is widely practised in Japan, where the size of the gift is codified according to the type of social exchange. Joy (2001) examined gift giving in Hong Kong, finding that it is embedded in sociocultural influences. She described a continuum that guides gift exchanges on the basis of the most intimate to the least intimate friendship. In other cultures, however, gift-giving practices may be less frequent, based on the view that it might embarrass the recipient, be necessary to reciprocate and finally both participants may resent being obliged to participate in the ritual.

Park (1998) investigated gift giving in Korea and the United States using focus groups and indepth interviews as well as a survey. The following is a quote from a Korean respondent (p. 580):

I do have a lot of occasions to give a gift for face saving. Because saving face is very important in social life, I should give a gift on those occasions in order not to lose face. But I can't afford them always. Actually, there are too many occasions to afford with my income. The most frequent gift occasions for face saving are weddings, funerals, New Year's Day and *Choo Suk* [Korean Thanksgiving]. When I receive a gift, I feel pressure to reciprocate sometime in the future. In fact, face saving gifts are not pleasant at all.

In his survey Park found that Korean and Americans both cited altruistic motivation more than 50 per cent of the time, but it was higher for the American sample (86 per cent). In addition, Koreans more often gave out of obligation (17 per cent), self-interest (11 per cent), group conformity (7 per cent) and face-saving (5 per cent).[8] (For other examples of cultural differences in learning see *WS4*. One such example is

Figure 4.1 Two different ways of learning how to read

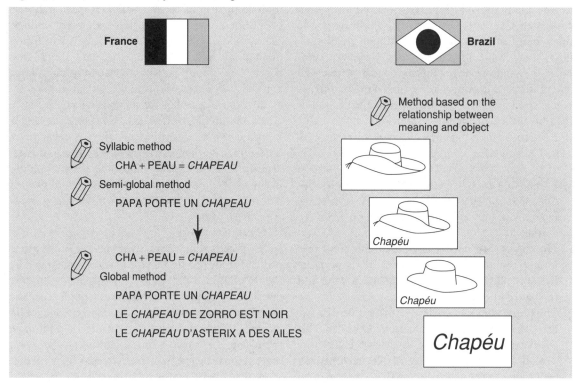

the difference between learning and memory in the French–Brazilian contrast, see Figure 4.1 and *WS A4.6.*)

4.4

Ethnic consumption

Ethnicity as a thwarted ingroup orientation

The reality of ethnic consumption is a strong component of modern consumption culture. Ethnic products have been popularized worldwide and ethnic food and restaurants are the fastest-growing segments in the food industry. Ethnicity reflects the internationalization of lifestyles in two respects: (1) because people move internationally through migrations and (2) by doing this they introduce new consumption opportunities.

Ethnic consumption also has a great deal to do with mixing consumption patterns of the home and host country. One of the most influential models of migrants'

adaptation and adjustment processes is Berry *et al.*'s (1987) acculturation model. This model is based on two dimensions: maintenance of their ethnic or home culture and their relationship with the host culture. These dimensions lead to four basic strategies:

1. *Assimilation* – acquiring the host culture while not maintaining their home culture.
2. *Integration* – acquiring the host culture while maintaining their home culture.
3. *Separation* – rejecting the host culture while maintaining their home culture.
4. *Marginalization* – rejecting both the host and home culture.

These strategies can be seen in the consumer behaviour of ethnic groups. For instance, elements of an *integration* strategy can be seen in the interesting description of an immigrant culture's eating and consumption habits given by Herbert Gans (1962) in his classic book *The Urban Villagers*, about the life of Italian-Americans in a New York neighbourhood, which he calls 'West End'.

Their actual diet, however, bears little resemblance to that of their Italian ancestors, for they have adopted American items that can be integrated into the overall tradition. For example, although their ancestors could not afford to eat meat, West Enders can, and they spend considerable sums on it. Typically American meats such as hot dogs, hamburger and steak are very popular indeed, but they are usually prepared with Italian spices, and accompanied by Italian side-dishes. The role of American culture is perhaps best illustrated by holiday fare. Turkey is eaten on Thanksgiving, but is preceded by a host of Italian anti-pastos, accompanied by Italian side-dishes, and followed by Italian desserts. This amalgamation of ethnic and American food is, of course, not exclusive to the West Enders, but can be found among all groups of foreign origin. (p. 184.)

On the maintenance of culture dimension, ethnic subcultures are based on shared beliefs and habits and the sense of belonging to a specific group of people, different from the society at large. Ingroup orientation is central to ethnicity, but to a large extent, the sense of belonging to the subcultural community is thwarted, because it is simultaneously necessary – and difficult – to identify with the values and behaviour of the dominant ingroup, the nationals of the country of residence. Hispanics in the United States have to cope with this dilemma: they have to adjust to a predominantly WASP (White Anglo-Saxon Protestant) culture, while their basic assumptions, interaction models and sense of belonging would drive them towards the Hispanic community.

Ethnicity is a matter of shared belief about a common ancestry. Bouchet (1995) lists six main attributes of ethnic community: (1) a collective proper name; (2) a myth of common ancestry; (3) shared historical memories; (4) one or more differentiating elements of common culture (e.g. language); (5) an association with a specific homeland; and (6) a sense of solidarity. Because ethnic belonging in the host country is taken from the culture's original territory and inhabitants, people often try to maintain their subculture by means of ethnic stereotyping. In marketing, this gives rise to opportunistic use where, for instance, 3M has used Scottish imagery to denote value in 'Scotch' tape, since the Scottish stereotype of supposed frugality is viewed favourably in the United States (Solomon, 1994).

Elements of a *separation* strategy can be seen in Ger and Østergaard's (1998, p. 49) description of Turkish students in Denmark as more 'Turkish' than those who live in Turkey:

Some families brought the curtains from Turkey, thinking that the curtains in Odense were too simple. Their furniture reminded the Turkish author of the 1960s urban middle class furnishings in Turkey: chandeliers, then a symbol of wealth, a prominent buffet, and 'Turkish' crochéed covers hanging from the shelves. They displayed many knick-knacks – small decorative souvenirs, currently sold for tourists in Turkey . . . Several homes had Turkish flags. One male informant, who displayed such a flag, in addition to posters of the Turkish national anthem and Istanbul, rosary beads, a Turkish soccer team key chain, and a Koran, and who was wearing a small flag pin on his sweater, explained that the Danes always have flags in their houses. Unlike 'some who try to hide the fact that they are Turks', he wants everyone to know that he is Turkish. His e-mail messages end with 'We Love Turkey'.

On the more negative side, Caetano *et al.* (1998) discuss the stresses related to social adjustments to the host culture leading to alcohol abuse. This resembles a *marginalization* strategy, where people may lack clear behavioural guidelines that can result in self-destructive tendencies.

The acculturation strategy

It may be wrong to equate consumers from a definite ethnic group to a specific market segment, which seeks specific products or service benefits; as noted in the section above it is more complex. Lee *et al.* (2002) questioned the usefulness of observable ethnicity as a market segmentation basis in international consumer marketing. They state that the dual cultural influences result in mixed schemas of cultural values, norms and behaviours. This reflects the *integration* strategy, but we also see an *assimilation* strategy reflected in consumer behaviour. For instance, Yankelovitch *et al.* (1982) found Hispanics to be more American than Anglo Americans in many characteristics. Similarly, Kim and Kang (2001) examined the effects of ethnicity among three main ethnic consumer groups in the United States: blacks, Hispanics and whites. They found that both blacks and Hispanics were more influenced by media in their purchase of clothing than whites, and concluded that ethnic minority groups look for symbolic cues from the media in their desire to belong to mainstream society.

Assimilation takes place when the relative influence of the culture of origin diminishes and immigrants hold faster to the values and behaviours of the country of residence. Assimilation is evidenced in the following areas: consumption patterns, employment, marriage with people originating from the host culture, participation in the political process as a candidate, and having acquaintances outside the ethnic community. The process of assimilation is a lengthy one, which may require several generations to be fully accomplished.

In the assimilation process, two mechanisms are at work (Wallendorf and Reilly, 1983). The first is based on structural constraints where compliance is compulsory, not voluntary: if people drive on the other side of the road, the individual will be obliged to adapt. The second is based on the newcomer's willingness to adjust to the new culture's behaviour and rules: it depends on the enthusiasm for what the new culture brings, in terms of increased freedom and improved material status. As Calantone *et al.* (1985, p. 208) explain it:

lack of availability may force some immigrants to make changes in the foods they purchase. Thus, behavioural change may occur without a concomitant change in values or beliefs. In making empirical comparisons, therefore, it is crucial to include only those behavioural patterns that reflect free choices by immigrants and to exclude adaptation to structural constraints.

Ethnicity as identity

When assimilation has fully taken place, probably by the third or fourth generation, those now assimilated may share much more with the society at large than with their subcultural group. However, there is often resurgence of ethnicity; as Bouchet (1995) remarks, ethnicity has more to do with the evolution of identity in general rather than with the origin of one's historical identity. For instance, Oswald (1999, p. 307) illustrates how Haitian consumers in the United States 'culture swap', using goods to move between one cultural identity and another as they negotiate relations between home and host cultures:

Odette insisted she was so mainstream as to provide nothing at all about Haitian culture, having lived in the United States for 30 years and having served in the U.S. Army . . . Odette planned to hold the children's party at Chuck E. Cheese, a pizzeria chain, but invited relatives to the home for a Haitian barbecue and the ubiquitous rice and beans.

Thus ethnic consumption should be considered as a complex and unstable reality, which marketers need to look at with quite an open mind (see *WS4.4* for examples of the effects of ethnicity on consumption).

It gives birth to strange mixtures, such as the Chino-Latino cuisine, a fusion of Asian and Cuban cuisine to be found in New York, which has its roots in the Chinese immigration to Cuba in the early 1900s (Straus, 1992).

When dealing with ethnic consumption, the following points must be kept in mind:

1. Translation or spelling mistakes or inadequate wordings may be resented as offending the group's honour. For instance, a *burrito* was mistakenly called in Spanish a *burrada*, which means 'big mistake' (Solomon, 1994). This results in minority group people having a sense of being rejected because their language is not used properly, or at least not understood, or *respected*.
2. In ethnic behaviour, the status of membership, that is, the claim of being 'different', is central and may be pushed to its extreme. Smaller ingroups are stronger platforms for identification. Hispanics will therefore break down further into Mexicans, Puerto-Ricans, Cubans, etc.
3. The level of acculturation, or the degree to which people have learned the ways of the host culture, influences ethnic consumption. Age is also significant: older people and less acculturated people tend to display a stronger attitude as ethnic consumers.
4. Identification needs are 'reversible', creating ambiguous and even contradictory demands. Most people belonging to ethnic communities strive for both integration into the society at large and maintenance of their specific cultural roots. In some areas of consumption, such as housing and furnishing, they may express their belonging to the larger national ingroup and in another area, such as food, they may maintain strong ethnic behaviour.

4.5

Marketing as an exchange of meanings

Consumers buy meanings and marketers communicate meanings through products and advertisements (see *WS4.5* for more information on semiotics). As suggested by McCracken (1991), consumer goods are vehicles of cultural meanings and consumers choose and then make use of these cultural meanings. In order to understand this, however, we have to look with other eyes. For instance, Penaloza (2001, p. 373) investigated the cultural meaning of the Old West in the United States, finding that it has different meaning for whites and non-whites: 'For whites, popular depictions of adventurous explorers, miners, and ranchers accompany those of land thieves, murderers, and forced religious converters. For Native Americans, popular depictions of hostile savages stand beside romantic naturalists and spiritualists, wealthy casino owners, and movement activists fighting ongoing battles for land, mineral, and water rights'. She uses this information to understand the workings of the contemporary Stock Show and Rodeo.

Marketing may be seen primarily as a process of exchange where communication, broadly defined, is central. As Richard Bagozzi (1975, p. 35) states:

In order to satisfy human needs, people and organizations are compelled to engage in social and economic exchanges with other people and organizations. This is true for primitive as well as highly developed societies. Social actors obtain satisfaction of their needs by complying with, or influencing, the behaviour of other actors. They do this by communicating and controlling the media of exchange, which in turn, comprise the links between one individual and another. Significantly, marketing exchanges harbour meanings for individuals that go beyond the mere use of media for obtaining results in interactions.

Many of the meanings in marketing exchanges are culture based: they are inter-subjectively shared by a social group (D'Andrade, 1987). Inter-subjective sharing of meanings signifies that each person in the group knows that everyone else knows the cognitive schema. Therefore in the process of exchange through buyer–seller relations, marketing communications or product consumption, interpretations are made spontaneously, as if they were obvious realities, and a great deal of information in the process of marketing as exchange and communication need not be made explicit. For instance, Kragh and Djursaa (2000) explored the meanings carried by Danish and English dining and living rooms by having respondents view photographs from the other country. They noted that:

The English respondents complain that Danish modernist rooms look old fashioned, . . . the English respondents also think the Danish rooms are boring and bare . . . Returning the complement, the Danes complain that the English rooms are tasteless, and pinpoint the syntactical features which convey this message: they find them overdone, with too many flowers and patterns. In addition, they find the room composition odd, missing their sofa groups with coffee tables which are integral to Danish ideas of togetherness (pp. 1314–15).

Culture, as noted by Bagozzi, may be considered as a sort of *meta-language* central to the marketing process when viewed as exchange and communication. It works as a kind of *game rule*, implicitly indicating how people will interact in an exchange relationship, influencing their constraints and their leeway in behaviour and decisions. The attitudinal differences toward market research between American and Japanese people (section 7.6) are a good example of this: what is the 'right' way (that is, legitimate or appropriate) to communicate with the market? What is the market (actual buyers versus potential consumers)? In each case the objective is seemingly the same: to collect relevant information and market data, in order to decide on marketing strategies.

Two examples will help illustrate the differences in marketing meta-communication: first, the role of emotions in Japanese marketing, and second, the emphasis on the symbolic relationship between person and object in the Italian style of marketing.

The role of emotions in Japanese marketing

There is wide range of books on Japanese marketing, which are unfortunately written only in Japanese *Kanji* and *Hiragana*, thereby limiting access for non-Japanese (*Gai-jin*) readers. But the Japanese provide details in English in the review of the largest Japanese advertising agency, *Dentsu Japan Marketing/Advertising*. Koichi Tanouchi, a professor of marketing at Hitotsubashi University, depicts the Japanese style of marketing as being fundamentally based on emotions and sensitivity. He first insists, as many authors do, that Japan is oriented towards rice production, and is not a nation of hunters and gatherers. This means more collective organization and interpersonal sensitivity: the cultivation of rice requires the simultaneous flooding of paddy fields, which cannot be decided by an isolated landowner. This involves a strong collective solidarity, serious planning and individual tenacity.

Tanouchi states that, in his opinion, 'masculine' values are less developed in Japan than 'feminine' values, which he illustrates by the example of marital relationships in household and personal spending (1983, p. 78):

In Japan, the husband is supposed to hand all his income over to his wife. If he doesn't, he is criticized by people around him. If she complains about this to his boss in his business company, the boss is very likely to take the wife's side, and advise him to give all his salary to his wife and add that that is the best way to keep peace at home and that everyone else is doing so. The wife has the right to decide how much money her husband can have for daily lunch and coffee. Regularly, about once in a half year, Japanese newspapers carry a research report about the average amount of the money the average husbands get from their wives. Wives decide about their husbands' lunch money watching these figures.

Tanouchi argues that sensitivity and emotions permeate most aspects of Japanese marketing. This is evidenced by the high level of sensitivity and response to *actual* consumer needs and by the search for social harmony between producers and distributors (see section 12.1 on *Keiretsu* distribution). It is also prominent in Japanese sales force compensation arrangements, where collective reward systems are often used. They foster cooperation, avoid threatening individual competition and promote social harmony in the sales team (section 15.4).

It needs to be borne in mind that traditional collectivist mindset in Japan is being tempered by the influence of more traditionally Western ideas. Research indicates profound changes occurring in Japanese society. Rose and Shoham (1999) examined the differences in the United States and Japan among mothers of young children. They found that: 'Self-respect, warm relationships with others, and security were cited as the most important values by American respondents. In contrast, Japanese respondents cited fun and enjoyment, followed by security, accomplishment, and self-fulfilment. These findings represent an intriguing contrast to the view of Japan as a monolithic collectivist culture, and illustrate the blending and inherent dualism of Japanese society . . . Thus, both individual and collectivist elements have been incorporated into Japanese society, particularly among the post Second World War II generations' (p. 58).

The role of the symbolic link between object and person through the medium of design in Italian marketing

It can be said that a specific Italian marketing style is emerging. This style is characterized by heavy emphasis (and corresponding financial commitment) devoted to product appearance and design. The article sold is intended to act as a link between the producer–seller and the consumer–purchaser: both appreciate the aesthetic qualities of the object. The Italians concentrate

---

Box 4.4

The functional form of the cigarette lighter

The stylized fluidity of the 'functional forms' testifies to the connotation of mental dynamics, the semblance of a lost relationship, in an attempt to reconstruct a purpose through the accumulation of signs. For example, a lighter in the shape of a pebble was successfully launched by advertising some years ago. The oblong, elliptic and asymmetrical form is 'highly functional', not because it provides a better light than another lighter, but because it fits exactly into the palm of the hand. 'The seas have polished it into the shape of the hand': it is an accomplished form. Its function is not to give a light, but to be easy to handle. Its form is, so to speak, predetermined by Nature (the sea) to be handled by man. This new purpose is the sole rhetoric of the lighter. The connotations are here twofold: as an industrial object, the cigarette lighter is supposed to recall one of the qualities of the handicraft object, the shape of which furthers the gesture and the body of man. Moreover the allusion to the sea brings us to the myth of Nature, itself cultured by man, which follows all his desires: the sea plays the cultural role of a polisher; it is the sublime handicraft of nature. As the stone rolled by the sea, furthered by the hand producing light, the cigarette lighter becomes a wonderful flint, a whole prehistoric and artisanate purpose comes into play in the very practical essence of an industrial object.

(Source: Baudrillard, 1968, pp. 82–3. Author's translation.)

on the style and functionality of the object, and its integration in the environment. The focal point is the symbolism of the object and its fit with the meaning attributed to it by consumers, as such increasing importance is given to qualitative studies. It is of course unrealistic to claim that the Italians are alone in having an awareness of the symbolic meaning of possessions for consumers. But they incorporate it at a very high level and make it an essential element of their marketing communication. Baudrillard (1968) and his 'system of objects' (see WS4.5 for a list of Baudrillard's works), which was fairly successful in France, ultimately achieved real success in Italy, where he is regarded as a guru of marketing semiology (Box 4.4).

4.6
Conclusion

The other side of the poster mentioned at the start of this chapter says '*Bei Mercedes bleibt alles anders*' ('With Mercedes everything remains different'). In international marketing, where similarities abound, it is wise to examine particular differences in consumer behaviour with *different* eyes. This will provide a method of enquiry which favours the discovery of significant differences in how consumers behave across cultures and offers insights into the way consumers invest meaning into their purchases.

Questions

1. What would you expect to be the relation of *consumer loyalty* with the following cultural variables? Argue why, in your opinion, consumers having a certain cultural trait would be more, or conversely less, loyal:
(a) strong future orientation;
(b) strong ingroup orientation;
(c) high individualism;
(d) high uncertainty avoidance.

2. Discuss how a strong emphasis on group belonging in a particular culture may influence buying decisions.

3. Discuss possible cross-cultural variability in the concept of 'status-seeking consumers'.

4. Why can 'word-of-mouth communication' among people be considered as a fairly robust consumer behaviour concept cross-culturally?

5. What is *ethnic consumption*?

Notes

1. *Potlach* still exists in modern societies, especially in the context of fund-raising where appreciation banquets, kick-off luncheons and campaign parties present ritualized, symbolic gift giving which induces participants into the social dynamics of philanthropy (Hanson, 1997).
2. Belk *et al.* (1997), illustrated evidence of substantial convergence across American, Danish and Turkish subjects on three dimensions: (1) desires are interpersonal, (2) desire can be dangerous and (3) desires follows a cycle where emotions and feelings differ in the 'before', 'during' and 'after' stages, suggesting that 'the thrill lies more in the desire than in its realization' (p. 26).
3. See for instance: Kushner (1982), Laurent (1982), Redding (1982), Yau (1988), Yang (1989) and Robinson (1996).
4. While there are 27 distinct scales that have been designed to measure aspects of individualism and collectivism (Oyserman *et al.*, 2002), three scales that been designed to measure the independent and interdependent self concepts: Gudykunst *et al.* (1994, 1996); Leung and Kim (1997) and earlier versions; and Singelis (1994).
5. See for instance Olsen (1995), who explains how brand loyalty builds on memories, past experiences and consumer nostalgia, with personal and family histories being deeply enmeshed in the cultural biography of brands.

6. Watkins and Liu (1996) offer a complete discussion of how collectivism, individualism and ingroup membership can have an impact on consumer complaining behaviour. This may be of assistance for exercise A4.2.

7. On cross-cultural differences in materialism see Ger and Belk (1996, 1999), Eastman *et al.* (1997) and Lundstrom *et al.* (1999).

8. Arunthanes *et al.* (1994) distinguish between high context cultures (to which Asian countries typically belong) where business gifts are imperative, accepted as a normal social practice and have reciprocal effects, and low context cultures (the prototype being the United States or Northern Europe) where they are optional, and even sometimes perceived as attempts at bribery. Some studies suggest major cultural differences between gift-giving behaviour in Oriental and Western cultures (Green and Alden, 1988; Beatty *et al.*, 1991). For instance, reciprocation and moral obligations are central in the Japanese gift-giving tradition. Japanese tourists travelling abroad must bring back home *omiyage*, that is, local specialities purchased as gifts for families and friends at home (Applbaum and Jordt, 1996). *Omiyage* are, for many Japanese tourists Louis Vuitton luggage or other French luxury brands, of which they are major purchasers when they stay as tourists in Paris. As emphasized by Wong and Ahuvia (1995, p. 81): 'Unlike souvenirs which are purchased for the self, *omiyage* are tokens for others to share in one's travel experience.' Buying gifts for oneself is more often a pattern to be found in societies that value an independent self, a typical statement about such purchases being that it is 'a present from me to me' (Mick and DeMoss, 1990, p. 322). Laroche *et al.* (2000) investigate in-store information search strategies for Christmas gifts.

9. Anonymous (2002) 'La télephonie Européne pour un recentrage sur le client', *Freesurf Actualité Hi Tech*, November 21, 2002. Retrieved April 30, 2003 from http://www.freesurf.fr/actualite_media/ap/technology/index.html.

10. Anonymous (2003) 'News', *Analysys News*, 26 March, 2003. Retrieved April 30, 2003 from http://www.analysys.com/default.asp?Mode=article&iLeftArticle=1192.

11. Phillips, Leigh (2003) 'Messaging and entertainment services to boost mobile operator revenue and ARPU, report' *Europemedia.net*, March 27, 2003. Retrieved April 30, 2003 from http://www.analysys.com/default_acl.asp?Mode=article&iLeftArticle=5&m=&n=.

12. Erkki Liikanen (2002) Conference address: Mobile Europe 2002 Conference, Bremen, Germany, *m-Travel.com*, March 22, 2002. Retrieved April 30, 2003 from http://europa.eu.int/rapid/start/cgi/guesten.ksh?p_action.gettxt=gt&doc=SPEECH/02/111|0|RAPID&lg=EN&display=.

13. Bruzzese, Stephanie (2002) 'European and Asian markets already riding high on teen profits', *M-Business Daily*, undated. Retrieved May 15 from http://www.mbusiness-daily.com/magazine/story/new/fe1_page1.

14. Anonymous (2002) 'Européen et mobile', *ORANGE Magazine*, Spring, 2002, No.4, pp.9–13.

15. Anonymous (2002) 'Européen et mobile', *ORANGE Magazine*, Spring, 2002, No.4, pp.9–13.

16. Delaney, Mark, Jeff McFarland, Gee Hong Yoon, and Tom Hardy (2002) 'Global design and cultural identity', *Innovation*, Summer 2002. Retrieved April 30, 2003 from http://www.idsa.org.

17. Delaney, Mark, Jeff McFarland, Gee Hong Yoon, and Tom Hardy (2002) 'Global design and cultural identity', *Innovation*, Summer 2002. Retrieved April 30, 2003 from http://www.idsa.org.

18. Eurescom (2001) 'c "ICT uses in everyday life"', *Eurescom P903 Newsletter*, page 3, May 2001.

19. Anonymous (2002) 'Européen et mobile', *ORANGE Magazine*, Spring, 2002, No.4, pp.9–13.

20. Ó hAnluain, Daithí (2002) 'They be jammin' in France', *Wired News*, March 23, 2002. Retrieved May 15 from http://www.wired.com/news/culture/0,1284,51273,00.html.

21. Chaterji, Chandra S. (2002) 'Wireless and internet technology adoption by consumers around the world', *Taylor Nelson Sofres Information Technology*, May, 2002.

22. Gartner Group (2002) 'SMS bigger than email in Europe', Nua Internet Surveys, November 5, 2002. Retrieved April 30, 2003 from http://www.qlinks.net/quicklinks/stats12.htm.

23. Nahmany, Peggy (2003) 'Y RN'T WE N2 SMS?', *PR Newswire*, February 12, 2003. Retrieved April 30, 2003 from http://www.findarticles.com.

24. Chaterji, Chandra S. (2002) 'Wireless and internet technology adoption by consumers around the world', *Taylor Nelson Sofres Information Technology*, May, 2002.

25. Phillips, Leigh (2003) 'Messaging and entertainment services to boost mobile operator revenue and ARPU, report' *Europemedia.net*, March 27, 2003.

26. Anonymous (2002) 'Européen et mobile', *ORANGE Magazine*, Spring, 2002, No.4, pp.9–13.

27. Laughlin, Kirk (2002) 'Revenue at risk: Why are ARPUs falling in North America, but rising in parts of Europe?', *America's Network*, March 1, 2002. Retrieved April 30, 2003 from http://news.com.com/2100-1023-979414.html?tag=cd_mh.

References

Aaker, Jennifer L. (2000), 'Accessibility or diagnosticity? Disentangling the influence of culture on persuasion processes and attitudes', *Journal of Consumer Research*, vol. 26, no. 4, pp. 340–57.

Aaker, Jennifer L. and Angela Y. Lee (2001), ' "I" seek pleasure and "we" avoid pains: The role of self-regulatory goals in information processing and persuasion', *Journal of Consumer Research*, vol. 28, no. 1, pp. 33–49.

Aaker, Jennifer L. and Bernd Schmitt (2001), 'Culture-dependent assimilation and differentiation of the self: preference for consumption symbols in the United States and China', *Journal of Cross-Cultural Psychology*, vol. 32, pp. 561–76.

Aaker, Jennifer L. and Patti Williams (1998), 'Empathy versus pride: the influence of emotional appeals across cultures', *Journal of Consumer Research*, vol. 25, no. 3, pp. 241–61.

Abe, Shuzo, Richard P. Bagozzi and Pradip Sadarangani (1996), 'An investigation of construct validity and generalizability of the self-concept: self-consciousness in Japan and the United States', *Journal of International Consumer Marketing*, vol. 8, nos 3/4, pp. 97–123.

Applbaum, Kalman and Ingrid Jordt (1996), 'Notes toward an application of McCracken's "cultural categories" for cross-cultural consumer research', *Journal of Consumer Research*, vol. 23, December, pp. 204–18.

Arunthanes, Wiboon, Patriya Tansujah and David J. Lemak (1994), 'Cross-cultural business gift giving: A new conceptualization and theoretical framework', *International Marketing Review*, vol. 11, no. 4, pp. 44–55.

Askegaard, Søren and Karen Brunsø (1999), 'Food-related lifestyles in Singapore: preliminary testing of a Western research instrument in Southeast Asia', *Journal of Euromarketing*, vol. 7, no. 4, pp. 65–86.

Bagozzi, Richard P. (1975), 'Marketing as exchange', *Journal of Marketing*, vol. 39, no. 4, pp. 32–9.

Bagozzi, Richard P. (2000), 'On the concept of intentional social action in consumer behavior', *Journal of Consumer Research*, vol. 27, pp. 388–96.

Bagozzi, Richard P. and K.-H. Lee (2002), 'Multiple routes for social influence: the role of compliance, internalization and social identity', *Social Psychology Quarterly*, vol. 65, no. 3, pp. 226–47.

Bagozzi, Richard P., Nancy Wong, Shuzo Abe and Massimo Bergami (2000), 'Cultural and situational contingencies and the theory of reasoned action: application to fast-food and restaurant consumption', *Journal of Consumer Psychology*, vol. 9, no. 2, pp. 97–106.

Ballah, R.N. (1970), *Tokugawa Religion*, Bencon Press: Boston.

Bao, Yeqing Bao, Kevin Zheng Zhou and Chenting Su (2003), 'Face consciousness and risk aversion: do they affect consumer decision-making?' *Psychology and Marketing*, vol. 20, no. 8, pp. 733–55.

Baudrillard, Jean (1968), *Le Système des objets*, Gallimard: Paris.

Beatty, Sharon E., Lynn R. Kahle and Pamela Homer (1991), 'Personal values and gift-giving behaviors: A study across cultures', *Journal of Business Research*, vol. 22, no. 2, pp. 149–57.

Belk, Russell W. (1988), 'Third World consumer culture', in E. Kumçu and A. Fuat Firat (eds), *Research in Marketing*, supplement 4, JAI Press: Greenwich, CT.

Belk, Russell W., Güliz Ger and Søren Askegaard (1997), 'Consumer desires in three cultures: Results from projective research', in Merrie Brucks and Debbie McInnis (eds), *Advances in Consumer Research*, vol. 24, Association for Consumer Research: Provo, UT, pp. 24–7.

Berry, J.W., U. Kim, T. Minde and D. Mok (1987), 'Comparative study of acculturation stress', *International Migration Review*, vol. 21, pp. 491–511.

Bouchet, Dominique (1995), 'Marketing and the redefinition of ethnicity', in Janeen Arnold Costa and Gary J. Bamossy (eds), *Marketing in a Multicultural World*, Sage: Thousand Oaks, CA, pp. 68–105.

Brunsø, K., K.G. Grunert and K. Kristensen (1996), 'An analysis of national and cross-national consumer segments using the food-related lifestyle instrument in Denmark, France, Germany, and Great Britain', *MAPP Working paper No. 35*, Aarhus: The Aarhus School of Business.

Caetano, Raul, Catherine L. Clark and Tammy Tam (1998), 'Alcohol consumption among racial/ethnic minorities: theory and research', *Alcohol Health and Research World*, vol. 22, no. 4, pp. 233–42.

Calantone, R., M. Morris and J. Johar (1985), 'A cross-cultural benefit segmentation analysis to evaluate the traditional assimilation model', *International Journal of Research in Marketing*, vol. 2, pp. 207–17.

Cavusgil, S. Tamer and Erdener Kaynak (1984), 'Critical issues in the cross-cultural measurement of consumer dissatisfaction: developed versus LDC practices', in Erdener Kaynak and Ronald Savitt (eds), *Comparative Marketing Systems*, Praeger: New York, pp. 114–30.

Chen, Cheng-Nan, Mengkuan Lai and David D.C. Tarn (1999), 'Feminism orientation, product attributes and husband-wife decision dominance: a Taiwan–Japan cross-cultural study', *Journal of Global Marketing*, vol. 12, no. 3, pp. 23–39.

Chien, M. (1979), *Chinese National Character and Chinese Culture: A historical perspective*, The Chinese University of Hong Kong Press: Shatin, Hong Kong (in Chinese).

Chiou, Jyh-Shen (1995), 'The process of social influences on new product adoption and retention in individualistic versus collectivistic cultural contexts', *Proceedings of the Second Conference on the Cultural Dimension of International Marketing*, Odense, pp. 107–27.

Chiou, Jyh-Shen (1999), 'Investigating the consumer social-adjustment and value-expressive perceived ends in product purchasing decisions', *Journal of International Consumer Marketing*, vol. 12, no. 2, pp. 87–109.

Cowley, Elizabeth (2002), 'East–west consumer confidence and accuracy in memory for product information', *Journal of Business Research*, vol. 55, no. 11, pp. 915–21.

Cundiff, Eward and Marye Tharp Hilger, *Marketing in the International Environment*, 2nd edn, Prentice Hall: Englewood Cliffs, NJ.

D'Andrade, Roy G. (1987), 'A folk model of the mind', in Dorothy Quinn and Naomi Holland (eds), *Cultural Models in Language and Thought*, Cambridge University Press: Cambridge, pp. 112–48.

de Mooij, Marieke (2000), 'The future is predictable for international marketers: converging incomes lead to diverging consumer behaviour', *International Marketing Review*, vol. 17, no. 2, pp. 103–13.

Dubois, Bernard (1987), 'Culture et marketing', *Recherche et Applications en Marketing*, vol. 2, no. 3, pp. 37–64.

Eastman, Jacqueline K., Bill Fredenberger, David Campbell and Stephen Calvert (1997), 'The relationship between status consumption and materialism: a cross-cultural comparison of Chinese, Mexican and American students', *Journal of Marketing Theory and Practice*, vol. 5, no. 1, pp. 52–66.

Engel, James F., Roger D. Blackwell and Paul W. Miniard (1986), *Consumer Behavior*, 5th edn, Holt, Rhinehart & Winston: New York.

Fei, X.T. (1948), *Rural China*, Guancha She: Shangai (in Chinese).

Gans, Herbert (1962), *The Urban Villagers*, The Free Press: New York.

Ger, Güliz and Russell W. Belk (1996), 'Cross-cultural differences in materialism', *Journal of Economic Psychology*, vol. 17, no. 1, pp. 55–77.

Ger, Güliz and Russell W. Belk (1999), 'Accounting for materialism in four cultures', *Journal of Material Culture*, vol. 4, no. 2, pp. 183–204.

Ger, Güliz and Per Østergaard (1998), 'Constructing immigrant identities in consumption: appearance among the Turko-Danes', *Advances in Consumer Research*, vol. 25, pp. 48–52.

Green, Robert T. and Dana L. Alden (1988), 'Functional equivalence in cross-cultural consumer behavior: gift giving in Japan and the United States', *Psychology and Marketing*, vol. 5, pp. 155–68.

Gudykunst, William B., Y. Matsumoto, S. Ting-Toomey, T. Nishida, K. Kim and S. Heyman (1994), 'Measuring self construals across cultures', paper presented at the annual meeting of the International Communication Association, Sydney, Australia, July 1994.

Gudykunst, William B., Y. Matsumoto, S. Ting-Toomey, T. Nishida, K. Kim and S. Heyman (1996), 'The influence of cultural individualism-collectivism, self construals, and individual values on communication styles across cultures', *Human Communication Research*, vol. 22, pp. 510–43.

Hanson, John H. (1997), 'Power, philanthropy, and potlatch: what tribal exchange rituals can tell us about giving', *Fund Raising Management*, vol. 27, no. 12, pp. 16–19.

Hirschmann, Elisabeth C. (1985), 'Primitive aspects of consumption in modern American Society', *Journal of Consumer Research*, vol. 12, September, pp. 142–54.

Howard, J. and J.N. Sheth (1969), *The Theory of Buyer Behaviour*, John Wiley: New York.

Hsieh, Y.W. (1967), 'Filial piety and Chinese society', in C.A. Moore (ed.), *The Chinese Mind*, University of Hawaii Press: Honolulu, pp. 167–87.

Hsu, F.L.K. (1971), 'Philosophical homeostasis and jen: conceptual tools for advancing psychological anthropology', *American Anthropologist*, vol. 73, pp. 23–44.

Joy, Annamma (2001), 'Gift giving in Hong Kong and the continuum of social ties', *Journal of Consumer Research*, vol. 28, pp. 239–56.

Kacen, Jacqueline J. and Julie Anne Lee (2002), 'The influence of culture on consumer impulsive buying behavior', *Journal of Consumer Psychology*, vol. 12, no. 2, pp. 163–76.

Kim, Jai-Ok, Sandra Forsythe, Quingliang Gu and Sook Jae Moon (2002), 'Cross-cultural consumer behavior, needs and purchase behavior', *Journal of Consumer Marketing*, vol. 19, no. 6, pp. 481–502.

Kim, Youn-Kyung and Jikyeong Kang (2001), 'The effects of ethnicity and product on purchase decision making', *Journal of Advertising Research*, 41, March, pp. 39–48.

Kluckhohn, Florence R. and Frederick L. Strodtbeck (1961), *Variations in Value Orientations*, Greenwood Press: Westport, CT.

Kolettis, Helen (2001), 'E-commerce: who's buying in?', *Security Distributing and Marketing*, vol. 31, no. 1, pp. 52–5.

Kotler, Philip (2003), *Marketing Management*, 11th edn, Pearson Education International.

Kragh, Simon Ulrik and Malene Djursaa (2001), 'Product syntax and cross-cultural marketing strategies', *European Journal of Marketing*, vol. 35, no. 11/12, pp. 1301–19.

Kushner, J.M. (1982), 'Market research in a non-Western context: the Asian example', *Journal of the Market Research Society*, vol. 24, no. 2, pp. 116–22.

Laroche, Michel, Gad Saad, Chankon Kim and Elizabeth Browne (2000), 'A cross-cultural study of in-store information search strategies for Christmas gift', *Journal of Business Research*, vol. 49, no. 2, pp. 113–26.

Laurent, Clint R. (1982), 'An investigation of the family life cycle in a modern Asian society', *Journal of the Market Research Society*, vol. 24, no. 2, pp. 140–50.

Lazer, William, Shoji Murata and Hiroshi Kosaka (1985), 'Japanese marketing: towards a better understanding', *Journal of Marketing*, vol. 49, Spring, pp. 69–81.

Lee, Chol and Robert T. Green (1991), 'Cross-cultural examination of the fishbein behavioural intentions model', *Journal of International Business Studies*, pp. 289–305.

Lee, Eun-Ju, Ann Fairhurst and Susan Diallard (2002), 'Usefulness of ethnicity in international consumer marketing', *Journal of International Consumer Marketing*, vol. 14, no. 4, pp. 25–48.

Lee, Julie Anne (2000), 'Adapting Triandis's model of subjective culture and social behaviour relations to consumer behaviour', *Journal of Consumer Psychology*, vol. 9, no. 2, pp. 117–26.

Lee, Julie Anne and Jacqueline J. Kacen (1999), 'The relationship between independent and interdependent self-concepts and reasons for purchase', *Journal of Euro-Marketing*, vol. 8, no. 1/2, pp. 83–99.

Lee, Julie Anne and Geoffrey Soutar (2004), 'Singaporeans I- and We-intentions to come to Australia', *Australian and New Zealand Marketing Academy Conference (ANZMAC) Proceedings 2004*, Victoria University: Wellington, New Zealand.

Leung, T. and M.S. Kim (1997), 'A revised self-construal scale', Unpublished manuscript, University of Hawaii at Manoa, Honolulu.

Levitt, Theodore (1983), 'The globalization of markets', *Harvard Business Review*, vol. 61, May–June, pp. 92–102.

Liefeld, John P., Marjorie Wall and Louise A. Heslop (1999), 'Cross cultural comparison of consumer information processing styles', *Journal of Euro-Marketing*, vol. 8, no. 1/2, pp. 29–43.

Liu, Raymond R. and Peter McClure (2001), 'Recognizing cross-cultural differences in consumer complaint behavior and intentions: an empirical examination', *The Journal of Consumer Marketing*, vol. 18, no. 1, pp. 54–75.

Luna, David, and Susan Forquer Gupta (2001), 'An integrative framework for cross-cultural consumer behavior', *International Marketing Review*, vol. 18, no. 1, pp. 45–69.

Lundstrom, William J. and D. Steven White (1999), 'Intergenerational and cultural differences in materialism: An empirical investigation of consumers from France and the U.S.A.', *Journal of Euro-Marketing*, vol. 7, no. 2, pp. 47–65.

Malhotra, Naresh K. and J. Daniel McCort (2001), 'A cross-cultural comparison of behavioral intention models', *International Marketing Review*, vol. 18, no. 3, pp. 235–69.

Markus, Hazel Rose and Shinobu Kitayama (1991), 'Culture and the self: implications for cognition, emotion and motivation', *Psychological Review*, vol. 98, no. 2, pp. 224–53.

Maslow, Abraham H. (1954), *Motivation and Personality*, Harper and Row: New York.

McCracken, Grant (1991), 'Culture and consumer behaviour: an anthropological perspective', *Journal of the Market Research Society*, vol. 32, no. 1, pp. 3–11.

Mendenhall, Mark, Betty Jane Punnett and David Ricks (1995), *Global Management*, Blackwell: Cambridge, MA.

Mick, David Glen and Michelle DeMoss (1990), 'Self-gifts: phenomenological insights from four contexts', *Journal of Consumer Research*, vol. 17, December, pp. 322–32.

Miller, J.A. (1977), 'Studying satisfaction modifying models, eliciting expectations, posing problems and making meaningful measurements', in H.K. Hunt (ed.), *Conceptualization and Measurement of Customer Satisfaction and Dissatisfaction*, Marketing Science Institute: Cambridge, MA, pp. 72–91.

Mitchell, V.W., M. Yamin and B. Pichene (1996), 'A cross-cultural analysis of perceived risk in British and French CD purchasing', *Journal of Euromarketing*, vol. 6, no. 1, pp. 5–24.

Olsen, Barbara (1995), 'Brand loyalty and consumption patterns', in John F. Sherry, Jr. (ed.), *Contemporary Marketing and Consumer Behavior*, Sage Publications: Thousand Oaks, CA, pp. 245–81.

Oswald, Laura R. (1999), 'Culture swapping: consumption and the ethnogenesis of middle-class Haitian immigrants', *Journal of Consumer Research*, vol. 25, March, pp. 303–18.

Oyserman, Daphna, Heather M. Coon and Markus Kemmelmeier (2002), 'Rethinking individualism and collectivism: evaluation of theoretical assumptions and meta-analyses', *Psychological Bulletin*, vol. 128, pp. 3–72.

Park, Seong-Yeon (1998), 'A comparison of Korean and American gift-giving behaviors', *Psychology and Marketing*, vol. 15, no. 6, pp. 577–93.

Penaloza, Lisa (2001), 'Consuming the American West: animating cultural meaning and memory at a stock show and rodeo', *Journal of Consumer Research*, vol. 28, no. 3, pp. 369–98.

Redding, S. Gordon (1982), 'Cultural effects on the marketing process in Southeast Asia', *Journal of the Market Research Society*, vol. 24, no. 2, pp. 98–114.

Reynolds, Nina L. and Antonis Simintiras (2000), 'Establishing cross-national equivalence of the customer staisfaction construct', EBMS Working Paper, 2000/7.

Richins, M. (1983), 'Negative word-of-mouth by dissatisfied consumers: a pilot study', *Journal of Marketing*, vol. 47, Winter, pp. 68–78.

Richins, Marsha (1994), 'Valuing things: the public and private meaning of possessions', *Journal of Consumer Research*, vol. 21, no. 3, December, pp. 504–21.

Richins, M. and B. Verhage (1985), 'Cross-cultural differences in consumer attitudes and their implications for complaint management', *International Journal of Research in Marketing*, vol. 2, pp. 197–205.

Robinson, Chris (1996), 'Asian cultures: the marketing consequences', *Journal of the Market Research Society*, vol. 38, no. 1, pp. 55–62.

Rose, Gregory M. (1999), 'Consumer socialization, parental style, and developement timetables in the United States and Japan', *Journal of Marketing*, vol. 63, July, pp. 105–19.

Rose, Gregory M. and Aviv Shoham (1999), 'The values of American and Japanese mothers: an application of LOV in the U.S. and Japan', *Journal of Euro-Marketing*, vol. 8, no. 1/2, pp. 45–62.

Sin, Leo Y.M., Gordon W.H. Cheung and Ruby Lee (1999), 'Methodology in cross-cultural consumer research: a review and critical assessment', *Journal of International Consumer Marketing*, vol. 11, no. 4, pp. 75–96.

Singelis, T.M. (1994), 'The measurement of independent and interdependent self-construals', *Personality and Social Psychology Bulletin*, vol. 20, pp. 580–91.

Singh, Jagdip (1988), 'Consumer complaint intentions and behavior: definitions and taxonomical issues', *Journal of Marketing*, vol. 52, January, pp. 93–107.

Solomon, Michael R. (1999), *Consumer Behavior*, 4th edn, Prentice Hall: New Jersey.

Steenkamp, Jan-Benedikt E.M., Frenkel ter Hofstede and Michel Wedel (1999), 'A cross-national investigation into the individual and national cultural antecedents of consumer innovativeness', *Journal of Marketing*, vol. 63, April, pp. 55–69.

Straughan, Robert D. and Nancy D. Albers-Miller (2001), 'An international investigation of cultural and demographic effects on domestic retail loyalty', *International Marketing Review*, vol. 18, no. 5, pp. 521–41.

Straus, Karen (1992), 'Go hog wild with Chino-Latino pork dishes', *Restaurants and Institutions*, vol. 102, no. 19, pp. 43–57.

Tanouchi, Koichi (1983), 'Japanese-style marketing based on sensitivity', *Dentsu Japan Marketing/Advertising*, vol. 23, July, pp. 77–81.

Triandis, Harry (1994) *Culture and Social Behavior*, McGraw Hill: New York.

Van Raaij, W.F. (1978), 'Cross-cultural methodology as a case of construct validity', in M.K. Hunt (ed.), *Advances in Consumer Research*, Association for Consumer Research: Ann Arbor, vol. 5, pp. 693–701.

Viswanathan, Madhubalan, Terry L. Childers and Elizabeth S. Moore (2000), 'The measurement of intergenerational communication and influence on consumption: development, validation, and cross-cultural comparison of the IGEN scale', *Journal of the Academy of Marketing Science*, vol. 28, no. 3, pp. 406–24.

Wallendorf, Melanie and Michael D. Reilly (1983), Ethnic migration, assimilation and consumption', *Journal of Consumer Research*, vol. 10, December, pp. 292–302.

Watkins, Harry S. and Raymond Liu (1996), 'Collectivism, individualism, and in-group membership: implications for consumer complaining behaviors in multicultural contexts', *Journal of International Consumer Marketing*, vol. 8, nos 3/4, pp. 69–96.

Wilk, Richard (1995), 'Real Belizean food: building local identity in the transnational Caribbean', *Proceedings of the Second Conference on the Cultural Dimension of International Marketing*, Odense, pp. 372–91.

Wimalasiri, Jayantha (2000), 'A comparison of children's purchase influence and parental response in Fiji and the United States, *Journal of International Consumer Marketing*, vol. 12, no. 4, pp. 55–73.

Wong, Nancy and Aaron Ahuvia (1995), 'From tofu to caviar: conspicuous consumption, materialism and self-concepts in east-Asian and Western cultures', *Proceedings of the Second Conference on the Cultural Dimension of International Marketing*, Odense, pp. 68–89.

Yang, Chung-Fang (1989), 'Une conception du comportement du consommateur chinois', *Recherche et Applications en Marketing*, vol. IV, no.1, pp. 17–36.

Yang, M.C. (1972), 'Familism and Chinese national character', in Y.Y. Lee and K.S. Yang (eds), *Symposium on the Character of the Chinese*, Institute of Ethnology, Academia Sinica (in Chinese), pp. 127–74.

Yankelovitch, Skelly and White (1982), *Spanish USA: A study of the Hispanic market in the U.S.*, for Spanish Television Networks.

Yau, Oliver H.M. (1988), 'Chinese cultural values: their dimensions and marketing implications', *European Journal of Marketing*, vol. 22, no. 5, pp. 44–57.

Appendix 4

Teaching materials

A4.1 Exercise

'Dichter's consumption motives'

Question

Discuss the cross-cultural variability of the major motives for consumption as identified by Ernest Dichter some 30 years ago. Choose five associations between motives and associated products for your discussion.

Motive	Associated products
Power, masculinity, virility	Power: Sugary products and large breakfasts, bowling, electric trains, pistols, power tools.
	Masculinity, virility: Coffee, red meat, heavy shoes, toy guns; buying fur coats for women, shaving with a razor.
Security	Ice-cream, full drawer of neatly ironed shirts, real plaster walls, home baking, hospital care.
Eroticism	Sweets, gloves, a man lighting a woman's cigarette.
Moral purity, cleanliness	White bread, cotton fabric, harsh household cleaning chemicals, bathing, oatmeal.
Social acceptance	Companionship: ice-cream (fun to share), coffee.
	Love and affection: toys, sugar and honey.
	Acceptance: soap, beauty products.
Individuality	Gourmet foods, foreign cars, cigarette holders, vodka, perfume, fountain pens.
Status	Scotch [whisky], ulcers, heart attacks, indigestion, carpets.
Femininity	Cakes and cookies, dolls, silk, tea, household curios.
Reward	Cigarettes, candy, alcohol, ice-cream, cookies.
Mastery over environment	Kitchen appliances, boats, sporting goods, cigarette lighters.
Disalienation (a desire to feel connectedness to things)	Home decorating, skiing, morning radio broadcasts.
Magic, mystery	Soups (have healing powers), paints (change the mood of a room), carbonated drinks (magical effervescent property), vodka (romantic history), unwrapping of gifts.

(Source: Solomon, 1999, p. 168.)

A4.2 Exercise

Investigating the cross-cultural applicability of a consumer complaint scale

A scale of consumer complaint behaviour (CCB) developed by Singh (1988) is portrayed below. US respondents were asked to express their degree of agreement or disagreement on a six-point Likert scale on the items listed below (possible behavioural responses to dissatisfaction with a consumption experience). Factor analysis allowed three dimensions to be distinguished for CCB.

1. *Voice CCB*
   (a) Forget about the incident and do nothing.
   (b) Definitely complain to the store manager on your next trip.
   (c) Go back or call the repair shop immediately and ask them to take care of your problem.

2. *Private CCB*
   (a) Decide not to use that repair shop again.
   (b) Speak to your friends and relatives about your bad experience.
   (c) Convince your friends and relatives not to use that repair shop.

3. *Third party CCB*
   (a) Complain to a consumer agency and ask them to make the repair shop take care of your problem.
   (b) Write a letter to the local newspaper about your bad experience.
   (c) Report to the consumer agency so that they can warn other consumers.
   (d) Take some legal action against the repair shop/manufacturer.

Question

Investigate the cross-cultural applicability of such a scale. Since you cannot do this with a full psychometric design, conduct your investigation mostly into the meaning, situations, institutions and behaviours depicted by the items.

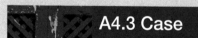

A4.3 Case

Mobile phones in the European Union

European mobile telecommunications are in a crisis, stated Jean-Michel Hubert, director of the French Telecoms Regulation Authority at an international mobile technology conference. The main reason is a relatively saturated market, and low average revenue per user (ARPU), at 29 euros in Europe versus 50 euros in the USA.[9] According to the Western European Mobile Forecasts and Analysis 2003–2008 report, the number of active subscribers is forecast to grow just five percent in 2003 to 309 million.[10]

There is still ARPU growth in France, Germany, Spain, and the UK, but ARPU in Italy is static, and in Sweden it is declining.[11] Mobile sector growth has been exponential in the European Union (current penetration at 70%, see Table 4.4), and linear in the USA (current penetration at 50%) and Japan. In China, growth is exponential but penetration is still relatively low, partly due to the size of the population.[12] Penetration is mainly dependent on age: in Finland, for instance, penetration among youth aged 13–18 is 90 per cent.[13] In terms of new subscribers, the European market is near saturation point. For an understanding of this phenomenon, one must look to cultural differences among European countries.

The cultural roots of the European mobile phone predicament

Zbigniew Smoreda, sociologist at *France Telecom* and researcher on the Eurescom P903 study that examined mobile habits in nine countries, explains that overall, in countries like Denmark, Germany, and the UK, the primary reason for obtaining a mobile subscription was to keep one's life organized. For the French, the primary reason was to be available at all times.[14]

However, the most striking differences were found between urban and rural settings. The city user, whether in Copenhagen or Rome, is likely to use the phone often – perhaps partly due to the complications of city life, and partly due to age (they tend to be younger).[15] From an aesthetic perspective, Samsung handset designers speak of 'global localization' and the balance of 'reason and feeling' attributes that govern the design, then subsequently the marketing process[16] (see Table 4.3).

Table 4.3 Samsung's 'reason and feeling' attributes for mobile phone design

Region	Attribute: 'reason'	Attribute: 'feeling'
Asia	high tech	Cuteness
Europe	Minimal	Emotion
North America	Durable	Dynamic

(Source: Mark Delaney *et al.*, 'Global design and cultural identity', *Innovation* (Industrial Designers Society of America), Summer 2002.[17])

According to the Eurescom P903 study, Italians were the fastest adopters of the mobile telephone, quickly overtaking the Nordic countries where the standard was first launched. Italian youth take the credit for this; age being the 'most important factor for predicting the adoption of the mobile phone'.[18] It is not a cliché to say that Italians are talkative, according to Alessandra Bianchini, communications head at Italian mobile operator *Wind*, it is one of the reasons that mobile phones are ubiquitous in Italy. She goes on to say that another cliché about Italians – love of family – is another reason: the mobile phone is ideal for keeping in touch with relatives and friends. In fact, mobile technology was promoted more as a tool of rather than business from the outset in Italy. It is not a rare sight to see young Italians chatting on their phones, perched on the back of a scooter in the midst of city traffic – phones are used everywhere. In 2002, there were 50 million mobile numbers in Italy owned by 86 per cent of the population, and one quarter of these have multiple subscriptions. The Netherlands, where 76.6 per cent of the population is a mobile user, presents a contrast to the Italian attitudes towards mobile use. In accordance with clichés about the Dutch, their use of the technology is economical: they are one of the least talkative on their mobile phone in Europe, partly due to concern over talk rates. According to Marc Gommers of mobile operator *Dutchtone*, another reason for this is the precision of the Dutch language that allows them to express themselves rapidly. There are also social norms that frown upon over-use of the phone in public; in restaurants they are banned, as they are in Denmark.[19] In France, the lack of such social norms triggered increasing frustration about the inconsiderate use of mobile phones, inciting the government to legalize mobile phone jamming in public places – a measure agreed with by 85 per cent of the population.[20]

Table 4.4 Mobile phone penetration in Europe

Penetration	≥ 74%	62%–73%	45%–61%	≤ 44%
Western Europe	Finland Italy Netherlands Norway	Belgium Denmark Germany Portugal UK	France Spain	
Eastern Europe			Czech Republic Estonia	Hungary Latvia Lithuania Poland Ukraine

(Source: Taylor Nelson Sofres *Global E-Commerce Report*, 2001; TNS A-P M-Commerce Report, 2001.[21])

According to a Gartner G2 report, 41 per cent of European adults use SMS, even more than those who use email (30%). That figure rises in Germany, where 43 per cent of adults prefer SMS to using email (29%).[22] Britons send more SMS than other Europeans (31 versus 26 per month on average). Europeans overall use SMS much more than Americans. Schuyler Brown of Euro RSCG Worldwide's S.T.A.R. (Strategic Trendspotting and Research) team believes that commuting and PC use determine SMS use. European teenagers tend to use public transport, an ideal situation for chatting via SMS, whereas American teens tend to drive to school and work. Likewise, the European teen spends more time in public spaces, where time can be spent sending and receiving SMS, compared with the American teen who is more likely to be sitting at home which is likely to be equipped with a PC, wide-screen TV, and games consoles, competitors for time and attention deviated to SMS in Europe.[23]

Third Generation (3G) applications

Regarding mobile applications in addition to voice and text messaging, there is interest in Europe in so-called third-generation (3G) (or UMTS) capability for specific applications, such as information (including maps and directions, news, and financial), m-banking, and m-trading.[24] Most of the year-on-year growth in phone sales is attributed to these 'smart phones'.

However, overall interest is tepid. A Taylor Nelson Sofres study of 7,000 subscribers in 10 European countries found that Poland and Turkey were the most likely countries to adopt 3G, while 58 per cent 'other' Europeans, and 66 per cent Britons were 'not interested' in 3G phones. Britain, one of the most mature mobile markets in world, is mainly happy with 2G phones, and is not interested in going beyond pre-pay. The implication is that Europeans are likely to keep their trusty old handsets, and only a minority will be interested in purchasing 3G phones.

In order to develop the 3G market, operators have ideas to increase non-voice revenue, forecast to attain 24 per cent of mobile service revenue by 2005. Most of this revenue now comes from person-to-person messaging, and increasingly includes downloadable music and games.[25] Web logging (known as blogging) is now offered for mobile phone users whereby a personal webpage (known as a Foneblog by its Irish creator, www.newbay.com), complete with photos and even short videos, is created and may be viewed by other mobile phone users via WAP or a standard web browser. Many games are already available, like Sweden's Botfighters game that combines SMS and Global Positioning Systems (GPS), informing players via SMS that they are approaching another player. The first to respond to the message receives extra 'life' game points.[26] More simple games based on the sports, driving, puzzle, and arcade formats are affordable and easy to procure. A realistic example of a phone game is the Finnish football team Helsinki PK-35 pay-per-shot game whereby their approximately 3,000 fans may send text suggestions from their mobile phones for game strategy, including defense and substitutions.[27] If only mobile phone users could send text suggestions regarding strategy to their mobile operators, they could help these companies at a crossroads to navigate an uncertain future.

Questions

1. How can mobile operators, software designers, and handset producers inspire Europeans to use their mobile phones for longer lengths of time and for more applications?

2. Using the cultural differences highlighted in the case, outline a 3G strategy targeted to one northern and one southern European country, that will explicitly take these differences into account.

3. Taking the case of mobile operator Orange (see www.orange.com), what would you advise as a pan-European 3G marketing strategy?

A4.4 Exercise

Cross-cultural consumer behaviour and the standardization/adaptation of service offers

Based on a discussion of variations in consumer behaviour across countries, review arguments in favour of standardizing or adapting service operations in one or several of the following service industries:

- private banking,
- telecommunications,
- hairdresser,
- motor insurance,

- life insurance,
- hotels,
- Haute Cuisine restaurants,
- satellite launch.

You may distinguish different subsets of the service industry or different market segments within this service industry; consider two aspects in each industry:

1. whether the service and its characteristics are more or less standard world-wide;
2. whether consumer behaviour and especially the service encounter differs across domestic markets;

You may take into account the following issues in your discussion of the cross-cultural variability of service encounters and consumer behaviour:

- Does language have an influence on the service encounter?
- Does religion have an influence on attitudes towards the service and on the service encounter itself?
- Do time attitudes (waiting, long term orientation, fatalism, linear vs. cyclical views of time, etc.) have an influence on the service encounter (pre-process, in-process, post-process)?
- Are there standards for this service industry? What is their reach?
- How does culture influence both the service customer and the service provider?

You may Google to get some additional insights on the issues above.

 ## A4.5 Exercise

Multidomestic versus Global

For the following industries or products discuss to what extent:

1. a world **consumer** exists (in terms of tastes and preferences, consumption habits, social taboos, local regulations influencing consumer behaviour, differences related to language, consumer learning, etc.)
2. the **products or services** offered are themselves global (similar world-wide): you may distinguish major product types within the generic product (e.g. high-fermentation versus low-fermentation beer); and
3. the **industry** itself can be considered as global (players tend to be global ones and competition takes place on a global rather than multi-local basis).

- Airlines
- Beer
- Pharmaceuticals (ethical/prescription drugs)
- Pharmaceuticals (non-prescription/over-the-counter drugs)
- Tobacco (cigarettes, cigars, other tobacco-based products)
- Meat-based foods
- Automatic blood analyzers
- Mail services (delivery of letters and parcels)
- Sheets and pillows

- Ski lifts
- Portable computers
- Writing instruments (you may distinguish between pencils, ball-point pens and fountain pens)
- Micro-chips
- Toilet tissues
- Washing machines (for cloth)
- Auditing services

This exercise can be used in relation to contents in Chapter 5 and 8 (where the concepts of multidomestic and global market are explained).

5

Local consumers and the globalization of consumption

IKEA is often cited as an example of successful marketing strategy given the globalization of world markets. However, consumption habits and way of life regarding household equipment, furniture and related items remain significantly different, according to whether people sleep with duvets or sheets, the size of pillowcases, or the kind of materials they use for their bathrooms. In Germany, for instance, most homes have no cupboards, and when Germans are interviewed, it becomes clear that their underlying assumption is that only lower-class people have cupboards because they cannot afford nice wardrobes. This traditional value in the Germanic world extends to Alsace but stops in France and the Latin countries, where both cupboards and wardrobes are considered convenient, and there is no implied meaning in terms of the perceived wealth of the household. This illustrates the paradox of globalization, based on the rather harmonious coexistence of global and local patterns. Thus IKEA succeeds globally while maintaining a strong Swedish brand image, with waitresses in traditional Swedish costume serving *glögg* to its customers, and branding its items of furniture with names that sound strongly Nordic (see Warnaby, 1999).

While globalization is a key issue for designing international marketing strategies, it is a difficult phenomenon to examine because demand occurs in actual markets and can never be fully separated from supply. The central paradox of globalization is the encounter between companies that are increasingly global and consumers who remain largely local. The general line of argument developed by this chapter is that consumption styles converge only at a macroscopic level. Consumption patterns resemble Russian dolls, building up from home to city, from community to region, and from nation to globe (Bell and Valentine, 1997).[1] Paradoxically, it has never been so urgent to take a close look at differences, that is, unique elements of meaning invested by local consumers in the products and services they buy and in their consumption experiences.

In order to scrutinize the apparent trend toward homogenization, three aspects of globalization processes must be distinguished. The first aspect is the globalization of demand, that is, the convergence of consumer behaviour (in this chapter), and marketing environments worldwide (in the next chapter). The second aspect is the globalization of supply and competition, with the progressive shift from domestic industries operating in national markets protected by non-tariff barriers to global industries. Many of these changes were initiated through the successive rounds of the General Agreement on Tariffs and Trade (GATT) and implemented by the World Trade Organization (WTO) and by regional trade organizations such as the European Union (EU) or the North American Free Trade Agreement (NAFTA) (see Chapter 6). The third aspect deals with the globalization of products and marketing offerings. Companies react to globalization partly by shaping new strategies and partly by refining their organizational design. They do this under cost constraints, given the potential for the experience effect of available technologies and the impact of transportation costs (see Chapter 8).

The first section of this chapter explains how traditional models of international trade have been strong drivers for the partisans of globalization. These models largely deny local consumers' tastes and differences across products with local design and manufacturing, and focus on merely utilitarian needs for undifferentiated generic products. These traditional models have been used as justification by those who argue in favour of worldwide similarity. In section 5.2, the global convergence of consumption patterns is discussed. The basic argument is that there may be convergence at the macro level for broad, generic product categories, but it is much less obvious when one adopts a micro-level of analysis looking at specific products and the minutiae of consumer behaviour. In section 5.3, an examination of the emergence of a global consumer culture, based on the values of 'modern culture' is made, in which a world standard package of goods might result. Section 5.4 delves back into the local level and examines precisely how products are to various degrees culture bound, and how goods and services are integrated into local meanings and lived as unique consumption experiences. Section 5.5 documents the issue of consumers' resistance to global products and consumption patterns, when these are resented as harmful to the local cultural or economic interests. The final section (5.6) tries to give an idea of the complex, kaleidoscopic patterns of local consumption in a globalizing world, that is, how consumers mix globalized products and local items in a grand *bricolage*.

5.1

Free trade doctrine and the denial of cultural variety in consumers' tastes

Ricardo's hypothesis

Traditional international trade doctrine has laid the foundations for a denial of culture in international marketing. One of the seminal texts on international trade is the seventh chapter of David Ricardo's *On the Principles of Political Economy and Taxation* (1817), which deals with foreign trade. His text basically explains why countries (and their traders) may derive benefits from developing international trade, instead of simply producing and trading within their own domestic market. Ricardo considers the case of two countries, England and Portugal, and two types of goods, wine and sheets (see *WS5.1*). This law, which

is called *the law of comparative or relative advantage*, conveys a very powerful message: a country that would be at a competitive disadvantage for both products (wine and sheets) would still benefit from participating in international trade. By trading internationally, each country finds a better exchange ratio for the goods than that provided by its domestic market. By concentrating efforts and resources on products where they have a relative advantage, both countries probably increase their national welfare and certainly global welfare. In Ricardo's text, which is both visionary and confused, many implicit assumptions are not clearly spelled out: (1) gains from trading internationally must offset transportation, customs duties and trading costs; (2) there are constant returns to scale; (3) products are identical, or at least are perceived as such by both consumers and merchants; (4) information must be easily available and efficient enough so that merchants in the two countries may be aware of the potential gains to be derived from international trade; and (5) there must be no other financial or government restriction or market barrier that limits international trade for these products.

The implicit assumption that products and consumers' tastes, habits and preferences are perfectly identical in the two countries (and accordingly by logical extension throughout the world) is a strong one. England produced almost no wine at the time and it is doubtful that British wine had the same physical characteristics, the same alcoholic content or the same taste as the Portuguese wine. Regarding the bed linen, the preferences of the English and the Portuguese were probably distinct enough to enable them to recognize clearly which were 'their' sheets. They certainly had different fabric and embroidery, and natives of the two countries would have been fully aware of the origin of the sheets on which they were sleeping. Furthermore, in Britain beer tends to be the drink of choice in pubs, whereas *vinho verde* or *porto* are the favourite drinks of the Portuguese while they listen to *fado* (guitar music). Ricardo's full negation of consumer culture, and of non-utilitarian motives, is based on the assumption that products have no reality as cultural artefacts. Only quantity and price matter. Exchange is purely economic: goods and services are commoditized, generic, indefinitely marketable and without cultural meaning.

These 'wine and sheet' considerations probably appeared as rather anecdotal and naive. The cultural variable – related to national culture and local ways – has been neglected in international trade theory, which is almost purely economics based, whether on theoretical grounds or for practical purposes. Classical economists and their successors are not fond of national culture, which has an aura of inertia and resistance to change attached to it. Their theories favour commonalities, not differences. They are based on utility maximization rather than on identity building through non-utilitarian motives.

Ricardo's theory was contemporaneous with a major decision in Britain's economic policy: the Corn Laws. Ricardo demonstrated that Britain should reduce its customs duties, thereby opening up its domestic market to foreign agricultural commodities – especially those from the colonies that were more cost competitive – and specialize in certain manufactured goods that it should export worldwide. The rationale behind this type of decision appears rather simplistic when real people are facing real-world consequences: rapid rural depopulation, social inequality, consumer frustration, stress, materialism, lack of self-sufficiency in food supplies, and threats to health and the environment (Ger and Belk, 1996).

The increase in global welfare predicted by international trade theorists has been used to label as 'nationalistic' and 'resistant to inevitable change' those local groups whose jobs were endangered by the progressive opening of the world economy over the last century. From this initial assumption, it was apparently axiomatic that the defence of cultural identity was inextricably linked to protectionist attitudes in international trade. This is illustrated in France by the *Lois Méline* introduced at the end of the nineteenth century out of a desire to protect French food supplies and French farmers, even though this meant higher costs for the consumer. This was also true in Germany where the writings of Friedrich List promoted a nationalistic approach to economic growth. (For more information on anti-globalization movements, such as ATTAC or Global Trade Watch see *WS5.1*.)

In practice it is difficult, except on the basis of questionable arguments, to make a sharp distinction between the protection of national/cultural interests (one's own identity being largely enhanced by what one consumes) and the interests of some industries which may deprive consumers of some bargains, or even of the opportunity to buy particular products.

Hence there is a natural tendency to ignore culture or to consider it as an anecdotal and residual explanatory variable, defending local, narrow interests rather than promoting global welfare. This tendency of international trade theory has been largely adopted or inherited by international business and international marketing, where culture remains a subsidiary explanation, with a weak explanatory power. This is exactly how partisans of the globalization of markets such as Levitt (1983) see the cultural variable: a reminder of the past, a vestige in a world where we all tend to adopt a sort of 'modern' lifestyle, at best a bunch of anecdotes and at worst useless constraints. Ultimately, it takes on a macro-perspective rather than a multifaceted approach where all actors are considered (Aulakh and Schechter, 2000).

The dismal treatment of diversity in global marketing

The global products philosophy is characterized by a lack of consideration for meanings invested by consumers at the local level. This is because price is a universal concern and low-cost arguments make sense. In this utilitarian view, products are commoditized in a worldwide sphere of exchange. As explained by Kopytoff (1986, p. 68): 'A commodity is a thing that has use value and that can be exchanged in a discrete transaction for a counterpart, the very fact of exchange indicating that the counterpart [most often, money] has, in the immediate context, an equivalent value.' As advocated by Levitt, and then continually repeated, rephrased and promoted by many other authors in the area of international marketing, we might expect to see the emergence of global markets for standardized consumer products on a previously unimagined scale. In Levitt's words it would 'not [be] a matter of opinion but of necessity' (1983, p. 97). Traditional differences in national tastes would disappear, while local consumer preferences and national product standards would become 'vestiges of the past'. Consumers worldwide would look for good quality/ low-cost products and global competitors would seek to standardize their offerings everywhere. Farewell diversity: we will not mourn your passing!

This world-view contains a number of assumptions to be discussed here and in other chapters. The first concerns the strong ideology of 'standard' in the

American mind. What dominates consumption is the utilitarian and materialistic side: people strive for a large quantity of fair-quality, low-cost products. Levitt rightly argues that low cost and high quality are not incompatible. However, this refers only to the quantitative definition of product quality, based on reliability, performance and durability. Here, quality is meant only in the sense of the word contained in the first of nine definitions given by *Collins English Dictionary*, 6th edn, 2003, p. 1325: '*a distinguishing characteristic, property or attribute*', this does not necessarily mean superior quality to other products. Quality in the sense of '*having or showing excellence or superiority*' is only the ninth and last meaning in the dictionary.

Levitt's text incorporates a section entitled 'vindication of the model T', where he clearly explains his view that 'consumption fordism' [which values assembly-line organization and continuous processes] is the only possible pattern. The second assumption deals with the continuum between traditional and modern societies.[2] 'Traditional' is associated with the past, which is of low value in the American view; the past is mostly seen as an impediment to effective action. This naive view of world diversity states that we are all converging towards a 'modern' lifestyle marked by standard products and consumption patterns worldwide.

The anti-diversity discourse can be found in international marketing texts where the inevitability of global preferences is presented as a simple fact, not to be discussed: 'No longer an alternative, global marketing has become an imperative for business' (Czinkota and Ronkainen, 1995, p. 3). The main result is that, in most international marketing textbooks, diversity is treated as an anecdotal constraint. There are, however, non-utilitarian reasons for consumer behaviour, and cultural diversity at the international level is a reality, as has already been shown in the previous chapters. Moreover, for companies that reject the 'consumption fordism' of globalization, diversity presents an opportunity to create differentiation and gain a competitive advantage. For instance, in 2000, the new CEO of Coca-Cola, Douglas Daft, declared a repositioning strategy based on three fundamental principles. The second of the three was to 'think locally and act locally'. In an article adapted from his speech (Daft, 2000, p. 12), he stated that:

Ours is a local business – we will think locally and act locally. We became one of the best marketers in the world because we understood that no one drinks 'globally'. Local people get thirsty, go to their local retailer, and buy locally made Coke. To think locally and act locally, we must push decision making and accountability to the local level . . . Understanding the local culture and acting on that understanding is paramount to success.

5.2

The global convergence of consumption patterns

General convergence at the macro-level

As will be argued in more detail in Chapter 8, supply and competition is now largely globalized, with the progressive shift from domestic industries operating in national markets protected by non-tariff barriers to global industries. This alone is enough to explain a large part of the globalization of consumption.

In addition, there is some evidence at least at the macro-level of convergence in consumption patterns. For example, Leeflang and Van Raaij (1995) found significant demographic convergence in the European Union: (1) the age distribution of the population comprises more older persons; (2) the size of households is constantly decreasing, with an EU average of 2.7 persons, ranging from a low of 2 persons in Denmark to a high of 3.6 in Spain; (3) the proportion of immigrants is increasing with higher concentrations in large cities. Convergence is also to be observed in the sociocultural environment in terms of growing equality between men and women and increasing percentages of working women, while all over the EU, health and environment concerns are on the rise. In Hofstede's terms, there is a trend towards more *femininity*. Convergence in consumer behaviour can also be observed at a broad level: services tend to replace durables in household budgets and demand is growing for health-care, services and products that are environmentally friendly, fun and convenience products. (For more information on global convergence of consumption patterns see *WS5.2*.)

Most of the empirical studies on globalization are synchronic in design; they study cross-national similarity in consumption patterns at a precise point in time. The most logical way to study the convergence process is, however, to examine how consumption changes over several time periods. A good example for illustrating long-term convergence in consumption figures is that of wine, traditionally a southern European drink, and beer, traditionally a northern European drink. Wine consumption has decreased and beer consumption has increased in the south (in France, Greece, Italy, Portugal and Spain), whereas the opposite pattern has evolved in the north of Europe (in Austria, Belgium, Denmark, Germany, Luxembourg and the UK) leading to macro-level convergence (Smith and Solgaard, 2000). Smith and Solgaard also found a tendency toward drinks with lower alcohol content, stricter drink-driving laws, and higher quality products. Similarly, Clements and Chen (1996) provide evidence of increasing macro-level similarity in cross-national consumption patterns in broad commodity categories. Using a utility-maximizing framework, actual consumption figures are examined, rather than consumer motives and involvement in the purchase.[3]

Numerous detailed examples are cited in support of the globalization of consumption behaviour. Beef consumption in Japan, traditionally a fish-eating country, has developed considerably while there has been a rise in fish consumption in traditionally meat-eating countries. There have been similar changes in relation to rice and wheat between the West and the East (see Box 5.1 for other examples). But, as de Mooij (2000, p. 105) points out, though economic systems may converge: 'there is evidence that with converging income, people's habits diverge. More discretionary income will give people more freedom to express themselves and they will do that according to their own specific value patterns.'

Rather than discuss macro-level globalization, it makes more sense from an international marketing perspective, to try to understand the nature of this phenomenon. With decreasing barriers to international trade over the last century, and mostly in the last 50 years, more variety has been brought to consumers in most countries of the world. In this sense, globalization increases, not decreases, diversity in everyone's experience.

Box 5.1

Savoury snacks and global law: Two different routes for globalization

Globalization can occur even when local patterns do not disappear. In the two examples below local patterns work either as an opportunity or as a constraint for the emergence of globalized product or service use.

Japan has a long tradition of savoury snacks based on local ingredients such as rice crackers (*arare* and *senbei*), dried seafood snacks (*kozakana*) and *edamame* (green soybeans lightly boiled in salt). Although these snacks still have high consumption rates among elderly people, they have lost ground to potato and corn-based Western-style snacks: sales of traditional Japanese-style snacks decreased by 16.5 per cent between 1993 and 1997.

In a totally different field, legal practice, local legal systems have presented an opportunity for US and English law firms (Spar, 1997). Due to the political nature of law, most countries restrict the practice of law to their own nationals. However, US law firms have been following the globalization of US companies, which took them along as they expanded abroad, in particular to arrange cross-border deals that maximized advantages under US tax law. By learning the intricacies of local legal systems, US law firms have adjusted to local contexts while maintaining their comparative advantage in terms of common law (the prevailing legal tradition in the United Kingdom and the United States), by assisting foreign firms willing to enter the US market or drafting international business contracts based on common law.

(Source: Adapted from Spar, 1997 and *Euromonitor*, 1997.)

Evidence of consumers' globalization at a micro-level

De Mooij and Hofstede (2002, p. 62) point out that 'international marketers would like us to believe that in the "new Europe" with a single currency, consumers will become more similar, will increasingly eat the same food, wear jeans and cross-trainers, and watch the same television programs. Reality is likely to be different.'

Generally, at the micro-level researchers have found that culture influences consumption patterns (e.g. Eshghi and Sheth, 1985), but that this influence differs by the product type, product/service category, situational factors, and reasons for purchase. First, for product type Huszagh *et al.* (1986) found that durable, household and functional products varied more by culture than non-durable, sensory and personal products. Second, for product/service category, Zaichkowshy and Sood (1988) found that restaurants, air travel and hair shampoo are more influenced by culture than beer, jeans, going to the cinema, soft drinks and stereos. Agarwal and Teas (2002) in a replication-extension, found that wristwatches are more influenced by culture than consumer electronics, which were examined by Dawar and Parker (1994) in a previous study. Third, for situational factors Nicholls *et al.* (1999) found that frequency, time of day, where consumers shopped, the length of time and the reason varied by culture for food, but not for clothing. Fourth, for reasons for purchase Woods *et al.* (1985) found that maintenance, enjoyment and defence reasons differed by country. (For more information on these studies see *WS A5.4.*) Many other examples illustrating micro-level differences were elaborated on in Chapter 4.

Thus, evidence at a micro-level, that of specific products and aspects of consumer behaviour, is somewhat inconclusive about the globalization of consumer behaviour. Finding convincing proof of this process is difficult, since testing for it would include such issues as the pace and process of globalization, the market segments involved and the geographically significant cultural areas (Jain, 1989). The trend towards globalization depends partly on which aspect of consumer behaviour is concerned, whether buying behaviour, shopping behaviour, lifestyle, values, psychometrics and underlying attitudes, influence processes (in the family, word-of-mouth communication, etc.). The use of culturally unique concepts and research instruments (roughly translated as 'American') compresses differences, even when cross-cultural precautions have been taken. Since the concepts and theories of marketing are mostly US-culture based, their full ability to capture local patterns of consumer behaviour is questionable.

5.3
The emergence of a global consumer culture

According to Ger and Belk (1996) there are at least four ways to interpret global consumer culture: the proliferation of transnational corporations; the proliferation of global capitalism; global consumerism; and global consumption homogenization. As there is no doubt that transnational corporations and capitalism have proliferated, this section will focus on global consumerism and later on global consumption homogenization. Global consumerism is defined by Ger and Belk (1996, p. 275) as 'a widespread and unquenchable desire for material possessions'. It is a culture in which the majority of consumers avidly desire, and therefore try to acquire and display, goods and services that are valued for non-utilitarian reasons such as status seeking, envy provocation and novelty seeking (Belk, 1988). The rise of large-scale, democratized consumption as a legitimate and positively valued human activity (unlike say, war or monastic contemplation) in most countries has led to the emergence of a global consumer culture. Prahalad and Lieberthal (1998, p. 71) illustrate this: 'What is big and emerging in countries like China and India is a new consumer base consisting of hundreds of millions of people. Starved of choice for over 40 years, the rising middle class is hungry for consumer goods and a better quality of life and is ready to spend.' As Ger and Belk (1999, p. 199) suggest: 'Each culture finds a culturally appropriate way to justify its own high level consumption behaviour and aspiration.' Even in countries where purchasing power does not really allow access to goods and services, US films, with an approximate market share of 90 per cent worldwide[4] have been a major driver of desires and aspirations, fuelling consumers' needs and envy. (For more examples, see *WS5.3.*)

The standard world package and 'McDonaldized' consumption

A consumer culture guides people in defining their aspirations towards a certain set of possessions. The standard US package of goods has developed into a standard world package that includes a car and a home with electric lighting, a refrigerator and a television. The same holds true for services, since the fast-food restaurant has become part of the standard world package. Ritzer (1999, p. 70) describes how strongly people identify with McDonald's around the world:

In Taipei, the Golden Arches have come to have more symbolic meaning than the local temple. In Seoul, people are passionate about McDonald's as well as their opposition to it. In Tokyo, Japanese boy scouts were reported to be pleasantly surprised when during a trip they discovered that there was a McDonald's in Chicago.

In the emergence of a global consumer culture, a process that Ritzer (1993) calls *McDonaldization* of society, the word 'standard' is central. 'Standard' has three meanings: (1) the same for everybody; (2) the same everywhere in the world; (3) the same for all time. The paradoxical success of the 'Classic' Coke as against the 'new' Coke is an illustration of the last point. Standard also means that product quality remains the same unless new technological developments allow improvements which complement the previous attributes.

Ritzer (1993) distinguishes four elements in the McDonaldization process:

1. *Efficiency*: the McDonaldized product or service offers the optimum method for getting from one point (being hungry) to another (being fed). We are living in the 'Republic of Technology' as Levitt (1983) says. In contrast to traditional solutions, fordist consumption values assembly-line organization and continuous processes: with the parking areas adjacent to the fast-food restaurant, a short walk to the counter, a limited menu and quick choice, finger food and speedy disposal of leftovers.
2. *Systematic quantification and calculation*: McDonald's offers more 'bang for the buck' and provides its customers with 'value' meals. Rational economic calculations based on the emphasis of price and the size/weight given for each ingredient extols the utilitarian view. In this model, quantity becomes equivalent to quality: the view that larger quantities are a sign of better value is latent in such a conception.
3. *Predictability*: whether in Chicago, Los Angeles, Paris, Moscow or Tokyo, we find the same Big Mac and French Fries. Consumers find great comfort in this predictability which offers neither bad nor good surprises, and reduces perceived risk. There is not much surprise in the limited range of products offered, but we know that it will be consistent over time and place. Predictable food is based on predictable, often frozen ingredients and corporate guidelines that detail everything to be done in the fast-food outlet.
4. *Control through the substitution of non-human for human technology*: the system is operated so that there is limited human involvement in the whole production process: rules are fairly strict and automatic systems (e.g. soft drinks or ice-cream dispensers) control the exact quantity, in line with point 2. This also facilitates predictability by reassuring customers about the service to be obtained from McDonald's.

The globalized consumption experience is only one part of the real world of consumption but it plays a dominant role because it has been consistently and heavily portrayed as 'useful' and 'good for people'. It is also publicized in a somewhat deceitful way since there is much more local adaptation, both in Coca-Cola and in McDonald's, than affirmed by these global marketers. In addition, the same concept can mean something quite different when borrowed from another culture. As Anderson and He (1999, p. 92) point out: 'The fast-food concept that fits the US fast life style has adapted successfully to PRC's consumers' life style, because less waiting and fast service do not mean to eat fast.'

Globalization and 'modern' culture

The most disputable and debatable aspect of globalization is the implicit assumption that we are all converging towards a 'modern lifestyle'. This view of cross-cultural buyer behaviour has three main assumptions: (1) modernity is a given and technology is our path to a bigger and better future for all of us on our little planet; (2) even if they differ externally, all societies can be placed on a continuum of social change – from traditional to developed societies; and (3) the criterion for placing a society on the continuum is its degree of resistance to the changes brought about by modernity (Sheth and Sethi, 1977). Firat (1995, p. 106) explains that in modern culture the central idea is that scientific knowledge and technology could control nature and improve human existence: 'thus, modern culture was a driven one with its eyes on the future and its feet securely planted on the material ground, in reality. Reaching the goals . . . required commitment, order, and universal, valid principles'. Even though it may be argued that we have already entered the postmodern era (Bouchet, 1994), most people still live in a modern era, marked by a strong belief in the achievements of science, its unlimited problem-solving capacity through technology and its exclusive contribution to global welfare. The modern project is clear in Levitt's view of globalization, when, criticizing multinational companies for being medieval (by which he means pre-modern), he writes:

The multinational corporation knows a lot about a great many countries and congenially adapts to *supposed* differences. It willingly accepts vestigial national differences, not questioning the possibility of their transformation, not recognizing how the world is ready to and eager for the benefit of *modernity*, especially when the *price is right*. The multinational corporation accommodating mode to visible national differences is *medieval*. (Levitt, 1983, p. 97; emphasis added.)

The global values in modern culture emerge because consumers throughout the world inevitably have fairly similar responses to new technologies and product innovations. 'Modern' culture is characterized by: (1) an individualist orientation that is supported by the exercise of purchasing power as a manifestation of individual freedom; (2) a strong emphasis on material achievements and materialistic values, that is, a *doing/having* rather than a *being* orientation; (3) a strongly economic, 'commoditized' time; (4) a tendency to discard the past in favour of a future orientation, while expressing some frustration at not living in the present as much as one would like; and (5) a fairly high degree of utilitarianism. Household equipment, for instance, tends to individualize tasks and people are more and more freed from both the constraints and the pleasures of communal life, in a mostly urban environment where families are nuclear and the extended family separated by huge distances. An increased awareness of a clock-bound and universal time, at the expense of a local and nature-bound time, accompanies the enthusiasm for innovation and change. Modern culture posits a strong future orientation as a mere imperative: consumers dispose quickly of machines and products that are still recent but already obsolete. Environmental concerns, although varying in degree, are typical of modern cultures since the deterioration of the earth's environment through increased levels of pollution and depletion of the ozone layer are common to many countries. Although Germany, with its *grüne punkt*, (green point) still largely leads the movement, the interest in 'green' products is shared worldwide. Chan (1996) shows, for instance, that both Canadian and Hong Kong consumers are more and more interested in environmentally friendly products.

The controversial claim that the 'American way of life' would have universal appeal and extend progressively to backward nations is typical of the binary thinking of modern thought, opposing concepts such as past/future, traditional/modern, true/false and rational/emotional (Firat, 1995). For instance, Baines *et al.* (2001, p. 1009) examined the 'Americanization' of political campaigning in western Europe. They argue that: 'because of the very different contextual environments and their implications for campaign conduct, the potential for "Americanization" is limited through indirect export methods.' They found that direct export without customization is less likely to be successful in European markets.

In fact, the true globalization of consumption patterns would occur if the 'globalization route' ceased to be one-way: in a genuinely global consumer world, US consumers will have to import genuine, unpasteurized, French *foie gras* or crude milk cheese which contain some innocent bacteria but which also have real taste and consistency. Similarly, French consumers will have to develop a taste for peanut butter, American women take to wearing kimonos, and Australian men swap their shorts and thongs for Bavarian *lederhosen*, if the route to globalization is to be less unidirectional.

The emergence of a global 'modern' culture is often confused with the convergence of local cultures, leading to an incorrect description of the globalization phenomenon. A frequent mistake is to equate 'modern' with 'American': while it is true that the

United States and US multinational companies have been literally the champions and heralds of modern culture in consumer goods (consumption fordism) and services, globalization is not simply the world-wide extension of the 'American way of life'. The imitation of solutions that are 'Made in the USA' results mostly from the borrowing of answers to challenges that were largely common worldwide. American society values a pioneer spirit and has less resistance to change and fewer social impediments than more traditional societies. When the Japanese, French or Chinese change, it is not as a result of American pressure; rather, since these societies are less innovative in terms of social adaptation to technological developments, they borrow part of their responses from the United States, while often making the United States scapegoats for the drawbacks of modernity.

Modern culture, with both high individualism and structured time patterns, implies a kind of social organization centred on peer-age segments. Girls give up their Barbie dolls between the ages of 12 and 13 because it would be inappropriate to play with dolls – even sophisticated ones – when they reach adolescence. Each age class increasingly has its own identity, its own way of doing things, membership is signalled through consumption, and the shared values and behaviour transcend national borders. It is also possible that certain age groups, such as teenagers, are allowed a 'cultural time-out', where they are expected to rebel from their cultural restraints. For instance, we see Japanese youth wearing typical American teenage clothing such as baseball hats on backwards, watching MTV, etc. Later, when they join the workforce and begin families they are expected to re-adopt culturally appropriate behaviour.

The increased adoption of modern culture cross-nationally is erroneously interpreted as a sign of full convergence – and as testimony to the progressive disappearance of local cultures. Significant elements of local cultures, such as language, writing systems, religions and relational patterns, are still intact and quite visible in the global landscape. Cultural differences seem to matter little because they rarely appear as the key explanation for behaviour. However, local cultures allow a deeper understanding of consumption in a specific context. Interpretation must be close to the local reality: for instance drip/filter coffee taken 'to go' or drunk with a meal (as is common in the USA), is a widely different coffee-drinking experience from espresso enjoyed with friends at a local café in Europe or Australia. Local cultures do not really disappear; rather, a new layer of common culture is superimposed on them. The very fact that the Japanese and the Chinese are not willing to change their ideographic writing system, which from a purely utilitarian perspective makes little sense, demonstrates the very deep roots of local cultures.

5.4

Local products and consumption experiences

Not surprisingly, globalized fordist consumption has a striking preference for 'culture-free' products and consumption situations. A different perspective on consumer behaviour centred on cultural meanings ascribed to things (McCracken, 1986) may be useful despite its limited use in international marketing texts. For instance, Applbaum and Jordt (1996) suggest the need to centre on things, and on how they are used in context; they argue that by doing so, more insights are gained into the complex patterns of local consumer behaviour than through the national character approach, based on limited universal variables and the design of cultural ideals (i.e. high versus low scores on common dimensions). They observe, for instance, the services for dating and arranged marriages in Japan and note that a Japanese wedding ceremony would be practically incomprehensible to a westerner apart from the (now shared) appearance of diamond rings and white wedding dresses. They describe the *pro nakôdo*, a commercial go-between for marriage services as follows:

Through personal contacts – that is, not through advertising – a *pro nakôdo* is introduced to a young man or young woman interested in being set up for arranged marriage dates . . . The *pro nakôdo* association meets once a month to exchange information on new registrants. At the meeting each *pro nakôdo*'s new contribution will be photocopied and distributed among the other *pro nakôdo* . . . the *pro nakôdos* bring home and place in their loose-leaf notebooks between 100 and 200 new pages each month. At the end of five years, or on marriage, whichever comes first, a person's sheet is removed from the notebook. At the time of this study, the association had slightly more than 6,500 registered clients.

If consumer culture matters, then it is likely that consumers will invest more meaning in products and services that are more bound to cultural interpretation. The question is therefore: what is more culture-free and what more culture-bound, in terms of product and service categories on the one hand, and consumer behaviour on the other?

Culture-bound products

Culture bonds arise in a number of ways, some related to the consumption situation, others to product attributes. This complexity is due to the *peculiar qualities intrinsic to the encounter between things and people*. The first aspect to examine is whether a rich (or poor) cultural context surrounds the product: shopping for it, buying it and/or consuming it and disposing of it. Furniture, for instance, will be more culture-bound than consumer electronics, because there is often a local style and a local manufacturing tradition for these items. Furniture may not only be bought, but also inherited or restored, which makes less sense for a CD player. Consumer electronics are a typical culture-free product category because they are technology-based, low in cultural context and universally used. It comes as no surprise, therefore, that consumer behaviour is very similar cross-nationally for consumer electronics (Dawar and Parker, 1994). An exception is in developing economies where consumer electronics do tend to become culture-bound.

For example in China, where colour TV sets are vested with symbolic values that are rooted in the local context (see Box 5.2).

The more closely products relate to the *physical* environment, the more culture-bound they will be, as physical environment influences the local material culture, which is linked to climate, density of population, housing, flora and fauna, etc. The absence of visible cattle rearing on most Japanese islands, except Hokkaido, distances Japanese people from dairy products. Japanese people find cheese, the most sophisticated dairy product, quite a strange kind of food; cheese conveys little meaning except that of foreignness. Similarly, local ways of building are generally based on the availability of substitute building materials (wood, cement, stones, etc.), certain craft traditions (e.g. masonry versus carpentry), and constraints (e.g. earthquakes), which explain the dominance of local technical solutions. For instance, the use of steel in bridges and urban freeways is much higher in Japan than it is in Europe where bridges are mostly built with reinforced concrete. Similarly, wood is frequently used for housing construction in the United States, whereas it is quite marginal in western Europe except in Scandinavia.

Culture bonds are strong for a product or service when there is an investment of *cultural and national background and identity* in consumption. Consuming then becomes, consciously or unconsciously, more than a simple utilitarian purchase, resulting in a preference for products made in one's own country. In

---

Box 5.2

Colour television as a life statement

Television has made tremendous inroads into Chinese homes over the last ten years: penetration rates are reaching 80 per cent in rural areas and 98 per cent in cities. Television, more than any other good, represents freedom from oppression in the 'new China', and breaking with the past by access to information, in a country that has traditionally been wary of foreign influence. Ownership of a TV set plays an important role in establishing one's financial image and projects an image of personal success. Chinese people indicate that owning a colour television is a prerequisite to marriage and some couples indicate that they are willing to wait two years to be able to afford the best possible TV (a Japanese one, often several times more expensive than a Chinese colour TV). One respondent said: 'Buying a Chinese TV will give my marriage a poor start. I must wait until I can buy a Japanese TV to project the right image to my friends.'

(Source: Adapted from Doran, 1997.)

terms of product attributes, the use of local materials and production processes, recipes and craft techniques will reinforce the perception of compatibility, if they are known as such by consumers.

Language content is also a major constituent of the cultural content of a product, as in genuinely cultural products (e.g. songs, soap operas, films and novels), or just in written language used on or around the product, such as the packaging or brand name. The instructions for assembling IKEA furniture rely on pictures alone, thus avoiding complex multiple-language explanations. An additional benefit of pictures is the decreased degree of culture-boundedness, because visual elements are more culture free than written materials.

Products that involve a *relationship to others*, in terms of displaying/showing or giving/sharing, are likely to be culture bound, precisely because this relationship is culturally coded. That is the social situation is likely to moderate the influence of culture. The same consumer may choose different brands depending on who is involved in the decision-making process or likely to use the product (Han and Shavitt, 1994; Bagozzi *et al.*, 2000; Lee, 2000). Conspicuous-consumption items, and more generally goods having a high sign value, are culture bound, although many luxury products are globally branded, the nature of their consumption is largely local, depending at least on concepts of the self and others (Wong and Ahuvia, 1995). Products that have been consumed as a part of life since childhood are often marked by locality. Peanut butter from the USA and Vegemite from Australia are not global products and cannot be found in many countries. As such, American and Australian expatriates have difficulty obtaining them when assigned abroad.

Complex products, such as films, are logically culture bound, because they require a high level of interpretation and knowledge of the local context in order for the film to be fully understood and enjoyed. One of the reasons for the limited global success of most films, except for Hollywood's, is that they rely on local cues which are not easily understood by different local audiences. Conversely, the success of American movies is based on their low contextuality, simplified characters, reliance on the universal appeal of violence, love, and wealth, and their simple moral dichotomy, where good struggles against evil. Even so, many Hollywood films are modified during the

dubbing process to add the appropriate local context. For instance, many of the jokes were changed in the German version of the animated movie Aladdin. Comedy, it seems, is largely culture bound, due to a sense of shared understanding.

The very *nature of the product* has some influence on the level of universality of needs. *Non-durables* seem to appeal more to tastes, habits and customs; therefore they are more culture-bound. Clothing, confectionery, food and household cleaners are all culture-bound.

Empirical evidence (Peterson *et al.*, 1985) seems to suggest that industrial and high-technology products (for instance, computer hardware, machine tools and heavy equipment) are considered appropriate for global strategies, as they often offer significant benefits over the previous alternatives. While one could easily believe that industrial products are typically culture free, this view is largely mistaken because the contexts in which they are used, and the functionalities sought, depend on culture. The construction industry, for instance, is highly influenced by local cultural traditions as well as the attitude towards time (short-term versus long-term orientation) and the perceived trade-off between the price and durability of equipment varies. In Europe, the difference between national markets is considerable; for instance, the market estimate for clay water pipes is 460,000 tons/year in Germany, whereas it is only 11,000 tons/year in France. In fact, clay water pipes are two or three times more expensive than cast-iron pipes; however, their durability extends way beyond the lifetime of those who decide on the investment; they may last for a century, or even several centuries. The German local authorities and/or standard-setting bodies prefer a high investment cost/extended lifetime trade-off whereas the French seem to consider this as too costly and a lifetime of a century is beyond significance for public decision-makers. Furthermore, the major player in France for this kind of water pipe, Pont-à-Mousson, uses ductile cast iron, a solution it has promoted widely with the water utilities. Box 5.3 provides a further illustration of how benefits sought of equipment goods depend on local culture.

One framework for unravelling the degree and the nature of culture bonds for products is to undertake a 'cultural biography' of the goods surveyed (Kopytoff, 1986). Drawing on the analogy with the life of a person, the biography of an object allows one

Box 5.3

Time to wait

Market data were gathered for blood analysis equipment in several European countries (Germany, France, Italy, Spain, and the United Kingdom) in hospital labs. Doctors were asked to rate the importance of time to results, a reason for adopting automatic blood analysis equipment allowing speedier outcomes. Responses reflect different degrees of preoccupation with time, Germans being the most concerned with short time to results (86 per cent of German labs mentioned this as a major factor in their buying decision), followed by the British (72 per cent), the French (67 per cent), the Spaniards (55 per cent), and the Italians (37 per cent). Thus, even for organizational purchasing, underlying cultural values are different.

to understand how it ultimately nests itself within a cultural milieu.

The biography of a car in Africa would reveal a wealth of cultural data: the way it was acquired, how and from whom the money was assembled to pay for it, the relationship of the seller to the buyer, the uses to which the car is regularly put, the identity of its most frequent passengers and of those who borrow it, the frequency of borrowing, the garages to which it is taken and the owner's relation to the mechanics, the movement of the car from hand to hand over the years, and in the end, when the car collapses, the final disposition of its remains. All of these details would reveal an entirely different biography from that of a middle-class American, or Navajo, or French peasant car. (Kopytoff, 1986, p. 67.)

Unique consumption experiences

Consumption is still largely a local reality. Far from being uniquely culture related, local reality also reflects climate and customs, and the mere fact that much of our lives is still experienced, shared, perceived and interpreted with those nearby who share the same kind of 'local knowledge' in the Geertzian sense (Geertz, 1983). Consumption experiences remain local while much global influence is integrated in shared cultural meaning (McCracken, 1991). As noted by Applbaum and Jordt (1996, p. 207): 'Globalizing influences have bored intercultural tunnels around the world, but core meaning systems such as those wrapped up in the idea of the family, continue to differ significantly.' There are, for instance, still huge differences in the pattern of household expenditures across EU countries.[5] Consumers attribute meaning to products and services in context, especially what it means to desire, to search, to evaluate, to purchase, to consume, to share, to give, to spend, and to dispose of. Consumption experiences are full social facts in interaction with other players in the market game: manufacturers, distributors, salespeople and also other consumers. (For more information on local consumer experience see *WS5.4*.) Two illustrations are given below.

Consumption as disposal

Consumption involves our views of our relationship with the environment, the nexus between nature and culture, affecting our perceptions, such as what is clean or dirty and where the cleaning effort should be allocated. Many consumption acts lead to the final destruction of the good, even in the case of consumer durables when they are obsolete or out of order. Paper-based products are a good case in point: filters for drip-coffee machines are white in France and yellow-brown in Germany (*naturbraun*), paper handkerchiefs are generally white in France and yellow-brown in Germany and toilet paper is generally pink or white in France and greyish in Germany. The Germans express their willingness to be environmentally friendly (*umweltfreundlich*) by purchasing paper-based products whose colour exhibits their genuinely 'recycled' nature, that is, not bleached with chlorine-based chemicals that are used to whiten the paper. The same holds true for German writing and copying paper, which, because of its greyish and irregular appearance, would be generally considered by most French as 'dirty' and of poor quality. The difference in consumer experience lies in the difference of *continuity* in the ecological concern. Germans feel the necessity to be nearer to nature because they live in a country about three times more densely populated than France and they insist on strong coherence between their words and their deeds. The two peoples seem to have different ways of reconciling nature and culture: the contrast has often been made between Germans, perceived stereotypically as natural, deep and aggressive, and the French, who are thought of as more sophisticated. German culture finds its expression in love for nature and a preference for isolation, whereas French culture advocates social life and shows disdain for everything that is too nature-oriented (Gephart, 1990).

Offering wine

Offering wine is a different experience in southern Europe from what it is in the United States, Japan or northern Europe. Hosts who receive wine from their guests have to decide whether to keep it for later, or to open it immediately to share it with their guests. In France, unless the host states explicitly that the wine is not suitable to accompany the meal, the received wine will be drunk with the guests, because sharing is a must and keeping the wine for oneself would imply that it may not be good enough to drink now. In many other countries, it would be impolite to drink their gift with the guest, since it would mean the immediate destruction of a present that should be kept as a memory, at least for a time. The emphasis in each case is on different values: the sense of sharing on the one hand, and the sense of keeping a present as a memory of the donor on the other.

Habits, habitus and shared meaning

Rather than as a value system, culture may be viewed simply as shared habits and customs, and as shared meaning about how particular experiences are to be interpreted in context. This system of shared habits and interpretation is often encompassed under the general heading 'common sense' (shared meaning), which translates into French as 'good sense' (*bon sens*) with a clear value judgement, or into German as 'sound understanding' (*gesunder Menschenverstand*), showing that it is the appropriate solution. Habits are central in local consumer behaviour because they

reduce the universe of ways of acting, and enable people to form attitudes and to select interpretations or solutions as if they were self-evident. Habits facilitate choices in a multitude of everyday life situations. It would be exhausting to review all possible alternatives all the time. Habits give us self-assurance. However, they receive little treatment in accounts of consumer behaviour, probably because they are tainted negatively as passive behaviour. Interestingly, Triandis (1994) put forward a theory that habits are multiplied by arousal, meaning that when we are angry or very happy, it is more difficult to overcome a habit. It is possible that our purchases differ when we are more aroused emotionally.

A Chinese proverb says that 'habit starts with the first time'; a Western proverb that 'habit is a second nature'. To become fully built into a person, habits need support in child-rearing practices, schooling and education systems and the whole reward–sanction system that goes with the social game. Habits are ways of doing and behaving that have been reinforced by authorization and gratification, so that, once the programming is forgotten they appear to be legitimate. Three examples taken from diverse contexts may be used to illustrate this:

Kaffeetrinken

The German *Kaffeetrinken* is a traditional German form of enjoyment, organized mostly at week-ends or holiday afternoons with family or friends, at home or in a *Konditorei* (pastry shop serving coffee and tea) or a restaurant, at about three or four o'clock. The special relationship of Germans to coffee, sweets and cakes (*Kuchen*) has much to do with happy hours experienced since childhood when people relax in a somewhat tight society with a deeply internalized pressure for conforming to rules.

British fire safety systems

The United Kingdom is one of the largest markets for fire safety equipment in the world; fire alarms outside buildings are intended to attract people's attention quickly in case of fire. The excessive fire safety instructions in both public and private buildings is striking for many foreigners. The tradition of wood cased in buildings, and the Great Fire of London, are probably historical and objective reasons for this British phobia about fires. The United Kingdom logically follows the European norm EN52 on fire safety equipment, which, although compulsory, is not at present respected by the Italians and the Spaniards: not only would the implementation of this regulation in all public buildings involve massive investment that Italian and Spanish state budgets cannot afford, but also in Latin countries stone predominates over wood in construction and the anguish caused by building fires has traditionally been much lower than in the United Kingdom.

Drinking a beer

Individuals invest meaning into their consumption experiences: even if figures seem to demonstrate broad convergence, quantitative convergence in fact conceals huge qualitative divergence as far as experiences, context, perceptions and interpretations are concerned. Beer is indeed consumed in greater quantities in southern Europe than in the past, but the very experience of beer drinking still has a different meaning from that attributed to it in the north of Europe: the meaning differential has not yet diminished in the same proportion as the volume differential.

Shared situations, habits and stories around beer differ: the product is reincorporated in a universe of shared meaning, which surfaces mainly in details: the shape and size of the beer glass, for instance. The Bavarian *Krug* (a large jar) does not give the same 'taste' to beer as the French *demi* (a quarter-litre stemmed glass), the English pint glass or the Australian middie. Beer differs in terms of bitterness, froth, bubbles, sweetness and alcoholic content. Most British beers are high-fermentation beers with lower alcohol content than beers on the Continent. To drink a beer in Germany has a different meaning from what it has in the United Kingdom or in France. In Germany, beer is consumed in a *Kneipe* (tavern) or bought from a *Getränkeshop* (a side-store to a supermarket entirely dedicated to beverages, a nice combination of German and English). Local beers play a dominant role in the German beer scene. In the region of Cologne, for instance, the *Kölsch* beers, comprising some ten high-fermentation brands of beer, are seen as a reference to the place, a little like wines in France. The German returnable half-litre bottles suit a densely populated country where people are concerned with recycling glass. German beers always refer to the purity law (*Reinheitsgebot*) of 1516.

In a British pub, drinking a pint (0.57 litres) or half-pint of beer is a different experience; the pub is a comfortable place that invites people to stay as if they were at home. Since people often drink more than a single pint of beer, it must be low in alcohol. This beer can be drunk without 'getting plastered', especially if one stays for quite a long period of time. A pub is a totally different world from the French *café-bar*, with its tiled floor and its rather cold interior design; in France regular customers invest the place with their own sense of comfort and human warmth and do feel the need to have it materially invested in the place. But non-regular customers will never find in a *café-bar* the immediate comfort that they find in most British pubs.

This tour of European beer drinking is completed with Finland where, until recently, only low-alcohol beer has been allowed to be sold in supermarkets. For the sale of standard beer, and also of any other kind of alcoholic drink, the state chain Alko has a monopoly. Alko stores have limited opening hours and are generally remote from central shopping areas. To buy beer (apart from the low-alcohol type) one must go to a taboo store, openly manifesting a leaning which the society disapproves of. For a case study on Bass Plc (UK) and the European beer market, see Vrontis and Vignali (1999).

5.5 Local consumer cultures and resistance to change

The Danes dominate the world market for blue cheese with their Blue Castello: a decontextualized product with an Anglo-Italian name. It is a pasteurized, inoffensive, white soft cheese, palatable for every germ-phobic cheese-lover. As such it is a good candidate for promotion as a global product, and a typical progeny of fordist consumption. The British Stilton, the French Roquefort or the Italian Gorgonzola, all traditional blue cheeses, may in the long run be under threat from this global alternative. You may wonder how much autonomy consumers have in encouraging or limiting the movement towards globalization. Naturally, we may or may not buy globalized products and services – to this extent we 'vote with our feet'. But we also have little choice but to buy what is available, astutely brought to stores by sophisticated merchants. In this respect there could be some resistance to change, not at the level of the individual buying decision, but at more of a macro-level. What this amounts to is people asking to have their 'way of life' preserved, especially through some kind of protectionist measures. Even though they win as consumers, people may think they lose from globalization as citizens and workers, which leads to a preference for buying locally made products.

While some products may be global, there are strong arguments against the existence of a global consumer *per se*. Cannon and Yaprak (2002, p. 47) examine the many faces of cosmopolitan consumer behaviour and finding that the concept of cosmopolitanism has been over simplified: 'there are several different patterns of cosmopolitan behaviour, varying both with the situation and the consumer. For example, we have argued that cosmopolitans might or might not anchor their behaviour in local culture, depending on both the nature of the purchase motivation . . . and the personality/need structure of the individual cosmopolitan.' As shown above, consumers' motivations do not easily globalize.

Account managers working for large international advertising agencies face the complex task of managing a brand's images across several countries and accumulate detailed experience of consumers' responses to global product offerings. Harold Clark (1987) of J. Walter Thompson argues that: (1) consumers are not 'global' themselves; (2) they are not aware of buying 'global' brands or products and they do not care whether the brand is available elsewhere in the world; and (3) consumers value personal and individual expression in their purchases; they will naturally let their individuality affect the values they place on the brands they buy. They contribute actively in this way to the *persona* of the brand in their own situation (Clark, 1987).

Consumers always 'construct' the identity of brands, even for 'global products' and they do so, on the basis of their local culture and identity. Aaker (1997) investigated how brand personality (BP) dimensions may differ from human personality (HP) dimensions, using samples of consumers in the USA. Later, Aaker *et al.* (2001) used an emic–etic approach to investigate cross-cultural dimensions of brand personality using consumers in Japan and Spain. Aaker and her colleagues found that there is a subset of BP dimensions that remain relatively similar across cultures, while others appear to be indigenous to particular cultures. Specifically, excitement, sincerity

and sophistication were consistent dimensions across all three cultures (United States, Spain and Japan), and competence was consistent between the United States and Japan, but did not emerge in Spain. In addition, culture-specific BP dimensions were found that were consistent with individualism and collectivism. Specifically, in the more collectivist Japanese and Spanish samples the dimension of peacefulness emerged, being associated with values like dependence, naiveté, mildness and shyness. For the more individualist US sample, ruggedness emerged, being associated with values like outdoorsy, masculine, Western, tough and rugged (Aaker, 1997). In addition, the dimension of passion emerged only in the Spanish sample, including two facets: emotional intensity being fervent, passionate and intense; and spirituality being spiritual, mystical and bohemian. While there is not current theoretical dimension associated with this, it is certainly descriptive of Spanish culture. It is also interesting to note that even the apparent culturally consistent BP dimensions show differences in their emphasis. For instance, while excitement was related with being young, contemporary, spirited and daring across all three cultures, it also contained culture-specific elements. In Spain and North America excitement also included imaginativeness, uniqueness and independence, while in Japan, it included talkative, funny and optimistic. Thus, while companies might try to create a global brand personality (e.g. Coca-Cola), it may be perceived and interpreted differently in each culture.

'Global brands' in this sense are portfolios of local marketing assets, federated under a common, lexically identical name. Although Blue Castello builds on both an American referential (blue cheese dressing) and an Italian image, it is doubtful whether people in all countries have the same kind of buying motives, product use and product image. False 'global' consumers buy false 'global' products, which they reinvest with their own culture-bound motivations and purposes. This suggests that most of the resistance will be hidden from global marketers. Box 5.4 illustrates this point.

Will consumers resist the globalization process?

An implicit assumption about the globalization of consumption is that consumers are pleased with it

Box 5.4

Consumer resistance to McDonald's?

France, where cultural resistance to fast food and hamburgers exists as a matter of national pride, is McDonald's fastest growing market in Europe. Having first achieved great success with a limited number of successful 'luxury' (high end of the market) fast-food stores located in the centre of major towns in France, McDonald has now expanded to the suburbs and motorway junctions, and offers breakfast service. Anti-fast-food consumer associations have resisted the fast-food movement. Anti-globalization activists like José Bové have caused material damage to restaurants. Nutrition specialists have shown that traditional French meals (based on diverse foods, lasting one hour) are much better for the digestion and prevent cancer of the digestive tract. Despite all this, McDonald's is popular with the young generation, especially children who will be tomorrow's adults and parents.

McDonald's has been responsive to criticisms of nutritionists in the United States. It has reduced fat, salt and sugar in its products and introduced a lean Deluxe burger with only 10 grams of fat and 310 calories against 20 grams of fat and 410 calories for the Quarter Pounder. In May 2002, the French weekly *Femme Actuelle* carried a McDonald's advertorial advising families not to eat at the restaurant more than once per week for health reasons (Dolbeck, 2002). McDonald's has also responded to attacks from environmentalists and animal rights activists, by replacing the Styrofoam hamburger box in most countries with paper or a new starch-based alternative, and enforcing strict guidelines for animal husbandry. In Northern Europe, McDonald's now insists on sorting its own refuse so that it can be appropriately recycled. Resisted or beloved, fast food is now an institution.

because it means cheap, good-quality products and, therefore, they do not resist the process. Thus, the 'globalness' of a product may be a cue for other criteria, such as quality. Steenkamp *et al.* (2003) found that perceived brand 'globalness' was positively related to perceived quality and prestige and, through them, to purchase likelihood in the United States and Korea, but only for consumers with low ethnocentrism. Those with higher ethnocentrism resist globalization by paying a premium for locally made goods, voting for protectionist governments, or acting as consumer lobbyists to support public action (e.g. against fast food) in order to maintain or re-create entry barriers that protect local consumption. They may, nonetheless, be self-contradicting individuals – for instance, drinking Coke while complaining about the Americanization of society. Globalization obviously has some drawbacks: some have denounced the de-humanizing process in post-fordist consumption, and the possible decrease in consumption diversity which may result from the progressive replacement of local consumption by globalized offerings (Ritzer, 1993). Others have wondered whether globalization is not going too far: the continual opening up of national markets through the WTO may result in

increased worldwide competition across countries that have widely different levels of social security and therefore cannot compete on a fair basis because social insurance may raise the cost of goods subject to global competition. Globalization would favour the consumer, not the worker, and raise complex issues when these combine in one single citizen.

'Globalization' is exposing a deep fault line between groups that have the skills and mobility to flourish in global markets and those who either don't have these advantages or perceive the expansion of unregulated markets as inimical to social stability and deeply held norms. The result is severe tension between the market and social groups such as workers, pensioners, and environmentalists, with government stuck in the middle. (Rodrik, 1997, p. 30.)

There are two different issues here. The first is knowing whether there are intellectual, ethical and practical reasons for protecting local cultures and consumers from the globalization of consumption patterns. As Ger (1997) points out, opening up markets is not necessarily desirable: 'goods can delight or frustrate, cultivate or impoverish, empower or alienate, and nourish or destroy social relations for individual people and contribute to societal, cultural, health and environmental problems'. The second issue is whether resistance mechanisms to globalization actually occur at the individual and/or social level. For this issue, we can see a growing network of loosely associated individuals and groups opposed to 'globalization'. They could be seen rioting at the 1999 WTO summit in Seattle, and since then disrupting subsequent international financial and trade meetings in Washington, Davos, Nice, Bologna, Milan, Florence and Genoa. Activists fall into sometimes dissonant categories, including marxists, environmentalists, trade unionists, anarchists, cultural preservationists, advocates of fair trade, and, more recently, anti-war activists. (For more information on their arguments and ideals see WS5.5.)

Global marketing is often presented as a powerful tool for promoting economic development. As Kearney (2001), notes: 'emerging-market countries that are highly globalized (such as Poland, Israel, the Czech Republic and Hungary) exhibit a much more egalitarian distribution of income than emerging-market nations that rank near the bottom of the Globalization Index (such as Russia, China, and Argentina) . . . the general pattern of higher globalization and greater income equality holds for most countries, both in mature economies and emerging markets.' Thus, global marketing could enhance the needs and desires of badly treated consumers who live in sellers' economies. Marketing could then favour the creation of local industries to produce consumer goods and meet their demands. However, Ger and Belk (1996) describe a Third World consumer culture and emphasize the hedonistic attraction for conspicuous consumption, even when basic utilitarian needs have not been met. Thus a growing body of literature, relating to marketing and economic development, emphasizes a marketing system that 'must design, deliver, and legitimate products and services that increase the material welfare of the population by promoting equity, justice and self reliance without causing injury to tradition' (Dholakia et al., 1988, pp. 141–2). This means clearly resisting some of the uglier consequences of globalization, such as the problems caused by Nestlé infant formula in developing countries (see section 15.5). Global consumer culture encourages individuals to interpret their needs exclusively as utilitarian needs for commodities, but people may well have non-utilitarian needs to consume culture that are more tailored and localized

(Sherry, 1987), especially when it is embedded in local items, both local cultural products and products whose consumption process is part of the genuine local culture.[6]

In the case of Turkey, Ger (1992) explains that satisfaction depends on social comparison and is not an immediate response. Most of the modern packaged goods reach two groups of higher socio-economic status, representing respectively 1 per cent and 4 per cent of the Turkish population whereas international products such as Coca-Cola target a larger audience by including the lower-middle class (46 per cent). She describes the positive and negative effects of marketing on socio-economic development, pointing out that increased dynamism, optimism, aspirations, communications, employment and demand for education are observed, whereas marketing 'accelerates the change in the set of values . . . Rapid transmission of the consumption culture from the core to the periphery has increased the desirability of both products and anything "Western"' (Ger, 1992, p. 329). The emulation of the West leads to resource allocation in gadgets and appliances at the expense of the satisfaction of more basic needs.

Preference for national products

It has persistently been demonstrated that in most developed countries domestic products generally enjoy a more favourable evaluation than foreign-made products. This strong preference for domestic products has been clearly evidenced for US, British, French, (European in general), as well as Japanese consumers.[7] Conversely, in developing countries, national products are not preferred to imported goods. Iranian producers, for instance, were shown to prefer imported products (Bon and Ollivier, 1979). In Iran, a product was favourably rated when it had a foreign/imported label. Bon and Ollivier did, however, observe the emergence of a deep-rooted nationalistic feeling in purchasing situations.[8] In eastern European countries, similar attitudes related to nationality and brand-name images: for instance, the Hungarians generally evaluate foreign products more positively than domestic products, although their image of the latter is not particularly unfavourable (Papadopoulos et al. 1990). It is also important to note that this is not static. Yu and Albaum (2002) studied the changes in the preferences of Hong Kong and Chinese consumers since the handover of Hong Kong from the United Kingdom to China. They found that consumers in both countries now have a greater preference for their own products than foreign products, including UK-made.

Different explanations have been proposed to explain this preference for national products, especially in developed countries. For instance Sharma *et al.* (1995) found that ethnocentrism and factors such as patriotism, collectivism, and openness to foreign cultures were significant. Ethnocentrism is the belief among consumers that it is inappropriate, or even immoral, to purchase foreign products because it puts the national economy at risk, leads to job losses and is unpatriotic (Shimp and Sharma, 1987). Shimp and Sharma (1987) studied the level of consumer ethnocentrism in different regions within the United States that were affected to a greater or lesser extent by foreign competition: Detroit, Denver, Los Angeles, and North and South Carolina. They observed that consumer ethnocentrism was much stronger where the threat was perceived by individuals whose quality of life was affected by foreign competition, as in Detroit where unemployment in the automotive industry is adversely affected by Asian competition. More recently, higher levels of ethnocentrism have been found in the US in females of lower socio-economic status and education (Klein and Ettenson, 1999).

Tapping into nationalism, 'Buy National' campaigns have been used in many countries including the United States, Portugal, Japan, France, Canada, and Mexico (Granzin and Painter, 2001), as well as Australia. 'Buy National' campaigns should be used very cautiously as they are affected by country of origin (COO) perceptions, product categories and situations. First, we should consider the possible opposing influences of ethnocentrism and COO perceptions. For instance, Moon and Jain (2001) found that South Korean attitudes toward the buying proposal in foreign advertising was negatively affected by ethnocentrism and positively affected by COO perceptions. These campaigns are less likely to be effective when other countries products are seen to have a COO appeal, such as Italian shoes or Swiss watches. Second, the influence of nationalism is likely to differ by product category. Han (1998) found that it significantly influences quality perception for cars,

but not for television sets. Third, the influence is also likely to differ by usage situation or context. Ger *et al.* (1999, p. 167) found that coffee type differed by situation in Turkey, especially when convenience may be a factor: 'I have Nescafe all the time, all day, when I am studying. Nescafe is more practical, you can easily make it, but it takes time to prepare Turkish coffee. Turkish coffee is usually consumed after the meals. Turkish coffee reminds me of being with friends and chatting together. When you go to a neighbour or a friend, she prepares Turkish coffee and you chat while you drink. I almost always drink it with my mother or my friend. I never drink it alone (Zehra, female, 18).'

Ettenson *et al.* (1988) investigated the effectiveness of 'Buy National' advertising campaigns with the case of a 'Made in the USA' campaign carried out for American clothing manufacturers.[9] Respondents' attitudes towards domestic products failed to correspond with their purchasing behaviour. Consumers will probably remain fairly rational in their product evaluations; therefore an attempt to reinforce the quality perception of locally made products artificially could prove ineffective. The best approach to adopt would be to play clearly on nationalistic feelings, and not to attempt to influence consumers in their product evaluation.

5.6

Emergent patterns of a mixed local/global consumer behaviour

What emerges from the confrontation of global and local consumption is a complex pattern where the variety of consumption experiences reaches unprecedented levels. Global consumption patterns are reflected in local kaleidoscopes where myriad pieces of coloured glass are constantly rearranged in innumerable pictures.

Positioning the local *vis-à-vis* the global: Patchworks and kaleidoscopes

As Firat, (1995, p. 111) rightly observes, 'In an overwhelmingly marketized existence, individuals experience practically all aspects of their lives as consumers'. Whereas consumption was not always highly regarded by modern consumers, the postmodernist consumers pursue, with little afterthought, the construction of their self-image.[10]

Because the postmodern consumer experience is not one of committing to a single way of being, a single form of existence, the same consumers are willing to sample the different, fragmented artifacts. The consumer is ready to have Italian for lunch and Chinese for dinner, to wear Levi's 501 blue jeans for the outdoor party in the afternoon and to try the Gucci suit at night – changing not only diets and clothes but also the personas and selves that are to be (re)represented at each function. (Firat, 1995, p. 115.)

Whether people really change their self-image so quickly may be debatable. However, most consumers assemble diverse consumption items in a very opportunistic, fragmented and idiosyncratic way, not hesitating to mix local products and ways with global products and services. There is high pragmatism in postmodern consumption, in particular because budgetary constraints are still highly meaningful. Fordist consumption items have their place in the patchwork: they offer good value and are often shrewdly advertised so that the potentially negative aspects of standard offerings on the consumer's self-image are largely erased. High-touch products and luxury brands play a complementary role, being the shiniest and most colourful squares of the harlequin tights of postmodern consumption. Local products are also present: they make up the bulk of the patchwork with more discreet and less shiny pieces of fabric. As shown by Box 5.5, featuring our favourite example (beer), local products are candidates for promotion at a higher level of image in other countries where they are opportunistically re-interpreted, precisely because their foreignness allows it.

A process of creolization takes place when foreign goods are assigned new meanings and uses by the buyers' culture, even if they are transferred to it without change. For instance, Kragh and Djursaa (2001, p. 1306) observed that 'traditional furniture such as English furniture of the eighteenth century Chippendale and Hepplewhite mould is found in a number of especially elderly Danish homes and kept alive as a cultural expression through the exposure to especially English upper-class interiors depicted in television series and films'. In this sense one can contrast the creolization paradigm, where attention focuses on the reception and domestication process of global goods in local contexts, to the Coca-colonization paradigm, where emphasis is on uniformity (Howes, 1996). A good example of such localization of consumption is Disneyland Tokyo, which is a perfect replica of the American model, yet is completely 'Japanized', i.e. fully reinvested by local cultural codes (for this see the lively accounts of Tokyo Disneyland by Van Maanen and Laurent (1992) and Brannen (1992)).

Box 5.5

'European' beers

Typical of the diversity of the European brewing industry is how different brands in their segments are viewed from country to country. Brands which do not have their origin in a country, which are 'foreign', are invariably viewed as premium segment products. A good example of this is BSN's Kronenbourg 1664, which is sold in France as an ordinary segment beer, but is viewed in almost all other (European) markets as a premium product. As an Italian brewer puts it: 'Foreign brands command a premium price for their image of higher quality.'

However, potential hazards exist for brewers in pursuing this policy: 'In Great Britain, (Belgian) Stella Artois is a premium beer, one of the most expensive beers you can get there, and people buy it because it is expensive. It is marketed and promoted that way. The British are travelling people, so now when they come to Belgium, they discover that Stella Artois is a cheap beer. So they ask themselves if it is justified to pay so much for it in Great Britain' (French brewing manager).

(Source: Steele, 1991, p. 58.)

Central and peripheral consumption contexts

In the emergent consumption patterns, the consumption context is an important aspect of how consumers combine global 'fordist' goods and services, high-touch luxury brands and local items. Consumption contexts involve a certain space (i.e. certain rooms in a home), as well as particular time periods and people. A family dinner in a British dining-room or a ski vacation in the French Alps are consumption contexts. Djursaa and Kragh (1998) studied the fragmented nature of globalization by distinguishing central and peripheral consumption contexts, based on in-depth, direct observation for two highly culture-bound product categories: furnishings and food. The consumption contexts of furnishings were Britain and Denmark, and the consumption contexts of food were three Arab cities: Riyadh, Jeddah and Dubai. Centrality for food is defined in terms of time of the day when a meal is consumed whereas centrality in the case of furnishings is defined in spatial terms as the room where traditional cultural values are respected because this room carries a strong culture-bound meaning. British informants clearly expressed the dining-room as a central consumption context and, when presented with modernist furniture for dining-rooms, indicated that:

they would be OK for kitchens or breakfast rooms but not for 'proper' dining rooms, which for the majority of English respondents had to be traditional to carry the proper cultural message of identity. In Denmark, by contrast, modernism is the cultural norm and carries out notions of identity perfectly adequately in central rooms as well as in main homes. (Djursaa and Kragh, 1998.)

In peripheral consumption contexts, it is easier for a consumer to innovate, to borrow from foreign cultural contexts. Informants from the three Arab cities noted that dinner, a peripheral meal, was increasingly taken in fast-food outlets, unlike their lunch, which for Arabs is the 'central' meal. A common pattern for Emiris is to go out for dinner at Pizza Hut, McDonald's or Harvey's, which have compartments for male and female members of the family to eat together, separated from other guests. In the case of dinner taken at home, 'global products also play a very significant part in the meal; as one respondent said, "Dinner is pizza and Pepsi"' (Djursaa and Kragh, 1998).

Kaleidoscopic borrowing and the assemblage of local and global items is only possible if marketers are flexible enough to introduce some adaptations to their offerings, ignoring the Levittian (1983) criticism of adjustment to local ways. For instance, when McDonald's in Egypt suffered an anti-American boycott for its support of Israel in 2001, the company introduced the McFalafel, promoted by the singer of the hit *I Hate Israel* by Sha'ban Abdel Rahim (Dabbous, 2001).

Global marketers should first target, peripheral consumption contexts to successfully introduce foreign products not rooted in the local culture. Eckhardt and Houston (2002) found that in China, McDonald's is appropriate for a date, but not for a celebration. McDonald's is not appropriate for a celebration because the prices and seating arrangements are standardized and offer no opportunity to make a special display of face to the guest of honour. Conversely, it is the standardized offering that makes it more appropriate for a date, as the man does not need to worry about the lavishness of a meal.

Borrowing can then be progressive: McDonald's has started in many countries without being open at breakfast time as it is in the United States. It is now trying worldwide to introduce breakfast offerings, which will result – from a fordist perspective – in increased efficiency in terms of covering overhead costs by prolonging demand patterns over 14 or more hours. McDonald's and other fast-food outlets have succeeded in extending fordist consumption throughout the world because they have been pragmatically adaptive, partly tailoring their offering to local habits.

Complexity and ambivalence in globalized consumption patterns

Consumers search for and create meaning because they need constantly to re-build their self-image. For this reason, their search for identity through consumption must be a key concern for marketers. In a globalized world, identity-seeking consumers can pick up products from two different shelves: one that favours the locality and the ingroup orientation and another that displays desirable values, meanings and signs offered by foreign, outgroup cultures. How consumers combine local and global meanings is complex. There is much ambivalence in the search for identity in a radically modern world where local diversity based on linguistic and religious differences will not disappear for centuries.

Globalized consumption has a threefold pattern. The first component is based on modernity and on fordist consumption; it corresponds to low-cost/fair-quality, weakly differentiated, utilitarian products, embedded in fairly low-context consumption experiences. Its highest potential for success is reached when products and consumption experiences are culture-free, or consumption contexts are peripheral. Examples range from the film *Titanic* to Camay soap. Families, because they often face stricter budgetary constraints than singles, are likely to be adept in modern fordist consumption. Despite appearances and discourse, fordist marketers show major adaptations and flexibility in facing local consumption. They display much more sensitivity to local ways than is described in textbooks, and their success is more pragmatic than ideological. The second element is a postmodernist type of consumption: fragmented, continually re-assembled and re-interpreted. This can be particularly true for big brands, conspicuous consumption, younger people and yuppies. The third element corresponds to people who are aware that consumption is now a key driver for culture and that their choices as consumers will influence their culture. This radically modern type of person behaves both opportunistically and critically, with a willingness to display diversity in consumption (Ritzer, 1993). For these consumers McDonald's is an ethnic, American restaurant.

In concluding this chapter, it may be wondered why companies should try to ignore local diversity. Rather than being a liability, it can also act as a superb opportunity for building competitive advantages based on differentiation, which are easier to defend against competitors than low-cost advantages.

Questions

1. Take mineral water as a product example and outline how 'global' mineral waters such as Perrier or Evian can coexist with quite local ones.

2. Is there a 'modern' lifestyle, common to many cultures around the world? How could it be described? What could be its principal *raisons d'être*?

3. 'Dating' is a very curious concept for many people. In any case it cannot be fully translated into many languages and simply means 'making an appointment'. Compare what dating means to Americans with what it means in other cultures, demonstrating how the complex process of finding a partner for life can be commercialized in different contexts.

4. List some arguments and evidence that may show that globalization of consumption and lifestyles is under way. Outline the limitations and discuss the counterarguments.

5. To what extent are 'modern culture' and individualism primary inputs in the process of globalization of consumer preferences and lifestyles?

6. Discuss to what extent 'Buy National' advertising campaigns are effective. What can they achieve? What can they not achieve?

7. The FDA (US Food and Drug Administration) prohibits the import of traditionally prepared French *foie gras*. FDA inspectors visit French *foie gras* laboratories and refuse most of them the right to export to the United States since hygiene standards are not met. For the French too much antiseptic would kill the taste and for the Americans such unpasteurized products are dangerous to one's health. Discuss the difference in understanding of what 'good food' is.

8. Compare a global film (e.g. *Spiderman* or *Lord of the Rings* or *Titanic*) and a local film on a number of aspects: story, characters, situations, atmosphere, key appeals for the viewer (action, love, violence, etc.), combination of music and sound, rhythm, type of ending, etc. Explain why local films are most often not good candidates for reaching a global audience.

Notes

1. In their book entitled *Consuming Geographies*, Bell and Valentine (1997) explain how food consumption is understood at different levels, body–home–community–region–nation–global, and how culinary cultures map across space with discourses and food practices being developed simultaneously at different levels.

2. Such a distinction is now abandoned in comparative management (Usunier, 1998).

3. Clements and Chen study very broad consumption categories (food, clothing, housing, durables, medicine, transport, recreation and 'other'), comparing the OECD countries and a group of less developed countries (LDC). Income elasticities are fairly similar across groups of countries and consumption categories except for transport and food (broadly confirming Engel's law that food as a percentage of total budget decreases with increases in income). Differences in price elasticities are significant only for clothing and transport across the two groups, OECD and LDC. In its highly macroscopic approach, this article offers spurious support to the 'homogeneity of tastes' thesis, which the authors partly acknowledge (p. 750), stating that, 'first, we are only dealing with commodities that are broad aggregates and it might be reasonable to expect more idiosyncrasy and heterogeneity for goods which are more narrowly defined. Second, the analysis deals with *groups* of countries, rather than individual countries (let alone individual consumers), and, again heterogeneity may rise as the unit of analysis becomes smaller.' That is precisely what makes the huge difference between marketing and economics.

4. In France, one of the few countries (with Japan and India) where the local film industry is still active, the market share of American movie films is generally between 55 and 60 per cent. In many countries of the world, with relatively small populations and their own language, the cost of making local movies is difficult to amortize on the sole basis of local audiences alone. Adding subtitles or dubbing foreign movie films is considerably less expensive. This explains why in many countries, for instance Scandinavian countries, the American market share of films is 90 per cent or more.

5. Despite convergence, it is easy to find much evidence of remaining differences; see for instance *Euromonitor* (1997), or the special issue of the *International Journal of Research in Marketing* edited by Leeflang and Van Raaij (1995). The percentages spent by households in various EU countries on food in general, on vegetables, chocolate or cheese still widely differ. See also section 6.4.

6. Sherry (1987, p. 189) states the culturally respectful marketing strategy as follows: 'the guiding rule of such a marketing strategy, as in any ethically invasive procedure, is *primum non nocere*: first do not harm. In the rush to globalization, the preservation of local culture has been considered primarily as an opportunity cost. If cultural integrity is epiphenomenal to business practice, splendid; if not, social disorganization is frequently the cost of progress.'

7. Reierson, 1966; Gaedeke, 1973; Lillis and Narayana, 1974; Baumgartner and Jolibert, 1977; Morello, 1984; Heslop *et al.* 1987. The preference for nationally made products in industrialized countries has been corroborated by several other studies (Nagashima, 1977 in the case of Japan; Bannister and Saunders, 1978, in the case of the United Kingdom; Graby, 1980a and 1980b, in the case of France; Cattin *et al.*, 1982, in the case of France and the United States. See also Samiee (1994). Schweiger *et al.* (1995) show that European consumers have a better evaluation of their domestic products ('Made in Europe') than products originating from both the United States and Japan on a wide range of items. See also section 10.2.

8. They noted that there was at the time no 'Buy Iranian' campaign in the style of state-sponsored advertising campaigns for the purchase of national products, such as occur regularly in European countries, Australia and the United States, or as are permanently undertaken in India. Despite that, some Iranian buyers expressed a nationalistic tendency by buying primarily local products.

9. It was forecast that, in 1995, 65 per cent of clothing sold in the United States would be cheap imported products. The CWPC (Crafted with Pride in the USA Council) provided a budget of $40 million that initially funded a series of television commercials showing American stars praising the superiority of American clothing. Consumers were subsequently questioned to determine the audience for and the effect of the campaign. They proved reluctant to reveal themselves to be unpatriotic.

10. For more about the postmodern consumer see Bouchet (1994).

11. Wildposting is the placement of stickers, flyers, rubber stamps or posters on outdoor surfaces of public or private property in public view, for marketing communications purposes. Often the effect is achieved by multiple postings. In practice, flyers are often stuck on construction sites, lampposts, buildings, the pavement, trees, bus stops, and so on. Rave promoters were the first to use wildposting to publicize their events. The practice is sometimes assimilated with so-called guerrilla marketing, alternative advertising and street marketing, as well as other tactics including 'street spam', 'brandalism' and 'bandit signs'. For the word in use go to: **www.wildposting.biz, www. mangomoose.ca/start.htm** and **www.npawildposting. com/pages/1/index.htm** (all North American sites).

References

Aaker, Jennifer, Veronica Benet-Martínez and Jordi Garolera (2001), 'Consumption symbols as carriers of culture: a study of Japanese and Spanish brand personality constructs', *Journal of Personality and Social Psychology*, vol. 81, no. 3, pp. 492–508.

Agarwal, Sanjeev and R. Kenneth Teas (2002), 'Cross-national applicability of a perceived quality model', *The Journal of Product and Brand Management*, vol. 11, no. 4/5, pp. 213–36.

Anderson, Patricia M. and Xiahong He (1999), 'Culture and fast-food marketing mix in the People's Republic of China and the USA: implications for research and marketing', *Journal of International Consumer Marketing*, vol. 11, no. 1, pp. 77–95.

Applbaum, Kalman and Ingrid Jordt (1996), 'Notes toward an application of McCracken's "cultural categories" for cross-cultural consumer research', *Journal of Consumer Research*, vol. 23, December, pp. 204–18.

Assaoui, Mohammed (2002), 'Disneyland Paris, 2ème Edition', Etude de Cas (case study), *Le Figaro* Entreprises, 11 March, 2002.

Aulakh, Preet S. and Michael G. Schlechter (eds) (2000), *Rethinking Globalization(s): From Corporate Transnationalism to Local interventions*, St Martin's Press: New York (review in *JIM*, vol. 8, no. 4, 2000, pp. 122–4).

Aupperle, Kenneth E. and Grigorios Karimalis (2001), 'Using metaphors to facilitate cooperation and resolve conflict: examining the case of Disneyland Paris', *Journal of Change Management*, vol. 2, no.1, pp. 23–32.

Bagozzi, Richard P., Nancy Wong, Shuzo Abe and Massimo Bergami (2000), 'Cultural and situational contingencies and the theory of reasoned action: application to fast food restaurant consumption', *Journal of Consumer Psychology*, vol. 9, no. 2, pp. 97–106.

Baines, Paul R., Christian Scheucher and Fritz Plasser (2001), 'The "Americanization" myth in European political markets – a focus on the United Kingdom', *European Journal of Marketing*, vol. 35, nos 9/10, pp. 1099–117.

Bannister, J.P. and J.A. Saunders (1978), 'UK consumers' attitudes toward imports: the measurement of national stereotype image', *European Journal of Marketing*, vol. 12, no. 8, pp. 562–70.

Baumgartner, Gary and Alain Jolibert (1977), 'The perception of foreign products in France', *Advances in Consumer Research*, vol. 16, pp. 103–5.

BBC News World Edition (2003), 'IKEA founder worried over growth', 3 January.

Beeler, Amanda (2000), 'Virus without a cure', *Advertising Age*, 17 April.

Belk, Russel W. (1988), 'Third World consumer culture', in E. Kumçu and A. Fuat Firat (eds), *Marketing and Development: Toward broader dimensions*, JAI Press: Greenwich, CT, pp. 103–27.

Bell, David and Gill Valentine (1997), *Consuming Geographies*, Routledge: London.

Bon, Jérôme and Alain Ollivier (1979), 'L'influence de l'origine d'un produit sur son image à l'étranger', *Revue Française du Marketing*, 1979/2, Cahier 77, pp. 101–14.

Bouchet, Dominique (1994), 'Rails without ties: The social imaginary and postmodern culture: Can post-modern consumption replace modern questioning?', *International Journal of Research in Marketing*, vol. 11, no. 4, pp. 405–22.

Brannen, Mary Yoko (1992), ' "Bwana Mickey": constructing cultural consumption at Tokyo Disneyland', in Joseph J. Tobin (ed.), *Re-made in Japan*, Yale University Press: New Haven, CT, pp. 216–34.

Business Times (2002), 'IKEA aims to double revenue in region', 26 November.

Cannon, Hugh M. and Attila Yaprak (2002), 'Will the real-world citizen please stand-up! The many faces of cosmopolitan consumer behavior', *Journal of International Marketing*, vol. 10, no. 4, pp. 30–52.

Cattin, Philippe, Alain Jolibert and Colleen Lohnes (1982), 'A cross-cultural study of "made-in" concepts', *Journal of International Business Studies*, Winter, pp. 131–41.

Chan, T.S. (1996), 'Concerns for environmental issues and consumer purchase preferences: a two-country study', *Journal of International Consumer Marketing*, vol. 9, no. 1, pp. 43–55.

Chu, Jeff (2002a), 'Happily ever after?', *TIME Europe*, 25 March, vol. 159, no. 12.

Chu, Jeff (2002b), 'Room for the imagination', *TIME Europe*, 25 March, vol. 129, no. 12.

Clark, Harold F. Jr (1987), 'Consumer and corporate values: yet another view on global marketing', *International Journal of Advertising*, vol. 6, pp. 29–42.

Clements, Kenneth W. and Dongling Chen (1996), 'Fundamental similarities in consumer behaviour', *Applied Economics*, vol. 28, no. 6, pp. 747–57.

Collins Dictionary and Thesaurus (1990), William T. McLeod (ed.), William Collins: Glasgow.

Czinkota, Michael R. and Illka A. Ronkainen (1990), *International Marketing*, 2nd edn, Dryden Press: Hinsdale, IL.

Czinkota, Michael R. and Illka A. Ronkainen (1995), 'Global Marketing 2000: a marketing survival guide', in Michael R. Czinkota and Illka A. Ronkainen (eds), *Readings in Global Marketing*, Dryden Press: Hinsdale, IL.

D'Hautesserre, Anne-Marie (2001), 'Destination branding in a hostile environment', *Journal of Travel Research*, vol. 39, no. 3, pp. 300–7.

Dabbous, Dalia (2001), 'Sing a song of conflict', *Cairo Times*, vol. 5, no. 20, 19–25 July.

Daft, Douglas N. (2000), 'Connecting with global consumers', *Executive Excellence*, vol. 17, no. 10, October, pp. 11–12.

Dawar, Niraj and Philip M. Parker (1994), 'Marketing universals: consumers' use of brand name, price, physical appearance, and retailer reputation as signals of product quality', *Journal of Marketing*, vol. 58, no. 2, pp. 81–95.

Dawson, Chester (2001), 'Will Tokyo embrace another mouse?', *Business Week Online*, 10 September.

De Mooij, Marieke (2000), 'The future is predictable for international marketers: converging incomes lead to diverging consumer behaviour', *International Marketing Review*, vol. 17, no. 2, pp. 103–13.

De Mooij, Marieke and Geert Hofstede (2002), 'Convergence and divergence in consumer behavior: implications for international retailing', *Journal of Retailing*, vol. 78, no. 1, pp. 61–9.

Dholakia, Ruby Roy, Mohammed Sharif and Labdhi Bhandari (1988), 'Consumption in the Third World: challenges for marketing and economic development', in E. Kumçu and A. Fuat Firat (eds), *Marketing and Development: Toward broader dimensions*, JAI Press: Greenwich, CT, pp. 129–47.

Djursaa, Malene and Simon Ulrik Kragh (1998), 'Central and peripheral consumption contexts: the uneven globalization of consumer behaviour', *International Business Review*, vol. 7, no. 1.

Dolbeck, Andrew (2002), 'A quick taste of the fast food industry', *Weekly Corporate Growth Report*, 1050320X, 11/11/2002, issue 1214.

Doran, Kathleen Brewer (1997), 'Symbolic consumption in China: the colour television as a life statement', in Merrie Brucks and Debbie McInnis (eds), *Advances in Consumer Research*, vol. 24, Association for Consumer Research: Provo, UT, pp. 128–31.

Eckhardt, Giana M. and Michael J. Houston (2002), 'Cultural paradoxes reflected in brand meaning: McDonald's in Shanghai, China', *Journal of International Marketing*, vol. 10, no. 2, pp. 68–82.

Eshghi, Abdolezra and Jagdish N. Sheth (1985), 'The globalization of consumption patterns: an empirical investigation', in Erdener Kaynak (ed.), *Global Perspectives in Marketing*, Praeger: New York, pp. 133–48.

Ettenson, R., J. Wagner and G. Gaeth (1988), 'Evaluating the effect of country-of-origin and the 'Made in the USA' campaign: a conjoint approach', *Journal of Retailing*, vol. 64, no. 1, pp. 85–100.

Euromonitor (1997), 'Market report Japan: savoury snacks', *Market Research International*, vol. XXXVIII, December, pp. 111–13.

Evening Standard London (2003), 'IKEA's flat pack revolution changing rooms in Russia', 24 April.

Family Business (2003), 'The world's largest family businesses', (undated).

Firat, A. Fuat (1995), 'Consumer culture or culture consumed?', in Janeen Arnold Costa and Gary J. Bamossy (eds), *Marketing in a Multicultural World*, Sage: Thousand Oaks, CA, pp. 105–25.

Furniture World (2001), 'IKEA takes art to a new height with its Suite Home Chicago entry', June–July.

Gaedeke, Ralph (1973), 'Consumer attitudes towards products "made in" developing countries', *Journal of Retailing*, vol. 49, Summer, pp. 13–24.

Geertz, Clifford (1983), *Local Knowledge*, Basic Books: New York.

Gentleman, Amelia (2003), 'Iraq fallout, strikes and forest fires have kept Americans and Europeans away', *Guardian*, 9 August.

Gephart, Werner (1990), 'Nature-environment', in Jacques Leenhardt and Robert Picht (eds), *Au Jardin des Malentendus, le Commerce Franco-Allemand des Idées*, Arles: Actes Sud, pp. 353–5.

Ger, Güliz (1992), 'The positive and negative effects of marketing on socioeconomic development', *Journal of Consumer Policy*, vol. 15, pp. 229–54.

Ger, Güliz (1997), 'Human development and humane consumption: well-being beyond the "good life"', *Journal of Public Policy & Marketing*, vol. 16, no. 1, pp. 110–25.

Ger, Güliz and Russell W. Belk (1996), 'I'd like to buy the world a Coke: consumptionscapes of the "less affluent world"', *Journal of Consumer Policy*, vol. 19, no. 3, pp. 271–305.

Ger, Güliz and Russell W. Belk (1999), 'Accounting for materialism in four cultures', *Journal of Material Culture*, vol. 4, no. 2, pp. 183–204.

Ger, Güliz, Søren Askegaard and Ania Christensen (1999), 'Experiential nature of product-place images: image as a narrative', *Advances in Consumer Research*, vol. 26, pp. 165–9.

Gilbert, Alorie (2000), 'IKEA to build supplier portal', *CNET.COM*, 26 March.

Gilligan, Gregory J. (2002), 'IKEA on the move', *Siam Future*, 28 July.

Graby, Françoise (1980a), 'Consumérisme et produits étrangers' *Coopération-Distribution-Consommation*, no. 5, pp. 17–23.

Graby, Françoise (1980b), 'Le consommateur français et les produits étrangers' *Coopération-Distribution-Consommation*, no. 5, pp. 31–40.

Granzin, Kent L. and John J. Painter (2001), 'Motivational influences on "buy domestic" purchasing: marketing management implications from a study of two nations', *Journal of International Marketing*, vol. 9, no. 2, pp. 73–96.

Gregerson, Hal B. (1998), 'Developing leaders for the global frontier', *Sloan Management Review*, vol. 40, no. 1, pp. 21–32.

Guardian (2002), 'Universal Studios, Shanghai Sign deal', 7 December.

Guyotat, Régis (2001), 'Un grand salon au rez de chaussée', *Le Monde Diplomatique*, December.

Han, C. Min (1988), 'The role of consumer patriotism in the choice of domestic versus foreign products', *Journal of Advertising Research*, June–July, pp. 25–32.

Han, S.-P. and S. Shavitt (1994), 'Persuasion and culture: advertising appeals in individualistic and collectivistic societies', *Journal of Experimental Social Psychology*, vol. 30, pp. 326–50.

Hatch, Denny (2003), 'Case Study, IKEA, Sweden's Jewel', *Target Marketing* (online), 18 May.

Heslop, L., N. Papadopoulos, G. Avlonitis, G. Bamossy, J. Beracs, F. Bliemel, F. Graby, G. Hampton and P. Malliaris (1987), in Leeflang and Rice (eds), 'A cross-national study of consumer views about domestic versus imported products', Proceedings of the European Marketing Academy Conference, Toronto.

Hill, Jim (2002), 'It's déjà vu all over again', *Orlando Weekly*, 3 March.

Hopkins, Nic (2003), 'Saudi Prince in talks with EuroDisney over rescue', *The Times*, 6 September.

Howes, David (1996), 'Commodities and cultural borders', in David Howes (ed.), *Cross-cultural Consumption*, London: Routledge, pp. 1–18.

Huszagh, Sandra M., Richard J. Fox and Ellen Day (1986), 'Global marketing: an empirical investigation', *Columbia Journal of World Business*, vol. XX, no. 4, pp. 31–43.

Ishibashi, Asako (2002), 'IKEA brings back Scandinavian design' (interview of Tommy Kullberg of IKEA, with Asako Ishibashi), *Nikkei Weekly Page*, published online by the Danish Furniture Promotion Centre, 22 July.

Jain, Subhash C. (1989), 'Standardization of international marketing strategy: some research hypotheses', *Journal of Marketing*, vol. 53, January, pp. 70–9.

Kauth, Robert K. Jr. (1988), 'The myth of cultural imperialism', *The Freeman*, vol. 38, no. 11.

Kearney, A.T. (2001), 'Measuring globalization', *Foreign Policy*, Globalization at work, pp. 56–64.

Klein, Jill Gabrielle and Richard Ettenson (1999), 'Consumer animosity and consumer ethnocentrism: An analysis of unique antecedents', *Journal of International Consumer Marketing*, vol. 11, no. 4, pp. 5–24.

Kopytoff, Igor (1986), 'The cultural biography of things: commoditization as process', in Arjun Appadurai (ed.), *The Social Life of Things, Commodities in Cultural Perspective*, Cambridge University Press: Cambridge, pp. 64–91.

Koranteng, Julia (2001), 'European park owners bullish about future', *Amusement Business*, 20 August, vol. 113, no. 33.

Koranteng, Julia (2002), 'Disney embarks on European marketing push', *Amusement Business*, 18 March, vol. 114, no. 11.

Kragh, Simon Ulrik and Malene Djursaa (2001), 'Product syntax and cross-cultural marketing strategies', *European Journal of Marketing*, vol. 35, no. 11/12, pp. 1301–21.

Lee, Julie Anne (2000), 'Adapting Triandis's model of subjective culture and social behaviour relations to consumer behavior', *Journal of Consumer Psychology*, vol. 9, no. 2, pp. 117–26.

Leeflang, Peter S.H. and W. Fred Van Raaij (1995), 'The changing consumer in the European Union: A "meta-analysis"', *International Journal of Research in Marketing*, vol. 12, pp. 373–87.

Levitt, Theodore (1983), 'The globalization of markets', *Harvard Business Review*, vol. 61, May–June, pp. 92–102.

Lillis, Charles M. and Chem L. Narayana (1974), 'Analysis of "made in" product images: an exploratory study', *Journal of International Business Studies*, Spring, pp. 119–27.

Margonelli, Lisa (2002), *Business 2.0*, vol. 3, no. 10, pp. 106–13.

Martenson, Rita (1987), 'Is standardization of marketing feasible in culture-bound industries? A European case study', *International Marketing Review*, vol. 4, Autumn, p. 14.

McCracken, Grant (1986), 'Culture and consumption: a theoretical account of the structure and movement of the cultural meaning of consumer goods', *Journal of Consumer Research*, vol. 13, June, pp. 71–84.

McCracken, Grant (1991), 'Culture and consumer behaviour: an anthropological perspective', *Journal of the Market Research Society*, vol. 32, no. 1, pp. 3–11.

Milhomme, Albert J. (1993), 'Customized or global, the strategy may not work at Euro Disney', in Tom K. Massey, Jr. (ed.), *Marketing: Satisfying a diverse customerplace*, Proceedings of the Southern Marketing Association, New-Orleans, LA, November, pp. 91–4.

Moon, Byeong Joon and Subhash C. Jain (2001), 'Consumer processing of international advertising: the roles of country of origin and consumer ethnocentrism', *Journal of International Consumer Marketing*, vol. 14, no. 1, pp. 89–109.

Morello, G. (1984), 'The made-in issue: a comparative research on the image of domestic and foreign products', *European Research*, vol. 5, no. 21, pp. 68–74.

Moscow Times (2002), 'Eastern Europe's largest mall opens on MKAD', 17 December.

Nagashima, Akira (1977), 'A comparative "made in" product image survey among Japanese businessmen', *Journal of Marketing*, July, pp. 95–100.

Nicholls, J.A.F., Tiger Li and Sychey Roslow (1999), 'Oceans apart: the influence of situational factor in Grenada and Cyprus', *Journal of International Consumer Marketing*, vol. 12, no. 1, pp. 57–72.

O'Brien, Tim (2000), 'Parc Asterix', *Amusement Business*, 16 October, vol. 112, no. 42.

Papadopoulos, Nicolas, Louise A. Heslop and Jozsef Beracs (1990), 'National stereotypes and product evaluations in a socialist country', *International Marketing Review*, vol. 7, no. 1, pp. 32–47.

Peterson, Blyth, Cato Associates Inc. and Cheskin Masten (1985), 'Survey on global brands and global marketing', Empirical Report, New York.

Pew Charitable Trust (2002), 'What the world thinks in 2002: how global publics view their lives, their countries, the World, America', 4 December.

Porter, Michael E. (1986), 'Changing patterns of international competition', *California Management Review*, vol. XXVIII, no. 2, pp. 9–39.

Prahalad, C.K. and K. Lieberthal (1998), 'The end of corporate imperialism', *Harvard Business Review*, July–August, pp. 70–9.

Pulley, Brett (2002), 'Disney the sequel', *Forbes*, 9 December, vol. 170, no. 12, pp. 106–12.

Reierson, Curtis (1966), 'Are foreign products seen as national stereotypes?', *Journal of Retailing*, Fall, pp. 33–40.

Ricardo, David (1817), *On the Principles of Political Economy and Taxation*, chapter XXII, 'Bounties on Exportation and Prohibitions on Importation', in *The Works and Correspondence of David Ricardo*, edited by Piero Sraffa, Cambridge University Press, Cambridge, 1951.

Ritzer, George (1993), *The McDonaldization of Society*, Pine Forge Press: Newbury Park, CA.

Ritzer, George (1999), 'Contemporary urban Japan: a sociology of consumption/The sociology of consumption: an introduction/Golden Arches East: McDonald's in East Asia', *Contemporary Sociology*, vol. 28, no. 1, pp. 68–70.

Rodrik, Dani (1997), 'Has globalization gone too far?', *California Management Review*, vol. 39, no. 3, pp. 29–53.

Samiee, Saeed (1994), 'Customer evaluation of products in a global market', *Journal of International Business Studies*, vol. 25, no. 3, pp. 579–604.

Schweiger, Günther, Gerald Häubl and Geroen Friederes (1995), 'Consumers' evaluations of product labeled "Made in Europe"', *Marketing and research Today*, vol. 23, no. 1, pp. 25–34.

Sharma, Subbash, Terence A. Shimp and J. Shin (1987), 'Consumer ethnocentrism: construction and validation of the CETSCALE', *Journal of Marketing Research*, vol. 24, pp. 280–9.

Sharma, Subbash, Terence A. Shimp and Jeonghsin Shin (1995), 'Consumer ethnocentrism: a test of antecedents and moderators', *Academy of Marketing Science Journal*, vol. 23, no. 1, pp. 26–38.

Sherry, John F. (1987), 'Cultural propriety in a global marketplace', in A. Fuat Firat, Nikhilesh Dholakhia and Richard P. Bagozzi (eds), *Philosophical and Radical Thought in Marketing*, Lexington Books: Lexington, MA.

Sheth, Jagdish N. and S. Prakash Sethi (1977), *A Theory of Cross-cultural Buyer Behavior*, North Holland Publishing: New York.

Shimp, Terence A. and Subbash Sharma (1987), 'Consumer ethnocentrism: construction and validation of the CETSCALE', *Journal of Marketing Research*, vol. 26, August, pp. 280–9.

Slavin, Terry (2001), 'IKEA in pre-fabs plan for low-paid', *Guardian* (online), 25 November.

Smith, David E. and Hans Stubbe Solgaard (2000), 'The dynamics of shifts in European alcoholic drinks consumption', *Journal of International Consumer Marketing*, vol. 12, no. 3, pp. 85–109.

Spar, Deborah L. (1997), 'Lawyers abroad: The internationalization of legal practice', *California Management Review*, vol. 39, no. 3, pp. 8–28.

St Petersburg Times (2002), 'IKEA plans five Russian stores by 2006', 12 November.

Steele, Murray (1991), 'European brewing industry', in Roland Calori and Peter Lawrence (eds), *The Business of Europe*, Sage: London.

Steenkamp, Jan-Bendict E.M. (1989), *Product Quality*, Van Gorcum: Assen, The Netherlands.

Steenkamp, Jan-Benedict E.M., Rajeev Batra and Dana L. Alden (2003), 'How perceived brand globalness creates brand value', *Journal of International Business Studies*, vol. 34, no. 1, pp. 53–65.

Triandis, Harry (1994), *Culture and Social Behavior*, McGraw Hill: New York.

Universal Mediterranea (2003), *Press Dossier*, Universal Mediterranea.

US Commercial Service (2002), *Welcome to the French market*, France, 2002.

Usunier, Jean-Claude (1998), *International and Cross-Cultural Management Research*, London: Sage Publications.

Usunier, Jean-Claude (2000), *Marketing Across Cultures*, 3rd edn, Prentice Hall: London.

Van Maanen, John and André Laurent (1992), 'The flow of culture: some notes on globalization and the multinational corporation', in S. Ghoshal and D.E. Westney (eds), *Organization Theory and the Multinational Corporation*, St Martin Press: New York, pp. 275–312.

Vrontis, Demetris and Claudio Vignali (1999), 'Bass plc, an assessment, evaluation and recommendations for their strategic approach in entering foreign beer markets', *International Marketing Review*, vol. 16, no. 4/5, pp. 391–405.

Warnaby, Gary (1999), 'Strategic consequences of retail acquisition: IKEA and Habitat', *International Marketing Review*, vol. 16, no. 4/5, pp. 406–16.

Wheatley, Malcolm (2001), 'IKEA's financial furnishings', *CIO Magazine* (online), 1 September.

Wong, Nancy and Aaron Ahuvia (1995), 'From tofu to caviar: conspicuous consumption, materialism and self-concepts in east-Asian and Western cultures', *Proceedings of the Second Conference on the Cultural Dimension of International Marketing*, Odense, pp. 68–89.

Woods, Walter A., Emmanuel J. Chéron and Dong Han Kim (1985), 'Strategic implications of differences in consumer purposes in three global markets', in Erdener Kaynak (ed.), *Global Perspectives in Marketing*, Praeger: New York, pp. 155–70.

Yu, Julie H. and Gerald Albaum (2002), 'Sovereignty change influences on consumer ethnocentrism and product preferences: Hong Kong Revisited one year later', *Journal of Business Research*, vol. 55, no. 11, pp. 891.

Zaichkowsky, Judith L. and James H. Sood (1988), 'A global look at consumer involvement and use of products', *International Marketing Review*, vol. 6, no. 1, pp. 20–33.

A5.1 Case

Setting the stage – Disneyland Resort Paris

Disney is the biggest entertainment company in the world with a market value of US$38 billion, and one of the oldest, continuously operating since 1923. Today it is comprised of filmed entertainment businesses, major media networks, publishing, theme parks, resorts, a cruiseline, real estate, and consumer products. Disney's first international park opened in Tokyo, Japan in 1983. Tokyo Disneyland opened with a flourish and continued to do well until the softening of Japan's economy in the 1990s, from which it has yet to recover. In an effort to boost attendance, the older male-oriented Tokyo DisneySea Park opened in 2001 (Dawson, 2001). Disney is currently building Hong Kong Disneyland, which is scheduled to open in 2005 – about the time that Universal Studios will open China's first world-standard theme park in Shanghai (*Guardian*, 2002). There has been criticism of value-for-money at Disney parks, which total ten worldwide, with an average admission fee of US$50. The company recently spent five billion dollars to address this concern and to build new rides and attractions to bolster falling attendance at the parks. The parks account for US$1.2 billion in operating income, which is 41 per cent of Disney's total – a significant business unit for the company (Pulley, 2002).

After their initial success with the Japanese park in the mid 1980s, Disney entered into negotiations with the Spanish and French governments. The French bid 'won' by enticing Disney with tax breaks, loans, and below-cost land. Disney was determined to profit more from the Paris park than they did in Tokyo, where a local operator, Oriental Land, took most of the initial risk and currently takes most of the profits. Therefore, the company staked a 39 per cent ownership in EuroDisney to operate the park, and to receive 10 per cent of admission fees, 5 per cent of food and merchandise sales, and 49 per cent of the profits.

EuroDisneyland opened in April 1992 to a host of problems, which were to continue until Disney loosened corporate constraints to fit the desires of local and European visitors. Disney's admissions and pricing policies were in the 'premium' bracket, even higher than US parks. At first, spending per visitor was half that of Japan, and hotel occupancy rates were 37 per cent (Gregerson, 1998). French intellectuals and artists had criticized the park since its embryonic planning stages (Aupperle and Karimalis, 2001). Notably, theatre director Ariane Mnouchkine coined the term 'Cultural Chernobyl' in the early 1990s, an enduring sobriquet applied to the park and other Disney ventures even today. Cries of cultural imperialism were heard from the intelligentsia, the media, and farmers who protested against the expropriation of agricultural land by the government for the park. However, the French had enjoyed Disney cartoons for more than 60 years, and some supporters of the project were very enthusiastic, such as film-star/singer Yves Montand who declared: 'T-shirts, jeans, hamburgers – nobody imposes these things on us. We like them' (Kauth, 1988).

It's a small world – or is it?

The EuroDisney park lost US\$515 million during its first year (Pulley, 2002). In the early days of EuroDisney, the management structure was rigid and little provision was made for local or employee participation, the prevailing Disney attitude formed by their self-ascribed infallible experience (D'Hauteserre, 2001). Many American managers in Paris were unaware of the many local and Asian adaptations made in Tokyo, and accepted at face value the relatively short psychic and cultural distance between the United States and France as signifying that the two cultures where similar (D'Hauteserre, 2001). Therefore, Disney implemented the same amusements, policies and plans in France as they did in the United States with some architectural changes due to the cooler weather (Usunier, 2000). In response to local criticism, Disney took steps to 'Europeanize' the park by adding a Discoveryland based on the writings of nineteenth-century French author Jules Verne, and by emphasizing characters of European origin such as Pinocchio (Italian), Cinderella (French) and Peter Pan (British). French managers were recruited as the issues became increasingly critical, such as the disputes with French employees, who being rather individualistic resented strict codes of conduct and dress. After a series of adaptations to the local and European markets, Disneyland Paris first became profitable in 1995, going on to become the 'number one tourist destination in Europe' in 2001, with 12.3 million visitors. Disneyland Paris follows Tokyo, Orlando, Florida and Anaheim, California, to rank fourth place in terms of attendance per year (International Association of Amusement Parks and Attractions, 2001). French visitors currently make up 40 per cent of the park's total, while 18 per cent come from the United Kingdom, 8 per cent from Germany, 8 per cent from Belgium, 8 per cent from the Netherlands and Luxembourg, 8 per cent from Spain and Italy, and 10 per cent from other countries.

There are seven on-site themed hotels with occupancy averaging 86 per cent in 2001, and about 22 others in the local area. Disneyland Paris concluded joint ventures for the construction of the three hotels that opened in Spring 2003. The hotel partners are Airtours UK Leisure Group (tour operator), Holiday Inn, and the French hospitality group Envergure. These hotels will add 1,100 more rooms to the 5,800-room capacity currently within the resort's seven Disney hotels. The design and décor of the new hotels draws its inspiration from the many château of the local region.

Learning from mistakes

As EuroDisney's CEO Jay Rasulo admitted, 'We had not yet had an on-the-ground experience in a multicultural environment. It was really the first park that had the majority of its guests coming from very diverse cultural backgrounds.' After near-catastrophic losses, Disney was quick to respond to customers' demands. The company reversed its ban on alcoholic beverages, adding wine to the menu. They developed more table-service restaurants, of which two employ chefs with 'Meilleur Ouvrier de France' status. Restaurants open earlier in the evening for early-bird German guests, and stay open later for Spanish night owls. Disneyland Paris is now working closely with French and European tour operators, travel agents, and transport operators who were formerly disregarded (Assaoui, 2002). The company has forged better relations with the local and national government, to the point where it is Mickey Mouse who concludes the French national tourism advertisement with the declaration, 'J'aime la France!' The Resort still needs to exercise great care in setting its prices, because continental Europeans with six weeks' paid holidays per year are necessarily more thrifty on holiday expenditures than Americans with their two-week, often unpaid holidays. Europeans therefore have less to spend at the park than Disney would like. As Milhomme emphasizes: 'In short the theme park is a short duration recreational means, with a high density spending pattern at the opposite of the recreational European pattern which aims at long duration recreational means with low density spending pattern.' (Milhomme, 1993, p. 94).

Act two: Disney Studios

Disney Studios opened in March, 2001, after a three-month 'soft opening' to test the reactions of visitors. The park is divided into four areas: the Front Lot, Animation Courtyard, Production Courtyard and Back Lot, the whole comprising ten attractions. Front Lot includes a studio mock-up, complemented by film props, a restaurant and boutiques. Animation Courtyard offers visitors the chance to learn about animation, while 'Animagique' showcases clips from Disney films, and 'Aladdin' is the backdrop for a magic carpet ride. Production Courtyard is the home of the Disney Channel and allows visitors a backstage glimpse of production through the Studio Tram Tour, while Catastrophe Canyon puts visitors through an imaginary film shoot. Back Lot includes notably the Rock 'n' Roller Coaster Starring Aerosmith and the Stunt Show Spectacular featuring Rémy Julienne. Visible efforts were made to adapt the primarily American material to local and European tastes. In the Tram tour, for instance, the following actors lend their voices to the eight languages used during narration: Jeremy Irons (English), Irène Jacob (French), Isabella Rossellini (Italian), Inès Sastre (Spanish), Famke Janssen (Dutch) and Nastassja Kinski (German). An effort was made in the décor and content to include European references, for instance to the French classics *Les Enfants du Paradis* and *Les Parapluies de Cherbourg*.

Aims of the new park

Disney Studios expected to attract guests from further away, such as Scandinavia and Spain, more likely to consider the distance travelled as offset by the increased benefits. According to EuroDisney Chairperson Jay Rasulo, the Studios should increase visitor counts to 17 million yearly, up 36 per cent from 12.3 million in 2001. The park should increase the average length of stay per visitor from today's 2.4 days to 3.4, and increase return visits from 41.5 per cent (Koranteng, 2001). The visitors attending the opening of Disney Studios could observe the improvements implemented over the past decade, including the expansion of Disney Village, and the dedicated rail station (with RER and TGV trains) bringing Paris within 20 minutes and Belgium or the United Kingdom within less than three hours. Within the immediate vicinity is an outlet mall that is open seven days per week. Disney Studios was not designed to deal with the SARS epidemic, the Iraq conflict, fears of terrorism, a disastrous summer heat wave, massive strikes and destructive forest fires, all of which increased cancellations and prompted holidaymakers to go elsewhere (Gentleman, 2003).

Financial matters: Some day my prince will come . . .

EuroDisney is still plagued with troubles. In September 2003, *The Times* reported that the park was asking one of its major investors, Saudi prince Alwaleed bin Talal, for a refinancing deal. Due to low park admissions, the company was expecting to have difficulty meeting its debt payments in 2004 (Hopkins, 2003). Walt Disney Studios reportedly cost the company US$600 million. The company reported a profit of €30.5 million for the financial year ending September 2001, 20 per cent less than the previous year (Assaoui, 2002). Stock analysts do not appear to be interested in Disney stock. Contributing factors include a debt load that is two times equity at US$13 billion (Pulley, 2002), and a stock price of about €1 – one tenth of its value a decade ago (Chu, 2002a). There are concerns that a debt-loaded park that is managing approximately 50 per cent more capacity in a time of slowing economies and a fast-growing theme park sector may be putting itself in danger (Chu, 2002a). The average visitor spends €43 per day at Disneyland Paris, which is 20 per cent lower than the figures for Orlando or Anaheim. This figure is worrying, given that theme parks make their profits from their hotels and merchandise (Chu, 2002a). In addition, France began in 2001 to see a slowdown in GDP growth (down to 1.9 per cent that year), caused by a climate of uncertainty and softer global economic conditions that slowed exports. At home, this has translated into higher un-employment (up to 9.8 per cent in 2002), lower inventory levels, and a lower level of business confidence (US Commercial Service, 2002). Although analysts are concerned with the park's launch during an economic downturn, some point out that as an accessible, full-service, short-break destination, Disney Studios could even benefit from a softer economy (Chu, 2002a).

Marketing the Studios

A massive campaign for Disney Studios started in December 2001 with the slogan 'Come and live the magic of cinema.' Advertising agency Publicis focused on television, print, billboard and online advertising. The ads were rolled out in the United Kingdom, Germany, France, Belgium, the Netherlands, Spain and Italy, and were designed to differentiate the new park from the resort, which was accordingly renamed 'Disneyland Resort Paris'. According to Disneyland Paris central marketing director, Christian Darquier, Disney Studios is positioned as 'a journey behind the screen to understand how the magic of movies, television, and anima-tion is made' whereas the resort was 'designed to make guests live out the stories behind Disney entertainment.' In an unusual move, Disney used direct marketing in the United Kingdom and the Netherlands (Koranteng, 2002). The Disney Channel, with its headquarters within Disney Studios, is working to raise awareness of the park, just as the channel success-fully did for the resort in the 1990s.

Not everybody loves Disney Studios

Disney Studios has drawn criticism from visitors who claim that the ten attractions are not enough to keep a family entertained for one half day. Other criticisms stemmed from the three rides cloned from Walt Disney World, as well as the 'tame' nature of some of the other rides (Hill, 2002). Other journalists refer to the new park as 'dull', and boring for children (Chu, 2002a). In addition, there is continuing wider criticism of 'Hollywood' and American culture by French intellectuals and the media. A new wave of concern is sweeping France regarding American imperialism, cultural or otherwise, at a time when geopolitical consider-ations have focused scrutiny on the global actions of the United States. Anti-globalization activist José Bové, who went from destroying a McDonald's restaurant in the south of France to global fame as a leader of the 'altermondialiste' movement, considers himself a spokesper-son for France's ambivalent attitude towards globalization. Even for those within the global-ization camp, France and the United States have had several rancorous disputes over trade and foreign policy, most recently over Iraq. On a smaller scale, a journalist voiced his concern for the impacts of a tour operator's decision to change from 'Paris and the Chateaux de la Loire' to 'Paris and Disneyland' (Guyotat, 2001). Placed within the framework of more quantitative terms, however, according to an international comparative study, the French give the United States the lowest ratings in Europe. Other nations whose citizens have flocked to the park in the past have been equally alienated by the policies of the US government (Pew Charitable Trust, 2002). This may give cause for concern that the Disney complex continues to operate in a culturally sensitive environment.

Competing with a better mousetrap

There is stiff competition among amusement/theme parks throughout Europe, of which France has its share. Parc Astérix, located 30 minutes away in Plailly, offers a unique blend of humor, thrills, history, and French and European culture. Parc Astérix has doubled its attendance, from 950,000 in 1992 to 2 million in less than a decade (O'Brien, 2000). Two Astérix films and the release of a new Astérix album have fuelled the enduring popularity of the character in Europe, to the likely benefit of the park. The identification of Astérix as a plucky Gallic villager, standing up to the evils of empire may even inspire goodwill towards the park in times of complex international politics. Planète Futuroscope, a unique park in Poitiers, is an intense audiovisual and amusement experience themed on high technology run by a former EuroDisney executive. Three other large regional parks opened in 2003 (Chu, 2002b). The French company Vivendi-Universal owns Universal Mediterranea, two clustered theme parks near Barcelona, Spain. The new water-themed park, Costa Caribe, boasts a new ride that attracted 1.5 million new visitors within its first four months (Koranteng, 2001). The addition of the new park and two new hotels are part of the positioning of the park as 'the most complete family resort in Europe' (Universal Mediterrania, 2003) thereby bringing the park into more direct competition with Disneyland Resort Paris (Chu, 2002a). Paramount Parks owns Terra Mitica, a history- and mythology-themed park near Benidorm, Spain. There are two Warner Bros. Movie World parks featuring Looney Tunes and Superheroes like Batman – one in Madrid, Spain and the other near Bottrop-Kirchhellen, Germany. There are two European Six Flags parks, located at Flevo, Netherlands and Wavre, Belgium. Growing competition may not be a threat in itself, however, because it is likely that tougher competition in Europe may benefit Disney in the long term, by habituating Europeans to Disney-style parks.

All company specific information and additional information can be found at the Disneyland Resort Paris corporate website: **http://www.Disneylandparis.com/uk**

Questions

1. More than a decade later, has Disney's top management completely addressed the lack of cultural sensitivity observed at the opening of the first park in 1992?

2. Comment in more detail on the issue of holiday regulations in Europe, the United States and Japan (duration, paid versus unpaid holiday) and their impact on leisure consumption.

3. How will changing geopolitical situations affect park attendance? What can be the repercussions of a US-led conflict in the Middle or Far East?

4. Based on the case study, use cultural factors to explain why visitors from Germany make up only 8 per cent of total Disneyland Resort Paris visitors. Do you think that Disney Studios will attract more Germans than the other park? What steps could management take in order to increase the German share of the market?

5. Do you consider that the company made a wise decision in incurring debt to develop Disney Studios? Given the state of the economy, the need to continually spend on new attractions, and the rapid rate of development for other competing theme parks in Europe, do you believe this investment is justified in the long term?

Saskia Faulk and Jean-Claude Usunier prepared this case solely to provide material for class discussion. The authors do not intend to illustrate either effective or ineffective handling of a business situation. The authors may have disguised certain names and other identifying information to protect confidentiality.

(©IUMI, reprinted with kind permission.)

A5.2 Case

Papa Ingvar's worries

Who can successfully market products around the world with names like 'snuttig', 'droppen', 'grimo', 'moren', 'jerker', 'mård' or 'slugis'? IKEA, the world's biggest home furnishings retail chain can use names that break some 'rules' of branding, and make a healthy profit out of it. Quirky and identifiably Swedish, the names mirror the company's image.

Small-town entrepreneur Ingvar Kamprad founded IKEA as a furniture mail-order company in Almhult, Sweden, in 1943. Since then, IKEA has expanded far from its pastoral headquarters to worldwide sales of €11.3 billion (*BBC News World Edition*, 2003) from 175 outlets in 32 countries and territories (*Business Times*, 2002). IKEA is now one of the world's largest family-owned companies. Although well past retirement age, Kamprad remains active in the business, reportedly travelling to IKEA stores by economy class and public transport, in order to listen to the concerns of ordinary people – and to save a little money. His three sons have worked at the company (*Family Business*, 2003). Since 1997, revenues have grown at a rate of 20 per cent and a new IKEA store is opened, on average, each month (Wheatley, 2001). Today, IKEA operates retail stores in countries as diverse as Austria, Australia, Canary Islands, France, Hungary, Iceland, Israel, Malaysia, Russia and Saudi Arabia, with 31 outlets in Germany, and 16 in the United States.

At the insistence of founder Kamprad, IKEA expanded rapidly, without adapting its core concept to local conditions. Starting in the early 1960s, IKEA took a foothold in Sweden, then Denmark. In 1973, the company took its high-design, good quality, reasonably priced goods throughout Europe and Australasia. Today, four out of IKEA's top five markets are in Europe, the fifth is the USA. Although IKEA has concentrated on company-owned, larger scale outlets, franchising has been used in fourteen countries and all stores operate on a franchising basis, regardless of ownership.

During 2003, store openings were scheduled in Germany, Australia, Hungary and Spain. There are currently two IKEA stores in Moscow, and one planned to open this year in St Petersburg (*Moscow Times*, 2002). In Moscow, IKEA is branching out to develop a mega-shopping mall (including an *Auchan* hypermarket) and hotel complex adjacent to its southern Moscow store (*Evening Standard London*, 2003). In the near future IKEA plans to open seventeen stores in Russia, with the majority in provincial cities, and two or three more in Moscow (*St Petersburg Times*, 2002). In 1974, the North American expansion began, a venture that continues with plans to open 50 stores in the USA by 2013.

Recent expansion in the Asia-Pacific region is projected to continue at a significant rate. IKEA aims to double its Asia-Pacific region revenue, currently 3.5 per cent of the global figure, to US$770 million by 2005 (*Business Times*, 2002). Within the next three or four years, IKEA expects to open 15–20 new stores in the area, including two in Japan. IKEA currently operates the largest warehouse in South-East Asia, which is poised to fill the expected demand (*Business Times*, 2002).

The nuts and bolts of IKEA

Founder Ingvar Kamprad formulated IKEA's vision to 'offer a wide range of home furnishings with good design and function at prices so low that as many people as possible will be able to afford them'. IKEA carries approximately 10,000 different home furnishings, garden items, plants, lighting, office furniture and supplies, household textiles, decorative items, kitchen cabinetry, toys and children's equipment, crockery and flatware, and seasonal decorations.

Product strategy

IKEA follows a standardized product strategy with an identical assortment around the world. IKEA designs all of its product lines and products, then uses a bidding process among hundreds of agreed suppliers, contracts the manufacturing job out under stiff quality-controlled conditions. Furniture and accessories are designed to fit four categories (Margonelli, 2002):

■ *Scandinavian*: simply styled, streamlined, light wood.
■ *Modern*: minimalist and funky.
■ *Country*: a new take on traditional European styles.
■ *Young Swede*: totally simple, but functional and stylish.

IKEA's office-supply division offers office furnishings that also fit into the four categories. It operates on a business-to-business as well as a retail level, in some areas publishing its own catalogue and employing its own call-centre employees. IKEA pioneered the idea of flat-pack merchandising, which means that buyers do the final assembly for most items. It has been estimated that six times more freight space would be needed if its products were shipped already assembled, a significant cost point especially when increasing numbers of items are made in the Asia-Pacific region and control of shipping times and costs becomes critical (Margonelli, 2002).

IKEA's shopping experience is a unique element in the marketing mix. In addition to the items they buy, shoppers have an experience at IKEA's self-contained shops. The largest stores feature a self-service restaurant with Swedish menu items, a snack bar, Swedish food boutique and a child-care centre for customers. The restaurant and café have been given central status at newer USA stores built on a clover-leaf shape, with sales floors radiating off from the food-service facilities.

Pricing strategy

The IKEA concept is based on low price, and products are designed to offer prices that are 30 to 50 per cent lower than fully assembled competing products (Margonelli, 2002). Keeping within this constraint, IKEA responds to different customer needs using a three-level pricing strategy: low, medium and high (Margonelli, 2002). The affordability of IKEA products is due to several business practices, including target-pricing, whereby a product is priced first then designed and sourced accordingly. Other elements of IKEA business that keep prices low are: high volume purchasing; low-cost logistics (hence the flat-packs), and inexpensive retail space, mainly in suburban areas. IKEA's prices do vary from market to market, largely because of fluctuations in exchange rates and differences in taxation and tariff regimes, but price positioning is kept as standardized as possible (Margonelli, 2002).

Communications strategy

IKEA's promotions are effected mainly through its catalogs, websites, and the IKEA family loyalty program. All stores follow a communications prototype, with catalogues, printed materials and websites designed to conform to the IKEA look. Websites (**www.IKEA.com**) are examples of tailored uniformity, featuring the same type of information on all 26 websites and seven mini-sites. However, the sites feature different photos and colours, and information based on the location and market familiarity with the concept, and many feature a choice of several languages. The seven mini-sites are standardized, simply offering contact information and map/directions (such as IKEA Saudi Arabia). The company has turned increasingly to online marketing, and has even indulged in the 'viral marketing' fad, whereby customers forwarded a promotional message to friends via e-mail and SMS (Beeler, 2000). Primary communications are centred on IKEA catalogues, of which 45 editions are printed in 23 languages with a worldwide circulation of over 118 million copies. The catalogues are uniform in layout except for minor regional differences. Other specialized publications include 'Smart Kitchen', 'IKEA View', 'Professional Office Furniture' and 'IKEA Summer' (Hatch, 2003).

IKEA advertising is designed to be unique and provocative. The company's communications goal is to generate word-of-mouth publicity through innovative and sometimes ground-breaking approaches. IKEA has featured ground-breaking advertising in several markets, earning the ire of some conservative groups. For instance, the company has used homosexual couples, just-divorced women, teenage pregnancy and marijuana as a topic in its ads. Perhaps the most controversy was sparked by IKEA's Netherlands campaign featuring a male homosexual couple with their daughter. For a view of IKEA's portrayals of lesbian and gay worlds, visit: **www.commercialcloset.org** (a review of gay advertising) or **www.gfn.com** (the Gay Financial Network).

According to Irena Vanenkova, IKEA's head of public relations in Russia, a good example of innovative communications by IKEA was a competition to find a handsome cat with a Swedish heritage to enter the new Russian showroom on opening day (cats are considered to bring Russians good luck), generating publicity and good-will through 20 publications and websites that would have otherwise cost thousands of rubles (Hatch, 2003). IKEA's thirtieth birthday celebrations in Switzerland were characterized by a thought-provoking use of the Swiss flag on a sombre and staid background, emblazoned with '30 years of democracy in Swiss home furnishings'. The official-looking artwork was counterbalanced by pricing offers using the number '30', such as sofas normally priced at 900 Swiss Francs selling for 30 Swiss Francs.

On a quieter front in communications, IKEA is active on environmental and social-responsibility programs, providing the company with exposure in the press, and a themed emphasis in their communications materials.

Target market

IKEA executives tend to be vague about their target markets, and the comment on the topic from the country manager for Japan, Tommy Kullberg, is typical. In an interview with *Nikkei Weekly*'s Asako Ishibashi, he stated that the company targets families with young children and young people starting a home, from virtually all social categories. These are people who tend to have a young 'mental age' (Ishibashi, 2002). Industry analysts refer consistently to first-time home buyers, young families and people renting their homes.

Distribution

IKEA has a division devoted to business travel logistics, primarily to allow company representatives to visit manufacturers in order to ensure that working conditions are optimal, and that products are made in accordance with IKEA's code of environmental and social responsibility. The primary countries of origin of IKEA products are: Sweden (14 per cent), China (14 per cent), Poland (8 per cent), Germany (8 per cent) and Italy (6 per cent). Manufacturers ship the components or finished products to large warehouses, such as the central one in Almhult, or to one of the other 25 distribution centres in 15 countries. About 30 per cent of the products are shipped directly to the stores, which are, in effect, warehouses (Margonelli,

2002). To facilitate the shipping, IKEA developed IKEA RAIL, the only private rail freight forwarding company in Europe. The network of subcontracted manufacturers numbers nearly 1,800 in 55 different countries, with 42 trading services offices in 33 countries, for which the company uses an online suppliers' portal to negotiate bids and order supplies, such as nuts and bolts from IKEA's internal supplier-to-supplier division (Gilbert, 2000). IKEA does not offer home delivery but IKEA stores cooperate with local companies that offer small trucks for rent, or delivery and even furniture assembly services. IKEA offers a mail order service and very recently introduced an online ordering facility in some countries; however, in its first stages the cumbersome system was not well received.

IKEA's competitors?

There is no global competitor for IKEA. The company has used its relatively low prices, stylish design and offbeat image, environmental performance (no PVC products, no sweatshop workers) and immediate gratification via do-it-yourself delivery in order to attain a unique positioning. No other large company in this sector has pioneered so many supply chain innovations, including long-term and online collaboration that is spiced up with civilized competition between suppliers. No other international furniture company offers such a universal appeal. Competitors are inevitably smaller than IKEA, and may be able to compete with the Swedish monolith on one of the above points, such as low price, but not simultaneously on all of them. The experience of shopping at IKEA is likewise unique: although lacking in salespeople, store facilities present many opportunities for the shopper to maximize the benefits of shopping IKEA-style. Measuring tapes, pencils, handy order forms, desks to write on, realistic mini-showrooms, and user-friendly merchandising are examples of this. IKEA's day-trip dimension is also inimitable, with signature food service, children's entertainment and even child care.

It's a big country. Someone's got to furnish it . . . IKEA in the United States

IKEA entered the US market in 1985, quickly establishing three outlets in the north-east, and experiencing such success that a major warehouse near Philadelphia was followed by others around the country. Since 1985, sixteen more stores have been opened in the United States and the company has grown to become the seventh largest furniture retailer in the country (Margonelli, 2002). Plans call for 50 stores across the country by 2013, with nine scheduled to open or re-open within the next year or so (Margonelli, 2002). IKEA quickly learned from its early experiences in North America. First, people considered their glasses to be too small in order to add ice – a singularly American habit. In addition, bed sizes needed to be changed according to standard North American measurements. Generally, furniture was made wider and larger for the USA, changing IKEA's conception of a worldwide appeal. In terms of merchandising, IKEA stores tend to display easily identifiable colour and design combinations, to guide the customer a bit more than they were accustomed to doing in Europe (Gilligan, 2002).

To gain awareness in a relatively new market, IKEA has been inventive, including among its promotions the 'Living Works of Art' exhibit as part of downtown Chicago's 'Home Suite Home' campaign. Three couples 'lived' in the heart-shaped exhibit, made up of IKEA furniture for several days, thereby earning US$15,000 for charitable causes (*Furniture World*, 2001). Another example is the recent 'unböring' campaign in the USA that included a dedicated website, television, print, direct, outdoor and wildpostings.[11] The 'unböring' campaign's 'manifesto' clearly places IKEA as an idiosyncratic company of Swedes, fighting 'for liberty and beauty for all'. For more on the campaign, see **www.unboring.com**.

IKEA is a complex business, comprising retail businesses, franchising, product development and design, supply-chain businesses like Schwedwood, and manufacturing management, distribution using conventional channels and IKEA RAIL, massive warehouse operations, real estate, food service operations, and even the ownership of local competitors like Habitat in the UK and France. The pan-European IKANO Bank and real estate services company is also owned by the Kamprad family. In Sweden in the 1990s, IKEA designed and sold houses. The 'Bo Klok Project' ('live smart' in Swedish) wood-frame houses were prefabricated and built with Swedish developer Skanska, in two Swedish cities. Efforts have been made to bring the project to the UK and other markets. Of course, home-buyers were given a 3000 SEK gift certificate for IKEA merchandise (Slavin, 2001). As a reflection of this complexity, IKEA founder Ingvar Kamprad told the Swedish newspaper *Smaalandposten* in an interview that, contrary to his earlier position as an 'engine' of growth, he now worries that the firm is expanding too quickly. In particular, he cites concern that in an economic downturn, some IKEA stores may have to close. 'Papa Ingvar', as he is known to many IKEA employees, said that he felt the responsibility for potential lost jobs was a very heavy burden (*BBC News World Edition*, 2003).

All IKEA company information and addition information can be found at the IKEA corporate website: **http://www.ikea.com**.

Questions

1. Furniture styles and home trends are usually thought to be linked to cultural attitudes and perceptions. How can a global company like IKEA successfully market its standardized products in so many countries? Based on your visit to IKEA websites for a variety of countries, give some suggestions for improvement to the communications director.

2. Why do IKEA products receive Swedish-sounding names? What is the role of IKEA's Swedish image, and its Swedish country of origin in the company's image policy?

3. How can IKEA continue long-term to market its wares to young-minded people around the world? Can the company remain true to its original mission, culture, and mass-appeal?

4. Regarding Ingvar Kamprad's worries about the firm's expansion, do you agree that the company is expanding too quickly or into too many different sectors? What marketing problems do you expect this growth will cause in the short and long term?

Saskia Faulk and Jean-Claude Usunier prepared this case solely to provide material for class discussion, originally adapted from a case prepared by Czinkota and Ronkainen, 1990, pp. 203–7. The authors do not intend to illustrate either effective or ineffective handling of a business situation. The authors may have disguised certain names and other identifying information to protect confidentiality. The full version of this case is available at *WS5.A*.

(©IUMI, reprinted with kind permission.)

6

The convergence of marketing environments worldwide

Consumers are immersed in local marketing environments that tend progressively to converge. There are three major components of a local marketing environment that have a more or less direct influence on how marketing strategy can be defined and implemented: the environment, institutions and local marketing knowledge. The first component deals with the general environment and its economical, political, legal, social, cultural and linguistic elements, which, although seemingly fuzzy and indirect, are pervasive. Section 6.1 deals with this components, although many chapters include one or the other of these environmental elements, especially the linguistic element (Chapter 13).

The second component of the marketing environment deals with marketing institutions and infrastructures, such as professional associations (marketing, salespeople, advertisers, etc.), regulatory bodies and how marketing regulations are enforced (codes of conduct or the law). Section (6.1) deals with this component, which surrounds marketing decisions.

The third component of the marketing environment deals with local marketing knowledge. This is generally overlooked, if not blatantly ignored, by international marketing textbooks. Local knowledge indubitably matters: if people, as employees, consumers or viewers, do not know, misunderstand and/or do not accept marketing concepts and practices, it is possible that strategies will be hard to implement. Section 6.2 deals with the issue of how marketing concepts and practices have been imported locally, especially how marketing is treated in the education system and in higher education programmes.

The remaining sections of this chapter deal with the regionalization of marketing environments.

Section 6.3 discusses the regional convergence of marketing environments through integration in the GATT framework and now under the World Trade Organization (WTO). Section 6.4 focuses on diversity in a marketing environment of the European Union (EU) focusing on western Europe. This section shows how a seemingly unified marketing environment is still highly diverse and needs tailored approaches; at the very least, much caution is needed when considering Europe as a single market area. Section 6.5 examines the case of eastern Europe and the former USSR, where there are fundamental changes at all levels of the marketing environment. Section 6.6 deals with challenges when an environment is both difficult to understand and needs much adaptation; it highlights the case of East Asian countries, which, despite major diversity among them, share some common traits when compared with the West. A concluding section (6.7) outlines some limitations to the worldwide convergence of marketing environments.

6.1

Local marketing environments

When trying to understand local marketing environments, self-criticism is a necessary perspective because we understand our local environment from our own ethnocentric perspective. There is always a reference point that makes judgements implicitly comparative (Usunier, 1998). For example, if local people do not properly understand or appreciate the interviewing process in market research, a value judgement would be to say that they are underdeveloped and need to be educated. An entirely different attitude is to try and understand their viewpoint, that is, scientific methods are not the only way of collecting data on how products and services are used by people. F.A. Hayek formulates the question of which knowledge should be used when we want to plan a complex set of interrelated decisions about resource allocation (e.g. an international marketing strategy) as follows:

the answer to our question will therefore largely turn on the relative importance of the different kinds of knowledge; those more likely to be at the disposal of particular individuals and those which we should with greater confidence expect to find in the possession of an authority made up of suitably chosen experts. If it is today so widely assumed that the latter will be in a better position, this is because one kind of knowledge, namely, scientific knowledge occupies now so prominent a place in public imagination that we tend to forget that it is not the only kind that is relevant . . . Today it is almost heresy to suggest that scientific knowledge is not the sum of all knowledge. But a little reflection will show that there is beyond question a body of very important but unorganized knowledge which cannot possibly be called scientific in the sense of knowledge of general rules: the knowledge of the particular circumstances of time and place. (Hayek, 1945, p. 521.)

From this perspective, local knowledge is important because it is operational, although at times it may be difficult to access because it is tacit rather than explicit. Taking note of local knowledge, as an outsider, produces a long list of caveats that may seem at times tedious, but make sense when implementing marketing decisions. High-context international marketing is infused with local knowledge. In contrast, low-context marketing strategies in foreign markets, which use supposedly universal marketing knowledge, treat locality as a constraint rather than as an opportunity. Figure 6.1 shows how local marketing knowledge should be considered as a fully fledged dimension of a national marketing environment.

Economic and political aspects of the local marketing environment

Culture and language are only part of the marketing environment.[1] The economic, political and legal environments have influence on marketing decisions and their implementation, as do social and cultural characteristics. For this reason, marketers have to

Figure 6.1 Dimensions of a local marketing environment

understand the local marketing environment before preparing their strategy.

The economic environment

A key economic characteristic of a marketing environment is the purchasing power per capita, because it sets the *average* level of budgetary constraints. United Nations or International Monetary Fund statistics give accurate data and most of the aggregate economic data for countries is available on the Internet and easy to access. (There are links to these statistics at *WS6.1*.)

To a certain extent prices are adapted by global marketers so that they fit with local purchasing power. However, there are some cases where low purchasing power simply excludes the sale of items, which are felt to be unnecessary. For instance, in North African countries, where international television is received via satellite dishes, people are quite shocked by pet food advertisements, which they view as showing contempt for human beings, who should be given priority over animals. Similarly, the strong emotional bond between an old lady and her beloved Yorkshire Terrier in a Parisian flat is beyond the bounds of their imagination.

Often more important than average income is the distribution of national income across social groups and individuals. Income and wealth inequalities are closely related to power distance, as explained in Chapter 3. In many developing countries such as Brazil, Indonesia or Egypt, a fairly small segment of the population has high per capita purchasing power, but much larger numbers are still moving towards middle-class status. The well-off tend to develop similar consumer behaviour to that of the corresponding social class in more developed countries. However, even among the poorer strata of the population, economic desires and achievements may be greater than they seem at first sight. For instance, real estate development takes place in Brazilian *favellas*, even though the sale of housing units is obviously not conducted by Century 21 real estate agencies.

The unemployment rate requires careful consideration, and the official statistics should be investigated thoroughly. The existence of a large informal sector in some economies, based on moonlighting and non-registered entrepreneurs, causes unemployment to be somewhat overestimated (Berger, 1991). For instance, in Africa we might discount the car repair industry, where informal (unregistered) car repair shops make up the bulk of the sector. Product substitution and more general substitution solutions (buy or repair, make or buy, acquire or rent, share or fully own) largely depend on the relative price and taxation levels of goods and services.

The political environment

As far as political institutions are concerned, democracy is generally considered as *the* most favourable marketing environment, in that the citizens, who are consumers, are given freedom of choice. However, although liberal democracy is clearly favourable, it is not an absolute imperative. The way marketing is developing in China shows that a US-style democracy and full respect for individual human rights are not absolute prerequisites for the growth of a consumer- and market-oriented society (Ho, 1997; Doran, 1997).

Political aspects of the local environment are generally associated with political risk or negative consequences for foreign companies: nationalization, contract revocation, repatriation of funds, threats to expatriate personnel, etc. These might come about due to political events such as revolution, riots, coups or, more generally, severe political instability in the host country. From a low power distance perspective, that of most international marketing textbooks,

political risk is a major problem for foreign operations. However, from a high power distance perspective, the most important issue is to pragmatically develop relationships with those holding the power, provided that their expected time in power will be significant. Thus, a major task in scanning an environment is to appreciate the racial, social and ethnic distinctions within a country and the relationships between diverse groups. For instance, the Malaysian marketing environment cannot be understood without reference to the Malay majority and the Chinese minority and the consensus between the two groups which gives political power to Malays and economic influence to the Chinese. Similarly, Sri Lanka cannot be understood without reference to the large Tamil minority in the northern part of the island which has been in constant struggle against the Singhalese majority for many years. The low power distance outgroupist assumption of international business and marketing knowledge is rather misleading in this respect. However, once again real-world global companies do not act as they might in textbooks examples. For some years, Procter & Gamble has defined a market environment, called 'Balkan', which embraces countries that, until recently, have had very difficult political relationships with one another: Bosnia, Bulgaria, Croatia, Macedonia, Romania, Serbia and Slovenia. Russell Miller, in his 1998 book on selling to emerging markets, examines some of the advantages of participating in newly emerging marketing, including increased volume, profits and economies of scale and reduced market dependence, competition, cyclical fluctuations, market dependence and saturation.

The legal environment

The legal environment is extremely important because sales and marketing are based on agreements and/or formal contracts. Understanding a local legal environment begins by ascertaining which main legal tradition it belongs to. In Europe whether a country uses code law, starting from general principles, or common law, based on precedents, will influence a wide variety of laws relating to marketing, such as those dealing with advertising, sales promotion, labelling, product liability, sales contracts, contracts with agents and dealers (e.g. termination payments). Section 6.4 explains some consequences of the legal diversity in European environments that hinder the development of a unified marketing environment in

Europe. Ethics are also influenced by the legal tradition (see sections 15.6 and 15.7). For instance, common law countries do not generally like to regulate excessively, but prefer to leave more room to allow for business self-discipline in the form of professional codes of conduct. In contrast, code law countries like to legislate on many matters. In France, a typical code law country, contracts for work and rental leases are framed by law and people simply fill in the blanks. In addition, contracts with consumers or between business partners may lead to litigation. This is not true in other world cultures where contracts may not be binding and litigation may be seen as evil, inasmuch as it shows that former business friends are now enemies and have proved unable to manage their relationship in harmony (see section 16.7). For instance, Lloyd (2000, p. 23) interviewed Coca-Cola's chief executive Mr Daft, who admitted that Coca-Cola mishandled a product recall in Europe when it 'fought the European Commission on competition issues . . . In the US, the reflex is to throw the whole thing into the courts and let the lawyers sort it out. It isn't the case in Europe: it's more of a negotiation culture.'

Local marketing institutions and infrastructures

The whole marketing process is based on a series of steps or processes that need to be applied locally, either in preparing for decisions (market research), developing strategy and implementing it (e.g. advertising campaigns or placing the product in distribution channels). The feasibility of marketing decisions and, more often, details of their execution are affected by local marketing institutions and infrastructures.

Market research can naturally be undertaken in most countries of the world and international marketers will find subsidiaries of major international market research organizations or local or regional companies that offer good research services almost everywhere. However, quite apart from its technicalities, which are explained at great length in specialist textbooks, market research is a human activity that generally involves interviewers/researchers and informants/respondents as human beings. The kind of neutral, objective stance that is required from informants, who must speak their true mind without any

influence from the interviewing person, is difficult enough to find in countries where market research, polls and panels are well established. It is all the more difficult to find in many local environments, where willingness to answer or more generally to deliver information is low, since interviewers are seen to be hidden sellers or impolite intruders. Similarly, motivation to answer will be low when there is no local belief that answering will benefit consumers as a community, because the feedback loop that links consumer research information to product improvement and to personal interest is uncertain and complex. Chapter 7 provides many examples that call for the adaptation of market research methods in local environments.

Distribution channel organization is influenced by national culture, legal requirements concerning store size and the opening of new stores, physical constraints, and established social and economic practices between manufacturers and middlemen in the distribution channels. Section 12.1 presents the example of the Japanese distribution system, which is often misunderstood and criticized because its locality is misunderstood.

Direct marketing, although its techniques are fairly consistent worldwide, needs access to mailing lists, the provision of which may conflict with protection of personal data and individual privacy. For instance, the German provisions concerning customer lists and their use are extremely strict: *Datenschutz*, as the Germans call it, may be an obstacle for foreign catalogue sales operators, if they do not adjust. Section 12.4 gives indications of how global direct marketing must be adjusted to local environments.

Advertising agencies are probably the most significant institutions in a local marketing environment. Local advertising agencies, whether subsidiaries of international groups or merely local companies, are likely to have knowledge of local consumers and viewers, since communication is a 'code business' based on linguistic and visual cues that are interpreted/ decoded on the basis of local cultures. Chapter 14 explains how both advertising strategy and execution need to be responsive to local conditions. The local advertising profession is likely to use a mix of universal knowledge about strategy and execution of advertisements and local knowledge based on a deep understanding of what attracts people as viewers and potential consumers. For instance, Budweiser hired a global advertising agency to develop several advertisements for its beer, with various versions to be shown worldwide during the World Cup Soccer in France. When they conducted market research to assess the effectiveness of the advertisements, they found that the young hedonistic theme was not well received by UK soccer fans. For them, soccer is a serious sport, steeped in history. To reach this market they engaged a UK company to develop advertisements that better reflected their culture.

Taylor *et al.* (1996) explain how French advertising professionals work with two distinct models for developing campaigns, one labelled the American model and the other built on the French preference for semiotics and linguistics. They cite the following comments from French advertising professionals, which represent the two different knowledge bases, one relying on tests and the other on experience and intuitive decisions, the use of which depends on the client's background (pp. 6–7):

I respect research but generally it's experience that tells you if it will work in France. I would say that 80 per cent of the time we do not need tests . . . When I look at the way American people approach [planning], they investigate ten different ways of doing it, . . . and they enjoy it. In France we would rather say 'We think this is the way to do it, and we try it.'

Similarly, Johansson (1994, pp. 21–2) explains that Japanese TV advertising is soft-sell oriented because of the uneasiness of the Japanese with the rough instrumentality of business transactions and imposition of direct messages:

The polite advertiser needs at some level to justify to the audience why the commercials interrupt the program, and a hard sell approach is not conducive to such an apology . . . It is not uncommon to hear 'gomen kudasai' ('I am sorry') in the audio of Japanese TV commercials.

Another significant characteristic of a marketing environment that needs to be studied are payments, especially the availability of electronic payment, local customs in terms of payment dates and customer credit practices, and (possibly) consumer complaints. As explained in Chapter 4, consumerism varies greatly across contexts because of the degree of legitimacy of consumer complaints, the focus of the complaint, whether broad or narrow, and the expectations of the consumer as to the outcome of the complaint.

In addition to general marketing institutions, product-specific infrastructures need to be examined in order to understand the local marketing environment, such as medical doctors and pharmacists for the marketing of drugs, libraries and bookstores for the marketing of books, etc. The marketing knowledge of local consumers is also significant and can be assessed by looking at various indicators, including courses taught in higher education, textbooks, student enrolment in marketing courses, television programmes dedicated to buying, consumption and advertising on TV channels.

Learning local cues is in fact a key issue for companies marketing internationally because they have to develop a fit with local culture. A marketing environment must always be studied before choosing a marketing strategy because decisions cannot be divorced from their implementation: if a 'good' strategy proves difficult to implement, it is in fact a bad strategy.

6.2
Marketing: Borrowed concepts and practices

The first basic link between culture and marketing, which is almost never mentioned, is the initial entrenchment of marketing in one particular national culture: that of the USA. These marketing concepts and practices have been enthusiastically adopted in many other countries, even those that do not share the same cultural background. All countries have their traders and merchants, and since marketing is a powerful tool for developing and controlling existing and new businesses, they may rightfully borrow it. But in doing so, they transform it and then integrate it into their own culture.

Marketing: US-based vocabulary, information sources and concepts

Marketing concepts and practices were initially and for the most part developed in the USA and have continued to spread because of the success of large US-based multinational companies in worldwide consumer markets. They have been popularized by

Philip Kotler's *Marketing Management* in its numerous translations and editions. Still, nowhere is their influence as strong as in the USA. In France, where much has been borrowed from the USA, about twenty thousand students attend a basic course in marketing each year. This compares with three hundred thousand in the USA. Even after taking into consideration the population differences, the *marketing intensity* of the USA is still about four times that of France. The same ratios hold true for most developed countries outside the USA. In addition to quantitative differences in marketing intensity, there are also qualitative differences across countries, in content, style and practices.

In Japan, most of the books on marketing management were borrowed from the USA and then translated directly without much adaptation. Moreover, market survey techniques, the underlying concepts and the wording of questions, as well as questionnaire, interview and sampling techniques, were all widely imported. As Van Raaij (1978, p. 699) points out: 'Consumer research is largely "made in the U.S.A." with all the risks that Western American or middle-class biases pervade this type of research in the research questions we address, the concepts and theories we use and the interpretations we give.' This type of direct export is still practiced today as Schultz (2002, p. 8) notes: 'Chinese companies have tried to copy those Western marketing approaches . . . assuming that they are "world-class." And, while some have worked, many haven't.'

Data, information sources (Nielsen panels, for instance) and consultancy businesses (advertising agencies, market consultants) are mostly of US origin, even if they are by no means all American. Marketing journals and academic reviews, such as the *Journal of Marketing*, the *Journal of Marketing Research* and *Advertising Age*, are largely from the United States. Of course, many other countries of the world also have marketing journals, but most of our research and many new advances for practitioners and scholars have been influenced by these imported materials. For instance, the percentage of US references on specialized topics in the bibliographies of British, German or French reviews of marketing is often as much as 90 per cent. A similar situation currently prevails in Japan, as Lazer *et al.* point out (1985, p. 71): 'what has occurred [in Japan] is the modification and adaptation of selected American constructs, ideas and practices to adjust them to the Japanese culture, that remains intact'. (For links to academic marketing associations worldwide see *WS2.1*.)

Marketing vocabulary is now used worldwide: 'mailing', 'media planning' and 'merchandising' are all familiar words. Even though efforts have been made in some countries to localize these words, they have generally failed. For instance, in France hardly anyone uses the official word *la mercatique* (it sounds ugly; see *WS A6.3* for more information on the controversy surrounding this word in France).

It is legitimate and often wise to retain an imported word in its original form until its total integration as a concept has been realized, which allows the foreign origin of the concept to be kept in mind and this, paradoxically, improves its chances of successful localization. Here, the transplant has all the more chance of being successful because there is a strong fascination for what is made abroad. This fascination and the availability of the Internet has meant faster dissemination of marketing concepts, even in less developed countries.

The success of the word 'marketing' gave a new image to trade and sales activities in many countries where it had often previously been socially and intellectually devalued, especially in Latin countries, due to the relative lack of interest on the part of Catholicism in trade and business. In Ancient Greece, Hermes, messenger of the Olympian gods, was also the god of communication, exchange, trade, merchants and even thieves.

Despite the success and the seemingly general acceptance of the term 'marketing', many examples indicate that there have been some basic misconceptions of it in many countries, especially developing countries (Amine and Cavusgil, 1986). For instance, a survey of Egyptian business people indicates a clear lack of understanding of the meaning of marketing (El Haddad, 1985). Either managers do not understand what marketing is all about or, if they do, they tend to believe that it has no application to their business. In fact they see marketing as the mere fact of selling, or the promotion of sales. It is normal to find large gaps between the rhetoric of marketing and the actual selling practices adopted by companies. Marketing did not really replace long-established commercial enterprises in many countries: it superimposed itself on local selling practices and merged with them.

A progressive integration

In many countries marketing knowledge has been progressively imported, at first simply, as universal and explicit knowledge, later merging with local tacit knowledge and ways of doing. In the case of Japan, Johansson and Nonaka (1996, p. 4) point out that marketing skills are expected to be assimilated throughout an organization:

Japanese marketers are not professionals in a technical sense; they seem to consider marketing too important to leave to experts . . . The common Japanese practice of entry-level hiring and subsequent rotation of job positions is predicated on the lack of position-specific skills. These practices help account for the fact that many individuals with engineering backgrounds are involved in marketing in Japanese manufacturing firms . . . Even though a rising number of managers are educated in marketing abroad, and Japan is also developing business schools, the entry-level hiring practices and the development of company-specific skills have made MBAs difficult to assimilate, and they are mainly used as internationalization (*kokusaika*) catalysts, rather than as skilled professionals.

A similar situation is also found in France, where adaptation to the cultural context has now been broadly achieved. French textbooks on marketing management, strategy and tactics are now widely available. Continuous efforts have been made to enable 'marketing' to appear as a '*rationalisation de la démarche commerciale*' ('rationalization of trade and sales practices'). It is seen as confronting the traditional *commercial* style with new concepts that are better suited to international competition (Dayan *et al.* 1988, p. 14):

In a [French] company, at the beginning of the industrial revolution . . . selling was not considered to be an honourable activity. The essence of trading – bargaining with the client – is seen as not being codifiable; it is an *art*, based on individual talents, intuitions and experience. Consequently commercial activities do not follow the standards of the company as a whole, which are based on rationality, logic, and organisation. With the advent of *marketing*, brand image activities have been improved, and they have been better integrated to the company as a whole. A full scale *direction de marketing* (marketing department) attracts significant areas of the human, intellectual, and financial resources of a company: it often has a critical influence on strategic decisions, it uses more and more sophisticated techniques, and it adopts a rational approach, which raises the *direction de marketing* to the level of other functional areas.

In this small passage (from the introduction to a French *marketing* textbook) several elements typify the importation process and its limits: the expression 'full scale' (*à part entière*) suggests that there are still many *directions de marketing* that cover only a part of the marketing function; the *power* of marketing within the organization is an important issue *per se*; the dialectic opposition of irrationality and art, versus logic and rationalization. In French society, only Cartesian logic may give legitimacy and credibility to marketing.

In French companies one often finds a *directeur du marketing* (vice president, marketing) and a *directeur commercial* (vice president, sales) whereas in the United States a vice president, marketing, would more commonly deal with marketing strategy as well as sales and advertising. The French *directeur commercial* is actually responsible for a large part of what Americans call 'marketing' as a functional area. The duties of a *directeur commercial* are primarily the supervision of sales, distribution outlets and sales representatives, as well as the management of customer relations; a *directeur du marketing* will most often be responsible for marketing surveys and/or communication. The organizational relationship between the *directeur du marketing* and the *directeur commercial*, whether parallel or hierarchical, will not encourage them to collaborate, especially when marketing is subordinate to the sales department. Many managers still tend to view marketing as somewhat 'intellectual', having little practical orientation, directed towards long-range targets and market strategy, and some even confuse it with advertising as a rather 'indirect' method of influencing the market.

In order to assess how marketing has been integrated in a local environment, it is advisable to use both quantitative and qualitative cues. The quantitative cues have been described above: student enrolment in marketing courses, the membership of professional and academic marketing associations, the number of marketing-related books published, the circulation of marketing journals, etc. The qualitative side of the integration process is more difficult to uncover because it deals with how broad cultural values and well-entrenched local practices conflict with some of the values underlying marketing (pragmatism, money orientation, expert knowledge, materialism). They are reconciled by flatly ignoring certain dimensions (marketing as expert knowledge), by over-emphasizing some of its positive aspects (marketing can also serve non-profit operations) or by maintaining, somewhat schizophrenically, two systems, one based on explicit, official marketing, and the other based on tacit, local knowledge of the appropriate ways to interact with customers and markets.

6.3

Regional convergence

The WTO and regional integration

Regional integration is now under way, based mostly on trade agreements. The basic assumptions, interaction models and attitudes described in Chapters 2 and 3 are located at too deep a level to be taken into account in negotiations between nation-states. Therefore, convergence is basically economic (as in the case of the North American Free Trade Agreement, NAFTA), more rarely political (as in the case of the EU, and this with obvious pains). Cultural convergence is a more difficult process: it certainly happens but over a very long period and with people largely unaware of it. Groups of countries can be identified for the purpose of marketing strategy on the basis of key elements in the regional environment, taking account of both similarities (which unite them against the rest of the world) and differences (which account for the intraregional diversity).

The WTO came into being at the beginning of 1995, after the Uruguay Round of GATT. Its achievements have been considerable. The WTO is now a full international organization with 147 members as at 1 April, 2004. It has adopted the pragmatic stance of the GATT and the basic treaty has largely been retained, including the philosophy of self-enforceable rules. Its purpose is to liberalize trade, allowing governments to negotiate agreements about trade in goods, services, inventions, creations and designs. Thus, the WTO does not take into account the cultural variable. Its fundamental principles are based on quite opposite premises. The principle of 'Trade without Discrimination' includes two aspects: Most-favoured-nation (MFN) and National treatment. First, the MFN principle states that, 'countries cannot normally discriminate between their trading partners. Grant someone a special favour (such as a lower

customs duty rate for one of their products) and you have to do the same for all other WTO members' (WTO, 2003, p. 10). Second, the National treatment principle is focused on 'giving others the same treatment as one's own nationals,' (WTO, 2003, p. 11). This is clearly a multilateral view, based on strong outgroup orientation, whereby the whole world is seen as being open to international trade and not covered, as it currently is, by a dense network of bilateral trade agreements. However, it was necessary to make an exception for those countries which, by virtue of their geographical proximity, had a natural interest in establishing closer links, basically by setting customs duties between them to zero, as long as they do not raise barriers to trade from the outside world.

Regional trade agreements would seem to contradict the WTO's principle of equal treatment for all, but Article 24 allows various forms of regional integration with the proviso that they 'should help trade flow more freely among the countries in the group without barriers being raised on trade with the outside world' (WTO, 2003, p. 64). In fact, by May 2003 there were over 265 regional trade agreements registered with the WTO with this number expected to approach 300 by 2005 (WTO, 2003). These encompass most of the globe, including the EU, NAFTA, Association of Southeast Asian Nations, the South Asian Association for Regional Cooperation, the Common Market of the South (MERCOSUR), the Australia-New Zealand Closer Economic Relations Agreement, and so on. These agreements take various forms of regional integration, the simplest being that of a free trade area (e.g. NAFTA), where countries have abolished customs duties between members but maintain their own external tariffs and customs procedures *vis-à-vis* third countries. A much stronger form is the customs union (e.g. EU), which adds to the former situation a common external tariff and customs procedures. Here, member countries commit themselves to coordinate and even integrate their economic policy. The EU has been an economic union since the Maastricht Treaty came into force, in January 1994. Part of the integration of economic policy has meant that no individual EU country is represented in the WTO. The EU itself negotiates agreements, after a discussion between member states has produced a common position. (For more information on regional integration see *WS3.3*.)

Table 6.1 Contrasts across large regional areas

Variable / Region	European Union (EU)	ASEAN (AFTA)	NAFTA
Type of regional agreement	Customs & economic union	Informal group of nations	Free-trade area
Linguistic diversity	Very large (many different official languages)	medium	Bi-polar (English + Spanish/French), with a predominance of English
Political system	Bureaucratic & transitional democracies	Authoritarian pluralism	Liberal democracy
Time orientations	Past orientation + linear time: West Present time: East	Cyclical/integrated/arrowed time	Economic time dominant
Individualism/ collectivism	Individualist Collectivist	Collectivist	Individualist except in Mexico
Power distance	Low: Northern EU High: Rest EU	High	Low except in Mexico
Masculinity/ Femininity	Predominantly feminine	Neutral	Masculine
Uncertainty avoidance	High: Roman-Germanic nations Low: Britain and Nordic countries	Weak	Weak
Dominant type of organization (Hofstede, 1991)	A mix of pyramids, machines, markets. No cross-national organizational consensus	'Families'	Markets

Comparison across regional areas

There is obviously convergence in regional areas of the world, but as argued above it is economic rather than cultural. For instance, while the recent signing of trade agreements between Brazil, Mexico and Chile is likely to yield significant economic benefit with an estimated 900,000 additional vehicle exports from Brazil over the next four years (Evans, 2003), there is still a lack of cultural convergence. That is, market barriers based on cultural differences rather than legal dispositions remain. Table 6.1 gives an idea of the significant differences that exist across regional areas. The next two sections discuss some features of the regional environment in the European Union and East Asian countries. But, as noted above there are literally hundreds of different regional agreements worldwide.

6.4

A diverse marketing environment: The European Union

The EU is based on the Treaty of Rome, which was signed by six original member countries (Belgium, France, Italy, Germany, Luxembourg and the Netherlands), all of which belonged to the Roman-Germanic legal tradition (also called the *code law* or *civil law* tradition). In 1973 Ireland, Denmark and the UK joined, in 1981 Greece, in 1986 Spain and Portugal, in 1995 Austria, Finland and Sweden, and in 2004 ten more countries in eastern and southern Europe joined (Cyprus, the Czech Republic, Estonia, Hungary, Latvia, Lithuania, Malta, Poland, Slovakia and Slovenia), expanding the list to 25 countries with very different histories. Notably, all but two of the ten newest members had socialist economies at least until 1989. While they have made huge changes toward a market economy, their living standards are well below that of the other EU members. As Wolf (2004, p. 18) notes: 'If real GDP per head rose two percentage points a year faster in the new members than in France, it would take 21 years for Slovenia and 57 years for Lithuania to catch up.' While the new European Union will eventually converge in terms of the economic environment, linguistic and cultural diversity in the EU is likely to remain very high.

The institutional basis of the European Union

There are four basic principles underlying the Treaty of Rome: the free movement of goods, the free movement of capital, the free movement of persons and the free movement of services. Understandably, such broad statements needed to be clarified, as has been done by issuing tens of thousands of regulations since its inception! Furthermore, the European Court of Justice issued thousands of rulings that have, to a certain extent, clarified the implementation of rules in precise cases. For countries such as the UK and Denmark, which entered in 1973, it has never been easy to accept this strong legislative orientation. They are low power distance societies, which favour more pragmatic and 'near-to-the-people' ways of solving problems.

The state interventionism tradition has historically been strong everywhere in Europe, although it is stronger in Latin Europe (see Lessem and Neubauer, 1994) and stronger again in the new eastern European EU members (Smith and Hills, 2003). This tradition is challenged by a general trend towards the privatization or disinvolvement of state and public authorities in money-losing businesses that do not necessarily fall under their obvious competence. EU policies have a very wide impact on companies, in areas such as industrial standards policy, taxation policy, antitrust policy (Articles 85 and 86 of the Treaty), monitoring of public subsidies to industry, R&D policy and EU legislation on public procurement.

But contrary to what is often said, the EU is not a large bureaucracy. It had a budget of €99.7bn in 2003, which was equivalent to 1 per cent of the total GNP of the 15 member states at the time. Of this, the budget is spent on agriculture (45 per cent), struc-

tural funding for less developed regions (35 per cent), internal policies (7 per cent), external policies (5 per cent), administration (5 per cent) and aid to future member states (3 per cent). This partly explains the lack of control over the use of European funds.

The decision system works on the basis of weighted votes per country as set out in the Nice Treaty: ranging from 29 for Germany, the United Kingdom, France and Italy to 3 for Malta. In terms of the differences between code law and common law (explained in section 3.4), the legal approach in the EU is completely based on code law. The Roman-Germanic legal tradition was fully shared by the six original members, but not by all of the member states that have since joined. It is interesting to note that even with this basic commonality, company laws between the six original members were quite divergent. German rules were quite strict, and the English comparatively liberal, but since the adoption of the SE (*Societas Europea*) there is now a greater convergence of policy.

An example of EU policy: The free movement of goods

Among the numerous EU policies, one deserves special attention, because it is aimed at the free movement of goods. There were many obstacles at the beginning of the 1980s on the road to a real 'common market', especially fiscal barriers, related to different indirect tax rates, and technical barriers due to different industrial standards in the EU. This made the elimination of physical borders problematic (Cecchini, 1988). Fragmented national markets resulted in smaller volumes of production and cost inefficiencies at the European level, especially in comparison with the United States and Japan. The EC White Paper of 1985 set out a full programme of 300 European directives to be adopted by 1992. Many of them dealt with common industrial standards at the European level, for which specific standardization bodies were established in order to coordinate the setting of standards (e.g. Comité Européen de Normalisation (CEN), Comité Européen de Normalisation Electro-technique (CENELEC) and European Telecommunications Standards Institute (ETSI)). The process was based on several possible means of standardization: (1) approximation of regulations (for instance, EU countries design common legislation

Box 6.1

Concrete, yoghurts and sewage plates: The shock of culture and climates

The conditions of use of concrete vary according to climate. The Greeks have no interest in concrete specifications concerning frost except in a few mountain villages. The Finns need concrete which can endure minus 40 degrees Celsius, but they are not preoccupied with the number of frost–defrost cycles. The French will prefer a concrete which can resist at least twenty frost–defrost cycles. That is why the classes for each use cannot be seen as quality classes.

Similarly, there is no common European definition of what is a yoghurt. Latin countries require that they are produced with living micro-organisms, whereas the Anglo-Saxons favour their sterilisation. This lack of harmonisation is a hindrance for the producers' European marketing strategies.

The Germans wanted to impose a minimal weight for sewage plates. Pont-à-Mousson, a French producer, uses ductile cast-iron instead of grey cast-iron for the Germans, with the result that French sewage plates weigh 50 to 60 kilos (so that they can be manoeuvred by a sewerage worker) instead of 100 to 120 kilos for the German (so that they are very steady on the roads). Different industrial traditions exist; corresponding to different functional benefits looked for by each country. The French company succeeded to have the minimal weight not mentioned in the European standard. It saved a billion dollar European business.

(Source: Esposito, 1994.)

Europe-wide for car exhausts); (2) mutual recognition (member states recognize another member state's legislation on a bilateral and reciprocal basis); and (3) the 'home country rule', based on the *Cassis de Dijon* ruling of the European Court of Justice: products that had been manufactured according to the standards and regulations of a particular member state could not be barred from entering any other EU national market, unless the local regulation did not meet the minimal compulsory EU standards. Although much has been achieved in the area of common standards, there still remain some discrepancies owing to climate and industrial traditions (see Box 6.1).

Is there a European consumer?

More than 30 years ago Fournis (1962) remarked that there cannot be such an individual as a 'European consumer' since customs and traditions tend to persist. European countries and cultures are deeply rooted in the past. Furthermore, a long history of wars and conflicts has ensured the persistence of strong feelings of national identity. In a 2003 poll, Europeans were asked about the strength of their National verses European identity. Of the 25 EU countries,

only 3 per cent gave their identity as European only, while 39 per cent gave their identity as National only (*Eurobarometer*, 2003).

Naturally, European cultures share some common cultural values: the majority of them share a set of values related to major life events (birth, marriage and death) and this differentiates them from Asian cultures. Patterns of displaying emotion for instance, differ widely between Europeans and Asians; and where Asians tend to prize group harmony, Europeans tend to favour self-esteem and respect for individuals. Nevertheless, this apparent cultural homogeneity of Europe, when compared to Asia, ceases to be so clear when we look at cultural variance inside Europe. Family relation patterns, religion, organization of everyday life – as regards meals, social, family and business life – tend to be quite heterogeneous. In the same vein, Wierenga *et al.* (1996, p. 52) show that there is much variation in the qualities considered important in the education of children in EU countries. While most countries value honesty, Spanish parents do not emphasize it; independence is valued by the Germans but not by the French; politeness is a French value while tolerance is highest with the British.

Marketing strategies for culture-bound products still need tailoring to each national market, or to groups of countries, despite the introduction of a common currency, which makes life easier for cross-border comparison and purchase. Beer, for instance, is subject to differences in national tastes, and is judged according to how bitter, frothy, bubbly, sweet and alcoholic it is. The leading brewer in Europe, Heineken, continues to tailor its products and marketing policies to different countries, since beer distribution systems vary across Europe. For another case in point, Nivea skin care cream, produced by the German multinational company Beiersdorff (BDF), has a leading edge in each national market in Europe. Nevertheless, its consistency has to be changed and its formula has to be adapted, depending on whether it is sold in northern or southern Europe (Mourier and Burgaud, 1989), and the Single Market has not changed this.

Wierenga *et al.* (1996) also argue in favour of largely customized strategies in Europe, given the dissimilarity of EU markets on a number of aspects of the marketing environment. Income allocation patterns across major domains of expenditure (food, clothing, energy, furniture and household equipment, health care, transport, leisure) vary significantly across member states according to Eurostats. Although converging, as noted in the previous chapter, the number of persons per household still ranges from a low of 2.2 in Germany to a high of 3.1 in Slovakia and Poland. The marketing infrastructure also still differs: the number of points of sale per 100 inhabitants ranges from a low of 0.8 in the Netherlands to a high of 4.0 in Portugal; distribution is highly concentrated in France where 9 per cent of all shops account for 89 per cent of the retail volume but it is not at all concentrated in Portugal, Italy or Spain. And, it is not just the structure but also the value of the experience that differs. For instance, assumptions that are valid for Western consumers, such as the higher levels of shopping value that result from more luxurious surroundings, do not necessarily hold true in eastern European countries (Griffin *et al.*, 2000). Although some have argued that convergence in Europe has already largely been achieved (Leeflang and Van Raaij, 1995), a close look at their data shows differences across EU countries in significant elements of the marketing environment such as the share of private labels in retail food stores, per-capita expenses on direct marketing, or the share of the print, TV, radio and other media in total advertising expenditures.

Is cultural convergence possible without a common language?

The introduction of the euro in 2001 as a common European currency has made life easier for cross-border purchases and allows a much simpler price comparison than previously. However, as de Mooij (2000, p. 104) emphasizes:

International marketers would like us to believe that in the 'new Europe' with a single currency, people will become more similar, will increasingly eat the same food, wear jeans and sports shoes and watch the same television programs. Reality is different. Few people watch international (English language) television programs regularly. Understanding the English language still varies widely and few Europeans, apart from the British and the Irish, regularly watch English language television without translation or subtitles.

An implicit, but extremely strong and enduring assumption underlying the treaties that created the EU is the respect for national languages, cultures and identities. However, it is phrased in Article 128, section 1 of the Maastricht Treaty in terms which introduce a compromise on relation to the promotion of members' cultures or the common European culture: 'The Community shall contribute to the flowering of the cultures of the Member States, while respecting their national and regional diversity, and at the same time bringing the common cultural heritage to the fore' (Council of the European Communities, 1992, p. 48). A fundamental element of culture is language, covered in Chapter 13. Language has a strong influence on our world-views and partly shapes our individual and collective behaviour. Even if this assumption in its strongest version (called the Whorfian hypothesis) has been challenged by linguists, it remains a useful metaphor for illustrating its influence on behaviours. Europeans are committed to their language as a social and cultural asset. In most European countries there is much stronger emphasis than in the United States on grammatical appropriateness, and correct pronunciation is often a social prerequisite for the holding of a number of posts.

The six original EU countries had four different languages. From 1986 there were 12 countries with 10 languages, and since May 2004, there are 25 countries with 20 different official languages. This 'Tower of Babel' situation makes communication difficult and an army of more than 3,000 full-time translators

BOX 6.2

French fears about English as the common European language

There is great pride in the French language in France. It is recognized as one of the two official languages of the United Nations, on a par-basis with English. French people have a rather defensive attitude towards English, and since the 1970s the French authorities have regularly issued official decrees prohibiting the use of English words, especially business words, in French texts (Usunier, 1990).

French fears typify resistance to globalization, since it is believed that through consumption patterns the whole of French society and culture could be 'Americanized'. The French are fascinated by the 'American way of life' as an exotic item. But many French people, including politicians, would be horrified to have it 'at home'. If the fears are, perhaps, legitimate, the defensive measures are certainly inadequate. The example of northern European countries shows that it is quite feasible to have a double-language culture. One is the local culture; it corresponds to ways of life and consumption patterns that are not globalized. The other is in English; it corresponds to an international lifestyle and globalized consumption patterns. Television channels in English such as MTV, Sky Channel and Super Channel can be seen in many northern European countries, although not in France, where the development of cable television has been stringently restricted. A few years ago the number of householders with cable television in France was half that of Ireland, a country with a population one-fifteenth the size of that of France and a much lower per capita purchasing power.

Most people believe that satellite TV in Europe, and other new communication technologies, will help to standardize the profile of the European consumer. But the conditions for achieving this will be much better if there is a common language through which to build a common European culture, sustaining new European consumption patterns.

are employed on the EU staff. The issue of a common language for Europe has never been addressed, at least publicly. It is practically an absolute taboo. In the European Single Act of 1987, Article 34 states that: 'This act [is] drawn up in a single original in the Danish, Dutch, English, French, German, Greek, Irish, Italian, Portuguese and Spanish languages, the texts in each of these languages being equally authentic' (European Communities, 1987, p. 574). One of the main proponents of keeping taboo the common language issue is France (see Box 6.2), but the Germans are very keen to have their language spoken, since there are now almost 90 million German speakers in the EU, as a result of the reunification of East and West Germany and the addition of Austria to the EU.

In a recent poll, young Europeans were asked to list the most useful factors for finding a good job. The most commonly cited factor was a command of languages (63 per cent of respondents from the fifteen EU member countries and 81 per cent from the new 2004 EU member countries).

However, it is clear that resistance to change will not prevent English from being the common language, if not the first language, then the standard second language. This is already true for business all over Europe. Even in the publishing business where linguistic differences between countries were traditionally viewed as powerful barriers to internationalization, English is more and more considered the standard language, especially for scientific and technical publications. Sinatra and Dubini (1991, p. 99) quote an English publisher as saying, 'All is published in English. In general publishing, anything significant is published in English, regardless of the mother language of the author. Higher level academic journals, they will all be in English.' A Dutch publisher gives a slightly different view: 'I don't think language will be a problem in the near future. I do not adhere to the idea of a common language for all countries of the community, but I think that soon all European citizens will be able to read three or four different languages. People will be citizens of Europe in the next century.'

A good example of how English will spread over the whole community is given by the new European Credit Transfer System (ECTS), sponsored by the EU Commission and designed for facilitating cross-border higher education. The ECTS information package that each university must prepare has to be written in two languages (they are not specified!). Naturally all of the universities involved have chosen their own national language plus English.

Another aspect of communication is technology. There appears to be a good deal of convergence in the use of technology among young Europeans. For instance, more than 75 per cent of people across the 25 EU member countries use mobile phones and more than 30 per cent use e-mail each week (*Eurobarometer*, 2003). But the way it is used appears to vary across cultures. As de Mooij (2000, p. 111) states:

The Internet is basically an unstructured means of communication. This is more difficult to accept in cultures of strong than of weak uncertainty avoidance. The latter will be later adopters of the Internet for regular communication and mail purposes. This explains relatively low daily use of e-mail in France and Germany, as compared with the UK and Scandinavian countries.

6.5

A changing marketing environment: Eastern Europe

The inclusion of eight east European countries (in total ten but Cyprus and Malta are not from eastern Europe) into the European Union is very important. Eastern Europe and Russia have huge raw material production and reserves including metal ores, coal, oil, gas and agricultural products, while western Europe has the technology.

The heritage

Communism meant collective ownership of the means of production. In most countries, except Poland, a large part of agriculture was state-owned and managed. The same was true for foreign trade, which was the monopoly of sectoral agencies. Administered trade was the rule where both production and trade were centrally organized. Ikarus buses were made in Hungary for the whole of eastern Europe and similarly Balkancar forklifts were made by the Bulgarians. As Naor (1986) emphasized in the case of Romania, distribution was as cost efficient as possible, that is, direct distribution from producer to retailers was advocated to the greatest extent possible. But distribution was very poor and parallel, informal distribution often replaced state-run retail outlets where people had to wait to find the few products available. Although the concept of marketing has long been known in countries such as Hungary and Poland, there was an absence of real marketing infrastructures, such as market research consultants, panels, advertising agencies, etc. Communism, having existed for between 40 and 70 years, has left its mark on culture. Consumers have been used to facing systematic undersupply moderated by queues rather than prices. In Bulgaria, for instance, people had to wait several years to obtain a car, which they finally paid for at a price so low that it could not be compared with a market price elsewhere. Managers, if taking any initiative, had to take into account political and ideological, rather than management, criteria.

Today there are democratically elected governments in most of eastern Europe, which are committed to establishing market economies based on free competition. The most important difference between the West and eastern Europe is the fact that there exists a gap of at least two or three generations in terms of productivity and infrastructure. In the most advanced countries, Hungary, Poland and the Czech Republic, there has been progress in maintaining property rights and removing some market imperfections, but this progress is far behind the West.

Although most countries in eastern Europe are committed to improving their economies, there are still many interrelated obstacles to be dealt with in the path to growth. Issues such as trade barriers, the development of banking and loan systems, pricing mechanisms, property and contract law all need attention. Privatization is considered a means to achieve market economies and growth, but there is no easy way to achieve privatization in eastern Europe. Over-optimistic estimates are now being revised and people have started realizing that it might take a decade or two before a privatized market economy is achieved.

The transition: Opportunism and misconceptions

Reactions from Western companies to market developments in eastern Europe have been rather cautious. However, in spite of this reluctance, most multinationals had entered these markets by the early 1990s (Tietz, 1994). Companies such as McDonald's, Pepsi-Cola, Coca-Cola, Statoil, Ericsson, Ikea, Fiat, Nokia, Volkswagen, Estée Lauder, Philip Morris, almost all pharmaceutical firms and several small and medium-sized companies have already established operations in these markets. The governments are providing a number of incentives to foreign companies to invest in their countries. In spite of the reluctance from Western companies to invest, there has been a considerable increase in registered joint ventures. By March 1992, there were 34,121 registered joint ventures between Western companies and organizations from eastern Europe and by 1994 it had reached 106,295 (Ghauri and Usunier, 1996).

A big comparative advantage of ex-communist countries is their good level of general education, with a high percentage of university graduates, and the proximity of eastern European values to those of western Europe. This is evidenced by the rapid implementation of Western-style training programs and the quick adjustment of local consumer behaviour to western European lifestyles (Djarova, 1999). Another comparative advantage of eastern Europe is a favourable ratio between labour costs and productivity. A study by the European Bank for Reconstruction and Development showed that the salaries of skilled workers in export investments were at 16 per cent of their Western parent-company level, while average productivity level was reported to be at 72 per cent of the Western level (EBRD, 1997). This is a key advantage, which, combined with qualified engineering staff, explains the success of some industrial takeovers such as that of the Czech Skoda by Volkswagen.

A fundamental condition for the development of markets and marketing is the change in ownership structure. The highly centralized organizational forms in eastern Europe do not stimulate a market orientation. Western companies are generally attracted by the core businesses of eastern European companies, but are uninterested in under-performing peripheral activities. As a consequence the take over of such companies often means immediate restructuring and selling the loss-making parts of the company (e.g. the case of Sara Lee/Douwe Egberts in Hungary). Privatization programmes have therefore been a major challenge for the governments, with major problems related to their implementation such as valuing companies, establishing a stock exchange, creating notaries and specialized intermediaries for real estate. One of the trickiest problems was to find local shareholders in countries where capitalism had long been associated with exploitation. Private ownership presupposes rules and institutions such as contract law, bankruptcy law, or courts for settling business disputes. The absence of such infrastructure created massive opportunism, as in the case of the former Soviet Asian republics (Box 6.3).

The eastern European countries comprise two groups; the northern countries have formed an alliance called the Visegrad group (Hungary, the Czech Republic, Slovakia and Poland). These countries are now part of the EU but the value structure of consumers differs widely across the region. Thus, a regiocentric approach to marketing must be used cautiously, since the belief systems have been shaped by different environmental influences. For instance, Poland and Hungary have a long tradition of marketing education which makes them more comparable in terms of local marketing knowledge to France or Germany than to Bulgaria or Romania. The Polish journal of marketing can be consulted on the world wide web. Since 1991, US trade with Poland has been increasing by more than 100 per cent per year. Polish imports from the United States reached more than $1.8 billion in 2000. However, nationalistic feelings are always strong in Poland as well as in other eastern European countries, especially when they are neighbouring countries where war and conflicts have featured in past centuries.

The group of southern Balkan states has traditionally been less developed and highly compartmentalized. Here, national identity takes priority over cooperation in an area where ethnic and religious diversity has always been quite strong. The Bulgarians, for instance, have poor relations with all their neighbours except the Serbs. Eastern Europe, and more generally the ex-communist countries, is experiencing rapid changes. Countries such as Romania and Bulgaria are standing in queue to enter the EU in the next

Box 6.3

Cotton story

In April 1994, a commodity trader was discussing the purchase of raw cotton in the former Soviet Asia (mainly Uzbekistan, Turkmenistan and Tadjikistan): 'For two years, the market for raw cotton has been tense, mainly for the three following reasons: (1) climatic hazards in certain producing regions which thus became net importers instead of net exporters, especially China; (2) reduction of cultivated zones in Uzbekistan; (3) to this, you must add that salespeople break their word in the former Soviet Asia. Last year, the Uzbeks sold their crops twice or thrice; this year, they seem to be a little more serious; but the worst is to be experienced in Turkmenistan. Last year, I signed several contracts for 20,000 tonnes, one of them for 4,000 tonnes, with an official export licence, a ministerial approval and a shipment certificate; I have never received anything!'

This failure appears all the more striking when one takes into account that in worldwide cotton trading it is a well-established custom that the professional who does not respect a contract not only must pay damages but also is blacklisted by the whole trading community.

(Source: M.O. Ancel, commodity trader at Louis Dreyfus & Co., Paris, 1994.)

---

round that can start as early as 2007. Many countries in this region started from a situation where people had no idea of what a contract, a price and delivery times were. (For information on marketing textbooks from the Russian Republic see *WS A6.4*.)

Generally, the ex-communist countries have a good level of general education. But as Griffin (2000, p. 34) notes, international marketers still have to live a very adventurous life:

Based on the marketplace realities, Russian consumers have a word that is used at times in place of 'buying' something.

The word *dostats*, best interpreted as 'to acquire with great difficulty,' was used by another Russian consumer we interviewed when he described his ability to 'dostats' almost 40 per cent of building materials for minor home repairs in only a few months.

Anecdotally, western European business people who take their own cars to these countries are told to take the wipers with them each time they park their car so that they will not be stolen. If they have to take a taxi, some precautions must be taken, as evidenced by Box 6.4.

Box 6.4

Taking a taxi in Moscow

A Belgian engineer, with no particular knowledge of 1994 Russia, was due to go to a construction site in Siberia for the German contractor he worked for. When he arrived in Moscow, he was transferred from the international to the national airport by a chauffeur of the German company. After working on the site in Siberia, a much quieter area than Moscow, he decided to return on his own, and earlier than initially planned, because the job had been done more quickly. When in Moscow, he took a taxi to the local offices of the German company.

Taking the first available car, he negotiated the fare at $50. At first, all seemed to be normal, but after a while, the taxi stopped in a fairly remote, deserted and unfriendly area. The driver then explained that he needed an additional $50 to continue to transport him. He paid without discussion and reached the company offices with no problem. He was lucky: it could have been much worse.

(Source: M.O. Ancel, commodity trader at Louis Dreyfus & Co., Paris, 1994.)

A challenging marketing environment: East Asia

East Asia is challenging for westerners because the values and mindsets are different. East Asians are perceived as economic rivals by westerners and their path to success has been often stereotypically attributed to imitative behaviour (at best) or counterfeiting (at worst). The challenge is to overcome stereotypes and misunderstandings. Despite the 1997 economic downturn in Asia (affecting, in particular, South Korea, Thailand and Indonesia), the uncertainties surrounding the Iraq war and the outbreak of Severe Acute Respiratory Syndrome (SARS), ASEAN countries posted a GDP growth of over 4 per cent in 2002 and 2003.

High rates of economic growth have been combined with increasing shares in world trade (approx 25 per cent for emerging Asia). However, in the mid-1960s, there was extensive pessimism about the future of Asia, considered to be overpopulated and unable to achieve proper development: a book published in 1968, by Gunnar Myrdal, a Nobel Prize winner, was entitled *Asian Drama, An Enquiry into the Poverty of Nations*. This pessimistic view has been largely discounted by facts.

Asian commonalities, in contrast to those of westerners, were viewed as a drawback, as not conducive to business initiative; such characteristics included the lack of individualism. Hofstede (1980) established a correlation between individualism and GNP per capita which seemed to suggest that individualism was a precondition for high levels of economic development. Now the perspective has been totally reversed. The issue is now for the West to understand why the collectivist values of many Asian nations help them to achieve much more than individualistic European countries, which have had lower rates of economic growth and higher unemployment rates over the same period of time.

The Confucian values have been said to be an essential driving force behind such dynamism (see Box 6.5; see also *WS6.6* on Asian values). Some have argued that, at the society level, they are backed by a system of *authoritarian pluralism* (Pohl, 1995) quite different from the liberal democracies in the West. Drug trafficking, for instance, is heavily penalized in countries such as Singapore, Malaysia and Thailand. A Dutch prime minister who recently travelled to one of these countries to plead for one of his countrymen

---

Box 6.5

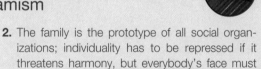

The fifth dimension: Confucian dynamism

This new dimension, mentioned in Chapter 2, has been added to Hofstede's four dimensions. Michael Bond, a researcher based in Hong Kong, designed a questionnaire called the Chinese Value Survey (CVS), which was administered in 23 countries. It is based on basic values as seen by native Chinese social scientists. A new dimension was discovered through the CVS. Bond coined the term 'Confucian dynamism' to emphasize the importance of Confucian practical ethics, based on the following principles:

1. The stability of society is based on unequal relationships, expressing mutual and complementary obligations as between father and son, older brother and younger brother, ruler and subject.

2. The family is the prototype of all social organizations; individuality has to be repressed if it threatens harmony, but everybody's face must be maintained by preserving others' dignity.

3. 'Virtuous behaviour' towards others consists of not treating others as one would not like to be treated oneself.

4. Virtue with regard to one's tasks in life consists of trying to acquire skills and education, working hard, not spending more than necessary, being patient and persevering.

Hofstede (2001) refers to this as long and short term orientation.

(Source: Adapted from Hofstede and Bond, 1988, and Hofstede, 2001, p. 354.)

who had been sentenced to death for drug trafficking, discovered that the rules were applied with much less leniency than in the United States or in Europe: he did not obtain mercy for the condemned man. Australia has had similar experiences, and was unable to prevent the execution of two Australian citizens in Kuala Lumpur in 1986. Since then some convicted traffickers, for example in Bangkok, have benefited from diplomatic negotiations between the respective countries resulting in prisoner exchanges. The components of authoritarian pluralism are as follows:

1. A negation of individualism: group belonging and consequent obligations are more important than individual human rights; persons try to be in unison rather than in discordance with society.
2. Family, as already emphasized in Chapter 4, is the basic building block. Divorce rates are much lower than in the West; family is a form of social insurance that efficiently replaces the costly impersonal welfare systems of Western countries.
3. Education is highly valued and people are ready to make financial sacrifices and efforts to obtain it.
4. Thrift, modesty and renunciation are the rule until somebody can show through conspicuous consumption that he or she has really deserved personal enjoyment (Asia is the dominant market for French XO cognac at $80 per bottle).
5. The strong work orientation is facilitated by the collective ambience of effort.
6. A 'national teamwork' orientation: trade unions, businesses and the government strive more in the same direction than in the West, although conflicts of interests also exist.
7. The Asian form of *contrat social*: the role of the state is mostly to provide *law and order*, as in Singapore. Citizens follow the rules in as far as the state is *fair and humane.*
8. The state is a company and the citizens its shareholders.
9. An orientation towards a 'morally clean environment': unbridled representations of sex and crime are not tolerated; attacks on other beliefs are inexorably pursued, since most of the societies comprise several religions.
10. The press is free, but is not a 'fourth estate'. Asian states believe in the necessity of a free press as a condition of good governance. But the press has no absolute right and must blend with the national consensus.

However, *Asian diversity* remains very strong, at least in terms of perceived inter-Asian differences. For instance, Ooi (2002, pp. 6–9) describes tensions between Singapore and its Muslim neighbours, such as Indonesia: 'B.J. Habibie, when he was president of Indonesia, reminded Singapore that the island city-state is only a little red dot in the vast green Malay–Islamic world. Green is the colour of Islam . . . national boundaries are still significant, and forces of globalisation have not eroded national patriotism.' Similarly, the Chinese perceive themselves as totally different from the Japanese, the Vietnamese or the Koreans. The Chinese Diaspora is present in several countries, with extended economic power and sometimes with difficult relationships with the native populations. The consensus is at society level: some strong conflicts between ingroups, for instance between Chinese and Malays in Malaysia, although still very present, have been overcome in favour of cooperation.

These cultural differences have been found to extend to differences in management style. For instance, at the country level Neelankavil *et al.* (2000) found that self confidence/charisma was very important for Chinese managers, but of low importance for Filipino and Indian managers. Similarly at the regional level, Ralston *et al.* (1999) found that managers in North Vietnam exhibited a more Western orientation toward Individualism, while managers in the South seem to hold a more traditionally Asian collectivist bent. The North is apparently embracing both Collectivism and Individualism. They suggest that 'similarities in economic evaluation between the Vietnamese and Chinese suggest that this paradox may be a developing economy paradox – at least an Asian paradox' (p. 670).

To illustrate the different attitudes and values of East Asians, Rosalie Tung (1996, pp. 369–70) recounts the following hypothetical situation presented to her by a Korean professor: two cars, driven by two Korean males, approach each other from the opposite ends of a narrow bridge; only one vehicle can pass at a time. He asks her what the two Koreans would do, and what two Japanese or two Chinese drivers would do in their place.

My response was as follows: 'the two Koreans would most probably step out of their cars and fight it out'. 'Correct', said my Korean colleague. 'In the case of the two Japanese drivers, each person would most probably ask the other to go first', I continued. 'Right you are again', nodded the Korean professor. I hesitated about the response to the possible reaction of the Chinese because China is a much larger country and there can be lots of regional differences. I told my Korean friend that I will venture an answer which is more characteristic of inhabitants in southern China. 'Each driver will most probably pull out the newspaper and start reading.' 'Correct again', my Korean friend said.

The formidable rise of China as a marketing environment is a special case in many respects because it is both an East Asian and a former communist country, while also a continent. Sethuraman (2004, p. 2) comments on the emergence of consumer power in China: 'China's rising demand for primary products and metals is boosting world commodity prices. Intra-regional trade now accounts for 40 per cent of total exports of the countries within.' China had an annual growth of 8.5 per cent in 2004. Now the sixth-largest country in the world in term of total advertising expenses at US$8.5 billion. China has more than 80,000 official advertising agencies (Madden, 2004). How China will import and develop marketing knowledge over the coming years is probably the greatest challenge faced by international marketers in the East Asian region. Business dealings with China need to be mindful of corruption throughout the government, military and business communities, and the impact politics can have on even the most basic business transactions. Legal concepts in China also rarely match Western ideals (Dixon and Newman, 1998). Because China is still a developing country, the majority of fast-growing Chinese companies that have become big are not those with the latest technology, but those that have the best management skills, effective business model, and successful branding strategy (Miao, 2003).

6.7

Limitations to the worldwide convergence of marketing environments

The political environment worldwide has clearly converged, with the steady decline of communist regimes. It is more and more difficult, given the powerful means of telecommunications, including satellite television and the Internet, to block the access of citizens to information on what is happening in their own country and in the world. Only a very few countries deny their citizens access to the Internet while some, like China and Tunisia, try to control access. The general economic environment is to a certain extent converging, but there are major limitations in a number of areas that are important for marketing. While economic systems are converging towards a market economy, the degree of poverty of a significant group of developing countries has been increasing over the years. Legal integration has limits since legal traditions continue to differ greatly. Some legal materials are duplicated and become complex, as in the EU where laws pertaining to marketing are regulated both at EU level and at the level of member states, sometimes resulting in discrepancies, even if local regulation is supposed to comply with Europe-wide directives.

Buying and consumption patterns in affluent counties appear to have in fact diverged as much as converged. Interestingly de Mooij (2001) found that preference for new cars over second-hand cars depended more on culture than on wealth, across 15 European countries. Today, consumers have more opportunities for choice and are often affected by social needs. As de Mooij (1998, pp. 58–9) states:

Clothes satisfy a functional need, whereas fashion satisfies a social need. Some personal care products serve functional needs, but others serve social needs. A house serves a functional need and a home, a social need. Culture influences the type of house in which people live, how they relate to their homes, and how they tend to their homes. A car may satisfy a functional need, but the type of car for most people satisfies a social need. Social needs are cultural-bound.

Marketing infrastructures are converging, because the standards of the marketing profession are fairly consistent worldwide. Multinational companies have heavily influenced the widespread adoption of similar practices even if to some extent tailored to local environments.

Marketing knowledge is probably the most controversial issue. It is based on Anglo-American cultural premises and seems to have been widely adopted worldwide. However, a multitude of differences, both local and cultural, reflect how marketing knowledge has been understood, sometimes misunderstood, and often transformed. Hence, management expectations about both consumers' responses and the performance of marketing tasks can be partly disproved, even in an environment to which they are apparently suited, because there has not been enough awareness and understanding of the local marketing environment. Thus, US-based consumer behaviour theories are not necessarily valid for other cultures.

Lastly, it is important to note that the heightened security following the terrorist attack on New York in September 2001, the war in Iraq and SARS have compelled nations to tighten their borders. Kearney (2002) discusses this in relation to the effect of government warnings, restrictions and public anxiety leading to a decline in global tourism for the first time in 50 years. While people may be shying away from travelling, other aspects of globalization such as mobile phones and the Internet are likely to increase our contact with people in other nations.

Questions

1. Why is local marketing knowledge important for designing marketing strategies?

2. In Sweden, the consumerist movement is particularly strong as compared with France, Italy and Spain. Discuss why in the light of Hofstede's four dimensions (see Table 3.3).

3. What are the common values shared by people in the first 15 countries in the European Union? Conversely, what may be the differences?

4. To what extent does 'Confucian dynamism' explain the economic success of South-East Asian countries?

5. Based on the case of eastern European, and more generally the ex-communist, countries, explain what a 'transition culture' is.

6. What are the values shared by US, Mexican and Canadian societies? Conversely, on which aspects do they differ?

7. Discuss the limitations of the following statement: 'In the future there will be three major trading blocs: North America, Western Europe and East Asia'.

Note

1. See for instance the four volumes published by Philip Parker (1997a, 1997b, 1997c and 1997d), which give detailed statistical references for the religious, linguistic, ethnic and national cultures of the world.

References

Amine, Lyn S. and S. Tamer Cavusgil (1986), 'Demand estimation in a developing country environment: Difficulties, and examples', *Journal of the Market Research Society*, vol. 28, no. 5, pp. 43–65.

Anonymous (2002), 'Iran takes on cola giants', *Asia Times* (online), 17 October.

Anonymous (2003), 'Qibla shows its bottle', *The Publican* (online), 7 May.

Berger, Brigitte (ed.) (1991), *The Culture of Entrepreneurship*, ICS Press: San Francisco.

Business World (2003), 'Anti-war, consumer groups launch boycott of 10 leading US products', *Business World* (*Manila*), 27 March, p. 1.

Cecchini, Paolo (1988), *The European Challenge 1992*, Wildwood House: Aldershot.

Council of the European Communities (1992), *Treaty on European Union*, Office for Official Publications: Luxemburg.

Cowen, Richard (2003), 'EU official sees boycotts if US files biotech suit', *Forbes* (online), 6 May.

Darbelet, Michel and Jean-Marcel Lauginié (1988), *Economie d'Entreprise*, vol. 1, Editions Foucher: Paris.

Datson, Trevor (2003), 'Muslim Cola – idealism or marketing froth?', *Reuters* (online), 30 April.

Dayan, Armand, Jérôme Bon, Alain Cadix, Renaud de Maricourt, Christian Michon and Alain Ollivier (1988), *Marketing*, Collection PUF Fondamental, Presses Universitaires de France: Paris.

de Mooij, Marieke (1998), 'Masculinity/femininity and consumer behavior', in G. Hofstede & Associates (eds), *Masculinity and Femininity: The taboo dimension of national cultures*, pp. 55–73, Sage: Thousand Oaks, CA.

de Mooij, Marieke (2000), 'The future is predictable for international marketers', *International Marketing Review*, vol. 17, no. 2, pp. 103–13.

de Mooij, Marieke (2001), *Convergence-Divergence*, unpublished doctoral dissertation, Universidad de Navarra.

Dixon, John and David Newman (1998), *Entering the Chinese Market: The risks and discounted rewards*, Quorum Books: Westport, CT. (Review in *Journal of International Marketing*, vol. 7, no. 3, pp. 126–7.)

Djarova, Julia G. (1999), 'Foreign investment strategies and the attractiveness of Central and Eastern Europe', *International Studies of Management & Organization*, vol. 29, no. 1, pp. 14–33.

Doran, Kathleen Brewer (1997), 'Symbolic consumption in China: the color television as a life statement', in Merrie Brucks and Debbie McInnis (eds), *Advances in Consumer Research*, vol. 24, Association for consumer research: Provo, UT, pp. 128–31.

El Haddad, Awad B. (1985), 'An analysis of the current status of marketing in the Middle East', in Erdener Kaynak (ed.), *International Business in the Middle East*, de Gruyter: New York, pp. 177–97.

Esposito, Odile (1994), 'Concurrence: l'arme des normes', *L'Usine Nouvelle*, 25 August.

Eurobarometer (2003), 'Comparative Highlights', Autumn.

European Bank for Reconstruction and Development (1997), *Transitional Report Update*, EBRD: London, April.

European Communities (1987), *Treaties Establishing the European Communities*, Office for Official Publications of the European Communities: Luxemburg.

Evans, John (2003), 'Brazil's automakers count on expanding overseas market,' *Automotive News*, vol. 77, no. 6023, pp. 22–5.

Fernandez-Fanjul, Eufrasio (2002), 'ZamZam Cola crece con la ola Antiyanqui', *El Mundo* (online), 8 September.

Fournis, Y. (1962), 'The markets of Europe or the European market?' *Business Horizons*, vol. 5, Winter, pp. 77–83.

GATT (1986), *Le Commerce International en 1985–1986*, GATT: Geneva.

Ghauri, Pervez N. and Jean-Claude Usunier (1996), *International Business Negotiations*, Pergamon/Elsevier: Oxford.

Griffin, Mitch, Barry J. Babin and Doan Modianos (2000), 'Shopping values of Russian consumers; the impact of habituation in a developing economy', *Journal of Retailing*, vol. 76, no. 1, pp. 33–52.

Hayek, F.A. (1945), 'The use of knowledge in society', *The American Economic Review*, vol. XXXV, no. 4, September, pp. 519–30.

Ho, Suk-Ching (1997), 'The emergence of consumer power in China', *Business Horizons*, vol. 40, no. 5, pp. 15–21.

Hofstede, Geert (1980), *Culture's Consequences: International differences in work-related values*, Sage Publications: Beverly Hills, CA.

Hofstede, Geert (1991), *Culture and Organizations: Software of the mind*, McGraw-Hill (UK): Maidenhead.

Hofstede, Geert (2001), *Culture Consequences*, 2nd edn, Sage Publications: Thousand Oaks, CA.

Hofstede, Geert and Michael Harris Bond (1988), 'The Confucius connection: from cultural roots to economic growth', *Organizational Dynamics*, vol. 16, no. 4, pp. 4–21.

Holden, Nigel (1995), 'A diachronic view of Russian misconceptions of marketing', *Proceedings of the Second Conference on the Cultural Dimension of International Marketing*, Odense, 27–31 May, pp. 30–52.

Hundley, Tom (2003), 'New colas hope to make money off Muslim rancor', *Chicago Tribune* (online), 5 February.

Jeffery, Simon (2003), 'Is it the real thing?' *The Guardian* (online), 5 February.

Johansson, Johny K. (1994), 'The sense of "Nonsense": Japanese TV advertising', *Journal of Advertising*, vol. XXIII, no. 1, pp. 17–26.

Johansson, Johny K. and Ikujiro Nonaka (1996), *Relentless: The Japanese way of marketing*, HarperCollins: New York.

Kearney, A.T./Foreign Policy (2002), 'Globalization's last hurrah?', *Foreign Policy*, Globalization at work, pp. 38–50.

Khrutskogo, V.E. (ed.) (1991), *Sovremennyi Marketing*, Financy i Statistika: Moscow.

Kotler, Philip (1994), *Marketing Management*, 8th edn, Prentice Hall: Englewood Cliffs, NJ.

Lazer, William, Shoji Murata and Hiroshi Kosaka (1985), 'Japanese marketing: towards a better understanding', *Journal of Marketing*, vol. 49, Spring, pp. 69–81.

Leeflang, Peter S.H. and W. Fred Van Raaij (1995), 'The changing consumer in the European Union: a "meta-analysis"', *International Journal of Research in Marketing*, vol. 12, pp. 373–87.

Lessem, Ronnie and Fred Neubauer (1994), *European Management Systems*, Maidenhead: McGraw-Hill.

Lloyd, John (2000), 'Cultivating the world: the heads of four global companies discuss with John Lloyd the pressure on them to balance the demands of international expansion with more sensitivity to local and environmental issues', *Financial Times*, 20 September, pp. 22–24.

Madden, Normandy (2004), 'Culture clash thwarts shops from enjoying China's boom', *Advertising Age*, vol. 75, no. 18, p. 20.

Majidi, Nassim and Christina Passariello (2003), 'After Iraq, Cola wars heat up', *BusinessWeek Online*, 17 April.

Miao, Jiawen (2003), 'Private equity investment in China', on the webpage '100 questions and Answers about Venture Capital in China', available at: **www.chinaupdate.net/Industries/DL/PrivateEquityHow.htm**

Mourier, Pascal and Didier Burgaud (1989), *Euromarketing*, Les Editions d'Organisation: Paris.

Mussey, Dagmar (1997), 'Marketing director provides SmithKline reasons to smile', *Advertising Age International*, November, p. 24.

Myrdal, Gunnar (1968), *Asian Drama, An enquiry into the poverty of nations*, Pantheon Books: New York.

Naor, Jacob (1986), 'Towards a socialist marketing concept – the case of Romania', *Journal of Marketing*, vol. 50, January, pp. 28–39.

Neelankavil, James P., Anil Mathur and Yong Zhang (2000), 'Determinants of managerial performance: a cross-cultural comparison of the perceptions of middle-level managers in four countries', *Journal of International Business Studies*, vol. 31, no. 1, pp. 121–40.

O'Flynn, Kevin (2003), 'Americans and Dollars not welcome', *Moscow Times* (online), 26 March.

Ooi, Can-Seng (2002), 'National economic policies: Singapore, AFTA and FTA', *Newsletter of the Asia Research Centre*, no. 12, pp. 3–12.

Parker, Philip (1997a), *Religious Cultures of the World*, Greenwood Publishing: London.

Parker, Philip (1997b), *Linguistic Cultures of the World*, Greenwood Publishing: London.

Parker, Philip (1997c), *Ethnic Cultures of the World*, Greenwood Publishing: London.

Parker, Philip (1997d), *National Cultures of the World*, Greenwood Publishing: London.

Pohl, Manfred (1995), 'Südostasien: Autoritärer Pluralismus und witschaftliche Dynamik', *Entwicklung und Zusammenarbeit*, vol. 36, no. 2, pp. 40–3.

Qibla Cola (2003), 'Qibla Cola Company Ltd. . . . Liberate your taste', Qibla Cola website homepage (undated).

Ralston David A., Nguyen Van Thang and Nancy K. Napier (1999), 'A comparative study of the work values of North and South Vietnamese managers', *Journal of International Business Studies*, vol. 30, no. 4, pp. 655–72.

Ries, Al (2003), 'Coca Cola gets it right with "Real"', *Advertising Age* (online), 20 January.

Russell, Miller R. (1998), *Selling to Newly Emerging Markets*, Quorum Books: Greenwich, CT. (Review in *Journal of International Marketing*, vol. 7, no. 2, pp. 93–5.)

Schultz, Don E. (2002), 'China may leapfrog the West in Marketing', *Marketing News*, vol. 36, no. 17, pp. 8–10.

Sethuraman, S. (2004), 'IMF on world economy: will the recovery "spring" eternal?', *Businessline*, 29 April, p. 1.

Sinatra, Alexandro and Paola Dubini (1991), 'Book publishing', in Roland Calori and Peter Lawrence (eds), *The Business of Europe*, Sage: London, pp. 94–115.

Smith, Charles G. and Stephen M. Hills (2003), 'Political economy and the transition from planned to marked economies', *European Business Review*, vol. 15, no. 2, pp. 116–22.

Taylor, Ronald E., Mariea Grubbs Hoy and Eric Haley (1996), 'How French advertising professionals develop creative strategy', *Journal of Advertising*, vol. XXV, no. 1, pp. 1–14.

Theodoulou, Michael, Charles Bremner and Daniel McGrory (2002) 'Cola wars as Islam shuns the real thing', *The Times Online*, 11 October.

Tietz, B. (1994), 'The opening up of eastern Europe: the implications for western businesses', in P. Buckley and P. Ghauri (eds), *The Economics of change in East and Central Europe: Its impact on international business*, Academic Press: London.

Tudor, Jan Davis (2001), 'Going online overseas', *Searcher*, vol. 9, no. 9, pp. 36–7.

Tung, Rosalie (1996), 'Negotiating with East Asians', in P.N. Ghauri and J.-C. Usunier (eds), *International Business Negotiations*, Pergamon/Elsevier: Oxford, pp. 369–81.

Usunier, Jean-Claude (1990), 'Some contextual aspects of the French international business education system: a pessimistic view', *European Management Journal*, vol. 8, no. 3, pp. 388–93.

Usunier, Jean-Claude (1998), *International and Cross-Cultural Management Research*, Sage Publications: London.

Van Raaij, W.F. (1978), 'Cross-cultural methodology as a case of construct validity', in M.K. Hunt (ed.), *Advances in Consumer Research*, Association for Consumer Research: Ann Arbor, MI, vol. 5, pp. 693–701.

Wierenga, Berend, Ad Pruyn and Eric Waarts (1996), 'The key to successful Euromarketing: standardization or customization?', *International Journal of Consumer Marketing*, vol. 8, nos 3/4, pp. 39–67.

Wolf, Martin (2004), 'Coming together: a small step for Europe's economy but a giant leap for the continent', *Financial Times*, 26 April, pp. 17–20.

World Trade Organization (2003), *Understanding the WTO*, 3rd edn, WTO Information and Media Relations Division: Switzerland.

Zayavlov, P.S. and V.E. Demidov, (1991), *Formula Uspekha – Marketing*, Mezhdunarodniye Otnosheniya: Moscow.

Teaching materials

A6.1 Case

Muslim Cola: Cola wars or cola crusades?

During the prelude to the recent American-led invasion of Iraq, some consumers boycotted American products and brands. In the Philippines, ten leading products were targeted, including Coke, McDonald's, Citibank and Starbucks. Among the reasons given by boycott leaders was 'disgust and revulsion' at the invasion (*Business World*, 2003). In some Russian and German cities, restaurant patrons were told that Coke was unavailable because of the current political situation (O'Flynn, 2003). Other countries with active boycotts discussed in the press included Argentina, Egypt, France, Greece, India, Indonesia, Italy, Malaysia, Pakistan, Saudi Arabia, Tunisia and Yemen. Almost without exception, Coca-Cola figures prominently in the boycotted product lists. Coca-Cola has itself been targeted in a long-standing boycott over its bottling plant in occupied Palestine (Anon, 2003). For years boycotts in support of the Palestinian Intifada have been in effect, as well as boycott threats in opposition to the Bush Administration's international trade stance on biotech foods and other issues (Cowen, 2003).

Coke's prominence on boycott lists points to its paradigmatic status as an American brand. Variations on the Coca-Cola logo have been used as an image on anti-war posters, and in puns, as in 'COLA-teral Damage' by the Belgian group STOPUSA.

Muslim colas

Mecca Cola (www.meccacola.com) was launched by Tunisian-born entrepreneur Tawfik Mathlouthi in November, 2002. Although its packaging is similar in colour and style to that of Coca-Cola, its philosophy is diametrically opposed to the drinks monolith: its logo is 'No more drinking stupid – drink with commitment!', and 'Don't shake me, shake your conscience!' The French company claims that 10 per cent of its net profits will be sent to Palestinian children's charities, plus another 10 per cent to European charities favouring international peace and Palestinian causes. Mecca drinks (including Tonic, Classic, Mentha and Vanilly) are distributed in Australia, Belgium, Canada, France, Germany and the United Kingdom, according to the company (Hundley, 2003). In Great Britain, orders are brisk at over two million bottles per month (Jeffery, 2003). Mecca Cola 'sponsored' the million-strong peace march in London in February, 2003, handing out 'Not in my name' t-shirts and Mecca Cola.

Across the Channel, Qibla Cola made its appearance in February, 2003. According to the Qibla Cola website (www.Qibla-cola.com), British entrepreneur Zahida Parveen founded the company to offer 'real alternatives to global consumer brands that support unjust policies' (Qibla Cola, 2003). Like Mecca Cola, Qibla's offerings resemble those of Coca-Cola, and Qibla is the Arabic word for the direction to pray to Mecca, but the company is more than a nod at Mecca Cola. The company promotes Qibla Cola, Qibla Fantasy (orange and mango), Qibla 5 (lemon and lime, named for the five pillars of Islam), and spring water to 2.5 million Muslims in Britain, with an eye on Indonesia, Pakistan and Bangladesh (Hundley, 2003). The company works with Islamic Aid, a registered charity that is to receive 10 per cent of net profits. Qibla notes that it broke even after only two months, an exceptional performance for a start-up (Datsun, 2003). In an interview, Qibla CEO Zafer Iqbal proffered that the products' packaging and taste parallels with Coca-Cola were intended to 'leverage' Coke's global image and make consumers aware of Islamic alternatives like Qibla (Datson, 2003). Company spokesperson Abdul Hamid Ebrahim stated that the company's inspiration came from Iran's ZamZam Cola, a company that profited from a leading Iranian cleric's ruling that Coke and Pepsi were 'un-Islamic' (Hundley, 2003).

ZamZam cola has a leading market share of 47 per cent in its home country Iran, a net income of US$176 million last year and more than 7,000 employees in 17 factories (Fernandez-Fanjul, 2002). It is distributed throughout the Middle East, and in some African and European countries, notably Denmark. The company was Coke's long-term partner in Iran, prior to the Islamic Revolution. In the autumn of 2002, ZamZam produced more than ten million bottles to meet rising demand in Saudi Arabia, spurred on by anger over American support for Israel (Anon, 2002). As a consequence of boycotts and the advent of competitors like ZamZam, sales of Coca-Cola and Pepsi-Cola fell from 20–40 per cent in some Middle Eastern countries in 2002 (Theodoulou *et al.*, 2002).

There are other Muslim Colas dedicated to taking market share from Coke, including Pakistan's Salsabeen (promoted through pamphlets distributed after Friday prayers), Morocco's Star Cola, and French MuslimUp (**www.muslim-up.com**). All these cola companies face similar problems. They are up against the world's most valuable brand, Coca-Cola, valued at more than US$70 billion (Ries, 2003). For all but ZamZam, securing capacity contracts with bottling plants has proven difficult. Distribution is a problem, with supermarkets often reluctant to take on a new 'niche' product with an unsure future. Distributors are also concerned about the capacity of cola suppliers to meet demand at a consistent quality level. As a result, these alternative colas are often sold in small family owned shops in areas populated by immigrants (Majidi and Passariello, 2003). It is unlikely that any of the Muslim colas poses a real threat to the entrenched hegemony of Coke, however. As one consultant has put it, if the market for Muslim colas gets too big, Coke will simply buy them up, just as it did with start-up cola company Thumbs Up in India (Majidi and Passariello, 2003).

Questions

1. Some analysts believe that companies like Qibla and Mecca are not capable of long-term market share, and that their initial success is due to publicity that will quickly fizzle out. Is this a likely scenario, given the competitive environment in which they operate?

2. Some Muslims object to the 'commercialization' of Islam, as represented by these cola companies' marketing strategies. Should these Muslim cola companies target a wider audience? If so, how? Give them some marketing ideas.

3. If you were the CEO of the leading company (Coca-Cola) how would you react to the emergence of Muslim colas? In non-Muslim countries? In Muslim countries? Same question if you were the CEO of the longstanding challenger (Pepsi-Cola)?

A6.2 Case

Odol

When Manfred Hansen took over as marketing director of Lingner and Fischer in 1985, the company held a meagre 15 per cent of the oral care market in Germany – half of what the leader, Procter & Gamble, could claim. Known since 1997 as SmithKline Beecham, the company now commands a 30.4 per cent share of oral care while P & G's slice has shrunk to 13.8 per cent according to AC Nielsen. And Mr Hansen has kept his promise to be the leading oral care company in Germany, while becoming No. 1 in Switzerland and Austria as well.

SmithKline managed this turnaround through savvy marketing, including extending the familiar Odol and Dr Best brand names, bringing a fresh positioning to whitening products and paying close attention to consumer needs in areas such as packaging, where it eliminated wasteful wrapping entirely. The company also achieved its success in Germany by keeping an eye on global strategies while giving local managers some autonomy. 'SmithKline Beecham is acting much faster and takes greater risks than P & G,' said a marketing manager at the now pacesetting company. 'We are in constant touch with headquarters in order to understand market situations in other countries, [but] fortunately headquarters leaves us freedom to act in our market, taking into consideration the local situation.'

Becoming the market leader in toothpaste, a $545 million category in Germany and hotly contested by rivals P & G, Colgate-Palmolive Co. and Elidda-Gibbs hasn't been easy. Newcomers barely get a chance to survive; Henkel's thera-med, launched in 1979 is a rare exception. So SmithKline and Mr Hansen proceeded cautiously, testing its toothpaste in a year long test in two German cities, Bad Kreuznach and Buxtehude, of the names Odol med 3, Aquafresh med 3 and – extending the name of its existing toothbrush line – Dr Best med 3. It soon became evident that consumers favoured Odol med 3, a brand name under which the company had marketed a mouthwash concentrate since 1893. Not coincidentally, Odol is category leader in mouthwash with a 70 per cent share in Germany, 80 per cent in Austria, and 60 per cent in Switzerland. 'Odol's brand name is extremely strong; consumers have had confidence in the product for 100 years,' Mr Hansen said. 'We used this name because of the brand capital it has. Our headquarters ensures that each subsidiary uses international experience, but if we can be more successful with a local brand name, we use it.' For example, in Spain, the Aquafresh brand is marketed under the name Binaca Med 3.

SmithKline's eventual success in toothpaste was an even harder-won fight considering Odol med 3's premium price. The toothpaste was marketed for 25 per cent more than ten average in Germany, but the price was justified by its attributes, such as three-prong protection against cavities, plaque and periodontal disease. After notching a 4 per cent market share in 1989, its first year, Odol med 3 climbed to 6 per cent in 1990 with the introduction of a mint line extension. By 1993, share was still climbing despite the fact that SmithKline was spending only $8 million to $10 million on advertising – half of what P & G was laying out for its Blend-a-Med brand. Odol also got a boost from SmithKline's move in 1991 to strip away cumbersome packaging and sell the tubes without an outer box. 'We take our consumers very seriously,' Mr Hansen said 'When we noticed that consumers were reacting to unnecessary packaging, we acted immediately.'

The stripped-down package was touted in an amusing campaign from Grey Advertising, Düsseldorf, SmithKline's agency of record in oral care for 15 years. The spot mimicked a strip-tease act with the toothpaste unburdening itself of its outer wrapper as an audience of animated teeth yelled out cheers and catcalls. Mr Hansen, in fact, said its close relationship with Grey was a major reason for its conquest of German-speaking countries. 'We are one team,' he said. 'We have integrated the agency – the account people as well as the creative team – totally in our marketing, and we discuss with them everything from product policy to marketing strategy, prices and distribution.' Grey, then, was part of SmithKline's decision to create a special package shaped like a tooth for Odol med 3 in Germany. This development also helped the base brand reach its current 9 per cent market share in Germany neck-to-neck with Blend-a-Med. The package is being used as a template in other markets, Mr Hansen said.

What put SmithKline finally over the top was its whitening line extension, Odol med 3 samtweiss. At the time of its introduction, in 1996, whitening toothpastes were considered an also-ran in the category, used mainly by smokers and coffee and tea drinkers, and they claimed only a 5 per cent segment of the total toothpaste market in Germany. Mr Hansen and his team aimed to change that with advertising that argued against consumers' notions that whiteners damage teeth and are abrasive. Further, the message was that everyone with yellowing teeth should try Odol med 3 samtweiss. In a single year the strategy propelled the toothpaste's German share to 6.8 per cent share and rocketed SmithKline's overall toothpaste share to 15.8 per cent. That sent competitors, including Henkel and Colgate, scrambling to introduce whiteners, which are just now about to hit store shelves.

But SmithKline's wasn't finished yet. There were still toothbrushes to consider. Although the company had sold a toothbrush under the Dr Best name since 1953, the brand's share languished at 5 per cent of the German market in the mid-1980s, and Mr Hansen said the company was considering spinning it off. 'We even discussed selling the brand,' he revealed, 'but I fought for its survival because market research showed us the Dr Best name had a recognition level of over 70 per cent. What we needed was a product advantage.' The break came in 1988, in the form of a new brush with a floating neck and a flexible handle that massaged the gums without injuring them. Grey then set to work: the agency sought, and found, a real Dr Best, a dental professional from the US who appeared in TV ads that showed the toothbrush working on a tomato without damaging its delicate skin.

Not surprisingly, P & G and Colgate followed with products of their own – but not until SmithKline had leapt into the leadership position in toothbrushes with a 39.8 per cent share, up from a mere 5 per cent in 1985 when Mr Hansen began his initial assault.

(Source: Reprinted with permission from the November 1997 issue of *Advertising Age*. International copyright © Crain Communication Inc. 1997.)

Questions

1. Which aspects of the German marketing environment explain the success of Odol med 3 in terms of consumer response to the brand's innovations?

2. Why can a market like Germany be a lead market for packaging innovation in general?

3. Discuss the issues involved in transferring part of Odol's recipe for success to near national markets (France, the United Kingdom), especially the tooth-like packaging.

Cross-cultural market research

Companies will often encounter problems when undertaking market research across national/cultural boundaries. One European syrup maker ordered a survey of the Swedish market from a large international market research company. Unfortunately, syrup, a solution of sugar dissolved in water and flavoured with fruit juice, was incorrectly translated as *blandsaft*, a Swedish term for concentrated fruit juice, a local substitute for syrup with much less sugar. Thus, when the results came in, they were of no use, because it was a local product rather than the product category at large that had been surveyed. This simple translation mistake may have cost the company the money allocated to the research, but had they not discovered the mistake and acted on an answer to the wrong problem, it could have cost them dearly in market share as well.

The previous example is just one of many possible hazards engendered by the lack of timely, relevant information. For instance, the simultaneous launch of new products into several different national markets requires research to be undertaken in multiple locations at the same time. Typical research questions may be similar to the following:

1. How should one undertake a market survey for instant coffee in a traditionally tea-drinking country like the United Kingdom or Japan? What information and data must be sought? How should the data be collected?
2. Which information-gathering technique should be used for personal care products in a country where, for instance, potential respondents resent interviews as an intrusion into their privacy?
3. Where the starting point is a questionnaire that was originally designed for a specific country/culture, how should it be translated and adapted to the cultural specificity of other countries in which it is to be administered?

Even slight differences in the research question may require a different emphasis or even a different research technique to uncover the required answers. For instance, we might want to know how to increase market share, but we need to make sure that the problem (and not just the symptom) is correctly specified. Using instant coffee as an example, we might ask one of the following:

1. How can we recover the market share lost by instant coffee to ground coffee in a traditionally coffee-drinking country? This requires the investigation of consumption patterns in certain social and family situations, and the times at which people drink specific coffee-based beverages.[1]
2. How can we increase the market share for instant coffee out of the total hot beverages market in a traditionally tea-drinking country?

Cultural differences are the main characteristic of interest when contrasting countries, now that non-tariff barriers are easing. An understanding of the cross-cultural environment is a basic requirement in setting the research objective: therefore the objectives cannot be the same as those for domestic market research. Given the multinationalization of business, establishing the quality of research instruments, the consistency of behavioural/attitudinal constructs and the equivalence of samples are of paramount concern to the marketer. This chapter aims to provide the reader with some basic insights, drawn mostly from cross-cultural methodology in the social sciences, on how to solve these problems.

This chapter presents the main limits to equivalence across national/cultural contexts when one undertakes cross-cultural market research, and in particular the issue of conceptual and functional equivalence (section 7.1), translation problems (section 7.2), measure equivalence related to different units being used cross-culturally (section 7.3), the comparability of samples and sampling procedures (section 7.4) and the equivalence problems in data-collection procedures resulting from interviewers' and respondents' attitudes towards surveys (section 7.5). The last section (section 7.6) discusses whether international market research should use a different approach from traditional, positivistic market research techniques.

7.1
Equivalence in cross-cultural research

If the type of data sought and the research procedures implemented are considered to be of general application, the main difference between domestic and cross-cultural market research lies in the difficulty in establishing equivalence at the various stages of the research process.[2] It is not self-evident, as the Japanese style of market research shows (see section 7.6), that research procedures and the type of data sought are completely independent of the cultural context of the researcher. But this chapter first emphasizes dependence on the researched context.

The complexity of the research design is greatly increased when working in an international, multicultural and multilinguistic environment (Durvasula *et al.* 1993; Van de Vijver and Leung, 1997; Baumgartner and Steenkamp, 2001; Craig and Douglas, 2001a), not to mention the difficulties in establishing comparability and equivalence of data.

Even larger problems may arise when differences in sociocultural or psychographic variables imply different attitudes and behaviour when using particular types of product. For instance, in Singapore, Askegaard and Brunsø (1999) tested a food-related lifestyle instrument that had been developed in western

Europe. Out of the five areas in the survey (ways of shopping, quality aspects, cooking methods, consumption situations and purchasing motives), only consumption situations and purchasing motives showed even a minimal level of cross-cultural validity, with quality aspects and cooking methods having the most problems. Many possible reasons were given for this including (a) different cooking patterns in Singapore, where the use of maids and eating out are more prevalent, (b) lower involvement in cooking, (c) a broader concept of convenience, (d) different beliefs in health properties of food, and (e) different use of information in the highly competitive Singaporean food sector. Thus, questionnaires need to be adapted to the context in each country (see the hair shampoo exercise in section A7.2).

Research approaches: Emic versus etic

The classic distinction in cross-cultural research approaches, between *emic* and *etic*, was originated by Sapir (1929) and further developed by Pike (1966). The emic approach holds that attitudinal or behavioural phenomena are expressed in a unique way in each culture. Taken to its extreme, this approach states that no comparisons are possible. The etic approach, on the other hand, is primarily concerned with identifying universals. The difference arises from linguistics where phon*etic* is universal and depicts universal sounds that are common to several languages, and phon*emic* stresses unique sound patterns in languages.

In general, market research measurement instruments adapted to each national culture (the emic approach) offer more reliability and provide data with greater internal validity than tests applicable to several cultures (the etic approach, or 'culture-free tests'). But use of such instruments is at the expense of cross-national comparability and external validity: results are not transposable to other cultural contexts. This is why we need to examine cross-national equivalence, which is inspired by the etic rather than the emic perspective.[3] In terms of Table 4.1 the issue would be very much at the centre of the four cells; it lies somewhere between looking with the same eye at an object that is supposed to be different and changing to a slightly different eye in order to have a better look.

Levels of cross-cultural equivalence

Management must provide guidelines for the systematic collection of data, either domestic or international. It is important to follow a precise plan that outlines the various steps of the research process (Green *et al.* 1988), starting with a clear and concise statement of the research problem. The literature now includes many papers exploring the issue of cross-cultural equivalence (e.g. Green and Langeard, 1979; Leung, 1989; Poortinga, 1989; Durvasula *et al.* 1993; Van Herk and Verhallen, 1995; Cavusgil and Das, 1997; Van de Vijver and Leung, 1997; Steenkamp and Baumgartner, 1998; Bensaou *et al.*, 1999). Craig and Douglas (2001b) identify areas where non-equivalence, causing non-comparability, may arise in comparative consumer research. The various levels of cross-cultural equivalence displayed in Table 7.1 are explained in the text of the chapter, with six main categories and sixteen subcategories that are further discussed in this text. (For more information on cross-cultural equivalence see *WS7.1.*)

Conceptual equivalence

A basic issue in cross-cultural research is the determination of whether the concepts used have similar meaning across the social units studied. Problems of *conceptual equivalence* are more frequent when testing the influence of certain constructs on consumer behaviour. For instance, the hypothesis of the cognitive theory that people do not willingly behave inconsistently may hold true in the United States while not being applicable to some other countries (conceptual equivalence).

The following statement from the anthropologist Clifford Geertz (1983, p. 59) gives us some sense of how difficult it may be to reach true conceptual equivalence between cultures:

> The Western conception of a person as a bounded, unique, more or less integrated, motivational and cognitive universe, a dynamic center of awareness, emotions, judgement and action, organized in a distinctive whole . . . is, however incorrigible it may seem, a rather peculiar idea, within the context of world's cultures.

Such basic concepts as beauty, youth, friendliness, wealth, well-being, sex appeal, and so on, are often used in market research questionnaires where motivation for buying many products is related to self-image, interaction with other people in a particular society and social values. They are seemingly universal. However, it is always advisable to question the conceptual equivalence of all these basic words when designing a cross-cultural questionnaire survey. Even the very concept of 'household', widely used in market research, is subject to possible inequivalence: Mytton (1996) cites the case of Northern Nigeria where people often live in large extended family compounds or *gida* which are difficult to compare with the prevalent concept of household that reflects the living unit of a nuclear family.

Many examples in previous chapters illustrate the practical difficulties in dealing with the conceptual equivalence of constructs used in a survey. When

Table 7.1 Categories of cross-cultural equivalence

A. Conceptual equivalence	B. Functional equivalence
C. Translation equivalence ■ Lexical equivalence ■ Idiomatic equivalence ■ Grammatical–syntactical equivalence ■ Experiential equivalence	**D. Measure equivalence** ■ Perceptual equivalence ■ Metric equivalence ■ Calibration equivalence ■ Temporal equivalence
E. Sample equivalence ■ Sampling unit equivalence ■ Frame equivalence ■ Sample selection equivalence	**F. Data collection equivalence** ■ Respondents' cooperation equivalence ■ Data collection context equivalence ■ Response style equivalence

(Source: Adapted from Craig and Douglas, 2001b. Reprinted with permission.)

looking at the underlying dimensions across countries, it can often be seen that they are not equivalently weighted or articulated in the total construct. For instance, in the construct 'waiting in line' (to be served), the dimension of 'wasting one's time' may be emphasized in a time-conscious culture, whereas it may be almost non-existent in one that is not economically time-minded. In line with this, Chen *et al.* (2003) found that Americans were more impatient than Singaporeans, and that this led them to be willing to pay more for items that are available for immediate consumption.

Often the conceptual equivalence of several basic interrelated constructs has to be questioned, inasmuch as they relate to consumer behaviour idiosyncrasies for the specific type of product or service surveyed. Box 7.1 shows some construct equivalence problems in the case of life insurance policies.

Many popular marketing constructs have been used in cross-cultural research settings (perceived

---

Box 7.1

A multinational survey on life insurance: Conceptual equivalence problems in Islamic countries

In Islam it is considered evil to talk about death. Nevertheless, Muslim people do not fear death. On the contrary, they are probably much less frightened by the prospect of death than most people in Western/Christian countries. But the notion of destiny is of the utmost importance: humans may not decide about their own death, nor are they entitled to control the process of it. One is not allowed to challenge the course of destiny, and therefore one should not speculate on one's own life and death. A verse of the Koran says approximately this: 'Behave each day as if your life will be very long, and for your after life, behave as if you will die tomorrow.' In Saudi Arabia, life insurance is forbidden. But some high-risk industries, such as oil production, bypass this prohibition by insuring their local employees through foreign life-insurance companies, with policies located abroad.

In the Islamic world people do not like to invest and bet on the long term. Effort must be rewarded quickly if it is to be maintained. The concept of a financial product such as life insurance needs a long-term orientation and a strong individual capacity to imagine the future. Projection towards the future is a culture-related trait (see section 2.2). In Islam, you may certainly imagine how you will be tomorrow, but not at a particular place or moment. The future tense exists, but it is certainly not as accurate or meticulous as that of the English or European languages. Moreover, protection of the family and solidarity within the extended family are highly valued and work effectively. If a man dies, his brother will care for his wife and children.

The concept of life insurance is related to culture in at least the following four aspects: protection of the family and/or the individual; future orientation; betting on one's own life and death; the degree of solidarity in the family and extended family group. In Islamic countries it is important not to offend interviewees at first contact. It is better to rely on in-depth non-directive interviews and focus groups carried out principally by briefed local researchers who have a thorough personal knowledge of Islam and the local culture (the Islamic world spreads from black Africa to China). Some research questions will have to be addressed in order to prepare an adequate marketing strategy. Which is the appropriate mix, for the design of the life insurance policies offered to potential consumers, in terms of death benefit (amount of money to be paid when a person under a life insurance policy dies) and annuities (a series of payments made at regular intervals on the basis of the premiums previously paid)? Which term(s) should be proposed for people before they receive the benefits of their life insurance policy? How should the beneficiaries be designated? How should this offer be communicated to potential consumers through advertisement: which brand name should be adopted and which themes and advertising style should be favoured in the advertising campaign?

risk, brand loyalty, Rokeach value survey, lifestyles, etc.). Generally speaking, conceptual equivalence is an obstacle to the direct use of constructs that have been specifically designed for the US culture. The perceived risk construct, for instance, may differ in its components across cultures. It may be broken down into several subdimensions: social risk, physical risk, financial risk (Van Raaij, 1978). The emphasis placed on these subdimensions may vary across cultures: when buying cars, for example, people in some cultures may give more value to social risk because their purchase and use of car is mostly status oriented, whereas in other cultures people may be more concerned with physical safety because death in accidents is greatly feared. Further, it would be important to know if it was the perceptions of risk in the specific situation or the more generalized attitude toward risk that differed. Weber and Hsee (1998) found that Chinese students were less risk-averse than Americans, but that the difference was in the perceptions of the risk, rather than the attitude towards perceived risk.

Therefore it is necessary to investigate, far more frequently than is actually done, the construct validity in each culture where a cross-cultural consumer behaviour study is undertaken. This should be done by following recognized procedures to assess the validity of the underlying constructs at the conceptual level and reliability at the empirical/measurement instrument level (Grunert et al., 1993).[4]

Functional equivalence: Similar products and activities performing different functions

If similar activities perform different functions in different societies, their measures cannot be used for the purpose of comparison (Frijda and Jahoda, 1966). Concepts frequently used in market surveys, such as preparing a meal, are not necessarily functionally equivalent across countries. When asked: 'What dishes do you cook, or prepare with tomato juice?', Italians and Danes give different answers. Stanton et al. (1982) illustrate functional equivalence problems by taking the example of hot milk-based chocolate drinks. Whereas in the USA and the UK they are considered an evening drink, best before going to sleep, in much of Latin America a 'Chocolate Caliente' is a

morning drink. Functional equivalence is not reached due to differences in the consumption time period and in the purpose for use: waking/energizer versus sleep/relaxer. Similarly, functional equivalence will be a problem if we compare bicycle purchases in China where they are used mainly for transportation with other countries where they are mainly used for leisure (Roy et al., 2001).

A watch may be used as wrist jewellery, a status symbol, or an instrument for handling time and daily schedules. The same holds true for a fountain pen. In some countries its function may be as a simple general-purpose writing instrument; in others it may be regarded mostly as an instrument for signing documents. Elsewhere it may be considered purely non-functional since it needs time and care to refill it, and often leaks over one's fingers. Many other examples could be given, such as wine (everyday beverage accompanying meals versus beverage for special occasions), beer (summer refresher versus all-year standard 'non-water' beverage), mixed spirit drinks (a man's versus a woman's drink) and perfumes (masking bodily odours versus adding a pleasant smell after a shower).

The simple word 'coffee' covers a whole range of beverages that are enjoyed in very different social settings (at home, at the workplace, during leisure time, in the morning, or at particular times during the day), in quite different forms (in terms of quantity, concentration, with or without milk, cold or hot), prepared from different forms of coffee base (beans, ground beans, instant). The function of the Brazilian *cafezinho*, very small cups of coffee, rather strong and drunk every hour in informal exchanges with colleagues, cannot be compared with that of the US *coffee*, which is in large cups, very light, and drunk mostly at home and in restaurants. One of the best ways to investigate functional equivalence is to examine the social settings in which a product is consumed.

7.2

Translation equivalence

For many reasons, which are outlined principally in Chapter 13 on language, culture and communication, translation techniques, no matter how sophisticated, might prove incapable of achieving full comparability of data. Let us first make a small review of translation equivalence problems. (For more information on translation equivalence issues and additional examples see *WS7.2*.)

Categories of translation equivalence

Translation equivalence may be divided into the following subcategories:

1. *Lexical equivalence.* This is what dictionaries can provide us with: for instance, one may discover that the English adjective *warm* translates into the French *chaud*.
2. *Idiomatic equivalence.* The problem of idiomatic equivalence comes when you try to translate a sentence such as *'it's warm'*: French has two expressions for it, either *'il fait chaud'* (literally, 'it makes warm' meaning 'it's warm [today]') or *'c'est chaud'* (meaning 'it [this object] is warm'). An idiom is a linguistic usage that is natural to native speakers. Idioms are most often non-equivalent: the present continuous (i.e. I am *doing*) has no equivalent in French, except *je suis en train de ...* , which is highly colloquial, not to be used in correct French written language. This may also be problematic for regions within a country, as Roy *et al.* (2001, p. 207) states:

   The English phrase 'high risk' can be translated as 'qiang feng xian' in the middle and northern China but as 'gao feng xian' in southern China. To Chinese from the south, the word 'qiang' has two meanings, one is related to the 'magnitude' and the other to 'strength'; as such, it can be difficult to interpret the concept 'qiang feng xian'.

3. *Grammatical–syntactical equivalence.* This refers to the way words are ordered, sentences are constructed and meaning is expressed in language. English generally proceeds in an active way, starting with the subject, followed by the verb and then the complement, avoiding abstractions as well as convoluted sentences. Many languages, including German and French, start by explaining the circumstances in relative clauses, before they proceed into the action. This makes for complex sentences starting with relative clauses based on *when, where, even though, although,* and so on. The Japanese

language has a quite different ordering of words from Western languages: verbs are always at the end of the sentence: *'Gurunoburu no daigaku no sensei desu'* means: *'Grenoble of [the] university of professor [I] am'*, that is, *'I am a professor at the university of Grenoble'*.

4. *Experiential equivalence* (Sechrest *et al.* 1972). Experiential equivalence is about what words and sentences mean for people in their everyday experience. Coming back to *'chaud'*, it translates into two English words *'warm'* and *'hot'*: the French do not experience 'warmth' with two concepts as the English, the Germans and many others do. Similarly, the special experience of coldness in the word 'chilly' cannot be adequately rendered in French. Translated terms must refer to real items and real experiences, which are familiar in the source as well as the target cultures. An expression such as 'dish-washing machine' may face experiential equivalence problems when people, even if they know what it is, have never actually seen this type of household appliance nor experienced it. Another example of experiential non-equivalence is given by the Japanese numbering system, which reflects a special experience of counting, where the numbers cannot be fully abstracted from the object being counted. Most often the Japanese add a particle indicating which objects are counted. *Nin*, for instance, is used to count human beings: *yo-nin* is four (persons). *Hiki* is used for counting animals but not birds, for which *wa*, meaning *feather*, is used, *satsu* is used for books, *hon* for round and long objects, *mai* for flat things such as a sheet of paper, textiles, coins, etc., and *hai* for cups and bowls and liquid containers in general. As a vivid illustration of translation problems, Box 7.2 shows the translation errors in the case of a major concept, 'reproductive health', for the UN World Conference on Population Development, held in Cairo in 1994.

Back-translation and related techniques

The back-translation technique (Campbell and Werner, 1970) is the most widely employed method for reaching translation equivalence (mainly lexical and idiomatic) in cross-cultural research. This procedure helps to identify probable translation errors.

Box 7.2

'Reproductive health'

Cultural discrepancies are not only evidenced in factual themes, they also manifest themselves in translation difficulties: the concept of 'reproductive health' was translated into German as '*Gesundheit der Fortpflanzung*' (health of propagation). The Arabic translators invented the formula: 'spouses take a break from each other after childbirth', the Russian translators worded this in despair as 'The whole family goes on holiday' and the Chinese translators elevated themselves to the almost brilliant formula 'a holiday at the farm'. This shows that the new word-monsters, elegantly coined by the Americans, are almost non-translatable worldwide; on the other hand, they infuse international conferences with a lot of humour.

(Source: Bohnet, 1994.)

One translator translates from the source language (S) into a target language (T). Then another translator, ignorant of the source-language text, translates the first translator's target language text back into the source language (S'). Then the two source-language versions, S and S', are compared.

For instance, when translating '*un repas d'affaires*' ('*a business meal*' in English) from French to Portuguese in the preparation of a questionnaire for Brazil, it is translated as *jantar de negocios*. When back-translated, it becomes a '*dîner d'affaires*' ('business dinner'). In Brazilian Portuguese, there is no specific expression for '*repas d'affaires*'. It is either a 'business lunch' ('*almoço de negocios*') or a 'business dinner'. One has to choose which situation to elicit in the Brazilian questionnaire (as would be the case in English): the 'business meal' has to be either at noon or in the evening in the Portuguese version. When back-translating, discrepancies may arise from translation mistakes in either of the two directions or they may derive from real translation equivalence problems that are uncovered. Then a final target-language questionnaire (T_f) is discussed and prepared by the researcher (who speaks the source language) and the two translators. In practice it is advisable to have one translator who is a native speaker of the target language and the other one a native speaker of the source language. It means that they are translating *into* their native language rather than *from* it, which is always more difficult and less reliable.

However, back-translation can also instil a false sense of security in the investigator by demonstrating a spurious lexical equivalence (Deutscher, 1973).

Simply knowing that words are equivalent is not enough. It is necessary to know to what extent those literally equivalent words and phrases convey equivalent meanings in the two languages or cultures. Another technique, blind parallel translation (Mayer, 1978), consists of having several translators translate simultaneously and independently, from the source language into the target language. The different versions are then compared and a final version is written.

Combined translation techniques, limits of translation

Parallel and back-translation can be merged, as shown in Figure 7.1. When two languages and cultures present wide variations, such as Korean and French, combining parallel and back-translation provides a higher level of equivalence (Marchetti and Usunier, 1990).

For example, two Koreans translate the same French questionnaire F into two Korean versions, K1 and K2. A third Korean translator, who is unfamiliar with the original French text F, translates K1 and K2 into F1 and F2. A final Korean questionnaire, K3, is then prepared by comparing the two back-translated French versions F1 and F2. English is used to help compare them as it is widely used and more precise than either French or Korean. This example could be refined: the number of parallel translations may be increased, or back-translation processes may be independently performed (Usunier, 1991).

Figure 7.1 Examples of translation techniques

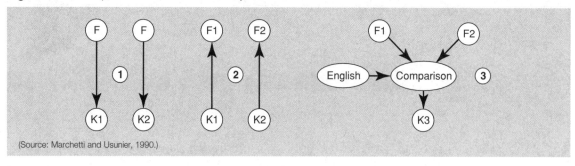

(Source: Marchetti and Usunier, 1990.)

A more sophisticated solution to the problem of translation has been suggested by Campbell and Werner (1970). Research instruments should be developed by collaborators in the two cultures, and items, questions or other survey materials should be generated jointly in the two cultures. After back-translation, or after any initial translation process has been performed, there is an opportunity to change the source-language wording. This technique, called *decentring*, not only changes the target language, as in the previous techniques, but also allows the words in the source language to be changed, if this provides enhanced accuracy. The ultimate words and phrases employed will depend on which common/similar meaning is sought in both languages simultaneously, without regard to whether words and phrases originate in the source or the target languages. In the above example of the business meal, choosing the decentring method would imply changing the words in the source questionnaire to 'business lunch'. In any case, it remains absolutely necessary to pre-test the translated research instrument in the target culture until satisfactory levels of reliability on conceptual and measurement equivalences are attained (Sood, 1990). Table 7.2 presents a synthesis of translation techniques as well as their advantages and drawbacks.

Table 7.2 Advantages and drawbacks of translation techniques

Technique ⇨	Direct translation	Back-translation	Parallel translation	Combined techniques
Process	S ⇨ T	S ⇨ T; T ⇨ S' comparison S to S' ⇨ final version T_f	S ⇨ T; S ⇨ T' Comparison T to T' ⇨ final version T_f	S ⇨ T; S ⇨ T' T ⇨ S'; T' ⇨ S" comparison S' and S", decentring of S ⇨ final version T_f
Advantages	Easy to implement	Ensures the discovery of most inadequacies	Easier to implement in S country with T translators	Ensures the best fit between source and target versions
Drawbacks/ Constraints	Leads to translation errors and discrepancies between S and T	Requires the availability of two translators, one native in S and one native in T languages	Leads to good wording in T, but does not ensure that specific meaning in S is fully rendered	Costly to implement Difficult to find the translators Implies readiness to change source-language version

Key: S = source language, T = target language (translators or versions).

Measure equivalence

Variations in the reliability of research instruments

Variation in cross-cultural reliability of underlying instruments has already been assessed, and Davis *et al.* (1981) claim that measurement unreliability is a threat to cross-national comparability. They investigated the problem of measurement reliability in cross-cultural marketing research for three types of consumer behaviour measures (demographics, household decision involvement and psychographics) across five country-markets, utilizing three different reliability assessment methods. Their findings show that it is easier to obtain measurement equivalence between demographic variables than between psychographic variables such as lifestyles. For psychographic variables it may be necessary to use a more in-depth assessment method to gain a better understanding of the variable, as well as potential linkages to products. For instance, Durgee *et al.* (1996) suggest a 'means-ends', which begins with the core values. First, they ask respondents which values are important in their life. Then, they ask respondents to indicate which of a list of products make the value or feeling possible. Finally, they ask how each product facilitates the value or feeling. Through this technique they found that the value *family security* is not only defined in terms of physical safety but also in terms of financial security. That is, *family security* is linked to alarm systems through the means of safety and linked to mutual funds through financial security. Both the assessment method and the nature of the construct may cause measurement unreliability across countries. (For more information on measurement equivalence issues see *WS7.3.*)

Variations in knowledge and familiarity with products, concepts or attitudes also impact on the equivalence of measures. Erevelles *et al.* (1998) found a warranty to be perceived in a different manner in China than in the United States. In China it is viewed as an extrinsic cue of little value to the potential buyer, due to their lack of familiarity with the concept. Similarly, Parameswaran and Yaprak (1987) compared the attitudes of respondents in two countries (the United States and Turkey) towards the people and products from three countries of origin (West Germany, Japan and Italy) using three products (cars, cameras and electronic calculators). They demonstrate that the same scale may have differing reliabilities when used by the same individual in evaluating products from differing cultures:[5]

differing levels of awareness, knowledge, familiarity and affect with the peoples, products in general, and specific brands from a chosen country-of-origin may result in differentials in the reliability of similar scales when used in multiple national markets . . . Two alternative courses of action may alleviate this problem. Measures to be used in cross-national market comparisons may be pre-tested in each of the markets of interest until they elicit similar (and high) levels of reliability . . . Alternatively, one might devise a method to develop confidence interval (akin to statistical spreads based on sample sizes) around the value of the measure based on its reliability. (Parameswaran and Yaprak, 1987, pp. 45–6.)

Therefore, comparison of results across countries should be made while simultaneously analyzing and checking for the reliability measures of the rating scales.

Perceptual equivalence

As emphasized in sections 1.4 and 9.4, perception varies across cultures. Colours are perceived differently according to a culture, that is cultures do not have equivalent sensitivity to the various parts of the colour spectrum and the corresponding languages do not qualify colours in exactly the same way. In addition, the symbolic interpretation of colour varies widely (Box 9.5). The same is true for smells: the first issue in equivalence is whether people perceive them physically and mentally in the same manner; the second issue deals with the kind of interpretation they vest in these smells. When conducting research about packaging, perfumes for washing liquids, etc., where perceptive clues are important for product evaluation, it is a key research issue to formulate questions so that interviewees can express their native views on the smell or the colours. Rather than ask them whether they like a lavender smell, it is better to ask them first to recognize the smell, then to comment on what it evokes.

Metric equivalence

If the scores given by respondents do not have the same meaning, then metric equivalence is a problem. Scores may differ across culture for a variety of reasons including the avoidance of extreme responses, humility or social desirability (Van der Vijver and Poortinga, 1982). Unfortunately, these differences can only be checked after the data is collected, limiting the validity of cross-cultural comparisons. There are several techniques available to researchers to assess metric equivalence, the most popular being multiple-group structural equation modelling (Mullen, 1995; Singh, 1995; Steenkamp and Baumgartner, 1998; Myers *et al.* 2000).[6]

The validity of a rating scale in a cross-cultural study is affected by the equivalence of the scales and by the homogeneity of meanings. For instance, Roy *et al.* (2001) discussed the problems with the use of scales in China. They emphasized the difficulty in determining lexical equivalents across languages for verbal descriptions of a scale, as the Chinese language does not readily provide good antonyms (see Table 7.3). It is also difficult to ensure that the distances between scale points, especially verbal scales, are equivalent across languages (metric equivalence). For instance, they found that Chinese managers do not understand the terms 'agree/disagree' adequately.[7] Thus, it is naive to use a differential semantic scale originally written in English, French or any other language and translate it lexically (simply with dictionary-equivalent words) into other languages. In this case decentred measurement is preferable, which means construct-ing reliable and valid scales for all the countries under survey. In this way the original wording of the scale may be changed if it provides better measurement equivalence across countries/cultures.

Sood (1990) studied the metric equivalence of nine scale terms (from 'excellent' to 'very bad') across eight languages (English, Arabic, Chinese, Farsi, French, German, Korean and Spanish). He found that: (1) some languages have fewer terms to express gradation in evaluation (e.g. Korean), whereas others have a multitude (French); and (2) there are large discrepancies in the 'value' of these adjectives, measured on a scale from 0 to 100: for instance, the Spanish '*muy malo*' rated 58 per cent higher than its supposed English equivalent of 'very bad'. Therefore the best solution is not to translate scale terms but rather to start from local wordings based on scales used by local researchers. Also we need to be wary about the meaning of numbers across cultures. For instance, the numbers 2, 8 and 9 are considered lucky in China and as such may be chosen more frequently (Roy *et al.*, 2001). Thus, it may be advisable in some cultures to only number the end points.

One promising avenue for cross-cultural research is the use of purely visual scales that avoid the verbocentric nature of most market research instruments, which are based on words and sentences that never translate perfectly. Zaltman (1997) argues in favour of 'putting people back in': most communication relies on images and is non-verbal, whereas thinking processes rely on metaphors to elicit hidden knowledge. Instruments that allow respondents to express the mix between emotions and reason may be more

Table 7.3 Adjectives which have the same level of meaning in two languages and provide similar distances between the point of the scale

Colloquial rating scale				Formal rating scale			
US adjectives			**French adjectives**	**US adjectives**			**French adjectives**
Fantastic	20	20	Extraordinaire	Remarkably good	17	17	Très bon
Delightful	17	17	Superbe	Good	14	14	Bon
Pleasant	14	14	Très correct	Neutral	10	10	Moyen
Neutral	10	10	Moyen	Reasonably poor	6	6	Faible
Moderately poor	7	7	Assez faible	Extremely poor	3	3	Très mauvais
Bad	4	4	Remarquablement faible				
Horrible	2	2	Terriblement mauvais				

(Source: Pras and Anglemar, 1978, p. 76.)

useful. For instance, the use of 'smiling faces' as scales should not be limited to children, on the basis of the (unconscious) view that adults *should* use words, not pictures, and should not express their views metaphorically. Similarly, Bergami and Bagozzi (2000) developed a visual and verbal representation of the overlap between a person's self-identity and the identity of the group to increase equivalence across cultures. More sophisticated visually oriented scales, such as the self-assessment manikin (SAM), allow cross-cultural measurement with less biases than verbal scales; they further enable a better apprehension of the respondents' emotions (Morris, 1995).

Calibration equivalence

Calibration equivalence problems arise from different *basic* units being used as well as from *compound units* when they are based on different computation systems (see Box 7.3). For instance, a typical calibration equivalence problem relates to differences in monetary units; this is especially true in high-inflation contexts where daily prices over a year cannot be directly compared with those of a low-inflation country. Naturally, exchange rates and units of weight, distance and volume cause calibration equivalence problems. Calibration equivalence mixes with perceptual equivalence: for instance, how many colour classes are recognized by people from a particular country? This might prove useful for a packaging test

or a product test. Western subjects, for example, have more colour classes than African subjects, and some primitive people have only a two-term colour language. The Bantu of South Africa, for example, do not distinguish between blue and green. Consequently they do not discriminate between objects or symbols in these colours (Douglas and Craig, 1984, p. 100).

Temporal equivalence

Temporal equivalence is similar to calibration equivalence, in terms of calibrating dates and time periods. Information, for instance, ages at different speeds across countries: in a country where the annual inflation rate is minimal, income and price data are comparable across years; whereas in a Latin American country such as Venezuela with a 30–40 per cent annual inflation rate forecast from 2002–2004 (see WS7.3), it is necessary to indicate on which day the data were collected and what the price indexes and exchange rates were at that time. Temporal equivalence also deals with differences in development levels and technological advancement: certain countries are 'equivalent' to what others were 20 years ago. Assessing time lags may be useful for making analogies: such a market may develop in South Africa now as it did in the United States 15 or 20 years ago and the product life cycle may be similar even though the two countries are at different points on the curve.

Box 7.3

Measuring fuel efficiency across cultures

Most Europeans use the metric system, an international standard. They measure distances in kilometres and liquid volumes in litres (one cubic decimetre). When looking at fuel consumption, they calculate how many litres are necessary for driving a hundred kilometres, at a particular average speed. Fuel consumption is measured in litres/100 km. In the USA, 'gas mileage' is based on a reverse concept: given a definite fuel volume, namely a gallon, how many miles can one drive with it? For Europeans trying to understand what

miles per gallon means is somewhat nightmarish. First, they have to know which gallon it is: the British or Imperial gallon (4.55 litres) or the US gallon (3.79 litres) and whether it is a statute mile (1.609 kilometres) or a nautical mile. When they understand that it is a US gallon and a statute mile, they still have to make an inverse calculation and try to finish with 100 kilometres in the denominator in order to know whether the car has high petrol consumption or poor gas mileage. Fortunately, gasoline is cheap in the United States.

7.4

Comparability of samples

When secondary data – especially published statistical data – are sought, there may be some difficulties in comparing these data across countries (see also WS7.4):

1. Differences in categories: for instance, for age brackets, income brackets or professions.
2. Difference in base years, when some countries have no recent data.
3. Unavailable or unreliable data, the data collection procedure by the local census bureau being biased for certain reasons (non-exhaustive census, inadequate sampling procedure).
4. Sampling unit (who should the respondent be?).

Choice of respondents (sampling unit equivalence)

An important criterion for sampling is the choice of respondents. Selecting a unit of analysis is a key issue in the conceptualization of comparative research design. The role of respondents in the buying decision process (organizational buying, family buying, information and influence patterns, etc.) may vary across countries. Several studies have found differing parental influence over children's purchases across countries. For instance, parents have a greater influence over their children's purchasing in Fiji (Wimalasiri, 2000), Japan (Rose, 1999) and Thailand (Viswanathan *et al.*, 2000), when compared to the United States. In the United States, it is not uncommon for children to have a strong influence when buying cereals, desserts, toys or other items, whereas in countries that are less child-oriented, children's influence on the buying decision will be much smaller (Craig and Douglas, 2001b). It is therefore crucially important to assess, first, the basic equivalent sampling units. This statement is as relevant for industrial markets as for consumer goods markets: when researching industrial products, it is important to compare the position, role and responsibility of industrial buyers throughout different countries.

Representativeness and comparability of national/cultural samples

Sampling is a basic step in most market surveys. A complete census, where the whole population of interest is researched, generally proves too costly. Therefore it is advisable to infer the characteristics of the whole population from a limited sample. In this process the following tasks must be carried out:

1. Finding a sampling frame or list, where the basic population characteristics are known (a telephone directory, an electoral list, etc.).
2. Drawing a sample from this frame, by a method which may be either probabilistic or non-probabilistic.
3. Checking that the selected sample is representative of the population under study.

The main problem in the cross-cultural sampling process is the selection of comparable samples across countries. Reaching perfect comparability is very difficult, if not impossible. These limitations should be considered when interpreting research findings.

In cross-cultural research, there are often two levels of sampling to consider. The first level is a sample of countries or cultures and the second level is based on samples of individuals within the chosen countries or cultures. At the first level, the research question is directly comparative. Hofstede (2001) clearly explains that samples of cultures should not be confused with samples of individuals. He draws attention to the risk of abusive stereotyping, whereby country characteristics are considered as individual characteristics. He compares mean values for each country, calculated from the scores on each question for the respondents from that country.

Samples of countries can be used to compute the average influence of cultural values on certain consumption patterns. For instance, what are the main cultural variables that, in combination with socio-demographic and economic variables, determine the per capita consumption of a particular product or service: motor insurance, telephones, milk powder, etc.?[8] Strategic marketing decision making often needs such research for selecting target national markets and markets with low actual demand but high growth potential, and for deciding where to locate efforts for the future.

A cross-cultural/cross-national design may also be useful when one tries to derive an estimated market demand figure in a country where statistical sources are scarce and unreliable. Amine and Cavusgil (1986) give examples of methods for estimating market potential when limited data are available. They take the case of the Moroccan demand for wallpaper. For instance, it is possible to estimate a regression equation explaining per capita annual wallpaper consumption, with explanatory variables such as income per capita, percentage of home ownership, frequency of use of other wall-covering materials, etc. To estimate the parameters it is possible to use a cross-section sample (data for a sample of countries, for the same year), or a pooled cross-section/time series sample, when the countries' data are available for several years. For a country where wallpaper consumption is unknown, it is then possible to compute it with the values of the explanatory variables.

A second issue is the representativeness of each sample in each unit of analysis, which may be a country, a culture, or a common language group which shares similar patterns of social interaction and communication (Douglas and Craig, 1997). Countries are often used as proxies for cultural units. In cross-cultural research it seems *a priori* relevant to follow a systematic procedure, the same in every country, to achieve reliability and comparability of data. Unfortunately, demographic definitions do not correspond exactly from one country to another. Age does, of course, as long as people know their birth dates, but occupation, education and socio-economic status usually do not. If data are presented in categories, say for income or age bracket, these categories will most likely not correspond exactly across countries (category equivalence). Religion and tribal membership will also have to be added to traditional demographics as they are of the utmost importance in some less developed countries (Goodyear, 1982).

A representative sample?

A researcher may construct a sample which represents the population of interest. However, a sample split into 50 per cent men and 50 per cent women conveys a different meaning in a country where women's rights are recognized from that in more traditional countries where women's status is lower. The expression 'representative sample' therefore makes little sense if one does not clarify which traits and characteristic this sample actually represents. For instance, shopping behaviour is very different worldwide: in some places men tend to do most of the shopping, in other countries it is mostly women; this also depends on various other factors (income level, type of product, etc.). In this case the samples must represent actual shoppers, rather than a representative number of men and women in the general population of potential shoppers.

In order to define a sampling procedure for cross-cultural research, a method must be selected so that each national sample is fully representative of the population of interest, and which furthermore provides comparable data across countries. Craig and Douglas (2001a) stress the limited availability of an exhaustive sampling framework which corresponds exactly to the characteristics of the population at a global (multi-country) level. This extends to the Internet. While the Internet might seem attractive to researchers due to lower costs and faster speed in data collection, Internet sampling frames are limited by the technological capabilities of the populations of interest.

In fact, sampling frames are often biased. Mytton (1996), doing audience research for the BBC worldwide, stresses the frequent lack of reliable or recent census data in many developing countries, in the former Soviet Union and in eastern Europe. A sample drawn from the electoral list in Bolivia may over-represent men, since women are not as likely to vote (Stanton *et al.*, 1982). Similarly, Tuncalp (1988) states that most sampling frames in Saudi Arabia are inadequate: there is no official census of the population, no elections and therefore no voter registration records, and telephone directories tend to be incomplete. Tuncalp suggests that non-probability sampling is a necessary evil in many countries. Often sampling frames for businesses are of better quality, since most businesses want their number on lists, such as the telephone directory, but Roy *et al.* (2001) points out that in China these directories are often out of date and lists are likely to only include the businesses or people associated with the list supplier.

Estimating sample size is also a critical step. The use of traditional statistical procedures, such as constructing confidence intervals around sample means, or hypothesis testing, is difficult to implement since such procedures require precise estimates of the variance of the population. This variance estimate is often unavailable in countries that have poor census data.[9] The most frequently used procedure is therefore the selection of sample size, country by country, taking into account their respective peculiarities.

Reynolds *et al.* (2003) developed a framework to determine which sampling approach should be used for international studies. They stress that the objective of the research should guide the technique. For instance, if the objective is to examine similarities and differences across cultures and cross-national comparability is important, non-probability samples may be a better method to allow the researcher to create homogeneous samples. Conversely, when the objective is to describe attitudes or behaviour within specific countries, within-country representativeness is important and probability samples should be used to enable the researcher to estimate the sampling error.

Taylor (1995) explains how survey firms in different countries measure public opinion and survey markets with different methods; he shows for instance that quota sampling, considered as unacceptable since the 1950s in the United States, is used in most of Europe. Similarly the use of RDD (random digit dialling) to construct phone samples, which is standard practice in the United States for telephone surveys, in order to include both unlisted people and recent movers, is not used in phone samples in many other countries.

Finally, one may conclude that representativeness and comparability of cross-cultural samples can be better achieved by using different samples and sampling techniques that produce equivalent levels of reliability, than by using the same procedure with all samples. For example, Doran (2002) used different screening criteria in North America and China to ensure that the samples were comparable. In North America the objective was to sample mainstream consumers. Here, the screening criteria included being a native English speaker, born in North America to North American parents. In China the objective was to sample respondents who had access to consumer markets. Here, the screening criteria included an education level that would allow a literate information search and an income level that would allow consumption.

The main problem (before any statistical procedure is implemented) is to secure equivalence in meaning: does it make sense to represent the same populations across various countries? Do the samples actually represent these populations in the same way?

7.5
Data-collection equivalence

Where primary data are concerned, discrepancies in response patterns across countries may cause data unreliability and so limit direct comparison. Let us assume that through any of the translation procedures described above we are able to develop equivalent national versions of a common questionnaire for a cross-cultural market research study, and that we have consistent and equivalent samples. We may still have to overcome response equivalence, such as the following:

1. Secrecy/unwillingness to answer (respondents' cooperation equivalence).
2. Response biases (data-collection context equivalence).
3. Differences in response style (response-style equivalence).

Sources of error measurement related to response styles are multiple and may directly create discrepancies between observed measurement and true measurement. Some basic precautions may help to avoid the generation of data with a great deal of measurement error (see *WS7.5*).

Reluctance to answer: Respondents' cooperation equivalence

Respondents sometimes feel that the interviewer is intruding into their privacy. They prefer not to answer, or they consciously bias their answers, fearing that their opinion could later be used against them (Stanton *et al.*, 1982). Many countries have strong privacy/intimacy patterns, where the family group is protected from external, impersonal interference. Tuncalp (1988) explains that the very private and reserved nature of Saudis is not conducive to personal interviews. Being independent, Saudis do not want to be exposed to justifying or explaining their actions when answering a barrage of questions. In the case of Afghanistan and Mozambique, Mytton (1996, p. 26) explains that:

Protocol demands that the most senior woman of the house should be interviewed before any other female . . . In some areas of Afghanistan, women cannot be used as interviewers. In others the reverse is the case; a male stranger coming to a house would be regarded as a possible threat . . . As in Afghanistan, many respondents in Mozambique did not know their own age or that of other members of the household . . . In several areas the presence of strangers writing down information on pieces of paper while talking to people, started rumours. One rumour suggested that the survey team was registering the number of children in each household with the intention to return later and kidnap them. Research had to be delayed for meetings to be held with the local authorities in order for them to reassure people living in the area.

Similarly, there are also differences in response rate from business surveys. Harzing (2000) found that response rates to industrial mail surveyed differed dramatically across 22 countries: ranging from over 40 per cent in Denmark and Norway to 7 per cent in Hong Kong and 11 per cent in the United States. This was in spite of the efforts to motivate respondents (CEOs and Human Resource managers), including a reminder mailing, letter, photograph of the researcher and a tea bag or coffee satchel with the message 'Why don't you take a short break, have a nice cup of tea and fill out the questionnaire right now, it will only take 10–15 minutes' (p. 245).

Context equivalence of data collection

Questions are never culture-free: there is inevitably a social and cultural context built into them. Contextual equivalence relates to elements in the context of the data-collection process that have an influence on responses. As Douglas and Craig explain (1984, p. 109): 'In the Scandinavian countries, for example, respondents are considerably more willing to admit overdrinking than in Latin America. In India, sex tends to be a taboo topic.' Any question that deals, directly or indirectly, with social prescription needs to be worded so that people can elaborate a response without feeling too embarrassed, and responses have to be screened in order to know if the responses reflect actual reality or a view of what is socially desirable.

Some well-disposed and open-minded interviewees may be questioned further to deliver their true view on the question.

It is possible to measure individual social desirability bias and to then use this information to adjust the results of a survey. For instance, Hult et al. (1999) used items from the Marlowe-Crowne Social Desirability Scale to assess differences in convenience samples from the United States, Japan and Sweden. They found that the US respondents showed a higher level of social desirability than the Japanese or Swedish respondents. Similarly, Keillor et al. (2001) measured social desirability, as well as the source or influencers for respondents intercepted in shopping areas in the United States, France and Malaysia. They found that Malaysian respondents had a higher level of social desirability bias than the US or French respondents. In addition, Malaysian respondents were more strongly influenced by personal sources, such as family and friends, and US respondents more strongly influence by impersonal sources such as the media and government.

Biases resulting from the relationship with the interviewer

Sexual biases between interviewer and respondent are also an important source of the reluctance to grant interviews. In many traditional countries, housewives are reluctant to grant interviews to male interviewers. Ethnic bias may also exist between the interviewer and the respondent: a Chinese person may feel uncomfortable when interviewed by a Malay (Kushner, 1982). Much response bias may result from the interviewees not understanding that the process of interviewing them is in order to generate objective data. Informants may perceive the purpose of research as a very long-winded form of selling, especially in developing countries (Goodyear, 1982). The objective and the process of the interview must often be explained at the beginning. When briefing native interviewers (management students) in Mauritania, I was asked the following question: 'What do you want us to tell the interviewee to answer?' It was necessary to explain to the interviewers that interviewing was a distanced and objective process, where interviewees had complete freedom of response. The idea of objective truth, external to personal relations, is unfamiliar to Mauritanians

(Box 7.4). Furthermore, among the Mauritanian interviewers, the *Maures*, of Arabic descent, clearly explained that they would not interview black Africans. Fortunately, there were some black Africans who were potential interviewers for their own ethnic group. Strong ingroup orientation implies that group membership has to be shared between interviewer and interviewee for the process to take place.

Maruyama (1990) explains in the same vein that Japanese managers in Indonesia tend to recruit Bataks, because their characteristics resemble those of the Japanese, although they are not necessarily liked by other Indonesians and they may perform poorly as data collectors. This ethnicity-of-interviewer bias has been shown to exist even within the United States where both Hispanic and Anglo-American respondents significantly bias their responses to items pertaining to the interviewer's culture; therefore it seems more appropriate to match respondent's and interviewer's ethnicity, especially for Anglo-Americans (Webster, 1996).

Some respondents, especially in Latin-American countries (Stanton *et al.*, 1982) tend to present a 'courtesy bias' by answering in order to please the interviewer. Respondents tend to tell the interviewer what they think the interviewer would like to hear. This response pattern probably takes place in countries where people tend to have difficulty in answering opinion surveys and market research questionnaires. When they agree to participate, it can be from a personal feeling of goodwill towards the interviewer.

Response-style equivalence

Response-style equivalence is the final step. All the rest may be equivalent; yet our respondents may offer non-equivalent responses. The three main concerns in relation to response-style equivalence are:

1. Yea-saying pattern (and, conversely, a nay-saying pattern).

Box 7.4

The weaknesses and strengths of the 'local researcher'

1. Weaknesses

(a) Often of lower intellectual ability and research experience than his or her equivalent in developed countries.

(b) Often finds it difficult to adopt neutral, objective stance with reference to informants or clients. May want to be didactic in groups and may well prefer to distort findings to reflect a more educated picture of his countrymen than exists in reality. Alternatively, may seek to distance himself from the 'average consumer' by exaggerating their foibles and lack of sophistication. He himself, especially if he is from an educated family, may be out of touch with his countrymen.

(c) He may be unwilling or unable, even for business reasons, to cross traditional barriers of class, religion or tribe.

(d) He rarely has the Puritan work ethic and does not always see the value of objective truth. Delays, shortcuts and distortion are likely.

2. Strengths

(a) He knows the country and its people. He can usually establish rapport easily and understands what is said. If he knows the Western country he can also interpret the significance of what is said, to explain differences.

(b) He knows the language. Language can be an enormous barrier, as anyone who has tried to interview through interpreters must recognise.

(c) He is immune to local ailments and is physically comfortable in the (research) environment. He can cope, through familiarity, with common problems.

(Source: Goodyear, 1982, pp. 90–1.)

2. Extreme response style/response range.
3. Non-contingent responding (careless, random or non-purposeful).
4. Item non-response pattern.

Baumgartner and Steenkamp (2001) analyzed mail survey data from 11 European countries to assess the amount of response-style bias in five-point (strongly disagree to strongly agree) Likert scales. Generally, they found that all of the above forms of response-style responding influenced some of the scales, but that there was no evidence of more severe response-styles in some countries than others. Specifically, the scales with the most contamination measured health consciousness, consumer ethnocentrism, quality consciousness and environmental consciousness.

First, 'yea-saying' or acquiescence is the tendency to agree with items and nay-saying or disacquiescence is the tendency to disagree with items regardless of content (Baumgartner and Steenkamp 2001). For acquiescence the response scores tend to be inflated with the mean score of the respondents being biased towards the positive end of the scale, and for disacquiescence the reverse occurs. Van Herk and Verhallen (1995) found this bias when interviewing Greek and Italian housewives on their cooking behaviour: there is systematic tendency in the Greek sample to give more positive answers in psychographics as well as in product-related questions, than in the Italian sample. The yea-saying bias translates into a higher mean score on almost all questions.

Standardizing scores across cultures allows the 'yea-saying' pattern to be eliminated, although it is fairly difficult to differentiate whether people were generally striving to give answers towards the positive end of the scale or were agreeing strongly with a particular item. Thus the 'yea-saying' pattern is diagnosed only when it is consistent across almost all the questions. Baumgartner and Steenkamp (2001) suggest balancing the items so that some are positively worded and others are negatively worded, but Wong et al. (2003) caution that this approach may affect other aspects of equivalence across countries as East Asians do not see positively and negatively worded items as opposites.

Second, extreme response style is the tendency to choose the most extreme response regardless of content, while response range is the tendency to either use a narrow or wide range of categories around the mean (Baumgartner and Steenkamp, 2001). This response pattern is systematically marked by a higher or lower standard deviation. For instance, in the United States people tend to respond with more enthusiasm, and therefore present a more extreme response style in answering, than the Japanese (Zax and Takashi, 1967) or Koreans (Chun et al., 1974). This could produce a bias in the standard deviation of data, increasing it artificially in cultures where people tend to overreact to questions, compared to other cultures where people may tend to suppress their opinions, either positive or negative. Clarke (2000) studied responses given to scales ranging in format (3- to 10-point) from university students in Australia, France, Singapore and the United States. He found that the amount of extreme response differed by country, with France exhibiting the highest level, followed by the United States, followed by Australia and Singapore. The scales with the least extreme response style were 5- to 7-point response formats (Clarke, 2000, 2001).

Third, non-contingent responding is the tendency to respond carelessly, randomly or non-purposefully (Baumgartner and Steenkamp, 2001). This may happen if respondents are not very motivated to answer the questionnaire.

Fourth, item non-response is an important source of bias in cross-national surveys. Respondents may be unwilling to respond to some questions, such as those relating to income or age. Douglas and Shoemaker (1981), studying non-response to different items in a public opinion survey in eight European countries, found evidence of non-response in relation to income being higher in the United Kingdom and Ireland, whereas the willingness to respond to political questions was highest in Germany and Italy.

Encouraging feedback from the informant on cultural adequacy

As Maruyama (1990) emphasized, humans are not simple response machines. Maruyama cites 'criticality dissonance', where respondents disguise and transform responses because they fear that information may be misused. As shown above, international market research is full of criticality dissonance. The basic process affecting the truthfulness of responses is 'relevance dissonance': 'the purpose of the questionnaire survey as perceived by the respondent differs from the respondent's own purpose. The questionnaire is perceived as irrelevant and useless. In such a case counterexploitation takes place. The respondent looks for a way to manipulate the survey or interview to produce some benefit' (1990, p. 30).

For these reasons, it seems necessary to design research procedures where feedback from the informant is possible: for instance, focus groups, in-depth interviews and open-ended questions. Unique features of cultural behaviour cause non-equivalence. It is impossible to uncover these levels of non-equivalence if the instrument and methodology prevent them from appearing. A pragmatic solution is to ask interviewees their opinion of the relevance of questions, words and concepts used in the questionnaire at the end of the normal interview process (post-test). A pre-test of questionnaires is also necessary. As an example, Doran (2002) used multiple methods to elicit feedback from respondents, including a preliminary study using in-depth interviews, focus groups to identify the appropriate product categories and help define the interview, and, after the main study, follow-up interviews to clarify unclear issues and investigate new issues.

A questionnaire forced upon interviewees does not elicit information (see the hair shampoo exercise in section A7.2). If emic feedback is to be introduced, both interviewers (especially when they have not been personally involved in compiling the questionnaire) and interviewees must be put in a situation where they may comment on the questions themselves and explain what is culturally meaningful in their own context and what is not. Interviewees should be given the opportunity after the normal answering process to elaborate freely on what they think of the questions, the situations described, and so on. This orientation is slightly different from the traditional one where interviewed people are simply required to answer, not to 'criticize' the questions. Emic feedback allows an improvement in the adequacy of the source culture's constructs and instruments.[10]

Informants should be neither overestimated nor underestimated. They cannot respond to a barrage of questions alien to their knowledge and frame of reference. Therefore the content of the research must somehow be strictly controlled and must focus on really significant issues; surveys should be parsimonious and should not ask too much from informants. On the other hand, informants need to be carefully

listened to because it is they who, as insiders, have the relevant pieces of information. The same care has to be taken with interviewers: they must be properly controlled (some – not all – may cheat by guessing responses or even filling in questionnaires themselves), and adequately briefed (professional interviewers may not be found everywhere – see Box 7.4).

7.6

Researching internationally

For various reasons, apart from the equivalence issues reviewed previously, international research is different from domestic research: (1) it is more difficult and more costly to implement, and the stakes are often smaller than those in the domestic market; and (2) information often needs to be fed more directly into action, thus a 'hands-on' approach is to be recommended. (See WS7.6 for information on market research companies worldwide.)

The Japanese style of market research

Johansson and Nonaka (1987) show that Japanese firms use market survey techniques that are quite distinct from those used by US companies. Japanese do survey markets, but decide what to do afterwards fairly independently of the survey conclusions. For example, research was presented to Akio Morita, founder and president of the Sony Corporation, which suggested that the Walkman would not be bought by consumers: they would not buy a tape player that does not record, even a portable one. Trusting his intuition, though undoubtedly after fairly wide consultation, Akio Morita and Sony took the decision to launch the Walkman, with the success we all know. It is likely that an American boss would not have taken such a decision.

In fact Japanese firms take a direct interest in the realities of the market-place and outlets. They look for information from the actual *buyers* (not the potential consumers), who are interviewed about the products they want, and how the products themselves could be better tailored to consumers' needs. Johansson and Nonaka cite the example of the chief executive officer of Canon USA. He spent six weeks visiting Canon distribution networks, chatting to sales executives, customers and store managers, in order to find out why Canon cameras were not selling as well as the competition.

This attitude is quite different from the prescriptions of traditional market research, which are as follows:

1. Market research has to be representative; therefore a representative sample must be used.
2. Market research must be scientifically objective. A questionnaire (that is, a systematic but not necessarily *open-ended* information retrieval instrument) should be administered by non-participating researchers (they should not be personally involved in the consequences of the responses given by interviewees).
3. Research has to study the *potential* market, not the *actual* market (that is, real buyers and real users).
4. As far as possible, the people who undertake market research should not be the same people who ultimately decide on the marketing strategy to be adopted. There is a potential danger that the boss of Canon USA could be manipulated by customers and distributors, who might take the opportunity to demand lower prices or other benefits by overstating competitors' strengths. There is also the risk that by focusing on the actual market, as yet untargeted market segments could be ignored or neglected.

As Johansson and Nonaka emphasize (1987, p. 16):

Japanese-style market research relies heavily on two kinds of information: 'soft data' obtained from visits to dealers and other channel members, and 'hard data' about shipments, inventory levels, and retail sales. Japanese managers believe that these data better reflect the behaviour and intentions of flesh-and-blood consumers. Japanese companies want information that is context specific rather than context free – that is, data directly relevant to consumer attitudes about the product, or to the way buyers have used or will use specific products, rather than research results that are too remote from the actual consumer to be useful.[11]

Market research as images of reality: Atomistic versus organic views

In fact, market surveys are, at best, 'photographs' of the market; they are not the market itself. At the Los Angeles County Museum of Art there is a painting by the Belgian Painter René Magritte, called 'La pipe'. It simply shows a pipe, with a thin trail of smoke coming out of it. That is (almost) all. Then: there is a short subtitle at the bottom of the painting, saying *ceci n'est pas une pipe* ('*this is not a pipe*'): a very 'down to earth' way of reminding us that *images of reality* should not be confused with reality itself. We may create images of reality, especially through the media (for instance, a war reported on a TV screen) but we may also ignore large chunks of reality (especially its experiential elements).

On the other hand, we should not underestimate the power of the process of designing images of reality, especially for decision-making purposes. Scientific market research provides marketing decision-makers with an image of the actual and/or potential market, consumer behaviour and the competition. Large parts of reality are beyond our limited perceptual apparatus. Let us take another example: at the Mount Wilson observatory in California, there are photographs of the stars taken using a special quality of film, with a shutter exposure of four hours. The stars in the sky are far more numerous than we will ever see with our limited vision. The same holds true for market research: from panels or, more generally, from a large and representative sample of consumers, we may derive images of the market that we will never match simply by talking with anyone who is around.

Our argument is that, across countries, marketing decision-makers do not use exactly the same information for a similar decision process, and that, to a certain extent, culture influences the scope and nature of researched information, and the use of the results in the process of marketing decision making. Two basic approaches to reality may be contrasted, as ideal types, the atomistic and the organic approaches (Table 7.4), which we all share, across individuals and cultures. In terms of research traditions, the atomistic view is close to distanced positivistic research, the organic view is nearer to humanistic enquiry (Hirschmann, 1986) and action research.[12]

In the atomistic view we consider ourselves as being outside the real world, as observers, able to depict with a certain degree of precision workable images of the real world (atomistic), and then to use them to interact with this external world. The atomistic approach leads us to consider reality as fundamentally divisible into units that display enough independence that, operationally, we can ignore the interrelations between pieces of it.

Table 7.4 Atomistic versus organic approaches

Approach to reality	Atomistic	Organic
Nature of reality	Divisibility/independence	Global/indivisible/dependent
Time	Linear/divisible	Cyclical/integrative
Communication style	Explicit/low context	Implicit/high context
Interpersonal relations	Individualist/reciprocal	Collectivist/loyal
Intellectual style	Data/measurement oriented	Intellectual modesty
Proof	Validated theory (truth)	Virtue/conviction
Space	Universalist	Localist
Decision making	Formalized	Weakly structured

Conversely, one may emphasize that we are an integral part of this reality, to which we belong so inextricably that it is not really possible to separate oneself from the reality. We are so deeply immersed in it that it would make no sense. The organic approach assumes the indivisible nature of reality, its elements (if there are any) being fundamentally interdependent. Reality is global, rather than piecemeal.

These two approaches are complementary, rather than antagonistic. However, one approach can be dominant among a group of people or a culture, or in an individual or an area of knowledge (Usunier, 1997).[13] Table 7.4, which builds on Tables 2.1 to 3.5, illustrates how these approaches are linked to major categories of cultural differences, although the difference between atomism and organism is not a cultural difference.

The atomistic belief in *divisibility* favours the view that time is divisible, that the basic unit of interpersonal relations is the individual, and that communication can and must be explicit (that is, clearly separated, 'divided' from surrounding issues, topics and preoccupations). Separating emotions from actions, friendship from business, is typically an atomistic attitude towards reality, seen as divisible. Very naturally, the atomistic approach favours the perception that data orientation and measurement are the proof that a piece of reality is divisible and (therefore) exists. To illustrate the importance of measurement in the atomistic approach, let us take the case of a company that is trying to improve service *within* the company, so that it is not only front-line service providers who are concerned with service to customers. In addressing such an issue, a typical atomistic statement would be: 'To arrive at a position where excellent service is achieved will be a difficult

enterprise. This primarily results from the lack of service measurement knowledge *within* the company.' In fact, scales exist only to measure service quality *vis-à-vis* customers, so that the atomistic solution is to try and develop a measurement instrument, because the reality of within-company service cannot be tackled in the absence of measurement instruments. The organic approach holds the contrary assumption: it is precisely because measurement is difficult that the two issues are considered as non-separate and to be treated as a joint piece of reality. The research approach will be quite different.

On the other hand, a dominance of the organic approach favours collectivism in its strongest sense: people do not consider themselves as being separate from the group to which they belong. Their sense of belonging includes the implicit view that they are not really separable from their group. The communication style is more implicit and contextual, because the sense of the interdependence of pieces of reality is much stronger. In interpersonal relationships, loyalty is characteristic of the organic approach, whereas reciprocity, based on tabulated favours (time, amount and persons being clearly defined), is linked to the atomistic approach. To this list can be added that proof (in the sense of making it work; be accepted and be considered as a necessary piece of reality) is based on validated theory, for the atomistic approach, and on arguments favouring conviction and virtue, for the organic approach.

With divisible reality, linear time and individual emphasis, the atomistic approach conceives of decision making as a highly formalized process, followed by implementation, control and feedback. It is a time sequence such as we see in many managerial textbooks. Conversely, the organic approach emphasizes circularity in time and the integration of time horizons. Preparing, making decisions and implementing them are not easily seen as completely separated pieces of time reality, leading to a fairly unstructured decision-making process. Finally, the organic approach does favour 'localism', local solutions, because solutions are built within a context and there is a difficulty in conceiving universal solutions. Conversely, the data and theory orientation in the atomistic approach favours universalism, because reality, when reduced to figures, shows a fairly high degree of universality.[14]

The case of research on international markets: Doing research with limited data availability and limited resources

International business and marketing requires a greater focus on the external environmental, since this differs more across countries, than within countries. For instance, Ya-Fei (2000) discusses the need for research into government in China. Specifically, her firm has divided their research into vertical and horizontal studies. First, vertical market studies research the governing structures relating to the client's business including government policies, organization, and influences. For instance, an international chemical firm commissioned them to interview government officials to obtain their position on a new regulation, 'China's Environmental Regulations for Chemical Products Imports and Exports', that was threatening their business operations, so that they could develop a strategy to lobby for adoption of internationally accepted practices. Second, horizontal market surveys are more industry-specific, such as studying market opportunities, the competitive environment and consumer preferences, etc. Similarly, Tan and Lui (2002, p. 803) discuss trends in international marketing research in Asia, pointing out that:

there is also a growing realization that it is not enough to monitor shifts in brand perceptions or market share. It is, in fact, far more important to possess a holistic understanding of the total operating environment (including political and economic issues) and have better appreciation of the competitors' plans and activities. This understanding results in the clients' increasing dissatisfaction with traditional marketing research as being too narrowly focused on marketing issues: research techniques and an overriding concern with data rather than analysed information . . .

Market research should therefore not just be conducted in response to one apparent market threat or opportunity, but rather on an ongoing basis in order to achieve a sustainable advantage.

As explained in the sections above, when research is conducted internationally, the basic conditions of market research are different from those prevailing in the domestic market. For instance, Wood and Robertson (2000) found that export managers in the United States most highly value information that provides market potential, followed by legal, political, infrastructure, economics and, finally, culture: they first have to establish that the country has the necessary demand, is open, will remain open, is conducive to entry, and is evolving, and then they can seek the cultural information that will improve the success. Market experience, market share and availability of people and resources are generally much higher in the domestic environment than in international markets (Grønhaug and Graham, 1987).

Cavusgil and Godiwalla (1982) stress the high level of uncertainty in international markets and the limited availability of objective information, both in quantity and in quality. This may explain why international marketing decisions are dominated by the influence of subjective and perceptual factors. In fact, the same information can be used in different ways. For instance, Daimantopoulos and Souchon (1999) found that information was used either for 'instrumental and conceptual' use or for 'symbolic' use. The first category is the direct application of the research to a specific problem (instrumental use) or for general enlightenment or future use (conceptual use). The second category is really a misuse of information (symbolic use), such as using it out of context, selectively disclosing information that confirms a previously held conviction or ignoring facts. Daimantopoulos *et al.* (2003) surveyed exporting companies from Austria, Germany, New Zealand, the United Kingdom and the United States, finding that information (relating to export marketing research, export assistance and export marketing intelligence) was more likely to be used instrumentally/conceptually than symbolically, although there were differences across countries. For instance, US exporters were more likely to use information symbolically than the other countries; conversely, Austrian exporters were less likely to use information symbolically than the other countries.

Instrumental or conceptual use of information is more likely to increase market knowledge and performance, than symbolic use (Toften and Olsen, 2003).

The less sophisticated nature of international marketing research is also evidenced by Cavusgil (1984). Officials of 70 companies from Wisconsin and Illinois, involved in international business, were interviewed. Mostly simple survey techniques were used: foreign market research is generally informal, with no standard procedures. Furthermore, the frequency of identifying and analyzing foreign markets is much less than once a year. Sophistication increases with the higher degree of involvement in foreign markets, as measured by the percentage of export profits to total company profits. A study by Koh (1991) confirms these findings: a large proportion of US exporters, approximately two-thirds of the companies surveyed, do not adopt a formalized marketing plan. But when they do, they tend to focus on issues similar to those researched domestically and to neglect 'strategic issues relating to risks appraisal, environmental issues, cultural considerations . . . which require close contact with the foreign environment' (Koh, 1991, p. 17).

The acceptance of intuition in the decision-making process is a key element of those differences. Should we continue with very in-depth research, if the final decision is taken by somebody who may or may not follow the conclusions of the research? Should the researcher and the decision-maker be different people or the same? These questions are raised by the cross-cultural comparison of marketing research practices.

Research on the Internet

The Internet offers many opportunities to access both secondary and primary research. First, for secondary research the Internet makes it easy to locate preliminary information about a region or country of interest, including the macro environmental factors, such as political, legal, geographical, economical and cultural information, as well as the micro environmental factors, such as market size, distribution systems, presence of local and global competition and consumer information. Kumar (2000) provides examples of information search on competitive intelligence analysis, industry analysis, buyer behaviour and new

business-to-business markets, which can help in the initial stages of market consideration. Access to secondary information over the Internet is fast, easy and low cost, but it is also difficult to compare and validate the data and the authenticity of sources of information.

Second, for primary research the Internet offers the ability to conduct traditional surveys via e-mail, online surveys and focus groups. It also allows tracking exposure to websites, product, advertising, company information and patterns of use, such as information search patterns. The Internet's capacity for interactivity also means that it is easy to communicate directly with customers and respondents through chat rooms and bulletin boards (Tan and Lui, 2002). Access to primary information over the Internet is relatively easy and cheap, but it is usually limited to Internet/e-mail users. This may be especially problematic in countries where there is low Internet access (Craig and Douglas, 2001a).

7.7

Conclusion

It is dangerous to prepare an international market survey by simply transposing domestic research. The nature and scope of researched market information, the ways of collecting it, the accuracy of the data as well as the criteria of reliability of the data present cross-cultural variance. This holds true even when these factors are perceived as normatively quite universal. International market researchers have to reveal their own ethnocentric biases, by giving feedback opportunities to their informants or to local collaborators. From this point on, a systematic search for formal equivalence may appear dangerous. Equivalence of constructs and instruments has to be established first. As Craig and Douglas (2001a, p. 85) put it, international marketing researchers 'are being challenged to conduct research that is of the highest possible quality, as quickly as possible, in multiple diverse settings'.

The final recommendation is to search for the meaning, bearing in mind this advice:

1. Scientific methods provide pictures which otherwise would not be available (the 'Mount Wilson' argument).

2. But images of reality are not reality itself (the '*la pipe*' argument).
3. Address the relevant questions (only those that can be articulated into decision and action).
4. Respect your informants and consider their competence as insiders as superior to yours as an outsider; but interview only those people who have something to say.
5. Keep a 'hands-on' approach to market research.
6. Culture must be examined at each step of the research process: questions, survey methods, interviews and questionnaires, informants.

Questions

1. Define the following terms:
(a) conceptual equivalence;
(b) temporal equivalence;
(c) sexual bias.

2. Discuss the functional equivalence of the following products or consumption experiences. For this, choose countries/culture with which you have familiarity and experience and think in terms of benefits and those that are particularly emphasized in certain cultures:
(a) a bicycle;
(b) drinking a beer;
(c) red wine;
(d) a watch.

3. What are the obstacles for a sample of consumers to be cross-culturally representative?

4. Discuss how market size can be estimated in a country where there is little or poor statistical data available.

5. List possible benefits for a washing powder or liquid and suggest possible cross-cultural variability in the dominance of certain benefits as compared with others.

6. Suggest ways of obtaining relevant market and consumer behaviour information where potential informants are not accustomed to questionnaires and interviews.

7. How does the individualism/collectivism difference have an impact on the drafting of market research questionnaires?

8. Which constraints does strong ingroup orientation put on the data-collection process?

Notes

1. See for this Weiss (1996) who compares European coffee experiences to that of the Haya community in Tanzania, a coffee-producing country. He explores the meaning of coffee for Haya people who produce it and consume it in ways that remain largely distinct from the meanings attributed to coffee in the global economy.
2. The issue of cross-cultural equivalence was initially developed in psychology (see Frijda and Jahoda, 1966; Poortinga, 1989) and was later borrowed by international market research (see Van Herk, 2000).

3. Wind and Douglas (1982) propose a hybrid approach, which they define in the following way: 'The proposed approach develops country, culture or sub-culture specific concepts and measures. These are compared, combined or modified, and wherever possible common "pan-cultural" concepts, which do not have a specific cultural bias, and which reflect the idiosyncratic characteristics of each country, culture or sub-culture are identified. Country-specific measures of the "pan-cultural" and country idiosyncratic concepts are developed and compared. To the extent

possible they are combined and country-specific measures are administered, generating the secondary data for the comparison.'

4. Green *et al.* (1988) give the following definitions of validity and reliability of measurement: 'By validity the behavioural scientist means that the data must be unbiased and relevant to the characteristic being measured . . .'. By reliability 'the behavioural scientist means the extent to which scaling results are free from experimental error' (pp. 249 and 253). Validity is then broken down into content, criterion and construct validation: see Green *et al.* (1988, ch. 7, 'Measurement in marketing research', pp. 240–79).

5. The cars reviewed are the Volkswagen Golf (VW Rabbit, West Germany), the Honda Civic (Japan) and the Fiat 128 (Italy). Cameras considered are Leica (West Germany), Canon (Japan) and Ferrania (Italy). The brands of electronic calculator used are Royal (West Germany), Canon (Japan) and Olivetti (Italy).

6. Myers *et al.* (2000) suggest an extension of Mullen (1995) and Steenkamp and Baumgartner's (1998) methods to test whether there is bias in the overall cross-cultural measurement model at an item-specific level. Their method assesses whether the constructs are composed and interpreted in the same way through a series of constrained and unconstrained models. Specifically this method can assess which constructs work as well as which individual items may be problematic across cultures.

7. Similar problems have been found in Japanese (Johnson *et al.*, 1993) and French (Pras and Angelmar, 1978).

8. For instance, de Mooij and Hofstede (2002) compared 26 developed countries, finding that national wealth explained most of the variance in country-level adoption of faxes, mobile phones, cable television, personal computers and the Internet. But they also found that uncertainty avoidance is related to ownership of personal computers and mobile phones.

9. Sentell and Philpot (1984) propose a method for evaluating the representativeness of samples taken from imperfectly known parent populations. Their method is based on the comparison of proportions estimated from two independent samples, focusing on situations where the larger sample size is unknown. Their method is implemented by testing two sets of sample statistics of Thai households.

10. Badhuri *et al.* (1993) provide a quite interesting and lively review of how local market research agencies can co-operate, in the conduct of qualitative research, with client companies who undertake research from the United States in several European countries, coordination being done by a European research company. They distinguish six approaches ('the hands-on approach', 'client as expert', 'we know best', 'the democratic approach', 'the colonial approach' and 'cheap and cheerful approach') and show to what extent the client's ethnocentric views and the worldviews of the local informants find their expression in the research process undertaken in each approach.

11. Naumann *et al.* (1994) provide somewhat contrary evidence to that of Johansson and Nonaka (1987) when they compare the practices of US and Japanese market research firms. Based on mail surveys sent to research firms in both countries, they show that in most areas Japanese and American market research practices seem to be similar. Research firms in both countries survey similar research issues, with the exception of competitor analysis and distribution where Japanese research is more intense. There appears to be no difference in the use of quantitative versus qualitative research between the two countries. However, information is based on self-reports by respondents, who may be concerned with the image of professionalism; this may bias Japanese answers towards the positive response style, which could explain why there systematically appears to be a higher percentage of Japanese firms than US firms using any type of quantitative data analysis techniques. Johansson and Nonaka's views are based on insiders' views and backed by ch. 3 in their recent book, *Relentless: The Japanese Way of Marketing* (Johansson and Nonaka, 1996).

12. For a clarification of these terms see Easterby-Smith *et al.* (1993).

13. The distinction we make here is typical and can cross the borders of the two national groups that we use, with some exaggeration and some simplification, as archetypes. Let us quote a keynote address, given by the chairman of Heineken, at an ESOMAR (European Society for Opinion and Marketing Research) meeting: 'Decision making itself is about making choices, about taking risks, about looking ahead . . . Research is about describing, about facts, about analysing . . . I believe that the rational paradigm of collecting data, analysing them and acting upon them is not sufficient for the issues decision makers are confronted with . . . I am trying to make an argument for a more responsible use of research. A less absolute and more relative approach to its findings, one that leaves room for the more undefined factor in decision making. That of personal insight, judgement and intuition. And I think we should give a somewhat higher priority to this factor.' (Vuursten, 1996, p. 44.)

14. It is tempting to say that a typical atomistic culture is the United States and that Japan is a typical organistic culture. This is possible, but only as a modal characteristic, since the organistic approach also exists in the United States.

15. Language of translation is optional. Instructors will decide this according to their teaching objectives and to the language competencies of students. Cultural and linguistic contexts may be varied *ad libitum*, in relation to the participants themselves (nationalities, language skills, personal experiences in various countries, etc.). The participants are one of the main resources as far as cultural and language expertise is concerned. Students may also try to obtain information on foreign cultural contexts either by using secondary data, or by interviewing members of a particular group.

References

Amine, Lyn S. and S. Tamer Cavusgil (1986), 'Demand estimation in a developing country environment: difficulties, and examples', *Journal of the Market Research Society*, vol. 28, no. 5, pp. 43–65.

Askegaard, Søren and Karen Brunsø (1999), 'Food-related lifestyles in Singapore: preliminary testing of a Western research instrument in Southeast Asia,' *Journal of Euromarketing*, vol. 7, no. 4, pp. 65–86.

Badhuri, Monika, Marianne de Souza and Tim Sweeney (1993), 'International qualitative research: a critical review of different approaches', *Marketing and Research Today*, vol. 21, no. 3, pp. 171–8.

Baumgartner, Hans and Jan-Bendict E.M. Steenkamp (2001), 'Response styles in marketing research: a cross-national investigation', *Journal of Marketing Research*, vol. 38, no. 2, pp. 143–56.

Bensaou, M., Michael Coyne and N. Venkatraman (1999), 'Testing metric equivalence in cross-national strategy research: an empirical test across the United States and Japan', *Strategic Management Journal*, vol. 20, no. 7, pp. 671–89.

Bergami, Massimo and Richard P. Bagozzi (2000), 'Self-categorization, affective commitment, and group self-esteem as distinct aspects of social identity in the organization', *British Journal of Social Psychology*, vol. 39, pp. 555–77.

Bohnet, Michael (1994), 'Was wurde in Kairo wirklich beschlossen', *Eine Welt* (BMZ, Bonn), October.

Campbell, D.T. and O. Werner (1970), 'Translating, working through interpreters and the problem of decentering', in R. Naroll and R. Cohen (eds), *A Handbook of Method in Cultural Anthropology*, The Natural History Press: New York, pp. 398–420.

Cavusgil, S. Tamer and Yezdi M. Godiwalla (1982), 'Decision-making for international marketing: a comparative review', *Management Decision*, vol. 20, no. 4, pp. 47–54.

Cavusgil, S. Tamer (1984), 'International marketing research: insights into company practices', in *Research in Marketing*, vol. 7, JAI Press: Greenwich, CT, pp. 261–88.

Cavusgil, S. Tamer and Ajay Das (1997), 'Methodological issues in empirical cross-cultural research: a survey of the management literature and a framework', *Management International Review*, vol. 37, no. 1, pp. 71–96.

Chen, Haipeng Allen, Sharon Ng and Akshay R. Rao (2003), 'Cultural differences in consumer impatience', *Marketing Science Institute*, no. 03–122.

Chun, K.T., J.B. Campbell and J. Hao (1974), 'Extreme response style in cross-cultural research: a reminder', *Journal of Cross-Cultural Psychology*, vol. 5, pp. 464–80.

Clarke, Irvine III (2000), 'Global marketing research: is extreme response style influencing your results?', *Journal of International Consumer Marketing*, vol. 12, no. 4, p. 2000.

Clarke, Irvine III (2001), 'Extreme response style in cross-cultural research', *International Marketing Review*, vol. 18, no. 3, pp. 301–24.

Craig, C. Samuel and Susan P. Douglas (2001a), 'Conducting international marketing research in the twenty-first century', *International Marketing Review*, vol. 18, no. 1, pp. 80–90.

Craig, C. Samuel and Susan P. Douglas (2001b), *International Marketing Research*, Wiley: Chichester.

Davis, H.L., S.P. Douglas and A.J. Silk (1981), 'Measure unreliability: a hidden threat to cross-national research?', *American Marketing Association Attitude Research Conference*, March, Carlsbad, CA, pp. 1–40.

de Mooij, Marieke and Geert Hofstede (2002), 'Convergence and divergence in consumer behavior: implications for international retailing', *Journal of Retailing*, vol. 78, no. 1, pp. 61–9.

Deutscher, I. (1973), 'Asking questions cross culturally: some problems of linguistic comparability', in Donald P. Warwick and Samuel Osherson (eds), *Comparative Research Methods*, Prentice Hall: Englewood Cliffs, NJ, pp. 163–86.

Diamantopoulos, Adamantios and Anne L. Souchon (1999), 'Measuring export information use: scale development and validation', *Journal of Business Research*, vol. 46, September, pp. 1–15.

Diamantopoulos, Adamantios, Anne L. Souchon, Geoffrey R. Durden, Catherine N. Axinn and Hartmut H. Holzmuller (2003), 'Towards an understanding of cross-national similarities and differences in export information utilization: a perceptual mapping approach', *International Marketing Review*, vol. 20, no. 1, pp. 17–43.

Doran, Kathleen Brewer (2002), 'Lessons learned from cross-cultural research of Chinese and North American consumers', *Journal of Business Research*, vol. 55, no. 10, pp. 823–9.

Douglas, Susan P. and C. Samuel Craig (1984), 'Establishing equivalence in comparative consumer research', in Erdener Kaynak and Ronald Savitt (eds), *Comparative Marketing Systems*, Praeger: New York, pp. 93–113.

Douglas, Susan P. and C. Samuel Craig (1997), 'The changing nature of consumer behavior: implications for cross-cultural research', *International Journal of Research in Marketing*, vol. 14, no. 4, pp. 379–95.

Douglas, Susan P. and Robert Shoemaker (1981), 'Item non-response in cross-national surveys', *European Research*, vol. 9, July, pp. 124–32.

Durgee, Jeffrey F., Gina Colarelli O'Connor and Robert W. Veryzer (1996), 'Translating values into product wants',

Journal of Advertising Research, vol. 36, no. 6, pp. 90–100.

Durvasula, Srinivas., J. Craig Andrews, Steven Lysonski and Richard G. Netemeyer (1993), 'Assessing the cross-national applicability of consumer behaviour models: a model of attitude towards advertising in general', *Journal of Consumer Research*, vol. 19, no. 4, pp. 626–36.

Easterby-Smith, Mark, Richard Thorpe and Andy Lowe (1993), *Management Research: An introduction*, Sage: London.

Erevelles, S., A. Roy and L.S.C. Yip (1998), 'Prices and warranties as signals of quality: an investigation of Chinese consumers', Working paper, University of California-Riverside.

Frijda, N. and G. Jahoda (1966), 'On the scope and methods of cross-cultural research', *International Journal of Psychology*, vol. 1, no. 2, pp. 109–27.

Geertz, Clifford (1983), *Local Knowledge*, Basic Books: New York.

Goodyear, Mary (1982), 'Qualitative research in developing countries', *Journal of the Market Research Society*, vol. 24, no. 2, pp. 86–96.

Green, Paul E., Donald S. Tull and Gerald Albaum (1988), *Research for Marketing Decisions*, 5th edn, Prentice Hall: Englewood Cliffs, NJ.

Green, Robert T. and Eric Langeard (1979), 'Comments and recommendations on the practice of cross-cultural marketing research', paper presented at the International Marketing Workshop, *E.I.A.S.M.*, Brussels, November, pp. 1–16.

Grønhaug, Kjell and John L. Graham (1987), 'International market research revisited', in S. Tamer Cavusgil (ed.), *Advances in International Marketing*, JAI Press: Greenwich, CT, pp. 121–37.

Grunert, Suzanne C., Klaus G. Grunert and Kai Kristensen (1993), 'Une méthode d'estimation de la validité interculturelle des instruments de mesure: le cas de la mesure des valeurs des consommateurs par la liste des valeurs LOV', *Recherche et Applications en Marketing*, vol. 8, no. 4, pp. 5–28.

Harzing, Anne-Wil (2000), 'Cross-national industrial mail surveys: why do response rates differ between countries?', *Industrial Marketing Management*, vol. 29, pp. 243–54.

Hirschmann, Elisabeth (1986), 'Humanistic inquiry in marketing research: philosophy, method and criteria', *Journal of Marketing Research*, vol. 13, August, pp. 237–49.

Hofstede, Geert (2001), *Culture Consequences*, 2nd edn, Sage Publications: Thousand Oaks, CA.

Hult, G. Tomas, M., Bruce D. Keillor and Barbara A. Lafferty (1999), 'A cross-national assessment of social desirability bias and consumer ethnocentrism', *Journal of Global Marketing*, vol. 12, no. 4, pp. 29–43.

Johansson, Johny K. and Ikujiro Nonaka (1987), 'Market research the Japanese way', *Harvard Business Review*, May–June, pp. 16–22.

Johansson, Johny K. and Ikujiro Nonaka (1996), *Relentless: The Japanese Way of Marketing*, HarperCollins: New York.

Johnson, J.L., T. Sakano, J.A. Cote and N. Onzo (1993), 'The exercise of interfirm power and its repercussions in US–Japanese channel relationships', *Journal of Marketing*, vol. 57, April, pp. 1–10.

Keillor, Bruce D., Deborah Owens and Charles Pettijohn (2001), A cross-cultural/cross-national study of influencing factors and socially desirable biases', *International Journal of Market Research*, vol. 43, no. 1, pp. 63–84.

Koh, Anthony C. (1991), 'An evaluation of international marketing research planning in United States export firms', *Journal of Global Marketing*, vol. 4, no. 3, pp. 7–25.

Kumar, V. (2000), *International Marketing Research*, Upper Saddle river, NJ: Prentice Hall.

Kushner, J.M. (1982), 'Market research in a non-Western context: the Asian example', *Journal of the Market Research Society*, vol. 24, no. 2, pp. 116–22.

Leung, K. (1989), 'Cross-cultural differences: individual level vs culture-level analysis', *International Journal of Psychology*, vol. 24, pp. 703–19.

Marchetti, Renato and Jean-Claude Usunier (1990), 'Les problèmes de l'étude de marché dans un contexte interculturel', *Revue Française du Marketing*, no. 130, 1990/5, pp. 167–84.

Maruyama, Magoroh (1990), 'International meta-marketing: strategic judo, foreign user habits and interactive invention', *Human Systems Management*, vol. 9, pp. 29–42.

Mayer, Charles S. (1978), 'Multinational marketing research: the magnifying glass of methodological problems', *European Research*, March, pp. 77–84.

Morris, Jon D. (1995), 'SAM: The self-assessment manikin, an efficient cross-cultural measurement of emotional response', *Journal of Advertising Research*, vol. 35, no. 6, pp. 63–8.

Mullen, Michael R. (1995), 'Diagnosing measurement equivalence in cross-national research', vol. 26, no. 3, pp. 573–96.

Myers, Matthew B., Roger J. Calantone, Thomas J. Page Jr. and Charles R. Taylor (2000), 'An application of multiple-group causal models in assessing cross-cultural measurement equivalence', *Journal of International Marketing*, vol. 8, no. 4, pp. 108–21.

Mytton, Graham (1996), 'Research in new fields', *Journal of the Market Research Society*, vol. 38, no. 1, pp. 19–32.

Naumann, Earl, Donald W. Jackson Jr. and William G. Wolfe (1994), 'Examining the practices of United States and Japanese market research firms', *California Management Review*, vol. 36, no. 4, pp. 49–69.

Parameswaran, Ravi and Attila Yaprak (1987), 'A cross-national comparison of consumer research measures', *Journal of International Business Studies*, Spring, pp. 35–49.

Pike, Kenneth (1966), *Language in Relation To a Unified Theory of the Structure of Human Behavior*, Mouton: The Hague.

Poortinga, Ype H. (1989), 'Equivalence in cross-cultural data: an overview of basic issues', *International Journal of Psychology*, vol. 24, pp. 737–56.

Pras, Bernard and Reinhard Angelmar (1978), 'Verbal rating scales for multinational research', *European Research*, March, pp. 62–7.

Reynolds, N.L., A.C. Simintiras and A. Diamantopoulos (2003), 'Theoretical justification of sampling choices in international marketing research: key issues and guidelines for researchers', *Journal of International Business Studies*, vol. 34, no. 1, pp. 80–9.

Rose, Gregory M. (1999), 'Consumer socialization, parental style, and development timetables in the United States and Japan', *Journal of Marketing*, vol. 63, July, pp. 105–19.

Roy, Abhik, Peter G.P. Walters and Sherriff T.K. Luk (2001), 'Chinese puzzles and paradoxes: conducting business research in China,' *Journal of Business Research*, vol. 52, no. 2, pp. 203–10.

Sapir, Edward (1929), 'The status of linguistics as a science', *Language*, vol. 5, pp. 207–14.

Sechrest, L., T. Fay and S.M. Zaidi (1972), 'Problems of translation in cross-cultural research', *Journal of Cross-cultural Psychology*, vol. 3, no. 1, pp. 41–56.

Sentell, G.D. and J.W. Philpot (1984), 'A note on evaluating the representativity of samples taken in less developed countries', *International Journal of Research in Marketing*, vol. 1, pp. 81–4.

Singh, Jagdip (1995), 'Measurement issues in cross-national research', *Journal of International Business Studies*, vol. 26, no. 3, pp. 597–619.

Sood, James H. (1990), 'Equivalent measurement in international market research: is it really a problem?', *Journal of International Consumer Marketing*, vol. 2, no. 2, pp. 25–41.

Souchon, Anne L. and Adamantios Diamantopoulos (1999), 'Export information acquisition modes: measure development and validation', *International Marketing Review*, vol. 16, no. 2, pp. 143–68.

Stanton, J.L., R. Chandran and S. Hernandez (1982), 'Marketing research problems in Latin America', *Journal of the Market Research Society*, vol. 24, no. 2, pp. 124–39.

Steenkamp, Jan-Bendict E.M. and Hans Baumgartner (1998), 'Assessing measurement invariance in cross-national research', *Journal of Consumer Research*, vol. 25, no. 1, June, pp. 78–90.

Tan, Thomas Tsu Wee and Tan Jee Lui (2002), 'Globalization and trends in international market research in China', *Journal of Business Research*, vol. 55, no. 10, pp. 799–804.

Taylor, Humphrey (1995), 'Horses for courses: how survey firms in different countries measure public opinion with different methods', *Journal of the Market Research Society*, vol. 37, no. 3.

Toften, Kjell and Svein Ottar Olsen (2003), 'Export market information use, organizational knowledge, and firm performance: a conceptual framework', *International Marketing Review*, vol. 20, no. 1.

Tuncalp, Secil (1988), 'The marketing research scene in Saudi Arabia', *European Journal of Marketing*, vol. 22, no. 5, pp. 15–22.

Usunier, Jean-Claude (1991), 'Business time perceptions and national cultures: a comparative survey', *Management International Review*, vol. 31, no. 3, pp. 197–217.

Usunier, Jean-Claude (1997), 'Atomistic versus organistic approaches: an illustration through cross-national differences in market research', *International Studies of Management & Organization*, vol. 26, no. 4, pp. 90–112.

Van de Vijver, F.J.R. and Kenneth Leung (1997) *Methods and Data Analysis for Cross-cultural Research*. Sage: Thousand Oaks, CA.

Van der Vijver, F.J.R. and Ype H. Poortinga (1982), 'Cross-cultural generalization and universality', *Journal of Cross-Cultural Psychology*, vol. 13, pp. 387–408.

Van Herk, Hester and Theo M. Verhallen (1995), 'Equivalence in empirical international research in the food area', *Proceedings of the Second Conference on the Cultural Dimension of International Marketing*, Odense, pp. 392–402.

Van Raaij, W.F. (1978), 'Cross-cultural research methodology as a case of construct validity', in H.K. Hunt (ed.), *Advances in Consumer Research*, vol. 5, Association for Consumer Research, Ann Arbor, MI, pp. 693–701.

Viswanathan, Madhubalan, Terry L. Childers and Elizabeth S. Moore (2000), 'The measurement of intergenerational communication and influence on consumption: development, validation, and cross-cultural comparison of the IGEN scale', *Journal of the Academy of Marketing Science*, vol. 28, no. 3, pp. 406–24.

Vuursten, Karel (1996), 'Decision making at Heineken', *Marketing and Research Today*, vol. 24, no. 1, pp. 42–5.

Weber, Elke U. and Christopher Yr Hsee (1998), 'Cross-cultural differences in risk perception, but cross-cultural similarities in attitudes towards perceived risk', *Management Science*, vol. 44, no. 9, pp. 1205–17.

Webster, Cynthia (1996), 'Hispanic and Anglo interviewer and respondent ethnicity and gender: the impact on survey response quality', *Journal of Marketing Research*, vol. 33, February, pp. 62–72.

Weiss, Brad (1996), 'Coffee breaks and connections: the lived experience of a commodity in Tanzanian and European world', in David Howes (ed.), *Cross-cultural Consumption*, Routledge: London, pp. 93–123.

Wimalasiri, Jayantha (2000), 'A comparison of children's purchasing influence and parental response in Fiji and the United States', *Journal of International Consumer Marketing*, vol. 12, no. 4, pp. 55–74.

Wind, Yoram and Susan P. Douglas (1982), 'Comparative consumer research: the next frontier', *Management Decision*, vol. 20, no. 4, pp. 24–35.

Wong, Nancy, Aric Rindfleisch and James E. Burroughs (2003), 'Do reverse-worded items confound measures in cross-cultural consumer research? The case of the material values scales', *Journal of Consumer Research*, vol. 30, no. 1, pp. 72–91.

Wood, Van R. and Kim R. Robertson (2000), 'Evaluating international markets: the importance of information by industry, by country of destination, and by type of export transaction', *International Marketing Review*, vol. 17, no. 1, pp. 34–55.

Ya-Fei (2000), 'Putting the PR in PRC', *Asia Pacific Management Forum*, July/August, available at: **www.apmforum.com/columns/china5.htm**

Zaltman, Gerald (1997), 'Rethinking market research: putting people back in', *Journal of Marketing Research*, vol. 34, November, pp. 424–37.

Zax, M. and S. Takashi (1967), 'Cultural influences on response style: comparison of Japanese and American college students', *Journal of Social Psychology*, vol. 71, pp. 3–10.

Appendix 7

Teaching materials

A7.1 Case

Mobile phones in the European Union

Questions

Using the same text as in Chapter 4 (see section A4.3), answer the following questions:

1. Assuming that Orange has decided to undertake an in-depth market survey in order to decide whether to develop its market penetration in a southern European market (e.g. France or Spain), versus a northern European market (e.g. Germany or Denmark), how would you design such a survey?

2. What information is needed?

3. How would you collect it?

A7.2 Exercise

Hair shampoo questionnaire

You will find below a market survey questionnaire, administered by interviewers to women interviewees between the ages of 18 and 30. It was originally designed for the US market. A similar market survey, as far as the objectives are concerned, will be undertaken in other countries. Suggest cross-cultural adaptations to this instrument. In particular,

1. Review the possible problems related to the translation of the questionnaire. Suggest solutions and translate it into. . . .[15]
2. Review the data-collection procedure, from the point of view of the interviewer as well as that of the interviewee.
3. Suggest changes in the questionnaire design and/or wording, and/or modification in survey methods, if:
   (a) the information sought is meaningless in the local context;
   (b) the required information is meaningful but the data-collection procedures are inadequate; either they will not enable you to collect the information, or else this information will be biased.

- You must do this for at least 3 of the following countries: Algeria, Brazil, France, Germany, Thailand.
- You should then propose a 'central' version of the questionnaire, that is, a survey instrument which enables you to collect the maximum amount of information, which could be retrieved in a reliable manner, in the largest possible number of countries. This questionnaire would then help the meaningful comparison of countries.

Questionnaire used in hair shampoo study

	Time Interview Started ....
	Ended ....
Respondent Name	Respondent No. ....
Address	
City	State ....
Telephone No	
Interviewer	
Name	
Interview Date	

Screening Questions (Part S)

'Hello, I'm .... of the Wharton School, University of Pennsylvania. We're conducting a survey on women's attitudes and opinions about hair care products.'

1. On average, how often do you shampoo your hair at home?

More than twice a week	....
Once or twice a week	....
Once or twice every two weeks	....
Once or twice every three weeks	....
Twice a month	....
Less than twice a month	....

IF LESS THAN TWICE A MONTH, TERMINATE

2. What is your age? ....
(IF UNDER 18 OR OVER 30 TERMINATE)

Part A

'First I'm going to show you a set of 16 cards. Each card contains the name of a benefit that a hair shampoo might provide.' (PLACE SET OF WHITE CARDS* ON TABLE IN FRONT OF RESPONDENT.)

'Please take a few moments to look over these benefits.' (ALLOW TIME FOR RESPONDENT TO STUDY THE CARDS.)

'Now, thinking about various brands of hair shampoo that you have tried or heard about, pick out those benefits that you think are most likely to be found in almost any hair shampoo that one could buy today.' (RECORD CARD NUMBERS IN FIRST COLUMN OF RESPONSE FORM A AND TURN SELECTED CARDS FACE DOWN.)

* For the wording on the cards, see p. 213.

'Next, select all of those remaining benefits that you think are available in at least some hair shampoo – but not necessarily all in a single brand – that's currently on the market.' (RECORD CARD NUMBERS IN SECOND COLUMN OF RESPONSE FORM A. RECORD REMAINING CARD NUMBERS IN THIRD COLUMN. THEN RETURN ALL CARDS TO TABLE.)

'Next, imagine that you could make up an ideal type of shampoo – one that might not be available on today's market. Suppose, however, that you were restricted to only 4 of the 16 benefits shown on the cards in front of you. Which 4 of the 16 benefits would you most like to have?' (RECORD CARD NUMBERS IN FOURTH COLUMN OF RESPONSE FORM A.)

RESPONSE FORM A

(1)	(2)	(3)	(4)
Benefits Most Likely to be Found in Almost Any Hair Shampoo – Card Numbers	Benefits Available in Some Shampoo – Card Numbers	Remaining Benefits – Card Numbers	Four Benefit Ideal Set – Card Numbers

Part B

'Now, let's again return to some of the shampoo benefits you have already dealt with.' (SELECT WHITE CARD NUMBERS 1 THROUGH 10: PULL OUT CARD 4 AND PLACE IT IN FRONT OF RESPONDENT.)

'Suppose a shampoo were on the market that primarily stressed this benefit – "produces hair that has body". If you could get a shampoo that made good on this claim, which one of the remaining nine benefits would you most like to have as well?' (RECORD NUMBER IN RESPONSE FORM B.)

'Which next most?' (RECORD.)

'Please continue until all of the nine benefits have been ranked.'

RESPONSE FORM B

(Enter Card Numbers 1 Through 10 Excluding Card #4)	
( ) Most Like to Have	( )
( ) Next Most	( )
( )	( )
( )	( )
( )	( ) Least Most

Part C

'Now, I am going to read to you some short phrases about hair. Listen to each phrase carefully and then tell me what single words first come to your mind when you hear each phrase.' (RECORD UP TO THE FIRST THREE 'ASSOCIATIVE-TYPE' WORDS THE RESPONDENT SAYS AFTER EACH PHRASE IN RESPONSE FORM C.)

RESPONSE FORM C

(a)   Hair that has body

_____   _____   _____

(b)   Hair with fullness

_____   _____   _____

(c)   Hair that holds a set

_____   _____   _____

(d)   Bouncy hair

_____   _____   _____

(e)   Hair that's not limp

_____   _____   _____

(f)   Manageable hair

_____   _____   _____

(g)   Zesty hair

_____   _____   _____

(h)   Natural hair

_____   _____   _____

Part D

'At this point I would like to ask you a few questions about your hair.'

1. Does your hair have enough body?
    Yes _____   No _____

2. Do you have any special problems with your hair?
    Yes _____   No _____
    If yes, what types of problems?
    _____
    _____

3. How would you describe your hair?
    My hair type is:
    Dry _____   Normal _____   Oily _____

4. The texture of my hair is:
    Fine _____   Normal _____   Coarse _____

5. My hair style (the way I wear my hair) is:
    Straight _____
    Slightly wavy or curly _____
    Very wavy or curly _____

6. The length of my hair is:
Short (to ear lobes) _____
Medium (ear lobes to shoulder) _____
Long (below shoulder) _____

7. How would you describe the thickness of your hair?
Thick _____   Medium _____   Thin _____

Part E
'Now I would like to ask you a few background questions.'

1. Are you working (at least twenty hours per week, for compensation)?
Yes _____   No _____

2. Are you married?
Yes _____   No _____

3. What is your level of education?
Some high school _____
Completed high school _____
Some college _____
Completed college _____

4. (HAND RESPONDENT INCOME CARD.) Which letter on this card comes closest to describing your total annual family income before taxes? (CIRCLE APPROPRIATE LETTER.)

A.	Under $9,000	E.	$30,001–45,000
B.	$9,001–15,000	F.	$45,001–60,000
C.	$15,001–20,000	G.	Over $60,000
D.	$20,001–30,000		

'Thanks very much for your help.'

Appendix
Text of the 16 benefits cards (original text in English + my translation into French overleaf):

1. Hair stays clean a long time
2. Hair stays free of dandruff or flaking
3. Hair that looks and feels natural
4. Hair that has body
5. Manageable hair that goes where you want it
6. Hair with sheen or luster
7. Hair with no split ends
8. Hair with enough protein
9. Hair that doesn't get oily fast
10. Hair that's not too dry
11. Hair with fullness
12. Hair that's not frizzy
13. Hair that holds a set
14. Hair with texture
15. Hair that's easy to comb when it dries
16. Hair that looks free and casual

Example of a translation into French. Below are my suggestions:

1. *Des Cheveux qui restent propre longtemps*
2. *Des Cheveux sans pellicules ni noeuds*
3. *Des Cheveux respirant le naturel*
4. *Des Cheveux qui ont du volume*
5. *Des Cheveux souples que l'on peut coiffer à son gré*
6. *Des Cheveux brillants et chatoyants*
7. *Des Cheveux qui ne se cassent pas*
8. *Des Cheveux assez riches en protéines*
9. *Des Cheveux ne devenant pas gras trop vite*
10. *Des Cheveux pas trop secs*
11. *Des Cheveux qui ont de la plénitude*
12. *Des Cheveux qui ne sont pas frisottés*
13. *Des Cheveux tenant la mise en plis*
14. *Des Cheveux ayant une bonne texture*
15. *Des Cheveux faciles à coiffer lorsqu'ils sèchent*
16. *Des Cheveux naturels, en liberté*

(Source: Adapted from Green *et al.*, 1988, pp. 359–62.)

Part 3 Marketing decisions for the intercultural environment

Introduction to Part 3

For some decades, the '4Ps' model of marketing management has been widely used for designing marketing strategies and, to a lesser extent, for implementing them. Like most international marketing textbooks, this book follows the '4Ps' model: *product*, *price*, *place*, and *promotion*. Part 3 explains how the first three Ps, product, price and place, should be managed internationally with a view to generating the best possible compromise between large-scale operations and adaptation to local markets. The last 'P', promotion, is largely treated in Part 4 since marketing communications deserve special treatment in an international context where communication needs to be tailored because of language differences.

Multinational companies respond to the globalization of competition by designing international marketing strategies that try to create experience effects within the constraint of transport costs. They also use a number of production systems, such as flexible manufacturing, in order to gain differentiation advantages that are related to the customization of product offerings to local market needs. Chapter 8 deals first with the supply side by examining how cost arguments explain the emergence of global strategies and the globalization of competition. On the demand side, cross-border segments can be targeted in order to generate larger-scale operations; Chapter 8 explains how geographical and demographic segmentation criteria can be combined in order to segment international markets optimally.

Chapter 9 documents the strategic choice between adaptation or standardization of products across national markets. It starts therefore with a review of key arguments in favour of the standardization or the adaptation of physical attributes. Physical attributes are the most sensitive to scale economies and at the same time they often require customization because of climate and other objective features of local markets. Service attributes also need to be tailored because consumers' expectations regarding service quality and service performance vary across national contexts. Finally, symbolic attributes linked to product design and packaging are examined in a cross-cultural perspective that highlights the diversity of cultural interpretations of symbols looking at attributes such as colour, figure, shape, etc.

Among the symbolic attributes that diffuse meaning, two of great importance are the country of origin of products and their brand names. Chapter 10 deals therefore with the management of images diffused by these attributes. It reviews how consumers evaluate products according to their country of origin, taking into account perceived risk related to goods produced in other countries, which may be cheaper or less prestigious in terms of design and/or manufacture, as well as the nationalistic tendencies of consumers who prefer to buy products made in their own country. The final section deals with the linguistic constraints of transferring national brand names on to the international scene and outlines the managerial limitations involved in the development of global brands.

Rather than seeing price merely as *the* objective factor in the economics of international marketing, Chapter 11 examines the role of price as a central element of relational exchange, that is, as a signal conveying meaning between buyer and seller, marketers and consumers, and between companies and their middlemen. It also presents and documents the main pricing decisions that a company has to face when it sells internationally. The first perspective developed is that of bargaining, which is still widely in use in many markets and remains a key ritual in buyer–seller relationships because it mixes economics and human intercourse in a subtle way. Then cross-cultural variation in the use of price by consumers to evaluate and choose products is discussed. The three last sections of the chapter are devoted to managerial issues in international price policy, that is, how multinational companies may use price policy to conquer new markets, how to enter markets where competition is avoided through cartels and price agreements, how to fight against parallel imports by unauthorized dealers, and how prices should be managed in unstable environments, which often combine high inflation, administered prices and strict foreign exchange control.

Chapter 12 is concerned mostly with the 'place' variable in the 4Ps model and deals consequently with international distribution. The case of Japanese *Keiretsu* distribution is used to exemplify the cultural embedding of distribution channels and the difficulty of entering foreign channels as a 'cultural outsider'. It shows how relationships between channel members are deeply rooted in local patterns of human and economic relationships and highlights the role of distribution as a 'cultural filter', which must be carefully considered (along with other criteria) before choosing a foreign distribution channel. Direct marketing worldwide, especially through catalogue sales and through the Internet, is developing fast: the section dealing with direct marketing explains which products best suit direct overseas distribution and outlines some linguistic and cultural limitations that must be carefully considered before designing and implementing cross-border direct marketing. The final section examines cross-national variations in sales promotion methods and explains which aspects need to be customized when transferring promotional techniques across borders.

Intercultural marketing strategy

Globalization can occur at the market, organization and/or consumer level. Globalization occurs mostly at the level of markets where supply, demand and competition are becoming increasingly global. Regional agreements worldwide and the World Trade Organization (WTO) have brought tariff and non-tariff barriers down. These are progressively being replaced by entry barriers related to scale and experience at the organizational level. Consumer behaviour, a natural entry barrier related to culture, will diminish very gradually and only over a long period: there are still many very different marketing 'villages', not a global one. This chapter defends the ideas that strategic management has to be 'global', whereas marketing management largely needs to be tailored to local contexts; therefore, an intercultural orientation to international marketing best serves a global strategic view.

The strategic dilemma for international marketers is to achieve both low cost and differentiation in the minds of consumer's *vis-à-vis* competitors. While differentiation, a key tenet of this book, may result in cost increases, there are possible compromises. Cost efficiency can be obtained in three major areas: production, transport and marketing. In order to minimize costs and unnecessary differentiation, and to maximize relevant differentiation, customers should be clustered in groups sharing common characteristics. Culture is naturally one of the main cues for clustering, but not the only one; sociodemographic criteria are also significant in an international perspective.

We need to consider the *scale* of global operations, their geographical *scope* and relevant *segments* (national versus transnational). The first section of this chapter discusses scale, concentrating on cost arguments. Global strategies are very significant from a pure cost perspective. The second section discusses scope, concentrating on how global competition has progressively become the rule, due to the liberalization of world trade. The third section shows how companies have reacted to these major changes during the last 20 years and how they were forced by the pressure of worldwide competition to standardize marketing strategies while keeping an eye on very dissimilar consumer environments. The final section deals with the segmentation of world markets and discusses the respective place of cross-border segments based on sociodemographics and lifestyles and geography-based cultural segments.

8.1

Cost arguments and global strategies

Trends towards global (competitive) markets

The distinction between the multidomestic and the global market, identified by Michael Porter, has been widely applied since the beginning of the 1980s. According to Porter, competition becomes global when 'a firm's competitive position is significantly affected by its position in other countries and vice-versa' (1986, p. 18). When an industry is multidomestic, separate strategies are pursued in different national markets, and the competitive scene remains basically a domestic one. While there are forces moving us toward a global competition, such as those cited by Sheth (2001) including regional integration, ideology-free world, technological advances and borderless markets, the movement is not as fast it may seem, as there are other forces that have slowed the process. In fact, Rugman (2001, p. 583) suggests that globalization 'does not, and has never, existed in terms of a single world market with free trade . . . Government regulations and cultural differences divide the world into the triad blocks of North America, the European Union and Japan'. He argues that the move has been to regionalization rather than globalization, as most global companies earn the majority of their revenue within their home triad and adapt their products to the local market. For example: 'More than 85 per cent of all automobiles produced in North America are built in North American factories . . . over 90 per cent of the cars produced in the EU are sold there; and more than 93 per cent of all cars registered in Japan are manufactured domestically' (pp. 584–5).

There are some fundamental reasons for industries to remain multidomestic, including wide differences in consumer needs and attitudes across markets, legal barriers resulting from domestic regulations (which have long been in place in the case of banking and insurance), and non-tariff barriers, which artificially maintain competition between purely national competitors (food and drug health regulations, for instance). Accordingly, the basic preoccupation of a global strategy, very briefly defined, is the configuration and coordination of activities, including marketing, across national markets.

The trends towards global markets differ fairly widely, depending on the industry. First, the influence of national regulations and non-tariff barriers varies largely across product categories. Second, the potential for experience effects also differs across product categories: for example, there is less potential for cost reduction due to volume increase in the case of perishables, such as cheeses, than for microchips. Third, there are different degrees of international 'transportability', that is, the extent to which transportation costs impinge on the degree and patterns of globalization of an industry. Thus, exporting may be the dominant internationalization pattern for easily transportable products such as semiconductors, and foreign direct investment may be the prevailing pattern for industries whose products are expensive

to transport long distance (e.g. cement). Fourth, the trend towards globalization may be curbed in the case of culture-bound products: the globalization of foods such as cheese, although such a trend clearly exists, is slower than in the microchip industry.

In addition, globalization may not be the most profitable route for a company to take. For instance, Qian and Li (2001, pp. 326–7) caution that; 'no definitive conclusions can be drawn from past research on the relationship between foreign operations and profitability'. Quin and Li hypothesize that increasing the scope of foreign operation should increase profits. Using data from 125 large US firms, they found that a medium global market diversification strategy performed better than a high one.

As previously mentioned, pure cost efficiency can be obtained in three major areas: production, transport and marketing. Each of these is discussed below.

Production and experience effects

The potential for experience effects differs widely across product categories. The Boston Consulting Group has isolated one of the main reasons for this through research into the success of various companies, including Japanese companies, in global markets. Experience effects provide companies with the ability to reduce unit costs dramatically through an increase in product quantity. The experience effects determine the relationship of unit cost to cumulated production volume according to the following formula:

$$C_n = C_1 n^{-\lambda}$$

where C_n is the cost of the nth unit; C_1 is the cost of the first unit; n is the cumulated number of units produced; and λ is the elasticity of the unit cost with respect to the cumulated production volume.

The form of the function reflects a constant elasticity. Let us call k the effect of elasticity. When production is doubled, the cost (and therefore, to a certain extent, the price) will decrease by $1 - k = 1 - 2^{-\lambda}$ per cent each time the experience doubles. If, for example, k equals 70 per cent, the cost will decrease by 30 per cent on a doubling of the cumulated production (1 − 70 per cent = 30 per cent). Experience effects theory has been supported by empirical verification (e.g., Day and Montgomery, 1983).

Experience effects have been estimated for such diverse products and services as long-distance telephone calls in the United States, bottle tops in West Germany, refrigerators in Great Britain, and motorcycles in Japan. (For more information on cost, experience effects and the learning curve see *WS8.1.*)

The source of experience effects is fourfold:

1. The effects of *learning by doing*. The more times one carries out a task or manufactures a component or a product, the more efficiently and quickly it can be done.
2. *Scale effects*. By increasing the scale of production, the average cost can be reduced. Many industrial products, such as pocket calculators, require a large amount of research and development for product design, yet only a small quantity of raw materials for their manufacture.
3. *Technological advances*. The increase in cumulated production offers a dual possibility for technological improvements. On one hand, production equipment may be refined; on the other hand, the product itself can be simplified and rendered cheaper to produce. These product simplifications usually result from reducing the number of component parts, rather than a reduction in the number of functions and the degree of sophistication, which would adversely affect the consumer.
4. *Economies of scope*. Component parts may be shared by different products. For instance, the same basic diesel engine may be used for a fork-lift truck, a small truck, a van, a car, or as an inboard motor for a boat, with a few slight adaptations. The increase in the production scale of shared components (or shared overhead costs, or any kind of shared common inputs) results in economies of scope.

Not every product has the same potential for experience effects. The potential is clearly smaller for cheese or books than for hi-fi systems or microcomputers. An examination of Japanese successes in world markets demonstrates that the Japanese have concentrated on goods that have very high experience effects, such as motorcycles, motor cars, photocopiers, video and DVD equipment, hi-fi systems, television sets, outboard motors, musical instruments and cameras. Right from the start, Japanese companies opted for global markets, even though their domestic market for such products was itself very substantial.

Competitors have struggled to resist the competitive pressure of Japanese companies. For instance, the motorcycle industry in Europe illustrates how a lack of experience effects can inhibit innovation. In an attempt to compete with the Japanese (Honda, Yamaha, Suzuki, Kawasaki), Motobécane, a French manufacturer, launched a 125cc motorcycle 20-odd years ago. This model had a two-stroke engine that operated on a mixture of petrol and oil, since Motobécane was unable to make a four-stroke engine, like Honda, or an 'oil lube' (a device for mixing oil and petrol automatically), like Yamaha, Suzuki and Kawasaki. This motorcycle emitted a thick cloud of white smoke through its exhaust. The range of models offered has remained very limited, as with other French motorcycles. The 350cc Motobécane, which could have enjoyed a lucrative local market by supplying the French police, was not fast or reliable enough. The lack of experience effects in the company was a barrier to technological improvements. Motobécane is now renamed MBK and is a subsidiary of Yamaha.

Local players however, can use experience effects to maintain the upper hand over transnationals by using their local identity advantage. As noted by Ger (1999, p. 65), 'Rather than operating in the already highly competitive markets shared and dominated by the TNCs [transnational corporations], local firms can better take advantage of their potential by operating in alternative domains and "out-localizing" the TNCs, in both global and local markets'.

International transportability

The unit weight, that is, dollar price per kilogram or per pound, differs widely across categories of goods, and therefore across the industries that manufacture them. The price of cement or basic ordinary steel products ranges from 50 cents per kilogram to several dollars per kilogram, whereas that of cars ranges from 10 dollars per kilogram (for example, a small family car at the bottom end of the market) to 60 or 70 dollars per kilogram for luxury cars at the top end of the market (large Mercedes, BMWs or Jaguars). A portable computer may reach a price of 750 dollars per kilogram (or even more), not to mention its component chips, which may climb to several thousand dollars per kilogram.

In the international transportation system, shipping charges do not follow a simple tariff, which would be directly proportional to weight. They are calculated on the basis of a mix of criteria, depending on the nature of goods to be shipped and on the shipping line. Shipping lines are also subject to economies of scale. Transportation cost factors are influenced by the forces of competition between transportation companies, and also by the method of transportation (ship, aeroplane, truck or train). The mix of criteria includes weight, volume, dimensions, ease of loading and unloading, perishability, packaging and speed of delivery. Of these, weight, volume and perishability are clearly the most detrimental factors to international transportation.

Some markets will remain almost exclusively multidomestic, because goods and services cannot be transported – services such as hairdressing, for instance. Although transportability may have a negative influence on cross-border transactions of goods and services, it does not hamper the globalization of an industry where cross-border investments are possible. For instance, the cement industry still competes on a global basis, through foreign direct investment and the sale and licensing of technology, despite the markets being regionally segmented within countries due to the high cost of transportation in proportion to basic unit price.

Transportability relates also to consumers, who may be more 'transportable' than the products or services that are offered to them. Ski resorts are a good example: ski slopes, buildings and equipment are not transportable, nor is snow. But potential skiers may be transported at low cost on charter flights, from countries without mountains, snow or ski resorts (but with some purchasing power). Thus we may observe in the international ski-resorts industry a twofold pattern of globalization. On the one hand, some world-famous ski resorts, such as Val d'Isère in France, Kitzbühl in Austria, Zermatt in Switzerland and Thredbo in Australia enjoy a global market. People arrive from many parts of the world, often on package holidays sold by tour operators or travel agencies. On the other hand, there remains in most ski-oriented countries a large number of purely local ski resorts ('ski villages'), which compete on a more domestic basis. This part of the industry is multidomestic. Between these two segments, one globalized, one multidomestic, there are in fact many intermediate ski resorts, which compete on a regionally globalized basis. This is the case with most medium-size ski resorts in the European Alps: in Austria, France, Germany, Italy, Switzerland and some eastern European countries, which compete for European skiers.

The Internet has also increased the transportability in many markets. Forrester Research (2000) predicts that global e-commerce will reach US $6.8 trillion in 2004. According to Prasad et al. (2001, p. 83): 'Benefits sought by marketers in using the Internet include improved efficiency and lower costs across supply and demand chains; improved speed, flexibility, and responsiveness in meeting customer needs; greater market access; and enhanced ability to overcome time and distance barriers of global markets'. While the Internet cannot transport most physical products, it can affect communication, transactional and distribution channels (Prasad et al., 2001).

The disconnection between sourcing and marketing

The countries where sourcing and marketing take place may be geographically distant in industries which compete on a global basis. The sites of most cost-efficient production are often export processing zones in newly industrialized countries. Consumer markets may be located in distant and remote places. The same brand may be 'made in' multiple countries, generating different country-of-origin (COO) images (see section 10.2). This multinational production causes a 'blurring effect' for COO. Consumers, who still use country of origin as an information cue for comparing brands, are now becoming more and more aware of the actual disconnection between sourcing and marketing. Usunier (2002) recently found that actual knowledge about a product's origin and its influence on preference for local products is relatively small.

A world-view versus a local view

There is clearly a difference between customer orientation, which puts customers' needs first, and market orientation, which focuses on a larger view of satisfying customers' current and future needs throughout the marketing value chain (Hult et al., 2001). Market orientation gives 'system-wide attention to markets (customers, competitors and other entities in the environment) throughout the organization' (Hult and Ketchen, 2001, p. 901). Thus, a 'global strategy' clearly implies a world-view of competition and competitive advantage, not simply a belief that consumers and markets are themselves global. The issue of global strategies has been extensively documented in the strategic management literature; it is clearly beyond the scope of this book (which emphasizes the cultural dimensions of international marketing) to discuss in detail the specific issues related to global strategies.

In cultural terms, the ethnocentrism of the managing team of any company is shown by the way in which it treats the domestic/national market on the one hand and 'foreign' markets on the other. This issue is not purely academic; it permeates the ways in which a company organizes its international activities and the nationalities of its top executives as well as other more practical considerations such as the choice of the language(s) to be spoken between subsidiaries and head office.

Once the company has achieved a certain level of development in foreign markets, the 'export' view and the 'international development' view can no longer coexist effectively. They are dependent on four different perspectives: ethnocentrism, polycentrism, regiocentrism and geocentrism (Perlmutter, 1969; Wind et al., 1973). (For more information on these perspectives see WS8.1.) Two of these (ethno- and geocentrism) are somewhat irreconcilable. In terms of set theory, the domestic market is perceived as disjointed from foreign markets. Ethnocentric companies view international operations as secondary to their domestic operations. A company that considers its national base as its top priority will impose its own language on its foreign subsidiaries. It will supply the domestic market first when production capacity is overstretched. It will never invite a non-national on to the board of directors unless this person shares the company's native language and culture. Conversely, a geocentric company, which considers its domestic market belonging to the world market in the same way as any other domestic market, will make the opposite choices. Sheth and Parvatiyar (2001, p. 21) argue that the nine determinants of international marketing cycles are gradually declining: political stability, government policy, ideology-driven economy, fear of colonialism, marketing transfer issues, lack of

infrastructure, North–South dichotomy, East–West dichotomy and product life. A geocentric perspective is dependent on a truly borderless world.

Regiocentrism and polycentrism are more moderate perspectives. A regiocentric company is more open to global marketing than an ethnocentric one. But, this perspective also recognizes that regional marketing strategies may be necessary to better meet customer needs. Malhotra et al. (1998) argue that cultural factors still strongly inhibit the development of a homogeneous market. They emphasize a regional perspective, using regional trading blocs as building blocks to world trade. They also recognize the importance of acknowledging differences within the bloc. Finally, a polycentric company recognizes that differences occur in overseas markets. Each country is accepted as one of many ethnocentric places which may have their own marketing policies and programmes.

When companies distance themselves from an ethnocentric attitude and adopt one of the other perspectives, by virtue of their management style and corporate culture, they develop genuinely offensive and defensive marketing strategies in foreign markets. Such a strategy manifests itself in flexible reallocation of resources from one market to another. For instance, a company will relocate into market Y, where it holds a solid position, as a reaction to one large competitor launching a price offensive in country X. This type of situation is conceivable in strongly oligopolistic markets where several (five to ten) large multinationals control the world market, as happens in the food industry or the liquefied gases industry.

Nevertheless, it seems that stiff competition may give way to forms of cooperation between large companies from developed countries. The theory developed by Kenichi Ohmae, head of the Tokyo office of McKinsey Consultants, in his book *Triad Power: The coming shape of global competition* (1985), emphasizes the need for companies that want to survive international competition to have a solid base in the market area of each of the three major industrialized regions' collectively known as the 'triad': North America, Japan and Europe. Ohmae further suggests that in each of these regions, companies should establish links of international division of labour with neighbouring developing countries. Companies in Latin America are natural subcontractors for North American companies. South-East Asian countries subcontract for Japanese firms. The same cooperation pattern should occur between African countries and European companies. To ensure this necessary tripolar presence, Ohmae advocates that alliances should be built between companies belonging to one of the developed market areas. Most of these companies, even large ones, cannot individually afford to make the necessary investment that would ensure a full presence in each of the three regions.

Prioritized markets often remain undisguised. To avoid the trap of 'collective unconsciousness', companies must reflect on how prioritized markets relate to corporate culture, as well as to the search for market and business opportunities, and to the decision-making process. Some European companies still supply their domestic market as a priority, on the basis that this market is the 'home base'. This attitude has two dangerous consequences:

1. It leads to a bias in *product design*. The modest sales records of certain European cars, mainly French and Italian, in the North American (principally US) market is, at least partly, attributable to local French and Italian motor regulations which bias the design of cars, and make them inappropriate for use in America. In France, the speed restrictions on motorways, and a high road tax that largely increases with the size of the engine, has discouraged the production of large cars and sports cars. The same holds true in Italy, where the high cost of petrol has encouraged the production of small cars, too small in fact for US consumers. This has dissuaded car manufacturers in those countries from building high-speed luxury saloons, a gap in the market that was mostly filled by the Germans and the Swedes, before the Japanese came with their Lexus and Acuras.

2. Home-base-oriented companies often suffer the unfortunate reputation abroad of unreliability with respect to *delivery dates*. This is due to marginalization of foreign markets, which are considered as a provisional outlet to be approached when the home market is depressed. It leads to a consistent preference for supplying a domestic customer rather than a foreign customer. Even though such foreign customers may have ordered earlier, they will be forced to wait and will only receive delivery after domestic customers have been satisfied. A genuine respect for delivery dates should have led to a different outcome.

As soon as domestic demand increases, the prioritization of national markets implies that production capacity will cease to be used for supplying foreign customers. As a consequence, there is a general risk that attempts to set up stable business relationships with customers and intermediaries in foreign markets will be hampered. Typically, foreign agents will only be visited when business at home is slack, and will be let down (as will foreign customers) as soon as the home market situation improves. This attitude fails to satisfy the essential precondition for effective international development.

The world market share concept: Global size and the diagnosis of economic market share

Calculating its world market share helps to prevent a company from being ethnocentric when defining its position *vis-à-vis* the competition. Competition is seen from the outset as global. Box 8.1 illustrates the dangers of overemphasizing domestic market share.

A diagnosis of a particular company's situation within world markets requires the following evaluations (even though estimates may be only approximate):

1. What is the size of the world market (volume, units, sales figures)?
2. What is the company's production size?
3. What is the company's share of the world market?
4. What is the minimum world market share necessary to remain competitive, considering potential experience effects?

The world market for fork-lift trucks was roughly 200,000 units per year. Fenwick held only 2 per cent of this market. 'Competitive' market share could be estimated to have been 10 per cent, or 20,000 trucks a year. Fenwick was therefore well below the required global size. In view of this, it should have reduced its range to either diesel or electric fork-lifts and to a limited range of sizes so that production could have been much greater in a more specialized world market.

There is no precise rule for estimating the 'competitive' world market share. This figure depends on the optimum size of production, which in turn depends on the potential for experience effects for a specific

Box 8.1

Fenwick, a synonym for fork-lift

Fenwick, the leading company for fork-lift trucks in France, is also a word used in everyday speech as a synonym for fork-lift trucks. A few years ago the company controlled 40–50 per cent of the French market, but nearly went bankrupt because it lacked international size. This company only produced 4,000 fork-lift trucks per year, whereas its global competitor, Toyota, produced 35,000 and its main east European competitor, Balkankar (a Bulgarian company), 70,000. This had a negative effect on Fenwick's unit costs. Fenwick should have adapted its marketing strategy, by reducing the depth of its product range, thereby increasing production size within this narrower product range. Toyota was in a position to offer a very wide product range (diesel or electric, with varying loading capacities, etc.). Fenwick, on the other hand, should have restricted its range albeit at the risk of losing customers who expect to find a single supplier capable of dealing with all their requirements.

product or service. Experience effects are, though, much stronger under the following conditions:

1. When the product/service is mass produced.
2. When the product/service involves a production process with large initial fixed costs (in R & D, and/or in production facilities investment, and/or in initial marketing costs).
3. When the added value of the product/service is high, in relation to the whole production cycle.
4. When the product/service is in a fairly open international market; any producer may sell throughout the world without facing prohibitive transport costs, customs barriers, statutory restrictions or market barriers (e.g. differences in taste).

The easiest empirical solution for the evaluation of 'competitive' market share is to examine the competitors and determine the size of those who operate most effectively. Limitations on international size arise in various areas; for example cement (very high transport costs compared to its price), pharmaceuticals (statutory restrictions), foodstuffs (taste differences), etc. As far as services are concerned, the potential for experience effects is much smaller, since in many cases services must be performed in a direct relationship with the consumer and are often intangible, which means they cannot be held in stock. In addition, their market area is often fairly localized and they are subject to local customs and ways of life, such as the type of food and service found in a restaurant or the kind of treat offered by hotels.

Global markets as learning opportunities

Global markets work as a set of coherent opportunities, through markets being at different product life-cycle (PLC) stages and through experience cumulated across national markets. According to PLC theory (Vernon, 1966), national markets at different development stages offer different kinds of opportunities. If, for instance, the market for wallpaper is saturated in developed economies, it may be opening up in newly industrialized countries. PLC theory clearly indicates the way in which sourcing and marketing activities should be disconnected. PLC theory, in conjunction with the world market share concept, assists in the identification of what to supply and from where, and in which countries to market.

Global markets are also full of learning opportunities; the internationalization process has been presented mostly as a learning and experiencing process (Johanson and Vahlne, 1977). Since the cultural variable is fundamental to this learning process, some markets may be used almost purely as learning opportunities. When Procter & Gamble attacked the Japanese market for baby nappies (diapers) it initially achieved great success. Its market share subsequently dropped sharply against the main Japanese competitor Kao. P & G did its best to survive in the face of harsh competition from Kao and other Japanese producers, to satisfy the exigent Japanese consumers and to make its way through the Japanese *Keiretsu* distribution system (see Chapter 12). P & G's experience

Box 8.2

Stimorol and Hollywood

A Danish chewing-gum company, Dandy A/S, which produces Stimorol, encountered difficulties in selling its products in France. Dandy was particularly successful at producing chewing gum *dragée*. Hollywood France (owned by the US company General Foods/Kraft) was less successful in the production of this type of product, but had better access to the major distribution outlets (hypermarkets). In fact, only large companies are able to have their products referenced, that is, registered as products accepted for sale by the channel.

Referencing requires the payment of large 'entry fees' to the hypermarkets, which are only semi-legitimate. Dandy of Denmark and Hollywood ended up forging a cross-competence alliance whereby Dandy produces Hollywood *dragée* products and markets Hollywood products through Dandy's international sales organization, and Hollywood markets Dandy's Stimorol brand in France and produces the Dandy stick products.

(Source: Hollensen, 1991, p. 736.)

in Japan has made it aware of the competitive threat of the Japanese producers. P & G realized that it would face harsh competition if Japanese producers were to decide to expand in world markets. This has already helped P & G resist the internationalization of Kao, which, to date, has not succeeded in becoming a global competitor to P & G.

Global markets may also be seen as partnership opportunities: with local consumers, with distributors and (why not?) with competitors (Box 8.2).

Opportunities exist for local firms to find niche markets, where their local identity and culture is an advantage. Ger (1999) outlines three localization strategies by concentrating on: (1) local as an alternative to modern global; (2) information goods; or (3) goods for the less affluent world. For the first strategy Ger (1999, p. 76) suggests that: 'Local firms can reinvent, reconstruct, and repackage local products, services, and places . . . They can produce a variety of "toys" for the global consumer seeking diversity (the affluent cosmopolitans in modernizing domestic markets as well as in foreign markets). LCs [local companies] can offer alternative products for the non-conformist or ethically concerned consumers. LCs can offer prestige by providing the unique, the exotic, the unusual.' In this way a local company can become a global player, but Ger suggests that they should aim to start in a foreign market or simultaneously in local and foreign markets. They need to think and act both locally and globally, either as by creating a niche at home or an alliance as a global player

(Ger, 1999). For example, Wilkinson and Cheng (1999) cited several examples from winning entries in the annual Australian Multicultural Marketing Awards. 'Techmeat Australia, an award winner in 1994, was started by a Korean immigrant who realized that Australian butchers and abattoirs were discarding cuts of meat considered delicacies in his home country. He now exports A\$2 million worth of meat to Korea every year' (Wilkinson and Cheng, 1999, p. 118).

Another opportunity is to go global via the Internet. As Susan Douglas (2001) points out, the Internet is radically changing existing business models and established ways of doing business in international markets. 'Firms can instantly "go global", targeting a specific market segment worldwide, or reach customers by building a network of Internet sites in different languages throughout the world' (p. 106).

8.2

The globalization of competition

Evidence from macroeconomic data over long periods of time

There is little doubt about the globalization of competition. Market areas do not depend mainly on consumer preferences. Their reach is influenced much more by potential supply and by trade barriers, whether tariff or non-tariff, and also by the opportunities of economies of scale and experience effects. Clear evidence from macroeconomic figures shows that competition is globalizing both at a world-wide level and at a regional level.

International trade continues to expand despite the outbreak of severe acute respiratory syndrome (SARS) and the tension in the Middle East. From 1984 to 1994, the annual rate of increase for world trade was 5.8 per cent, compared with 2.7 per cent for world production (Focus, 1995). Despite the problems mentioned, this comparison has remained fairly constant. From 1995 to 2003 the annual rate of increase for world trade was 4.5 per cent, compared with 2.5 per cent for world production (WTO, 2004). Since 1995, there has only been one year, 2001, when merchandise exports grew less than the World gross national product (GNP) of the nations involved in international trade (WTO, 2004). This points to a long-term trend: an increase in the scale of production. Industrial productivity accompanies the freeing of international markets and the growth of international trade. The value of world merchandise trade rose by 16 per cent to $7.3 trillion in 2003 (WTO, 2004).

The economic linkage between countries and therefore competition between companies has continued to grow. A comparable evolution may be observed, at an even greater pace, at the regional level. Distances are becoming less important and the move to worldwide globalization has its roots at regional level.

During the 1960s and 1970s, the growth of intra-regional international trade within Europe was much faster than the overall world trade growth (Usunier, 1980). In more recent years Asia and the transitional economies have been doing much better than Europe with double-digit import and export expansion in merchandise trade, in real terms (WTO, 2004). In 2003, western Europe's merchandise imports increased by less than 1 per cent and exports by almost 2 per cent. This shows a relative slowdown of the globalization of competition in Europe from the 1980s onwards and, as a consequence, a deterioration of its competitive position worldwide. The entry of the transitional economies into the EU is likely to change this trend. See Chapter 6 for more information on the EU.

Evidence from business and industries

Many companies have been compelled to globalize their business, one example being Black & Decker, because of fierce competition with the Japanese power-tool maker Makita. The reasons for this are stated by *Fortune* magazine, reporting the strategic move of Black & Decker towards globalization: 'Makita is Black & Decker's first competitor with a global strategy. It doesn't care that Germans prefer high powered, heavy-duty drills, and that Yanks want everything lighter. Make a good drill at a low price, the company reasons, and it will sell from Baden-Baden to Brooklyn' (Saporito, 1984, p. 24). For another example of a global strategy, see the DaimlerChrysler website regarding their commitment to global social responsibility (*WS8.2*).

Michael Porter (1986) analyzed the change in patterns of international competition. At the industry level, where competitive advantage is won or lost, there is a shift from multidomestic industries to global ones. Porter is not referring to consumer-led globalization but to a strategic move by companies trying to integrate activities on a worldwide basis, to gain competitive advantage over their competitors at various levels of the value chain.

Nevertheless, globalization remains conditional on the maintenance of the freeing of trade barriers. The establishment of the WTO (World Trade Organization) in 1995 was a major move towards freeing trade in products and services and improving the institutional mechanisms for solving trade disputes between countries.

The globalization of the Japanese economy and other Asian countries has posed some real threats to both the United States and Europe. Therefore, free trade can be maintained and expanded only if a certain equilibrium of the balance of trade between nation-states permits the maintenance of a low-trade-barriers environment that favours globalization at the industry level. The WTO seems, in this respect, to have been established as an organizing framework for international competition, building on the rules of the GATT treaty, rather than a major breakthrough towards free trade worldwide. It provides increased competition in the area of services, by relaxing national barriers in a number of service industries (telecommunications, insurance, banking, etc.). It also provides more homogeneous rules concerning industrial property (patents and trade marks), thereby making it easier for brands to achieve global coverage. (See *WS11.5* on the globalization of competition and antitrust policy.)

It is important to globalize in an efficient and controllable manner (Matthyssens and Pauwels, 2000). Research into cultural closeness has found that cultural similarity can assist with the level of affinity (Swift, 1999), communication, trust and relationship development (Anderson and Weitz, 1989), successful cooperation (Van Oudenhoven and Van der Zee, 2002), a tendency to consume similar goods (Yu and Zietlow, 1995), a more positive country of origin image (Wong and Lamb, 1983) and a lower cost of doing business (Yu and Zietlow, 1995). Xu and Shenkar (2002) further break down the distance to regulative, normative and cognitive levels.

8.3

Globalization of international marketing strategies

While artificial entry barriers are disappearing, global markets remain more apparent than real when one looks at consumption patterns. So how can products and marketing strategies be globalized in the face of the fierce pressure of the globalization of competition, while under the constraint of consumers who tend to resist the globalization movement, at least in part? With respect to this question, two major issues have to be considered:

1. The standardization of marketing programmes: what should be the degree of similarity in marketing strategies from one country to another?
2. Organizational issues: what is required to implement a standardized marketing strategy successfully?

Standardization of international marketing programmes

Before the classic article of Buzzell (1968), 'Can you standardize multinational marketing?', natural entry barriers related to culture were seen as very high, requiring adaptation to national markets and offsetting the potential advantages of scale economies. Buzzell showed clearly that, with the decrease of purely artificial trade barriers, large international companies could create natural entry barriers unrelated to culture through economies of scale. Since then there have been numerous texts that have sought to advise business people how to make the best choices between standardization and adaptation of marketing policies to foreign markets. This literature advocates either 'hard' or 'soft' globalization:

1. 'Hard globalizers' see globalization as a new 'paradigm' for international marketing (Hampton and Buske, 1987). 'Consumers in increasing numbers demonstrate that they are willing to sacrifice specific preferences in product features, function and design for a globally standardized product that carries a lower price' (p. 263). According to Hampton and Buske there is a shift to the global marketing paradigm since the process of adapting products to national wants and needs contradicts their global convergence.
2. 'Soft' partisans of globalization see it as a necessary trend, but constrained by the environment. The physical conditions of a country as well as the laws relating to product standards, sales promotion, taxes, or other aspects of production, may affect standardization of marketing programmes, especially in developing countries (Hill and Still, 1984).

With both soft and hard globalization, what consumers actually want in various national markets is not really considered: differences are either denied (hard) or treated as an external constraint (soft). Behind the globalization debate there is a quite practical issue in terms of the everyday life of companies: the traditional dilemma between production flexibility and marketing's tendency to customize products to diversified needs. Factory managers prefer to be inflexible, for low-cost purposes, whereas marketing managers favour as much tailoring to customers' needs as possible. Developments in factory automation nowadays allow product customization without major cost implications (Wind, 1986). New strategies have been found to serve diversified needs, to customize products and at the same time to maintain low costs owing to economies of scale and experience effects. A modular conception of products permits shared economies of scale at the components level, whereas lagged differentiation maintains a high scale of production as long as possible in the production process and organizes cheap final customization either in the factory or in the distribution network

(Stobaugh and Telesio, 1983; Deher, 1986; Gilmore and Pine, 1997; see Box 8.3). So why maintain such a strong 'paradigm for action' emphasis on globalization if consumption patterns are not clearly globalizing and if adjusting to global competition is reconcilable with tailoring products and marketing strategies to national markets?

First, many companies believe that standardization will result in higher performance. Zou and Cavusgil (2002) surveyed companies in the United States to assess the influence of self-reported standardization on perceived performance (both strategic and financial). The standardization of promotions and product are perceived to affect both aspects of performance. However, Theodosious and Leonidou (2003) assessed empirical research in the area, finding that a firm's performance is indifferent to standardization versus adaptation. They argue that this relationship is more complicated, being dependent on the fit between strategy and context.

Box 8.3

Standardized components and mass customization

In the same way as the modular design of products, the use of standardized components in the production process enables manufacturers to postpone final product differentiation. Identical components may be shared by diverse end-consumer products: for example the same plug will fit various appliances. 'Modules' are standardized components designed to be suitable for a wide variety of possible uses, allowing a significant reduction in the numbers of components.

Lagged differentiation is illustrated by the crystal glassworks at Saint Louis which have only a limited number of basic moulds for producing all their glassware while finishes (size, engraving, decoration, etc.) are applied at the end of the line to plain glasses. Unfinished glasses of different sizes and shapes are mass produced.

Similarly, the same basic cream cheese Tartare is packaged in different ways, right at the end of the production line: packed in aluminium foil in individual servings, in a plastic tub, canned or wrapped. In other cases, a basic cheese will be flavoured differently (cherry, walnut, port wine, rose or other flower perfumes, etc.). Some packagings are standardized such as plastic containers which can be used for melted cheese as well as various types of fresh cheese.

Canson & Montgolfier manufacture papers of different weights on rolls 2.20 metres wide and several hundred metres long. This 'upstream' operation requires large-scale investment and a high level of technology, and has limited flexibility. As far as possible, each type of roll is manufactured in batches (several times a year) and stored before its final processing. Cutting, shaping and finishing is carried out on standard rolls, which are then customized to the required formats and styles of each country. At Petit-Bateau, which manufactures traditional knitwear, the knitting is done on unbleached yarn. Dying is applied to the yarn subsequently. Likewise, standardized patterns permit the creation of a large number of different clothes. At Dim, a lingerie manufacturer, tights are produced undyed. The dye, which is subcontracted, is applied at the last possible opportunity on untreated standard tights. This allows flexible tailoring to the different shades sought by consumers. Irons by SEB-Calor are all manufactured on the same moulding, which gives rise to 100 different models, according to function, colour, casing, voltage and brand name. Christofle's Arab cafetières, designed exclusively for the Middle East, are manufactured with the same stamping moulds as other cafetières.[*]

The Planter's Company, a unit of Nabisco, chose cosmetic customization when it retooled its old plant in Suffolk, Virginia, in order to satisfy the increasingly diverse demand of its retail customers. Wal-Mart wanted to sell peanuts and mixed nuts in larger quantities than Safeway or 7-Eleven did, and Jewel wanted different promotional packages than Dominick's did. In the past, Planter's could produce only long batches of small, medium, and large cans; as a result, customers had to choose from a few standard packages to find the one that most closely met their requirements. Today the company can switch quickly between different sizes.[**]

(Sources: *Deher, 1986, p. 66, and **Gilmore and Pine, 1997, p. 94.)

Second, these beliefs are often acted upon. For example, Schuh (2000) analyzed case studies of western European and US companies operating in central eastern European countries. He concluded that Western companies rely heavily on standardization even when market conditions seemed to favour localization.

Third, many companies place more importance on their home markets. For example, Wright (2001, p. 352) interviewed managers of US and Japanese companies, finding the 'existence of ethnocentric orientations in both US and Japanese firms because of the prevailing assumptions by headquarter firms about the importance of their home markets'.

Globalization as a way to change the organizational design of international marketing activities

The reasons for globalizing marketing activities are largely organizational ones. Although there is evidence of some savings at the level of manufacturing costs, the financial pay-offs for hard globalization have been at best dubious when one considers the financial performance of companies as a whole (Samiee and Roth, 1992; Whitelock and Pimblett, 1997; see also case A5.3). MNCs that grew fast worldwide in the 1960s and 1970s did so by granting a large degree of decision-making autonomy to their subsidiaries in their home markets. Subsidiaries were asked to replicate the corporate values and organizational practices of the parent company and also encouraged to adjust completely to the local market. Later on, subsidiary managers used the message of 'our market is unique' to defend specific, nationally designed marketing policies. Hence they defended their autonomy even at the expense of sometimes rather fallacious arguments. MNCs probably needed at the beginning of the 1980s to shift their organizational design towards more centralization. Parent companies wanted to have a more unified implementation scheme of new, more centrally designed international marketing strategies, responding to the globalization of competition. Procter & Gamble did this in Europe by introducing the Eurobrand concept, consisting of a common brand name and a basic marketing strategy for most western European countries (see Box 8.4). In recent years, after a long

---

Box 8.4

Reactions from European managers of Procter & Gamble to Eurobrands

Comments of some managers in national subsidiaries:

'We have to listen to the consumer. In blind tests in my market that perfume cannot even achieve breakeven.'

'The whole detergent market is in 2-kilo packs in Holland. To go to a European standard of 3 kg and 5 kg sizes would be a disaster for us.'

'We have low phosphate in Italy that constrains our product formula. And we just don't have hypermarkets like France and Germany where you can drop off pallet loads.'

Comments of a general managers to P & G European headquarters:

'There is no such thing as a Eurocustomer so it makes no sense to talk about Eurobrands. We have an English housewife whose needs are different from a German Hausfrau. If we move to a system that allows us to blur our thinking, we will have big problems.

Product standardisation sets up pressures to try to meet everybody's needs (in which case you build a Rolls-Royce that nobody can afford) and countervailing pressures to find the lowest common denominator product (in which case you make a product that satisfies nobody and which cannot compete in any market). These decisions probably result in the foul middle compromise that is so often the outcome of committee decision.'

(Source: Bartlett, 1983.)

period of standardization/centralization, P & G gives now slightly more weight to localization, especially with regard to advertising and branding.

Global companies willing to recentralize their operations, since the 1980s tend towards some authoritarianism from headquarters, especially when they adopt the 'hard' version of the globalization creed. Often the globalization of consumption is presented as an unquestionable postulate, because it is much easier to 'sell' the recentralization policy within the organization. Kashani (1989) gives the example of the Danish toy company Lego, which was facing a leading competitor in the United States. The competitor, Tyco, sold its toys in plastic buckets instead of Lego's elegant see-through cartons, standardized worldwide. When asked by the management of the US subsidiary to package in buckets like Tyco, who was gaining market share, the head office rejected the request. After two years and a massive loss of share of the US market, Lego's headquarters in Billund (Denmark) decided to create a newly designed bucket. Not only was the share erosion in the US stopped, but the bucket was introduced worldwide and proved to be a great success.

The relationship between headquarters and subsidiaries in the defining of marketing strategy is complex. Too much autonomy results in purely local solutions with few economies of scale and an absence of worldwide coordination; at that point, strong action is needed. This was the case in Black & Decker's gamble on globalization (Saporito, 1984, p. 26):

Globalization did not go down well in Europe for one good reason: Black & Decker owned half the market on the continent, and an astounding 80 per cent in the U.K. European managers asked: 'Why tamper with success?' But Farley (B & D new chairman) believed that the company was treading water in Europe – sales failed to grow last year – and that Makita's strategy made globalization inevitable . . . Those who don't share Farley's vision usually don't stay around long. Last year he fired all of his European managers.

This was combined with a complete turnaround: Black & Decker acquired the GE small appliance division and a Swedish company producing woodworking tools, and changed the company name to B & D as well as the logo. B & D recentred a large part of its business on self powered tools with built-in batteries; finally it achieved a strong comeback (Li, 1990).

It is the patterns of globalization of competition which impose changes in organizational design

(recentralization), rather than the globalization of consumption patterns. In this process, negotiations and compromises between headquarters and subsidiaries are constant. As Kashani emphasized (1989, p. 92): 'the way global decisions are conceptualized, refined, internally communicated, and, finally implemented in the company's international network have a great deal to do with their performance'. Local managers naturally tend to emphasize the uniqueness of local consumption patterns and marketing environment (legal, distribution networks, sales promotion methods and so on). The Headquarters of successful global companies are flexible rather than authoritarian in dealing with their subsidiaries' assumed or real uniqueness; for instance, they commission research rather than flatly ignore a subsidiary's arguments; they take new ideas and suggestions from the most talented and dynamic subsidiaries, rather than rejecting their advice outright.

In fact, international marketing programmes have experienced a trend towards greater standardization, but this needs to be differentiated, according to: (1) the elements of the marketing mix considered; (2) the type of market: whether it is a developed or undeveloped country; (3) the type of product: consumer or industrial goods; and (4) the control exerted over the subsidiary, whether it is wholly owned or a joint venture. Ozsomer et al. (1991) investigated the degree of marketing standardization for 33 multinationals operating in Turkey: product characteristics, brand name, positioning and packaging are the least adapted elements; price, promotion and distribution are more tailored to the local environment. Similarly, Schuh (2000) found that adaptations mainly occur in non-core elements, including labelling, instructions, and selection of the appropriate product-mix and creative execution. Picard et al. (1989) found that the level of standardization of US multinational companies operating in Europe varied by product category. Between 1973 and 1983 there was a decrease in the degree of standardization for consumer durables and industrial goods, and an increase for consumer non-durables. More recently, O'Donnell (2000) examined performance implications of global standardization within high-tech, industrial products. She found that for these global industries, global standardization was positively related to organizational performance. Finally, Alden et al. (1999) sampled advertising in seven countries, both Asian and Western, to assess their global, local and foreign positioning. They found that 59 per cent of advertising emphasized associations with the local culture, while 22 per cent emphasized globally shared meaning and only 4 per cent emphasized foreign culture.

The degree of standardization is larger in wholly-owned subsidiaries than in joint ventures (Ozsomer *et al.*, 1991). In many cases, standardization is often done incrementally by transferring existing products at headquarters level or in important subsidiaries. Hill and James (1991) show that there remains a considerable degree of power at subsidiary level in relation to product and promotion transfer in consumer goods multinationals. In most cases market needs are assessed by the subsidiary itself, which then uses the worldwide product portfolio as a resource base. In developing countries, subsidiaries initiate product transfer in 85 per cent of the cases, whereas in developed markets they do it in only 63 per cent of the cases. This suggests that world or regional headquarters exert more authoritative pressure for standardization across developed markets, especially in Europe. In the transfer process some adaptation is made to local requirements (see Chapter 9 on this issue). In addition, cultural differences between headquarters and subsidiaries can affect performance. For instance, Hewett and Bearden (2001, p. 60) found that 'in more collectivistic cultures, trust takes on greater importance in motivating cooperative behaviours' as compared to more economic type rewards.

Artificial entry barriers, related to duties and standards, are now being progressively replaced by natural entry barriers related to scale and experience. For international marketing, culture-related experience is all the more important since the natural entry barriers relating to consumer behaviour and marketing environments will diminish very gradually and only in the long term. Language-related differences, for instance, will remain. Therefore, global marketing strategies must be implemented cautiously, especially in culture-bound industries: local knowledge has to be generated, by research, by organizational learning, by hiring 'cultural' insiders or by acquiring local companies with culture-specific business experience. (For more information on global marketing strategies see WS8.3.)

Globalization belongs to the realm of organizational discourse rather than to actual international marketing. Rather than a 'hard' global marketing strategy, it is possible to adopt an intercultural marketing strategy which has basically the same goals but

is more respectful of local culture and attempts to serve purely national as well as transnational market segments.

8.4
Market segments

Intercultural marketing is about localizing as much as globalizing: it aims to customize product and marketing strategies to customer needs within the framework of a global strategy. Intercultural marketing tries to balance cross-national differences requiring mandatory local adaptation and cross-national commonalities which enable the building of size and experience effects. To do this, the international marketer needs to define country clusters where similar marketing policies can be followed (for a review of country clustering, see Holzmüller and Stöllnberger, 1994).

Taking advantage of the desire for assimilation and cultural identification: The case of cultural products

Cultural products such as music, literature and movie films are strongly suffused with local particularism. Books, records and films are, however, three products where global marketing has been successfully employed. The success of Harlequin romantic novels, Harry Potter and *The Lord of the Rings* films has been remarkable: profound attraction has bypassed the filter of national cultures. The romantic and melodramatic adventures of Harlequin heroes found a lonely female public eager for tenderness in the majority of urban centres. Similarly, the meanings conveyed by the adventures of Harry Potter extend far beyond British culture.

Cultural products that build on fairly universal feelings and ways of being are the ones to which standardized marketing policy can be applied. In the recording industry, marketing techniques, particularly with regard to collections of popular music, have generally evolved in a similar fashion across industrialized nations, with increased large-scale distribution or specialized chains, similar promotion channels and advertising, and a global standardization of product presentation. The recipe for global success is, however, less easily applicable than it seems: American country music has failed in its attempt to achieve major success in continental Europe. Its only real international development occurred in Australia, despite some success in the United Kingdom. A reason for this is that no significant segment of the European population can identify itself with the images evoked by the music of the American West and the symbols of a pioneer tradition. On the other hand, the Australian outback, with its jackaroos and jillaroos, is similar in many respects to the American West with its cowboys and cowgirls, and has given birth to an Australian musical tradition whose roots are in country music.

Intercultural marketing is facilitated when the conditions for product identification are present in the target market. Consumers buy the meaning that they find in products for the purpose of cultural identification, based on the desire for assimilation in a certain civilization, as in the case of ethnic consumption (see section 4.4). Such identification was the reason that record companies began to market classical music on a large scale in the form of collections. In the 1980s, market surveys showed that owning a collection of classical music recordings, combined with a superficial knowledge of the most famous pieces, promoted a personal image of stability and respectability for people aged between 25 and 40, projecting an image of successful integration in professional and social lives. As a result, certain record companies launched mass-market compilations of classical music; their marketing strategy was to implement the strict rules of global marketing: same product, same packaging, same price and same type of communication. These compilations, however, became less successful in the 1990s when classical music ceased to be a major element in the acquisition of respectability.

Apart from their utilitarian aspects, McDonald's Big Mac and Coca-Cola are sources of meanings that provide their buyers with fantasized cultural adaptation to a desired way of life. Rock music represents a tolerant and leisurely way of life for many young Europeans and Asians. Identification with these symbols is one of the necessary conditions for being *trendy*, or 'cool'. The international marketing of rock music achieves even greater success where certain values (e.g. individualism, strong desire for equality) are already present in the market segment to be con-

quered, in this case young people between the ages of 10 and 25.

The process of cultural identification functions in two ways: that of *identity* (the reproduction of national culture as it used to be, the desire to be 'at home'), and that of *exoticism* (the desire to escape from one's own culture, to experience different values and ways of life). These two ways are intermingled in a quite ambivalent fashion in the process of cultural identification. This ambivalence prohibits any simplistic approach; it is therefore necessary to cluster countries or consumers who share certain meaningful cultural characteristics. Such clusters form cultural affinity zones and cultural affinity classes.

Cultural affinity classes and zones

The intercultural marketing approach not only concentrates on geography- and nationality-based criteria but also takes into account consumer attitudes, preferences and lifestyles that are linked to age, class and ethnicity, occupation, and so on. Many studies have used these bases to identify international market segments, including demographics (Anderson and He, 1999), psychographics and values (Hofstede, 1976; Boote, 1983; Kamakura et al., 1993; Kale, 1995; Wedel et al., 1998; Kahle et al., 1999; Kropp et al., 1999; Steenkamp, 2001), quality of life (Peterson and Malhotra, 2000), attitudes (Verhage et al., 1989), behaviour (Askegaard and Madsen, 1998), brand loyalty (Yavas et al., 1992) and situation (Gehrt and Shim, 2003).

Geographical cultural affinity zones correspond to a large extent to national cultural groups, while cultural affinity classes exist in terms of other segmentation bases. For instance, people between the ages of 15 and 20 in Japan, Europe and the United States form a cultural affinity class. They have a tendency to share common values, behaviour and interests, and tend to present common traits as a consumer segment; their lifestyles converge worldwide irrespective of national borders. As such, we see lifestyle convergence in teenagers in Europe who spend time watching MTV. Carey et al. (1997) surveyed 7- to 12-year-olds around the world in the ABC Global Kids Study, tracking their lifestyle and consumption patterns. A pictorial response scale was used when interviewing children on emotions and preferences while product usage was reported more frequently by mothers, rather than children. World-wide, children basically seem to share many common dreams and aspirations; they tend to have significant purchasing power and participate actively in family decision making for a number of product categories. (See *WS8.4* for examples of lifestyle segmentation studies and methods.)

De Mooij and Keegan (1991) reviewed com-parative lifestyle research in Europe and Asia, finding multinational target groups across the United Kingdom, France, Italy and Germany. 'Each of these target groups represents a distinctive segment across the different nations. Members of the social milieus within a multinational target group sometimes have more in common than with many of their fellow countrymen. In spite of these similarities, there are of course, differences. Similar values may translate differently at the local level' (De Mooij and Keegan, 1991, pp. 118–19). Attempts at monitoring cross-border changes in lifestyles are made in Asia by the Survey Research Group (SRG), which conducts lifestyle surveys in Hong Kong, Malaysia, the Philip-pines, Singapore, Thailand and Taiwan. Similarly, changes in lifestyles across social milieus in European countries are monitored through extensive surveys, such as the ACE (Anticipating Change in Europe) study, CCA (Centre de Communication Avancée), Eurostyles and Sinus Gmbh 'Social Milieus'.

Lifestyle convergence can also be observed for gender-based segments on a worldwide basis; Tai and Tam (1997) review the change in lifestyles of female consumers in Hong Kong, Taiwan and China on a number of issues such as the perception of women and their roles, family and home orientation, health and environment. They find that women in the People's Republic of China tend to be quickly influenced by Western values and are increasingly becoming sim-ilar to both Hong Kong and Taiwanese female con-sumers. Similarly, Koc (2002) found that gender was a useful segmentation criterion for travel agencies in Turkey.

The practical difficulty is in combining geography-based cultural affinity zones and demographics and lifestyle segmentation criteria (cultural affinity classes). One may wonder for instance, in relation to a specific product or service, whether consumption behaviour, values and lifestyles among the 15- to 20-year-olds are more homogeneous across Europe or

Asia than among the 30- to 40-year-olds in the same zones. Steenkamp and Ter Hofstede (2002) reviewed the international marketing segmentation literature. They found that only eight of the 25 studies reviewed used responses from individual consumers. In addi-tion, they described a number of conceptual and methodological issues that need to be addressed in future studies including construct equivalence, level of aggregation, and choice of segmentation basis.

Cultural affinity classes are probably an ideal means of defining an international target for standardized products, in so far as they create a sense of belonging to a common age, gender or income group across dif-ferent countries. Many different methods have been suggested for international market segmentation based on some form of cultural affinity, including those by Kale and Sudharshan (1987), Kreutzer (1988), Ter Hofstede *et al.* (1999), Souiden (2002) and others. Furthermore, the development of new media such as the Internet and satellite television channels will help the international launch of prod-ucts targeted at the same cultural affinity classes across different countries.

Accordingly, market research should survey con-sumer segments as cells in a matrix, with countries in columns and cultural affinity classes in rows. If similar behaviour is observed by market researchers for a particular row across the different cells of the matrix with regard to key consumer behaviour figures (e.g. consumption of soft drinks, organization of personal time, time spent listening to the radio or watching television, etc.), the emergence of a common consumption culture and a cross-national segment can be detected. If, on the other hand, dif-ferent cultural affinity classes in different countries adopt similar behaviour at the international level, marketing communication will have to be modified to facilitate the process of diffusion from one country to another. If a drink, for example, is popular among 25- to 30-year-olds in one country and among 50- to 60-year-olds in another country, this indicates a weak affinity of national cultures.

Attempts to market products on a global level also highlight cultural affinity zones in which the same marketing strategy with the same type of products can be successfully implemented. In Europe, for example, two of these zones are quite separate (see Figure 8.1) – Scandinavia and the Mediterranean countries. A third zone encompasses the central

Figure 8.1 A hypothetical map of the zones of cultural affinities in Europe

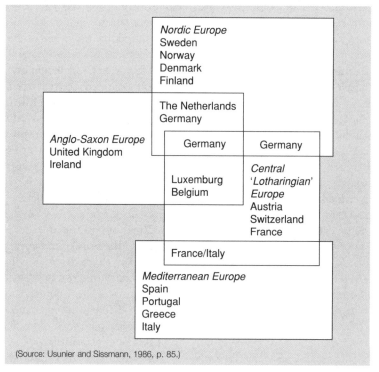

(Source: Usunier and Sissmann, 1986, p. 85.)

European countries and Great Britain, which serve as a bridge between northern and southern Europe, while retaining their own distinct personality. Despite the traditional isolation of the United Kingdom, there are fewer differences between the United Kingdom and Denmark or Sweden than between the UK and Italy or Spain. Accordingly, an item successfully marketed in the United Kingdom is more likely to repeat this success in The Netherlands or Denmark than in southern Europe. The long established differences between Anglo-Saxon and Latin culture are reinforced by the religious divide between Protestants and Catholics. Cultural affinity zones display similar characteristics for easily identifiable criteria such as language, religion, family life patterns, work relations and consumption patterns. Intercultural marketing begins by choosing one of the main countries from a cultural affinity zone as a 'lead country' that will be used as a base for market entry and diffusion of strategy, with only minor adaptation for other countries throughout the zone. Marketing teams can interact with each other across zones within a regional area, especially when countries lie at the border of two zones. As an

example, Figure 8.1 offers a *hypothetical map* of the zones of cultural affinities for western Europe.

The operational mapping of cultural affinity zones can be based on cultural as well as marketing criteria related to the product category, such as consumer behaviour, price levels, attitude towards innovation, opening hours in distribution outlets, etc. When a product is launched internationally, the new product will be launched first in lead countries and subsequently marketed in other countries in the zones. For instance, a record successful in Latin countries during the summer, when waves of holiday-makers come from all over Europe, will have a greater chance of spreading into Nordic countries once people return home and go into music stores to buy the songs they have heard on holiday. Equally, a band may be so successful in a single country, such as Germany, that its music spreads into neighbouring countries. It spreads rapidly in the border regions, for example in Belgium, because of media overlap. The launch of a new product through cultural affinity zones can take from 18 months to two years, which is a relatively long period of time compared with the standard life cycle of a song, generally a few months (Usunier and Sissmann, 1986). The concept of 'lead country' has been used successfully by multinational companies such as Procter & Gamble when they developed the Eurobrand concept in the mid-1980s.

In addition, we also need to recognize that product information can now be more rapidly disseminated than ever via the Internet, which may influence the stability of the segment membership (Kumar and Nagpal, 2001). Austin and Reed (1999) stated that: 'Almost 10 million (14 per cent) of America's 69 million children are now online with over 4 million children accessing the Internet from school and 5.7 million children going online from home' (p. 590). This may dramatically affect convergence in segmentation in the future.

National versus regional differences

Sovereign states have very dissimilar sizes: China (9,600,000 km²) is more than 232 times the size of Switzerland (49,293 km²), even though both countries are significant international players on the world scene. Geographical location has a relation to culture: for instance, on average, islands tend to develop more homogeneity than continental countries. A special case is that of mega-countries such as the United States, Canada, Brazil, China and India because their internal diversity is fairly large. Even smaller countries, such as the United Kingdom, Spain, Italy, Sweden and France, exhibit a strong North/South paradigm which is reversed in the southern hemisphere for countries such as Argentina, Australia and New Zealand. Even tiny Switzerland also displays significant internal diversity, especially between the French- and the German-speaking communities, which respectively account for 20 per cent and 75 per cent of the population. Therefore, national differences are not the only source of variance in consumer behaviour across different geographical locations.

Regional differences in large countries with multi-ethnic and multicultural backgrounds can explain differences in consumer behaviour (Garreau, 1981). Researchers have consistently found significant within-country differences (e.g., Kahle, 1986; Muller, 1989; Ralston et al., 1994; Schwartz, 1994; Januszewska et al., 2000; Lenartowics and Roth, 2001; Lenartowics et al., 2003). Most of these have to do with geograph-

ical divisions where geography, a shared history and a common ethnic background has served to create homogeneous groupings within countries (Lenartowicz et al., 2003).

The case of the United States is well documented. In the USA, Kahle (1986) found regional differences in consumers' values and Gentry et al. (1987) found regional differences in innovativeness and perceived risk, as well as cultural adherence, religious commitment, and fate-orientation. In South America, both regional differences within countries and value similarity across countries were found. Lenartowicz et al. (2003) used the Rokeach Value Survey (RVS) to examine the importance of regional subcultures in Brazil and Colombia and their value similarity with consumers in Uruguay and Venezuela. They found significant differences between regions in the relative importance of values, concluding that 'geography, a shared history and a common ethnic background might be as important in defining cultural subgroups as religion and language' (p. 1006). In Canada, differences have been found between English and French speakers in the same location. Laroche et al. (2002) investigated consumers in Montreal, Canada finding differences in pro-environmental knowledge, attitudes and behaviours between primarily French and primarily English speakers. They found that French-Canadians know more and are more concerned about environmental issues, whereas English-Canadians are more likely to recycle and are willing to pay more for environmentally friendly products.

However, regional differences within countries, even if perceived more clearly by nationals than by foreigners, are most often much smaller than international differences. For instance, Januszewska et al. (2000) studied the perceptions of chocolate among Belgian and Polish consumers, and found that at least two of the five segments were driven by nationality: the first segment was made up of 87 per cent Belgium consumers and third one made up of 91 per cent Polish consumers. In addition, they found that a subcultural design was not appropriate for Poland. Similarly, Calantone et al. (1985) find English Quebecois women to be more similar to French Quebecois women than to Ontario English women (all of these people being Canadians) in the benefits they seek from a brassiere. Their findings support the idea of the assimilation model, where the cultural values of the immigrants tend to merge with those of the locally dominant cultural group. This supports geography as an operational basis for international marketing segmentation. (For more information on geographic versus demographic segmentation see *WS8.4*.)

8.5

Conclusion

When building clusters of countries ('cultural affinity zones') that can be approached with a regionally stand-ardized marketing strategy, marketing professionals have to take into account basic cultural variables such as language, institutions, membership in a regional grouping, and basic cultural traits as described in Chapters 2 and 3. However, some sociodemographic characteristics such as sex, age and income also provide a sound basis for transnational marketing strategies in terms of 'cultural affinity classes'. Thus international marketing segments must be defined in order to allow for the best possible compromise between national/cultural and sociodemographic characteristics.

Questions

1. Describe how experience effects induce firms to standardize products. Give examples.

2. Select a multinational company annual report and find evidence of globalization (global decisions, global products, globalization of competition, consumption patterns, management procedures, etc.).

3. Why is globalization taking place more clearly on the supply side than on the demand side?

4. For the following industries/products discuss to what extent: (a) a world consumer exists; (b) the product or services offered are themselves global (similar worldwide); and (c) the industry itself can be considered as global:
   - airlines;
   - tobacco;
   - meat-based foods;
   - sheets and pillows;
   - pharmaceuticals.

5. What are zones of cultural affinity?

6. Discuss the relative importance for segmentation purposes of sociodemographic variables, such as age, sex, income, habitat, etc., in comparison with cultural variables based either on nationality or values.

References

Alden, Dana L., Jan-Benedict E.M. Steenkamp and Rajeev Batra (1999), 'Brand positioning through advertising in Asia, North America, and Europe: the role of global consumer culture', *Journal of Marketing*, vol. 63, pp. 75–87.

Amdur, Meredith (2003), 'Koch Lorber lines up Bollywood DVD series', *Variety*, 10 July.

Anderson, Erin and Barton Weitz (1989), 'Determinants of continuity in conventional industrial channel dyads', *Marketing Science*, vol. 8, pp. 310–23.

Anderson, Patricia M. and Xiahong He (1999), 'Culture and fast-food marketing mix in the People's republic of China and the USA: implications for research and marketing', *Journal of International Consumer Marketing*, vol. 11, no. 1, pp. 77–95.

Askegaard, Søren and T.K. Madsen (1998), 'The local and the global: exploring traits of homogeneity and hetero-geneity in European food cultures', *International Business Review*, vol. 7, no. 6, pp. 549–68.

Austin, M. Jill and Mary Lynn Reed (1999), 'Targeting children online: Internet Advertising issues,' *Journal of Consumer Marketing*, vol. 16, no. 6, pp. 590–602.

Bartlett, Christopher (1983), 'Procter & Gamble Europe: Vizir launch', *Harvard Business School Case* 9-384-139.

BBC News (2001), 'Bollywood eyes Afghan market', online, 27 November.

BBC News (2002a), 'Lagaan scoops Bollywood awards', *Entertainment*, online, 6 April.

BBC News (2002b), 'Bollywood's hopes for Oscar dollars', online, 13 February.

Boote, A.S. (1983), 'Psychographic segmentation in Europe', *Journal of Advertising Research*, vol. 22, December–January, pp. 19–25.

Business Standard (2002), 'Movie marketing comes of age', New Delhi, 21 March.

Businessweek (2002), 'Bollywood VS. Hollywood', 2 December.

Buzzell, Robert D. (1968), 'Can you standardize multinational marketing?', *Harvard Business Review*, November–December, pp. 102–13.

Calantone, R., M. Morris and J. Johar (1985), 'A cross-cultural benefit segmentation analysis to evaluate the traditional assimilation model', *International Journal of Research in Marketing*, vol. 2, pp. 207–17.

Carey, George, Xiaoyan Zhao, Joan Chiaramonte and David Eden (1997), 'Is there one global village for our future generation? Talking to 7–12 year olds around the world', *Marketing & Research Today*, vol. 25, no. 1, pp. 12–16.

Chabra, Aseem (2002), 'How original is Bollywood?', *Rediff on the Net*, online, 31 October, available at: http://rediff.com/entertai/2002/oct/31bolly.htm.

Cooper, Louise (2003), 'Bollywood struck by horror', *BBC News*, online, 23 April, available at: http://news.bbc.co.uk/1/hi/business/2969101.stm.

Czinkota, Michael R. and Illka A. Ronkainen (1990), *International Marketing*, 2nd edn, Dryden Press: Hinsdale, IL.

Day, George S. and David B. Montgomery (1983), 'Diagnosing the experience curve', *Journal of Marketing*, Spring, pp. 44–58.

De Mooij, Marieke K. and Warren Keegan (1991), *Advertising Worldwide*, Prentice Hall: Hemel Hempstead.

Deher, Odile (1986), 'Quelques facteurs de succès pour la politique de produits de l'entreprise exportatrice: les liens entre marketing et production', *Recherche et applications en marketing*, vol. 1, no. 3, pp. 55–74.

Dentsu Young and Rubicam, Inc. (2000) *New York Marketing Information. The Indian Influence*, Dentsu Young and Rubicam, Inc. (Japan), 10 July.

Douglas, Susan P. (2001), 'Exploring new worlds: the challenge of global marketing', *Journal of Marketing*, vol. 65, no. 1, pp. 103–7.

Episcopo, Jo (2001), 'Bollywood comes to Cannes', *BBC News World Edition*, online, 15 May, available at: http://news.bbc.co.uk/1/hi/entertainment/film/1331700.stm.

Focus (1995), Information bulletin of the World Trade Organization, January–February, no. 1, pp. 4–5.

Gahlot, Deepa (1999), 'Why the world loves Hindi movies', *Himal: The South Asian Magazine*, September, 1999.

Garreau, J. (1981), *The Nine Nations of North America*, Houghton Mifflin: Boston, MA.

GATT (1986), *Le Commerce International en 1985–1986*, GATT: Geneva.

Gehrt, Kenneth C. and Soyeon Shim (2003), Situational segmentation in the international marketplace: the Japanese snack market', *International Marketing Review*, vol. 20, no. 2, pp. 180–94.

Gentry, J.W., P. Tansujah, L. Lee Manzer and J. John (1987), 'Do geographic subcultures vary culturally?', in Michael J. Houston (ed.), *Advances in Consumer Research*, vol. 15, Association for Consumer Research: Provo, UT.

Ger, Güliz (1999), 'Localizing in the global village: local firms competing in global markets', *California Management Review*, vol. 41, no. 4, pp. 64–83.

Gilmore, James H. and B. Joseph Pine II (1997), 'The four faces of mass customization', *Harvard Business Review*, vol. 75, no. 1, January–February, pp. 91–101.

Hampton, Gerald M. and Erwin Buske (1987), 'The global marketing perspective', in S. Tamer Cavusgil (ed.), *Advances in International Marketing*, JAI Press: Greenwich, CT, vol. 2, pp. 259–77.

Hewett, Kelly and William O. Bearden (2001), 'Dependence, trust, and relational behavior on the part of foreign subsidiary marketing operations: implications for managing global marketing operations,' *Journal of Marketing*, vol. 65, October, pp. 51–66.

Hill, John S. and Richard R. Still (1984), 'Adapting products to L.D.C. tastes', *Harvard Business Review*, March–April, pp. 92–101.

Hill, John S. and William L. James (1991), 'Product and promotion transfers in consumer goods multinationals', *International Marketing Review*, vol. 8, no. 4, pp. 6–17.

Hofstede, Geert (1976), 'Nationality and espoused values of managers', *Journal of Applied Psychology*, vol. 61, no. 2, pp. 148–55.

Hollensen, Svend (1991), 'Shift of market servicing organization in international markets: a Danish case study', in Harald Vestergaard (ed.), *An Enlarged Europe in the Global Economy*, proceedings of the 17th Annual Conference of the European International Business Association, Copenhagen Business School: Copenhagen, pp. 732–42.

Holzmüller, Hartmut H. and Barbara Stöllnberger (1994), 'A conceptual framework for country selection in cross-national export studies', *Advances in International Marketing*, vol. 6, pp. 3–24.

Hult, G. Thomas M., David W. Cravens and Jagdish Sheth (2001), 'Competitive advantage in the global marketplace: a focus on marketing strategy', *Journal of Business Research*, vol. 51, pp. 1–3.

Hult, G. Thomas M. and David J. Ketchen, Jr. (2001), 'Does market orientation matter? A test of the relationship between positional advantage and performance', *Strategic Management Journal*, vol. 22, no. 9, pp. 899–906.

Januszewska, Renata, Jacques Viaene and Wim Verbeke (2000), 'Market segmentation for Chocolate in Belgium and Poland', *Journal of Euromarketing*, vol. 9, no. 3, pp. 1–25.

Jatania, Lynn (2002), 'Hollywood/Bollywood', *Sidekick Magazine*, January, issue 51.

Jha, Subhash K. (2002), 'Hollywood, Bollywood-style!', *Rediff on the Net*, online, 28 March, available at: **www. rediff.com/entertai/2002/mar/28bolly.htm**.

Johanson, Jan and Jan-Erik Vahlne (1977), 'The internationalisation process of the firm: a model of knowledge development and increased market commitments,' *Journal of International Business Studies*, vol. 8, no. 1, pp. 23–32.

Kahle, Lynn R. (1986), 'The nine nations of North America and the value basis of geographic segmentation', *Journal of Marketing*, vol. 50, April, pp. 37–47.

Kahle, Lynn R., Gregory Rose and Aviv Shoham (1999), 'Findings of LOV throughout the world, and other evidence of cross-national consumer psychographics: Introduction', *Journal of Euromarketing*, vol. 8, no. 1/2, pp. 1–13.

Kale, Sudhir. H. (1995), 'Grouping Euroconsumers: a culture-based clustering approach', *Journal of International Marketing*, vol. 3, no. 3, pp. 35–48.

Kale, Sudhir. H. and D. Sudharshan (1987), 'A strategic approach to international segmentation', *International Marketing Review*, vol. 4, no. 2, pp. 60–70.

Kamakura, Wagner. A., Thomas P. Novak, Jan-Benedikt E.M. Steenkamp and Theo M.M. Verhallen (1993), 'Identification de segments de valeurs pan-Europe´ens par un mode`le logit sur les rangs avec regroupements successifs (Identifying pan-European value segments with a clusterwise rank-logit model)', *Recherche et Applications en Marketing*, vol. 8, no. 4, pp. 30–55.

Kashani, Kamran (1989), 'Beware the pitfalls of global marketing', *Harvard Business Review*, vol. 67, September–October, pp. 91–8.

Kaushal, Raj (2003), 'The rise and rise of "desi" beats', *Telegraph*, 13 September.

Koc, Erdogan (2002), 'The impact of gender in marketing communications: The role of cognitive and affective cues', *Journal of Marketing Communications*, vol. 8, pp. 257–75.

Kreutzer, R.T. (1988), 'Marketing mix standardization: an integrated approach in global marketing', *European Journal of Marketing*, vol. 22, no. 10, pp. 19–30.

Kripalani, Manjeet and Ron Grover (2002), 'Bollywood: can new money create a world-class film industry in India?', *Businessweek*, 2 December.

Kropp, Fredric, Marylin Jones, Gregory Rose, Aviv Shoham, Bella Florenthal and Bongjin Cho (1999), 'Group identities: a cross-cultural comparison of values and group influences', *Journal of Euromarketing*, vol. 8, no. 1/2, pp. 117–31.

Kumar, V. and Anish Nagpal (2001), 'Segmenting global markets: look before you leap', *Marketing Research*, vol. 13, no. 1, pp. 8–13.

Laroche, Michel, Marc-Alexandre Tomiuk, Jasmin Bergeron and Guido Barbaro-Forleo (2002), 'Cultural differences in environmental knowledge, attitudes, and behaviours of Canadian consumers', *Canadian Journal of Administrative Sciences*, vol. 19, no. 3, pp. 267–83.

Lenartowicz, Thomasz, James P. Johnson and Carolyn T. White (2003), 'The neglect of intracultural variation in international management research', *Journal of Business Research*, vol. 56, no. 12, pp. 999–1008.

Lenartowicz, Thomasz and Kendall Roth (2001), 'Does subculture within a country matter? A cross-national study of motivational domains and business performance in Brazil', *Journal of International Business Studies*, vol. 32, no. 2, pp. 305–25.

Li, Tiger (1990), 'Black and Decker's turnaround strategy', in Hans B. Thorelli and S. Tamer Cavusgil (eds), *International Marketing Strategy*, Pergamon Press: Oxford, pp. 495–8.

Malcolm, Derek (2001), 'A song and a dance', *Guardian*, 25 October.

Malhotra, Naresh K., James Agarwal and Imad Baalbaki (1998), 'Heterogeneity of regional trading blocks and global marketing strategies: a multicultural perspective', *International Marketing Review*, vol. 15, no. 6, pp. 476–506.

Mather, Anne (1966), *Dangerous Enchantment*, Harlequin: London.

Mathur, Arti (2003), 'India looks to UK to stem piracy', *Variety*, 29 May.

Matthyssens, Paul and Pieter Pauwels (2000), 'Uncovering international market-exit processes: a comparative case study', *Psychology & Marketing*, vol. 17, no. 8, pp. 697–719.

O'Donnell, Sharon and Insik Jeong (2000), 'Marketing standardization within global industries', *International Marketing Review*, vol. 17, no. 1, pp. 19–33.

Ohmae, Kenichi (1985), *Triad Power: The coming shape of global competition*, Free Press: New York.

Ozsomer, Aysegul, Muzzafer Bodur and S. Tamer Cavusgil (1991), 'Marketing standardisation by multinationals in an emerging market,' *European Journal of Marketing*, vol. 25, no. 12, pp. 50–64.

Pearson, Bryan (2003a), 'Analyst sez Bollywood's on track to bounce back', *Variety*, 23 March.

Pearson, Bryan (2003b), 'Love, song, dance . . . and suspense', *Variety*, 16 February.

Perlmutter, H. (1969), 'The tortuous evolution of the multinational corporation', *Columbia Journal of World Business*, vol. 4, no. 1, pp. 9–18.

Peterson, Mark and Naresh K. Malhotra (2000), 'Country segmentation based on objective quality-of-life measures', *International Marketing Review*, vol. 17, no. 1, pp. 56–73.

Picard Jacques, Jean-Jacques Boddewyn and Robin Soehl (1989), 'U.S. marketing policies in the European Economic Community: a longitudinal study, 1973–1983', in Reijo Luostarinen (ed.), *Dynamics of International Business*, Proceedings of the 15th Annual Conference of the European International Business Association, Helsinki, vol. 1, pp. 551–79.

Porter, Michael E. (1986), 'Changing patterns of international competition', *California Management Review*, vol. XXVIII, no. 2, pp. 9–39.

Prasad, V. Kanti, K. Ramamurthy and G.M. Naidu (2001), 'The influence of Internet-marketing integration on marketing competencies and export performance', *Journal of International Marketing*, vol. 9, no. 4, pp. 82–110.

Qian, Gongming and Ji Li (2002), 'Multinationality, global market diversification and profitability among the largest US firms', *Journal of Business Research*, vol. 55, no. 4, pp. 325–35.

Rose, Steve (2001), 'Sheer Khan', *Guardian*, 20 October.

Rugman, Alan (2001), 'The myth of global strategy', *International Marketing Review*, vol. 18, no. 6, pp. 583–8.

Samiee, Saeed and Kendall Roth (1994), 'The influence of global marketing standardization on performance', *Journal of Marketing*, vol. 56, April, pp. 1–17.

Samli, A. Coskun and John S. Hill (1999), *Marketing Globally: Planning and practice*, NTC Publishing: Lincolnwood, IL. (Review in *Journal of International Marketing*, vol. 7, no. 2, 1999.)

Saporito, William (1984), 'Black & Decker's gamble on globalization', *Fortune*, 14 May, pp. 24–32.

Schuh, Arnold (2000), 'Global standardization as a success formula for marketing in central eastern Europe', *Journal of World Business*, vol. 35, no. 2, pp. 133–48.

Shah, Deepa (2002), 'Hooray for Bollywood', *Observer*, 24 March.

Sheth, Jagdish N. (2001), 'From international to integrated marketing', *Journal of Business Research*, vol. 51, pp. 5–9.

Sheth, Jagdish N. and Atul Parvatiyar (2001), 'The antecedents and consequences of integrated global marketing', *International Marketing Review*, vol. 18, no. 1, pp. 16–29.

Souiden, Nizar (2002), 'Segmenting the Arab markets on the basis of marketing stimuli', *International Marketing Review*, vol. 19, no. 6.

Steenkamp, Jan-Benedikt E.M. (2001), 'The role of national culture in international marketing research', *International Marketing Review*, vol. 18, no. 1, pp. 30–44.

Steenkamp, Jan-Benedikt E.M. and Frenkel Ter Hofstede (2002), 'International market segmentation: Issues and perspectives', *International Journal of Research in Marketing*, vol. 19, no. 3, pp. 185–213.

Sternstein, Aliya (2003), 'Bully for Bollywood!', *Forbes Global*, 28 April.

Stobaugh, Robert and Piero Telesio (1983), 'Assortir la politique de fabrication à la stratégie des produits', *Harvard-L'Expansion*, Summer, pp. 77–85.

Swift, Jonathan B. (1999), 'Cultural closeness as a facet of cultural affinity', *International Marketing Review*, vol. 16, no. 3, pp. 182–201.

Tai, Susan H.C. and Jackie L.M. Tam (1997), 'A lifestyle analysis of female consumers in greater China', *Psychology and Marketing*, vol. 14, no. 3, pp. 287–307.

Ter Hofstede, Frenkel, Jan-Benedikt E.M. Steenkamp and Michel Wedel (1999), 'International market segmentation based on consumer-product relations', *Journal of Marketing Research*, vol. XXXVI, February, pp. 1–17.

Theodosiou, Marios and Leonidas C. Leonidou (2003), 'Standardization versus adaptation of international marketing strategy: an integrative assessment of the empirical research', *International Business Review*, vol. 12, no. 2, pp. 141–71.

Usunier, Jean-Claude (1980), 'Les Lois de déformation des réseaux du commerce international', unpublished doctoral thesis, University of Paris II.

Usunier, Jean-Claude (2002), 'Le pays d'origine du bien influence-t-il encore les évaluations des consommateurs?', *Revue Française du Marketing*, no.189/190, 2002/4–5, pp. 49–65.

Usunier, Jean-Claude and Pierre Sissmann (1986), 'L'interculturel au service du marketing', *Harvard-L'Expansion*, no. 40, Spring, pp. 80–92.

Van Oudenhoven, Jan Pieter and Karen I. Van der Zee (2002), 'Successful international cooperation: the influence of cultural similarity, strategic differences, and international experience', *Applied Psychology*, vol. 51, no. 4, p. 633.

Verhage, Bronislaw J., Lee D. Dahringer and Edward W. Cundiff (1989), 'Will a global strategy work? An energy conservation perspective', *Journal of the Academy of Marketing Science*, vol. 17, no. 2, pp. 129–36.

Vernon, Raymond P. (1966), 'International investment and international trade in the product life cycle', *Quarterly Journal of Economics*, vol. 80, no. 2, pp. 191–207.

Wedel, Michael, Frenkel Ter Hofstede and Jan-Benedikt E.M. Steenkamp (1998), 'Mixture model analysis of complex samples', *Journal of Classification*, vol. 15, no. 2, pp. 225–44.

Whitelock, Jeryl and Carole Pimblett (1997), 'The standardization debate in international marketing', *Journal of Global Marketing*, vol. 10, no. 3, pp. 45–65.

Wilkinson, Ian F. and Constant Cheng (1999), 'Multicultural marketing in Australia: synergy in diversity', *Journal of International Marketing*, vol. 7, no. 3, pp. 106–25.

Wind, Yoram (1986), 'The myth of globalization', *Journal of Consumer Marketing*, vol. 3, Spring, pp. 23–6.

Wind, Yoram, Susan P. Douglas and Howard V. Perlmutter (1973), 'Guidelines for developing international marketing strategies', *Journal of Marketing*, vol. 37, April, pp. 14–23.

Wong, C. and C. Lamb, Jr. (1983), 'The impact of selected environmental forces upon consumers' willingness to buy foreign products', *Journal of the Academy of Marketing Science*, vol. 11, no. 2, pp. 71–84.

World Trade Organization (2004), 'Stronger than expected growth spurs modest trade recovery', available at: **www.wto.org/english/news_e/pres04_e/pr373_e.htm** [accessed 18 May 2004].

Wright, Len Tiu (2001), 'Intercontinental comparisons in marketing strategy', *International Marketing Review*, vol. 18, no. 3, pp. 344–54.

Xu Dean and Oded Shenkar (2002), 'Institutional distance and the multinational enterprise', *Academy of Management Review*, vol. 27, no. 4, pp. 608–18.

Yavas, Ugur, Bronislaw J. Verhage and Robert T. Green (1992), 'Global consumer segmentation versus local market orientation: empirical findings', *Management International Review*, vol. 32, no. 3, pp. 265–73.

Yu, C.J. and D.S. Zietlow (1995), 'The determinants of bilateral trade among Asia-Pacific countries', *Asean Economic Bulletin*, vol. 11, no. 3, pp. 298–305.

Zou, Shaoming and Tamir Cavusgil (2002), 'The GMS: a broad conceptualization of global marketing strategy and its effect on firm performance', *Journal of Marketing*, vol. 66, no. 4, pp. 40–56.

Teaching materials

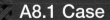

A8.1 Case

Bollywood

'Why me?' grumbled Nico Rogosky, account executive for Pentagram Asian films North America. When Bollywood producer Anjali Kumar called to ask him to take over the marketing and distribution of two new 'Bollywood' films, he suggested she contact a South Asian film marketing expert like *Eros*. 'No, no,' she had breezily said, 'we don't want to plug the films to your Indian minority market as usual. We want to make crossover films to appeal to other ethnic groups and the general public. I called you for a different approach.'

Nico had spent the entire afternoon viewing two Bollywood hits with his Indian equivalent, just to get an idea of the genre. So, he mused, sipping a searing-hot green tea, they want us to market their movies, then DVDs and videos, and maybe cable. The company also asked for advice on producing films directly for the North American market. Nico had enjoyed talking over dinner with his Indian counterpart from Kumar Film, a sophisticated chain-smoker named Rishi, who had studied business in Florida. Now sitting comfortably at his home office, Nico listened to the conversation he had recorded.

Nico's conversation with Rishi

Nico: I could see the actors were lip-synching, it was embarrassingly obvious!

Rishi: We'll cut the singing out of the films for you. Everyone knows that actors can't sing, and a handful of back-up singers sing for all the Bollywood stars. Actually, no one cares: back-up singer Lata Mangeshkar has more worldwide sales than the Beatles. Actors Shah Rukh Khan and Aamir Khan sold out London's Wembley Arena with backup singers singing 100 per cent of the concert!

Nico: It was incongruous, though, all those songs interfering with the story line.

Rishi: Actor and film producer Shahrukh Khan famously said that if he had produced *Gladiator*, he would have Russell Crowe singing songs in it [Rose, 2001]. Film star Aamir Khan said that in a movie, the songs hold an emotion, and squeeze the juice from it . . . It's just pure Bollywood.

Nico: The sexual tension between the lovers was unbearable, but the most we saw was some kissing. I would have expected them to, like, hop in bed at that point.

Rishi: Yeah, some say we're prudes, that we're censored. We're conservative, but not prudish. So metaphor, imagery and song/dance routines express sexual undercurrents. That film was quite explicit, actually. You have a lot of people here in the US who would appreciate our level of modesty in films.

Nico: The movies were fabulous, but the story and character development were weak.

Rishi: When I've spoken with film critics from your country, from England, and from France, they all say we're 'exuberant', 'melodramatic', 'earthy'. But film snobs prefer 'over the top', 'predictable', 'unrealistic', and 'superficial'. Our films are life, only more pretty. We don't pretend we're intellectuals or artists. A lot of our audiences are in far-flung villages, workers who spend a day's wage at the ticket office. We give them beauty, glamour, romance, music . . . escape. That is what your troubled people are now seeking too.

Nico had seen *Bend it like Beckham*, *Monsoon Wedding*, and other 'Asian' films that were hits in the USA and the UK, like *Crouching Tiger, Hidden Dragon*, but nothing like this. They want to appeal to Americans? For the art-house crowd there shouldn't be an issue, thought Nico. Indian style is 'in', henna, piercing, yoga, ayurveda, tattoos, and so on have become mainstream, and South-Asian inspired music like Bhangra and Asian Underground are played regularly in dance clubs (Kaushal, 2003). But what will the archetypal housewife in Idaho think of Bollywood movies? On the other hand, the conservative right should love the movies. Nico smiled, remembering their recent boycotts of Hollywood stars for their political stances and the boycotts for alleged sexual and homosexual allusions in Disney children's films.

What about the growing communities of immigrants who tend to be more conservative (at least where their families are concerned) than mainstream Americans. A lot of them have felt marginalized over the past few years, and may be seeking self-affirmation elsewhere than Hollywood. *You know, Rishi and his colleagues might just stand a chance with a little help from us*, was Nico's surprising thought before sitting down to read more about Bollywood.

Bollywood: A preview

In the world of film, there are two giants: the United States and India. In terms of films produced per year, India's Mumbai (formerly Bombay, hence 'Bollywood') is the leading lady. In 2001, India produced 1,013 films, while Hollywood films numbered 739 (*Businessweek*, 2002). Any similarities between the two end there. It is estimated that Mumbai alone produces about 800 Hindi films per year, with other Indian cities producing the rest. Worldwide revenues for Bollywood in 2002 were estimated at US$1.3 billion, while Hollywood totalled US$51 billion (*Businessweek*, 2002).

According to the legend, Bollywood films resemble the fragrant, heady *masala* mixture of black pepper, cumin, cloves, cardamom, and other spices used in cooking. *Masala* films are a mixture of elements to keep audiences interested: song, dance, action, romance and comedy. It is a film genre unto itself: the product of Indian village theatre, Victorian drama, and opera. Films commonly comprise three hours of romance, travel, courtship, marriage, tragedy and redemption, played to the backdrop of sumptuously appointed and colourful sets. (For more information, go to **www.bollywhat.com**.)

The stars, like Madhuri Dixit, Rani Mukherjee and Hrithik Roshan are gorgeous, and they express their emotions with a frantic sincerity in words and in lip-synched songs that appear to put the plot on hold. The music uses primal rhythms, and the tunes are catchy, accompanied by sinuous dances featuring dozens of costumed dancers. The plot may shift from place to place, with surprising interludes shot in beautiful locations like Scotland, Australia, Switzerland or New Zealand.

The storyline usually begins with a boy meets girl premise, however one of the two is from the 'wrong' social background. There is a coincidence that brings star-crossed lovers together, then fate thwarts them with death. Weeping mothers, archetypal families, giggling sisters, stereotypical characters and slapstick roles complete the *masala* film recipe. That is the legend. The reality of Bollywood films has changed in recent years, for artistic and more prosaic business and marketing reasons.

Bollywood is often accused of taking 'inspiration' from Hollywood productions partly because Hollywood is India's primary recognizable reference for wealth, style, and coolness. This perception only works one way, however: Bollywood films have yet to cross over from the 'ethnic' South Asian cinema to the main street cinema. Leading producer Ashok Amritraj does not believe that a Hindi film can have mass appeal in the USA (Chabra, 2002).

Others point to *Lagaan* and *Monsoon Wedding*, two Indian films with critical and box-office success. *Lagaan* (2001) featured a cricket game that put oppression into play between poor Indian villagers and their sneering colonial overlords (go to **http://www.lagaan.com** for more information). It was short listed for the Best Foreign Film Award at the Oscars, nominated Best Foreign Language Film at the Academy Awards, and won seven India International Film Awards (*BBC News*, 2002a). It made money also: US$2 million at US and UK box offices (*BBC News*, 2002b). *Monsoon Wedding* (2001), which featured an arranged marriage in New Delhi, won a Golden Lion at the Venice Film Festival. The film earned over US$30 million worldwide, and was the highest grossing Indian film to date in the United States at US$13,882,786. In a development likely to increase acceptance of Bollywood films, Sir Andrew Lloyd Webber's musical *Bombay Dreams* will probably be as much of a hit on Broadway as it has been in London.

Bollywood holds obvious potential, with an annual growth rate of 12.6 per cent (compared to Hollywood's 5.6 per cent). Some Bollywood hits boast of a return on investment of 25 per cent or more. Possibly the most persuasive argument in favour of Bollywood is the general claim that 'half of humanity' views Bollywood films – in 2001, 3.6 billion tickets were sold worldwide. By way of comparison, Hollywood sold 2.6 billion tickets. New forms of distribution are adding Bollywood's profitability: in 2001, DVD, video and satellite television sales totalled US$108 million, an increase of 25 per cent from the previous year (*Businessweek*, 2002).

Bootlegged DVDs and videos inundate India's domestic and expatriate markets worldwide within days of a Bollywood film release, costing the Indian film industry US$75 million in 2002, or 60 per cent of the market value (Sternstein, 2003). From pirated soundtracks, Bollywood lost over US$140 million (Mathur, 2003). However, management consultants KPMG International predict that gross revenue should rise to US$1.97 billion by 2007 due to consolidation and quality over quantity in films (Pearson, 2003a).

Up until 2001, film making was not recognized as an 'industry' in India, therefore about 40 per cent of Bollywood's finances originated in organized crime, according to the police (Kripalani and Grover, 2002). A string of film-worthy murders and scandals made clear that Bollywood glamour, power and money laundering were attractive to the mob. Producers now seek funding from banks and international corporations, forcing a new professionalism that includes proper marketing plans and newer marketing tools like in-film product placements and 'marketing the film like a brand' activities and public relations, and merchandising (*Business Standard*, 2002). (To get an idea of some Bollywood marketing tactics, visit **http://www.indiafm.com**.)

Hollywood itself believes in the potential of Bollywood: Columbia TriStar Motion Picture Group distributed *Lagaan* and *Mission Kashmir* in the United States, and is slated to distribute many more. Twentieth Century Fox has committed to marketing and distributing Hindi films by Bollywood producer Ram Gopal Verma. Hyperion Pictures is collaborating in a US–Bollywood feature called *Marigold* (Kripalani and Grover, 2002). Bollywood film, video and DVD distributors in the United States target the 'Desi' communities (Indian, Pakistani, Sri Lankan and Bangladeshi), and increasingly the Middle Eastern and Russian communities there where the genre has a huge following (Amdur, 2003).

Indian films have slowly but surely become an international commodity. An estimated 10–15 million Indian expatriates known as Non Resident Indians (NRIs) live in the United Kingdom, the United States, Asia and Africa. Their annual income totals approximately US$375 billion, and they are said to account for 40 per cent of any Bollywood production's profits. The large South Asian communities in the USA and UK account for 55 per cent of international ticket sales and, understandably, Bollywood films incorporate NRIs into their stories in an effort to keep the interest of expatriates (Dentsu Young and Rubicam Inc., 2000; Shah, 2002). This apparently alienates the average viewer in India, however.

Hindi cinema has for years enjoyed a strong following independent of the South Asian expatriate communities in the Gulf region, Egypt, Russia and certain eastern European countries, and some African nations. Afghanistan was once one of the biggest markets for Hindi films, and the first films to play after the fall of the Taliban were Hindi (*BBC News*, 2001). Because of their relatively modest and subtle portrayal of the female body and sexual acts, Hindi films have long had the favour of distributors in Arab countries (Dentsu Young and Rubicam Inc., 2000). The fact that many Bollywood stars are Muslim is also helpful. Indian films have long had a 'cult' or 'art house' following in wealthy countries as well (Gahlot, 1999). Since 2001, the Indian government has demonstrated greater commitment to export efforts, and has participated in more film festivals and exhibitions (Episcopo, 2001). Technological change has played a role in the 'internationalization' of Bollywood films, with satellite television beaming around the globe.

However, at the moment Bollywood was poised to achieve respectability, things started to go wrong. Some reports estimate that only 7 per cent of films in 2001 made a profit (Jatania, 2002). In 2002, 98 per cent of films were box office failures, with the notable exception of horror film *Raaz*, incurring a loss of US$58 million (Cooper, 2003; Pearson, 2003b). (For a survey of Bollywood's lucrative 'horror' phase, go to **http://sify.com/entertainment/movies/ horror/index.php**.) The Indian government announced that it was to loosen its protectionist laws on cinema imports, opening the floodgates to Hollywood films. Across India, 500 cinemas closed in 2002 and in the first half of 2003, the industry was thought to have lost US$2 million to US$8 million (Pearson, 2003b). Bollywood appeared to be at a crucial juncture.

As actor Akshay Kumar observed, Indian audiences no longer imperatively seek *rohadhona* (tears and family-oriented emotion) at the cinema because they receive high doses of it from television soap operas (Jha, 2002). Analysts have reported audience fatigue with rehashed formulas and high ticket prices (Pearson, 2003b). Producers have responded to a perception that audiences want a change by making thrillers and horror films (all containing some song and dance routines). Suspense films have all but taken over from the well-worn Bollywood romantic formula. However, they are conducive to good music, and romance may be integrated into the plot to keep the audience happy, according to trade analyst Vindo Mirani (Pearson, 2003b).

In a nod to 'Western' films, some recent films have included fewer songs or no songs at all, in addition to far away locations – such as Los Angeles where Sanjay Gupta directed *Kaante*, a US$2.2 million thriller featuring four Bollywood idols and an all-American cast and crew. The film, recorded in English and Hindi, opened to mixed reviews in India. The film was closely modelled on Hollywood hits *Usual Suspects* and *Reservoir Dogs*. According to reports, the producers of *Kaante* plan two US releases of the film: a full-length version intended for South Asian expatriates, and a shorter one (minus songs) for the general public (Chabra, 2002). Other films have met the same cut before release abroad – *Asoka*, the story of the emperor-turned-Buddhist monk is an example where songs and dances have been cut for European release (Malcolm, 2001).

Questions

1. What is culture specific and what is universal in Indian movie films? Which features of Indian films may not fit with a Western audience?

2. Is there a market for Indian movies in the United States? In Europe? What are the target audiences (ethnic groups versus general audience)?

3. Should Nico Rogosky and Pentagram accept the offer of Anjali Kumar to take over the marketing and distribution of two new 'Bollywood' films? If yes, what should Nico ask from Anjali and Rishi if he wants to minimize the risk of a failure?

For images and profiles on some major Bollywood stars, go to the following sites:

www.amitabh4u.com
www.bollywhat.com/Biographies/RANI_bio.html
www.khoj.com/Entertainment/Films/Hindi/Actresses/Madhuri_Dixit/

Saskia Faulk and Jean-Claude Usunier prepared this case solely to provide material for class discussion. The authors do not intend to illustrate either effective or ineffective handling of a business situation. The authors may have disguised certain names and other identifying information to protect confidentiality.

(©IUMI, reprinted with kind permission.)

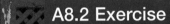

A8.2 Exercise

Dangerous Enchantment

First read the short extract from *Dangerous Enchantment,* the evocative title of the novel by Anne Mather (1966). Harlequin books are a worldwide success. They are translated into 15 languages and read in many countries. Therefore they can be considered as a truly 'global' cultural product. This short extract has been chosen for its capacity to illustrate the style of Harlequin books.

The next day Julie had collected herself. She was glad in a way that she had seen the woman with Manuel. At least it brought home to her more strongly than any words could have done the completely amoral attitude he possessed.

Marilyn had seen the television as well, however, and said: 'I say, Julie, did you see that Manuel Cortez is back in England?'

Julie managed a casual shrug. 'So what?'

'Darling, really!' Marilyn gave her an old-fashioned look. 'Surely you aren't as indifferent as all that! I know you refused a date with him, but I'm sure that was more because of Paul Bannister than anything else.'

Julie tossed her head. 'I really can't see what all the fuss is about. Paul would make four of him!'

'You must be joking!' Marilyn giggled. 'Get you! I didn't know Paul was becoming such a dish all of a sudden. Why? What's changed him?'

Julie refrained from replying. She had no desire to get involved in an argument about Paul when it meant her stating things that in actual fact were not true. It was no use pretending about Paul's attractions; he was handsome, yes, and tall, yes, and young; but there was nothing particularly exciting about him and Julie could never understand girls who thought men's looks were enough. She had known many men, and in her small experience personality mattered far more than mere good looks.

However, during her lunch break she did borrow a newspaper from Miss Fatherstone in the hope that there might be more particulars about the woman with Manuel, but there was not. There was a picture of him at the airport, and a small article, and that was all.

When they left the building that evening it was snowing, and an icy wind was blowing, chilling them to the bone. Julie, wrapped in a loose dark blue mohair coat, hugged her handbag to her as she started along towards the main thoroughfare accompanied by Donna and Marilyn. She wore knee-length white boots, but between the place where her boots ended and the place where her skirt began she felt frozen, and she wondered whether for the winter at least she should go back to normal-length skirts.

Her hair was blowing about her face, for she was wearing no hat, and she walked straight into the man who stood purposely in her way.

'I'm sorry . . .' she began hastily, a smile lightening her face, and then: 'You!'

Manuel smiled, and her heart leapt treacherously into her throat. She had let go of Donna's arm in her confusion, but both Marilyn and Donna were staring open-mouthed. Manuel took Julie's arm, and said smoothly: 'You will excuse me, ladies,' in a mocking tone, and drew Julie across the pavement to the familiar green Ferrari.

'No, wait!' began Julie, but it was no use. Manuel had the car door open and was propelling her inside, his hard fingers biting cruelly into her arm.

'Don't argue,' he said, for all the world as though it was a natural occurrence that he should meet her from work.

Julie did not want to create a scene in the street, so she climbed into the luxurious warmth of the car and sliding across out of the driver's seat, she allowed him to slide in beside her. He slammed the door, flicked the ignition, and the car moved silently forward, purring like a sated panther.

She stole a glance at him as they turned into the main thoroughfare, and saw, with a sense of inevitability, that far from changing he was much more attractive than she remembered. He turned for a moment to look at her as they stopped at some traffic lights, and said: 'How have you been?'

Julie contemplated her fingernails. 'Fine. And you?'

He shrugged, and did not reply, and she felt like hitting him. How dared he sit there knowing that she must have seen him with that girl yesterday! She looked out of the car window, suddenly realizing that she was allowing him to drive her heaven knows where, and she was making no comment.

'Where are you taking me?' she asked in a tight little voice.

'Home,' he said lazily. 'Where do you think? I thought I would save you the journey on such a ghastly night. Tell me, how do you stand this climate? It's terrible. Me, I like the sun, and the sea, and warm water to swim in.'

'Don't we all?' remarked Julie dryly. 'This will do.' They had reached the end of Faulkner Road.

Manuel shook his head. 'What number?'

'Forty-seven. But please, I'd rather you didn't drive along there. It would only cause speculation, and if you should be recognized . . .' Her voice trailed away.

'That's hardly likely tonight,' remarked Manuel coolly, and drove smoothly to her gate where he halted the car.

'Thank you, señor.' Julie gave a slight bow of her head, and made to get out, but Manuel stopped her, his fingers biting into her arm.

'Aren't you pleased to see me?' he asked mockingly. Julie looked at him fully. 'No, not really.'

'Why?'

'Surely that's obvious. We have nothing to say to one another.'

'No?'

'No.' Julie brushed back her hair as it fell in waves over her eyes. It glistened with tiny drops of melted snow and she was unaware of how lovely she was looking.

Manuel shrugged, and lay back in his seat. 'Go, then.'

Julie felt furious. It always ended this way, with herself feeling the guilty one. Well, he wasn't going to get away with it! She swung round on him.

'Don't imagine for one moment that I've been brought home believing your little tales', she cried angrily. 'I know perfectly well that the reason you have brought me home is because you could hardly take me to the apartment when you already have one female in residence!'

Manuel stared at her, a dull flush just visible in the muted light of the car rising up his cheeks.

(Source: Mather, 1966, *Dangerous Enchantment*, pp. 89–92. © 1966 Anne Mather. Used by permission of the publisher, Harlequin Enterprises II BV.)

Questions

1. Identify the main sociodemographic characteristics of the target audience of such books.

2. Identify from the text (situation, characters and the relations between them) how, and to what extent, this text moves people in such way as to touch feelings and emotions that are widely shared in the world population.

3. Define the target audience of Harlequin books, in terms of cultural affinity class(es).

9

Product policy 1:
Physical, service and symbolic attributes

A central issue in international marketing strategy is the decision whether to adapt products for foreign markets after the consumer, the national markets and their particular characteristics have been surveyed, or to standardize products, which is a simplified strategy based on experience effects and cost reduction. For instance, part of the UK's loss of dominant position in the Arabian Gulf countries to the Japanese during the 1960s was due to a lack of product adaptation. In contrast to the British, the Japanese adapted their products to the needs of local markets, after careful research into demographic, economic, sociocultural, political-legal and physical environments (Tuncalp, 1990).

The real issue is not a dichotomous choice, as most companies do not exclusively adapt or standardize across their marketing mix elements (Vrontis, 2003). Around a core product offering that is standard worldwide, most global companies such as Coca-Cola or McDonald's customize when needed. Export performance has been shown to be a combination of both adaptation and standardization strategies (Shoham, 1996) and to depend on a large number of factors related to the four components of the marketing mix (Baalbaki and Malhotra, 1995). It has been shown that the industry's potential for standardization dictates a company's strategy: in global industries that emphasize high-tech, firms that respond by standardizing show superior performance (O'Donnell and Jeong, 2000); conversely, within a particular industry, firms that customize have better performance (Samiee and Roth, 1992). Product customization may also result in market differentiation, thus creating a competitive advantage *vis-à-vis* actual

competitors, raising entry barriers for potential competitors. Therefore the message is: standardize as much as feasible and customize as much as needed. This is supported by Theodosiou and Leonidou (2003, p. 167) who after reviewing the empirical research in the area report that: 'international marketing strategy (whether standardized or adapted) will lead to superior performance only to the extent that it properly matches the unique set of circumstances that the firm is confronted by within a particular overseas market'.

This chapter and the next (which is devoted to the product's brand name and national image) propose a decision-making framework for the adaptation/standardization of various product attributes: physical characteristics, design, form, colour, functions, packaging, brand name and 'made-in' label. An assessment will be made of the potential for adaptation and standardization at different levels of product attributes: physical attributes, service attributes and symbolic attributes (through its colour, shape, country of origin, brand name and so on).

The first section of this chapter sets out a systematic model to clarify the choice between adaptation and standardization of product policy. It can be applied successively to each existing national market as well as to markets where a company intends to set up new business. The second section is devoted to the physical attributes of the product. The third section deals with the standardization/adaptation of service attributes. The fourth section relates to symbolic attributes.

The etymology of the word 'symbol' derives from Ancient Greece, where the symbol was originally an object cut into two. The two halves were retained by the host and the guest and later passed on to their children. When these two halves were reunited, this enabled the owners to be recognized and served as proof of the bond of hospitality previously created. The symbol therefore replaces, represents and denotes some other entity by means of a conventional relationship or a suggestion, the evidence of which has usually been lost. The connotative meanings of symbols are, of course, culture based. They are interpreted differently across countries.

Other important symbolic attributes are the brand name and the national images linked to the product and its country of manufacture. The conversion of a national brand into an international one, and the linguistic problems that may occur, are dealt with in Chapter 10. The issue of global brands, either worldwide or regional ones, is also considered in Chapter 10.

9.1
Adaptation or standardization of product attributes

The product element of the marketing mix is often cited as the most standardized element, but within the product element there are various attributes that are more or less likely to be standardized. For instance, Vrontis (2003) surveyed 500 large UK multinational companies in five sectors, including manufacturing, services, transportation and communication, construction, and retail and wholesale, to find out what elements of the marketing mix were most standardized. For the product element, most companies reported standardizing product quality (78 per cent), brand name (72 per cent), image (71 per cent), performance (67 per cent), size and colour (54 per cent) and packaging and styling (52 per cent), while fewer standardize variety, design and features (48 per cent), pre-sales service (45 per cent), after-sales service and warrantees (43 per cent), and delivery and installation (42 per cent). The same companies reported that the most important reasons for adapting the marketing mix included culture (92 per cent), market development (87 per cent), competition (84 per cent), laws (82 per cent), economic differences (78 per cent), sociological consideration (74 per cent), customer perceptions (71 per cent), technological consideration (60 per cent), political environment (53 per cent), level of customer similarity (49 per cent), marketing infrastructure (44 per cent) and differences in physical conditions (39 per cent).

From a consumer point of view, Hult *et al.* (2000) compared the importance consumers place on sixteen product attributes in France (a developed market) and Malaysia (an emerging market), finding that only two attributes (product quality and appearance) received high emphasis on both samples. In Malaysia consumers relied more on the core product attributes and in France on the image and service attributes when evaluating grocery products and clothing. In fact, one may state that consumers are not buying the product itself, but the benefits they hope to derive from the product. A product can be defined as a set of attributes that provide the purchaser/user with actual benefits. Consumers from different countries may assign different weights to similar product attributes. For instance, German consumers place more importance on ecological attributes than British consumers (Diamantopoulos *et al.*, 1995).

There are three layers of product attributes that lend themselves more or less to standardization:

1. The physical attributes (size, weight, colour, etc.). Standardization of these attributes affords the greatest potential for cost benefits since economies of scale are made principally at the manufacturing stage.
2. Service attributes (maintenance, after-sales service, spare parts availability, etc.). These attributes are fairly difficult to standardize, as circumstances for service delivery differ widely from one country to another. It should further be emphasized that most services are performed in direct relation to *local* customers. Service attributes are more dependent on culture.
3. Symbolic attributes. These often comprise the interpretive element of the physical attributes. A colour is simultaneously a chemical formula for a painting or a coat, and also the symbolic meaning conveyed by the material. Symbolic attributes affect the choice between adaptation and standardization in a fairly ambiguous manner. It is confusing when consumers show a strong liking for domestic goods based on nationalism and also show a penchant or fascination for foreign cultures and their goods. Therefore, when adapting or standardizing

Table 9.1 Factors influencing adaptation or standardization of product attributes

Product attributes	Arguments in favour of adaptation	Arguments in favour of standardization
Physical attributes	**1** Cost-reducing adaptations Local standards, hygiene and safety regulations, local marketing knowledge, consumer behaviour, marketing and physical environments	**2** Experience effects Economies of scale International standards International product use
Services attributes	**3** Limited savings related to scale Local peculiarities in service, maintenance and distribution	**4** Significant learning effects 'Mobile' clientele
Symbolic attributes	**5** Unfavourable image of imported products, company, nationality or brand name Inadequate meaning conveyed by colour, shape, etc.	**6** Favourable image of imported products, company, nationality or brand Exotic or ethnic appeal Demands for 'universals'

symbolic attributes, the requirements for national identity symbols will sometimes intermingle with those for symbols of exoticism.

Table 9.1 proposes a systematic description of the arguments in favour of adaptation on the one hand and standardization on the other. Distinctions can be made according to the different levels of physical, service and symbolic attributes. Some arguments in favour of either adaptation or standardization originate from within the company, which can benefit from changing its way of operating. Other arguments are related to external constraints imposed by the environment, market characteristics and consumer behaviour. The influence of these factors may require that a company either adapts or standardizes its offerings. In Table 9.1 each internal cell is numbered and these cell numbers will be referred to in the text to elaborate on each concept. (See *WS9.1* for more information on adaptation and standardization.)

9.2

Physical attributes

As we saw in Chapter 8, experience effects, and accordingly the cost reductions related to cumulated production, clearly weigh in favour of standardization

(cell 2). Despite this, empirical studies report mixed results for standardization. In a comprehensive review of the literature, Theodosiou and Leonidou (2003) found that quality, design and features were the most standardized product-related elements, while product lines, branding and packaging were at least partially adapted for foreign markets. Furthermore, while only a few studies examined the relationship between standardization and performance, they report that: 'Standardizing product quality did not have a significant effect on either static or growth measures of profit performance (Shoham, 1996), and the same was true with respect to adapting product positioning (Albaum and Tse, 2001).' Since quality is one of the two product attributes that Hult *et al.* (2000) found to be equally important to consumers in a developed and an emerging market, this offers little support for the standardization argument.

However one can investigate the opportunity of supplying an adapted 'simplified' product, if there is local demand. For instance, Littrell and Miller (2001) examined Indian inspired garment sales in the United States, finding that the level of complexity of the garments had little impact on consumers' acceptance or purchase, although the level of compatibility and familiarity with the silhouette and fasteners was important.

Cost-reduction adaptations may compensate for the loss in cumulated volume (cell 1). For instance, the success of Japanese pick-up trucks in developing countries was due to product simplifications in suspension, engine and gearbox, which the Japanese achieved at a lower cost level. However, this situation is rare. More commonly, product simplifications have failed to achieve their goals. Historically, Ford and General Motors developed a 'bare bones' model T type of vehicle to sell in developing countries, both of which were failures. Similarly, a computer specially designed for developing countries was developed in the 1980s by Jean-Jacques Servan-Schreiber with French government funding. It was a total failure. In these cases, the advantages resulting from 'simplifications' did not reduce costs enough to offset a reduction in economies of scale and the loss of product functionality was not appreciated by consumers. Since simplified products may not be advantageous in terms of cost, it is the learning process of local consumers and how the local context affects this learning process which may become the central concerns for the international marketer (Wills *et al.*, 1991; Amine, 1993).

Compulsory adaptation

Compulsory adaptation of physical attributes is often related to national regulations and standards (cell 1). Certain countries use standards which seem to operate as non-tariff trade barriers. For instance, Germany is known for its use of an exhaustive system of over 30,000 industrial standards (DIN), which are determined by standard-setting committees. German manufacturers are strongly represented on the boards of these committees. Nevertheless, DIN standards are by no means intended as non-tariff barriers. (For more information on ISO and regional standards organizations see *WS9.2.*) Some examples include:

1. *The industrial standards for the supply of electricity*: the voltage, the frequency of the alternating current (50 versus 60 Hz), the shape of plugs, etc. differ by region if not by country.
2. *Safety standards*: in the motor industry lighting, brake systems and vehicle safety often differ by country. For instance, the Corsa has become one of the best selling cars around the world. It is sold in approximately 80 countries and manufactured on 5 continents, where its name, body style, suspension or engines are changed to meet local standards. The Corsa is called a Vauxhall/Opel Corsa in Germany, a Chevrolet Chevy (Corsa) in Mexico, a Buick Sail in China and a Holden Barina in Australia. Obviously the changes increase production costs, documentation and country-specific spare parts. Control of marketing management becomes difficult.
3. *Hygiene regulations*: the food processing, chemicals and pharmaceutical industries must carry out adaptations to comply with hygiene legislation. The producers of *foie gras* which is exported to the United States have to obtain FDA (Food and Drug Administration) hygiene certification. For this they have to allow the FDA to inspect their laboratories for bacteria as well as their methods of production. FDA inspectors often require *foie gras* to be pasteurized and the laboratories disinfected with an antiseptic detergent. This inevitably affects the taste and conflicts with the traditional image of a home-made quality product. Many of the French *foie gras* producers have set up laboratories in the USA where the product is prepared according to US hygiene standards. Even a product as common as Coca-Cola faces different regulations, including very different requirements for the use of artificial sweeteners across countries and the necessity to include an expiry date in some countries (e.g. France), but not others (e.g. Holland) (Dana and Oldfield, 1999).

A huge variety of regulations influence the need for adaptation (packaging, labelling, sizes, advertising, sales promotion, etc.). In many countries, public or mutual bodies offer to assist companies by examining the problems of conforming to the technical aspects of foreign standards. Despite this, a good number of companies, for reasons relating to ethnocentrism, fail to consider the problem of adaptation of products for foreign markets. Newcomers to the export business often do not start by considering the loss of standardization; their first consideration is the obligatory adaptation to technical standards.

In fact, obligatory adaptations are often minor in comparison to the required adaptations to differences in consumer behaviour and in the national marketing environment. Three main issues should be considered:

Box 9.1

'Pizza relativity'

There is, in the real world, a lot of 'pizza relativity'. During in-depth interviews at Hewlett Packard in France, some American expatriates told me that they had travelled to Geneva, Switzerland, 100 miles (160 km) from the site where they were located, in order to have a meal at Pizza Hut. Although in Grenoble there are a large number of 'authentic' pizzerias (the town has a very large Italian presence), some Hewlett-Packard American expatriates preferred the taste, crustiness, toppings and cooking style of the American pizza. When attending a congress in Milan, I discovered that the Italian pizza (at least at the restaurant where I ate it) was not at all like those I am used to eating in Grenoble (made by cooks of Italian origin): the crust was much thicker and there was less topping. My last memory is of the oily Brazilian pizzas (which I tried only twice).

Conclusion: pizzas, like 'Chinese' food, are largely localized, often because of the lack of genuine ingredients, but also because taste is localized. Local views of what is 'genuine' are mostly based on fantasies about the 'true' pizza or the 'genuine' Peking duck.

1. *Consumption patterns*: consumer tastes, frequency of consumption, the amount consumed per helping, etc. will differ. The size of a cereal box and the style of packaging that preserves the product, will depend in part on whether consumers eat 50 grams of cereal a day, or if they consume larger amounts but less often. Even products which are supposed to be the epitome of international standardization are subject to customization for local tastes (see Box 9.1). Dana and Oldfield (1999) examine the various adaptations that Coca-Cola has made across countries. They found that: 'Consumers in different countries drink Coca-Cola for different reasons. In China, it is a luxury item, served on silver trays at government functions. In Spain, it is used as a mixer with wine, for example. In California, it is kept in coolers to be used as refreshment; in Tromso, Norway, it is kept in warmers, rather than coolers' (p. 294). While there are definite national trends, it is also important to remember that market segments exist within and across countries. Allio and Allio (2002) described the success of Coors introduction into Puerto Rico, after they used local market research knowledge to identify the segment with the most potential (young, upper income, urban). Their major competitor, Budweiser lost market share because they continued to target the entire market, and ignored unique aspects of local Hispanic culture. In fact, van Mesdag (1999) argues that food is one of a group of products (visual arts, music, architecture, social behaviour, clothing, etc.) that are not easily globalized. He proposes the 'duration-of-usage' hypothesis, where products that evolved in times when countries did not readily communicate are more difficult to standardize.

2. *Climate and the physical environment* in general are important, and sometimes neglected, factors behind further obligatory adaptation (cell 1). Motor vehicles must be specifically designed to withstand the harsh Scandinavian winters or the warmth and humidity of the Ivory Coast. The possible range of physical environments where the product will be used must be taken into account: for example, the quality of road surfaces and the existence of tracks suitable for vehicles. The diversity of physical environments is often the cause of unexpected failure (Box 9.2). One should take into account in advance the range of elements that constitute potential demands for adaptation. This is not always such an obvious step to take. Ethnocentrism is often the rule in product design.

3. *Adapting products to local product usage*. A number of variables have to be considered in order to ensure buyers use the product properly, such as level of literacy, technical knowledge and ability to use written information (such as ingredients list or instructions for use). Lack of attention to such variables caused problems for Nestlé in the Third World with its infant formula: the addition of

Box 9.2

Adaptations to the physical environment

A European drinks manufacturer decided to widen the range of one of its product lines with a giant-size version, with the purpose of its active promotion in several markets, the United States in particular. After completion of production facilities, the new model was launched. The company then realized to its horror that it had forgotten one small detail: the giant-size bottle was a couple of inches too tall for the shelves in the vast majority of the American stores. You can imagine the result: the sales promotion activities that were planned had to be cancelled, there was discontent among the distributors and the sales force lost a great deal of motivation while a new mould was hastily manufactured.[a]

Quaker Oats has an established share of the Cameroon market: it has been carefully adapted in line with consumption habits. It is easily made into the gruel that the Cameroons call *paf* or *pap*. It is usually eaten with maize or tapioca. In addition, Quaker uses metallic packaging which is perfectly suited to the preservation of the product in the Cameroon climate. The shelf life of the box is about ten years, even in a tropical country. Cameroon itself is not a wholly typical tropical country since in Douala, for instance, there is an annual rainfall of 7 metres. The metallic box ensures that the product is preserved despite the humidity. It does, however, rust, and even though the product itself is not affected, certain retailers refuse to repurchase Quaker Oats because their previous stock rusted.[b]

(Sources: [a]Adapted from Giordan, 1988, p. 110; [b]adapted from Camphuis, 1984.)

impure water and the failure to boil the water made the product dangerous for babies, even though the powder that left Nestlé's factories was perfect. Consumers, on average, tend not to read instructions for use thoroughly enough and to try to use items, especially consumer durables, too quickly, before they have learned the basics of how to operate them. The Germans make special adaptations designed to guard against misuse by consumers; for instance, when the knob of a dish-washing machine is turned anti-clockwise, whereas it should be turned only clockwise, or when the machine is switched on when the water tap is off. In Germany, where the sense of uncertainty avoidance is quite strong (section 3.2), a product is called *idiotensicher* ('idiot proof') when all possible product design adaptations have been made to avoid the negative consequences of any imaginable misuse. Adaptation to possible misuses is related to the issue of product liability, where quite different legal solutions are found from one country to another. Windshield sun protectors made in Spain and sold there do not need to bear a special warning, reminding the user not to drive with the protector in place, because it is supposed that Spanish drivers are not fools. For export, especially to the United States, they must display such an explicit warning: in the case of an incident, the manufacturer could be held liable. Essayist Rod Usher in Time Magazine gives several instances of how litigiously paranoid American businesses are: one dessert product warns that 'Product will be hot after heating'; and a birthday badge reading 'Happy 50th Birthday' carries a warning 'Unsuitable for children under 5' (1998, p. 84).

Requirements for international standardization

Yet national requirements sometimes lean toward international standardization (cell 2). This may occur in four situations:

1. There are industries where international standards tend to develop from technical standards originating in individual countries. For instance, in the field of oil drilling, the API (American Petroleum Institute) standards are in force worldwide. Every oil company, whether American or not, must follow the API standards. Oil-drilling equipment manufacturers are also obliged to design their

products in accordance with these standards. However, the number of industries with worldwide standards remains limited. The adoption of foreign/international standards can even prove to be problematic for selling in the country of origin. For instance, a European iron and steel company obtained certification from ASME (the American Society of Mechanical Engineers) for the very thick steel plate used in nuclear and petrochemical plants. In this small industry, they had a quite substantial world market share. ASME certification was recognized worldwide since most nuclear plants use licensed American technology. When they subsequently came to sell their heavy steel plates for plants intended for German and French electricity utilities, the US standards were not considered acceptable and they were forced to adapt to German and French standards.

2. Some products achieve 'international usage' such as aircraft suitcases (Samsonite of Belgium and Delsey of France), portable computers, duty-free articles, etc.

3. Innovative products often experience an international diffusion process (Rogers, 1983). Large R & D expenses are initially incurred for many innovative products, and the benefits from many technical products are not greatly affected by culture (e.g. DVDs). The pace of the diffusion of innovations is largely enhanced by the strength of the groups of 'early adopters'. These groups may also have a high level of exposure to international travel and to new products in the countries where they are first launched. By word-of-mouth communication, they transfer knowledge of the product to their non-travelling compatriots. They facilitate positive reactions from other consumers without exposure to these new products, in the first phases of the adoption process: awareness, interest, evaluation, testing. More generally, international travel accelerates the process of diffusion of standardized innovations. There is also some evidence that consumer innovativeness is higher for people from countries with lower uncertainty avoidance, higher individualism and more masculinity (Baumgartner and Steenkamp 1996).

4. The final point in cell 2 encompasses the basis of Levitt's (1983) assertions about the globalization of markets. According to Levitt, certain aspects of ways of life would tend towards uniformity with differences in cultural preferences, national taste, standards and the institutional business environment being remnants of the past. Levitt argues that the so-called ethnic markets are a good example: Chinese food, country music, pizzas and jazz now tend to be found worldwide. Although Levitt claims that he is not advocating systematic disregard for local or national differences, he overestimates the worldwide convergence of taste for global products as emphasized in Chapters 5 and 6. Whatever value judgements are made about the all-inclusive tendency towards homogenization of world cultures, consumer segments and product categories, this issue must be raised for each company, on the basis of careful research on its product, consumers and markets. For instance, Schuh (2000) points out that while market conditions favour customization in central eastern Europe, the extra cost may not pay off as many of these countries have small markets which are rapidly changing due to the huge investment from Western retailers, media, banks, etc.

The trend towards international standards

The costs required for adapting to national standards are very high since adaptation also implies the replication of test and certification procedures in many countries. In the pharmaceuticals industry, the cost of bringing a new drug on to the market is estimated at US$230 million in the United States, $150 million in Europe and $125 million in Japan. Countries still follow somewhat different routes for granting market entry to new pharmaceuticals. For instance Japan, requiring only 18 months, appears liberal in contrast with the US Food and Drug Administration; given the relative brevity of initial trials in Japan, approval covers only the first six years, after which the manufacturer must reapply (Pahud de Mortanges et al., 1997).

Fortunately, there is a definite trend towards common standardization worldwide, especially with ISO (International Organization for Standardization) standards; some of these are now widely applied, such as the standards on quality, the ISO 9000 family. European technical standardization is participating in this movement, which stems from the EC Treaty, especially Article 30, which prohibits quantitative restrictions on imports from other member states and measures having an equivalent effect (that is, this is mainly a form of protectionist standardization). As explained in Chapter 6, the *Cassis de Dijon* ruling firmly established the 'home country rule', whereby a product should not be barred from importation into an EU country when it conforms to the standards of the EU country in which it is produced. The EU countries are engaged in a European standardization process, through three Brussels-based organizations: CEN, CENELEC and ETSI. This largely stems from the 1985 EC White Paper, which identified technical barriers as one of the main obstacles to the achievement of a single market in Europe (see section 6.4).

Product standards are in fact a very complex strategic issue (much more so than depicted here), since they have a definite influence on the competitive strategy of the firm. In high-technology industries, for instance computers, consumer electronics and telecommunications, the issue of compatibility of standards over time (multi-vintage compatibility) and across competitors is a very important one. There are examples where promoting a standard and licensing it to competitors (the VHS of Matsushita) proved a better strategy than keeping a monopoly on one's own standard (the Betamax VCR of Sony – now defunct). Other examples show that it was more efficient to keep the technology under total control, as Xerox did for its proprietary photocopying technology before the patent expired. But technology products are not the only items for which product standards need to be considered as part of their marketing strategy. For instance, Vertinsky and Zhou (2000) examined forest product firms, finding that their choice to obtain FSC certification 'was to defend or create market access to markets with influential buyers' groups (e.g. the UK) or markets where environmental groups have strong influence on public opinion and the government (e.g. The Netherlands and Germany)'.

9.3 Service attributes

World trade in commercial services rose by 12 per cent in 2003 to US$1.8 trillion dollars (WTO, 2004).

While the US was the leading exporter (16 per cent) and importer (12.5 per cent) of services, the top ten exporters consist of a wide range of countries including the UK, Germany, France, Spain Italy, Japan, Netherlands, China and Hong Kong. Many factors are driving this expansion including the WTO, protective measures (intellectual property rights, copyrights, trademarks, etc.), changing government attitudes, trading blocks, technology and changing demographics (e.g. more women in the workforce) (Javalgi and White, 2002). Despite this, there are still many barriers for companies that wish to export services. In fact, the export of services is more highly regulated than the export of products. According to Kostecki and Nowakowski (2002) managers cite regulatory barriers as more important than barriers internal to the firm (e.g. limited resources) or unfavourable markets (e.g. competitive environment or weak demand). Many of these barriers are not transparent to outsiders and difficult to negotiation. Kostecki and Nowakowski identified that informal barriers, such as official harassment to support local policy objectives (e.g. delays in delivery of work permits or excessive administrative fees to ease local unemployment), private harassment for personal gain (e.g. customs delays alleviated by 'fees' and 'donations' to family members of high ranking civil servants) and red tape for no apparent reason (e.g. inefficient public administration) are more problematic to managers than formal barriers. In light of this, they urge service exporters to adopt 'world class' practices from corporate structure and process to information networks and public relations strategies in order to copy with the regulatory environment.

Services may stand alone, or be part of a product offering. Service attributes include the following:

1. Repair and maintenance, after-sales service.
2. Installation.
3. Instruction manuals, information and guidance on how to use the item.
4. Other related services (demonstrations, technical assistance).
5. Waiting time, delivery dates (and respect for them).
6. Guarantees (repair or replacement of goods).
7. Spare parts availability.
8. Return of goods, whether defective or not.

Adaptation of service in the light of local conditions

The extent of service attributes differs according to the type of good being serviced. Service attributes are essential for industrial equipment and many consumer durables. Although it might not seem so, they also have a significant role to play in the field of consumer non-durables. Service requirements differ widely from country to country (cell 3) because they are related to environmental factors such as the following:

1. The level of technical expertise.
2. The level of labour costs, which is decisive in the balance between durability and reparability. For instance, Africans are experts at repairing and even revamping totally worn-out cars.
3. The level of literacy (this may render instruction manuals useless).
4. Climatic differences: certain climates increase the difficulty of performing maintenance operations because of temperature, humidity, etc.

5. The remoteness of locations, which can render services difficult and costly to perform (e.g. servicing a gas turbine in the middle of the Amazonian forest).
6. Different ways of performing a seemingly identical service (see Box 9.3).

Actual services in developing countries are more traditional and of a limited technical level, at least when viewed by technologically developed countries. In societies where shortages are common, recycling is essential: African shoemakers, for instance, are experts at making shoe soles from used tyres. Technical expertise and craftsmanship is not lacking in developing countries; it is expressed differently, and relates to the prevailing economic conditions. In many African countries for instance, a lot of maintenance is done by small mechanical workshops, which succeed in repairing cars but take a long time to do so; although not orthodox, their repair methods work. Service instructions issued by car manufacturers naturally need some adaptation. It is better to show mechanics how to do a job than to send them a free 800-page

Box 9.3

Who's afraid of injections?

What is more standard in appearance than a syringe and an injection? There are, however, significant differences in the methods used to avoid causing pain to the patient. For intra muscular syringes, there are two different ways of administering an injection. They correspond to two basic service attributes (correct injection of the substance, avoidance of pain):

1. Only the needle itself is stuck in, then the body of the syringe (the cylinder containing the substance and the plunger driving it) is fixed into the base of the needle, in accordance with a technique known as *luerslip* (this method is used in America). The first question asked by an American nurse is: how does it come apart? (Service attribute.)
2. French, Italian and Spanish doctors and nurses prefer (and are used to) using the fully assembled syringe. The American method would probably

involve the risk of more pain to the patient when connecting the two parts of the syringe after the needle has been implanted (an operation they are not used to doing). The service attribute required of the syringe is therefore based on its lightness and being in one piece, which is provided by a bolt system (*luerlock*). The first question asked by a French, Italian or Spanish nurse is: does it hold tight?

Further service attributes relate to who is legally permitted and professionally qualified to administer an injection and where it is possible to buy syringes. In Italy – in contrast to other European countries – syringes are on general sale, even in corner shops. They are available in blister packaging at the supermarket. Traditionally, many housewives actually give injections to members of their family.

(Source: Excerpt from a discussion with Beckton Dickinson, a world leader in single-use medical items-consumables.)

book on maintenance operations. Services are generally delegated to distribution channels. The shortage of available and/or adequate channels and the small size of distribution outlets are obstacles to services, particularly in developing countries.

Even across developed countries, differences in the service offered by distribution channels are much greater than one might expect. The daily and weekly shop-opening hours vary widely. They may range from less than 60 hours per week total opening time in northern Europe and Australia to more than 100 hours per week in southern Europe and the United States. This affects attitudes towards distribution services; for example, where weekly store-opening hours are limited, people tend to turn to the Internet or mail order. Where a husband and wife are at work during shop-opening hours, an elderly parent with different service requirements may have to do the shopping for them.

A number of dimensions of the service encounter are common cross-culturally, but the way in which they are valued and interpreted by customers varies. First, several studies have shown consistency in the dimensions that are important to service quality and the relationship between service quality and satisfaction. For instance, Brady and Robertson (2001) surveyed consumers in the United States and Ecuador, finding that the influence of service quality on intentions is moderated by the level of satisfaction in both countries. In addition, Witkowski and Wolfinbarger (2002) found that the SERVQUAL instrument, which includes the dimensions of reliability, empathy, responsiveness, assurance and tangibles explained over half the variance for both German and US samples.

Second, several studies have reported marked differences in the strength of the relationships and value placed on different elements of service. For instance, van Birgelen et al. (2002) found that national culture moderated the service quality–customer satisfaction relationship when the service encounter was over the phone or computer in Europe. Specifically, for over the phone encounters they found customers from individualist countries were less bothered by the absence of personal contact and those from more uncertainty avoidant culture held a weaker service quality–customer satisfaction relationship. The culture effects were even stronger for the electronic service encounter, where all four national culture dimensions influenced the service encounter. Kathryn Frazer

Winsted (1999) lists common service encounter dimensions to explain satisfaction for restaurants (control, courtesy, formality and promptness) and medical (authenticity, caring, friendliness and personalization). She surveyed students in Japan and the United States, finding that personalization is more important to consumers in the United States (more individualist) than Japan (more collectivist), while formality is more important in Japan (more status conscious) than the United States (more egalitarian). Similarly, Witkowski and Wolfinbarger (2002) found differences between German and US students' (and their friends) ratings of service quality in banks, medical care, retail clothing stores, postal facilities and restaurants. Generally, the German respondents had lower service expectations than US respondents in all settings, as well as lower satisfaction for banks, clothing stores and postal facilities. In the context of museum visits and in the case of two much closer cultures, Sweden and The Netherlands, De Ruyter et al. (1997) find few differences in the value dimensions of satisfaction in both countries. Visitors from both nations place emotional value on pleasant treatment at the museum entrance, and attribute logical value to the museum restaurant (value for money); however, they differ noticeably in their valuation of the permanent collection: emotional value is the most important determinant of satisfaction for the Swedes (a good atmosphere) and logical value (satisfactory information) for the Dutch.

Differences have also been found across cultures in other outcomes to the service encounter. For instance, Liu et al. (2001) found that customers from more collectivist or uncertainty avoidant countries have a higher intention to give positive word-of-mouth after a positive service encounter, but if they receive a negative service encounter they tend not to give negative word-of-mouth, complain, or even switch. The reverse was true for consumers from more individualist and lower uncertainty avoidant countries. In a business setting, Money et al. (1998) found that word-of-mouth may be more important in Japan than in the United States. They studied the number of personal information sources buyers from Japanese and US firms used when they searched for a service in Japan and in the United States. They found that Japanese companies used 340 per cent more referral sources than US firms when they purchased a service in the United States. While US firms used more referral sources when they purchased in Japan, the Japanese firms still used 78 per cent more referral sources overall.

Culture and the waiting experience

An important aspect of service is waiting to be served (to obtain maintenance or spare parts, to receive cash in a bank or to be served in a restaurant). In waiting, people have to deal with time, rules and power. The cultural assumptions concerning time are central in the waiting experience: people with a strong economic time pattern (see section 2.2) may experience waiting as a waste of time, a painful moment with negative emotions. Waiting is organized in queues to varying degrees and the rules concerning the waiting process are more or less respected according to culture (see section 3.6). Another important aspect of waiting is power: where power distance is strong, it seems almost legitimate to let the least powerful wait, with jumping the queue as standard behaviour for the most powerful. In fact, rather than jumped, the waiting line is bypassed: important consumers have a direct access to the service. On the contrary, in the United States, where low power distance and strong economic time prevail, waiting lines are well organized and everybody is treated fairly, following the principle of 'first come, first served'. Box 9.4 presents the Japanese attitude towards waiting in various service situations.

Waiting time can be reduced or increased according to the level of service personnel available; it can therefore be adapted according to the locally prevailing assumptions about time. In Europe, where time is, on average, slightly less economic than in North America, the fast-food outlets are not as quick as they are in America (where the formula was invented). People are not as preoccupied with the waiting time. In the USA, Pizza Hut gives a free pizza to customers who have waited more than ten minutes; in most European countries this practice does not need to be transferred, because people do not resent waiting and may even value waiting time in a restaurant as a sign of careful preparation. Similarly, Rowley and Slack (1999, p. 375) found differences in the environment in airport departure lounges across countries: 'US airports have much more of a sense of urgency and activity (or a "buzz") than airports in other parts of

the world. Elsewhere the sense is more one of leisure and luxury, calm and relaxation. These messages are subtly conveyed through the way in which retail outlets are arranged, the attitudes of service agents and the nature of promotional messages.'

Another service attribute is the type of rules that apply to waiting and the degree to which the waiting lines are organized. In many countries, waiting is not organized at all and the principle 'first come, first served' finds no translation. Since people are used to unorganized waiting they know that they will have to fight those who will jump the queue, by shouting, threatening them or themselves jumping the queue. For instance, the contrast between French and Swiss ski resorts, especially at peak time, is striking: whereas in France the absence of waiting corridors results in untidy crowds, in Switzerland the waiting process remains fairly peaceful and organized even if the waiting time is slightly longer. It comes as no surprise that for American tourists travelling to Europe the service quality image of French ski resorts appears significantly lower than that of the Swiss and Austrian ski resorts, particularly as concerns honesty and friendliness (Ofir and Lehmann, 1986).

Cultural assumptions and the service encounter

The service encounter implies a person-to-person relationship, in maintenance as well as in restaurant or other services. To this extent, the prevailing cultural norms will apply in service encounters as they apply in any social interaction. Even though much is shared, especially from a normative point of view (availability, courtesy, willingness to give information), social codes concerning adequate service vary according to culture. Edward Hall (1976, pp. 58–9), for instance, explains how, when staying in a hotel in downtown Tokyo, he was completely mystified by a problem with his room:

I had been a guest for about ten days and was returning to my room in the middle of an afternoon. Entering the room I immediately sensed that something was wrong. Out of place. Different. I was in the wrong room. Someone else's things were distributed around the head of the bed and the table . . . I checked my key again. Yes, it really was mine . . . At the desk, I was told by the clerk, as he sucked in his breath in deference (and embarrassment?) that indeed they

Box 9.4

Sabisu (the Japanese concept of service)

Misako Kamamoto, chief conductor of the Japan Travel bureau recounts her experience guiding Japanese tourists overseas:

'When I take a group of Japanese tourists to a restaurant in Europe for the first time, I make a point to advise them in advance as follows: "Quite apart from the problem of whether the food suits the Japanese palate, you must be resigned to the fact that it takes a good deal of time to have a meal in a European restaurant." . . . some members of the party are bound to start complaining despite the warning that I have given them. "Why are European restaurants so slow in serving us? Please ask them to speed up the service." Some get so impatient that they stand up and leave, saying, "I don't want to wait for dessert or coffee. I can't stand a restaurant which gives such bad service." In a European restaurant, the essence of good service is to give the guests plenty of time to enjoy conversation together with the meal. So it makes sense that dishes are served with long intervals in between.

Japanese tourists who go shopping in Paris invariably return full of complaints because they were not treated like "gods" as in Japan. "The sales clerks take the attitude that they are doing you a favor by 'allowing you to buy'. They are so curt. What do they think customers are, anyway? The sales clerks have absolutely no interest in doing business. When I asked a clerk to show me something of a different color or different size, she acted annoyed and said brusquely, 'We have none.' She didn't even try to search."

In a Japanese bank, the clerk counts the notes by himself and puts them all together in a tray for the client, . . . few Japanese take the trouble of counting the notes on the spot . . . The Japanese usually consider that it is impolite to distrust anyone and believe that the other party will most naturally live up to the trust placed in him. In restaurants and hotels, Westerners do not make payment until they have thoroughly examined the bill, item by item and make sure that the sum is correctly totalled. In contrast the Japanese have always believed that restaurant and hotel bills are correct. Therefore, even when they are overseas, they assume the same and make payment without examining the bill. This habit sometimes becomes a trouble.

When they travel by train in Europe, the Japanese are struck by the quietness of the stations which are so unlike the noisy Japanese stations. There is no bell or loudspeaker signaling the departure of a train. Their first reaction is, "It's so nice and quiet." But this soon gives way to anxiety. "Why is it that there is no bell notifying us of the departure? It would be a lot of trouble if we missed the train," some say. . . . Whereas European railways give priority to silence and their rule is to have travelers enjoy a quiet journey, Japanese railways seem to think that their mission is to provide passengers with all kinds of information via blaring loudspeakers.'

(Source: Kamamoto, 1984, pp. 26–7.)

had moved me. My particular room had been reserved in advance by somebody else. I was given the key to my new room and discovered that all my personal effects were distributed around the new room almost as though I had done it myself.

Later Hall was to discover that, in contrast to the United States where being moved in such a way is almost an insult, in Japan it was tangible evidence that, after some days, he was treated as a family member, somebody belonging to the group of familiar clients, who can be treated in a relaxed and unceremonious way.

There are many situations where 'good' service is not self-evident. A case in point is when people are asleep on a plane when a meal is served. Kamamoto (1984) explains that, as far as the Japanese are concerned, the steward must wake those who are asleep so that they do not miss the meal, whereas westerners prefer not to be disturbed in their sleep. Naturally, the best solution, whatever the culture, would be for

Table 9.2 Cultural dimensions and automated service

Dimensions		High	
		Being	Doing
	Affectivity	1. Strong preference for personnel in contact	3. Like the machine but would like personnel also
	Neutrality	2. Do not like the machine but do not like people either	4. Strongest preference for purely automated service

the steward to wait and serve the sleeping person as soon as he or she awakes; but such treatment is rarely possible because of schedule constraints.

An important cultural aspect of the service encounter is the *doing/being* divide. Hall (1976, p. 109), contrasts the French and the Americans: 'The French as a rule are much more involved [than the Americans] with their employees and with their customers and clients as well. They do not feel they can serve them adequately unless they know them well.' The first sentence is questionable: to many foreigners, service quality in France (as in other Latin countries) appears poor in comparison with the United States. Many American visitors perceive the commitment of French service providers towards their clients as quite small. The real key is in Hall's second sentence: 'unless they know them well'. In societies where *doing* is strongly emphasized, as in the United States, waiters and other service providers are task centred rather than person or relationship centred. It is no real problem for them to serve *unknown* people. To many French or Latin eyes, North American service appears the exact opposite of Hall's judgement, friendlier, more attentive and more dedicated than in European countries, especially in southern Europe. Stereotypically stated, in a *being*-oriented society, the situation in service encounters is dichotomic: dedication and friendliness towards known customers, absence of real commitment towards customers when they *are unknown*.

Another interesting question is whether customers prefer automated service, which is widely expanding (e.g. automatic teller machines, ticket machines, etc.), or to be served by real, flesh-and-blood people. A *being* orientation implies a preference for personnel in contact whereas the doing orientation favours automated service, which is purely task oriented. The dimension of affectivity versus neutrality (see section 3.5), an important aspect of Trompenaars' (1993) relational orientation, can be combined with the *doing–being* divide for describing possible preferences, as in Table 9.2: affectivity will create a preference for personnel in contact, because human relationships in the service encounter are preferred to service automation. Naturally, all this is based on cultural ideal types; other factors, such as age and level of education, have a strong influence on individual acceptance of automated service; older people and less educated persons have more difficulties in dealing with automated service devices, which they consider user unfriendly.

Factors in favour of service standardization

The decision to adapt services to diversified international requirements implies little cost (cell 3), since it is far easier to reach increasing returns from economies of scale for the physical attributes than for the service attributes of a product. On the other hand, there can be substantial learning effects with service attributes. For example, various management procedures such as the stocking of spare parts or hotel laundering may be standardized.

In certain cases (cell 3) the adaptation of service attributes will lead to cost savings because locally supplied services will be far less comprehensive than in the country of origin. This is feasible either when local service requirements are less demanding or when the product has been expressly constructed to be almost maintenance free. In this case it will also be designed to stand up to 'untrained' users. Physical attributes will then interact with service attributes within the product as a whole.

However, service standardization (cell 4) will be required when the clientele are internationally 'mobile'. Customers move with their service requirements. The global success of truck manufacturers from northern Europe (DAF, Volvo, Scania, Mercedes) is due in part to their ability to offer a standardized service in a range of countries and on sites along the routes that are most commonly taken by international lorry drivers. For instance, an engine or a gearbox can be completely overhauled within a specified period of time at any location on the route. The same holds true for McDonald's restaurants where service is to a large extent standardized worldwide: customers know what they will find in term of service, whether they enter a McDonald's in Tampere, Finland, Osaka, Japan or Montauban, France.

9.4

Symbolic attributes

The symbol can be defined linguistically as the sign that designates a relationship which is non-causal (as opposed to the *indicator*) and non-analogous (as opposed to the *icon*).

The *Oxford English Dictionary Online* defines 'symbol' as 'Something that stands for, represents, or denotes something else (not by exact resemblance, but by vague suggestion, or by some accidental or conventional relation)'. Any animate or inanimate object may be a basis for making a symbolic association. A fox may be a symbol of cunning, whereas an oak may be a symbol of strength. The use of the words 'may be' recognizes the fact that not every culture makes such associations. Either there are no foxes or oaks, or other interpretative meanings are applied. Symbols work as a powerful means of suggestion and evocation. The symbolic aspects of consumption are important to consumers: the social meaning of many products is more important than their functional utility or at least as important, e.g. clothes or perfumes. As Solomon emphasized (1983, p. 320): 'Symbolic interactionism focuses on the process by which individuals understand their world. It assumes that people interpret the actions of others

rather than simply react to them.' Most symbols are not universal; they may be understood and used by a large part, but not all, of the world population. One of the rare symbols to transcend cross-cultural boundaries is that of left and right, with a positive value put on the 'right' side, which is seen as the adequate way, as correct and true, or as being in accordance with moral or legal behaviour (Cohen, 1996). In French (*droit*) or German (*Recht*) the same word is used for designating both the right side and law.

In terms of adaptation/standardization, two different issues will be addressed:

1. The relationship between symbolic attitudes and national product images, with respect to product category, company and brand names and country of manufacture (see Chapter 10).
2. Divergent symbolic interpretations. Meanings are principally conveyed by the packaging and outward appearance of a product. If a symbolic attribute which was ethnocentrically conceived has a very different and highly negative interpretation in the target culture, adaptation is required (cell 5). For instance, symbolic associations linked to objects or colours may vary considerably across countries and cultures. Carlsberg had to add a third elephant to its label in Africa, since two elephants seen together are considered an ominous sign (McCornell, 1971).

The link between symbols and culture

The link between symbols and culture comprises seven successive steps. The starting point is a conceptual one: colours, for example, are wavelengths of light reflected by objects; a set of waves of different frequencies produces a colour spectrum. If it is stated that an object is red, this means the following:

1. It soaks up all received light except red.
2. The language has the term called 'red', which designates a certain part of the spectrum that reflects the object (which has no colour as such).
3. Our perceptual apparatus – eyes, retinas, optical nerves, brains – are capable of identifying the wavelengths.
4. Through a learning mechanism, both linguistic and visual, we have learnt to recognize this colour

as 'red' since early childhood; that is, to qualify it by imitation of all the other people who also designate this colour as 'red'.

Perception results from a culture-based adaptive process (points 2 and 4 above). Numerous experimental studies have shown that certain peoples have a less discriminating perception of colour (their vocabulary and identification is more restricted). They 'mix up' certain 'colours' that other peoples can distinguish. It has also been shown that sensitivity to visual illusions (shapes and length) varies according to culture, particularly as a result of the effects of syncretism. Suggestive visual associations result from our daily environment. Our native physical environment shapes our perceptual universe (see section 1.4). In the case of pictorial perception, Cohen (1995) distinguishes two questions: (1) 'What do people see when they look at this picture?' and (2) 'What does the picture mean?' The second question refers to meaning, interpretation and symbolism, but the first question, which has to be answered first, refers to what people *actually see*. Western pictorial conventions representing three dimensionality on a plane, for instance, are based on arbitrary codes: smaller objects, and higher objects in the picture plane, are meant to be farther away; an overlapped object is supposed to be farther away, and the rules of 'perspective' are applied in the form of convergence of lines. As explained by Cohen (1995, p. 219):

A picture of an empty bowl in front of a child was supposed to show that the child was hungry and malnourished. The two cues which should have indicated three-dimensionality were overlap and size. But when individuals in the target market were shown the picture, they thought the bowl was an empty washbowl. This was because the bowl was in the foreground and was large in size compared with the child.

In order to move on from the *percept* (i.e. the subjects are able to formulate verbally what has been shown to them) to the *symbolic image*, three steps must be added to the four previously set out. The cultural process intervenes at each of these three final steps:

5. An association has been established between a certain colour, form, smell, shape, etc. and a suggested meaning, as in the two parts of the Greek symbol (see the etymological definition of the symbol given in the introduction). Initially there

can be a highly tangible link: for example, the colour brown may be tainted by a negative sense in the connotation of waste, since it may be concretely associated with excrement.

6. This link is ignored; there are two complementary parts but the way they are related has been forgotten: why in most Western countries is blue the colour for little boys and pink for little girls? The association is important for choices in baby-related markets.

7. Then there is social overspill through education, advertising, the mass media, literature, magazines – in short, throughout society and indeed even to packaging and marketing communication in general. The symbol shares the characteristics of a language. It conveys rich and diversified meanings, full of nuances, and its messages are often implicit. It conjures up a set of evocations, suggestions and interpretations that are almost subconscious yet still very real in the minds of consumers. Indeed, this set of interpretations is to a large extent specific to each national culture. For example, does orange juice have to be yellow, orange or slightly red, full of pulp or clear, thick or very fluid, in order to evoke different product attributes: the sense of its being a nature-based/non-artificial drink, its dietary qualities, an image of refreshment, healthy for children as opposed to being intended for adults?

Images diffused by symbolic attributes

Symbols, in their capacity as signs with suggestive power that is non-causal and non analogous, rely on natural elements: colours, shapes, locations, materials, everyday objects, animals, countryside and elements of nature, famous characters, etc. In certain cultures the lake is a symbol of love, the blue of virginity. Most commonly the 'natural' backgrounds of symbols appear fairly arbitrary, in so far as the original link has often been lost or transformed, as and when the symbol became widely used. The interpretation of symbolic messages conveyed by attributes, such as colour, shape and consistency, may differ significantly between the marketer's culture and the consumer's culture. Williams and Longworth (1989) cite the case of Coral Sea tuna fishery in Australia, where the government spent money to

Figure 9.1 An example of diverging symbolic interpretations

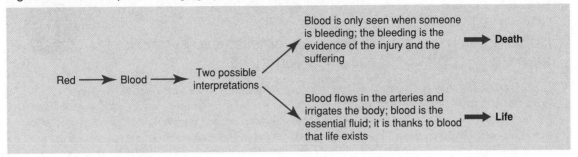

develop exports to Japan. The fishing operation was unable to obtain a high price for its fresh tuna air-freighted to Japan, because the Japanese had a problem with the colour of the fish. After investigations were conducted in the Tsukiji central wholesale market, it appeared that the negative interpretation was related to the meat colour, which evidenced a non-Japanese origin; this resulted in the Australian tuna consistently being sold at a discount. Today, Australia selects and sends only the more compatibly coloured Southern Bluefin tuna into the high priced sashimi (raw fish) market in Japan. Exports of tuna have grown from A\$6.6 million in 1990–91 to over A\$331 million in 2000–01 (Austrade, 2004).

Ethnocentrism is instinctive in all symbolic thought. It is therefore quite inevitable, especially when it is present in the consumer's culture. In the case of ethnic products, it may even be of some use to marketers, in order to maintain genuineness. However, inappropriate (or even poor) use of backgrounds that diffuse symbolic images that are not adapted to the local consumer presents a danger for international marketers. Inappropriate use of symbolic meanings may be based on the best possible intentions on the part of the marketer but may result in the worst consequences for users: for example, the skull and crossbones symbol, used in most Western countries to represent lethal dangers posed by electricity, poison, steam, etc., is a symbol of potency in many African countries.

The symbolism of colours, shapes, numbers, etc.

White is the colour of birth and in the West usually celebrates a happy life event, whereas in China it symbolizes mourning. Conversely, the colour black symbolizes death in the West, perhaps because its darkness suggests fears that the sun will not return, whereas it is an everyday colour in China.

Hidden behind each symbol is one or more material support. Red, for example, is the colour of blood: it can evoke and suggest meanings that differ widely depending on the culture (see Figure 9.1). Every culture has an image of blood, which feeds part of the symbolic content of the colour red (see Box 9.5). Naturally, the colour red can be linked to substances other than blood – certain flowers, for instance. Use of red as the dominant colour on a product or its packaging must therefore be very carefully considered beforehand (cell 5 in Table 9.1).

Associating symbols

The following examples illustrate symbolic associations. Symbols which are diffused by the design of a product or its packaging may be associated with the intrinsic qualities of the product itself.

The Italian company Olivetti produced a typewriter that was such a beautiful object that a New York museum displayed it in its modern art collection. This typewriter proved to be a commercial failure in the United States even though the Americans liked its appearance. Potential purchasers found that its design did not inspire an image of robustness (cell 5). Furthermore, in Anglo-Saxon societies there is often a puritanical attitude that work is an activity required by duty, which is sometimes arduous and should be more painful than enjoyable. This beautiful and enjoyable object was incompatible with such an attitude.

Coca-Cola decided to adapt the name 'Diet Coke' to 'Coke Light' or 'Coca-Cola Light' when it found

Box 9.5

Colours, things, numbers and even smells have symbolic meanings . . . often not the ones you think!

Green, America's favorite color for suggesting freshness and good health is often associated with disease in countries with dense green jungles; it is a favorite color among Arabs but forbidden in portions of Indonesia. In Japan green is a good high-tech color, but Americans would shy away from green electronic equipment. Black is not universal for mourning: in many Asian countries it is white; in Brazil it is purple, yellow in Mexico, and dark red in the Ivory Coast. Americans think of blue as the most masculine color, but red is more manly in the United Kingdom or France. While pink is the most feminine color in America, yellow is more feminine in most of the world. Red suggests good fortune in China but death in Turkey. In America, a candy wrapped in blue or green is probably a mint;

in Africa the same candy would be wrapped in red, our color for cinnamon . . . in every culture, things, numbers and even smells have meanings. Lemon scent in the United States suggests freshness; in the Philippines lemon scent is associated with illness. In Japan the number 4 is like our 13; and 7 is unlucky in Ghana, Kenya and Singapore. The owl in India is bad luck, like our black cat. In Japan a fox is associated with witches. In China a green hat is like a dunce cap; specifically it marks a man with an unfaithful wife. The stork symbolizes maternal death in Singapore, not the kind of message you want to send to a new mother.

(Source: Copeland and Griggs, 1986, p. 63.)

---

that the word *diet* connoted the need for weight-reduction rather than minimizing weight gain in some countries (Dana and Oldfield, 1999). In other countries, legal issues with the word *diet* have aided the trend (Coleman, 1999). Now Coca-Cola uses the word 'Light' in almost one-third of countries, including Germany, Spain, Argentina, Mexico and Brazil.

In many cases, symbolic associations may work even though, from a rational point of view, individual symbols are somewhat contradictory: consumers' interpretation of symbolic associations take the form of an impressionistic halo rather than a detailed content analysis. An example is a German *Weissbier* (a beer brewed with wheat instead of barley), called Oberdorfer. It claims on one side of its label to be brewed according to the Bavarian purity law of the year 1516, whereas the other side of the label boasts 'ice-rifing' (sic), 'our new *coole* art to brew beer' (*coole* is a germanification of 'cool', which evokes positive values of quietness and relaxation in many non-English speaking cultures, and 'ice-rifing' probably evokes a late crop of hops which provides a

more bitter taste). Associating (local) tradition and (foreign) modernity is in general no major problem: consumers themselves experience in their daily life the complex mix of modern and traditional, local and foreign values and behaviours.

A French company exported to West Germany a cheese from the Pyrénées. On the packaging was a shepherd surrounded by his sheep. This picture was directly related to what was shown in the television commercial. In France this image conveyed the idea of a natural manufacturing process and home-made qualities. A consumer test carried out in Germany, after the initial failure of the product, showed that the shepherd was associated by the Germans with dirt. The shepherd was withdrawn and subsequently replaced with a picture of mountain scenery. The product was then able to undergo a successful relaunch. In this example the problem stems from the association of symbolic opposites: country/mountain, dirty/clean, natural/artificial. Clearly in this case, the symbolic associations of the French and the Germans are very different.

Colours may also be associated with particular product categories or product attributes. Purple, for instance, is perceived as expensive in Asian cultures, but inexpensive in the United States. Black is perceived as demonstrating trustworthiness and high quality in China (Jacobs *et al.*, 1991). Colours may also be associated with countries, the products of which are supposed to be the most likely to have this colour dominant on their packaging. By gathering data in four countries (China, South Korea, Japan and the United States), Jacobs *et al.* (1991) show that Asian nations associate red with the United States, but US people do not associate their country with red; purple is associated with France, and the four cultures reviewed associate both France and Italy with the colour green.

Madden *et al.* (2000) explored the extent to which students from East Asia, Europe, North America and South America like various colours, the meanings they associate with colours and how they would match colours for a logo by testing. They found that blue, green and white share similar meanings and are well liked across countries, while black and red, although also liked, hold different meanings across countries. For instance, red was perceived as active, hot and vibrant across all countries, but in the PRC and Taiwan it was also perceived as pleasant. In addition, when students were asked to match colours for a product logo, the colours paired with red differed considerably. It was paired with black (for the United States and Brazil), with white (Colombia, Hong Kong, China and Taiwan) and with yellow (Austria, Canada and China).

Exotic, ethnic and universal appeals

Certain factors weigh in favour of the standardization of symbolic attributes (cell 6 in Table 9.1): favourable perception of imported products, positive association with the country of origin (perfume with France, fast food with the United States, etc.) and other factors are examined in detail in the next chapter. Many people buy a small slice of American life when they enter a McDonald's restaurant, a touch of French romance when they buy a Cacharel perfume, or an instant of German *gemütlichkeit* when they drink a Löwenbräu beer. In these consumption experiences, ethnic product symbolism is associated with exotic appeal for the consumer; thus, symbolic attributes must be kept standardized even though the product or its surrounding services are to a certain extent adapted to local markets.

A good example of a purely standardized product is the 'Classic Christmas Cake' sold worldwide through mail order by Collin Street Bakery from Corsicana, Texas (see *WS9.4*). The advertisement, sent by mail worldwide, emphasizes that they still bake the 'Deluxe cake true to the Old-World recipe brought to Corsicana, Texas from Wiesbaden, Germany in 1896, by master baker Gus Weidmann'; it boasts the richness of the ingredients ('a full 27 per cent rich pecans') and claims to deliver in 196 countries. Associating symbols of tradition (Old World), genuineness and American richness, they have a full register of images that work worldwide (and claim to do so!). Some brands try also to build on universal symbols: Coca-Cola has always successfully avoided being associated too strongly with an American image, by creating a strong brand association with youth, sports and leisure situations, all universal themes. Packaging consistency is a solution for products that want to diffuse a universal image and build on a highly standardized offering: Coke uses the same red and white logo in each country, and its bottle design is consistent across markets. Similarly, McDonald's never strays from its yellow arches. The symbolic interpretation then shifts from the parts to the whole: rather than relating to interpretations of yellow and arches in particular cultures, it diffuses a message about McDonald's worldwide.

For the designer of product attributes that convey appropriate symbolic meanings, the following recommendations can be made:

1. When conducting research on possible standardization before a product launch, it is preferable to choose symbols that have a universal or near-universal value (as far as they exist).
2. Since there is very great diversity in the interpretations and associations of symbols, product and packaging standardization must be systematically preceded by product and packaging tests carried out in each national market, using local informants.

Questions

1. List basic attributes of a perfume at the three levels (physical, service and symbolic). Indicate how the interpretation of symbolic attributes of perfumes may differ cross culturally.

2. What are basic attributes of Coca-Cola (physical, service and symbolic) in its original US context? Coca-Cola is adapted to suit local tastes and its advertising, although based on core advertising themes and guidelines, is customized for local audiences. Why?

3. How can a company make compromises between worldwide product standardization and customization to local markets?

4. Why is service adaptation across markets necessary? Outline basic reasons.

5. People in a queue may be told how long they still have to wait before being served. What are the possible interpretations by consumers of such information?

6. You have to choose a colour and a design for a fire extinguisher. What are the standard colour and signs used in your native culture. Assess whether they are cross-culturally transferable. Answer the same question for a coffee package.

7. Are there universal, or near-universal, symbols? To what extent can they be used in a marketing strategy? Provide examples.

Notes

1. Fast food scenario created from compiled articles including: Smucker, Philip, and Nicholas Blandford (2002) 'Arab states vent rising wrath', *Christian Science Monitor*, April 22, 2002. Retrieved January 5, 2004 from http://www.csmonitor.com/2002/0422/p01s04-wome.html. Kilani, Hala (2002) 'Grassroots campaign takes aim at U.S. economy', *The Daily Star* (Beirut), April 13, 2002. Retrieved January 5, 2004 from http://www.lebanonwire.com/0204/02041306DS.htm Blandford, Nicholas (2002) 'Arab citizens seize boycott banner', *Christian Science Monitor*, May 7, 2002. Retrieved January 5, 2004 from http://www.csmonitor.com/2002/0507/p06s01-wome.html.

2. Henry, Clement (2003) 'Clash of civilizations', *Harvard International Review*, Vol. 25, Issue 1 (2003). Retrieved January 5, 2004 from http://www.hir.harvard.edu/articles/index.html?id=1101&page=1.

3. Springborg, Robert (2003) 'Identity in crisis: Egyptian political identity in the face of globalisation', *Harvard International Review*, Fall, 2003. Retrieved January 2, 2004 from http://www.hir.harvard.edu/articles/index.html?id=1101&page=2

4. Barber, Benjamin R. (1992) 'Jihad vs. McWorld', *The Atlantic Online*, March, 1992. Retrieved January 5, 2004 from http://www.theatlantic.com/politics/foreign/barberf.htm.

5. Springborg, Robert (2003) 'Identity in crisis: Egyptian political identity in the face of globalisation', *Harvard*

International Review, Fall, 2003. Retrieved January 2, 2004 from http://www.hir.harvard.edu/articles/index.html?id=1101&page=2

6. McNulty, Brian (2002) 'The food service market in Saudi Arabia', *IMES Ireland*, 16 February, 2002. Retrieved May 5, 2004 from http://www.imes.co.uk/pages/fsarticle.htm.

7. Zayed, Dahlia (2004) 'Fast food still sells in Egypt', *AME Info*, August 26, 2004. Retrieved September 7, 2004 from http://www.ameinfo.com/news/Detailed/42253.html.

8. http://www.kfcindonesia.com

9. http://www.kfc.com.my/outlets/index.html

10. http://www.egyptyellowpages.com.eg/index.asp

11. http://www.pizzahutsaudia.com

12. http://www.baskinrobbins.com

13. http://www.subway.com

14. Abdel-Halim, Mustafa (2003) 'Muslims rally against U.S. products, Big Mac feels backlash', *Islam Online*, February 8, 2003. Retrieved January 5, 2004 from http://www.islamonline.net/English/News/2003-02/08/article03.shtml

15. Taja, Waheed (2002) 'Buying locally made U.S. products not permissible: Scholar', *Islam Online*, July 3, 2002. Retrieved January 5, 2004 from http://www.islamonline.net/English/News/2002-07/03/article09.shtml.

16. Abdel-Halim, Mustafa (2003) 'Muslims rally against U.S. products, Big Mac feels backlash', *Islam Online*, February 8, 2003. Retrieved January 5, 2004 from

http://www.islamonline.net/English/News/2003-02/08/article03.shtml

17. Taja, Waheed (2002) 'Buying locally made U.S. products not permissible: Scholar', *Islam Online*, July 3, 2002. Retrieved January 5, 2004 from http://www.islamonline.net/English/News/2002-07/03/article09.shtml.

18. Ibid.

19. Cox, James (2002) 'Arab nations see boycotts of U.S. products', *USA Today*, June 26, 2002. Retrieved January 24, 2004 from http://www.usatoday.com/money/world/2002-06-26-arab-boycott.htm

20. Murphy, Dan (2003) 'U.S. multinational companies wary of backlash', *Christian Science Monitor*, April 21, 2003. Retrieved November 30, 2003 from http://www.csmonitor.com/2003/0421/p12s01-woap.html.

21. Cox, James (2002) 'Arab nations see boycotts of U.S. products', *USA Today*, June 26, 2002. Retrieved January 24, 2004 from http://www.usatoday.com/money/world/2002-06-26-arab-boycott.htm

22. Murphy, Dan (2003) 'U.S. multinational companies wary of backlash', *Christian Science Monitor*, April 21, 2003. Retrieved November 30, 2003 from http://www.csmonitor.com/2003/0421/p12s01-woap.html.

23. Laksamana.net (2003) 'Anti-war protesters close *KFC* outlet', *Laksamana.net*, March 18, 2003. Retrieved January 5, 2004 from http://www.kabar-irian.com/pipermail/kabar-indonesia/2003-March/000284.html.

24. Ibid.

25. Shehzad, Waseem (2003) 'American companies feeling the impact of Muslim boycotts', *Crescent International* (Toronto), undated. Retrieved January 5, 2004 from http://www.aljazeerah.info.

26. Zia, Amir (2003) 'U.S. food sells fast in Pakistan despite boycott', *Reuters U.K. Top 100*, July 31, 2003.

27. Abdel-Halim, Mustafa (2003) 'Muslims rally against U.S. products, Big Mac feels backlash', *Islam Online*, February 8, 2003. http://www.islamonline.net/English/News/2003-02/08/article03.shtml

28. Zia, Amir (2003) 'U.S. food sells fast in Pakistan despite boycott', *Reuters U.K. Top 100*, July 31, 2003.

29. Kennedy, Miranda (2003) 'America off our soil', *The Nation*, May 19, 2003. Retrieved March 1, 2003 from http://www.thenation.com/docprint.mhtml?i=20030602&s=kennedy.

30. For more information about *Halal* foods and the food industry go to: http://www.eat-*Halal*.com and http://www.zabihah.com/ (global directory of *Halal* restaurants), and http://www.ifanca.org/faq/fastfood.htm (Islamic Food and Nutrition Council of America)

31. Eliasi, Jennifer R. and Johanna T. Dwyer (2002) 'Kosher and *Halal*: Religious observances affecting dietary intake', *Journal of the American Dietetic Association*, July, 2002.

32. Mathiot, Cédric (2004) 'L'éclosion fulgurante du poulet *Halal*', *Libération*, February 14, 2004. Retrieved February 30, 2004 from http://www.liberation.fr/page.php?Article=178769.

33. Muslim Consumer Group (2003) 'MCG criteria for Zabiha meat', *News Alerts*, Muslim Consumer Group for

Food Products, August 10, 2003. Retrieved September 7, 2004 from http://www.muslimconsumergroup.com/news.htm.

34. Eat-*Halal*.com (undated) 'Eating out', *Eat-Halal.com*, undated. Retrieved January 14, 2004 from http://www.eat-*Halal*.com/eatingout.shtml.

35. Eat-*Halal*.com 'Eating out', (web page) *EatHalal.com* (Canada), 2004. Retrieved February 30, 2004 from http://www.eat-*Halal*.com/eatingout.shtml.

36. Mathiot, Cédric (2004) 'L'éclosion fulgurante du poulet *Halal*', *Libération*, February 14, 2004. Retrieved February 30, 2004 from http://www.liberation.fr/page.php?Article=178769

37. Eurofood (2002) 'Western food firms eyeing slice of growing *Halal* food market', *Eurofood*, August 1, 2002.

38. Eliasi, Jennifer R. and Johanna T. Dwyer (2002) 'Kosher and *Halal*: Religious observances affecting dietary intake', *Journal of the American Dietetic Association*, July, 2002.

39. Islamic Food and Nutrition Council of America (undated) '*What is Halal?*' (web page), Islamic Food and Nutrition Council of America. Retrieved March 5, 2004 from http://www.ifanca.org/*Halal*.htm

40. Mathiot, Cédric (2004) 'L'éclosion fulgurante du poulet *Halal*', *Libération*, February 14, 2004. Retrieved February 30, 2004 from http://www.liberation.fr/page.php?Article=178769.

41. Chicken Cottage (undated) 'About Chicken Cottage' (web page), Chicken Cottage International, undated, http://www.chicken-cottage.co.uk/2003/contact.htm.

42. Wax, Emily (2003) 'In Egypt, anger at U.S. displaces admiration', *Washington Post*, March 24, 2003. Retrieved January 17, 2004 from http://www.commondreams.org/headlines03/0324-07.htm.

43. Abdel-Halim, Mustafa (2003) Muslims rally against U.S. products, Big Mac feels backlash', *Islam Online*, February 8, 2003. http://www.islamonline.net/English/News/2003-02/08/article03.shtml.

44. Classic Cairo (2002) 'Ceramics and sandwiches', *Classic Cairo*, February 26, 2002. Retrieved January 5, 2004 from http://www.cairolive.com/newcairolive/classic/26-2-2002.html.

45. KFC Holdings Malaysia (2004) *Syariah Advisory Council of KFCH* (webpage), KFC Holdings Malaysia, 2004. Retrieved September 7, 2004 from http://www.kfcholdings.com.my/sac.htm.

46. For more information on politico-religious activism against fast food companies go to: http://www.proislam.com/muslim_boycott.htm and http://www.petitiononline.com/sb2002/petition.html.

47. Taja, Waheed (2002) 'Buying locally made U.S. products not permissible: Scholar', *Islam Online*, July 3, 2002. Retrieved January 5, 2004 from http://www.islamonline.net/English/News/2002-07/03/article09.shtml.

48. MacFarquhar, Niel (2002) 'An anti-American boycott is growing in the Arab world', *New York Times*, May 10, 2002.

49. Zia, Amir (2003) 'U.S. food sells fast in Pakistan despite boycott', *Reuters U.K. Top 100*, July 31, 2003.

50. Business Today (2002) 'The road to hell', *Business Today* (Egypt), June 1, 2002. Retrieved January 11, 2004 from http://www.epnet.com.

51. Taja, Waheed (2002) 'Buying locally made U.S. products not permissible: Scholar', *Islam Online*, July 3, 2002. Retrieved January 5, 2004 from http://www.islamonline.net/English/News/2002-07/03/article09.shtml.

52. Bard, Mitchell (2004) *The Arab Boycott*, American-Israeli Cooperative Enterprise, undated, 2004. Retrieved January 11, 2004 from http://www.us-israel.org/jsource/History/Arab_boycott.html.

53. Bard, Mitchell (2004) *The Arab Boycott*, American-Israeli Cooperative Enterprise, undated, 2004. Retrieved January 11, 2004 from http://www.us-israel.org/jsource/History/Arab_boycott.html.

54. Arnold, Michael S. (1999) 'Boycott wars with burgers', *Jerusalem Post*, 13 September, 1999. Retrieved January 5, 2004 from http://www.jpost.com/com/Archive/13.Sep.1999/Features/Article-7.html.

55. Arnold, Michael S. (1999) 'Boycott wars with burgers', *Jerusalem Post*, 13 September, 1999. Retrieved January 5, 2004 from http://www.jpost.com/com/Archive/13.Sep.1999/Features/Article-7.html.

56. Bard, Mitchell (2004) *The Arab Boycott*, American-Israeli Cooperative Enterprise, undated, 2004. Retrieved January 11, 2004 from http://www.us-israel.org/jsource/History/Arab_boycott.html

57. Arnold, Michael S. (1999) 'Boycott wars with burgers', *Jerusalem Post*, 13 September, 1999. Retrieved January 5, 2004 from http://www.jpost.com/com/Archive/13.Sep.1999/Features/Article-7.html.

58. Bard, Mitchell (2004) *The Arab Boycott*, American-Israeli Cooperative Enterprise, undated, 2004. Retrieved January 11, 2004 from http://www.us-israel.org/jsource/History/Arab_boycott.html.

59. Anonymous (2002) 'U.S. warns companies over Israel boycott', *BBC News*, November 5, 2002.

60. Ganley, Elaine (2004) 'Thousands march around the world in headscarf protest' *Al-Jazeera.info*, January 18, 2004.

61. Robinson, Francis (2002) 'Islam and the West', *Asian Affairs*, Royal Society for Asian Affairs, October, 2002. Retrieved January 5, 2004 from http://www.rsaa.org.uk/Robinson.pdf.

62. Ibid.

63. Ibid.

64. Modood, Tariq (2003) 'Muslims and the politics of difference', The Political Quarterly, (undated, 2003). Retrieved January 5, 2004 from http://www.blackwellpublishing.com/journal.asp?ref=0032-3179&site=1

65. Zubaida, Sami (1998) 'Muslim societies: Unity or diversity?' *International Institute for the Study of Islam in the Modern World Newsletter*, October, 1998. Retrieved January 5, 2004 from http://www.isim.nl/files/newsl_1.pdf.

66. Shadid, Anthony (2003) 'Old Arab friends turn away from U.S.', *Washington Post*, February 26, 2003. Retrieved January 23, 2004 from http://www.washingtonpost.com.

67. Friedland, Roger (2001) *Money, sex, and god: the erotic logic of religious nationalism*, (speech) Center for Comparative Studies, Department of Religious Studies and Sociology, Yale University, September 20, 2001. Retrieved January 5, 2004 from http://www.yale.edu/ccr/friedland.doc.

68. Robinson, Francis (2002) 'Islam and the West', *Asian Affairs*, Royal Society for Asian Affairs, October, 2002. Retrieved January 5, 2004 from http://www.rsaa.org.uk/Robinson.pdf.

69. Cox, James (2002) 'Arab nations see boycotts of U.S. products', *USA Today*, June 26, 2002. Retrieved January 24, 2004 from http://www.usatoday.com/money/world/2002-06-26-arab-boycott.htm.

70. See for instance, the Palestinian Initiative for the Promotion of Global Dialogue and Democracy (MIFTAH), headed by Dr Hanan Ashrawi, Palestinian Member of Parliament. Contains news, research studies, historical documents, social and economic information on the Middle East. http://www.miftah.org.

71. Aide Sanitaire Suisse aux Palestiniens (undated) *Chronologie 2000–2001*, Aide Sanitaire Suisse aux Palestiniens, undated. Retrieved January 11, 2004 from http://www.assp.ch/page/history/hist11.html.

72. Shearman and Sterling (2001) *Arab League Boycott of Israel*, Shearman and Sterling Client Publication, April, 2001. Retrieved January 11, 2004 from http://www.shearman.com/documents/LIT_0401.pdf.

73. Egyptian State Information Service (2002) 'Economists say boycott best weapon against U.S., Israel', *Egyptian State Information Service*, April 13, 2002. Retrieved January 11, 2004 from http://www.sis.gov.eg/online/html7/o130422c.htm.

74. Cox, James (2002) 'Arab nations see boycotts of U.S. products', *USA Today*, June 26, 2002. Retrieved January 24, 2004 from http://www.usatoday.com/money/world/2002-06-26-arab-boycott.htm.

75. MacFarquhar, Niel (2002) 'An anti-American boycott is growing in the Arab world', *New York Times*, May 10, 2002.

References

ABN Amro (2000), 'Filmspace: Behind the Scenes', ABN Amro (internal magazine), 12 September.

Albaum, Gerald and David K. Tse (2001), 'Adaptation of international marketing strategy components, competitive advantage, and firm performance: a study of Hong Kong exporters', *Journal of International Marketing*, vol. 9, no. 4, pp. 59–71.

Allio, David J. and Robert J. Allio (2002), 'Coors light in Puerto Rico: battling for local dominance in a global market', *Strategy and Leadership*, vol. 30, no. 6, pp. 13–17.

Amine, Lyn S. (1993), 'Linking consumer behavior constructs to international marketing strategy: a comment on Wills, Samli, and Jacobs and an extension', *Journal of the Academy of Marketing Science*, vol. 21, no. 1, pp. 71–7.

Anholt, Simon (1999), 'Getting on the brandwagon', presentation by International Finance Corporation, Autumn, 1999.

Anonymous (2003a), 'Movie culture in Italy and Egypt', *The Power of Love*, undated, available at: **http://kvc. minbuza.nl**

Anonymous (2003b), 'In 2002 European films were unable to repeat the exceptional performance achieved in 2001', *LUMIERE* press release, 21 March.

Arlidge, John (2003), 'Harry Potter and the crock of gold', *Observer* (London), 8 June.

Austrade (2004), 'Aquaculture overview', Australian Government Austrade website, available at: **www. austrade.gov.au/australia/layout/0,,0_S2-1_CLNTXID 0019-2_-3_PWB1104076-4_tradestat-5_-6_-7_,00.html** [accessed 24 July 2004].

Baalbaki, Imad B. and Naresh K. Malhotra (1995), 'Standardization versus customization in international marketing: an investigation using bridging conjoint analysis', *Journal of the Academy of Marketing Science*, vol. 23, no. 3, pp. 182–94.

Baumgartner, Hans and Jan-Benedict E.M. Steenkamp (1996), 'Exploratory consumer buying behavior: conceptualization and measurement', *International Journal of Research in Marketing*, vol. 13, no. 2, pp. 121–37.

Brady, Michael K. and Christopher J. Robertson (2001), 'Searching for a consensus on the antecedent role of service quality and satisfaction: an exploratory cross-national study', *Journal of Business Research*, vol. 51, no. 1, pp. 53–60.

Camphuis, Pierre-Arnold (1984), 'Launching a product on the Cameroon market', Internship report, Ecole Supérieure de Commerce de Paris.

Center for Strategic and International Studies (2001), 'Culture and globalisation', *Global Connections*, undated.

Chew, Eugene (1999), 'Life goes on: the 1999 Hong Kong Film Festival', *Toto Cinema Matters*, undated.

Cohen, Judy (1995), 'Toward a theoretical understanding of the impact of culture on pictorial perception', *Proceedings of the Second Conference on the Cultural Dimension of International Marketing*, Odense, pp. 213–45.

Cohen, Judy (1996), 'The search for universal symbols: the case of right and left', *Journal of International Consumer Marketing*, vol. 8, no. 3/4, pp. 187–210.

Coleman, Zach (1999), 'Foreign markets develop taste for Coke Light', *Atlanta Business Chronicle*, 10 May.

Copeland, Lennie and Lewis Griggs (1986), *Going International*, Plume Books/New American Library: New York.

Dana, Leo-Paul and Brenda M. Oldfield (1999), 'Lublin Coco-Cola Bottlers Ltd', *International Marketing Review*, vol. 16, no. 4/5, pp. 291–8.

De Ruyter, Ko, Martin Wetzels, Jos Lemmink and Jan Mattsson (1997), 'The dynamics of the service delivery process: a value-based approach, *International Journal of Research in Marketing*, vol. 14, no. 3, pp. 231–43.

Diamantopoulos, A., B.B. Schlegelmilch and J.P. Du Preez (1995), 'Lessons for pan-European marketing? The role of consumer preferences in fine-tuning the product-market fit', *International Marketing Review*, vol. 12, no. 2, pp. 38–52.

Dollt, Andreas (2003), 'Cinema Statistics', *Statistics in Focus: Industry, trade, and services*, Eurostat, Theme 4-8/2003.

Fitzgerald, Kate (2003), 'Hollywood and the demographic revolution', *AdAge.com*, 15 July.

Frazer Winsted, Kathryn (1997), 'The service experience in two cultures: a behavioral perspective', *Journal of Retailing*, vol. 73, no. 3, pp. 337–60.

Frazer Winsted, Kathryn (1999), 'Evaluating service encounters: a cross-cultural and cross-industry exploration', *Journal of Marketing Theory and Practice*, vol. 7, no. 2, pp. 106–23.

Freedman, Michael (2003), 'Supreme court upholds copyright extension', *Forbes.com*, 15 January.

Frontline (2001), 'Interview with Howard Stringer, Chairman and CEO of Sony America', *Frontline*, Public Broadcasting Service (USA), undated.

Fuma Shapiro, Simona (2000), 'The culture thief', *The New Rules*, Fall.

Garncarz, Joseph (2002), 'Germany goes global: challenging the theory of Hollywood's dominance on international markets', *Media in Transition, Globalisation and Convergence: An international conference*, 10–12 May.

Gaydos, Steven (2000), 'Forman brings Euro touch . . .', *Variety*, 10 January.

Giordan, Alain-Eric (1988), *Exporter Plus 2*, Economica: Paris.

Groves, Don (1999), 'Disney goes ape with *Tarzan* dubs', *Variety*, 14 June.

Guider, Elisabeth (2003), 'Warner Bros. hits $1 billion B.O. overseas', *Variety*, 22 July.

Hall, Edward T. (1976), *Beyond Culture*, Doubleday: New York.

Hooper, John, *et al.* (2002), 'World Wide Wizard (Harry Potter)', *Guardian*, 8 November.

Hult, G. Tomas M., Bruce D. Keillor and Roscoe Hightower (2000), 'Valued product attributes in an emerging market: a comparison between French and Malaysian consumers', *Journal of World Business*, vol. 35, no. 2, pp. 206–20.

Jacobs, Laurence, Charles Keown, Reginald Worthley and Ghymn Kyung-Il (1991), 'Cross-cultural colour comparisons: global marketers beware!', *International Marketing Review*, vol. 8, no. 3, pp. 21–30.

Javalgi, Rajshekhar G. and D. Steven White (2002), 'Strategic challenges for the marketing of services internationally', *International Marketing Review*, vol. 19, no. 6, pp. 563–81.

Kamamoto, Mitsuko (1984), 'Japanese concept of service', *Dentsu Japan Marketing/Advertising*, January, pp. 26–9.

Kapur, Shekhar (2002), 'Dying cowboy, pouncing tiger', *Mail & Guardian* online (South Africa), 30 August.

Kariuki, John (2003), 'Africa at large: Hollywood goes to war in Africa', *The East African* (Kenya), The Norwegian Council for Africa, 23 June.

Koc, Erdogan (2003), 'The role and potential of travel agency staff as a marketing communications tool', *Tourism Analysis*, vol. 8, pp. 105–11.

Kostecki, Michel Maciej and Marcin Nowakowski (2002), 'Regulatory barriers to export of services: a managerial view from Poland-based export firms', *Argumenta Oeconomica*, vol. 12, no. 1, pp. 17–51.

Lange, André (2003), 'Harry, Billy, Amélie . . . and the others?' *Focus 2002 – New: Focus 2003*, Marché du Film, Cannesmarket.com, available at: **www.cannesmarket.com** [accessed 30 July 2003].

Lange, André and Susan Newmann-Baudais (2003), *World film market trends, Focus 2003*, Marché du Film, Observatoire Européen de l'Audiovisuel, May, available at: **www.obs.coe.int/online_publications/reports/focus2003-pdf** [accessed 30 August 2004].

Levitt, Theodore (1983), 'The globalization of markets', *Harvard Business Review*, vol. 61, no. 3, May–June, pp. 92–102.

Littrell, Mary A. and Nancy J. Miller (2001), 'Marketing across cultures: consumers' perceptions of product complexity, familiarity and compatibility', *Journal of Global Marketing*, vol. 15, no. 1, pp. 67–86.

Liu, Ben Shaw-Ching, Olivier Furrer and D. Sudharshan (2001), 'The relationships between culture and behavioral intentions toward services', *Journal of Service Research*, vol. 4, no. 2, pp. 118–29.

Madden, Thomas J., Kelly Hewett and Martin S. Roth (2000), 'Managing images in different cultures: A cross-national study of color meanings and preferences', *Journal of International Marketing*, vol. 8, no. 4, pp. 90–107.

McCornell, J.D. (1971), 'The economics of behavioral factors in the multinational corporation', in Fred E. Allvine (ed.), *Combined Proceedings of the American Marketing Association*, p. 260.

Money, R.B., M.C. Gilly and J.L. Graham (1998), 'Explorations of national culture and word-of-mouth referral behavior in the purchase of industrial services in the US and Japan', *Journal of Marketing*, vol. 62, October, pp. 76–87.

O'Donnell, Sharon and Insik Jeong (2000), 'Marketing standardization within global industries', *International Marketing Review*, vol. 17, no. 1, pp. 19–33.

Ofir, Chezy and Donald R. Lehmannn (1986), 'Measuring images of foreign products', *Columbia Journal of World Business*, Summer, pp. 105–8.

Pahud de Mortanges, Charles, Jan-Willem Rietbroek and Cort MacLean Johns (1997), 'Marketing pharmaceuticals in Japan: background and the experience of US firms', *European Journal of Marketing*, vol. 31, no. 8, pp. 561–82.

Pells, Richard (2002), 'American culture goes global, or does it?', *The Chronicle Review*, 12 April, p. B7.

Riding, Alan (2003), 'Filmmakers seek protection from US dominance', *New York Times*, 5 February.

Rogers, Everett M. (1983), *Diffusion of Innovations*, 3rd edn, Free Press: New York.

Rowley, Jennifer and Frances Slack (1999), 'The retail experience in airport departure lounges: Reaching for timeless and placelessness', *International Marketing Review*, vol. 16, no. 4/5, pp. 363–75.

Samiee, Saeed and Kendall Roth (1994), 'The influence of global marketing standardization on performance', *Journal of Marketing*, vol. 56, April, pp. 1–17.

Schuh, Arnold (2000), 'Global standardization as a success formula for marketing in central eastern Europe', *Journal of World Business*, vol. 35, no. 2 pp. 133–48.

Shoham, Aviv (1996) 'Marketing-mix standardization: determinants of export performance', *Journal of Global Marketing*, vol. 10, no. 2, pp. 53–73.

Solomon, Michael R. (1983), 'The role of products as social stimuli: a symbolic interactionism perspective,' *Journal of Consumer Research*, vol. 10, December, pp. 319–29.

Telegraph (2001), 'Hey, world! Hollywood's coming!', *Telegraph* (London), 31 March.

Theodosiou, Marios and Leonidas C. Leonidou (2003), 'Standardization versus adaptation of international marketing strategy: an integrative assessment of the empirical research', *International Business Review*, vol. 12, no. 2, pp. 141–71.

Trompenaars, Fons (1993), *Riding the Waves of Culture*, Nicholas Brealey: London.

Tuncalp, Secil (1990), 'Export marketing strategy to Saudi Arabia: the case of British exporters', *Quarterly Review of Marketing*, vol. 15, no. 2, pp. 13–18.

Usher, Rod (1998), 'Uncommon sense', *Time Magazine*, 26 October, p. 84.

van Birgelen, Marcel, Ko de Ruyter, Ad de Jong and Martin Wetzels (2002), 'Customer evaluations of after-sales service contact modes: an empirical analysis of national cultural consequences', *International Journal of Research in Marketing*, vol. 19, no. 1, pp. 43–64.

van Mesdag, Martin (2000), 'Culture-sensitive adaptation or global standardization – the duration-of-usage hypothesis', *International Marketing Review*, vol. 17, no. 1, pp. 74–84.

Vertinsky, Ilan and Dongsheng Zhou (2000), 'Product and process certification: systems, regulations and international marketing strategies', *International Marketing Review*, vol. 17, no. 3, pp. 231–52.

Vrontis, Demetris (2003), 'Integrating adaptation and standardisation in international marketing: the AdaptStand modelling process', *Journal of Marketing Management*, vol. 19, pp. 283–305.

Wattenberg, Ben and Daniel Wattenberg (1999), 'Hollywood is sharing the spotlight', *Jewish World Review*, 13 April, 1999.

Waxman, Sharon (1998), 'Hollywood attuned to world markets', *Washington Post*, 26 October, p. A1.

Williams, Stephen C. and John W. Longworth (1989), 'Factors influencing tuna prices in Japan and implications for the development of the coral sea tuna fishery', *European Journal of Marketing*, vol. 23, no. 4, pp. 5–24.

Wills, James, A. Coskun Samli and Laurence Jacobs (1991), 'Developing global products and marketing strategies: a construct and a research agenda', *Journal of the Academy of Marketing Science*, vol. 19, no. 1, pp. 1–10.

Witkowski, Terrence H. and Mary F. Wolfinbarger (2002), 'Comparative service quality: German and American ratings across service settings', *Journal of Business Research*, vol. 55, no. 11, pp. 875–81.

World Trade Organization (2004), 'Stronger than expected growth spurs modest trade recovery', available at: **www.wto.org/english/news_e/pres04_e/pr373_e.htm** [accessed 18 May 2004].

Appendix 9

Teaching materials

A9.1 Case

Movies worldwide

The world market for feature films has been dominated by the United States for more than 50 years. Hollywood, MGM, Warner Bros and the roaring 20th Century Fox lion are names, images and sounds with worldwide recognition. Examples of 60 years of creative work by US studios may be seen on TCM/TNT Turner Classic Movies (**www.turnerclassicmovies.com**). Despite the criticism that films are too commercialized, with scenarios overly influenced by focus groups, the average Hollywood release remains a worldwide success. *Ben Hur*, *Star Wars* and *Titanic* are examples of global hits that have done more than sell tickets around the world. They also reached the status of artistic myths in their categories (epic, science fiction and disaster, respectively). The *Harry Potter* films (released by Warner Bros.) are a more recent example of Hollywood's massive impact around the world. The film is the third highest international grosser in history (Guider, 2003). In Norway, one in five people saw the second film, having booked weeks in advance of the opening night. Twelve million Germans have seen the film. In Japan, adults, to whom the film is primarily marketed, are as fanatical about it as children (Hooper *et al.*, 2002). *Harry Potter*, as a franchise, is more profitable than blockbusters *Star Wars*, *Titanic* and *The Matrix* (Arlidge, 2003) (see **www.harrypotter.warnerbros.co.uk/**).

What many non-American US movie viewers ignore is that some films succeed at home but not abroad, and vice versa. Robin Williams did very well globally in *Good Morning Vietnam*, *Mrs Doubtfire* and *The Dead Poets Society*. However, his US health system drama *Patch Adams* failed overseas. According to Duncan Clark, international theatrical department head at Sony, certain formats are thought to fail abroad, such as black, urban and historical themes, as well as baseball and football films (Waxman, 1998). At home, film makers try to target different ethnic markets in addition to the mainstream. Since marketers are targeting youth, English now is the language of ethnic-oriented films (Spanish or Chinese subtitles may be available, so as not to alienate older viewers), however the theme of the screenplay may differ. Action and adventure movies are more successful among Asian-American audiences, for example (Fitzgerald, 2003). Film makers tend to select their cast, and particularly their stars, with a view to attracting international interest in their films. A respected source for directors is the Hollywood Reporter's 'Star Power' classification for the international box office. In 2002, the top five actors were Tom Cruise, Julia Roberts, Tom Hanks, Mel Gibson and Jim Carrey. Non-white actors are thought to hold little attraction for overseas markets, apart from Will Smith, Denzel Washington and Jackie Chan (Waxman, 1998).

Movie imports

In most cinema markets around the world, the majority of films are imported, reaching 78 per cent in Italy and 93 per cent in Egypt (Anon, 2003a). The market share of American movie films is very high (most often above 50 per cent). They reach peaks of 90 per cent in Scandinavia, and for the European Union as a whole, 78 per cent in 2002, up from 66 per cent in 2001 (Anon, 2003b; Lange, 2003). Even in supposedly 'resistant' countries like France, the share of American films is above 50 per cent, or approximately eight times the value of the combined imports of films made in other European countries (Center for Strategic and International Studies, 2001). In Spain, domestic film production is stagnant, accounting for 12.5 per cent of admissions, while American films accounted for 70 per cent (Riding, 2003). Films from central and eastern Europe, the Mediterranean Basin and Latin America generally account for a market share of about 1 per cent in the European Union, making the EU more impenetrable to film makers other than those from the United States, Canada, Australia and Japan. It is likely that a combination of cultural protectionism and poor distribution systems create conditions for market dominance of US films in Europe (Lange, 2003). Interestingly, there are historical differences. In the 1950s, German, French, and Italian audiences had a marked preference for their own national productions. Up until the 1980s, it was rare that the same film would share top ten status in Germany, France and Italy. However, since that time, 40 per cent of the top ten films in these three continental European countries are the same Hollywood films (Garncarz, 2002). Between 1996 and 2002, the top five films in terms of box office receipts were either British or British-American co-productions like *Bridget Jones's Diary* (2001), *Notting Hill* (1999), *James Bond: The World is Not Enough* (1999) and *Bean – the Ultimate Disaster Movie* (1997) (Lange and Newmann-Baudais, 2003).

Hollywood's hegemony

Hollywood's hegemony was won primarily thanks to its massive home market, which allowed studios to recover their costs domestically, freeing up resources for expensive stars, special effects and marketing (which averages US$25 million per film) (Fuma Shapiro, 2000). Having recovered production costs in their home markets, Hollywood studios can sell their films relatively cheaply to foreign distributors. In fact, three quarters of film distributors around the world are American-owned, making the top ten film studios also the top ten global distributors (ABN Amro, 2000). Around the world, US Distributors have the leverage to do what is illegal at home: 'Blockbooking', forcing theatres or distributors they do not own to buy packages of lower quality films in order to obtain a desirable hit film (Fuma Shapiro, 2000). The appeal of Hollywood films around the world is not so surprising considering that Hollywood producers have always had to appeal to different ethnic, religious and social groups in their heterogeneous home market. In addition, many 'Hollywood' directors of the present and past are not American at all. Examples are many, including Taiwanese Ang Lee (*Hulk*, *The Wedding Banquet*), British Sam Mendes (*American Beauty*), German Roland Emmerich (*Independence Day*, *The Patriot*) and British Ridley Scott (*Gladiator*, *Alien*). Another element that increased acceptance of US films among non-native speakers of English was the adoption of an introspective, non-verbal style in interpreting roles. This style (known as the 'Method') originated in nineteenth century Russian theatre and is diametrically opposed to the Shakespearean tradition that emphasises eloquence. As a by-product of the 'Method' style of Marlon Brando, James Dean, Robert DeNiro, and others, Hollywood films are easily understood even when one's knowledge of English – or the quality of subtitles – is poor (Pells, 2002). It is helpful that Hollywood's American-ness can tap into the most prominent country-brand equity in the world, to increase its potency (Anholt, 1999).

Table 9.3 Top two films by gross box office receipts per country/region 1996–2002

Country	Top grossing film	Second grossing film
Australia (2002 only)	*Star Wars: Episode 2* (USA)	*Lord of the Rings: Fellowship of the Ring* (USA/New Zealand)
European Union (1996–2002)	*Titanic*, 1997 (USA)	*Harry Potter and the Sorcerer's Stone*, 2001 (USA)
France (2002 only)	*Astérix et Obelix: Mission Cléopatre* (France/Germany)	*Harry Potter and the Chamber of Secrets* (USA)
Italy (2002 only)	*Pinocchio* (Italy/France/Germany)	*Lord of the Rings: Fellowship of the Ring* (USA/New Zealand)
Japan (2002 only)	*Harry Potter and the Sorcerer's Stone* (USA)	*Monsters, Inc.* (USA)
Korea (2002 only)	*Marrying the Mafia* (Korean)	*The Way Home* (Korean)
Latin America (1996–2002)	*Central do Brasil*, 1998 (Brazil/France)	*El Hijo de la Novia*, 2001 (Argentina/Spain)
Spain (2002 only)	*Spider-Man* (USA)	*Harry Potter and the Chamber of Secrets* (USA)
USA (2002 only)	*Spider-Man* (USA)	*Star Wars: Episode 2* (USA)

(Source: Based on Lange and Newman-Baudais (2003) 'World film market trends', *Focus 2003*, Marché du Film, Observatoire Européen de l'Audiovisuel, **www.obs.coe.int**. Reproduced with permission.)

US concerns about declining share of global movie market

Although American film productions account for about 85 per cent of world film audiences, some in Hollywood are increasingly concerned about dependence on world markets (Riding, 2003). In 2001, market share of American films fell by 16 per cent against local films around the world, and local films were bigger hits than US films in Korea, France, India, and other countries. Hollywood has its sights trained on the Asian markets (Japan, India and China) and related markets (Arab countries, North Africa, East Africa, Indonesia, Iran and South Asia), comprising over 75 per cent of the world's population (Kapur, 2002). Hollywood is actively seeking to acquire films from around the world with a more global appeal and to this end Sony and Miramax have acquisition executives seeking Chinese-language films in Hong Kong (*Telegraph*, 2001). More and more Hollywood studios are giving a more international flavor (and appeal) to their films by co-producing abroad or by filming extensively on location in target markets. Africa, for example, is considered to be a safe bet by some Hollywood studios due to an almost total lack of cultural protectionist measures, and little resentment of America and the concept of an 'American Hero'. *Tears of the Sun* and *Emma's War* were filmed on location, and Disney's *Lafiya* is intended to interest Africans and Black Americans (Kariuki, 2003).

Cultural protectionism

American film marketers need to take into account the cultural protectionism in some European countries and others, including Indonesia, Brazil and Korea. Protective duties, import quotas, and screening time quotas are common tools used to protect local film production (Garncarz, 2002). The French film industry receives approximately US$400 million per year in subsidies, an amount that has been growing each year. Other European countries with a cultural subsidy structure, such as Spain and Italy, are with France the most prolific of Europe's film producers (Dollt, 2003). In an effort to preserve the smaller, fragmented film industries around the world, Canada and 35 other countries have joined trailblazing France to negotiate a 'cultural exception' within the World Trade Organization, and the adoption of UNESCO's global convention on cultural diversity (Riding, 2003). Hollywood has paid for protectionism of its own, too. The massive motion picture industry lobbying of Washington pushed hard for a decision favouring copyright extensions for creations like Disney's Mickey Mouse in *Steamboat Willie* (soon to expire). The US Supreme Court recently upheld a law extending to a total of 70 years after the creator's death, or 95 years in the case of creations owned by corporations (Freedman, 2003).

Non-American films are beginning to attain better acceptance in the United States. *Crouching Tiger, Hidden Dragon* won the second highest number of Oscar awards, grossed US$100 million in North America despite American's traditional dislike for subtitled films. *Crouching Tiger, Hidden Dragon* is one of the 'breakthrough' films signalling the increasing acceptance of foreign films in the United States. Another such film is *Life is Beautiful*, the surprising humorous drama directed by Italian Roberto Benigni, where again a subtitled, foreign-language film succeeded in mainstream cinemas across North America to become the top grossing foreign language film in history, with more than US$43 million in receipts (Wattenberg and Wattenberg, 2001).

The film's key cultural components

Traditionally the movie industry is local. It is a multidomestic industry, dealing with local actors, local scripts, and the indigenous language. Most films produced worldwide are targeted for local or regional audiences. Egypt and India are major movie film producers. Indian films are viewed from the Middle-East to East Asia. Apart from the work of well-known film makers like Satyajit Ray, the majority of Indian films are unknown to a non-Asian audience. Films essentially reflect the local cultural scene of the country where they were made. The local scene means familiar landscapes, clothing, institutions, scenes, urban sites, and ways of interacting between people. A film also features products because product placement has become a way of increasing film budgets everywhere, resulting in the presentation of local products or global ones distinguished by a local touch. In Hong Kong, films feature the names of companies that purchased product placement more prominently than they do the names of the film stars (Chew, 1999). Local cues portrayed in films, such as the US legal system inherent to courtroom dramas, are most often unfamiliar to foreign viewers and generate an impression of the unknown, which may be positive (exoticism) but is usually viewed negatively. Films that are popular usually reflect the values held by the audience. In Germany, for instance, a rather collectivist and duty-oriented society gradually evolved post-war into one that valued self-determination and pleasure-seeking. This change in value orientation was reflected in the increasing popularity of the *James Bond* series, John Wayne films, *Jaws* and *Superman* where the protagonist drives the narrative to fulfill his own goals and the main values of the work are 'fun' (Garncarz, 2002).

Films are about storytelling (e.g. drama, comedy), through a visual and spoken narrative based primarily on language. This causes one of the key problems when selling films worldwide: how will speakers from other linguistic contexts understand a Mexican or a Japanese film if it is still in its original language. Generally, when Hollywood studios produce films intended for international markets, they intentionally minimize the dialogue and simplify it, so translations are easier to make, and narrative cues are embedded in the context (Frontline, 2001). Partly for this reason, film makers emphasize the visuals of a film when the overseas market is targeted. Most countries either use dubbing or subtitles. Dubbing is more costly to implement because it requires specialized professionals to draft a text that fits, as well as actors to dub the voiceover that replaces the original voice soundtrack. In the case of Disney's animated films like *Tarzan*, musical soundtrack dubbing may bankroll international stars like Phil Collins singing in five major languages, including two types of Spanish (Castilian and American), with local stars doing the dubbing in smaller markets (Groves, 1999). Dubbing is very popular in most European countries, where industries have grown up around the activity in large countries like Italy, Germany, France and Spain. Dubbing is also popular in Asia. Viewers of dubbed films are accustomed to the inevitable mismatch between actors' lips and their dubbed pronouncements. Smaller countries tend to use subtitles because the dubbing process is too costly. In Finland for instance, most films are subtitled in Finnish and Swedish, the two official languages. US viewers have never accepted dubbed films, with *Crouching Tiger*, *Hidden Dragon* and *Amélie* being notable exceptions. They also dislike watching subtitled foreign language films. Perhaps more importantly, US distributors consider foreign-language films as more suited to the niche 'art-house' cinema circuit than the mainstream. This, among other factors, explains the very low market share of foreign films on the US market, where more than 97 per cent of the films viewed are locally produced (Center for Strategic and International Studies, 2001).

Story-telling is also culturally meaningful, whether scripts put emphasis on fine-grained psychological relationships between characters (e.g. Swedish films by Ingmar Bergman), historical topics, action films, mob and gangster films, kung fu, or any kind of drama that is meaningful to the audience. The film script may finish with a happy ending or not. According to Czech-born Hollywood director Milos Forman (*One Flew over the Cuckoo's Nest*, *Ragtime*), the main difference between US and European films is that Hollywood likes happy endings and 'macho fairy tales', while Europeans prefer more ambiguity and realism (Gaydos, 2000).

There are also a number of other components for a film, including music, soundtrack and images. The most significant cultural component in a film is in the interaction between the key characters: their communication style typically reflects a context-bound interaction style. When people with Al Pacino interact in *The Godfather*, it cannot at all be compared with people interacting with Toshiro Mifune in the *Seven Samurai*. (For more information, go to **www.sprout.org**.)

The global film: The exception rather than the rule

The market for films is not *per se* a global market. There still will remain some important market barriers related to language and culture. However, the market is far from being a purely multidomestic one. As noted above, imports are considerable and viewers are eager to watch foreign films. Many spectators like both national films (identity enhancing) and foreign (mostly American) films. A film has a greater chance of reaching a worldwide audience if its story is rather simple and universal, relatively context-free and easy to capture. An example of this is Japanese filmmaker Akiro Kurosawa's *Seven Samurai*, a global success later adapted by Hollywood as *The Magnificent Seven*, a Western removed from its Japanese context, with a larger global reach than the original film. Film maker Jean-Jacques Annaud (**www.jjannaud.com/**) has produced films that reached a worldwide audience because, apart from their artistic quality, they eluded certain cultural obstacles (such as *La Guerre du Feu*, devoid of language, as was an interpretation of Jack London's *The Bear*. The popularity of animated films, such as *Finding Nemo* and *The Lion King*, may in part be due to their lack of particularistic cultural cues. *The Lord of the Rings* series (**www.lordoftherings.net/**), although filmed on location in the Southern Island of New Zealand, has no context-bound cues for the spectator apart from those from J.R.R. Tolkien's fantasy works. Appeals are also important to establish when targeting wider audiences: violence, action, science fiction, sex and eroticism, and suspense are likely to appeal broadly and in different cultures. In an international business analysis of film, six characteristics of American films were identified as: a fast pace, sexual tension, graphic violence, repetition of a fable or storyline, and a happy or spectacular ending (Fuma Shapiro, 2000). Less likely to appeal worldwide are family intrigues, psychological dramas, social criticism and moral narratives – more likely to characterize European films.

Questions

In order to answer the questions, you may use the web-based information contained in the links under 'A9.1 Movies Worldwide' on the website. For more information, a key word search on **www.google.com** *generally will find it.*

1. Why have American films been so successful over the last half century? Outline what you consider to be the key success factors for a film (type of story and genre; actors; directors, pace, music, and so on). Was the fascination for the American culture and way of life the prominent reason for that success? What was the contribution of the American melting pot with its huge diversity of migrants' origins to the creativity and global outlook of the American movie film industry?

2. What is the future of local films? Should they still target a local language and culture audience? Is there any future for local movie industries? Why? Take country examples if you wish.

3. If you were a ROW (rest-of-the-world, that is, non US) film director, willing to reach a wider audience, how would you go about increasing your chances to be accepted by the audience in a larger number of countries?

4. Are films primarily artistic pieces or are they mere commodities? Should film making be seen as an industry or as an art? If compromises are possible how would you devise them?

Saskia Faulk and Jean-Claude Usunier prepared this case solely to provide material for class discussion. The authors do not intend to illustrate either effective or ineffective handling of a business situation.

(©IUMI, reprinted with kind permission.)

A9.2 Case

Fastfood: *Halal* or *Haram*?

It was a crowded table at this noisy North African *KFC* outlet. Kader and four of his friends lounged comfortably in their chairs, eating and talking at a leisurely pace. After a range of references to France, movies, friends, and cars, the lunch companions launched into a discussion of the calls for an American boycott.

'I've been boycotting Israeli products for ages, that's why I don't drink *Coke*', stated Ahmed. 'Oh, come on: that's just one of a million rumors going around by email, you can look at any "rumors" website to find out the truth', retorted Fadi, 'As for me I drink *Pepsi* because they refused to go into Israel while others did.'

Kader sensed an opportunity: 'Look at you both, if you really are so politically aware, why are you wearing *Nike* shoes and smoking *Marlboro*s? You should be embarrassed!' Ahmed laughed as he answered 'Mr Kader, my friend, what are you doing enjoying your *KFC* food, then? It's an American company isn't it?' 'We all know that, what a lot of people don't realise is that everyone in that kitchen is an Arab, all the food comes from Arab suppliers, all . . .' Fadi interrupted, 'How do you know? How do any of us know? You believe what they say in their ads? Did you check with their suppliers? My friend, you, and all of us, are in the dark'. Taking a deep puff on his cigarette, Ahmed stated emphatically: 'I agree with all the calls to boycott, I don't want to support the Americans. As they say "by buying American products you cause Palestinian blood to flow", but what would I smoke, what would I wear, where would I eat? You tell me where there are some good local "light" cigarettes'. He squashed the cigarette in the ashtray. 'And where are the great Arab clothes designers and shoe manufacturers? When I'm at home I like *Starbucks* even though the head of the company's a Zionist, and THAT's not a rumor, bro'. Let's face it, we don't have a choice. Look, my shoes are counterfeit *Nike's*, and at least I don't go to *McDonald's*.'

Fadi snorted, and pointed his finger at Kader. 'Look, Ahmed, you are my friend, I wouldn't say anything bad about you, but you think that not going to *McDonald's* is going to help the Palestinians? The Iraqis? You know I don't normally eat here, you invited me. I don't believe that by wearing a *Tommy Hilfiger* shirt I'm oppressing Palestinians. Why don't you start your own clothes and shoes company, then I would know it's really "Arab",' he added quietly. Kader shook his head, and said 'Come on guys, let's not wear each other out. It's true, though, that instead of *Hilfiger* you could choose a European company, at least they're not as bad. *Diesel* is cool. *Puma* is cool. I read that the guy who runs *Hilfiger* is a racist, did you know that? *Marlboro* addicts should switch to smokes like *Gauloises Blondes*.' Then he lightly touched each friend on their arm, adding 'Guys, guys, we can do better, the point is we don't have to be slaves to American marketing. What's the big deal? We can make a little sacrifice on favorite brands compared with the price that Palestinians pay in blood.' Fadi had been quiet for a while. Suddenly, he spoke out 'You know, I heard this Lebanese girl speaking, she started a pro-boycott organization. She said that boycotting American products isn't just about hurting the American economy, she said it's more about getting the Americans to understand that their interests lie with us, 200 million Arabs, instead of the four million Israelis!'[1]

Fast food restaurants in the Middle East and other sensitive parts of the world have been hit by boycotts, criticism, and direct violence. *Starbucks*, *McDonald's*, *Pizza Hut*, *KFC*, and others are pawns in the global game of traditionalists versus progressives, of conservatives versus liberals, of protectionism versus globalization. Fast food companies have been the target of religious edicts, protests, vandalism, and aggressive competitive tactics, some of which have been openly supported by governments.

Globalization in the Middle East

The Middle East is a particular case of development. Most economies in the Middle East are state-controlled. Many are young states with a colonial legacy, and some were Cold War battlefields. The concept of Arab nationalism restricts some countries in an inflexible frame of reference. In some cases, the legitimacy of Middle East governments is challenged by their peoples' perception that they are passive in the face of the regularly televised humiliations of Palestinians, and foreign influence in countries like Afghanistan and Iraq. Various conflicts have justified large expenditures on arms, reducing resources for education and social benefits. These factors combine to create a polarized ideological environment where pro-globalization pragmatists may be in opposition to Islamists. Such conditions are not conducive to good business.[2]

As Arab nationalism has worn thin over the last two decades, the opposing forces in Arab societies have become more visible. Those likely to welcome globalization and its manifestations like *McDonald's* into their countries tend to be more affluent. Those on the lower end of the social scale are more likely to embrace ancient identities based on cultural, religious, ethnic, or linguistic differences.[3] In his book *Jihad vs. McWorld*, Benjamin Barber attempts to understand these opposing forces. 'McWorld', or globalism, offers integration into a larger economic system, and access to credit, markets and technology. 'Jihad', a term Barber uses loosely to describe tribalism, represents the fragmentation of societal identities, with 'Jihad' offering its proponents a local identity, sense of community, and solidarity against perceived outsiders.[4] Jihad being the compelling ideology of the 'losers' of a capitalist economic system, it is also the ideology of the majority, of the masses. With the cosmopolitan exception of Dubai, these two axes describe the tensions within which foreign-owned or -influenced businesses must operate in the Middle East,[5] representing a complex marketing environment.

Fast food has quickly established itself as a growing trend in the Middle East. In Saudi Arabia, for example, fast food outlets account for 15 per cent of all foodservice sales, compared with 32 per cent in the US However, sales by fast food outlets have grown by 10 per cent per year over five years. The following chart gives an idea of the fast growth rate of the fast food market in Saudi Arabia.

Table 9.4 Number of fast food outlets in Saudi Arabia (1990–2002)

Food type	1990	1997	2002
Burger	95	181	268
Chicken	17	70	151
Coffee/baked goods	16	61	244
Ice cream	24	174	309
Pizza	49	136	209
Sandwich/Arabic	11	50	112

(Source: IMES Research (2002) The food service market in Saudi Arabia.[6])

In Egypt, fast food has become a part of daily life. According to a recent study done in Cairo, 23 per cent of the city's population buy foreign branded fast food at least twice per week. The main consumers were teenagers and adult males, and consumption mainly took place via home or office delivery.[7] Fast food outlets have become ubiquitous in the Middle East with the exception of Syria. The following table gives an idea of the degree to which fast food outlets have become part of the landscape.

Table 9.5 Non-exhaustive list of fast food outlets in predominantly Muslim countries

	Domino's Pizza	Hardee's Restaurants	Subway	Burger King	McDonald's
Bahrain	4	6	–	3	8
Egypt	8	14	–	–	50
Indonesia	–	–	–	–	108
Jordan	1	–	–	5	–
Kuwait	5	–	16	47	34
Lebanon	4	10	3	8	–
Malaysia	19	–	2	21	–
Oman	–	–	1	–	–
Pakistan	1	–	9	–	21
Qatar		4	6	6	–
Saudi Arabia	36	24	13	35	71
Turkey	32	–	3	98	111
United Arab Emirates	6	21	32	21	25

(Sources: www.dominospizza.com, www.hardeesrestaurants.com, www.subway.com, www.bk.com, www.mcdonalds.com.)

Other foodservice chains with significant presence included, at the time of writing, *KFC* with 207 units in Indonesia,[8] 128 in Malaysia,[9] and 36 in Egypt[10] and *Pizza Hut* with 66 units in Saudi Arabia[11] and a strong presence elsewhere. Allied-Domecq-owned *Baskin Robbins* developed 133 units in Saudi Arabia.[12] According to the website, *Subway* has 9 units in Iraq, although most were temporarily closed.[13]

Religious edicts (fatwa)

Prominent Muslim scholars have issued religious edicts against the consumption of American products in Egypt, Qatar, Syria, Kuwait, and other countries. Sheikh Youssef Al-Qaradawi, Muslim scholar and president of the European Council for Fatwa and Research, has issued several fatwas calling for a Muslim boycott of Israeli and American products, stating that 'To buy their goods is to support tyranny and oppression. It's a duty not to do that'.[14] The Grand Imam of Islam's highest authority, Al-Azhar, stated that it is 'forbidden' not to follow the boycott of Israel and the supporters of Israel ('America is a second Israel'[15]), issuing a fatwa on the subject.[16] In a more precisely-worded fatwa regarding franchises, Dr. Mohammad Saeed Al-Bouti of Damascus University's Sharia school said that 'American products which must be boycotted are those whose revenues go to the US such as American cigarettes and restaurants. There are too many of these companies in our countries.' He specified that products produced in Islamic countries according to franchise agreements were forbidden because a portion of revenues from these products was given to the American company.[17] Other fatwas issued regarding the anti-Israel/anti US boycotts have been issued by Dr. Fu'ad Mukhaymar, head of the Egyptian Sunni Egyptian Institutions, and Dr. As-Sayed Nuh, Kuwait University professor.[18]

Vandalism, protests and violence

The destruction of a fast food outlet, defacing of its facade, breaking windows, and graffiti are common ways of expressing one's disagreement with all that is represented by US fast food operations. McDonald's windows were broken by angry pro-Palestinian demonstrators in Oman, and an outlet in Bahrain was defaced by stone-throwing youth.[19] *KFC* was attacked in Pakistan, Indonesia, Lebanon, and Greece.[20]

Burger King, *McDonald's*, and *Starbucks* were the sites for sit-ins and protests in Beirut where they blocked access to the counters and held pro-Palestinian messages.[21] *Pizza Hut* was bombed in Lebanon.[22] *KFC* was bombed in 2001 in Makassar, Indonesia.[23] In 2003, protesters closed the *KFC* outlet in Palu, Indonesia to express their resistance to a war in Iraq.[24] Students in Beirut protested in front of Starbucks outlets and handed out leaflets to inform people of Starbucks' chief executive's pro-Israel stance.[25] A bomb exploded outside *KFC* in Pakistan in December, 2001, causing no injuries.[26] A *KFC* outlet was destroyed in Cairo by anti-American protesters.[27] Mobs attacked several *KFC* outlets in Karachi, Pakistan in 2003. The company decided against further expansion in Pakistan in the short term, preferring to invest in less risky locations.[28] At *McDonald's* in New Delhi, protesters closed the outlet, screaming 'America off our soil!'[29]

Muslim food prescriptions

'*Halal*' is the Arabic word for 'Lawful', being food that is produced in the manner stipulated in Muslim Holy texts. In the case of restaurants, '*Halal*' mainly applies to meats, dairy products, and other items contaminated by meat[30]. *Halal* directives pertain mainly to slaughter, when the animal should be killed by a Muslim who invokes the name of Allah as the animal dies. Death should be caused by a slit throat causing the animal to bleed to death. The slaughterhouse should be supervised by a pious Muslim man.[31] In Europe, the largest *Halal* meat processing plants are in Belgium.[32] Some Muslims insist that meats be *Zabihah* in addition to *Halal*: that the owner of the meat-processing business be a Muslim, that the animal was fed exclusively on a vegetable diet and not treated with growth hormones, that the animal be hand-slaughtered and not stunned.[33] Devout Muslims are generally advised by Muslim organizations to avoid 'most items' at fast food outlets, although some fast-food chains attempt to purchase some *Halal* ingredients.[34] Muslims are advised to particularly avoid non-*Halal* pizza restaurants where there is a 'high risk' of contamination from pork products and meat by-products in cheese toppings.[35] In France the many Muslim patrons often justify *KFC* purchasing *Halal* meat, although the company does not publicize the fact nor do they display their *Halal* certificate (which is on hand in the kitchen if a Muslim wanted to inspect it), in fear of alienating other customer segments.[36] The *Halal* market was estimated at US$ 150 billion in 2002. Food industry experts have predicted that the *Halal* food trend will grow, with demand rising and increasing numbers of food suppliers and restaurant operators seek *Halal* certification.[37] The following table puts Muslim food restrictions in the context of the world's other major religions.

New Muslim-based competition

In some countries, local Muslim and *Halal* operators have stepped in to attract Muslim customers, due to the expressed reluctance of some Muslims to frequent fast-food outlets. Reasons cited by Muslims for avoiding fast food and prepared foods generally include preparation and service by non-Muslim staff, contamination of vegetarian and vegetable/fruit offerings by unlawful ('Haram') meat products, animal fat, gelatin, wine vinegar, enzymes, emulsifiers, non-*Halal* rennet[38,39] (as used in cheese and other dairy products), and vanilla-laced sweets because vanilla essence may contain alcohol. In France, there is a definite trend towards offering *Halal* fast-food on the American fried chicken and hamburger model. The kitchen equipment and menu at outlets named among others 'ChickenSpot' and 'Paris Fried Chicken' resembles that of *KFC* and *McDonald's*, and the equipment identical to that used by *KFC*.[40] A similar phenomenon is visible in Canada, Singapore, Australasia, and the UK. In the UK, for example, *Chicken Cottage*, a *Halal* fast food chain, currently has 62 outlets and has doubled in size within the past two years.[41] In Egypt, a local entrepreneur started *Mo'men* ('believer' in Arabic) in 1998 as a substitute for *McDonald's*. The chain, reported to be 'doing well' with outlets that are 'always packed' serves burgers and chicken nuggets, along with some traditional Egyptian items.[42] All machines and equipment used by *Mo'men* restaurants are American-made.[43] *Mo'men* offers vegetarian items that cater to Christians fasting for Lent, and a variety of festive menu items following the Muslim Eid festival.[44] In other countries, such as Malaysia and Singapore, restaurants apply for *Halal* certification from an official Muslim organization. In Malaysia, for example, *KFC* and *Pizza Hut* are advised by a 'Syariah Council' that oversees the supply chain and food production and service to ensure that all are *Halal*.[45] http://www.kfcholdings.com.my/sac.htm In Singapore, the Majlis Ugama Islam Singapura inspects and provides certificates for *Halal* products and services (http://www.muis.gov.sg).

Boycotts targeting fast-food chains

As stated in several reports, fast food is often a target of boycotts because it is far from being a necessity, particularly when there are local brands as alternatives. Recent Arab boycotts are considered to be an extension of the original anti-Israel boycott, which is still technically in force in some countries.[46] Boycotts intensified and took on different forms in the run-up to the hostilities in Iraq, with Malaysians focusing on *Coca-Cola* and *Pepsi*, Thai Muslims setting up 'US product free zones', Moroccans calling for a US dollar boycott, and Egyptians boycotting *McDonald's* specifically for its alleged Jewish ties.[47] In Bahrain, a major super-market chain removed American products from the shelves, replacing them with alternatives produced by companies not affiliated with the US[48] In Pakistan, *KFC* chief executive Rafiq Rangoonwala said that during the beginning of hostilities in Afghanistan and Iraq, sales at *KFC* outlets dropped by five to ten per cent, but soon regained earlier levels.[49] In Egypt, Jordan, and some Gulf countries, in-store sales were down but home delivery stayed the same or even rose, suggesting that some customers were simply avoiding the social pressure of being seen at the restaurant.[50]

Some people supported boycotts for their perceived cultural benefits, such as protecting local culture from 'American culture'. Regarding fast-food franchises, Muslim economist Dr. Monzer Kahf bemoaned American fast food replacing; 'Our traditional hommos, fool, sharwerma, falafel/ta'miyyah, kebab, booza, and other traditional fast food you see all over the Muslim land from Morocco to Malaysia and Indonesia'.[51]

The context of fast-food chain boycotts

In its original form the anti-Israel boycott was initiated on 2 December, 1945, as a means of refusing any kind of Arab support to Israel. The original goal of the boycott was to isolate Israel from other countries, particularly its geographic neighbors.[52] The boycott originally operated on three levels: companies trading directly with Israel, companies that do business with Israel, and companies that do business with companies trading with Israel.[53] Companies allegedly operating on all or some of these three levels were listed by Arab governments to facilitate their identification by local traders. The boycott of Israel was designed to destroy the state, according to Yoram Sheni, Israeli Foreign Ministry division head. Companies were forced to choose between trading with Israel or the more populous Arab countries.[54] In one example, *Coca-Cola* traded with Israel starting in the mid-1960s (earning blacklist status in the Arab world until 1992) while *Pespi-Cola* traded with the Arab world and was barred from trading with Israel until 1992.[55] In 1977, during the Carter Administration, the Congress made it illegal for US companies to participate in the boycott.[56] Since then, contrary to expectations, trade between Arab countries and the US continued to improve.

In 1994, six Gulf Cooperation Council states announced that they would no longer follow the secondary boycott. The beginnings of the peace process reduced the power of the boycott, and indeed dismantling the boycott was one of the conditions set out in peace treaties between Israel, Egypt, Jordan, and the Palestinian Authority. The boycott was estimated to have cost Israel some US$40 billion in lost trade as well as a 'psychological impact'.[57] As a result of Israel's violent response to the Intifada in 2001, the Arab League's Boycott Office revived its activities at the behest of Arab leaders in Damascus, with the notable absence of influential Arab countries like Egypt and Jordan.[58] The statement they issued said that the boycott was a 'peaceful, legal and noble' action to support Palestinians.[59]

Why do they care? The transnational aspect of Muslim cultures

When the French government declared in January, 2004 that Muslim headscarves were to be banned from schools, there were vocal demonstrations all over the world. Muslim women and men in Egypt, Indonesia, Lebanon, Palestine, Syria, UK, and U.S.A. joined French demonstrators to protest the ban.[60] This recent event illustrated the solidarity felt by Muslims around the world on certain issues, particularly where Islam meets the 'West'. In what some thinkers have referred to as the transnational nature of Islam, or 'active pan-Islamic con-sciousness',[61] Muslims tend to be concerned for the welfare of Muslims in other countries. Founder of Pakistan and poet Sir Muhammad Iqbal wrote on the topic: 'Our essence is not bound to any place; . . . Nor any fatherland do we profess except Islam'.[62] Partly for this reason, there is widespread concern among Muslims everywhere about the Palestinian issue, and the US-led invasion of Iraq.

The Muslim world, which will comprise one third of humanity by 2025,[63] is far from mono-lithic. Ethnic, racial, and nationalist differences often bedevil efforts at unity. Within Islam the religious distinctions, such as those between Sunni and Shi'a, are divisive. Differences aside, Muslims generally hold themselves to be members of a global community, or *Ummah*.[64] Despite the manifold historical, regional, and national differences in Islamic institutions and interpretations of the Koran, Shari'a (Islamic Law) and Hadith (Traditions of the Prophet), there are commonalities in the stated beliefs of politicized Islam centered on the rejection of material capitalism. The rise of Islamist beliefs and the search for an Islamic foundation for political and economic life is likely a reaction to the perceived secularization brought on by 'Modernity'.[65]

Political Islamic movements appear to agree on protesting the invasion of foreign capital, culture, and goods. The founder of the internationally active Muslim Brotherhood and father of political Islam, Egyptian Hasan Al-Bana, declared in 1928 that Europeans were using mater-ialism and other devices to foster atheism among Muslims. Today, the Muslim Brotherhood is considered to represent mainstream Islam in Egypt and Jordan, providing a credible opposi-tion.[66] In a similar vein, the Iranian Ayatollah Khomeini said that the pro-capitalist policies of the Shah allowed American capitalists to enslave Iranians and aimed to destroy Islam and its sacred laws.[67] In his book *America and the Third World War*, Osama Bin Laden challenged Muslims to rise up against the intentional spread of Westernisation, which he said destroys Muslim rights.[68] Organizers of anti-American boycotts, such as activists, religious leaders, and students, argue that Israel is the beneficiary of taxes paid by US corporations via US foreign aid.[69]

An issue that appears to unite Muslims the world over is support for the Palestinians[70], hence their vocal, political, and economic support for Palestinian and anti-Israeli causes. Both rejection of Western material culture and support for Palestine have been important in understanding a backlash against *McDonald's* and other overtly 'Western' and American brands which intensified during Israeli campaigns in the West Bank and Gaza following the beginning of the so-called 'Second' or '*Al-Aqsa*' Intifada, initiated on 29 September, 2000.[71] Support for the Palestinian struggle is often cited by Muslims around the world as reasons to reject Israel and perceived supporters of the state of Israel. The Palestinian issue has united the 21 members of the Cairo-based League of Arab States (known as the Arab League) for years, notably through its support of the Israel boycott.[72] Apart from media reports of Muslim statements to this effect, official sources confirm this view, such as the pronouncements of clerics and political leaders in Iran. The Egyptian State Information Service published a report in English, for example, making economic arguments that the best way to condemn Israel is via a boycott.[73] In the United Arab Emirates and elsewhere in the Arab world, phrases like this are common on websites, leaflets, and email messages: 'The penny you spend to buy these products amounts to another [Israeli] bullet for the body of our brave Palestinian brothers'.[74]

As a result of Israel's repressive response to the Intifada, the Arab League's Boycott Office revived its activities at the behest of Arab leaders in 2001. When a boycott was announced in Saudi Arabia, lists were circulated of American products and their non-American substitutes. As in many recent boycotts, news of the boycott spread via the internet, email messages, SMS, voice mail messages, newspaper editorials (even in state-run newspapers) mosque sermons, and fliers.[75] In a related development, *Burger King* opened an outlet in the Ma'aleh Adumim

Mall in 1999. The mall was located in a settlement in the occupied territories. After an Arab boycott and letter-writing campaign to *Burger King*, the company closed its controversial outlet. *McDonald's* has so far refused to open branches in the West Bank.

Questions

1. Why have fast-food restaurants been so successful outside their country of origin, the United States? Consider basic, universal aspects of consumer behaviour in your arguments.

2. How does religion affect consumer behaviour, especially as concerns eating habits, food products and beverages? Take examples from different great religions. What kinds of problems are involved for fast-food restaurants to take into account religious prescriptions concerning food? What kind of responses are given by fastfood companies in terms of product and service adaptation?

3. To what extent are fast-food in general and fast-food restaurants in particular associated with a) globalization; b) Westernization; c) modernization; d) threats to local cultural identities? How could fast-food restaurant chains handle their marketing communications in order to avoid boycotts and reduce violence against their outlets?

4. Comment about the ambivalence of Muslim-based fast-food competition.

Saskia Faulk and Jean-Claude Usunier prepared this case solely to provide material for class discussion. The authors do not intend to illustrate either effective or ineffective handling of a business situation. The authors may have disguised certain names and other identifying information to protect confidentiality.

This case was designed to present a complex marketing situation. It presents sensitive political, cultural, economic, and religious issues, and was in no way intended to offend, nor to advocate, the cause of any party.

(© IUMI/HEC, 2004.)

10

Product policy 2: Managing meaning

Brand equity is a measure of the overall value of a brand (Keller, 1998). The set of associations that surround a brand is referred to as customer based brand equity. Thus, a name can convey a great deal of information and make a substantial contribution to brand equity, as Leclerc *et al.* (1994, p. 263) point out:

What do Klarbrunn waters, Giorgio di St Angelo design wear and Häagen-Dazs ice cream have in common? All three are successful brands, and all are not what they seem. Klarbrunn is not the clear mountain-spring mineral water from the German Alps that its brand name suggests; it is American water bottled in Wisconsin. Giorgio di St. Angelo design wear is not the latest fashion from Milan but the product of U.S. designer Martin Price. And Häagen-Dazs is not Danish or Hungarian ice cream; it is American ice cream made by Pillsbury with headquarters in Minneapolis.

This chapter directly complements the preceding one as it deals with the symbolic attributes that are linked to brands and national images. These issues are more significant for a company that does not as yet have an established brand on the international market. It is easier to avoid basic errors in relation to the choice of a brand name when starting from scratch. Correcting mistakes once brand goodwill has been created can prove a costly and tricky operation. A brand, even one that has a poor impact, may be an asset due to a marketing investment, which may have resulted in brand awareness and associations. Consumers are often confused by changes in a brand name. Changes

to brand names, if they are possible, risk wasting time and incurring expenditure.

This chapter begins by discussing the interplay of images – those of the product's country of origin, the company name and/or the brand name of its products. This complex interplay of images warrants closer analysis. When one starts without an established brand, there is the potential for an intentional diffusion of favourable images, suitable for the product category and the national segments targeted.

The evaluation of product quality by consumers has been documented by a great number of empirical studies, as has been the perception of certain product attributes, according to their country of origin (COO). While the impact of COO has often been overestimated, it is still an important variable that can be used to convey information about a brand. The second section of this chapter reviews studies dealing with the country-of-origin paradigm. These studies suggest consistent answers to such questions as the following: Are 'Buy British' or 'Buy American' advertising campaigns successful? Do consumers have strong preferences for their national products? Which countries are best perceived, and on which attributes? Do countries' images change over time?

Section 10.3 addresses the issue of the conversion of national brands into international brands. The linguistic obstacles that are met in this conversion are examined. The question of the so-called 'global' brands is also documented since this is becoming a significant issue in international marketing.

10.1

National images diffused by the product's origin and by its brand name

The complexity of national images diffused by the product

There is an important relationship between images of products and the symbols diffused by their nationality. For instance, for the purchasers of Swedish cars who pay twice as much as comparable cars from other countries, the symbolic label 'Made in Sweden' suggests reliability and long life, removing fear of mechanical failure. The relationships between product and nationality in consumers' evaluations were first studied with respect to the 'made in' label, that is, the origin label put on products. But the 'made in' label is not the only element that contributes to consumer perception of product nationality. The following elements all contribute to perceptions of product nationality (Figure 10.1):

1. The image of national products versus imported or international products.
2. National images of generic products: yoghurt calls to mind the Balkans, perfume evokes France, a pair of jeans the United States, etc.

Figure 10.1 Several layers of country-, company- and brand-related product image

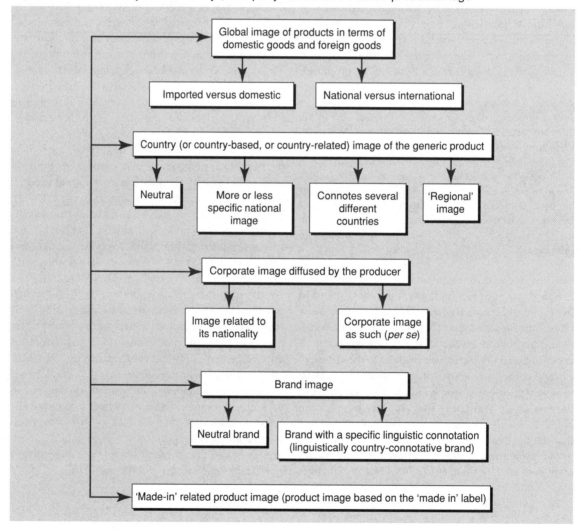

3. The national image of the manufacturing company.
4. The image diffused by the brand name.
5. The image of the 'made in' label depicting the manufacturing origin; origin labelling is mandatory in international trade.

In most cases, a product category is not clearly associated with only one country: wine is not associated with France only, but also with other European countries (Germany, Italy, Spain, Portugal) and with California, Australia, Argentina and Chile. There are also regional associations: in Europe furniture made of natural pine wood is often associated with Scandinavia as a whole. However, the desirability of products associated with a country or region can differ by product category and consumer group, so companies must be careful about the image they wish to convey. For example, Loeffler (2002) found that, for France, Germany, Italy and Spain, the quality of foreign cars are judged to be significantly lower than for corresponding domestic cars. However, Loeffler also found that foreign cars are evaluated in a different way to domestic cars in Germany: they are seen as lower quality, but superior in emotional aspects (more interesting and fascinating). This may help explain why Harris *et al.* (1994) in an experiment found that German-named burger restaurants were preferred by US respondents over their domestic (American) ones.

The stereotypes associated with national images are not confined to Western cultures. For instance, Japanese consumers associate Germany and France with long history and tradition, Switzerland and Australia with rich nature, California and Brazil with plentiful agricultural products, the United States and Germany with advanced industrial technology, and France with sense of design and high-class products (Nishina, 1990). These associations can lead to higher perceptions of quality for compatible products.

As can be seen from Table 10.1, national images operate on multiple levels and as such can send confusing messages to consumers. The following broad normative guidelines for management of a product's national image are developed for the four levels illustrated in Table 10.1:

Table 10.1 Some examples of the combined influence of brand name and country of origin on product image

Product	National image of the generic product	National image of the manufacturer	Country evoked by the brand name label	Country image diffused by the 'Made in' label
Shalimar (perfume by Guerlain)	French	French	India/Orient	French
Kinder (milk chocolate bars made by Ferrero)	Swiss and other countries	Italian (but the manufacturer's name, Ferrero, rarely appears)	German (means 'children' in German)	'Made in' hardly visible – often Italy
National (vacuum cleaner made by Matsushita)	Neutral	The manufacturer's name (Matsushita) does not appear	The National brand makes people believe that is a local product	'Made in' label hardly visible – different national origins
Coca-Cola	International	American	America	Neutral
Kremly (yoghurt by Chambourcy, part of Nestlé)	Balkan/Bulgarian Slav	Looks French, but is a worldwide brand of the Swiss Nestlé	Kremly (name and graphics) evokes the Kremlin, a Slav image	The 'Made in' label is a local one
Brother (typewriters by Brother)	Neutral	English/American (in fact a Japanese company)	International	The 'Made in' label indicates the origin

1. *National image of the generic product*: one should diffuse an image which corresponds in each country to what is locally valued (imported or national) in the product category concerned. This can lead to the adoption of a name from the target country, imposed by prevailing nationalistic feelings.
2. *National image of the manufacturer*: if the product category is generally associated with a specific country of origin, one should change the brand name accordingly. For example, a manufacturer of machine tools should not be reluctant to adopt a German name, because of the favourable association of German-sounding names with technical reliability.
3. *Country evoked by the brand name label*: the visibility of the company name, the brand name and the 'made in' label should be adjusted depending on their respective ability to convey the desired symbolic meanings.
4. *Country image diffused by the 'made in' label*: it is often advisable to reduce the physical size of the 'made in' label if the perception of the country of origin proves negative for local consumers (provided such reduction is permitted, or ignored, by local regulations). On the other hand, one should enlarge it in the cases where the opposite perception prevails.

10.2

Consumer product evaluation according to country of origin

The use of the 'country of origin' attribute

Consumers use the manufacturer's country of origin (COO) on a symbolic level. In other words, they use it as an associative link: Germany – robustness, France – luxury, Italy – beauty, etc. Leclerc *et al.* (1994) found that the French pronunciation of a brand name positively affects the perceived hedonism of the product and negatively affects its perceived utility. They further demonstrate that, in an actual product taste test where consumers have direct sensory experience of the product, foreign branding changes consumers' perceptions of the product (in this case yoghurt). The cognitive processes that lead to these evaluations are therefore worth examination.

More than 300 articles have been published on COO over the last 35 years (Nebenzahl *et al.*, 2003), with a great deal of diversity in countries (as origins), product categories and consumers surveyed (in terms of demographics and nationality). A comprehensive bibliography is provided on the book's website (see *WS10.0*).

In the early years COO effects were often assessed in isolation: it was the only factor that differed between product choices in early experiments. The basic objective of many of the early studies was to demonstrate that the COO cue actually influenced consumers' evaluations. Attempting to determine in which direction and why, was only a secondary objective in the first studies (Bilkey and Nes, 1982).[1] This made the effects seem stronger than they would be under more realistic circumstances (Bilkey and Nes, 1982). During the early 80s to early 90s researchers began to review the effects of COO in relation to other extrinsic and intrinsic product attributes, such as price, perceived risk, etc. (Bilkey and Nes, 1982; Papadopoulos and Heslop, 1993; Samiee, 1994).

During the late 90s and early 2000s several integrative reviews were published (Peterson and Jolibert, 1995; Nebenzahl *et al.*, 1997; Verlegh and Steenkamp, 1999; Jaffé and Nebenzahl, 2001). These reviews provide some important insights regarding the transfer of influence to the real world. First, in the real world consumers are likely to be influenced by multiple intrinsic and extrinsic cues. The effect of COO is less when COO information is included along with other cues, such as product, price, and warrantee information (Verlegh and Steenkamp, 1999). Peterson and Jolibert (1995) found that the average effect of COO on perceptions of quality and reliability was 0.30 when single cue countries were considered, but it dropped to 0.16 when multiple attributes or cues were added to the COO information.

Second, COO has a stronger influence at the earlier stages of the decision-making process. The effect is stronger perceptions of brand quality than attitude toward the product or purchase intention (Peterson and Jolibert, 1995; Verlegh and Steenkamp, 1999). For instance, Peterson and Jolibert (1995), based on a meta-analysis of 52 COO studies, reported that the average effect of COO on quality/reliability was 0.30, whereas its average effect on purchase intentions was 0.19 for single-cue studies and only 0.03 for multi-cue studies. It is likely to have a much smaller effect on action purchasing behaviour. Thus, as the consumer moves closer to a choice the effect of COO is less important.

Third, COO is more often used as a reliable cue of brand quality than it is used to infer quality (Agrawal and Kamakura, 1999). Agrawal and Kamakura (1999) examined the objective quality of 13 products (chosen from the 1980–94 US Consumer Reports) to assess whether perceived differences were due to actual differences in objective quality across firms representing different countries or to a halo effect in favour of products made in some countries. First, they found that countries differed in the objective quality of their durable consumer electronic goods: products originating in Japan had significantly higher objective quality than those originating in the United States, Europe and Korea, and that the Korean products had significantly lower objective quality than those from the United States, Japan and Europe. They then used this information to re-examine 12 previous COO studies that reported the perceived quality of similar products, adding the objective quality scores. They found that COO had no significant impact on the prices companies charged, after controlling for the objective quality of the goods. This gives support to COO being used as a reliable cue or summary for brand quality, rather than as a halo effect.

In addition to COO being used as a product quality cue, Verlegh and Steenkamp (1999) also suggest that COO information is used as a cue conveying symbolic and emotional value (see Askegaard and Ger, 1998; Batra et al., 2000), and as a right or normative way to do things (see Smith, 1990; Klein, et al. 1998).

Stereotypical country images

Throughout to COO studies one finds a relatively small number of stereotypical images that are fairly consistent across nationalities of consumers: the image of the robustness of German products, the image of France as associated with luxury goods, the image of Korean products as being cheap. However, even these shared perceptions are restricted and unstable: for instance, the Italians do not have the same image of their products as do consumers from other countries, and the image of Korean products as cheap is changing.

In addition, there are many perceptions of COO that are not shared by consumers of different national cultures. Often, minimal differences in relationships between countries (similarity of culture and language, past colonial links, etc.) lead to differences in the perceptions of the others products (e.g. Yaprak, 1987).[2]

The image of a country, in political, economic, cultural and social terms, may influence the willingness of foreign consumers to purchase that country's products independently of their perceived quality.[3] That was the case of the international boycott of French ethnic products during the French nuclear tests in 1995–6. Consumers may be unwilling to purchase products originating from a country under a dictatorship or one that acts in contravention of certain internationally recognized rules (as with countries that use child workers), even if these products fit their needs. Wang and Lamb (1983) asked 94 people, all US nationals, about their readiness to purchase products from different countries (36 in all). They also asked them to identify the political, cultural and economic environment of each country. In this way they were able to demonstrate that variables related to the socio-political image of a country partially explained consumers' readiness to purchase products from that country. The American consumers were more prepared to buy products from politically democratic countries such as those in Europe, Australia and New Zealand. Crawford and Lamb (1981) sought to determine whether purchasers of industrial products were prepared to purchase foreign products and what their preferred sources were in terms of nationality. According to them, 'willingness to buy foreign products is influenced not only by the individual country, but also by the existing levels of economic development and political freedom' (Crawford and Lamb, 1981, pp. 30–1).

One may also wonder whether the overall level of industrial development influences the evaluations of a particular COO and of its products by foreign consumers. Ahmed et al. (2002) found that Canadian male consumers evaluated products from highly industrialized countries more positively than from newly industrialized countries. Thorelli and Glowacka (1995) examine US industrial buyers sourcing internationally, and contrast the willingness of these buyers to source from industrializing (e.g. Brazil, China, Mexico, Poland) as opposed to industrialized (e.g. Japan, Sweden, Taiwan, West Germany) countries. US purchasers were found to be more willing to source from industrialized countries, except in the case of Mexico where buyers experienced with this trade partner, rated them much better than for other industrializing countries. US purchasers were also more ready to buy from foreign suppliers who had established warehouses or sales offices in the United States, irrespective of the COO. The very fact of having already done business with industrial suppliers from less favourably perceived COO, such as Latin American countries, causes experienced purchasers to hold a higher image of their products and quality than that held by inexperienced industrial importers (Saghafi et al., 1991).[4] Khanna (1986) demonstrates that among the products of four countries from Asia (India, Japan, Taiwan and South Korea), evaluated by consumers from the same four countries, the Indian products had the poorest image in terms of quality, creativity, design and technological level. Nevertheless it remains clear that vendors located in less favourable foreign environments may be cheap and reliable suppliers, so long as they are carefully evaluated and given a fair opportunity to perform. That is, the cost of their *learning* should be shared with their customer, and afterwards both will benefit.

However, country images may become partly divorced from the image of their products. Imagine, for instance, the case of a country under a non-democratic governing regime that nevertheless produces some excellent goods which are exported to democratic countries, as is the case with China.

How does the image of products from certain countries change over time?

Another important issue in relation to COO image is whether there are changes in these images over time and, if there are, at what rate they occur. The response to this question seems to be yes, and the rate seems to be fairly rapid. This was particularly true for products originating from Japan and the new industrial countries of Asia, such as Korea and Taiwan (Jaffé and Nebenzahl, 1989).[5]

Many studies confirm the dramatic improvement of the image of Japan as a COO (Kraft and Chung, 1992; Kamins and Nagashima, 1995).[6] According to Darling and Kraft (1977), the image that the Finnish consumers held of Japanese products was in the process of changing in 1977. At the beginning of

the 1970s, Japanese products were seen as being of dubious quality; they were backed by rather restricted guarantees and poor after-sales service. By the end of the 1970s, however, they were seen by Finnish consumers as having improved significantly as far as quality was concerned. This improvement has been confirmed in recent times in the case of Saudi consumers, who tend to rate Japanese products as the highest with respect to central product attributes, followed by American and German products, whereas products from the United Kingdom, France and Italy tend to be perceived as lower quality (Bhuian, 1997).

There was also a very clear improvement in the acceptance of South Korean products in the United States in the space of just over two years. Khera (1986) compared the results of a May 1982 study (Khera et al., 1983) with those of a November 1984 replication (Khera et al., 1985). In the first study only one-third of consumers declared themselves satisfied with Korean products, while in the second the satisfied numbered almost two-thirds (65.3 per cent). The perception of the general level of Korea's industrial development (specifically in comparison with Taiwan and Brazil) improved similarly.

Nebenzahl et al. (1997) have provided a conceptual framework for accounting for the dynamic aspects of COO evaluations by consumers who revise their image according to the observed performance of product from a particular COO in comparison to the performance of products from competing COO over the same period. The length of time required for image revision depends on the efforts made by a country and its manufacturers to improve image. (See WS A10.4, 'Confession of a purchaser of Italian products', for an example of COO-related buying behaviours.)

COO and moderator effects

Many factors may moderate the influence of COO on consumer evaluation including: (1) customer awareness of COO, which may be quite limited or even non-existent if the COO is neither advertised nor labelled, (2) consumer knowledge of and familiarity with the product category all have an influence, (3) consumers ethnocentric tendencies, (4) the product category and (5) perceptions of risk.

The effect of multinational production and COO consumer awareness

As a result of the expansion of multinational firms, companies sell the same products under identical brand names in different countries throughout the world. These products actually have widely differing national origins, not necessarily that of the COO of the parent company. Sony products, for example, can be just as easily 'Made in France', 'Made in Germany' or 'Made in Thailand' as 'Made in Japan'. In this sense, one must increasingly distinguish between COO and country of manufacture (Samiee, 1994) as consumer evaluations may differ (Johansson and Thorelli, 1985). For instance, Chao (2001) found that consumer attitudes and intentions toward televisions and stereos are more positive when the product is assembled in the United States, if US parts are also used, than if Mexican parts are used.

Han and Terpstra (1988, p. 244) sought to determine whether the brand name or the COO had more influence on consumers, and their conclusion was that: 'the sourcing country has greater effects on consumer evaluations of product quality than does the brand name'. Similarly, in the case of Russian, Hungarian and Polish consumers, that is, emerging market economies, brand name plays a limited role in comparison to COO (Ettenson, 1993). However, Eroglu and Machleit (1989) concluded that consumers accord a similar influence to brand and country of manufacture respectively. More recently, Lee and Ganesh (1999) found that consumers depend more on brand image than country image in their evaluation of binational brands. And, in the case of industrial products, Ahmed *et al.* (1994) found that country of design is a more important cue in organizational purchase decisions than country of assembly and brand name. Although complex, these factors can be used to guide strategy. For instance, Ahmed *et al.* (2002) looked at the interaction between brand and COO. They found that a positive COO perception can compensate for a weak brand, but when the COO perception was negative a strong brand did not compensate in the service industry.

The corollary question deserves consideration: what price reduction do consumers require to 'accept' a less favourable origin, in relation to a specific brand? Johansson and Nebenzahl (1986, p. 120) determined the levels of monetary discounts (dollar values) at which consumers were prepared to purchase products from a 'less favourable' COO. They were, for example, willing to buy a Buick manufactured in the United States for $10,258 rather than pay $7,351 for the same car made in the Philippines. Nebenzahl and Jaffé (1989) measured such elasticity of demand in the country of production with Israeli consumers (and Usunier *et al.*, 1993, did likewise with French consumers), for three possible countries of production (South Korea, Japan and West Germany) and for three brands (Sanyo, Grundig and Sony). A discount of 30–40 per cent was necessary to sell Japanese or German brand products when they had been manufactured in South Korea. It was shown (Usunier, 1994) that consumers belonging to lower social classes (who are favourite targets for lower-priced goods) did not ask for a larger price discount than consumers of higher social status when it was proposed to shift production to a less favourable country of manufacture (South Korea). Furthermore, consumers from lower social classes evaluate Korea more positively as a COO than do higher social status consumers. Thus, it would be wise for the marketing strategy for 'cheap'-origin goods in highly developed markets to put emphasis on quality rather than price, especially when consumers with modest means and from lower socio-economic classes are targeted.

Today, it is even more important to understand the interplay of these images, as multinational companies have much more scope in their decisions to use these effects or not. Originally, the GATT treaty left each member state free to define its own rules of origin, but since the creation of the World Trade Organization (WTO) in 1995, the global harmonization of rules of origin started. The freedom of each member state to define its own rules of origin was progressively curtailed. According to WTO policy, rules of origin should not be used as protectionist trade instruments; in particular, origin labelling should not discriminate against the exports of particular countries, nor should it create distortions in international trade flows. Origin labelling for countries with weaker images as manufacturing nations (which is the case of developing nations) is increasingly associated with discrimination against the exports of newly industrialized countries. Compulsory origin labelling on the product itself may therefore be considered a type of non-tariff barrier. As a consequence, there is less and less marking of origin labels on products in world trade. Furthermore, multinational corporations often prefer consumers to remain uninformed of the origin of goods since their system of global sourcing is partly based on low-cost manufacturing countries with weaker quality images.

Consequently 'country of origin' information is increasingly fuzzy and ambiguous in international trade. For customs officers, it is now enough to have the origin mentioned in custom documents rather than on the merchandise itself. Consequently, consumers see less and less the origin of products, especially when it is unfavourable. Many Multinational Companies de-emphasize manufacturing origin as much as possible and emphasize country-of-brand. For instance, Daimler-Benz emphasizes in its corporate advertising 'being at home in more than 200 countries'. New, uninformative labels emerge such as 'made in Europe', or 'made in Asia' as well as humorous origin labels such as 'made in nowhere', or complex indications such as 'assembled in . . .' or 'U.S. made . . . (Components/raw materials)' (Samiee, 1994, p. 594).

Familiarity and knowledge

The influence of the COO evaluation cue is stronger where the consumer is unfamiliar, lacks knowledge or is not motivated to process the information about a product category. Schaefer (1997) examined the influence of brand familiarity and consumer knowledge on the evaluation of COO by British consumers for lager beers imported from Australia, Belgium, the former Czechoslovakia, Denmark, Germany and The Netherlands in comparison with British brands. Objective product knowledge based on attribute information leads to an increased reliance on COO in product evaluations if the brand name is unfamiliar, but not if the brand is familiar. Expert consumers base their evaluation on the strength of actual product attributes, whereas novices tend to rely more on the COO cue as such (Maheswaran, 1994). Han (1990) tested the 'halo effect', which affects consumers' beliefs and (only indirectly) their evaluations, against the 'summary effect', where the COO cue directly influences consumers, in the form of a global evaluation. He found that the 'halo effect' is used more when consumers are unfamiliar with the product category, whereas the 'summary effect' is used once they have achieved familiarity.[7] Similarly, motivation to process product related information is also likely to influence the effect of COO (Ahmed et al., 2002;

Gürhan-Canli and Maheswaran, 2000). For instance, Gürhan-Canli and Maheswaran (2000) found that COO perception is more favourable under low motivation because consumers engage more in attribute processing under high-motivation situations. It has also been proposed that such situational characteristics as severe time limitations would lead consumers to make greater use of the COO stereotypical images (Swinder and Rao, 1997).

Ethnocentric and cultural tendencies

Consumer ethnocentrism represents 'the beliefs held by consumers about the appropriateness of purchasing products originating in a foreign country' (Shimp and Sharma, 1987, p. 280). It represents the beliefs held by consumers about the appropriateness, indeed morality, of purchasing foreign products (Shimp and Sharma, 1987; Sharma et al., 1995). Thus, highly ethnocentric consumers are likely to believe that purchasing imported products harms the domestic economy and causes unemployment. In addition, consumer age has been identified as a variable that significantly correlates with ethnocentrism. In particular, older consumers were found to be much more ethnocentric than younger ones (Witkowski, 1998).[8]

Consumer ethnocentrism has been shown to influence consumers' attitudes and perceptions about foreign products (Sharma et al., 1995; Mascarenhas and Kujawa, 1998; Witkowski, 1998; Balabanis and Daimantopoulos, 2004). For instance, Balabanis and Daimantopoulos (2004) found that ethnocentrism was positively related to preferences for domestic products and negatively, although less so, related to foreign products. Thus, domestic companies may benefit from ethnocentrism, but foreign companies may not necessarily find resistance to their offerings. They found that the relationship between ethnocentrism and preference depends on the product category.

Gürhan-Canli and Maheswaran (2000) found that COO also varies across cultures, after controlling for consumer ethnocentrism. They studied consumers in Japan and the United States, concluding that 'individualists evaluated the home country product more favourably only when it was superior to competition. In contrast, collectivists evaluated the home country product more favourably regardless of its superiority' (p. 315). Similarly, Balabanis et al. (2002) found support for collectivist values, such as conformity (for the Czech sample) and benevolence and tradition (for the Turkish sample) being negatively associated with COO evaluations, but only mixed support for individualist values being associated with COO.

Product categories

Various studies have evidenced perceptual linkage between COO and product types; the relative influence of the COO cue varies according to product category (Kaynak and Cavusgil, 1983; Manrai *et al.*, 1998; Balabanis and Diamantopoulos, 2004) and to the type of attribute considered (Eroglu and Machleit, 1989). Even different products coming from the same country have produced varying patterns acceptability (e.g. Herche, 1992; Sharma *et al.*, 1995). For example, people from Australia might like French perfume, but dislike French cameras, or even French wine, as Australia generally produces a heavier wine. Certain products are considered more 'ethnic', more typical of certain countries; consumers tend to associate countries and products: Italy and pizza, Germany and machine tools, Britain and puddings.[9]

In their meta-analysis Verlegh and Steenkamp (1999) found that the COO effect is no larger for consumer goods than for industrial goods, despite many researchers arguing that this would be the case, on the basis that industrial buyers are more informed and as such less likely to be susceptible to country information (Ahmed and d'Astous, 1995). Several studies have reported a favourable image of German industrial products even within the United States, where American purchasers regard German industrial products as being of higher quality than their own (Jolibert, 1979; Cattin *et al.*, 1982).[10] A similar favourable image is now found for Japanese industrial products, which receive better overall ratings from Korean importers than American products (Kraft and Chung, 1992; Chang and Rim, 1995).

Perceptions of risk

A sound hypothesis which has been proposed by several studies is the mediation of perceived risk to explain the influence of the COO on consumer evaluations. Either consumers perceive a lesser risk for national products, which would explain the preference for national products, or they perceive a lesser risk for the products of certain countries with a favourable image.[11] Accordingly, consumers would tend to prefer certain sources because they perceive a reduced risk in purchasing that country's products (Lumpkin *et al.*, 1985).

In their study of the risk perceived by Americans for clothing – clothes and shoes made abroad versus those made in the United States – Lumpkin *et al.* (1985) confirm that the perceived risk is weaker for a product of national origin. They showed that perceived risk only has a strong influence when consumers are aware of the foreign origin of the clothes. They also detected differences according to the categories of products: certain countries (China, Korea) presented the same perceived risk whatever the product, whereas Italy offered a weak perceived risk for shoe purchases and France offered a high perceived risk when buying jeans.

Also using clothing in their experimental setting, Baumgartner and Jolibert (1977) found that certain traits of a foreign country may reduce the perceived risk if the consumers (French, in this case) hold the belief that a foreign country, by virtue of its physical, climatic or social environment, is particularly suitable for the manufacture of a particular product: for instance, an English overcoat for the winter. Generally, the overall level of perceived risk for a specific national origin is less for its *ethnic* products.

Issues related to the measurement of country of origin images

The results of COO studies can be affected by many factors including the quality of the samples used, choice of methodology, product categories and level of complexity. Originally many studies used samples of students to represent the overall population of consumers/evaluators, interviewing them about products of different origins. This was thought to bias the results as students differ in their socio-demographic characteristics (being younger and more highly educated) and are generally more homogeneous than the average consumer. However, Usunier (2003) found that student samples are used in only 23 per cent of COO studies, while the general consumer population were used in 56 per cent of the studies and professional buyers in 21 per cent, when he reviewed a 35-year span of COO studies.

Second, measurement instruments, such as questionnaires, psychometric scales and the categories of products chosen or brands mentioned, may create problems of cross-cultural equivalence (see Chapter 7). For instance, Jaffé and Nebenzahl (1984) tested the validity and accuracy of alternative questionnaire formats with the same respondents. They listed the same information in two different ways: the scales in Q1 were listed according to attribute and in Q2 according to country. The resultant scores were significantly different, which tends to suggest that images of COO may not be completely comparable across studies, but depend on the presentation of the questionnaire. In a similar vein, Han *et al.* (1994) show that the survey mode, whether personal interview, telephone survey or self-administered questionnaire, influences the ratings of COO. Personal interviews may be susceptible to demand artefacts (the subject distorts his answer in the direction intended to fulfil the researcher's expectations), and self-administered questionnaires to haloing biases (the lack of involvement results in all responses being based on a common stereotype). Social desirability biases (the subject responds in the same way as the 'average man' would) may be more likely to occur when interviews are conducted by telephone.

Third, the product categories represented in COO research may limit the generalizability of the results. There is an over-representation of consumer electronics (31 per cent), cars (35 per cent) and clothing and accessories (30 per cent), with more than 75 per cent of the articles mentioning these product categories (Usunier, 2003). On the other hand, luxury products were only cited in less than 5 per cent of articles.

Fourth, the level of complexity may bias the results of COO research, as few studies have used complex research designs involving both multiple product attributes and different types of country images. There is a growing complexity in the market-place in terms distinguishing the effects of the country of origin (COO), country of manufacture (COM), country of brand (COB), country of design (COD) and country image (CI). Usunier (2003) found that COO is present in 95 per cent of the articles, while COM and COB were in 24 per cent, CI in 16 per cent and COD in only 9 per cent.

Fifth, do consumers still attach importance to the country where a product is manufactured? Hugstad and Durr (1986) have shown that 60 per cent of American consumers (70 per cent under 35) consider

it unimportant to assess where their purchases come from. However, this varies across product categories: 74 per cent of the sampled consumers consider country of origin as relevant when buying cars, but only 20 per cent for the purchase of tee-shirts. Hester and Yuen (1987) have assessed the degree of knowledge of American and Canadian consumers as concerns the manufacturing origin of goods (clothes) just after they had been purchased. Only 25 per cent of Canadian and 20 per cent of American consumers were aware of the origin of their purchases. Sixty-five per cent of the Canadians and 52 per cent of the Americans surveyed had no idea of the manufacturing origin. Overall, only a small number of consumers (11 per cent) were both concerned that their purchase was made in their own country and knew where the piece of cloth they had just bought was manufactured. In a survey based on consumer electronics and a sample of French consumers only 35 per cent knew the origin of the last purchase they had made and only 16 per cent of them had a preference for the national manufacture at the same time (Usunier, 2003). Despite this, the variability across product categories means that for at least some products, COO will remain an important influence.

10.3

National, international and global brands

Branding is an important tool used to differentiate products. The recognized benefits include expanding sales, increased profits, greater longevity, greater power with distributors and the ability to survive adverse economic conditions (Kotler *et al.*, 2003). However, there are also possible negative consequences that need to be acknowledged. For instance, Naomi Klein in her 2002 book *No Logo: No space, no choice, no jobs* argues that the focus on branding led to significant downsizing and outsourcing that is displacing manufacturing with the service sector and reshaping the world of work. She cites this as one of the reasons behind the backlash against the 'brand bullies' such as McDonald's and Nike. Interestingly, she also comments on the branding of activism and the need to point out that: 'there are more than two worlds available, to expose all the invisible worlds between the economic fundamentalist of 'McWorld' and the religious fundamentalism of '*Jihad*' (Klein, 2002, p. 10).

The majority of brands throughout the world were originally conceived on a national level and not as international brands. Even among US brands, only a small number have achieved international recognition. In an empirical survey of US brands as global brands, Rosen *et al.* (1989) studied 650 US brands and their international scope (in how many countries, the age of the brand, etc.) and their general conclusion is that 'despite all the talk about the internationalisation of marketing efforts, the international diffusion of US brands is actually rather limited and . . . that most US brands are not marketed abroad' (p. 17).

Most brands are related to a specific linguistic context. Their evocative power is dependent on the language of the country and markets where they were originally launched. In Europe, at least 99 per cent of all brands were still national, if not purely local, in their appeal (Wilsher, 1992).[12] However, certain brands were launched right from the start for their capacity to convey meaning internationally. In the 1960s a Japanese car manufacturer with increasing export sales, decided it was necessary to have a name suitable for international markets: Toyota, with its three syllables which can be pronounced in any language, was the name finally selected. Similarly, the oil-refining and distribution brand name ELF was created at the time of the merger of the petroleum groups ERAP and SNPA.

International companies face three situations in terms of international brand names:

1. The *ex nihilo* creation of a brand name, especially for new products with high global potential. The name must be pronounced and understood in a similar way across diverse linguistic and cultural contexts.
2. The management of a large brand portfolio resulting from both external growth by acquisitions of local players and multiple layers of branding (e.g. corporate names, category brands, product names). Such a brand portfolio is increasingly being simplified, in order to avoid spreading brand advertising budgets too thinly over a large number of names. Only a few of these names will become transnational brands. The appropriate course of action is to nominate the best applicants in translinguistic terms, taking into account local brand equity and the attachment of both local consumers and local marketing teams to brands that often have a rich history.
3. Assessment of the potential for an international extension of regional brands developed by a subsidiary based in the lead country for a region.

Transposition of a national brand name to an international level

Often the brand name of products is the name of the company that manufactures them. Since the brand name is historically related to the founders of the company, symbolically it would be difficult to change. Companies such as Procter & Gamble (with names that are difficult to pronounce in many languages) have followed a twofold brand strategy. Product brand names, such as Ivory, Camay, Pampers, Vizir and Tide, have been promoted almost independently from the Procter & Gamble company name (look at the respective sizes of the names on the packaging) and the Procter & Gamble name has been colloquially simplified so that it can be more easily memorized and verbalized, either to simply Procter or to P & G.

An example of lack of adaptation is offered by the leading French company for iron and steel and heavy mechanical equipment during the 1970s and 1980s, Creusot-Loire. It branded and sold its products under the company's name in many countries in the world, including the United States. Unfortunately American customers found this name difficult to pronounce, for the following reasons:

1. The throaty French 'CR' sound hardly exists in English.
2. 'EU' is a typically French diphthong, unpronounceable for Americans.
3. 'S' must be pronounced 'Z' because it is located between two vowels (French rule!).
4. 'O' is a very open sound.
5. 'T' is, here, a mute consonant and must therefore be ignored in pronunciation.
6. 'OI': once again a typically French diphthong (unknown in English).
7. 'R' is a hard 'r', almost unused in English.
8. 'E' is, at the end of the word, a mute vowel, and therefore must be ignored in pronunciation.

Naturally such a brand name is difficult to memorize for most customers in many countries. Moreover, such difficult brand names can be a serious obstacle to clear communication between buyer and seller, creating confusion when discussing business on the phone. It is therefore necessary to be prepared to carry out the necessary brand name modification. (For more information on corporate brand names see *WS10.3*.)

While there may be limited benefits from global standardization for many aspects of communications, there seem to be strong arguments for corporate branding, including increased market efficiency, reduced advertising and inventory costs, and convenient identification for people travelling internationally (Onkvisit and Shaw, 1989). For instance, Melewar and Saunders (1998) examined the benefits sought from a global corporate visual identity system (CVIS), which consists of the companies name, symbol/logo, typography, colour and slogan. They surveyed British MNCs with subsidiaries in Malaysia, finding that the perceived benefits of CVIS standardization include increased sales, consumer goodwill, consumer familiarity, consumer awareness and market share. However, the diversity of national regulations and the rarity of brands with similar spellings in most national markets make it difficult to register a standardized brand across a large number of countries.

The options for the transposition of an existing name range from translation, to transliteration, to creating a new transparent brand. First, simple translation is rarely used as it may result in a disaster in relation to meaning,[13] scattered brand image, and inability to create international brand recognition. *Transliteration* is better as it attempts to reconstitute in the target language the connotative meaning that exists in the source language (i.e. the language of the country of origin of the brand). In this way the American hair care product *Silkience* (Gillette) is sold under the same brand name in Germany, under the brand name *Soyance* in France and under the brand name *Sientel* in Italy (Czinkota and Ronkainen, 1990). However, the best type of brand is the *transparent* brand, such as Sony, which is suitable everywhere. The name Sony arose from a real 'shooting down' of the company name by the brand name of its products (Yoshimori, 1989). The original name of the firm (Tokyo Tsuhin Kogyo – Tokyo Industrial

Telecommunication Company) was changed to Sony as soon as the brand name of its products proved to be successful.

Linguistic aspects of the brand

Brands are signs based on sounds, written signs (letters or pictographs) and visual elements (logotype, brand design). The linguistic content of a brand name has an influence on its verbal, auditory and intellectual meaning, and its interpretation by consumers. The brand name is often associated with a copyrighted design. Visual elements also comprise how a brand is written (alphabet, characters, ideographs). Table 10.2 shows which branch of linguistics should be used to appreciate how the sound, spelling and design of a brand name travel from a source to a target linguistic context.[14] A brand name should generally be relatively easy to pronounce. A simple rule is that the brand name should not exceed three syllables, each composed of one consonant and one vowel. Chinese mostly has such simple successions of one consonant and one or two vowels (Huang and Chan, 1997), whereas German and Dutch often have many successive consonants (up to seven in a row in German) and French sometimes has long strings of vowels.

When considering the sound or phonological aspects of an international brand, one should check that the sound pattern corresponds to phonemes that are pronounced in all major languages (phonetics) and that it does not use unique sound patterns of the source language (phonemics). The name Hewlett-Packard, for instance, is far from perfect and is better when shortened to HP. The English 'th' or the French nasalized triphthong 'oin' (don't try it!) are among such difficult combinations. Japanese, on the other hand, is a formidable language for international brands because it is exclusively composed of phonemes that are recognized by virtually all languages in the world, and it eschews successive consonants.[15] Denotative meaning, such as that of *Milka* chocolate, which directly relates to milk, is lost in most other languages; understanding of this meaning is limited to Anglo-Saxon and Germanic languages which use this root (etymology) and to speakers of English as a second language. Similarly, connotative meaning is generally lost when a product crosses borders: the detergent *Tide* was once sold in France (the name

Table 10.2 Brand cues and meaning transfer

Brand cue	Element of meaning		Branch of linguistics concerned
Sound		L	
– Assemblage (vowels	⇨ Pure sound	I	Phonology (phonemics/phonetics)
and consonants)	⇨ Denotative meaning	N	
	⇨ Connotative meaning	G	
– Tonality		U	Etymology
		I	Semantics / Rhetoric
Written name		S	
– Alphabetic letters ⇨ sounds	Sounds ⇨ words ⇨ ideas	T	Semantics
– Pictographic writing	Pictograph design ⇨ ideas	I	Semiology
	Pictograph design ⇨ symbols	C	
Design			
– Assemblage of words (brands	– Descriptive	F	Grammar
and slogans)	– Suggestive	I	Rhetoric
– Icons (causal and analogous sign)	– Humorous	L	Semantics
– Symbols (untraceable linkage)	– Claim supportive	T	Semiology
	– Oneiric	E	
	– Ethnic	R	

being pronounced *teed*) but nobody had the slightest knowledge of the idea of powerful tidal waves washing clothes that was evoked by the brand in English-speaking markets. Evidence suggests that meaningful names are easier to recall than meaningless ones (Robertson, 1989).

Written brand names are generally based on the alphabet: people first read sounds, then decode words and finish with ideas. A third of the consumers in the world use ideographic writing systems; they go directly from pictographs to ideas. Sounds for a definite written item vary: people in various parts of China and Japan use similar ideographs which they recognize as having the same meaning but pronounce quite differently.[16] However, even with the Roman alphabet, the use of identical letters may result in a brand sounding different, according to the linguistic context: the Danone brand of yoghurt is spelled Dannon in the United States because consistency of pronunciation is preferred to consistency of spelling (Colombat, 1997). Given the wide differences in tonicity across languages, a brand such as Coca-Cola cannot be considered global, so far as sound patterns are concerned, e.g. when Jean-Claude orders a Coke in Brazil in his flat French accent (there is very little tonicity in French) people have trouble understanding him.

The design of a brand also has an influence on its verbal, auditory and intellectual meaning: for instance, Whiskas (a Mars brand) has a translinguistic iconic value because it uses a cat's head to suggest its favourite user; but the colours are probably interpreted differently across cultures. Brand names are usually associated with a copyright design and the graphic composition of a logo conveys as much meaning as the letters of the brand name. Similarly, the IBM trademark is inseparable from its graphics in its evocative ability to communicate with the consumer:

The letters of the IBM logo are actually obtained by the superimposition of characters known as 'Mecanes' and of a 'blind' (alternate slats of coloured bands). The blind is in this case the informative image of the letters IBM, their morphological determinant . . . It thereby becomes the sign of computer language, binary-based. The 'Mecanes' are typesetting characters whose square serif evokes industrial production and rooting in the mechanical world. (Cabat, 1989, p. 344.)

The imagery of the IBM brand logo is translinguistic, and therefore offers a truly international ability to convey meaning. The link between brand and drawing is an intimate one. How, for instance, is the Coca-Cola brand name stored in consumers' minds? As eight letters, as the traditional design of the Coca-Cola words or the Coke bottle, or as a combination of them? Trademark legislation around the world varies in this respect. In some countries trademarks can only be composed of alphabetic letters and their design must be separately registered under the design and pattern laws if they are to be effectively protected; in the United States a trademark may be bereft of any linguistic content and can be registered solely under the trademark laws. There is no systematic need, in the United States and many other countries, for additional registration of a trademark's design.

Linguistic devices for brand names

Table 10.3 shows various linguistic devices that can be used in creating brand names. Whether by accident or design, advertisers and marketers strive to give

Table 10.3 Linguistic characteristics of brands

Characteristics	Definitions and/or examples
I Phonetic devices	
1. Alliteration	Consonant repetition (**Co**ca **C**ola, **Coc**oon)
2. Assonance	Vowel repetition (K**a**l K**a**n, V**i**z**i**r, **O**m**o**)
3. Consonance	Consonant repetition with intervening vowel changes (**W**eigh**t W**a**t**chers, Tic Tac)
4. Masculine rhyme	Rhyme with end of syllable stress (Max Pax)
5. Feminine rhyme	Unaccented syllable followed by accented syllable (Americ**an** Airl**ines**)
6. Weak/imperfect/slant rhyme	Vowels differ or consonants similar, not identical (Bl**ack** & D**eck**er)
7. Onomatopoeia	Use of syllable phonetics to resemble the object itself (Wisk, Cif, Wizzard)
8. Clipping	Product names shortened (*Chevy* for a Chevrolet, *Deuche* for a Citroen Deux Chevaux, *Rabbit* for a Volkswagen)
9. Blending	Morphemic combination, usually with elision (Aspergum, Duracell)
10. Initial plosives[a]	/b/, /c-hard/, /d/, /g-hard/, /k/, /q/, /t/, (Bic, Dash, Pliz, Pim's)
II Orthographic devices	
1. Unusual or incorrect spellings	Kool-Aid, Decap'Four
2. Abbreviations	7-Up for Seven-Up
3. Acronyms	Amoco, Amro, DB, Cofinoga, Lu, BSN
III Morphological devices	
1. Affixation	Jell-O, Tipp-Ex
2. Compounding	Janitor-in-a-Drum, Vache-qui-rit
IV Semantic devices	
1. Metaphor	Representing something as if it were something else (Arrid); simile was included with metaphor when a name described a likeness and not an equality (Aqua Fresh, Longeurs et Pointes, Head and Shoulders, Tendres Promesses)
2. Metonymy	Application of one object or quality for another (Midas, Ajax, Uncle Ben's, Bounty)
3. Synecdoche	Substitution of a part for the whole (Red Lobster)
4. Personification/pathetic fallacy	Humanizing the non-human or ascription of human emotions to the inanimate (Betty Crocker, Clio, Kinder)
5. Oxymoron	Conjunction of opposites (Easy-Off, Crème de peinture)
6. Paranomasia	Pun and word plays (Hawaiian Punch, Raid – insecticide, Fédor – orange juice)
7. Semantic appositeness	Fit of name with object (Bufferin, Nutella)

[a] An initial is said to be plosive if, to produce this sound, one needs first to stop the flow of air completely, then audibly release the air previously compressed.

(Source: Adapted from Vanden Bergh *et al.*, 1987.)

some punch and evocative capacity to their brand names. Of course this is done, as far as possible, in line with the symbolic connotations that they intend to communicate in relation to product attributes and, inevitably, it is done in a particular source language. There are four main categories of linguistic device: phonetic devices (sound, perceived by the ears), orthographic devices (relating to writing, perceived by the eyes), morphological devices (adding morphemes to the brand-name root) and semantic devices (the figure produces meaning, perceived through culture-based interpretations).

The linguistic devices set out in Table 10.3 help one to understand what constitutes the pure linguistic capacity of a brand, independently of the established goodwill (brand recognition may be high for linguistically unadapted but long-standing brand names). The issue for brand marketers is whether these advantages are transposable into other linguistic contexts. The alliteration of Coca-Cola transposes well, but the composition of the words Janitor-in-a-Drum, or even the juxtaposition of opposites (Easy-Off), do not. This is because Coca-Cola does not require a basic comprehension of the words that make up the brand name. Where understanding of complex linguistic figures is required, brand names are difficult to translate and, more generally, to transpose. As a rule, the linguistic devices in categories I and II are the more 'translinguistic'. A good number of the devices in category IV are not at all translinguistic, especially nos 1, 4, 5, 6 and 7.

Semantic issues: Intended versus unintended meaning

As shown above, meaning can be lost when a brand crosses borders. Nestlé (*Nestele*: 'little nest' in the Alemanic dialects of the southern German-speaking area) is lost in most of the world's languages and people probably cannot understand why the logo presents a bird in a nest. Beiersdorff's 'Uhu' brand for glue sticks is based on the German name for eagle owl. Most intended meaning does not extend much beyond the source language area. It is, however, not a major problem if consumers in other linguistic areas memorize the sound of brand names easily and invest them with new, positive meanings.

Unintended negative meaning is the most dangerous. The brand name should not have an unfortunate meaning in a different linguistic/cultural context. However, checking the translinguistic capacity of a brand name is by no means universal practice. There is no shortage of examples: the German hair spray Caby-Net launched on the French market (*cabinet* is a toilet in French); the Japanese gun, Miroku, the name of which has several meanings including 'look at your arse' in French. The examples of certain American cars in South American markets are also famous. The Chevrolet (Chevy) Nova (the intended meaning was 'new') translates into Spanish as 'does not work'. The Ford Pinto meant 'tiny male genitals' in Brazil. Kellogg's renamed its *Frosted Flakes* as *Sucrilhos* for Brazil, and its *Cocoa Krispies* as *Crokinhos*; similarly it had to change its *Bran Buds* brand name in Sweden, so that Swedish people did not read that they were to be served 'grilled farmer' in their breakfast bowls (Giordan, 1988). The type of research that must be carried out is straightforward: it is necessary to interview a group of consumers from the target country about the perceptual effects of the intended names and sometimes it is necessary to interview several depending on the number of dialects with potential for unintended meanings.

The case of Asian ideographic writing systems

We have stayed up to now within the limited framework of languages based on the Roman alphabet where letters correspond to sounds and sounds to ideas, but almost one-fourth of the world's populations read logographic characters, including Chinese, Japanese and Korean (Tavassoli and Han, 2002). Reading logographs relies more on visual processes, which affects consumers' memory (Schmitt *et al.*, 1994; Tavassoli, 1999; Tavassoli and Han, 2002), as well as brand attitudes (Pan and Schmitt, 1995; Schmitt and Zhang, 1998; Zhang and Schmit, 2001). For instance, Schmitt *et al.* (1994) found better recall from Chinese who wrote words down and Americans who spoke the words during recall, suggesting that verbal information is encoded in a visual manner in Chinese and a phonological manner in English. Similarly Tavassoli and Han (2002) examined native speakers and bilinguals finding that visual branding is more easily integrated in memory for Chinese speakers, while auditory branding is more easily integrated for English speakers. Thus, certain types of translations are likely to work better in different cultural contexts. As such, Zhang and Schmitt (2001) put forward a framework to examine issues for the creation or translation of English to Chinese brand names. They explored the boundaries by examining the effects of the degree of emphasis on the English name compared with that placed on the Chinese name in a dual writing situation and the presence of prior types of brand translations in the same product category. Similarly, Hong *et al.* (2002) explored the effect of phonetic translations into Mandarin for familiar and unfamiliar brands on perceptions of quality in Singapore. They found that the phonetic translation performed better for an unfamiliar brand, but for a familiar brand it was better to keep the original name.

Global brands wanting to reach these markets face a difficult task. Even Coca-Cola is not known exactly by this name in China since the simple translated name would have a negative connotation; Coca-Cola is transliterated as 'ke kou ke le' in Mandarin and 'ho hau ho lohk' in Cantonese (in terms of approximate sound equivalence), which conveys the meaning of 'tasty and enjoyable/happy' (Wilke, 1994). In fact, Chinese characters are pronounced differently according to the dialect spoken (Mandarin, Cantonese, Hokkien, etc.), and there is a large number of homonyms (same pronunciation, but written differently to indicate the distinct meaning). For instance 'gong' corresponds to many different meanings ranging from work to attack to palace, depending on the characters (Schmitt and Pan, 1994). Thus there are many possibilities to select from when transposing Roman-letter brand names into Chinese characters.

In East Asia, and especially in China, calligraphy and meaning become much more important than in standard Western branding. A brand name must have a positive connotation that is a combination of: (1) characters with favourable sounds, which can be pronounced in about the same way in as many regions as possible, while avoiding the pitfalls due to tonality; (2) characters that convey favourable meaning, if possible related to the brand's advertised qualities; (3) a balance between *yin* (even number of strokes) and *yang* characters (odd number of strokes); (4) a favourable content in terms of lucky numbers such as 8; (5) suitable calligraphy for the brand; the calligraphy must convey certain visual signs that fit

with the brand imagery, such as in the case of the Volkswagen 'Cheep': a character was used that evoked an imaginary slope that the jeep had to climb (Schmitt and Pan, 1994).

Consequently, Pepsi-Cola is transposed into Chinese characters meaning 'hundred happy things' and Mercedes-Benz becomes 'Benchi', with two characters meaning 'striving forward fast'. However, such transposition is not possible for all brands. In some cases, when the transposition of sounds is deemed as more important than the transposition of meaning (it may be difficult to find a chain of characters that do both), the brand name may sound very similar to the sound of the Western version, such as 'nifeya' for Nivea, but the meaning level may be very poor. For Nivea the assemblage of characters means 'girl-not/Africa-second rank/Asia' (Wilke, 1994).

Francis *et al.* (2002) examined brand names used by 49 Fortune 500 companies who manufactured consumer products that were available in China or Hong Kong. They found that most brands were leveraged in some way. That is, 44 per cent sounded similar, 22 per cent had similar meanings, and 10 per cent used their English brand names. In addition, while most brand names attempted to convey benefits (74 per cent) only 11 per cent shared the same benefits across languages. Thus, firms appear to localize their brand names in China. Localization may be necessary when there are large linguistic and cultural differences. Ewing *et al.* (2002) examined data from ACNielsen Retail Audit in China to examine trends for domestic and multinational brands (MNBs). They found that domestic brands are increasing in sales and, while the average price is lower than for MNBs, the gap is narrowing.

In Japan the issue is both less and more complicated since the Japanese are familiar with the Western alphabet (*romaji*) but they use also the Chinese characters (*Kanji*), and two syllabaries, the *hiragana* for Japanese words and the *katakana* for foreign loanwords (which use the same syllables as the *hiragana*, but with a slightly different calligraphic style that signals the foreign origin). These alternative writing systems carry different associative meanings which must be carefully monitored in order to convey appropriate subliminal messages: (1) as to the origin of the product: *kanji* and *hiragana* will look more Japanese while *romaji* and *katakana* signal foreignness; (2) as to the product category: high-tech products will best be written in *katakana* which connotes modernity, whereas traditional products are best served by *Kanji*; (3) as to the consumer universe implied by the writing style: *hiragana* have a feminine image and are used frequently for beauty products and cosmetics (Schmitt and Pan, 1994).

Functions of the brand according to national contexts

The trade name has a number of functions for the consumer such as *identity* (it guides consumers when making their choice), *practicality* (it works as a summary of information about product characteristics), *guarantee* ('signature of the manufacturer'), *personalization* (the brand name allows consumers to express their individuality through their purchases) and an *entertainment* function because the brand allows the exercise of free choice and enables consumers to satisfy their needs for freshness, arousal, and surprise (Lambin, 1989). For the producer, the brand fulfils two essential functions: *positioning* within the competitive scene and *capitalization* of image and advertising expenditure over the long term.

These functions are very differently valued across countries, to the extent that some functions of the brand can be almost non-existent in certain national contexts. Accordingly in France there is a certain social mistrust of brands, especially by public authorities: they supposedly increase prices, constituting entry barriers to possible competitors and thereby limiting competition (Contensou, 1989). Furthermore, being set up on the basis of large cumulative advertising expenditure, they are said to increase the price of the product to the detriment of the consumer. Contensou shows that in fact these fears are groundless and further points out that (1989, p. 246) 'inflationary tendencies have no connection to brand development and the multiplication of products sold under brand names'. Kapferer (1989), taking the same defensive attitude towards brand names, has shown that they support the actual intentions of the manufacturers, their achievements to the benefit of consumers and that without effective attempts to foster product quality, brand images cannot be sustained.

In contrast to France, Japan seems to be a country where the brand is very highly valued. Yoshimori (1989, pp. 277–8) explains this:

In feudal Japan, the brand was not distinct from the name of the ancestral house itself. This name had great importance, to the extent that everything was done to protect its good image, and above all to perpetuate it. Anyone who tarnished that reputation even through mere carelessness was obliged to rectify the damage through dying... [Yoshimori then gives examples of Japanese executives who have recently committed suicide because they believed that through their actions or negligence they had tarnished the reputation of their company]...a trading company, or any such firm, was not merely an economic entity; it also constituted a religious community which transcended the physical life of the family that controlled it. Ancestors occupied an almost divine place: it was therefore believed that the preservation and advancement of *kamei*, the name of the ancestral house, was an almost religious obligation since it (*kamei*) was the concrete translation of the presence of ancestors.

The brand in Japan is a real figurehead of competitive struggle. Abbeglen and Stalk (1986) show how, during the 1950s, the Honda brand name destroyed the Tohatsu brand (which today is completely unknown). They also describe in great detail the episodes in the Homeric quarrel between Honda and Yamaha at the start of the 1980s, which ended with a victory for Honda. In the United States, as in Japan, brands are central to competition. Brand marketing occupies a stable position in the strategies of US companies, but also one which is constantly changing, as are market shares. The vigour of the brand can only be built on 'tidal waves' of sales promotion and advertising as well as on consistent efforts towards improvement of product quality. Dupuy and Thoenig (1989) compared brand status in the United States, France and Japan. They noted that brands in France have a much weaker status than in Japan and the United States.

Differences in national distribution systems explain to a large extent the degree of brand-related competition. In Japan, the *Keiretsu* distribution system (see section 12.1) enables producers to control distribution channels and therefore to direct the brand name principally towards the relationship with the consumer. Alpert *et al.* (2001) surveyed buyers about their behaviour toward pioneer and me-too follower brands. While they found that both Japanese and US buyers accepted about the same proportion of pioneer brands (~63 per cent), they reported being offered dramatically different numbers by the manufacturers: In Japan about half of all new brands offered were pioneer brands, while in the United States only 14 per cent were pioneers. A possible explanation is that the Japanese suppliers better understand the retailers' preferences and try to meet them.

In France, where large-scale distribution is involved in conflicts with producers, the channels develop their own brands. For instance, large-scale retailers in France (hypermarkets) have created their own private labels over the last 20 years (*produits libres*). Distributors' brands do not need any product-related advertising expenditure and tend to compete with manufacturers' brands. This leads to an inflation of distributors' brands and private labels, which compete against established manufacturers' brands.

International and global brands

International brands share a common trait of long-term orientation. The main objective of the brand is to establish brand goodwill or equity over time through consumer brand awareness and recognition. When products share very similar attributes and performance, a well-known brand may have the edge by virtue of its reputation and the consumer loyalty it has created. Accordingly, Procter & Gamble has retained some brands such as Ivory soap for more than a century. Camay soap is also nearing this age: the brand name that is, not the formula of the product, which has been regularly updated. Thus, international brands' public recognition has usually been based on *considerable cumulative advertising expenditure*. They are often supported by the history of a prestigious company (for cars, Mercedes, Jaguar, Ferrari, Cadillac, etc.). For instance, Hsieh (2002) investigated the degree of brand globalization in terms of brand image cohesiveness across countries with responses to a survey from car owners in 20 countries. He found that most of the brands with a high degree of globalization are luxury brands from prestigious companies, such as Mercedes, Porche, BMW, Lexus and Jaguar. He also found that respondents from countries that are geographically close tend to perceive a similar brand image. Zaimou *et al.* (1999) found that in addition to geographic proximity, historical and cultural factors (e.g. common religion, historical links, similar customs and habits) also explain why Bulgarians are just as likely to buy

Greek products as German and Italian ones that are perceived as superior.

Brands can be aligned with the local consumer culture, a foreign consumer culture or a global consumer culture (Alden *et al.* 1999). Alden *et al.* (1999) examined advertisements from India, Thailand, Korea, Germany, The Netherlands, France and the United States, finding that most advertisements associate the brand with the local consumer culture (59 per cent), or global consumer culture (22 per cent), while only 4 per cent aligned the brand with a foreign consumer culture. Their definition of foreign consumer culture is fairly strict, in the sense that an association was only classified in this category if it was clearly from an identifiable country. If it was seen as 'Western' for instance, it would be classified as a global association, as it was 'not associated with a single country (local or foreign), but rather a larger group generally recognized as international and transcending individual national cultures' (p. 80). Which associations are more effective is a more difficult question. For instance, Fan (2002) points out consumers may value both localized international brand names as well as international brands that convey foreign benefits. He cites two successful examples in China: Reebok customizes its image to national differences with a meaningful name (translated as *dashing step*) which has no foreign image; while Nike maintains a standardized image of 'fitness and performance' in all markets. The brand name Nike has no special meaning in Chinese, but it does have a distinctly Western image which sounds appealing.

In order to be successfully aligned with a foreign consumer culture, brands need to have a *basic credibility which is based on a national image* (Shalofsky, 1987). Coca-Cola is seen as a typical American drink and Marlboro (cigarettes) is associated with an American image, the Marlboro cowboy. Similarly, Chanel No. 5 is based on the image of French *luxe* and *haute couture*, conveyed by the character of Gabrielle Chanel (Coco). Buitoni is understood as Italian pasta and Johnny Walker as whisky from Scotland. Despite this, Clark (1987) argues, in each country, consumers 'repaint' the supposed international brand image with their own local images.

As noted in the introduction to this chapter, the interplay between brands and national images is a game of complex meanings (Table 10.1): one needs to be cautious before saying that a brand is universal.

Coca-Cola's name is adapted in Chinese to avoid negative connotations. Low-calorie sugar-free Coke is called Diet Coke in the US, but Coca Light is becoming more prevalent around the world. The word *diète* conjures up the image of a strict diet or the need to lose weight. Brand images combine with the product's origin and the manufacturer's name, which is also a brand. A name like Brother offers a fairly good combination of interpretive meanings because the Brother name diffuses an English/international image that hides the Japanese origin of the manufacturer. Brother manufactures electronic typewriters and items with no 'ethnic' relation to a specific country. Finally, the concept of brotherhood supports the image of reliability, faithfulness and loyalty of an object with which people may work closely.

A basic condition for belonging to the very narrow club of global brands is to have built brand equity over a number of years by considerable advertising spending based on consistent core themes (consistent both over time and across countries). Building a global brand is expensive, but valuable. The value of the Coca-Cola brand is estimated at US$70.5 billion, Microsoft at $65 billion, and the Marlboro brand name at $22 billion (Interbrand, 2003). Advertising remains the key investment for developing brand awareness, although advertising spending has been claimed not to be an absolute necessity for creating brand equity, with such examples as the Body Shop or Haågen Dazs having developed their brands through events, sponsoring and retail shops (Joachimsthaler and Aaker, 1997).

The second condition is that the brand's image must have been carefully monitored over time. This requires considerable sophistication in the management of meaning. According to Kish *et al.* (2001), PepsiCo assesses their brand by examining recognition (awareness) and regard, which is made up of four components (brand reputation, affiliation, momentum and differentiation). They survey consumers in 14 countries to guide their marketing strategies. For instance, in Spain they found that awareness is increasing and among those who are aware regard is growing (i.e. a healthy brand), but in Australia, there is little increase in awareness, even though regard is growing among those who are aware. Thus, using this model, Pepsi can identify the aspects of their brand they need to address, such as increasing brand awareness in Australia. Similarly,

Macrae (1991) explains that Coca-Cola, a world-class brand that celebrated its 100th anniversary in 1986, monitors consumer sentiment generally, as well as brand specific sentiment. It used the favourable image of American soldiers just after the Second World War but avoided having the brand's image damaged by the Vietnam War by launching, in 1971, the 'Hill top' advertising campaign worldwide. Young people of all nations and races, dressed in national costumes, were grouped together on a hillside, singing about peace and harmony; the song became a hit at record stores.

Although some people try to defend the idea of global brands (Peebles, 1989), it is a somewhat blurred and probably even deceptive concept. There can only be a limited number of brands known by consumers in several countries throughout the world simultaneously (a few dozen, perhaps one or two hundred at most). As such, there is still hope for local brands: 'The essence of local brands' strength is their being local, which means a considerably-felt proximity that goes far beyond the local brands' advantage to an extensive and well-known distribution network developed through time, by canvassing the country and delivering a faster service to customers' (Kapferer, 2002, p. 169).

Many companies promote both global and local elements. Contrary to the global-brand building of McDonald's, Ronald McDonald is used as a point of differentiation in each market: he celebrates Christmas in Europe, Chinese New Year in Hong Kong, promotes wine in France and fish filets in Australia (Lundstrom, 2000).

But it is the perceptions of globalness that often drive consumer behaviour. For instance, Steenkamp *et al.* (2003) surveyed consumers in the United States and Korea to assess perceived brand globalness (PBG). They found that PBG influences the likelihood of brand purchase through three sets of beliefs, that 'globalness' (a) signifies better quality, (b) provides status and prestige, or (c) provides a way to become part of a global consumer culture.

As was pointed out in Chapter 5, global brands are more likely to be portfolios of basically localized marketing assets (consumer franchise and goodwill based on images which are in fact heterogeneous), a mere collection of local brands, federated under a *lexically equivalent single name*. The brand name may not even be pronounced similarly in different linguistic areas, a factor which can be critical for radio advertising, for example.

The management of global brands is complex. As such, Douglas *et al.* (2001) propose a brand architecture framework, based on the geographic scope, product scope and the level in the organization at which the brand is used. This framework is designed to search for ways to reduce the number of brands and improved efficiency and harmonize brand strategy across product lines and country markets.

The global brand, like the global campaign, requires a large amount of creative time and investment. A brand is a *sensitive asset of symbols*, suggested and maintained by diversified marketing communications: sponsoring, advertising, communication, public relations, communication through the product itself or even the style of outlets. This mix of marketing communications must be carefully managed, so that the public never feels betrayed in those beliefs that have been invested in the brand. Alain Etchegoyen (1990, p. 55, emphasis added) describes in the following way the brand image of Louis Vuitton:

There is no mythology without gods or demi-gods. That is why one must not expect gods to collapse into the melting pot of the market. Some products have to keep at a distance so that other products appear to come from *somewhere else. The brand can only remain influential at the expense of maintaining a sacred fire.* The imaginary Eden of carefully tended [brand] images will not withstand the boorish hell of bar codes [products].

Furthermore, the complexity of trademark law must be considered on an international level. Despite the move toward a standard of foreign trademark protection which binds WTO member countries, there are still many differences across countries. Gillespie *et al.* (2002) examined the patterns of protection internationally. They found that groups of countries differed in their treaty participation and varied in their local trademark legislation. For participation in foreign treaties, developed countries (83 per cent) and transitional economies (79 per cent) had a higher rate (83 per cent) than NICs (53 per cent) or LDCs (45 per cent). There were also differences in trademark legislation, such as procedures to contest the application before it is approved, the legitimacy of prior use to stop a potential preempter, and the necessity to use the product to maintain the trademark after approval. Here, developed countries and NICs rated higher than LDCs and transitional economies. (For information on intellectual property and the World Intellectual Property Organization see *WS10.3.*)

In short, the costs and the legal complexity of managing a global brand remain extremely high. When one is starting from scratch, the creation of an international brand is an undertaking that should be considered as a long-term target. In this respect Yoshimori (1989, p. 279) quotes the reply of Sony's chairman, Akio Morita, in 1955 to an American client who was requesting Sony to manufacture for him as a subcontractor. Morita refused to manufacture 100,000 transistor radios and, allegedly, said:

Fifty years ago your brand name was probably as unknown as ours is today . . . Today I decide the first stage for the next fifty years of my company. In fifty years I can promise that our name [Sony] will be just as famous as your company's is today.

Questions

1. Discuss the international transferability of the following assemblages (product, company, country of manufacture, brand name).

Generic product	Company name	Brand name	Made in
Pizza	Dr Oetker	Pizza Rustica	Germany
Computer chip	Intel	Pentium	United States
Drilling tool	Bosch	Fuchsschwanz	Spain
Car	Daewoo	Daewoo / Nexia	South Korea
Tomato sauce	Mars	Dolmio	The Netherlands
Insecticide	Bayer	Baygon	Germany

2. A very large German food company, Dr Oetker, still sells its products in France under the name *Ancel* (the brand name of a French company taken over many years ago). Why?

3. Discuss the relationship between a country's image (through its people, its history, its political and social situation, etc.) and the image of products known to be made in this country.

4. Discuss the possible international extension of the following company and/or brand names:
   - *Müller* (German yoghurts)
   - *Barilla* (Italian pastas and cookies)
   - *Procter & Gamble*
   - *Teysseire* (French syrups)
   - *Kuoni* (a Swiss tour operator)
   - *Schimmelpenninck* (Dutch cigars and cigarillos)
   - *Ishikawajima Harima Heavy Industries* (a Japanese industrial equipment company)
   - *Roi des Montagnes* (French dried mushrooms)
   - *Hewlett-Packard*
   - *Douwe-Egberts* (a large Dutch food and tobacco company)
   - *Club Méditerrannée* (a French tour operator)

5. Given the increasing importance of China as a consumer market, Nestlé has decided to stop using the category brand name for milk-based products it has used worldwide, Chambourcy, a brand with great recognition in Europe and Latin America. The name was deemed too difficult to transfer in the Chinese linguistic context. Furthermore, Nestlé maintained advertising spending at three levels (corporate name, category name and product name) and decided to use the Nestlé name directly for all its milk-based products in addition to a brand name for the particular product in some cases. Discuss the marketing and management implications of such a decision.

Notes

1. Some of the first studies include Schooler, 1965, 1971; Reierson, 1966; Schooler and Sunoo, 1969; Etzel and Walker, 1974; Wang and Lamb, 1980. For instance, Schooler and Wildt (1968) showed their subjects identical products (drinking glasses). Some drinking glasses were supposed to have been 'Made in USA' whereas the others claimed to be 'Made in Japan'. They clearly evidenced an evaluation bias due to the effect of the country of origin. But price discounts may lead the consumer to purchase the 'worst' product – the Japanese one in this case and at that time. However, considering the *country of origin* as the only criterion in consumer evaluation of quality leads to an exaggeration of the importance of the 'made in' label.

2. Krishnakumar (1974) has, for instance, shown that Indian students evaluate British products more positively than do students from Taiwan, a difference attributable to the past colonial links between the United Kingdom and India. Yavas and Alpay (1986) demonstrated that in two neighbouring countries, Saudi Arabia and Bahrain, consumers hold the same views of products originating from abroad.

3. Martin and Eroglu (1993) developed the construct of country image by showing that it can be divided into three subdimensions: political, economic and technological.

4. Similarly a study undertaken for industrial goods from eight South American countries (Crawford, 1985) showed that the degree of industrial development (not only based on objective data, but also as perceived by partially uninformed consumers) has an influence on the image of products.

5. Dornoff *et al.* (1974) observed a change in American consumers' perception of imports from Asian countries over a few years towards a more favourable attitude.

6. By replicating a 1967 study eight years later, Nagashima (1970, 1977) showed that Japanese businessmen's perceptions of their own products had become more favourable and that their image of the Japanese 'made in' label had significantly improved. The Japanese stopped seeing their products modestly as simply 'cheap' and 'unreliable'.

7. Johansson (1989) suggests two different interpretations of the cognitive effect of the COO: (1) consumers use the

COO in order to simplify the decision-making process. Consumers use this choice attribute as a summary criterion, which provides them with a 'ready-made' global evaluation. It facilitates their choice, particularly when time is limited; (2) consumers use the COO as a salient choice attribute when they have feelings towards and knowledge of a particular country.

8. Several studies have shown that gender is not a discriminating factor (Anderson and Cunningham, 1972; Tongberg, 1972; Graby, 1982), but Ettenson *et al.* (1988) found that men are generally more influenced by 'Buy national' campaigns. Generally, it would seem that the readiness to purchase foreign products decreases with age (Schooler, 1971; Tongberg, 1972; Dornoff *et al.*, 1974; Graby, 1982). Dogmatism, greater nationalism and stabilized consumption habits are probably the result of ageing, and explain the reluctance to buy foreign goods. However, inconclusive results have been reached by other researchers, who have shown that age has no influence (Johansson *et al.*, 1985; Morganosky and Lazarde, 1987; Usunier, 1994). Generally a more favourable evaluation of foreign products is made by consumers when they have a higher level of education (Anderson and Cunningham, 1972; Dornoff *et al.*, 1974; Wang, 1978) or a higher income level (Wang, 1978), or when they have travelled abroad and are therefore more familiar with the products of these foreign countries (Graby, 1982).

9. Gaedeke (1973), for example, found that tinned meat produced in Brazil is much more highly regarded than televisions made there, and that video recorders that are 'Made in South Korea' were more highly regarded than shoes from the same country. Hooley *et al.* (1988) find clear associations in the minds of British consumers about fruit and vegetables with different origins: grapes and tomatoes were associated with Italy, apples were associated with France, citrus fruits with Spain, and potatoes with Britain.

10. French and UK industrial products are regarded as being of equivalent quality to US ones, and Italian industrial products as being of inferior quality to American products (White, 1979). In addition, Perrin *et al.* (1981) showed in a study of the International Marketing and Purchasing European group that different national markets across Europe are not equally demanding as a whole and furthermore do not emphasize the same requirements. German and Swedish industrial purchasers prove to be more demanding, whereas the Italian and British purchasers are less so. German and Swedish suppliers have the same image of good technical quality and punctual delivery across all European markets. It appears that French industrial companies are unique in respect of one achievement: the exceptional quality of the relationships they construct over time with their French clients: 'actually, in no other country do purchasers accord such an advantage on this point to their national suppliers' (Perrin *et al.*, 1981, p. 102).

11. Hampton (1977) considered the situation where American goods are manufactured either in the United States or abroad in selected countries. In the sample were some strong-perceived-risk countries (Algeria, Pakistan, Turkey), some moderate-perceived-risk countries (the Philippines, Hong Kong) and some weak-perceived-risk countries (Canada, Japan, West Germany). In the questionnaire these origins were combined with a sample of products that offered diverse levels of perceived risk. Overall the results confirmed that consumers perceived less risk for goods manufactured in the United States than for the same products when foreign made, whatever the level of perceived risk of the foreign country of manufacture. In several instances, product–country connections were clearly established in consumers' minds, such as the colour television and Japan, the calculator and Hong Kong, or even instant coffee and Brazil, thereby reducing the level of perceived risk of a country as a general place of manufacture. For these specific products, these were considered favourable manufacturing countries.

12. For an examination of how companies can develop euro-brands and the obstacles they face in such an endeavour, see Littler and Schlieper (1995).

13. Let us imagine the case of the detergent *Tide*, translated as *Marée* in French, a term that connotes strong smells and dirt rather than strength, washing power and cleanliness. Such examples are endless.

14. Definitions of the words used in Table 10.2: etymology: the study of the sources and development of words; grammar: the branch of linguistics that deals with syntax and morphology; phonology: the study of the sound system of language(s); phonemics: aspects of phonology concerned with the classification and analysis of the phonemes of a language; phonetics: study of speech processes, including the production, perception and analysis of speech sounds; rhetoric: the art of using speech to persuade or influence; semantics: the branch of linguistics that deals with the study of meaning; semiotics: the study of signs and symbols, especially the relations between written or spoken signs and their referents in the physical world or the world of ideas.

15. When transcribed in the Roman alphabet (*romaji*), which is not their natural written form.

16. I remember travelling in Tokyo with a Chinese friend who was able to understand all the road signs but did not know how to pronounce them in Japanese.

References

Abegglen, James and George Stalk Jr (1986), 'The Japanese corporation as competitor', *California Management Review*, vol. XXVIII, no. 3, Spring, pp. 9–37.

Agrawal, Jagdish and Wagner A. Kamakura (1999), 'Country of origin: a competitive advantage?', *International Journal of Research in Marketing*, vol. 16, no. 4, pp. 255–67.

Ahmed, Sadrudin A. and Alain d'Astous (1995), 'Comparison of country-of-origin effects on household and organizational buyers' product perceptions', *European Journal of Marketing*, vol. 29, pp. 35–51.

Ahmed, Sadrudin A. and Alain d'Astous (1999), 'Product-country images in Canada and in the People's Republic of China', *Journal of International Consumer Marketing*, vol. 11, no. 1, pp. 5–22.

Ahmed, Sadrudin A., Alain d'Astous and Mostafa El Adraoui (1994), 'Country-of-origin effects on purchasing managers' product perceptions', *Industrial Marketing Management*, vol. 23, no. 4, pp. 323–32.

Ahmed, Sadrudin A., Alain d'Astous and Jelloul Eljabri (2002a), 'The impact of technological complexity on consumers' perceptions of products made in highly and newly industrialised countries', *International Marketing Review*, vol. 19, no. 4, pp. 387–407.

Ahmed, Zafar U., James P. Johnson, Chew Pei Ling, Tan Wai Fang and Ang Kah Hui (2002b), 'Country-of-origin and brand effects on consumers' evaluations of cruise lines', *International Marketing Review*, vol. 19, no. 3.

Ahmed, Zafar U., James P. Johnson, Xia Yang, Cheng Kheng Fatt, Han Sack Teng and Lim Chee Boon (2002c), 'Does country of origin matter for low-involvement products?', *International Marketing Review*, vol. 21, no. 1, pp. 102–20.

Alden, D.L., J.-B. E.M. Steenkamp and R. Batra (1999), 'Brand positioning through advertising in Asia, North America and Europe: the role of global consumer culture', *Journal of Marketing*, vol. 63, January, pp. 75–87.

Alpert, Frank, Michael Kamins, Tomoaki Sakano, Naoto Onzo and John Graham (2001), 'Retail buyer beliefs, attitude and behaviour toward pioneer and me-too follower brands: a comparative study of Japan and the USA', *International Marketing Review*, vol. 18, no. 2, pp. 160–87.

Anderson, William T. and William H. Cunningham (1972), 'Gauging foreign product promotion', *Journal of Advertising Research*, vol. 12, no. 1, pp. 29–34.

Askegaard, S. and Guliz Ger (1998), 'Product-country images: toward a contextualized approach', *European Advances in Consumer Research*, vol. 3, pp. 50–8.

Balabanis, George and A. Diamantopoulos (2004), 'Domestic country bias, country-of-origin effects, and consumer ethnocentrism: a multidimensional unfolding approach, vol. 32, no. 1, pp. 582–610.

Balabanis, George, Rene Mueller and T.C. Melewar (2002), 'The human values' lenses of country of origin images', *International Marketing Review*, vol. 19, no. 6.

Batra, Rajeev, Venkatram Ramaswamy, Dana L. Alden, Jan-Benedict E.M. Steenkamp and S. Ramachander (2000), 'Effects of brand local and nonlocal origin on consumer attitudes in developing countries', *Journal of Consumer Psychology*, vol. 9, no. 2, pp. 83–96.

Baumgartner, Gary and Alain Jolibert (1977), 'The perception of foreign products in France', *Advances in Consumer Research*, vol. 7, pp. 103–5.

Bhuian, Shahid N. (1997), 'Saudi consumers' attitudes towards European, US and Japanese products and marketing practices', *European Journal of Marketing*, vol. 31, no. 7, pp. 467–86.

Bilkey, Warren J. and Erik Nes (1982), 'Country-of-origin effects on product evaluations', *Journal of International Business Studies*, Spring–Summer, pp. 89–99.

Cabat, Odilon (1989), 'Archéologie de la marque moderne', in Jean-Noel Kapferer and Jean-Claude Thoenig (eds), *La Marque*, MacGraw-Hill: Paris, pp. 307–53.

Cattin, Philippe, Alain Jolibert and Colleen Lohnes (1982), 'A cross-cultural study of "made-in" concepts', *Journal of International Business Studies*, Winter, pp. 131–41.

Chang, Dae Ryun and Ik-Tae Rim (1995), 'A study on the rating of import sources for industrial products in a newly industrialized country: the case of South Korea', *Journal of Business Research*, vol. 32, pp. 31–9.

Chao, Paul (2001), 'The moderating effects of country of assembly, country of parts, and country of design on hybrid product evaluations', *Journal of Advertising*, vol. 30, no. 4, pp. 67–81.

Clark, Harold F. Jr (1987), 'Consumer and corporate values: yet another view on global marketing', *International Journal of Advertising*, vol. 6, pp. 29–42.

Colombat, Catherine (1997), 'Danone imprime sa marque sur la planète', *L'Essentiel du Management*, April, pp. 74–80.

Contensou, François (1989), 'La Marque, l'efficience économique et la formation des prix', in Jean-Noel Kapferer and Jean-Claude Thoenig (eds), *La Marque*, McGraw-Hill: Paris, pp. 231–73.

Crawford, John C. and Charles W. Lamb Jr (1981), 'Source preferences for imported products', *Journal of Purchasing and Materials Management*, Winter, pp. 28–33.

Crawford, John C. (1985), 'Attitudes toward Latin American products', in Erdener Kaynak (ed.), *Global Perspectives in Marketing*, Praeger: New York, pp. 149–54.

Cundiff, Edward W. and Marye Tharp Hilger (1988), *Marketing in the International Environment*, 2nd edn, Prentice Hall: Englewood Cliffs, NJ.

Czinkota, Michael R. and Illka A. Ronkainen (1990), *International Marketing*, 2nd edn, Dryden Press: Hinsdale, IL.

Darling, John B. and F. Kraft (1977), 'A competitive profile of products and associated marketing practices of selected European and non-European countries', *European Journal of Marketing*, vol. 11, no. 7, pp. 519–37.

Dornoff, Ronald J., Clint B. Tankersley and Gregory P. White (1974), 'Consumers' perceptions of imports', *Akron Business and Economic Review*, vol. 5, Summer, pp. 26–9.

Douglas, Susan P., C. Samuel Craig and Edwin J. Nijssen (2001), 'Executive insights: integrating branding strategy across markets: Building international brand architecture', *Journal of International Marketing*, vol. 9, no. 2, pp. 97–114.

Dupuy, François and Jean-Claude Thoenig (1989), 'La Marque et l'échange', in Jean-Noel Kapferer and Jean-Claude Thoenig (eds), *La Marque*, McGraw-Hill: Paris, pp. 159–89.

Eroglu, S.A. and K.A. Machleit (1989), 'Effects of individual and product specific variables on utilizing country of origin as a product quality cue', *International Marketing Review*, vol. 6, no. 6, pp. 27–41.

Etchegoyen, Alain (1990), *Les Entreprises ont-elles une âme?*, Editions François Bourin: Paris.

Ettenson, R., J. Wagner and G. Gaeth (1988), 'Evaluating the effect of country-of-origin and the "Made in the USA" campaign: a conjoint approach', *Journal of Retailing*, vol. 64, no. 1, pp. 85–100.

Ettenson, Richard (1993), 'Brand name and country of origin effects in the emerging market economies of Russia, Poland and Hungary', *International Marketing Review*, vol. 10, no. 5, pp. 14–36.

Etzel, Michael J. and Bruce J. Walker (1974), 'Advertising strategy for foreign products', *Journal of Advertising Research*, vol. 14, June, pp. 41–4.

Ewing, Michael T., Julie Napoli, Leyland F. Pitt and Alistair Watts (2002), 'On the renaissance of Chinese brands', *International Journal of Advertising*, vol. 21, no. 2.

Fan, Ying (2002), 'The national image of global brands', *Journal of Brand Management*, vol. 9, no. 3, pp. 180–92.

Francis, June N.P., Janet P.Y. Lam and Jan Walls (2002), 'Executive insights: the impact of linguistic differences on international brand name standardization: a comparison of English and Chinese brand names of Fortune-500 companies', *Journal of International Marketing*, vol. 10, no. 1, pp. 98–116.

Gaedeke, Ralph (1973), 'Consumer attitudes towards products "made in" developing countries', *Journal of Retailing*, vol. 49, Summer, pp. 13–24.

Gillespie, Kate, Kishore Krishna and Susan Jarvis (2002), 'Protecting global brands: toward a global norm', *Journal of International Marketing*, vol. 10, no. 2, pp. 99–112.

Giordan, Alain-Eric (1988), *Exporter Plus 2*, Economica: Paris.

Graby, Françoise (1982), 'Les consommateurs et les produits étrangers: application au marché français', *Proceedings of the 7th Seminar on Research in Marketing*, IAE: Aix en Provence, Lalonde des Maures.

Gürhan-Canli, Zeynep and Durairaj Maheswarm (2000), 'Cultural variations in country of origin effects', *Journal of Marketing Research*, vol. 37, pp. 309–17.

Hampton, Gerald M. (1977), 'Perceived risk in buying products made abroad by American firms', *Baylor Business Studies*, October, pp. 53–64.

Han, C. Min (1990), 'Country image: halo or summary construct?', *Journal of Marketing Research*, vol. XXVI, May, pp. 222–9.

Han, C. Min and Vern Terpstra (1988), 'Country of origin effects for uni-national and bi-national products', *Journal of International Business Studies*, vol. 19, no. 2, Summer, pp. 235–55.

Han, C. Min, Byoung-Woo Lee and Kong-Kyun Ro (1994), 'The choice of a survey mode in country image studies', *Journal of Business Research*, vol. 29, no. 2, pp. 151–62.

Harris, Richard Jackson, Bettina Garner-Earl, Sara J. Sprick and Collette Carroll (1994), 'Effects of foreign product names and country-of-origin attributions on advertisement evaluations', *Psychology and Marketing*, vol. 11, no. 2, March/April, pp. 129–44.

Herche, Joel (1992), 'A note on the predictive validity of CETSCALE', *Journal of the Academy of Marketing Science*, vol. 20, no. 3, pp. 261–4.

Hester, Susan B. and Mary Yuen (1987), 'The influence of country of origin on consumer attitude and buying behavior in the United States and Canada', in Melanie Wallendorf and Paul Anderson (eds), *Advances in Consumer Research*, vol. 14, Association for Consumer Research: Provo, UT, pp. 538–43.

Hong, F.C., Anthony Pecotich and Clifford J. Schultz (2002), 'Brand name translation: Language constraints, product attributes, and consumer perceptions in East and Southeast Asia', *Journal of International Marketing*, vol. 10, no. 2, pp. 29–45.

Hooley, Graham J., David Shipley and Nathalie Krieger (1988), 'A method for modelling consumer perceptions of country of origin', *International Marketing Review*, vol. 5, no. 3, pp. 67–76.

Hsieh, Ming H. (2002), 'Identifying brand image dimensionality and measuring the degree of brand globalization: a cross-national study', *Journal of International Marketing*, vol. 10, no. 2, pp. 46–67.

Huang, Yue Yuan and Allan K.K. Chan (1997), 'Chinese branding name: from general principles to specific rules', *International Journal of Advertising*, vol. 16, no. 4, pp. 320–35.

Hugstad, Paul S. and Michael Durr (1986), 'A study of country of manufacturer impact on consumer perceptions', in Naresh Malhotra and John Hawes (eds), *Developments in Marketing Science*, vol. 9, Academy of Marketing Science: Coral Gables, FL.

Interbrand (2003), 'Best global brands', *Business Week*, 2 August.

Jaffé, Eugene D. and Israel D. Nebenzahl (1984), 'Alternative questionnaire formats for country image studies', *Journal of Marketing Research*, vol. 21, pp. 463–71.

Jaffé, Eugene D. and Israel D. Nebenzahl (1989), 'Global promotion of country image: the case of the 1988 Korean Olympic Games', in Reijo Luostarinen (ed.), *Dynamics of International Business*, vol. 1, proceedings of the 15th annual conference of the European International Business Association, Helsinki, Finland, pp. 358–85.

Jaffé, Eugene D. and Israel D. Nebenzahl (2001), *National Image and Competitive Advantage: The theory and practice of country-of-origin effects*, Copenhagen: Copenhagen Business School Press.

Joachimsthaler, Erich and David A. Aaker (1997), 'Building brands without mass media', *Harvard Business Review*, vol. 75, no. 1, January–February, pp. 39–50.

Johansson, Johny K. (1989), 'Determinants and effects of the use of "made in" labels', *International Marketing Review*, vol. 6, no. 1, pp. 47–58.

Johansson, Johny K. and Hans B. Thorelli (1985), 'International product positioning', *Journal of International Business Studies*, vol. 16, Fall, pp. 57–75.

Johansson, Johny K. and Israel D. Nebenzahl (1986), 'Multinational production: effect on brand value', *Journal of International Business Studies*, vol. 17, no. 3, pp. 101–26.

Johansson, Johny K., Susan P. Douglas and Ikujiro Nonaka (1985), 'Assessing the impact of country of origin on product evaluations: a new methodological perspective', *Journal of International Business Studies*, vol. 16, Fall, pp. 57–75.

Jolibert, Alain (1979), 'Quand les directeurs d'approvisionnement français et américains évaluent l'image des produits fabriqués dans cinq pays industriels', *Revue Française de Gestion*, January–February, pp. 94–101.

Kamins, Michael A. and Akira Nagashima (1995), 'Perceptions of products made in Japan versus those made in the United States among Japanese and American executives: a longitudinal perspective', *Asia Pacific Journal of Management*, vol. 12, no. 1, pp. 49–68.

Kapferer, Jean-Noel (1989), 'La face cachée des marques', in Jean-Noel Kapferer and Jean-Claude Thoenig (eds), *La Marque*, McGraw-Hill: Paris, pp. 9–44.

Kapferer, Jean-Noel (2002), 'Is there really no hope for local brands?', *Journal of Brand Management*, vol. 9, no. 3, pp. 163–70.

Kaynak, E. and T.S. Cavusgil (1983), 'Consumer attitudes toward products of foreign origin: Do they vary across product classes', *International Journal of Advertising*, vol. 2, pp. 147–57.

Keller, K.L. (1998), *Strategic brand management: Building, measuring and managing brand equity*, Prentice Hall: Upper Saddle River, NJ.

Khanna, Sri Ram (1986), 'Asian companies and the country stereotype paradox: an empirical study', *Columbia Journal of World Business*, Summer, pp. 29–38.

Khera, I., B. Anderson and C.Y. Kim (1983), 'Made in India versus Hong-Kong/Korea/Taiwan', *Foreign Trade Review*, January–March, pp. 362–81.

Khera, Inder (1986), 'A broadening base of US consumer acceptance of Korean products', in Kenneth D. Bahn and M. Joseph Sirgy (eds), *World Marketing Congress*, Academy of Marketing Science: Blacksburg, VA, pp. 136–41.

Khera, Inder, David Karns and C.Y. Kim (1985), 'U.S. consumers' perceptions of Korean products and brands', Pan-Pacific Conference II, Seoul, Korea, 12–18 May.

Kish, Paulette, Dwight R. Riskey and Roger A. Kerin (2001), 'Measurement and tracking of brand equity in the global marketplace', *International Marketing Review*, vol. 18, no. 1, pp. 91–6.

Klein, Jill Gabrielle, Richard Ettenson and Marlene D. Morris (1998), 'The animosity model of foreign product purchase: an empirical test in the People's Republic of China,' *Journal of Marketing*, vol. 62, January, pp. 89–100.

Klein, Naomi (2002), 'Between McWorld and Jihad', *Development*, vol. 45, no. 2, pp. 6–10.

Kotler, Philip, Ang Swee Hoon, Leong Siew Meng and Tan Chin Tiong (2003), *Marketing Management: An Asian perspective*, 3rd edn, Pearson: Singapore.

Kraft, Frederick B. and Kae H. Chung (1992), 'Korean importer perceptions of US and Japanese industrial goods', *International Marketing Review*, vol. 9, no. 2, pp. 59–73.

Krishnakumar, Parameswar (1974), 'An exploratory study of the influence of country of origin on the product images of persons from selected countries', PhD Dissertation, University of Florida.

Lambin, Jean-Jacques (1989), 'La marque et le comportement de choix de l'acheteur', in Jean-Noel Kapferer and Jean-Claude Thoenig (eds), *La Marque*, McGraw-Hill: Paris, pp. 125–58.

Leclerc, France, Bernd H. Schmitt and Laurette Dubé (1994), 'Foreign branding and its effects on product perceptions and attitudes', *Journal of Marketing Research*, vol. 31, no. 2, May, pp. 263–70.

Lee, Dongdae and Gopala Ganesh (1999), 'Effect of partitioned country image in the context of brand image and familiarity: a categorization theory perspective', *International Marketing Review*, vol. 16, no. 1, pp. 18–39.

Lindstrom, Martin (2000), 'Global branding versus local marketing', Clickz Network Solutions for Marketers, online, 23-11-2000, available at: **www.clickz.com/brand/brand_mkt/print.php/832711**

Littler, Dale and Katrin Schlieper (1995), 'The development of the Eurobrand', *International Marketing Review*, vol. 12, no. 2, pp. 22–37.

Loeffler, Michael (2002), 'A multinational examination of the "(non-) domestic product" effect', *International Marketing Review*, vol. 19, no. 5, pp. 482–98.

Lumpkin, J.R, J.C Crawford and G. Kim (1985), 'Perceived risk as a factor in buying foreign clothes', *International Journal of Advertising*, vol. 4, pp. 157–71.

Macrae, Chris (1991), *World Class Brands*, Addison-Wesley: Wokingham.

Maheswaran, Durairaj (1994), 'Country of origin as a stereotype: effects of consumer expertise and attribute strength on product evaluations', *Journal of Consumer Research*, vol. 21, September, pp. 354–65.

Manrai, Lalita A., Dana-Nicoleta Lascu and Ajay K. Manrai (1998), 'Interactive effects of country of origin and product category on product evaluations', *International Business Review*, vol. 7, no. 6, pp. 591–616.

Martin, Ingrid M. and Sevgin Eroglu (1993), 'Measuring a multi-dimensional construct: country image', *Journal of Business Research*, vol. 28, pp. 191–210.

Mascarenhas, O.A.D. and D. Kujawa (1998), 'American consumer attitude toward foreign direct investments and their products', *Multinational Business Review*, vol. 6, Autumn, pp. 1–9.

Melewar, T.C. and John Saunders (1998), 'Global corporate visual identity systems: standardization, control, and benefits', *International Marketing Review*, vol. 15, no. 4, pp. 291–308.

Morganosky, Michelle A. and Michelle M. Lazarde (1987), 'Foreign-made apparel: influence on consumers' perceptions of brand and store quality', *International Journal of Advertising*, vol. 6, no. 4, pp. 339–47.

Nagashima, Akira (1970), 'A comparison of Japanese and U.S. attitudes towards foreign products', *Journal of Marketing*, vol. 34, January, pp. 68–74.

Nagashima, Akira (1977), 'A comparative "made in" product image survey among Japanese businessmen', *Journal of Marketing*, July, pp. 95–100.

Nebenzahl, Israel D., Eugene D. Jaffé and Jean-Claude Usunier (2003), 'Personifying country-of-origin research', *Management International Review*, vol. 43, no. 4, pp. 383–406.

Nebenzahl, Israel D. and Eugene D. Jaffé (1989), 'A methodological approach to the estimation of demand functions from country-of-origin effects', in Reijo Luostarinien (ed.), *Dynamics of International Business*, vol. 1, proceedings of the 15th Annual Conference of the European International Business Association, Helsinki, Finland, pp. 386–414.

Nebenzahl, Israel D., Eugene D. Jaffé and Shlomo I. Lampert (1997), 'Towards a theory of country image effect on product evaluation', *Management International Review*, vol. 37, no. 1, pp. 27–49.

Nishina, Sadafumi (1990), 'Japanese consumers: Introducing foreign products/brands into the Japanese market', *Journal of Advertising Research*, vol. 30, no. 2, pp. 35–45.

Onkvisit, Sak and John J. Shaw (1989), 'The international dimension of branding: strategic considerations and decisions', *International Marketing Review*, vol. 6, no. 2, pp. 22–34.

Pan, Yigang and Bernd H. Schmitt (1995), 'What's in a name? An empirical comparison of Chinese and Western brand names', *Asian Journal of Marketing*, vol. 4, no. 1, pp. 7–16.

Papadopoulos, Nicholas and Louise A. Heslop (1993), *Product and Country Images: Research and strategy*, The Haworth Press: New York.

Peebles, Dean M. (1989), 'Don't write off global advertising: a commentary', *International Marketing Review*, vol. 6, no. 1, pp. 73–8.

Perrin, Michel, Claude Marcel, Robert Salles and Jean-Paul Valla (1981), 'L'image des biens industriels français en Europe', *Revue Française de Gestion*, January–February, pp. 97–107.

Peterson, Robert A. and Alain Jolibert (1995), 'A meta-analysis of country-of-origin effects', *Journal of International Business Studies*, vol. 26, no. 4, pp. 883–900.

Reierson, Curtis (1966), 'Are foreign products seen as national stereotypes?', *Journal of Retailing*, Fall, pp. 33–40.

Robertson, K. (1989), 'Strategically desirable brand name characteristics', *Journal of Consumer Marketing*, vol. 6, Fall, pp. 61–71.

Robson, Matthew J. and Mark A.J. Dunk (1999), 'Developing a pan-European co-marketing alliance: the case of BP-Mobil', *International Marketing Review*, vol. 16, no. 3, pp. 216–30.

Rosen, Barry Nathan, Jean J. Boddewyn and Ernst A. Louis (1989), 'US brands abroad: an empirical study of global branding', *International Marketing Review*, vol. 6, no. 1, pp. 7–19.

Saghafi, Massoud M., Fanis Varvoglis and Tomas Vega (1991), 'Why US firms don't buy from Latin American companies', *Industrial Marketing Management*, vol. 20, pp. 207–13.

Samiee, Saeed (1994), 'Customer evaluation of products in a global market', *Journal of International Business Studies*, vol. 25, no. 3, pp. 579–604.

Schaefer, Anja (1997), 'Consumer knowledge and country of origin effects', *European Journal of Marketing*, vol. 31, no. 1, pp. 56–72.

Schmitt, Bernd H. and Yigang Pan (1994), 'Managing corporate and brand identities in the Asia-Pacific region', *California Management Review*, vol. 36, no. 4, Summer, pp. 32–47.

Schmitt, Bernd H, Yigang Pan and Nader Tavassoli (1994), 'Language and consumer memory: the impact of linguistic differences between Chinese and English', *Journal of Consumer Research*, vol. 21, no. 3, pp. 419–31.

Schmitt, Bernd H. and Shi Zhang (1998), 'Language structure and categorization: a study of classifiers in consumer cognition, judgement and choice', *Journal of Consumer Research*, vol. 25, no. 2, pp. 108–22.

Schooler, Robert D. (1965), 'Product bias in the Central American common market', *Journal of Marketing Research*, vol. 2, November, pp. 394–7.

Schooler, Robert D. (1971), 'Bias phenomena attendant to the marketing of foreign goods in the US', *Journal of International Business Studies*, Spring, pp. 71–80.

Schooler, Robert D. and A.R. Wildt (1968), 'Elasticity of product bias', *Journal of Marketing Research*, vol. 5, February, pp. 78–81.

Schooler, Robert D. and D.H. Sunoo (1969), 'Consumer perceptions of international products: Regional versus national labeling', *Social Science Quarterly*, vol. 49, no. 4, pp. 886–90.

Shalofsky, Ivor (1987), 'Research for global brands', *European Research*, May, pp. 88–93.

Sharma, Subash, Terence A. Shimp and J. Shin (1995), 'Consumer ethnocentrism: a test of antecedents and moderators', *Journal of the Academy of Marketing Science*, vol. 23, no. 1, pp. 26–37.

Shimp, Terence A. and Subash Sharma (1987), 'Consumer ethnocentrism: construction and validation of the CETSCALE', *Journal of Marketing Research*, vol. 24, August, pp. 280–9.

Smith, N. (1990), *Morality and the Market*, London: Routledge.

Solomon, Michael R. (1994), *Consumer Behavior*, 2nd edn, Allyn and Bacon: Needham Heights.

Steenkamp, Jan-Benedict E.M., Rajeev Batra and Dana L. Alden (2003), 'How perceived brand globalness creates brand value', *Journal of International Business Studies*, vol. 34, no. 1, pp. 53–65.

Swinder, Janda and C.P. Rao (1997), 'The effect of country-of-origin related stereotypes and personal beliefs on product evaluation', *Psychology and Marketing*, vol. 14, no. 7, pp. 689–702.

Tavassoli, Nader T. (1999), 'Temporal and associative memory in Chinese and English', *Journal of Consumer Research*, vol. 26, no. 2, pp. 170–81.

Tavassoli, Nader T. and Jin K. Han (2002), 'Auditory and visual brand identifiers in Chinese and English', *Journal of International Marketing*, vol. 10, no. 2, pp. 13–28.

Thorelli, Hans B. and Aleksandra E. Glowacka (1995), 'Willingness of American industrial buyers to source internationally', *Journal of Business Research*, vol. 32, pp. 21–30.

Tongberg, R.C. (1972), 'An empirical study of relationships between dogmatism and consumer attitudes toward foreign products', PhD. dissertation, Pennsylvania State University.

Usunier, Jean-Claude (1994), 'Social status and country-of-origin preferences', *Journal of Marketing Management*, vol. 10, pp. 765–83.

Usunier, Jean-Claude (2003), 'Relevance versus convenience in business research: the case of country-of-origin research and marketing', IUMI Working Paper 0301, University of Lausanne, Switzerland, May, p. 311.

Usunier, Jean-Claude, Israel D. Nebenzahl and Eugene D. Jaffé (1993), 'Pays d'origine et stratégie de prix', *Revue Française du Marketing*, 1993/1, no. 141, pp. 35–47.

Vanden Bergh, Bruce, Keith Adler and Lauren Oliver (1987), 'Linguistic distinction among top brand names', *Journal of Advertising Research*, vol. 27, no. 4, pp. 39–44.

Verlegh, Peeter W.J. and Jan-Benedikt E.M. Steenkamp (1999), 'A review and meta-analysis of country of origin research', *Journal of Economic Psychology*, vol. 20, pp. 521–46.

Wang, Chih-Kang (1978), 'The effect of foreign economic, political and cultural environment on consumers' willingness to buy foreign products', PhD dissertation, Texas A & M University.

Wang, Chih-Kang and Charles W. Lamb Jr (1980), 'Foreign environmental factors influencing American consumers predispositions toward European products', *Journal of the Academy of Marketing Science*, vol. 8, Fall, pp. 345–56.

Wang, Chih-Kang and Charles W. Lamb Jr (1983), 'The impact of selected environmental forces upon consumers' willingness to buy foreign products', *Journal of the Academy of Marketing Science*, vol. 11, Winter, pp. 71–84.

White, Phillip D. (1979), 'Attitudes of U.S. purchasing managers toward industrial products manufactured in selected Western European nations', *Journal of International Business Studies*, Spring/Summer, pp. 81–90.

Wilke, Margaritha (1994), 'Der werte name – die marke auf Chinesisch', *Der Neue China*, vol. 21, no. 3, September, pp. 15–16.

Wilsher, Peter (1992), 'Diverse and perverse', *Management Today*, July, pp. 32–5.

Witkowski, T.H. (1998), 'Consumer ethnocentrism in two emerging markets: determinants and predictive validity', *Advances in Consumer Research*, vol. 25, pp. 258–63.

Yaprak, Attila (1987), 'The country of origin paradigm in cross-national consumer behavior: the state of the art', in Kenneth D. Bahn and M. Joseph Sirgy (eds), *World Marketing Congress*, Academy of Marketing Science: Blacksburg, VA, pp. 142–5.

Yavas, Ugur and Guvenc Alpay (1986), 'Does an exporting nation enjoy the same cross-national image?', *International Journal of Advertising*, vol. 5, pp. 109–19.

Yoshimori, Masaru (1989), 'Concepts et stratégies de marques au Japon', in Jean-Noel Kapferer and Jean-Claude Thoenig (eds), *La Marque*, McGraw-Hill: Paris, pp. 275–304.

Zeithaml, Valarie A. (1988), 'Consumer perceptions of price, quality and value: a means-end model and synthesis of evidence', *Journal of Marketing*, vol. 52, July, pp. 2–22.

Zhang, Shi and Bernd H. Schmitt (2001), 'Creating local brands in multilingual international markets', *Journal of Marketing Research*, vol. XXXVIII, August, pp. 313–25.

Ziamou, Paschalina, Yorgos Zotos, Steven Lysonski and Costas Zafiropoulos (1999), 'Selling exports to consumers in Bulgaria: attitudes towards foreign products', *Journal of Euromarketing*, vol. 7, no. 3, pp. 59–77.

Appendix 10

Teaching materials

A10.1 Exercise

Interpreting symbolic attributes

For the following products, you are given possible physical attributes; try to imagine how they could be diversely interpreted at a symbolic level in different cultures (you do not need to precisely relate a definite interpretation to a particular culture, but simply to emphasize probable divergence of interpretation across cultures in general).

- A car/colour black
- Orange juice/thick (with pulp)
- Cheese/with traces of blue (*Penicillium glaucum*)
- Beer/frothy
- Orange juice/colour deep orange
- Car/automatic gear-box
- Apple juice/vitamins added
- Refrigerator/ice-cube distributor
- Cheese/packed in wooden case
- Car/diesel engine

For further guidance, see Zeithaml (1988), and also Solomon (1994, pp. 67–73).

A10.2 Case

Soshi Sumsin Ltd

Sammy Soshi's first assignment for his new job with Soshi Sumshin Ltd was to recommend a new name for the firm's line of electronic products. Sammy had completed his MBA at Emory University in May 1995 and had returned to Seoul, Korea, to work in his father's firm. Soshi Sumsin manufactured a line of electronic products, which included VCRs, stereos and televisions. The senior Mr Soshi got involved in electronics manufacturing when he agreed in 1980 to manufacture television components for an American manufacturer. Eventually, he was producing a full line of television sets, as well as VCRs and stereo equipment for three American firms. In addition, since 1992, he had been marketing his own line of products in the Korean market under the Sumsin brand name.

Mr Soshi felt that his firm was now ready, both in terms of manufacturing know-how and capital, to enter international markets under his own brand name. The American market was chosen as the first target because of its size and buying power, and an introduction date of April 1996 had been tentatively set. Having little familiarity with the American market, Mr Soshi was relying heavily on his son, Sammy, to help with marketing decisions.

The first problem to which Sammy addressed himself was the selection of a brand name for the line. His father had planned to use the Sumsin name in the American market. Sammy pointed out that a failure to give careful consideration to the effect of a brand name in a different culture could cause major marketing difficulties later. He cited the experience of Tatung as a case in point. Tatung was a Taiwanese maker of televisions, fans and computer terminals. When the company entered the American market it did not even consider changing its brand name. The Tatung company had a favourable connotation in Chinese and was known in the company's oriental markets. However, in the United States, not only was the name meaningless, but it was difficult to know how to pronounce it.

Because of these difficulties, Tatung's American advertising agency finally decided to emphasize the strangeness of the name, and it launched a campaign based on a play on words which might help customers to pronounce Tatung. Each ad carried the query, 'Cat Got Your Tatung?' Sammy believed that a lot of effort that should have been placed on the product itself had been expended to overcome a bad trade name.

Sammy cited a second example of problems resulting from a poorly chosen brand name. Another Taiwanese company, Kunnan Lo, introduced its own brand of tennis rackets in the American market in 1987. Recognizing that their own name would present problems in the American market, they decided to select an American name. Ultimately, they decided on the name Kennedy; it was quite similar to their company name, and it was certainly familiar in the United States. However, after initial promotional efforts, it quickly became apparent that Kennedy was not a neutral name. Many tennis players were Republicans, and for them the Kennedy name had negative connotations. As a result, the name was changed to Kennex, a neutral, artificial word that was still similar to the company name. However, Kennex also quickly proved to be unsatisfactory, because of some confusion with the name Kleenex. To eliminate this confusion, the name was finally changed to Pro-Kennex, which provided both a tennis tie-in and retention of a root similar to Kunnan Lo. The waste of resources in the series of name changes would have been better avoided.

Determined to avoid the mistakes of these other companies entering the American market, Sammy Soshi carefully evaluated the alternatives available to his company. The first was his father's preference – to use a company family name. However, Sumsin was somewhat difficult for English-speaking people to pronounce and seemed meaningless and foreign. Soshi was equally unfamiliar and meaningless, but he was also afraid that Americans would confuse it with the Japanese raw fish, *sushi*.

A second alternative was to acquire ownership of an existing American brand name, preferably one with market recognition. After considerable research, he chose the name Monarch. The Monarch company had started manufacturing radios in Chicago in 1932 and Monarch radios had been nationally known in the 1940s. The company was badly hurt by television in the 1950s, which reduced the size of the radio market appreciably. The company was finally wiped out by the invasion of inexpensive transistor radios from Asia in the 1960s. The company filed for bankruptcy in 1972. Sammy found that he could buy the rights to the Monarch name for $50,000. The name was tied in with electronics products in the public's mind, but he wondered how many people still remembered or recognized the Monarch name. He also wondered whether this recognition might be more negative than positive because of the company's failure in the market.

A third alternative would be to select a new name and build market recognition through promotion. Such a name would need to be politically and socially neutral in the American market and ultimately in other foreign markets. It should be easy to pronounce and remember and have neutral meaning or favourable meaning to the public. The possibilities might be considered.

The first was Proteus, the name of an ancient Greek sea god. This name would be easy to pronounce in most European languages, but was almost too neutral to help sell the product. The other alternative was Blue Streak, again, an easy name in English, but not necessarily in other European languages. Sammy felt that the favourable connotation of speed and progress might provide a boost for the products to which it was applied.

(Source: Adapted from Cundiff and Hilger, 1988, pp. 440–2. Reproduced with kind permission.)

Questions

1. Evaluate the alternative names being considered by Sammy Soshi. Which name would you recommend?

2. Whatever new name is chosen, should Soshi Sumsin adopt the same name in the Korean market?

3. What are the advantages of selecting different brand names, as appropriate, in each foreign market?

4. Enumerate the characteristics that should be possessed by a good international brand name.

 A10.3 Case

Derivados de Leche SA

Derivados de Leche SA, founded in 1968, was the first firm to market yoghurt in Mexico. It distributed yoghurt under the brand name Delsa only in Mexico City, primarily in a limited number of upper-income areas. The company was family owned, and the capital was all local. For the first five years, Delsa was sold in food stores, particularly in the newly developing supermarkets, without any advertising or other promotion. Yoghurt was a new, unfamiliar food product in the Mexican market, but Delsa depended primarily on word of mouth to provide product recognition.

In 1973, a number of laws regulating foreign investment in Mexico were modified under a single new 'regulation of foreign investment' law. According to this law foreign investors were welcome in Mexico on a joint labour basis so long as the foreign ownership share did not exceed 49 per cent. Labour-intensive industries that helped to decentralize population were particularly welcome. It was many years before this affected the yoghurt market, but eventually, three multinationals entered on this joint venture basis, changing the structure of the market dramatically.

The first new brand, Chambourcy, was introduced by a joint venture subsidiary of Nestlé which had operated in Mexico since 1935. This company, Industrias Alimentacias Club SA, was a major Mexican food producer with 7,000 employees. Chambourcy was launched with a strong promotional campaign and wide distribution. The following year, in 1989, a subsidiary of the French food firm, BSN-Gervais, launched their Danone yoghurt in the

Mexican market. Danone was also heavily supported with promotion. Finally, in 1991, a third multinational entered the market. Productos de Leche SA was 51 per cent owned by Mexican capital and 49 per cent by the Borden Company of the United States; it entered the Mexican market with two brands of yoghurt, Darel and Bonafina.

By 1997, the management of Derivados de Leche SA was becoming concerned about its future position in the yoghurt market. All three of the multinational competitors were aggressive marketers and promoters and were strong financially. Although the foreign ownership was a minority (49 per cent), management was dominated in each case by the minority ownership, so that management was competent and professional. In the short term, Delsa benefited from the primary demand creation activities of the multinationals. In 1994, Delsa sales almost reached 1600 tons, and by 1997, grew to 3,800 tons. But Delsa's market share had dropped from over 95 per cent in 1988 (there were some other, very small, Mexican owned competitors) to only 21 per cent in 1997.

The three multinationals divided 77.5 per cent of the market among them. If the trend continued, it was feared that Delsa's share of the market might drop so low that it would provide very little product recognition. And it was possible that ultimately sales volume would stabilize and perhaps even decline.

By 1998, Delsa management was faced with the grim reality of competition from financially strong and aggressive, professionally managed multinationals. Delsa managers felt that pricing could not be blamed for this loss in market share; in 1997, the sales price of Delsa was slightly below that of its competitors. A major handicap for Delsa was its failure to promote recognition of its brand name. Although Delsa had been pulled along in the market by the initial marketing efforts which were designed to create a primary demand for yoghurt, the marketing efforts of the competitors were now focused almost entirely on selective brand name promotion. Delsa management had concentrated its efforts on getting the product into retail outlets and maintaining good relationships with dealers; no effort had been made to create consumer recognition and franchises through advertising and other promotion. Management was made up of the family members who owned the company; they brought little professional training to the job.

Owner-managers of small and medium-sized firms in Mexico tended to run their businesses for quick, short-term profit rather than long-term development. New capital investment was needed to enlarge the production capacity, and serious consideration needed to be given to investing in a promotional campaign to build and maintain Delsa brand recognition.

Delsa was considering applying for a government-subsidized loan to double its production capacity from 4,000 tons per year to 8,000 tons. These loans were available only to 100 per cent Mexican-owned manufacturers, but were limited to the financing of manufacturing facilities. Delsa's marketing manager wanted to emphasize the local Mexican ownership of Delsa and to increase the firm's advertising budget from $40,000 to about $200,000. He also wanted to redesign the package so as to include some statement that indicated the brand was of pure Mexican origin. Delsa's owners wanted to put pressure on the Mexican government to limit the food processing industry to 100 per cent Mexican-owned firms. It was not known what the possibilities were of getting such legislation passed.

(Source: Adapted from Cundiff and Hilger, 1988, pp. 335–6. Reproduced with kind permission.)

Questions

1. What are Delsa's strengths and weaknesses in competing with multinationals?

2. What is the impact of 'country of origin' on demand for yoghurt?

3. What recommendations can you make to strengthen Delsa's market position?

The critical role of price in relational exchange

At first sight, price appears to be anything but 'cultural'. In appearance, it is usually a figure, a number or a unit. And so price is often assumed to be an intrinsically objective element of exchange and an issue reserved for rational economic factors. But price has a more subjective element. It is a signal that conveys meaning and as such it is perceived in quite different ways across cultures and across individuals. The subjective and perceptual aspects of price are examined in section 11.1.

Price is an important component of communication between buyers and sellers. It is also an element in short-term or long-term bonding. Price is a decisive element of social interaction between buyer and seller; it is a way of evaluating offerings, it endorses their agreement and shapes their relationship, whether short or long term. In section 11.2 bargaining is examined as a classical, primitive and widespread relationship between buyer and seller, particularly prevalent where there is no compulsory price labelling. In modern mass markets, the primary influence wielded by customers on price usually takes the form of a 'take it or leave it' bargain with quasi-anonymous sellers. This dichotomous attitude (i.e. choice/no choice) is contrary to the purpose of bargaining and relational exchange, where price is supposed to be a 'friendly price', even a 'friend's price'. Each party wants to make a good deal, that is, *human relations are practically inseparable from economic transactions.* Section 11.3 deals with situations where the price is clearly marked and hence known by customers, who are then in a position to appraise the price–quality ratio.

The last three sections of the chapter present company attitudes in international market pricing decisions.

An anthropomorphic approach is used whereby companies and markets are considered as interacting parties to an exchange. Companies are led to distort and manipulate prices between domestic markets, either to increase consumer brand loyalty in certain markets through offensive strategic pricing, or to avoid parallel imports which undermine their local distribution system (see section 11.4). Price can also be used as a tactical weapon *vis-à-vis* competitors in particular national markets (see section 11.5). Finally, price can be manipulated because of an inflationary environment or by over- or under-invoicing in order to close price-sensitive deals (see section 11.6).

This chapter does not consider the strictly economic aspects of price, such as the relationship between price and costs in international marketing or the law of one price, which states that, in the absence of transport, transaction-related costs and price discrimination, trade takes place in only one market and only one market prevails. Nor does it discuss the influence of exchange rate variance on price strategies in international marketing. However, you will find some information on these issues on the website, including an interesting paper by Froot and colleagues analyzing volatility over the last 700 years (see *WS11.1*).

11.1

Price as a signal conveying meaning

Prices may be considered to be fairly objective in most consumer goods and consumer durables markets where goods are sold in mass distribution outlets that

Table 11.1 Price-based signals

Meaning conveyed by price in	by . . .	Section
Buyer–seller interactions	Bargaining rituals, price offers and relationship development	11.2
Consumer behaviour	Differences in consumer price-mindedness across cultures	11.3
Product evaluation	To what extent is quality inferred from price?	11.3
(Tough) competition	Signalling willingness to compete by dumping prices	11.4
Target market(s)	Showing commitment to customers in a target market through attractive pricing	11.4
Distributors (grey markets)	Signalling desire to avoid parallel imports from opportunistic distributors who disturb international price policy and may damage brand image	11.4
(Peaceful) competition	Signalling willingness to enter 'peacefully' in a market with cartels	11.5
Price increase policy	Meaning conveyed by price in high-inflation contexts	11.6
Relationship to suppliers	Overcoming the barriers for the supplier to receive the real price by over- or under-invoicing	11.6

allow price comparison between stores. In that case, the meaning conveyed by the price centres mostly on the value of the good and the money transfer.

Prices become more central to the relationship between buyers and sellers, and to companies and their customers, distributors or competitors in the following conditions:

1. The price is not displayed.
2. It is not necessarily the seller who announces the first price.
3. There is no clear market reference for what would be a 'fair price'.
4. A particular price is understood by both the seller and the buyer as taking place within a series of transactions (i.e. past, present and future).
5. Prices for particular transactions are not necessarily meant to cover even marginal cost.
6. Prices may be distorted by inflation and government price regulation.
7. The total price is a combination of direct and indirect prices (e.g. a product's price plus the price of maintenance, spare parts, updates, etc.).

The seven points above are examples of situations where price is more 'relational' than 'economic'. As shown in Table 11.1, price can convey meaning and be an object of interaction between the various participants of the market situation, that is, manufacturers, distributors, consumers and competitors (see *WS11.1*).

11.2

Bargaining

The limits of price as an element of social relations: Bargaining versus no bargaining

The importance of bargaining is often underestimated because, in many countries, consumers are used to prices that are clearly displayed. If we do not find satisfactory prices, we simply do not buy the product. In most cases, people no longer bargain – or at least, they appear not to. Bargaining is either legally prohibited or strictly controlled in most developed countries. Most sales of consumer products take place within oligopolistic distribution channels offering merchandise from producers also organized in oligopolies. In direct relations with customers, prices are unilaterally set by vendors and are therefore nonnegotiable. Bargaining at the supermarket checkout is rare and liable to expose one to the colourful epithets vented by other customers.

Yet, once the price reaches a substantial level, people return to bargaining because of one of its irreplaceable functions, which is splitting the surplus between buyer and seller. In many markets exchange still takes place through bargaining, either legally or from necessity (e.g. those for consumer durables and equipment for firms and households such as new and second-hand cars, furniture, property and industrial machinery).

In most developing countries bargaining is still the rule, even for items of low value or little vital interest. Weak purchasing power considerably increases the importance of bargaining. In certain African markets (e.g. Mauritania), where sugar is sold by the lump and carrots by the slice, and island economies (e.g. Marshal Islands), where cigarettes are sold by the 'stick', bargaining is essential for survival. Moreover, people may not be pressed for time; the rewards of bargaining in relation to its cost are fundamentally different in developing and industrialized nations. Finally, bargaining has a fun dimension as well as a human one, possibly because of its similarity to role-playing. The human dimension exists because bargaining and commerce generally are contemplated with more seriousness in developing countries than in industrialized ones where commercial intercourse has been largely 'depersonalized', particularly in the case of consumer goods (see *WS11.2*). This is in fact one of the major reasons that bargaining is either legally prohibited or socially restricted in developed countries. As stated by Allen (1971, p. 49):

It has conventionally been supposed that bargaining is socially disadvantageous, on the grounds that it breeds hostility, rivalry and distrust ... While it is true that there is always an element of suspicion as to the real value of the commodity (and subsequently of the price), this suspicion never turns into an open conflict if the bargainers intend to conclude the sale. Any bargainer, whether seller or buyer, is careful not to offend his partner, for fear of putting an end to the transaction. Thus, though initiated by suspicion, bargaining tends rather to eliminate it, instituting instead an atmosphere of common interest and trust, which often leads to a lasting client relationship. In this way it cements community relations, rather than subverts them.

Ritual aspects of bargaining

Brand marketing is, by definition, not conducive to bargaining. Self-service and other non-personalized services do not allow people living in modern societies with advanced distribution systems to experience the rituals involved in bargaining. These rituals pose challenges to the uninitiated. They are independent of, yet complementary to, the price negotiation. People

who bargain more are no less rational – they are rational in a different way.

A Lebanese anthropologist, Khuri (1968, p. 701), described the rituals involved in bargaining in the Middle East by emphasizing that such intercourse always begins with standard signs of respect, affection, common interest and trust. As soon as a potential buyer shows interest in an item and requests information, the seller replies vaguely:

Between us there is no difference; we share the same interest, price is not what pleases me, what pleases me is to find out what pleases you; pay as much as you want; brothers do not disagree on price; for you it is free; it is a gift.

Nothing in the above quote should be taken literally. No potential customer from the same culture would do so. This introductory incantation signals a social bond of mutual interest and trust through metaphorical kinship, likely to create an impression of friendliness and fraternity. The potential customer then insists that a price be indicated. The vendor hesitates and, perhaps, proposes a price after having presented and lauded the merits of his product at great length. Contrary to Western bargaining, potential customers should not pretend to doubt the qualities of the item because that could make them seem ignorant and therefore more vulnerable. The discussion continues with each party holding a price (i.e. maximum for sellers and minimum for customers) below or above which no transaction can take place. The potential buyer suggests a price, but is not necessarily willing to pay it. After an agreement has been reached, the transaction then takes place and the buyer purchases the item for cash. However, the bargaining operation could have been conducted just to seek information on the price. This is one instance where the bargaining activity is partly disconnected from the sales activity.

Bargaining may be disconcerting for people who are used to displayed prices and who, as a result, *do not envisage entering into any sort of pleasant economic intercourse* merely to obtain information. When prices are not displayed it may be embarrassing for potential buyers to ask for them, because doing so may latently signal their difficulties affording the purchase thus exposing their low purchasing power. Roeber (1994, p. 49) explains how asking the price is associated with class perception in the context of Zambia:

Working people, I was told, were 'sufferers'. The meaning of that word was best explained by the man who stated vehemently, 'If you have to ask the price of something, you are automatically a sufferer'... there was another category of people, the *apamwamba* or 'big shots', who did not have to ask for the price of commodities. They always had money to buy what they needed.

The relationship between bargaining and price display is obvious. Wherever the law forces the vendor to display prices clearly, the practice of bargaining will diminish. It is understandable that people who have lost the habit of personalized commercial relations – if indeed they ever had it – may be embarrassed in these situations where affection and economics, and friendship and self-interest, are implicitly communicated, almost simultaneously. The novice bargainer also risks provoking the seller's hostility if the seller gets the impression or wishes to give the impression of being 'taken for a ride' by the buyer. In fact, what remains of bargaining in Western societies is disguised behind 'rational' arguments such as quantity and cash discounts, stock liquidation operations and auctions of discontinued items. Moreover, bargaining could smear the image of the distribution channel as well as that of the goods it sells. Prus (1989, p. 146) quotes certain remarks made by Canadian vendors:

'We're flexible, where if they're getting a larger order and they suggest it, we'll give a little . . . Some customers feel that they have to have a discount to buy it.' (*Sales manageress, luggage.*)

'You can dicker in furniture, appliances, carpeting, something like that, here. But not on the smaller things, like clothing, giftware, shoes.' (*Department store salesman.*)

'Normally I try not to dicker. I am quite firm on the prices. I've found that dickering can be rather awkward. It is awkward for the merchant and the customer. And it is especially awkward if other people are around. If you can stay away from dickering, you can also avoid an image as someone who will go down. I have been known to dicker, but it is something I try to avoid.' (*Women's clothing.*)

Declaring prices

Cavusgil (1990) noted that international pricing is not a topic that lends itself to easy generalization. Export pricing must first address the unique nature of the individual firm or buyer with whom one is dealing. He takes the example of the Middle East where 'Regal Ware, a producer of kitchen appliances and cookware, uses a higher list price in such markets to leave a margin of discretion' (p. 505). (A short guide to doing business and bargaining in the Middle East can be found in *WS11.2*.)

In a culture where bargaining is expected, proposing a price is a tug-of-war exercise. Who will give way, the seller or the customer? Who should be the first to make concessions by virtue of the position of strength that is internalized within the society? At least four items play a major role in answering these questions:

1. The initial power position of each party.
2. The degree of urgency for either the buyer or the seller to close the deal.
3. The importance of the negotiation margin from the start. The initial suggested price must leave room for further discussion. It could be in the vendor's interest to exaggerate the first price in order to leave the customer some room to manoeuvre. For instance when dealing with a buyer whose performance is subject to confirmation by superiors, that buyer is supposed to obtain a discount. The buyer's job is to reduce the price so, ironically, the vendor would be wise to open negotiations with an exaggerated price (see Box 11.1).
4. The type of social process by which buyer and seller progressively adjust their price. In the case of competitive bidding situations based on a tender offer an excessively high price would eliminate that vendor from the short list of pre-selected candidates.

11.3

Price and consumer evaluations

Culture-based appraisal of quality and price

Consumers tend to use price as a proxy or cue for quality, especially when other criteria are absent. Price plays a major subjective role in the assessment of quality (Zeithaml, 1988), when:

1. It is very difficult to measure quality objectively. There is no generally accepted method of measuring the objective quality of a product, and much less so for a service.

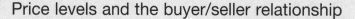

Box 11.1

Price levels and the buyer/seller relationship

Scenario 1

The seller wishes to offer a fair price from the start, close to the final price, expecting it will win the customer's loyalty. This should convince the buyer of the vendor's honesty, openness and genuine desire to do business. If the customer shares these European, American or Australasian values and decides to cooperate, an agreement is quickly reached and each party is satisfied.

Scenario 2

The same vendor suggests the same price, close to the final price, as a sign of goodwill towards the buyer. The buyer who comes from a different culture (such as India or Pakistan) is embarrassed: his boss expects him to obtain the greatest pos-

sible discount from the seller. His role centres on the price rebate rather than on the price level. The announced price, close to the final price, leaves buyer and seller with little satisfactory negotiating room, therefore no deal is made.

Scenario 3

The vendor announces a much higher initial price, leaving room for negotiation from the start. This allows the buyer to demonstrate skill in a mutually beneficial bargaining exercise and enables both parties to increase the long-term value of their social relationship. The final agreed price is very close to that in Scenario 1. With the buyer interested mostly in the rebate and the seller in the price level, both can achieve greater satisfaction than in Scenario 1.

---

2. The perceived quality of a product is even more difficult to measure than quality itself. The concept of quality is subjective but not irrational, in that it is based on an evaluation of both intrinsic product attributes such as taste or physical characteristics, and extrinsic product attributes such as advertising, the brand, and price.
3. Perceived quality combines with other evaluation criteria (e.g. perceived monetary and non monetary prices) to form a perceived value that shapes and determines the consumer's decision to buy or not.

Price perceptions include both monetary and non-monetary aspects. Perceived monetary price means that consumers may not recall the exact price, but may have framed in their minds a simplified, general impression (i.e. 'it is expensive' or 'it is not so expensive after all') in comparison to a reference price range. This price impression needs to be sufficiently close to consumer expectations if they are to buy (Jacoby and Olson, 1977). Maxwell (2001) found support for this in India and the United States. In both countries the perceived acceptability of price influenced the probability of purchase by increasing the perceived value of the jeans.

Consumers' perceptions of a non-monetary price may be better understood in terms of Becker's (1965) conclusion that the objective price is not the only *sacrifice* accepted by consumers when purchasing a product. Other *sacrifices*, such as the time spent shopping or cooking are often included in the perceived price. Maxwell (2001) also measured the acceptability of other costs, including discussing the purchase with friends and travelling on buses for long periods of time. Interestingly, these other costs were less acceptable to Indians than Americans.

Consumers do not build these subjective evaluations of quality and monetary and non-monetary price through irrational individual idiosyncrasies but through unconscious submission, in their everyday lives, to social representations dictated by their cultural upbringing. For instance, Erevelles *et al.* (1999, p. 67) examined the influence of price on perceived risk as part of a larger study with students from Hong Kong and the United States. They found that price perceptions had more influence on risk perceptions in the United States in relation to a car purchase. Becker's model is firmly rooted in American society and culture. Therefore, some elements are not cross-culturally equivalent; what is a costly 'sacrifice' in one country may be true enjoyment in another. To cite a few examples of common aphorisms (note: the reverse of each is also defensible):

1. 'It is important to measure time, time is money' (see section 2.2): therefore, perceived non-monetary price will be higher in general for economic-time minded consumers.
2. 'Home-made food is the best': this maxim could, for instance, influence the perceived quality of frozen foods even though there is no reason why their objective qualities (e.g. taste and nutritional value) should not be better.
3. 'Where there is pleasure, time doesn't count' (French proverb).

Certain representations directly influence the perceived non-monetary price of a product, particularly the desirability/non-desirability or the convenience/inconvenience of an element of the perceived non-monetary price. Put simply, the price of a nail is not easily separable from the non-monetary price involved in driving it in, including the risk of hitting one's finger in the process. Non-monetary price reflects costs related to time spent, the search itself, psychological risk, etc. These costs shape the consumer's perception of the sacrifice involved in the consumption experience in exchange for the satisfaction to be derived from it.

Non-monetary price varies a great deal across cultures. A trip to buy a product or the preparation of meals may be perceived as enjoyable in certain cultures and reflects no perception of sacrifice or non-monetary price awareness. However, the same task may be perceived as being tedious in other cultures. Ackerman and Tellis (2001) argue Chinese consumers place more importance on the monetary sacrifice and less on the time sacrifice than US consumers, due to the Chinese social norm of frugality and sophistication in money. It is also likely that time is more important than money to many US consumers, especially for small purchases like grocery items. Similarly, the rapid expansion of the 'do-it-yourself' market in France, in comparison to other neighbouring countries, is related to a marked preference for doing small jobs oneself instead of requesting the services of a professional. This preference can be traced to a social representation in a high power distance society where being served is negatively valued: the French concept of *égalité* tends to associate service with servitude and humiliation. The French fiscal system has long corroborated this by offering tax rebates to people engaging in 'do-it-yourself', while restricting the opportunity of hiring domestics to the very upper classes.

Relationships between objective quality and price, and choice strategies

One might expect in a competitive market that price and quality strongly correlate. However, many empirical studies show that the actual relationship between price and objective quality is fairly low, probably because consumers are imperfectly informed about the price and quality of competing products (for a review, see Fauld *et al.*, 1994). Quality is often revealed through product use, that is, through post-purchase rather than pre-purchase information cues. Objective quality is based on characteristics that can be measured by consumer tests like those carried out by *Consumer Reports* magazine such as durability, performance and safety features (see *WS11.3* for information on price comparison sites and consumer associations). Measures of the price–quality relation are based on correlations between quality evaluations, carried out by consumer magazines, and the price of the product.

In the United States, Oxenfeldt (1950), in the earliest study on the topic, ranked 35 products from best to worst based on two dimensions (price and quality) in comparative product tests in *Consumer Reports* between 1939 and 1949. Price and quality were rather weakly related with a rank correlation of 0.25. Sproles (1977) found a positive correlation for 51 per cent of the 135 products retained in the study. In other words, high price was not necessarily related to high quality. However, for 35 per cent of the products he found no correlation and for 14 per cent a higher price was related to low quality. Similarly, Riesz (1978) found a positive rank correlation of 0.26 between price and objective quality among 685 categories of product. Curry and Riesz (1988) studied price quality over the product life cycle for 62 durable products; their findings indicate that when both low-quality/high-price and high-quality/low-price brands were introduced early in the product life cycle, the inconsistent relationship between price and quality tended to stabilize over time.

The same conclusion has been reached cross-nationally: in Japan, the mean price–quality relationship reached −0.06 (Yamada and Ackerman, 1984) and −0.18 in the automobile industry (Johansson and Erickson, 1985). In the case of consumer durables, Fauld *et al.* (1994), comparing Australia, Canada, New Zealand, the United Kingdom and the United States, find slightly positive price–quality correlations across the five countries, ranging from 0.18 to 0.35. All this confirms that there exists cross-nationally a positive but weak correlation between objective price and objective quality.

More concretely, it is not possible for consumers to assess whether a German *Miele* washing machine, which is three times more expensive than a machine branded by *Zanussi* – Italian arm of the Swedish *Electrolux* group – lasts three times longer before they purchase one. In fact, Lilien and Yoon (1989) found that, for personal computers, performance only explained 30–40 per cent of the deviation in price. At issue is how consumers perceive quality and how they use price to infer quality. In the case of consumer durables and specifically consumer electronics, Dawar and Parker (1994) have shown that price is a universal signal for quality. The formation of beliefs about price and quality may seem to be similar across nations and culture. Veeck and Burns (1995) found that for urban Chinese, the price–quality relationship is stronger for durables than for non-durables, and inexperienced consumers tend to infer more quality from price than experienced ones. Yucelt and Firoz (1993) showed that in Turkey, price is considered a good or fair indicator of quality for 75 per cent of the consumers they surveyed – a high price is relied upon as an indication of higher quality. Moore *et al.* (2003) found that Polish consumers perceived price in a similar manner to US consumers. The only difference was in the perception of the sale concept, which is not well developed in Poland.

When the consumption experience is immediate, as it often is for non-durable consumer goods, quality can be assessed instantly and the price may not be a salient cue for inferring quality. This is particularly true when price differentials for non-durables are small. Sjolander (1992), for instance, showed that when evaluating the quality of the same ice-cream, Polish and Swedish consumers do not differ in their evaluations. That is, whether high, medium or low priced, consumers rated the ice-cream quality at the same level.

Consumers therefore appear to have difficulty establishing a clear price–quality relationship, especially when quality is revealed by the post-purchase experience and takes place over a long period of time. Furthermore, in order to form their perceptual evaluation of total price – monetary as well as non-monetary – consumers need a better understanding of the costs involved in using the product (Zeithaml, 1988). Often, in the absence of information based on actual product use, they are forced to resort to simplified formulae to guide their choice. The results of an experiment by Schindler and Kibarian (2001) illustrate a simplified influence of price by varying the price endings (using 99 or 00) in a controlled advertising experiment. They found that consumers were more likely to perceive the price as relatively low if it had a 99-ending versus 00-ending. In addition, the 99-ending also had a negative effect on perceptions of quality.

Tellis and Gaeth (1990) depict three basic choice strategies when the consumer has a better knowledge of price than of quality. In the first strategy, *best value*, people use a rational standpoint to choose the brand with the least overall cost in terms of price and expected quality to maximize the utility that will be derived. In the second strategy, *price seeking*, price is used as a proxy for the unknown quality, leading the consumer to choose the highest-price brand (i.e. the consumer makes an attribution of quality from the price). In the third strategy, *price aversion*, people choose the lowest-price brand in order to minimize immediate costs (i.e. they are risk averse). The salience of these three models depends on the consumer's situation, that is, the amount of information they have, their capacity to establish price–quality relations, and their experiences. These relations and strategies were observed in the United States, but we would expect different attitudes in making a strategic choice, according to the consumer's national culture.

Cultural dimensions of price–quality evaluation and consumer choice strategies

McGowan and Sternquist (1998) suggest that some dimensions of price are fairly universal. They surveyed US and Japanese university students, finding that price–quality relationships, prestige sensitivity, and value-consciousness are similar across the two samples. They explained that:

'The Japanese trade press has maintained that domestic consumers only consider price as a proxy for quality. That is, high price is a cue for high quality. Until the recent recession, however, Japanese consumers did not have many price options. The economic downturn has brought price competition to Japan, and the most profitable retailers in 1997 were discounters.'

That consumers are rational and attempt to evaluate, as objectively as they can, price–quality relations is a generally accepted idea. Yet, this idea of the best price–quality relationship is depicted in various ways, for example, by minimum levels of quality and maximum levels of price, below or above which consumers will eliminate a product from the set of products they will consider.

1. *Northern European consumers*: one may be surprised at the price levels in northern European shops but also by the robustness and durability of products. A possible explanation is that these countries are primarily Lutheran, a religion favouring a lifestyle imbued with a certain austerity in terms of material well-being. On the one hand, goods should be expensive in order to limit their consumption (see Box 11.2). On the other hand, people prefer lasting goods in line with an austere, thrifty and utilitarian outlook on life. For instance to furnish homes, they prefer sturdy, long-lasting furniture. This means looking for the best price–quality relation where the minimal level of quality is relatively high, thus eliminating a range of possibilities even where the price is low enough to enhance the price–quality relationship. IKEA's strategy corresponds to this type of choice (see the case study A5.2 at the end of Chapter 5).

2. *Southern European consumers*: purchasing power in southern Europe is somewhat lower than the north European average. People stay outdoors more because the climate is warmer. Social life often takes place outdoors and is materially much less austere, hence the more pronounced taste for seasonal fashions and for appearance and show. In addition, the Catholic doctrine is rather ambiguous about money, and has little to say about the price–quality ratio. Moreover, the Catholic Church has never been preoccupied, either explicitly or implicitly, with the price and quality of material possessions. The Catholic religion is not a 'lover of money' and could be said to therefore implicitly support spending. Like all idealistic systems with a worldly dimension, the Catholic doctrine manages to sustain the paradox of being anti-money but not anti-expenditure. This is the complete opposite of the Protestant paradox of thrift that considers expenditure as a catalyst for poor morality but still favours the accumulation of wealth. The

---

Box 11.2

The Puritan paradox

I fear, wherever riches have increased, the essence of religion has decreased in the same proportion. Therefore I do not see how it is possible, in the nature of things, for any revival of true religion to continue long. For religion must necessarily produce both industry and frugality, and these cannot but produce riches. But as riches increase, so will pride, anger, and love of the world in all its branches. How then is it possible that Methodism, that is, a religion of the heart, though it flourishes now as a green bay tree, should continue in this state? For the Methodists in every place grow diligent and frugal; consequently they increase in goods. Hence they proportionately increase in pride, in anger, in the desire of the flesh, the desire of the eyes, and the pride of life. So, although the form of religion remains, the spirit is swiftly vanishing away. Is there no way to prevent this – this continual decay of pure religion? *We ought not to prevent people from being diligent and frugal; we must exhort all Christians to gain all they can, and to save all they can; that is, in effect, to grow rich.*

(Source: Speech by Methodist minister John Wesley at the end of the eighteenth century, a few years before the Industrial Revolution in Britain. Quoted by Weber, 1958, last sentence italicized by Weber.)

difference exists in where the shame lies: for the Catholic, spending is not really shameful, but money is, and the religion rejects money while accepting its pleasures. For the Protestant, excessive or conspicuous spending is shameful.

Max Weber (1958, p. 31) emphasized the relative beneficence of the Catholic Church, 'punishing the heretic, but being lenient with the sinner', in contrast to the Reform Church, which imposes stricter rules and regulations. The Catholic influence lacks the austerity and rigour of Protestantism. In a way, it accords free will to material choice, as in the famous quotation from the Bible, 'Render unto Caesar the things that are Caesar's' [Mathew 22:15]. Consequently, the Latin (Catholic) consumer is more diverse, particularly in relation to displaying social class. In Latin society, social classes are more distinct and buying has the function of reinforcing one's social image. Given that there are marked differences in buying power, one would expect diversified choice strategies among consumers – for example:

1. Snobbish consumers who, by definition, buy the most expensive foods (i.e. the Veblen effect of preferring high prices).
2. Consumers who are more concerned about price and who would automatically buy the least expensive items (i.e. price-averse consumers).
3. Consumers who use price–quality relations, in line with the Latin temperament that includes a propensity for intellectual logic and rationality.

11.4

International price tactics

Price manipulation

Vendors may use pricing to serve three interrelated objectives: (1) profits, (2) sales, and (3) market interactions. While profits and sales objectives are clear, marketing interactions are also profit objectives as their focus is on relations with other market actors (i.e. customers, distributors, competitors, regulatory authorities) in order, ultimately, to make a profit. Table 11.2 identifies 11 pricing objectives under these three categories.

Price is a tactical tool in local markets and a strategic tool in face of global competition. Price tactics in domestic markets must take their place within a global strategy of cost domination based on the search for economies of scale and experience effects (see Chapter 8) or differentiation, which is obtained by designing a product offering that has been differentiated from competitors or tailored to local markets (see Chapter 9).

Keegan (1984) described three possible positions for international strategic pricing:

1. *The extension/ethnocentric position*: a single global price based on the factory price of the goods, the customer being charged for insurance, freight and customs costs.

Table 11.2 Pricing objectives

	Objectives		
Profit	(1)	Maximize company profits	
	(2)	Reach target profits	
Sales	(3)	Increasing unit volume	
	(4)	Attain sales figures	
	(5)	Increase cash flows	
Interaction	(6)	Develop new markets	
	(7)	Maintain customer loyalty	
	(8)	Achieve greater market stability	
	(9)	Attain price parity with competitors	
	(10)	Eliminate competitors	
	(11)	Promote the image of the company and/or its products and/or brands	

2. *The polycentric adaptation position*: local subsidiaries fix their own prices according to local market conditions.

3. *The intermediate geocentric inventive position*: the subsidiary takes into account local competition and seeks to maximize the firm's total income through international coordination of tactical pricing.

These positions can be related somewhat simplistically to Stöttinger's (2001) results. Stöttinger interviewed 45 seasoned European international business managers to assess 'best practices', finding that all but three firms set international prices centrally, in line with an extension/ethnocentric position. The others decentralized pricing decisions for different reasons. Stöttinger explained that one company holds different strategic positions in their domestic and international markets: 'domestically the firm is known as a low-price, mass market manufacturer, internationally it is positioned in the premium segment' (p. 49), in line with the intermediate geocentric inventive position. The other two companies are mainly active in Eastern Europe, 'as respondents put it – in-depth knowledge of the market situation and the customer's financial conditions govern the pricing policy' (p. 50), in line with a polycentric adaptation position.

Price can be used against competitors. Prices can be manipulated and distorted between markets as long as customer or distributor disputes can be avoided. In fact, consumers cannot always arbitrate, because of transaction costs, complexities of international trade operations for private people, customs regulations and technical standards. However, agents are often tempted to arbitrate for consumers. Agents can reduce the transaction costs and rapidly gain experience in such practice. For example, certain agents may specialize in re-importing products sold at lower prices in a neighbouring market.

Suppliers face many difficulties in pricing goods and services. For instance, large international customers are placing increasing pressure on suppliers to offer them a global-pricing contract to reduce inefficiencies in obtaining prices in multiple locations (Naryandas *et al.*, 2000). This poses many problems for suppliers, who may have difficulty in passing on their full costs, especially when parts or services are also transferred among divisions that may be located in different countries. Stevenson and Cabell (2002)

suggest a two-staged approach that first identifies the cost-drivers that cause costs to increase or decrease and then allocates costs to products, or regions, by the drivers. 'For example, in marketing a cost driver would be the number of shipments made to a particular region, number of orders entered, or sales calls made in a region; these drivers are used to allocate costs' (p. 81). After all of the costs are accumulated, they can then be allocated to products and regions.

Signalling willingness to compete: Domestic markets, export markets and dumping

Who gets the lowest prices? This question requires consideration when a company operates in different national markets, where the opportunity exists to increase profits through price discrimination. It naturally presupposes that buyers or distributors do not have the possibility of arbitrage. That is, buying where cheapest, either for consumption or for resale at a higher price in another national market. Other reasons for price discrimination across national markets may be found among the 11 pricing objectives in Table 11.2.

A basic international pricing issue is price discrimination between domestic and foreign markets, which depends on the positions of the respective markets on the company's cost curve. For a firm to maximize its profit, it must sell its products at a price greater than or equal to the marginal cost (i.e. the addition to the total cost of producing one extra unit). In practice, people refer to the cost price based on total costs. However, in industries where overheads are high – such as aerospace, chemicals and steel – direct costing (i.e. variable costs directly related to production) may be used.

When a completely new aircraft is launched with initial fixed expenses of US$5 billion, or a new car with overhead costs of US$1 billion, is the domestic market or the export market supposed to 'pay' for the depreciation of these sunk costs? This is a very important question and calls for a number of subjective considerations. Should the domestic market or other exclusive markets pay for its loyalty or, on the contrary, should it benefit from price cuts as compensation and encouragement for loyalty? If potential car purchasers in Britain were aware of the surcharge

Figure 11.1 Dumping and the relationship between unit costs and cumulated production

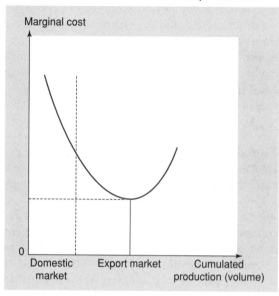

they pay, about 20 per cent higher than the European average, perhaps they would show less loyalty to their national carmakers.

Figure 11.1 addresses the problem of where to situate the domestic and export markets respectively on the horizontal axis of the cost curve. Because sales, whether domestic or export, usually take place simultaneously, the problem is one of subjective (but stable) conceptualization of the bases of the cost curve, as it corresponds to exported quantities. It is this concept that leads directly to the practice of dumping. Article VI of the General Agreement on Tariffs and Trade (GATT) prohibits dumping where it prejudices the production of one of the contracting parties (see WS11.4). It allows certain countries to impose anti-dumping taxes on dumping prices. The United States has regularly exercised this clause, especially on European and Japanese steel exports. Dumping is based on the following assumptions:

1. One role of the domestic market or other exclusive markets is to recover sunk costs. These markets should therefore be situated on the ascending part of the cost curve in relation to the x-axis signifying quantity.
2. In placing the home market in this zone, the remaining zone where marginal costs decrease

would be reserved for foreign markets where competition is supposed to be more open or where prices that are more attractive are offered. It should, however, be remembered that the company's home market is its competitors' foreign market.
3. Dumping assumes that foreign markets are like rubbish bins. This is true except in the situation where the aim is to assume the role of a predator, momentarily flooding the market with the intention of raising prices after a sizeable market share has been secured.

Showing commitment in a target market: Gaining market share through pricing

Slashing prices in the short term may appear to be an attractive strategy for obtaining new clients, building customer loyalty, and increasing market share. This could even result in the consumer being trapped if prices are subsequently raised and if competitors, who have lost market share, are not prepared to engage in a price war to regain their previous share. Competitors will therefore often accept the new status quo and products will be priced high.

Slashing prices is a price tactic when viewed from the perspective of a single market. Across markets, however, it is the implementation of a global strategy. The Japanese are unsurpassed in the art of initially penetrating a market through price rebates in order to obtain a sizeable share in it. Johansson and Nonaka (1990, p. 592) described the pricing strategies of Japanese firms as follows:

The general theme was one of seeing the entry into a market as a long-term 'investment' and market penetration was accordingly a much more important pricing objective than quick profit taking with a skimming approach. Several of the firms employed a version of the 'experience curve pricing strategy' where a relatively low price was expected to lead to large volume and future cost savings. It became rather clear that individual markets were not seen as 'profit centres' but rather as pieces in one large global puzzle. By generating sufficient funds at home and in selected country markets where the share positions were strong, the lower returns emanating from a low price penetration strategy in newer markets could be sustained over a relatively long period.

Thus, in many African countries, Japanese car manufacturers entered the European-dominated market about 30 years ago offering relatively cheap, reliable, air-conditioned cars. Because their objective was not to eliminate competitors, the Japanese left room for European cars after having acquired the lion's share of the market, which they did by raising prices. The benefits of this strategy were threefold: they calmed hard-pressed rivals, raised their profit margins, and finally avoided the risk that their relatively low pricing would lead to a lasting unfavourable image of their products.

Avoiding parallel imports: Combating grey markets and opportunistic distributors

A grey market occurs when 'an exporter knowingly or unknowing sells to an unauthorized agent who competes directly with the sole agent appointed by the exporter within the same territory' (Palia and Keown, 1991, p. 47). Grey markets are based on parallel imports that hamper the effectiveness of marketing strategies in certain national markets. For instance, if a company sells at a discount to a Central American distributor because local consumers cannot afford European or US price levels, goods risk being shipped back from Central America to the United States and sold there through unofficial channels (Weigand, 1991). For more information, see WS11.4, which examines grey markets in terms of American music CDs exported to China (Gough, 2003).

Fragmented national markets are geographically proximate in regions including Europe, West Africa, Latin America, and South-East Asia. Once different price levels are set in neighbouring countries, consumers and some distributors seek cheaper supplies across the border, making the manufacturer compete with its own products. If the price differential is large enough to offset transaction costs, unauthorized intermediaries may compete with sole agents or exclusive dealers in national markets where a specific marketing strategy has been defined (see case A11.2). They therefore benefit from brand advertising and marketing strategies carried out by the company and its regular dealers, without having to contribute to cover these costs and are thus able to cut their own prices and margins (Tan et al., 1997).

Interestingly, Myers (1999) found that the number of markets served and monetary issues such as the form of currency and inflation rate fluctuations did not have impact grey market activity. They did, however, find that internal and external control issues such as distribution control and integration of channels, centralization of decision making and product standardization (i.e. a lack of interesting adaptations) were all related to lower grey market activity. After reviewing the legal controls for grey marketing, Clarke and Owens (2000, p. 285) suggest that: 'Marketers may be best served by minimizing the conditions which create gray markets or looking for nonlegal response alternatives.'

Many companies that manufacture home appliances and consumer durables struggle to control the ultimate destinations of their products. For instance, Belgian, Dutch and French agents in cities close to the German border sometimes buy from German wholesalers instead of their domestic distributor, who may sell at a higher price. When price policies implement country-specific prices, they should consider all the opportunities that may exist for consumer and/or distributor arbitrage. As Weigand (1991, p. 53) emphasized, consumer arbitrage is often effected through holiday travelling, for instance, 'An English tourist taking a holiday in Miami bought a place setting of bone china made in Britain. She didn't pay Britain's substantial value added tax. Further the dollar was cheaper that day.' Weigand also noted that British manufacturers recognize that these personal imports affect their domestic sales. However, they have not found a way to stop them.

The same problem applies to products whose novelty is their major selling point. For example, a new DVD movie may be released in the United States prior to its European release, therefore creating a potential grey market in Europe. In such cases, this will be difficult to avoid because a segment of European movie buffs will know when the DVD becomes available and will happily pay a premium to be among the first to own it. Opportunists who organize the parallel market pocket the inflated profit margin. To combat this, distributors place region specific code restrictions on DVDs, although this has been only marginally successful due to the introduction of multi-region DVD players. Similarly, in China censors restrict the import of foreign music. In 2001 censors only approved about 700 titles (Gough, 2003). This increased the opportunity for grey markets. Gough (2003) suggests that more than 90 per cent of CDs sold on mainland China may be illegal copies. They contend that the music industry is partly responsible as most of the CDs are not pirated but resold old stock that did not sell in the United States. While several companies, including Warner and Atlantic, now destroy all unsold albums in-house, the difficulties with piracy remain.

Piracy is extremely difficult to combat worldwide (Green and Smith 2002). Brand counterfeiting of consumer goods not only costs the brand owners monetary sales, but also has the effect of eroding the brand's value as the counterfeit products are of inferior quality (Green and Smith, 2002). Claims by the global software and music industry indicate that up to US$14 billion was lost due to piracy in 2001 (Van Wijk, 2002). While the costs of lost sales are obviously massive, the industry has yet to find a cost-effective way of restricting digital duplication of their intellectual property. Most attempts at copy-protecting music CDs have been either circumvented by consumers or caused consumer backlash due to incompatibility with audio systems (Van Wijk, 2002).

The objective of monitoring product price positioning across markets is a difficult issue. In some countries, agents may be forced to sell at prices lawfully dictated by producers. In others, however, legislators may consider such practices contrary to effective competition. Resale price maintenance laws prohibit the imposition of prices by the producer on an agent, even though this may be required by marketing strategy. Firms then manoeuvre around these laws through recommended retail price labelling, thus controlling agents' discretionary margin. Even so, the agent could still sell the product at an offer price (e.g. to promote the agent's store) and conflict with the producer's pricing strategy.

Exclusive distribution agreements in home markets would appear to be a plausible solution to the problems of the grey market. But the implementation of such clauses of exclusivity is somewhat difficult. In the United States, there is some reluctance to limit competition by granting enforceable exclusivity rights to dealers. Parallel importers, competing with authorized dealers in leading brands, like Cartier and Seiko, were accorded an almost complete victory by the K-Mart ruling handed down by the US Supreme Court (Kmart Corp. v. Cartier, Inc., 486 U.S. 281 [1988]). However, in 1998 the Supreme Court clarified its opinion in the L'Anza case, where it ruled that after the first legal sale, the copyrights owner no longer has the right to control distribution, which means they cannot prevent unauthorized importation

of products bearing their brand name (Clarke and Owens, 2000).

European Union legislation also restricts exclusive distribution agreements. EU competition rules (e.g. Article 85 of the Treaty of Rome) prohibit any kind of market-sharing agreement by which a company could limit the sales of its distributors exclusively to a domestic market. In order to increase competition across EU countries, Article 85 and several jurisdictional decisions of the European Court of Justice have legitimized parallel imports. A company cannot prevent its 'exclusive' German distributor from selling to Italian customers, even if the company has also appointed an 'exclusive' distributor in Italy. Because it is difficult to prevent distributors from seeking arbitrage opportunities, grey markets have developed in Europe and other areas, seeking to overcome the many non-tariff barriers whenever price differentials offset the costs of parallel importing. Chaudhry and Walsh (1995) reviewed the price and legal environments of the pharmaceutical industry in the EU, concluding that the European Court of Justice 'will continue to use Article 30 and the Exhaustion of Rights Doctrine to support the gray market' (p. 18). In general, we expect that grey marketers will be able to continue to obtain their licenses.

Possible solutions to the problems of grey markets, that is, solutions that may counter parallel imports, are as follows (see *WS11.4* for more information):

1. *Reduce the price differentials between markets*: lower the price in a national market where it is too high and/or inflate it where it is too low, in order to offset enough of the price differential, so that there is no longer any profit in parallel importing. This, however, may be at the expense of the global coherence of the marketing strategy in either one or both countries. Authorized dealers, provided that they have a cost advantage, could be encouraged to engage in a price war with parallel importers in order to drive them out of the market (Tan *et al.*, 1997). Similarly, authorized dealers could scale down their promotional expenses in order to regain advantage over the grey dealers.

2. *Materially alter the product*: the official product should be favourably differentiated against the parallel imported product. If changes are only superficial, importers and consumers will not be fooled. If changes are more significant, economies

of scale are lost. Other possibilities entail changing minor product attributes: extended warranties can be granted only to authorized dealers, so that parallel importers will offer products with little or no after-sales service and guarantee (Tan *et al.*, 1997). A label 'not for export' or 'for domestic sale only' may be attached to the packaging (which also clearly identifies the national origin). This may prevent some dealers from re-exporting, but the effectiveness of these labels is very limited, since in most countries it is not legal for a manufacturer to prohibit the export sales of its own products.

3. *Educate the dealer* (Cavusgil and Sikora, 1988): weaker dealers may be prime targets for grey markets attacks and may, at first, react with an outburst of anger, because it may seem to them that the manufacturer is making excess profit at their expense. Explaining why such price differences exist is part of the manufacturer's role although the dealer may not consider such explanations to be credible.

4. *Terminate the dealer agreements* (or threaten to do so) when the dealer buys from unauthorized parallel sources. Weigand (1991) cites the case of Apple, which prints the following statement: 'Any Apple dealer or VAR (Value Added Retailer) found to be in violation of the mail-order or transhipping prohibitions will be stripped of its authorized status.'

5. *Buy back the grey market goods*: this is positively perceived by authorized dealers, who feel actively protected by the brand owner. Generally, this solution is possible only when a permanent solution to parallel imports has been found and is quickly implemented after a short – and costly – period of buy-back.

6. *Sell products under a different name*, leaving the foreign distributors to promote the products, or develop a unique trademark in each country (Clarke and Owens, 2000). The danger here is loss of benefits from a global trademark.

7. *Target different consumer segments*, determined on the basis of degree of risk aversion (Tan *et al.*, 1997).

Finally, it is important to emphasize the risk that consumer perceptions of product positioning may be adversely affected by discrepancies in price for the same good across markets. Ibison (2001, p. 13) described the problem for Daimler Chrysler in Japan:

There was surprise at Daimler Chrysler Japan when executives saw a television advertisement promoting a model they were not due to launch in Japan for another four months. The advertisement – for the C-class Mercedes – was not part of the German/US auto group's planned marketing strategy. Nor were the prices, which were 30 per cent cheaper than they were planning to charge. In fact, the commercials, the press conference and the news stories were all generated by a savvy Japanese car dealer who had latched on to one of last year's most tempting arbitrage opportunities: the weak euro. The dealer had travelled to Europe, where C-classes had already been launched, bought 20 from a dealer in Germany, shipped them back to Japan and put them on his forecourt.

Not only has the perception of the reference price and positioning for Mercedes changed, but there will be real difficulties if there is a product recall, as there will be no way to trace the purchasers. In addition, it is estimated that it reduced the potential sales by up to 12 per cent, decreasing profitability and potentially the services that can be offered.

For informed consumers – currently a rather rare species – buying in the home market is no longer attractive when they become aware that home-market prices are artificially inflated. Despite the ubiquitous Internet, average consumers tend to be ignorant of international price differentials, and even when informed, they resign themselves to the tariff and non-tariff barriers that 'imprison' customers in their home market. This situation is changing rapidly however as regional integration speeds up in South America, Europe and South-East Asia. Consumers are slowly becoming aware of the price levels for similar goods and services in neighbouring countries. They are also being offered increased opportunities for buying abroad, with no customs duties or clearance formalities.

Pricing and the Internet

Forrester Research predicts that global e-commerce will reach US$6.8 trillion in 2004, including nearly $3.5 trillion in North America (Forrester Research, 2000). The industries that have taken the most advantage of this new economy include financial services, retailing and the news industry; in addition, health care and pharmaceuticals, automobile manufacturers, energy suppliers and distributors, and agriculture and food are all emerging industries that are at early stages of e-commerce development (Penbera, 1999).

Undoubtedly the Internet offers consumers easier access to comparative information. But, Baker *et al.* (2001) report that the vast majority of online consumers purchase from the first site they visit, including 89 per cent for books, 84 per cent for toys, 81 per cent for music and 76 per cent for electronics. They also report that price is not the main consideration for business buyers, as only 30 per cent of business buyers reported lower prices as the key benefit of online purchasing. Other key factors they list include lower transaction search costs and automating information to track inventory and make better decisions.

The Internet is slowly becoming a necessity, rather than an advantage for firms. According to Porter (2001, p. 78): 'The more robust competitive advantages will arise instead from traditional strengths such as unique products, proprietary content, distinctive physical activities, superior product knowledge, and strong personal service and relationships.' Similarly, Ancarani (2002) cautions firms to avoid the 'commodity trap' by taking advantage of the increased information and advances in technology rather than being pressed by the potential power of consumers. These factors will allow firms to better differentiate their products. For instance, the increased ability to track and profile online customers presents the opportunity for firms to refine market segmentation, and use 'price discrimination, dynamic and smart pricing, product and price versioning, price bundling and unbundling' (Ancarani, 2002, p. 680).

11.5

Market situations, competition and price agreements

Ideal versus actual competition

The status of price in the exchange process may be viewed in different ways: (1) as an objective equilibrium point of a contract between two parties, or (2) as the instrument of a social relationship, a subjective equilibrium resulting from the interaction between buyer and seller. In classical economic terms, the social exchange relationship disappears behind Adam Smith's 'invisible hand' of the market. However, it is debatable whether human nature tends more to alliance or competition; both are aspects of human

nature. The invisible hand assumes that the nature of competitors is to battle each other fiercely; however, human nature may well tend, at least sometimes, more towards agreement to divide territory between companies and sign pacts, albeit of limited duration.

On the worldwide market for household care products five main firms compete strongly against each other: Procter & Gamble, Colgate-Palmolive, Unilever, Henkel and the Kao Corporation of Japan. They are competing head-to-head for market share on some segments, brands and national markets, whereas in other areas and for other brands armistices have been implicitly signed. Competition patterns should therefore be surveyed case-by-case. A complex reality hides behind the normative position 'it is essential to be competitive'. To varying degrees, competition and alliances between companies will always occur (see *WS11.5* on US antitrust and competition policy). Even more complex is the code that constrains newcomers to the competitive scene (e.g. a national market), determining how they should behave towards already established players. Large newcomers frequently face a combined attack from all the firms, whether domestic or foreign, already present in a national market. The current incumbents may, for instance, lower their prices or spread rumours about the newcomer's product/service policies and long-term commitment to local customers. This results in poor competition, which may be detrimental to customers. An example of such hidden agreements existed in the French fire safety market, where a norm stricter than the European standard (EN 54) barred outsiders from entering the market. As a result, prices for fire detectors in France are double those in Britain. For all these reasons, the customization of marketing strategies must be carried out according to *actual* rather than *ideal* competition patterns.

Market situations and competition-avoidance patterns

Competition is not necessarily self-perpetuating. The dynamics of competition may lead to the concentration of supply amongst a limited number of companies and therefore to an actual decrease in the sum total of competing forces. For instance the trend toward concentration has been seen throughout western Europe, with the combined market share exceeding 50 per cent for the top three in grocery retailing (Aalto-Setälä, 2002). Aalto-Setälä found that, in Finland, a high market share locally and an increasing number of industry-wide stores were associated with higher mark-ups.

The United States, which is the archetype of enacted liberalism, has been much more realistic in this regard than other countries because it introduced effective institutions at an early stage (e.g. see WS11.5 for details of US anti-trust legislation and the Sherman Act) to oversee the proper functioning of competition, to discourage dominant positions and the establishment of monopolies through mergers and acquisitions. However, as Cateora emphasized, perhaps with some exaggeration (1983, p. 128): 'Except in the United States, 20th century orientation toward competition has been to avoid it whenever possible.'

Conversely, DeMarco (2001) argues that while monopolies should be monitored for exclusivities and discrimination including prices and supplies, we have insufficient evidence to condemn them. Prior to the Second World War, one of the large German cartels, Interessen Gemeinschaft Farben, brought together three major chemical companies, Bayer, BASF and Hoechst, which now operates under the Aventis logo. All three are now at the forefront of the world chemical industry. Japanese *zaibatsus*, such as Mitsui and Company, Mitsubishi Group and Sumitomo Group have existed for centuries. Typically, one extended family controls groups of companies that may encompass businesses as diverse as banking, car production, trading and shipbuilding. The Americans prohibited *zaibatsus* after their victory over the Japanese in 1945, which simply caused them to evolve into today's *keiretsus* (WS12.1).

Competition between companies in Japan is often savage. Abegglen and Stalk (1986) demonstrated this using the motorcycle industry as a case-in-point. Honda was far behind Tohatsu in the 1950s but completely overtook them; in 1964 Tohatsu went bankrupt. After entering the motor vehicle sector during the 1960s, Honda's motorcycle business suffered a relative loss of competitiveness because of Yamaha, which achieved almost the same market share in 1981. At the beginning of the 1980s, Honda decided to attack Yamaha. Whereas Honda introduced 81 new models and ceased production of 32,

reflecting 113 changes in product range in all, Yamaha 'only' introduced 34 new models and withdrew three, reflecting 37 changes. This strategy, in combination with a fierce attack on prices and distribution led to the collapse of Yamaha at the start of 1983. In addition to substantial losses, Yamaha announced redundancies and a restructuring programme, as well as a reduction in stocks. Yamaha's chairperson was forced to publicly acknowledge his failure. Foreign companies seeking to establish themselves in Japan often underestimate this fierce domestic competition (for illustration see case A9.1 and Tsurumi and Tsurumi (1999) for the case of Fujifilm and Kodak). This competitive strategy is one of the principal sources of Japanese strength when they enter foreign markets.

An industrialist's vocation is not to enjoy competition as an end in itself. Competition is imposed by the public sector opening up frontiers and ultimately by competitors themselves. If companies possess the legal and informal means to reduce competition, they will do so. This perspective remains true as long as the type of agreement is stable and the conditions remain mutually beneficial.

A German economist, Von Stackelberg (1940), had the idea of combining supply and demand situations to construct a typology of markets. He distinguished buyer and seller according to whether they number one, several or many (see Table 11.3).

Every country has a few monopolies and some markets where pure and perfect competition reigns. In addition, each country has a large number of oligopolies that are usually producers of large-scale consumption and durable consumer goods, oligopolies, and bilateral oligopolies that are usually producers of industrial input goods, such as steel, chemicals, rubber, and capital goods. What varies, as a function of culture, is the social approval or disapproval of these market forms. Local decision-makers need to determine whether monopolies may be desirable or dangerous for the community. Foreign intruders will be seen positively, from the consumer's point of view, or negatively, from the local competitor's point of view, because ultimately consumers are often also employees whose employment may be put at risk by the competition.

Indeed Americans are often shocked by the amount of protection European governments provide to their flagship companies. The Airbus–Boeing

Table 11.3 Basic forms of markets according to Von Stackelberg

		Sellers		
		One	Some	Many
Buyers	One	Bilateral monopoly	Contradicted monopsony	Monopsony
	Some	Contradicted monopoly	Bilateral oligopoly	Oligopsony
	Many	Monopoly	Oligopoly	Pure competition

saga is typical of conceptual differences that partly derive their roots from culture. The Europeans consider that government loans – often viewed as sunk costs – were used wisely in view of the success of the Airbus aircraft, the number of jobs created, the positive effects on the trade balance and the preservation of a previously threatened European civil aeronautic industry. However, for the Americans it was a costly mess that helped no one: Boeing's success was challenged by disloyal competition, European taxpayers were burdened and international trade rules were distorted. Without Airbus, Boeing would be in quasi-monopoly situation, exacerbated by the McDonnell Douglas merger in 1997; a potential problem caused by lack of competition.

11.6

Managing prices in highly regulated environments

Over the last 20 years or so, the annual inflation rate attained double digits in some countries, sometimes exceeding 100 per cent per year, causing monthly or daily changes in prices. High inflation may constrain pricing policies somewhat, because prices cannot be increased daily or weekly to adjust for inflation.

The case of high-inflation countries

At the national level, price stability is based on macroeconomic policies as well as cultural values. The requisite discipline is based on: (1) future time orientation, which provides the monetary authorities

with a perspective of continuity in fighting inflation; (2) control of the creation of money and credit; and (3) a belief in free market forces that may keep price increases under control because of active competition. Such a belief is, in general, related to individualism and low power distance.

One of the main reasons for persistently high inflation is that it benefits some actors in the economic system. Inflation transfers wealth fairly smoothly from some social strata to others. It appears that high inflation countries are also high in power distance (see Table 3.3). With some notable exceptions (such as Japan), the higher a country's power distance, the higher its inflation rate. The typical case for high inflation is a developing country with a semi-authoritarian government and heavy financial regulation (e.g. price controls on most goods, foreign exchange control, strict import controls and high duties). High power distance at the societal level is expressed in bureaucratic controls and restricted freedom for businesses, unless they have the appropriate connections at the top.

High inflation rates cause the local non-convertible currencies to weaken systematically against stable and convertible foreign currencies, because of constantly decreasing nominal purchasing power. Furthermore, the exchange rate is maintained at unrealistic levels. This results in a parallel foreign exchange market, illegal but generally tolerated by the authorities. In comparison with official exchange rates, parallel rates are favourable to foreign currency sellers and unfavourable to buyers. In Iran in 1993, following a period of very high inflation, the official exchange rate was about 1,500 rials more than the grey market exchange rate, before it was decided to align the official rate. In such situations, foreign exchange controls serve the purpose of enriching the most powerful who can buy foreign currencies at the favourable official rate, while restricting the capacity of local exporters to receive a real price, because exporters are obliged to sell export receipts in hard currencies at the usually overvalued official rate.

Inflation is supposed to be combated by price control, an expression of the power of regulatory authorities over companies. Where there is high power distance, there tend to be oppressive rules (see section 3.6). Price increases, so vital for a company's survival, may be delayed by public authorities even though last month's or last week's inflation rate caused the entire industry to go into the red – costs soared while sales stagnated because of controlled prices. For instance, the Brazilian automobile industry is subject to 'staircase' price increases by which Volkswagen, Fiat or Ford are suddenly allowed to increase their price by 50 per cent or more. The strong present orientation of the Brazilian public authorities' action favours high inflation, as is the case in many Latin American countries.

Such countries possess a high-inflation culture, where consumers and companies adapt to the changing situation. Consumers delay buying after price increases occur and buy very large quantities just before they are thought to occur, because price increases are not officially announced. If possible, they stock up with items bought during favourable periods. The threat of an imminent price increase is used to motivate customers to buy 'now'. Customers must also have a present orientation and a readiness to buy at the best possible moment, for instance purchasing 'inflation bargains' because they are currently cheap, rather than because they are actually needed. Such customer opportunism may be a problem for the consumers themselves, because they tend to be too price-minded, neglecting other important criteria in their decision-making process. Contrarily, companies do not depend on consumers for defining prices. The key for price policy, which is mostly short term, is to negotiate price increases with public authorities. Pricing depends more on government authorization than on customers and competition.

The terms of discussion with price regulatory authorities is highly relational and manipulative, rather than strictly economic. In order to obtain optimal price increases, companies argue about losses incurred because of price limitation for which they have to be compensated. Cost prices declared to regulatory authorities tend to be systematically overestimated and losses exaggerated in order to obtain as favourable a new price as possible. A company will argue for a substantial price increase so as to have a 'reserve' before the next increase. Naturally, this whole process fosters inflation rather than slows it down. Another way of obtaining the necessary price allowances – although illegal and unethical – is to propose a 'baksheesh' (i.e. kickback) or some favours to the civil servants in charge of price control within the public administration.

Over- and under-invoicing

As explained above, many high-inflation countries have legislation aimed at controlling prices. The control may take effect at retail, wholesale or production levels, or at several levels simultaneously. Price increases may be curbed, limited or even frozen. Trade profit margins may be monitored. The rationale for price control is usually a basic mistrust of free market mechanisms, often augmented by a long-established tradition of state intervention in the economy.

Foreign exchange regulations also influence the practice of over- and under-invoicing. When countries experience balance of trade and balance of payments problems, they often use administrative decrees aimed at stopping the outflow of foreign currency. Local exporters are often forced to repatriate their earnings in foreign currencies as soon as possible and to exchange them for local currency at sometimes derisory exchange rates. Local importers are also under close scrutiny. The necessity of purchasing abroad is assessed before they may receive foreign currency to pay suppliers. Furthermore, they are often obliged to deposit a guarantee that may be more than the equivalent of their foreign purchase. This sum is deposited at the central bank for a specified period prior to payment, with little or no interest. Where strict foreign exchange controls are enforced, local currency may not be converted into foreign 'hard' currencies.

Two reasons induce firms to practise under- or over-invoicing. First, where there is a high level of political risk, as is the case with many developing countries, local business people seek to transfer funds to foreign banks as fears of political upheaval increase. Second, local business people may wish to expatriate money through under-invoicing, simply because they need cash to buy a prohibited or scarce product or equipment for their production facilities and particularly for the manufacture of products for export.

Verna (1989) described various cases of over- and under-invoicing in international trade, relating to differences in currency convertibility. A totally convertible currency may be used in all international commercial and financial operations, irrespective of the object, place, or sum. Only a limited number of countries enjoy total convertibility of their currencies. Where the local currency is non-convertible, over- and under-invoicing is likely to occur (Verna, 1989), whereas when quantitative restrictions are put in place, smuggling is more likely. Local business people ask foreign customers to under-invoice, foreign suppliers to over-invoice, and then wait for the extra money to be paid into their bank account abroad.

Currency black markets thrive in countries where the national currency is totally non-convertible. For this reason, there may be huge discrepancies between the black-market exchange rate and the official central bank rate. Exporters who are obliged to go through official channels lose major benefits from their transactions. Either they must sell foreign currency at the abnormally low official rate, or they must buy foreign currency for their purchases at the abnormally high parallel rate. Hence the temptation

for local exporters to under-invoice and have the fully convertible balance transferred to a foreign bank account. To ensure these machinations work smoothly, the local exporter should have complete confidence in the foreign customers or an effective means of pressurizing them (see *WS11.6* for an example of trade mis-invoicing in Turkey).

Over-invoicing works in a symmetrical way for imports. When local importers ask for an import licence from their national authorities, the face value should be as high as possible to increase the allowance for buying foreign currency. Importers ask their suppliers to over-invoice and to transfer the extra money into a convertible foreign account to maximize their overall profits. For example, Verna noted (1989, p. 115):

An import licence will authorize the importer to order goods from a foreign supplier; a specified amount in foreign currency is paid by the local authorities in the name of the importer. In return, the importer should refund the authorities in local currency, at the official rate, and also pay customs duties on arrival of the goods. To obtain such an import licence may be a sort of 'windfall' because it allows the importer to buy foreign goods at a better price than is offered on the free market, mainly through the (favourable) exchange rate differential between the official and black markets . . . import licences can sometimes be transferable. They then become objects of exchange and even the subject of an auction . . . to the extent that some governments, which have become aware of this trade, sell import licences to the highest bidder.

Questions

1. To what extent does price bargaining involve friendship?

2. What is the relationship between bargaining and 'modern culture'?

3. Discuss 'economic rationality' from a cultural point of view.

4. How may price levels reflect Protestant as opposed to Catholic values?

5. What are the limitations on a consumer in displaying obvious price-mindedness when shopping? How do these limitations relate to culture?

6. In certain countries, smuggling is fairly legitimate: customs officers are not very concerned with arresting smugglers, consumers buy smuggled products knowingly, and smugglers are known by everyone for what they do. Why and under which circumstances is this so? What are the consequences of smuggling being accepted as a legitimate activity?

7. With the abolition of duty free shopping in 1999, increasingly rapid travel to France by car (including train–car travel by Eurostar), and the loosening of import 'allowances' for wine and spirits, UK citizens continue to buy massive quantities of drinks in Calais, France. In Calais, just 33 km (20 miles) from Dover, French stores have special areas for these British day-trippers. Excise duties on alcohol are higher in the United Kingdom than in France. What are the consequences for the UK brewing industry and its distribution channels? How could the brewing industry respond?

8. Is over- or under-invoicing legal? Why is it sometimes unavoidable?

References

Aalto-Setälä, Ville (2002), 'The effect of concentration and market power on food prices: Evidence from Finland', *Journal of Retailing*, vol. 78, no. 3, pp. 207–16.

Abegglen, James and George Stalk Jr. (1986), 'The Japanese corporation as competitor', *California Management Review*, vol. 28, no. 3, Spring, pp. 9–7.

Ackerman, David and Gerard Tellis (2001), 'Can culture affect prices? A cross-cultural study of shopping and retail prices', *Journal of Retailing*, vol. 77, no. 1, pp. 57–82.

Allen, David Elliston (1971), 'Anthropological insights into customer behavior', *European Journal of Marketing*, vol. 5, no. 3, pp. 45–57.

Ancarani, Fabio (2002), 'Pricing and the Internet: Frictionless commerce or pricer's paradise', *European Management Journal*, vol. 20, no. 6, pp. 680–7.

Baker, Walter, Mike Marn and Craig Zawada (2001), 'Price smarter on the net', *Harvard Business Review*, February, pp. 122–7.

Becker, Gary S. (1965), 'A theory of the allocation of time', *Economic Journal*, vol. 75, September, pp. 493–517.

Cateora, Philip R. (1983), *International Marketing*, 5th edn, Richard D. Irwin: Homewood, IL.

Cavusgil, S. Tamer (1990), 'Unravelling the mystique of export pricing', in Hans B. Thorelli and S. Tamer Cavusgil (eds), *International Marketing Strategy*, 3rd edn, Pergamon: Oxford, pp. 503–21.

Cavusgil, S. Tamer and Ed Sikora (1988), 'How multinationals can counter grey market imports', *Columbia Journal of World Business*, vol. 23, no. 4, Winter, pp. 75–85.

Chaudry, Peggy E. and Michael J. Walsh (1995), Managing the gray market in the European Union: The case of the pharmaceutical industry', *Journal of International Marketing*, vol. 3, no. 3, pp. 11–33.

Clarke, Irvine III and Margaret Owens (2000), 'Trademark rights in gray markets', *International Marketing Review*, vol. 17, no. 3, pp. 272–86.

Curry, David J. and Peter C. Riesz (1988), 'Price and price–quality relationships: a longitudinal analysis', *Journal of Marketing*, vol. 52, January, pp. 36–51.

Dawar, Niraj and Philip M. Parker (1994), 'Marketing universals: consumers' use of brand name, price, physical appearance, and retailer reputation as signals of product quality', *Journal of Marketing*, vol. 58, no. 2, pp. 81–95.

DeMarco, C.W. (2001), 'Knee deep in technique: the ethics of monopoly capital', *Journal of Business Ethics*, no. 31, pp. 151–64.

Erevelles, Sunil, Abhik Roy and Stephen L. Vargo (1999), 'The use of price and warranty cues in product evaluation: a comparison of U.S. and Hong Kong consumers', *Journal of International Consumer Marketing*, vol. 11, no. 3, pp. 67–91.

Fauld, David J., Orlen Grunewald and Denise Johnson (1994), 'A cross-national investigation of the relationship between the price and quality of consumer products: 1970–1990', *Journal of Global Marketing*, vol. 8, no. 1, pp. 7–25.

Forrester Research, Inc. (2000), 'North America will lead global eCommerce to $6.8 trillion in 2004 (press release)', 19 April, available at: **www.forrester.com/er/press/release/0,1769,281,00.htm**.

Froot, Kenneth, Michael Kim and Kenneth Rogoff (2001), 'The law of one price over 700 years', revised version of NBER Working Paper no. 5132.

Gough, Neil (2003), 'Zombie discs: retail companies and retailers dump them on scrap dealers, but unwanted "saw-gash" music CDs find a ready market in China', *Time Asia*, vol. 161, no. 3.

Green, Robert T. and Tasman Smith (2002), 'Executive insights: countering brand counterfeiters', *Journal of International Marketing*, vol. 10, no. 4, pp. 89–106.

Ibison, David (2001), 'Weak euro lets top car dealers go far in Japan: parallel imports luxury prices cut', *Financial Times* (London), 10 January, p. 13.

Jacoby, Jacob R. and Jerry C. Olson (1977), 'Consumer response to price: an attitudinal, information processing perspective', in Y. Wind and P. Greenberg (eds), *Moving Ahead with Attitude Research*, American Marketing Association: Chicago, pp. 73–86.

Johansson, Johny K. and Gary Erickson (1985), 'Price–quality relationships and trade barriers', *International Marketing review*, vol. 2, no. 3, pp. 52–63.

Johansson, Johny K. and Ikujiro Nonaka (1990), 'Japanese export marketing: Structures, strategies, counterstrategies', in Hans B. Thorelli and S. Tamer Cavusgil (eds), *International Marketing Strategy*, 3rd edn, Pergamon: Oxford, pp. 585–600.

Keegan, Warren J. (1984), *Multinational Marketing Management*, Prentice-Hall: Englewood Cliffs, NJ.

Khuri, Fuad I. (1968), 'The etiquette of bargaining in the Middle-East', *American Anthropologist*, vol. 70, pp. 693–706.

Lilien, Gary and Eunsang Yoon (1989), 'Success and failure in innovation – a review of the literature', *IEEE Transactions on Engineering management*, vol. 36, no. 1, pp. 3–10.

Maxwell, Sarah (2001), 'An expanded price/brand effect model: a demonstration of heterogeneity in global consumption', *International Marketing Review*, vol. 18, no. 3, pp. 325–43.

McGowan, Karen M. and Brenda J. Sternquist (1998), 'Dimensions of price as a marketing universal: A comparison of Japanese and U.S. consumers', *Journal of International Marketing*, vol. 6, no. 4, pp. 49–65.

Moore, Marguerite, Karen McGowan Kennedy and Ann Fairhurst (2003), 'Cross-cultural equivalence of price perceptions between US and Polish consumers', *International Journal of Retail & Distribution Management*, vol. 31, no. 4/5, pp. 268–79.

Myers, Matthew B. (1999), 'Incidents of grey market activity among U.S. exporters: occurrences, characteristics and consequences', *Journal of International Business Studies*, vol. 30, no. 1, pp. 105–26.

Narayandas, Das, John Quelch and Gordon Swartz (2000), 'Prepare your company for global pricing', *MIT Sloan Management Review*, vol. 42, no. 1, pp. 61–70.

Oxenfeldt, A.R. (1950), 'Consumer knowledge: its measurement and extent', *Review of Economics and Statistics*, vol. 32, no. 4, November, pp. 300–16.

Palia, Aspy P. and Charles F. Keown (1991), 'Combating parallel importing: views of US exporters to the Asia-Pacific region', *International Marketing Review*, vol. 8, no. 1, pp. 47–56.

Penbera, Joseph J. (1999), 'E-commerce: Economics and regulation', *S.A.M. Advanced Management Journal*, vol. 64, no. 4, pp. 39–47.

Porter, Michael E. (2001), 'Strategy and the Internet', *Harvard Business Review*, March, pp. 63–78.

Prus, Robert C. (1989), *Making Sales: Influence as interpersonal accomplishment*, Sage Publications: Newbury Park, CA.

Riesz, P. (1978), 'Price versus quality in the marketplace', *Journal of Retailing*, vol. 54, no. 4, pp. 15–28.

Roeber, Carter A. (1994), 'Moneylending, trust, and the culture of commerce in Kabwe, Zambia', *Research in Economic Anthropology*, vol. 15, JAI Press: Greenwich, CT, pp. 39–61.

Saito Duerr, Mitsuko (1989) in Gerald Albaum, Jesper Strandskov, Edwin Duerr and Lawrence Dowd, *International Marketing and Export Management*, Addison-Wesley, Reading, MA.

Schindler, Robert M. and Thomas M. Kibarian (2001), 'Image communicated by the use of 99 endings in advertised prices', *Journal of Advertising*, vol. 30, no. 4, pp. 95–9.

Sjolander, Richard (1992), 'Cross-cultural effects of price on perceived quality', *European Journal of Marketing*, vol. 26, no. 7, pp. 34–44.

Sproles, George B. (1977), 'New evidence on price and quality', *Journal of Consumer Affairs*, vol. 11, Summer, pp. 63–77.

Stevenson, Thomas H. and David W.E. Cabell (2002), 'Integrating transfer pricing policy and activity-based costing', *Journal of International Marketing*, vol. 10, no. 4, pp. 77–88.

Stöttinger, Barbara (2001), 'Strategic export pricing: a long and winding road', *Journal of International Marketing*, vol. 9, no. 1, pp. 40–63.

Tan, Soo J., Guan H. Lim and Khai S. Lee (1997), 'Strategic responses to parallel importing', *Journal of Global Marketing*, vol. 10, no. 4, pp. 45–66.

Tellis, Gerard J. and Gary J. Gaeth (1990), 'Best value, price-seeking, and price aversion: the impact of information and learning on consumer choices', *Journal of Marketing*, vol. 54, April, pp. 34–45.

Tsurumi, Yoshi and Hiroki Tsurumi (1999), 'Fujifilm-Kodak duopolistic competition in Japan and the United States', *Journal of International Business Studies*, vol. 30, no. 4, pp. 813–30.

Van Wijk, Jeroen (2002), 'Dealing with piracy: intellectual asset management in music and software', *European Management Journal*, vol. 20, no. 6, pp. 689–98.

Veeck, Ann and Alvin C. Burns (1995), 'The formation of beliefs in a price–quality relationship: a study of urban Chinese consumers', *Asian Journal of Marketing*, vol. 4, no. 1, pp. 47–61.

Verna, Gérard (1989), 'Fausses facturations et commerce international', *Harvard-l'Expansion*, no. 52, Spring, pp. 110–20.

Von Stackelberg, H. (1940), *Die Grundlagen der Nationalökonomie*, Springer Verlag: Berlin.

Weber, Max (1958), *The Protestant Ethic and the Spirit of Capitalism*, Charles Scribner's Sons: New York.

Weigand, Robert E. (1991), 'Parallel import channels: options for preserving territorial integrity', *Columbia Journal of World Business*, vol. 26, no. 1, pp. 53–60.

Yamada, Y. and N. Ackerman (1984), 'Price–quality correlations in the Japanese market', *Journal of Consumer Affairs*, vol. 18, no. 2, pp. 51–65.

Yucelt, Ugur and Nadeem M. Firoz (1993), 'Buyers' perception of the price–quality relationship: the Turkish case', *Proceedings of the 6th World Marketing Congress*, Istanbul: Academy of Marketing Science, pp. 564–8.

Zeithaml, Valarie A. (1988), 'Consumer perceptions of price, quality and value: a means-end model and synthesis of evidence', *Journal of Marketing*, vol. 52, July, pp. 2–22.

Teaching materials

A11.1 Case

Saito Importing Company

Some years ago, Saito Importing Company, located in California, USA, brought in a shipment of wood carving from Bali in Indonesia. At the time, the official exchange rate was 78 Indonesian rupias per US dollar. The 'black market' rate (as viewed by the Indonesian government), or 'free market' rate (as viewed by most of the rest of the world), was approximately 1,300 Indonesian rupias per US dollar.

The seller requested a letter of credit for one-half the value of the shipment, to be provided by a US bank and confirmed by an Indonesian bank, and stipulated that the balance be wired to a New York bank account.

Obviously, the 'half' that was received in New York had many times the value of that received in Indonesia. The money in the bank account in New York was available for the seller to invest, to purchase goods for shipment to Indonesia or elsewhere, or to use if leaving Indonesia. Money held in Indonesia at that time, could be used for such purposes only with the approval of the government. What the Indonesian exporter did was, of course, illegal under Indonesian law.

Saito Importing Company did not receive the goods until over a year later. Since Bali does not have a port which will accommodate ocean-going vessels, the letter of credit specified that transhipment was allowed. In the process of transhipment, the goods travelled around much of the world and were delayed while waiting for on-going vessels at points of transhipment.

When the wood carvings finally arrived in the US, Saito Importing Company declared the actual price paid for the goods, and indicated to customs why there was a discrepancy between purchase price and the value shown on the documents. The American company did not do anything illegal under US law.

(Source: Duerr, 1989, p. 310. Reproduced with kind permission.)

Questions

1. Should the US company have refused to agree to make the payments as requested by the Indonesian exporter? What would have been the expected effect on the Indonesian exporter's price?

2. What effects would you expect the unrealistic official exchange rates had on Indonesian exports?

A11.2 Case

Riva International

Françoise Gain, the *directrice du marketing* at Riva in Brussels, Belgium, received astonishing results from the consumer panels and distributor panels for September and October 2004. It appeared that sales in Belgium and France of one of its main products, the *Nutrifying Complex Crème* Riva, were 20 per cent lower than the production level in the Belgian factory, which supplied both markets. No signs of excess inventories in the distribution in France or Belgium were noticed by the sales force during visits to the distributors.

Riva Belgium was the subsidiary of Riva Products Corporation, a large US-based multinational, whose main business lines were related to the cosmetics and beauty care industry. The Belgian subsidiary was in charge of both the French and the Belgian markets. In 1999 a scientific breakthrough by the corporate R&D laboratories had led to the development of a new skin care cream. Several patents had been filed and registered to protect the property. In Europe, the industrial use of these patents had been licensed to Riva Belgium, which began producing and selling the new skin care cream in February 2001. Sales increased quickly, and Belgian and French consumers received the new product, liking both its efficiency and good price–quality ratio. Following instructions from international headquarters, the output of Riva Belgium was intended exclusively for supplying the Belgian and French markets as well as the markets of French-speaking Africa.

In January 2004 the English subsidiary of Riva, UK Riva Ltd, started producing the same *Nutrifying Complex Crème* product. Hefty investments had been made in the English factory to ensure the best quality and a large production capacity. This product had been launched at the top end of the market for skin care cream. It was priced high and supported by heavy advertising and promotional expenses. After a promising start, deliveries had been falling off since August 2004. Actual deliveries to English distributors steadily diverged from target sales.

Françoise Gain knew about this situation as she had been engaged as an internal consultant in the launching of *Nutrifying Complex Crème* Riva in the United Kingdom. However, what worried her most in November 2004 was the gap between sales to consumers in France and Belgium and ex-works shipments. She informed Jacques Graff, chief executive of Riva Belgium and a member of the international board.

At first he did not seem to be bothered by such a gap, and showed little interest in the issue: 'Françoise, you know: panel data, what does it mean really? Our product sells well and that is all that matters! Tell your panel company to reconsider their samples and their data collection procedures, and you will see that everything is in fact normal.'

Françoise Gain nevertheless took the decision to undertake an audit by an external consultant. His findings exactly confirmed those of the panels and brought evidence of no sizeable excess inventory at the distribution level. It followed from the auditor's investigations that deviations were ascribed mostly to deliveries to two large wholesalers, who ranked among the five largest customers of Riva Belgium.

One month after his talks with Françoise Gain, Graff received a confidential note, issued by the chief executive of UK Riva Ltd. It stated that a member of his sales force had accidentally seen, at an English wholesaler, a carton containing *Nutrifying Complex Crème* Riva with country-of-origin label 'Made in Belgium'. The wholesaler had been evasive if not reluctant to tell the sales representative where it came from. Jacques Graff asked Françoise Gain to come to his office, and handed her the note without comment.

'I am not surprised by this note', answered Françoise. 'On the contrary, it is evidence for my suspicions about parallel imports of our Belgian products to England. I have noticed that the sales figures that vanished from Belgium and France precisely equalled the drop in deliveries of UK Riva Ltd. It is now quite clear that some of our wholesalers export to English distributors and that, before doing this, they did not warn our sales and marketing group. I examined the cost structure of UK Riva production and found that our product made in Belgium could be sold by Belgian wholesalers to English distributors at a profit. Belgian distributors may price it at 15 per cent below the English list price, even though there are transport costs.'

'How is that possible?' asked Graff, amazed.

'The English *Nutrifying Complex Crème* Riva was launched with heavy production and promotion costs,' explained Françoise Gain. 'It is positioned at the high end of the market. It is priced higher than any of the competing products. I told them, before the launch, that this retail price level was too high. They disapproved. The finance department at UK Riva Ltd wanted a quick return on investment, taking into account the large cash outflows at the start. The marketing people, backed by the advertising agency, claimed the opportunity to seize a segment which was at the very top end of the market and which had been, up to then, neglected by competitors. Consequently my opinion was put aside.'

Jacques Graff started to pace back and forth. 'As a chief executive of the Belgian subsidiary, I am delighted. Our plant works at full capacity. But, as a member of the international board, I cannot let the English subsidiary plunge. What can we do?'

'One thing is certain', answered Françoise Gain. 'We cannot prevent our customers, namely independent wholesalers, from exporting to England if they wish to do so. As for the English distributors, one cannot blame them for seizing a better-priced offer and simultaneously taking advantage of the promotional effort of UK Riva! I know it is more easily said than done, but you should have defined, a long time ago, an international pricing strategy at the international board level.'

'It is never too late to do the right thing! Françoise, please prepare a report on your suggestions to cope with this parallel import problem of *Nutrifying Complex Crème* Riva', said Graff in conclusion.

Questions

1. What are the reasons for these parallel import problems?

2. What can be done to stop wholesalers exporting to the UK?

3. Is it necessary to change the marketing strategy of *Nutrifying Complex Crème* Riva, particularly its price? If so, where and how should it be implemented?

4. How should one organize a coordinated international marketing strategy across national markets? Prepare the report requested by Graff.

(Source: Adapted from a case written by Alain Ollivier, Ecole Supérieure de Commerce de Paris.)

A11.3 Case

Taman SA

At Taman SA, a Spanish company, orders systematically exceed production. Is this a result of the marketing and sales department's expertise, the lack of production capacity, or the inability of the production department to plan demand peaks effectively? Nobody knows the exact answer.

To tell the truth, one should excuse both the production department and the sales department. The market for high-technology products, in which Taman has built a strong European share, is growing rapidly, at about 50 per cent per year. Taman's competitors face similar problems.

In spite of a rather elaborate cost accounting system, accountants may endlessly argue about the real direct and total cost price of a given order. Diverse and changing factors tend to blur the calculation of costs, such as the allocation of R&D expenses, the cost of components, shared expenses between different orders, the price–volume relation, etc.

The director of marketing and sales and the director of production and operations are constantly in conflict. Conflicts focus on such cases as that of Magnusson AB. Magnusson AB is a new customer from whom Taman has never, up to now, received an order. Following technical tests of Taman products by Magnusson people at their factory, and after a successful certification procedure, Magnusson is ready to place a fairly large order.

The marketing and sales director argues that getting a new client is something you have to pay for. The director of production and operations considers that the largely positive margin that this order brings is smaller than that of other orders. Besides, he fears that it could disturb the production schedule for the coming weeks and consequently that it could result in numerous delivery delays.

Question

Describe this problem in about 30 lines. What ways and means would you suggest to these two directors for solving their conflict and/or serving their customer base better?

A11.4 Case

AIDS – Global ethics and the pricing of AIDS drugs

This case can be found on the book's website (see *WS A11.4*).

12

International distribution and sales promotion

This chapter considers, from a cross-cultural perspective, those elements of the marketing mix which are crucial in 'pushing' the product towards the customer. Nonetheless, it does acknowledge that some elements of channel and sales promotion apply universally across countries and cultures. The elements that help to 'push' the product to the customer are as follows: (1) the distribution channels; (2) sales promotion; and (3) the sales force (examined in Chapter 15).

As exhaustiveness is impossible, an eclectic approach has once again been taken. We have chosen to present the Japanese distribution system, which is reputed to be complex and difficult to deal with. Western distribution channels tend to be depersonalized, simplified, and efficient. Section 12.1 describes how the Japanese *Keiretsu* distribution system is physically rooted in the Japanese landscape and explains how it also depends on the Japanese national character. Although the distribution channels provoke negative reactions from the non-Japanese, or *Gai-jin*, they are so deeply embedded in Japanese business customs that criticism is virtually pointless. Non-Japanese companies have condemned the channels on the grounds that they favour Japanese goods and producers and they are reputed to act as a barrier to the entry of imported goods. Some of these disparaging comments have been frequently voiced at the WTO and GATT international negotiations; however, these comments reveal ignorance of the deep roots of *Keiretsu* in the Japanese culture. Since channels involve a direct relationship with final customers, servicing and informing them, they deeply reflect cultural idiosyncrasies. The next two sections

present the criteria for selecting foreign distribution channels (section 12.2) and examine the role of distribution as a 'cultural filter' (section 12.3). Section 12.4 relates to the considerable expansion of direct marketing worldwide; it explains how catalogues and direct marketing tools must be adapted for cross-border use and discusses how the world wide web can be used for direct marketing, the Internet serving as an electronic platform for the international distribution of goods and services.

The last topic in this chapter, sales promotion (section 12.5), has some universal objectives: to let potential consumers try the product, to facilitate repurchasing, to increase the frequency of purchases, to reach a new segment of consumers, to reinforce brand loyalty, and so on. Sales promotion has developed a number of techniques, which have been well documented. Although this whole range of techniques is known in most countries, there is wide variation in their degree of local legitimacy and legal acceptance.

12.1

The cultural dimension of distribution channels: The case of Japanese *Keiretsus*

Distribution and Japan

Japan is an insular and heavily populated country, with only a small proportion of inhabitable land. A population of over 127 million people is effectively concentrated into an area of roughly 60,000 square kilometres. Despite this, there are more retail outlets in Japan (1.62 million) than in the United States (1.5 million), while the average number of employees per retail outlet is 12 in the United States versus only 4 in Japan (Johansson, 1997). The distribution system is highly fragmented: numerous retail firms with many levels of wholesale and semi-wholesale operations form a complex, and seemingly confused, illogical network.

The wholesalers and semi-wholesalers play a central role in Japan, where the distribution system was very fragmented. Historically, the manufacturing sector was made up of small businesses which lacked sufficient marketing and management capabilities. This sector was supported by distributors who provided outlets, funding, raw materials and working capital. Similarly, at the other end of the chain, the wholesalers and semi-wholesalers added their expertise to the retail sector which was very fragmented. Kuribayashi (1991) and Montgomery (1991) noted a change in the growth trend of retail stores: whereas it grew at 1–2 per cent p.a. until 1982, it has since been declining at about the same annual rate (1 per cent). However, this process was largely slowed down by the 1974 large-scale retail store law, which was revised and in fact strengthened in 1979: the law limits the size of stores and requires the approval from smaller-scale retail stores, before a new large store (500 square metres or more) may open.

The retail trader has a close relationship with the customer. Many consumers go shopping on foot or by bicycle, a very viable option considering the level of traffic congestion, town centre speed limits of 20 kilometres per hour, and an absence of car parks due to shortage of space (Dupuis and de Maricourt, 1989). As a result, the relationship between the consumer and the retailer is a close one and they get to know each other well.

The high level of purchasing power in Japan contrasts with the quantitative limitations on consumption due to the lack of space. The area available actually restricts many forms of consumption: it is not possible to drive long distances as in Europe or the United States simply because roads and motorways would become completely jammed. The purchase of items of furniture or household goods is also limited by the availability of inhabitable space. However, as a means of reinforcing this restriction

in a positive way, the Japanese are extremely keen on detail, aesthetics, quality and service (Turcq and Usunier, 1985). They demand extensive services from their retailers, even if they have to pay for them. Accordingly, they have the benefit of a wide range of services, which, although straightforward, do make life easier for the Japanese consumer:

1. Daily opening times of up to 12 or 13 hours.
2. Very restricted periods of closure during the year, for both weekly and annual holidays.
3. Availability of free home delivery.
4. Easy acceptance of returned goods, even though the goods may not be defective.
5. Credit accounts with monthly payments for regular customers.

The compensation for the retailer is in higher gross profit margins; about 30 per cent higher than the European average (Dupuis and de Maricourt, 1989, p. 129).

The Japanese system

This strong relationship – service and loyalty, willingness to pay for the retailers, commitment to their customers – is passed along the entire distribution structure right through the wholesalers and semi-wholesalers to the producers. Shimaguchi (1978) describes the principal characteristics of the relationships within the Japanese system of distribution by distinguishing both the practice of and the philosophy behind the system of vertical control in the distribution system known as *Keiretsuka ryutsu*, or *Keiretsus*. This may be approximately translated into English as 'distribution channel arrangements' or 'integrated marketing networks' (Czinkota and Woronoff, 1991, p. 57).

The practical aspects revolve around a widespread and extremely complicated system of discounts. Rebates operate on three levels: (1) to encourage sales promotion (to increase new consumers, support for products that are selling badly, clearing expensive stocks); (2) as rewards (for the favourable product placement in the shop window or on the counter); and (3) as a means of control (limitation of sales of competing products, reductions in the rate of returns, payments in cash or within a short period of time, respect for 'recommended' prices, etc.). These rebates are calculated either on a percentage basis or on a flat rate. Rebates are often confidential to encourage retailers to believe that they are receiving more than the others. However, to avoid frustration and jealousy, many producers have encouraged more explicit systems of rebate.

The system of *tegata* is the second aspect of these sales practices. *Tegatas* are deferred payment systems, based on promissory notes which allow the offer of extended credit periods to the operator at the next stage of the channel. The relationship between two successive layers in this vertical distribution network can be described as (financially) 'protected/obliged'. Trade credit is largely and liberally extended throughout the whole distribution system, rather like in Italy and France, but unlike the United States and Germany, where payment times are much shorter. Payment periods range from 60 to 120 days and sometimes to 180 days. Glazer (1968, p. 20) remarks that 'everybody uses them [promissory notes] and some are referred to as "pregnancy" notes, in that they may not become due for nine months and more'. The practice of deferred payments has a snowball effect, whereby everybody in the network, financially strong or not, is threatened by notes that become uncollectable. Accounts receivable are made more onerous by the *tegata* practices. Financial reliance becomes not only an individual, but also a collective issue: if one member fails, this may lead to a chain reaction of bankruptcies.

The Japanese distribution system is heavily influenced by the nation's cultural traditions and legal systems. As Pirog *et al.* (1997, p. 3) point out: 'a culture that extols individualism will place fewer social obligations on the dyad than one emphasizing social reciprocity.' They also cite difficulties in using the courts to uphold the law, which is: 'typified by the absence of discovery, prohibiting class action suits, contingency fees, and limited damage awards tend to make "arms length" deals risky' (p. 5). This facilitates long-term relationships bound by trust.

Japanese distribution's commitment *vis-à-vis* service to consumers

The right to return unsold products is extremely liberal because consumer complaints are seen as opportunities for learning rather than as a problem.

Learning begins with the consumers at the end of the chain because retailers cannot afford to hold in stock products that have been returned by customers. The dedication *vis-à-vis* consumer complaints is real:

In Japan, when a customer complains, the sales clerk realizes that the customer has a problem, and then tries to understand exactly what it is. She first empathizes with the customer and adopts the customer's viewpoint to gain a clear understanding of what the customer's problem is. This means listening more than talking, and avoiding judgemental or critical remarks. (Johansson and Nonaka, 1996, p. 33.)

Since distributors receive products to sell rather than order them, they must be given the capacity to provide full feed back from the consumer to the manufacturer. If the producer does not receive an explicit order from the distributor, the producer will send a *mihakarai-okuri*, which is a delivery based on the producer's estimate of the level of stock held by the intermediary. The wholesalers accept these deliveries, although sometimes grudgingly. They then have to try to sell these extra consignments further on down the line within the network. This presupposes the fairly liberal right the intermediary and consumers have to return goods even when they are not defective.

A further aspect of the Japanese method of distribution is the high frequency of deliveries. Shimaguchi (1978) explains this high frequency (retailers and wholesalers are in contact daily) in terms of limited financial resources, powerful competition and a tradition of wide personal contact between those who trade with each other. As a result the wholesalers are obliged to sell to retailers in small quantities and at short and regular intervals. Although wholesalers have a tendency to regard the system as inefficient, they accept it because on a global level, it achieves an economic compromise between increased delivery costs and decreased inventory costs. It is worth noticing the similarities with the *kanban* system of just-in-time deliveries in the field of industrial procurement and subcontracting. One might expect these quasi-affective relationships between channel members to translate into non-aggressive price negotiations and ultimately into non-competitive pricing. Nothing of the kind occurs: the whole distribution system is very much concerned with price levels. Distributors enforce competition, without the need to shift frequently from one supplier to another in order to compel them to keep product prices low. Thus Weigand (1970, p. 24) notes:

As a consequence of the Japanese commitment toward their employees, Japanese sellers must view prices as a highly flexible marketing instrument. The notion of marginal pricing and the importance of selling at prices that contribute to costs is well understood both by businessmen and by academicians ... Prices may be cut at any level in the marketing channel by firms that must have sufficient immediate income to meet their unavoidable costs, but the move ultimately will affect the retailers' cost of goods.

Furthermore, the setting of an initial price in Japan is a key decision. Raising the price afterwards may be as difficult as reducing it. The Japanese place a high symbolic meaning on prices; a price reduction may spoil the image of the product, especially when it is intended as a gift (Montgomery, 1991). In fact, Japanese traders in the distribution system fight over price a great deal, in spite of their loyalty to each other; this, in turn, stimulates demand.

'Traders ... try to resolve their disputes flexibly, not necessarily based on formal contacts but on their mutual trust and confidence which has been built up by human relationships and a long, stable continuity of transaction' (Kuribayashi, 1991, p. 55). The personal relationship and human association between the members of the system clearly introduce an emotive element. It is further supported by the practice of gifts. Twice a year, in July at *ochugen* and in December at *oseibo*, the companies send out an enormous number of presents (Shimaguchi, 1978) whose cost, importance and nature conform to a complex code. This practice is further reinforced by business lunches and trips with clients, occasions that aim to win their friendship rather than to discuss business, which would be considered the height of bad manners.

In addition to the practices cited above, producers often give support to the distribution channels in the area of sales promotion, for example by sending out extra demonstrators and salespeople to supermarkets, or 'kits' for product presentation within the department. There are incentive schemes for retailers, who are offered bonuses such as a *kabuki* show, a weekend in Hong Kong or even a week in Hawaii. Although such practices do exist in other countries to

varying degrees (see Box 12.1), sources agree that in Japan they exist in the strongest and most systematic form (Weigand, 1970; Shimaguchi, 1978; Kuribayashi, 1991).

Traditional *Gai-jin* criticisms of the Japanese system of distribution

Numerous converging criticisms of the Japanese distribution networks are made by foreign firms. There are, first, complaints about the distribution system being in collusion with Japanese public authorities trying to protect local business. Cateora, for instance, explains the case of the Coca-Cola company when it introduced Fresca in Japan: 'The Japan Soft Drink Bottlers Association staged an anti Coca-Cola campaign in which they charged unfair marketing practices. Then, when the Coca-Cola company applied to introduce Fresca, the association put so much pressure on various Japanese ministries that the company withdrew the application' (Cateora, 1983, p. 622).

A second argument against *Keiretsu* distribution is that it creates such a chain of affective relationships operating vertically between producers, wholesalers and retailers that foreign producers find the systems impenetrable. One of the most heavily criticized aspects is the *itten itchoai* system ('single outlet, single account'), which requires retailers to order only from specified wholesalers and prohibits these same wholesalers from selling to other retailers, thus restricting competition to the wholesale stage. In the same way, numerous territorial restrictions (exclusive distribution arrangements) are reinforced by the setting up of dealerships for specified areas, which cooperate amongst themselves and increase the producers' ability to impose their marketing strategies (Ishida, 1983). As a consequence, Japanese distribution systems are resented as one of the main obstacles encountered by foreign firms seeking to penetrate the Japanese market and even a cause of failure.

Third, Japanese channels are supposed to be inefficient: long, costly, complex and imposing an ultimate surcharge on the consumer. The main reason for their continued existence, despite their inefficiency, must be the Japanese wish to exclude foreign competition, to protect 'Japan Inc.'. For this reason, the Japanese system of distribution has become a major target of criticism from abroad.

Is the Japanese system of distribution impenetrable?

Czinkota and Woronoff (1991) emphasize that the *Keiretsus*, which also exist in the production system, aim to 'keep it all in the family': subcontracting networks are institutionalized, whereas elsewhere they would be fluid and informal. Shimaguchi (1978) has described the main factors, deeply ingrained in the Japanese mentality, which underlie the *Keiretsu* distribution system:

A well-known Japanese psychoanalyst, Doi, wrote a famous book in 1973, entitled *Amae-no-kozo*, that is 'the anatomy of dependence'. Apparently *amae* is a unique feature of Japanese society, which is diffused throughout society, including the distribution channels. Amae is 'the indulgent, passive love which surrounds and supports the individual in a group, whether family, neighbourhood, or the world at large. Close dependency and high expectancy of others in a group seems to be the way of life in Japan' (Shimaguchi, 1978, p. 58).

Nakane (1973) has also emphasized the role of *amae* in the building and the maintenance of group bonds in Japanese society. It means that relationships between channel members are not depersonalized ones, even when members belong to different companies. Frequent visits of suppliers (producers and/or wholesalers) to retailers are required for maintaining close human relationships in the channels and fostering the quality of the services rendered to the ultimate consumers.

A vertical structure is virtually inevitable in view of the Japanese mentality. The notion of social status is central to Japanese culture. In the field of interpersonal relationships there are three distinct levels: the *sempai* are people of advanced years, highly respected,

---

Box 12.1

'Master's' retailers at Dunlop France (a subsidiary of Sumitomo Rubber): *Keiretsu* distribution in France

The sports division of Dunlop France (a subsidiary of the Japanese Sumitomo Rubber) manufactures and markets tennis balls. It has developed a system of privileged relationships with its dealers, which is very much like the *keiretsu* system.

The object is to select a limited number of retail shops that procure their articles from Dunlop France. In exchange for certain commitments, retailers receive advantages from Dunlop France. Dunlop aims to improve its brand image and to increase consumer brand awareness. Which retailers may apply for the 'Master's' label? They must be independent retail stores; this excludes large specialized sportshops and hypermarkets. They should have a good reputation with potential buyers and be recognized as experts in tennis equipment; they must also offer product lines for golf and squash. Moreover, they must enjoy total freedom of procurement.

'Master's' retailers enjoy beneficial trading conditions, as in *Keiretsu* distribution. Dunlop France is committed to informing them of new products before other retail stores, and supplying them with the new products first. Finally, Dunlop France publishes a complete list of the 'Master's' points of sale in the specialized tennis press (*Tennis de France* and *Tennis Magazine*). These benefits naturally imply some obligations for retail stores. Retail stores commit themselves to maintaining a defined level of inventory and products on display, both tennis rackets and tennis balls as well as lines for golf and squash. They also commit themselves to sell at least 70 per cent of their tennis balls annually under the Dunlop brand name.

Moreover, the retailer must report to Dunlop France any remarks made by consumers that may lead to improvements in the quality of new products. Ultimately, the retail store manager provides a sponsor (usually a well-known tennis professional) with Dunlop France rackets and balls. Presently about 150 stores bear the 'Master's' label. Dunlop France carefully ensures that the selected stores fulfil their obligations. The outcome, as far as brand awareness and brand image are concerned, proves quite satisfactory, especially for tennis rackets.

(Source: Adapted from Eric Zeller, 1989, pp. 33–4.)

addressed by their name and the suffix *san*; younger, less experienced people (the *kohai*) are addressed by their name with the suffix *kun*; colleagues on the same level in the hierarchy (same age, experience and seniority) are the *doryo* and should be addressed without a suffix. The determination of social status is extremely important and is one of the major reasons behind the widespread practice of exchanging business cards. Vertical relationships exist between organizations in much the same way as between individuals.

The Japanese are fairly long term oriented and their sense of time (*Makimono* time, see section 2.2) emphasizes continuity, stability and perseverance. According to Inagaki (quoted in Turpin, 1990) persistence is instilled into Japanese people by their mothers from early childhood. A survey based on a representative sample of 3,600 Japanese (over 16 years old) has shown that, among the ten preferred words of the Japanese, *doryoku* (effort) ranks first, *nintai* (persistence) second and *kanjo* (tenacity) ranks fifth. As a consequence of its long-term orientation, Japanese business is much more turnover oriented than profit oriented. Japanese companies tend, as far as possible, to accept business as soon as the sales price covers direct costs and begins to cover fixed costs. This fact is illustrated by Hanawa (quoted by Shimaguchi, 1978): '*Kami yori usui Kosen* (margins thinner than paper) is a common saying in Japanese business circles. In certain cases, with a complete disregard for producers' price lists, Japanese distributors end up bargaining machines after harsh negotiations at a price lower than list. Why such low margins? There is a Japanese business philosophy which believes that "A deal done is better than none".'

The Japanese themselves (Yoshino, 1971; Shimaguchi, 1978; Ishida, 1983; Kuribayashi, 1991) admit that the *Keiretsu* system is infused with a sense of conservatism, and that it does not lead to innovation. They probably appreciate in the distribution system (a very relational and human sector, everywhere in the world), the warm, sensitive and emotional tradition which permeates marketing and business in Japan.

The question of whether *Keiretsu* distribution is intentionally a barrier to the entry of foreign goods on the Japanese market is a difficult one. It seems to be an accusation against the Japanese for what is essentially their way of being. As stated above they are themselves quite critical of their distribution system. According to Ishida (1983, p. 322):

the formation of distribution keiretsu in oligopolistic markets for highly differentiated products has the following consequences: (1) elimination or reduction of interbrand and intra brand price competition, (2) strengthening of barriers against new entrants to the market, (3) restriction of dealer independence with a consequent loss of business enthusiasm, innovation, and rationalisation, and (4) preservation and strengthening of oligopolies.

It may be argued that the above aims to accord tokens of goodwill to the American negotiators (in the Americans' relations with their Japanese counterparts, and in the GATT arena in general), greatly irritated by the Japanese distribution channels which Americans clearly do not understand. This does not prevent the Japanese from recognizing the way in which they may be seen by the *Gai-jin*. But they are not really prepared to change that part of the system which is authentically Japanese, and which constitutes the major barrier resented by non-Japanese business people.

Whether Japan is becoming less *Keiretsu*-bound is a controversial issue. Dedoussis (2001, p. 7) notes: 'the continuing enthusiasm for certain Japanese practices such as loose functional, and even hierarchical, demarcations, and development of Keiretsu-like inter-firm alliances in other countries attests to the need for scrutinizing the "end of Japanese management" argument.' On the other hand, Pirog *et al.* (1997) note that younger consumers are more likely to shop at large discount stores, because they are more price-conscious, less tied to traditional bonds and able to access cars. These new discount stores cut out the middle of the distribution channels, determine their own merchandise assortments and pay in cash rather than depending on credit.

Recent opportunities have allowed access to shopping outside of the *Keiretsu* system. The long economic slump provided opportunities for foreign retailers to acquire the operations of failed Japanese retailers, giving them access to the market. Recently, discount retailers, such as Wal-Mart and Costco (USA) and Carrefour (France) have entered the Japanese retail system. Online shopping has also gained popularity with young consumers.

Overcoming the barrier of Japanese distribution

Do real-life examples indicate that foreign companies have achieved original and efficient market entry?

Box 12.2

Rosenthal in Japan

Rosenthal, a German company, exports porcelain items, fine glassware and trinkets, which sell quite well on the Japanese market, more as gifts than for the buyer's use. The range of products offered in Japan is somewhat different to that in other countries: emphasis is put more on tea drinking items, which may be offered as presents, than on dishes. Rosenthal constantly surveys the Japanese market, in order to adapt its product range to Japanese tastes and to find those items which could best be sold in Japan. Over the last twenty years, Rosenthal has established close relations with its Japanese distributors. They are frequently invited to visit Rosenthal's production facilities in Germany.

Rosenthal assists them a great deal in the display of its products on the shelves and maintains a full-time team of window dressers in Japan. The main dealers, that is large department stores, are visited at least once a week. Moreover, Rosenthal has initiated a special training session for Japanese retailers: each year a group of Japanese retailers is invited to a ten-day session in Germany, with all expenses paid by Rosenthal, in order to learn how to advise customers. Retailers greatly appreciate this support, and they willingly push Rosenthal's products, especially since margins are hefty.

(Source: Dupuis and de Maricourt, 1989, p. 152.)

Many instances tend to show that the barriers imposed by Japanese distribution channels may be overcome. Ohmae (1985) quotes the case of the US pharmaceutical company Shaklee, which has directly transferred its door-to-door sales system from the United States to Japan. Shaklee had noticed that there was no legal rule requiring vitamins and nutritive pills to be sold only through medical doctors or pharmacists. It was only a custom: no regulation had formally imposed it. The Japanese pharmaceutical companies observed the phenomenal growth of Shaklee's sales but were unable to react. They were afraid of damaging relations with their traditional intermediaries, especially wholesalers and retail pharmacists. They were still obliged to rely on them for the sales of their drugs. Another US-based pharmaceutical company, Bristol-Myers, also implemented such a door-to-door sales programme, with their Japanese joint-venture partner (Cateora, 1983). The product was sold in a box that contained toothpaste, analgesics and other home remedies, and was offered to households on the basis of consignment sale: every six months a salesperson visited the household, replenished the collection and collected the payment for the products that had been used. Pahud de Mortanges *et al.* (1997) explain how many large pharmaceutical companies from Western countries have been able successfully to enter the Japanese market. They have adapted to local selling practices,

with one salesperson promoting pharmaceuticals per 2.5 practising physicians whereas the ratio is one salesperson to every ten physicians in the United States.

Such cases as Rosenthal (see Box 12.2) or ComputerLand (case A12.1) clearly prove that Japanese distribution channels are penetrable by foreign companies. Montgomery (1991) also provides evidence of US companies, such as Williams Sonoma, successfully circumventing the *Keiretsu* distribution system, via catalogue sales and limited retail stores of their own. Moreover, the Japanese distribution system does change, especially under the harsh competitive forces of the Japanese market. As Ohmae (1985) stated, it is not a 'stone statue', nor are there written rules that prohibit its change.

How to deal with the Japanese distribution system

What are the stages that must be followed to permit successful entry into Japanese channels while respecting the uniqueness of Japanese culture? It may be a slow process, but a five-stage approach for the successful introduction of a foreign product into Japanese distribution channels can be recommended (Shimaguchi and Rosenberg, 1979; Montgomery, 1991; Pirog *et al.* 1997):

1. Find a Japanese partner; this is the key to securing adaptability to the unique cultural environment. The *sogoshosha* (trading companies) are potential partners, provided that they do not represent a competing Japanese producer or export the products of a Japanese competitor, and are not related to a larger group (*zaibatsu*) which has competing lines of products. An important choice is to decide whether to ally with a company in the same industry or in a non-related industry. Whereas one may tend naturally to the former in order to ensure a smooth start (in that the two partners share the same business culture), it may prove much more dangerous in the long run. The Japanese local partner may become a competitor on world markets through new products originally designed by the joint venture and then transferred to the Japanese partner's main operations (Czinkota and Woronoff, 1991).

2. Find an original position in the market, either by offering a significantly higher level of quality or a significant price advantage, or by emphasizing the exoticism of the product as being foreign and imported.

3. Identify alternative opportunities for distribution channels. Philips, for instance, has succeeded in splitting its sales of electric shavers and small household appliances between two different types of channel: large department stores and chains on the one hand, small retailers on the other.

4. Be patient, aim for the long term and be prepared to wait for a long pay-back period (probably five to ten years).

5. Be aware that it is necessary to adopt the mentality of Japanese distribution channels. Build a network of personal relationships, develop loyalty, spend time and resources building relationships of trust.

12.2

Criteria for choosing foreign distribution channels

Goldman (2001) studied the transfer of retail formats in China, finding that six transfer strategies were appropriate under different conditions: for companies with a global orientation, strategies included niche protection and a format-pioneering opportunity (leading edge); for companies with a host country orientation, strategies include opportunism (exploit connections), formal extension (home to compatible countries), portfolio transfer (formats from most similar country) and superior competitive position. Which of these strategies is more appropriate is based on many factors both inside (e.g. ethnocentric versus geocentric perspectives; see Alexander and Myers, 2000) and outside a firm, in terms of other companies and relationships (Ford, 2002).

McNaughton and Bell (2000) surveyed Canadian firms with export sales, finding that 63 per cent used the same channel as in their home market. They stress that firms need to fully evaluate alternative before extending their existing change. The method for selecting channels abroad is based on a checklist of issues that have to be dealt with in the choice of foreign distribution channels (Cateora, 1993; Czinkota and Ronkainen, 1990). The '9-Cs' criteria that seem most significant are as follows:

1. *Consumers and their characteristics*. Some geographical segments in a foreign market may be, for instance, more import oriented. Channels serving these segments should therefore be preferred. The French beer Kronenbourg, for example, entered the United States and was initially available only in the centre of New York, then went on to reach the whole metropolis including the suburbs. The reason for this is that people within this area consume large quantities of imported as well as US beer. It was not until five years later that Kronenbourg became available throughout the whole of the United States. De Mooij and Hofstede (2002) suggest that cultural dimensions point to groups of countries likely to differ in their propensity for certain retail functions. For instance, they suggest that one of the consequences of long-term orientation is being sparing with resources. This leads to a preference to pick up merchandise and may lead to lower acceptability of e-commerce.

2. *Culture*. This point has already been considered in relation to Japanese distribution networks. Distribution is the element of the marketing mix what is most deeply rooted in culture, because it is closely related to everyday life and human relationships (even in large-scale, self service, apparently depersonalized stores). For instance, Griffith (1998) studied the meanings of the market bazaar in

Amman, Jordan. He found that the ties to culture and self-identification were so strong, that this created a barrier to newer distribution techniques. The next section describes in more detail the impact of culture on selected aspects of distribution.

3. *Character*. It is important that the image projected by the channel, its sales methods, shop locations and clientele as well as appearance, should correspond to the image and character that the product is intended to convey. An important reason for the success of Louis Vuitton Malletier is the large-scale investment in a global network of exclusive retail outlets, located in high-profile areas in major cities throughout the world. Conversely, Blockbuster failed in Germany when they tried to fight the pre-established image of video rental stores to create a family-oriented image: in Germany video stores are not places children enter, as one-third of the titles are pornographic (Simmonds, 1999). Retail stores need to fully understand the importance of image and positioning overseas. Transferring an image from one country to another can be diffcult. Burt and Carralero-Encinas (2000) surveyed consumers in the United Kingdom and Spain on their perceptions of the traditional British retailer Marks & Spencer, which for several years has had outlets in Spain. They found that the image as a conservative, middle-class store was very similar in the two countries, but other aspects did not transfer as well, including store reputation, quality and range, which were more positive in Britain.

Local consumers may also remain faithful to their traditional distribution outlets for specific segments of consumption, precisely because of their traditional character. In Spain, for instance, Nueno and Bennett (1997) explain that, despite the continuous development of hypermarkets, consumers make a clear distinction between the products sold in the different distribution channels and prefer to purchase perishable goods such as fish, fresh fruit and vegetables, meat and bread in traditional stores.

4. Necessary *capital* relates to the issue of what financial resources are necessary to start and maintain the channel (e.g. fixed capital, working capital, possible initial losses that will need to be financed).

5. *Cost*. This criterion is strongly linked to the previous one, but relates more to trade margins than to overhead costs. It depends largely on the respective positions of strength of producers and distributors. In the United Kingdom, for instance, food distribution is in the hands of a very limited number of large store chains such as Tesco, Sainsbury and Asda (see Child, 2002 for information about Tesco's strategy). These giants exert pressure on major manufacturers to make them bear part of the cost, in particular those relating to storage; they also request smaller, more frequent deliveries with mixed items. A similar situation exists in France where the powerful hypermarkets impose numerous constraints on the producers, increasing their overheads: payments of fixed commissions in return for the right to carry the reference number, layout of the counter displays by the producer's own staff, direct help in sales promotion, etc.

6. *Competition* arises in channels either through competing products being placed side by side on shelves, or through competitors refusing other producers access to the distribution channels. For instance, Czinkota and Ronkainen (1990) cite the case of the American manufacturers of caustic soda, which is used in the manufacture of glass, steel and chemical products, who were incapable of successful entry into the Japanese market despite their price advantage. The Japanese union of manufacturers of caustic soda formed a cartel that apparently set the level of imports, specified which trading company was to work with which American supplier and bought up the cheap American imports in order to sell them through the intermediary of its members. The success of the operation was twofold, since they received the profit in place of the American exporter and still managed to keep control of their market. The American exporters were equally unsuccessful in their attempts to deal directly through small distributors, since the industrial users of the product were concerned about the risk of cutting themselves out from their main source of supply (the Japanese) if they placed orders directly with the American exporters.

The power of competition will somewhat depend on the concentration of retailers, which is likely to differ across cultures. For instance, in Australia two department stores account for 82 per cent of the market, in the United States the top five account for 65 per cent and in Japan the top three only account for 32 per cent (Euromonitor, 2003a,

2003b, 2004). Larger retail groups hold more power in the channel. Aalto-Setala (2002) found that, at least in Finland, this leads to higher price mark-ups.

7. *Coverage* is another important element. It is important to cover markets that are widely scattered. Furthermore, markets that are very concentrated tend also to concentrate maximum competition, since demand attracts supply. The coverage in terms of product range, sizes and options must also be considered, especially when channel members look for complementary products, spare parts and so on. The product coverage according to channel type varies across countries: a French *droguerie* doesn't sell the same products as a US *drugstore* or a German *Drogerie*, although there is overlap between the product ranges.

8. *Continuity.* It is vital that the channel in which investment is to be made does not turn out to be unusable for some reason (e.g. bankruptcy or financial difficulties, recapture of market share by more aggressive competition, the introduction of legal prohibitions on the sale of products through the channel, etc.). Continuity may be hampered by slick competitors. Cateora (1983) cites the example of an American firm that lost roughly half its local sales in South America. Two of its European competitors had unofficially agreed to force the American company out of the market. One of the two, which was selling a wide range of products, forced the distributors to stop representing the even wider range marketed by the American. The other competitor purchased shares in the company that distributed the American company's products.

Continuity makes intitial channel choice that much more important. Research seems to show that consumers make the choice about where to shop based on similar criteria across cultures. For instance, Severin *et al.* (2001) examined shopping centre choice in Canada, the United States and Norway, finding that good service, wide selection, low prices and good quality all had a significant influence on the choice of shopping centre.

9. *Control.* The ideal situation of course is where the company creates its own distribution network. This ensures maximum control. It appears that integrating the company's own distribution abroad should be considered, particularly when the product differentiation is large (i.e. where there are few

substitutes) or where the network assets are transaction specific, such as a product which requires lengthy training for the consumer as well as the seller (Anderson and Coughlan, 1987). Another alternative is to control by equity, via a carefully drafted contract (the written base), or preferably through long-established trusting relationships with the local distributor (personal verbal base). For example, the Caterpillar company sells worldwide without sales subsidiary companies, by using a system of dealers. Some Caterpillar dealers have been in business for more than half a century. If ownership is not practical, control of marketing may be kept. Gabrielsson *et al.* (2002) found that a hybrid channel strategy, where sales and distribution are managed by foreign channels, but sales promotion is managed by the producer, is the most favoured option in the personal computer industry in Europe.

12.3

The role of distribution as a 'cultural filter'

Culture at the interface between shoppers and the stores

Distribution forms subtle relationships with consumers by means of direct contact. People get into the habit of buying certain products which are backed by fixed services, at clearly defined times, in particular shops. Table 12.1 presents guidelines for exploring how distribution is affected by the prevailing cultural patterns in a definite country/culture context. The table refers to specific sections in other chapters where some of the underlying rationales have already been exposed. Naturally, culture explains only part of the variance in distribution systems; another part is related to shoppers and their sociodemographic characteristics, or to economic conditions.

Shopping behaviour differs in many ways according to culture. The first point to take into consideration is whether the shopping experience is partly experienced as a waste of time in the whole consumption process, as may be the case in countries where time is strongly economic. The differences in opening hours in northern and southern Europe clearly illustrate the

Table 12.1 Influence of culture on some aspects of distribution *vis-à-vis* shoppers

Selected aspects of distribution	Traits that *may* differ according to country/culture
(1) Shopping behaviour	Is time spent shopping experienced as wasted? (economic time; section 2.2) Is return of goods standard behaviour? (complaining behaviour; section 4.3) Who is the shopper? (sex roles, age, etc.) Degree of loyalty to the shop and the shopkeeper (section 4.2)
(2) Opening hours	Religion-based arguments in favour of restricted store opening hours Femininity-based arguments (store personnel should not be exploited)
(3) Product range	Products may be banned because of religious or legal prescriptions
(4) Willingness to service consumers	Human nature is good (friendliness towards shoppers) versus bad (indifference)/negative view of service to others (section 9.3)
(5) Waiting lines	Compliance with rules (see Tables 3.3 and 3.6 and section 9.3)
(6) Thefts by consumers or personnel	Ethical behaviour – ingroup orientation (see sections 2.3, 3.6 and 15.6)
(7) Self-service versus personnel in contact	See section 9.3

influence of culture on the distribution system: in northern Europe, Sunday is sacred and a prevailing feminine orientation strives towards protecting store employees' quality of life (which would be spoilt by long opening hours). Griffin *et al.* (2000) discuss the affect of product scarcity and lack of selection on the meaning of the shopping experience in Russia. They found that Russian consumers rated the utility of their shopping system lower than US consumers, while their hedonic experience was similar. It seems that Russian consumers may be happy to get a product they need and therefore less concerned about the retail environment. Straughan and Albers-Miller (2001) found that many aspects of culture influence domestic store loyalty across a sample of consumers from the United States, Australia, France and South Korea. For instance, consumers were found to be more loyal if they were from a strong uncertainty avoidance or collectivist culture, or if they were male.

Certain products may be banned from particular outlets for legal dispositions based on religious or social beliefs. In France, for instance, basic drugs, and more generally non-ethical drugs such as aspirin, can be sold only through pharmacies; in the United States, as in many countries, drugstores sell basic medicines. These practices correspond to differing views on whether people can have recourse to self-medication. The French legislators do not trust patients and require them to proceed in all cases through doctors and pharmacists, whereas the US system is confident of people's common sense and ability to distinguish what is a flu and what is a serious illness.

Another example concerns the distribution of beer in Turkey, a Muslim country: up to June 1984, beer was considered a non-alcoholic beverage and thus sold in coffee-houses; beer consumption increased sixfold between 1969 and 1983. Under pressure from religious authorities, the government reclassified beer as an alcoholic beverage (which it undeniably is), banned its advertising on radio and television, and prohibited its sales in outlets lacking alcohol licences. The prohibition of sales through the channel of coffee-houses resulted in a dramatic drop in beer sales in Turkey (Miller and Demirel, 1988).

Wide differences also exist in the waiting and service conditions at the cashier's desk: in the United States and Japan it is standard practice in supermarkets to help customers pack their purchases; an employee is often specifically in charge of packing; in most of Europe, where mass distribution is oriented towards low price rather than service, customers have to pack their things in a hurry while paying their bill (Turcq and Usunier, 1985).

Theft, either by customers or store employees, is an important phenomenon in distribution that has to be deciphered, country by country, in light of cultural differences. Naturally, economic constraints (purchasing power per capita) play a certain role but they do not explain all: in France and Italy, theft is more developed than in Greece which has a much lower per capita income. In some countries, theft is not a problem because it is clearly understood as evil by everybody. The kind of consensus which brings about this favourable result is hard to explain, and probably even harder to replicate. Where the rate of theft to sales amounts to several per cent, it cannot be explained simply by economic conditions, namely poverty. Theft is regarded by some as a sport and is implicitly understood as a legitimate way of social redistribution. Another explanation is strong ingroup orientation whereby ethical behaviour is limited to the ingroup: in countries where retailers are immigrants belonging to a particular foreign group, thieving from a store that belongs to a foreigner may not be felt to be evil but rather as a way to recover one's own goods from this 'outlander'. Theft may also be situation specific, as in the case of digital music and video downloading via the Internet. Generally, taking a music CD from a store would be considered stealing, while, in contrast, downloading the same CD off the Internet is considered acceptable by many. The only difference is in the method of obtaining the product rather than the principle. (For articles concerning digital piracy see WS12.3.)

The influence of culture on the relationship between channel members

Depending on the country concerned, the relationships between domestic producers and distributors may be stronger, more loyal and collaborative, or weaker, more unstable and conflictual. Strongly established links between members of domestic channels generally make entry more difficult for foreign firms. France, which largely invented the concept of the hypermarket, benefits from a distribution set-up that is effective, powerful and strongly independent of producers. It is so strong that products bearing the store name compete head to head with the producers' brands, creating an atmosphere of conflict between producers and distributors where loyalty is difficult to maintain. The system is inherently susceptible to penetration by imports: foreign suppliers are perceived as more flexible and a good alternative to domestic producers. At the other extreme, Japan is the place where links between producers and distributors are traditionally very strong and positive. Central to this are the *Keiretsus* of distribution, true vertical relationships, mixing business and emotion in typically Japanese fashion, as described in section 12.1. These networks are based on a powerful sense of loyalty, with many services being rendered by one party for the other, and therefore more difficult for foreign companies to penetrate. Kim and Oh (2002) surveyed distributors in Japan and the United States, finding that long-term orientation, which is more prevalent in Japan, positively affects distributor commitment. They also found that the level of total interdependence was more important than interdependence asymmetry for Japanese distributors. Skarmeas and Katsikeas (2001) also found that higher levels of interdependence, investment, relational norms and trust characterized high performance UK importers.

Kale and McIntyre (1991) posit a series of hypotheses on channel relationship based on Hofstede's (1980) four cultural dimensions. They first consider the initiation process where firms try to draft the distribution agreement. According to them, companies coming from high uncertainty avoidance (UA) societies will be biased in favour of finding partners who have a solid reputation and can offer written performance guarantees; conversely, in the case of weak UA, partners will be sought more informally and more flexibility will be shown in negotiations. Firms in highly individualist and masculine cultures (typically the United States) will tend to choose partners on objective criteria, negotiate the terms of the agreement from an adversarial standpoint, and engage in new relationships as well as divorce themselves from the old ones on the basis of economic criteria. Conversely, partners coming from collectivist and relatively feminine societies (for instance South Korea, Taiwan, Thailand) will be more relationship centred and will expect more harmony in the partnership, and dissolution will be less aggressive and less frequent.

During the implementation process, Kale and McIntyre hypothesize that high power distance (PD) will lead firms to use coercion in their influence attempts, whereas low PD firms will avoid coercion, will prefer face-to-face communication to memos and will engage in consultative rather than unilateral decision making. High individualism and masculinity will result in more frequent and manifest conflicts between channel members, as well as lower levels of cooperation. In contrast to these orientations, they cite a senior executive of Coca-Cola in Japan explaining that: 'Once the partnership was in place, it wasn't just the Coca-Cola company selling in Japan; it became a family, a spirit of togetherness, of common purpose.'

Merrilees and Miller (1999) examined the roles of product and relationship (*guanxi*) in direct selling (Amway) in Australia (individualist) and compared their results to Luk *et al.* (1996) from China (collectivist). They found that in both countries relationship elements affect direct selling effectiveness, but in China, relationship elements are more important and more coherent in line with *guanxi*. Similarly, O'Grady and Lane (1992), interviewed chief executive officers of almost 300 companies, finding that Canadian retailers when they enter the US market have to face different values. Americans are significantly more competition oriented (more achievement oriented, more risk taking) and more oriented towards a Protestant work ethic than the Canadians. The Canadian retailers are less individualistic and masculine and higher in power distance and risk avoidance than the American distributors. These findings are largely consistent with the hypotheses of Kale and McIntyre in distinguishing competitive/confrontational distribution scenes from collaborative ones: 'The executives frequently commented that Americans were found to be much more competitive than Canadians. Frequently the executives voiced comments typically used to describe battles such as "It was all out war" or "Their arsenal was impressive"' (O'Grady and Lane, 1992, p. 8).

Shoham *et al.* (1997) have studied conflicts in international channels of distribution, that is, when channels members belong to different cultures and are separated by cultural distance. They show very clearly that the degree of channel conflict increases with cultural distance, whereas a high quality distribution system, in the form of visiting foreign markets frequently and providing channel support, tends to decrease channel conflicts. In the case of Greek exporters (collectivist/high UA and PD) and their British importers (individualistic/low UA and PD), Katsikeas and Piercy (1991) show that the relationships are fairly stable with a low degree of conflict and few communication problems, except on pricing issues. This is reinforced by the fact that, among the British importers, there are a good number of Greeks or Cypriots, which shows the strong value of having one's own countrymen as 'beachheads' in the target market.

There is also evidence that leadership styles are not transferable across cultures. For instance, Mehta *et al.* (2001) found that in the United States a supportive leadership style led to higher cooperation, followed by a participative and directive style. In Finland the participative style led to the most cooperation, followed by supportive and directive leadership styles. Finally, in Poland a supportive leadership style was positively related to cooperation, while a directive style was negatively related to cooperation. They suggest that in Poland the directive style may be too closely related to the previous communist system.

12.4
Direct marketing worldwide

One among millions of direct marketing purchasers in the world, Jean-Claude buys the family Christmas cake (a Deluxe medium, 2 3/4 pounds) from Collin Street Bakery in Corsicana, Texas, which is baked following the traditional recipe of Gus Weidman, a Bavarian who went to the United States at the end of the nineteenth century. Bought by credit card, the cake reaches his home in France within one month. Catalogue sales have been expanding worldwide at a very fast rate over the last 10 to 15 years. In 1993, *Catalog Age* reported that 37 per cent of US mail-order companies had international operations while another 20 per cent were considering the possibility of an overseas programme (Robles and Akhter, 1997). Lands' End, one of the leading US direct marketers worldwide, sends its products to more than 170 countries, while large European mail-order companies such as Otto Versand, Quelle, Bertelsmann and La Redoute have developed important cross-border operations, especially in Europe (Akhter, 1996). The development of international credit cards and the consequent facilitation of international payments have greatly decreased the transaction costs for both consumers and cataloguers. Restrictive legislation opening hours for stores may be an incentive for consumers to buy direct: Germany and Austria, two countries where store opening hours have been historically strictly limited in comparison to other developed countries, rank first and fourth worldwide as regards catalogue sales per capita (Mühlbacher *et al.*, 1997); the German catalogue industry is the strongest in the world relative to country size.

There are several problems involved in selling direct cross-border. First, logistics issues: direct mail can be sent from the domestic country, from within the target country, or from a third country, with the objective of minimizing mailing costs while keeping speed and security of delivery at a fair level. Although it may seem the easiest solution to mail from within the target country because the local language and culture will be better understood, there may be constraints in the local postal service that make it more advantageous to mail from a third-country; This can prove cheaper in terms of mailing costs (Desmet and Xardel, 1996).

The second major issue about cross-border direct marketing deals with regulation, mainly postal regulations, customs and privacy issues, all of which are largely country-specific (Rawwas *et al.*, 1996). However, regulations are becoming more and more standardized at the regional level, as in the EU where a European Union Postal Service was implemented in 1998 after six years of preparation. Customs may be a problem, since goods sent to reach the foreign customer for a specific date (e.g. Christmas) can be delayed by customs authorities; this will not be the case when goods are shipped to industrialized nations.

The third issue is the availability of mailing lists, and their degree of reliability in terms of names and addresses, especially when they are not regularly updated. Rosenfield (1994) makes an international comparison of US direct marketing in the USA and in other countries, and states that US marketing is different rather than better. Mailing costs in the USA are comparatively low, but mailing lists are sometimes of marginal quality, causing a low net response rate. Among the European countries, France appears as the most high-tech country in the world for direct mail but with expensive lists; Germany also has very high standards and world-class technology but German lists are subject to stringent privacy rules (*Datenschutz*); Italy, on the other hand, with its inefficient postal service, is a relatively difficult context for direct marketing. In Latin America, Argentina and Chile are favourable countries with fairly good infrastructure, but Brazil lags behind because of postal and phone problems.

Direct marketing has to be adapted for language and cultural reasons. The text, for catalogues, letters and so on, is generally prepared with the help of locals or even directly in the target country to ensure appropriateness of language. Some catalogues advertise directly worldwide in English. Examples are *the World's Best*, from Baltimore, or *Shepplers*, which sells Western wear; they target an affluent English-speaking audience and use international mailing lists or selective national mailing lists. The Lands' End catalogue contains a four-page leaflet called 'Lands' End Glossary' which explains the basics in Arabic, German, Japanese and Spanish. Language adaptation must also target the addressee's name: 'Jean', a boy's first name in French, is a girl's first name in English, so that sometimes Jean-Claude receives international direct mail adressed to 'Mrs' or 'Ms'.

The source culture is often indicated by the origin of the mail, the letter or the stamp, and it may be desirable to emphasize the culture if it is positively valued in the target country (there is a strong association of the source country with the products sold and a positive evaluation of it as a country of origin). Conversely, it may be better to fully localize operations when the name must be local: Germany's Bertelsmann sells books and records direct in France, under the name 'France Loisirs', because the original company name is not positively associated with cultural products in France. The Bertelsmann's book club operates in various European countries (Germany, France, the UK) and adapts its operations to suit each country, within the same basic formula (a two-year subscription with a minimum purchase of one book every three months): the catalogues are adapted for each market; in France it sells through 500 salespeople, a method that is totally ineffective in the UK; there are no shops in the UK but France and Germany maintain a network of 200 and 300 shops respectively (Desmet and Xardel, 1996).

Ethics are a problem in international direct mail; concerns with privacy, and the possible fraudulent uses of mailing lists, are major concerns in a number of countries: Germany and New Zealand have very strict privacy regulations but some other countries are more lenient. Even in neighbouring countries, such as the United States and Canada, ethical views on direct marketing differ: Canadians tend to have more power distance than Americans and resent letters written in too direct a style; therefore, letters have to be written differently for Canadian audiences (Graves, 1997).

Direct marketing and the Internet

Today, most countries have access to the Internet. According to Direct Marketing (2001): 'Nearly 1 billion Internet users, about 15 per cent of the world's population, will generate more than $5 trillion in Internet commerce by 2005' and the number is increasing. Saskin (2001) estimates that there is a new Internet user every two seconds. It is forecast that retail sales of goods and services online will be upwards of $269 billion in 2005 (Bakos, 2001).

Direct marketing is increasingly using the Internet as a global medium. Many, such as Urban Outfitters (see WS12) use their website to provide detailed product information along with the ability to make online purchases. Some companies are entirely Internet based, with no bricks-and-mortar shopfronts at all. Amazon.com, perhaps the most widely recognized of these companies, started as an online bookstore and is now more like an online department store (see WS12.4). Lands' End, like many other direct mail companies, have a website from which everything in the catalogue can be ordered: it checks the inventory in real time, totals the order and provides for payment and shipment. CatalogSite, for instance, offers catalogues online to both end customers and catalogue distributors, and 3M's website gives information on a growing number of its 60,000 products, provides access to further information on its products and worldwide operations, and offers items for sale.

Some companies have flourished on the Internet, such as the book distributor/online department store Amazon.com, the leading bookseller on the Internet, which devotes a webpage to each product offered. The Internet allows companies to display a considerable amount of information on their products: the AMP connect web catalogue enables users to navigate among 70,000 different spare parts. Toyota's website offers text screens with detailed product specifications and dealer locations; potential consumers can also test a variety of colours and view their future car from a variety of vantage points as well as look at interiors (Hodges, 1997).

Although a fascinating instrument for international marketing, the Internet has a number of limitations, in terms of extensive use. The first key issue is that of the network infrastructure which was initially built for US national defence purposes and was then developed by academic users. The commercial development of the web is a formidable challenge because the numbers of servers have to be regularly increased and jams on the web can be a reality. The second issue concerns the safety of payments by credit card on the Internet; specifically, the need to ensure that the card number is not used fraudulently by opportunistic Internet navigators. Although many potential customers see this as a problem, the use of encryption and the presence of specialized intermediaries between supplier and customers makes fraud more and more unlikely. Payment will be less of a problem in the future since it is now possible to load one's bank card with cash value using one's regular bank's website, and use electronic cash anonymously for online purchases (Hodges, 1997).

Quelch and Klein (1996) foresaw that the main uses of the Internet for international marketing would be sending company information to internal customers (employees and intermediaries), sending product information to and conducting transactions with customers, and providing marketing and sales support and information to internal users. Only a limited number of products can be sold on the Internet, because virtual shopping lacks the full-scale experience of real shopping, especially the human encounter and the opportunity to see and buy the product directly. According to Tian and Emery (2002), speciality consumer goods are the most likely to be successfully marketed over the Internet considering the likelihood that consumers will already be well informed about the product. For example, the website americanaexchange.com specializes in finding and selling antique and rare books. In addition, Kwak et al. (2002, p. 35) discuss some of the unique aspects of the Internet that allow certain products to be successfully experienced prior to purchase: 'over the past few years, new internet music startups like CDNow, N2K, MP3.com, and Liquid Audio have revolutionized the way the industry and consumers transact . . . Via numerous product trials and free information for the product on the web that are not typically available offline.

The lack of ability to really experience some types of products over the Internet explains the failure of some virtual shopping galleries which ceased operating within a few months. The word 'virtual', often advertised as if it were an 'open sesame', is far from inoffensive:

The technology of virtual simulation cannot but reinforce this risk of de-realization by giving a pseudo-concrete and pseudo-palpable character to imaginary entities . . . On one hand, thus, they constitute tools to command complexity, propitiating a better intelligibility, on the other they have a certain propensity to encourage latent forms of illusion and even schizophrenia. The more we recur to simulation as a scriptural means and as a way of inventing the world, the greater the risk to confound the world with the representations we make of it. (Queau, 1993, pp. 98–9, cited by Ribeiro, 1997, p. 499.)

Due to the US background and technology used for the world wide web, the majority of webpages are currently in English (Tian and Emery, 2002), but this is changing. Many major international organizations and companies are producing websites in multiple languages (see *WS12* for examples of multilanguage sites). Cutitta (2002) notes that in little over a year the per cent of those accessing the web with English as their first language dropped from 50 per cent to 43 per cent.

Cox (2000) highlights further logistic EU Internet hurdles: 'The challenge for the EU is to come up with meaningful rules for financial services and e-commerce without strangling the nascent Internet economy in the cradle. A case in point: if a company wants to set up accounts with the same bank in different EU countries, as many as 900 signatures are required' (p. 64).

Naturally, the Internet is not free of problems. As an article in the *Economist* (2000, p. 18) put it,

Here is this amazingly useful, if disruptive, thing, built from the bottom up by idealists, largely self-regulated and beyond the reach of governments or big companies. It is a nice idea. Sadly, the Internet is neither as different nor as 'naturally' free as wired Utopians claim. The sheer pervasiveness of the Internet makes it impossible for even the best-intentioned of regulators to keep out. Such issues as privacy, consumer protection, intellectual property rights, contracts and taxation cannot be left entirely to self regulation if e-commerce is to flourish. And, as the judge's ruling in favour of a break-up of Microsoft has just confirmed . . . antitrust action may be even more important online than off.

Both domestic and international legal issues are difficult to manage on the Internet. For instance, what constitutes a contract in cyberspace, how do countries collect taxes for online transactions, how do we protect intellectual property, how do we stop certain types of information from appearing, and how do we protect consumers, where is the legal jurisdiction – the location of the buyer, the seller, or both (Zugelder *et al.*, 2000)? Recently, Internet taxation issues have been attracting more attention (Waltner, 1999). Malaysia has shown concern about losing tax revenues from e-commerce transactions (Kasim and Ravendran, 2001). In 2001, the United Kingdom vetoed plans to introduce legislation on e-commerce in the EU as it will be impossible to enforce the VAT on non-EU companies' (*International Tax Review*, 2001). For now we will have to wait and see.

12.5

Sales promotion: Other customs, other manners

Sales promotion techniques are fairly universal, but in their use and the conditions of their implementation they vary cross-nationally and depend on cultural variables (see Box 12.3). Sales promotion targets some basic marketing objectives that are cross-culturally valid. It aims to engage the consumer in any of the following: (1) a first trial; (2) a first purchase; (3) an immediate purchase; (4) re-purchase; (5) an increase in frequency of purchase; and (6) entering a point of sale. Promotional techniques combine the sales proposal with the following:

1. Discounts or rebates of various kinds: coupons, 'in-pack' money-off, reimbursement offers, etc., mostly directed at immediate purchase.
2. Competitions: games, contests, lotteries, sweepstakes, etc.
3. Collection devices of various kinds (stamps and continuity plans), oriented towards increasing the frequency of purchase and building consumer loyalty.
4. Free samples or some kind of cross-product offer, for the purpose of consumer trial especially.
5. Gifts: 'in-pack' gifts, purchase with purchase, reusable packaging, product bonus, etc.

Box 12.3

Global transferability of sales promotions: Lego examples

A case in point is Lego A/S, the Danish toy marketer which undertook American-style consumer promotion in Japan some years ago. Earlier, the company had measurably improved its penetration of U.S. households by employing 'bonus' packs and gift promotions. Encouraged by that success, it decided to transfer these tactics unaltered to other markets, including Japan, where penetration had stalled. But these lures left Japanese consumers unmoved. Subsequent investigation showed that consumers considered the promotions to be wasteful, expensive, and not very appealing. Similar reactions were recorded in other countries. Lego's marketers thus got their first lesson on the limitations of the global transferability of sales promotions.

In 1997, Lego was involved in a global promotion with Shell Oil, since promotional Lego toys were designed exclusively to be distributed at Shell's 44,000 service stations world-wide. The material for this global promotion was the same world-wide but the tactics used, including giveaways, cash-back coupons and discount coupons, were decided locally.

(Source: Kashani, 1989, pp. 92–3 and Koranteng, 1997.)

Cross-national differences in the use of sales promotion techniques

The first question to be addressed is: who is the target? It is not solely the end consumer. Sales promotion may also address store personnel by encouraging them to stock a product or to display it in a favourable position, or to promote the product directly. In some countries, the success of some batteries derives from the fact that store personnel put one brand in a more favourable display position than others; they do so because of the gifts they receive from the batteries' manufacturers, ranging from a camera to vacations abroad. In less developed countries, where retailers in rural areas lack resources, they may be more appropriate targets for sales promotion than the final consumers who have little choice but to buy what is actually in the only store available. Similarly, where people have servants who shop for food and household supplies, it may be better to target them, the actual buyers, rather than the members of the family who employs them (Foxman *et al.* 1988).

A second question is whether a technique is considered ethical: sales promotion regulations differ cross-nationally according to various assumptions about what is moral or immoral and what is fair or unfair in the relationship between a merchandiser/sales promoter and a customer/shopper. Most developed countries strictly regulate sales promotion in order to prevent abuses (Boddewyn and Leardi, 1989). There is also some fear, as with advertising, that sales promotion costs could result in overpricing of products. Czinkota and Ronkainen (1990) cite the example of AC Nielsen, which tried to introduce money-off coupons in Chile that had to be sent to the manufacturer for reimbursement. The supermarket union opposed the promotion on the grounds that it would raise costs unnecessarily and recommended its members not to accept the coupons.

The areas in which ethical issues are mostly raised are competitions, gifts and cross-product offers. The United Kingdom and the United States are the most favourable countries for sales promotions (Boddewyn and Leardi, 1989). Anglo-Saxon countries are generally more liberal than other countries, especially for competitions: most kinds of lotteries, free draws and sweepstakes are legally permitted. In most Anglo-Saxon countries, private betting (bookmakers) organizations are permitted whereas in most other countries, betting (horse races, lotteries) is state controlled, since it is seen as immoral for private individuals to profit from organizing lotteries and betting games. Italy authorizes lotteries and sweepstakes where prizes are not in cash but in kind. Prizes in competitions are often limited to small amounts: The Netherlands limits prizes to 250 guilders, which severely restricts the attractiveness of sales promotion competitions. France allows competitions, but they are carefully controlled so that no purchase is needed to enter the competition. This leads in many countries to precisely drafted regulations where terms such as 'purchase obligation' and 'chance' are strictly defined (see Box 12.4 which describes the regulation of sales promotion competitions in the canton of Geneva, Switzerland, where Swiss precision leaves little room for ambiguity).

Many national regulations prohibit gifts or limit their value. In France, the value of a promotional gift cannot be higher than 4 per cent of the retail price and must not exceed FFr. 10 (US$1.87). The idea behind this prohibition is that consumers should buy products, not gifts. If the value of the gift is too high in comparison to the total price of the item, this could result in the consumers being fooled by the merchandiser. Collectors' items, as gifts, are subject to the same kind of regulatory ceiling: the value of the collector's item associated with the purchase is often legally limited. Sales promotions encouraging a first trial, such as cross-product offers and purchase with purchase offers, are often controlled by national legislation because, when consumers pay for two products at the same time they cannot clearly assess the one for which they actually pay. A description of the sales promotion rules of the main countries (which are regularly updated) may be found in Boddewyn (1992).

Some sales promotion techniques are fairly resistant cross-culturally, since they appear less questionable: free samples as a way to induce people to try the product; money off the next purchase as a way to induce consumers to repeat their purchase; point-of-purchase materials, product demonstrations as a way to increase consumer knowledge of the product, free

---

Box 12.4

Sales promotion through competitions in Switzerland (Geneva)

Competitions for sales promotion are governed by the law on lotteries. The basic principle is fairly simple: *chance cannot be linked with an obligation to purchase*. On this basis there are three situations where a competition is considered lawful:

1. There is no purchase obligation and the right answers are not to be found by chance.
2. There is a purchase obligation and the right answers are not to be found by chance.
3. There is no purchase obligation and the right answers are to be found by chance.

Consequently, it is necessary to define the two expressions 'purchase obligation' and 'chance'.

Definition of 'purchase obligation'
1. A label, a cap, or any part of a packaging has to be sent by post.
2. The entry form for the competition is printed on the reverse of a label.
3. The entry form is inside the packaging.
4. There is a participation fee for the competition.
5. The competition is announced in a place where people are attending a paying performance.

6. Where the competition is organized by a newspaper and is publicly advertised and the newspaper or magazine has to be bought in order to cut out the entry form.
7. A piece of information is required which is on the label or packaging, and cannot be found by simply looking at the product on the shelves.
8. If, to obtain such information, people are compelled to enter a sales room where they cannot 'escape' the salesperson, the judge may consider that there is a 'moral constraint' on the purchase.

Definition of 'chance'
1. Random draw.
2. Random draw in the event of tied entries.
3. A question which cannot be answered by skill, science, calculus or knowledge, for instance: time taken by winner of a race; flight time of a plane; number of cigarettes or matches which have to be put end to end in order to cover the distance between two cities; to be the tenth visitor to an exhibition, the twentieth buyer of a product, and so on.

(Source: Adapted from Gambiez *et al.*, 1988, pp. 12–13.)

food tastings, etc. However, some countries object to sales promotion techniques in general because of the risk of consumers being misled. Whereas some countries believe in the personal responsibility and trust consumers to seek and evaluate information (the United Kingdom, the United States), others have less confidence in the capacities of individual to make free and responsible choices (Latin-European and northern European countries). In Scandinavian countries, sales promotions face the greatest obstacles, since every promotion has to be approved by an official body.

Sociocultural factors influencing the implementation of sales promotion techniques

Table 12.2 presents a series of sociocultural factors, some of them already mentioned above, which influence the implementation of sales promotion techniques. The level of literacy is obviously an important variable to be considered since promotion is often associated with text; if the target market is largely illiterate, people will not respond to a coupon campaign for instance. Level of literacy becomes crucial when the purpose of the campaign is consumer education. Visual and oral promotion should be given preference over written materials wherever the literacy rate is low. Promotional campaigns in some African countries travel from village to village showing a promotional movie film while the operator hands free samples of the product to the audience. Conversely, an increasing level of education and political awareness may be favourable for promotion that has a higher ambition: Thailand's state-owned oil company Bang Chak Petroleum, which offered

two oranges or a copy of the Thai constitution as promotional gifts, was more successful with the constitution booklet (Wentz, 1997).

Retailer sophistication is required when the promotional techniques need some follow-up, such as redeeming coupons or dealing with stamps or collectors' devices, that is, the retailer needs to be an intermediary between the manufacturer and the final consumer in a fairly organized way (stocking coupons, reckoning, ordering premiums, etc.). If prizes are given, they must suit the target market's tastes: this is especially important in competitions where the prizes are advertised. Cars, trips, various household equipment or goods, or cash are possible prizes: whenever legally possible, cash is the most universally acceptable prize, since it allows further free spending.

Unethical trade behaviour *vis-à-vis* the manufacturer is possible in a number of cases: retailers can decide to sell what were supposed to be free samples or they can pocket money-off offers by increasing prices. Retailers' employees can put aside samples, gifts or premiums for themselves or others. Strict control of the retailers involved in a promotion is required wherever such opportunistic attitudes are possible.

Promotional techniques can be associated with images of social status. Foxman *et al.* (1988) give the example of Hong Kong where the response to coupons is very positive, whereas the use of stamps is popular in Thailand, both of these locally popular techniques being associated with middle-class status. In many countries coupons or money-off offers can be associated with low-class status, because the implied price consciousness mediates an image of low purchasing power. On the other hand, promotional techniques based on a price reduction cannot be

Table 12.2 Cross-cultural adequacy problems for selected sales promotion techniques

Technique	Culture-related features that may affect implementation
Coupons	Level of literacy, consumer and retailer sophistication/low social status implied
Contests and sweepstakes	Legal requirements/Prizes must suit target market tastes
Price-offers	Absence of price labelling and display/bargaining/trade misuse
Stamps and collections	Future orientation needed/high inflation/level of channel sophistication
Free samples	Interpretation of gratuity/trade misuse/theft of sampled products
Gifts (in, on or near packs)	Legal requirements/theft by channel employees or customers

implemented in countries where basic prices are not displayed and bargaining is the rule: the rebate has a meaning only in as much as a clear market price is known by the consumer. Once again, in such cases, it is better to target channel members rather than the end user, for instance by offering retailers a rebate for quantity sold after a certain period of time, as they will be obliged to make sales in advance to customers in order to build volume.

Some promotional techniques require extended involvement, such as collectors' devices, stamps or self-liquidating premiums, refunds after a series of purchases, etc. Cultures with a present time orientation respond poorly to these techniques which require future orientation because of delayed gratification (Foxman *et al.*, 1988). Similarly, high inflation is very detrimental to any sales promotion whose rewards are not virtually immediate: the face value of coupons, price-off offers and other rebates may have little meaning after the passage of the few

weeks, necessary for printing, distribution and claiming of the rebates.

The final caveat is that it is necessary to check that the purpose of the promotional technique is locally understood (this is a problem of conceptual equivalence). For instance, in many societies being given a free sample is difficult to interpret. The basic rationale, that a producer wants consumers to try a product in order to have them buy it, is not self-evident. A free sample is understood either as a sign of poor quality ('they give it because they cannot sell it') or as a sign of the naivety of the manufacturer ('let's take as much as possible'). P & G, which is now expanding rapidly in eastern Europe, experienced major problems with free samples in Poland in 1993, where some people ignored them whereas others broke mailboxes to steal as many samples as they could. In any case, it must be kept in mind that price reductions are by far the most popular sales promotion techniques (Boddewyn and Leardi, 1989).

Questions

1. A distribution formula is successful in the United States; you are asked to extend it through a franchise system to several countries around the world. How would you devise a policy for those franchisees who want adaptation to the standard recipe for their home market, in the following areas: size of the store, personnel recruitment, servicing, stocking, brands represented, display, store name, etc.?

2. What are the ways in which retailing know-how is transferred internationally?

3. Discuss the distinguishing features of the Japanese distribution system.

4. Why do exporting firms tend to have somewhat different distribution channels abroad compared to their domestic market, apart from the peculiarities of the local distribution systems?

5. Up to recently, the typical store in Germany was open each day, from Monday to Friday, from 9 a.m. to 6.30 p.m. On Saturdays, German shops closed at 2 p.m., and they all closed on Sundays. Once a month there was a special shopping Thursday when stores were open till 8.30 p.m. Conversely, opening hours in the United States are much longer and some supermarkets have 24-hour opening, seven days a week. Stores employees in Germany are highly unionized and unions have traditionally opposed any increase in opening hours. To what extent do time-related cultural differences explain the huge difference in store opening hours between Germany and the United States?

6. Using a local catalogue (from your own country), explain how (in terms of language, size, photographs, prices, product information, delivery and payment conditions, etc.) it should be adapted to be sent to a culturally remote market with a similar level of economic development (choose the target market).

7. Discuss how store size can be related to culture.

8. Explain how cultural values can have a negative impact on self-service and automated service in general (that is, without personnel in contact with the shopper/consumer).

9. Based on available statistics, review key differences in the retailing systems in the countries of the European Union.

References

Aalto-Setala, Ville (2002), 'The effect of concentration and market power on food prices: Evidence from Finland', *Journal of Retailing*, vol. 78, no. 3, pp. 207–16.

Akhter, Syed H. (1996), 'International direct marketing: export value chain, transaction cost, and the triad', *Journal of Direct Marketing*, vol. 10, no. 2, pp. 13–23.

Alberta Agriculture, Food and Rural Development (2001), *Competition for World Honey Markets: An Alberta Perspective, Report Two*, prepared by Competitive Intelligence Unit, April.

Alexander, Nicholas and Hayley Myers (2000), 'The retail internationalisation process', *International Marketing Review*, vol. 17, no. 4/5, pp. 334–53.

Anderson, Erin T. and Anne T. Coughlan (1987), 'International market entry and expansion via independent or integrated channels of distribution', *Journal of Marketing*, vol. 51, January, pp. 71–82.

Bakos, Yannis (2001), 'The emerging landscape for retail e-commerce', *Journal of Economic Perspectives*, vol. 15, no. 1, pp. 69–80.

Boddewyn, J.J. and M. Leardi (1989), 'Sales promotion: practices, regulation and self-regulation around the world, *International Journal of Advertising*, vol. 8, no. 4, pp. 363–74.

Boddewyn, Jean-Jacques (1992), *Premiums, Gifts and Competitions*, International Advertising Association: New York.

Burt, Steve and Jose Carralero-Encinas (2000), 'The role of store image in retail internationalisation', *International Marketing Review*, vol. 17, no. 4/5, pp. 433–53.

BusinessWorld (1999), 'The EuroConsumer: curious law', 21 December, p. 1.

Cateora, Philip R. (1983), *International Marketing*, 5th edn, Richard D. Irwin: Homewood, IL.

Cateora, Philip R. (1993), *International Marketing*, 8th edn, Richard D. Irwin: Homewood, IL.

Child, Peter N. (2002), 'Taking Tesco global,' *The McKinsey Quarterly*, 3, available at: **www.mckinseyquarterly.com.**

Cox, Anthony (2000), 'Europe EU faces tall task in regulating e-commerce', *Bank Technology News*, vol. 13, no. 6, pp. 63–4.

Cundiff, Edward W. and Marye Tharp Hilger (1988), *Marketing in the International Environment*, 2nd edn, Prentice Hall: Englewood Cliffs, NJ.

Cutitta, Frank (2002), 'Language matters', *Target Marketing*, vol. 25, no. 2, pp. 40–4.

Czinkota, Michael R. and Illka A. Ronkainen (1990), *International Marketing*, 2nd edn, Dryden Press: Hinsdale, IL.

Czinkota, Michael R. and Jon Woronoff (1991), *Unlocking Japan's Markets*, Probus Publishing: Chicago, IL.

De Mooij, Marieke and Geert Hofstede (2002), 'Convergence and divergence in consumer behavior: Implications for international retailing', *Journal of Retailing*, vol. 78, no. 1, pp. 61–9.

Dedoussis, Vagelis (2001), 'Keiretsu and management practices in Japan – resilience amid change', *Journal of Managerial Psychology*, vol. 16, no. 2, pp. 173–88.

Desmet, Pierre and Dominique Xardel (1996), 'Challenges and pitfalls for direct mail across borders: The European example', *Journal of Direct Marketing*, vol. 10, no. 3, pp. 48–60.

Direct Marketing (2001), '1 billion Internet users to fuel $5 trillion in E-commerce by 2005', vol. 64, no. 5, p. 12.

Doi, T. (1973), *The Anatomy of Dependence*, Kodansha: Tokyo.

Dupuis, Marc and Renaud de Maricourt (1989), '*France/Etats-Unis/Japon, trois mondes, trois distributions*', Cahier ESCP no. 89–81, Ecole Supérieure de Commerce de Paris.

Economist (2000), 'Leaders: regulating the Internet', 10 June, pp. 18–20.

Euromonitor (2003a), 'Department stores in Japan', Euromonitor International, available at: **www.marketresearch.com.**

Euromonitor (2003b) 'Department stores in Australia', Euromonitor International, available at: **www.marketresearch.com.**

Euromonitor (2004) 'Department stores in USA', Euromonitor International, available at: **www.marketresearch.com.**

Ford, David (2002), 'Solving old problems, learning new things and forgetting most of them: distribution, internationalisation and networks', *International Marketing Review*, vol. 19, no. 3, pp. 225–35.

Foreign Agricultural Service (1998), *Honey Situation and Outlook in Selected Countries*, Foreign Agricultural Service, November.

Foxman, Ellen R., Patriya S. Tansuhaj and John K. Wong (1988), 'Evaluating cross-national sales promotion approach strategy: an audit approach', *International Marketing Review*, vol. 5, Winter, pp. 7–15.

Gabrielsson, Mika, V.H. Manek Kirpalani and Reijo Luostarinen (2002), 'Multiple channel strategies in the European personal computer industry', *Journal of International Marketing*, vol. 10, no. 3, pp. 73–95.

Gambiez, Chantal, Hélène Lelièvre and Véronique Surget (1988), 'La Promotion des Ventes en Suisse', Research paper for the International Marketing Seminar, Ecole Supérieure des Affaires, University of Grenoble.

Glazer, Herbert (1968), *The International Business in Japan: The Japanese image*, Sophia University: Tokyo.

Goldman, Arieh (2001), 'The transfer of retail formats into developing economies: the example of China', *Journal of Retailing*, vol. 77, no. 2, pp. 221–42.

Graves, Roger (1997), 'Dear Friend' (?): culture and genre in American and Canadian direct marketing letters', *Journal of Business Communication*, vol. 34, no. 3, pp. 235–52.

Griffin, Mitch, Barry J. Babin and Doan Modianos (2000), 'Shopping values of Russian consumers: the impact of habituation in a developing economy', *Journal of Retailing*, vol. 76, no. 1, pp. 33–52.

Griffith, David A. (1998), 'Cultural meaning of retail institutions: a tradition-based culture examination', *Journal of Global Marketing*, vol. 12, no. 1, pp. 47–59.

Hodges, Mark (1997), 'Is Web business good business?' *Technology Review*, vol. 100, no. 6, August/September, pp. 23–32.

Hofstede, Geert (1980), *Culture's Consequences: International differences in work related values*, Sage: Beverly Hills, CA.

International Tax Review (2001), 'UK delays EU web tax', vol. 12, no. 6, p. 5.

Ishida, Hideto (1983), 'Anticompetitive practices in the distribution of goods and services in Japan: the problem of distribution Keiretsu', *Journal of Japanese Studies*, vol. 9, no. 2, pp. 319–34.

Johansson, Johny K. (1997), *Global Marketing*, Irwin: Chicago, IL.

Johansson, Johny K. and Ikujiro Nonaka (1996), *Relentless: The Japanese Way of Marketing*, HarperCollins: New York.

Kale, Sudhir H. and Roger P. McIntyre (1991), 'Distribution channel relationships in diverse cultures', *International Marketing Review*, vol. 8, no. 3, pp. 31–45.

Karg, Pamela J. (1999), 'Taking flight', *Rural Cooperatives*, 10888845, September–October, vol. 66, no. 5.

Kashani, Kamran (1989), 'Beware the pitfalls of global marketing', *Harvard Business Review*, September–October, pp. 91–8.

Kasim, Sharifah and Anuja Ravendran (2001), 'Tackling tax issues in e-commerce activities (HL)', *Computimes Malaysia*, July, 9, p. 1.

Katsikeas, Constantine S. and Nigel F. Piercy (1991), 'The relationship between exporters from a developing country and importers based in a developed country: conflict considerations', *European Journal of Marketing*, vol. 25, no. 1, pp. 6–25.

Kim, Keysuk (2002), 'On distributor commitment in marketing channels for industrial products: contrast between the United States and Japan', *Journal of International Marketing*, vol. 10, no. 1, pp. 72–97.

Kim, Keysuk and Changho Oh (2002), 'On distributor commitment in marketing channels for industrial products: contrast between the United States and Japan', *Journal of International Marketing*, vol. 10, no. 1, pp. 72–97.

Koranteng, Juliana (1997), 'If the web is so worldwide why is it mainly in English?', *Advertising Age International*, May, p. 16.

Kuribayashi, S. (1991), 'Present situation and future prospects of Japan's distribution system', *Japan and the World Economy*, vol. 3, no. 1, pp. 39–60.

Kwak, Hyokjin, Richard J. Fox and George M. Zinkhan (2002), 'What products can be successfully promoted and sold via the Internet?' *Journal of Advertising Research*, vol. 42, no. 1, pp. 23–38.

Luk, S., L. Fullgrabe and S. Li (1996), 'Managing direct selling activities in China: a cultural explanation', paper presented to *EIRASS, Third Recent Advances in Retailing and Consumer Sciences Conference*, Telfs, Austria, June, pp. 1–18.

McNaughton, Rod B. and Jim Bell (2001), 'Channel switching between domestic and foreign markets', *Journal of International Marketing*, vol. 9, no. 1, pp. 24–39.

Mehta, Rajiv, Trina Larsen, Bert Rosenbloom, Jolanta Mazur and Pia Polsa (2001), 'Leadership and cooperation in marketing channels: a comparative empirical analysis of the USA, Finland and Poland', *International Marketing Review*, vol. 18, no. 6, pp. 633–66.

Merrilees, Bill and Dale Miller (1999), 'Direct selling in the West and East: the relative roles of product and relationship (Guanxi) drivers', *Journal of Business Research*, vol. 45, pp. 267–73.

Miller, Fred and A. Hamdi Demirel (1988), 'Efes pilsen in the Turkish beer market: marketing consumer goods in developing countries', *International Marketing Review*, vol. 5, Spring, pp. 7–19.

Montgomery, David B. (1991), 'Understanding the Japanese as customers, competitors and collaborators', *Japan and the World Economy*, vol. 3, no. 1, pp. 61–91.

Mühlbacher, Hans, Martina Botschen and Werner Beutelmeyer (1997), 'The changing consumer in Austria', *International Journal of Research in Marketing*, vol. 14, pp. 309–19.

Nakane, Chie (1973), *Japanese Society*, University of California Press, Berkeley.

National Honey Board (2001a), *National Honey Board Positioning Report Phase II*, report prepared by rose research (r2), Boca Raton, FL, for National Honey Board,

September. Retrieved 23 February, 2003 from www.nhb.org/download/industry/positioning_report_2.pdf

National Honey Board (2001b), *2000 Strategic Plan* (online), National Honey Board. Retrieved 23 February, 2003 from www.nhb.org/info-pub/board/SP/SP2000.pdf

National Honey Board (2002a), *Honey Industry Facts*, press release, National Honey Board, March, available at www.nhb.org/intl/4country

National Honey Board (2002b), *Exports from the United States* (Domestic merchandise only), National Honey Board, available at www.nhb.org/domestic

Nueno, José Luis and Harvey Bennett (1997), 'The changing Spanish consumer', *International Journal of Research in Marketing*, vol. 14, pp. 19–33.

O'Grady, Shawna and Henry W. Lane (1992), 'Culture: an unnoticed barrier to Canadian retail performance in the United States', paper presented at Academy of International Business Annual Conference, Brussels, 22 November.

Ohmae, Kenichi (1985), *La Triade, Emergence d'une stratégie mondiale de l'entreprise*, Flammarion: Paris.

Pahud de Mortanges, Charles, Jan-Willem Rietbroek and Cort MacLean Johns (1997), 'Marketing pharmaceuticals in Japan: background and the experience of US firms', *European Journal of Marketing*, vol. 31, no. 8, pp. 561–82.

Pirog, Stephen F., Peter A. Schneider and Danny K.K. Lam (1997), 'Cohesiveness in Japanese distribution: a sociocultural framework', *International Marketing Review*, vol. 14, no. 2, pp. 124–34.

Queau, Philippe (1993), 'O tempo do virtual', in André Parente (ed.), *Imagem-Maquina*, Editora 34: Rio de Janeiro, pp. 91–9.

Quelch, John A. and Lisa R. Klein (1996), 'The Internet and international marketing', *Sloan Management Review*, vol. 37, no. 3, Spring, pp. 60–77.

Rawwas, Mohammed Y., David Strutton and Lester W. Johnson (1996), 'An exploratory investigation of the ethical values of American and Australian consumers: direct marketing implications', *Journal of Direct Marketing*, vol. 10, no. 4, pp. 52–63.

Ribeiro, Gustavo Lins (1997), 'Transnational virtual community? Exploring implications for culture, power and language', *Organization*, vol. 4, no. 4, pp. 486–505.

Robles, Fernando and Syed H. Akhter (1997), 'International catalog mix adaptation: an empirical study', *Journal of Global Marketing*, vol. 11, no. 2, pp. 65–91.

Rosenfield, James R. (1994), 'Direct Marketing worldwide: one man's perspective', *Journal of Direct Marketing*, vol. 8, no. 1, pp. 79–82.

Sanford, M.T. (2002), 'Selling honey on the world wide web', *Bee Culture*, March.

Saskin, Rose (2001), 'Beyond multilingualism', *World Trade*, vol. 14, no. 6, p. 52.

Severin, Valerie, Jordan J. Louviere and Adam Finn (2001), 'The stability of retail shopping choices over time and across countries', *Journal of Retailing*, vol. 77, no. 2, pp. 185–202.

Shimaguchi, Mitsuaki (1978), *Marketing Channels in Japan*, UMI Research Press: Ann Arbor, MI.

Shimaguchi, Mitsuaki and Larry J. Rosenberg (1979), 'Demystifying Japanese distribution', *Columbia Journal of World Business*, Spring, pp. 38–41.

Shoham, Aviv, Gregory M. Rose and Fredric Kropp (1997), 'Conflicts in international channels of distribution', *Journal of Global Marketing*, vol. 11, no. 2, pp. 5–27.

Simmonds, Kenneth (1999), 'International marketing: avoiding the seven deadly traps', *Journal of International Marketing*, vol. 7, no. 2, pp. 51–62.

Skarmeas, Dionisis A. and Constantine S. Katsikeas (2001), 'Drivers of Superior Importer Performance in Cross-Cultural Supplier-Reseller Relationships', *Industrial Marketing Management*, vol. 30. no. 2, pp. 227–41.

Straughan, Robert B. and Nancy D. Albers-Miller (2001), 'An international investigation of cultural and demographic effects on domestic retail', *International Marketing Review*, vol. 18, no. 5, pp. 521–41.

Tian, Robert G. and Charles Emery (2002), 'Cross-cultural issues in Internet marketing', *Journal of American Academy of Business*, vol. 1, no. 2, pp. 217–24.

Turcq, Dominique and Jean-Claude Usunier (1985), 'Les Services au Japon: l'efficacité . . . par la non-productivité', *Revue Française de Gestion*, May–June, pp. 12–15.

Turpin, Dominique (1990), *World Competitiveness Report*, IMD/World Economic Forum: Lausanne.

Waltner, Charles (1999), 'Web's days as tax-free zone are numbered – as e-commerce booms, the battle over Internet taxation standards starts heating up', *InternetWeek*, 6 December, pp. 26–30.

Weigand, Robert E. (1970), 'Aspects of retail pricing in Japan', *MSU Business Topics*, vol. 18, Winter, pp. 23–30.

Wentz, Laurel (1997), 'Global Village', *Advertising Age International*, October, pp. 1–3.

Yoshino, Michael Y. (1971), *Marketing in Japan: A management guide*, Praeger: New York.

Zeller, Eric (1989), Masters thesis, Ecole Supérieure de Commerce de Paris, pp. 33–4.

Zugelder, Michael T., Theresa B. Flaherty and James P. Johnson (2000), 'Legal issues associated with international internet marketing', *International Marketing Review*, vol. 17, no. 3, pp. 253–71.

Teaching materials

A12.1 Case

ComputerLand in Japan

ComputerLand recognized that they would need a Japanese partner in order to enter the Japanese market. Because of government regulations and attitude, it probably would not have been possible to obtain permission to establish a wholly owned subsidiary. Additionally, the complexities of the Japanese market would have made development of franchises there very difficult. (Both McDonald's and Kentucky Fried Chicken entered the market with Japanese partners.)

ComputerLand wanted a partner who had experience in both procurement and distribution of computer products. Though they talked with a number of companies, Kanematsu-Gosho Ltd emerged as the top candidate. Kanematsu-Gosho was a major trading company, had experience in the desired areas, and already had business dealings with IBM. ComputerLand entered into negotiations with the Japanese company in order to try to develop a joint venture. The discussions, which lasted for nine months, were detailed and difficult. The Chairman of ComputerLand was concerned that if his vice-president went to Japan to negotiate, he would be at a disadvantage trying to operate in the different culture. He therefore insisted that the negotiations be done in the United States by telephone from Japan.

This made it difficult for the Japanese to negotiate. The Japanese decision-making process requires much more consultation and agreement with the company than would normally be necessary in European and American firms. There were long delays and a lot that had to be done through telex correspondence. Among other things, the Japanese government had to be persuaded to allow the American partner to have a 50 per cent ownership rather than the customary (at the time) minority position. The agreement was finally concluded with ComputerLand contributing knowledge, trade mark and technology and Kanematsu-Gosho contributing cash to start the joint venture, ComputerLand Japan Ltd. The Vice-President of ComputerLand then went to Japan to head the operation as Vice-President and Resident Director. A number of policy and operational problems had to be solved.

In the United States, franchisees were required to pay cash before merchandise would be shipped to them. An attempt was made to follow this policy in Japan. Retailers in Japan, however, are used to receiving credit from wholesalers – often for 0 to 90 days or even longer. A cash-in-advance policy proved to be impossible in Japan, so the company eventually went to a 10-day-open-credit policy.

In the United States, franchises were given only to individuals, not to corporations or other businesses. This was done so that the stores would be personally managed by the owners. ComputerLand Japan was not able to find a sufficient number of individuals who had or could obtain the necessary cash. Eventually the policy was changed to allow a company to own a minority interest. As in Europe, store locations and format were also a problem. Within the United States, ComputerLand insisted on a minimum size for a store of 2,000 square feet (185 m²), a location with a large amount of traffic going by, and a parking lot in the rear. This was simply not possible in most locations in Japan.

It was also difficult to attract top-quality people as employees to work for a foreign company in Japan. Finally, there were simple problems of coordination between proprietor-owned ComputerLand and large, publicly owned Kanematsu-Gosho. In spite of these difficulties, ComputerLand Japan was very successful, growing to 50 franchises with annual sales of US$50 million. It was assisted greatly by the fact that, for the first two years of operation, ComputerLand had the exclusive distribution right in Japan for the IBM PC.

Over the years, Kanematsu-Gosho found it increasingly difficult to continue to accept some of ComputerLand's policy. Additionally, they felt that the American partner was simply exercising too much control. When ComputerLand offered to buy them out, Kanematsu-Gosho agreed. The operation then became a wholly owned subsidiary of the United States corporation. Eventually, this subsidiary was sold to one of the franchisees who continues to operate it under a license agreement with ComputerLand.

(Source: Written by John T. Sakai, Director, AZCA Inc., former Vice-President of ComputerLand. Reproduced with the kind permission of the author.)

Questions

1. Was it wise for ComputerLand to insist on holding the negotiations in the United States? What were the advantages and disadvantages to each of the parties? Why did Kanematsu-Gosho agree to the location?

2. Analyze the differences between the Japanese and American distribution systems as they appear in this case. Which elements of the 'ComputerLand model' are transferable to Japan?

3. When exporting to another country or setting up a joint venture there, how can you decide which of the local customs and business practices you should accept, and which of your home country practices you should introduce?

A12.2 Case

The virtual beehive: The online marketing of US honey

The first official record of beekeeping stretches back 5,000 years, to Ancient Egypt, where beekeepers navigated their bees up or down the Nile, depending on the season. Today, itinerant Chinese families and their bees track blooming flora for thousands of kilometers across the country in rented vans. Rural poor women in Malaysia cultivate the bees that pollinate coffee plantations and provide pungent honey. American beekeepers winter with their bees in Texas, and summer with them in the North Dakota plains. Argentinean landowners use low-cost labour to keep bees on their extensive lands.

Beekeeping has always been a specialized business. The demand for bee products, including honey, bee pollen, royal jelly, propolis (adhesive used for comb placement and repair) and beeswax has been quite steady throughout history. In the past beekeeping was prized because of the sweetening and medicinal properties of honey, medicinal uses for other hive products, as well as the wax used in a myriad of ways, including candles, adhesive and hairdressing. The beekeeper's life today is in some ways more difficult than it was in the past, without the steady patronage of the religious and medical orders. Today, there are more competing products, such as corn syrup and aspartame. There are more low-cost producers, many in developing countries. The rationalized business practices of international retail conglomerates demand massive quantities, making packers and intermediaries necessary for small producers. However, now in their fifth millennium, beekeepers may finally have found through the Internet a way to keep more of their scanty margins for themselves, instead of profiting packers, agents and exporters.

Beekeeping, a fragmented sector

Supply is subject to weather, the length of the flower blooming season and bee disease control. Smaller beekeepers tend to leave the field because costly technology is increasingly needed for pest control, management of newly immigrated bees and pesticide use in the environment (Foreign Agricultural Service, 1998). For these reasons, among others, beekeepers tend to consolidate, although they remain a small agricultural grouping with little political muscle and low bargaining power. Under these conditions, prices tend not to be stable and currently follow a downward trend: US prices in 2000 were half those in 1997 (Karg, 1999). Yet, in the USA, 40 per cent of honey produced comes from smaller beekeepers, hobbyists and part-timers (National Honey Board, 2002a). Smaller producers may improve their chances for survival by joining a cooperative, like the almost 90-year-old Sioux Honey Association, from Sioux City, Iowa.

Risk management in a risky business: The cooperative

The oldest beekeepers' cooperative is best known under its 'Sue Bee' brand (from 'Sioux'), and is the largest honey marketer in the world (second to Sue Bee in terms of market share is a German company) (Karg, 1999). In addition to continuing sales to retail outlets and online, the cooperative is focusing on manufactured food plus the food service segment (Karg, 1999). By featuring the Sue Bee logo on its label, a food-processing company is likely to boost the image of its sauces, prepared foods, condiments or beverages. Use of honey in these products is at an all-time high (Karg, 1999). Visit Sue Bee Honey at **www.suebee.com**.

Biggest importers of US honey 2001

The US National Honey Board (NBH) is concerned with promoting sales of US honey abroad. It has collected the following data concerning the ranking of US honey export sales (National Honey Board, 2002b):

1. Germany
2. Korea
3. Canada
4. Yemen
5. Saudi Arabia
6. United Arab Emirates

The marketing environment for honey

Before the rise of the Internet, buyers and honey processors/packers spent a great deal of time negotiating their bulk honey contracts. What may have then taken up to 30 days may now be concluded during a 30-minute online bidding process (Alberta Agriculture, 2001). Increased consolidation of retail businesses and food suppliers has placed bulk honey sellers at a disadvantage. For instance, retail buyers often demand slotting fees (to get the product on the shelf and, often, to keep competitors off) and pay-to-stay fees (to keep the product on the shelf). It is estimated that some Canadian packers pay 10 per cent of their total costs on these fees (Alberta Agriculture, 2001). Retail buyers expect to pay a low price for high volume, with accompanying food safety assurances in writing (Alberta Agriculture, 2001).

The honey market is diverging between a high-end, speciality product and a low-end, low-cost, relatively undifferentiated, 'generic'-type product (Alberta Agriculture, 2001). Honey is assailed by direct and indirect competitors for sweeteners (such as sugars, fruit concentrates, rice sweetener and molasses) and spreads (such as fruit-, nut- or chocolate-based spreads), which often make their own health- and nutrient-related claims. The entry of low-cost producers like China, Argentina and Mexico onto the honey stage has made retail buyers even more cost-conscious (Table 12.3), as is the increased market share of countries like India, Vietnam, Turkey and Hungary. The participation of China and Argentina in the US market has lessened due to fees that raise prices. Both countries allegedly were dumping honey on the US market within the past decade and now pay anti-dumping fees, and, in the case of Argentina, countervailing fees.

Table 12.3 USA honey imports from China, Argentina, Canada, Mexico and other: pounds (lbs) imported to December 2002

Country	Pounds (lbs) imported		
	2000	2001	2002
Argentina	98,918,160	53,950,832	13,174,534
China	53,546,855	48,603,333	17,097,663
Canada	29,289,354	21,083,039	44,430,094
Mexico	4,550,132	8,735,508	23,283,075
Other	7,883,157	24,627,842	93,840,265

(Source: National Honey Board 2002a.)

The positioning of honey in the USA

The US National Honey Board (NBH at **www.nhb.org**) used in-depth face-to-face interviews to determine the positioning of honey in the USA. Respondents were asked questions regarding factors such as interest/intent, believability and uniqueness relating to three positioning statements, 'Livens up the Flavor of Any Meal', 'Nature's Healer' and 'Nature's Original Sweetener'. The top performer in the tests was 'Nature's Healer', a positioning that successfully differentiates honey from other options due to respondents' beliefs in its 'healthiness' (35 per cent), 'providing more benefits than artificial sweeteners' (27 per cent) and 'promoting healing' (25 per cent) (National Honey Board, 2001a). Despite performing well otherwise, the 'Nature's Healer' positioning elicited the lowest 'believability' score of the three positioning statements tested, however media reports of scientific findings relating to honey should increase believability over time. The findings show that, on average, honey is used in US households 1–$\frac{1}{2}$ times per week and that most honey consumers buy honey 2–3 times per year. It appears that many consumers would like to use honey more often, but do not know of ways to do so. Based on the research findings, the positioning strategy was refined. The new statement was 'Honey: the natural daily choice to enhance health and well being', a positioning concept designed to address food and 'pharmacological' uses (National Honey Board, 2001b). To support this, the NHB committed its resources to encourage research on honey-related issues (including honey's antimicrobial, antioxidant and healing properties, and its nutrient content) to communicate the findings to targeted consumer segments as well as the food-processing industry.

Whatever the positioning of the product, online marketing may help smaller and biggest producers alike, particularly in challenging marketing conditions. In the USA, the National Honey Board's **www.honeylocator.com** offers the potential honey purchaser 300 types of US honey on its menu, while the producers' sub-sites offer even more (Sanford, 2002). The types of honey depend on the flora where bees collected nectar. This determines the colour (white to dark brown), taste and aroma. Thus nectar collected from mesquite results in a different honey from that collected from lavender. A search for 'orange blossom', for instance, returned 55 companies.

Buyers may search the site using honey variety, market segment, or postal code. The pages located display contact information, product lists (usually pollen, royal jelly, kosher honey, organic honey), markets (bakery, retail, foodservice, wholesale, for export, brewery, food manufacturing) and export markets. As is vital with a searchable data base, the suppliers are encouraged to stay current through various means, such as the bi-weekly 'Beemail' news-letter, contests for suppliers like 'Show me the honey', and supplier links. Canadian cooper-ative Beemaid Honey is Canada's biggest and one of the oldest honey marketers. The company maintains a large site in its worldwide marketing efforts at **www.beemaid.com**.

Honey exporters may list themselves on online commercial directories, such as usaexporters.net, where company profiles and links may be provided. On a simpler level, such as the Panhellenic Confederation of Agricultural Cooperatives at **www.paseges.gr**, interested importers may find a list with links to email addresses for more information. Honey producers or marketers may opt for banner advertising on other related sites, such as the US-based **www.localhoneyforsale.com**, or even a cooking or tourism site. In addition to export-oriented sites, the web boasts many informative beekeeping sites, some of which offer advice on apiculture problems, such as **www.gardenweb.com** where beekeepers may solicit comments about how to clean a hive or which queen bees to purchase. A vast resource for beekeepers and honey purchasers is **www.beehoo.com**, a site in English and French with linked directories to exporters and hive suppliers. Another resource in English, French, Spanish and German is Apiservices at **www.beekeeping.com**, where one may access academic journals, exporter directories, classified ads, and a honey web ring. With all the possibilities offered online, rural Spanish beekeepers, beekeeping apprentices in Nepal, and isolated Australian apiaries have the potential to sell directly to buyers, anywhere in the world . . . or do they?

Questions

1. Visit sites in at least four different languages from the list below, or from your own searches. Comment on the obstacles of selling honey internationally online, in terms of language, shipping, trust, hygiene and import regulations, etc.
France: **www.lunedemiel.fr, www.abeillestore.com**
Canada: **www.intermiel.com**
Argentina/Mexico: **www.cipsa.com.ar, www.apicultura.com.ar/miel, www.naturalhoney.com, www.tiatrini.com.mx**
Germany: **www.honig.de, www.schwarzwaldhonig.de**
Italy: **www.montioni.com**
Netherlands: **www.export.nl**
USA: **www.honeylocator.com, www.suebee.com**
Greece: **www.add.gr**

2. Of the sites you visited, which did you consider to be most effective at selling honey long-term? Discuss the reasons for your choice, keeping in mind that in the long run, the site is only as good as its suppliers.

Saskia Faulk and Jean-Claude Usunier prepared this case solely to provide material for class discussion. The authors do not intend to illustrate either effective or ineffective handling of a business situation. The authors may have disguised certain names and other identifying information to protect confidentiality.

(©IUMI, reprinted with kind permission.)

Part 4 Intercultural marketing communications

Introduction to Part 4

Language plays a central role in marketing communications when they take place in an international and multilingual context since communication styles as well as world views are deeply influenced by the structure of languages. This part reviews four major types of marketing communication tools which are successively examined: advertising, personal selling, public relations, marketing and business negotiations. These tools not only aim to communicate with customers but also with all stakeholders in the market, including middlemen, business partners, public authorities, and even competitors.

Communication is never language-free. That is why Chapter 13 presents intercultural communication, both verbal and non-verbal and explains how language shapes our world-views in as much as the words we use and the way we assemble them in speech correspond to particular assumptions and experiences about the world in which we live. This naturally results in ethnocentrism: a spontaneous tendency to refer to our own beliefs and values when interpreting situations and trying to make sense out of experience. Stereotyping is part of the game of reducing unfamiliarity to familiarity by oversimplifying foreign traits. It comes therefore as no surprise that misunderstandings in intercultural communication are quite frequent. The last section in this chapter explains how to avoid cultural misunderstandings and improve communication effectiveness in international business, especially when using interpreters.

The main tool for communicating marketing messages to customer audiences is advertising. For reasons of image consistency, many companies want to promote their products globally through standardized advertising campaigns that use the same advertising strategy and execution worldwide. Thus, the question to be answered before transferring campaigns cross-nationally is: which elements should be localized and which ones can be similar worldwide? Chapter 14 first examines the general influence of culture on attitudes towards the social utility of advertising, especially when advertising adopts a comparative stance. International companies have to make decisions in two main areas, advertising strategy (information content, advertising appeals, etc.) and advertising execution (characters and roles represented, visual and textual elements, etc.). Based on a review of cross-cultural studies of advertisements, the chapter explains the extent to which both strategy and execution can be standardized or should be localized. The focus is then on the development of global media resources and the globalization of advertising agencies.

A lot of marketing information is also communicated directly to market stakeholders, that is, presented and explained directly by the sales force or indirectly through intermediaries or business partners in foreign markets. Chapter 15 starts by explaining what 'commerce' means from an intercultural perspective, that is, the ways and means to effectively communicate with the market in both directions, rather than in a one-sided exchange as is largely the case with advertising. The chapter therefore develops a number of issues that are central to personal selling in an international perspective: how to network in business markets, buyer–seller interactions, how cultural differences affect the management of the sales force, public relations across cultures, and last but not least, the issue of bribery and business ethics in an international context.

The last two chapters in this book are dedicated to a topic that is generally left aside by international marketing textbooks, that of negotiating sales and business agreements. Good communication with business partners must be a key concern when marketing across borders, languages and cultures. Chapter 16 explains how trust is a sensitive asset in relational marketing and reviews the influence of culture on international marketing negotiations using the framework developed in part one of the book. It explains how divergence in the underlying concepts of negotiation, the preferred outcomes, the attitudes towards time, etc., may result in misunderstandings during the negotiation process. Chapter 17 presents some elements of the national style of business negotiation for different cultural groupings and proposes guidelines for effective international marketing negotiations.

13

Language, culture and communication

Glen Fisher, a distinguished scholar in the field of inter-cultural relations, has described a conversation with a Latin-American friend about the words used in English and Spanish for business relations. His friend first remarks that in English the word 'business' is positive. It connotes the fact of being 'busy' and emphasizes doing things. Expressions such as 'getting down to business' highlight people who have a responsible concern for their work. Fisher further explains that:

In Spanish the word is 'negocio' . . . The key is the 'ocio' part of the word, which connotes leisure, serenity, time to enjoy and contemplate as the preferred human condition and circumstance. But when harsh reality forces one from one's 'ocio,' when it is negated, then one has to attend to 'negocio'. The subjective meaning is obviously much less positive than in English. (Fisher, 1988, pp. 148–9.)

In this chapter, several such examples show how a linguistic/cultural group, through words or language structure, expresses a definite world-view, *eine Weltanschauung* as the Germans express it. The anthropologist and linguist Benjamin Lee Whorf went even further, arguing that language shapes our world-views, our behaviour toward others and our manner of acting. Language is obviously a major – though not the only – component of culture. However, it is for many reasons underemphasized in international business literature. First, language seems to be trans-latable: there are dictionaries and, if need be, professional translators. Unfortunately this ignores the fact that a part of the message which is culturally unique is lost in the translation process (as the Italian proverb says *traduttore traditore*, translator betrayer). Second, international business literature is in general centred

on decision making and strategy formulation rather than the implementation of decisions. Language is important mostly in the implementation phase because implementation is largely based on communicating with others: buyers, employees, colleagues, superiors. The logic of the planning stage can overlook the significance of language and communication, because these items are related to implementation. The third argument is that language differences have been systematically underestimated in international business literature because of an understandable bias in American culture: since English has traditionally been the *lingua franca* of international business there were no major reasons for native speakers of English to learn foreign languages. There is much more motivation for people from Germany, Japan, France and Italy to take the question of language seriously.

In this chapter we will review the main aspects of language and communication that have both a direct and an indirect impact on international business operations:

1. Verbal communication styles and their relationship to contextual factors.
2. Non-verbal communication, especially through gestures and eye and body language.
3. The way language shapes and reflects particular world-views.[1]
4. Ways of dealing with language differences in international business.

Awareness is even more necessary than knowledge in relation to the impact of language and communication differences on international business. Given the variety of national and regional languages, one cannot expect to be able to speak and write them all. Even multilingual business people will frequently be faced with language contexts in which they have little or no proficiency. What is needed then is an awareness that large chunks of reality will always be partly hidden from us because we are not native speakers.

13.1

Verbal communication: The role of context

'Verbal' implies words and sentences and, in most of what follows, spoken discourse, rather than written communication. Written communication is a special case and it is treated in more detail in other sections of this book devoted to advertising and international negotiation and contracts. Verbal may be opposed to non-verbal communication, which is often said to occupy a dominant place in actual communication flows. However, language is legitimately seen as having a prominent place in communication, perhaps because it is largely explicit and therefore more easily amenable to consciousness. Thus linguistic differences are perceived as one of the main causes of intercultural communication misunderstandings, though certainly not the only one. Where differences in the coding/decoding process are ignored by the communicators, they may persist throughout the whole interaction process; instead of disappearing, they may become more marked, even when people seem to be better acquainted with each other.

A first distinction in language-based communication is whether the messages sent by the speaker are explicit; that is, to be taken literally and not necessarily to be set 'in context.' Setting messages 'in context' would imply that what is literally said has to be in some way reinterpreted using various cues taken from the context, particularly the cultural context of the speaker.

The context of language-based communication

The use of the word 'context' and the emphasis that is put on the role of context in communication derive from Edward T. Hall, an American anthropologist (see Bluedorn, 1998 for an interesting interview with

Hall). During the 1940s Hall studied the culture and social integration of Hopi and Navajo Indians. He first advised diplomats in the 1960s, and then, later on, business people in their dealings with other cultures. This naturally led him to an interest in intercultural communication, a field where he has been a major contributor during the last 40 years. Hall is the kind of individual who is fascinated by foreign cultures, sometimes showing a certain prejudice in their favour and against his own native culture.[2] (For more information on intercultural communications see *WS13.1*.)

The communication mode that first springs to mind is the verbal mode. Phrases and words in a single language have (more or less) a precise meaning; in any case, we live with the necessary assumption that words and their combinations have a particular meaning, and that the listener gets a clear message from the speaker. This assumption allows us to avoid the time-consuming task of constantly verifying that the message received is the same message that was sent. However, the communication mechanism incorporates several elements:

1. Even in an exchange that is primarily verbal, part of the message is non-verbal: gestures, gesticulations, attitudes, etc. The issue then is to know to what extent non-verbal/implicit messages (which will be discussed in the next section) *mix* with verbal/explicit messages.

2. Communication integrates feedback mechanisms to verify or improve the clarity of messages. In many cultures, the accuracy of the communication process needs to be checked by various means, including repetition, paraphrases, interruption, etc.

3. In most cases, communication is dependent on its context: who says it and where and when it is said. Contextual factors may distort what actually seems to be said literally.

Although Edward Hall does not define context precisely, the following components can reasonably be presumed: location, people involved (age, sex, dress, social standing, etc.), the context of the conversation itself (at the workplace, in a showroom, during a round of labour negotiations, during a sales visit). He contrasts *high context* (HC) and *low context* (LC) in the following way: 'a high-context (HC) communication or message is one in which most of the information is either in the physical context or internalized in the person, while very little is in the coded, explicit, transmitted part of the message. A low-context (LC) communication is just the opposite; i.e. the mass of the information is vested in the explicit code' (Hall, 1976).

Context will often influence communication without the participants being aware of it. For example, cultural prejudices may intervene, with such unspoken questions as: does this young speaker deserve trust? The relationship assumed by a particular culture between age and credibility may be positive, negative or neutral, and therefore have an impact on the flow of communication. Another important issue is whether it is necessary to know one's conversation partner relatively well to be able to talk seriously to him or her about business. This relates to the intensity of the personalization, or conversely the depersonalization of the communication process.

Context brings together the sum of interpretation mechanisms that originate within a culture and allow the message to be explained. In his collection *The Snows of Kilimanjaro*, Ernest Hemingway (1976, p. 33) tells a story, entitled 'A day's wait', in which a young boy is told that he has a fever of 102 – in degrees Fahrenheit – though he does not know that the temperature was measured on this scale. Since he had previously been in France, he thinks of the temperature as being on the Celsius temperature scale, and asks: 'About how long will it be before I die?' His mother does not know what is the matter with him and explains that people do not die of a fever of 102. The young boy goes on arguing: 'I know they do. At school in France, the boys told me you can't live with 44 degrees. I've got 102.' Finally his mother understands that he has been waiting all day to die and she explains that, like kilometres and miles, temperature can be measured on different scales, and what is 37 degrees on one thermometer is 98 on another.

Low-context cultures and explicit communication

As explained above, in certain cultures, communication is based on low context and explicit messages. These messages are almost 'digital' and could be translated into simple computer units (bytes). The Swiss, for instance, have a reputation for talking quite literally, with explicit messages and low context. This implies a great deal of precision in the verbal aspect of communication, implying precision with respect to time commitments and so on. Thus, in Switzerland a speed limit is interpreted literally as just that. The speed limit on motorways is 120 kilometres an hour, and when a driver is caught speeding by the police, a speedometer error of 6 per cent is allowed and then the fine is given in proportion to the speed violation. When a patient arrives late for a doctor's appointment in certain Swiss cantons, he or she has to pay a cash penalty and reschedule the appointment if the doctor is unavailable.[3]

These two examples should be taken for what they are: not as illustrations of an unhealthy preoccupation with punctuality, exactness and respect for rules, but as evidence of a tight social order, a highly organized social system that is costly to run but is also greatly beneficial for all. In the case of the health service, a Swiss doctor who has made a preliminary assessment over the phone with a patient will schedule their time together very precisely. If each party makes an effort to keep the appointment, the result is a genuine saving. The patient will also avoid a long period in the waiting room, exposed to the germs of the other patients.

Appointments are one example of explicit messages that in low-context cultures must be taken literally. Another would be an arrangement such as: 'I can offer you a price of $140 per package of 12, to be delivered in cases of 144 within five weeks': an example of a seller's explicit message to a potential buyer. Among the cultures with explicit communication and low context are the North American cultures (United States and Canada), together with the Germanic cultures (Germany, Switzerland and Austria), the Scandinavians, Australia and New Zealand.[4]

Contextuality of communication is partly related to whether the language itself expresses ideas and facts more or less explicitly. Japanese, for instance, is in general less precise than English or French: personal pronouns are often not explicitly expressed in Japanese, and the number of tenses is much smaller, especially in comparison to French. In Japanese, both spoken words (that is sounds) and written words (based on *kanji*, or pictographs) often have multiple meanings, so that the listener needs some kind of contextual clarification. Sometimes, Japanese people write the *kanji* (ideographs) briefly on their hand to make clear what they are saying.

Naturally it would be a mistake to say that certain languages are vague and others precise. The real world is more complex. This has to be strongly nuanced when one looks more carefully at the *structure* of the language. German has many verbs that have quite different meanings according to context. It is easy to discover such examples just by consulting a German–English dictionary. For instance, the verb *absetzen* means, according to context, to deposit or deduct a sum, to take off a hat, to dismiss an official, to depose a king, to drop a passenger, to sell goods, to stop or pause, or to take off (a play).[5] The same holds true for the Finnish language: even though the Finns, like many northern Europeans, have a reputation for their explicitness in communication, Finnish has a very special language structure which renders context useful in communication. They use 16 cases which virtually replace all the prepositions used in other languages. Even proper nouns can be declined using these cases.

All languages share a common objective: they have a common problem to solve, which is conveying meaning in an appropriate way from people to people. But they achieve it differently, relying to varying degrees on precise words, structured grammar or, in contrast, on contextual indications of how ambiguous meanings should be made precise. English is a precise and fairly context-free language. This holds especially true for 'international English'. The *lingua franca* of international business is context free, rendering it impoverished, but at the same time precise.

High-context cultures favour a more diffuse communication style

A notion that helps in the understanding of the differences in context-related communication styles is the distinction between specific and diffuse. In low-context cultures, people tend to focus on specific issues and address their counterpart in a specific role (as a buyer for instance), not really impersonally but with a specific view of what the person before them has to do. In high-context cultures, people generally address broader issues and move easily between different conceptions of their counterpart (as a private person, as a buyer, as a potential friend). Diffuse in style should not be equated with 'confused' in communication, but it is clear that to speakers from low-context cultures,

communication with people from high-context cultures may at times appear complicated.

Among the high-context cultures, according to Hall, we find the Latin American, the middle Eastern and the Japanese.[6] In Japan, context plays a significant role. One example is the rules of politeness; the manner of speaking perceptibly shifts in register between more than 20 subtly different forms according to the age, sex and social position of the conversation partner, as well as the relative positions of the speakers in the social hierarchy (pupil/teacher, buyer/seller, employee/employer). The word 'no' practically does not exist in the Japanese vocabulary – a '*yes*' in certain circumstances can actually mean 'no'. Keiko Ueda (1974) distinguishes 16 ways to avoid saying 'no' in Japanese. The range of possible solutions varies from a vague 'no', to a vague and ambiguous 'yes,' a mere silence, a counterquestion, a tangential response, exiting (leaving), making an excuse such as sickness or a previous obligation, criticizing or refusing the question itself, saying 'No, but . . .' or 'Yes, but . . .', delaying answers ('We will write you a letter') and making apologies. Woodward, (1999) illustrates how this virtual absence of 'no' in Japan manifests itself in e-mail contacts. She quotes Hans Boehm, managing director of the German Association for Personnel Management in Dusseldorf: '"I know that Japanese people are very, very polite and never say 'No' . . . So, I encourage them to say 'No' when they mean no. And I double-check with them to make sure when they say 'Yes' they mean yes." The nuances in the tone of voice are lost in e-mail messages, so when dealing on important issues with Japanese associates, Boehm always follows up with a phone call.' (p. 15)

No one belonging to cultures of this sort which use implicit messages and high context can communicate without a fairly good understanding of their conversation partner. Impersonal dealings (such as the style of an American businessman who comes for a day to discuss a contract, rapidly gets to the heart of the matter, and uses the limited time available for discussion, insisting on concentrating on crucial matters) will make a person from those cultures ill at ease and impede their conversation. Kim *et al.* (1998) found that people from high-context cultures (China and Korea) are more socially oriented, less confrontational, and more complacent about life than people from a low-context culture (United States).

A misunderstanding between the two communicators may come up over their differences of opinion as to what is truly important. The person from a high-context/diffuse communication culture will prefer spending some time chatting about life in general with the very purpose of getting to know their negotiating partner. The person from a low-context/specific communication culture, on the other hand, will prefer to get straight down to business with the aim of avoiding wasting time on chatting and proceeding directly to a rational discussion of the project.

Occasionally, some cultures, which fall in the middle range, may shift from an explicit/specific to an implicit/diffuse communication style, and vice versa. The United Kingdom and France are examples of such a tendency. The British practice of 'understatement' values complicity between people at the expense of clarity. French has often been considered as a good language for diplomacy because it can be alternately vague and precise, according to the kinds of words and style chosen. Sometimes French can be written with very precise words, with simple sentences (subject verb complement), but it can also, if the occasion demands, be styled in a very vague manner, starting with long dependent clauses describing circumstances and possibilities.

Communication on the Internet

The Internet is far from being immune to the language-based difficulties wrought by high- versus low-context cultures. For instance, MacLeod (2000, p. 37) notes: 'Sentences written in Japanese need to be formal, whereas an informal tone is suitable for the U.S. translation also throws up questions of length. Each page of English may need up to two pages in German. In some Asian languages, not only are the characters larger than in English, they also read from right to left.' Woodward (1999) states that a common mistake in the United States is to automatically address others by their first name. The same is true in Iceland and Canada (Axtell, 1993), as well as Australia. Axtell (1993) cautions that in more formal countries, such as Germany, Austria, Switzerland and Sweden as well as many Asian countries, you would never address a new contact by their first name unless invited to do so.

Moreover, high-context languages are the ones that are growing most rapidly on the Internet, including Japanese, Chinese and Korean. Cutitta (2002, p. 41) reports that the percentage of English language online is dropping: in 2000 it dropped from 49 per cent in September to 43 per cent in December. Thus the context in e-mail conversation is becoming more important. For instance, Woodward (1999, p. 15) quoted Jeanne Poole, manager of international HRM benefits and systems for PQ Corp:

You should be very careful [in e-mails] not just start out in a cold business-like manner with some cultures . . . If I am dealing with the Dutch, I don't have to be so careful; I can just get right to the point in my e-mail. If, on the other hand, I am dealing with our Chinese or Latin American friends, I am always more careful about how I begin my message to them. I build up to the topic by saying things such as, 'I hope you are doing well. We haven't talked in a while. I just wanted to take a minute to chat with you about something that came up.'

The environment of the Internet allows marketers to customize information targeted at different cultures. For instance, Luna *et al.* (2002) stresses that websites should strive to achieve cultural congruity with the inclusion of both verbal and nonverbal content that is congruent with specific cultures. The use of a visitor's language symbolizes respect for the culture (Koslow *et al.*, 1994), increasing the potential bond (Luna *et al.*, 2002). In addition, they note the malleability of the website for non-verbal communication (p. 408):

Nike could develop a global image as an athletic equipment band standing for the values of hard work and success common across many cultures. However, depending on the domain of its visitors, nike.com could expose them either to Michael Jordan or to the soccer player Rivaldo. Paying close attention to the manifestations of culture, such as values and symbols, can enhance the navigation experience of visitors.

The cultural context of communication styles

So far, the discussion has been mostly about low- and high-context communication and their relationship to precision in languages, as well as to the specificity or the diffuseness of the communication focus. However, verbal communication styles include a series of other elements: tone of voice, frequency and nature of conversational overlap, speed of speech, degree of apparent involvement in what one says, emphasis on talking versus emphasis on listening, digressive and indirect speech styles, etc. These are marked by cultural norms which implicitly define what is 'good' communication ('good' meaning appropriate between members of the cultural community in so far as they share the same code). There are at least three areas where communication style is strongly culture bound:

1. The style may reflect a self-concept. In cultures where the self-concept is strong, one may expect a communication style based on talking and self-assertion; where, on the contrary, suppression of the self is valued, a modest, listening communication style is likely in a participant, all other things being equal (especially purely individual personality characteristics).

2. Communication styles reflect a view of what is appropriate interaction. The Latin style of interruption, for instance, is a lot about showing interest. Latins often find themselves speaking when others have not finished their sentence, and those who have some familiarity with the Anglo-Saxon and the Nordic communication styles may feel sorry about what could seem an overlap or even an interruption, although it is really well intentioned and positive. In Latin cultures, interruption and overlap show empathy with the other speaker and shared interest in the topic. Furthermore, Latins are (or they believe they are) able to speak and listen at the same time.

3. Communication styles also reflect the appropriate emphasis put, according to cultural norms, on talking and listening respectively. Japanese top executives often behave like a 'sphinx': they are almost pure listeners. Their role is to hear people. With some exceptions, Japanese bosses often display a mediocre talent for making public speeches and appear to be poor spokesmen. In contrast with Latin cultures, for instance, where interactions may appear to be held between 'two speakers', the Japanese have often a tendency to display a 'two listeners' communication culture. Silence is in fact valued as a full element of communication. It conveys messages, which, although implicit, may be interpreted through contextual factors. In a novel entitled *Shiosai*, the Japanese writer Yukio Mishima features a young fisherman, Shinji, who takes his salary back to his mother, a widow with another, younger son. Shinji's salary is the family's

only resource. Mishima recounts: 'Shinji liked to give his pay envelope to his mother without uttering a word. As a mother, she understood and always behaved as if she did not remember it was pay day. She knew that her son liked to see her looking surprised' (Mishima, 1969, p. 57).

Many messages are included in silent communication, and, in general, Europeans and Americans tend to fear them much more than Asians do. The issue of shared meaning attributed to communication behaviour inside the cultural group is important, whether the values are positive or negative. Silence may be experienced positively, as a moment for listening (especially to what is 'not said'), or negatively as a sign of possible loss of interaction, as a time-waster, or even as a sign of possible animosity on the part of the conversation partner. Similarly, conversational overlap may be seen as diluting the clarity of exchange, mere impoliteness, a lack of interest in what one says, or as fatuous on the part of the overlapper. Conversely, it may be interpreted as a sign of empathy, a quick feedback saving time, or even a necessary sign for pursuing the exchange.

As we hope to have shown, the rules for achieving 'good' communication are largely cultural. The feeling that the flow of messages is going smoothly between two conversation partners is based on their ability to avoid a 'bad' conversation, where messages would be altered or interrupted. The value judgement on the means that are 'good' or 'bad,' appropriate or inappropriate, is largely based on unconscious cultural standards. In a domestic setting, people agree implicitly on the appropriate rules of communication. In an intercultural situation, people have to allow themselves the informal opportunity to discuss and establish the rules of their communication (what is called meta-communication). It is quite clearly a difficult task. Box 13.1 illustrates the substantial difficulties involved in clarifying the rules of communication about what friendship means and involves.

Simintiras (2000) stresses that the in-equivalence of argument patterns are barriers to cross-cultural sales encounters. He puts forward that arguments need to be equivalent in both the statements and the inferences if they are to be comparable: 'Establishing statement equivalence requires examination of, among other things, conceptual, functional, category, language, temporal, contextual and response style equivalence'

Box 13.1

The language of friendship

The American finds his friends next door and among those with whom he works. It has been noted that we take people up quickly and drop them just as quickly. Occasionally a friendship formed during school days will persist, but this is rare. For us (Americans) there are few well-defined rules governing the obligations of friendship. It is difficult to say at which point our friendship gives way to business opportunism or pressure from above. In this we differ from many other people in the world. As a general rule, in foreign countries friendships are not formed as quickly as in the United States, but go much deeper, last longer and involve real obligations. For example, it is important to stress that in the Middle East and Latin America your 'friends' will not let you down. The fact that they personally are feeling the pinch is never an excuse for failing their friends. They are supposed to look out for your interests. Friends and family around the world represent a sort of social insurance that would be difficult to find in the United States. We do not use friends to help us out of disaster as much as we do as a means of getting ahead – or, at least, of getting the job done. The United States systems work by means of a series of closely tabulated favors and obligations carefully doled out where they will do the most good. And the least that we expect in exchange for a favour is gratitude.

The opposite is the case in India, where the friend's role is to 'sense' a person's need and to do something about it. The idea of reciprocity as we know it is unheard of. An American in India will have difficulty if he attempts to follow American friendship patterns. He gains nothing by extending himself in behalf of others, least of all gratitude, because the Indian assumes that what he does he does for the good of his own psyche. He will find it impossible to make friends quickly and is unlikely to allow sufficient time for friendships to ripen. He will also note that as he gets to know people better, they may become more critical of him, a fact that he finds hard to take. What he does not know is that one sign of friendship in India is speaking one's mind.

(Source: Hall, 1960. Reproduced with permission.)

(p. 41). While this is difficult, there are some possible solutions for people who need to communicate with those from high-context language cultures including repeating the message, clarifying and asking for clarification, trying to understand, or, as Simintiras suggests, using culture-free, logical arguments (i.e. logically valid sentential statement patterns).

13.2

Non-verbal communication

Since much of what is exchanged in communication is only implicitly meant and agreed on, not talked about, non-verbal communication is largely used as an additional interpretative framework which allows people to overcome the shortcomings of verbal communication. The rules, rites and usage of non-verbal communication are also culture bound (see *WS13.2*).

When business people from different cultures communicate, they also exchange elements of non-verbal communication. This constitutes a large part of what Edward Hall calls 'context', which is used in the decoding of implicit messages. The elements of context can be separated into four levels:

1. Non-verbal communication such as gestures, gesticulations, eye contacts, etc.
2. The analogical components of verbal messages,[7] such as a way of saying 'yes' that makes it mean 'no', profuse thank-yous that contain a meaning other than their 'digital' content precisely because of their excess, etc.
3. Messages that are often emitted unknowingly by the speakers according to their personal characteristics of age, size, weight, sex, dress, and so on. All of these characteristics are encoded in the culture of the speaker, and decoded by the listener using his or her own cultural programme.

4. Elements of interpretation dictated by the circumstances of the conversation, including type of place, atmosphere of the meeting, how the space is organized in the office,[8] time, etc.

Although all four of these elements interact, this section focuses on the first aspect, non-verbal communication, while recognizing that status, circumstances and the other aspects of context combine with it in bringing about culture-bound interpretations.

Communication through gestures

Body language is an infinite source of differences and misunderstandings (see *WS13.2*). Condon and Youssef (1975) give the following account. A professor who was of English origin and taught at the University of Cairo was sitting on his chair with his feet in front of him, the soles of his shoes facing toward his Egyptian students. A Muslim considers this to be one of the worst possible insults. A student demonstration followed, and it was taken up by the newspapers, which denounced British arrogance and demanded that the professor be sent back to his home country.

Ways of greeting people differ greatly between cultures. While the French have the custom of shaking hands the first time they meet a person each day, the Anglo-Saxon cultures use this custom much less extensively. They are surprised by what for them is an excessive use of the handshake by the French. In Japan, a bow is the appropriate manner of greeting. In certain large Japanese department stores there are hostesses whose sole job is to bow to each customer who comes into the store. Anyone who has observed bowing rituals in Japanese railway stations or airports cannot help but be struck by the complexity of these bowing ceremonies, where the number, depth and synchronization are accurately codified. As Ferraro emphasizes: 'In fact it is possible to tell the relative social status of the two communicators by the depth of their bows (the deeper the bow, the lower the status) . . . The person of lower status is supposed to initiate the bow, and the person of higher status determines when the bow is completed' (Ferraro, 1990, p. 73).

A challenge in intercultural communication is to understand what hand gestures mean in a particular culture. As Box 13.2 shows, a simple piece of advice would be to avoid gesturing with the hand for fear of being misunderstood. Yet there are circumstance and places where it may be adequate.

The meaning of head gestures is also a point of great cultural difference. Moving the head back and forth means yes in most western European countries, but it means no in Greece and Bulgaria, and moving the head from left to right is a sign of negation for some and affirmation for others. In many Western countries it is considered a gesture of affection to pat a child on the head, but in Malaysia and many Islamic countries the head is considered to be the source of spiritual and intellectual activity and is therefore sacred (Harris and Moran, 1987).

Box 13.2

Avoid gesturing with the hand, and yet . . .

In general, avoid gesturing with the hand. Many people take offence at being beckoned this way, or pointed at, even if only conversationally. In parts of Asia, gestures and even slight movements can make people nervous. If you jab your finger in the air or on a table to make a point, you might find that your movements have been so distracting that you have not made your point at all. Unintentionally, Americans come across as aggressive and pushy. Yet, in other parts of the world, particularly in Latin America or Italy, gesturing is important for self-expression, and the person who does not move a lot while talking comes across as bland or uninteresting. As always, watch what local people do. Or ask. While in England we once asked, 'How do you point out someone without pointing?' Our companion dropped a shoulder, raised his eyebrows and jerked his head to the side, as though tossing it in the direction he meant to point. Clear as day, he pointed without pointing.

(Source: Copeland and Griggs, 1986, p. 111.)

Another area of non-verbal communication where the importance of cultural variations cannot be denied is that of physical contact and proxemics (see WS13.2 for more information on proxemics). Ferraro (1990) offers a complete description of forms of non-verbal communication involving physical contact: various groups kiss (the cheek, lips, hand, foot), take a person by the arm, clasp the shoulders, pinch the cheek, shake hands, tickle, stroke, give a little pat, etc. These gestures, running over into the realm of familiarity and sexual conduct, are subject to extremely varied codes of use. The kiss, regarded as normal between Russian men or Arab men, who also hold hands in the streets, may appear shocking to Anglo-Saxons. Ferraro (1990, pp. 85–6) recounts his own experience while conducting anthropological field research in Kenya:

After several months of living and working with Kikuyu, I was walking through a village in Kiambu district with a local headman who had become a key informant and a close personal acquaintance. As we walked side by side my friend took my hand in his. Within less than 30 seconds my palm was perspiring all over his. Despite the fact that I knew cognitively that it was a perfectly legitimate Kikuyu gesture of friendship, my own cultural values (that is, that 'real men' don't hold hands) were so ingrained that it was impossible for me not to communicate to my friend that I was very uncomfortable.

The significance of communication codes is complex, and it would be wrong to see as opposites peoples who are reserved in their physical contact (including Anglo-Saxons) and those who are more liberal. Nowhere does there exist true freedom from customs. The way in which American and European men and women show their feelings for each other by kissing in public may seem to be the shocking demonstration of something that should be kept private when seen by other peoples. Dancing, which is part of many cultures' social gatherings, may seem indecent to some and perfectly innocent to others.

Facial expressions and communication with the eyes

Laughing and smiling, frowning and knitting one's brow express communication. A smile can be a sign of satisfaction, of agreement, of embarrassment . . . or even not a sign at all. Certain cultures consider the spontaneous expression of attitudes and emotions by a facial expression to be normal. The reverse is true in other cultures, particularly in Asia where it is considered desirable not to show emotion; this has given rise to the impression of Asians as inscrutable and stoic. According to Morschbach (1982):

Self control, thought of as highly desirable in Japan, demands that a man of virtue will not show a negative emotion in his face when shocked or upset by sudden bad news; and, if successful, is lauded as *taizen jijaku to shite* (perfectly calm and collected) or *mayu hitotsu ugokasazu ni* (without even moving an eyebrow) . . . The idea of an expression-less face in situations of great anxiety was strongly emphasized in the *bushido* (way of the warrior) which was the guide-line for samurai and the ideal for many others.

Visual contacts, such as looking someone straight in the eyes, or, conversely, looking away, or lowering the eyes, or turning them away when they meet someone else's eyes, are all given different meanings in different cultures. This is proof that the same conduct (innocent as it may be) can be arbitrarily given totally opposite meanings. As Harris *et al.* (2004) remarked, Arabs often look each other straight in the eyes because they believe that the eyes are the windows of the soul and that it is important to know the heart and soul of those one is working with. By contrast, Japanese children are taught in school not to look their teacher in the eyes, but to look at the level of the neck. When they become adults, it is considered a gesture of respect to lower their eyes in front of their superiors. Europeans have a tendency to look people straight in the eyes; like the Americans and Australians, they tend to associate a lack of honesty with someone who looks away, and see it as potentially signalling an unfriendly, defiant, impersonal or inattentive attitude.

Dealing with unknown communication styles, especially non-verbal ones, is not an easy task. It is impossible to have an exhaustive knowledge of the full range of cultural interpretations of physical behaviour, gestures and contact. Although it is clear that one can avoid major behavioural mistakes, it is more difficult to develop adequate behaviour oneself unless one stays long enough in a particular country to have time to learn. Besides, part of the locally 'adequate' behaviour was learned in childhood, through rearing and education practices, and it translates into a physical demeanour that is profoundly ingrained. Once again, knowledge appears not to be enough. Awareness begins with the capacity to *unlearn*, that is, to discover progressively the cultural relativity of one's own verbal and non-verbal communication behaviour. The *unlearning process* is a key point, a condition, for the learning process to take place.

In everyday adjustment, courtesy can not be ignored in international business. Politeness and courtesy are based on linguistic indirection used to show social consideration (Morand, 1996), by not being direct. Thus politeness is always a high-context communication in every culture. It has a certain core of universal rules such as not spitting at a person or slapping another's face. However, the degree of contextuality varies according to language and culture. The word *courtesy* is derived from the word 'court', meaning the residence of a king or emperor. It emphasizes the kind of noble behaviour that enhances self-respect through the respect of others. Most languages have such a word. German, for instance, has the word *höflich* (polite), based on the German word for court, *Hof*. Much is forgiven foreigners provided that they are not arrogant and that they show consideration for their hosts, even if ignorant of their customs. Modest, though firm, behaviour facilitates the acceptance of cultural mistakes by the other party.

13.3

Language shaping our world-views

Language contains pre-shaped images of the real world that partly condition our experiences. In this section, we give examples that show that language shapes and reflects different assumptions in terms of time, emotions and feelings, attitude to action, social hierarchy, and how this is expressed in the colloquial phrases used in marketing communications. That language actually shapes culture, and therefore cultural behaviour, is a major causal assumption that can be challenged, for often all that language does is simply reflect culture. That is why we set the limits of this assumption in the second part of this section.

Language influencing culture

The first proponent of the idea that language has a decisive influence on culture was the linguist Edward Sapir (see *WS13.3* for information on Sapir). Language creates categories in our minds, which in their turn directly influence the things we judge to be similar and those that *deserve* to be differentiated. It is our *Weltanschauung* that will be determined: our way of observing, of describing, of interacting and finally the way in which we construct our reality. Sapir (1929, p. 214) writes:

The fact of the matter is that the real world is to a large extent unconsciously built up on the language habits of the group. No two languages are ever sufficiently similar as to be considered as representing the same social reality. The worlds in which different societies live are distinct worlds, not merely the same world with different labels attached.

The linguist and anthropologist Benjamin Lee Whorf developed and extended Sapir's hypothesis. The Whorf–Sapir hypothesis contends that the structure of language has a significant influence on perception and categorization. But although the empirical testing of this hypothesis seems to have been fairly thorough,[9] it is not considered valid by many linguists. For example, the gender given to words is not necessarily indicative of a particular cultural meaning (e.g. the gender of the Earth, the sun and the moon, of vices and virtues); for most it often seems to reflect an arbitrary choice. It may be the case however that this attribution of gender had a certain meaning at the genesis of the language, but that the meaning has since been lost.

Spoken languages are not the only ones to evolve. For instance, Lanksheer and Knobel (2003) discuss the '*new literacies*' that are mediated by computing and communications technologies. These include the development of semiotic languages, such as emoticons in e-mail or online chat space, or instant messaging, using and constructing hyperlinks, identifying software that will 'read' files and the many other aspects of language developed to navigate the world of 'bits'. Lankshear and Knobel (2001) describe the difficulties (for those not born to this culture) in understanding these new ways of thinking in a world that is not based on physical space where value is related to scarcity, but on information space where value is related to familiarity and attention to data. They cite Barlow (the co-founder of the Electronic Frontier Foundation and a writer for the Grateful Dead) as follows:

Barlow's third distinction is between people who have been born into and have grown up in the context of cyberspace, on the one hand, and those who come to this new world from the standpoint of a life-long socialization in physical space, on the other. We will refer here to the former as 'insiders' and the latter as 'outsider-newcomers'. This distinction marks off those who 'understand the Internet, virtual concepts and the IT world generally' from those who do not . . . New comers to cyberspace don't have the experiences, history and resources available to draw on that insiders do. And so, to that extent, they cannot understand the space as insiders do. Barlow believes this distinction falls very much along age lines . . . people over the age of twenty-five (in 1995) are outsider-newcomers.

Similarly, the language of marketing can be difficult for those 'not born to it'. Holden (1998) comments on the fact that the vast majority of marketing text is written in English and translated into other languages. It rarely happens the other way around. He illustrates the difficulties in translating these largely *American* concepts into languages such as Russian where the product life cycle can not be easily illustrated and segmentation is literally translated into '*segmentatsiya*', which means little to Russians. On the positive side, Holden (p. 88) points out that scholars from non-English speaking countries 'acquire in effect two separate world-views about their academic discipline. But more than that . . . the experience of synthesising two professional world-views gives them, not necessarily a fully-fledged third world-view as such, but unquestionably new insights which would not have arisen without this experience-commingling process mediated through the knowledge of another foreign language.'

Box 13.3 illustrates how languages reflect different patterns of time. Levine and Norenzayan (1999) investigated the pace of life in large cities in 31 countries by examining the average walking speed, the time postal clerks completed a request and the accuracy of public clocks. Overall, the speed was faster in stronger economies and individualist cultures. Specifically they found that eight of the nine overall fastest countries were from western Europe: the top three Switzerland, Ireland and Germany were closely followed by Japan.

the slowest speeds were in the nonindustrialized Third World. The very slowest were in three countries popularly associated with a relaxed pace of life: Brazil (where the stereotype of '*amanha*' [literally, 'tomorrow'] holds that, whenever it is conceivably possible, people will put off the business of today until tomorrow); Indonesia (where the hour on the clock is often addressed as '*jam kerat*' ['rubber time']); and, slowest of all, the archetypical land of a *manana*, Mexico.

Languages in relation to actions, thoughts and emotions

Another example may be given of the language–culture link by the way – linguistic as well as cultural – in which an Anglo-American deals with action, especially in business. There is a rich vocabulary to be used, which is often difficult to translate into many other languages, if real equivalence of meaning is sought. The words might include, for instance: *problem solving, issue, matter of fact, down to earth, (empirical) evidence, completed, feed-back, to perform, achievement, individual, data, to check, to plan, deadline, cognitive, emotional, successful,* and so on. Even such an elementary word as *fact* contains a rather demanding content: in English it must be an *established* piece of reality; its French equivalent, *fait*, is less demanding in terms of unanimously agreed-on reality (*les faits peuvent être discutés*, corresponding to a spirit of the facts being 'challenged' rather than just discussed); in German, a fact may be translated by *Tatsache, Wirklichkeit, Wahrheit* or *Tat* – it can mean equally a piece of *reality*, a piece of *truth* or a piece of *action*.

The following short passage caricatures the English way of acting:

This man is achievement and deadline oriented. He first reviews the issues at stake. Then he tries hard to gather data, to verify, measure. As much as possible he will bring hard facts, empirical evidence, not simple opinions. If and when his thoughts and his emotions are conflicting, he will choose to behave as a matter-of-fact and down-to-earth guy. Being individually rewarded, he is therefore eager to perform the task and complete the job. He (almost) always meets his schedule.

When trying to translate this small text into other languages,[10] the difficulties extend far beyond the pure lexical and grammatical ones. They are *cultural translation* difficulties. These problems correspond to what is often called the *spirit* of a language (in French, *Le génie de la langue*): far from being merely a linking of a chain of words, a language contains a series of stands taken on the nature of our relationship to reality.

Let us compare, for instance, the respective qualities of the three most prolific western European languages. By 'qualities of languages' we mean that one of these languages may be better at expressing ideas, facts, or moods, than the others. A comparison between English, French and German[11] suggests that German is stronger

Box 13.3

Time patterns revealed by language

Representations of time are conveyed through the medium of language, as a means of communication and therefore collective action. Whorf comments about the Hopi language in the following terms:

After long and careful study and analysis, the Hopi language is seen to contain no words, grammatical forms, constructions or expressions, that refer directly to what we call 'time', or to past, present, and future, or to motion as kinematic rather than dynamic (i.e. as a continuous translation in space and time rather than as an exhibition of a dynamic effort in a certain process), or that even refer to space in such a way as to exclude that element of extension or existence that we call 'time', and so by implication leave a residue that could be referred to as 'time'. Hence, the Hopi language contains no reference to 'time', either implicit or explicit. (Carroll, 1956, pp. 57–8.)

The vocabulary of time reveals much about the linkage between language and cultural representations. For those who have doubts about the existence of differences in cultural representations of time that are revealed, conveyed and reproduced by language, the example of the English/US word 'deadline' is very illustrative. A quick translation into French would give 'échéance [temporelle]' or 'délai de rigueur' (Langenscheidt, 1989) but would not render the intensity of this word. Taken literally, it seems to suggest something like 'beyond this (temporal) line, you will (there is a danger of) die (dying)'. It therefore gives a genuine notion of urgency to what was originally a very abstract notion (a point which has been agreed upon on a line of time). The word deadline is used in French by many businesspeople as such (*un deadline*), even though it is not in the official dictionary, because it conveys a typically Anglo-American sense of urgency that French people do not find in their own language.

Language also reflects (and pre-shapes) how people envision the future. In some African languages (Kamba and Kikuyu), there are three future tenses which express (1) action in two to six months; (2) action that will take place immediately; and (3) action 'in the foreseeable future, after this or that event.' Commenting on the uses of these African tenses, M'biti demonstrates how coherence and sophistication in the accurate use of the near future, are important to people.

You have these tenses before you: just try to imagine the tense into which you would translate passages of the New Testament concerning the Parousia of Our Lord Jesus Christ, or how you would teach eschatology . . . If you use tense no. 1, you are speaking about something that will take place in the next two to six months, or in any case within two years at most. If you use no. 2, you are referring to something that will take place in the immediate future, and if it does not take place you are exposed as a liar in people's eyes. Should you use no. 3 you are telling people that the event concerned will definitely take place, but when something else has happened first. In all these tenses, the event must be very near to the present moment: if, however, it lies in the far distant future – beyond the two-year limit – you are neither understood nor taken seriously. (M'biti, 1968, quoted in Doob (1971), pp. 74–5.)

Levine, conducting research on Brazilian versus US time, highlights the way concepts of punctuality are reflected in the language. He takes the example of the translation from English to Portuguese of a questionnaire containing the verb 'to wait':

Several of our questions were concerned with how long the respondent would *wait* for someone to arrive versus when they *hoped* the person would arrive versus when they actually *expected* the person would come. Unfortunately, it turns out that the terms *to wait*, *to hope* and *to expect* are all typically translated as the single verb *esperar* in Portuguese. In many ways our translation difficulties taught us more about Brazilian–Anglo differences in time conception than did the subjects' answers to the questions. (Levine, 1988, pp. 48–9.)

There is a sort of continuum across languages in the accuracy of description of the waiting phenomenon (a fundamental issue in time experience!). French language, which lies somewhere between English and Portuguese in terms of temporal accuracy, uses two words: *attendre* (to wait) and *espérer* (to hope). To expect has no direct equivalent in French and must be translated by a lengthy circumlocution ('*compter sur l'arrivée de . . .*').

than English in the expression of abstractions.[12] In German, word endings such as -heit, -keit, -ung, -schaft, -tum and -nis allow the 'abstractification' of concrete notions. English is not only less able to express pure concepts, it is also less prone to. English is more action and more outward oriented, and takes the view that data-oriented and objective approaches to issues allow a separation between internal feelings and external actions. French expresses inner states more accurately, with an emphasis on emotions rather than pure thoughts, describing the self and others. This corresponds to a view that any action is related to affectivity. Stereotypically, we could say that English is a language of action, French a language of emotions and German a language of thoughts. Thus, while it is possible and very desirable to remove language barriers it is still difficult to understand the emphasis on actions, thoughts and emotions.

Language and cultural skills are becoming increasingly important for multinational firms. Howard (2001) states that the replacement costs for an employee who leaves an overseas post averages US$1 million. The most common reasons for leaving is the inability to adjust to cultural and language differences.

Interestingly, the Internet may offer a less contextual format, which may be more amenable to language translation. Translation software is now available that can automatically translate text, so that real time chatting is possible over the Internet. But of course there are still problems with accuracy: even error rates of 1 per cent can cause serious problems in international business (*Business Korea*, 2000).

Language as a reflection of status, hierarchy and a vision of appropriate social relationships

The way we address other people is another example of how language shapes or reflects a social hierarchy. There is only one word used in English for 'you', even when accompanying a first name, and this is most often considered as reflecting a society that has strong assumptions about equality between people. It is said to reflect informality. By contrast, the French often use the formal *vous* for people they do not know very well instead of the informal *tu*, which they reserve for family and friends. Thus the French are reputed to be more formal. The Germans use *du* (second person

singular) in informal and personal settings and *Sie* (third person plural) in formal address. The Germans, like the Spaniards, have three forms of address: while the second person plural (*ihr*) has been lost in practice in German, it remains in Spanish.

In fact, a closer look at these forms shows that the English 'you' was not originally a second person singular, which was 'thou' in old English (as in Shakespeare's plays), but the more polite second person plural. That means that the only address kept in English is based on an assumption of full respect and formality and not on the everyday and less formal form of 'thou'. In fact, the assumed informality of English address, advocated by many native English speakers, is difficult to grasp for a Latin. The addressing of people by their first name and the use of 'you' appears to the Latin as a different kind of formalism rather than true informality. Language reflects quite complex assumptions about equality between people. It is true that the French use of *vous* reflects the strong emphasis on hierarchical and status differences in French society. But it can be very diversely nuanced, with the addition for instance, of *Monsieur* (formal *vous*) or simply the first name (informal *vous*). Of course it is not simply because they have used the polite form for so long that the French have a fairly hierarchical society. But the language context contributes to a constant reframing of culture-bound assumptions about hierarchy in a society.

Sugimoto (1998) studied cross-cultural norms of apologies. He describes the two forms of apology in Japan, the *sunao* apology, which is a sort of gently submissive apology given with good grace, and a sincere form of apology, which is more from the heart. These apologies are codified in Japanese conduct manuals, which provide many readily usable apology expressions. Conversely, Americans tend to favour direct, spontaneous and unformulaic apologies, and sincerity is conveyed through original expressions. (For other examples of politeness, courtesy and etiquette see *WS13.3*.)

Language used in writing advertising messages

A function of language is to convey messages. A common problem for advertisers worldwide is how to use language in order to describe consumer benefits,

Box 13.4

Global marketing communications?

The slogan 'Put a Tiger in your Tank', although often taken as the most perfect example of a standardized advertising campaign, is not as standardized as it might seem. It has been argued that it is standardized, because at first reading it looks as if it were fully equivalent across countries. However, studying the advertisements more closely, one sees that in some countries the power is located in the tank (northern Europeans: '*Pack den Tiger in den Tank*' in Germany, '*Stop'n Tiger in uw Tank*' in Holland). In other countries, the powerful tiger is located in the engine (in French, '*Mettez un Tigre dans votre moteur*', in Italian, '*Metti un Tigre Nel Motore*'). The interpretation, as to where the power source is located differs. Note, however, that an engine cannot work without fuel and vice versa. Nobody is really right, it is simply the interpretations that differ, the Anglo interpretation (tank) being more passive and the Latin interpretation (engine) more active. In Thailand and some neighbouring countries the tiger is experienced quite differently from how it is viewed in Europe, America or Japan. Until recently the tiger was a danger for the local population, especially in the countryside; therefore its image is that of jungle danger rather than of power. The image expressed by the word 'tiger' is not the same in a country where the tiger is experienced as a physical threat and sometimes as a source of terror for the local population as it is in countries where tigers have only been seen in books, films and zoos.

suggest product qualities and convince potential buyers. It must be done using words that represent local world-views. That is why international advertising is very 'Whorfian', even if advertisers and their agencies are not conscious of it (see Box 13.4). The language input in marketing communications is much more significant than it may seem at first. It is directly useful, in designing copy strategy, and indirectly useful, when one is trying to understand consumer moods or viewers' emotions. For example, life insurance advertising implies the evocation of death, which may be taboo in certain cultures, or subject to the use of a particular vocabulary and subdued style. Advertising – especially when it comes to targets and strategies – is never as standardized as it appears to be at first sight.

In addition to vocabulary, accents can also affect perceptions of advertising. For instance, Lwin and Wee (1999) examined the influence of various English accents in advertising for three Asia Pacific countries: Australia, Myanmar and Singapore. The results showed that Western-sounding English accents had the greatest positive influence on advertising effectiveness, followed by a familiar Asian accent, and finally by less familiar accents. In Box 13.4 we illustrate the diverging cultural interpretations of a sign that *prima facie* seems universal (but is not so).

Languages and new international cultures

People have a great deal of leeway in using language. This is more clearly expressed in French than in English since two words correspond to 'language': *la langue* (in English, literally, 'tongue' – the same word serving in French to express both the physical organ and what it helps to create) and *le langage*. *La langue* is the language itself and *le langage* is largely how people use *la langue*, and possibly other means, in order to communicate.

The most obvious influence of culture on language is that of a vocabulary with its own particular capacities and limits. Specific examples of this are the new technological vocabularies from computer science, nuclear technology, audiovisual communication, aerospace technology, etc., which are largely borrowed and exchanged between linguistic and national cultures, the benefit being the creation of a nearly universal technical culture. There are also vocabularies that have been enriched because of physical occurrences that demand precise description, as in the huge number of terms for different types of snow that exist in the language of Eskimos and all peoples who live near the Arctic Circle. Another example is the rich culinary vocabulary in France, where a preoccupation with good food is an element of society that strongly influences daily life.

We do not intend to enter into a debate on the causality of language and culture, which is scientifically very complex and which also risks turning into a 'chicken and egg' argument. However, common-sense reasoning reveals limitations to the Whorfian hypothesis in relation to those who speak many languages, or those who were raised in various linguistic and cultural environments, or the Swiss who share a strong national culture in spite of language differences.[13] In a static scenario, that is, one where an individual or a certain group has been educated in a totally homogeneous cultural environment, language can have an influence on world-view and on one's actions when confronted with reality. But the theory is much less valid in a dynamic scenario, that is, one where language changes from generation to generation or where people travel abroad. Then they will encounter opportunities to borrow language and culture. Interaction between language and culture is reciprocal, in particular in the light of cultural borrowing.

Choosing the correct vocabulary is one of the limitations with the automated translation technologies currently being developed. These automated translation technologies offer the possibility of bringing us closer to a universal communication system that preserves the richness of linguistic and cultural diversity (Lehman-Wilzig, 2001). It is anticipated that the first primitive automated system providing instantaneous translation (rather than waiting for a human interpreter to finish) will be in use by 2015. But even with such amazing technology, there exist culture-specific hazards in the linguistic minefield: homonyms, for example, words with the same spelling that have multiple meanings, are quite common in English, and many other languages. Lu (2001) experimented with three of the currently available tools of translation on the web, which allow people to search the Internet in both English and Asian languages, and compose e-mail messages in your own language and send them in another. He found that homonyms still cause errors for machine translators: 'EWSurf misunderstood the name of the Japanese electronics giant Sony as a term of endearment for a male child, and missed the true meaning of an MP3 player. So visitors to Sony's website are exhorted in Chinese to "enjoy your son's digital new music . . . using an MP3 contestant"' (p. 39). Similarly, Castelluccio (1999) explains that

the word *dog* may mean a four-legged mammal in a strictly lexical definition, but it may also be used as verb meaning to persistently pursue, or a bad investment, or an ugly person, or ruin (as in 'going to the dogs'). Thus, all of these definitions need to be entered before *dog* can be associated their foreign equivalents. Rudich (1999, p. 32) suggests that the companies consider 'hiring a professional to massage the idiosyncrasies of translated syntax and semantics'.

13.4

Ethnocentrism, stereotypes and misunderstandings in intercultural communication

One may add that the cultural mechanism (living according to one's culture in one's daily life) is almost an unconscious action. The cost of adopting the cultural traits of the environment in which one lives is minimal. But there are generally high costs associated with the identification and adoption of the traits of another culture. This is shown clearly by the difficulties encountered by immigrants in integrating, even those who have immigrated voluntarily.

Ethnocentrism

Owing to the high cost of changing one's culture, most people live without even envisaging such a possibility. This causes what James Lee (1966) calls the SRC (Self-Reference Criterion): we all have an automatic and unconscious tendency to refer to our own thought framework, which is mainly tied to our national culture (which in general we did not choose), to interpret situations, evaluate people, communicate, negotiate or decide which attitude to take. This framework is generally modelled by ethnocentrism, which was discussed in Chapter 10 in relation to country of origin effects (see *WS13.4* for further examples of ethnocentrism).

The concept of ethnocentrism was first introduced by G. A. Sumner (1906) more than 80 years ago, to distinguish between *ingroups* (those groups with which an individual identifies) and *outgroups* (those regarded as antithetical to the *ingroup*). Ethnocentrism has been extended by psychologists at the level of the individual, where it relates to the natural tendency of people to refer themselves spontaneously to the symbols, values and ways of thinking of their own ethnic or national group (their ingroup). Ethnocentrism may lead to disinterest and even contempt for the culture of other groups (Levine and Campbell, 1972). Lee (1966) suggests the following steps in order to try to eliminate the decisional bias related to the SRC when dealing with international operations:

1. Define the problem or the objectives, as would be done according to the customs, behavioural standards and ways of thinking of the decision-maker's country.
2. Similarly, define the problem or the objectives as would be done according to the customs, behavioural standards and ways of thinking of the foreign country (where the decision will be implemented).
3. Isolate the influence of the self-reference criterion on the problem, and identify the extent to which it complicates the decision-making problem.
4. Redefine the problem (and often the objectives), without the bias related to the SRC and then find the solutions and make decisions that fit with the cultural context of the foreign market.

In this way one can imagine the following situation. People are standing in line at an amusement park, such as Disneyland, where there are some very popular attractions. In the original context in the United States, discipline with respect to queues is strong. They are usually well organized and there are even tangible indications for this (yellow line on the ground indicating to people where to stop to queue, visible corridors for queuing in line, etc.). In the foreign context of France, where there is a developed sense of 'free-for-all' and less of a habit of organized queues, combined with a reluctance towards anything that seems too socially structured, the problem will not present itself in the same terms.

Although it constitutes the first practical framework that allows us to attribute all operational value to cultural representation, the SRC also comprises a degree of naivety and inadequacy. It presupposes that it is possible easily to penetrate the mysteries of a culture without being a native. Cultural expertise is a complex reality. Sometimes neither marketing experts from the original country (in total ignorance) nor foreigners (through lack of consciousness of their

own culture) are capable of diagnosis in the second and third phases. The effect of the effort of bias removal and the results achieved by the use of the SRC are not immediate. For instance, Billikopf (1993) describes his first trip to Russia. He was tutored on Russian culture, talking to interpreters about what was the correct thing in various situations. On one of these occasions the interpreter explained that a gentleman will always show courtesies to ladies, such as pouring her *limonad*. Later, he tried to use this reasoning when he offered his host's wife a banana. When she smiled and said yes without reaching for one, he picked one for her and peeled it half way before he handed it to her. His host's smile told him he had done the right thing. On a later trip he was informed that: 'In Russian, when a man peels a banana for a lady it means he has a romantic interest in her' (p. 1). Billikopf cautions that generalizations about eye-contact, personal space, touch and interest in participation, especially based on faulty observation, can be dangerous.

Stereotypes

As pointed out by Gauthey and Xardel (1990, p. 20), if the French perceive Americans as being arrogant and tough in business, and see the British as insincere, it is for the most part due to stereotypes, which give a distorted view. American arrogance is, in fact, related to a different hierarchy of values: professional relations are centred on the task at hand, the object of discussion, to the exclusion of personal relations with the other party.

Stereotypes, although sometimes representing a simplification that is intellectually useful, nonetheless have the function of reducing and conserving our differences, which can make them dangerous. Soutar *et al.* (1999) surveyed Australians and Japanese who had business dealings with people from the other country or lived in that country. They asked them to estimate the values (using the List of Values scale) of their own and the other culture. In general, they found that the Japanese respondents' views of Australians were closer to Australians' views than the other way around, although exposure through living there tended to bring the Australians' views closer. For example, relationships with others was the most important value for Japanese, but Australians felt this was much less important to the Japanese than other values such as being well respected, having a sense of belonging and having security. This illustrates that our stereotypes of other cultures can be quite different from their reality. Thus, even those who immerse themselves in another culture will not fully understand the nuances.

Gauthey (1989, p. 63) notes the personal aspect: 'It seems a thousand times easier to stay attached to our own values and to transfer onto the foreigner the responsibility to change his point of view than to decenter ourselves, that is to leave our system of reference and put ourselves in the place of the other.' Characteristic of stereotypes are a cognitive function (wherein they work as a simplified intellectual representation of other people) and also an emotional function (self-defence against a difference that provokes anxiety). Michel Droit, in his book *Chez les Mangeurs d'hommes* (With the Man eaters), exposes the stereotype of the sorcerer in primitive societies. He describes the people of Papua New Guinea as seen by civilized observers who are necessarily their ideological enemies (1952, p. 124, author's translation):

Armed with tamed snakes which they use to execute their victims, with poisons, enchanted prayers and medicinal herbs known only to them, sorcerers, through well-organized propaganda and strong co-operative solidarity, let entire populations live in fear and sometimes in terror of their '*nepou*', that is their evil powers.

The point is not to suggest that Michel Droit's description of the sorcerer is false. His reading partially reveals reality but also ignores how the sorcerer is integrated into the Papuan community. Stereotypes are often used to capture the salient traits of a 'foreign' national character. For instance, Yoshida (2000, p. 1) relates a very amusing anecdote of a European professor who assigned students from different nationalities to submit a report on the elephant. Stereotypical submissions included: 'A philosophical analysis of the existence of the elephant' from a German student, 'How to raise an elephant in your backyard for money and fun without risk of litigation' from an American student, 'A comparative analysis of elephant studies in foreign countries, particularly Europe and America: what the Elephant thinks of us Japanese' from a Japanese student, and a Chinese student just submitted a recipe. Box 13.5 shows how French people are viewed (at least stereotypically) by people of other nations. (See WS13.4 for a bibliography of stereotype literature.)

Box 13.5

Some stereotypes of the French (undeserved?)

How various nationalities perceive the French:

- The Germans: Pretentious and offhand. Fashionable, womanizing, frivolous, fickle, well-mannered, resourceful.
- The British: Nationalistic, chauvinistic, intransigent, centralist, dependent on the state, polite but not open-minded, humourless, short-tempered.
- The Dutch: Cultured, fond of good living, fidgety, talkative, not very serious, feelings of superiority.
- The Spanish: Pretentious, early sleepers, cold and distant, hypocritical, impolite, patronizing, hard working.
- The Swedish: In-built superiority complex, scornful, boastful, talkative, immoral, dirty, neo-colonialists, disorganized, cultured gastronomy, suffocating hierarchy.

- The Finns: Xenophobic, superficial, scornful, chauvinistic, courteous, romantic, enjoying life, patriotic, chaotic.
- The Americans: Chauvinistic, well-mannered. Combination of good food and good conversation, Paris. Curious about foreign people, pretentious, talkative, pleasant, intelligent.
- The Russians: Talkative, self-satisfied, lazy. Luxury, inequality, culture. Pleasant, intelligent, resourceful.
- The North Africans: Fairly racist, a little stingy, reasonably honest. Good education and good food. Selfish.
- The Asians: Exhibitionist, indiscreet. Reticent in making friends. Bureaucracy and red tape.
- The Black Africans: Racist, honest, lacking respect for elders and betters. At odds with themselves and nature. Not spontaneously hospitable.

(Source: Gruère and Morel, 1991, p. 51.)

Self-shock

It is necessary to acknowledge that the problem of cultural representation is more complex than simply 'getting to know the other'. As shown by Zaharna (1989) in a review article on the culture shock experienced by people of different cultures, the problematic representation of the 'other' may evolve into a confrontation (equally problematic) with oneself. Zaharna calls this process 'self-shock'. Experiencing how others actually are may be somewhat destabilizing: identity confusion is a typical feature of culture shock (Oberg, 1960). Self-shock is probably one of the principal causes of stereotyping. Stereotypes often protect 'the self', much more than they really provide information on 'the other'.

When people from different cultures meet, as when expatriate managers meet local executives or international sellers meet local buyers, the encounter is an intercultural one where the absence of previous knowledge of the other's culture makes for uncertainty. At first, one might think that the basic problem is 'getting to know the other'. But in the intercultural encounter, there is in fact a 'progressive unfolding of the self', which can be attributed to 'a set of intensive and evocative situations in which the individual perceives and experiences other people in a distinctly new manner and, as a consequence, experiences new facets and dimensions of existence' (Adler, 1975, p. 18). In intercultural encounters, the necessary introduction of the 'other' risks disturbing one's personal identity, which is placed in question by the 'mirror effect'.

Within our own cultural context, we have unconsciously built our 'self-image'. We necessarily construct an image of ourselves from the observations that we make, based on the responses of others to our conduct. This is emphasized by Erikson (1950, p. 13): 'Identity is the confidence gathered from the fact that our own ability to maintain interior resemblance and continuity equals the resemblance and continuity of the image and the sense that others have of us.' But the process of the creation and maintenance of personal identity has two characteristics that make it problematic in the intercultural encounter: (1) it happens for the most part outside our consciousness, and (2) it requires a good capacity for interpersonal communication.

According to Zaharna 'self-shock', unlike culture shock, which is seen as a reaction to difference between oneself and the other, is a concept that extends to differences with and inside the self. The root of 'self-shock' lies in the intimate workings of the relationship between the ego (that is, personal identity), our behaviour, and the 'other' (as the 'other' actually is, and as the other is perceived by us), and also in forcing us to reflect upon ourselves. Self-shock emerges as a deep imbalance between our need to confirm our identity and our ability to do so. In one way, this situation places the individual in a position of 'double-bind' (Bateson, 1971). The self-shock situation increases our need for the reinforcement of our personal identity, while at the same time resulting in a loss of ability to satisfy this need. Thus, one can understand more easily that certain stereotypes or abrupt judgements about foreigners result almost directly from our attempts to defend ourselves by avoiding the painful double constraint of self-shock.

Gauthey (1989, p. 64) cites the case of the general manager of a software company, a subsidiary of a French advertising and communications group, who says: 'I can't stand the English, and when I go to London, I never leave the airport.' This attitude is clearly defensive: in refusing to leave the airport, he stays on neutral international ground, with no risk of being confronted by the image of himself that he will be shown by the English.

International empathy: A naive concept

In the concept of international empathy we can catch a glimpse of the immense naivety of those who argue in favour of cultural empathy (being open-minded, sincerely interested in the other, ready to listen, etc.). This communication tactic, although well meant, may only last for a brief period – the time during which the personal identity of the 'empathizer' has not yet come into play. There are a series of concrete issues at stake, which are important for people involved in intercultural communication in business:

1. Which personality types and/or personal backgrounds are best suited to intercultural communication?

2. Related questions are: Are we able to communicate better with particular countries and cultures? How can we increase our abilities in this respect?

3. A question rarely dealt with is: If an adjustment must be made during the intercultural encounter, who should be the one to adapt? Quite apart from personal capacities, empathy or the position of strength, can the intercultural learning situation be led other than bilaterally? In other words, why learn if the other does not learn too? Why not learn simultaneously, rather than in two parallel learning situations that may never meet?

13.5

How to improve communication effectiveness in international business

A 'reasonable' version of the use of the Whorfian hypothesis

The first consequence of the Whorf–Sapir hypothesis, in so far as one chooses to adhere to it, is that business people from different cultures not only communicate in different ways, but also perceive, categorize and construct their realities differently. This therefore supposes a 'state of alert' in communication, a readiness to accept that words, even those that are translated with no apparent difficulty, offer only an illusion of sharing in the same vision of reality. It is necessary to retain as many foreign words as possible in their original form, in the following ways:

1. By forcing oneself to recognize their unique nature and therefore keeping culturally unique concepts in the native language form to signal their uniqueness.

2. By questioning the interpreters, or even one's foreign business partners, about the precise meaning of words or expressions in the context of a particular culture.[14]

3. By clearly identifying areas of shared meaning.

For instance, in the examination of contract clauses, it is necessary to try to extricate the true meaning of each clause, starting from the perspective that they are never exactly equivalent. This is true even in the case where a dictionary seems to indicate (falsely) that an English term is a strict equivalent of a French term, such as *act of God* and *force majeure*.[15]

Internet and language

It has already been observed in this chapter that languages other than English are assuming a highly prominent place on the Internet. Abas (2002, pp. 1–2) noted that 'about 146.2 million individuals access Web sites in the Asian languages (Arabic, Chinese, Hebrew, Japanese, Korean, Malay and Thai) . . . This was in contrast to only 25.5 million individuals doing the same three years ago, a jump of 5.73 times.' Statistics like this seem to support Heppner and Farré's (2001) assertion that English is no longer the *lingua franca* of the Internet: translators have never had more work.

There are many problems with translation on the Internet, including making sure software can accept foreign language features, such as double-byte Asian characters (Yunker, 2000), and overcoming the subtleties with ever-expanding translation dictionaries (Bisby, 1999) and cost (Heuberger, 2001). Translation techniques are also evolving alongside dictionary size and hardware horsepower. Many translation software packages, rely on example-based translation: 'If the program learns that French people write adjectives after nouns ("vin rouge" means "red wine" rather than "wine red"), it can use this knowledge to guess that "riviere rouge" means "red river", not "river red"' (Bisby, 1999, p. 17). Despite this, it can cost upwards of US$20,000 to translate a website of 100 pages: software can only go so far – translation is still very much a human process (Heuberger, 2001).

Linguistic ethnocentrism versus linguistic polycentrism

An unfortunate consequence of the Whorf–Sapir hypothesis is that linguistic ethnocentrism is largely inevitable. One might wonder whether it would be a more realistic approach to have only natives of a language and culture write about cultural topics for their fellow citizens. If we think of anthropology, a discipline with a high record of reporting on other cultures, it seems that the answer would be 'yes'. Famous anthropologists generally belonged to the cultures of their publishers and readers, not to the cultures they observed. The same holds true for area specialists. For instance, the two specialists of French culture who are best known are Theodore Zeldin of Harvard

University and John Ardagh, a British journalist. Similarly, the most prominent specialist in Germany on French contemporary civilization is a German, Ulrich Wickert. It is often useful to be an outsider in relation to what is observed and, culturally and in language terms, an insider in reporting what has been observed. This evokes the issue of *cultural mediation*, which is discussed briefly in section 2.3. However paradoxical and provocative it may seem, it is sometimes more important to be understood than to understand, inasmuch as the *understanding* depends on the mindset of the observer as well as on the object to be understood. What is said by mere cultural insiders is often difficult to understand unless it has been in some way recalibrated in the linguistic background of the reader, which means more than simply translated.

For international business people to be linguistically non-ethnocentric does not mean that they have to have a full command of several foreign languages. It is more important, and in fact much easier, to catch what is unique in the structure of the foreign language and some of its words than trying to become fluent in that language. A look at a book of basic grammar and careful attention to specific words are a good start. Very often authors of books on Japanese business customs or management style keep Japanese words as they are originally pronounced when they want to signal a culturally specific meaning.[16] Sometimes words are forged that partly bridge the cultural divide. Boye de Mente cites for instance the Japanese word *nomination*, which is made up of the first part of the Japanese word *nomimasu* (to drink) and the last half of 'communication': 'This Japlish word refers to business conversations and socializing that takes place in bars, cabarets, and other drinking establishments, and it is one of the institutionalized ways of "wisdom gathering" in Japan' (de Mente, 1990, p. 261).

Culturally unique life concepts have a major impact on decision-making processes inside companies and especially on the issue of labour–management relationships. They are signalled by words such as *Management by objectives* for the Americans, *ringi* for the Japanese, *mitbestimmung* for the Germans and *concertation* for the French. The same holds for the managing institutions of a company: a German *Aufsichtsrat*, often translated into English as 'supervisory board', should be considered a specific institution, typical of German business culture, with particular consequences in the real life of real businesses (Schneider-Lenné, 1993). Although linguistic ethnocentrism is largely inevitable, we must strive for linguistic polycentrism, by trying to keep original words, understanding meaningful elements in the grammar (such as gender, tenses and sentence construction), and trying to behave as 'explorers' of the meanings and world-views expressed by different languages.

Taking the true measure of language and communication abilities in international business

In considering English as the *lingua franca* of international business, we have to differentiate two groups: native and non-native English speakers. Their positions are clearly different. For non-native English-speaking business people, learning English and often one or two other languages is a must. For instance, the Swedes, Finns, Danes and Norwegians often speak three or four foreign languages: English, another Nordic language and French, German or Spanish. The situation is very different for native English speakers. Simon (1980, p. 2) observes: 'The US continues to be the only nation where you can graduate from college without having had one year of a foreign language'. Australia also falls into this category. Although regrettable, this may be explained and understood. The United States and Australia are vast, linguistically homogeneous countries where nearly everyone shares the common language of English. Australia is also geographically quite remote from much of the world. There is no real need to learn foreign languages, whereas in Europe most large cities are located less than 200 miles (330 km) from a foreign-speaking area and a foreign language is an asset. Although the USA is now the fourth-largest Spanish-speaking country in the world and more than half the population of Miami is of Spanish-speaking origin, this does not necessarily require Americans to learn Spanish. Rather, Hispanics have to learn English. Moreover, there may be differences in the amount of effort required to learn certain foreign languages. If an American or a European wants to really learn Japanese, the characters have to be learned, which implies a much larger effort than for the Japanese to learn the Roman alphabet: the *gai-jin* (non-Japanese) has to learn two syllabaries of about 100 characters each (*hiragana* and *katakana*, phonetic symbols) and about 1,850 *kanjis* (ideographic symbols), whereas the Roman alphabet to be learned by the Japanese has only 26 phonetic characters, not a large addition given the skill needed to master Japanese writing. Lastly, Americans can fairly easily find English speakers during their travels, and they can count on their foreign business partners having – at least superficially – a good command of English. Furthermore, Americans are tolerant and lenient towards the mistakes of their non-native counterparts: 'international English' sometimes has little to do with real English grammar and words.

These are good reasons why native English speakers are somewhat lazy about foreign languages. Understandably, therefore, the impact of language differences has been systematically underestimated in international business literature because of an 'English-only' bias in Anglo-American culture. Most international business textbooks do not include a single reference in a foreign language. Even a text devoted to the cultural dimension of international business such as Ferraro (1990) does not have (among about 200 references) a single *truly* foreign reference, that is, from a foreign author in a foreign language, although some works by foreign authors are listed when they have been published in English.[17] This may imply a substantial bias, since these authors would not be read in their own linguistic contexts and any foreign authors who have not been translated into English are not even considered. However, there are naturally good and practical reasons for maintaining language homogeneity in sources, namely that the reader would not be able either to find or to read these references, so this should not be considered only as a reflection of linguistic ethnocentrism.

What is unfortunate, however, is that native English speakers are at a disadvantage, although the opposite may appear to be true. The main disadvantage for them is that they cannot grasp the features of the foreign language in terms of world-view and communication style. Furthermore, many native English speakers cannot imagine what it means or is like to express oneself in a language with little proficiency unless they themselves have tried to learn and speak a foreign language. Thus native English speakers have to develop an awareness of their paradoxical competitive disadvantage in terms of language. However, the message to be conveyed cannot be simply and plainly to learn foreign languages. It is a different thing to understand and speak a foreign language as such and to understand the consequences of languages being different. Absolute proficiency in many languages is not needed. International business people do not have to be multilingual; they do, however, need to have an awareness of what language differences imply.

On the other hand, non-native English speakers must not deceive those with whom they deal. Although many foreign business people seem to have a good command of English, they still have the kind of worldview that has been shaped by their native language and culture. Thus proficient non-native English speakers may be somewhat misleading partners for their opposite numbers: they look quite the same, but they are quite different. This may be especially true for northern Europeans. They may seem quite similar, especially to Americans, since their English pronunciation has largely been shaped by television viewing. Nevertheless, they may have in reality a different mindset and also a much greater proficiency for oral than for written communication, which can cause problems when the written details of business contracts are discussed.

Some guidelines for effective communication in international business

The following are some guidelines for effective communication in international business (see *WS13.5* for practical examples of these guidelines in action):

1. Start by assessing as accurately as you can the possible intercultural obstacles that exist, such as language and problems of communication in general. Business people often underestimate or even completely overlook this point, since they often share a technical culture with their conversation partner. They are also deceived by an almost international atmosphere that can be quite misleading. Glen Fisher points out:

   Obviously, the modern intensity of international interaction, especially in business and in technological, communication and educational fields, has produced something of an internationalized 'culture' which reduces the clash of cultural backgrounds and stereotyped images. Happily for us this *modus vivendi* is largely based on Western practices and even on the English language, so many otherwise 'foreign' counterparts are accommodating to the American style of negotiation. (Fisher, 1980, p. 8.)

Unfortunately, in the real world, the person who does not feel the need to adapt, especially as far as language is concerned, may be indulging in indolence. The result will be the mistaken impression that one's partner is just like oneself. That is to say that often similarities are illusions, especially when foreigners seemingly share the same 'international culture'. Those who adapt are aware of differences, whereas those who must be adapted to remain unaware.

2. Be aware that what is explicitly said is not necessarily what is implicitly meant. Check, verify. Spend time on checking communication accuracy, especially when the stakes are high (orders, delivery dates, contractual involvement in general).

3. Learning the non-verbal communication style of other cultures may prove very difficult. Deep cultural learning in this area is very hard after childhood. It is better to aim for a state of alertness so that one does not decode non-verbal messages erroneously, rather than try to gain full command of different types of non-verbal communication.

4. In many cases interpreters may serve a crucial purpose; they may be transposers of meaning. They do not work 'like a dictionary', translating literally. They may translate better from one language to another than in the reverse direction, and this will depend not only on which language is their native one, but also on a personal leaning that they may have towards one party. It is also necessary to make sure that they are truly loyal to the party who has hired them. It may be advisable to hire several interpreters when the business at stake justifies it.

5. It must be clearly appreciated that there is always a part of the language that cannot be translated. Culture-specific meaning is conveyed by language as it reflects the culture. Always keep in mind the Italian adage, cited above, *traduttore/traditore* (translator/traitor).

6. Develop a 'bomb squad' ability to defuse a conflict based on negative stereotypes. Subjective misunderstandings in intercultural communication often snowball and mix with purely interest-based objective conflicts, resulting in confrontations that may not be productive. There are sometimes necessary conflicts, and even good ones, where confrontation should not be avoided. In many other cases, however, cultural misunderstandings may have a purely negative influence on the dealings that follow, possibly even leading to the breaking off of negotiations.

7. Keep in mind that all this depends on advance preparation, and unfortunately cannot be improvised. An effort to help the other intelligently and agreeably to understand one's own culture is a prerequisite, and may often involve 'wine and dine' situations. When formal business negotiations or even preliminary business talks start and one side lacks even the barest knowledge of the partner's culture, relations will often turn sour. It will soon be too late to approach basic issues affected by common understandings and cultural differences. Then the only way to negotiate is to discuss on the substantive ground of 'business is business'. In this light, training in intercultural business seems more like a preliminary investment to improve the effectiveness of business deals than a way of resolving urgent problems. In medical terms, cultural understanding in business appears as the prevention rather than the cure.

Questions

1. Comment on the following sentences:

   It is the subjective meaning of words and expressions that needs to be captured. Time spent exploring why a given utterance does not translate well may be more productive for the one who is actually trying to communicate than concentration on technical excellence. (Fisher, 1988, p. 172.)

2. Give examples of low-context versus high-context communication, explaining what is meant by low and high contexts.

3. Transform the following buyer's remark into low-context and high-context sentences: 'Your price is too high compared with that of the competitors'.

4. Discuss the following statements from the perspective of stereotyping:

Many Germans, for instance, do not like to converse much during their meals. Germans will ordinarily begin their meals by taking a sip of beer or soda and then picking up and holding knives and forks throughout the meal, putting them down only when they are finished eating. For many Germans eating is a serious business that is not to be disturbed by trivial comments and animated conversation. (Gannon, 1994, p. 5.)

Germans also frequent the symphony on a regular basis; the former West Germany with its population of 62 millions boasts approximately 80 symphony orchestras . . . This societal and cultural love of music has produced some of the finest composers of classical symphonic music. In fact, many experts agree that the classical symphony reached its highest level of attainment and maturity in the works of Haydn and Mozart. (Gannon, 1994, p. 68.)

5. Why can the obvious showing of emotions be considered dangerous? Why do cultures vary in the degree of emotional restraint?

6. Consider the gender aspect of words in the following languages. In English almost everything is neutral except persons and some animals, and exceptionally an object such as a ship. French has feminine and masculine but no neutral. In German, persons, objects and concepts can be feminine, masculine or neutral. For instance 'sun', 'earth' and 'moon' are all neutral words in English; in French they are respectively masculine (*le soleil*) and feminine (*la terre, la lune*); in German the same words are feminine (*die Sonne, die Erde*) and masculine (*der Mond*). Elaborate on the possible cultural meanings of attributing gender to words. To what extent can we speak of more or less 'sexualized' languages (I mean here 'sexualized' and not simply 'gendered')? Outline the limitations of such an interpretive approach.

7. In Japanese there are no articles either definite or indefinite. *Hon*, for instance, means 'the book', 'a book', 'the books' or 'books'. What does this imply for the Japanese when they want to express their thoughts?

8. Consider gift-giving practices as an element of communication. What are the main dimensions of gift giving (consider the donor, the receiver, the size and nature of the gift, the circumstances and its meaning for either side)? How would cultural interpretations differ? Take into account the values involved. (You can base your discussion on elements found in articles about gift giving.)

9. Can you describe at least one circumstance when you had an ethnocentric attitude? If you find it hard, can you explain why?

Notes

1. Depending on your own linguistic background, in reading this chapter you may be wondering how the linguistic mix (original French text, English translation) has influenced the kind of arguments put forward and the way in which they have been expounded. The Whorfian hypothesis, briefly explained in section 13.3, is presented in detail in the writings of Benjamin Whorf, collected after his death by John B. Carroll (1956).

2. A good example is the following assertion in Hall (1966, p. 50): 'In the Northern European tradition most Americans have cut themselves off from a powerful communication channel: olfaction. Our cities lack both olfactory and visual variety . . . During World War II in France I observed that the aroma of French bread freshly removed from the oven at 4:00 A.M. could bring a speeding jeep to a screaming halt . . . In the typical French town, one may savor the smell

of coffee, spices, vegetables, freshly plucked fowl, clean laundry, and the characteristic odor of outdoor cafés.' Although there is some truth in Hall's words, we are not so sure that France is so odourful and the Americans so cut off from olfactive communication.

3. The example took place in Geneva, where the penalty was 15 Swiss Francs (about $12).

4. We are not arguing that these national cultures have a great deal in common. The concept of low context/explicit messages relates only to communication; in other aspects they may differ widely.

5. Langenscheidt, *German–English Dictionary* (Pocket Books: New York, 1970).

6. Hall posits the American as being more HC (or less LC) than the Swiss, the Germans and the Scandinavians (1976, p. 91), and the French and the English as more HC than the Americans but less than the Japanese. A possible tentative ranking on a scale starting with LC and moving across to HC would be: Swiss-Germans, Germans, Scandinavians, Americans, English, French, other southern Europeans, Latin Americans, Middle Easterners, Japanese.

7. Analogical components of verbal messages are those that work by imitation of existing models or regular patterns, but which cannot be reduced to binary, digital information. First, a 'yes' is '1', as opposed to 'no', which is '0' (digital component); second, the meaning derived from how this 'yes' is said is the analogical component of the message.

8. In this chapter, we have not paid special attention to the 'language of space'. This includes the codes concerning social distance: how far should one stay from another person in order to respect their area of private space and does such an area even exist? A complete approach to these relations of space was proposed by Hall (1966) in *The Hidden Dimension*, where he developed the concept of 'proxemics' – the grouping of observations and theories dealing with the use of space by human beings, especially as far as private space and social space are concerned. Hall further developed an interesting cross-cultural comparison of proxemics between the Germans, the English, the French, the Japanese and the Arabs.

9. The verifications of the Whorf–Sapir hypothesis seem to have been fairly conclusive, in particular those related to the comparative experiments based on Navajo children on the one hand and Anglo-Americans on the other. They shared all the principal socio-cultural characteristics (education, family income, religion, etc.) except language (see the experiments reported by Ferraro, 1990, pp. 54–5).

10. Jean-Claude wrote this short English text himself, therefore it is not a 'valid text' but a caricature or exercise in reflection. Native anglophones will notice the 'Gallic' style with respect to idioms.

11. This is related to English, French and German intellectual styles, which are described in more detail in Chapter 3, using the typology of Galtung (1981).

12. What is said here is fairly tentative; there are no definitive proofs, and so there are at best illustrations, and many people may disagree with what we say here. Think of it as proposed rather than imposed.

13. However, in Japan Jean-Claude had a student who was the son of the Turkish ambassador to the United Nations. Having been raised in France, Belgium, Italy and Brazil, he was studying for a Master's Degree in International Management at the American Graduate School of International Management in Phoenix, Arizona. Already a fluent speaker of Turkish, French, English, Italian and Portuguese, he was learning Japanese. But he was quite unable to move with ease from any one of these languages to another. When in the middle of a conversation Jean-Claude asked him for the English translation of a French word (He taught in English), he could never do this without a considerable delay. In fact *he thought separately in each one of these languages*, which is fairly consistent with the Whorfian hypothesis.

14. Sussman and Johnson (1996), based on a qualitative analysis of critical incidents provided by professional interpreters (in German, French, Japanese and Spanish), highlight three major roles for interpreters: editor, cultural coach and monitor/checker. In their view, international executives should be informed consumers of interpretation services. Executives conducting business through the services of an interpreter should hire an interpreter with proven or accredited skills and try to avoid using multiple interpreters since the use of many interpreters results in confused and protracted business transactions. It is also necessary to determine whether the interpreter should be a passive or an active participant taking on more than the strict interpreting role.

15. To investigate the equivalence/non-equivalence of terms, take two dictionaries and look in each of them at the translations in both directions. The Langenscheidt compact dictionary translates *act of God* as *force majeure*, but it translates *force majeure* as *overpowering circumstances*; *Harrap's Concise Dictionary* does not include the expression *act of God* in the English section and translates *force majeure* as 'circumstances outside one's control'. The next step is to consult a lawyer to arrive at the meanings of all these expressions, and find their respective legal consequences. *Force majeure* is used, as such, in English and US contracts.

16. It is naturally impossible to keep Japanese words in their original, spoken and written, form; they need to be transliterated into the Roman alphabet. The system often used is the *Hyojunshiki* (standard system), which is an adaptation of the Hepburn system.

17. The total unawareness of language differences in intercultural encounters is a general feature of the English-speaking cross-cultural literature. In an article about cross-cultural groups at work, Smith and Berg (1997, pp. 9–10) give many cues about how to improve intercultural effectiveness, but totally ignore language. People have to 'learn how to learn together', to discover 'other members' unique cultural contributions', to 'explore group polarities'. That native language is our main asset, learnt spontaneously, and is a main cultural differentiator across different linguistic areas is ethnocentrically ignored because everyone in the global world is supposed to speak fluent English. Language diversity as an opportunity for improving intercultural encounters is denied. Period.

References

Abas, Zoraini Wati (2002), 'Internet growth based on languages', *Computimes Malaysia*, May, vol. 16, p. 1.

Adler, Peter S. (1975), 'The transitional experience: an alternative view of culture shock', *Journal of Humanistic Psychology*, vol. 15, pp. 13–23.

Anonymous (2003), 'China's online community hits 68 million', *Silicon.com*, online, 22 July, available at: **http://networks.silicon.com/broadband/0,39024661, 10005249,00.htm/**.

Axtell, Roger E. (1993), *Do's and Taboos Around the World*, Wiley: New York.

Bateson, Gregory (1971), introduction to *The Natural History of an Interview*, University of Chicago Library Microfilm Collection of Manuscripts in Cultural Anthropology, Series 15, Nos 95–8.

Billikopf Encina, Gregorio (1999), 'Cultural differences?', online, available at: **www.cnr.berkeley.edu/ucce50/ ag-labor/7article/article01.htm**

Bisby, Adam (1999), 'Translation tools speak globally', *Computer Dealer News*, vol. 15, no. 15, p. 17.

Bluedorn, Allen C. (1998), 'An interview with anthropologist Edward T. Hall', *Journal of Management Inquiry*, vol. 7, no. 2, pp. 109–15.

Business Korea (2000), 'Removing language barriers', vol. 17, no. 12, pp. 58–9.

Carroll, John B. (1956), *Language, Thought and Reality: Selected writings of Benjamin Lee Whorf*, MIT: Cambridge, MA.

Castellucio, Michael (1999), 'Hey, can anybody read this?' *Strategic Finance*, vol. 81, no. 1, pp. 63–4.

Chowdhry, Amitav (2000), 'India bursting at the linguistic seams', *The UNESCO Courier*, April.

Condon, John C. and Fahti Youssef (1975), *Introduction to Intercultural Communication*, Bobbs Merrill: Indianapolis.

Copeland, Lennie and Lewis Griggs (1986), *Going International*, Plume Books/New American Library: New York.

Correll, Sharon (2003), '*Examples of Complex Rendering*', Non-Roman Scripts Initiative, Summer Institute of Linguistics (SIL), 21 April.

Cutitta, Frank (2002), 'Language matters', *Target Marketing*, vol. 25, no. 2, pp. 40–4.

de Mente, Boye (1990), *How to Do Business with the Japanese*, NTC Books: Chicago, IL.

Droit, Michel (1952), *Chez les Mangeurs d'hommes*, La Table Ronde: Paris.

Erikson, Erik (1950), *Childhood and Society*, Norton: New York.

Ethnologue (1992), 12th edn, Dallas, TX.

Ferraro, Gary P. (1990), *The Cultural Dimension of International Business*, Prentice Hall: Englewood Cliffs, NJ.

Fisher, Glen (1980), *International Negotiation: A cross-cultural perspective*, Intercultural Press: Yarmouth, ME.

Fisher, Glen (1988), *Mindsets*, Intercultural Press: Yarmouth, ME.

Galtung, Johan (1981), 'Structure, culture and intellectual style: an essay comparing Saxonic, Teutonic, Gallic and Nipponic Approaches', *Social Science Information*, vol. 20, no. 6, pp. 817–56.

Gannon, Martin J. (1994), *Understanding Global Cultures: Metaphorical journeys through 17 countries*, Sage Publications: Thousand Oaks, CA.

Gauthey, Franck (1989), 'Gérer les différences dans l'entreprise internationale', *Intercultures*, no. 6, April, pp. 59–66.

Gauthey, Franck and Dominique Xardel (1990), *Le Management Interculturel*, PUF, Collection 'Que Sais-Je?': Paris.

Gruère, Jean-Pierre and Pierre Morel (1991), *Cadres Français et Communications Interculturelles*, Eyrolles: Paris.

Hall, Edward T. (1960), 'The silent language in overseas business', *Harvard Business Review*, May–June, pp. 87–96.

Hall, Edward T. (1966), *The Hidden Dimension*, Doubleday: New York.

Hall, Edward T. (1976), *Beyond Culture*, Doubleday: New York.

Hall, Patrick A.V. (2002), 'Bridging the digital divide', *Electronic Journal of Information Systems in Developing Countries*, vol. 8, no. 1, pp. 1–9.

Harris, Philip R. and Robert T. Moran (1987), *Managing Cultural Differences*, 2nd edn, Gulf Publishing Company: Houston, TX.

Harris, Philip R., Robert T. Moran and Sarah Moran (2004), *Managing Cultural Differences: Global Leadership Strategies for the 21st Century*, Butterworth-Heinemann: Oxford.

Hemingway, Ernest (1976), *The Snows of Kilimanjaro and Other Stories*, Charles Scribner's and Sons: New York.

Heppner, Janet and Maria Eugenia Farre (2001), 'Of two minds: is English the lingua franca for global e-business?', *Internet World*, vol. 7, no. 12, p. 14.

Heuberger, Andres (2001), 'Manage your global WWW brand', *World Trade*, vol. 14, no. 11, pp. 56–60.

Holden, Nigel (1998), 'Viewpoint: international marketing studies – time to break the English-language strangle-hold?', *International Marketing Review*, vol. 15, no. 2, pp. 86–100.

Howard, David (2001), 'Lost in translation', *Ziff Davis Smart Business*, vol. 14, no. 11, p. 44.

Kang, Kyeong Soon and Brian Corbett (2001), 'Effectiveness of graphical components in web site e-commerce application: a cultural perspective', *Electronic Journal of Information Systems in Developing Countries*, vol. 7, no. 2, pp. 1–6.

Kim, Donghoon, Yigang Pan and Heung Soo Park (1998), 'High-versus low-context culture: a comparison of Chinese, Korean, and American cultures, *Psychology and Marketing*, vol. 15, no. 6, pp. 507–21.

Koslow, Scott, Prem Shamdasani and Ellen Touchstone (1994), 'Exploring language effects in ethic advertising: a sociolinguistic perspective', *Journal of Consumer Research*, vol. 20, March, pp. 575–85.

Langenscheidt (1989), *Compact Dictionary French–English/ English–French*, by Kenneth Urwin Publishers, New York.

Lankshear, Colin and Michele Knobel (2001), 'New technologies, social practices and the challenge of mindsets', *AERA 2001*, available at: **www.geocities.com/c.lankshear/ mindsets.html**

Lankshear, Colin and Michele Knobel (2003), *New Literacies: Changing knowledge and classroom learning*, Open University Press: Buckingham.

Lee, James A. (1966), 'Cultural analysis in overseas operations', *Harvard Business Review*, March–April, pp. 106–11.

Lehman-Wilzig, Sam (2001), 'Babbling our way to a new Babel: erasing the language barriers', *The Futurist*, May–June, pp. 16–23.

Levine, Robert V. (1988), 'The pace of life across cultures', in Joseph E. McGrath (ed.), *The Social Psychology of Time*, Sage Publications: Newbury Park, CA, pp. 39–60.

Levine, Robert A. and Donald T. Campbell (1972), *Ethnocentrism: Theories of conflicts, ethnic attitudes, and group behavior*, John Wiley: New York.

Levine, Robert V. and Ara Norenzayan (1999), 'The pace of life in 31 countries,' *Journal of Cross-Cultural Psychology*, vol. 30, no. 2, pp. 178–205.

Lu, Caixia (2001), 'Chinese, or just Chinglish?', *Far Eastern Economic Review*, vol. 164, no. 15, p. 39.

Luna, David, Laura A. Peracchio and Maria D. de Juan (2002), 'Cross-cultural and cognitive aspects of Web site navigation', *Journal of the Academy of Marketing Science*, vol. 30, no. 4, pp. 397–410.

Lwin, May and Chow-Hou Wee (1999), 'The effect of an audio-stimulus: accents in English language on cross-cultural consumer response to advertising', *Journal of International Consumer Marketing*, vol. 11, no. 2, pp. 5–37.

MacLeod, Marcia (2000), 'Language barriers', *Supply Management*, vol. 5, no. 14, pp. 37–8.

Maroto, Jésus (2003), 'Return on investment in multilingual websites from a marketing perspective', *LISA newsletter*, 7 April, vol. XII, no. 2.1.

M'biti, John (1968), 'African concept of time', *Africa Theological Journal*, vol. 1, pp. 8–20.

Mishima, Yukio (1969), *Le Tumulte des flots* [Shiosai], translated from Japanese, Gallimard: Paris (original edition 1954).

Morand, David A. (1996), 'Politeness as a universal variable in cross-cultural managerial communication', *International Journal of Organizational Analysis*, vol. 4, no. 1, pp. 52–74.

Morschbach, Helmut (1982), 'Aspects of non-verbal communication in Japan', in Larry Samovar and R.E. Porter (eds), *Intercultural Communication: A reader*, 3rd edn, Wadsworth: Belmont, CA.

Nielsen/NetRatings (2003), 'Global internet population grows an average of four per cent year-over-year', *Nielsen/NetRatings*, online, 20 February, available at: **www.nielsen-netratings.com/pr/pr_030220_hk.pdf/**.

Oberg, Kalvero (1960), 'Culture shock: adjustment to new cultural environments', *Practical Anthropology*, vol. 7, pp. 177–82.

Pastore, Michael (2000), 'Web pages by language', *Cyberatlas*, online, 5 July, available at: **www.clickz.com./stats/ big_picture/demographics/article.php/408521/**.

Rudich, Joe (1999), 'Language translation', *Link-up*, vol. 16, no. 6, November/December, pp. 32–4.

Saito Duerr, Mitsuko (1989) in Gerald Albaum, Jesper Strandskov, Edwin Duerr and Laurence Dowd, *International Marketing and Export Management*, Addison-Wesley: Reading, MA.

Sapir, Edward (1929), 'The status of linguistics as a science', *Language*, vol. 5, pp. 207–14.

Schneider-Lenné, E. (1993), 'The governance of good business', *Business Strategy Review*, vol. 4, no. 1, Spring, pp. 75–85.

Simintiras, Antonis C. (2000), 'The role of tautological equivalence in cross-cultural sales negotiations', *Journal of International Consumer Marketing*, vol. 12, no. 4, pp. 33–53.

Simon, Paul (1980), *The Tongue Tied American*, Continuum Press: New York.

Smith, Kenwin and David Berg (1997), 'Cross-cultural groups at work', *European Management Journal*, vol. 15, no. 1, pp. 8–15.

Soutar, Geoffrey N., Richard Grainger and Pamela Hedges (1999), 'Australian and Japanese value stereotypes: a two country study', *Journal of International Business Studies*, vol. 30, no. 1, pp. 203–16.

Sugimoto, Naomi (1998), 'Norms of apology depicted in U.S. American and Japanese literature on manners and etiquette', *International Journal of Intercultural Relations*, vol. 22, no. 3, pp. 251–76.

Sumner, G.A. (1906), *Folk Ways*, Ginn Custom Publishing: New York.

Sussman, Lyle and Denise Johnson (1996), 'Dynamics of the interpreter's role: implications for international executives', *Journal of Language for International Business*, vol. 7, no. 2, pp. 1–14.

Ueda Keiko (1974), 'Sixteen ways to avoid saying "no" in Japan', in J.C. Condon and M. Saito (eds), *Intercultural Encounters in Japan*, Simul Press: Tokyo, pp. 185–92.

UNCTAD Secretariat (2002), *E-commerce and Development Report 2002*, UNCTAD Secretariat, United Nations, UNCTAD/SDTE/ECB/2.

Woodward, Nancy Hatch (1999), 'Do you speak Internet?', *HRMagazine*, vol. 44, no. 4, pp. 12–16.

Yoshida, Susumu (2000), 'Can the West understand the East? And vice-versa? Issues of cross-cultural communication', *Management Japan*, vol. 33, pp. 1–13.

Yunker, John (2000), 'Going global', *Pharmaceutical Executive*, vol. 20, no. 7, pp. 138–46.

Zaharna, R.S. (1989), 'Self shock: the double-binding challenge of identity', *International Journal of Intercultural Relations*, vol. 13, no. 4, pp. 501–26.

Appendix 13

Teaching materials

A13.1 Exercise

Multicultural class

Look at the person seated next to you in class, or anyone with whom you have frequent interaction. Then select somebody originating from a foreign culture. List three examples of non-verbal communication that she or he uses, describe them accurately and decode their meaning. Now ask this person to look at you and do the same. Then work together and compare both interpretations and try to understand why meaning was shared or, possibly, not shared.

(*This exercise can be implemented only with a good degree of cultural diversity within the student group.*)

A13.2 Exercise

I 'love' cake

Start from the English verb 'to like' and find its equivalents in French, German and Spanish. Do not hesitate to translate them back into English in order to detect differences in meaning. Include in your search some basic etymological grounds (e.g. *gusto* in Spanish is based on the word for 'taste'). What differences in terms of world-views are suggested by the different conceptual dimensions of 'liking' (preference, affective, pleasure, love, enjoyment, eating/ingesting, etc.) and their attributions to people, things or situations? Suggest possible consequences for international marketing and advertising strategies.

A13.3 Case

Longcloud – Languages in cyberspace

Language is a steed that carries one into a far country. (Arabic proverb.)

Brushing through green pastures in her rugged truck, Longcloud marketing director Sarah Elder mused over what she would say at this afternoon's meeting. Longcloud Lamb was a young company, specializing in chilled and frozen New Zealand lamb and goat products with a difference: it was organic and exceeded animal welfare stipulations in major export markets. With already five established export partners in the USA and Japan, and 32 regular customers in the area, Sarah and her colleagues were pleasantly surprised by the phenomenal demand growth in only seven years of operations. Accelerated global growth for Longcloud was now imperative, to recoup costs of the recent acquisition of new lands, 42 per cent more stock, and an updated processing plant with EU and USDA certification and Halal capability.

Given that the company managed current wholesale customers in export markets using an e-commerce platform, it seemed obvious that a better website was the answer. In addition, the latest processing and shipping technology made it possible to send chilled cuts to smaller export customers on an individual basis. Most New Zealand exporters were beefing up their sites too, although Canadian-born Sarah had been surprised that most were English-only. Longcloud aimed to capture certain European markets for organic chilled lamb and goat products, as well as niche markets around the world, such as organic restaurants, schools, and religious and non-profit organizations. The lamb meat cuts market was global, and interest in organic meats was a growing phenomenon. First in interest for organic lamb was the European Union, primarily Britain, France and Germany, followed by the USA. Then, there were smaller markets throughout North Africa, the Middle East and India, many with a particular interest in Longcloud's Halal capacity. There was a growing interest for organic goat meat in fragmented Latin American markets, also.

'Because we must differentiate ourselves from mainstream chilled lamb producers, we need to demonstrate our difference in our communications materials. What better way than to talk to customers and prospects in their own language?' Sarah would argue later that day in the meeting. Her colleagues then made a chorus of objections, such as: 'The fact that Longcloud is organic is difference enough, we don't need to bother with languages', and: 'Translating is so costly, can't we just put one of those Altavista Babelfish translation icons on each page? How are you going to decide which languages to use anyways?' Jumping into the fray, general manager Linden Carmody stated, 'Fine, so we publish our multilingual site, but all we can speak is bad French . . . so what happens to our customer relationship beyond on-site ordering and payments? Right, and what about e-mails, how will we understand and answer them?' Each one had a point, Sarah conceded, however it was well established that customers appreciated the ease of conducting business in their own languages, at least for most of the transactions. Especially if Longcloud was to be dealing with niche markets, she opined, a more personalized approach would be necessary. She believed that was the case even if just two other languages were used, such as French for the ten or more countries that speak the language and seek organic lamb, and Arabic for countries with a Halal market and some organic sensitivities. With potentially wider and more diverse business contacts around the world, Sarah argued further, Longcloud's medium-term goal to grow its own tanned organic lambskin and organic wool products businesses was more likely to be realized. In the website language debate, Longcloud was not alone: innumerable companies and organizations faced the same problem, and could find no easy solution.

According to *Global Reach*, more than 63 per cent of people accessing the Internet do not do so in English. That figure should be up to 75 per cent by 2005, according to projections (Maroto, 2003). An online study by *Vilaweb* in 2000 found that 68.39 per cent of total webpages were in English, followed by Japanese (5.85 per cent), German (5.77 per cent), and Chinese (3.87 per cent) (Pastore, 2000). There are manifold difficulties of estimating language use on webpages; however, it is clear that English dominates the web although it does not dominate the world's languages, as Table 13.1 illustrates. English is spoken by approximately half the number of those who speak Chinese, yet Chinese is vastly underrepresented on webpages.

China has one of the world's fastest-growing online populations. According to the Chinese Internet Network Information Center, 68 million people have Internet subscriptions, indicating a much higher number with online access – an increase of 6.8 million over six months. The number of Chinese Internet users doubles every 12–18 months (Anon, 2003). German, Japanese and French appear to be relatively present on the Internet; however, the languages themselves do not have a correspondingly large population of speakers, as is clear from Table 13.1.

Table 13.1 Ranking of languages according to number of speakers

Language	Principal countries or regions spoken	Estimated speakers (in millions)
Chinese	China, Taiwan, the diaspora	885
English	Australasia, North America, South Africa, British Isles	450
Hindi/Urdu	Indian sub-continent, the diaspora	333
Spanish	Latin America, Spain	266
Portuguese	Angola, Brazil, Mozambique, Portugal	175
Bengali	Indian sub-continent	162
Russian	Former Soviet Union	153
Arabic	Middle East, North Africa	150
Japanese	Japan	126
French	Belgium, Canada, France, North Africa, Sub-Saharan Africa, Switzerland	122

(Source: *Ethnologue*, 12th edn, Dallas, TX, 1992.)

According to *Nielsen/NetRatings*, 580 million people worldwide had access to the Internet in the fourth quarter of 2002. This compares with 563 million online in the last quarter of 2001. The country experiencing the biggest year on year growth in terms of population was Spain, at 22 per cent, while the United States experienced a corresponding increase of 3 per cent. The United States still had the largest number online at 168.6 million, followed by Germany (41.8 million), the UK (30.4 million) and Italy (25.3 million). Spain also led in Internet use of e-mail, chat rooms and instant messaging. In terms of online access populations, the USA remains the leader, although the margins are narrowing (see Table 13.2).

Table 13.2 Online access in terms of percentage of the total online population

Country or region	Share of world online population (per cent)
USA	29%
Europe	23%
Asia-Pacific	13%
Latin America	2%
Rest of world (countries not under Nielsen/NetRatings)	33%

(Source: Nielsen/NetRatings, 20 February, 2003.)

The role of e-commerce

In a best-case projection for 2006, e-commerce should comprise 18 per cent of the world's business-to-business and retail transactions (UNCTAD Secretariat, 2002). This growth presupposes the participation of a diverse language base, and the adaptation of e-commerce platforms to linguistic and cultural conditions. Many multinational corporations have websites that are entirely in English, however, and the number of major global businesses who have adapted their sites is growing slowly.

How to adapt a website – more than just a translation

When adapting software to local contexts, the following elements need to be considered: language, literacy and culture. For organizations looking to adapt their message locally around the globe, the same elements are pertinent in website and e-commerce platforms design. Apart from translations, which alone may account for half the localization costs for software, the choice of language or dialect may be critical. Should one select an 'Official language' to the detriment of a language spoken unofficially by large numbers of the target audience? Elements of website design that need to be adapted according to the culture of the target audience include colours used, text versus graphics, a 'busy' screen versus a minimalist one, animations, symbols and icons (Kang, 2001). Currently, there are software facilities for dealing with cultural variations in number formats, sort orders, and times and dates formats. At this time, technology is not well prepared to implement non-Gregorian calendar types. The correct and locally adapted use of proper names is also problematic (Hall, 2002).

Which language?

When deciding which languages to use in adapting a regionally targeted website, certain social and economic factors should be considered independently of the number of speakers of the languages under consideration. Predominant among these are literacy, language use and access. Indian languages are a case in point. India, with one billion people, has two official languages: English and Hindi. There are 18 major languages and 418 other languages spoken by 10,000 or more people (Chowdhry, 2000). First, there may be a large number of speakers for some languages, although the corresponding literacy rate may be quite low. Where this is the case the complexity of the language used and the share of online graphics may reflect this. In addition, it is now possible to integrate speech or speech recognition systems (currently only available for the world's 'main' languages) on the site's capabilities (Hall, 2002).

Secondly, many people around the world are accustomed to using languages other than their own for business or general communication purposes. As in many developing countries, some Indians may feel uneasy conducting business in any language other than English, yet they may feel similar unease communicating at home in English. The user's website language of preference may depend on whether the Internet is accessed from home or from work. English may be more acceptable for work-access, while a local language may be preferable for use from the home computer. For this reason, the company with international ambitions needs to determine the likely point of access for its target audiences.

Thirdly, access to the Internet may be uneven. For instance, raw Internet access numbers may be low in some rural areas; however, one entrepreneur with a computer and Internet access may allow many others to access the net using the most basic equipment, in exchange for a user fee. Internet access may in this case be higher than initially assumed. Similarly, when looking at the size of the Internet audience in targeted nations, one should be wary of dismissing a small audience, such as the 0.1 per cent of Nigerians online. That small percentage represents 100,000 of the country's most affluent, and likely the same people who make major decisions in government and its bureaucracies (International Federation of Red Cross and Red Crescent Societies, 2001).

Complicating the issue of adapting (or not) to a locally understood language are social factors that have imbued English with its status as the language of preference for business in some countries. At the same time, there are fierce debates over the use and even the survival of some Indian languages (Chowdhry, 2000). One should not assume that English is generally a safe choice: it is vital to gauge the attitudes of the target audience towards the language because in some regions there may be historical or political reasons for polite hostility towards those who use English.

Those who decide to localize their websites should be aware of several software complexities involved in online publishing of non-Roman scripts, including Arabic, Bengali, Greek, Thai and Hebrew, that have only recently been addressed. One of the problems caused by fonts online is the correct use of diacritics, the accents placed above and below letters – small symbols that can often change the meaning of a word depending on its orientation – used in some Nordic languages, Greek, French, Turkish and some eastern European languages, to name a few. The directionality of symbols is another issue. The fact that numerals are ordered from left to right in Arabic and Hebrew scripts, which themselves are oriented from right to left, is another example of online font problems (Correll, 2003). In addition, some non-Latin scripts require two bits in processing, which complicates encoding and may considerably slow down an e-commerce site. The first program to address these problems was produced by the Unicode Consortium, with the goal of eventually codifying all characters produced by humans, anywhere and at any time in history. Currently in its fourth version, the Unicode Standard addresses issues like vertical script (as in East Asian languages) or the right–left orientation of Semitic scripts. Although there are other means of dealing with language representation, the Unicode Consortium has developed the only system to be accepted by the International Standards Organization, as well as the most widely used code within html format. The entire text of Unicode 4.0, as well as useful guidance and information, is available at **www.unicode.com**.

Questions

1. Assess in which ways culture, religion and language may influence foreign marketing operations in the organic meat business. Does it differ whether marketing and sales are implemented through traditional marketing or by e-commerce?

2. Investigate the possibility of using automatic translation programs for non-English speaking visitors of a website. For this, you can make your own trials on websites that offer free sample translation, such as **www.freetranslation.com/**, **www.softissimo.com/** or **www.linguatec.de/news.en.shtml**.

3. Assess the approximate cost of developing a different language version of an English-based website.

4. Should Longcloud develop its website in languages other than English? If yes, which language(s)? Argue about the pros and cons of such decisions.

Saskia Faulk and Jean-Claude Usunier prepared this case solely to provide material for class discussion. The authors do not intend to illustrate either effective or ineffective handling of a business situation. The authors may have disguised certain names and other identifying information to protect confidentiality.

(©IUMI, reprinted with kind permission.)

A13.4 Case

Supreme Canning

The Supreme Canning Company (the true name of the company is disguised) is an independent US packer of tomato products (whole peeled tomatoes, chopped tomatoes, katsup, paste, pizza and other sauces, and tomatoes and zucchini). The company is located in the State of California. Although it produces some cans with its own brand label, much of its output is canned for others and their brand names and labels put on the cans. It produces shelf-size cans for eventual sale at retail, gallon-size cans for use by restaurants and industrial users, and 55 gallon drums for use by others for repacking or further processing. Its annual processing capacity is in excess of 100,000 tons of tomatoes (processed during an operating season of approximately three months in length).

The California canning industry had suffered from heavy competition from abroad and inadequate local demand. A somewhat increasing domestic demand for specialty tomato products, especially pizza and other sauces, was not adequate to absorb increasing imports. The high value of the US dollar had made it difficult for US companies to sell abroad. Excess capacity and the resulting depressed prices had led to bankruptcy for a number of Californian canners. With the decline of the value of the dollar and the efforts of Japan to reduce its trade barriers and increase imports, it appeared that Supreme Canning Company might be able to get into the Japanese market. An inquiry received from a foodpacker and distributor in Japan indicated interest from that side. The Japanese firm produced and distributed a large number of products, was well known in Japan, and was much larger than the US company.

Since Supreme Canning Company did not have well-known brand names of its own, the company was interested in acting as a large-scale supplier of products made to customer specifications for use by the customer or distribution under the customer's label. Thus, the inquiry from Japan was most welcome.

The Japanese company invited senior executives of the American firm to visit their production facilities and offices in Japan. Both the president and chairman of the board of Supreme Canning Company had a four-day visit with the executives of the company in Japan. The president of the US company, who had some knowledge of Japanese business practice from studies at Stanford University and from his widespread reading, attempted to act as a guide to Japanese business practice. The chairman of the board had little knowledge of Japan, and viewed himself as a decisive man of action. Although there were a few minor misunderstandings, the visit was concluded successfully and the Americans invited the Japanese to visit their plant in California for four days.

The Japanese indicated their interest in the signing of a mutual letter of cooperation. The American chairman of the board was not interested in this, but rather wanted some specific agreements and contracts. As the time for the Japanese visit to the US drew near, the Japanese indicated that their president would not be able to come. Some senior executives would be able to meet, but they would only be able to spend two days instead of four. The vice-chairman of the board of the California company wrote asking why the Japanese were not going to send their president, and inquiring why they could not spend four days instead of two, 'as we did in Japan'. The letter was frank and direct. The tone was that of a person talking to an equal, but not with any great deal of politeness. The Japanese company decided to cancel the visit, and no further negotiations or serious contacts were made.

Some months later, a local businessman of Japanese extraction asked the president of Supreme Canning Company if some representatives of another (and even larger) Japanese food products producer and distributor could visit the plant. Four Japanese showed up along with the local businessman, who acted as interpreter and go-between. The three middle-aged Japanese produced their *meishi* (business cards) and introduced themselves. Each spoke some English. The older man did not present a card and was not introduced. When the president of the American company asked who he was, the go-between said, 'He's just one of the company's directors'. The visit concluded without discussion of any business possibilities, but this was to be expected in an initial visit from Japanese businessmen.

Supreme's president later found out the family name of the unknown visitor and immediately recognized it as being that of the president of the Japanese company. He assumed that the president of the Japanese company had come but had hidden the fact. He felt that he had been taken advantage of. He telephoned the go-between and told him that he never wanted anyone from that company in his plant again. From a description of the unknown visitor, a consultant to the company realized that the visitor was not the president of the Japanese company. Rather, it was the semi-retired father of the president. The father retained a position on the board of directors and maintained an active interest in company activities, but was not active in day-to-day affairs. Unlike his son who was fluent in English, he spoke only Japanese.

(Source: Duerr, 1989, pp. 85–7.)

Questions

1. Was the chairman of the American company wrong for not having found out in advance about Japanese business practices? Why did he not do so? (Answer the same questions in relation to the Japanese companies and US business practices.)

2. What are the principal cultural mistakes made (a) by the Americans from the Japanese perspective, and (b) by the Japanese from the American perspective?

3. What should the president of the American company do now?

 ## A13.5 Critical incident

Scandinavian Tools Company

A major Swedish company that specialized in metal tools and factory equipment had created a French subsidiary a few years ago, based in Lyons, France. This plant was at first supplied with inputs (specialty steels, high-speed steels for blades and saws, etc.) from Sweden. It mostly produced and sold for the French markets and for exports to southern European markets, namely Italy, Spain and Portugal. The drive and energy for creating this new venture came from a young Swedish executive, Bo Svensson. Svensson had spent part of his time as a student, and then as a young engineer, in France. Thereafter he had been in a position to convince the top management of this large Swedish multinational company to launch a new subsidiary in France.

Svensson was very enthusiastic about France. He liked the country very much and had learnt the language, which he spoke fluently with a slight northern European accent. In the rush of starting the new company everything went smoothly. Svensson, who was chief executive officer of the French venture, knew how to secure customers and make them loyal; he also knew how to deal with the headquarters in Sweden. The market was growing quickly and competition was not particularly fierce. At the beginning, products were made in Sweden and then exported to France, where Svensson and the subsidiary dealt with marketing and distribution.

After a few years demand began to swell, so the parent company in Sweden decided to build a production plant in France. Machines and factory equipment for the new plant came from Sweden, and the factory was quickly operating at normal capacity. Svensson then hired a vice-president for administration, André Ribaud, an ambitious young executive, also in his thirties, with a law background. The two men got on well together, although their backgrounds and personal profiles were quite different. They shared the work and responsibilities: Svensson was in charge of relations with headquarters, marketing and the monitoring of financial performance; as plant manager, Ribaud was in charge of production operations, human resource management, cost accounting, monitoring cost prices and delivery delays.

After a few years it appeared that Svensson felt more and more relaxed in his job. Quite independent in his profitable subsidiary of (at that time) 200 employees located in a place remote from Sweden, he was able to have a very flexible timetable. He was also very free with personal expenses, which he was entitled to have reimbursed by the subsidiary: he simply had to sign his own expenses receipts. Svensson did not hesitate to use this facility: he did not make a clear distinction between his own money and the company's money. Svensson gradually got into the habit of abusing company-paid personal expenses. Ribaud was shocked. Svensson even went so far as to have the expenses of his mistress paid by the subsidiary.

Meanwhile, Ribaud was still working as efficiently as during the initial years. Growth had been impressive. Starting with a few employees in a two-room office in Lyons, the subsidiary had grown to a dynamic medium-sized company with more than 500 people on the payroll; Scandinavian Tools France had bought two plants from competitors. Following these changes, Ribaud's responsibilities quickly increased. He had involved himself completely and passionately with the company. He knew each member of staff personally and was respected by them.

Over time the relationship between the two men had considerably worsened. Svensson saw that Ribaud was winning more and more influence and power inside the company, and was well known by the customers. He felt jealous of him and tried his best to make Ribaud's life in the company difficult. Ribaud, on the other hand, increasingly resented the excessive expenses and the catty remarks of his boss, for whom he no longer felt any esteem. Svensson was a complex, energetic and whimsical character. His charisma and stamina had enabled him to seduce the French clients as well as the management staff at the headquarters in Sweden. The excellent financial performance of the French subsidiary had enabled him to retain the confidence of his superiors, who were also Swedish compatriots. They had trust in his management talents and therefore they allowed him a large degree of freedom. He had also established friendships with some of the senior directors at headquarters, especially with the director in charge of public relations. Svensson was well known at headquarters level, and he understood company 'politics' quite well.

After 15 years of almost steady growth, the market was reaching the stage of maturity. With the removal of borders within the EU, there were many acquisitions by large European and American competitors. The French subsidiary had lost some of its profitability. The middle managers were complaining to Ribaud about Svensson's lack of interest in the subsidiary and his mismanagement. Everybody believed that emergency decisions had to be taken before the situation got even worse. But Svensson turned a deaf ear to their complaints and remained unwilling to enter into discussion with either Ribaud or the other executives. The French were also amazed, and somewhat shocked, to see that there was no reaction from headquarters. It looked as if headquarters had little interest in the destiny of the French subsidiary. People at headquarters still seemed to have confidence in Svensson, who knew how to make them feel secure.

Ribaud did not feel comfortable in this situation. He felt that the financial balance of the subsidiary was threatened and that one factory would probably have to close in the near future. It also seemed to him that the interests of Swedish shareholders were not being adequately taken into account. Relations between Svensson and Ribaud were so damaged that Svensson was convinced that Ribaud was plotting against him. Svensson therefore systematically took a contradictory stance to Ribaud, at the risk of making inappropriate decisions that could possibly lead the subsidiary almost to the brink of bankruptcy.

Each time Ribaud brought up these problems during meetings with people from headquarters, Svensson abruptly interrupted him, shifting from English to Swedish in order to keep him out of the conversation. Under heavy pressure from some of the executives of the subsidiary who were about to resign and leave the company, Ribaud felt obliged to react. He had tried, during visits by members of the Swedish headquarters, to give them, indirectly, an idea of the situation. But he got the impression that he was not being heard. They had their own image of the chief executive officer which was clearly different.

In desperation, Ribaud decided to send an official note to the top management in Stockholm, in which he told them that he would be obliged to resign if nothing was done to put an end to the present disorder. He tried to write it as objectively as possible in a matter-of-fact style, citing evidence and hard facts. This was not an easy task since objectivity may prove difficult in such circumstances and, moreover, he was denouncing his boss, which is never very pleasant. He called one of the members of the top management in Stockholm whom he knew a little better than the others, explained about the letter and sent him a copy.

Question

What answer could he expect?

14

Intercultural marketing communications 1: Advertising

Advertising, which is based on language and communication, is the most culture-bound element of the marketing mix. When Polaroid introduced its cameras to Europe in the mid-1970s, it used the same advertising strategy as in the United States, including TV commercials and print advertisements. These campaigns achieved little impact in raising awareness of instant photography and failed to pull customers into the stores. Later, the company developed very successful European campaigns on the basis of the strategy of Polaroid Switzerland, one of its smallest subsidiaries, located in a multicultural, central European country. The strategy of Polaroid Switzerland was to promote the functional uses of instant photography as a way to communicate with family and friends, which proved to be transferable in European countries (Kashani, 1989).

This chapter could be subtitled 'national cultures, technological advances and the globalization of marketing communications'. Indeed it attempts to show, as did Chapters 5 to 8, that globalization is not the very simple process it is often believed to be. The first sections of this chapter describe cultural differences as they pertain to various aspects of advertising: what are the general attitudes *vis-à-vis* advertising (14.1)? How are advertising strategy (14.2) and creative standards (14.3) affected by local culture? How is media selection affected by differences in media availability and style (14.4)? Section 14.5 examines the globalization of advertising.

Since advertising is largely based on language and images, it is influenced by culture. Cross-national differences continue to exist, for the simple reason that we have not yet ceased to have different languages.

Moreover language, be it through words or images, is the strongest link between advertisers and their potential audiences in marketing communications. The management process for marketing communication *per se* does not depend on the particular country where the advertising campaign is launched. It is composed of six steps (Figure 14.1). Logically, these steps should be taken in order, although feedback at any step is possible and often necessary, especially after testing the campaign. The six basic steps are as follows:

1. Isolate the communication problem to be solved: increase brand awareness, change the brand image, increase sales, differentiate from rival brands, take market share from the competition, etc.
2. Identify the relevant target population: which consumer segments? What are their sociodemographic characteristics, consumption habits, psychographic characteristics (consumer lifestyles and values), etc.?
3. Define the marketing communication objective in terms of influencing the target population, at either the attitudinal or the behavioural level. Communication objectives may be, for instance, to convince consumers that they like the product (to improve product acceptance), to let people try a product again (to increase sales by building consumer loyalty), to let people act, or to educate the consumer, etc.
4. Select the advertising themes and a creative strategy: how will the brand name be emphasized? Which copy strategy should be used?
5. Design a media plan: which media to use, how to optimize the best media to reach the target audience, etc.

Figure 14.1 Main steps in the management of advertising communication

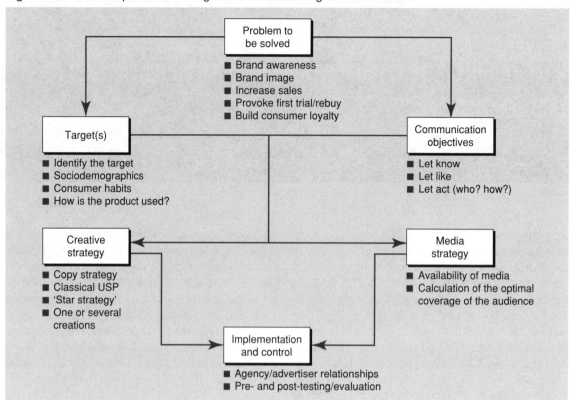

6. Implement and monitor the advertising campaign: pre- and post-tests of advertisement effectiveness; research on different aspects (message recall, brand recall, aided brand recognition, actual influence on sales); etc.

The international dimension naturally has an influence on the implementation of each of these steps, but not an equal influence on each step. Let us take an example: to advertise life insurance in Tunisia, it should be taken into account that the life insurance market is a new one, where consumers have little knowledge of this kind of financial service. For this reason, the message shows a man and a woman watering a tree which grows by leaps and bounds. Finally, a large pine tree protects them with its branches, while they sit happily in its shade. Certainly culture will influence the objective: the education of the consumer would be a basic objective in a country where life insurance is almost unknown. But the changes caused by cultural differences are most obvious with respect to the creative strategy

(step 4). One should acknowledge and respect the values of Tunisian consumers who belong to an Arab-Muslim culture which is nevertheless strongly linked to two European cultures (Italy and France). The complex mix of Muslim and Western culture has to be considered, since values that involve important matters (life and death, protecting one's family, betting on the future) are at stake.

The media plan will also be strongly influenced by local idiosyncrasies: media availability, viewing habits and media regulations still differ greatly across countries. Conversely, the other steps in Figure 14.1 are not strongly affected by local factors: defining a communication problem or a communication objective, or testing the effectiveness of a campaign, calls for a similar approach in each country. Although the first three sections of this chapter favour customization of advertising, section 14.4 may appear to be in contrast to this. Technological advances such as satellite television and the global reach of the media have an undeniable impact on local attitudes and purchasing behaviour. The emergence of worldwide advertising media partly breaks down cultural resistance. In fact, it opens different lines of communication between cultures that previously were geographically and culturally separated, such as western and eastern Europe, or southern Europe and North Africa. Furthermore, it opens the way to new marketing communications in areas of the world which are culturally fragmented, for ethnic, linguistic or political reasons: Europe, South-East Asia, Central and Latin America. In this new style of international marketing communication, strictly national segments and audiences must be differentiated from cross-border regional segments and audiences. The choice of the appropriate media as well as the choice of the language in which to advertise are therefore key success factors. The final section of this chapter deals with the issue of advertising globalization.

14.1

Influence of culture on attitudes towards advertising

General attitudes towards the role and functions of advertising

Advertising, which is a large part of marketing communications, is a field that is constantly changing. On the one hand it is closely dependent on the cultural and linguistic attitudes of the local target population. On the other hand, in so far as social representations are not fixed, advertising is a privileged method of cultural borrowing; advertising mirrors changing social behaviour. The relative freedom of advertising creation and the need to capture the audience imply that advertising is sometimes challenging and often innovative. It is therefore the ground for societal debates. This is illustrated below by several advertising-related issues, e.g. 'publiphobia' (social criticism and rejection of advertising) and attitudes towards comparative advertising.

General attitudes towards publicity and 'publiphobia'

One view that has always existed is that advertising is nothing more than wasted money. This negative view of advertising is vaguely rooted in the ideas of the Saint-Simonist doctrine,[1] in which anything that does not involve the production of material goods is considered to be socially unproductive. Retail sales and the service industry, including advertising, are considered to be parasitic activities. This view is often reinforced by the (misleading) argument that consumers pay for advertising costs, which are included in the price of the product they buy.

This social representation was a part of the Marxist doctrine, and its influence on real socialism often produced disastrous consequences, such as shortages of basic staple items. This was largely caused by the absence of any effective distribution system through which products would have been made available to consumers. The shortage was further reinforced by the absence of a marketing communication system to inform people which goods and services were available to them, when, where and at what price (traditional and useful functions!).

In many European countries, especially in northern Europe and in France, there are still some traces of 'publiphobia'. The advertising profession in France was even forced to launch a huge poster and billboard campaign about 15 years ago, against those known as 'publiphobes'. In certain countries such as Kuwait, advertisements for pharmaceutical products are strictly controlled or even forbidden. It is often considered immoral to spend too much on advertisements and sales promotions for ethical drugs, on the assumption that it unduly increases the final price of a drug and thereby reduces the chances of the poorest people to buy essential medical supplies and regain their health. As a consequence, many countries put a ceiling on pharmaceutical advertising, or subject it to a special tax.

At the international level, more attention is now being given to the idea that advertising, though undeniably useful to society, can also have negative results such as the encouragement of conspicuous consumption and the creation of wants that cannot be satisfied, or that advertising may be deceptive. Therefore the economic and social committee of the UN (United Nations) has proposed a resolution that would protect consumers in developing nations. Wills and Ryans (1982) have looked at how consumers, students, academics and managers differ in their attitudes towards advertising, across 14 countries. They show that, across all the countries, the views held by consumers and managers are quite different. Managers often find advertising to be quite factual (75 per cent), providing important information about products or services (71 per cent) and both entertaining and informative (78 per cent), whereas consumers rate it at a lower level on these dimensions (61, 48 and 50 per cent respectively). More than 50 per cent of the consumers, on average (across the 14 countries), tend to have a negative opinion about the information content of advertising. On the other hand, the attitudes of consumers and managers do not differ significantly on various aspects of advertising: whether the advertisements are humorous, aesthetically pleasing or informative about prices.

Andrews *et al.* (1991) show that there are substantial differences among young people from various countries (the United States, Denmark, Greece, India and New Zealand) in the perception of advertising in general. US students had more affective responses towards advertising, using statements such as 'stupid', 'entertaining', 'annoying'. They were also the least critical of advertising among the five nations surveyed. The potentially negative effects of advertising, in economic as well as social terms, represented only 22 per cent of US students' statements, compared with 60 per cent for Greeks and 51 per cent for the Indians. New Zealand students, who come from a country where advertising regulation is quite strict, had the most negative views of advertisements: They emphasized the view that advertisements were 'meaningless repetition' or that they 'interrupt good programmes'. In another study Darley and Johnson (1994) found that people from developing countries are more critical of advertising and more concerned with the impact of advertising on product costs than people from developed countries.

More recently, Waller and Pollonsky (1999) studied the views held by Australian and US youths on political advertising. They found that their views were similar: political advertising, especially negative spots, were felt to exert a great deal of influence on voters and their emotions. They also believe that political advertisements are frequently misleading and caused people to become cynical about politics.

Attitudes towards comparative advertising

Attitudes towards comparative advertising basically depend on the responses that are given in a particular society to the following questions:

1. What is the social function of comparative advertising?
2. What are the prevailing arguments concerning the legitimacy of comparative advertising?
3. How should competition between brands be facilitated?
4. Does comparative advertising result in fooling the consumer by using disputable information to praise one's own brand and put down others?

Socially dominant responses to these questions directly influence comparative advertising regulations in a given country. In some countries, comparative advertising is held in low esteem. This is the case in France, where it has traditionally been considered a denigration of competing brands. It is therefore forbidden under Article 1382 of the Civil Code. In order for the advertisement to be considered comparative, there need only be a comparison of two competing products, even if the terms are not inaccurate, tendentious or antagonistic. For instance, about 20 years ago Lip, the top French watchmaker, was under attack by Timex, the top company in the American watch industry. The main feature of Timex's Kelton brand was its distribution through tobacconists, whereas Lip was confined to the more traditional channel of watch and jewellery stores. With the purpose of counter-attacking in order to regain market share Lip began an advertising campaign that showed a broken watch in an ashtray surrounded by a thick cloud of smoke, with a slogan that read: 'The watches sold in tobacconists are like cigarettes: they go up in smoke.' As a consequence, Lip was forced to pay heavy penalties to Timex.

Belgium, Italy and Germany are some other European countries that forbid comparative advertising. It is sometimes argued that some countries forbid comparative advertising as an indirect way of protecting their national products from unfavourable comparisons with imported goods. According to Boddewyn (1984) the French authorities, who were about to legalize comparative advertising, took a step backwards when they changed their mind due to fear that Japanese car manufacturers would use comparative advertising to aggressively communicate the advantages of their cars; thereby increasing their share of the French market where competition with other European producers is already active.

Allowed in the United States, but forbidden in many countries, comparative advertising is in a process of change at the European level. It is already permitted in some European countries, and a European Union directive has allowed comparison under definite constraints. Legislation requires that advertising be based on features of the competing products or services that are material, relevant, verifiable and fairly chosen. Comparisons should be objective and should not discredit competitors or their brands.

The basic arguments in favour of comparative advertising seem to make sense: it facilitates consumer information, choice and competition between brands. Hence automobile advertising frequently gives performance statistics of competing models, such as fuel consumption, speed and comfort. Opponents of comparative advertising argue that truly objective comparisons would need to be handled by completely independent testing organizations. As a consequence, comparative advertising would often end up giving either no information at all or partly misleading information to the consumer. Opponents of comparative advertising also implicitly support the idea that it is necessary to enforce moral business relationships between competitors. The role of marketing communications, by means of advertising, is to praise the virtues of their own product, not to put down the virtues of competing products (however indirectly).

James and Hensel (1991, p. 55) emphasize the possibility that malicious comparative advertising can be negative. They take the example of a Kentucky Fried Chicken advertisement that made explicit reference to McDonald's:

The first ad, sponsored by Kentucky Fried Chicken, opens with a red-haired Ronald McDonald surrogate (sans clown outfit) being interrogated by a Senate 'subcommittee' rivalling the likes of that faced by Oliver North. Allegations are raised as to the defendant's lack of expertise and questionable ability to provide quality chicken (McNuggets) to the public. When pressed as to how he expects to be able to sell chicken given this lack of expertise, 'Ronald' responds, 'Toys, lots of toys!', while the man who appears to be his legal counsel buries his head in his hands.

Jeon and Beatty (2002) conducted an experiment to assess the persuasiveness of three types of advertisements in Korea and the United States: direct comparative (to another specific brand), indirect comparative (to 'a leading brand') and non-comparative. They found that comparative advertisements were generally more persuasive than non-comparative advertisements in both countries. But there were differences in the type

of comparative advertisement that was most effective: in the United States the indirectly comparative advertisements were most effective, while in Korea the direct comparative advertisements were more effective. They argued that these differences were due to novelty effects (see Aaker and Williams, 1998): in Korea, direct comparative ads were only recently encouraged, while in the United States indirect comparisons were less common.

14.2 Culture and advertising strategy

The function of an advertisement is to communicate a message to an audience based on two major elements: strategy and execution. While there is some overlap between these categories, advertising strategy comprises 'what is said' and execution concerns more 'how it is said'. Advertising strategy relates to the types of appeals used, the themes developed and the overall communication style, whether (1) direct or indirect, (2) explicit or implicit or (3) rational or emotional. Advertising style in communicating with the audiences of viewers, readers or listeners can be roughly divided into three basic categories: (1) persuasive, (2) informative and (3) oneiric, that is dream-oriented.

Advertising appeals

A limited number of different advertising appeals can be identified based on common themes and concepts. Although all of them are used worldwide, cultural sensitivity is portrayed through the varying usage of these same appeals (Agrawal, 1995). A comparison of US and Japanese advertising strategies shows, for instance, that the same ten basic appeals are used. The Japanese preference for implicit, indirect communication is reflected by a relative lack of hard-sell appeals. Instead, there are four times as many soft-sell appeals in Japanese as in US advertisements. In accordance with Japanese values, there also are more advertisements that stress tradition and the veneration of the elderly (Javalgi *et al.*, 1995). The product-merit appeal, on the other hand, is dominant in US advertisements (Mueller, 1987). As stated by Lin (1993, pp. 44–5), Japanese cultural values stress status symbols in advertising whereas Americans place emphasis on individual determinism:

Japanese advertisements reveal an indulgence with sensitive crafting of product image and appearance slated within a subtle frame of reference. This contrasts sharply with the American fixation on presenting facts and attributes to showcase product superiority . . . [In Japan] 'boasting' of product quality and 'bribing' consumers into submission are not in line with the custom of respectful treatment of consumers and respectable projection of company image. These same rationales explain why comparative and testimonial messages are not a desirable form of advertising in Japan.

Lin (2001) found that the Chinese more often use soft-sell, veneration of the elderly and tradition, oneness with nature and group consensus and status appeals, than in the United States, where there is more frequent use of the hard-sell appeal, time-oriented and individualist appeals, as well as product merit appeals. Similarly, Chiou (2002) found that in Taiwan transformational (e.g. user image, brand image, usage occasion) and traditional appeals (e.g. consensus, soft-sell, veneration of elderly and traditional) were more effective than informational (e.g. comparative, unique, pre-emptive) and westernized appeals (e.g. independence, modernity, product merit).

Several other characteristics have been noted which distinguish Japanese from US creative strategy: little relationship between advertisement content and the advertised product, only brief dialogue in TV commercials with minimal explanatory content, priority placed on company trust rather than product quality, etc. (Kishii, 1988; Di Benedetto et al., 1992). Different advertising strategies in Japan and the USA are also observed with regard to corporate advertisements (McLeod and Kunita, 1994).

Differences in the use of symbolic and informational appeals have been found in many countries. For instance, symbolic advertising is more often used in France, descriptive appeals in Korea and associative appeals in the USA and Asian countries (Cutler et al., 1992). Similarly, Zandpour et al. (1992) found more symbolic strategies in French advertising, more argument and imitation in US commercials and more information and obligation strategies in Taiwan. Swedish ads also depend more on symbolic associations than US advertisements (Martenson, 1987).

Italian and French advertisements often appear as very dream oriented: viewers and readers are supposedly willing to escape from the real world. This oneiric style of advertisement enhances the fantasy of the consumer and emphasizes the imagination of satisfaction and enjoyment. It does so in a rather holistic way (the product and its benefits tend to be implied rather than actually shown). The oneiric style does not really concentrate on actual buying and consumption experiences. The dream-like dimension that surrounds the product is favoured at any price. Relying on the dream-oriented part of the advertising audience is typical of the 'Séguéla' doctrine.

Germans, unlike the French or the Italians, are known to have a taste for highly informative advertising. A young German advertising specialist, Konstantin Jacoby (quoted in *Communication et Business*, 1988, p. 18) criticizes French advertising, and especially the most well-known publicist Jacques Séguéla (co-founder of the RSCG agency, reputed for oneiric, dream-oriented copy strategies):

Certainly it [French advertising] is better than German advertising, but the French should take care not to sink in art for art's sake or in *séguélomania*. The message of the Citroen advertising campaign is horrible. What is the link between the Great Wall of China and Citroen? Are Citroen cars manufactured there now?

A significant degree of similarity in advertising strategies only appears in culturally close countries like the United States, the United Kingdom and Canada. Overall, advertising agencies in all three places use the same strategies in the same number of cases. Problem solution is most popular, followed by USP (unique selling proposition), emotion, brand image and brand identity (West, 1993; Appelbaum and Halliburton, 1993).

At least some of the differences in emphasis across cultures may be due to a difference in the diagnosticity of information. For instance, there is evidence that the informational value or diagnosticity is greater for consensus information (Aaker and Maheswaren, 1997) and source expertise (Pornpitakpan and Francis, 2001) in more collectivist cultures than it is in more individualist cultures.

The information content of advertising: Cross-national differences

The information content of advertising is a key issue since it shows whether the strategy follows the informative option, rather than the persuasion or dream-orientation avenues. The information content will naturally be lower when the two last avenues are followed. Ever since the first systematic evaluation of information content by Resnik and Stern (1977), the informativeness of advertising has received considerable attention all over the world. Many researchers compared their country's advertising situation to that of the United States. The most important findings of these studies are that information content varies by country – but also by broadcast time, product type and medium. Stern and Resnik (1991), based on a review of existing evidence, found that the information content (the number of information cues contained in advertisements) varies cross-nationally.

Overall, it appears that US television advertising is less informative than most other television advertising worldwide. US television advertising contains less information than Australian (Dowling, 1980), French-Canadian (Johnstone *et al.*, 1987), Spanish (Bigne *et al.*, 1993), Ecuadorian (Renforth and Raveed, 1982), Irish (Ward and McQuirk, 1987), French and German (Schroeder, 1991) and Japanese television advertising (Lin and Salwen, 1995). Only British TV advertisements seem to contain less information than US advertisements (Weinberger and Spotts, 1989a). However, Keown *et al.* (1992), comparing the information content of television, radio and print advertising across four countries (the United States, Japan, South Korea and the People's Republic of China) found the highest level of information cues in the United States, followed by Japan and the People's Republic of China, whereas South Korean advertising scores lowest in informative content. In all countries, television and radio advertising were generally less informative than print advertising. Cross-culturally, print media are more informative than radio and television: comparing the information content of media in the United States, Japan, China and South Korea, it was found that magazine and newspaper advertisements have a larger number of information cues than television and radio advertisements (Keown *et al.*, 1992). Similarly, Rita Martenson (1987) shows that Swedish advertisements have less information elements than American advertisements. She attributes this fact to the atmosphere of intense competition for the attention of television viewers that exists in the United States where consumers change channels to avoid commercials, use commercial breaks to look at the programmes on other channels, etc. 'This means that [in the US] any commercial that does not have a very clear and simple message will strongly reduce its chances of getting the slightest amount of attention' (Martenson, 1987, p. 141).

In a meta-analysis of 59 studies about information content, an interesting result from a cross-cultural perspective is that advertising in developed countries is more informative than in developing countries (Abernethy and Franke, 1996). When comparing advertising practices in Turkey, Canada and Sweden, Kaynak and Ghauri (1986, p. 127) explain that in developed countries advertising copy in general contains more writing and technical information, because most consumers have a high level of literacy and education: 'Unlike Canada and Sweden, most of the advertising copy used by the Turkish agencies is persuasive in nature rather than informative.' The Turkish word for advertising is *Reklam*: this corresponds to a more traditional vision of advertising, where persuasion and slogans are the key issues. Callow and Schiffman (2002) investigated how students process visual images in print ads. They found that students from the Philippines (a higher context culture) were more able to derive the implicit meaning from the visual images than those from the United States.

A closer look at some of the studies quoted above offers additional valuable insights. Information content varies strongly from one country to another. Although product types and other environmental factors such as the competitive environment have an influence on information content, culture is the most important factor in explaining how much and what kind of information can be found in advertising. Both the types of information cues and the quantity of information are culture bound. Whereas some targets prefer more rational, tangible cues – as in the USA – others expect emotional and more 'subjective' information. This is why many Japanese advertisements present 'company-sponsored research', an element that is much less important in Western countries. Even in neighbouring countries with a similar economic environment, such as France and Germany, information content varies fundamentally (Schroeder, 1991). Because information reduces uncertainty, cultures known to avoid uncertainty such as the German culture (Hofstede, 1991) will always have a tendency to ask for more information than cultures that have lower uncertainty avoidance. Furthermore, communication in Germany is based on explicit messages. It thus naturally scores high on the Resnik and Stern procedure, which counts explicit information cues.

Assuming that consumers are rational information seekers (which is not true in most cultural contexts), advertising content should be related to information sought by consumers in order to improve the relevance of their choices. If for any reason consumers are not 'good' (motivated and educated) information seekers, they will be less sensitive to the information content of an advertisement. This is the case if they do not directly use advertising information in their brand evaluations in order to reduce perceived risks when purchasing. Hoover *et al.* (1978) compared Mexican consumers with their American neighbours: they found that Mexicans generally displayed a much lower level of perceived risk related to their purchases. Hoover *et al.* argue that the lower level of perceived risk is related to a somewhat fatalistic tradition which exists in Mexican society. Conversely, in the United States a more 'master-of-destiny' orientation implies a greater perceived risk of being disappointed by any purchase. Thus Mexican consumers and, more generally, consumers belonging to fatalistic-oriented societies react more easily to persuasive message (the brand name repeated numerous times) and also oneiric messages (a dream that allows one to escape from a daily life that is not always bright).

Finally, it should be noted that the types of information cues vary by country. While Japanese advertisements, for example, have very few price, warranty and guarantee cues compared to US advertisements, they carry a much higher number of packaging cues (Lin, 1993; Lin and Salwen, 1995; Javalgi *et al.*, 1995). Korean advertisements include the price 38 per cent of the time, whereas in other countries the average is between 8 per cent (India) and 16 per cent (France) (Cutler *et al.*, 1992). While 'The British don't even want to mention money' (Reinhard and Philips, 1985, p. 46), French commercials present more quality information and new ideas, and in Taiwan information about product availability and special offers are significantly higher than average (Zandpour *et al.*, 1992).

As a general rule, advertising strategy must fit with the local orientation concerning information content and style of advertising. Advertising strategies that follow purely informative, oneiric or persuasive routes will have to be considered cautiously as applicants for cross-border transfer.

14.3

Culture and advertising execution

Once the advertising is strategy defined, execution remains a quite significant cross-cultural 'filter', since meaning transfer is fine-tuned through executional details, most of which are strongly culture bound. This section reviews the empirical literature in the following domains of advertising execution: (1) language; (2) humour; (3) characters and roles represented; (4) the influence of mores and religion, and (5) visual elements of advertising.[2]

Language

Advertisements usually have several text elements (catch-phrase, product description, slogan) and use colloquial language, very subtle yet precise in meaning. The character and structure of these elements heavily influence the advertisement's effectiveness, while language differences are the strongest barrier to effective communication. Duncan and Ramaprasad (1995) show that companies who tend to favour standardized international advertising strategy (68 per cent) and standardized execution (54 per cent), standardize language much less (11 per cent) across all countries. In order to be effective in a French context, for example, 50 per cent of all words in an advertisement should be nouns and verbs, the percentage of words exceeding three syllables should not be higher than 10 per cent, most of the long words should be familiar words, and sentences should have an average length of about 10–13 words (Tixier, 1992). Furthermore, advertising language often uses colloquial words or slang, which are particular to local people and as such difficult to find in dictionaries. The viewer or the listener understands messages all the more readily when colloquial speech expresses the delicate messages of daily life – sentiments, sensations, family relations, friendships, love affairs – that are reflected in advertising. Translating colloquial speech is difficult since it uses idiomatic expressions, which change from one language to another.

Marcel Bleustein Blanchet (quoted in *Reader's Digest*, 1987, pp. 42–3) a publicist for more than 60 years, notes a change in the role of slogans, which have become both simpler and more sophisticated, and less frequently used. He explains that 'when the public was less demanding and less blasé, slogans were the best means of launching a brand. Especially when radio began to advertise . . . pre-war slogans were a sort of *comptines* [little nursery rhymes]. They were assonant forms that the ear picked up instinctively.'

Effective textual elements, including the use of foreign vocabulary in an advertisement, are defined differently from one culture to another. A very large percentage of Asian advertisements contains English – and in some rare cases French – words (i.e. Mueller, 1992; Sherry and Camargo, 1987). Since the most important function of this foreign vocabulary ultimately is to achieve positive country-of-origin effects, its use depends on product type and product origin. Within a sample of ads from Hong Kong, Japan, South Korea and Taiwan, the likelihood of encountering foreign words is highest for advertisements in Hong Kong and Taiwan featuring Western-made personal care products (Neelankavil *et al.*, 1995). However, it would be fundamentally wrong to conclude from the heavy use of foreign words in Asian countries that there is a trend towards a globalization of advertising language. The Japanese culture in particular has demonstrated that English loanwords are used for their symbolic weight but are embedded in Japanese traditions. 'The loanwords are Japanized, becoming a distinctive communication neither entirely alien nor entirely traditional' (Sherry and Camargo, 1987, p. 185).

Since only a minority of persons worldwide can understand English, there will be problems with the comprehension of foreign words. In cases where translations lead to the desired associations, space considerations have to be taken into account when conceiving an advertisement. Differing language structures means that the textual part of advertisements grows by about 25 per cent when English is translated into Roman languages, and by 30 per cent when translated into Germanic languages (Grüber, 1987). This can alter the overall layout of the advertisement, and possibly decrease the relative impact of visual elements.

As argued in the previous chapter, the slogan 'Put a tiger in your tank' is not as standardized as it might seem. At first reading, it seems as if it would be fully equivalent across countries, but the interpretation differs as to where the power source is located, engine or tank. Examples of translation and

conceptual equivalence problems abound, especially for advertising campaigns in which message standardization has been attempted (for examples see Ricks *et al.*, 1979). A full rewrite is usually needed to transpose slogans from one language to another. This implies a thorough search for words that have the same intended meaning as in the source language, provided that these can be found (see section 7.2).

Even translating a message into each target country's language does not guarantee uniform comprehension. The meaning attributed to certain words depends on association norms that differ cross-culturally. According to Kroeber-Riel (1992), if the English word 'quiet' is translated into German (*ruhig*) and French (*tranquille*), German consumers mostly think of a forest (41 per cent), sleep (35 per cent), church (20 per cent), but also of a cemetery (13 per cent) and a bed (8 per cent). The pictorial associations of their French counterparts are fundamentally different and less homogeneous (countryside: 13 per cent; forest: 11 per cent; house: 9 per cent; library: 5 per cent, etc.). The congruency coefficient between both groups for the word 'quiet' is only 0.17 (Kroeber-Riel, 1992).

For advertisements that must be easily internationalized, one should avoid at all costs any problems related to language, for instance by using a merely visual TV commercial on which a voice-over in the local language can be added for each country. Television commercials aimed at a European audience often use a script where the characters speak neither to the audience nor to each other. Then a voice-over message on a sound track can be added to the image track. This avoids the drawbacks associated with dubbing. Most people lip-read unconsciously, at least in part. When watching a dubbed commercial, many people feel uneasy about the lag between lip movements and sounds.

Written communication should also be avoided in messages targeted at a multilingual audience. For instance, a commercial for a detergent where a housewife is handed a packet of '*Waschpulver*' will be identified by British, Italian or French viewers as foreign or German. A few years ago, IBM used the character of Charlie Chaplin and the mode of a silent film in a multinational campaign, the goal of which was to foster corporate image. This allowed the advertisement to be used in any country of the world. The same can be applied to magazine advertisements where the text can be reduced or even virtually deleted. It may sometimes be kept in its original language in ads for ethnic products. The text must be short and must strongly support an ethnic image (French for perfume, English for a large international newspaper, Italian for luxury leather shoes, etc.). The text must be universally understood, although not necessarily in full detail; the message should at least make sense with respect to the halo of meanings around the product proposal.

Several studies have focused on how bilinguals process information in advertising. For instance, Luna and Peracchio (2001) conducted two experiments with Spanish–English bilinguals. Their results suggest that a high level of congruity between picture and text increases memory for second-language advertisements. Toffoli and Laroche (2002) studied bilingual students from Hong Kong, finding that when they were exposed to the English advertisement and responded in English their reactions were more similar to the Canadian sample than when they reacted to the Chinese version. Specifically, they perceived greater source honesty, less forcefulness on the part of the source and reported a more positive attitude toward the brand, than those who were exposed to the Chinese advertisement and responded in Chinese.

Humour

Humour can be based on gestures, situations, or words. It is sometimes involuntary. For instance, when Charles De Gaulle decided to retire from public life, the British ambassador and his wife threw a gala dinner party in his honor. At the dinner table the Ambassador's wife was talking with Madame De Gaulle: 'Your husband has been such a prominent public figure, such a presence on the French and International scene for so many years! How quiet retirement will seem in comparison. What are you most looking forward to in these retirement years?' 'A penis', replied Madame De Gaulle. A huge hush fell over the table. Everyone heard her answer . . . and no one knew what to say next. Le Grand Charles leaned over to his wife and said: 'Ma chérie, I believe ze English pronounce zat word, "appiness !" ' (retrieved from http://www.gdargaud.net/Humor/French.html).

The basic concept of humour is universal since it can be found in every culture and in any country's

advertising; however, preferences for types of humour vary cross-culturally (McCullough and Taylor, 1993). Globally, most humour has an incongruity-resolution structure: people develop expectations based on category norms that are capable of being violated, sometimes in a humorous way (Suls, 1983); a naked businessman or a clothed ape speaking to the audience are examples of incongruity-based humour. Some cross-cultural support exists for a positive affect-based effect of humour in advertising. For groups of Finnish and US students a linkage between perceived funniness of an advertisement, liking the advertisement, and liking the product can be established (Unger, 1995). However, a closer look at the use of humour also reveals notable cultural differences.

First, the percentage of advertisements intending to be humorous varies across countries. There is for example a significantly higher percentage of humorous advertisements in television commercials in the UK than in the United States whereas French commercials use humour about as frequently as US spots but clearly more often than German spots (Weinberger and Spotts, 1989b; Appelbaum and Halliburton, 1993).

Second, although the incongruity principle can be found in the advertising of different countries, the relative importance of such humour varies. Alden *et al.* (1993) related Hofstede's values to the use of humour in advertising, by comparing two individualist cultures (the United States and Germany) with two collectivist and high-power-distance cultures (Thailand and South Korea). More incongruent contrasts are found in German (92 per cent) and Thai (82 per cent) than in American (69 per cent) and Korean ads (57 per cent). Additionally, in countries with high collectivism scores, significantly more characters are depicted in humorous advertisements than in more individualistic countries. Similarly, in countries high on the power distance dimension (i.e. Korea, Thailand) characters portrayed in humorous advertisements are much more likely to have an unequal status than in low-power-distance countries such as the USA and Germany (Alden *et al.*, 1993).

Third, the kind of humour preferred by each target culture differs: while English people are known for their black humour, Germans seem to prefer humour based on gloating (Huth and Unger, 1988). The latter would not be much appreciated in Japan where slapstick or demeaning humour is seldom seen in advertising. Instead the Japanese make humorous dramatizations of situations involving family members, colleagues, neighbours, etc., to create a bond of mutual feelings between the advertiser and the viewer (Hanna *et al.*, 1994). Additionally, black and earthy humour is also present in Japanese commercials. Subjects such as diseases, wars or funerals, which are taboo themes in the United States, are treated with humour in some Japanese advertisements (Di Benedetto *et al.*, 1992). Thus it appears that humour can be an element of standardization in cross-cultural advertising, especially when it is based on the incongruity principle which has a fairly global appeal. Nevertheless, the creative presentation of humour in advertisements needs considerable adaptation to be effective (Alden *et al.*, 1993).

Characters and roles represented in advertisements

When depicting characters, advertising must be extremely careful. Whether it is the age, dress or situation of a character that is represented, nothing should be left to chance in advertising messages. In general, target audiences prefer characters with which they can identify. Since the physique of a person – and even more so a hero-like person depicted in an advertisement – is a clear manifestation of a particular culture, the choice of characters needs particular attention in cross-cultural advertising.

Advertising is often accused of perpetuating traditional social roles, sometimes even acting as a vehicle for outdated ideas. However, the real situation is much more ambiguous: in most countries advertising acts as an agent of both social change and social maintenance. Advertising creation sometimes acts as an agent of change because social challenge is a method of capturing the attention of the audience, and because social innovators are also opinion leaders for new products and new ways of life. Advertising also reinforces traditional and sometimes old-fashioned social patterns: it is the mirror of society as a whole. Potential dangers are brought home by Prendergast *et al.* (2002). They examined the relationship between the 'ideal woman' depicted advertising and self-reports of eating disorders and body image dissatisfaction among females in Hong Kong. The study found that exposure to advertising was linked to eating disorders and body image dissatisfaction.

Another important issue related to characters in advertising is the portrayal of gender role. Several cross-cultural investigations have examined role portrayal in magazine and TV advertising. They all found that advertising reflects traditional stereotypes of male and female roles to varying degrees. Overall, women for example are mostly shown in non-working roles, often in the home, and in decorative roles. When women appear in working roles, they are more likely than men to be depicted in clerical, blue-collar or secretarial roles.

Although the studies show that sex role stereotypes are found in all cultures, differences exist. Some of the factors we would expect sex role stereotyping to differ by include masculinity, tradition and religion. First, several researchers have found that sex role stereotyping differs between countries classed as more masculine and those classed as more feminine. For instance, Huang (1995) shows that in a more masculine society (the United States) there is more sex role stereotyping, women are less frequently portrayed in working situations and there is less frequent use of female voice-over than in a feminine society (Taiwan). Similarly, Yeung and Lau (1993), found that Japan (a more masculine society) showed men in working roles 94 per cent of the time, while in Hong Kong and Taiwan magazine advertising treat gender role similarly, putting half of the men in working roles. However, Siu (1996) found that males are more likely to be portrayed as product authorities and females as product users in both Hong Kong and Singapore (Siu, 1996). Similarly, Tan *et al.* (2002) found that in Malaysia and Singapore men were more often shown in occupational roles or engaged in relaxing activities such as reading the newspapers and eating or, while women were more often shown in non-occupational roles or as homemakers.

In Swedish (more feminine) magazine advertisements, women are more likely to be depicted in working roles, far more likely to be portrayed in recreational roles, and far less likely to be depicted in decorative roles than in US (more masculine) magazine advertisements (Wiles and Tjernlund, 1991). In addition, women were never depicted in housework and childcare activities in Swedish advertisements whereas they were shown twice as often as males in such situations in US advertisements (Wiles *et al.*, 1996). Rose *et al.* (1993), show that German and Japanese (more masculine) people emphasize more traditional roles for women than do people in Denmark, France, New Zealand and the United States. However, across all six countries, the traditional view of female roles decreases from older to younger generations, which shows consistent cross-national convergence.

Second, sex role stereotyping appears to be more prevalent in more traditional and religious cultures. For instance, a Malaysian television channel, oriented towards a mostly Muslim target audience, typically depicts men in exciting and independent top executive roles and women as housewives who stay home to look after the family (Wee *et al.*, 1995, p. 62). In contrast, on Singapore television men were more likely to be depicted in middle management roles, while women were depicted in white-collar and service occupations or in a more modern context: as young, attractive and concerned with beauty. Interestingly, the portrayal of women on a second Malaysian channel targeted both to Malaysian and to Singaporean audiences, is a compromise between the stereotypes held by both audiences. However, this is not always the case. In a comparative study of three fairly masculine countries (Australia, Mexico, the United States), we might expect tradition to play a role. That is, we might expect a more traditional image in Mexico and a more modern image in the United States and Australia. Mary Gilly (1988) analyzed 12 hours of programmes for each country: 275 American, 204 Mexican and 138 Australian commercials were viewed. In both the United States and Mexico (as opposed to Australia) men, more often than women, were shown in roles of authority or expertise with respect to the product, whereas women were more often shown in the role of the consumer. In addition, in the United States a woman was more likely to be shown at home.

However, these generalizations do not always exist. For instance, Odekerken-Schröder *et al.* (2002) examined whether gender stereotyping in advertising is related to a country's level of masculinity, using the UK and The Netherlands, but no convincing support was found. Similarly, Al-Olayan and Karande (2000) investigated differences in the content of magazine advertisements between the United States and the more traditional Arab world (comprising 12 Middle-Eastern countries and ten African countries). They found that people are depicted less frequently in Arabic magazine ads. However, 'when ads picture men and/or women, men and women are portrayed to

the same degree both in the U.S. and the Arab world' (p. 80). The portrayal of women did differ, however, as women were used mainly when their presence related to the advertised product.

We need to check our intuition with facts from the country. It seems that Australia and Sweden have a more balanced and non-traditional representation of men and women in their advertising than for example the United States and Singapore. Malaysia, and to a lesser extent Mexico, where religious values and tradition are more important, display the biggest sex-role differences in advertising. Whereas on Malaysian (Muslim) television the portrayal of the sexes lags behind changes in society (i.e. the number of housewives is grossly exaggerated – Wee *et al.*, 1995), marketers in countries like Sweden have a more proactive approach in defining sex roles, thus creating new trends. Even across countries with quite similar levels of development, stronger traditional values in the society, such as in Japan compared with the United States, cause women's roles to be portrayed more traditionally (Javalgi *et al.*, 1995).

There is room for some standardization if both genders are depicted in recreational (men more than women) or decorative roles (women more than men). This is likely to be acceptable, for example, in the United States, Sweden and The Netherlands (J. Wiles *et al.*, 1995). Generally, in any country's advertising, women should ideally be young. However, the preference for beauty-types presented in advertising differs across societies (Bjerke, 1995). For instance, the Wash & Go shampoo advertising campaign by Procter & Gamble was standardized across Europe in terms of its core theme, but it was adapted locally using different beauty presenters appropriate for each country.

Similarly, a certain degree of standardization can be found regarding the use of Western models in Asian countries. Such models can be found in more than one-third of magazine advertisements in Hong Kong, Taiwan, Japan and South Korea, and they are particularly frequent in advertisements for products from the West, notably personal care products (Neelankavil *et al.*, 1995). At the same time however, many advertisements reviewed in those countries had a completely local character.

Cross-cultural differences are also observed with regard to the portrayal of the elderly in advertising. A country's degree of orientation towards traditional values has an impact on the portrayal of the elderly in advertising messages. For instance, Japanese magazine advertisements show more respect towards the elderly than their American counterparts (Mueller, 1987; Javalgi *et al.*, 1995). However, common stereotypes are not always confirmed. For example, in Latin America the elderly are not presented more frequently in a family setting or as celebrity endorsers, nor is there a greater proportion of elderly males than in the United States (Bates and Renforth, 1987).

Traditional roles that are not present in the source culture may unintentionally appear when they are interpreted by the target culture. A 'spurious' meaning may appear in the target culture which was not intended by the advertiser in the source culture. For instance, Douglas and Dubois (1980) give the example of a brandy advertisement that was targeted at the South African Bantu market. It showed a couple seated at a table with a bottle superimposed over them. Many Bantus thought that the woman was carrying the bottle on her head, as many traditional African women do. This created an unintended and confusing contrast between the traditional, local aspect of the characters and situation and the modern, imported aspect of the product. It therefore prevented clear and effective marketing communication.

As a consequence, one should study a representative sample of local advertising messages, whether commercials or magazine advertisements. This will give a better idea of the sex roles, age roles, typical everyday situations and social relations in a particular country. It can be achieved by conducting a systematic content analysis of newspaper, magazine and television advertisements (at least several dozen of each). An advertisement should always be created in cooperation with a native of the target culture, who acts as a test audience; in the case of internationally standardized advertisements, messages in the various linguistic/cultural contexts should be reviewed by natives of each target culture or subcultures.

In order to avoid creating spurious associations, the advertising script may go so far as to avoid presenting any characters at all, especially if the target audience is not clearly defined or too large, making the choice of characters a difficult one. For instance, in a Renault advertisement, a car without a driver was shown moving in the middle of a scale-model city. This avoided the choice of a specific character, whose age, sex or appearance would influence the product's positioning undesirably. A car without a driver may, however, be negatively interpreted in countries where such a situation is associated with a safety issue (runaway car) or a distortion of reality (how can a car drive without a driver?). This may inhibit a positive response to the message.

The influence of mores and religion

It is crucial to choose the appropriate symbolic elements by which cultural meanings about products and services may be communicated to the audience. Mores and religion act as filters of advertising messages, transforming factual information into culturally interpreted meaning (e.g. a naked woman washing her hair in her bathroom) into elements of culture-based meaning (it incites people to sexual debauchery). If one focuses on information rather than meaning, it is difficult to become aware of the influence of mores and religion on advertising messages. This point is illustrated by the example of advertising in Saudi Arabia (Box 14.1).

Al-Mossawi and Michell (1992) measured the influence of the degree of strictness versus Islamic rules on attitudes towards contentious and non-contentious commercials in Gulf countries. Their findings show that strict Muslims are more interested in, and especially have a higher recall of, non-contentious advertisements whereas lenient Muslims show no difference between advertisement containing elements considered to be against the principles of Islam or not. The influence of religion on advertising, exemplified by the Muslim religion, although strong, is not uniform across countries or individual viewers within a particular country (see Al-Makaty *et al.* (1996) in the case of Saudi Arabia). Furthermore, sensitive issues such as family planning can be treated successfully if creation adequately goes beyond traditional beliefs and taboos (Wafai and El Tigi, 1994).

Many of us are superstitious, even though we may deny it. Rarely will advertisements show people walking under ladders, unless, for the sake of humour, something happens to them. This is proof of the force of superstition. The social habits of daily life also play a role, particularly those that are related to what is (locally) considered polite, courteous or hospitable. In this way, a well-known brand of tea alienated the Saudi public when it showed a Saudi host using his

---

Box 14.1

The influence of religion on advertising in Saudi Arabia

The Saudi legal system is unique in the sense that it identifies law with the personal command of the 'one and only god, the Almighty'. The Islamic laws known as *Sharia* are the master framework to which all legislation, existing and proposed, is referred and with which it must be compatible. The *Sharia* is a comprehensive code governing the duties, morals and behaviour of all Muslims, individually and collectively in all areas of life, including commerce. *Sharia* is derived from two basic sources, the Quran or Holy Book, and the *Hadith*, based on the life, sayings, and practices of the Prophet Muhammed . . . At the very minimum, an understanding of fundamental *Sharia* laws as contained in Quranic injunctions is necessary in order to gain insights into advertising regulation and content . . .

Three sets of Quranic messages have special significance for advertising regulation. First there are strict taboos (*haraam*), such as alcohol, gambling, cheating, idol worship, usury, adultery and 'immodest' exposure . . . For example alcoholic products are banned. There are no local advertisements, and foreign print media are only allowed into the country after all advertisements of alcoholic beverages have been censored. Promotions involving games of chance are illegal . . .

Other dangers for advertisers include messages which may be considered as deceptive by religious standards. According to Islam, fraud may occur if the seller fails to deliver everything promised, and advertisers may need to use factual appeal, based on real rather than perceived product benefits. Statuary should not appear in advertising, since it may be perceived as a symbol of idol worship. Since religious norms require women to be covered, international print advertisements may have to be modified by superimposing long dresses on models or by shading their legs with black. Advertisers of cosmetics in Saudi Arabia refrain from picturing sensuous females; instead, in typical advertisements a pleasant-looking woman appears in a robe and headdress, with only her face showing . . . A second set of Quranic injunctions governs the duties a Muslim must perform, such as praying five times daily, fasting during the month of Ramadhan, giving *zakaat* (charity) to the poor, and respecting and caring for parents and the disadvantaged. Advertisers have to ensure that they do not hinder the performance of these obligations. For example, during the five prayer times, which last from 10 to 20 minutes, products cannot be promoted on radio or TV, retail shops close, and no commercial or official transactions are permitted. Advertisements should not depict, even humorously, children being disrespectful to parents and elders, whereas the image of a product could be enhanced by advertisements that stress parental advice or approval . . .

A third set of Quranic injunctions remind the faithful of God's bounties and enjoins them to thank Him for such blessings as good health, peace of mind, food, water and children. It is legal and sometimes recommended practice for advertisers to introduce their messages with Quranic words: 'In the Name of Allah, the Most Gracious, the Most Merciful'; 'By the Grace of God'; 'God is Great (Allah-o-Akbar)'; Al-Rabiah and Nasser, a manufacturer of water pumps, uses a Quranic verse: 'We made from water every living thing.' Such verses may also be used to legitimise operations or to assure that services are in accord with Islamic principles.

(Source: Luqmani *et al.*, 1988, pp. 61–4. Reproduced with permission.)

---

left hand to serve tea to one of his guests. Moreover, the guest was wearing shoes, which is considered in Saudi Arabia to be the height of rudeness.

Generally the relationship between men and women, depicted by advertising, is a ticklish problem. For instance, Miller and Demirel (1988) depict advertising for beer on the Turkish market which portrays men and women drinking the beer in a social setting at home. Emphasizing a family setting as the consumption situation is a response to the problem of showing men and women together in the predominantly male institutions of coffee houses and beer pubs, which would violate Turkish customs of courtship and social interaction.

Attitudes towards nudity differ from one country to another. French advertising is considered to have more nudity than most other countries. It is well accepted in French society, since the meaning conveyed by nudity is very much related to beauty, excellence and nature. To contrast this, we give the example of the Guy Laroche perfume Drakkar Noir in France and Saudi Arabia (Czinkota and Ronkainen, 1990, p. 616). The original French advertisement showed a man's bare forearm, held at the wrist by a woman's hand, with the man's hand holding a bottle of cologne. The Saudi advertisement showed the man's forearm covered by a suit jacket, with only the cuff of the shirt showing, while the woman lightly touched his hand with one of her fingers. Respect for the existing social conventions in the target society will long remain a prerequisite for the localization of advertising messages. Furthermore, the role of advertising has never been (at least officially) to change a society's mores, but rather to sell a product.

Visual elements

Advertising copy is complex and inevitably tends to reflect the cultural background of those who have created it. For instance, Clarke and Honeycutt (2000) compared the use of colour in advertisements in France, the United States and Venezuela. They found black and brown were more common in France and the United States, while red, orange and green were more common in Venezuelan advertisements. They gave examples where the meanings of colour differs between these countries: a masculine colour in the United States is blue, while in France it is red; mourning is represented by black in France and the United States, while in Venezuela it is purple; green is associated with money in the United States while in France it is pharmacies. Similarly, Huang (1993) showed that colour is used differently in US and Taiwanese industrial advertising: yellow, a favourite colour of the Chinese (the colour of royalty), is found more often in Taiwanese advertisements, whereas brown was preferred in many American advertisements.

Background themes, the setting and roles depicted are also important aspects of the copy. By systematically comparing Brazilian and US advertisements for cars over a ten-year period, Tansey *et al.* (1990) showed that Brazilian advertisements use significantly more urban themes and depict more leisure situations than US advertisements. The setting or product use conditions that are most often depicted by the advertising visual also differ. For instance, individualistic as compared with collectivist settings for product use have been shown to be significant elements of contrast between Chinese and American advertising (Han and Shavitt, 1994; Zhang and Gelb, 1996; Zhang and Neelankavil, 1997) and Colombian and American advertising (Gregory *et al.* 2002).

Many visual elements commonly found in print advertisements (size of the visual, use of photographs, use of black and white advertisements, presentation of children) vary across countries. Cutler *et al.* (1992) investigated the visual component of print advertising across five countries (the United States, the United Kingdom, France, Korea and India) through a detailed content analysis of about 250 advertisements per country. Indian advertisements use significantly more black and white and show more children than those in any other country; Korean advertisements show price two or three times as frequently as those in other countries, and represent more elderly persons whose wisdom is valued in Far Eastern cultures; French advertisements are by far the most oriented towards aesthetics: five times more than US, Korean or Indian advertisements, but only twice as much as British advertisements. US advertisements appear by far the most comparative, ten times more frequently than those in France for instance. Furthermore, US advertisements depict children in more idealistic settings – clean and smiling – than French advertisements, where they are more likely to appear quite realistic (Hall and Hall, 1989).

Standardization of magazine advertisements in the countries mentioned will not be easy for durable or non-durable products since there are more differences than similarities for product types. Each country is unique on one or several visual characteristics. Overall, however, no systematic differences between industrialized and developing countries appear. Interestingly, within the Western countries analyzed, the use of visual elements in the United Kingdom more closely resembles practice in the United States than in France. This means that there may be standardization barriers within the European Community (Cutler and Javalgi, 1992; Cutler *et al.*, 1992).

When comparing language to pictorial elements in advertising, many pretend that pictures are understood everywhere. This is certainly true but does not help the international advertiser much since the issue is not *whether* pictures are understood but rather *how* they are understood. As with language elements, pictures also present culture-specific association norms (Hung and Rice, 1995). While rain evokes freshness for certain persons, it is associated with coldness by others. This certainly can not be characterized as a positive factor for global advertising (Kroeber-Riel, 1992). In fact, people from different cultural origins have different attitudinal reactions when exposed to foreign television commercials (Martenson, 1987). People from different cultures do not evaluate information in the same way. Hornik (1980) has emphasized that, while concepts like product attributes are probably universal and the product function similar across nations, the exact form of attribute perception in each society might differ considerably. After being exposed to a verbal briefing and photographs of a new car, British, German, French and Swedish respondents had different perceptions of the product. The car's styling scored well in Germany and Sweden, but poorly in Britain and France. With regard to safety, the new car scored well only in Britain. At the same time it was perceived as particularly unreliable in Sweden (Colvin *et al.*, 1980). Walle (1997, p. 702) explains how the Marlboro man, a global promotional icon, is understood differently worldwide and re-invested with local meanings; it is, for instance, considered as a symbol of wealth and prosperity by Africans and was a symbol of freedom to East Germans in the time of communism:

To this East German woman, the Marlboro man was a seductive icon, but to her it did not represent the heritage of the American frontier. Juxtaposing the image of a man who lives without fences to the realities of her own life and the shadow of the Berlin wall, she viewed the Marlboro man as an alternative to the oppressive dictatorship in which she lived. We both saw the same ad; I interpreted it as an American while she processed it in ways which fit into her life. The product and promotion were homogeneous; the meaning and response were not.

Advertising in societies experiencing rapid change

China has witnessed a dramatic change in the place of advertising in the overall business and social scene.[3]

In societies where people have been told for a long time that advertising is simply capitalist propaganda and as such evil and deceptive, advertisers today still face some degree of distrust and cannot just use the same approach as elsewhere. Many consumers still feel that good products sell themselves and that only bad products need advertising. Zhou *et al.* (2002) compared the results of a 1999 survey of consumers from China with that of a previous study in the United States. They found that while general attitudes toward advertising were similar, fewer Chinese respondents trusted the messages and believed in industry regulation. In such a context, foreign companies have to target long-run acceptance, stressing product availability and building brand reputation (Liang and Jacobs, 1994). They cannot just imitate what is done elsewhere.

The case of China also illustrates that product meaning changes over time. Luxury goods evolved from hated symbols of decadent capitalism to consumption incentives for those who work hard (Tse *et al.*, 1989; Swanson, 1996). This goes along with a shift in the dominant values in Chinese advertising. Between 1982 and 1992, utilitarian values decreased and more symbolic values – with both Eastern and Western origins – increased (Cheng, 1994). Cultural values depicted by Chinese advertisements tend to reflect both Chinese culture and Western imports and have much to do with product categories and country of origin. The value of 'tradition', for instance, is more often used for food and drink whereas 'modernity' is found in a large number of Chinese advertisements that promote products for the new affluent society (Cheng and Schweitzer, 1996). Over time, product availability as the main emphasis in Chinese advertisements has decreased. Simultaneously, emphasis on brand superiority and comparative advertising has become more frequent (Zhou and Belk, 1993).

Cross-national transferability of advertising copy

The transfer of promotional materials is practiced frequently in multinationals (Hill and James, 1991): they are adapted as necessary. When attempts are made to transfer advertising copy cross-culturally, the first issue is the grouping of countries within which cross-national transfers are easier. For instance, Zandpour and Harich (1996) grouped countries according to whether they value more rational (think) or more emotional (feel) advertising appeals. The second issue deals with the precautions to be taken when transferring copy. Even between countries that look culturally very similar, such as the United States and the United Kingdom there are very significant differences in the style of advertising copy. The first obvious difference is that broadcast television is more commercialized in the United States than in the UK. Studies have found that the frequency of advertising differs by product category in Europe: Katz and Lee (1992) personal care, travel and cars are more frequently advertised in the US and services are more frequently advertised in the UK; Koudelova and Whitelock (2001) found that cars and accessories, retail outlets and service advertising are more frequently advertised in the UK, while household cleaning agents were more frequent in the Czech Republic. Even within Europe there is no evidence that the content of advertising copy is converging: on the contrary, the cultural content, specific to each country, appears to be increasing over long periods of time (Snyder *et al.* 1991).

An interesting approach is to try to cluster countries according to cultural values (e.g. Hofstede's dimensions or Schwartz values) in order to determine whether it is possible to transfer part or the whole of an advertising creation or even a full campaign. Kale (1991) gives the example of the promotion of India as a tourist destination for the US market. When trying to adapt, both the target (United States) and the source (India) cultures have to be considered: they differ mostly on Hofstede's power distance (40 versus 77) and individualism (91 versus 48). Kale insists that the (Indian) message must be targeted to the (US) individual: the message must reflect friendliness and informality, and it must value autonomy, variety and pleasure, all positive values for highly individualistic cultures, such as that of the United States. He further suggests that, since democracies are perceived as small-power-distance institutions, the message should emphasize that India has a democratic government, which would help bridge the gap of power distance between the source and the target country. Albers-Miller and Gelb (1996) have shown that advertising appeals used in business advertising largely match cultural values represented by Hofstede's four cultural dimensions. For instance status appeals in advertisements are more often used in a high-power-distance

society such as Korea than in a low-power-distance society such as the United States (Cutler *et al.*, 1995). Masculinity in Mexico (*Machismo*) seems to be an influential force in the advertisements for traditional male-oriented products such as automobiles (Gregory and Munch, 1997, 115).

Since Hofstede's dimensions seem to be meaningful, it is interesting to try to cluster countries according to them. Sriram and Gopalakrishna (1991) combined these dimensions with economic and demographic as well as media availability indicators (televisions per 1,000 people, radios per 1,000 people, advertising spending per capita, etc.). They clustered countries into six groups: Japan is isolated in one group, and most other groups are fairly heterogeneous geographically, except northern Europe and a sort of central Asian area extending from Iran to the Philippines. The two Hofstede dimensions that discriminate significantly between these groups are once again power distance and individualism. They should be used with caution however, as they have a broad rather than a precise influence on advertising and should be used for defining strategy rather than executional details.

If a transfer has been decided upon, the following elements should always be carefully checked to ensure the cultural adequacy of the final copy: (1) comparative advertising or not; (2) degree and type of informative content and style; (3) adequacy of basic copy themes in relation to local mores and customs; (4) execution: background themes, colour, use of words (puns, suggestive words), use of humour, use of symbols, type of characters and roles (age, sex, status), situations and types of relationship depicted; and (5) implementation constraints, such as lack of a medium available locally.

14.4

Media worldwide: Technological advances and cultural convergence

Worldwide differences in advertising expenditure

One cannot help but be struck by the difference in advertising expenses across countries, even though these countries may have comparable levels of economic development. This can be partially attributed to media availability (radio, television, newspapers, magazines, film, billboards). Where some media are non-existent or their availability is limited, expenses are automatically restricted by the lack of space for advertising. In the mid-1990s, the world average per capita advertising expenditure was about US$60. In 2001, the United States has the leading edge with US$465 advertisement spending per capita, followed by Japan with US$322, the United Kingdom with US$256 and Germany with US$210 per capita. Despite the September 11 terrorist attacks and a recession, the United States still spent the most on advertising (US$135.7 billion), followed by Japan ($45.5 billion), Germany ($17.2 billion), United Kingdom ($15.2 billion), France ($9 billion) and Italy ($7 billion), followed by Brazil, South Korea, Canada and China. Per capita advertising expenditure is much lower in developing nations. For instance, China only reached a per capita spend of $4.2 billion despite its rank of tenth for total advertisement spending (*Ad Age Global*, 2002).

Cross-cultural differences in media availability and use

The availability of advertising media is influenced by the level of a country's economic development and also by its view of the appropriate mix between business/commercial activities, on the one hand, and cultural/recreational activities on the other hand. Tuncalp (1992, 1994) gives the example of Saudi Arabia, where traditional values do not permit the showing of films to public gatherings; as a result, the cinema medium does not exist in Saudi Arabia. Ethical debates about whether certain products can be advertised have an influence on regulations, for instance about media space available for cigarette and alcohol.

Prior to the European Unions ban on tobacco advertising and sponsorship, all member states prohibited television advertising of tobacco, but other restrictions varied by country. For instance, in Spain, tobacco advertising was only banned from the TV and in places where sales or consumption was prohibited. In Luxembourg advertising was allowed in sales outlets, in the press and on posters, although there were restrictions on advertising content and health warnings were compulsory. In France, Italy and Portugal

there was a total ban on tobacco advertising, although some exceptions were permitted under strict conditions. In 2001, the EU outlawed tobacco advertising in the print media, on the radio and the Internet. In addition, it banned sponsorship of cross-border events, although national or local events are not covered by the directive.

Today, anti-smoking advertising is becoming more prevalent and there is growing evidence of the effectiveness of anti-smoking advertising. With two experiments Pechmann and Shih (1999) showed that in the United States ninth graders' attitudes to smoking can be influenced by advertising. First, they showed them films with smokers in them, which led to elevated levels of arousal, enhanced their perceptions of a smoker's stature and increased their intent to smoke. Next, they showed the same film but placed anti-smoking advertisements in it, which led to negative thoughts about the movie characters who smoked. Quester (1999) surveyed young adult students in Australia and Malaysia finding that anti-smoking advertisements result in less favourable attitudes toward smoking.

Advertising is largely based on news and entertainment media. The communication support systems such as television and audiovisual equipment, printing presses, photographic equipment, etc. are costly and need to be balanced by sales, advertising or other sources of revenue. Financial support in countries where banks have limited lending capacity is often based on political influence (which may prove unstable). In many countries the press is even more dependent on politics than on advertisers.

Apart from purely economic factors, the availability of the media is also influenced by two social representations concerned with the relationship between the media and its audience. The first deals with what is considered a reasonable ratio between advertising and entertainment time (news and programmes) by the local audience and what they consider the appropriate sequencing between advertising and entertainment, for instance in terms of television movies being sliced up by advertising. The second social representation is whether advertising is considered an entertainment in itself. If entertaining the target audience is a necessary condition for capturing their interest, creative effort may have to be devoted to entertainment rather than mere advertising messages. This may reduce the effectiveness of the advertisement because the viewers' attention is attracted by the creative side of the message and diverted from the product that is being presented. Responses to the issue of how entertainment and advertising interrelate probably differ in the United States and Europe.

Many countries have instituted rules that place limits on television advertising. Sweden has no advertising on its national channels. Germany limited advertising to 20 minutes per day over three to five time periods. There are now several private television stations such as Sat 1, Pro 7 or Vox, with no limitation on advertising time, while the limitations on public channels (ARD and ZDF) have been loosened. France controls all its channels, public and private, with regulations (*cahier des charges*) that limit television commercials to about an hour per day. New Zealand has two state-controlled television stations, which forbid advertising on Sunday, and a third station, totally commercial (Andrews *et al.*, 1991).

Conversely, where little or even no advertising regulation exists, there can sometimes be such an invasion by advertising that viewing television programmes becomes little more than watching advertisements, a reproach frequently addressed by Europeans to American, Brazilian or Canadian television channels. The general contrast here seems to be between the Americas (the United States, Mexico, Brazil and Canada), with liberal advertising regulations, and most other countries, where audiovisual media availability is more limited by regulation. For instance, while Saudi Arabia lifted the ban on commercial advertising on radio, all broadcasts are screened, in order to ensure that they conform to Islamic moral and religious standards.

In many countries, radio stations have flourished with extensive advertising space, that is, up to 20 minutes of commercials per hour; programmes are constantly interrupted by advertising. This hectic schedule may be resented by listeners who constantly change stations, obliging advertisers to buy media space for the same time blocks across several radio stations. The question of finding the acceptable proportion of advertising to total time is an important one. Studies have shown that in the United States an increasing number of consumers consider that television advertising is sometimes stupid and tends to be less intelligent than previously. US television viewers are therefore dissatisfied (Martenson, 1987). The situation is fairly paradoxical: as the number of media channels increase, it becomes more difficult to reach and monitor a target audience since viewers' saturation with advertisements reduces their ability to listen to advertising and to zapping. It is surprising that the issue of whether the viewer/listener is entertained by advertising is rarely addressed, given its practical importance. Zapping has been widely studied, but most studies have only sought to demonstrate how an advertiser can avoid its unfortunate results. It is taken for granted that the audience has no saturation threshold, or at the very least an extremely high one. This assumption suggests the absolute legitimacy of mass advertising communication within a society that willingly portrays itself as being free-market oriented. In contrast, many European countries started from the opposite assumption, and advertising therefore took a long time to assert itself on television.

The emergence of global media

The previous sections have placed emphasis upon differences in advertising across countries. These differences do not offset certain similarities and convergence. Diverse media combine into a 'media landscape' which is primarily shaped by the freedom of choice of the audience. Some media have achieved almost worldwide recognition and a truly global audience. Among the international advertising media that have achieved the most impressive worldwide reach is the monthly *Reader's Digest*. It is the world's most widely read magazine, with a circulation of 21 million with over 100 million readers worldwide. It is published in 48 editions and 19 languages and is sold in more than 60 countries. It was founded in 1920 by DeWitt Wallace and his wife Lila Acheson. The first issue came out in February 1922 (see Box 14.2).

There are now some 'global' newspapers such as the *International Herald Tribune*, the *Wall Street Journal* and the *National Geographic* magazine. Their circulation covers almost the entire world. *Time* magazine publishes more than 400 geographic and demographic editions, reaching 30 million readers worldwide, which enables advertisers to reach precise target audiences in a large number of locations throughout the world. Many French magazines such as *L'Express*, *Le Point* and *Elle* and German magazines such as *Der Spiegel* and *Burda Moden* also publish international editions. The advertising clientele of these worldwide publications

Box 14.2

The internationalization of the *Reader's Digest*

'Since the formula of the Digest is so effective in the United States, why not attempt to repeat it elsewhere?' thought DeWitt Wallace. But exporting the formula of a magazine requires that the obstacle of language be overcome. The simplest solution was to begin in England, which could serve as a gateway into Europe. Accordingly, the first foreign edition of the *Reader's Digest* appeared in Great Britain in 1937. The second foreign edition, however, did not appear in Europe. In 1940, in the midst of the Second World War, the first issue of *Selecciones del Reader's Digest*, the Spanish-American edition, came out in Cuba. Why Cuba? The long-term objective was to attack the South American market, even if sales had to be made at a loss (as indeed occurred for many years). But for the time being, DeWitt Wallace's objective was more of a missionary one, for he sought to combat the Nazi advance. In 1942, a Portuguese edition in Brazil followed. This edition reached a print run of 300,000 copies. In 1943, there was a return to Europe with the publication of a Swedish edition. The war was not yet over, but DeWitt Wallace was

already contemplating market entry into Europe. He offered cut-price subscriptions of the *Digest* to families of young Americans who had been called up. Along with chewing gum and nylon stockings, the *Reader's Digest* was to arouse the interest of young Europeans. After the war, in 1947, *Sélection du Reader's Digest* finally appeared in France under the management of General Thompson. There was an initial print run of 275,397 copies, which almost doubled for the second issue. The global expansion of the *Reader's Digest* did not stop . . . Germany, Italy, Switzerland and Belgium, as well as India, South Africa, Australia and New Zealand, were all in turn to have their edition of the magazine. Today, thirty-nine editions of the *Reader's Digest* are published, including one for schoolchildren, another in large type for those with sight problems and an edition in Braille. It can justifiably claim the distinction inscribed on every cover of being the most widely read magazine in the world.

(Source: Adapted from *Reader's Digest*, 1987, pp. 10–11, and *Reader's Digest* news release 'Products and services', June 1988.)

nevertheless remains fairly limited. It consists of 'global' advertisers who themselves are mostly targeting a global clientele, namely a segment of well-off consumers who travel internationally. Industries that use media with global reach are basically airlines, cars, banks and financial services, consumer electronics and telecommunications, tobacco and alcohol, pharmaceuticals, perfumes and luxury products. Such is the case in Asia where pan-Asian advertising media reach an upper-scale audience composed of affluent business people and travellers (Ha, 1997). However, advertisers should be cautious when using similar media globally since media perception, in terms of being enjoyable, informative, annoying and offensive, has been shown to vary cross-culturally (Somasundaran and Light, 1994).

The global media landscape has two facets: while local media survive because language differences remain a pervasive reality, a globalized supply of media is emerging which greatly serves the globalization of advertising. The best example of such breakthroughs

in international telecommunications is the growth of the world wide web as an advertising medium. The web is most attractive for reaching people under 35, called 'generation X', who have over US$200 billion purchasing power worldwide and comprise nearly 75 per cent of web users. Industries such as telecommunications, computers, electronic entertainment equipment, publishing and financial services are the most intense users of the web as a global medium (Kassaye, 1997).

The influence of television satellites

Television satellites now offer media with regional or global coverage. The United States is a pioneer in this field – no fewer than 30 satellites were in service in the United States in 1990 (Mariet, 1990) serving an impressive number of television channels. Examples in this section mostly focus on Europe and Asia, which tend to remain fragmented audiences because of language diversity. Previously, television channels were purely national, mostly state owned, and with some development of private hertzian (transmission of hertzian waves by ground stations) and cable channels during recent years. Europe is now following the United States. Programmes such as MTV, CNN, TNT Cartoon and BBC Worldwide now reach millions of homes on all continents through satellite television.[4]

Many satellites covering most of Europe are now available for transmission, such as Astra (Luxemburg) and TDF and TVSAT (French-German). Daily newspapers are also becoming globalized as a result of information transmitted by satellites and computerized type setting; the core parts of the global newspaper are common to all local editions and are sent as digital information to local printing workshops, which add local news and advertising. Whereas satellite television has developed considerably in Europe, its penetration rate is still low in Asia, despite some inroads made by the Hong Kong-based Star TV satellite (Ha, 1997). There are different possibilities for the use of television satellites. They can transmit images that will be used to make up programmes (primarily news and sports) that are then re-broadcast in a traditional form, e.g. hertzian ground television. The broadcasting of satellite images to viewers can be achieved via a cable network. An infrastructure of ground receiving stations is then needed, before the images are sent to viewers through the cable. Ground stations can receive signals of minimal strength, amplify them and redirect them through cable to private homes. Cable channels can be scrambled and paid for with the purchase of a decoder, by subscription or hourly fees. The third solution is a broadcast that is directly received by the viewer with a parabolic antenna (dish). In this case the satellite must broadcast much stronger signals so that they can be picked up on the ground.

The problem of the satellite and cable network infrastructure is just as complex as the creation of new programmes to fill the screens of the new television channels. For the television industry the problem is acute: television channels cannot show just news from international news agencies and cheap talk shows, with the overall purpose of reducing the hourly cost of programmes. Television channels must set up some really entertaining programmes in order to attract viewers who then have a reason to watch the commercials. Europeans as well as Asians have difficulties creating

and selling television series and soap operas internationally in comparison to the United States (Sarathy, 1991). It is estimated, for instance, that the changes in the European televisual industry necessitate over 50,000 hours of new programmes per year. In 1987 the rights to one hour of the *Dallas* series cost US$32,000, compared to US$400,000 for the production of one episode of the series *Chateauvallon* by a European consortium led by the French state-owned station Antenne 2. In 1989, the re-broadcast rights to an American television film cost US$70,000, compared with almost a million dollars for the production of a comparable European film (Sarathy, 1991). This situation has not changed over the last ten years: the American TV industry still has a leading edge on prices.

Media giants have emerged which are likely to take control of large parts of the global media industry, such as Ted Turner, Berlusconi, Leo Kirsch, Springer, Bertelsmann, Hachette, the Luxemburg television company (RTL), Australian press magnate Rupert Murdoch and the Canadian ITC group. The bulk of these groups are multimedia interests and are equally engaged in the development of the press media covering regional areas. Many countries have invested in cable systems, which are competing with direct television (DBS). Some countries are already equipped with dense cable networks, such as Ireland, Belgium and Germany, where more than half of all households are linked in. Other countries such as France are lagging behind and attempting to catch up. In general, there has been little European consensus on standards for telecommunication technologies such as high-definition television (HDTV), fibre optic networks, electronic transmission standards, etc. Technological, industrial, media, cultural and legal interests overlap in a realm of complex influences, where national state influence is still strong, as is the tradition in the European media and television industries.

Certain European regulations aim to protect the cultural identity of European audiovisual networks. The French, in particular, were somewhat disturbed by the invasion of American programmes, to the detriment of European culture and creation. (Once again, self-contradiction is possible: some people may be both faithful viewers of American television series and opponents of imported television programmes as a whole.) This implies an increasing influence of the English language, which the French and other Europeans fear could further damage the influence and reach of their own languages. In May 1989, the EU adopted a directive that required at least half of the programmes on European television to be produced in Europe. Nevertheless the text of this directive was fairly vague and allowed loose interpretation by the member countries. Similarly, some Asian countries tend to protect their cultural identity often by prohibiting or discouraging the installation of satellite dishes, thus limiting the potential coverage of pan-Asian media.

Enlargement and overlapping of media

The influence on marketing communications of media globalization and potential media overlap is quite significant. There is a large increase in the available media space on television; the new channels are almost all private, and must finance their operations either by advertising or by subscription (cable and/or scrambler/decoder). Satellites such as Astra cover a significant number of countries in western Europe. This produces great overlap zones where viewers are able to receive a large number of channels with a simple dish and decoder. This phenomenon can be observed worldwide, especially in Europe and Asia. However, it is questionable whether media overlapping has been a problem in Europe for advertisers, especially since 1993, when the physical borders between the then 12 member states of the EU were progressively abolished. Some people tend to underrate the importance of media overlapping:

Much is made of overlapping media particularly in classroom situations. Yet the impact of imported overlapping media has only a marginal beneficial effect on audiences. Evidence from Ireland, Austria and Switzerland indicates that where advertising comes in from adjacent countries it is largely ignored unless the product is also advertised locally, thus undermining the increased coverage potential. There is a need to harmonize creative presentation where overlaps occur to prevent confusion in the minds of potential customers. (Dudley, 1989, pp. 287 and 290.)

One has to address the issue of whether media overlapping in Europe may lead to a compulsory standardization of brands and of the creative themes and presentation of ads. Sarathy (1991) illustrates this issue by citing Unilever's difficulties in creating Euro-advertising for its household cleanser, which is called Vif in Switzerland, Viss in Germany, Jif in the United Kingdom and Greece and Cif in France.

Mourier and Burgaud (1989) suggest that companies that adapt marketing plans to each European market risk being misunderstood by consumers. Indeed in switching channels, consumers would be disturbed if the same product were advertised under different brand names and had diversified packagings, and if different product uses and benefits were emphasized. However, not all viewers watch foreign channels, and not all products are marketed throughout Europe.

Technological and social changes open the door for more specific and segmented marketing

There are increasing numbers of standard brand names across Europe, especially within industries that are potential candidates for regional marketing globalization in Europe – such as banks and financial services for private clients, airlines, mass market consumer goods, as well as many consumer durables such as cars, household appliances, stereo and video systems and photographic equipment. Until now, domestic markets were considered to be the most likely units to be segmented; however, complex segments emerge where country is not necessarily the segmentable unit *par excellence* (see section 8.4 on intercultural marketing strategies based on cultural affinity zones and classes).

Some pan-European market segments include a homogeneous population across countries – for example, age groups. This is the case in relation to products for young people. Television stations such as MTV and Sky are well prepared for this. The rock radio image, supported by the emergence of European rock, is carefully cultivated by MTV. As pointed out by Tom Freston, the president of MTV: 'Music crosses borders very easily, and the lingua franca of rock'n'roll is English. Rock is an Anglo-American form.' Freston further indicates what he considers to be the mission of MTV: 'We want to be the global rock and roll village, where we can talk to youth world-wide' (cited by Sarathy, 1991).

Ethnicity plays an increasing role in Europe, and pan-European market segments may be fairly effective when cultural and linguistic minorities are targeted. At the national level, these minorities do not reach the critical numbers that could justify the creation of specific media, since they are scattered all over the countries of Europe. But minorities may be more significantly served at the European level. Mariet (1990) cites the case of the development of Hispanic television in the United States. There are two principal networks: Univision-SIN, started in 1961, now reaches 5.1 million households, that is, 85 per cent of Spanish-speaking Americans; the other large Hispanic network, Telemundo, covers 77 per cent of these households and is present in 35 states. Such initiatives are also likely to flourish in Europe, in that they can fulfil the need for television communication of Arabic-speaking North African immigrants, Turks, Armenians or Jews. Erbil (1995) describes the case of ethnic community viewers in Germany: the largest foreign group is the Turks, with 1.9 million people and seven channels (one on cable); the Italians number 560,000 and have three channels available; the Greeks 350,000 with two channels; the Poles 260,000 with five channels; the Spaniards 135,000 with six channels (four on cable); the Japanese community has 27,000 members and can have access to a Japanese-speaking channel (JSTV) both on cable and by satellite. Despite this, Holland and Gentry (1999) caution that high levels of ethnic identification in advertising may not necessarily lead to positive responses from the targeted consumers, it depends on how the accommodation is interpreted. They suggest a model of intercultural accommodation that provides insight about how different minority groups may react to advertising.

Cross-border segments may also be based on classes of cultural affinity (section 8.4). In these groupings, consumers share similar buying habits or a common language; segments may be further divided on the basis of traditional criteria such as sociodemographics (age, sex, income, etc.). For example, a relevant segment may consist of beer drinkers in the zone of cultural affinity of Mediterranean Europe, identified by several common sociodemographic characteristics and/or by criteria linked to their consumption habits and psychographics. MTV, TNT Cartoon and Eurosport are typical media for reaching classes of cultural affinity. Alden *et al.* (1999, p. 77) gives examples of the global consumer positioning for the globally cosmopolitan segments including:

Sony ('My First Sony'), which positioned one of its products as appropriate for young people around the world; Phillips ('Let's Make Things Better'), whose advertisements explicitly feature people from different countries; and Benetton ('The United Colors of Benetton'), whose slogan emphasizes the unity of humankind.

Some market segments and advertising audiences will remain mostly domestic ones. As a consequence, they will be only slightly influenced by market globalization in Europe. Ethnic food products such as the German *Knödel* would fall into this category. Regional and local marketing have developed alongside global marketing and are able to target very precise and quite small populations through local radio stations which have emerged over the past ten years. The marketing strategy of small segments of the service industry could be supported by emerging local media, for instance for local cultural products such as sports events, shows, private tutoring, etc. When marketing at the local level, cross-border geographical segments can be designed such as a county in northern France grouped with a neighbouring county in French-speaking Belgium (Walloon).

14.5

The globalization of advertising

Agencies internationalize

Advertising agencies are nowadays largely internationalized. The largest agencies, including McCann-Erickson, Grey, Ogilvy & Mather, Euro RSCG, Saatchi and Saatchi, BBDO, Y&R Advertising, Publicis and J. Walter Thompson, have built up a network of subsidiaries covering most countries over the last 20 or 30 years. The largest advertising agency in the world, Dentsu Inc., is Japanese, while the largest Japanese agencies are now present in a growing number of countries, mostly in Asia. The Japanese advertising market is a large one: it remains very attractive to Japanese agencies, which then target South-East Asia and Australia in the first stages of their international expansion.

Large national agencies are compelled to follow the route towards the internationalization of marketing communications, media and audiences. As well as having to be able to organize cross-border campaigns for advertisers, they also try to remain knowledgeable experts on local idiosyncrasies in the implementation of marketing communication strategies. National agencies, because of limited financial resources, may acquire minority stakes in agencies in neighbouring foreign countries or may build international networks of national agencies through alliances or joint ventures. In 2003 the top four marketing organizations reported the following revenues: Omnicom Group (US$8.62 billion); WPP Group ($6.76 billion); IPG ($5.86 billion); and the French Publicis group ($4.41 billion), according to *Advertising Age*'s 60th annual *Agency Report* (Ad Age, 2004).

Relationships between advertisers and agencies

Following the internationalization of advertisers, agencies have increased their foreign operations. In large multinational corporations with diversified product lines, this can lead to a complex advertiser/agency organization. The various organizational levels (national, regional and worldwide) within both the multinational agency and the multinational advertiser must be in constant contact with each other, increasing the usual communication problems within large international organizations. Different approaches may be chosen for the organization of international marketing communication with respect to the agency/advertiser relationship (see Case A14.1). One possibility is to use just one large international advertising agency, which allows for centralization of communication; this can be implemented for each product division separately, or for large brands or for the purpose of managing the corporate image worldwide. An opposite solution is to hire local agencies that are well acquainted with local constraints as they affect media and consumers. Intermediate solutions between these two extremes attempt to find an effective trade-off between worldwide coordination and the local tailoring of advertising campaigns. Ford has decided to regionalize its brand advertising in Europe with central coordination and five sub-regional teams which adapt advertising strategy to clusters of local European markets (*Advertising Age International*, 1997).

Advertising standardization: Feasibility and desirability

After a review of arguments for and against advertising standardization worldwide, Onkvisit and Shaw (1987) conclude that a more meaningful question is whether standardized advertising should be used or not, even if it is feasible. Harvey (1993) considers the following arguments in favour of standardized advertising: (1) provides consistent image across markets; (2) avoids confusing mobile consumers; (3) may decrease the cost of preparing campaign themes, copy and materials; and (4) enables firmer control over the planning and execution of campaigns across markets. He gives a complete checklist of factors to be considered in order to assess whether the standardized approach is appropriate. These include product factors, competition, organization variables, media infrastructure, regulations and market/societal variables; some aspects of the advertising process may be standardized while others are not. The danger of this approach is that it does not distinguish desirability of standardization (which has to be assessed first) from its feasibility; he states initially that 'given the strong economic and administrative rationale it is assumed that, if possible, advertisers would prefer to standardize advertising' (Harvey, 1993, p. 58). Interestingly, Solberg (2002) surveyed 150 Norwegian exporters, finding that knowledge of the local market led to more standardization: the more they learned about local conditions the more similarities they perceived and the more they felt able to standardize the marketing mix.

Evidence from companies concerning advertising standardization shows a mixed picture. Ryans and Ratz (1987) analyzed 34 usable responses from international advertising and marketing managers. They found relatively high levels of advertising standardization for campaign themes, creative execution and media execution. Only parent company managers were interviewed and their quantitative reports (based on levels of agreement or disagreement on a rating scale) may be rather distanced from actual local decisions. An interpretive key to their findings is offered by Ryans and Ratz themselves (1987, p. 157) who observe that 'the majority of respondents thought that usage situations for their products were very similar worldwide . . . [an] explanation is that international advertising managers have adopted the position of the globalists and assume it holds true for their products'. However, it seems that advertising standardization, as reported by major international agencies, has increased over the last 30 years especially under pressure from clients (Rosenthal, 1994).

In order to determine the level of standardization, Mueller (1991) analyzed print and television campaigns for American consumer goods and services advertised in the United States and either in Germany or Japan (for which market distance with the United States is larger than for Germany). Between the United States and Germany, the highest level of advertising standardization was exhibited by Mars Candy bars, followed by Marlboro cigarettes; the lowest levels were associated with Camel cigarettes and credit cards. In the case of Japan the level of adaptation was on average much larger, signalling the more important role of market distance compared with product type. Across Chinese-speaking countries, standardization is feasible only for some strategic decisions (target segments, positioning, core themes) but cannot be used for tactical decisions such as executional style and media planning (Tai, 1997). In a medium where we might expect more standardization Ju-Pak (1999) found significant differences. Ju-Pak examined advertising on the web across the United States, the United Kingdom and South Korea. The study showed all three nations use similar creative approaches and information cues, but they were distinctly different in their creative strategy and information content, even between the United States and the United Kingdom. This illustrates that standardization even between two relatively similar countries may not be easy.

Interestingly, Backhaus *et al.* (2001) assessed the degree of standardization from the consumers' perspective. Using students from Germany, The Netherlands and France they found that the strongest influence on the perceived similarity of advertising was the picture used, followed by the general layout, advertising topic and language.

The global campaign concept

One cannot underestimate the complexity of managing an international campaign (Clark, 1987), especially in the realm of agency/advertiser relations, which are often difficult to manage even when both agency and advertiser are excellent companies. For instance, Procter & Gamble has always had a reputation as a demanding advertiser for its agencies, but also for being very loyal to them. P & G, like many large companies, has had very stable relationships (sometimes

for 40 years or more) with a group of agencies; some of them have worldwide responsibility for a product line and/or a major brand (*Advertising Age*, 1987). But the creative work is sometimes a source of conflict between major advertisers and their agencies when their views diverge as to the strategy to be followed. Most advertisers then try to adopt a democratic style, by discussing opinions, facts, data and drafts of potential advertising campaigns. The final say always comes when campaigns are actually launched and their impact on various objectives may be monitored (brand awareness, brand image, sales increase, etc.). Van Raaij (1997) adopts the view that the globalization of marketing communications is less pervasive than it seems at first sight; therefore the necessary degree of adaptation should increase over a continuum of four levels: *mission* (long term, identity and vision of the communicator), *proposition* (campaign themes), creative *concepts* (how themes are translated in the language and cultures of the target groups) and *execution*. While mission can rather easily be globalized, execution will need much local tailoring. Kanso and Nelson (2002) examined the role of American and non-American subsidiaries in designing and implementing campaigns for non-domestic markets. Their findings indicated '(1) the advertising theme should not be the same across countries; (2) even the use of similar appeals and symbols in advertising campaigns targeting foreign markets is ill advised; (3) the choice of illustrations and colours must tie well with consumers' aesthetic sense; and (4) the integration of local communication expertise is a necessity to overcome language and cultural barriers in worldwide markets' (p. 86).

The objective of a global advertising campaign has to be clearly defined: it does not seek to save on creative costs. It aims to promote a global brand name and image. Accordingly, the creative director for McCann-Erickson worldwide, Marcio Moreira, emphasizes that an advertiser should not pursue a global advertising strategy as a way of saving money, trying to achieve in only one campaign what may in fact require 12. The correct implementation of a global campaign requires a great deal of effort and creative time, and ultimately its cost may prove higher than the sum total of individual campaigns (Marcio Moreira, quoted by Hill and Winski, 1987). Dean M. Peebles (1988), who was for many years the manager of international communications for Goodyear, the world's leading tyre manufacturer, recommends the following steps for the design and implementation of a global advertising campaign:

1. Choose a large advertising agency with subsidiaries all over the world; select in this agency an international account manager, who reports to the advertiser's headquarters.
2. Establish multinational planning meetings between the client and the agency, as well as a multinational creative team.
3. Brand managers and headquarters level should conduct and supervise consumer research and the pre-tests of the draft communication.
4. The resulting draft global campaign should be sufficiently finalized in order to facilitate discussion, but flexible enough to be transposed (rather than translated) into the various cultures and lifestyles of the target audiences.

Figure 14.2 presents a flowchart of headquarters–subsidiary relations for the planning and coordination

Figure 14.2 Flowchart for the management of multinational advertising campaigns at Goodyear

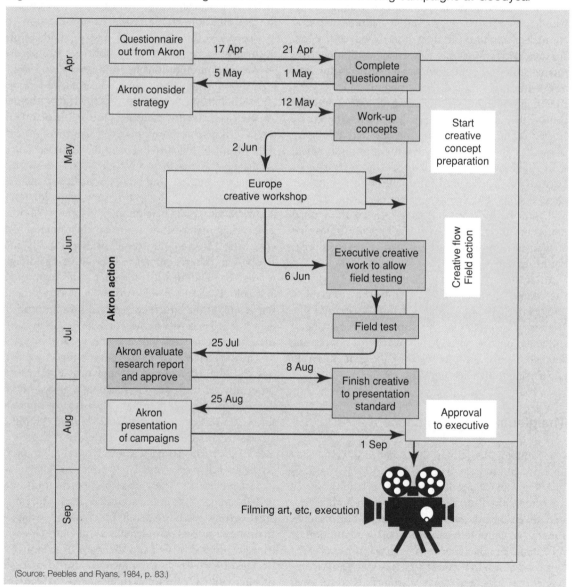

(Source: Peebles and Ryans, 1984, p. 83.)

of worldwide advertising at Goodyear. This flow-chart indicates the tasks to be performed and the (tight) time schedule imposed (Peebles and Ryans, 1984, p. 83).

Practical implementation of global advertising campaigns is not an easy task. The organization must be completely interactive and use both bottom-up and top-down communication flows. Communication between headquarters and subsidiaries should not be a 'sham' dialogue in which decisions already taken at the very top level would have to be accepted by local executives as if they were their own. This issue is all the more complex because interaction problems between various levels within the multinational advertiser (international headquarters, regional headquarters, country subsidiaries) may snowball, leading to difficulties of communication and coordination with the international agency.

Global communication is primarily intended to establish the corporate image of a company or to foster recognition of one of its major brands across a large number of countries (e.g. McDonald's, Goodyear, Michelin, Nestlé). For instance, the Subtitles campaign of IBM was introduced globally in 1995 with the aim of promoting the universality of the brand imagery of IBM. The message was that IBM delivers simple and powerful solutions anywhere, at any time and for anyone; the use of subtitles and voice-overs allowed for both a global message and a localized communication (McCullough, 1996). The next step is to advertise the products themselves, and at this point the creative input of local subsidiaries and regional headquarters, as well as their influence on the advertising strategy, is much more significant. But local campaigns, even if they advertise local products and local brand names, must be carefully coordinated so that they make a positive contribution to the global message. The core values which are conveyed by the company's corporate image (e.g. high technology, robustness, innovativeness, style, social responsibility) should also be recognizable in its brand and product advertising at the local level. Finally, communication with market segments which remain specific to certain countries should be fully delegated to the local level. Not every piece of communication can be globalized.

Questions

1. The English word 'hair' corresponds to two totally different French words: *cheveux* (of head) or *poil* (on body). Interpret the difference in concepts of what 'hair' is. What might be the consequences in terms of marketing for personal care products?

2. Describe the respective cultural adequacy of persuasive, informative and oneiric messages.

3. Why does the acceptance of comparative advertising vary cross-culturally?

4. What are the target audiences of satellite television in Europe?

5. Give examples of mores which vary cross-culturally and outline their possible consequences in terms of advertising adaptation.

6. What are the real benefits of a global advertising campaign?

7. Wella, a German giant in personal hair care, has recently decided to globalize a brand of its subsidiary Mühlens in Cologne (Germany) 4711, which is the original *Eau de Cologne* perfumed water. The 4711 brand, although well known in the German-speaking area, has an old image and *Eau de Cologne* seems to be associated in the minds of consumers in many countries with cheap perfume rather than tradition or luxury. How would you tackle this issue?

Notes

1. Saint Simon was a nineteenth-century social philosopher who advocated the view that distribution and services in general were economically unproductive activities.
2. We do not comment here about music and lyrics because it is widely used cross-nationally and necessarily borrows somewhat to local style of music while using quite often global music, ranging from classic to pop, disco, reggae, etc. Murray and Murray (1996) show for instance a small difference in frequency of music in commercials between the United States (84.5 per cent) versus the Dominican Republic (94.3 per cent). International advertisers in the Dominican republic tend to use more fast tempo/non-Latin music while domestic advertisers made a larger use of lyrics with Latin music, especially the local *merengue*.
3. See for instance the striking contrast between Ho and Sin (1986) or Stewart and Campbell (1986) and Swanson (1996, 1997).
4. For statistics on the global reach of TV channels, and media in general, see *Advertising Age International*, which regularly publishes data on satellite TV, major advertising spenders worldwide and major ad agencies.

References

Aaker, Jennifer L. and Durairaj Maheswaran (1997), 'The effect of cultural orientation on persuasion', *Journal of Consumer Research*, vol. 24, December, pp. 315–28.

Aaker, Jennifer L. and Patti Williams (1998), 'Empathy versus pride: the influence of emotional appeals across cultures', *Journal of Consumer Research*, vol. 25, no. 3, pp. 241–61.

Abernethy, Avery M. and George R. Franke (1996), 'The information content of advertising: a meta-analysis', *Journal of Advertising*, vol. 25, no. 2, pp. 1–17.

Ad Age (2004), *2004 Advertising Age Agency Income Report* (online), available at: **www.adage.com/news.cms? newsld=40256**

Ad Age Global (2002), 'Top 10 global ad markets', vol. 2 no. 8, pp. 18–20.

Advertising Age (1987), 'The house that built ivory', 20 August, pp. 26–7.

Advertising Age International (1997), 'Brand management goes regional at Ford', October, p. i2.

Agrawal, Madhu (1995), 'Review of 40-year debate in international advertising: practitioner and academician perspectives to the standardization/adaptation issue', *International Marketing Review*, vol. 12, no. 1, pp. 26–48.

Albers-Miller, Nancy D. and Betsy D. Gelb (1996), 'Business advertising as a mirror of cultural dimensions: a study of eleven countries', *Journal of Advertising*, vol. XXV, no. 4, Winter, pp. 57–70.

Alden, Dana L., Jan-Benedict E.M. Steenkamp and Rajeev Batra (1999), 'Brand positioning through advertising in Asia, North America, and Europe: the role of global consumer culture', *Journal of Marketing*, vol. 63, pp. 75–87.

Alden, Dana L., Wayne D. Hoyer and Chol Lee (1993), 'Identifying global and culture-specific dimensions of humor in advertising: a multinational analysis', *Journal of Marketing*, vol. 57, April, pp. 64–75.

Al-Makaty, Safran S., G. Norman Van Tubergen, S. Scott Whitlow and Douglas A. Boyd (1996), 'Attitudes towards advertising in Islam', *Journal of Advertising Research*, vol. 36, no. 3, pp. 16–26.

Al-Mossawi, Mohammed and Paul Michell (1992), 'The impact of cultural factors on the response of viewers to TV commercials in the Gulf countries: an empirical study', *Proceedings of the first Conference on the Cultural Dimension of International Marketing*, Odense, pp. 443–69.

Al-Olayan, Fahad S. and Kiran Karande (2000), 'A content analysis of magazine advertisements from the United States and the Arab world', *Journal of Advertising*, vol. 29, no. 3, pp. 69–82.

American Foundation for AIDS Research (2002), *Global Initiatives Mexico*, American Foundation for AIDS Research Special Reports, undated.

Andrews, J. Craig, Steven Lysonski and Srinivas Durvasula (1991), 'Understanding cross-cultural student perceptions of advertising in general: implications for advertising educators and practitioners', *Journal of Advertising*, vol. 20, no. 2, pp. 15–28.

Appelbaum, Ullrich and Chris Halliburton (1993), 'How to develop international advertising campaigns that work: the example of the European food and beverage sector', *International Journal of Advertising*, vol. 12, pp. 223–41.

Backhaus, Klaus, Katrin Mühlfeld and Jenny Van Doorn (2001), 'Consumer perspectives on standardization in international advertising: a student sample', *Journal of Advertising Research*, vol. 31, September/October, pp. 53–61.

Bates, Constance and William Renforth (1987), 'The elderly in magazine advertising: an intercountry comparison between the U.S. and Latin America', in Charles F. Keown and Arch G. Woodside (eds), *Proceedings of the Second Symposium on Cross-Cultural Consumer and Business Studies*, Honolulu, Hawaii, 14–18 December, pp. 30–3.

Bautista, Sergio Antonio, *et al.* (2003), *Costing of HIV/AIDS treatment in Mexico*, Partners for Health Reform Plus, March.

Beers, Charlotte (2002), 'Funding for public diplomacy, Statement before the Subcommittee on Commerce, Justice, and State of the House Appropriations Committee', US Department of State, online, 24 April, available at: **www.stategov/r/us/9778.htm/**.

Bigne, Enrique, Marcelo Royo and Antonio C. Cuenca (1993), 'Information content analysis of TV advertising – the Spanish case', *Proceedings of the 6th World Marketing Congress*, Istanbul, pp. 324–29.

Bjerke, Rune (1995), 'An experimental study in standardisation of Euro advertising: a beauty type as advertising presenter', unpublished PhD thesis, University of Otago, New Zealand.

Boddewyn, Jean J. (1984), 'The regulation of advertising around the world in the 1980s and beyond', in Gerald M. Hampton and Aart P. Van Gent (eds), *Marketing Aspects of International Business*, Kluwer-Nijhoff Publishing: Boston, MA, pp. 73–83.

Callow, Michael and Leon Schiffman (2002), 'Implicit meaning in visual print advertisements: a cross-cultural examination of the contextual communication effect', *International Journal of Advertising*, vol. 21, no. 2., pp. 259–77.

Cateora, Philip R. (1983), *International Marketing*, 5th edn, Richard D. Irwin: Homewood, IL.

Cevallos, Diego (2002), 'Rural women with AIDS', *Inter Press Service*, AEGIS.

Cheng, Hong and John C. Schweitzer (1996), 'Cultural values reflected in Chinese and US television commercials', *Journal of Advertising Research*, vol. 36, no. 3, pp. 27–44.

Cheng, Hong (1994), 'Reflections of cultural values: a content analysis of Chinese magazine advertisements from 1982 and 1992', *International Journal of Advertising*, vol. 13, pp. 167–83.

Chiou, Jyh-shen (2002), 'The effectiveness of different advertising message appeals in the Eastern emerging society: using Taiwanese TV commercials as an example', *International Journal of Advertising*, vol. 21, no. 2, pp. 217–36.

Clark, Harold F. Jr (1987), 'Consumer and corporate values: yet another view on global marketing', *International Journal of Advertising*, vol. 6, pp. 29–42.

Clarke, Irvine III and Earl D. Honeycutt, Jr. (2000), 'Color usage in international business-to-business print advertising', *Industrial Marketing Management*, vol. 29, pp. 255–61.

Colvin, Michael, Roger Heeler and Jim Thorpe (1980), 'Developing international advertising strategy', *Journal of Marketing*, vol. 44, Fall, pp. 73–9.

Communication et Business (1988), *Numéro 'Spécial Europe'*, no. 70, 14 March.

Country profile HIV/AIDS: Mexico, US Agency for International Development, June, 2003.

Cutler, Bob D., Edward G. Thomas and S.R. Rao (2000), 'Informational/transformational differences in usage across media types, product categories, and national cultures', *Journal of International Consumer Marketing*, vol. 12, no. 3, pp. 69–83.

Cutler, Bob D., Rajshekhar G. Javalgi and M. Krishna Erramilli (1992), 'The visual component of print advertising: a five-country cross-cultural analysis', *European Journal of Marketing*, vol. 26, no. 4, pp. 7–20.

Cutler, Bob D., Rajshekhar G. Javalgi and Dongdae Lee (1995), 'The visual component of print advertising: a five-country cross-cultural analysis', *Journal of International Consumer Marketing*, vol. 8, no. 2, pp. 45–58.

Cutler, Bob D., S. Altan Erdem and Rajshekhar G. Javalgi (1997), 'Advertiser's relative reliance on collectivism-individualism appeals: a cross-cultural study', *Journal of International Consumer Marketing*, vol. 8, no. 2, pp. 43–55.

Czinkota, Michael R. and Illka A. Ronkainen (1990), *International Marketing*, 2nd edn, Dryden Press: Hinsdale, IL.

Darley, Willam K. and Denise M. Johnson (1994), 'An exploratory investigation of beliefs towards advertising in general: a comparative analysis of four developing countries', *Journal of International Consumer Marketing*, vol. 7, no. 1, pp. 5–21.

de Grazia, Victoria (2002), 'Bush team enlists Madison Avenue in war on terror', *International Herald Tribune*, (online), 26 August, available at: **www.iht.com/**.

Di Benedetto, C. Anthony, Mariko Tamate and Rajan Chandran (1992), 'Developing creative advertising strategy for the Japanese marketplace', *Journal of Advertising Research*, vol. 32, January–February, pp. 39–48.

Douglas, Susan and Bernard Dubois (1980), 'Looking at the cultural environment for international marketing opportunities', in P. Kotler and K. Cox (eds), *Marketing Management and Strategy: A reader*, Prentice Hall: Englewood Cliffs, NJ, pp. 388–96.

Dowling, G.R. (1980), 'Information content in U.S. and Australian television advertising', *Journal of Marketing*, vol. 44, no. 4, pp. 34–7.

Dudley, James W. (1989), *1992: Strategies for the Single Market*, Kogan Page: London.

Duncan, Tom and Jyotika Ramaprasad (1995), 'Standardized multinational advertising: the influencing factors', *Journal of Advertising*, vol. 24, no. 3, Autumn, pp. 55–68.

Erbil, Kurt (1995), 'Ein Stückchen Heimat', *TV Spielfim*, vol. 10, pp. 30–1.

Gannett News Service (2002), *History of Public Diplomacy*, Gannett News Service, 14 July.

Gilly, Mary (1988), 'Sex roles in advertising: a comparison of television advertisements in Australia, Mexico, and the United States', *Journal of Marketing*, vol. 52, April, pp. 75–85.

Gregory, Gary D. and James M. Munch (1997), 'Cultural values in international advertising: an examination of familial norms and roles in Mexico', *Psychology and Marketing*, vol. 14, no. 2, pp. 99–119.

Gregory, Gary D., James M. Munch and Mark Peterson (2002), 'Attitude functions in consumer research: comparing value-attitude relations in individualist and collectivist cultures', *Journal of Business Research*, vol. 55, pp. 933–42.

Grüber, Ursula (1987), 'La communication internationale a sa langue: l'adaptation', *Revue Française du Marketing*, no. 114, 1987/4, pp. 89–96.

Ha, Louise (1997), 'Limitations and strengths of Pan-Asian advertising media: a review for international advertisers', *International Journal of Advertising*, vol. 16, no. 2, pp. 148–63.

Hall, Edward T. and Mildred Reed Hall (1989), *Understanding Cultural Differences*, Intercultural Press: Yarmouth, ME.

Han, S.-P. and S. Shavitt (1994), 'Persuasion and culture: advertising appeals in individualistic and collectivistic societies', *Journal of Experimental Social Psychology*, vol. 30, pp. 326–50.

Hanna, Nessim, Geoffrey L. Gordon and Rick E. Ridnour (1994), 'The use of humor in Japanese advertising', *Journal of International Consumer Marketing*, vol. 7, no. 1, pp. 85–106.

Harris, Shane (2003), 'Brand U.S.A.', *Government Executive Magazine*, 1 October.

Harvey, Michael G. (1993), 'Point of view: a model to determine standardization of the advertising process in international markets', *Journal of Advertising Research*, vol. 33, no. 4, pp. 57–65.

Hill, J.S. and J.M. Winski (1987), 'Goodbye, global ads', *Advertising Age*, 16 November.

Hill, John S. and William L. James (1991), 'Product and promotion transfers in consumer goods multinationals', *International Marketing Review*, vol. 8, no. 4, pp. 6–17.

Ho, Suk-ching and Yat-ming Sin (1986), 'Advertising in China: looking back at looking forward', *International Journal of Advertising*, vol. 5, pp. 307–16.

Hofstede, Geert (1991), *Culture and Organizations: Software of the mind*, McGraw-Hill: Maidenhead, Berkshire.

Holland, Jonna and James W. Gentry (1999), 'Ethic consumer reaction to targeted marketing: a theory of intercultural accommodation', *Journal of Advertising*, vol. 28, no. 1, pp. 65–77.

Hoover, Robert J., Robert T. Green and Joel Saegert (1978), 'A cross-national study of perceived risk', *Journal of Marketing*, July, pp. 102–8.

Hornik, Jacob (1980), 'Comparative evaluation of international and national advertising strategies', *Columbia Journal of World Business*, vol. 15, no. 1, pp. 36–45.

Huang, Jen-Hung (1993), 'Color in US and Taiwanese industrial advertising', *Industrial Marketing Management*, vol. 22, pp. 195–8.

Huang, Jen-Hung (1995), 'National character and sex roles in advertising', *Journal of International Consumer Marketing*, vol. 7, no. 4, pp. 81–96.

Hung, Kineta and Marshall D. Rice (1995), 'A comparative examination of the perception of ad meanings in Hong Kong and Canada', in Scott M. Smith (ed.), *Proceedings of the 5th Symposium on Cross-Cultural Consumer and Business Studies*, Brigham Young University: Provo, UT, pp. 262–6.

Huth, Sabine and Fritz Unger (1988), 'Eine vergleichende Untersuchung zur humorvollen Werbung: BRD vs. USA', *Planung und Analyse*, vol. 5, pp. 197–200.

James, Karen E. and Paul J. Hensel (1991), 'Negative advertising: the malicious strain of comparative advertising', *Journal of Advertising*, vol. 20, no. 2, pp. 53–67.

Javalgi, Rajshekhar, Bob D. Cutler and Naresh K. Malhotra (1995), 'Print advertising at the component level: a cross-cultural comparison of the United States and Japan', *Journal of Business Research*, vol. 34, pp. 117–24.

Jeon, Jung Ok and Sharon E. Beatty (2002), 'Comparative advertising effectiveness in different national cultures', *Journal of Business Research*, vol. 55, no. 11, pp. 907–13.

Johnstone, Harvey, Erdener Kaynak and Richard M. Sparkman, Jr. (1987), 'A cross-cultural/cross-national study of the information content of television advertisements', *International Journal of Advertising*, vol. 6, pp. 223–36.

Jordan Times (2002), 'Lebanon bans TV spots aimed at improving U.S. image', *Jordan Times*, 20 December, available at: www.aljazeerah.info/.

Ju-Pak, Kuen-Hee (1999), 'Content dimensions of Web advertising: a cross-national comparison', *International Journal of Advertising*, vol. 18, no. 2, pp. 207–31.

Kale, Sudhir H. (1991), 'Culture-specific marketing communications: an analytical approach', *International Marketing Review*, vol. 8, no. 2, pp. 19–30.

Kanso, Ali and Richard Alan Nelson (2002), 'Advertising localisation overshadows standarization', *Journal of Advertising Research*, vol. 42, no. 1, pp. 79–89.

Kashani, Kamran (1989), 'Beware the pitfalls of global marketing', *Harvard Business Review*, September–October, pp. 91–8.

Kassaye, W. Wossen (1997), 'Global advertising and the World Wide Web', *Business Horizons*, vol. 40, no. 3, pp. 33–42.

Katz, Helen and Wei-Na Lee (1992), 'Oceans apart: an initial exploration of social communication differences in US and UK prime-time television advertising', *International Journal of Advertising*, vol. 11, pp. 69–82.

Kaynak, Erdener and Pervez N. Ghauri (1986), 'A comparative analysis of advertising practices in unlike environments: a study of agency–client relationships', *International Journal of Advertising*, vol. 5, pp. 121–46.

Keown, Charles F., Lawrence W. Jacobs, Richard W. Schmidt and Kyung-Il Ghymn (1992), 'Information content in advertising in the United States, Japan, South Korea, and the People's Republic of China', *International Journal of Advertising*, vol. 11, pp. 257–67.

Kishii, T. (1988), 'Message vs. mood: a look at some of the differences between Japanese and Western television commercials', *Dentsu Japan Marketing/Advertising Yearbook*, Dentsu: Tokyo.

Klein, Naomi (2002), 'Brand USA', *Alternet.org* (online), 13 March, available at: **www.altnet.org/story.html? StoryID=12617.**

Koudelova, Radka and Jeryl Whitelock (2001), 'A cross-cultural analysis of television advertising in the UK and Czech Republic', *International Marketing Review*, vol. 18, no. 3, pp. 286–300.

Kroeber-Riel, Werner (1992), 'Globalisierung der Euro-Werbung. Ein konzeptioneller Ansatz der Konsumentenforschung', *Marketing ZFP*, vol. 14, no. 4, pp. 261–7.

Leonard, Mark (2002), 'Velvet fist in an iron glove', *Observer*, (online), 16 June, available at: **http://observes.guardian. is.uk/comment/story/0,,738515,00.htm**

Liang, Kong and Laurence Jacobs (1994), 'China's advertising agencies: problems and relations', *International Journal of Advertising*, vol. 13, pp. 205–15.

Lin, Carolyn A. (1993), 'Cultural differences in message strategies: a comparison between American and Japanese TV commercials', *Journal of Advertising Research*, vol. 33, no. 4, pp. 40–8.

Lin, Carolyn A. (2001), 'Cultural values reflected in Chinese and American television advertising', *Journal of Advertising*, vol. 30, no. 4, pp. 83–94.

Lin, Carolyn A. and Michael B. Salwen (1995), 'Product information strategies of American and Japanese television advertisements', *International Journal of Advertising*, vol. 14, pp. 55–64.

Luqmani, Mushtag, Ugur Yavas and Zahir Quraeshi (1988), 'Advertising in Saudi Arabia: content and regulation', *International Marketing Review*, vol. 6, no. 1, pp. 59–71.

Luna, David and Laura A. Peracchio (2001), 'Moderators of language effects in advertising to bilinguals: A psycholinguistic approach', *Journal of Consumer Research*, 28, September, pp. 284–95.

Mariet, François (1990), *La Télévision Américaine*, Editions Economica: Paris.

Martenson, Rita (1987), 'Advertising strategies and information content in American and Swedish advertising: a comparative content analysis in cross-cultural copy research', *International Journal of Advertising*, vol. 6, pp. 133–44.

McCullough, Lynette S. and Ronald E. Taylor (1993), 'Humor in American, British and German ads', *Industrial Marketing Management*, vol. 22, pp. 17–28.

McCullough, Wayne R. (1996), 'Global advertising which acts locally: the IBM subtitles campaign', *Journal of Advertising Research*, vol. 36, no. 3, pp. 11–15.

McLeod, Douglas M. and Motoko Kunita (1994), 'A comparative analysis of the use of corporate advertising in the United States and Japan', *International Journal of Advertising*, vol. 13, pp. 137–52.

Mexico Child Link (2003), *Mexico Street Children Statistics*, Mexico Child Link, undated.

Miller, Fred and A. Hamdi Demirel (1988), 'Efes pilsen in the Turkish beer market: marketing consumer goods in developing countries', *International Marketing Review*, vol. 5, Spring, pp. 7–19.

Mourier, Pascal and Didier Burgaud (1989), *Euromarketing*, Editions d'Organisation: Paris.

Mueller, Barbara (1987), 'Reflections of culture: an analysis of Japanese and American advertising appeals', *Journal of Advertising Research*, vol. 27, no. 3, pp. 51–9.

Mueller, Barbara (1991), 'Multinational advertising: factors influencing the standardised vs. specialised approach', *International Marketing Review*, vol. 8, no. 1, pp. 7–18.

Mueller, Barbara (1992), 'Standardization vs. specialization: an examination of westernization in Japanese advertising', *Journal of Advertising Research*, vol. 32, January–February, pp. 15–23.

Murray, Noel M. and Sandra B. Murray (1996), 'Music and lyrics in commercials: a cross-cultural comparison between commercials run in the Dominican Republic and the United States', *Journal of Advertising*, vol. XXV, no. 2, Summer, pp. 51–63.

Neelankavil, James P., Venkatapparao Mummalaneni and David N. Sessions (1995), 'Use of foreign language and models in print advertisements in east Asian countries: a logit modelling approach', *European Journal of Marketing*, vol. 26, no. 4, pp. 24–38.

NewsHour Media Unit (2003), 'Undersecretary Charlotte Beers interviewed by Terence Smith', *NewsHour*, Public Broadcasting Service, January.

Odekerken-Schroder, Gaby, Kristof De Wulf and Natascha Hofstee (2002), 'Is gender stereotyping in advertising more prevalent in masculine countries? A cross-national analysis', *International Marketing Review*, vol. 19, no. 4, pp. 408–19.

Onkvisit, Sak and John J. Shaw (1987), 'Standardized international advertising: a review and critical evaluation of the theoretical and empirical evidence', *Columbia Journal of World Business*, Fall, pp. 43–55.

Orris, Michelle (2003), 'White House: better PR can reverse anti-American sentiment', *Austin American Statesman*, 1 August.

Pechmann, Cornelia and Chuan-Fong Shih (1999), 'Smoking scenes in movies and antismoking advertisements before movies: effects on youth', *Journal of Marketing*, vol. 63, no. 3, pp. 1–13.

Peebles, Dean M. (1988), 'Don't write-off global advertising: a commentary', *International Marketing Review*, vol. 6, no. 1, pp. 73–8.

Peebles, Dean M. and John K. Ryans (1984), *Management of International Advertising*, Allyn and Bacon: Boston, MA.

Perlez, Jane (2002), 'Muslim as apple pie video greeted with scepticism', *New York Times* (online), 30 October.

Pornpitakpan, Chantikha and June N.P. Francis (2001), 'The effect of cultural differences, source expertise, and argument strength on persuasion: an experiment with canadians and Thais', *Journal of International Consumer Marketing*, vol. 13, no. 1, pp. 77–101.

Prendergast, Gerard, Leung Kwok Yan, and Douglas C. West (2002), 'Role portrayal in advertising and editorial content, and eating disorders: an Asian perspective', *International Journal of Advertising*, vol. 21, no. 2, pp. 237–58.

Public Broadcasting Service (2003), *NOW with Bill Moyers, Politics and Economics*, 31 January.

Quester, Pascale (1999), 'A cross-cultural study of juvenile response to anti-smoking advertisements', *Journal of Euro-marketing*, vol. 7, no. 2, pp. 29–46.

Reader's Digest (1987), 40th anniversary special edition, *Sélection du Reader's Digest*, Paris.

Reinhard, K. and W.E. Phillips (1985), 'Global marketing: experts look at both sides', *Advertising Age*, vol. 56, no. 15, p. 46.

Renforth, W. and S. Raveed (1983), 'Consumer information cues in television advertising: a cross country analysis', *Journal of the Academy of Marketing Science*, vol. 11, no. 3, pp. 216–25.

Resnik, Alan J. and Bruce L. Stern (1977), 'An analysis of information content in television advertising', *Journal of Marketing*, vol. 44, no. 1, pp. 50–3.

Ricks, David A., Jeffrey S. Arpan and Marilyn Y. Fu (1979), 'Pitfalls in overseas advertising', *Journal of Advertising Research*, reprinted in S. Watson Dunn and E.S. Lorimer (eds), *International Advertising and Marketing*, Grid: Columbus, OH, pp. 87–93.

Rose, Gregory M., Lynn R. Kahle and Fredric G. Kropp (1993), 'A woman's place is in the home: a cross-cultural analysis of attitudes towards women', in Gerald Albaum *et al.* (eds), *Proceedings of the 4th Symposium on Cross-Cultural Consumer and Business Studies*, University of Hawaii, pp. 213–17.

Rosenshine, Allen (2002), 'Selling America to people who hate it', *Advertising Age*, 18 February.

Rosenthal, Walter (1994), 'Standardized international advertising: a view from the agency side', *Journal of International Consumer Marketing*, vol. 7, no. 1, pp. 39–62.

Ryans, John K. and David G. Ratz (1987), 'Advertising standardization: a re-examination', *International Journal of Advertising*, vol. 6, pp. 145–58.

Sarathy, Ravi (1991), 'European integration and global strategy in the media and entertainment industry', in Alan M. Rugman and Alain Verbeke (eds), *Global Competition and the European Community*, vol. 2, JAI Press: Greenwich, CT, pp. 125–48.

Satloff, Robert (2003), 'How to win friends and influence Arabs', *Weekly Standard*, 18 August.

Schroeder, Michael (1991), 'France-Allemagne: la publicité. L'existence de deux logiques de communication', *Recherche et Applications en Marketing*, vol. 6, no. 3, pp. 97–109.

Seiminski, Gregory C. (1995), 'The art of naming operations', *Parameters*, Autumn 1995, pp. 81–98.

Sherry, John F. jr. and Eduardo G. Camargo (1987), '"May your life be marvelous": English language labelling and the semiotics of Japanese promotion', *Journal of Consumer Research*, vol. 14, September, pp. 174–88.

Siu, Wai-Sum (1996), 'Gender portrayal in Hong Kong and Singapore television advertisements', *Journal of Asian Business*, vol. 12, no. 3, pp. 47–61.

Snyder, Leslie B., Bartjan Willenborg and James Watt (1991), 'Advertising and cross-cultural convergence in Europe, 1953–1989', *European Journal of Communication*, vol. 6, pp. 441–68.

Solberg, Carl Arthur (2002), 'The perennial issue of adaptation or standardization of international marketing communication: Organizational contingencies and performance', *Journal of International Marketing*, vol. 10, no. 3, pp. 1–21.

Solomon, Norman (2002), *Branding New and Improved Wars*, Fairness and Accuracy In Reporting (FAIR), 29 October.

Somasundaram, T.N. and C. David Light (1994), 'Rethinking a global media strategy: a four country comparison of young adults' perceptions of media-specific advertising', *Journal of International Consumer Marketing*, vol. 7, no. 1, pp. 23–38.

Sriram, Ven and Pradeep Gopalakrishna (1991), 'Can advertising be standardized among similar countries? A cluster-based analysis', *International Journal of Advertising*, vol. 10, pp. 137–40.

Stern, Bruce W. and Alan J. Resnik (1991), 'Information content in advertising: a replication and extension', *Journal of Advertising Research*, vol. 31, no. 3, pp. 36–46.

Stewart, Sally and Nigel Campbell (1986), 'Advertising in mainland China: a preliminary study', *International Journal of Advertising*, vol. 5, pp. 317–23.

Suls, J. (1983), 'Cognitive processes in humour appreciation', in J. Goldstein (ed.), *Handbook of Humour Research*, Springer: New York, pp. 39–57.

Swanson, Lauren A. (1996), 'People's advertising in China: a longitudinal content analysis of the *People's Daily* since 1949', *International Journal of Advertising*, vol. 15, pp. 222–38.

Swanson, Lauren A. (1997), 'China myths and advertising agencies', *International Journal of Advertising*, vol. 16, no. 4, pp. 277–83.

Sylvester, Rachel (2003), '*Brand USA* campaign attempts to win over UK', *The Age* (Australia), 25 January.

Tai, Susan H.C. (1997), 'Advertising in Asia: Localize or regionalize', *International Journal of Advertising*, vol. 16, no. 1, pp. 48–61.

Tan, Thomas Tsu Wee, Lee Boon Ling and Eleanor Phua Cheay Thengh (2002), 'Gender-role portrayals in Malaysian and Singaporean television commercials: an international advertising perspective', *Journal of Business Research*, vol. 55, pp. 853–61.

Tansey, Richard, Michael R. Hyman and George M. Zinkhan (1990), 'Cultural themes in Brazilian and U.S. auto ads: a cross-cultural comparison', *Journal of Advertising*, vol. 19, no. 2, pp. 30–9.

Teinowitz, Ira (2002), 'Charlotte Beers and the selling of America', *Advertising Age*, 23 September.

Teinowitz, Ira (2003), 'Charlotte Beers to resign from State Department', *Advertising Age*, 3 March.

Tixier, Maud (1992), 'Comparison of the linguistic message in advertisements according to the criteria of effective writing', *International Journal of Advertising*, vol. 11, pp. 139–55.

Toffoli, Roy and Michel Laroche (2002), 'Cultural and language effects on Chinese bilinguals' and Canadians' responses to advertising', *International Journal of Advertising*, vol. 21, pp. 505–34.

Tse, David K., Russell W. Belk and Nan Zhou (1989), 'Becoming a consumer society: a longitudinal and cross-cultural content analysis of print ads from Hong King, the People's Republic of China, and Taiwan', *Journal of Consumer Research*, vol. 15, March, pp. 457–71.

Tuncalp, Secil (1992), 'The audio-visual media in Saudi Arabia: problems and prospects', *International Journal of Advertising*, vol. 11, pp. 119–30.

Tuncalp, Secil (1994), 'Outdoor media planning in Saudi Arabia', *Marketing and Research Today*, vol. 22, no. 2, May, pp. 146–54.

UNAIDS (2002), *Global HIV/AIDS and STD Surveillance*, Epidemological fact sheets, UNAIDS and WHO, undated.

Unger, Lynette S. (1995), 'A cross-cultural study on the affect-based model of humor in advertising', *Journal of Advertising Research*, vol. 35, no. 1, January–February, pp. 66–71.

Usdin, S. (2001), 'Soul City', *Urban Health and Development Bulletin*, Medical Research Council of South Africa, vol. 3, no. 2, June, 2000.

Van Raaij, W. Fred (1997), 'Globalisation of marketing communications', *Journal of Economic Psychology*, vol. 18, pp. 259–70.

Wafai, Mohamed and Jehan El-Tigi (1994), 'Selling beyond belief – how to use advertising to promote non-traditional concepts', *Marketing and Research Today*, vol. 22, no. 2, May, pp. 128–38.

Walle, A.H. (1997), 'Global behaviour, unique responses: consumption within cultural frameworks', *Management Decision*, vol. 35, no. 10, pp. 700–8.

Waller, David S. and Michael Jay Polonsky (1999), 'Student attitudes towards political advertising and issues: a cross-cultural study', *Journal of International Consumer Marketing*, vol. 11, no. 2, pp. 79–98.

Wang, Gheng Lu and Allan K.K. Chan (2001), 'A content analysis of connectedness vs. separateness themes used in US and PRC print advertisements', *International Marketing Review*, vol. 18, no. 2, pp. 145–59.

Ward, James W. and Jim McQuirk (1987), 'Information content in television advertising: Ireland, United States and Australia', in C.F. Keown and A.G. Woodside (eds), *Proceedings of the Second Symposium on Cross-Cultural Consumer and Business Studies*, Honolulu, Hawaii, 14–18 December, pp. 37–40.

Wee, Chow Hou, Mei-Lan Choong and Siok-Kuan Tambyah (1995), 'Sex role portrayal in television advertising. A comparative study of Singapore and Malaysia', *International Marketing Review*, vol. 12, no. 1, pp. 49–64.

Weinberger, Marc G. and Harlan E. Spotts (1989a), 'A situational view of information content in TV advertising in the U.S. and U.K.', *Journal of Marketing*, vol. 53, no. 1, pp. 89–94.

Weinberger, Marc G. and Harlan E. Spotts (1989b), 'Humour in U.S. versus U.K. TV commercials: a comparison', *Journal of Advertising*, vol. 18, no. 2, pp. 39–44.

Weiser, Carl (2003), *U.S. losing battle worldwide on public relations front*, Gannett News Service, 31 March.

Wells, Robert A. (2002), 'Mobilizing public support for war: An analysis of American propaganda During World War I', paper presented at the Annual Meeting of the International Studies Association, 24–27 March.

West, Douglas C. (1993), 'Cross-national creative personalities, processes, and agency philosophies', *Journal of Advertising Research*, vol. 33, no. 5, September–October, pp. 53–62.

Wiles, Charles R. and Anders Tjernlund (1991), 'A comparison of role portrayal of men and women in magazine advertising in the USA and Sweden', *International Journal of Advertising*, vol. 10, no. 3, pp. 259–67.

Wiles, Charles R., Judith A. Wiles and Anders Tjernlund (1996), 'The Ideology of advertising: the United States and Sweden', *Journal of Advertising Research*, vol. 36, no. 3, pp. 57–66.

Wiles, Judith A., Charles R. Wiles and Anders Tjernlund (1995), 'A comparison of gender role portrayals in magazine advertising: the Netherlands, Sweden and the USA', *European Journal of Marketing*, vol. 29, no. 11, 35–49.

Wills, James R. and John K. Ryans Jr (1982), 'Attitudes toward advertising: a multinational study', *Journal of International Business Studies*, Winter, pp. 121–41.

World Health Organization (2002), *Infectious Diseases Report 2002*, World Health Organization, available at: **www.who.int/infectious-disease-report/2002/**.

Yeung, Kevin and K.F. Lau (1993), 'Gender role stereotyping in print advertisements: a comparison of Hong Kong, Taiwan and Japan', in Gerald Albaum *et al.* (eds), *Proceedings of the 4th Symposium on Cross-Cultural Consumer and Business Studies*, University of Hawaii, pp. 225–31.

Zandpour, Fred and Katrin Harich (1996), 'Think and feel country clusters: a new approach to international advertising standardization', *International Journal of Advertising*, vol. 15, no. 4, pp. 325–44.

Zandpour, Fred, Cypress Chang and Joelle Catalano (1992), 'Stories, symbols and straight talk: a comparative analysis of French, Taiwanese and U.S. TV commercials', *Journal of Advertising Research*, vol. 32, January–February, pp. 25–37.

Zhang, Yong and Betsy D. Gelb (1996), 'Matching advertising appeals to culture: the influence of products' use conditions', *Journal of Advertising*, vol. XXV, no. 4, Winter, pp. 29–40.

Zhang, Yong and James P. Neelankavil (1997), 'The influence of culture on advertising effectiveness in China and the USA: a cross-cultural study', *European Journal of Marketing*, vol. 31, no. 2, pp. 134–49.

Zhou, Nan and Russell W. Belk (1993), 'China's advertising and the export marketing learning curve', *Journal of Advertising Research*, vol. 33, no. 6, November–December, pp. 50–66.

Zhou, Dongsheng, Weijiong Zhang and Ilan Vertinsky (2002), 'Advertising trends in urban China', *Journal of Advertising Research*, vol. 42, May/Jane, pp. 73–81.

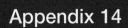

Appendix 14

Teaching materials

A14.1 Case

BrandUSA – Selling Uncle Sam like Uncle Ben's

'One does not need to destroy one's enemy, one need only destroy his willingness to engage,' wrote the ancient Chinese strategist Sun Tzu, as quoted on the US Psychological Operations Veterans Association website (**www.psyop.com**). Using this rationale, nations throughout history have attempted to persuade potential adversaries of the justness of their cause, the certainty of their victory, or the reasons for war that do not justify the death and destruction it would cause. Although written more than 2,500 years ago, Sun Tzu's thoughts are strikingly relevant in a world ever more dependent on the mass media for information.

It appears that the US government adopted Sun Tzu's rationale in the wake of the terrorist attacks of 11 September 2001, when it appointed Charlotte Beers as undersecretary of state for public diplomacy and public affairs (State Department). Charlotte Beers, the 'Queen of Branding', formerly chairperson of J. Walter Thompson Worldwide and executive at Ogilvy Mather, architect of brands ranging from IBM to top dog food and credit card brands (Klein, 2002).

When facing criticism for filling the post with someone lacking diplomatic experience, Colin Powell personally defended Beers by crediting her advertising skills for his preference for Uncle Ben's brand rice. These were exactly the sales skills he thought useful in selling American policies worldwide, thereby lessening the well-documented hatred of the United States (Sylvester, 2003). The US Congress apparently agreed, granting a congressional appropriation of US$520 million for Beers' projects (de Grazia, 2002). Upon announcing her appointment, Colin Powell advocated that the United States must change from 'selling U.S. . . . to really branding foreign policy' (Teinowitz, 2002).

Allen Rosenshine, Chairman-CEO of agency BBDO Worldwide, expressed his views about Charlotte Beers' appointment thus: branding precepts are just as appropriate for the American government as they are for commercial purposes because they may be effective in persuading people who 'hate' America to respect America's social, economic and political systems. The theory is that branding creates a psychological bond between user and product that enhances the value of that product. In the same manner, branding a country can create 'something people can value and aspire to with their minds and hearts' (Rosenshine, 2002). Naomi Klein deconstructed the prevailing branding emphasis in government in her article 'Brand USA' (Klein, 2002).

Beers was to hinge her campaigns on the underlying belief that Americans and foreign Muslims share fundamental values – home, family and religion – and interests like pop music and sports (Satloff, 2003). The most public face of her work at the State Department was the US$15 million 'Shared values' campaign, designed by McCann-Erickson. According to a State Department official interviewed by the *New York Times*, the target audience for the advertising campaign was the 'non-elite', in 'disaffected countries', aged 15–59 years (Perlez, 2002). The ads were based on focus group research among Muslim Americans, resulting in a film of American Muslims, including a teacher, a broadcasting student, a paramedic and a banker, each speaking of the goodwill and respect for Islam they experienced from Americans (listen to video clips at: **www.opendialogue.org/english/bios.html**). The video was aired during Ramadan 2002 in several Arab countries, then pulled due to criticism and the reticence of the Lebanese government to allow the ad on government-owned television stations concerned that the video constituted propaganda (*Jordan Times*, 2002).

The campaign was part of an effort to address the perceived misperception of the USA. Beers stated in a television interview that Muslims view the United States as 'anti-Islam' and not a fitting environment for Muslims to live and work (NewsHour Media Unit, 2003). She told Congress members that 'a poor perception of the US leads to unrest, and unrest has proven to be a threat to our national and international security' (Beers, 2002). Her job was publicly perceived as an effort to explain the foreign policy of the Bush administration, particularly the 'war on terrorism' to the world (de Grazia, 2002). In a speech, Beers cited a February 2002 Gallup poll of nine predominantly Muslim countries, where less than 50 per cent of the population expressed a favourable view of the USA. In the case of Kuwait, Morocco and Saudi Arabia, the number expressing a favourable opinion was 28 per cent, 22 per cent, and 18 per cent respectively (Beers, 2002). A number of misconceptions in the so-called 'Arab Street' were also to be addressed, such as the belief held by some that Israel planned the terrorist attacks of September 11.

In support of the 'Shared Values' campaign, a website was launched along the lines of the video (**www.opendialogue.org**), and video characters were made available for satellite interviews. Beers' team produced a booklet on the September 11 terrorist attacks, replete with photos and Ossama Bin Laden's own admissions regarding the attacks in 1.3 million copies and 36 languages, distributed in predominantly Muslim countries, and notably as a supplement in Arab *Newsweek* (Beers, 2002).

In December, 2002, Beers re-branded the US government-controlled Voice of America (VOA) Arabic radio station as Radio Sawa (**www.radiosawa.com**), broadcasting so-called '*pop*oganda', complete with Western and Arab pop music and zippy news bulletins instead of the usual VOA fare (Leonard, 2002). The initial success was such that the station's cross-cultural and news format were quickly copied by the army of Jordan, and other Arab countries (Leonard, 2002). The State Department also launched similar Radio Farda, in the Farsi language. Radio Sawa was an attempt to win the ears and hearts of those who would otherwise get their news from Al-Jazeera (**www.english.aljazeera.net**) or, in the case of Iraq, from Iranian radio stations (Harris, 2003). In a similar effort, on a more traditional bent, Beers expanded the almost defunct US educational and cultural exchanges. She also started a program to disseminate pro-American films and programming materials to Arab countries, and provided American spokespeople to work with foreign television stations to produce programming that showcases US aid to their country. She was quick to locate speakers who could rebut foreign media attacks on the United States, most notably in the case of former US ambassador to Syria, Arabic-speaking Chris Ross, whom she sent frequently to speak on the pan-Arab network Al-Jazeera.

The US government is conscious that effective branding is also necessary in the military. According to Army Chief of Public Affairs, Major General Charles McClain, the perception of a military operation can be as important to its success as the execution itself (Soloman, 2002). Since the 1980s, military operations have been named self-consciously to please various audiences, in contrast with earlier names such as 'Operation Killer' in Korea or 'Operation Paperclip' in the Second World War (Table 14.1).

Table 14.1 Names of prominent US military operations and military/humanitarian operations conducted by the military that reflect a branding emphasis

Date and location	Name of operation reflecting branding emphasis
1987–1988 – Persian Gulf	Earnest Will
1989–1990 – Panama	Just Cause
1991 – Gulf War phases I and II	Desert Shield/Desert Storm
1991–1996 – Northern Iraq	Provide Comfort
1998 – Sudan and Afghanistan	Infinite Reach
2001 – Afghanistan 'War against Terrorism'	Infinite Justice (oops) name hastily changed after Muslim advisors warn that only Allah is 'infinite'
2001 – Afghanistan	Enduring Freedom

(Source: Norman Solomon (2002) in Fairness and Accuracy in Reporting (FAIR) and Gregory Seiminski (1995).)

During the past century, there were two government offices dedicated to swaying opinions on war at home and abroad. The first, The Committee on Public Information, was founded at the behest of President Woodrow Wilson during the First World War. J. Walter Thompson executives used pamphlets to convince German soldiers on the Western Front that their defeat was inevitable (Wells, 2002). (To view leaflets used in the recent Iraq conflict, go to **www.centcom.mil/galleries/leaflets/showleaflets.asp.**) In the Second World War, the US Government called its wartime propaganda a 'strategy of truth' executed by The Office of Strategic Services for American allies and others. The war was portrayed in leaflets, press releases and short films as a battle between Good and Evil (Public Broadcasting Service, 2003). The Foreign Information Service broadcast news in Europe and Asia to counter the war-time propaganda run by other governments, a service called Voice of America, the precursor of today's service of the same name (Gannet News Service, 2002). J. Walter Thompson continued to advise the government on the Marshall Plan, and was subsequently assigned to communications for NATO (de Grazia, 2002). Throughout the Cold War the United States Information Agency and Radio Free Europe continued working towards the mission of understanding and influencing international public opinion – an effort culminating in the hiring of Charlotte Beers. The effort to influence the attitudes of the general public (as opposed to diplomats) in other countries is termed 'public diplomacy'. According to Harold Pachios, chair of the Advisory Commission on Public Diplomacy, public diplomacy is more important than the traditional type practiced between diplomats because all governments (whether allies of the United States or not) are sensitive to domestic public opinion regarding their stance relative to American policies (Weiser, 2003). (For more on public diplomacy visit **www.publicdiplomacy.org/.**)

Public diplomacy activities receive a budget of US$1 billion per year. Those who believe the USA faces a public relations problem in dealing with the world are advocating for more money. Richard Lugar, chair of the Senate Foreign Relations Committee stated that for each dollar spent on the US military, seven cents are spent on diplomacy and one quarter of a cent is spent on public diplomacy (Weiser, 2003). Some believe that rising hostility towards the United States may be a consequence of the cuts to the US$70 million spent after the 11 September 2001 attacks on US-sponsored international news services (Orris, 2003). Like a marketing-minded company, the State Department's International Information Programs monitors the reaction of foreign media to US-influenced international issues (**http://usinfo.state.gov/products/medreac.htm**). The State Department then works to correct any perceived misconceptions or biases in international media. Most other public relations efforts are carried out as in any commercial communications program; however there is lack of coordination between the different functions within the State Department, according to former US Information Agency comptroller Stan Silverman. Silverman also stated his belief that advertising agency tactics, like those used by Charlotte Beers in her public diplomacy campaigns, are too 'simplistic' for other cultures (Orris, 2003).

Since 11 September 2001, American politicians believe that hatred for the USA may come from envy, or perhaps ignorance of what their country represents. As a possible expression of that belief, September 11 is now known as 'Patriot Day' (go to **www.hallmark.com** and click on 'browse free e-cards' to view expressions of 'Patriot Day' sentiment). However, as Naomi Klein pointed out in her article 'Brand USA', children around the world are all too familiar with America's perceived high ground in terms of 'liberty and justice for all'. Hollywood has beamed American films and television programming all over the world, while CNN and other news sources disseminate the American perspective on reality. Therefore non-Americans are well versed in American values, however they are angry about the incompatibility of these stated values and United States' actual foreign policy on the Israel–Palestine conflict, Iraq and many others. Charlotte Beers resigned in March, 2003 due to health reasons (Teinowitz, 2003). As American popularity plummeted around the world and analysts and politicians argued over the best approach to public diplomacy, the department sought a new direction. Beers and her 'Shared Values' campaign may have clearly communicated that the USA is a good country for Muslims to live in. Her perception that the problems between the world and the USA are simply image or branding-related problems were likely too simplistic: as with any advertised product, the world is waiting for a foreign policy 'product' consistent with advertised American values like freedom, justice and equality. The search for a solution to the American public diplomacy problem has become urgent: a Pew Research Center study found that evaluations of the USA in 20 countries and the Palestinian Authority are markedly lower than a year previously. In only seven countries did a majority of people express a favourable opinion of the United States, of which the leader was Israel with 79 per cent approval ratings. In seven out of eight Muslim countries, the majority of people believe that the United States is a military threat to their nation.

Following the replacement of Charlotte Beers by Margaret Tutwiler towards the end of 2003, there was much speculation as to the future of 'Brand USA'. Tutwiler, a former ambassador and State Department Assistant Secretary for Public Affairs under the first President Bush, was widely thought to be less brand-oriented than Beers. Public diplomacy continued, however, with Middle East Television Network (MTN) planned for launch in December 2003 to 'End the deafening silence from America'. Also continuing were other targeted communications efforts including *Hi* magazine, a glossy youth-oriented magazine that attempts to focus on lifestyle and avoid politics altogether (Harris, 2003). The magazine's Arabic-only website offers interactive boxes for readers to 'Ask America' questions, in the spirit of promoting dialogue (**www.himag.com**). MTN, a 24-hour news nemesis of Al-Jazeera is designed to work harder than Fox or CNN to 'discredit' the perceived anti-American stance of Arab news networks. The network has been outsourced to an independent media company by the State Department, with the mission to 'Sell America' in the crowded media markets of the Middle East (Harris, 2003).

Questions

1. It is often said that marketing is about discovering what target audiences want and making it available. Consider what the United States could 'offer' to its 'target audiences', giving three examples of possible audiences.

2. Is it ethical for political leaders to use marketing strategies to persuade a nation to go to war, and to persuade others, including the enemy, that the war is going well?

3. Should a government market itself across cultures like Coca-Cola or Nike have done?

4. Is it likely that the Bush Administration, in constructing branded communications, may have increased loathing and distrust in the Arab world?

5. What is the difference between diplomacy and propaganda?

Saskia Faulk and Jean-Claude Usunier prepared this case solely to provide material for class discussion. The authors do not intend to illustrate either effective or ineffective handling of a business situation. The authors may have disguised certain names and other identifying information to protect confidentiality.

(©IUMI, reprinted with kind permission.)

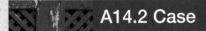

A14.2 Case

Excel and the Italian advertising campaign

Excel is a multinational company, based in northern Europe, which produces television sets, video recorders and other consumer electronics. In the 1980s it went through a phase of external growth by the take-over of the German and French subsidiaries of a large US-based company that had decided to divest itself of this industry. Within two years this Nordic company tripled in size. It changed from having a mainly Scandinavian base to having a complete European spread, with an 11 per cent share of the European market. The group, built in successive layers, inherited numerous local brands, namely those of the companies taken over. These brands are basically localized marketing assets, with only national coverage and brand recognition. Excel plans to have only one pan-European brand in the long run, with one local brand for each individual country.

The European headquarters were installed in Switzerland, near Lausanne. This location was chosen so that headquarters would be situated in central Europe but not in a country where Excel already had a plant, as this might imply some sort of 'national preference'. Over a period of two years an important reshaping of the industrial base was undertaken, with massive lay-offs in some plants and industrial investment aimed at increasing productivity.

Excel wanted to minimize advertising expenses while simultaneously giving its brand a strong, similar image across Europe. In fact it inherited some very diverse brand names, which were those of the companies most recently acquired in their home markets. Excel was therefore willing to design a pan-European advertising campaign. The national subsidiaries were invited either to join this campaign or to design their own campaign. In the latter case, they would have to finance it with their own money. The campaign was scheduled for autumn 1990. Because of the World Cup which was taking place in Italy in June 1990, the Italian subsidiary decided that it could not wait until the autumn, as this type of sports event usually generates increased demand for television sets and video recorders. They managed to go ahead by themselves: they made an advertisement which proved to be a real hit and generated a significant sales increase. A television commercial was created and a poster also. The same advertising theme was used for sales promotion. The advertisement showed a superb television set with a video recorder as an integral part, encircled by a red ribbon which largely hid the screen. The slogan was '*Venite a veder lo; dal vero*' (come and see it; for real).

This campaign was a success soon after it started, and was presented to the general managers of the subsidiaries, who met for a residential seminar in Switzerland with the people at European headquarters in Geneva. Reactions were very positive. They proposed the idea of using the same campaign, themes and creation in other European markets. At the beginning of March, Mr Makinen, in charge of marketing communications at the European headquarters, decided to send a memo to the marketing/advertising managers of each subsidiary. A poster and a video presenting the Italian campaign were also enclosed. This memo made a concrete suggestion to the subsidiaries that they should adopt the themes and creation of this campaign. It asked them for their opinions. Makinen invited them to study the feasibility of using such a campaign in their home market and to send their comments back quickly, so that a pan-European campaign could possibly be launched in August. The Italian advertising manager, Signor Ragoli, was available if the European headquarters or national subsidiaries wanted any additional information.

Responses from the subsidiaries (that is, the answers plus the course of action finally adopted) were as follows. It took quite a long time for answers to come back, which could be explained by the overload of work experienced by people in the subsidiaries during this period of reorganization. Some countries never answered the proposal. Otherwise reactions were quite positive, except for that of France. The Spanish answer came quickly. The advertising and public relations manager, Senor Gonzales, sent a copy of the letter to his Italian colleague at European headquarters. He wrote that Spain had decided to use the campaign created in Italy, in order to unify Excel marketing communication. The Spanish wanted to use five different television channels for a total of 22 slots. They supported this with a press campaign and sales promotion in distribution channels. They needed the original version of the Italian television commercial, with music on one track and speech on another (one image track plus two sound tracks). In Spain the final version of the Excel campaign was launched in May 1990. The image track remained unchanged, but the music had been modified and there were several other minor changes. What seemed, at first sight, to be a straight copy of the Italian concept, finally turned out to be a largely modified version. Nevertheless Spain was the only country where the marketing team made the decision to use the experience of their Italian colleagues.

Sweden and Norway also responded quickly to the memo in similar terms. In neither of these two countries was advertising allowed on national television channels; furthermore, they traded under the Scandinavian brand name Scantel, rather than Excel. The Swedish response explained that the subsidiary did not advertise on television, since TVl and TV2 did not offer any space; but with the growth of satellite television the Italian proposal might be interesting for the future. The Swedes thought that the Italian campaign was well designed and implemented. The model presented (Excel 7181) was usable with their brand name since they had the same make. The Norwegians' answer had also been very positive. They promised to keep in mind the concepts of the Italian campaign and further indicated that they would recommend its implementation for 1991.

In France the advertising and public relations manager, Monsieur Dubois, initially contacted by telephone, expressed a positive but rather cautious opinion. He said that he had first to discuss the themes and creation with his advertising agency. He called back to make it clear that even if he had any advertising funds left (in fact they were already entirely spent), he considered that the Italian campaign was not appropriate for Ariane (the brand name of the recently acquired French subsidiary). According to him, it did not fit in with the French criteria of what actually makes good advertising. In his opinion Ariane had a fairly traditional image in France, and French consumers would need more serious arguments to change their views. Consequently 'good' advertising for the Ariane brand had to emphasize, first of all, the high-technology image. Ultimately, he thought that the Italian campaign was not sophisticated enough, and that French people prefer more in-depth, sophisticated and detailed campaigns.

Question

How can the failure of the European headquarters to have the Italian campaign adopted by the other European subsidiaries be explained? What is the right way to go about this in the future? What has to be changed?

A14.3 Exercise

Borovets – a Bulgarian ski resort

Compare the two short texts below (each dated the beginning of 1990). Both depict the Bulgarian ski resort Borovets. The first one is an extract from the magazine *Actuel* (no. 122), from an article entitled 'Guide des bons plans à l'Est' (A guide to travelling in Eastern countries), p. 69. The other is an extract from the trade brochure of the Bulgarian state tourist corporation, *Balkanturist*, entitled 'Bulgaria welcomes you', p. 10. This short exercise is not meant to serve any other purpose than as a pedagogical exercise; it does not aim to describe any real situation and should not prejudice readers concerning holidays in Bulgaria.

Text 1: A charter flight to Bulgaria

The phenomenon already exists, it never stops swelling. Bulgaria is a hospitable place for exhausted proletarians in quest of cheap snow and sun. For the time being, most of the troop comes from Britain: 75 per cent of the tourists are English, 20 per cent are German, the remaining 5 per cent are Dutch, Swedish or French.

The Bulgarian government rubs its hands. The blaze of freedom which blasts through the East has already brought hordes of capitalist tourists. Bulgaria is in urgent need of foreign currencies. The country hopes to have its holiday resorts working at full capacity. Borovets is the most famous resort: in fact, it is a concrete boil encrusted on the mountains. The eight hotels, of luxurious appearance, offer limited comfort: water shortages, telephones out of order, ghost reception desks, bad-tempered staff and rooms where the cleanliness is somewhat dubious. Infrastructure, equipment and service do not meet minimum requirements.

Bulgarian tourism turns out dissatisfied customers. Like Franco's Spain of the 1970s, it is the same reinforced concrete everywhere. Varna and Burgas on the Black Sea coast look like Benidorm. The sea coast is built up with concrete rabbit hutches which swarm with Bulgarian city-dwellers, Greek spendthrifts or drunk Britons. Apocalypse! The rare night-clubs are inaccessible. Meals in the 300-place restaurants have all the style and allure of gymnasium banquets.

Text 2: Borovets

In Bulgarian, Borovets literally means 'beautiful place'. Borovets during the winter has pure, ozone-rich air; it has 150 days of snow cover which provides exceptional ski slopes, from 1,300 to 2,500 meters high.

Each year Borovets is host to numerous international ski championships. Ingemar Stenmark, the Mahre brothers, Girardelli and many other famous skiers have spoken highly of this resort which welcomes everyone.

It is a very fashionable ski resort, with its numerous comfortable and cosy hotels, its enticing restaurants and various entertainment facilities for day and night. Borovets is located 50 miles from Sofia, and it has been enjoyed by children and adults since the end of the nineteenth century, when it was only a small holiday centre.

It is no exaggeration to say that Borovets can compete with the Swiss or the French ski resorts. Now why wait any longer to visit us? We wish only to welcome you.

Questions

1. Why is there such a difference between these two pictures? Do these two articles refer to the same reality?

2. How can one get an idea of the level of service in this resort?

3. How should the state company for Bulgarian tourism (which manages the resort) communicate? What prevents them from doing so?

A14.4 Exercise

Slogans and colloquial speech

Marketing communications (advertising copy, slogans, promotional offers, text on coupons, etc.) are language based. The quality of reception of the marketing messages by the target audience is very sensitive to the accuracy of the wording. Marketing communication is based on everyday – colloquial – speech, often very idiomatic.

The basic purpose of this exercise is fairly simple: it may be implemented with a group of people who have different linguistic backgrounds, but yet have a capacity to communicate with each other since some of them speak several languages. It does not imply that total fluency is necessary. Participants should simply take care to translate *into* the language(s) which they speak fluently (not *from*).

The exercise consists of the following:

1. Collecting slogans (and, more generally, short marketing communication texts) from magazines, billboards, posters, television commercials, sponsor announcements or short texts such as those found in greeting cards; translating them into other languages, with the objective of finding the equivalent meaning and local wording. The translation techniques explained in section 7.2 (back-translation, parallel translation and a combination of the two) should be used.

2. Collecting 'identical' slogans (again, generally any short marketing communication text) that are pushing the same international brand in different countries, then analyzing and comparing how similar propositions and concepts are conveyed in the different languages. Bookshops that sell foreign newspapers and magazines will be useful places to find the basic data.

A14.5 Case

AIDS (2) – Designing a communication campaign for Mexico

It was late when Pilar Quiñones returned to her office after a meeting with Dr Perez-Bustamante, Director of the Centro Nacional Para la Prevención y Control de VIH/SIDA (CENSIDA), the Mexican Health Ministry's official HIV/AIDS organization. *Muy difícil*, she thought, looking at the mass of paperwork on her desk. UNAIDS reports and campaigns, Pan American Health Organization charts, internal CENSIDA statistics and scientific journal clippings occupied the space normally taken by glowing product reviews, colour-coded consumer research reports and shiny product samples.

Quiñones, Vice President of Mexico's largest advertising agency, had just agreed to design a national AIDS awareness campaign. At first, she had resisted the idea, arguing that the government should design its own AIDS programs because an advertising agency does not have the specialized knowledge that is needed. Dr Perez-Bustamante of CENSIDA eventually persuaded her by saying that all governments that succeeded in their fight against AIDS have used advertising agencies.

As Quiñones worked on the project over the next few days, her interest deepened. She personally had never known anyone with AIDS, however she had heard of friends-of-friends who had it, and had read about several high-profile cases in the press. Mexico's AIDS infection rate among adults was relatively low at 0.3 per cent, the same as Canada's and much less than neighbouring Guatemala (1 per cent), Belize (2 per cent) and the USA (0.6 per cent) (UNAIDS, 2002). HIV/AIDS cases were estimated at about 177,000, the 16th leading cause of death in Mexico and fourth leading cause of death among young men. The very poor, of which nine million are children living in absolute poverty, are unlikely to have access to anti-retroviral treatment for the disease (Bautista *et al.*, 2003). Infection rates were not stabilizing and, more worrying, the raw data on infections were probably under-representing reality, reflecting a mobile population, highly dissuasive stigma, corruption and an inefficient health-recording system.

Why were the vast majority of drug-related AIDS cases in the north, close to the US border? Why were women taking up more and more of the AIDS burden? Why were homosexuals again starting to practice unsafe sex? Quiñones jotted down a list of 'barriers' to communication that appeared to be quite significant in Mexico, presented in Table 14.2.

Since stigma is such an important factor in AIDS prevention and treatment, what would be the best way to reduce it? Quiñones sat back in her leather and steel chair, pondering the realization that her campaign should create social norms for less risky behaviours and less stigma. *Aren't all campaigns like that, though, to create a social norm for product adoption and evaluation behaviours*, she mused, *to get people to value a particular brand is not so different from getting people to value safer sex practices. So, what is the need here?* The scientists and policy-makers at Centro Nacional Para la Prevención y Control de VIH/SIDA (CENSIDA) had simply said her mandate was to raise awareness and reduce infections. She would need to quantify those goals so as to measure the success of the campaign later on. She started making another list, influenced by her discussions with HIV/AIDS experts, to be discussed later with the strategy people and the creative people within the agency. The list of 'needs' that should be satisfied by the country's HIV/AIDS program is represented in Table 14.3.

Table 14.2 Informal notes on barriers to HIV/AIDS social marketing in Mexico

Literacy:	We need a message that sounds powerful when said on radio/tv, looks powerful when represented in image form, and can be expressed simply
Language:	Campaign in Spanish and some major native languages, such as Mayan or Nahuatl? It appears that indigenous peoples not much affected by HIV . . . yet. Or is it not diagnosed/not reported? HIV/AIDS has tended to establish itself among the dispossessed, the poor, the marginalized in other countries
Religion (Catholic):	The Pope has frequently condemned the use of condoms, and Mexican First Lady Marta Sahagun Fox was publicly attacked by bishops for exhorting Mexicans to use condoms (they stated that condom use was an invitation to depravity)
Demographic:	Massive undocumented flows of migrants (how to reach them?): ■ from south to north, some in transit from Central America en route to the USA; ■ Mexicans leaving for temporary, usually agricultural, work in the USA or manufacturing work on the northern border; ■ Jobless/dispossessed farmers leaving the countryside to go to cities; ■ migrants returning from the USA, usually to homes in rural areas.
Cultural:	Male value of *machismo*, whereby men should be seen as invincible, not sick, not seeking help (*how can we break through that?*)

Table 14.3 Possible needs identified for HIV/AIDS infections reduction campaign

Simply to re-open public dialogue about HIV/AIDS:	A study in Peru (with some cultural similarities to Mexico) found that teachers and parents needed help to bring sexual issues out into the open. Doctors say that many rural Mexicans have never heard of the disease, partly because it is so difficult to talk openly about sex.
Reduce stigma:	There is anecdotal evidence that stigma is so strong in rural Mexican contexts that people refuse to be tested, and do not even tell their spouses if they suspect they have the disease for fear of reprisals by neighbours on their entire family.
Get Tested:	Pregnant women who visit clinics are tested for the disease, and there is some mandatory, but illegal testing in the private sector. Many young people believe that HIV/AIDS only happens to prostitutes, sexually promiscuous people and homosexuals.
Behaviour Change Communication (BCC):	use condoms. Condom use is low; UNAIDS pinpointed condom use at about 59 per cent in a sample of Mexican men in 2001.

Quiñones wondered whether to segment the campaign geographically to reflect the large cultural differences between the northern states, the central cities and the south. On the other hand, it would be important to mirror the large differences in the urban and rural attitudes and access to testing, information and treatment. There were also specific groups common to different geographic areas, such as gay men. The affluent gay communities had often been profiled by the ad agency in the past, as a favoured target market for travel and luxury goods. She opened a new page on her laptop to list the ever-growing questions posed by this HIV/AIDS campaign, one of the major ones being 'who are we trying to reach?' Targets are identified in Table 14.4.

Table 14.4 Potential target audiences identified in informal study

Residents of the big cities? e.g. in Mexico City 28 per cent of reported HIV/AIDS cases in 2001, other big cities smaller but still significant share.

Rural populations? Disease is spreading much faster in rural areas than in cities, yet there is less awareness, testing, and information about the disease, and more stigma related to it (American Foundation for HIV Research, 2002). In rural areas, women comprise 21.3 per cent of those with HIV/AIDS, while in cities the percentage is closer to 14 per cent (Cevallos, 2002). Rural populations may require a more conservative format.

Age segments? Street children used for prostitution and pornography, numbers estimated at two million by the government (Mexico Child Link, 2003). Most danger for street children from sexual exploitation is in areas close to the US border. About 90 per cent of them are addicted to glue and solvents, also a low literacy level according to Casa Alianza, street children's charity.

Gender segments? Women comprised one-sixth of AIDS cases, whereas in the 1980s, they comprised one-twentieth. In some southern states (with high concentrations of indigenous peoples), heterosexual transmission is the predominant mode, implying that women are increasingly victims of the disease (Country Profile HIV/AIDS: Mexico, 2003).

Migrants in transit from neighbouring countries with high rates of the disease. An estimated 30 per cent of HIV/AIDS cases are temporary migrant workers returning home from the USA with the disease (American Foundation for HIV Research, 2002).

Intravenous drug users make up a relatively small portion of HIV/AIDS cases. If targeted, geographic factors to be accounted for: vast majority in states bordering the United States.

Her assistant knocked at the door with his results of searching for ideas in other campaigns from around the world. He tabulated his preliminary findings in Table 14.5.

Quiñones was impressed by the range of social marketing strategies implemented in other countries, and particularly by the work in the area of international organizations and advocacy groups. The World Health Organization (WHO) provided a good example of this. Using a historical perspective in the publication 'Mobilizing for healthy behaviour', for instance, there was a comprehensive social marketing model named C.A.U.S.E. This model was inspired by the anti-apartheid movement in South Africa, the fight for civil rights in the USA, and the struggle for independence in India. The central idea is to roll out as many elements of C.A.U.S.E. as possible, including:

■ Celebrity (such as Princess Diana against landmines)
■ Activity (such as pacifist rallies and demonstrations)
■ Unexpected event/story (such as the media reports on contaminated blood)
■ Symbol (such as a flag, ribbon, or logo)
■ Event (such as World Aids Day) (WHO, 2002)

Table 14.5 Non-inclusive survey of communications ideas implemented in other countries

Country/organization	Communications idea
UNAIDS 2002–03	'Live and let live' reducing AIDS-related stigma (mass media)
UNAIDS 2001–02	'I care . . . do you?' targeting men (mass media)
Several African countries	'A,B,C: Abstain, Be faithful, Condomise' simple reminder (billboard)
Several African countries	'Graze close to home' and cattle image: non-offensive allegory (billboard)
USA, France	Youth identification in 'slice of life' shots: public service announcements encouraging testing, condom use (television)
USA	Magic Johnson, ex-basketball player (spokesperson, events, press, public service announcements) Patti Labelle, singer: signature campaign 'Live long, sugar' (spokesperson, events, songs, public service announcements targeted at male homosexuals)
Brazil	Ronaldo, football player (spokesperson, events, press, public service announcements)
Many countries	'Myth breakers' mosaic of faces or photos, can you tell which one has AIDS? (Billboard, public service announcements)
South Africa	'Soul City', award-winning 'soap opera' type edutainment series based on television episodes, supported by radio shows, press discussions of issues, and high quality booklets (Usdin, 2001)
Brazil	Condom use promotion: condoms emblazoned with football team emblems

From her experience with product launches and media campaigns, Quiñones knew that more research was needed. There was no need to reinvent the wheel, much effective work has already been done in other Latin American countries. For example, the output of groundbreaking activist communicators 'Calandria' in Peru included many ideas in media planning and products for social marketing of health and development programs (see **www.accionensida.org.pe**).

The information she needed in order to design the campaign was of three types:

1. Profiles of targeted segments of the population. The advertising agency had many such profiles, however none that looked at sexual behaviour and attitudes. Quiñones would need a clear view of who these targeted audiences are, what they believe about HIV/AIDS, and what are the themes that resonate with them that would help get the message across.
2. Literature review of AIDS-related behavioural change intervention research. There have been many critical analyses of AIDS behavioural change programs. Ideally, each time such a program is carried out, the results are monitored, results that could be useful to Quiñones in designing her campaign. Because much of this work is conducted by non-profit organizations and charities, it is easily accessible and will not bite too much out of the budget. A good resource to begin with is **www.comminit.com** (The Communication Initiative).
3. The final type of information that would be helpful in designing the campaign is a survey of current and past campaigns from around the world. *Why reinvent the wheel?* Surely Quiñones and her creative team could find some inspiring ideas, particularly ones that have proved their effectiveness in other settings. See Table 14.5 for her findings.

Table 14.6 Potential partners for the HIV/AIDS campaign

Potential partner	Quick summary of top advantages/disadvantages
Mexican film industry	Less reach over certain target audiences than television, possibly more impact on public relations; many possible spokespeople, although costly.
Family Health International (**www.fhi.org**)	As one of the primary female reproductive health providers, it is well entrenched at local/community levels around the country.
Casa Alianza (**www.casa-alianza.org**)	Prize-winning charity working with street children in Mexico and three other countries. Their 'Luna Project' focuses on HIV and AIDS. May be useful in sub-campaign targeted at street children and may give more credibility than a program run by the Ministry of Health.
US Agency for International Development (**www.usaid.gov**)	USAID is a highly visible, credible and financially powerful organization. It is the largest donor on HIV and AIDS to Mexico, well-known for social marketing of condoms. However, with Mexicans having such high levels of 'national pride' it would be better to keep the project as local as possible.
Radio stations	A multitude of radio stations, already well segmented in terms of audiences, listened to as background noise all day by many Mexicans. May lack the attention-getting power for a long message, however may be effective for 'edutainment' formats.
MTV	MTV has a well-established track record in AIDS activism.
Mexican passions	Football (everyone but mainly males), bullfighting (mainly older males) and *telenovelas*, soap-operas or social dramas (mainly females of all ages, and some gay men). A spokesperson may be found from one of these areas, or sporting events may be used to educate the 'captive audience'.

Quiñones was aware that an isolated program would get few results. It would be imperative to partner with a highly visible organization or company. She made a short list and handed it to her assistant to solicit ideas from other executives for cause-related marketing efforts (see Table 14.6).

In order to understand the best ways to reach the targeted audiences, Quiñones drew up a list of possible media and supporting vehicles to carry the message, and a quick note about the kind of information needed.

1. *Mass media*: readership of newspaper, magazines and frequency of exposure.
2. *Internet*: access to the Internet, frequency of use:
   - e-zines, weblogs, chat rooms, subscription material: type and frequency of use;
   - e-mail: access to and frequency of use;
   - Internet games: e.g. HIV/AIDS game by activists at **www.SuperShagLand.com**.
3. *Television*:
   - advertising spots/public service announcements;
   - edutainment show on the lines of Soul City (see Table 14.5);
   - insertion of AIDS issues into *telenovelas* (social dramas), comedies or talk shows.
4. *Radio*:
   - advertising spots/public service announcements;
   - programming including music/talk/interviews/*radionovela* (social dramas).

5. *Mobile and fixed line phones*:
   - new hotline for young people;
   - SMS and even MMS (short and media messages) to phone users, perhaps as a game.
6. *Minibus stickers*: minibus being the most common means of transport.
7. *Leaflets*, possibly to support television, radio and Internet efforts.
8. *Logo t-shirts, caps, pens, condoms, etc.*
9. *Youth mobilization programme*: festivals, street theatre, street football, popular song, video.

For an idea of the type of vehicle Quiñones might decide to use as one part of her campaign, go to the site of Media For Development International (MFDI) to watch a free 48-minute Ugandan AIDS prevention film using Real Player (**www.mfdi.org**).

Questions

1. How should sensitive messages about AIDS issues be conveyed to a Mexican audience given the cultural traits of Mexico? What is the best strategy: direct or indirect? Emotional or rational? Informative? Persuasive?

2. What should be the target audience(s) of the Mexican AIDS campaign?

3. Make propositions as concerns the copy strategy and media planning of the campaign.

4. Which potential partners would you approach for this campaign? Do you recommend that Quiñones uses sponsoring and other forms of marketing communication? If yes, how would you design an integrated marketing communications plan?

Saskia Faulk and Jean-Claude Usunier prepared this case solely to provide material for class discussion. The authors do not intend to illustrate either effective or ineffective handling of a business situation. The authors may have disguised certain names and other identifying information to protect confidentiality.

(©IUMI, reprinted with kind permission.)

15

Intercultural marketing communications 2: Personal selling, networking and public relations

In Ghana there is a saying: 'Mouth smiles, money smiles better'. Money is always at the very centre of personal selling. Both personal selling and public relations also focus on human interaction. These person-to-person relationships are at stake in this part of marketing communications, as we mix rational and non-rational arguments, hard business facts and human relationships.

There are four ways of achieving marketing communications: advertising (examined in the previous chapter), sales promotion (section 12.5), personal selling and public relations. Understandably enough, cultural differences (time and space assumptions, interaction models and attitudes towards action, as described in Chapters 2 and 3) have a major impact on how relationships start and develop. It is argued in section 15.1 that people who want to take into account cultural differences have to be *relationship* centred rather than purely *deal* centred (commerce rather than simply marketing). Section 15.2 develops this argument by comparing the Western view of business networks to the Chinese *guanxi*. We then discuss how culture impacts on buyer–seller interactions (section 15.3), which involves personal contact, and as such is more culture bound. Personal selling issues are then examined from an organizational perspective focusing on how a sales force can be managed in a cross-cultural context (15.4). Section 15.5 deals with public relations, which, even though it does not directly contribute to sales, may be of prime concern for defending corporate image before various publics. In the last two sections we examine ethical issues related to selling, first by presenting facts about bribery (15.6) and second by suggesting

some ways of appreciating the cultural relativity of ethical attitudes (15.7).

15.1

Intercultural commerce

Commerce as implementation of marketing programmes

Commerce is about personal selling and establishing continuity in the relationship with individual customers, organizational buyers and intermediaries. Commerce is defined by the *Collins Dictionary* as follows: '1. the activity embracing all forms of the purchase and sale of goods and services; 2. social relationships; 3. *Arch.* sexual intercourse.' Commerce favours the social interaction between vendor (producer and/or distributor) and consumer. The quality of this social interaction, including marketing strategies that respect cultural integrity, guarantees the effective implementation of global strategies. Commerce is simply non-technocratic marketing.

The '4P's model (McCarthy, 1964) of the marketing mix (product, price, place and promotion) has been extensively used; as a paradigm it continues to assist greatly in the design of marketing strategies, serving to question their coherence and soundness. But little by little, it has led to rather ritualized marketing practices where functions and their content are seen as fairly independent. Market research specialists are not product managers, nor are they advertising managers or sales promoters; as we have argued in section 7.6, an atomistic view of reality leads to decisions made by experts, each one having precisely defined tasks. An issue that does not fall clearly within their explicit responsibility will not even be considered. For instance, when questions arise as to consumer complaints management, it is not always clear who should be in charge of it. The correct answer should be that *everybody* is in charge of consumer complaints and great care should be taken to avoid having *nobody* in charge of consumer complaints.

Technocratically oriented market research treats the customer too impersonally, like abstract units in a sample. Messages from consumers are filtered by close-ended questions, which pre-shape what people actually say. A large part of what they *would be willing to say* is in fact often ignored. The '4P's paradigm of marketing theory has led to practices that are sometimes totally ignorant of the company environment (Zeithaml and Zeithaml, 1984). Various segments of the public (consumers, actual buyers, competitors, etc.) are often ignored simply because there is no established communication channel to hear their voice.

The Internet has the ability to bring customers and suppliers closer, despite the challenges of distance, time and cultural separation in international business. Sharma (2002) suggests firms can better service the needs of their customers via the Internet to:

1. provide information instantaneously to employees, suppliers and customers;
2. increase instant and constant connectivity, reducing dependence on time zones;
3. create communities that share news and expertise;
4. increase the effectiveness of transactions by reducing time and errors; and
5. share cost reduction through self-service, and automated information systems.

However, Hulnick (2000) warns that cultures differ in the acceptability of initiating and managing relationships remotely: in South-East Asian countries the personal touch is still essential to build trust, while in other countries, such as Australia, people are more comfortable with remote relationships. Even in low context, more individualist cultures, such as the United States, the majority of people still want contact with a live customer service representative (Spiegelman, 2000).

Continuity in commercial relationships: Learning from consumers

Firms, and their employees, often have a tendency to try to maintain the *status quo*, thereby avoiding difficult choices: this process of 'knowledge disavowal' involves not being prepared to ask questions and avoiding exploratory and developmental research (Barabba and Zaltman, 1991; Fournier *et al.*, 1998). A new style of marketing, more consumer and relationship oriented, less strategy oriented, recommends that the voice of the market should be heard. For instance, Procter & Gamble recently shifted its focus toward its customers and renamed its trade department as 'Customer Business Development'.

Instead of focusing on market share, relationship marketing focuses on customer retention, customer commitment and share of the customer's business (Sheth and Parvatiyar, 2002). According to Sheth and Parvatiyar (2002) there are three unique aspects to relationship marketing: (1) it is a one-on-one relationship between the marketer and seller; (2) it is an interactive process, where boundaries of time, location and identity between the supplier and customers are blurring; and (3) it is a value-added activity, where there is collaboration and mutual interdependence.

There are indeed many reasons why the relationship and the lines of communication between a producer and the ultimate consumer may be broken. The preoccupation with *marketing continuity* is a directly operative one and Day (1994) explains that a company needs to activate sensors at the point of customer contact:

In most organizations front-line contact people – who handle the complaints, hear requests for new services, cope with lead users, or lose sales due to competitor initiative – are seldom motivated to inform management on a systematic basis. They may fear [to] have their job load increase, suspect the information won't be used, or not know where it should be sent . . . Channels for the upward flow of information need to be established and incentives need to be offered for useful insights.

Distribution often acts as a filter; consumers complain but there is no specific communication channel to the manufacturer and complaints are not taken seriously or are simply ignored (see Box 15.1). When the distributor is independent, located in a foreign country, and paid by commission on sales rather than

Box 15.1

'Tubeless tyres', you said . . .

A consumer bought a leading European make of tyre for his car. He asked his garage to fit the tyres. In fact they fitted tubeless tyres since they were supposed to be cheaper (as they did not need air chambers). These tyres, however, kept deflating. When complaining for the first time, the consumer was told by the garage to be slightly more careful in inflating the tyres. They had to be reinflated roughly twice a week. The customer contacted his garage again but was merely told that it 'didn't usually happen'. The customer asked if the tyre manufacturer would take back the defective tyres but the garage told him that that was impossible and that in any case the tyres did at least stay inflated for a couple of days.

Finally, after going backwards and forwards several times, the customer had air chambers put into the tyres. The problem immediately ceased. When he spoke to his garage, they informed him that the wheel rims had warped slightly owing to the 30,000 miles (48,000 km) that the car had done. Other cars (the garage mentioned a German make) had rims made out of a thicker steel which was more resistant and therefore did not warp. Such a car could have tubeless tyres fitted successfully, whatever its age. The customer asked the garage to pass on this information to the tyre manufacturer so that it could inform tyre centres which cars were not suitable for tubeless tyres after a certain mileage had been covered. The garage said that this was impossible. The information was not passed on. Tubeless tyres continue to deflate in a fairly large number of cases. Customers either fit air chambers or buy a different car . . . or they change their make of tyre.

---

rewarded for key consumer or competitor information, it is likely that the upward flow will be nil unless specific action is taken. A product may, for instance, be refused by distribution for substantive reasons which remain ignored, such as store employees experiencing difficulties in opening cardboard boxes which are stapled in such a way that they are injured when trying to open them. Similarly, a class of potential consumers may be neglected by marketing communications, since only actual buyers are targeted and research has failed to examine alternative segments.

The example of Japanese *Keiretsu*, presented in section 12.1, demonstrates the value of building communication channels which help in the design and implementation of marketing strategies. Where opportunities for the return of products are liberal, distributors may warn producers about defective products that consumers are simply not happy with. Conversely, when producers or retailers reject consumer complaints and therefore the return of products, they will often shift responsibility for the failure on to the consumers. They may, for instance, tell them that they have not read the instructions, or have misused the product, or fixed it incorrectly.

There may be cultural differences in people's willingness to complain. In a business setting Griffith

et al. (2000) compared distributors from Canada and the United States (Type 1: individualist, small power distance, weak uncertainty avoidance) with distributors from Chile and Mexico (Type 2: collectivist, large power distance, strong uncertainty avoidance). They found that there was a stronger positive relationship between commitment and satisfaction in intercultural relationships than in intracultural relationships: companies from Type 1 cultures may need to work harder to develop relationships with Type 2 cultures. In addition, they found that a negative relationship between conflict and satisfaction only exist in Type 1 cultures, suggesting that Type 2 cultures may be less likely to report conflict to maintain social harmony. Similarly, Song *et al.*'s (2000) findings suggest that avoiding behaviours adversely affects integration in both Western (the United States and the United Kingdom) and Eastern cultures (Japan and China), even in countries where conflict avoidance is the social norm.

In addition, people from different cultural backgrounds may prefer different remedies to dissatisfaction. For instance, Hui and Au (2001) conducted an experiment, finding that Canadian students perceived a higher level of fairness when they were given compensation for damages, whereas Chinese students perceived a higher level of fairness when they were able to express dissatisfaction and someone listened. Ho (1997) reported that dissatisfied customers are less likely to receive monetary or material remedies in China than in Canada.

A negotiation and human resource emphasis

A commerce orientation means that not only personnel but also clients should be seen by a company as its human resources. The frontiers of the organization should be less clear-cut. Most companies are very dichotomous in that they develop impermeable boundaries between their 'inside' and their 'outside'. Insiders are generally people listed on the payroll. It is often claimed in slogans emanating from within the company that consumers are 'kings' (to be found everywhere: *le client est roi*, *der Kunde ist König*, etc.), but in reality they are treated as pure *outsiders* and there is little personal knowledge of who the consumers actually are. A consumer who wants to meet a manager will generally not even be received, even if the intention is just to explain something about the product or the service, with a constructive view towards its improvement.

Very often distribution channels will be used as 'shock-absorbing mattresses'. As distribution channels are in direct contact with customers, if something goes wrong, it is *their* job to deal with it. Splendid isolation of manufacturers is too often the rule of non-commerce-oriented organizations, whenever they claim to be marketing oriented. To avoid this bias, consumers must be viewed as one of the key human resources of the company. They are not kings, but suitable people with whom to negotiate reasonable changes to the buyer–seller relationship. Personal selling is the main tool of commerce: it allows direct relationships and communications with distributors and final customers and must convey messages in both directions, from the manufacturer to the market and vice versa.

Making contacts

Commerce puts equal emphasis on the marketing offer (product, price, delivery dates, etc.) and on the quality of the social relationship between buyer and seller, manufacturer and consumer. That is why making appropriate contacts and developing relationships is an essential part of commerce, this being true for personal selling and public relations as well as marketing negotiations. The issue is at what level of the organization and with which people must contacts be made to maximize the chances of a successful outcome. When making contacts, in a cross-cultural perspective, people should be aware of the following: (1) status is not shown in the same way in all cultures; (2) influential persons are not the same and individual influence is not exerted in the same way; and (3) the decision-making process differs. Box 15.2 illustrates the first two points with an African example.

Credibility is an initial condition for building trust in relational marketing. According to Slatter (1987), the salesperson's job in competitive bidding situations (which are quite common in international sales of equipment, turnkey plants and in the case of public procurement) consists of five main tasks:

1. Establishing the salesperson's personal credibility.
2. Undertaking market research.
3. Influencing design and specifications.
4. Establishing the firm's credibility.
5. Establishing a communication system.

There are clearly two levels where credibility has to be established: personal and organizational. The credibility of a particular person is linked to cultural codes. People emit messages about their own credibility which are linked to physical, status and/or behavioural attributes (see sections 3.1 and 15.3). The vendor will try to become personally acquainted with key decision-makers in potential target companies. There may be some problems in clearly identifying the key decision-makers, and establishing one's credibility with them. They may resent dealing with 'mere salespeople', especially in countries where sales status is low and power distance is high, because it conflicts with their self-image and their organizational position. Hierarchical relationships *across* organizations are a very sensitive issue; all the more so because they supposedly exist only subjectively. Complex codes of interpersonal relationships govern the establishment of credibility: it is therefore often necessary to use sales assistants or market researchers as 'door-openers', who will quickly be succeeded by higher-ranking sales executives or sales managers (Box 15.3).

Box 15.2

The little man in rags and tatters

The story takes place in the corridor to the office of the minister of industry of the Popular Republic of Guinea at the beginning of the 1980s. Whether you had an appointment or you came to solicit a meeting, you had to be let in by the door-keeper. Besides, the door was locked and he had the key. This little man looked tired and wore worn out clothes; his appearance led foreign visitors to treat him as negligible and to pay little attention to him. When visitors had been waiting for a long time while seeing others being given quick access to the minister, they often spoke out unrestrainedly, voicing their impatience to the old man, who seemed to have only limited language proficiency. In fact, the door-keeper spoke perfect French and was the uncle of the minister, which gave him power over his nephew according to the African tradition. It was notorious that the minister placed great confidence in his uncle's recommendations. Thus some foreign contractors never understood why they did not make deals although they had been developing winning arguments with the minister himself.

(Source: Gérard Verna, Laval University, Québec.)

Box 15.3

The Japanese 'message-boy'

During research into the key factors surrounding the success of Japanese engineering companies in world markets, I had the opportunity to interview several Japanese engineering specialists. One of them had worked for C. Itoh, a large Japanese trading company, on the sale and project follow-up of an oil refinery in Algeria. He explained by the use of a diagram (Figure 15.1) the Japanese 'method' for selling turnkey factories.

He stressed the central role of the *sogoshosha* (GTC: general trading company) as an *organizer*, a function that includes the responsibilities of information source, business intermediary and co-ordinator. An *organizer* is roughly equivalent to a 'sales prospection expert before, during and after the sale of a large and highly complex item'. One of C. Itoh's small offices in Algiers, which specialized in import–export, principally of textile products, learned of the existence of a new tender for an oil refinery which was shortly to be published. The Algiers office sent a fairly detailed fax to Tokyo – step (1) in Figure 15.1 – where the engineering company(ies) and the manufacturing companies (MFG) who would be in a position to tender for the project were sought out – step (2).

Even at this early stage, a project team will begin to assemble from among the different companies involved (3). The trading company contacts the official bodies: first, the foreign insurance division of the Ministry of International Trade and Industry (GOV) to determine whether the project has a chance of being covered for political and commercial risk (4). The Japanese Exim-Bank, the public export-finance body (BKG), will also be contacted for a preliminary study into financing options. These bodies will not make any firm commitment, but they will give a preliminary response: if the project risks not being covered by official guarantees, or receiving only limited cover, the project team instituted by the trading company may decide to abandon the tender.

While all this is going on, and even before the bid documents are available, a preliminary team will be sent to the site to examine the possibilities of water and energy supply, transport facilities, etc. Already the Japanese are gaining time (5). Once the bid documents are available to companies (6), the trading company's local representative will go to collect them personally from the future owner and dispatch the documents to Tokyo after having summarized the main points in a long and detailed fax

Box 15.3 *(continud)*

Figure 15.1 The role of Japanese general trading companies as 'organizers' in the negotiation and implementation of international turnkey operations: a Japanese view

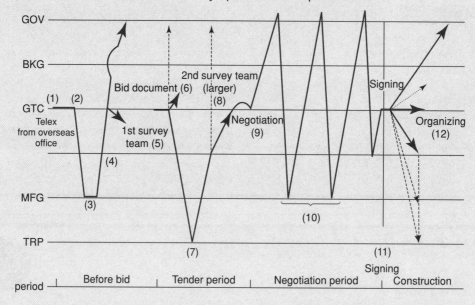

or e-mail. The representative will not hesitate to stay up most of the night to draft this text. By this stage, the Japanese have already gained 15 days on their international competitors (7).

Once the detailed fax or e-mail has been received, a larger team will go to examine the technical and economic conditions on site. The results of this survey, and the consultation with various engineering partners, heavy equipment manufacturers (MFG) and carriers (TRP), will enable the formulation of a detailed bid, which very often has to be submitted within a fairly short time span (30 days) after the publication of the tender. The bid will not be sent, but handed over by a young executive, who will be 25 to 30 years old: a 'message-boy' (8). His task is an important one: thanks to him, there is no risk of the documents being blocked by customs; he also has the job of 'sizing up' the people being dealt with and of discerning the people who will really make the final decision. Once more the Japanese have gained time; they are never late in submitting a tender, whereas a number of their foreign competitors submit theirs after the deadline. Although late delivery of a bid is usually accepted

(bidding times are fairly short), it does not necessarily reflect favourably on the capacity to meet delivery dates.

Now the negotiation phase begins (9). This will easily last several months and in extreme cases will stretch, with long interruptions, over several years. Much shuttling back and forth between the various levels (10) will allow the finalizing of an offer. If successful, the offer will lead to the signature of the contract for a large-scale project (11), in which the trading company and the engineering company will generally be joint contractors. As a result, the trading company will adopt the role of coordinator between the various companies carrying out the project (12).

According to my Japanese informant, Nobuhiko Suto, now a professor at Tokai University, who had been personally involved in the deal, the 'message-boy' is typical of the Japanese way of doing business. He is even requested to scrutinize the face of the people to whom he submits the offer to determine their reaction to the Japanese bid. In the West, it is difficult to conceive of such care being taken to assess subjective reactions objectively.

Any 'detail' may be of importance in establishing credibility in the absence of more profound informational cues, which come only when the relationship is more established. Business cards are important because they provide clear information on business persons: their family and first names, how to reach them, their status within the company, etc. A foreign-language card will also reflect sensitivity to the host culture (Freivalds, 1991) and when one is working mostly with a particular culture (e.g. a US business person exporting to Japan), it is advisable to have a card printed in English on the one side with the Japanese transliteration on the other side. Credibility is often based on first impressions: accent has been shown to influence the credibility and effectiveness of an international business person. Tsalikis *et al.* (1992) compared the effect of accent type on credibility of business people in a Latin American context: in Guatemala, for instance, Guatemalan Spanish evokes more favourable judgements than the same sales pitch in foreign-accented Spanish.

The decision-making process in the buyer's organization is a key issue for making adequate contact. Power distance (PD) plays an important role in the style of organizational decision making: the higher it is, the more centralized it is. In a French context, for instance, with high PD, individualism and uncertainty avoidance, decision making and budgetary power are located at the top of the organization. Most people cannot make a decision by themselves, including buying a pencil, without referring to the top. Thus for personal selling, one has to target contacts at the top while keeping friendly contacts with people at intermediate levels because they could resent their lack of power being openly manifested by the seller's attitude and could therefore obstruct. In countries where power distance is small, decision making is more decentralized, and there are financial thresholds for decisions at each level of the hierarchy, especially when there is also an individualistic orientation in the culture. In such a context the level of contact is roughly proportionate to the financial amount of the sales contract.

The Japanese style of reaching decisions by committee can disorientate people of other nationalities who are used to decisions being made by a boss, a great deal of power being thereby concentrated in one person's hands. There are many examples of companies that, after protracted negotiations with Japanese firms, heard nothing more for several months. They assumed that they had lost the deal, but to their surprise they ultimately received an agreement: the process of *ringi* had been at work in the Japanese company – a procedure of written consultation that requires the input of various interested parties, meetings and careful consideration of objections and suggestions. Box 15.3 shows how the Japanese manage the process of preliminary contacts in a situation where both the seller's and the buyer's organization are complex.

15.2
Networks in business markets

For many reasons, firms tend to develop networks; among these reasons is the long-term nature of business relationships between industrial suppliers and buyers (Dwyer *et al.*, 1987). For instance, an airline builds regular relationships with an aircraft company over the lifetime of the aircraft, which is often 25 years; similarly the aircraft company is closely connected to the engine manufacturer because the design of the aircraft includes specific engines. Industrial companies also build alliances for developing common R & D projects or to manage common assets such as jointly developed software or a joint distribution system. Therefore, since companies do not work in isolation, the term *network* refers to two or more organizations involved in long-term relationships.

Generically, a network may be viewed as consisting of 'nodes' or *positions* (occupied by firms, households, strategic business units inside a diversified concern, trade associations and other types of organization) and *links* manifested by interaction between the positions . . . Networks may be tight or loose, depending on the quantity (number), quality (intensity), and type (closeness to the core activity of the partners involved) of interactions between the positions or members. (Thorelli, 1986, p. 38.)

The network approach to business has been developed by the IMP group with the view that relationships between companies, built out of the history of the companies' dealings with each other, matter as much as mere elements of the deal itself, that is the hard data on product specifications, price and terms of contract (see Ford, 1990; Johansson and Mattsson, 1988). In business networks, personal contacts matter because they serve to reduce the uncertainty linked to complex deals by face-to-face exchange of information on technical, organizational and commercial issues. 'Mutual trust, respect and personal friendship between participants allows confidential information to be exchanged' (Ford, 1990, p. 81).

Mavondo and Rodrigo (2001) surveyed managers in Australia and China who have business ties in the other country. They found that social bonding (mutual personal friendship and liking) precedes the development of trust, face and cooperation. Personal contacts also enable interacting partners in the network to assess each other's competence, to negotiate implementation issues and beyond-the-letter-of-the-contract issues in the case of highly complex products and turnkey plants. If there is a critical problem, they offer a framework for the quick exchange of information and rapid decisions about corrective measures. Personal contacts also play a social role. However, market rationality and the 'doing' orientation maintain the lead in the Western view of networking. People are there to 'close the deal', not to enjoy the pleasures of social life:

companies are not likely to encourage interaction which is only socially based. There is an expectation that other elements of interaction (such as information exchange, product sales or purchases and adaptations) would also result. There is evidence from the research that buyers are more inclined to maintain 'good but distant' relationships than salesmen. Yet some suppliers see the dangers of too close an involvement of their salesmen with customers, in that they may lose their objectivity and take actions in the interests of the social relationships, rather than in the wider interests of their company. (Ford, 1990, p. 83.)

Broadly considered, business networks are a fairly universal reality. The very notion of *guanxi* can to a large extent be considered the Chinese, and more broadly the East Asian form of business connection, consisting in maintaining relationships with the appropriate organizations and individuals within these organizations. The Chinese *guanxi* corresponds to *Kankei* in Japan and *Kwankye* in Korea, that is, after-hours socialization, which become important forums for meeting and convincing key decision-makers in a socially more comfortable atmosphere (Tung, 1996). *Guanxi* mixes social behaviour and business practices in a complex set of disinterested and interested personal interactions. It is not necessarily directed at short-term results and consists of an

investment in relationships that may or may not be called upon in the future. The practice of *guanxi* translates into large sales forces for maintaining contacts and large accounts receivables (in a way similar to the liberal credit policy in Japan, see section 12.1). Firms engaged in a connected set of companies, called *guanxihu*, do their best to avoid embarrassing a business partner experiencing temporary financial problems. *Guanxi* has been shown to be strongly favourable to the performance of international joint ventures in China (Luo, 1995) as well as for foreign-invested enterprises in China and Chinese domestic firms (Luo, 1997; Luo and Chen, 1997).

The Chinese concept of *guanxi* shares some common traits with the Western concept of networking, especially the continuity of business relationships and a framework for understanding the relationships between firms engaged in cooperative rather than competitive behaviour. There are, however, some significant differences which Luo and Chen (1997, pp. 3–4) explain as follows:

guanxi primarily relates to personal, not to corporate, relations, and exchanges that take place amongst members of the *guanxi* network are not solely commercial, but also social, involving the exchange of *renqing* (social or humanized obligation) and the giving of *mianzi* (face in the society), or social status. This feature often leads *guanxi* to be named 'social capital'. In contrast, networking in Western marketing and management literature is the term primarily associated with commercially based corporate-to-corporate relations. Because of this difference, many Western business people are often in danger of overemphasizing the gift-giving and wining-and-dining components of a *guanxi* relationships, thereby coming dangerously close to crass bribery or to [being] perceived as 'meat and wine friends' which is a Chinese metaphor for mistrust.

Hutchings and Murray (2002) interviewed Australian expatriates in Shanghai, China to assess the implications of *guanxi* on networking. They found that managers from larger firms and those who had been there a longer time considered *guanxi* to be less important than those who were from smaller firms or had been there a shorter time. While the general opinion was that *guanxi* is similar to Western concepts of networking, they stressed the importance of face: 'to give face, to save face, and above all, to avoid causing loss of face. They highlighted the fact that in causing loss of face to another, then they automatically lost face themselves, and thus they viewed the saving and managing of face of others as essential to their own ongoing success in China' (p. 188).

As previously mentioned, the Internet is also an important tool for networking. The very basis of the Internet is a 'network' of interconnected computers and, as an extension of that, people. (For example of using the Internet as a network tool, see *WS15.2.*)

15.3

Buyer–seller interactions

Seller's status and the status of trade

In many countries sales work has a low status. Selling is implicitly associated with persuasion techniques and taking money from people rather than usefully bringing products and services to them. Trade has some negative connotations in Latin countries: for instance, where it was traditionally associated with exploitation, especially when buying for resale, leading to the view that distribution, and services in general, were economically unproductive activities. Those who adopt this view consider engineering and production to be noble activities in contrast to marketing and sales, which are devalued. Such poor status often makes people think that personal selling does not require formal training, just innate communication talents, a certain lack of scruple and a good deal of opportunism.

The value placed on money is also central to the status of trade, since sellers sell goods and services *against* money. Cultures differ in their beliefs about money (Ang, 2000). In fact most cultures have a problem with money, which is often implicitly viewed as depriving activities of a higher sense of purpose, making people *bassement intéressés* (meanly self-interested). A range of possible solutions are shown by the different values placed on price bargaining, presented in section 11.2: either explicit reference to price is avoided whenever possible, explicit discussions about price come quite late (which may at times be embarrassing), or a supposedly 'favourable' price is ritually associated with friendship or common belonging.

The seller's status is in fact often related to membership of a particular group such as the Chinese, who have been prominent merchants in many South-East Asian Nations, or the Lebanese in West Africa. The reader will recognize here some of the basic assumptions presented in Table 2.2, especially the being/doing divide. The status of a minority as 'commercial group', reflecting strong being orientation, is ambiguous: members of this minority may have taken this role because it was somewhat rejected by the majority, but their success and influence as tradespeople may be resented. On the other hand, in many countries, it is an absolute necessity for the seller to be personally acquainted with the buyer, and common membership in the same ingroup may be required. The buyer might find some personal characteristics of the seller difficult to accept, such as a European export saleswoman selling to a Saudi buyer.

Power distance also has an influence on the seller's status: in high-power-distance countries, the seller is often responsible for conveying the producer's conditions to the customer, with very limited leeway for negotiation – especially about price and delivery conditions. Jolibert and Tixier (1988, p. 11), both French, coming from a high-power-distance society, give a good example of the distinction between sales (understood as a low power/low status situation) and marketing negotiation (considered a high power/high status role):

During sale the business conditions are fixed by the vendor. The purchaser is not in a position to debate them . . . The job of the vendor therefore consists of convincing the purchaser of the worth of his offers, of the appropriateness of the product offered to meet the needs of the purchaser . . . Negotiation begins when there is a *possible discussion* about the terms of business between the purchaser and the vendor.

In this definition the salesperson's role is only to convince; he/she is given no role in representing the customer's needs and making them known to his or her company! More paradoxically, in this definition, the purchaser is also in a subordinate situation to the supplying company.

Selling styles: Arguments and presence

Let us begin with a question framed in radical terms: what must a salesperson do when asked to sell poor-quality products or, less radically, when the seller perceives the weaknesses of a product through clients' comments? Should the salesperson inform the company, in particular the production department,

Figure 15.2 Selling orientations

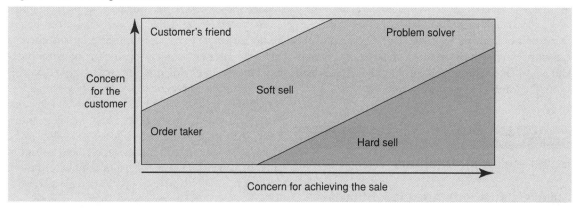

or merely consider the terms of the business offering as fixed and stick to the role of persuasion? In fact, when preparing arguments, a salesperson has two main concerns: one is for the customers and their needs; the other is for achieving the sale, for 'closing the deal'. Adcock *et al.* (1993, p. 306) combine these as shown in Figure 15.2.

If one regards the seller's role as strictly separate from that of the business negotiator, sales staff being supposed to obediently sell products as they are and not to debate the marketing mix, then the role of salespeople is principally that of persuasion, the art of persuasion being subject to highly significant cultural variations. The following questions outline possible ways of differentiating the sales persuasion technique:

1. How far can one take persuasion without becoming insistent, and irritating?
2. Is one persuasive merely by listening, where clients appreciate salespeople to whom they can talk, or by talking?
3. What arguments will be the best and the quickest for persuading the prospective purchaser?

Cateora (1983) proposes some stereotypes of selling styles:

1. In Asian countries, where people mind arrogance and the showing of extreme self-confidence, vendors should make modest, rational, down-to-earth points; they should avoid winning arguments against the buyer, who could suffer a 'loss of face', and react quite negatively.
2. In Italy, on the contrary, the lack of self-confidence would be perceived as a clear sign of

lack of personal credibility and reliability; thus one needs to argue strongly in order to be considered a serious partner.
3. In Switzerland, you have to speak precisely and your words will be taken quite literally.
4. In the United Kingdom, it is advisable to use the *soft sell* approach (do not be pushy with your prospective buyer). The very favourable position of the 'soft sell' approach in Figure 15.2 (which is drawn from British authors) gives some support to this.
5. In Germany, you should use the *hard sell* approach (make visits, offer trials, be very visible).
6. When selling to a Mexican buyer, one should emphasize the *price*.
7. In Venezuela, a vendor will have to emphasize the *quality*.

If a true variety of selling styles related to national culture exists, it is not to be denied that the style of selling depends also on the personality of the salesperson and the type of industry, from the market trader to the executive selling billion-dollar contracts, from the friend to the distant acquaintance. However, culture dictates assumptions about the role adopted by the majority of sellers. For instance if the view is that a good salesperson should be able to close the deal, then the job is that of short-term persuasion at any price. Conversely, if the seller is viewed as the representative of the client within the company, salespeople should have a long-term outlook, listen to the client and even be willing to lose an order once in a while. Selling styles also depend on which type of concrete results (winning new customers, reaching a sales target)

Table 15.1 A summary of the influence of culture on buyer–seller relationships

Cultural value	Influence on seller and buyer
Inferior status for trade	Poor status for sales; selling is reserved to a minority group
Being/doing	More personal relationship orientated; more impersonal deal orientated
Money	Price bargaining as friendship ritual
Ingroup orientation	Only people from a certain ingroup are considered as adequate for sales roles; transactions have to be made preferably across ingroup members
Family orientation	Buyer–seller relationships are viewed as an element of a larger family network
Short-term orientation	Achieving the sale is the paramount goal
Long-term orientation	Keeping the client is the paramount goal
Low/high power distance	Equality/inequality between buyer and seller
Listening versus talking	Soft sell versus hard sell

and/or more subjective achievements (getting on well with clients, maintaining a friendly atmosphere in the sales team) are considered as evidence of the seller's efficiency or inefficiency.

Equality in the buyer–seller relationship

Some of the basic conditions of the buyer–seller interaction are partially dictated by culture, especially the relative positions of strength of buyer and seller. Numerous empirical studies have been undertaken to determine which role, buyer or seller, holds the *ab initio* position of strength in intercultural marketing negotiations. Graham (1981) suggests that one of the reasons for the American trade deficit with Japan was the difference regarding the position of strength in the representation of the buyer–seller relationship. The Japanese believe that strength lies with the purchaser, whom the salesperson must do the utmost to satisfy, whereas the Americans envisage a more egalitarian position, as Graham (1981, p. 9) points out in his examination of which party adapts to the other in the relationship of intercultural business negotiation:

Anthropologists tell us that power relations usually determine who adopts and adapts behavior in a cross-cultural setting. Japanese executives in an American setting are likely to be the ones to modify their behavior . . . However, if an American seller takes his normative set of bargaining behavior to Japan, then negotiations are apt to end up abruptly. The American seller expects to be treated as an equal and acts accordingly. The Japanese buyer is likely to

view this rather brash behavior in a lower status seller as inappropriate and lacking in respect. The Japanese buyer is made to feel uncomfortable, and he politely shuts the door to trade, without explanation. The American seller never makes the first sale, never gets an opportunity to learn the Japanese system.

Table 15.1 gives a summary of the influence of culture on buyer–seller interactions. (*WS15.3* has a number of links to articles examining buyer–seller relationship dynamics.)

15.4

Sales force management in a cross-cultural perspective

Several authors in the field of international marketing have stressed the influence of cultural differences on sales force compensation systems (Still, 1981; Hill *et al.*, 1991; Cateora, 1993; Hempel, 1998; Money and Graham, 1999). Cross-cultural differentiation is an important variable for improving the effectiveness of the sales function: Lackman *et al.* (1997), based on data from four cultural groupings (western Europeans, Americans, Japanese and Latin Americans) have shown that substantial differentiation in line with Hofstede's parameters is required in the industrial sales function to generate effective marketing results.

The idea that the promotion of sales personnel is done on merit and that decisions are made on an objective basis is very strong in the United States. This is linked with the 'master of destiny' philosophy that underlies much of US management thinking (Cateora, 1993). People are in control of their own destiny and therefore responsible for the effective use of their own resources. In many cultures which have a more fatalistic approach to life, controlling individual performance does not seem to make sense. Uncontrollable higher-order forces largely shape our acts and future. Ali and Schwiercz (1985), for instance, report that Saudi Arabian performance and evaluation control systems work informally, without systematic controls, established criteria or definite procedures.

The question of the influence of culture on sales force management is not considered exhaustively here. Many of its facets are infused with human resource management and therefore subject to significant cross-cultural variance. For instance, many enquiries considered in the United States as discriminatory when recruiting salespeople according to a US 'affirmative action compliance program' (e.g. Chonko et al., 1992, p. 410) would never be considered as discriminatory in most countries. The birthplace of applicants, their marital status, age, citizenship or language competencies are standard, non-discriminatory enquiries in most cultures where there is still some *being* orientation. The 'affirmative action, equal opportunity' programme is derived from extremely strong *doing* and *outgroup* orientations, whereby it is seen as almost evil to describe persons as they *are*.

This section does not consider the question of whether to employ local or international sales representatives, the expatriation of sales and marketing personnel or companies that sell to international customers with highly qualified and often multilingual 'selling globe trotters' who deal with equipment, advanced technology or turnkey projects. This section relates to companies that sell durable or non-durable consumer goods, equipment for small businesses or intermediate industrial goods. In each country where they are established, such companies have a local consumer base and local sales representatives, and therefore the influence of culture on sales force compensation systems is much stronger. Problems arise when multinational companies try to unify the remuneration systems of local sales staff and when they attempt to apply a standardized incentive system linked to the parent company's culture to local sales representatives.

Incentives for sales representatives

Hofstede's (1991, 2001) parameters can be used (section 3.2) as well as Hall's theory of communication (1976) to clarify the incentives issue. The organization must encourage its sales representatives and/or the sales team to attain specific objectives (turnover target, profit target, promotion of certain products, gaining market share at the expense of competitors, etc.). There are therefore several steps, which are influenced by cultural differences:

1. Setting objectives.
2. Evaluation, i.e. setting up a system to calculate target-to-actual-sales deviation followed by feedback to the salespeople.
3. Compensating the sales force achievements: designing the incentive system and attempting to standardize it across countries.
4. Implementing the sales force compensation system.

Two incentive systems for monitoring the sales force (models 1 and 2 in Table 15.2) are described below. They are Weberian 'ideal types', not necessarily to be found in their pure form in the real world. Model 1 is appropriate for a firm belonging to an individualistic society where communication is fairly explicit (low context, see section 13.1), power distance is small and uncertainty avoidance is weak (e.g. the United States). Model 2 is appropriate for a company originating from a society where communication is implicit (high context), power distance is high and uncertainty avoidance is strong (e.g. Japan). One can hypothesize that the masculinity/femininity cultural dimension also influences the practical implementation of these two models of sales force compensation: assertive (masculine) and nurturing (feminine) feedback to low-performing salespeople and corrective actions are carried out differently.

Table 15.2 Contrast models

Cultural traits	Model 1	Model 2
Power distance	Low	High
Individualism	High	Low
Uncertainty avoidance	Low	High
Context of communication	Low	High

Attitudes towards the setting of objectives and their use in performance measurement

The first step is the setting of sales objectives. Here, differences in the preciseness and contextuality of communication style across societies (Hall, 1976) affect the setting of objectives. Objectives that are precisely set, quantified and openly negotiated correspond to societies where people communicate fairly explicitly with a weak context. On the other hand, the stronger the tendency to communicate with a high context, the poorer will seem a system based solely on numbers. 'Number crunching' is not a trait of high-context societies: figures are not assumed to depict correctly the complexities of the real world. In high-context societies, numbers are considered as efficient, but oversimplified. Despite that, some kind of quantified objectives are needed, but they are not considered as accurate and do not serve the same purpose. Depending on which model (1 or 2) is appropriate, objectives may have different roles.

The first role is that of *formal and realistic evaluation* (model 1), where the sellers must deserve their salary. In societies where relations have been relatively depersonalized people can be evaluated by figures: the bottom line is related to what an average seller is expected to attain. Target levels of sales are negotiated with the salesperson. Only results are relevant. The deviation of actual sales from target is measured precisely. Corrective actions, sanctions and rewards result from the monitoring of the salesperson's performance (carried out by the boss).

The second major role is that of *internal incentive* (model 2), where the situation is not as clear cut. In societies where the seller cannot easily be dismissed (e.g. lifetime employment and strong uncertainty avoidance, emphasizing a high level of job security), staff turnover is low and closer personal ties exist within a stable work force. The objective is not openly and truly negotiated, as in model 1, since high power distance clashes with the idea that task objectives should ideally be set by oneself. It is assumed that the boss knows what the sales staff should achieve, not the salespeople themselves. The objective then is not necessarily as realistic as in model 1. The boss may manipulate the situation by setting 'instrumental' objectives: excessively high target levels are set which serve as an ultimate level of attainment. Although everybody knows (implicitly) that a lower performance level will be achieved, this will still be a better performance than if such an ambitious objective had not been set. The risk is that sellers may seek security and lack personal initiative and drive.

Accuracy of goal setting

After objectives have been set, deviation from the target must be measured. The accuracy of systems of performance evaluation and incentive calculation is always higher in a situation of explicit communication, corresponding to model 1. This orientation rewards individual merits, even more so when the company emphasizes individual rather than team achievements. In other words, the individual is seen as the very source of the performance (see the individualism assumptions detailed in section 3.1). In the case of high context/implicit communication (model 2), the evaluation phase is not necessarily precisely and formally implemented since the objective may be significantly higher than that which can realistically be attained. In failing to attain the set objectives, sellers will, nonetheless, have made their very best efforts. If model 1 were applied at this step only, they would be considered as underperforming. However, owing to the implicit system of evaluation, they are not considered so. There is unspoken awareness in the organization that sales objectives are not wholly realistic. No formal and quantified evaluation is implemented. Furthermore, what constitutes a good sales performance is implicitly clear within the company, making it relatively useless to assess performance very precisely.

Individualism/collectivism, uncertainty avoidance and performance measurement

The individualist or collectivist orientation in a society is a meaningful axis of cultural differentiation (Hofstede, 1991). In the United States, where individualism is very strong, the cultural emphasis is put on individual achievements (Kotabe et al., 1992). It implies precise and individualized sales targets, fostering competition within the sales force. Competition between the salespeople, within the sales team, is considered legitimate, even though it may undermine the coherence of collective action when this is needed (e.g. in exchange of information on customers and accounts, training other salespeople in sales practices, transfer of experience from senior to junior salespeople, etc.).

More traditional societies tend not to engage in individual goal setting and variable commission rewarding. Still (1981) argues that, in Thailand, family background largely determines social position, much more than money, which confers only limited status. Fixed salaries demonstrate social status, stability and group belonging. As such, they are more desirable than a larger income that includes a substantial but variable commission component, as this emphasizes individualism and instability. Similarly, Hill *et al.* (1991, p. 23) point out:

Tradition is also an important determinant of Japanese compensation plans. Because their social system is based on hereditary and seniority criteria, salary raises, even for sales forces, are based on longevity with the company. Similarly commission systems are tied to the combined efforts of the entire sales force, fostering the Japanese team ethic and downplaying the economic aspirations of individuals.

Precise measurement of salespeople's performance may even be considered almost evil in some countries. In South-East Asia, the ethics of non-confrontation clearly clash with an objective review of performance. It could cause the subordinate to 'lose face' and would infringe a societal norm (Redding, 1982). Motivation theories, which in fact underlie sales force compensation systems, are culturally bound, because they were developed in the United States by Americans and for Americans (Adler, 1991). They put a strong emphasis on individualism and rationalism as bases for human behaviour.

According to Hofstede's empirical description of work-related values, collectivist societies such as Japan tend to favour global stimulation of the sales force as a team. Intrinsic rewards are favoured. Conversely, more individualistic societies such as the United States will favour individual performance variables (individual sales, profits per area, etc.) and extrinsic rewards. For instance, Money and Graham (1999) found that in the United States job satisfaction was primarily driven by satisfaction with their pay, whereas in Japan it was related to satisfaction with co-workers and happiness with work. Conversely,

Hanna and Srivastava (1998) found that in Japan the sales force had a preference for extrinsic, competition-oriented rewards, especially the younger salespeople. However, the extrinsic rewards were not only individual, but also included a component of group reward.

The marketing information systems needed to run these intrinsic/extrinsic stimulation methods are rather different. The same retrieved information may serve different functional purposes according to the country. In Germany, very detailed market information will be sought in an attempt to reduce uncertainty in decision making, since Germans fear uncertainty and try to avoid it (Hofstede, 1991). In the United States, where a high value is put on assertiveness and personal achievement (masculine society, with low uncertainty avoidance) the same detailed information will be used for the precise control of salespeople.

Femininity/masculinity and ways of remedying underperformance

When sellers are clearly underperforming, there are different methods to deal with the problem, particularly from the point of view of the immediate superiors. In a masculine society, the absence of results will be emphasized in a fairly crude manner. In a company where the individual is supposed to be efficient and to perform well, unsatisfactory achievements will probably lead first to a clear warning that performance must be improved. Then, if the salesperson fails to come up with arguments relating to factors outside his or her control and if underperformance continues, the employee will be dismissed. This hard-line method does not, on balance, lead to better sales performance than the methods employed by companies based in feminine countries.

In countries that are more femininity oriented (Sweden, northern European countries, France), values are placed more strongly on quality of life. There is a protective and maternal attitude on the part of the organization towards its members. This does not mean, however, that these societies strive less for efficiency than masculine societies. Sellers who underperform will simply be entitled to more understanding. Checks are initially made to see if there are any explanations, apart from their abilities as salespeople, which may excuse their weak performance, such as poor definition of a sales area with too small a potential, or particularly strong competition within the sector, etc. When the reasons for their underperformance have been assessed with them (formally or informally), they receive assistance from colleagues and from the organization (especially in the form of additional training). It is only after the organization has done everything within its power to help the salesperson to increase his or her performance that a final decision is taken.

Compensation systems based on cultural values and industry characteristics

Table 15.3 describes some basic sales force compensation systems according not only to the cultural values involved but also to the type of goods sold. Fixed salaries, for instance, will be preferred where uncertainty avoidance is high. Employees who enjoy job security have a preference for a fixed salary, possibly with a limited part of it related to variable commissions. Salespeople accept pure commission payments, with no fixed salary at all, only in model 1. Cultural dimensions combine with the type of industry, which also has a strong influence on the compensation system: sellers are not rewarded in the same way for the sale of nuclear plants, batteries and photocopiers. Large individual sales, requiring lengthy sales efforts and sales force teamwork, tend to be in line with straight salary compensation, as do the cultural values of model 2. Smaller individual sales, requiring

individually identifiable sales efforts, tend to correspond with commission payments and the cultural values of model 1.

The rewards can be intrinsic or extrinsic. Intrinsic rewards are related to the satisfaction of inner needs. They are rewards which individuals give to themselves (Anderson and Chambers, 1985). They involve no pecuniary element and have no influence on material life. People may be intrinsically motivated by a job well done, the esteem of their colleagues or even the securing of a contract *per se*.

On the other hand, extrinsic rewards are material and are generally made in cash or in kind. They involve different forms of bonuses and commissions. Extrinsic rewards can be linear (in direct proportion to sales exceeding the objective), progressive or retrospective, or can be triggered once a single objective has been attained; the criteria and formulae for calculating variable extrinsic rewards are very varied (Hill *et al.*, 1991; Chonko *et al.*, 1992). Purely extrinsic rewards, such as variable commissions on sales, are motivators which work 'from the outside'. Some rewards are on the fringe of intrinsic and extrinsic rewards: for example, medals or titles (best salesperson for the period). Rewards can be centred on the individual, on the group (e.g. a leisure trip for the whole sales team) or on a mix of both (e.g. awards for the best sales teams). As is frequently the case in Japan, group rewards may take the form of a joint holiday for the sales team, which is both an individual and a group reward simultaneously, contributing to the consolidation of the intra-group relationship. Various forms can be considered for rewarding

Table 15.3 Basic sales force compensation systems, sectors and the cultural values involved

Objectives/type of goods	Compensation plans	Values involved
Long-term sales efforts; equipment, turnkey sales	Fixed salary and promotions	Lifetime employment; cooperation within the sales team; collective performance
Reach precise sales quotas; consumer goods	Pure (or quasi-pure) commission	Own business: no loyalty to the company; individualistic and competitive
Achieve more precise goals (sales of certain products, new territories or segments)	Fixed salary, plus monetary and non-monetary incentives	Mixed values: contract and long-term orientation; loyalty but not unlimited commitment

individuals: short breaks or long holidays, presents to the sellers or their relatives, payment by the company of certain personal expenditures, etc.

Models 1 and 2 depict extreme characteristics, but real-world compensation systems combine intrinsic and extrinsic, individual and collective rewards. Rewards such as promotion and salary increases combine recognition (intrinsic) and money (extrinsic). A large range of possibilities for compensation exists, which can be used to design a sales force compensation system adapted to the local culture. Two caveats must be added: (1) model 2 is not the paradise of salespeople in contrast to the extreme pressure to achieve in model 1 – nothing may be derived from these models in terms of different salespeople's satisfaction across cultures, and/or perception of being treated fairly; and (2) standardization of sales-force compensation is possible at the regional level where cultural variance is limited.

Kotabe *et al.* (1992) show that US salespeople perceive that they are treated more fairly by their organizations than the Japanese or Koreans, especially in terms of the pace at which their sales managers require them to perform their tasks and assignments. Japanese employees, traditionally regarded as highly motivated and productive, are also under strong pressure to perform, as a way to maintain their place in the group. As for Koreans, Kotabe *et al.* (1992, p. 45) note that

many Korean employees appear to have little control over their destinies in their organizations because of the seemingly autocratic management style and the use of non-contingent reward-based systems. Management decisions, as they relate to employees, apparently are often predicated on criteria unrelated to an individual's performance. This kind of situation may lead employees to experience inequity.

Programmes aiming at the improvement of sales-force productivity can be standardized at the regional level, as shown by the example of Digital Equipment Corporation, for the 2,500-strong sales force of its 17 European subsidiaries (Kashani, 1989, p. 94); they must be prepared carefully, with respect for people and their cultures:

sales managers were at first predictably unenthusiastic about using the system. It was considered an infringement on their authority. What gradually sold them on it was the continuity of attention the program got in the two years after its highly visible launch, through watchful monitoring

of progress toward full implementation, coordinating sessions among local sales managers, and periodic messages of reinforcement from top management . . . The coordinating sessions for subsidiary sales managers were particularly helpful, highlighting the payoffs from use of the system and furnishing a forum for dealing with common problems.

15.5

Public relations across cultures

Public relations (PR) consists of a set of coordinated communication programmes between an organization and its publics, designed to improve, maintain or protect a company product or image. The 'publics' concerned by PR can be internal, such as employees, or external to the firm, such as the general public, customers, suppliers, distributors or the media. Other targets for PR actions are government, for the purpose of lobbying about new or existing legislation, or stockholders and the financial community. The function of PR in a cross-national, and therefore most often a cross-cultural context, is made difficult especially in terms of *mutual* understanding. The functions of PR are twofold: (1) in normal situations, to create and enhance a favourable corporate image with the various publics concerned, with the view that a foreign firm is particularly susceptible to nationalistic criticism; (2) in crisis situations such as boycotts, accidents, strikes, product recalls, and so on, to maintain goodwill by responding to criticism, explaining remedial action that is taken to overcome the problem, and anticipating and countering messages that may damage the corporate image.

Cross-cultural differences have been noted in the way companies react to disasters such as plane crashes, major pollution, etc. They reflect the prevailing sense of responsibility *vis-à-vis* the community but also the companies' sense of secrecy and the view of what is culturally appropriate for dealing with these events: adopting a very low profile and waiting for the tempest to calm down or adopting a high profile, pleading either guilty or not guilty. Swiss pharmaceutical companies, when confronted with major pollution incidents in the Rhine River, which were allegedly their fault, adopted an extremely low profile, engaging in very little communication, reflecting the Swiss penchant for secrecy and dislike of public display. When JAL suffered its worst-ever plane crash in 1985, with 520 dead, the JAL response was very elaborate, going far beyond what westerners would expect in such situations, including the dismissal of its president and public apologies to the Japanese people (Pinsdorf, 1991). Similarly, in 2004, when Mitsubishi Motors was found to have covered up truck defects, blamed for a series of accidents, the Japanese government made strong statements about how 'deplorable' their actions were and took action against Mitsubishi Motors (banning purchases of vehicles for at least one year), as well as the executives involved.

PR enters the scene as a very different form of communication: it is not advertising, or salesmanship. PR people, whether full-time officers or outside PR consultants, have nothing to sell. They use publicity as a means of conveying messages to the publics (whether by securing editorial space in the case of any kind of films, videotapes or slides), as well as the organization of events, meetings, conferences, sponsorship. The Channel Tunnel for instance, burdened with financial problems and construction delays, had to undertake PR with the two basic stockholder communities, French and British, and with the international banks financing the project. There may be many cross-cultural differences, including the very notion of PR, which is rooted in *modern* corporate culture, and may be unknown in some cultural contexts.

Cultural variance may occur in the following aspects of the PR process: (1) the recommendations for making contact are basically the same as in section 15.2, except that a PR officer is selling nothing, which may make the contact both easier (there being no money involved) and less efficient (PR may be considered purposeless); (2) managing relationships; (3) disclosing information, especially in the case of private, secret or sensitive information; (4) developing arguments, some of which cannot be understood locally; and (5) dealing with nationalistic feelings.

Managing relationships: Thinking locally

People from Western countries do not naturally think in terms of who is a member of which group: working with the key ethnic groups is, however, a key element for good PR in many foreign contexts. The model of a free press can not be assumed: in many countries its freedom is curtailed by the government, often in much more subtle ways than mere censorship. The influence of local competition should not be underestimated: the lack of antitrust laws in many countries reflects the legitimacy of making market-sharing or price agreements with competitors and the lack of concern with the benefits for consumers of 'fair trade'. Consequently, PR officers may be involved in talks with competing firms, a practice which would be considered unethical in the United States because it would infringe US antitrust legislation. Such discussions are all the more important when the local competitors are technologically inferior to the foreign firm but the local firm can use their nationality as a weapon against a foreign intruder.

When making agreements, PR officers should avoid: (1) unnecessarily disclosing information that local parties regard as secret, the sense of confidentiality being culturally relative; (2) using arguments that are not understood because their basic logic clashes with the host country culture; and (3) conveying messages about local people and culture that are perceived as negative.

Foreign firms have to face nationalism: being foreign makes things slightly worse for a company when it is under attack. When Audi cars faced the problem of sudden acceleration with its 5,000 series in the United States, the German company, a subsidiary of the Volkswagen group, did not adopt a low profile, convinced as it was of the high quality of its engineering. It took a very negative stance against the CBS television programme *60 minutes*, which showed the problems of sudden acceleration and interviewed drivers. Audi criticized the tests made for this programme and further, denied the allegations, attributing sudden acceleration to the negligence of the drivers. Finally, Audi took action too late and recalled 25,000 cars in January 1987. The market response was dramatic and sales in the US dropped from 74,000 in 1985 to 23,000 in 1988 (Czinkota and Ronkainen, 1990).

Ambiguous arguments are as much to be avoided as taking too strong a position. If the local employees of a multinational company receive better pay than the average worker in the country, this can be seen as beneficial to the recipients individually but detrimental to the community as a whole, because, for instance, it lures farmers to the industrial sector, or it causes merchants to raise their prices because of the purchasing power of a small affluent group.

Emphasizing local citizenship is always necessary: it must be done with unambiguous arguments. Hence in the mid-1980s IBM emphasized its importance in Europe as a local employer, citing the number of employees in each country and the local R & D efforts. Such a view of local citizenship embodied in a global attitude was expressed by Percy Barnevik, the Swedish-born president and chief executive officer of ABB (the merger of Asea (Sweden) and Brown Boveri (Switzerland)), when he was asked by William Taylor (1991, p. 91), the associate editor of the *Harvard Business Review*, what it means to be a global company:

ABB is a company with no geographic center, no national axe to grind. We are a federation of national companies with a global coordination center. Are we a Swiss company? Our headquarters is in Zurich, but only 100 professionals work at headquarters and we will not increase that number. Are we a Swedish company? I'm the CEO and I was born and educated in Sweden. But our headquarters is not in Sweden, and only two members of our board of directors are Swedes. Perhaps we are an American company. We report our financial results in U.S. dollars, and English is ABB's official language. We conduct all high-level meetings in English. My point is that ABB is none of those things – and all of those things. We are not homeless. We are a company with many homes.

The need for public relations not only varies due to actions of the firm, but also may vary due to actions of governments. For instance, Garten (2003) warns that American firms are underestimating the growing risks of anti-American sentiment. He points to surveys by RoperASW and DBB Worldwide that indicate the value of American brands is being eroded by this sentiment: 'U.S. corporations are increasingly seen as arrogant and insensitive to local cultures . . . attitudes that will harden as local opposition to U.S. foreign policy grows' (p. 30). Keith Reinhard, chairman of DBB Worldwide proposed a collective 'USA Inc.' effort to offset the damage.

The case of product liability

Product liability is an area where PR is needed. For instance, when Mitsubishi Motors was found to have covered-up truck defects, blamed for a series of accidents, their sales plummeted. According to Treece and

Yamaguchi (2004), Mitsubishi's sales dropped almost 39 per cent in May as compared to a year earlier and the drop is expected to worsen.

Nestlé, the Swiss food company, one of the largest in the world, faced a boycott because its infant-feeding formula had allegedly caused many deaths of babies in the Third World. In 1974, a report by a British journalist and a pamphlet entitled 'Nestlé kills babies' started an accusation process that developed during the mid-1970s. Nestlé withdrew its infant formula advertising and decided to participate in consumer education programmes. The key reasons for the problems experienced by Nestlé's Third World consumers' were cultural: the belief in the magic properties of Western products and the pressure to give what is the best, the most modern, as a sign of love for babies. A more down-to-earth reason was the poor use of the product, mixed with contaminated water. Nestlé should have anticipated the key reasons for misuses of its otherwise excellent product: (1) illiteracy – people just cannot read the instructions for use; (2) even when literate, people rarely rely on written materials, which have an abstract image; and (3) the inability to cope with ambiguous messages: the product is good but can be bad. This is a problem for pharmaceutical companies, in that most drugs have side effects. However, in many countries it is dangerous to mention them too explicitly since people will not believe in a drug whose manufacturer clearly acknowledges the potentially adverse consequences (most of which can be avoided by proper use!). (*WS15.5* has links to worldwide PR databases and companies.)

15.6

Bribery: Facts

Bribery is associated with selling, obtaining favours, making things work: it is a practice that can be found in almost all cultures. The Germans call it *Schmiergeld* ('grease money'), the French *pot-de-vin* (literally jug of wine), in the Middle East it is a baksheesh, in Italy a *Bastarella* (little envelope) and in Mexico a *mordida* (a bite). These practices know few borders and even the Japanese construction industry has been heavily plagued by bribery scandals in recent years. Naturally every country officially prohibits bribery, but laws are locally enforced. Principles are often universal, whereas their enforcement may be a matter of place (see Tables 3.6 and 3.7 on the types of rules; in addition, *WS15.6* contains a link to the *Global Corruption Report*, which examines corruption across different countries).

Types of bribery

Information and data on illegal payments are very sparse and often fragmentary. Such issues are sensitive and companies remain very secretive. Factual data have, however, been collected, both through the investigations carried out by financial journalists (Péan, 1988) and academic researchers (Walter, 1989) and, more systematically in the US, as a consequence of prosecutions under the Foreign Corrupt Practices Act 1977 (Gillespie, 1987).

The practice is too widespread to be ignored. It takes various forms:

1. *Small and large gifts*. A common practice is to offer influential foreign officials a trip, fully paid, at a four-star hotel with a limousine for the duration of their stay; the whole affair, including receptions, restaurants and pretty hostesses for evenings, quickly reaches a cost of $50,000.
2. *Percentages* paid based on the contract value. Here the illegal payments result in much larger sums being paid, in proportion to the size of the contract (whether it is for the sale of a squadron of fighter planes, or a turnkey plant, etc.). Indeed, in the United States, the public disclosure of the illegal payments involving American multinationals in the 1970s mentioned sums of up to US$70 million. The companies involved included Lockheed, United Brands and Gulf Oil. Many other firms were implicated, principally in the mining, aeronautical and engineering sectors. Today, corruption affairs still flourish in large international negotiations of turnkey projects. For instance, eight international construction companies were charged with bribery in Lesotho after they allegedly paid bribes to win contracts for an US$8 billion dam project that was partly funded by the World Bank. The alleged offenders were companies from France, Italy, the United Kingdom, Canada and South Africa (BBC News, 1999).
3. *Tips*. When civil servants are poorly paid, but hold authority and responsibility (e.g. a police officer, a customs officer or a tax inspector) it may be 'implicitly understood' that in exchange for carrying out poorly rewarded public duties, such officials may supplement their income. Thus to pass through customs or to obtain a tax form (for a mandatory declaration) requires a 'greasing' payment, which may be seen as a form of implicit salary, in so far as the authorities are perfectly well aware of the existence of such practices. In China in 1993, more than 60,000 cases of corruption of civil servants were revealed, with more than half a million people being under investigation and more than 10,000 already tried before a court (Galtung, 1994). In Ukraine, business activities are highly regulated and 32 different ministries are entitled to issue licences for various activities. Since inspectors from government bodies have the right to inspect companies at any time and for almost any reason, the average Ukrainian manager spends two days per week on inspections. The regulatory system offers a large leeway to inspectors in their dealings with enterprises; as a consequence, bribing inspectors is a quick and efficient path for Ukrainian managers to obtain official approval (Pidluska, 1998). A similar situation is depicted by Werner (2000, p. 18) as concerns another ex-Soviet republic Kazakstan, where 'nothing is allowed but everything is possible [provided that you pay for it !]'.

Methods

Whether illegal payments are made, and what sums are involved, varies widely from country to country. Payments are much more substantial, for example, in the construction industry or in Nigeria than in electronics or in Australia. An important caveat must be made: not everyone is corrupt. There is nothing worse than attempting to bribe someone who strongly disapproves of such immoral behaviour. This last point is clearly illustrated by Agpar (1977) who quotes the case of the managing director of a large American multinational who offered 500 Saudi Riyals in cash to a Saudi police officer (about US$140) so as to ensure that a decision on a fairly minor offence against labour law would be favourable. In a fury, the officer reported the attempted bribe to his superiors. After spending 20 days in prison, the businessman was fined 25,000 Riyals and was fortunate to escape a more serious penalty. As emphasized by Werner (2000), bribing is similar to gift exchange in that it follows a culturally coded etiquette that indicates who is willing to accept a bribe, where and when it can safely be given, and what to say and do when presenting the bribe to the recipient. This case clearly demonstrates the danger and also the ineffectiveness of the direct method (passing cash from one hand to another). Accordingly, more indirect methods exist instead:

1. Slush funds are set up to effect small payments by cheque, nominally as payment for services rendered. Systematically overstated expense reports are a commonly used device for funding slush funds: auditors may discover them when expense report copies are marked up from what the actual expense had been, with markups averaging 1,000 per cent of the actual expenses (Thompson, 2002). In the 1980s, for instance, Braniff Airlines sold 3,500 plane tickets in South America for a total of US$900,000 without making any record of the transactions in their accounts. This money was used to set up a slush fund that in turn fed a secret bank account. This money was mentioned neither in the parent company accounts, nor in those of the subsidiary. This secret account was used to pay additional commissions to organizers and travel agents in clear breach of the Federal Aviation Act.

2. The transfer of what the English call 'brown paper packets' or 'plain brown envelopes' is often made by an intermediate consultancy company. These companies often have their head office in Luxemburg or Liechtenstein, or in some other tax haven. The consultancy company is often involved right from the tender stage in the case of a factory or turnkey project. Consider the scenario where one of the key decision-makers for the final selection of the foreign contractor controls a local construction consultancy company. During a reception, this person will whisper to the head of the negotiating team of a large engineering or construction company he is dealing with that it would be advantageous if his consultancy

company were to be requested to carry out preliminary technical studies. These studies will in fact be largely fictitious. The fees paid for these studies will correspond to the commission. If these studies are further sub-contracted to a nominee company in Luxemburg, the baksheesh money will be transferred to a 'safe place'.

3. Nominee and local consultancy companies, to which 'phoney' consulting contracts are given, may be used in different ways. For example, an approach may be made to an adviser to the transport minister for country X who is well placed to influence the decision on an underground railway project in town Y. It will be suggested that he be made a part-time employee of the Luxemburg-based nominee company. Without having to move at all he will receive a salary each month which, for reasons of discretion and convenience, will be paid into an account in Switzerland. When he goes skiing with his family, the adviser/consultant will take the money out of his bank account in Geneva, then discreetly spend it in an exclusive ski resort. Money spent abroad is less compromising than money brought back home.

4. Two other accounting solutions are frequently employed: the over-invoicing of certain transactions, expenditure or receipts, and the recording of fictitious transactions. For example, the American Hospital Supply company was obliged to pay a 10 per cent commission to obtain the contract for the construction of a hospital in Saudi Arabia. AHS artificially inflated the price of the contract, then recorded a commission for consultancy fees, even though no service of this type had been rendered. This allowed the 10 per cent commission to become tax-deductible expenditure, and made the payment apparently legitimate, whereas in fact it remained illegal (Daniels *et al.*, 1982). Vogl (1998, p. 30) gives the example of a European supplier of pharmaceuticals negotiating with the minister of health of a developing country that has received emergency funds from an aid agency to purchase urgently required medicines: 'Instead of agreeing on the purchase of new drugs, the minister and the supplier conspire to use the aid funds to purchase out-of-date drugs which are far cheaper. The supplier consequently makes a handsome profit and places a portion of it in an offshore bank account set up by the minister.'

15.7

Bribery: Ethical aspects

Bribery is considered by most business people as a key ethical issue in international marketing. According to Mayo *et al.* (1991), more than one-third of a sample of US executives ranked bribery as the most serious of ten possible ethical problems that may arise in international marketing operations. Similarly, Australian and Canadian managers rank gifts, favours and entertainment, traditional small-scale bribery, and the confusing issue of whether gifts are intended as bribes or not in different cultures, as the three key ethical problems in international marketing out of a list of ten (Chan and Armstrong, 1999).

The first ethical position is that of cultural relativism: whether it is right or wrong, good or bad, depends on one's culture. This is based on the view that rules are applicable locally in the ingroup territory and thus when in Rome, one should do as the Romans do. In relativistic terms, words such as 'right' or 'wrong', 'good' or 'bad', only have a meaning within a specific cultural context. The first part of this section tries to give a view of cultural relativism in the case of Africa where corrupt money is largely, but not completely, redistributed in society. However, one cannot ignore the negative consequences of such widespread corrupt practices. Galtung (1994) and others show the heavy burden placed by corruption on economic development: for instance, the property of President Mobutu Sese Seko of Zaire is said to be equivalent to the whole of the external debt of the country. A second position is therefore cultural universalism, which is based on the view that there are core ethical principles which are universally applicable, whenever and to whomever, independently of territory and group membership. The US Foreign Corrupt Practices Act of 1977, revised in 1988, is an example of such a universalist approach to ethics *and* rules. The third possible view is a pragmatic and respectful view of how ethical behaviour can be developed in a cross-cultural context.

Cultural relativism: The bribe as bonanza

There is often a tendency to oversimplify the issue of international corruption to one of a face-to-face meeting between two people, a donor and a recipient. In reality the donor of the baksheesh often faces a group of recipients: an illegal payment rarely benefits one single person. As a result bribery is intermingled with a dense network of social relationships. Bonds of fraternity and complicity develop between people of the same ethnic background or tribe. These people are necessary intermediaries for ensuring that the influences, the information search and the handing over of the baksheesh may all be effectively implemented. The bonds built on everyday cooperation call for redistribution of small parts of the bribe: the secretary who guesses the existence of the baksheesh, the customs officer who intercepts a 'brown paper parcel', etc. However, each should take their share in proportion to their level of influence and power in the society and should take care not to exaggerate (Box 15.4).

Most of Kinshasa's residents, who were abandoned by the corrupt regime of Mobutu Sese Seko, had lived by roadside trading in order to feed their families. Article 15, a fictional clause in the constitution was a general licence to do whatever you liked, or 'Fend for Yourself' and almost nothing was outside its ambit. A cleanup campaign spearheaded by Kinshasa governor Theophile Memba, has attempted to transform Zaire. Tom Boland (1998) reports that small traders were alarmed by measures that would deny them their living. Boland says that 'With Article 15 still at the back of their minds, many of the traders who have been moved on in recent weeks, have bounced back and reappeared in nearby spaces.' One senior Kinshasa banker says 'It's only when the state has provided an alternative space for trading that this kind of operation has proved successful.'

Bonds may also be forged by the possibility of retaliation; those who have not requested a baksheesh, but who have a strong suspicion as to its existence, may either inform the authorities or exert a sort of implicit blackmail by demanding their 'cut'. They may even take no action by simply closing their eyes to what is happening. They are guided by their rationality: they can take the risk of participating in illegal remuneration and benefit personally; exert blackmail and thereby risk offending those in power leading to ultimate punishment; or lastly inform against the person who has accepted the bribe and suffer any adverse consequences that may result.

Primitive hunter/gatherer societies, as described by ethnologists, can be used as an archetype for the

Box 15.4

'Article 15'

On the banks of the large Zaire river just as in the province of Shaba, no one in Zaire is surprised to see a civil servant demanding a 'matabiche' in return for a passport or some other official document. On the contrary, people would be worried if such a request was not made. No Zairian would take offence at having to pay for an official hearing, or to have a letter sent to a department head. Seals and headed note paper are bought and are even sometimes forged. In Zaire, civil servants are 'resourceful people' and know how to supplement their income. The police set up roadblocks when they need money: drivers never have the requisite paper and are therefore obliged to put their hands in their pockets.

At the main post office in 'Kin' (Kinshasa, the capital), letters and parcels may – like anywhere else in the world – be posted in a box, but it is less than certain that they will ever arrive at their destination. The 'citizen' (in Zaire, the 'Supreme Guide' has brought into fashion this revolutionary title) greatly increases the chances of this occurring if he greases the palm of the postman. Likewise, a citizen may make a telephone call to the other end of the planet for the price of a tip. All this comes under 'Article 15' a shameful way of designating the small scale corruption practised by civil servants. This corruption is institutionalised and widespread; it also goes under the name of 'matabiche': bribe, backhander, a 'little something', brown paper packet.

The practice is so ingrained that President Mobutu did not shy away from encouraging it in a speech on the 20th May 1976: 'If you are going to steal, steal a small amount and do it intelligently, in a nice way. If you are going to steal so much that you become rich in a single night, you will be arrested.'

(Source: Excerpt from Péan, 1988, pp. 139–40.)

redistribution of a bribe considered as plunder. While the men hunt (symbolically: those who hold power and go 'hunting' for large sums), the women, children and the elderly devote their efforts instead to gathering wild fruits and vegetables (symbolically: those who collaborate at a menial level, but who are still aware of what is happening). Ultimately the bribe/plunder is divided up according to fairly precise rules. Redistributing plunder and crops among the members of one's tribe is basic moral behaviour in many countries (see Box 15.5). However, the tendency to think that developing countries have 'lower' ethical standards should be resisted, even though the extent of bribery in some developing nations and evidence from research would suggest it. For instance, Burns and Brady (1996), show lower ethical perceptions among Malaysian students than American students; Al-Khatib *et al.* (1996) show that Egyptians are more lenient towards 'questionable actions' than Americans. There is, however, a systemic effect: sellers' markets, high inflation, low wages and economic hardship explain questionable practices while they obviously do not excuse them. Very often, the bribery issue is not one of ethical standards, but a mere matter of survival. Arnould (1995, p. 130) gives the example of West African traders who refuse to pay the bribes asked for by customs agents or policemen: 'A truck and its contents were burned at the border between Benin and Togo under mysterious circumstances when the driver working for one onion trader in Lomé refused to pay.'

Average citizens unfortunately get used to the behaviour of officials securing special privileges for themselves and their close friends. In Bulgaria a survey showed that 57 per cent of the population believed that politicians were primarily interested in taking advantage of their power position (CIPE, 1998). Economic power is intermingled with political influence, such as in the tradition known as *coronelismo* in Brazilian politics, which corresponds to the case of wealthy landowners who can bribe, manipulate and pressure the local electorate to vote for the

Box 15.5

A good minister in Senegal

For the man in the street, a good minister is a demagogue, someone who is adept at by-passing the law and its rulings to keep the voters from his region, his parents and his friends happy. If you try to behave like a minister acting objectively by treating your cousins, your allies, members of the branch of your party in the same way as all other citizens, even political opponents, the people will be totally confused. You will not be understood. You are not respecting the rules of the game. You will be the object of public contempt. You are not a minister for the purpose of serving the nation or carrying out the policies of a government which is in power for the good of all its citizens. You are first and

foremost a minister for your own good, so that you may take advantage of your position, and enable your parents and allies, your friends and the members of your party to benefit too. No one will reproach you, everyone will understand. Those who are out of office are the only ones who will criticise this behaviour although if they were in office themselves they could not be sure of resisting the demands of their own tribe, family, or parents-in-law. There is nothing wrong in taking advantage of one's position to help out one's relatives; the ideal would be to consider all citizens as your own relatives.

(Source: Ndao, 1985, pp. 34–5.)

candidates they choose. *Coronelismo* still flourishes in isolated and impoverished regions of the Brazilian countryside (Gallant, 1997).

It is sometimes difficult to distinguish between a gift and a bribe. Both obey the norms of reciprocity that are linked to the local context. As emphasized by Steidelmeier (1999, p. 127) 'phenomenologically, it is difficult to distinguish a bribe from a tip or a commission or consulting fee. In the end, moral judgment depends upon the social understanding of the meaning of the action as derived from the analysis of means and ends, consequences and intentions.'

Werner (2000) also acknowledges the lack of clear boundary between gifts and bribes. She explains that in Kazakstan there are ten words for different types of gifts and ritual payments according to the context and the nature of the gift; for instance *kiit* and *minit* are gifts to in-laws, the first in the form of clothing, the second in livestock or money. However, the word for bribe, *para*, is used consistently to refer to illegal exchanges: 'a traffic policeman may extort a relatively small amount of money, the local equivalent of a few dollars, from an innocent driver. In a different context, a young man who needs a job might voluntarily pay a bribe of $500 to $1,500 to a military official, who in return will forge a document specifying that the young man was exempt from military service for health reasons ($500) or a document specifying that

the young man actually did complete military service ($1,500)' (p. 18).

Recent evolution in the fight against bribery in international contracts

Since the United States adopted the FCPA (Foreign Corrupt Practices Act) in 1977, they have been constantly fighting at the international level to have such legislation adopted by the major industrialized countries (Lewis, 1998). They have used different international organizations as forums for promoting global anti-bribery legislation, including the 8th International Conference Against Corruption, which issued the Lima Declaration Against Corruption, a blueprint for action. The major achievement is the OECD Convention on Combating Bribery of Foreign Public Officials in International Business Transactions, which is an extension of the principles contained in the FCPA among the OECD[1] countries.

The OECD convention

The convention was adopted on 21 November 1997. It is now progressively being ratified by the signatory countries[2] (the 29 OECD countries plus Argentina, Brazil, Bulgaria, Chile and Slovakia). The text obligates parties to criminalize bribery of foreign public officials. It does not specifically cover political parties; however, business-related bribes to foreign public officials made through political parties and party officials are covered. The negotiators agreed to apply 'effective, proportionate and dissuasive criminal penalties'. The convention requires that countries be able to seize the bribe or property of similar value or that they apply monetary sanctions of comparable effect.

The convention is not self-enforcing: countries have to modify their existing laws and enact new ones to comply with the provisions of the convention, which outlaws (Hamra, 2000):[3]

1. Kickbacks to obtain or retain government business.
2. The tax deductibility of bribes as business expenses.
3. Off-the-books accounting practices.
4. Loose public procurement procedures which facilitate bribes and collusion.
5. Bribing through intermediairies, consultants and agents.

Most developed countries have now ratified the convention and modified their national legislation so as to make it locally enforceable. In Tokyo, on 30 November 2001, the Third Annual Conference of the ADB/OECD[4] adopted an Anti-Corruption Initiative for Asia-Pacific, whereby 17 Asian and Pacific governments endorsed a regional action plan to fight corruption. However, some efforts are less successful: the Inter-American Convention against Corruption that was signed by 26 countries in 1996 has been ratified by only ten.

Other efforts at combating bribery

The International Chamber of Commerce (ICC) has also been playing an active role by drafting a self-regulation code for companies. The ICC 'Rules of Conduct to Combat Extortion and Bribery' deal with ethical issues in international business negotiations such as payments to sales agents and other intermediaries, business entertainment and gifts, and political contributions. Contrary to the OECD convention, it covers bribery within the private sector as well as to public officials (Brademas and Heimann, 1998).

At the corporate level, it appears that the formulation of global corporate ethics codes involves 95 per cent of CEOs and 78 per cent of company boards of

directors (Berenbeim, 1999). Bribery is a topic covered by a vast majority (92 per cent) of the ethics code. Many of them provide concrete operationalizations of what is a bribe and how to deal with it. Some, not all, target compliance by providing managers involved in foreign operations with precise procedures and guidelines. In relative terms, corruption tends to deter investors from negotiating foreign direct investment in countries with high levels of corruption (Habib and Zurawicki, 2002).

There are basically two sides in bribery: that of donors, which are principally concerned with the conventions and codes previously described, and that of the recipient countries, which are less directly concerned. Corruption in international deals will not cease by the simple virtue of donors becoming suddenly honest and drying up the supply of bribes. In most potential recipient countries no strong anti-bribery code exists or, if there is one, it is not actually enforced.

The level of corruption of particular countries can be measured, based on composite indicators of perception of corruption. They are published on a yearly basis by Transparency International (**www.transparency.org**), an NGO considered to be the most influential global anti-corruption organization (Transparency International, 2002). Data is based on mean scores of seven to nine surveys per country, rarely less. Highest scores correspond to the lowest levels of corruption, e.g. in 2002, Finland came top with 9.7; Denmark was next with 9.5; Switzerland ranked 12th with 8.5; the United States scored 7.6; Germany scored 7.3; while France ranked 25th with 6.3. Many developing countries and some eastern European countries plagued by endemic corruption scored low: Peru, Brazil and Bulgaria (all with 4), Romania and Zambia (2.6). The most corrupt countries (according to Transparency International) were Kenya, Indonesia, Nigeria, Angola, Madagascar, Paraguay (all below 2) and Bangladesh with the lowest score (1.2).

A number of countries where corruption is endemic show increased severity against offenders. China for instance (3.5 on the Transparency corruption scale) is combating bribery, going as far as the execution of senior officials, like the Vice Governor of Southern Jiangxi province who was convicted of having accumulated about US$850,000 in bribes (ABC news, 2002). A top banker was recently sentenced to

15 years imprisonment on bribery charges. He had been found to have taken about US$500,000 in bribes from 1997 to 1999 when he was chairman of the group that controls one of China's largest banks (Xinhua News Agency, 2002).

Comparison of ethical attitudes across industrial nations

Ethical attitudes within the major developed countries towards illegal payments are not uniform (Lee, 1981). Until recently, in France, Germany and Switzerland bribery was simply seen as a cost of doing business abroad and could be claimed as a corporate tax deduction. The French call it FCE, *frais commerciaux exceptionnels* ('exceptional sales expenses'), and it was not only deductible from corporate income but also eligible for export credit insurance in cases where the foreign client takes the bribe but does not pay for the contract (Usunier and Verna, 1994). US managers tend to adopt stronger ethical standpoints than their European and Japanese counterparts. Becker and Fritzsche (1987) suggested a scenario that posed a business ethics problem linked to an illegal payment. Three sample groups of businessmen were interviewed, one from the United States (124 respondents), one from West Germany (70 respondents) and one from France (72 respondents). The scenario was as follows:

The Rollfast Bicycle company has been barred from entering the market in a large Asian country by collusive efforts of the local bicycle manufacturers. Rollfast could expect to net 5 million dollars per year from sales if it could penetrate the market. Last week a business man from the country contacted the management of Rollfast and stated that he could smooth the way for the company to sell in his country for a price of US$500,000. If you were responsible, what are the chances that you would pay the price? (Becker and Fritzsche, 1987, p. 89.)

While the replies from the French and German managers differed little, those of the Americans indicated that they were, by and large, less prepared to pay the secret payment. Whereas 47 per cent of the American respondents gave as an explanation that this was unethical, illegal and contrary to the corporate code of conduct, 38 per cent of Germans and 55 per cent of the French thought either that 'the competition would force us to accept', or that 'it's simply the price you have to pay for doing business'.

France and West Germany have legislation prohibiting the bribing of public civil servants, but these regulations do not apply extraterritorially. French and German businessmen cannot be prosecuted for bribes effected outside their national territory. Conversely, the FCPA as well as numerous other American regulations (anti-trust, fiscal, and so on) do have extraterritorial application. Despite the fact that the FCPA increases the probability of disclosure, the corruption scandals in the Middle East by no means involved only the United States. Gillespie (1987) notes that the corruption affairs in the Middle East involving European or Asian multinationals were revealed either locally or by newspapers in the countries making the payments. For the period 1970–85, there were 42 involving American companies, 29 involving European or Asian companies: in not one of the scandals that she studied were Americans imprisoned, whereas Europeans or Asians were jailed in seven instances.

A pragmatic and respectful view of ethical behaviour in a cross-cultural context

As noted by Berenbeim (1997, p. 26) host country conditions have to be taken into account:

You cannot say to a country manager, 'Don't do this, don't do that, now here are your goals for country X where all of your competitors do this and that. I don't want to hear any excuses if these objectives are not met.' Under those circumstances, either rules will have to be broken or ambitious goals will not be achieved. The way to avoid this kind of impossible situation is to build a consensus among practitioners for enforceable rules . . . The example of the FCPA is a case in point. Although it would be more satisfying to punish the person who demands the bribe than the company that pays it, obtaining legal prohibitions in the major industrial countries and targeting the companies that bribe rather than the local citizens who demand payment is likely to have greater impact.

The first consideration is pragmatic: business people who make illegal payments take (real) personal risks for (potential) organizational benefits, either through company loyalty or personal interest (sales commission or promotion). Doing this, they (1) involve their company in the risk of being implicated in a scandal; and (2) themselves risk being implicated, indicted, and ultimately sentenced to a long term of imprisonment.

In the case of turnkey sales, the favourite domain for big bribes, it is important to clarify the mandate for negotiation that is given to the project negotiators by the engineering company or consortium of contractors. One may put it in straightforward terms: 'If you must grease palms do it right.' Unless the negotiators actually raise the bribery issue directly and openly, the exact extent of their powers and responsibility will be insufficiently clarified. The executives who sell factories or turnkey equipment often 'go into battle' with little prior warning or protection.

The payment of a baksheesh always involves the individual responsibility of the donor, even if his or her company, or the consortium that he or she represents, also risks being drawn into the scandal. As Graham (1983) states: 'From a legal standpoint, the recommendation is clear – avoid questionable deals. The loss of the few "questionable" contracts is not worth the risk of indictment, prosecution, conviction . . . Moreover, if you are indicted, will your company support you or opt to plead guilty and accept the fine?' A pragmatic view for an individual requires reference to a personal norm, not a corporate one.

Useful guidelines for those confronted with this issue are provided by the definition of a 'moral personality' proposed by John Rawls in his *A Theory of Justice* (1971). A moral personality is characterized by two capacities, namely the capacity to conceive good and the capacity to develop a sense of justice. The first is realized through a rational project for one's life. The second implies a continuing desire to act in a way that one believes is just. Thus for Rawls, a moral personality has chosen his or her own goals; and he or she prefers those conditions that enable him or her to fully express his or her nature as a rational, free and equal being. The unity of the person is then manifested by the coherence of his or her project. This unity is based on a higher order aspiration to follow the principles of rational choice in a manner that suits his or her sense of justice. It means that if you are asked to do something that violates your sense of right and wrong, it is better not to do it, even if it means not behaving as a Roman in Rome.

A final remark: Rawls' definition of a 'moral personality' remains a rather Western one, in that it emphasizes rationality, individualism and the sense of equality with others. In many other cultural contexts, where moral personalities actually exist, these traits would not be emphasized in such a definition.

There is unfortunately no common international legal framework which can circumvent bribery. Moreover, national based legal texts, since they simply prohibit or permit certain acts, do not explain how to behave in the real world. The only universal guides for behaviour stem from the UN codes or from several analyses of case studies that provide a basis for identifying ethical issues. Ethical conflicts must therefore largely be documented on a moral rather than purely legal basis, keeping in mind that moral judgements are in part universal, and in part culturally relative.

The final word may be given by Adam Smith who describes some key aspects of the 'character of virtue' in the following terms ([1759], 1984, p. 214):

The prudent man is always sincere, and feels horror at the very thought of exposing himself to the disgrace which attends upon the detection of falsehood. But though always sincere, he is not always frank and open; and though he never tells any thing but the truth, he does not always think himself bound, when not properly called upon, to tell the whole truth. As he is cautious in his actions, so he is reserved in his speech; and never rashly or unnecessarily obtrudes his opinion concerning either things or persons.

Questions

1. Indicate elements of variation in selling styles (including basic views of what is a buyer–seller interaction, the kind of arguments developed and the communication style).

2. Personal selling often plays a more important role in foreign than in domestic markets. Why?

3. Discuss the limitations to the standardization of a sales-force stimulation system.

4. Discuss how a strong emphasis on group belonging in a particular culture may influence the recruitment of salespeople.

5. Discuss the cultural relativity of the following statements about salespersons (excerpt from Hill *et al.*, 1993, pp. 68–9):
   ■ Our salespersons are very achievement-oriented.
   ■ Salespersons need patience to be successful.
   ■ Our salespersons consider the source of income, whether salary or commission, to be more important than the size of income.
   ■ Our sellers should have definite call schedules and planned routes.
   ■ Our salespersons are very time-oriented.
   ■ Our salespersons need a lot of supervision.
   ■ Selling is a prestigious job in the country.
   ■ Salespersons are regarded as future managers.
   ■ A salesperson's social class can limit his/her contacts and effectiveness.
   ■ Family connections often help salespersons in their work.
   ■ A salesperson's religious beliefs can limit his/her contacts and effectiveness.

6. What is the border line between a 'gift' and a 'bribe'? Outline possible criteria for defining such a border which allow for some cross-national flexibility.

7. How can bribery be related to space-related cultural assumptions?

8. WTD, a large US multinational chemical company, has been recently attacked in several large Latin American countries where it has plants. The company has been attacked by the local press for alleged pollution and poor safety conditions for employees. It has been argued that WTD has much lower standards in these areas than in the USA and that the company shows its Yankee and imperialist orientation in such choices. The company executive officers think these criticisms are largely wrong: inadequate local legislation and poor respect of safety rules by local employees have caused problems rather than a deliberate neglect on WTD's part. Advise the firm on a public relations programme.

9. Discuss the cultural relativity of the framework for a manager facing an ethical dilemma, who should ask the following questions:
   ■ What are the **facts**; what are my alternatives?
   ■ What parties will be affected?
   ■ What do **I** owe to each of these parties?
   ■ What would produce the greatest **benefits** for **all** parties?
   ■ What **rights** does each party have, and how can these rights best be **respected**?
   ■ Are all parties treated **fairly** and **justly**?
   ■ On balance, what is the most **ethical** alternative?
   ■ How do **I** best **implement** this alternative?

   The words in bold are those which offer the best route for questioning about the cultural relativity of this framework.

Notes

1. OECD is the Organisation for Economic Co-operation and Development.
2. See German, Peter M. (2002), for a detailed account of how the OECD Convention on bribery translates into national legislation, in the Canadian case.
3. Regular updates of steps taken to implement the Convention country-by-country can be found at **www.oecd.org/**.
4. ADB is the Asian Development Bank.

References

ABCnews (2002), 'Acting tough as part of anti-corruption stand, China executes official', *ABCnews* (online), 11 November, available at: **http://abcnews.go.com/sections/world/DailyNews/chinaexecute000308.html/**.

Adcock, Dennis, Ray Bradfield, Al Halborg and Caroline Ross (1993), *Marketing, Principles and Practice*, Pitman: London.

Adler, Nancy J. (1991), *International Dimensions of Organizational Behavior*, 2nd edn, PWS-Kent: Boston.

Agpar, M. (1977), 'Succeeding in Saudi Arabia', *Harvard Business Review*, January/February, pp. 14–33.

Ali, Abbas and Paul M. Schwiercz (1985), 'The relationship between managerial decision styles and work satisfaction in Saudi Arabia', in Erdener Kaynak (ed.), *International Business in the Middle East*, De Gruyter: New York, pp. 138–49.

Al-Khatib, Jamal A., Scott J. Vitell and Mohammed Y.A. Rawwas (1996), 'Consumer ethics: a cross-cultural investigation', *European Journal of Marketing*, vol. 31, no. 7, pp. 750–67.

Anderson, Paul F. and Terry M. Chambers (1985), 'A reward/measurement model of organizational buying behavior', *Journal of Marketing*, vol. 49, Spring, pp. 7–23.

Ang, Swee Hoon (2000), 'The power of money: a cross-cultural analysis of business-related beliefs', *Journal of World Business*, vol. 35, no. 1, pp. 43–60.

Arnould, Eric J. (1995), 'West African marketing channels', in John F. Sherry, Jr. (ed.), *Contemporary Marketing and Consumer Behavior*, Sage Publications: Thousand Oaks, CA, pp. 109–68.

Barabba, Vincent P. and Gerald Zaltman (1991), *Hearing the Voice of the Market*, Harvard Business School Press: Cambridge, MA.

BBC News (1999), 'Dam builders charged in bribery scandal', Friday, 19 November.

Becker, Helmut and David H. Fritzsche (1987), 'A comparison of the ethical behavior of American, French and German managers', *Columbia Journal of World Business*, Winter, pp. 87–95.

Berenbeim, Ronald E. (1999), 'Global Corporate ethics practice: a developing consensus', *The Conference Board*, Research Report no. 1243-99-RR.

Berenbein, Ronald E. (1997), 'Can multinational business agree on how to act ethically?', *Business and Society Review*, vol. 98, pp. 24–8.

Boland, Tom (1998), 'Street vendors: Congo war on Kinshasa's informal sector FWD', *CNN* (online), article taken from **http://cnn.com/WORLD/africa/9806/08/RB001417.reut.html** [accessed 8 June 1998, no longer available].

Brademas, John and Fritz Heimann (1998), 'Tackling international corruption: no longer taboo', *Foreign Affairs*, vol. 77, no. 5, pp. 17–22.

Burns, David J. and John T. Brady (1996), 'Retail ethics as appraised by future business personnel in Malaysia and the United States', *Journal of Consumer Affairs*, vol. 30, no. 1, pp. 195–217.

Cateora, Philip R. (1993), *International Marketing*, 8th edn, Richard D. Irwin: Burr Ridge, IL.

Chan, T.S. and Robert W. Armstrong (1999), 'Comparative ethical report card: a study of Australian and Canadian Manager's perception of international marketing ethics problems', *Journal of Business Ethics*, vol. 12, pp. 3–15.

Chonko, Lawrence B., Ben M. Enis and John F. Tanner (1992), *Managing Sales People*, Allyn and Bacon: Boston, MA.

CIPE (1998), 'Corruption in Bulgaria threatens social stability', *Economic Reform Today*, no. 2, p. 18.

Czinkota, Michael R. and Illka A. Ronkainen (1990), *International Marketing*, 2nd edn, Dryden Press: Hinsdale, IL.

Daniels, John D., Ernest W. Ogram and Lee H. Radebaugh (1982), *International Business: Environments and Operations*, 3rd edn, Addison-Wesley: Reading, MA.

Day, George S. (1994), 'Continuous learning about markets', *California Management Review*, vol. 36, no. 4, pp. 9–31.

Dwyer, Robert F., Paul H. Schurr and Sejo Oh (1987), 'Developing buyer–seller relationships', *Journal of Marketing*, vol. 51, April, pp. 11–27.

Ford, David (ed.) (1990), *Understanding Business Markets*, Academic Press: London.

Fournier, Susan, Susan Dobscha and David Glen Mick (1998), 'Preventing the premature death of relationship marketing', *Harvard Business Review*, vol. 76, no. 1, January–February, pp. 42–51.

Freivalds, John (1991), 'Foreign-language business cards', *Agri Marketing*, vol. 29, no. 3, pp. 48–9.

Gallant, Katheryn (1997), 'The art of stealing', *Brazzil* (online), available at: **www.brazzil.com/cvrmar97.htm.**

Galtung, Frederick (1994), *Korruption*, Göttingen: Lamuv Verlag.

Garten, Jeffrey E. (2003), 'Anger abroad is bad for business', *Business Week*, 10 November, p. 30.

Gillespie, Kate (1987), 'Middle East response to the US Foreign Corrupt Practices Ave', *California Management Review*, vol. 24, no. 4, Summer, pp. 9–30.

Graham, John L. (1981), 'A hidden cause of America's trade deficit with Japan', *Columbia Journal of World Business*, Fall, pp. 5–15.

Graham, John L. (1983), 'Foreign Corrupt Practices Act: a manager's guide', *Columbia Journal of World Business*, vol. 18, no. 3, pp. 89–94.

Griffith, David A., Michael Y. Hu and John K. Ryans Jr. (2000), 'Process standardization across intra- and inter-cultural relationships', *Journal of International Business Studies*, vol. 31, no. 2, pp. 303–23.

Habib, Mohsin and Leon Zurawicki (2002), 'Corruption and foreign direct investment', *Journal of International Business Studies*, vol. 33, no. 2, pp. 291–307.

Hall, Edward T. (1976), *Beyond Culture*, Doubleday: New York.

Hamra, Wayne (2000), 'Bribery in international business transactions and the OECD convention: benefits and limitations', *Business Economics*, October, pp. 33–46.

Hanna, Nessim and Tanuja Srivastava (1998), 'Modeling the motivational antecedents of the Japanese sales force: how relevant are western models', *Journal of Global Marketing*, vol. 11, no. 4, pp. 49–74.

Hempel, Paul S. (1998), 'Designing multinational benefits programs: the role of national culture', *Journal of World Business*, vol. 33, no. 3, pp. 277–94.

Hill, John S., Arthur W. Allaway, Colin Egan and Ünal O. Boya (1993), 'Perceptions of foreign field sales forces: an exploratory factor analysis of their characteristics, behaviors and sales', *Proceedings of the 6th World Marketing Congress*, Istambul, pp. 67–70.

Hill, John S., Richard R. Still and Ünal O. Boya (1991), 'Managing the multinational sales force', *International Marketing Review*, vol. 8, no. 1, pp. 19–31.

Ho, Suk-ching (1997), 'The emergence of consumer power in China', *Business Horizon*, September–October, pp. 15–21.

Hofstede, Geert (1991), *Culture and Organizations: Software of the mind*, McGraw-Hill: Maidenhead, Berkshire.

Hofstede, Geert (2001), *Culture Consequences*, 2nd edn, Sage Publications: Thousand Oaks, CA.

Hui, Michael K. and Kevin Au (2001), 'Justice perceptions of complaint handling: a cross-cultural comparison between PRC and Canadian customers', *Journal of Business Research*, vol. 52, pp. 161–73.

Hulnick, Gail (2000), 'Doing business virtually', *Communication World*, February–March, pp. 33–6.

Hutchings, Kate and Georgina Murray (2002), 'Working with Guanxi: an assessment of the implications of globalisation on business networking in China', *Creativity and Innovation Management*, vol. 11, no. 3, pp. 184–90.

Johansson, Jan and Lars-Gunnar Mattsson (1988), 'Internationalization in industrial systems – a network approach', in N. Hood and J.E. Vahlne (eds), *Strategies in Global Competition*, Croom Helm: New York.

Jolibert, Alain and Maud Tixier (1988), *La Négociation Commerciale*, Editions ESF: Paris.

Kashani, Kamran (1989), 'Beware the pitfalls of global marketing', *Harvard Business Review*, September–October, pp. 91–8.

Kotabe, Masaaki, Alan J. Dubinsky and Chae Un Lim (1992), 'Perceptions of organizational fairness: A cross-national perspective', *International Marketing Review*, vol. 9, no. 2, pp. 41–58.

Lackman, Conway L., David P. Hanson and John M. Lanasa (1997), 'Social relations in culture and marketing', *Journal of Marketing Theory and Practice*, vol. 5, no. 1, pp. 144–52.

Lee, K.H. (1981), 'Ethical beliefs in marketing management: a cross-cultural study', *European Journal of Marketing*, vol. 15, no. 1, pp. 58–67.

Lewis, Eleanor Roberts (1998), 'The OECD anti-corruption treaty: why is it needed? How will it work?', *Economic Perspectives*, vol. 3, no. 5, pp. 6–9.

Luo, Yadong (1995), 'Business strategy, market structure, and performance of IJV', *Management International Review*, vol. 35, no. 3, pp. 249–64.

Luo, Yadong (1997), 'Guanxi and performance of foreign-invested enterprises in China', *Management International Review*, vol. 37, no. 1, pp. 51–70.

Luo, Yadong and Min Chen (1997), 'Does guanxi influence firm performance?', *Asia Pacific Journal of Management*, vol. 14, pp. 1–16.

Mavondo, Felix T. and Elaine Rodrigo (2001), 'The effect of relationship dimensions on interpersonal and inter-organizational commitment in organizations conducting business between Australia and China', *Journal of Business Research*, vol. 52, no. 2, pp. 111–21.

Mayo, Michel A., Lawrence J. Marks and John K. Ryans Jr. (1991), 'Perceptions of ethical problems in international marketing', *International Marketing Review*, vol. 8, no. 3, pp. 61–75.

McCarthy, E. Jerome (1964), *Basic Marketing: A managerial approach*, Prentice Hall: Englewood Cliffs, NJ.

Money, R. Bruce and John L. Graham (1999), 'Salesperson performances, pay, and job satisfaction: tests of a model using data collected in the United States and Japan', *Journal of International Business Studies*, vol. 30, no. 1, pp. 149–72.

Ndao, Cheikh Alioune (1985), *Excellences, vos épouses!*, Les Nouvelles Editions Africaines: Dakar.

Péan, Pierre (1988), *L'Argent Noir*, Librairie Arthème Fayard: Paris.

Rawls, John (1971), *A Theory of Justice*, Belknap Press of Harvard University: Cambridge, MA.

Redding, S. Gordon (1982), 'Cultural effects of the marketing process in Southeast Asia', *Journal of the Market Research Society*, vol. 24, no. 2, pp. 98–114.

Sharma, Arun (2002), 'Trends in Internet-based business-to-business marketing', *Industrial Marketing Management*, vol. 31, pp. 77–84.

Sheth, Jagdish N. and Atul Parvatiyar (2002), 'Evolving relationship marketing into a discipline', *Journal of Relationship Marketing*, vol. 1, no. 1, pp. 16–94.

Slatter, Stuart St P. (1987), 'The salesman's job in competitive bidding situations', *Industrial Marketing Management*, vol. 16, pp. 201–5.

Smith, Adam (1759), *The Theory of Moral Sentiments*, London, A. Millar. 1984 edition by D.D. Raphael and A.L. MacFie, Indianapolis: Liberty Fund.

Song, Michael X., Jinhong Xie and Barbara Dyer (2000), 'Antecedents and consequences of marketing managers' conflict-handling behaviors', *Journal of Marketing*, vol. 63, July, pp. 105–19.

Spiegelman, Paul (2000), 'Live customer interaction and the Internet join in "internation"', *Direct Marketing*, vol. 63, no. 4, pp. 38–41.

Steidlmeier, P. (1999), 'Gift-giving, bribery and corruption: ethical management of business relationships in China', *Journal of Business Ethics*, vol. 20, pp. 121–32.

Still, Richard R. (1981), 'Cross-cultural aspects of sales force management', *Journal of Personal Selling and Sales Force Management*, vol. 1, no. 2, pp. 6–9.

Taylor, William (1991), 'The logic of global business: an interview with ABB's Percy Barnevik', *Harvard Business Review*, March–April, pp. 90–105.

Thompson, Courtenay (2002), 'Below the surface', *Internal Auditor*, October, pp. 67–9.

Thorelli, Hans B. (1986), 'Networks: between markets and hierarchies', *Strategic Management Journal*, vol. 7, pp. 37–51.

Transparency International (2002), *Transparency International Corruption Perceptions Index 2002*, available at: **www.transparency.org**.

Treece, James B. and Yuzo Yamaguchi (2004), 'Mitsubishi's Japan sales collapse in May', *Automotive News*, vol. 78, no. 6098, p. 44.

Tsalikis, John, Marta Ortiz-Buonafina and Michael S. Latour (1992), 'The role of accent on the credibility and effectiveness of the international business person: the case of Guatemala, *International Marketing Review*, vol. 9, no. 4, pp. 57–72.

Tung, Rosalie (1996), 'Negotiating with East Asians', in P.N. Ghauri and J.-C. Usunier (eds), *International Business Negotiations*, Oxford: Pergamon/Elsevier, pp. 369–81.

Usunier, Jean-Claude and Gérard Verna (1994), *La Grande Triche: Ethique, Corruption et Affaires Internationales*, Editions La Découverte: Paris.

Vogl, Frank (1998), 'The supply side of global bribery', *Finance & Development*, June, pp. 30–3.

Walter, Ingo (1989), *Secret Money*, 2nd edn, Unwin-Hyman: London.

Werner, Cynthia (2000), 'Gifts, bribes, and development in Post-Soviet Kazakstan', *Human Organization*, vol. 59, no. 1, Spring, pp. 11–22.

Xinhua News Agency (2002), 'Top banker sentenced on bribery charges', *China Through a Lens* (online), 11 October, available at: **www.china.org.cn/english/2002/Oct/45463.htm**.

Zeithaml, Carl P. and Valarie Zeithaml (1984), 'Environmental management: revising the perspective', *Journal of Marketing*, vol. 48, Spring, pp. 46–53.

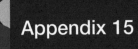

Appendix 15

Teaching materials

A15.1 Case

When international buyers and sellers disagree

No matter what line of business you're in, you can't escape sex. That may have been one conclusion drawn by an American exporter of meat products after a dispute with a German customer over a shipment of pork livers. Here's how the disagreement came about:

The American exporter was contracted to ship '30,000 lbs. of freshly frozen U.S. pork livers, customary merchandisable quality, first rate brands.' As the shipment that was prepared met the exacting standards of the American market, the exporter expected the transaction to be completed without any problem. But when the livers arrived in Germany, the purchaser raised an objection: 'We ordered pork livers of customary merchantable quality – what you sent us consisted of 40 per cent sow livers.'

'Who cares about the sex of the pig the liver came from?' the exporter asked.

'We do,' the German replied. 'Here in Germany we don't pass off spongy sow livers as the firmer livers of male pigs. This shipment wasn't merchantable at the price we expected to charge. The only way we were able to dispose of the meat without a total loss was to reduce the price. You owe us a price allowance of US$1,000.'

The American refused to reduce the price. The determined resistance may have been partly in reaction to the implied insult to the taste of the American consumer: 'If pork livers, whatever the sex of the animal, are palatable to Americans, they ought to be good enough for anyone,' the American thought.

It looked as if the buyer and seller could never agree on eating habits.

(Source: Dun and Bradstreet Corporation.)

Questions

1. What does 'customary merchandisable quality' mean? Where? In which language and cultural context?

2. Discuss how ethnocentrism and SRC (self-reference criterion) are at work in this case.

3. In this dispute, which country's law would apply, that of the United States or of Germany?

4. If the case were tried in US courts, who do you think would win? And if tried in German courts? Why?

5. Is formal litigation justified in such a case? How can one solve this problem? How can one avoid this type of conflict in the future?

A15.2 Case

Setco of Spain

Planning sales targets for the sales force is a universal practice. Nobody questions it. So it was when Mr Gonzales, a Spaniard, was recruited by Setco of Spain, the Spanish subsidiary of a large US multinational company. Soon after his job began, he was assigned a product line, of which he had some experience, in a new sales territory. The sales manager of Setco of Spain did not know precisely the market potential of this new area. Until then, potential customers in this area had never been regularly visited. Moreover few indicators were available in order to estimate the market potential of this new area in a quantified and precise manner.

When he first met the sales manager for Spain, Gonzales was amazed by his friendly tone; dialogue within the sales team and horizontal communication were the rule. Instead of being set an objective, he was invited to give his opinion on the matter. In fact, he could set his quarterly sales target himself, after visiting the area and making some preliminary contacts with prospects. Because of the newness of this area, the sales manager made no comment. Gonzales was confronted with a new freedom: in his previous positions as sales representative, he had never fixed his own sales targets by himself. He had always been given targets by his boss. His reaction was therefore to reduce significantly the objective relative to the sales he was reasonably expecting, in order to retain some leeway.

After four months, actual sales per area were released. Gonzales was used to this kind of report, since it provided basic data for computing possible bonuses. However, he was surprised to see that his actual sales figures was compared to target sales, and the difference between actual and target sales was explictly presented. It looked flattering. The individual achievements of the other members of the sales team were mentioned in this memo as well. They did not match that of Gonzales.

At the meeting of the sales force, quarterly sales were examined, as well as the targets for the next quarter and the marketing programme. Gonzales was surprised to see how embarrassing his 'performance' appeared to the other sales representatives. Never had any sales representative at Setco of Spain so largely overshot the mark. He was teased by his colleagues, who made some bittersweet remarks and jokes. He felt bad about it, especially because he had been trying hard. He had used all his skills as a salesman, which were considerable and had been proved in his previous positions.

During the discussions, he acknowledged that his area's market potential had been largely underestimated. His sales target was therefore revised and increased by a large amount. This was done in full agreement with all the members (including him) of the sales team, who democratically discussed targets and achievements together during the quarterly sales meetings.

In the companies for which he had worked before, sales objectives were settled in a somewhat hierarchic way. The objectives were, fortunately, too high to be achieved. Being out of reach, the objectives worked as a sort of line of sight, an ideal level. It worked as a way of forcing lazy people to do more and of motivating the achievers to surpass themselves. Logically enough, actual sales were not carefully monitored, nor were individual achievements calculated by comparisons of target sales and actual sales.

At the end of the third quarter, Gonzales began to think that he had been set too high an objective. He had been working extremely hard for almost six months, pushed by enthusiasm for his new job. Moreover an unusually large order from a company in his sales area had swollen his first quarterly sales. This did not happen during the second and third quarters.

When the quarterly sales meeting took place, Gonzales once again appeared as the 'star' of the meeting: he had a record shortfall. No sales representative at Setco of Spain had ever experienced such a wide negative gap between target and actual sales. His colleagues made fun of him. They were slightly relieved to see him bite the dust. Some days later he received a personal memo from the marketing director, who made it clear that he had to adapt quickly or leave the company. 'You should know that in our company a salesman has to be able to settle his own objectives in a precise, realistic and dynamic way. Targets are the result of negotiations with the sales manager: they are based on market data. Individual sales targets are summed up, at every level in the corporation. They are the basis for the quarterly corporate sales figure forecast. The stocks of our company are registered on the New York Stock Exchange. Operators on the Stock Exchange are extremely sensitive to this kind of data. If every salesman in this company performed like you, our forecasts at the corporate level would be meaningless. Our headquarters simply cannot accept this.'

Question

What should Gonzales do?

A15.3 Case

Union Carbide at Bhopal

In the 1970s, Union Carbide Corporation (UCC), one of America's largest chemical multi-nationals had established production facilities in India. Its Indian subsidiary, Union Carbide India Limited (UCIL), under pressure from the Indian authorities, had built a new factory in 1978 to produce pesticides in Bhopal, the capital of Madhya Pradesh, a town situated 375 miles (600 km) south of New Delhi. It produced Sevin, a pesticide composed primarily of methyl isocyanate, extremely dangerous for humans and to be carefully kept in liquid form below 25 degrees Celsius. The project was plagued by problems of safety from the outset: in 1978, its year of construction, a huge fire broke out. Five major gas leaks in 1981 and 1983 left one dead and 47 injured. In 1982, a detailed inspection by American experts uncovered ten serious faults in the factory's safety systems. In fact, the factory's alarm system was ringing so often that people living in the vicinity of the factory treated it almost as background noise.

The Indian government imposed restrictions on foreign companies, limiting their direct participation by requiring that they negotiate local partnerships. UCC was able to continue operating in India only by agreeing to the formation of a new company, Union Carbide India Limited (UCIL), in which UCC was reduced to a majority shareholder with 50.09 per cent of the share capital. A further 22 per cent went to the government and the remainder was divided amongst 23,500 private Indian investors. Bhopal's social and political environment developed rapidly as a result of the factory. Attracted by the availability of work and the water and electricity which were supplied to the site at reduced rates, people poured in to the surrounding area. As a consequence, the population grew from 385,000 in 1971 to 671,000 in 1981. By 1984, it stood at nearly 800,000. From its original position of isolation, the factory was soon totally enveloped by the town's growth. Creaking under the strain of this huge influx of population, the town struggled to accommodate everyone. In the absence of a better alternative, the poorest of the new arrivals congregated in 'Khasi Camp', a shanty town situated between the centre of Bhopal and the factory.

Links between UCIL and the local Indian political establishment were mutually rewarding in many ways. The factory's legal adviser, for instance, was a former local head of Indira Gandhi's Congress Party. The former local police chief magically won the contract to guard the factory. One of the nephews of the former state education minister was the head of public relations at the factory.

There were also financial difficulties. In 1982, a slump in sales of its products resulted in the factory suffering a dramatic reduction in profitability. UCC, the parent company of UCIL, even considered shutting the plant down completely, but the Indian government refused to countenance such a possibility for fear of frightening away potential foreign investors. To balance the books, UCIL determined to reduce the factory's overheads. They chose to make many of their most qualified personnel redundant. These vacant posts were then either filled by less experienced personnel or simply scrapped. The consequent loss of morale and expertise amongst the workforce adversely affected work at the factory. News of these unfortunate mishaps was carefully suppressed thanks to the close working relationship between UCIL and the local authorities. The Indian authorities even extended UCIL's operating licence for a further seven years despite objections from the Press and opposition members in the state parliament.

The incident took place in the night of 2 December 1984. Water in substantial quantities was mixed by error with methylisocyanate, causing high pressure, the explosion of the vessel and massive leaks of lethal gas in the surroundings of the factory. The local population had no idea of what to do in the event of a serious incident at the factory: simply putting a wet cloth on the face would have protected a great many people. Even the local doctors were completely ignorant about the effects of the product being manufactured on their doorsteps. Warren Anderson, the chief executive officer of UCC, courageously decided to go to India.

Following the disaster, the state government of Madhya Pradesh carefully drew up an initial list of the human cost of this night of horror. The toll was a heavy one: they estimated that 3,828 people had been killed and 358,712 injured. Of these, 22,955 were left with a permanent disability. A single night of tragedy in Bhopal had claimed 362,540 victims. Ten years later, the government believed that about 6,600 people were killed in the incident. Bhopal pressure groups put the death toll at 16,000 and still rising by a few each week. They claimed that up to 600,000 people – more than half the city – suffered damage to their lungs, eyes and immune systems.

On 4 December 1984, Warren Anderson flew to Bhopal with a team of experts to try and discover the cause of the tragedy. His efforts were in vain. Anderson was arrested and imprisoned, then finally expelled. It was not until 20 December that the Indian authorities allowed a commission of inquiry to begin its work on site. They arrived to find that the factory had been closed since 6 December and was already being dismantled.

Public relations in such a context were extremely difficult to organize since most 'hard facts' arguments might have seemed insults to the Indian management, public authorities, doctors or even to the general Indian public. The solution was found in complex litigation: each party argued that the case should be heard in the jurisdiction of the other. Finally, UCC came out with the favourable decision that the final judgements be made in India where relevant jurisprudence was almost non-existent. On 14 February 1989, the Indian Supreme Court rendered its judgement: the American defendants were found liable and ordered to pay a total of US$470 million, US$50 million was to be paid in rupees by UCIL and US$415 million by UCC; the remaining US$5 million had been paid under the previous order of the American Federal Court as first aid to the victims. Many people found that the final award was rather low. For example, if this sum represented only those killed in the incident, it would be roughly equivalent to US$130,000 per victim. If it included those permanently disabled, the amount would represent only US$18,000 per person and if it was intended to compensate every injured person, it would represent an average of US$1,350 per person.

Its reputation heavily tarnished by the Bhopal affair, UCC realized in 1986 that a great deal of time and effort would be needed to regain lost confidence. During a speech delivered to the Davos Economic Forum on 5 February 1991, the new Chief Executive Officer of UCC, Robert Kennedy, affirmed 'Care for the planet has become a critical business issue – central to our jobs as senior managers'. UCC prioritized respect for the environment and safety concerns and established a health, safety and environment committee staffed by independent outsiders and an executive vice-president was given specific responsibility for environmental issues. The global performance of UCC in tackling pollution and improving safety and respect for the environment is regularly checked by independent experts. The company now has drawn up a strategic environmental plan with specific verifiable goals.

Questions

1. What are the problems involved in facing social responsibility in a culturally alien context?

2. Was Warren Anderson's trip to Bhopal a 'good' decision? Why? On the basis of which behavioural standards, home or host country's, should a company react?

3. How would you describe Union Carbide's corporate responsibility in the Bhophal case?

 ## A15.4 Case

The *Brenzy nouveau* has arrived!

Legritte Company was founded just after the Second World War by a skilful engineer, Monsieur Legritte. Aided by the reconstruction boom which was followed by the rapid economic growth of the 1960s, the Legritte Company developed more by improving the quality of its products than by investing money in marketing and sales. The intrinsic quality of the products, namely electrical connections for industrial use, has been the strong point of the business from the very beginning.

The company is located near Lyons (France) and employs about 200 people, with an annual turnover of 80 million francs. Two years ago Legritte was taken over by a US-based multinational company, Brenzy. Monsieur Legritte, drawing near to retirement age and with no qualified successor, sold his property to the Brenzy Corporation, which now owns the full 100 per cent. Brenzy has progressively introduced more up-to-date management methods in this traditional family business. Inventory management, cost accounting and delivery systems have all been changed to fit with Brenzy's procedures.

Sales promotion in France, and Europe generally, is based on nicely printed catalogues, technical instructions and directions for use. Unit prices reduce according to the size of orders. Products are promoted through small gifts given to the purchasers. Thus the launch of a new pre-insulated line of products, recently certified by EDF (Electricité de France, the public utility for electricity), came with a free gift (electrical pliers) for any order higher than 10,000 francs. This offer was open for six months. In order to receive the gift, the buyer simply had to fill in the gift voucher and enclose it with the order, provided the amount was sufficient.

Brenzy-Legritte was a newcomer to advertising. Being a fairly traditional medium-sized industrial company, they had not up to now invested a lot of money in advertisements. When they decided for the first time to advertise their products they did it by promoting their products along with what they called '*le Brenzy nouveau*', with a play on words between Brenzy and Beaujolais, a freshly harvested red wine and a fashionable drink.

An advertisement in a specialist journal showed a bottle of Beaujolais nouveau, with the following slogan above the image: 'The Brenzy nouveau has arrived!' Text in bold characters at the bottom stated: 'You are thirsty and craving a new line of effective products! Brenzy-Legritte is happy to join you in ordering Beaujolais nouveau!' It was indicated that a minimum order of 500 Euros entitled buyers to receive three free bottles and a minimum order of 800 Euros entitled them to receive six free bottles. The expiry date for this offer was stipulated. The new line of Brenzy-Legritte products was shown on the label of the bottle of Beaujolais.

EDF, which is a large customer of Brenzy-Legritte, was not very happy about this humorous advertisement. It seems that EDF experienced problems amongst its personnel when the boxes of Beaujolais arrived at its offices.

Brenzy-Legritte is now undergoing drastic changes in its organization. Computers have been linked to the European headquarters in Brussels. Strictly defined management procedures have been imposed by headquarters. Brenzy has issued a professional code of conduct, the implementation of which is compulsory for the French subsidiary as well as for all the other subsidiaries around the world. It is a complete code of business ethics, comprising precise and detailed prescriptions. Below are some extracts.

Suffice it to say that this code of conduct is perceived by most people at Brenzy-Legritte, especially the salespeople, as largely inappropriate to the French context and a mere interference in their business. They prefer to disregard it.

Excerpts from the code of conduct at Brenzy-Legritte

Correct use of company funds

1. Company funds will not be used in order to make payments, or concealed loans, with the purpose of dishonestly influencing a supplier, a client or a civil servant. This prohibition applies not only to direct use of company money, but also to any kind of indirect payments, by the means of consultants/intermediaries, or by reimbursing to employees payments made by them.
2. No payment shall be made, for and in the name of the company or one of its subsidiaries, with the intent or knowledge that part of such a payment will serve other purposes than those described in the documents related to this payment.

Gifts, favours and entertainment
Small gifts of symbolic value, minor favours and modest receptions may be offered at the company's expense only when they meet all of the following conditions:

1. They must be compatible with the rules of the company and current business practices.
2. Their monetary worth must be limited; they must be presented in such a form as not to appear as a bribe or remuneration; they must not give rise to suspicions about the impartiality of the beneficiary.
3. They must be approved by the general manager of the subsidiary or by a vice-president at Brenzy Corporation; they must be compatible with the instructions previously approved by the direct superior, the managing director and a senior vice-president at Brenzy Corporation.

Gifts and entertainment for civil servants

As indicated above, gifts, other than symbolic ones or gifts of a very modest value, whatever their nature, or a sumptuous reception, whatever its motives, are not allowed.

Issues related to these procedures and their violations

1. Any employees who want to ask questions about this code and its implementation shall discuss it with the head of the department. If it entails legal or accounting matters, they shall refer to qualified personnel from the legal services and the accounting department, who shall be consulted.

2. The discovery of a case which is fraudulent, illegal, or which violates the rules of the company shall immediately be reported to the legal counsellor. If such cases are identified, which implicate senior executives in the corporation, this case shall be reported to the executive vice-president, for examination by the chairman of the board, the chief executive officer, and the chairman of the audit committee.

3. No derogation to this procedure will be accepted in these matters. There will probably be some 'business opportunities' in the future, when it would be necessary to make questionable payments in order to succeed against a competitor, for one reason or another. The duty of the employee, in this case, is to reject such 'opportunities'.

4. Any infringement of the above-mentioned principles will result in disciplinary sanctions, including dismissal, a suing of the employee and a detailed report to competent regulatory authorities.

5. Moreover, disciplinary sanctions will be directed against any executive who initiates or approves such actions, or knows about them, or may have known about them, and did not quickly act to rectify them in accordance with this code. Adequate disciplinary sanctions will also be directed against any executives who neglect their hierarchical responsibilities, by not ensuring that their subordinates have been properly informed about the rules established in this code.

Questions

1. Analyze cross-cultural differences in the perception of ethical behaviour as concerns sales promotion activities. Why is this code of conduct perceived by most people at Brenzy-Legritte as largely inappropriate?

2. Why was the American company legally obliged to introduce such a code of conduct in its subsidiary?

3. Analyze the border between gifts and bribes. How can they be clearly differentiated?

Intercultural marketing negotiations 1: People, trust and tasks

Cultural differences are generally acknowledged as having an impact on international business negotiations, though not all researchers agree on the magnitude of the impact. Some argue that negotiation is negotiation, irrespective of where and with whom it is conducted. Zartman's view (1993, p. 19) is that:

Culture is to negotiation what birds flying into engines are to flying airplanes or, at most, what weather is to aerodynamics – practical impediments that need to be taken into account (and avoided) once the basic process is fully understood and implemented.

There is much empirical support for the impact of culture on business negotiations (see for instance, Faure and Rubin, 1993; Graham *et al.*, 1994; Leung, 1997; Brett and Okumura, 1998; Bazerman *et al.*, 2000; Adair *et al.*, 2001; Adler, 2002; Wade-Benzoni *et al.*, 2002). There is additional support from authors actually involved in international negotiations (Foster, 1995; Cohen, 1997; Herbig, 1998; Schuster and Copeland, 1999; Saner, 2000).

In international marketing, negotiation skills are needed. Many agreements have to be negotiated, drafted, signed and finally implemented: sales contracts, licensing agreements, joint ventures and various kinds of partnerships, agency and distribution agreements, turnkey contracts, etc. Negotiation is based not only on legal and business matters, corresponding to the *doing* orientation, but also on the quality of human and social interactions, corresponding to the *being* orientation (section 2.3). Goldman (1994) for instance emphasizes the importance for the Japanese of *ningensei*, which literally translates as an all-encompassing and overriding concern for and

prioritizing of 'humanity' or *human beingness* (see Box 16.2). According to Japanese specialists in international marketing negotiations:

The North American and U.K. negotiators failed to communicate ningensei at the first table meeting. Rushing into bottom lines and demanding quick decisions on the pending contract they also overlooked the crucial need for ningensei in developing good will . . . Hard business facts alone are not enough . . . Ningensei is critical in getting Japanese to comply or in persuading Japanese negotiating partners. (Nippon Inc. Consultation, quoted in Goldman, 1994, p. 31.)

There are various kinds of 'distances' between the potential partners: physical distance certainly, but also economic, educational and cultural distance, which tend to inflate the cost of negotiating internationally. Negotiations for large contracts may take years, but fortunately not continuously. Most international deals incur transaction costs that are disproportionate to the costs related to domestic deals: people in the domestic market usually share the same language and cultural background, which acts as a common knowledge base. For instance, it is much easier within the native cultural setting to guess who will be a good payer, a reliable partner or a trustworthy supplier.

Thus it would be a mistake to go flitting about like a butterfly on the international market: always looking for new partners, new customers and new ventures, without following up. This results in a great deal of 'one-off' business. Business people and companies perform poorly if they do not understand the golden rule of international marketing negotiations, which is: have few partners and conduct few negotiations, but make the stakes meaningful. This will enable both parties to build a durable partnership. One should 'marry' well rather than often (section 16.1). This chapter seeks to develop two simple ideas. The first is that *trust* between buyer and seller is a key variable when structuring and developing any relational exchange. The second is that trust in an international sale or business venture is heavily dependent on *culturally coded signs*, and may ultimately be withdrawn precisely because these cultural codes have been ignored. These difficulties in interacting, negotiating sales, planning common ventures, working out agreements and achieving them together are deeply rooted in the cultural, human and social background of business people. They are not related to a superficial variance of business customs.

Empathy alone is not enough for the avoidance of misunderstandings. In fact, people with different cultural backgrounds often do not share the same basic assumptions, as we have shown in Chapters 2 and 3. This may undermine the process of building and maintaining trust between culturally uneven partners (section 16.2). Subsequent sections deal with the various aspects of cultural differences that affect the trust-building process, particularly misunderstandings about personal and institutional credibility (section 16.3); differences in the underlying concept of negotiation: cultural predispositions to integrative negotiation, that is, the preference for maximizing the common cake before looking at one's own portion, or to a distributive orientation – maximizing one's own portion of the cake, rather than the cake itself (section 16.4); time-based misunderstandings during the negotiation process (16.5); the existence of a common rationality between the parties (section 16.6). Section 16.7 outlines the possibility of differences in outcome orientation and compares oral and written agreements as support for trust between the parties. The following chapter complements this one by examining some elements of national negotiation styles.

16.1

The dynamics of trust in relational marketing

The motto of the Deutsche Bank, the largest German bank and a quite successful organization internationally, is '*Vertrauen ist der Anfang von allem*': trust is the beginning of everything. Trust is indeed a necessary condition for smooth and efficient business between partners, but is also a highly intangible, volatile asset, difficult to create, easy to destroy. Pursuing the Whorfian perspective introduced in Chapter 13, let us look first at how trust is expressed in various languages.

What is trust?

The English concept of *trust* is the reliance on and confidence in the truth, worth and reliability of a person or thing. Reliance is central in the Anglo-Saxon concept of trust, which is why the legal institution of trust has been highly developed in the common law tradition, whereas it was non-existent in the Roman-Germanic tradition until very recently. The German concept is based on two verbs: *trauen* and *vertrauen*, both of them meaning literally to 'trust'. But in fact the Germans use the first form, *trauen*, mostly in the negative sense, '*Ich traue Dir nicht*' ('I do not trust you'), and the second in the positive sense '*Ich vertraue Dir*' ('I trust you'). The prefix *Ver* indicates a transformation and this explains what lies behind the German concept of trust: (1) the initial position is distrust and (2) only after a favourable change has occurred can trust be established. The French notion of *confiance*, as in other Romance languages, is based on the Latin *confidentia*, a compound of *cum* (with, shared) and *fides* (faith, belief): the notion of sharing common beliefs is central to the Latin concept of trust. The Japanese word for trust is *shin-yô* meaning literally: sincere business; it is based on a compound of *shin*, a character for 'sincerity' and *yô*, which means literally 'something to do, a business' (Sakade, 1982).

Assuming that the very concept of trust is the same cross culturally and that languages only favour a facet of it, we have the following elements:

1. Trust is reliance on and confidence in people, words and things.
2. Trust is inseparable from distrust: since obvious showing of distrust is detrimental to the establishment of trust, every culture has to deal with the paradox of their inseparability.
3. Trust is about sharing common faith, beliefs, possibly education or group membership.
4. Trust is directed to the future and to common achievements, even though this does not deny the value of the lessons of the past.

Fukuyama (1994, p. 26) defines trust as 'the expectation that arises within a community of regular, honest, and cooperative behavior, based on commonly shared norms, on the part of other members of that community'.[1] Trust basically saves transaction costs in interpersonal and interorganizational relationships. The savings result from smooth communication: one does not need to write everything down, to invest in control systems; meetings are quicker: mutual understanding and consensus are reached more easily. But there are major obstacles to the establishment of trust in an *intercultural* perspective: (1) people do not always share the same communication style; (2) they may not share the same beliefs; (3) they do not necessarily agree on what are adequate control systems; and (4) their interpretation of a control system as signalling trust, distrust or a reasonable combination of both differs. Since the process of building and withdrawing trust is a very dynamic one – it can be killed in a few minutes – trust must be seen as an infant to be protected rather than an independent self.

A marriage between buyer and seller: The dimensions of relational marketing

Many successful international marketing partnerships share the following characteristics: (1) a long time span over which transactions occur, (2) a large size in terms of unit sales (i.e. compared to total turnover) and (3) a long-term relationship established between buyer and seller (Jackson, 1985). These characteristics all fit quite well with the concept of the 'domesticated market' (Arndt, 1979). In this type of market, 'transactions are planned and administered, instead of being conducted on an ad hoc basis' (p. 70). Marketing is viewed from this perspective as an ongoing exchange relationship. Exchange is no longer studied as if it were a time-series of independent, discrete transactions. Buyer–seller relationships are seen to extend far beyond the short time horizon of discrete, small-scale transactions. Relational exchange marketing is almost inevitable in industrial markets, especially in the large worldwide market for international turnkey projects and systems, ranging from the turnkey brewery to the ready-made airport. These contracts are international by nature since the contractor (or contracting consortium of companies) and the owner belong to different nationalities. Turnkey operations may even be seen as a continuous sales process when the owner is planning expansion or a new project, subject to the performance achieved by the contractor in the present project. Trust is then an asset of prime importance in that it enables negotiation partners to overcome short-term conflicts of interest, personal confrontations or even communication misunderstandings (Dwyer *et al.*, 1987). This holds true for the negotiation phase itself, that is, before the signing of the contract(s), as well as for the negotiation process during the implementation phase. Different national/cultural backgrounds are then the source of communication problems and possible misunderstandings. (See *WS16.1* for more information about trust in relational marketing.)

In relational marketing, switching from one supplier to another incurs high transaction costs. This may be contrasted with discrete-transactions marketing, the case traditionally considered in marketing, which applies mainly to consumer goods and is characterized by (1) oligopolistic markets, where a few vendors face a multitude of buyers, and (2) standardized obligations, which are often embedded in a unilateral contract where price cannot be challenged by the buyer. Each transaction in relational marketing may be viewed as having its own history as well as encompassing its future, in as far as it may be anticipated by each partner (Macneil, 1980). Future collaboration (new orders, future common ventures, an extension or revamping of the actual plant, etc.), as well as the conditions, atmosphere and end results of the actual cooperation, are dependent on the assumptions each partner makes about the *trustworthiness* of the other party.

One may easily argue that relational marketing is applicable far beyond the domain of industrial and equipment goods. The negotiations of consumer goods companies with their foreign agents, licensees and distributors for making agreements belong to relational marketing. For instance, some of the relations between the Coca-Cola Company and its foreign dealers, or Procter & Gamble and its advertising agencies, have been established for several decades. Even with the individual consumer, discrete transaction marketing is not the only type of possible relationship: one may form a more personalized relationship with individual consumers by establishing contact with them on a more personal basis through distributors and their employees, in order to build long-term consumer loyalty, which is for instance largely the goal of the Japanese *Keiretsu* distribution system.

Development stages in the process of relational exchange

There are five main phases in the development of a relational exchange (Scanzoni, 1979): (1) awareness; (2) exploration; (3) expansion; (4) commitment; and (5) dissolution. The practical interest of Scanzoni's model is its validity across cultures. It breaks down the exchange relationship into phases, where trust always appears as the 'central asset'. The first phase – awareness – deals with the recognition of the other party as a feasible partner for exchange. Short distances, whether cultural, geographic or linguistic, facilitate this process. It is easier to trade with 'local buyers' than with 'distant merchants'. The intercultural situation renders this phase more difficult: many deals fail at this level; for instance, if they receive a letter written by a non-native speaker in poor English, most native English speakers will fear further communication difficulties and decide to abandon the project as early as possible, before real costs have been incurred. Case A13.4 (Supreme Canning) illustrates such a failure in the awareness phase.

In the second phase – exploration – the exchange relation begins. It remains a tenuous one. Partners are exploring the potential benefits and costs of an exchange. Several means are possible: trial purchase, installing a prototype plant, lending a machine or offering a technical visit to an existing plant. Five subprocesses are at work in exploration: attraction, communication and bargaining, power and justice, norm development and expectations development. Most of these subprocesses are subject to a certain cultural variance. For instance, bargaining attitudes, functions and rites vary according to cultures (section 11.2). Moreover, the development of common norms is more easily attained if potential partners in the exchange share to the same cultural background. During the expansion phase, partners reap the benefits of their relationship and simultaneously

become increasingly interdependent. The subprocesses of the preceding phase are still at work during the expansion. If each party has a strong positive perception of the other party's performance, the motivation to maintain and increase the exchange relationship is strong. This in turn reduces the probability that parties are looking for alternative partners, because of a lack of confidence in the future of the present exchange relationship ('unfaithfulness').

Such a process of exploration took place in the case of Euro-Disney (now called Disneyland Paris), between the Disney Corporation and its European partners. Initially the decision was made to transfer the basic successful Disneyland recipe to France, the same amusements, themes and policy guidelines, including the no-alcohol policy. However, while the project was under way, from 1986 to 1992, strong criticism from some French media called Euro-Disney '*un Tchernobyl culturel*' (a cultural Chernobyl), invoking the risk of cultural invasion, while other French people were in favour of Euro-Disney. Progressively the park has been Europeanized, emphasizing European characters such as Pinocchio (Italian), Cinderella (French) and Peter Pan (British), as well as European history.

Signing one or more contracts is not a necessary step for the commitment phase. The parties exchange implicit or explicit signs (either written or oral) of their willingness to continue their exchange relationship. One of these signs may be the allocation by both partners of large resources to the joint venture, starting a pilot plant or sharing personnel.

Dissolution is a possibility at any moment of the exchange relationship. It rests on an internal evaluation made by each partner of the costs of discontinuing the exchange. If these costs outweigh the benefits, the partners may negotiate a dissolution. These costs are difficult to estimate. The potential benefits of a new exchange relationship are also fairly uncertain and difficult to forecast. Breaking off is a complex process, often related to a crisis initiated by one of the partners. If the other party is willing to enter this separation ritual, dissolution becomes feasible. This 'divorce' is the counterpart of the relational marriage. Ohmae (1989, p. 148) gives a lively example of a dissolution of a joint venture between a US firm (N.O. in Box 16.1) and its Japanese partner (the soon-to-be former partner, F.P., in Box 16.1).

Box 16.1

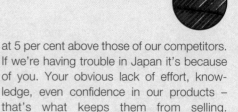

Intercultural discord

(Soon-to-be) New Owner: You guys never make decisions in time.

(Soon-to-be) Former Partner: Speedy decisions are not everything. Consensus is more important.

N.O.: Well, just tell the dealers that our products are the best in the world. Tell them that they sell everywhere except here.

F.P.: But the dealers complain that your products are just okay, not great. Even worse, they are not really tailored to the needs or aesthetic preferences of local customers.

N.O.: Nonsense. What customers buy, everywhere in the world, is the physical performance of the product. No one matches us in performance.

F.P.: Perhaps. Still the dealers report that your products are not neatly packaged and often have scratches on the surface.

N.O.: But that has no effect on performance.

F.P.: Tell that to the dealers. They say they cannot readily see – or sell – the performance difference you're talking about, so they have to fall back on aesthetics, where your products are weak. We will have to reduce the price.

N.O.: Don't you dare. We succeeded in the United States and in Europe by keeping our prices at 5 per cent above those of our competitors. If we're having trouble in Japan it's because of you. Your obvious lack of effort, knowledge, even confidence in our products – that's what keeps them from selling. Besides, your parent keeps on sending our joint venture group a bunch of bumbling old incompetents for managers. We rarely get the good people. Maybe the idea is to kill off our relationship entirely so they can start up a unit of their own making imitation products.

F.P.: Well, if you feel that way, there is not much point in our continuing on together.

N.O.: Glad you said that. We'll buy up the other 50 per cent of the equity and go it on our own.

F.P.: Good luck. By the way, how many Japanese-speaking managers do you have in your company – that is, after we pull out all the 'bumbling old incompetents' from our joint venture?

N.O.: None. But don't worry. We'll just hire a bunch of headhunters and get started up in record time.

(Source: Ohmae, 1989, p. 148.)

16.2

The influence of culture on marketing negotiations

Culture and negotiation examined in the academic literature

The influence of culture on international business negotiations has often been studied using a comparative and cross-cultural setting (Graham, 1985; Graham, 2003; Wade-Benzoni et al., 2002) based on a dyadic simulated negotiation[2] (Kelley, 1966) where nationality is a proxy and summary variable for culture. Each nationality's negotiation style is described, on the basis of the contrast between different national groups observed in the simulated negotiation. Caution is necessary in directly transposing data on the behaviour or negotiation strategies of people from a particular country, collected during intracultural negotiations (with their compatriots). For instance, when Italians negotiate together, or with the French, they may not adopt exactly the same behaviour and strategies as they do when negotiating with Americans. Adler and Graham (1989) address the issue of whether these simple international comparisons are fallacies, when and if researchers are trying to describe cross-cultural interactions accurately. They demonstrate that negotiators tend to adapt their behaviour in intercultural negotiation and do not behave completely as predicted from observations in intracultural settings. They show, for instance, that French-speaking Canadians are more problem-solving oriented when negotiating with English-speaking Canadians than they normally are between themselves. Therefore their behaviour as observed in intracultural negotiations can only serve as a partial basis for the prediction of their style and strategies when negotiating with people belonging to different cultures. Hence the word 'intercultural' in this text directly relates to the study of interaction between people with different cultural backgrounds. The word 'cross-cultural' relates to a research design that is generally comparative.

General influence of culture on business negotiations

Culture mostly has an indirect influence on the outcome of negotiations (see for instance the models of McCall and Warrington, 1990 and Graham and Sano, 1990; see also Bazerman *et al.*, 2000). It works through two basic groups of mediating variables: (1) the situational aspects of the negotiation (time and time pressure, power and exercise of power, number of participants, location, etc.) and (2) the characteristics of the negotiators (especially personality variables and cultural variables) (see *WS16.2*). These two groups of factors in turn influence the negotiation process, which ultimately determines the outcome. However, it is our contention that culture also has an influence on the outcome orientation: certain cultures are more deal/contract oriented whereas others favour relationship development. A census of the impact of culture on international business negotiations is given in Table 16.1. It indicates where in other chapters, especially Chapters 2 and 3, these topics are treated at more length.

Table 16.1 The impact of cultural differences on international marketing negotiations

Cultural difference	Impact on negotiations
(1) Behavioural predispositions of the parties	
Concept of the self and others	Impact on credibility in the awareness and exploration phases (Table 3.1 (b) and (c))
Interpersonal orientation	Individualism versus collectivism/Relationship versus deal orientation
Ingroup orientation	Similarity/'Limited good' concept (Table 2.2 (a) and (b))
Power orientation	Power distance/Roles in negotiation teams/Negotiators' leeway
Willingness to take risks	Uncertainty avoidance/Degree of self-reliance of negotiators (Table 3.2 (d))
(2) Underlying concept of negotiation/Negotiation strategies	
Distributive strategy	Related to ingroup orientation/Power distance/Individualism/Strong past orientation
Integrative strategy	Related to problem-solving approach and future orientation
Role of the negotiator	Buyer's and seller's respective positions of strength (section 15.2)
Strategic time frame	Continuous versus discontinuous/Temporal orientations (Table 2.1 (c) and (d))
(3) Negotiation process	
Agenda setting/Scheduling the negotiation process	Linear-separable time/Economicity of time/Monochronism/Negotiating globally versus negotiating clauses (Table 2.1 (a), (b), (c))
Existence of a common rationality between the partners	Ideologism versus pragmatism/Intellectual styles/Wishful thinking/ (Table 3.5 (b), (c) and (d))
Communication	Communication styles (Chapter 13)/degree of formality and informality
Negotiation tactics	Type and frequency of tactics/Mix of business with affectivity
(4) Outcome orientation	
Partnership as outcome	Making a new ingroup – marriage
Deal/Contract as outcome	Rules between the parties (Table 3.5 (g))/Legal systems
Profit as outcome	Accounting profit orientation (economicity)
Winning over the other party	Distributive orientation
Time line of negotiation	Continuous versus discontinuous/There is no real time line to negotiation

An intercultural approach to building trust in international business negotiations

Trust is the mediating variable in the influence of culture on the process of international business negotiations. Relevant issues for building trust in international business negotiations are as follows:

1. How partners use their own cultural codes, as people and as representatives of organizations, to rate each other's credibility.
2. Their respective preference for the adoption of a 'problem-solving' orientation, embedded in an integrative and collaborative rather than a distributive/competitive strategy.
3. How cultural patterns of time affect negotiation phases, scheduling, plans and deadlines.
4. The partners' approaches to formulating problems, identifying relevant issues and alternative solutions, and the extent to which this 'common rationality' is shared by both parties.
5. Differences in communication style and in the degree of formality/informality during the negotiation process.
6. The type of negotiation tactics used and the extent to which certain tactics can be misinterpreted and damage trust.
7. The basis for trust, whether is it oral ('my word is my bond') or written (only what has been laid down on paper and signed is viewed as binding).
8. The attitudes towards possible litigation; some cultures are litigation-oriented, which results in the 'get-it-in-writing' mentality.
9. Differences in business ethics concerning illegal payments (see sections 15.6 and 15.7).

16.3

Behavioural predispositions of the parties

Who is seen as a credible partner?

The issue of credibility has already been examined several times in this text. It is a key one in international marketing, depending on which personal attributes in a particular culture provide an individual with credibility for certain tasks and interactions (see section 3.1). Triandis (1983, p. 147) has emphasized three dimensions of the self-concept that may have a strong influence on the coding/decoding process of credibility: (1) self-esteem – the extent to which people think of themselves as very good or not too good; (2) perceived potency – the extent to which people view themselves as powerful, able to accomplish almost any task; and (3) perceived activity – the extent to which person sees the self as a doer, an active shaper of the world.

Since people generally live in homogeneous cultural settings (i.e. countries or regions within countries with one language, a dominant religion and shared values) they use the same cultural codes. When people do not share the same codes there may be problems in assessing their partner's credibility/trustworthiness. For example, the emitter (the decoder) may consider as a credible person somebody who shows a low self-concept profile (modest, patiently listening to partners, speaking little and cautiously, etc.); if, conversely, the receiver (the decoder) considers as a credible person somebody with a high self-concept profile (showing self-confidence, speaking arrogantly, not paying much attention to what the other is saying, etc.), there will be a credibility misunderstanding.

One of the main reasons for the seriousness of the Cuban missile crisis at the beginning of the 1960s was a misinterpretation by the Soviet leader Khrushchev of the credibility of the American president, John F. Kennedy. Kennedy and Khrushchev had held talks in Vienna, after the unsuccessful attack by US soldiers resulting in defeat at the Bay of Pigs. During their meeting, the young President Kennedy recognized that this attack had been a military and political mistake, which he regretted. Khrushchev saw this confession of error as a testimony of Kennedy's frank naivety and lack of character. He therefore inferred that it was possible to gain advantage by installing nuclear missiles in Cuba, which would have been targeted at the United States. This led the world to the brink of nuclear war between the superpowers. The events that followed showed that Khrushchev had been wrong in evaluating Kennedy's credibility. Ultimately, Kennedy showed great firmness and negotiating skill.

Khrushchev's mistake may be explained by differences in the cultural coding of credibility. Whereas in the United States, reaching a high position while still young is positively perceived, Soviet people associate age with the ability to carry responsibilities. More-over, the admission of a mistake or a misjudgement is also positively perceived in the United States. US ethics value frankness and honesty. It is further believed that individuals may improve their behaviour and decisions by taking into account the lessons of experience. On the other hand, in the Soviet Union, to admit errors was rare. It generally implied the very weak position of people subjected to the enforced confessions of the Stalinist trials.

Signs of credibility

Personal credibility is decoded through the filter of numerous physical traits, but these are not often considered as they seem to be only appearances or because we tend to use these reference points unconsciously. The credibility signs clearly have a symbolic dimension: the associative links between personal characteristics and credibility are, in part, fixed arbitrarily by culture. Being tall may, for instance, be perceived as a sign of strength and character. Stoutness may be considered a positive sign for a partner in societies where starvation is still a recent memory. Where malnutrition is a reality for a section of the population, it is better to be fat, that is, well nourished and therefore rich and powerful-looking. Naturally these signs have a relative value: weight, height, age and sex cannot be considered as adequate criteria for selecting negotiators. Furthermore, negotiators may in fact be partly aware of or even share the cultural code of their partner. Each of these basic signs plays a role in the initial building of a credibility profile: age, sex, height, stoutness, face, tone and strength of the voice, accent and fluency in a particular language, self-esteem, perceived potency, perceived activity, etc. This profile only influences credibility in early contacts, that is, in the awareness and exploration phases.

Collective credibility: Relating personal trustworthiness to institutional credentials

Collective (company and ingroup) credibility is complementary to personal credibility. There are objective elements which permit assessment of the credibility of the firm, such as its balance sheet, annual reports, reference lists, technical specifications and all those elements that allow assessment of the financial and technical quality of a potential partner. Data and information increase the objectivity of the exchange relationship, but are not enough. For instance the Japanese, like many Europeans, do not emphasize financial performance measured by profits or dividends as a sign of company credibility as strongly as the Americans do. The Japanese and Europeans tend to place more emphasis on turnover, the company's connection with the government, its social reputation and its history.

As emphasized in the previous chapter, finding the appropriate level to establish contact may be an important issue. In societies where decision making is decentralized, it may sometimes be better to contact the people who have the required authority for making decisions, even though they may be at intermediate hierarchical levels (small power distance). In more centralized societies credibility is established on both sides by the top decision-makers meeting. Where committee decision making is the rule, the firm's credibility must be developed by contacts with many people, since it is often impossible to identify who is the ultimate individual decision-maker. There may be no such person. US and European companies often believe that they have lost a deal negotiated with the Japanese because they do not receive a 'yes' for weeks or sometimes months. During this time, the *ringi* process has been at work in the Japanese company. Proposals are circulated among everyone involved in the deal, so that they can discuss it and ultimately affix their own seal of approval. Since (objective) credibility is based on power and decision making, a capacity to understand the influence process in the other party's decision making is therefore a key asset for effective negotiation.

In any national environment there are always some institutions which enable potential partners in joint ventures to assess each other as credible (business schools, engineering schools or law schools, professional associations and meetings, clubs, etc.). Laton McCartney (1989), for instance, describes 'The Grove', an annual three-day encampment, organized by the Bohemian Club of San Francisco, which has played a significant role in the growth of the Bechtel empire, the world leader in turnkey operations for many years:

But the real business of The Grove, where a favorite pastime was figuring out the corporate connections and interlocking directorates of incoming members, was just that: business. Not business by contract or by deal – both of which were barred on The Grove's grounds – but business by sheer association, by men spending time with, getting to know and like each other. 'Once you've spent three days with someone in an informal situation,' explained John D. Ehrlichman, who attended Grove encampments while a chief aide to Richard Nixon, 'you have a relationship – a relationship that opens doors and makes it easier to pick up the phone. (McCartney, 1989, p. 14.)

Interpersonal orientation

The reproach made to Western business people by the Japanese, quoted in the introduction of this chapter, illustrates differences in interpersonal orientation. The concept of *Ningensei* (Box 16.2) presented at the beginning of this chapter has to do with the Confucian ethics which favour smooth interactions and the underplaying of conflict to the benefit of social harmony; it is typical of collectivist values of interpersonal relationships. For instance, the interpersonal sensitivity of Japanese people and their sincere interest in foreign cultures and people may make them friendly hosts at business lunches or dinners. As pointed out by Hawrysh and Zaichkowsky (1990,

p. 42): 'Before entering serious negotiations, Japanese business men will spend considerable time and money entertaining foreign negotiating teams, in order to get to know their negotiating partners and establish with them a rapport built on friendship and trust.' But it should never be forgotten that Japanese negotiators remain down to earth: they are strongly aware of what their basic interests are.

Ingroup orientation

Concern for the other party's outcome is not necessarily to be found equally across cultures. Cultures place a stronger or weaker emphasis on group membership (the other party is/is not a member of the 'ingroup') as a prerequisite for being considered a trustworthy partner. In cultures where there is a clear-cut distinction between the 'ingroup' and the 'outgroup' (according to age, sex, race or kinship criteria), people tend to perceive the interests of both groups as diametrically opposed. This is related to what has been called the concept of 'limited good' (Foster, 1965).

According to the concept of 'limited good', if something positive happens in favour of the outgroup, the wealth and well-being of the ingroup will be threatened. Such reactions are largely the outcome of

---

Box 16.2

The Confucian logic in *Ningensei*

Ningensei exemplifies four interrelated principles of Confucian philosophy: *jen, shu, i* and *li*.

1. Based on active listening, *jen* is a form of humanism that translates into empathetic interaction and caring for the feelings of negotiating associates, and seeking out the other's views, sentiments and true intentions.
2. *Shu* emphasizes the importance of reciprocity in establishing human relationships and the cultivation of 'like-heartedness'; in Matsumoto's (1988) words it is 'belly communication', a means of coding messages within negotiating, social, and corporate channels that is highly contingent upon affective, intuitive and non-verbal channels.

3. The dimension *i*, also termed *amae*, is concerned with the welfare of the collectivity, directing human relationships to the betterment of the common good. 'The *i* component of *ningensei* surfaces in Japanese negotiators' commitment to the organization, group agendas, and a reciprocity (*shu*) and humanism (*jen*) that is long-term, consistent and looks beyond personal motivation.'
4. *Li* refers to the codes, corresponding to precise and formal manners, that facilitate the outer manifestation and social expression of *jen, shu* and *i*. The Japanese *meishi* ritual of exchanging business cards is typical of *li* coded etiquette.

(Source: Adapted from Goldman, 1994, pp. 32–3.)

culture-based collective subjectivity: they stem from the conservative idea that goods and riches are by their very nature restricted. If one yields to the other party even the tiniest concession, this will directly reduce what is left for the members of the ingroup. The concept of 'limited good' induces negotiators to adopt very territorial and distributive strategies. It is a view which clearly favours the idea of the zero sum game, where 'I will lose whatever you may win' and vice versa. In Mediterranean and Middle Eastern societies where the ingroup is highly valued (clan, tribe, extended family), the concept of 'limited good' is often to be found. It slows the adoption of a problem-solving orientation, since co-operative opportunities are simply difficult to envisage.

It has been in fact argued that members of collectivist cultures make a sharp distinction between ingroups and outgroups, a reason being that harmony enhancement is only viewed as possible with ingroup members (see Leung, 1997 for a review of the empirical support). However, there is always some free room for negotiating insider/outsider status not only within but also across cultures: Merriam *et al.* (2001) present a number of case studies showing how people can gain status as partial insiders by making use of common features that transcend the borders of cultures, such as gender or professional cultures. Haugland (1998) demonstrates the role of a shared professional culture in blurring the ingroup/outgroup borders in an increasingly globalized world. His findings show that there is no significant impact of cultural differences on the international buyer–seller relationship in the context of the fisheries industries, whether trading partners of Norwegian exporters are European or American (more ingroup) or Japanese (more outgroup). As he points out: 'It is not unlikely that industries or trades which are very international will develop a specific industry culture, serving the role of unifying persons and companies from different nations and ethnic groups' (p. 27).

Power orientation

One must distinguish between the formal power orientation on the one hand and the real power/decision-making orientation on the other. The first has to do with demonstrating status and how this may enhance credibility, especially in high-perceived-potency societies. It relates to the kinds of meetings, societies, clubs, alumni organizations and so on that unite potentially powerful people. Belonging to such circles gives an opportunity for socializing and getting to know each other. The simple fact of being a member of a certain *club* is the main credibility message. The signs of formal power orientation differ across cultures; they may range from education and titles (English public schools, French *Grandes Ecoles*, *Herr Doktor*, Ivy League alumni in the United States, Todai graduates in Japan, etc.) to belonging to a particular social class or caste as in India.

Real power orientation is a somewhat different issue. As evidenced by Box 15.2 ('The little man in rags and tatters'), there may be wide differences between formal and actual influence on the decision-making process. When making contacts, in a cross-cultural perspective, people should be aware that in different cultures: (1) status is shown in different ways; (2) influential persons are different and individual influence is exerted in different ways; and (3) the decision-making process differs.

Hofstede (1989), in an article about the cultural predictors of negotiation styles, hypothesizes that larger power distance will lead to a more centralized control and decision-making structure because key negotiations have to be concluded by the top authority. And in fact Fisher (1980) notes in the case of Mexico, a typically high-power-distance country (score of 81 on Hofstede's scale; see Table 3.3), that one finds relatively centralized decision making, based on individuals who have extended responsibility at the top of organization. They become frustrated when confronted by the Americans who tend to have several negotiators in charge of specific issues:

In another mismatch of the systems, the Americans find it hard to determine how much Mexican decision making authority goes with which designated authority. There, as in many of the more traditional systems, authority tends to reside somewhat more in the person than in the position, and an organization chart does little to tell the outsider just what leverage – *palanca* – the incumbent has. (Fisher, 1980, p. 29.)

Willingness to take risks

One of the things associated with negotiation activities is risk taking. Disclosing information, making concessions, or drafting clauses involve risk taking because there is always a certain degree of vulnerability to the other party's opportunistic actions. As shown by Weber and Hsee (1998) cultural differences exist in the perception of risk rather than in the attitudes towards perceived risk. They studied how respondents from China, the United States, Germany and Poland differed in risk preference for risky financial options and found the Chinese to be the less risk averse, with the Poles in the middle, and Germans and Americans showing the highest level of risk aversion. However, they show that attitudes towards perceived risk are shared cross-culturally, that is, people across cultures tend to be consistently willing to pay more for less risky options. What differs is the perception of risk itself. As emphasized by Weber and Hsee (1998, p. 1207): 'An understanding of the reasons *why* members of different groups (for example, different cultures) differ in preference or willingness-to-pay for risky options is crucial if one wants to leverage this differences into creative integrative bargaining solutions in inter-group negotiations.'

Risk taking is related to Hofstede's cultural dimension of uncertainty avoidance, which measures the extent to which people in a society tend to feel threatened by uncertain, ambiguous, risky or undefined situations. Where uncertainty avoidance is high, organizations promote stable careers, produce rules and procedures, etc. 'Nevertheless societies in which uncertainty avoidance is strong are also characterized by a higher level of anxiety and aggressiveness that creates, among other things, a strong inner urge to work hard' (Hofstede, 1980). Hofstede points out that 'uncertainty avoidance should not be confused with risk avoidance . . . even more than reducing risk, uncertainty avoidance leads to a reduction of *ambiguity*' (1991, p. 116).

Harnett and Cummings (1980), using a risk-aversion scale ranging from 16 to 48, have shown Americans to be risk takers (31.9) in comparison to the Thai who are highly risk averse (38.2) with the Japanese (34.1) and the Europeans (around 35.7) being in the middle.[3] A high level of uncertainty avoidance is noted by Hofstede as being associated with a more bureaucratic functioning and a lower tendency for individuals to take risks. This may be a problem for business negotiators when they have received a mandate from top management. For instance, the bureaucratic orientation in ex-communist

countries has imposed strong government control on industry. As a consequence, Chinese negotiators, for instance, tend not to be capable of individual decision making. Before any agreement is reached, official government approval must be sought by Chinese negotiators (Eiteman, 1990). The same has been noted in the case of Russian negotiators by Beliaev *et al.* (1985, p. 110): 'Throughout the process a series of ministries are involved . . . Such a process also limits the degree of risk taking that is possible . . . the American who does not see it from (the Soviet) perspective may well interpret it as being slow, lacking in initiative and unproductive.' Tse *et al.* (1994) confirm this tendency in the case of Chinese executives, who tend to consult their superior significantly more than Canadian executives, who belong to a low-uncertainty-avoidance society.

16.4

Underlying concepts of negotiation and negotiation strategies

Integrative orientation versus distributive orientation

In business negotiations the purchaser (or team of purchasers) and the vendor (or group of vendors) are mutually interdependent while their individual interests clash. The ability to choose an effective negotiation strategy largely explains the individual performance of each party on the one hand, and the joint outcome on the other. In pitting themselves against each other, the parties may develop opposing points of view towards the negotiation strategy they intend to adopt: distributive or integrative.

In the distributive strategy (or orientation), the negotiation process is seen as leading to the division of a fixed 'cake' that the parties feel they cannot enlarge even if they were willing to do so. This orientation is also termed 'competitive negotiation' or 'zero sum game'. It leads to a perception of negotiation as a war of positions – territorial in essence. These are negotiations of the 'win–lose' type: 'anything that isn't yours is mine' and vice versa. The negotiators hold attitudes and objectives that are quasi-conflictual: interdependence is minimized whereas adverseness is emphasized.

Table 16.2 Dual concern model

	Concern for one's own outcomes	
Concern for the other party's outcomes	Low	High
High	Yielding	Integrative strategy
Low	Inaction	Contending

At the opposite end of the spectrum is the integrative orientation (Walton and McKersie, 1965). The central assumption is that the size of the 'cake' (the joint outcome of the negotiations) can be increased if the parties adopt a cooperative attitude. Negotiators may not be concerned purely with their own objectives, but may also be interested in the other party's aspirations and results, seeing them as almost equally important. The integrative orientation has been termed 'cooperative' or 'collaborative'. It results in negotiation being seen as an attempt to maximize the joint outcome between the parties. The division of this outcome is to a certain extent secondary or is at least perceived as an important but later issue. Here negotiation is a 'positive sum game', where the joint outcome is greater than zero.

In practice, effective negotiation combines distributive and integrative orientations simultaneously, or at different stages in the negotiation process (Pruitt, 1981). The 'dual concern model', presented in Table 16.2 (Pruitt, 1983), explains negotiation strategies according to two basic variables: concern for one's own outcome and concern for the other party's outcome. This leads to four possible strategies. According to this model, the ability to envisage the other party's outcome is a prerequisite for the adoption of an integrative strategy.

Factors favouring an integrative strategy

The adoption of an integrative strategy is facilitated by the following:

1. A higher level of aspirations on both sides: the negotiators want to reach a better outcome or are under pressure from their principals who have defined increased outcome objectives while still allowing them explicit autonomy and room for manoeuvre (Pruitt and Lewis, 1975).

2. The ability to envisage the future; this permits the discovery or 'invention' of new solutions, which enables both partners to overcome the problem of the fixed size of the 'territorial cake'.

3. The existence of 'perceived common ground' (Pruitt, 1983); if sufficiently wide, this overlap between the interests of the two parties allows new solutions to be explored.

If one seeks to develop relational marketing, an integrative negotiating strategy is required. The nature of transactions imposes it. Business is fairly continuous and sometimes stretches over several years, and therefore implies a very strong buyer–seller interdependence. The performance level depends largely on the extent and quality of the collaboration between the partners. In studying the styles of negotiation of industrial purchasers, Perdue et al. (1986) have found, on the basis of a sample of 195 industrial purchasers, that the majority of them saw themselves as adopting an integrative strategy towards vendors.

A problem-solving approach

The integrative orientation is directly linked to a problem-solving approach in negotiation (Pruitt, 1983). The problem-solving approach (PSA) can be defined as an overall negotiating behaviour that is cooperative, integrative and oriented towards the exchange of information (Campbell et al., 1988). Fair communication and the exchange of information between negotiators are important. 'Problem solvers' exchange representative information, that is, honest and objective data. There is no desire to manipulate the partner, as in instrumental communication (Angelmar and Stern, 1978). Empirical studies (involving experimental negotiation stimulation) have shown that this orientation positively influences the common results of negotiation (Pruitt, 1983). Rubin and Carter (1990), for instance, demonstrate the general superiority of cooperative negotiation by developing a model whereby a new, more cooperative contract provides both the buyer and the seller with cost reduction, compared with a previous adversarial contract. There are, however, some conditions: the first is the availability of cost-related data, the second is the release of the data to the other party during negotiation. The sharing of data is obviously conditioned by culture, language and communication-related issues.

The very concept of PSA is based on culturally relative assumptions: the first one is that the *doing* orientation is very strong in PSA – to solve a problem is to *do* something – and quite often PSA is posited as the *task*-related part of negotiation. Second, it assumes that both partners are *fair*, an English word untranslatable in many languages – *fair play* is used as such in French, for instance; 'fair' means something like 'open and honest in communication and interaction', a value that is not shared by many other cultures, as shown in the next chapter on national negotiation styles. Third, PSA assumes a view of *reciprocity*, based on *quick* response to the other party's openings, on a give-and-take basis where concessions on each side are precisely *measured* and balanced.

As noted by Graham *et al.* (1994), PSA appears to make sense for American negotiators, but this framework may not work in all cases when applied to foreign negotiators. Graham *et al.* (1994) developed an empirical comparison across ten countries/cultures (the United States, Anglophone Canada, Francophone Canada, Mexico, the United Kingdom, France, Germany, the former USSR, Taiwan, China, Korea), starting from three rival hypotheses: (1) the PSA framework is universal; (2) there exist variations within the PSA framework when applied to foreign groups; and (3) the PSA framework does not work at all when applied to non-US negotiators. They show that on average the model works 'differently', and a claim for universality cannot be made. If we think in terms of *ningensei*, it is easy to imagine how, on the one hand, negotiation can be seen universally as problems to be solved, and on the other hand, the ways and means of problem solving may differ: PSA favours task orientation whereas *ningensei* favours a sense of being on the 'same wavelength', that is, a relationship orientation.

Cultural dispositions to being integrative

Even though one may accept the increased effectiveness of integrative strategies, in as far as they aim to maximize the joint outcome, the problem of how this joint outcome is divided between the two sides remains a key issue. Three questions then merit consideration:

1. Do the parties tend to perceive negotiations as being easier, and do they tend to adopt an integrative orientation more readily, when they both share the same culture?
2. Do negotiators who originate from particular cultures tend towards an integrative or a distributive orientation? Furthermore, do negotiators who originate from cultures which favour a problem-solving orientation risk seeing their personal results heavily diminished by a distributive partner who cynically exploits their 'goodwill'?
3. Do cultural differences and intercultural negotiation reduce the likelihood of an integrative strategy?

Greater difficulties in being integrative in an intercultural negotiation situation than in an intracultural negotiation situation

There is general agreement that the results of negotiation are less favourable when the negotiation is intercultural as opposed to intracultural, all other things being equal (Sawyer and Guetzkow, 1965; Ghauri and Usunier, 2003; Brett and Okumura, 1998; Bazerman *et al.*, 2000). Van Zandt (1970) suggests that negotiations between Americans and Japanese are six times as long and three times as difficult as those purely between Americans. This increases the costs of the transaction for American firms in Japan, owing to the relative inefficiency of communication. Brett and Okumura (1998) show that intercultural US–Japanese negotiations result in significantly lower joint gains than intracultural US or Japanese negotiations (in which both national groups achieve similar joint gains). It seems that an explanation is that intercultural negotiators lack sufficient skills to adapt successfully and need a lot more clarifying statements than do intracultural negotiators (Adair *et al.*, 2001). Another possible explanation is that American negotiators tend to use harder tactics, engaging in threats, demands and sanctions, when there is more cultural distance with their partners' culture (Rao and

Schmidt, 1998). The subjective satisfaction of the negotiators (measured by a questionnaire) in their result tends to be lower for intercultural negotiation than for intracultural negotiation (Weitz, 1979; Graham, 1985). However, recent empirical findings have disconfirmed this: in Brett and Okumura (1998) intercultural negotiators were more happy and satisfied with the negotiation than were intracultural negotiators. This can be explained either by the subjective reward effect of achieving an obviously more difficult negotiation task (i.e. inter- as compared with intra-cultural negotiation) or by people being satisfied in both cultural groups by different – and not competing – outcomes (joint gains for Americans versus outcome parity for the Chinese, as in Tinsley and Pillutla, 1998).

Problem solving depends on a collaborative attitude which is easier with a partner from the same culture: similarity leads to more trust and an enhanced level of interpersonal attraction (Evans, 1963; Graham, 1985). As emphasized by Pornpitakpan (1999), greater similarity between two parties will induce greater interpersonal attraction. People need to evaluate others before entering into interaction: similarity facilitates accurate appraisal in the process of social comparison. It facilitates awareness and exploration between parties and leads to more cooperative behaviour in negotiation. As a result, each side considers communication from the other as more representative, that is, objective information with little or no manipulative influences. *Perceived* as well as *actual* similarity can influence the parties: if similarity is perceived, but not based on strictly objective indications (such as shared nationality, language or educational background), a dissymmetrical view of similarity may arise between the buyer and the seller. For instance, many business people in the Middle East have a good command of either English or French. Middle Eastern business people are often perceived by their American or European counterparts as being similar to themselves, whereas Middle Eastern negotiators know that their Western counterparts are different.

The role adopted in negotiation, whether buyer or seller, combines with perceived similarity: if sellers perceive a greater similarity, this can lead to a stronger problem-solving orientation on their part. Although appealing, similarity-based hypotheses have been poorly validated by the empirical study carried out by Campbell *et al.* (1988). No significant relationship was found among American and British buyer/seller pairs: similarity did not favour problem-solving orientation. In the case of the French and the Germans, the perceived similarity only led to a stronger problem-solving orientation on the part of the seller. However, in Campbell *et al.* (1988), the actual dissimilarity between negotiators was strongly reduced by the fact that all the simulated negotiations were intracultural.

As noted above, in intercultural encounters, misunderstandings may arise from perceptions of similarity that are not shared by both parties, such as a negotiation where the seller (e.g. American, for instance) perceives the buyer as similar (e.g. a Westernized Arab buyer) while the reverse is not true: the Arab buyer is perfectly aware that the American seller knows very little about Arabic culture. The seller will adopt a problem-solving approach because of a fallacious perceived similarity, whereas the buyer may exploit the seller without feeling obliged to reciprocate and may ultimately maximize his personal outcome by adopting a covert distributive strategy. However, the *dynamics of similarity* (showing to the other side that one understands them and thus laying the foundation for an integrative attitude on both sides) can work in the other direction, and *adaptation* can bring a positive result. Harris and Moran (1987, p. 472) cite the case of a US banker from the Midwest invited by an Arab sheikh to a meeting in London. The banker demonstrates unusual patience and deep awareness of the other party's power:

The banker arrives in London and waits to meet the sheikh. After two days he is told to fly to Riyadh in Saudi Arabia, which he does. He waits. After three days in Riyadh, he meets the sheikh and the beginning of what was to become a very beneficial business relationship between the two persons and their organizations began.

National orientations favouring the integrative strategy

The second question concerns the adoption of integrative strategies by some nationalities more than others. Studies tend to show that American business people show trust more willingly and more spontaneously than other cultural groups and have a stronger tendency towards a problem-solving and integrative orientation (Druckman *et al.*, 1976; Harnett and Cummings, 1980; Tinsley and Pillutla, 1998). The level of their profits as sellers depends on the buyer's responding positively by also adopting a problem-solving approach (Campbell *et al.*, 1988).

American negotiators have a stronger tendency to exchange representative communication, making clear and explicit messages a priority, and to exhibit less suspicion towards the other party, than most other cultures (Harnett and Cummings, 1980). This is in line with the American appreciation of frankness and directness and their low-context communication style (see section 13.1) that Graham and Herberger (1983) call the 'John Wayne Style' (Box 16.3). They often encounter certain difficulties in cultures where people take more time in the preliminaries: getting to know each other, that is, talking generally and only actually getting down to business later. As a result, Americans may not foster feelings of trust in negotiators from other cultural groups who feel it necessary to get to know the person they are dealing with (Hall, 1976).

Graham and Meissner (1986) have shown in a study comparing five countries that the most integrative strategies are adopted by the Brazilians, followed by the Japanese. On the other hand the Americans, the Germans and the Koreans choose intermediate strategies that are more distributive. This is consistent in the case of the Germans who are reputed for using the hard-sell approach, where the seller is fairly pushy and adopts an instrumental communication and a distributive strategy (Campbell *et al.*, 1988).

There is no empirical study that has shown, for example, that the Arabs from the Middle East have a tendency to be more distributive than the Americans. Americans tend to see the world as problems to be solved whereas Arabs see it more as a creation of God. The concept of integrative strategy, like the problem-solving approach discussed above, is strongly culturally influenced by the American tradition of experimental research in social psychology applied to commercial negotiation. As explained by Leung (1997, p. 648): 'In individualist societies, negotiation is seen more as a task than as a social process. The primary role of negotiators is to work out a solution that is acceptable to both sides.' It is also based on a 'master of destiny' orientation, which feeds attitudes of problem resolution. This presupposes a simultaneous concern for one's own outcome as well as for that of the negotiating partner (the 'dual concern model').

A key issue in the integrative approach is whether parties should primarily strive for achieving a maximum joint gain or for reaching outcome parity between negotiators. Tinsley and Pillutla (1998) show that American negotiators consider problem solving as a more adequate strategy and are more satisfied with joint gain maximization than Hong Kong negotiators.

Box 16.3

The 'John Wayne Style': Just call me John

Americans, more than any other national group, value informality and equality in human relations. The emphasis on first names is only the beginning. We go out of our way to make our clients feel comfortable by playing down status distinctions such as titles and by eliminating 'unnecessary' formalities such as lengthy introductions. All too often, however, we succeed only in making ourselves feel comfortable while our clients become uneasy or even annoyed. For example, in Japanese society interpersonal relationships are vertical; in almost all two-person relationships a difference in status exists. The basis for such distinction may be one or several factors: age, sex, university attended, position in an organization, and even one's particular firm or company . . . Each Japanese is very much aware of his or her own position relative to others with whom he or she deals . . . The roles of the higher status position and the lower status position are quite different, even to the extent that Japanese use different words to express the same idea depending on which person makes the statement. For example a buyer would say *otaku* (your company), while a seller would say *on sha* (your great company). Status relations dictate not only what is said but also how it is said.

(Source: Graham and Herberger, 1983, p. 162.)

When presented with cooperative instructions, Hong Kong negotiators tend to interpret them as meaning that they should strive for equality and display more satisfaction than Americans when the goal of outcome parity is reached. The tendency to search for equality in outcomes and to share the burden by allocating resources equally is confirmed in the case of Japanese as compared to American negotiators by Wade-Benzoni *et al.* (2002).

The dilemma about maximizing joint gains versus outcome parity is precisely where the 'double-bind' situation in negotiation is at its peak and where cultures offer simplified, pre-framed solutions to the paradox of having to cooperate at the risk of being taken advantage of. As emphasized by Bazerman *et al.* (2000, p. 297) cross-cultural negotiation research has provided data 'consistent with the generalization that members of individualist cultures are more likely to handle conflicts directly through competition and problem solving, whereas members of collectivist cultures are more likely to handle conflict in indirect ways that attempt to preserve the relationship.' Leung (1997) explains that 'disintegration avoidance' (DA) is at the very heart of Chinese negotiation behaviour; as long as there is reason for maintaining the relationship, DA will result in a preference for conflict avoidance. However, when the conflict is perceived as caused by the other party's misbehaviour, DA ceases to be effective and Chinese negotiators are more likely to recommend discontinuing the negotiation.

Ignorance of the other party's culture as an obstacle to the implementation of an integrative strategy in negotiation

One of the most important obstacles to effective international business negotiation is ignorance of all or at least the basic elements of the other party's culture. This barrier should be obvious, but is often forgotten by international negotiators. It refers not only to cognitive ignorance of the main features of the other party's culture, but also to the unconscious prejudice that differences are minor (that is, ignorance as absence of awareness). This favours the natural tendency to refer implicitly to one's own cultural norms, especially for the coding/decoding process of communication (the self-reference criterion of Lee, 1966).

Lucian Pye (1986) and Tinsley and Pillutla (1998), in the case of business negotiations between American and Chinese people, and Rosalie Tung (1984a, 1984b), Hawrysh and Zaichkowsky (1990) and Brett and Okumura (1998) in relation to US–Japanese business negotiations, note the American negotiators' lack of prior knowledge of their partner's culture. Before they come to the negotiation table, Americans do not generally read books, nor do they train themselves for the foreign communication style, nor do they learn about the potential traps that could lead to misunderstandings. As Carlos Fuentes states (in a rather harsh aphorism): 'What the U.S. does best is understand itself. What it does worst is understand others' (Fuentes, 1986). French negotiators also tend to be underprepared in terms of cultural knowledge (see Chapter 17 on national negotiation styles), whereas the Japanese seemingly try to learn a lot more than the French or the Americans about the other party's culture before negotiation takes place.

The negotiation and implementation of many international ventures often imply ongoing negotiations that may last for several years. In this case, national cultures tend to disappear as the two teams partly merge their values and behaviour in a common 'venture culture'. In order to improve intercultural negotiation effectiveness, it is advisable to build this common culture between the partners/adversaries right from the start of the negotiation process. Adaptation should, however, be done cautiously: it does not mean wholesale adoption of strategies that work for natives, and the advice 'when in Rome do as the Romans do' has to be applied with due caution (Francis, 1991). It means rather establishing common rules and communication codes, and finding people on each side who will act as go-betweens. Parties should also try to agree on a common interpretation of basic issues, facts and solutions and on a joint decision-making process. This process is largely informal and built on implicit communication. Furthermore, it relies heavily on those individuals who have been involved in the joint venture over a long period of time and who get on well together. A core group of people is to be maintained on both sides over the necessary period of time in order to preserve the shared understanding. (For more information on the underlying concepts of negotiation and negotiation strategies see *WS16.4*.)

16.5

Time-based misunderstandings in international marketing negotiations

When reading this section, the reader should have in mind the time-related cultural differences presented in section 2.2 of this book.

A continuous versus a discontinuous view of time

Cultures that have a cyclical and integrative view of time will tend to have an underlying view of negotiation as only one round in a recurrent relational process, with little sequencing, as compared with people holding a linear/separable view of time. This differentiation is also to be found in the outcome orientation where the time line of negotiation is less important for people with a cyclical/integrative view of time: for them the fact that a contract has been signed is no real reason not to continue the negotiation process. The *strategic time frame* also depends on temporal orientations: the lack of future orientation, for instance, may be a serious impediment to the genuine involvement of a party. (*WS2.2* contains information about how different cultures view time.)

Time for preliminaries

The importance of spending time on establishing personal relationships, especially in Asia and South America, has been noted by many authors (Hall, 1983; Pye, 1986; Graham and Sano, 1990; Hawrysh and Zaichkowski, 1990). There are a number of reasons for needing a personal relationship: (1) establishing the context of communication (Hall, 1976), acquaintance with the other persons being part of the necessary context; (2) a less strict separation between personal and professional spheres than in the West; and (3) the importance of personal status: this necessitates spending time in exploring who is who in order to avoid offending partners. This is all summed up in Burt's comments (1984, p. 7) that an American negotiator will be well advised to develop personal relations away from the negotiation room: 'The usual intense and rather dry approach to doing business

must be supplemented with a social relationship. The Japanese are accustomed to the use of entertainment as a means of becoming better acquainted and of developing goodwill.'

The cultural time concept of Americans, strongly economic, partly explains why spending time in building personal relations is implicitly seen as bad. Time being seen as a resource not to be wasted, spending time on non-business matters, non-task-related issues, is experienced as a violation of their cultural norms. What Adler *et al.* (1987) call 'non-task sounding', that is, establishing rapport and getting to know each other, the first phase in the process of business negotiations, not only needs a relaxed sense of economic time but also some past orientation. The Japanese, for instance, feel that an understanding of their past is necessary in order to understand them as negotiation partners today; thus it will make sense to spend time visiting Japanese shrines or learning the basics about *Zen* or *Ikebana*, the Japanese floral art.

Setting the agenda *and* scheduling the negotiation process

Most negotiation literature considers setting the agenda and scheduling the negotiation process as necessary tasks for the second step in Graham's four-stage model: the task-related exchange of information. An agenda is a schedule and list of items to be discussed during the negotiation process. In many cultures the very notion of 'agenda setting' is unheard of: cutting the process into pieces in advance and allocating time lots to each 'task' is at best theoretical. Hall's (1983) differentiation between monochronic and polychronic use of time (see section 2.2) is highly relevant for the scheduling of negotiation. An agenda-oriented negotiation team, basically monochronic, tends to try to negotiate clauses sequentially, whereas the other party, polychronic, may skip from one issue to another, coming back to points which had apparently been already settled, because they tend to negotiate globally. Graham and Herberger (1983) call it 'One thing at a time': Americans usually attack a complex negotiation task sequentially, that is they separate the issues and try to settle them one at a time. As emphasized by the report of the United States Institute of Peace (2002, p. 5) about US negotiating behaviour: 'Americans tend to subscribe to a view of negotiation as a linear process, a sequence of stages, that typically begins with prenegotiation, advances to the opening moves of the formal negotiation, continues through a probing middle phase, and culminates in an end game and a binding agreement.'

Managing temporal clashes in intercultural business negotiations

Depending on the aim of a joint venture, partners from different cultures may be working together to develop a low-cost operation, or a new R & D project, or distribution and sales facilities. In such settings, issues to do with time will inevitably arise, both at an everyday level, simply in order to meet at the same time, and at a deeper level, that of assigning a common time frame to business operations.

Different time perspectives, be they organizational or cultural, result in temporal clashes. The conflicts that result from the inability to merge different ways of dealing with time may be located at an individual level, that of business people interacting with foreign partners and negotiating with them. Temporal clash at the level of individual interaction results from differing answers given to the following questions: How is somebody treated when he or she arrives half an hour late for a negotiation session? Do sessions have a finishing time in addition to their starting time? Is time also structured during the meeting by setting an agenda and a definite time limit for discussion on each point?

To illustrate the synchronization problem in negotiation, let us take the example of a French meeting versus a US one (a fairly polychronic versus a fairly monochronic culture; see section 2.2). In France some people arrive quarter of an hour late, and some half an hour late. Not only does the meeting not start on time, but those people who were on time have to wait for those who are late. Rarely do people who are late present apologies. Some, not all, simply explain why they are late. It is not unusual, when somebody arrives quite late, for most other people to halt their discussion and spend five or ten minutes explaining to the latecomer what has been said so far! Moreover, unlike US meetings, French meetings are almost never assigned a finishing time. This means that quite often, if there are several successive meetings, the reason why some people arrive late is that the previous meeting

finished one or two hours after the (more or less vaguely and implicitly) agreed-upon finishing time.

Time-based tactical moves: Exerting time pressures in the bargaining process

The effect of time pressure is contingent on the accountability of the negotiator: 'When negotiators are not accountable to a constituency, time pressure results in less competitive interaction and a higher proportion of agreements. In contrast, when negotiators are accountable to a constituency, time pressure results in more competitive interaction and in a higher proportion of impasses' (Mosterd and Rutte, 2000, p. 241). Suffice to say that international business negotiators are generally accountable to a constituency, the CEO or top-level executives in their organization. As a consequence, the effect of time pressure often translates in more competitive behaviour, the use of harder tactics (involving demands and threats) and a greater propensity to break negotiation talks.

Pressure can be exerted on economic-time minded negotiators by postponing the beginning of the negotiation, delaying meetings, concealing from them the time for concluding the negotiation, etc. Cohen (1980, p. 94) gives a classical example of how the Japanese manipulate their Western partner's excessive time consciousness. When he arrived at Tokyo airport the Japanese asked him:

'Are you concerned about getting back to your plane on time?' (Up to that moment I had not been concerned.) 'We can schedule this limousine to transport you back to the airport.' I thought to myself, 'how considerate.' Reaching into my pocket, I handed them my return flight ticket, so the limousine would know when to get me. I didn't realize it then, but they knew my deadline, whereas I didn't know theirs.

The place where the negotiation takes place has an obvious influence on time-scarcity. Those who are 'at home' can monitor their regular business tasks while also participating in the negotiations. Those who have left their home country to negotiate at their partner's location can be impatient to go home for many reasons, both professional and personal. The pressure of 'wasted time' can be used to take advantage of negotiators who have an economic pattern of time and are far from their home base.

The expression 'to waste time' has little meaning for many cultures, including the Bantus, whose time patterns were described in reading A2.4. One may lose something tangible, like a ring or a pencil. But in order for it to be wasted or lost, we would need to be able to conceive of time as a thing that we can separate from the events it is inextricably bound up with. Indeed the Bantus find it difficult to equate abstract time with a monetary unit of measurement. As outlined previously, within their culture Bantu people know nothing comparable to a linear Newtonian time, where events take place. There are events, and each one of these events carries its own desire and its own time. Time cannot be wasted or lost, because time has simply to be lived or experienced, whatever may be the way to experience it. No one can steal time, not even death.

The same quietness in the face of time may be seen in the Orient, in contrast to the Western anguish and guilt about time that might be wasted or lost. Several authors in the field of international business negotiations note that time pressure is strongly felt by American negotiators, whether they negotiate with the Chinese (Pye, 1982) or with the Japanese (Graham, 1981; Graham and Sano, 1990; Tung, 1984a, 1984b). American negotiators are eventually forced to yield because they view time as wasted or lost if not optimally allocated. When pushed to its extreme, this logic may result in total inefficiency. People spend their whole time thinking of alternative uses for their time and assessing which alternative offers the best marginal return. As noted by Adler (2002, p. 219):

Americans' sense of urgency disadvantages them with respect to less hurried bargaining partners. Negotiators from other countries recognize Americans' time consciousness, achievement orientation, and impatience. They know that Americans will make concessions close to their deadline (time consciousness) in order to get a signed contract (achievement orientation).

However, urgency has a two-sided value. As noted by careful observers of American negotiation style, 'Americans are not always looking at the clock' (USIP, 2002). They may use their own self-defined deadlines to put the other party under pressure. They may also let diplomatic negotiations stretch out for years when there is little interest in the American media for the issue under discussion.

Making plans together: Coordinating and planning the common venture

In many international negotiations planning a common venture, the various stages – the steps in the construction of a turnkey plant, or the implementation phases of a joint-venture or licence agreement – need explicit reference to dates, deadlines and the sequencing of interdependent tasks. In other words, planning is such a basic function of management that it is extremely difficult to admit that there are other models of time than those on which it implicitly stands. Naturally it would be naive to consider that business people have purely traditional time patterns. In fact, complex patterns of time-related behaviour may be used by people who share several cultural backgrounds, both the original in-depth background, and other more superficial backgrounds. Furthermore, the native cultural background may be undervalued because it is supposed to be 'inefficient' or it is unknown to foreigners. Accordingly, people belonging to non-linear/economic time cultures often tend to imitate the cultural way of life that they tend to favour as the 'best' way. It might result in buying a superb watch as an item of jewellery or a diary because it is fashionable. But the functional behaviour that is in line with the watch or the diary will not be adopted. After these objects have been bought, they lose their cultural value as practical tools of the economic, monochronic, linear or separable time pattern. People involved in such cultural borrowing might prove unable to take any appointment seriously and probably experience difficulties in following any preset schedule.

The fallacy of imported economic time: Ideal and actual temporal behaviour

Ideal patterns of time and actual temporal behaviour may differ widely for negotiators who apparently use their partners' time culture rather than their own. Bista (1990), in the case of Nepal, highlights the conflict between time-based behaviour related to foreign education and the traditional influence of fatalistic beliefs on the lack of future orientation and sense of planning:

Planning involves the detailing of the connections between resources, objects and events, and the determination of an efficient course of action to attain desired results . . . Control is placed in the hands of the planner. But fatalism does not allow this kind of control, and is inherently antithetical to pragmatic thought . . . Over the past few decades, many Nepali students have travelled abroad to study in other countries, and have returned with advanced degrees in various professional capacities . . . Upon their return many are placed in positions of authority, as they represent the cream of Nepal's manpower resources. Though they may be initially inspired by a high degree of idealism, the new values that they bring back with them immediately confront fatalism and are typically defeated by it . . . After forty years of planning and an accumulation of foreign trained graduates, Nepal, then, still has little manpower to effectively bridge the disparities between the culture of the foreign aid donors and that of their own. (1990, pp. 137–8.)

In many countries, there is much cultural borrowing in relation to time management, that is, appointments, scheduling and meetings: the actual patterns of time management in industrialized countries such as the United States or northern Europe have been imported by other nations as ideal patterns (Usunier, 1990). In Latin-European countries, the PERT technique, which is designed for the scheduling of interrelated tasks, has been implemented mostly for its intellectual appeal. PERT, which is based on graph theory and looks for the 'critical path' in a set of tasks, has an appealing US 'management science' look. In France, where many managers and top executives have been trained as engineers, there has been great interest in this scientific management technique. However, actual project planning in France and Latin-European countries often works with high discrepancies relative to PERT dates: French people tend to be intellectually monochronic but actually behave in a polychronic manner (Hall, 1983).

Sometimes people even use two completely different time-management systems in parallel. This somewhat schizophrenic situation is most easily recognized when one looks at the construction of some turnkey projects in developing countries. At first, during the negotiation process and on signature of the contract, everybody genuinely agrees about using an economic-time/monochronic pattern. In fact the partners share the same beliefs as to what 'appropriate' time management should be and do not discuss. This is, however, an ideal view on one side and actual behaviour on the other, and extreme confusion occurs when the project is being implemented.

16.6

Cultural misunderstandings during the negotiation process

Existence of a common rationality between the partners

As explained in section 3.4, people differ in their way of relating thinking to action: whereas ideologists tend to think broadly and relate to general principles, the pragmatist orientation values focusing on detailed issues that are to be solved one by one. Typical of pragmatists are the Americans, as noted by Weiss (1987, p. 31), in the case of the GM–Toyota negotiations for their joint venture in California: 'the Japanese tended to start talks with statements of general principle and usually did not respond to proposals before checking with their headquarters. The Americans preferred specific proposals and responses at the table.'

When negotiating a large contract (for a nuclear plant or a television satellite, for instance), ideologists see arguments that favour their 'global way of thinking': it is a unitary production, it is a complex multi-partner business, it often involves government financing and also has far-reaching social, economic and political consequences. Pragmatists, on the other hand, see many arguments that favour their way of thinking: the technicalities of the plant and its desired performance require an achievement and deadline orientation (pragmatist values).

Pragmatism is associated with a tendency to look at the details of facts, to measure, to validate empirically. Ideologists on the other hand have a liking for speech, words and ideas. They will be more oriented towards instrumental communication. Inasmuch as they aim to manipulate other people, ideologists may be as effective as pragmatists, since they may influence their counterparts through nicely worded general communications. In relational marketing, especially in the first two phases of the relational exchange, negotiation between ideologists and pragmatists may create misunderstandings (see Box 16.5) which will be difficult to overcome during subsequent phases.

Indeed, developing common norms will be fairly difficult, although necessary if partners want to be able to predict the other party's behaviour. A frequent comment in such situations will be: 'One never knows

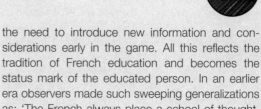

Box 16.5

Cartesian logic in negotiation

Rather imprecisely defined, the idea is that one reasons from a starting point based on what is known, and then pays careful attention to the logical way in which one point leads to the next, and finally reaches a conclusion regarding the issue at hand. The French also assign greater priority than Americans do to establishing the principles on which the reasoning process should be based. Once this reasoning process is under way, it becomes relatively difficult to introduce new evidence or facts, most especially during a negotiation. Hence the appearance of French inflexibility, and the need to introduce new information and considerations early in the game. All this reflects the tradition of French education and becomes the status mark of the educated person. In an earlier era observers made such sweeping generalizations as: 'The French always place a school of thought, a formula, convention, a priori arguments, abstraction, and artificiality above reality; they prefer clarity to truth, words to things, rhetoric to science . . .' [Quotation from Zeldin, 1977].

(Source: Fisher, 1980, p. 50.)

what these people have in mind; their behaviour is largely unpredictable.' An American (pragmatist oriented) describes negotiations with the French (more ideologist oriented) in the following terms (Burt, 1984, p. 6): 'The French are extremely difficult to negotiate with. Often they will not accept facts, no matter how convincing they may be.'

Communication

If negotiators want to promote an integrative approach, it is important for them to focus on sharing and seeking information. Communication has been shown to generate greater cooperation even among negotiation partners that display strong tendencies to self-interest (Wade-Benzoni et al., 2002). The language used for negotiation has its importance: the myth that any language can be translated into another language often causes English to be chosen as a central negotiation language and to add interpreters when proficiency is too low on one side.[4] As emphasized by Hoon-Halbauer (1999) in the case of Sino-Foreign joint ventures, few Chinese can speak a foreign language and all oral communication between the Chinese and their foreign partners has to pass through interpreters: 'When a third person is involved no genuine, direct communication between two persons can take place. In other words, "heart-to-heart" talks are unlikely to take place' (p. 359).

Furthermore, due to poor translation, it may be that only 30–40 per cent of the actual content of what is said in Chinese is conveyed to the non-Chinese speaking negotiation partners, resulting in the discarding of good ideas and suggestions made by the Chinese (Hoon-Halbauer, 1999). (WS16.6 offers some resources concerning intercultural communication in terms of negotiations.)

There are semantic differences in the words used and many misunderstandings can arise from ignoring the precise meaning of key concepts for the negotiation; Adachi (1998) gives the example of noticeable differences in the use of the word 'customer' by Japanese and American negotiators. She shows that cultural connotation is a crucial aspect of conversation which needs careful attention in understanding the meaning beyond the mere one-to-one translations of words. Moreover, speakers of certain languages (i.e. high-context languages such as Japanese, Chinese or Arabic) use more contextual cues to decode messages. The role of high-context versus low-context communication has been described by Hall (1960, 1976).

When messages are exchanged, the degree to which they should be interpreted has to be taken into account as well as the cross-cultural differences in linguistic styles, involving the use of silence or conversational overlap (George et al., 1998). For instance, silence is a full form of communication for the Japanese, and Graham (1985) reports twice as many silences in Japanese interactions as in American. Westerners often have the impression that they 'do all the talking'. Low-context negotiators, such as Americans, tend to be explicit, precise, legalistic, and direct in communication, sometimes forceful and even appearing as blunt to the other party (USIP, 2002). In a recent empirical survey of Japanese and US negotiators, Adair *et al.* (2001, p. 380) show that direct and indirect communication patterns are consistent with Hall's theory of low- versus high-context communication:

The U.S. negotiators relied on direct information to learn about each other's preferences and priorities and to integrate this information to generate joint gains. They were comfortable sharing information about priorities, comparing and contrasting their preferences with those of the other party, and giving specific feedback to offers and proposals. The Japanese negotiators relied on indirect information, inferring each other's preferences and priorities from multiple offers and counteroffers over time.

In terms of non-verbal communication a lack of eye contact for the Americans is a signal that something is amiss and 'American executives reported that the lack of eye contact was not only disconcerting but reduced their bargaining performance [with Japanese]' (Hawrysh and Zaichkowsky, 1990, p. 34).

Negotiators must be ready to hear true as well as false information, discourse based on facts as well as on wishful thinking or pure obedience to superiors. Frankness and sincerity are relative values: they can be interpreted as mere naivety, a lack of realism or a lack of self-control in speaking one's own mind. Furthermore, waiting for reciprocation when one has disclosed information useful for the other party makes little sense in an intercultural context. Frankness and directness are positive values for the Americans and to a lesser extent for the French, but they are not so for Mexicans in formal encounters, nor for the Japanese at any time (Fisher, 1980).

The issue of formality versus informality is a difficult one. Frequently a contrast is made between cultures that are supposed to value informality (e.g. American) and those that would be more formal (most cultures which have long historical roots and high power distance). 'Informality' may be simply another kind of formalism and the 'ice breaking' at the beginning of any typical US meeting between unknown people is generally an expected ritual. It is more important to understand the degree of formality required in particular circumstances. Away from formal negotiation sessions, people belonging to apparently quite formal cultures can become much more informal. Formalism in communication sometimes takes the form of diplomatic language, a highly coded type of speech, sometimes apparently quite remote from actual reality, known in French as *langue de bois* (literally 'wooden tongue' or 'wood language'). George Orwell, in *Animal Farm*, gives a good example of *langue de bois* concerning the pig Napoleon who had taken control of the farm and imposed its power on other animals.

Napoleon was now never spoken of simply as 'Napoleon'. He was always referred to in formal style as 'our Leader, Comrade Napoleon', and the pigs liked to invent for him such titles as Father of All Animals, Terror of Mankind, Protector of the Sheepfold, Ducklings' Friend, and the like. In his speeches Squealer would talk with the tears rolling down his cheeks of Napoleon's wisdom, the goodness of his heart, and the deep love he bore to all animals everywhere, even and especially the unhappy animals who still lived in ignorance and slavery on other farms. It had become usual to give Napoleon the credit for every successful achievement and every stroke of good fortune. You would often hear one hen remark to another, 'Under the guidance of our Leader, Comrade Napoleon, I have laid five eggs in six days'; or two cows, enjoying a drink at the pool would exclaim, 'Thanks to the leadership of Comrade Napoleon, how excellent this water tastes!' (1945, p. 62.)

Langue de bois, although a very non-American concept given the emphasis on direct, frank and honest speech in US culture, is practised in many organizations worldwide, either in relation to powerful people or groups, or concerning taboo issues; for instance, a previous failure with a foreign partner that would shed some useful light on actual negotiations.

Due to increased global communication through the Internet and the extensive use of computer-mediated communication, in particular e-mail, as well as to the rise of business-to-business marketplaces, there is an increasing use of global electronic media in negotiating international deals.[5] Contrary to traditional negotiation, which is assumed to be carried out almost exclusively via face-to-face communication, e-mail does not offer much of the non-verbal feedback that exists in other media. However, electronic communication is very useful for dispersed negotiations, when matters have to be discussed without incurring the high costs associated with face-to-face cross-border negotiation. Potter and Balthazard (2000) show that both Chinese and American managers prefer face-to-face over computer-mediated negotiation. However, both Chinese and Americans, negotiating intraculturally, do not perceive a significant difference between e-mail-based written negotiation and the same negotiation dealt with through a web-based threaded discussion even though the latter method seems to allow for more continuous interaction. Ulijn et al. (2001) based on a study involving 20 participants, use speech act theory and psycholinguistic analysis to show that culture affects non face-to-face communication as is the case of negotiation through e-mail. Kersten et al. (1999, 2002) also find a number of cultural differences between managers from Austria, Ecuador, Finland and Switzerland who negotiate electronically.[6] Finally, e-mail communication is often mixed with face-to-face encounters; e-mailing is widely affected by prior personal acquaintance of the people involved: if negotiators have started with some face-to-face activity, computer-mediated negotiation will be largely facilitated and communication misunderstandings arising from the 'dry style' of e-mails may largely be avoided.

Negotiation tactics

Graham (1993) has studied the negotiation tactics used in eight cultures, using videotaped negotiations where statements were classified into 12 categories using the framework of Angelmar and Stern (1978). His results show very similar negotiation tactics across cultures: most use a majority of tactics based on an exchange of information, either by self-disclosure or by means of asking questions (more than 50 per cent in all cases). The Chinese score highest on posing questions, an outcome that is consistent with Pye's comments about them: 'Once negotiation begins the Chinese seem passive. They simply ask questions, probe for information, and conceal any eagerness they may feel' (1986, p. 78). On the other hand, the Spaniards are the best at making promises. The proportion of 'negative' tactics, including threats, warnings, punishment and negative normative appeals (statements in which the source indicates that the target's behaviour is in violation of social norms) is fairly low in all cases, never exceeding 10 per cent of the

information exchange. Finally, the types of tactics and the frequency of their use do not vary as much cross-nationally as the level of their implementation.

The use of theatricality, threats of withdrawal and tactics based on time, such as waiting until the last moment to obtain further concessions by making new demands, are based in national styles of negotiations, discussed in the next chapter. Tactics are also related to the ambiguous atmosphere of business negotiations where implied warm human relations are supposed to be mixed with business. This relates to the divide between affective and neutral cultures (Trompenaars, 1993) presented at the end of section 3.5. Negotiations are always interspersed with friendship and enmity, which can have personal as well as cultural bases.

Emotions and conflict-handling styles in cross-cultural negotiations

Communication misunderstandings in intercultural negotiation quite often result in increased levels of emotions, that is, negotiators tend to depart from the rational and objective evaluation of issues at stake and to mix subjectivity and feelings with business matters. Morris et al. (1998, p. 730) outline two types of misunderstandings that frequently arise between Asian and American negotiators: 'In one type of misunderstanding, U.S. managers make the error of reading silence of their Asian counterpart as an indication of consent . . . A different type of misunderstanding occurs when Asian managers make the error of reading an U.S. colleague's direct adversarial arguments as indicating unreasonableness and lack of respect.' Emotions such as anger results in negotiators being less accurate in judging the interests at stake, more self-centred on their own interests; it also has a general effect of reducing joint gains (Bazerman et al., 2000).[7]

Kumar (1997) makes a sharp distinction between positive and negative emotions in negotiation. Emotions contain both an element of affect and an accompanying physiological arousal. For him, positive emotions result in being more flexible in negotiations, as well as helping negotiators to be more persistent, especially since a positive affective state increases the confidence level of negotiators. However, a positive affective state may also heighten expectations and result in negotiators' disappointment with actual outcomes.

Negative emotions, on the other hand, may result in conflict escalation, that is, actors take matters personally when they should see them with a more distanced attitude. Likely consequences are the attribution to the other side of the responsibility for conflict, and possibly the discontinuation of the relation. While negative emotions may serve to inform the parties that an existing situation is untenable, they may also be snowballing and result in a negative conflict spiral (Brett *et al.*, 1998; George *et al.*, 1998). Negative spirals are partly based on selectively choosing those information cues which will confirm the negative feelings of a negotiators leading her/him to an escalation of negative feelings toward the other party which are no more based on hard facts. They also result from systematic reciprocation of contentious communication. Negative spirals are particularly likely to occur in cross-cultural negotiations due to differences at three levels: differences in internalized values and norms, differences in emotional expression and differences in linguistic styles (George *et al.*, 1998). A conflict spiral appears as circular because it is based on repeated contentious communication whereby each side 'responds' to the other side's contentious communication with negative reciprocation (Brett *et al.*, 1998).

The way to solve problems of negative spirals in negotiation has to do with both models of conflict resolution and with strategic communication styles in negotiation which may help to manage discrepancies in process and outcomes of negotiation (Kumar and O'Nti, 1998). Tinsley (1998) shows that the Japanese, the Americans and the Germans use different models of conflict resolution. The Japanese tend to use what she calls the 'status model', that is, social interaction is viewed as governed by status and parties might solicit the advice of higher status figures to solve the conflict. The German display a preference for the 'regulations' model whereby conflict is seen as to be solved by applying standardized, universal and impersonal rules. Finally, Americans prefer the 'interest' model whereby parties exchange information on their interests, try to prioritize them and trade off interests. Another dimension of conflict resolution is whether people tend to avoid or to directly confront conflict. Morris *et al.* (1998) show that Chinese managers tend to display conflict avoidance

whereas American tend to develop a competing style. Moreover, negotiators who come from more traditional societies, where the dimension of social conservatism is high, tend to be more conflict averse (Morris *et al.*, 1998; Kozan and Ergin, 1999).

Monitoring emotions in negotiation has to do with the avoidance of negative spirals but also with the avoidance of being too systematically conflict avoidant. A number of communication strategies have been recommended for breaking negative spirals in cross-cultural negotiations. George *et al.* (1998) recommend that negotiators engage in what they call 'motivated information processing', that is, a process whereby information is selectively processed in ways that are supportive of motivational goals; motivation for certain outcomes, rather than affect, guides interpretation. Brett *et al.* (1998) show that a mix of reciprocation combined with non-contentious communication is likely to help in breaking negative spirals in negotiations.

16.7
Differences in outcome orientation: Oral versus written agreements as a basis for trust between the parties

It would be naive to believe that profits, especially future accounting profits for each party, are the only possible outcome of the negotiation process. Others include: relationship building, personal satisfaction, and alliances for future ventures. One reason that profits are not the sole possible outcome is that they are not fully foreseeable. However, since profits are often considered the sole motive, the negotiation partners are unaware of basic differences in outcome orientation. This can generate increased misunderstandings since many cultures are more relationship than deal oriented, as Weiss (1987) and Hawrysh and Zaichkowski (1990) in the case of the Japanese, and Pye (1986), Eiteman (1990) and Rotella *et al.* (2000) point out in the case of the Chinese. People from these cultures prefer the outcome of the negotiation process to be a gentleman's agreement, a loosely worded statement expressing mutual cooperation and trust between the parties, rather than a formal Western-style contract which embodies expected profits in words, numbers and clauses. The most crucial element of preparation for a negotiation with the Japanese is drafting an opening statement that seals the start of a relationship, in which the Western side may have the opportunity to seize the moment and set the tone for the rest of the negotiation (Corne, 1992).

Opportunism, misunderstandings, and the perceived degree of agreement

It is generally considered that agreements are mostly in writing. They are achieved by negotiation and by the signing of a written contract, which is often termed 'the law of the parties'. Unfortunately, this is not always true. Keegan (1984) points out that in some cultures 'my word is my bond', and trust is a personal matter, which he contrasts with the 'get-it-in-writing' mentality where trust is more impersonal. The former would be typical of the Middle East, whereas the latter would be found in the United States where hundreds of thousands of lawyers help people negotiate written agreements and litigate within the framework of these written agreements.

This does not mean, however, that people rely *entirely* on either an oral or a written base. The main problem in making the agreement work is to avoid opportunistic behaviour on one side which would exploit the other side, or, even worse, opportunism on both sides. Keeping one's word can be achieved by the taking of oaths and the existence of confidence between people who belong to a common group where perjury is considered a crime. Within the boundaries of such an ingroup-oriented business community, the indelicate merchant is punished by being outlawed as a potential partner.[8] But this works well only within the ingroup and on a personal basis. That is why, in an international setting where business people belong to different cultural communities, such 'words' cannot be considered as reliable enough for committing oneself. Written agreements, that is, formal contracts, offer a different avenue for avoiding opportunistic behaviour; they are more precise and more impersonal, both low-context and outgroup oriented. They offer predictability because details of each party's obligations and rights have been discussed and put on paper. The impersonal mediation of a third party, a national court or ICC arbitration, guarantees that disputes between the business partners will be examined on the basis of proven evidence and contradictory arguments. Provided that a party's behaviour can be observed (i.e. opportunistic behaviour cannot be hidden) and verified (proofs of breach of contract can be supplied), the court can oblige the infringing party to conform to a contract or to pay compensation. Generally, litigation serves only as a threat: even in the USA, only a very small proportion of lawyers in large law firms are involved in litigation (about 10 per cent).

Therefore, exploring, maintaining and checking the bases for trust is a complex process. An agreement may be non-symmetrical, such as when party A perceives that it agrees with B, but B does not agree with A; either B conceals the disagreement or there is some sort of misunderstanding, usually language-based. People may agree in broad terms but hold different views of 'executional details', and may not perceive their divergence which may relate to different interpretations of clauses or of a tacit part of the agreement. Although much may be written down, some aspects of the agreement will remain unwritten and will seem, to one but not the other party, obviously in line with a written clause. If the parties do not find an opportunity to discuss their interpretations, they will not be aware of such differences of opinion. A last caveat is that the agreement may not be understood by both parties as implying the same kind of commitment, the same stability over time of the exchange relationship; the parties may also be unaware that they do not share the same views of how precisely clauses should be interpreted in the future, whether broadly or to the letter.

Written documents as a basis for mutual trust between the parties

In written agreements there is a fundamental dialectic between distrust and confidence. At the beginning there is *distrust*. It is implicitly assumed that such distrust is natural. This has to be reduced in order to establish *confidence*. Trust is not achieved on a global and personal basis, but only by breaking down potential distrust in concrete situations where it may hamper common action. Trust is built step by step, with a view towards the future, and *real trust* is achieved only gradually. Trust is deprived of its personal aspects and, thanks to the written agreement, the parties may trust each other in business, although they do not trust each other as people. Trust is taken to its highest point when the parties sign a written agreement.

On the other hand, cultures that favour oral agreements tend not to hypothesize that trust is constructed by the negotiation process. They see trust more as a prerequisite to the negotiation of written agreements. Naturally they do not expect this prerequisite to be met in every case. Trust tends to be mostly personal and ingroup based. Establishing trust requires that people know each other. That is probably why many Far Eastern cultures (Chinese (Pye, 1982); Japanese (Graham and Sano, 1990; Tung, 1984; de Mente, 1987 and Corne, 1992)) need to make informal contacts, discuss general topics and spend time together before they get to the point, even though all this may not appear task related.

Subsequently, the negotiation process will be lengthy because another dialectic is at work. Since people are supposed to trust each other, the negotiation process should not damage or destroy the basic asset of their exchange relationship – trust. They will avoid direct confrontation on a specific clause, and therefore globalize the negotiation process. Global friends may be local foes, provided trust is not lost as the basic asset of the negotiation process.

The ambiguity of the cultural status of written materials as a basis for building trust between the parties

That one should always 'get it in writing' is not self-evident. The contrary idea may even emerge ('if they want it written down, it means that they don't trust me'). Regina Traoré Sérié (1986, quoted in Ollivier and de Maricourt, 1990, p. 145) explains, for instance, the respective roles of oral communication (spoken, transmitted through personal and concrete communication, passed from one generation to another by storytellers) and written materials (read, industrially printed, impersonally transmitted, with no concrete communication) in African culture.

Reading is an individual act, which does not easily incorporate itself into African culture. Written documents are presented as either irrelevant to everyday social practices, or as an anti-social practice. This is because someone who reads, is also isolating himself, which is resented by the other members of the community. But at the same time, people find books attractive, because they are the symbol of access to a certain kind of power. By reading, people appropriate foreign culture, they get to know 'the paper of the whites'. As a consequence, reading is coded as a positive activity in the collective ideal of Ivory Coast society, since it is a synonym for social success. This contradiction between 'alien' and 'fetish' written documents encapsulates the ambiguity of the status of books in African society.

Does writing produce irreversible commitments?

In cultures where relationships are very personalized, confidence cannot be separated from the person in whom it is placed. The basis for mutual trust is no longer the detailed written contractual documents, but a man's word, which is his bond. It is not 'just any word', but a special kind of word, which is heavily imbued with cultural codes (Hall, 1976). These words as bonds cannot easily be transferred from one culture to another. Adler (1980) describes the case of an Egyptian executive who, after entertaining his Canadian guest, offered him a joint partnership in a business venture. The Canadian was very keen to enter this venture with the Egyptian businessman. He therefore suggested that they meet again the next morning with their respective lawyers to fill in the details. The Egyptians never arrived. The Canadian businessman wondered whether this was caused by the lack of punctuality of the Egyptians, or by the Egyptian expecting a counteroffer, or even the absence of lawyers available in Cairo:

None of these explanations was true, although the Canadian executive suggested all of them. At issue was the perceived meaning of inviting lawyers. The Canadian saw the lawyer's presence as facilitating the successful completion of the negotiation; the Egyptian interpreted it as signalling the Canadian's mistrust of his verbal commitment. Canadians often use the impersonal formality of a lawyer's services to finalize an agreement. Egyptians more frequently depend on a personal relationship developed between bargaining partners for the same purposes. (Adler, 1980, p. 178.)

If agreements are mostly person based, then their written base may be less important. Thus the demand by a Middle Eastern buyer for renegotiation of clauses, in a contract already negotiated and signed, should not be seen as astonishing. It should not necessarily lead to litigation. Behind the demand for renegotiation is the assumption that, if people really trust each other, they should go much further than simple and literal implementation of their written agreements. This leads to the following question: to what extent should the contract signature date be considered a time line that signals the end of the negotiation?

Written agreements as a time line for negotiations

As noted above, there are two different ways to look at the influence of the written agreement on the time line of the exchange relationship. Those favouring written-based building of trust tend to see a written agreement as the key point in the exchange relationship. It completes a phase during which potential relations have been carefully discussed and explored. It establishes a strict contractual code, which has then to be implemented quite literally. Written words, sentences, numbers and formulas have to be strictly observed. If a party feels free to depart from what has been written down, the Damocles sword of litigation will hang over the parties – and nobody likes litigation, supposedly.

Those favouring oral-based personal trust consider the signing of a written agreement an important step, but only one of many in a continuous negotiation process. The negotiation process was active before signature and will be active afterwards. A continuous negotiation process, where the contract is only one step, not the major step, is seen as the best basis for maintaining trust. As Edward Hall (1960, p. 94) stated:

Americans consider that negotiations have more or less ceased when the contract is signed. With the Greeks, on the other hand, the contract is seen as a sort of way station on the route to negotiation, that will cease only when the work is completed. The contract is nothing more than a charter for serious negotiations. In the Arab world, once a man's word is given in a particular kind of way, it is just as binding as, if not more so than, most of our written contracts. The written contract therefore violates the Moslem's sensitivities and reflects on his honour. Unfortunately, the situation is now so hopelessly confused that neither system can be counted on to prevail consistently.

Different attitudes towards litigation

It is easy to understand that the function of litigation will be different for both sides. Recourse to litigation will be fairly easy for those favouring written-based agreements as the ultimate means of resolving breaches of contract. The oral and personal tradition is less litigation-prone because of its drawbacks: (1) it breaks the implicit assumption of trust, and (2) it breaches the required state of social harmony, especially in the Far Eastern countries, and may therefore be quite threatening for the community as a whole. As David (1987, p. 89, my translation) states:

... in Far Eastern countries, as well as in Black Africa and Madagascar ... subject to the westernization process which has been attempted, one does not find, as in Hinduism or Islam, a body of legal rules whose influence may be weakened by the recognized influence of other factors; it is the very notion of legal rules which is challenged. Despite authorities having sometimes established legal codes, it is well known and seems obvious that the prescriptions of these codes are not designed to be implemented literally. They should only be considered as simple patterns. The judge will be able to moderate their strictness and, moreover, it is hoped that this will not be necessary. The 'good judge', whether Chinese, Japanese or Vietnamese, is not concerned with making a good decision. The 'good judge' is the one who succeeds in not making any award, because he has been skilful enough to lead the opponents to reconciliation. Any dispute, as it is a threat to social harmony, has to be solved by a settlement through conciliation. The individual only has 'duties' towards the society. Recognition of 'subjective rights' in his favour is out of the question. Law as it is conceived in the West is seen as good for barbarians, and the occupation of lawyer, in the limited extent that it exists, is regarded with contempt by the society.

These remarks by a specialist in comparative law give a good idea of the differences in the tradition of litigation between the Far East and the West. The Western saying, 'the contract is the law of the parties', dominates the practices of international trade but this is in part window-dressing. In international marketing, a set of written contracts is always signed. This is not to say that people choose either oral or written agreements as a basis for trust. The real question is rather: how should the mix of written and oral bases for trust, as they are perceived by the parties, be interpreted? People do not deal with the real world in exactly the same way. Negotiating together requires changing one's views of reality. Not only differences in rationality and mental programmes, but also differences in time representations, may lead to a partner 'who thinks differently' being considered a partner 'who thinks wrongly'. (*WS16.7* has links to legal sites for a number of different countries.)

The greatest caution is recommended when interpreting the bases of trust, whether written documents or oral and personal bonds. Even in the Anglo-Saxon world, where it is preferred to 'get it in writing', a number of business deals, sometimes large ones – in the area of finance, for instance – are based on a simple telex or fax, or a phone agreement between two key decision-makers. It would be a mistake to believe that personal relationships do not exist in places where written contracts are generally required. Moreover, in cultures where 'my word is my bond', it should never be forgotten that it is difficult to trust outgroup people, regardless of whether the agreement is based on words or a contract. Trust has therefore to be established and monitored on both bases, while keeping in mind a clear awareness of the limits of each base.

Conclusion: Negotiating shared cultures

The process of intercultural encounter in negotiation has been described as akin to a dance in which one dancer dances a waltz when the other dances a tango (Tinsley *et al.*, 1999). There is, however, much adaptation in intercultural negotiation: negotiators tend to adjust to the other party's behaviour in ways that derive significantly from what would be the stereotypic attitude in their native culture (Adler and Graham, 1989; Bazerman *et al.*, 2000). It is naturally difficult to step out from one's own culture (Shapiro and Von Glinow, 1999). However, negotiators exchange masses of information during a full negotiation and they process it in complex ways that do not aim at an intellectual understanding of the beliefs and attitudes of the other party, but rather target mutual adjustment in view of maximizing outcomes. Negotiators therefore tend to adapt their behaviour to the other party, at least to the extent they perceive as useful for smoothing the process and improving the outcomes. On average, cultural adaptation, provided that it is done properly – without naive imitation – is positively experienced by the other side. Pornpitakpan

(1999) shows that neither the Japanese nor the Thais feel that their social identity is threatened by high adaptation coming from American sellers in sales negotiations. The Japanese buyers positively experience cultural adaptation by American sellers despite the marked tendency in Japan to make a clear-cut distinction between ingroup members (*nihon-jin*) and outgroup members (*gai-jin*).

Culture clash in negotiation may be strong at the very start, when negotiators expect behaviour from the other side that normatively corresponds to what they are used to as well as to what they consider as the most appropriate for effective negotiation. Cultural adaptation is not necessarily symmetrical. For instance, Japanese negotiators tend to adjust to Americans by using more direct information sharing and less indirect communication than in negotiations with their countrymen, whereas Americans adapt less to their Japanese counterparts (Adair *et al.*, 2001). A common professional culture may also help overcome the barriers related to cross-cultural understanding (Haugland, 1998). That is why culture often appears as a relatively poor predictor of the negotiation process and outcomes and should not be used directly to predict negotiation behaviour (Tinsley and Brett, 1997).

In complex international negotiations (see Chapters 7 and 15) there is a mix of antecedents constructs, based on national cultures, individual characteristics of negotiators, and organizational factors surrounding the negotiation (Money, 1998). Coalition building and emergent roles in the negotiation process transcend the borders of culture, leading to a re-design of the set of relationships. More extrovert negotiators and individuals who are proficient in the other side's language emerge as central figures in the negotiation process. Brannen and Salk (2000) show how a German and a Japanese company negotiate a common organizational culture within an International Joint Venture. This negotiated culture is not a blend of both cultures. It is rather an idiosyncratic whole, pragmatically defined for certain issues domains, containing parts of both parent cultures, but also new ways of doing that are specific to the common organization. Brannen and Salk take the example of problems related to working hours and summer vacations: the Germans tend to take three weeks vacation during the summer whereas the Japanese typically do not take more than five consecutive days of vacation, and this created conflicts between German and Japanese managers.

There was no possibility of a negotiated outcome with regard to the length of summer vacation because of Germany's legal climate; Japanese simply continued to take vacation time off as they were accustomed while Germans continued as they had always done. Over time, however, negotiated outcomes did evolve with regard to socializing and the length of working hours though they were reached in a more idiosyncratic fashion. Certain German managers began to stay later at work while many of the Japanese worked fewer hours than they were accustomed to in Japan. (Brannen and Salk, 2000, p. 472).

Questions

1. Discuss the principal foundations of trust and their cultural variability.

2. What is the role of time pressure in international marketing negotiations? How can you take advantage of time in the negotiation process?

3. Explain how frankness and directness in marketing negotiations can be diversely interpreted.

4. Why is seeing negotiation as a set of problems to be solved culturally relative?

5. How can the adoption of an integrative strategy be hindered by cultural factors?

6. To what extent is a written and detailed contract the basis of an agreement?

7. Discuss the value of introducing lawyers in intercultural negotiations.

8. Your company has signed a contract for a 10,000-student turnkey university in Saudi Arabia. A number of its facilities are designed for science and engineering schools and the remaining parts of the buildings will be designed for arts. The construction has not yet started. The Saudis send a fax telling you that an additional facility, a 500-student business school, is now planned and it must be integrated in the construction due to start in two months. What do you do?

Notes

1. Fukuyama's book, *Trust*, develops the idea that trust, or social capital as a propensity of people to cooperate beyond the borders of their limited ingroup (i.e. family, clan) is a key determinant of a nation's economic success. Fukuyama contrasts high-trust societies (prototypes: Germany, Japan) with low-trust societies (prototypes: China, France, Italy, Korea). In high-trust societies, economic actors can develop larger organizations, especially multinational firms, because people dare to trust 'strangers', that is professional managers and owners of other companies with which they merge their own business. In low-trust societies, the state is often obliged to intervene in order to create the large organizations needed for international competitiveness since local businesses find it difficult to create such organizations because they tend not to trust non-family associates. There is much more in Fukuyama's book than can be mentioned in these few lines. Suffice it to say that, after heavy criticism due to the alleged lack of empirical support, Fukuyama's theses have been strikingly confirmed on a sample of 40 nations by La Porta *et al.* (1997).

2. Kelley's game is a face-to-face simulated negotiation where a seller and a buyer negotiate a deal based on three products. Both buyer and seller have a profit sheet that they are instructed not to exchange. The rules can be learned quickly and this price-bargaining exercise lasts generally about half an hour. It allows measurement of a number of negotiation variables both in terms of outcomes (each player's profit and their joint profit; each negotiator's satisfaction based on post-exercise questions) and process (duration, tactics used and verbal exchanges are video taped and coded afterwards).

3. Although the national differences do not appear very large, the authors note that 'the difference between the Spanish (33.4) and the Greek managers (35.6) is large enough so that it could be expected to occur by chance less than one time in fifty if there were no real differences between these managers' (Harnett and Cummings, 1980, p. 22). Differences

are statistically significant between the Americans and the Thais but not between the Japanese and the Europeans.

4. Brannen and Salk (2000, pp. 473–5) give a detailed account of how language used is negotiated in the case of a German–Japanese joint venture: 'The negotiated outcome for language use [English as official venture language] was really the only one available. When a Japanese or German was confused or needed help, they would confer with members of their same cultural group in their mother tongue. This was done solely to expedite matters and clarify issues rather than as a means of excluding one or the other group from decision-making. One German manager spoke this way of the negotiation outcome: "The work language is English. But, during discussion, they would sometimes speak Japanese and I thought this was a good thing because you know your own language better and can understand better and can discuss things more precisely. One has to be tolerant . . .".' (p. 474).

5. For a review and discussion of non face-to-face negotiations, see the section entitled 'The case against face-to-face communication in bargaining', in Bazerman *et al.* (2000, pp. 295–6).

6. Full electronic negotiation systems have been proposed, such as INSPIRE (Kersten and Noronha, 1997, 1999) and Negoplan (Kersten and Szpakowicz, 1998).

7. For a review and discussion of the role of emotions on negotiation behaviour, see the section entitled 'Emotion and negotiation', in Bazerman *et al.* (2000, pp. 285–6).

8. Greif (1994) gives a very good account of how different societies solve the issue of trust and opportunism in business relationships, especially in the case of international trade. His analysis, both historical and based on game theory, relies on the comparison between two trading communities in the Mediterranean area during the late medieval area, the Maghribi traders and the Genoese merchants. Both faced the same kind of business environment and traded in similar goods; but they employed different solutions to the problem of agent's opportunism in the agency–principal relationship. While the Maghribis, a collectivist society, traded within their ingroup network and used the threat of collective economic punishment to reduce opportunistic behaviour, the individualistic Genoese 'ceased to use the ancient custom of entering contracts by a handshake and developed an extensive legal system for registration and enforcement of contracts' (p. 937).

9. There is a detailed teaching note available in the instructor's manual, which also contains personal and team role instructions, a standard contract form and an evaluation sheet for the negotiators.

References

Adachi, Yumi (1998), 'The effect of semantic difference on cross-cultural business negotiations: A Japanese and American case study', *Journal of Language for International Business*, vol. 9, no. 1, pp. 43–52.

Adair, Wendi L., Tetsushi Okumura and Jeanne M. Brett (2001), 'Negotiation behavior when cultures collide: the United States and Japan', *Journal of Applied Psychology*, vol. 86, no. 3, pp. 371–85.

Adler, Nancy J. (1980), 'Cultural synergy: the management of cross-cultural organizations', in W. Warner Burke and Leonard D. Goodstein (eds), *Trends and Issues in OD: Current theory and practice*, University Associates: San Diego, CA, pp. 163–84.

Adler, Nancy J. (1986), *International Dimensions of Organizational Behavior*, PWS-Kent: Boston.

Adler, Nancy J. (2002), *International Dimensions of Organizational Behavior*, 4th edn, South-Western: Cincinnati.

Adler, Nancy J. and John L. Graham (1989), 'Cross-cultural comparison: The international comparison fallacy?', *Journal of International Business Studies*, vol. 20, no. 3, pp. 515–37.

Adler, Nancy J., John L. Graham and Theodore Schwarz Gehrke (1987), 'Business negotiations in Canada, Mexico and the United States', *Journal of Business Research*, vol. 15, pp. 411–29.

Albaum, Gerald, Jesper Strandskov, Edwin Duerr and Laurence Dowd (1989), *International Marketing and Export Management*, Addison-Wesley: Wokingham.

Angelmar, Reinhardt and Louis W. Stern (1978), 'Development of a content analysis scheme for analysis of bargaining communication in marketing', *Journal of Marketing Research*, vol. 15, February, pp. 93–102.

Arndt, Johan (1979), 'Toward a concept of domesticated markets', *Journal of Marketing*, vol. 43, Fall, pp. 69–75.

Bazerman, Max H., Jared R. Curhan, Don A. Moore and Kathleen L. Valley (2000), 'Negotiation,' *Annual Review of Psychology*, vol. 51, pp. 279–314.

Beliaev, Edward, Thomas Mullen and Betty Jane Punnett (1985), 'Understanding the cultural environment: U.S.–U.S.S.R. trade negotiations', *California Management Review*, vol. 27, no. 2, pp. 100–12.

Bista, Dor Bahadur (1990), *Fatalism and Development*, Orient Longman: Calcutta.

Brannen, Mary Yoko and Jane E. Salk (2000), 'Partnering across borders: Negotiating organizational culture in a German-Japanese joint venture', *Human Relations*, vol. 53, no. 4, pp. 451–87.

Brett, Jeanne M. and Tetsushi Okumura (1998), 'Inter- and intra-cultural negotiations: US and Japanese negotiators', *Academic Management Journal*, vol. 41, no. 5, pp. 495–510.

Brett, Jeanne M., Debra L. Shapiro and Anne E. Lytle (1998), 'Breaking the bonds of reciprocity in negotiations', *Academy of Management Journal*, vol. 41, no. 4, pp. 410–24.

Brooke, Michael Z. (1985), *Selling Management Service Contracts in International Business*, Holt, Rinehart and Winston: London.

Burt, David N. (1984), 'The nuances of negotiating overseas', *Journal of Purchasing and Materials Management*, Winter, pp. 2–8.

Campbell, Nigel C.G., John L. Graham, Alain Jolibert and Hans Günther Meissner (1988), 'Marketing negotiations in France, Germany, the United Kingdom and United States', *Journal of Marketing*, vol. 52, April, pp. 49–62.

Cohen, Herb (1980), *You Can Negotiate Anything*, Bantam: New York.

Cohen, Raymond (1997), *Negotiating Across Cultures*, United States Institute of Peace Press: Washington, DC.

Corne, P.H. (1992), 'The complex art of negotiation between different cultures', *Dispute Resolution Journal*, vol. 47, pp. 46–50.

David, René (1987), *Le Droit du commerce international, réflexions d'un comparatiste sur le droit international privé*, Economica: Paris.

de Mente, Boye (1987), *How to do Business with the Japanese*, N.T.C. Publishing: Chicago, IL.

Druckman, D., A.A. Benton, F. Ali and J.S. Bagur (1976), 'Culture differences in bargaining behavior', *Journal of Conflict Resolution*, vol. 20, pp. 413–49.

Dwyer, Robert F., Paul H. Schurr and Sejo Oh (1987), 'Developing buyer–seller relationships', *Journal of Marketing*, vol. 51, April, pp. 11–27.

Eiteman, David K. (1990), 'American executives' perceptions of negotiating joint ventures with the People's Republic of China: lessons learned', *Columbia Journal of World Business*, Winter, pp. 59–67.

Evans, Franklin B. (1963), 'Selling as a dyadic relationship: a new approach', *American Behavioral Scientist*, vol. 6, May, pp. 76–9.

Faure, Guy Olivier and Jeffrey Z. Rubin (1993), *Culture and Negotiation*, Sage Publications: Newbury Park, CA.

Fisher, Glen (1980), *International Negotiation: A cross-cultural perspective*, Intercultural Press: Yarmouth, ME.

Foster, G.M. (1965), 'Peasant society and the image of limited good', *American Anthropologist*, vol. 67, pp. 293–315.

Foster, Dean Allen (1995), *Bargaining Across Borders*, New York: McGraw-Hill.

Francis, June P. (1991), 'When in Rome? The effects of cultural adaptation on intercultural business negotiations', *Journal of International Business Studies*, vol. 22, no. 3, pp. 403–28.

Fuentes, Carlos (1986), cited in 'To see ourselves as others see us', *Time*, 16 June, p. 52.

Fukuyama, Francis (1994), *Trust: The Social Virtues and the Creation of Prosperity*, Free Press: New York.

George, Jennifer M., Jones Gareth R. and Jorge A. Gonzalez (1998), 'The role of affect in cross-cultural negotiations', *Journal of International Business Studies*, vol. 29, no. 4, pp. 749–72.

Ghauri, Pervez N. and J.-C. Usunier (2003), *International Business Negotiations*, Pergamon/Elsevier: Oxford.

Goldman, Alan (1994), 'The centrality of "Ningensei" to Japanese negotiating and interpersonal relationships: implications for U.S.–Japanese communication', *International Journal of Intercultural Relations*, vol. 18, no. 1, pp. 29–54.

Graham, John L. (1981), 'A hidden cause of America's trade deficit with Japan', *Columbia Journal of World Business*, Fall, pp. 5–15.

Graham, John L. (1985), 'Cross-cultural marketing negotiations: a laboratory experiment', *Marketing Science*, vol. 4, no. 2, pp. 130–46.

Graham, John L. (1993), 'Business negotiations: generalisations about Latin America and East Asia are dangerous', *UC Irvine Research*, pp. 6–23.

Graham, John L. (2003), 'Vis-a-vis international business negotiations', in P.N. Ghauri and J.-C. Usunier (eds), *International Business Negotiations*, Pergamon/Elsevier: Oxford, pp. 23–50.

Graham, John L. and Hans G. Meissner (2003), 'Content analysis of business negotiations in five countries', Working Paper, University of Southern California.

Graham, John L. and Roy A. Herberger Jr (1983), 'Negotiators abroad: don't shoot from the hip', *Harvard Business Review*, vol. 61, no. 4, pp. 160–68.

Graham, John L. and Yoshihiro Sano (1990), *Smart Bargaining: Doing Business with the Japanese*, 2nd edn, Ballinger: Cambridge, MA.

Graham, John L., Alma T. Mintu and Waymond Rodgers (1994), 'Explorations of negotiation behaviors in ten foreign cultures using a model developed in the United States', *Management Science*, vol. 40, no. 1, January, pp. 72–95.

Greif, Avner (1994), 'Cultural beliefs and the organization of society: a historical and theoretical reflection on collectivist and individualist societies', *Journal of Political Economy*, vol. 102, no. 5, pp. 912–50.

Hall, Edward T. (1960), 'The silent language in overseas business', *Harvard Business Review*, May–June, pp. 87–96.

Hall, Edward T. (1976), *Beyond Culture*, Anchor Press/Doubleday: Garden City, NY.

Hall, Edward T. (1983), *The Dance of Life*, Anchor Press/Doubleday: Garden City, NY.

Harnett, Donald L. and L.L. Cummings (1980), *Bargaining Behavior: An international study*, Dame Publications: Houston, TX.

Harris, Philip R. and Robert T. Moran (1987), *Managing Cultural Differences*, 2nd edn, Gulf Publishing Company: Houston, TX.

Haugland, Sven (1998), 'The cultural dimension of international buyer-seller relationships', *Journal of Business-to-Business Marketing*, vol. 4, no. 4, pp. 3–33.

Hawrysh, Bryan Mark and Judith Lynn Zaichkowsky (1990), 'Cultural approaches to negotiations: understanding the Japanese', *International Marketing Review*, vol. 7, no. 2, pp. 28–42.

Herbig, Paul A. (1998), *Handbook of Cross-Cultural Marketing*, The Haworth Press: New York.

Hofstede, Geert (1980), *Culture's Consequences: International differences in work-related values*, Sage Publications: Beverly Hills, CA.

Hofstede, Geert (1989), 'Cultural predictors of national negotiation styles', in Frances Mautner-Markhof (ed.), *Processes of International Negotiations*, Westview Press: Boulder, CA, pp. 193–201.

Hofstede, Geert (1991), *Cultures and Organizations: Software of the mind*, McGraw-Hill: Maidenhead.

Hoon-Halbauer, Sing Keow (1999), 'Managing relationships within Sino-Foreign joint ventures', *Journal of World Business*, vol. 34, no. 4, pp. 344–71.

Jackson, Barbara B. (1985), *Winning and Keeping Industrial Customers: The dynamics of customer relationships*, D.C. Heath and Company: Lexington, MA.

Keegan, Warren J. (1984), *Multinational Marketing Management*, 3rd edn, Prentice Hall: Englewood Cliffs, NJ.

Kelley, Harold H. (1966), 'A classroom study of the dilemmas in interpersonal negotiations', in K. Archibald (ed.), *Strategic Interaction and Conflict*, Institute of International Studies, University of California: Berkeley, CA.

Kersten, Gregory E. and Sunil J. Noronha (1997), 'Supporting international negotiation with a WWW-Based system', *IIASA Interim Report* IR-97-49, August.

Kersten, Gregory E. and Sunil J. Noronha (1999), 'Negotiation via the world wide web: a cross-cultural study of decision making', *Group Decisions and Negotiations*, vol. 8, pp. 251–79.

Kersten, Gregory E. and S. Szpakowicz (1998), 'Modeling business negotiations for electronic commerce', *IIASA Interim Report* IR-98-015, March.

Kersten, Gregory E., Sabine Köszegi and Rudolf Vetschera (1999), 'The effect of culture in anonymous negotiations: a four countries experiment', *IIASA Interim Report* IR-99-023, July.

Kersten, Gregory E., Sabine Köszegi and Rudolf Vetschera (2002), 'Effect of culture in anonymous negotiations: an experiment in four countries', *35th Annual IEEE Conference on System Science*, vol. 1, pp. 7–10.

Kozan, M. Kamil and Canan Ergin (1999), 'The influence of intra-cultural value differences on conflict management practices', *The international Journal of Conflict Resolution*, vol. 10, no. 3, pp. 249–67.

Kumar, Rajesh (1997), 'The role of affect in negotiations: an integrative overview', *Journal of Applied Behavioral Science*, vol. 33, no. 1, pp. 84–100.

Kumar, Rajesh and Kofi O'Nti (1998), 'Differential learning and interaction in alliance dynamics: a process and outcome discrepancy model', *Organization Science*, vol. 9, no. 3, pp. 356–67.

La Porta, Rafael, Florencio Lopez-de-Silanes, Andrei Shleifer and Robert W Vishny (1997), 'Trust in large organizations', *American Economic Review*, vol. 87, no. 2, May, pp. 333–8.

Lee, James A. (1966), 'Cultural analysis in overseas operations', *Harvard Business Review*, March–April, pp. 106–11.

Leung Kwok (1997), 'Negotiation and reward allocations across cultures', in P.C. Earley and M Erez (eds), *New Perspectives on International Industrial/Organizational Psychology*, Jossey-Bass: San Francisco, pp. 640–75.

Macneil, Ian R. (1980), *The New Social Contract: An inquiry into modern contractual relations*, Yale University Press: New Haven, CT.

Matsumoto, M. (1988), *The Unspoken Way: Haragei – silence in Japanese business and society*, Kodansha International: New York.

McCall, J.B. and M.B. Warrington (1990), *Marketing by Agreement: A cross-cultural approach to business negotiations*, 2nd edn, John Wiley: Chichester.

McCartney, Laton (1989), *Friends in High Places: The Bechtel story*, Ballantine Books: New York.

Merriam, Sharan B., Juanita Johnson-Bailey, Ming-Yeh Lee, Youngwha Kee, Gabo Ntseane and Mazanah Muhamad (2001), 'Power and positionality: negotiating insider/outsider status within and across cultures', *International Journal of Lifelong Education*, vol. 20, no. 5, pp. 405–16.

Money, R. Bruce (1998), 'International multilateral negotiations and social networks', *Journal of International Business Studies*, vol. 29, no. 4, pp. 711–27.

Morris, Michael W., Williams Katherine Y., Leung Kwok, Larrick Richard, Mendoza M. Teresa, Bhatnagar Deepti, Li Jianfeng, Kondo Mari, Luo Jin-Lian and Jun-Chen Hu (1998), 'Conflict management style: accounting for cross-national differences', *Journal of International Business Studies*, vol. 29, no. 4, pp. 729–47.

Mosterd, Igor and Christel G. Rutte (2000), 'Effects of time pressure and accountability to constituents on negotiation', *International Journal of Conflict Management*, vol. 11, no. 3, pp. 227–47.

Ohmae, Kenichi (1989), 'The global logic of strategic alliances', *Harvard Business Review*, March–April, pp. 143–55.

Ollivier, Alain and Renaud de Maricourt (1990), *Pratique du marketing en Afrique*, Edicef/Aupelf: Paris.

Orwell, George (1945), *Animal Farm*, Penguin: London.

Perdue, B.C., R.L. Day and R.E. Michaels (1986), 'Negotiation styles of industrial buyers', *Industrial Marketing Management*, vol. 15, no. 3, pp. 171–6.

Pornpitakpan, Chantikha (1999), 'The effect of cultural adaptation on business relationships: Americans selling to Japanese and Thais', *Journal of International Business Studies*, vol. 30, no. 2, pp. 317–38.

Potter, Richard E. and Pierre A. Balthazard (2000), 'Supporting integrative negotiation via computer mediated communication technologies: an empirical example with geographically dispersed Chinese and American negotiators', *Journal of International Consumer Marketing*, vol. 12, no. 4, pp. 7–32.

Pruitt, Dean G. (1981), *Bargaining Behavior*, Academic Press: New York.

Pruitt, Dean G. (1983), 'Strategic choice in negotiation', *American Behavioral Scientist*, vol. 27, no. 2, pp. 167–94.

Pruitt, Dean G. and Steven A. Lewis (1975), 'Development of integrative solutions in bilateral negotiations', *Journal of Personality and Social Psychology*, vol. 31, no. 4, pp. 621–33.

Pye, Lucian (1982), *Chinese Commercial Negotiating Style*, Oelgeschlager, Gunn and Hain: Cambridge, MA.

Pye, Lucian (1986), 'The China trade: making the deal', *Harvard Business Review*, vol. 46, no. 4, pp. 74–84.

Rao, Asha and Stuart M. Schmidt (1998), 'A behavioral perspective on negotiating international alliances', *Journal of International Business Studies*, vol. 29, no. 4, pp. 665–94.

Rotella, Mark, Charlotte Abbott and Sarah Gold (2000), 'Chinese business etiquette and culture', *Publishers Weekly*, vol. 247, no. 25.

Rubin, Paul A. and J.R. Carter (1990), 'Joint optimality in buyer–seller negotiations', *Journal of Purchasing and Materials Management*, Spring, pp. 20–6.

Sakade, Florence (ed.) (1982), *A Guide to Reading and Writing Japanese*, Charles E. Tuttle: Tokyo.

Saner, Raymond (2000), *The Expert Negotiator*, Kluwer: The Hague.

Sawyer, J. and H. Guetzkow (1965), 'Bargaining and negotiation in international relations', in H. Kelman (ed.), *International Behavior*, Holt, Rinehart and Winston: New York.

Scanzoni, J. (1979), 'Social exchange and behavioral interdependence', in R.L. Burgess and T.L. Huston (eds), *Social Exchange in Developing Relationships*, Academic Press: New York.

Schuster, Camille P. and Michael J. Copeland (1999), 'Global business exchanges – similarities and differences around the world', *Journal of International Marketing*, vol. 7, no. 2, pp. 63–80.

Shapiro, D.L. and M.A. von Glinow (1999), 'Negotiation in multicultural teams: new world, old theories?', in *Research on Negotiation in Organizations*, vol. 7, JAI: Greenwich, CT.

Tinsley, Catherine H. (1998), 'Models of conflict resolution in Japanese, German and American cultures', *Journal of Applied Psychology*, vol. 83, pp. 316–23.

Tinsley, Catherine H. and Jeanne Brett (1997), 'Managing workplace conflict: a comparison of conflict frames and outcomes in the U.S. and Hong Kong', Paper presented at the Annual Meeting of the Academy of Management, Boston.

Tinsley, C., J. Curhan and R.S. Kwak (1999), 'Adopting a dual lens approach for overcoming the dilemma of difference in international business negotiations', *International Negotiations*, vol. 4, pp. 1–18.

Tinsley, Catherine H. and Madan M. Pittula (1998), 'Negotiating in the United States and Hong Kong',

Journal of International Business Studies, vol. 29, no. 4, pp. 711–27.

Triandis, Harry G. (1983), 'Dimensions of cultural variation as parameters of organizational theories', *International Studies of Management and Organization*, vol. 12, no. 4, pp. 139–69.

Trompenaars, Fons (1993), *Riding the Waves of Culture*, Nicholas Brealey: London.

Tse, David K., June Francis and Jan Walls (1994), 'Cultural differences in conducting intra- and inter-cultural negotiations: a Sino-Canadian perspective', *Journal of International Business Studies*, vol. 25, no. 3, pp. 537–55.

Tung, Rosalie L. (1984), 'How to negotiate with the Japanese', *California Management Review*, vol. 26, no. 4, pp. 62–77.

Ulijn, Jan M., Andreas Lincke and Yunus Karakaya (2001), 'Non-face-to-face international business negotiation: how is national culture reflected in this medium?', *IEEE Transactions on Professional Communication*, vol. 44, no. 2, pp. 126–37.

United States Institute of Peace (2002), *U.S. Negotiating Behavior*, Special Report 94, October, available at: **www.usip.org**.

Usunier, Jean-Claude (1990), 'Négociation commerciale des projets: une approche interculturelle', *Revue Française du Marketing*, nos 127–128, pp. 167–84.

Van Zandt, H.R. (1970), 'How to negotiate with the Japanese', *Harvard Business Review*, November–December, pp. 45–56.

Wade-Benzoni, Kimberly A., Tetsushi Okumura, Jeanne M. Brett, Don A. Moore, Ann E. Tenbrunsel and Max H. Bazerman (2002), 'Cognition and behavior in asymmetric social dilemmas: A comparison of two cultures', *Journal of Applied Psychology*, vol. 87, no. 1, pp. 87–95.

Walton, Richard E. and Robert B. McKersie (1965), *A Behavioral Theory of Labour Negotiations*, McGraw-Hill: New York.

Weber, E.U. and C.K. Hsee (1998), 'Cross-cultural differences in risk perception, but cross-cultural similarities in attitudes towards perceived risk', *Management Science*, vol. 44, no. 9, pp. 1205–17.

Weiss, Stephen E. (1987), 'Creating the GM–Toyota joint venture: a case in complex negotiation', *Columbia Journal of World Business*, vol. 22, no. 2, Summer, pp. 23–37.

Weitz, B. (1979), 'A critical review of personal selling research: the need for contingency approaches', in G. Albaum and G.A. Churchill Jr (eds), *Critical Issues in Sales Management: State of the art and future needs*, University of Oregon: Eugene.

Zartman, I. William (1993), 'A sceptic's view', in Guy Olivier Faure and Jeffrey Z. Rubin (eds), *Culture and Negotiation*, Newbury Park, CA: Sage Publications, pp. 17–21.

Zeldin, Theodore (1977), *France 1848–1945*, vol. 11, Oxford University Press: Oxford.

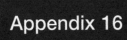

Appendix 16

Teaching materials

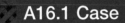

A16.1 Case

McFarlane Instruments

An American firm, the McFarlane Instruments Company, had delivered approximately US$400,000-worth of instruments to a People's Republic of China government agency. The agency refused to pay for the instruments, so the US company contacted the American Embassy in Beijing for assistance. The American commercial attaché arranged a meeting between the PRC industrial ministry representatives, company representatives, and himself.

In the meeting, the government officials stated that they would not pay because the instruments did not conform to the guarantee of accuracy of plus or minus 0.2 per cent. The US firm found this to be very strange since they had not encountered accuracy problems with their instruments sold in other countries. They finally inquired as to the temperatures at which the tests had been conducted. The Chinese officials indicated that tests had been conducted at 10°C and at 50°C.

The American firm replied that international practice and standards called for such tests to be conducted at 25°C. The instruments were normally used at approximately room temperature. Because of differential expansion and contraction coefficients of the materials in the instruments, use under much lower or higher ambient temperatures resulted in different levels of precision and need for recalibration.

The Chinese officials then produced a copy of the company's brochure which stated the plus or minus 0.2 per cent precision, but did not specify the test temperature. After approximately one hour of discussion, which consisted mainly of each side reiterating its position, the US firm attempted to break the deadlock. While avoiding any admission that the instruments failed to conform to international standards, they agreed to reduce the price by 30 per cent 'in order to maintain good relations'. Their only other choice was to attempt to reclaim the machines, and then attempt to re-export them through potentially difficult Chinese customs administration to the United States or elsewhere. The Chinese officials requested that a written proposal be submitted. This was done and the offer was made valid for a period of 60 days.

Three months later the Chinese government organization rejected the proposal, stating again that the instruments did not meet the promised precision. The US firm, after several more attempts at reconciliation, gave up and took back the machines. They now faced the difficult task of obtaining permission to re-export them, and the additional cost of doing that and paying for shipping costs.

Subsequent investigation indicated that the real problem had not had anything to do with the instruments themselves. Between the time the original contract had been signed and when the instruments were delivered, the PRC currency had been devalued. The contract was written in US dollars, and the Chinese organization had been allocated a given amount of the PRC currency, the '*renminbi*', to pay for it (through the appropriate foreign exchange agency). With the new exchange rate, the Chinese government organization did not have enough money to pay for the instruments. The discount offered by the American company had not been sufficient to make up for the difference in exchange rates. The Chinese found it easier to reject the instruments than to admit what had happened.

(Source: Adapted from Albaum *et al.*, 1989, pp. 388–9.)

Questions

1. How can you determine the real problems that impeded the negotiations? What are they, in your opinion?

2. Would you expect it to be easy to get appointments with Chinese government officials? Why or why not?

3. Would you expect it to be easy to obtain information from Chinese officials? Why or why not?

4. What important lesson for negotiations does this case illustrate? How would you have approached this problem?

A16.2 Negotiation game

Kumbele Power Plant

A consortium, BDH, has been established between a US-based engineering company, a French company belonging to the same sector and a German firm producing heavy industrial equipment. This consortium is in the final phase of negotiations to win a contract for building a turnkey electric power plant. The owner is the National Electricity Authority, a state-owned corporation which holds a monopoly on the transport and distribution of electricity in an English-speaking country in Africa. National Electricity Authority has issued the tender.

The tender procedure was initiated 18 months ago. At first there were about 20 potentially qualified contractors who submitted bids. Most of them were engineering companies originating from the main industrial countries, and some came from newly industrialized countries such as South Korea, Brazil and Turkey. After a preselection phase, the number of potential contractors was reduced to a short list of five companies or consortia. The final selection process lasted for several months, as bids that were technologically not comparable had to be taken into account.

The consortium created by Brown Engineering Corp. (US), Duponval SA (French) and Horst BauTechnik AG (German) was chosen as the organization with which the final negotiations would take place. But a Japanese competitor has also made a very attractive offer and is in a position to supplant BDH, if BDH should prove to be too demanding for National Electricity Authority. In fact BDH has a strong reference list, supported by similar plants it has built that are working effectively. Moreover, in addition to its offer, BDH provides a low-rate, long-term financing scheme for the buyer, which has been created by putting together export credits issued by public organizations from the countries of the three members of BDH: US Eximbank for Brown, BFCE (Banque Française du Commerce Extérieur) for Duponval and KfW (Kreditanstalt für Wiederaufbau) for Horst BauTechnik.

The final price has not yet been settled, as there are still some important clauses to be discussed:

1. The supply of basic materials by the consortium, during the start-up of the power plant.
2. The possibility of signing a 'B.O.T.' contract. A 'Buildings-Operate-Transfer' contract is a particular kind of turnkey operation, where part of the payment by the owner to the contractor is subject to the level of performance reached by the plant. After the start-up phase has been finished and individual pieces of equipment have been shown to work effectively, a phase begins where the contractor is assigned to operations. This means that a management contract has been signed. The variable fee may cover part or all of the turnkey operations as such and/or the management contract. In this case the consortium would agree to sign a management contract to run the operation until it reaches 100 per cent of its target capacity (400 megawatts).

The proposal that served as a starting base for the final bargaining process was priced at US$105 million. Each of the partners-to-be has naturally retained its right to improve its position, either by obtaining a rebate (the buyer) or by increasing this base price level by astutely negotiating supplementary services (the consortium).

Since the inception of this tender, National Electricity Authority has made it known that the first power plant will be followed by the construction of two similar plants, all this being stated in the ten-year plan for the electrification of the country. It seems very likely that the contractor selected to build the first unit, if effective, will be well positioned for the next two orders, which may possibly be placed by direct agreement between contractor and owner, that is, without a competitive bidding procedure.

At the negotiating table are three representatives of the buying organization and three representatives of the BDH consortium, each one an employee of one of the companies:

1. For the buyer:
(a) Mr Ozuwu, who is in charge of project financing for industrial development at the Ministry of Finance. He might be a useful and even necessary go-between for many red-tape problems related to administrative and financial issues that could arise when the project is under way: payments, clearing customs for imported equipment, fiscal and social problems of expatriates, etc.
(b) Mr Kempele, who is the director in charge of energy at the Ministry of Industry. He is concerned with the coordination of this project with the other industrialization projects being undertaken in the country. There have been many negative experiences of poor coordination in recent years: two years ago, some ships with a full load of cement were stranded in the main sea port of the country because there was not enough unloading equipment such as docks and cranes. This caused severe delay on several projects.
(c) Mr Bura, the third representative, is 38, much younger than both Ozuwu, who is about 50, and Kempele, who is 60. He has been trained in the United Kingdom and the United States and holds a Master of Science degree in Electrical Engineering. At National Electricity Authority he is in charge of new plants and investment projects. He is reputed to be ambitious but also capable and hard-headed. In the long run he is seen as a possible chief executive for National Electricity Authority. Bura has confidence in the country's development projects and in the capacities of local managers to run the new plants effectively.

2. For the consortium:
(a) Mr Smith, a project manager aged 42, who has worked for many years at Brown, the US member of the consortium. Brown will take charge of the boiler part and the plant

monitoring system. Brown is ranked among the leading US engineering companies. It has a high reputation for technical excellence as well as for cost control. Project managers at Brown are partly compensated with a bonus based on the profit generated by the project. A sophisticated cost accounting system monitors actual and forecast costs and margins regularly during the project. After the completion of projects lasting two to three years or more, final costs are calculated, with a minimal deviation from target costs.

(b) Mr Robin from Duponval SA, a French engineer who has worked for this company for the last ten years. Duponval has already formed several joint ventures with Brown, and Robin knows Smith because they have already worked together. Duponval SA is in charge of civil engineering and the total coordination of the work. This firm has established a good reputation worldwide for meeting delivery times.

(c) Mr Dietermeyer, a Doctor of Law, aged 55, has worked for the last 20 years for Horst BauTechnik. Although he has not been formally trained in engineering, he has built up a good knowledge of industrial engineering on the job. In addition to this he has attended many training sessions, which have provided him with an in-depth knowledge of the technologies of a large variety of turnkey plants. He is considered in his company a skilful, experienced and effective business negotiator. His law background is very useful in discussing precise clauses, understanding what is at stake and the possible legal consequences of a specific clause. Horst is in charge of supplying and installing turbo-alternators and all the electrical parts in the plant.

BDH consortium has been chosen as the contractor with which National Electricity Authority is willing to negotiate the final agreement under the supervision of the Ministry of Finance and the Ministry of Industry. A sum of US$105 million is the starting point for the discussion; until now it has been considered a lump sum for a turnkey operation contract. But things have not yet been fully settled.

The African team wishes to negotiate either a rebate on this price level, arguing that there will be future projects that could be awarded to BDH, or complementary services or guarantees, which could be granted at no cost. These might possibly be the following:

1. The free supply of materials required for production during the start-up phase, which will last one month.
2. Free technical assistance for the industrial management of the power plant, to ensure correct service to consumers and proper management of the electricity distribution network.
3. A commitment from BDH to subcontract part of the job locally, especially the less sophisticated part of the civil engineering work.

BDH naturally would prefer to maintain its price, for which it had been selected from harsh competition. In fact there were some cheaper competitors, whose bids were up to $15 million less. But neither their reference lists nor their financing deals matched BDH's bid.

BDH has one concern – the delay penalty clause that National Electricity Authority wants to include. The fine is supposed to be 1 per cent of the total price for each construction month beyond the agreed completion time. The consortium foresees that there could be some delay. It fears that it might be difficult to assign clear responsibilities to either the contractor or the owner (or the state authorities of the country, or a large subcontractor, especially if it was a local business). Usually turnkey contracts include a customs franchise for all the equipment imported in order to build the plant. But it is not particularly unusual for customs officers to fail to apply these rules immediately, thereby delaying customs clearance of components and equipment, and consequently delaying the completion of the plant.

The parties have agreed to discuss the issue of transforming this pure turnkey operation, paid for by a lump sum, into a 'Buildings-Operate-Transfer' contract. Under this scheme, part of the payment will be subject to a variable scale related to the level of capacity reached during the management contract period after the plant has been completed and started up. The possibility of a management contract has been discussed. It will probably be added to the turnkey contract (which includes the construction start-up phase, but no more). This management contract will encompass handling the industrial management procedures, the accounting system, setting salaries, customer service and providing training programmes for local executives. Progressively, local management is supposed to take over the management of the project. The basis on which the variable payment would be calculated has not been clearly settled up to now. This basis could be: the whole amount of the management contract, part of it, or the whole amount of the management contract plus part of the $105 million turnkey project.

The African proposal for this final negotiation includes the following elements:

1. The price of the management contract plus US$10 million (on top of the turnkey price) to become a variable and conditional payment, subject to the capacity level reached within a certain time span. This scheme would extend throughout the total 36 months of the management contract period.
2. For this variable part the proposed payment scheme is as follows:
   (a) 15 per cent after 6 months if the output reaches at least 50 per cent of the target capacity;
   (b) 15 per cent after 12 months if the output reaches at least 60 per cent of the target capacity;
   (c) 15 per cent after 18 months if the output reaches at least 70 per cent of the target capacity;
   (d) 15 per cent after 24 months if the output reaches at least 80 per cent of the target capacity;
   (e) 20 per cent after 30 months if the output reaches at least 90 per cent of the target capacity;
   (f) 20 per cent after 36 months if the output reaches 100 per cent of the target capacity.
3. The management contract may grant decision-making powers to the consortium in the following matters: recruiting personnel (workers, not the management), operating the plant and choosing supplies of appropriate quality and price. The selling price of the output as well as the operating costs are to remain the sole responsibility of National Electricity Authority.

The negotiation takes place at the headquarters of National Electricity Authority in Port Kumbele, where the power plant will be built. The talks simply aim at finalizing an agreement for beginning the construction as soon as possible. No detailed agenda has been prepared for the negotiations.

Discussion begins . . .

Recommendations for playing the Kumbele Power Plant negotiation game[9]

■ The objective is to simulate business negotiations for international turnkey operations. It may be played in four half-days, preferably in half-day sessions, with some time between them. Participants should first discuss between themselves as a team in order to prepare their negotiation strategies and tactics. The discussion should be centred on the business negotiation. Participants should not discuss technical matters related to the plant: this is because, first, the necessary information is not included in the text and, second, it is not meant to be an engineers' discussion.

■ The intercultural aspect may be adapted to suit the participants. The characters in the game may easily be changed to women.

■ This game may be played as a competitive game, where two teams compete for the contract with National Electricity Authority. One team representing BDH and one team representing the Japanese engineering company (let's call it Chikoda) will face the Kumbele team.

■ Participants should conduct research to obtain some information about selling turnkey projects and management services internationally. See for instance Brooke (1985).

A16.3 Case

Doing business in China – A failure in getting paid

In recent years, the People's Republic of China (PRC) has become much more open to trade with the West, and has also made substantial internal economic reforms. Companies in Japan, the western European countries, the United States and elsewhere have viewed the Chinese market as having enormous potential. With a population of a billion and a growing economy, it has appeared to many to be worthwhile to make a major effort to gain a foothold in the market. Both direct exports and joint ventures have been used.

In spite of the economic reforms, however, the PRC remains a tightly controlled, centrally directed economy. Most commercial enterprises and almost all production facilities are state owned and state run. Only a small number of designated organizations are allowed to engage in international trade, and all of these are state owned.

All contracts for trade must receive several government approvals. Larger contracts receive more approvals than smaller ones. It is not always apparent to the outsider, or perhaps even to some of the Chinese, what specific approvals will be required in particular cases. While letters of credit may be issued to companies exporting to China, these do not provide the same level of assurance that a letter of credit issued by, say, a London bank would. The Chinese bank will simply not release foreign exchange, regardless of the existence of a letter of credit, without the approval of appropriate government agencies. Foreign companies selling to the government may not receive a letter of credit, but may feel that they can rely on the good faith of the government.

A major United States exporter recently called upon the US Embassy in Beijing requesting assistance in solving a problem. About one year earlier they had sold approximately US$8.0 million-worth of equipment to the China National Technology Import Company for use by the Chinese Ministry of Petroleum Industries (MOPI). To date, no payment had been received, and the company did not seem to be getting anywhere in its attempts to collect. The commercial attaché at the embassy called the Technology Import and Export Department of the Ministry of Foreign Economic Relations and Trade (MOFERT), the Chinese department that appeared to be in charge of the transaction. MOFERT agreed to a meeting at 10.00 a.m. the next day. After the commercial attaché had briefed MOFERT representatives on the problem, they indicated that they were not in charge of the transaction; it came under the jurisdiction of the Import and Export Department, not the Technology Import and Export Department. Nevertheless they agreed to see what they could do to help. The commercial attaché expressed hope that the problem could be resolved as expeditiously as possible since the payment was already a year overdue.

At 2.00 p.m. the same afternoon, MOFERT officials called and informed the commercial attaché that the problem had been resolved and that payment would be forthcoming. They explained that MOPI had delayed submitting the request for initial contract approval and had sent that along with the request for payment. This had caused a delay. The rules had been changed so that, in addition to the approvals required when a contract is to be signed, an additional set of approvals is required from the same organizations when the goods are delivered. In the case of this contract, two separate sets of approvals were required from each of the following:

1. MOPI;
2. MOFERT;
3. the State Planning Commission;
4. the State Administration for Foreign Exchange Control.

(Source: George Lee of San Francisco State University, and formerly commercial attaché, US embassy, Beijing, PRC.)

Questions

1. Why does the People's Republic of China have a State Administration for Foreign Exchange Control, and so many approvals required for a purchase of goods from overseas?

2. Is the additional difficulty involved in trying to sell to the People's Republic of China, compared with trying to sell to France or Taiwan, worth the trouble? Why or why not?

3. If you wanted to export to the People's Republic of China, would you go to your own government or embassy in China for assistance? Why or why not?

4. If the United States company had a similar problem in France, is it likely they would have contacted their embassy for assistance? Why or why not?

Intercultural marketing negotiations 2:
Some elements of national styles of
business negotiation

One way to enhance negotiating power in International business deals is to identify a set of strategic archetypes used by foreign negotiators. For example, Asian negotiators, who are driven by low self-esteem and perceived potency, may benefit from dwelling on their company's vulnerability, small size and other alleged weaknesses, a tactic that is likely to swell the confidence of westerners, inducing them to ask for less and to yield more.

In marketing negotiation, the image of the other negotiating party is based on a collection of stereotypes, often meaningful, which amount to a portrait of that party's national culture. This exercise in mutual reflection has to be reciprocal and particular for each bilateral relationship. It is unlikely, for example, that Germans or Italians would have an identical perception of the French negotiation style. Similarly, the way the Japanese see westerners as lacking in *ningensei*, cannot be considered as simply inverse and complementary to the way US negotiators see their Japanese counterparts. You are unlikely to hear Americans complaining that their Japanese partners have an excessive *ningensei* orientation. It follows, therefore, that a matrix would be necessary if we were to delineate with any accuracy how the negotiating style of a particular country is perceived by other nationalities: for example, defining the Italian style in terms of how it is perceived by the Americans, the French, etc. Unfortunately, though, the use of multiple perspectives would be too complex. For the purposes of simplification, it must be conceded that archetypes of negotiation styles are generally an average of what is seen through Western eyes.

This chapter complements the previous one. It describes some elements of national or regional styles of business negotiation. At the risk of adopting what could be termed a Western stereotyping classification, this chapter describes salient traits of the following 'nationalities' (listed in alphabetical order): African, American, British, Chinese, French, German, Japanese, Mexican, Middle Eastern and Russian. Section 17.1 (and *WS17.1*) describes Oriental, section 17.2 (and *WS17.2*) Western negotiation style, section 17.3 (and *WS17.3*) deals with other areas of the world, and the last section proposes recommendations for effective intercultural marketing negotiations.

17.1

Orientals

Chinese style

One of the main experts on business negotiation with the Chinese, Lucian W. Pye (1982, 1986) lists the following factors, which combine to demonstrate that the Chinese are tactical, skilful and fairly tough negotiators:

1. 'As hosts, the Chinese take advantage of their control over the pace of negotiations. First they set the agenda, then they suggest that the Americans start the discussions . . . their proposals become the starting point from which all compromise follows' (Pye, 1986, p. 177).

2. The Chinese deliberately adopt a fairly passive attitude, taking care not to show enthusiasm,

concealing any feeling of impatience, playing their game impassively so as to force their opponents to be the first to show their hand.

3. They do not shy away from appearing very manipulative: with a view to disconcerting the other side and in the ultimate hope of obtaining further concessions, they will attribute an exaggerated importance to minor details, which in reality are of no consequence to them, or return to discussion of points where full agreement seemed to have previously been reached.

4. The bureaucratic orientation of the PRC is often noted: socialism has imposed strong government control on industry. As a consequence, Chinese negotiators tend not to be capable of individual decision making. Before any agreement is reached, official government approval must be sought by Chinese negotiators (Eiteman, 1990).

5. Chinese business people tend to overrate the advantage offered by their large population in terms of market opportunities. However, per capita purchasing power remains quite low. The Chinese promote their country as being 'the last big market on the planet' but underestimate the opportunities offered to their foreign partners by other countries (Eiteman, 1990).

6. Like the Japanese, the Chinese are less economic-time minded and less short-term oriented than westerners. 'The Chinese use time shrewdly. If they sense that business people are in a hurry to leave China, they may slow down negotiations and turn the deadline to their advantage' (Pye, 1986, p. 78).

7. The Chinese networking system, *guanxi* (see section 15.2; Luo, 1995; Luo and Chen, 1997), needs to be taken into account, as the development and maintenance of appropriate connections is key to business and may help in negotiating beyond the negotiation table itself. As emphasized by Tung (1996), most of these relationships are based on a combination of blood (immediate and extended families), educational ties and geography, that is, common membership in the same clan or village. Ingroup orientation is strong and people from outgroupist cultures must regard the Chinese networking activities without prejudice.

8. Pye also notes the role played by differences of attitude relating to the concept of 'friendship'. Thus it seems that whereas the Americans view friendship in terms of a feeling that rests on a natural mutual exchange, in other words on a principle of reciprocity, the Chinese view friendship in terms of loyalty. The idea is that of a long-lasting obligation:

What the Chinese neglect in terms of reciprocity they more than match in loyalty. They not only keep their commitments, but they also assume that any positive relationship can be permanent. A good example of this is the number of Chinese who have tried to establish pre-1949 ties with U.S. companies and individuals – as though nothing had happened in the intervening days. (Pye, 1986, p. 79.)

Japanese style

Numerous books are devoted to consideration of the Japanese style of negotiation and more generally to the Japanese mentality and style of management. Several major traits can be distinguished:

1. The Japanese are well prepared, especially when it comes to familiarizing themselves with the culture of the people they are dealing with (Tung, 1984). They are a highly ethnocentric people but, paradoxically, are also very conscious of this ethnocentrism. They are also well prepared in terms of defining their basic interests and are willing to defend them quite vigorously.

2. The purchaser's role is predominant. Vendors must be fully aware of this fact and adapt their behaviour accordingly (Graham, 1981).

3. Although at heart they are very sensitive and emotional, they seek to conceal their true emotions as far as possible (Burt, 1984; see also sections 3.5 and 13.2). Like all Asians they must not be made to 'lose face': in practice (at the very least) their foreign counterparts should avoid a style of communication that would be resented by the Japanese as being too direct.

4. Within a group of Japanese negotiators it is difficult to determine who really performs what function and who holds what power; it is always unwise to rely solely on 'who says what' as a clear indication of 'who holds power'.

5. Japanese negotiators display quite a high level of tolerance of ambiguity. Whereas Americans may perceive ambiguity to be a sign of weakness, or a lack of masculinity and assertiveness, for the

Japanese there is no conflict between masculinity and ambiguity (Hawrysh and Zaichkowsky, 1990).

6. Japanese people are very long-term oriented. In large companies lifetime employment is the rule. These companies are often backed by large banks, which, as the shareholders, do not strive for a quick return. They are more concerned with the soundness of the long-term business strategy of the company to which they lend. This partly explains why Japanese negotiators do not feel as strongly pressured by time lines as do their Western counterparts.

7. Like most Asians, the Japanese tend to prefer an agreement based on trust over a written contract. Even though this agreement may be loosely worded, in their view it is a better expression of the mutual trust that has developed between the parties (Oh, 1986).

8. The empathy of Japanese people may be very high: the interpersonal sensitivity of Japanese people and their sincere interest in foreign cultures and people makes them friendly hosts at business lunches or dinners. As noted earlier, Japanese businessmen spend time and money entertaining their negotiating partners to establish with them a rapport built on trust. However, Japanese negotiators remain strongly aware of what their basic interests are, and they are reputed to be tough negotiators.

Middle Eastern style (Arab-Islamic world)

If a 'Middle Eastern style' truly exists, the following caveat should be borne in mind. The countries considered here are almost exclusively Arab-Islamic countries, except for Iran, which is Shiite Islam but not Arab, and Turkey, which is Ottoman and Islamic but not Arab and has dominated the Arab world for centuries. Yet it would be a mistake to ignore the enormous diversity of the Middle East. Christian minorities (Lebanese Maronites, Egyptian Copts, Iraqi Nestorians, Armenians, members of the Orthodox churches, etc.) are present almost everywhere and influential in some countries. These religions are in fact fully integrated in the Middle East. It is therefore essential to be fully aware of the fact that a world that is somewhat hastily classified as Arab-Islamic is also composed of Arabs who are not Muslims and Muslims who are not Arabs.

Some of the characteristics of 'Middle Eastern style' are as follows:

1. The importance of 'concrete territorialities': knowledge of the subgroup to which the negotiator belongs is essential; the relationships between the parties must be explored with great care, to find out who is who and what relationship each negotiator has with the different groups.

2. The role of intermediaries ('sponsors' in Saudi Arabia) is very important. As a result of European colonization over the last two centuries, the majority of 'Middle Eastern' business people speak French or English and understand European civilization; whereas the reverse is rarely true. Intermediaries must be employed for a simple reason: we (the Europeans and Americans) systematically underestimate the cultural divide.

3. It must always be borne in mind that members of Middle Eastern civilizations were largely the founders of those in Europe. They have left many traces behind, and as far as art and culture are concerned, their influences were dominant for many centuries during the Middle Ages. The pride of the person with whom you are dealing must be – genuinely – respected.

4. One must expect a great deal of emotion, theatricality and demonstrativeness, interspersed with true pragmatism. The mixture is often bewildering. Friendship is sought, relationships are personalized, and the idea of a cold 'business-like' relationship is difficult to envisage. Once a true friend has been made (which is far from straightforward), the sense of loyalty can be very strong.

5. As has already been emphasized, Islamic values permeate daily life. For example, if the negotiations lead to consideration of a loan and interest rate, although this problem is not insurmountable, a great deal of caution is essential. The question of *riba*, which is usually translated as 'interest', never fails to pose problems for Koranic law and the different legislative assemblies entrusted with its interpretation. These assemblies have been more or less strict in their interpretation of *riba*, which is mentioned several times in the Koran, as being forbidden. Thus specific financial operations, excluding the imposition of a method of repayment for loans that is fixed in advance, have been settled in accordance with Islamic law and on the

basis of ancient practices. Rather than loans, they are joint operations where the banker brings the financing and clients their facilities and business talents. *Mudhâraba* corresponds to a project financing with no recourse for the banker; *musharaka* is similar except that the client brings part of the financing; *murabaha* is a sort of leasing agreement.

American style

The American style – individualism – is oriented towards several major aspects that are linked to the US national character, with the emphasis on ability, competence, professionalism, decision making and explicit communication. As a consequence, American negotiators usually exhibit the following qualities: seriousness, pragmatism and accuracy in writing clauses. American negotiators have fairly well-defined autonomy and room for manoeuvre, but clear limits are also set, and they have to report to their principals. In the negotiation process, Americans often consider that decisions have to be made on the spot by the individual who has the most expertise or responsibility in a given area (Beliaev *et al.*, 1985).

The following characteristics have been often noted:

1. Professionalism is a quality that is very widely recognized in Americans. In business negotiation, it means careful selection of the negotiators and methodical preparation of files.
2. In their failure to take sufficient account of the culture of other parties (Tung, 1984), the Americans, like the French, are an 'ethnocentric-missionary' people. They are quite convinced (as are the French) that their system is the 'one best way', and that the other peoples of the world would do well to adopt their system of values and behaviour.
3. A great deal of attention is (pragmatically) paid to precise issues to be debated, to facts and evidence, to an attitude oriented towards matter-of-fact discussions and to a tight negotiation time schedule. This renders them susceptible to becoming irritated by negotiating parties who are more interested in

general principles or even logical reasoning (the French, for example; Burt, 1984). This may also lead to their interpreting the attitudes of their negotiating counterparts who have a non-linear style as delaying tactics. They will resent global negotiation as a way of reconsidering what has already been decided and as a failure to respect a pre-set agenda.

4. A strong positive emphasis is placed on frankness and sincerity; Americans show willingness to make the first move by disclosing their position in the hope (sometimes unfulfilled) that their adversary will do likewise. They are also prepared to adopt the 'John Wayne Style' (Graham and Herberger, 1983; see Box 16.3), by pushing frankness to the bounds of arrogance. This can shock people from cultures where self-assertion must be contained within strict limits.
5. A genuine naivety, ingenuousness and a 'retarded adolescent' style (noted by Margaret Mead) can sometimes lead Americans to choose positions that are very tough because they are – genuinely – disappointed. This occurs mainly when, having demonstrated their quite genuine sincerity, they then feel that they have been badly treated, since their open-mindedness has been taken advantage of. However, sincerity and frankness are by no means universal cultural values, contrary to what a good number of Americans may believe.
6. Equality between purchaser and vendor, and 'let the best man win'. This can surprise people who deal with Americans, since Americans value personal assertiveness and so can appear tough, as there is little sympathy for anyone who loses. In the US business mentality, no consolation prizes are won by 'losers'.
7. The Americans are supposed to be informal in everyday life. In fact, compared to other peoples, they are formal in different areas. When it comes to negotiating agreements, they are quite formal and anxious about the preciseness and explicitness of written contracts, which are therefore drawn up with care. These contracts, the law between the parties, are also the basis for attitudes that are readily oriented towards recourse to litigation and legal battles with the assistance of lawyers.
8. As noted earlier, Americans tend to be short-term oriented. At the end of the Vietnam War, the Vietnamese were at a time advantage in the

US–Vietnamese peace talks in Paris, because they had rented a villa with a two and a half years' lease, whereas the Americans rented hotel rooms on a week-to-week basis. The US time pressure in business may be easily explained by the system of quarterly reporting to shareholders and the Stock Exchange. US companies depend heavily on the financial markets; labour mobility is high. Accordingly, people must get quick results and show a faster return than their foreign counterparts. This 'short-termism' tends to disadvantage them in negotiations.

British style

Like the French, the British have been strongly affected by their tradition of diplomatic negotiation and their country's position as head of a far-flung empire. The British style is characterized by the following:

1. A 'soft-sell' approach, which is essential for negotiating. British coolness is not an empty phrase. An air of confidence, restraint and calm is essential for any negotiators in the position of seller. They must never be seen to be pushy in negotiation.
2. The British have the reputation of being less motivated by money than the Americans; with the relative decline of Great Britain, they have become more inclined to make the most of their free time; companies are often filled with administrative personnel. This situation has a tendency to slow down the decision-making process significantly (Burt, 1984).
3. The study carried out by Campbell *et al.* (1988), using the vehicle of a simulated negotiation, demonstrates that the factor that has the strongest influence on negotiation in the United Kingdom is the role of negotiator (purchaser or vendor). In the negotiation simulation, British purchasers obtained slightly superior results to vendors of the same nationality. This is consistent with the British reputation of having a 'soft-sell' type of approach, where the vendor must take care not to annoy the purchaser by being too pushy, turning up too often, making too many proposals or by adopting an attitude that is too action oriented.
4. Although seemingly closest to the Americans, the British are not necessarily those who resemble them the most in the field of business practice.

They are usually more contextual and indirect in communication, so business negotiators need to be willing to try to interpret the British position.
5. Language-related issues (the style in which they write clauses, for instance) are treated very differently by the British and the Americans. Whereas US people easily accept a somewhat simplified 'international English' that will be used for drafting agreements, the British, like the French, take pride in correct language, and are sensitive to style for its own sake.

French style

1. The French are said to be somewhat difficult to negotiate with. As noted earlier, the French tend to be ideologists and find it difficult to 'accept facts, no matter how convincing they may be. Although they may consider themselves to be experts at negotiating, at times they tend to be amateurish and inadequately prepared' (Burt, 1984, p. 6).
2. The fact that the French are conflict prone, do not mind confrontation and sometimes even enjoy it, is confirmed by Weiss and Stripp (1985) who describe the French negotiating style as competitive and inherently confrontational. They also tend to use emotional and theatrical ways of behaving in negotiation.
3. In France (as in the United Kingdom) social class remains an important feature of society. Consciousness of social status is very strong in France, as is power distance (see Chapter 3). French negotiators are sensitive to the organizational status of their foreign counterparts, and require equivalence.
4. France is still one of the most centralized nations in the world, with a very long tradition of Paris-based decision making (inaugurated by Hughes Capet, in 987). High-ranking civil servants (*énarques* and *polytechniciens*) have a substantial say in business deals that involve large companies and their subsidiaries.
5. At times, some French negotiators may be resented as arrogant and disdainful: in a very high-power-distance society, which is at the same time individualistic, power display may be exacerbated, to the detriment of politeness and courtesy.
6. Burt (1984, pp. 6–7) complements his view of the French negotiation style as follows:

The French seem to enjoy negotiating for its own sake. When they are in the mood – sometimes for several days – very little progress is made. Sooner or later though, they tire of the game and want to reach closure. A careful count of the numbers of cigarettes consumed per hour serves as an indication of the restlessness and the willingness to make concessions in order to reach closure. Leisure time and the desire for the 'good life' are key motivators. An awareness of these motivators can be useful in reaching agreement, as is indicated in the following dialogue:

American: 'We need to reach agreement, since I've booked us at (the Frenchman's favourite restaurant). But we can't go until we reach agreement on these remaining issues.'

Frenchman: 'I agree. Let's go!'

German style

1. One of the striking aspects of the German national mentality is its relatively high level of uncertainty avoidance (score of 65 on Hofstede's index of uncertainty avoidance; see Table 3.3). A key term is *sicher* (sure, safe). The Germans do not like *unsicherheit*, a sense of insecurity, which makes them feel uneasy in business, as well as in their whole life. In front of partners who generate such uncertainty, Germans will quickly develop *Mißtrauen* (mistrust). They need to be *versichert*, that is, assured, and this cannot be done through superficial and wordy arguments, but only with hard facts, sound arguments, tests and so on.
2. The German love of formality is one thing that stands out clearly. For example, the title of *Doktor*, even *Professor Doktor*, is a recognized sign of ability and will be employed. Formality and the presence of constraining rules (which are generally respected) in the decision-making process on the German side are characteristics of the German system, which seeks to avoid uncertainty (as defined by Hofstede, 1980). These rules are often the end result of a reasonably solid consensus. The respect for accepted rules is more internalized by the Germans than forced upon them.
3. Decisions in a German company are taken at a fairly slow pace. The machine is 'well oiled', but it is also rather cumbersome. A fairly substantial number of signatures will be required for any final agreement.
4. Great pride is taken in the technical quality of products manufactured in Germany; thus a reaction of disbelief is instinctively provoked when a German is faced with something that originates from abroad and fails to conform, for example, to the DIN standards. As a result, readiness to participate in detailed discussions with technical experts is essential.
5. German earnestness is no myth. The Germans are people who keep their word, and who will respect the agreement made, whether it takes a written or an oral form. They loathe anything that approaches flippancy, in particular negotiation for negotiation's sake, or indeed the failure to keep appointments. Germans, when they negotiate with the Italians or the French, often resent their Latin counterparts' unreliability in keeping to their commitments.
6. They prefer explicit communication, and display a temporal style that is clearly monochronic. In negotiations, Germans wait for the schedule and agenda to be respected.
7. In the process of negotiations, the role of emotions and friendship is fairly limited; Germans keep their distance. They feel that a personal relationship could interfere with the result of their work (Schmidt, 1979).
8. There is ambivalence in the way Germans are perceived by others: they are both admired and disliked. As stated by Barzini (1983, p. 94), this 'has its roots not only in their less amiable traits – arrogance, tactlessness and obtuseness – but also in their great virtues, their excellence in almost all fields'. Germans should be considered as individuals more than any nationality in the world. This is the best way to avoid negative biases when negotiating with Germans, who, after all, are not personally responsible for every event of German history.

17.3

Negotiation styles in other areas of the world

Black African style

1. The way Black Africans love to just talk amazes those used to more purposeful speech. Africans simply do not have the same relationship to the universe as Europeans and Americans do. Differences relate to basic concepts such as time and space (see sections 2.2, 2.3 and A2.4). Poetry has a powerful meaning for Africans. The African is a very verbal

person: Africans are almost all polyglots; language is an instrument for the enjoyment of the pleasure of speaking. As a result, negotiations can sometimes seem to be rather ill directed, not just because Africans enjoy debating, but also simply because they enjoy speaking.

2. There is an absence of a strictly economic individual motivation:

Money does not have the same value as in Europe. Westerners are accustomed to an age-old tradition of exchange based on money which has acquired a strong symbolic value as reward for work, as a means of saving, as a measure of personal success and as the fair price of things . . . [in Africa] attitudes towards money follow different rules. Money is only a means of obtaining enough for survival and projection of self-image, whereas its other attributes fade into the background . . . this money is taken without remorse, and in good humour [the 'baksheesh' that is – see Chapter 15], and usually benefits, not just the person who receives it but also the whole family. The African system of distribution functions in such a way that money goes to the one who needs it: the employee whose salary does not allow him to live decently, the high-ranking civil servant who supports a large family in the village for example. (Gruère and Morel, 1991, pp. 122–3.)

3. The reality of tribes and the group is never to be ignored: during the process of business negotiations, the influence of the family and ethnic background will inevitably make its presence felt, whether through the participants or the beneficiaries of the negotiations.

4. The concept of time is simply not the same. This has a direct influence on the progress of business negotiations. As noted by Weiss and Stripp (1985, p. 39) in the case of Nigeria, 'Time is simply considered flexible. Lateness to meetings (even of several hours) is common. In the same vein, the foreigner who hurries through a negotiation – even after a very late start – will often be suspected of cheating.'

5. As Gruère and Morel (1991) emphasize, Black Africa is a mosaic, involving various characteristics of diversity: ethnic, religious (Christianity, Islam, animism) and linguistic. There too, as in the Middle East, a map of the 'human landscape' must be prepared in advance. In the West, we rarely consider people first as members of their tribe. People tend to be considered purely as individuals. The advantage of such a view has been growth in tolerance and reduction in violence between groups whose identity conflicts. The disadvantage has been the increase in individual isolation, since individuals are significantly less supported in their personal life by the ingroup.

Mexican style

1. As in many South American societies, family and political ties are extremely important in Mexico for determining individual influence. Strong ingroup orientation is expressed in bonds of loyalty and solidarity among the top people in both business and government. The dominant political party, PRI, is also a structure allowing patronage and networking in Mexican society, where relationships are a key issue. *Ubicacion*, that is, where one is plugged into the system, is important for determining a negotiator's status (Weiss and Stripp, 1985).

2. As noted earlier, Mexico is a high-power-distance country, ranking second or third highest worldwide, depending on the countries considered; as a consequence, decision making is fairly centralized and 'Mexicans logically prefer to deal abroad at the higher levels of government and business and on a personal and private basis' (Fisher, 1980, p. 28).

3. Personal leverage – *palanca* – is important and influential Mexican negotiators tend to be well positioned in their society, exhibiting their status and stamina.

4. Body language is important to most Latins: it conveys emotions, especially when a negotiator is trying to persuade the other party. To their American neighbours in particular, Mexicans appear at times overly dramatic, emotional and sentimental. Conversely, Mexican negotiators often resent their foreign partners for being reserved, inexpressive and cold.

5. Truthful communication is not to be expected always from Mexicans and frankness should not be taken for granted. Paz (1962) explains that: 'The Mexican tells lies because he delights in fantasy, or because he is desperate, or because he wants to rise above the sordid facts of his life' (quoted by Weiss and Stripp, 1985, p. 33). The use of instrumental strategies by Mexican negotiators is confirmed by Adler *et al.* (1987). This allows them to increase their profits, by manipulating their negotiation partner.

6. According to Graham (1993), in a comparative study across 17 countries, Mexicans appeared as

competitive negotiators (this being evidenced by a fairly low level of joint profits) and the Mexican buyers were those who obtained the lion's share of the profits (almost 57 per cent of the joint outcome), the highest position for buyers out of the 17 countries.

7. The Mexicans have a relaxed concept of time, expressing a polychronic pattern whereby schedules are not given precedence over relations with people. The *mañana* philosophy of time is based on a strong present orientation, which is detrimental to the accuracy of long-term planning and to real commitment *vis-à-vis* dates and deadlines. As the example of 'ocio' and 'negocio', at the beginning of Chapter 13 has shown, extreme activity, workaholism and high time consciousness are not strong values in Spanish-speaking Mexico.

8. Mexicans have a problematic identity problem with their big neighbour, the United States, and there is high sensitivity 'to their perceived dependent relationship with the U.S. and their long memory of patronizing and demeaning actions taken by the U.S. as a government, by American companies and by Americans as individuals' (Fisher, 1980, p. 40).

9. Although corruption has been combated by public authorities in recent years, bribery is still common in Mexico.

Russian style

1. Over 70 years of communism has left some deep impressions on Russian society. As noted in section 6.5, the results include a lack of understanding of basic economic concepts such as the free-market price, company valuation or balance sheet. Unfamiliarity with the free-market mechanisms is progressively being redressed by management education.

2. The low level of individual initiative and the strong aversion for risk taking are explained by Beliaev *et al.* (1985, p. 105) in the following terms:

Each negotiator will be well trained in the party discipline; obedient, with a well-developed sense of hierarchy; hard-working and trained for stress, but with narrow horizons; loyal to the state and fearful of mistakes because of the risk of falling to the level of the average Soviet citizen; cautious, tough, and inflexible because of the strictness of their instructions; and

willing to subordinate personal life to the demand of the position.

3. The Soviet style, still a part of the Russian style even after the disintegration of communism, has been described as fairly tough and unilateral. Negotiators tended to make extreme initial demands, to view adversaries' concessions as weakness, to make only minimal concessions and to ignore deadlines (Cohen, 1980). On the other hand, the Soviet-style Russians were good payers, and did respect contracts that were drafted in a very detailed way.

4. Graham *et al.* (1992) note the consensus of descriptions of Soviet negotiators as 'competitive' and 'uncompromising'. They show in a laboratory experiment that Russian negotiators tend to prefer a distributive strategy, and this with minimal negative effects on their (Russian) partner's satisfaction, which tends to suggest that such competitive behaviour is considered locally as standard practice.

5. The ethical system of Russians widely differs from that of Americans according to Lefebvre (1983):

Something that an American considers normative positive behavior (for example, negotiating and reaching a compromise with an enemy, and even any deal with another individual), a Soviet man perceives as showing Philistine cowardice, weakness, as something unworthy (the word 'deal' itself has a strong negative connotation in contemporary Russian). (Quoted in Graham *et al.*, 1992, p. 396.)

6. Communist centralized planning, based on detailed five-year plans, did not endow Soviet citizens with a sense of economic time (Beliaev *et al.*, 1985). Given the complexity of coordination between government bodies, the Soviet citizen gave up trying to meet exact schedules. In Russia today, this logically results in a highly present and short-term-oriented society.

7. Russia is now undergoing fundamental transition. The bureaucratic controls have progressively been relaxed, giving birth to a new society with deep contrasts. New entrepreneurs appear very different from former Soviets, and are almost Western in style, insofar as they are full of initiative and show great flexibility. These gains, however, are largely undermined by the prevailing lack of reliability, opportunistic behaviour, and the confusion between business and wild capitalism. Incidents involving payment defaults and failure to enforce negotiated contracts are now frequent. Many new

Russian entrepreneurs do not feel bound by business norms and contracts because either they ignore them or they view them as foreign and therefore inapplicable in their context.

17.4

Some basic rules for international marketing negotiations

In short, the international business negotiator should follow some basic rules:

1. Be well prepared; define in advance your basic interests, objectives and bottom line, and allow room for manoeuvre. Before participating in negotiation, learn the basics about the behavioural norms in your partner's culture, especially those concerning appointments, punctuality and planning.
2. Allow time for adequate preliminaries: getting to know the other party is often quite crucial. More time is needed than in domestic business negotiations, since cultural as well as personal knowledge has to be acquired. Allow yourself plenty of time, and then allow even more. Patience is an asset in negotiation and it is destroyed by time pressure.

3. Be flexible with the negotiation agenda if the other party does not stick to it.
4. If necessary, be prepared to withdraw from a negotiation if the stakes are too low, or send lower-level, less expensive executives. If possible, negotiate at home where you have a competitive advantage over your foreign partner, in terms of time control.
5. Be ready for different communication styles and be cautious in interpreting silence, emotionality, threats or any other kind of manipulative communication.
6. Never tell the other side when you are leaving, which would give them control over your time.
7. Respect the sensitivities of your partner in the area of (a) personal status; and (b) national pride.
8. Do not be deceived by the other party seeming to share your time pattern: try to set dates, deadlines and plans realistically and modestly. Tight deadlines may result into major delays that ruin the credibility of the whole planning process.
9. Try to balance relationship orientation and deal orientation: be prepared for the negotiation process to extend beyond the signature of the deal.

For different sets of guidelines and recommendations for international marketing negotiations see *WS17.4*.

Questions

1. What sort of cultural misunderstandings could arise from a negotiation between Japanese buyers and French sellers?

2. Discuss the influence of group orientation (as presented in Chapter 2 and illustrated in this chapter for some national groups) on behaviour during the negotiation process.

3. Negotiations between Russians and Chinese: are they easy? Why?

4. Imagine a negotiation between a (stereotypical) Mexican businessman and a (stereotypical) US businesswoman: which cultural misunderstandings may appear between them in the negotiation process?

5. Discuss similarities and differences between US and British business negotiation styles.

6. American business people meet potential Japanese partners in California to discuss a joint venture project. The joint venture would sell US-made products on the Japanese market. One of the Americans starts the first meeting by saying to his Japanese counterpart: 'Since we are going to work together in the future, we had better get to know each other now. My name is John. What is your name?' Is this form of address adequate? If so, why? If not, why not?

References

Adler, Nancy J., R. Brahm and John L. Graham (1992), 'Strategy implementation: a comparison of face-to-face negotiations in the People's Republic of China and the United States', *Strategic Management Journal*, vol. 13, no. 6, pp. 449–66.

Adler, Nancy J., John L. Graham and Theodore Schwarz-Gehrke (1987), 'Business negotiations in Canada, Mexico and the United States', *Journal of Business Research*, vol. 15, pp. 411–29.

Barzini, Luigi (1983), *The Europeans*, Penguin Books: London.

Bazerman, Max H., Jared R. Curhan, Don A. Moore and Kathleen L. Valley (2000), 'Negotiation', *Annual Review of Psychology*, vol. 51, pp. 279–314.

Beliaev, Edward, Thomas Mullen and Betty Jane Punnett (1985), 'Understanding the cultural environment: U.S.–U.S.S.R. trade negotiations', *California Management Review*, vol. 27, no. 2, pp. 100–12.

Brett, Jeanne M. and Tetsushi Okumura (1998), 'Inter- and intra-cultural negotiations: US and Japanese negotiators', *Academic Management Journal*, vol. 41, no. 5, pp. 495–510.

Burt, David N. (1984), 'The nuances of negotiating overseas', *Journal of Purchasing and Materials Management*, Winter, pp. 2–8.

Campbell, Nigel C.G., John L.Graham, Alain Jolibert and Hans Günther Meissner (1988), 'Marketing negotiations in France, Germany, the United Kingdom and United States', *Journal of Marketing*, vol. 52, April, pp. 49–62.

Cohen, Herb (1980), *You Can Negotiate Anything*, Bantam: New York.

Eiteman, David K. (1990), 'American executives' perceptions of negotiating joint ventures with the People's Republic of China: lessons learned', *Columbia Journal of World Business*, Winter, pp. 59–67.

Elgström, O. (1990), 'Norms, culture, and cognitive patterns in foreign-aid negotiations', *Negotiation Journal – On the Process of Dispute Settlement*, vol. 6, no. 2, pp. 147–59.

Fisher, Glen (1980), *International Negotiation: A cross-cultural perspective*, Intercultural Press: Yarmouth, ME.

Goldman, A. (1994), 'The centrality of "Ningensei" to Japanese negotiating and interpersonal relationships: implications for U.S.-Japanese communication', *International Journal of Intercultural Relations*, vol. 18, no. 1, pp. 29–54.

Graham, John L. (1981), 'A hidden cause of America's trade deficit with Japan', *Columbia Journal of World Business*, Fall, pp. 5–15.

Graham, John L. (1993), 'Business negotiations: generalisations about Latin America and East Asia are dangerous', *UCI Irvine/Research*, pp. 6–23.

Graham, John L. and Roy A. Herberger Jr (1983), 'Negotiators abroad: don't shoot from the hip', *Harvard Business Review*, vol. 61, no. 4, pp. 160–8.

Graham, John L., Leonid I. Ivenko and Mahesh N. Rajan (1992), 'An empirical comparison of Soviet and American business negotiations', *Journal of International Business Studies*, vol. 23, no. 3, pp. 387–418.

Graham, John L., A.T. Mintu and W. Rodgers (1994), 'Explorations of negotiation behaviors in ten foreign cultures using a model developed in the United States', *Management Science*, vol. 40, no. 1 (January), pp. 72–95.

Gruère, Jean-Pierre and Pierre Morel (1991), *Cadres Français et Communications Interculturelles*, Eyrolles: Paris.

Gudykunst, W.B. and S. Ting-Toomey (1988), 'Culture and affective communication', *American Behavioral Scientist*, vol. 31, pp. 384–400.

Hawrysh, Bryan Mark and Judith Lynn Zaichkowsky (1990), 'Cultural approaches to negotiations: understanding the Japanese', *International Marketing Review*, vol. 7, no. 2, pp. 28–42.

Hofstede, Geert (1980), 'Motivation, leadership and organization: do American theories apply abroad?', *Organizational Dynamics*, Summer, pp. 42–63.

Hofstede, Geert (1989), 'Cultural predictors of national negotiation styles', in Frances Mautner-Markhof, *Processes of International Negotiations*, Westview Press: Boulder, CO, pp. 193–201.

Hofstede, Geert (1991), *Cultures and Organizations: Software of the Mind*, McGraw-Hill: Maidenhead, Berkshire.

Kale, S.H. and J.W. Barnes (1992), 'Understanding the domain of cross-national buyer–seller interactions', *Journal of International Business Studies*, vol. 23, no. 1, pp. 101–32.

Kirkbride, P.S., S.F.Y. Tang and R.I. Westwood (1991), 'Chinese conflict preferences and negotiating behavior – cultural and psychological influences', *Organization Studies*, vol. 12, no. 3, pp. 365–86.

Lefebvre, Victorina D. (1983), 'Ethical features of the normative hero in Soviet children's literature of the 1960s–70s', *Studies of Cognitive Sciences*, vol. 20, School of Social Sciences: Irvine, CA.

Leung, K. (1997), 'Negotiation and reward allocations across cultures', in P.C. Early and M. Erez (eds), *New Perspectives on International Industrial/Organizational Psychology*, Jossey-Bass: San Francisco, pp. 640–75.

Luo, Yadong (1995), 'Business strategy, market structure, and performance of IJV', *Management International Review*, vol. 35, no. 3, pp. 249–64.

Luo, Yadong and Min Chen (1997), 'Does guanxi influence firm performance?', *Asia Pacific Journal of Management*, vol. 14, pp. 1–16.

Markus, Hazel Rose and Shinobu Kitayama (1991), 'Culture and the self: implications for cognition, emotion and motivation', *Psychological Review*, vol. 98, no. 2, pp. 224–53.

Morris, Michael W., Katherine Y. Williams, Kwok Leung, Richard Larrick, Teresa M. Mendoza, Deepti Bhatnagar, Jianfeng Li, Mari Kondo, Jin-Lian Luo and Hu Jun-Chen (1998), 'Conflict management style: accounting for cross-national differences', *Journal of International Business Studies*, vol. 29, no. 4, pp. 729–47.

Oh, T.K. (1986), 'Selling to the Japanese', *Nation's Business*, October, pp. 37–8.

Paz, Octavio (1962), *The Labyrinth of Solitude*, Grove: New York.

Potter, Richard E. and Pierre A. Balthazard (2000), 'Supporting integrative negotiation via computer mediated communication technologies: an empirical example with geographically dispersed Chinese and American negotiators', *Journal of International Consumer Marketing*, vol. 12, no. 4, pp. 7–32.

Pye, Lucian W. (1982), *Chinese Commercial Negotiating Style*, Oelgeschlager, Gunn & Hain: Cambridge, MA.

Pye, Lucian W. (1986), 'The China trade: making the deal work', *Harvard Business Review*, vol. 46, no. 4, pp. 75–84.

Schmidt, Klaus D. (1979), *Doing Business in France, Germany and the United Kingdom*, pamphlets published by the Business Intelligence Program, SRI International: Menlo Park, CA.

Shenkar, O. and S. Ronen (1987), 'The cultural context of negotiations – the implications of Chinese interpersonal norms', *Journal of Applied Behavioral Science*, vol. 23, no. 2, pp. 263–75.

Tinsley, Catherine H. and Jeanne Brett (1997), 'Managing workplace conflict: a comparison of conflict frames and outcomes in the U.S. and Hong Kong', Paper presented at the Annual Meeting of the Academy of Management, Boston.

Tinsley, Catherine H. and Madan M. Pittula (1998), 'Negotiating in the United States and Hong Kong', *Journal of International Business Studies*, vol. 29, no. 4, pp. 711–27.

Tse, D.K., J. Francis and J. Walls (1994), 'Cultural differences in conducting intra- and inter-cultural negotiations: a Sino-Canadian perspective', *Journal of International Business Studies*, vol. 25, no. 3, pp. 537–55.

Tung, Rosalie L. (1984), 'How to negotiate with the Japanese', *California Management Review*, vol. XXVI, no. 4, pp. 62–77.

Tung, Rosalie (1996), 'Negotiating with East Asians', in P.N. Ghauri and J.-C. Usunier (eds), *International Business Negotiations*, Pergamon/Elsevier: Oxford, pp. 369–81.

Wade-Benzoni, Kimberly A., Tetsushi Okumura, Jeanne M. Brett, Don A. Moore, Ann E. Tenbrunsel and Max H. Bazerman (2002), 'Cognition and behavior in asymmetric social dilemmas: a comparison of two cultures', *Journal of Applied Psychology*, vol. 87, no. 1, pp. 87–95.

Weiss, Stephen E. (1993), 'Analysis of complex negotiations in international business – the RBC perspective', *Organization Science*, vol. 4, no. 2, pp. 269–300.

Weiss, Stephen E. (1994), 'Negotiating with Romans: 2', *Sloan Management Review*, vol. 35, no. 3, pp. 85–9.

Weiss, Stephen E. and William Stripp (1985), 'Negotiating with foreign businesspersons: an introduction for Americans with propositions for six cultures', Working Paper no. 85–6, Graduate School of Business, New York University: New York.

Appendix 17

Teaching materials

A17.1 Case

Tremonti SpA

Tremonti SpA was a small company located in the suburbs of Milan. Like many small and medium enterprises in the northern part of Italy, it specialized in special machines and mechanical engineering. Tremonti SpA had developed a sophisticated knowledge in the production of machines for assembling electronic components.

The company had been founded by an engineer, Mr Stefanini, who owned the business and gave it its technological drive. Until now he had always made the choice to invest more money in R & D than in production operations. The company therefore cared more about prototypes than about mass production (if that means anything in an industry where world-wide markets rarely exceed tens or hundreds of machines).

A large part of the production was in fact subcontracted. This made factory investments lighter and gave production flexibility in the face of unsteady demand. But subcontracting about 60–80 per cent of the parts and a large amount of the assembly work was not satisfactory in that it made it difficult to follow and monitor production schedules accurately.

The export manager, Mr Lesca, had considerably increased export sales during the last five years. Export sales at Tremonti SpA were 80 per cent of the total corporate sales figure. Clients were mostly located in the US and in Europe, with a very small proportion in Japan. Lesca's team was composed of two export salesmen, who had a technical background and provided maintenance for machines located abroad, and two English-speaking secretaries who were in charge of export logistics and paperwork.

I

Lesca was worried by a problem with an American customer. The American had already bought one machine from Tremonti SpA and was very satisfied with it. It worked at full capacity, it had been delivered on time and it was reliable. Then he ordered a second machine, which was now in the production process.

Unfortunately, according to the manufacturing department, the production of this machine seemed to be delayed by four to six weeks from the agreed delivery date. Yet the American customer was willing to order a third machine, since the first one had been working satisfactorily for the last six months. He did not know about a possible delay to the second machine.

Lesca wondered what he should do:

1. Should he tell the American customer about the delivery delay of the second machine during his next visit to negotiate the sale of the third machine? The agreed delivery date for the second machine is six weeks after the next visit of Lesca to his American customer.
2. If yes, how should he announce it?

II

Finally, after the visit had taken place, Lesca was satisfied with the tactics he had adopted. He felt a need to extract some more widely applicable principles out of this communication experience. When flying back from the United States he wondered how he should have acted with people from the following national/cultural backgrounds: German, Japanese and Saudi Arabian.

III

Demand had been growing quickly. Since Tremonti SpA's machines were up-to-date and reliable, they were especially sought out. But delivery delays were increasing. A conversation with a German customer, Herr Weisslinger, gave him another opportunity to become aware of the high level of sensitivity of clients to their suppliers meeting delivery dates.

'You Italians,' began Weisslinger, 'you do not really know what a delivery date is. There are huge differences between the delivery date agreed upon when signing the contract and the actual delivery date. And you wait until the last minute to tell us that you won't be able to meet your delivery date. Sometimes you do not even report it and we have to send you a fax to try to find out when the machine will be delivered. Yet it should already have been delivered, and we are not even informed.'

'No, you carry it too far,' answered Lesca. 'I do not believe that we deliberately miss delivery dates. You have to understand: a delivery date is indicative. When ordering, a date is fixed that best suits the client. We indicate the delivery date that we think we are able to meet. Numerous hazards may then occur. Our suppliers and subcontractors do not adhere strictly to their delivery dates, and this causes a large part of our own delays.'

'If I understand you correctly, we have to accept things as they are,' said Weisslinger.

'I am afraid so,' replied Lesca. 'I am the personal advocate of our clients within the company. But, you know, my authority is limited, and the Italian national character values deadlines and time precision far less than Anglo-Saxons do. Moreover it is an organizational problem: everybody has to feel committed if we want to achieve a greater respect for delivery dates.'

'Yes indeed,' said Weisslinger, 'I think your machines are of good quality and your maintenance and after-sales service are OK. But your competitors provide equal qualities and they meet their deadlines. We have to make rational choices. You do not meet your delivery dates.'

Mr Lesca is now wondering how he should allocate his efforts. Should he go on playing the role of a 'trade ambassador', trying diplomatically to make the foreign clients accept delays? Should he, on the other hand, spend more time in the company and undertake action to improve the organizational functioning for delivery dates? How should he tackle the issue with Stefanini? What ways and means would be sufficient to improve the commitment to delivery dates?

IV

Some time after this conversation with Weisslinger, Lesca went to Japan on a business trip, and had the opportunity to present Tremonti SpA's technical achievements. On his return from Japan, he went to Stefanini's office to discuss the potential of the Japanese market. 'We did place some orders there, but they are small compared with the total Japanese market, and particularly small when compared with the sales we achieved in the United States. I have had preliminary talks with a large electronics company called Nokan. We examined the possibility of a marketing joint venture, which would be responsible for selling and servicing our machines on the Japanese market. It looks fine; but I know that Japanese people are not easy to deal with. They are extremely polite, courteous and gentle, but what are their real intentions? Frankly, I do not trust them. Besides, they have a reputation for ransacking technologies, and it is a fundamental that we protect our knowledge base.' Stefanini wanted to prepare for the negotiation of this marketing joint venture. He asked Lesca the following questions:

1. 'How can we get information about Japanese culture?'
2. 'Which aspects are relevant to our problem?'

Postscript

Globalization as 'modernism' brought to backward nations

According to Ernest Dichter, in an article entitled 'The World Customer', which is considered a seminal article in the field of international marketing, particularly as it was the first to picture the phenomenon of the globalization of world markets:[1]

Only one Frenchman out of three brushes his teeth. Automobiles have become a must for the self-esteem of even the lowliest postal clerk in Naples or the Bantu street cleaner in Durban . . . Four out of five Germans change their shirts but once a week. (1962, p. 113.)

The explanation is to be found some pages later: 'The fact that 64 per cent of the Frenchmen don't brush their teeth is in part caused by the lack of running water in many communities' (p. 116). The Germans rank first in terms of the illusions a nation can have about itself. Dichter proposes the following illustration: 'Germans still refer to themselves as a nation of poets and thinkers; yet the largest selling newspaper, the *Bildzeitung*, has a circulation of 2 million based largely on sensationalism and tabloid treatment of news' (p. 117). According to Dichter, at the beginning of the 1960s, Dutch housewives would serve instant coffee, making the verbal excuse that instant coffee is used only in an emergency. 'What happens, however, is that the number of emergencies has increased amazingly' (p. 117).

One might think that globalization emerged from the advances in modernity and cleanliness accomplished by these backward people when they overcame their resistance to change. One may also wonder whether there is any real connection between Goethe, Schiller, Kant and Heidegger on the one hand and the *Bildzeitung* on the other, other than the fact that they are all German. It is necessary to highlight the first paradox in this approach: many arguments in favour of the globalization of markets are totally ethnocentric; as such, they are in contradiction with the spirit of globalization, which is based on the rejection of ethnocentrism.

Some true reasons for the globalization of markets

Globalization is, first of all, based on technological advances, which in turn explain globalization on the supply side: economies of scale and experience effects, drastic changes over the past 40 years in transportation and also new telecommunications technologies. The globalization of consumers and demand will certainly occur in the future, but it will happen much later than its early defenders imagined. Moreover the process of worldwide globalization of demand may be quite different from what they visualized: a steady extension of the 'American way of life' throughout the world which would contribute to the global happiness of humankind.

But cultural coherence should not be forgotten and marketers still have to be aware of it. Consumers buy meanings, not just products. Meaning is intersubjectively shared in the cultural community. The process of globalization of demand will be long term because of the local nature of culture and its contribution to collective identity. Moreover, this evolution can be achieved only by individuals who *learn*. Learning is a large part of culture. Globalization implies that consumers throughout the world have to borrow foreign ways of life, experience new behaviours and construct shared meanings with people from other cultures. At present, a great many things are shared among the cultures of the world, but just as many remain culture specific. *Amnesty International*, the practice of *judo*, playing or listening to *jazz*, the *Olympics* and many other cultural artefacts, even though they were born in particular cultures, are probably bearers of future universal values. Obviously each national culture has a specific contribution to make to the movement towards globalization. If there is any true (and sincere) way of being *global* it is not by denying differences, but by being aware of and responsive to them. We face a second paradox, the two sides of which must be constantly kept in mind: on the one hand, lifestyles are apparently tending to become global; on the other, the claims for recovering cultural identity are stronger than ever. Numerous peoples who have been denied a sovereign state are demanding their independence as nations, emphasizing the uniqueness of their culture. The concept of a nation-state, although a fairly recent one historically,[2] remains very strong for many individuals. Although it is not the only way of protecting cultural identity, it is still the most elaborate and the most efficient one.

The law of comparative advantage, in Chapter 5, has almost completely eliminated the concept of culture from international trade theory. One may remark, as Galtung (1990) does, that: 'In short, this "law" [of comparative advantage] is a piece of cultural violence buried in the very core of economics.'[3] Ignoring cultural differences, the law of comparative advantage imposes a paradigm of international trade, which is excessively utilitarian: it assumes the *complete pre-eminence of utility over identity*. Yet real people do not live only with what is useful to them, they also live out of the maintenance and self-actualization of their identity, of which their cultural identity is a significant part. Thus it is necessary to integrate the dimension of culture in marketing strategies and in their implementation, when they focus on international markets.

Designing tailored marketing strategies and implementing them with respect for the local context

As this book (it is hoped) shows: marketing strategies tailored to national/cultural markets are not in contradiction with the choice of a global business strategy. On the contrary, *cultural tailoring* is a basic element of a global business strategy. The reality of cultural exchanges worldwide is now so complex and so inextricable that any oversimplification is dangerous. Let us take a concrete example: using instant coffee does not imply that one has, once and for all, adopted ready-made standardized consumer goods. Coffee beans and ground coffee have made a tremendous come-back against instant coffee, regaining lost market share in most coffee-drinking countries. No evolution is fixed; consumers change from 'tradition' to 'modernism', but also back to (almost) traditional ways of consuming. Among the segments targeted in an intercultural marketing strategy there will be both transnational market segments and national market segments, to which specific offers will be made. National culture will continue to influence strongly many aspects of the implementation of marketing strategies, choice of distribution channels and trade partners, setting of prices, sales and marketing negotiations, etc.

This is fortunate because, if cultural differences were to disappear, we suspect that life would be boring.

Notes

1. We are sorry for the unkind words used in some sentences in this article. It is a superb example of sincere ethnocentrism, as well as of relative lack of long-term vision. The article does, however, contain many insightful remarks.
2. The concept of a nation-state emerged clearly at the end of the seventeenth century and developed further during the nineteenth century. Germany and Italy, for instance, were not united as nation-states before the end of the nineteenth century, under the auspices of Bismarck in Germany and Cavour in Italy. Decolonization was the heyday of the concept of the nation-state: many countries were formed which corresponded not to a nation, not to a shared culture among the various groups of citizens, not even to a geographical unit.
3. Johan Galtung thoroughly defines what the process of cultural violence encompasses. In particular, one section of his article (4.5) argues that Ricardo's doctrine (developed further by Heckscher and Ohlin, and others) justifies the world division of labour: 'The principle of comparative advantage sentences countries to stay where the production-factor profile has landed them, for geographical and historical reasons' (p. 300). However, marketers are not economists: their pragmatism may induce them to choose *culturally non-violent* marketing strategies, if they prove successful.

References

Dichter, E. (1962), 'The world customer', *Harvard Business Review*, vol. 40, no. 4, pp. 113–22.

Galtung, J. (1990), 'Cultural violence', *Journal of Peace Research*, vol. 27, no. 3, pp. 291–305.

Author index

Aaker, David A., 303
Aaker, Jennifer L., 91, 132, 413, 414
Aalto-Setälä, Ville, 331, 350
Abas, Zoraini Wati, 392
Abbott, Charlotte, 517
Abdel-Halim, Mustafa, 266
Abe, Shuzo, 87, 128
Abegglen, James C., 301, 331
Abernethy, Avery M., 415
Ackerman(n), N., 322
Ackerman, David, 321
Ad Age, 432
Adachi, Yumi, 514
Adair, Wendi L., 494, 506, 515, 521
Adcock, Dennis, 466
Adler, Keith, 298
Adler, Nancy J., 57, 77, 470, 494, 498, 510, 512, 519, 521, 540
Adler, Peter S., 391
Agarwal, James, 222
Agarwal, Sanjeev, 123
Agpar, M., 475
Agrawal, Jagdish, 289
Agrawal, Madhu, 413
Ahmed, Sadrudin A., 289, 291, 293
Ahmed, Zafar U., 291, 292
Ahuvia, Aaron, 51, 53, 91, 106, 128
Akhter, Syed H., 353
Albaum, Gerald, 134, 183, 204, 209–14, 250, 528
Albers-Miller, Nancy D., 93, 351, 425
Alberta Agriculture, 366–7
Alden, Dana L., 106, 133, 230, 289, 302, 303, 418, 419, 431
Alexander, Nicholas, 348
Ali, Abbas, 468
Al-Khatib, Jamal A., 478
Allaway, Arthur W., 483
Allen, David Elliston, 318
Allio, David J., 252
Allio, Robert J., 252
Al-Makaty, Safran S., 421
Al-Mossawi, Mohammed, 420
Al-Olayan, Fahad S., 420

Alpay, Guvenc, 305
Alpert, Frank, 301
Amdur, Meredith, 243
American Foundation for HIV Research, 453
Amine, Lyn S., 160, 193, 251
Ancarani, Fabio, 330
Ancel, Marie-Odile, 170
Anderson, B., 290
Anderson, Erin T., 38, 227, 350
Anderson, Patricia M., 124, 232
Anderson, Paul F., 471
Anderson, W. T., 306
Andrews, J. Craig, 182, 183, 412, 427
Ang, Swee Hoon, 465
Angelmar, Reinhard, 190, 204, 505, 516
Anholt, Simon, 273
Appelbaum, Ullrich, 414, 418
Applbaum, Kalman, 106, 126, 129
Arlidge, John, 272
Armstrong, Robert W., 477
Arndt, Johan, 496
Arnold, Michael S., 268
Arnould, Eric J., 478
Arpan, Jeffrey S., 417
Arunthanes, Wiboon, 106
Askegaard, Søren, 92, 105, 135, 182, 232, 289
Assaoui, Mohammed, 146
Attali, Jacques, 24
Au, Kevin, 459
Aulakh, Preet S., 120
Aupperle, Kenneth E., 145
Austin, M. Jill, 235
Austrade, 263
Avlonitis, G., 139
Axinn, Catherine N., 201
Axtell, Roger, E., 378

Baalbaki, Imad B., 222, 248
Babin, Barry J., 166, 351
Backhaus, Klaus, 433
Badhuri, Monika, 204
Bagozzi, Richard P., 87, 89, 103, 128, 191

Bagur, F. Ali, 507
Bagur, J. S., 507
Baines, Paul R., 125
Baker, Walter, 330
Bakos, Yannis, 355
Balabanis, George, 292, 293
Ballah, R. N., 90
Ballon, Robert J., 28, 33
Balthazard, Pierre A., 516
Bamossy G. J., 139
Bannister, J. P., 139
Bao, Yeqing Bao, 95
Barabba, Vincent P., 458
Barbaro-Forleo, Guido, 235
Barber, Benjamin R., 266
Bard, Mitchell, 268
Bartlett, Christopher, 229
Barzini, Luigi, 539
Bates, Constance, 421
Bateson, Gregory, 391
Batra, Rajeev, 133, 230, 289, 302, 303, 431
Baudrillard, Jean, 104, 105
Baumgartner, Gary, 139, 293
Baumgartner, Hans, 182, 183, 190, 197, 254
Bautista, Sergio Antonio, 451
Bazerman, Max H., 494, 498, 499, 506, 509, 514, 516,
    521, 523
BBC News, 150, 154, 243, 244
Bearden, William O., 231
Beatty, Sharon E., 106
Becker, Gary S., 320
Becker, Helmut, 481
Beeler, Amanda, 152
Beers, Charlotte, 444
Beliaev, Edward, 504, 537, 540
Belk, Russell W., 51, 55, 88, 105, 106, 120, 123, 134, 424
Bell, David, 118, 139
Bell, Jim, 348
Benet-Martinez, Veronica, 132
Bennett, Harvey, 349
Bensaou, M., 182, 183
Benton, A. A., 507
Beracs, Joszef, 134, 139
Berenbein, Ronald E., 480, 481
Berg, David, 397
Bergami, Massimo, 87, 128, 191
Berger, Brigitte, 157
Bergeron, Jasmin, 235
Berne, Eric, 63, 78
Berning, Carol K., 24, 42
Berry, John W., 15, 17, 39, 42, 100
Beutelmeyer, Werner, 354
Bhandari, Labdhi, 134

Bhatnagar, Deepti, 516, 517
Bhuian, Shahid N., 290
Bigne, Enrique, 415
Bilkey, Warren J., 288
Billikopf Encina, Gregorio, 389
Bisby, Adam, 392
Bista, Dor Bahadur, 54, 512
Bitterli, Urs, 17
Bjerke, Rune, 420
Blackwell Roger D., 95
Bliemel, F., 139
Bluedorn, Allen C., 26, 375
Boas, Franz, 15
Boddewyn, Jean Jacques, 230, 295, 357, 358, 360, 412
Bodur, Muzzafer, 230, 231
Bohnet, Michael, 187
Boland, Tom, 477
Bon, Jérôme, 134, 161
Bond, Michael Harris, 27, 56, 171
Boote, A. S., 232
Borenstein, Severin, 38
Botschen, Martina, 354
Bouchet, Dominique, 102, 125, 139
Boya, Unal 0., 467, 470, 471, 483
Boyd, Douglas A., 421
Bradfield, Ray, 466
Brady, Michael K., 257
Brady, John T., 478
Brannen, Mary Yoko, 136, 521, 522, 523
Bremner, Charles, 178
Brett, Jeanne M., 494, 498, 506, 507, 509, 514, 515, 517, 521
Brislin, Richard W., 19–20, 45–6, 48–9, 81, 82
Brooke, Michael Z., 532
Browne, Elizabeth, 106
Brunsø, Karen, 92, 182
Bruzzese, Stephanie, 106, 113
Burgaud, Didier, 430
Burns, Alvin C., 322
Burns, David J., 478
Burroughs, James E., 197
Burt, David N., 510, 514, 535, 537, 538
Burt, Steve, 349
Business Standard, 243
Business Times, 150
Business Today, 268
Business Week, 242, 243
Business World, 177
Buske, Erwin, 227
Buzzell, Robert D., 227

Cabat, Odilon, 297–8
Cabell, David W. E., 325
Cadix, Alain, 161

Caetano, Raul, 101
Calantone, R., 102, 190, 204, 235
Callow, Michael, 415
Calvert, Stephen, 106
Camargo, Eduardo, 37, 417
Campbell, David, 106
Campbell, Donald T., 186, 188, 389
Campbell, J. B., 197
Campbell, Nigel C. G., 77, 436, 505, 507, 508, 538
Cannon, Hugh M., 132
Carey, George, 232
Carralero-Encinas, Jose, 349
Carroll, Collette, 287
Carroll, John B., 6, 396
Carter, J. R., 506
Castellucio, Michael, 388
Catalano, Joelle, 414, 416
Cateora, Philip R., 331, 344, 347, 348, 350, 466, 467, 468
Cattin, Philippe, 139, 293
Cavusgil, S. Tamer, 98, 160, 183, 193, 201, 202, 228, 230, 231, 293, 319, 329
Cecchini, Paolo, 164
Center for Strategic and International Studies, 276
Cevallos, Diago, 453
Chabra, Aseem, 243, 244
Chambers, Terry M., 471
Chan, Allan K. K., 296
Chan, T. S., 125, 477
Chandran, R., 185, 193, 194, 196, 414, 419
Chang, Cypress, 414, 416
Chang, Dae Ryun, 293
Chao, Paul, 291
Chapman, Malcolm, 30, 34
Chaterji, Chandra S., 112
Chaudry, Peggy E., 328
Chen, Chao C., 55
Chen, Cheng-Nan, 89
Chen, Dongling, 122, 139
Chen, Haipeng Allen, 184
Chen, Min, 464, 535
Chen, Xiao-Ping, 55
Cheng, Constant, 225
Cheng, Hong, 424
Chéron, Emmanuel, 123
Cherrie, Craig, 45–6, 182
Cheung, Gordon W. H., 93
Chew, Eugene, 275
Chiaramonte, Joan, 232
Chien, M., 90
Child, John, 5
Childers, Terry L., 89, 192
Chinese Cultural Connection, 27
Chiou, Jyh-Shen, 91, 93, 414

Cho, Bongjin, 232
Choe, Soonkyoo, 76
Chonko, Lawrence B., 468, 471
Choong, Mei-Lan, 420
Chowdhry, Amitav, 403, 404
Christensen, Ania, 135
Chu, Jeff, 147, 148, 149
Chun, K. T., 197
Chung, Kae H., 290, 293
Clark, Catherine L., 101
Clark, Harold F. Jr, 132, 302, 433
Clarke, Irvine III, 197, 327, 329, 423
Clement, Henry, 266
Clements, Kenneth W., 122, 139
Cohen, Herb, 511, 541
Cohen, Judy, 261, 262
Cohen, Raymond, 494
Coleman, Zach, 264
Colombat, Catherine, 297
Colvin, Michael, 424
Condon, John C., 381
Contensou, François, 301
Coon, Heather M., 105
Cooper, Louise, 244
Copeland, Lennie, 264, 381
Copeland, Michael J., 494
Corne, P. H., 518, 519
Correll, Sharon, 404
Cote, J. A., 204
Coughlan, Anne T., 350
Council of the European Communities, 166
Cowen, Richard, 177
Cox, Anthony, 356
Cox, James, 267
Coyne, Michael, 183
Craig, C. Samuel, 182, 183, 191, 192, 193, 195, 202, 304
Cravens, David W., 221
Cravens, Karen S., 62
Crawford, John C., 289, 293, 305
Cuenca, Antonio C., 415
Cummings, L. L., 504, 507, 508, 522
Cundiff, Edward W., 232, 312–5
Cunningham, William H., 306
Curhan, Jared R., 494, 499, 506, 509, 516, 521, 523
Curry, David J., 321
Cutitta, Frank, 378
Cutler, Bob D., 413, 414, 416, 420, 421, 423, 425
Czinkota, Michael R., 121, 296, 342, 345, 348, 349, 357, 423, 473

D'Andrade, Roy G., 103
D'Astous, Alain, 291
D'Hauteserre, Anne-Marie, 146

Dabbous, Dalia, 137
Daft, Douglas N., 121
Dahringer, Lee D., 232
Dana, Leo-Paul, 251, 252, 264
Daniels, John D., 467
Darley, William K., 412
Darling, John B., 290
Das, Ajay, 183
Dasen, Pierre R., 15, 17, 38, 42
Datson, Trevor, 178
David, René, 520
Davis, H. L., 189
Dawar, Niraj, 123, 127, 322
Dawson, Chester, 145
Day, Ellen, 123
Day, G. S., 458
Day, R. L., 505
Dayan, Armand, 161
De Grazia, Victoria, 443, 444, 445
De Jong, Ad, 257
De Juan, Maria D., 378
De Maricourt, Renaud, 161, 342, 347, 519
De Mente, Boye, 393, 519
De Mooij, Marieke K., 57, 87, 122, 123, 166, 168, 173, 204, 233, 348
De Mortanges, Pahud, 347
De Ruyter, Ko, 257
De Souza, Marianne, 204
De Wulf, Kristof, 420
Dedoussis, Vagelis, 346
Deher, Odile, 228
Delaney, Mark, 106, 113
DeMarco, C. W., 331
Demirel, A. Hamdi, 351, 422
DeMoss, Michelle, 106
Dentsu Young and Rubican Inc., 244
Derr, C. B., 75
Desmet, Pierre, 345
Deutscher, I., 187
Dholakia, Ruby Roy, 134
Di Benedetto, C. Anthony, 414, 419
Diallard, Susan, 101
Diamantopoulos, A., 194, 201, 249, 292, 293
Diaz Del Castillo, Bernal, 17
Dichter, E., 111, 548
Dixon, John, 173
Djarova, Julia G., 169
Djursaa, Malene, 103, 136, 137
Dobscha, Susan, 458
Doi, T., 345
Dolbeck, Andrew, 133
Dollt, Andreas, 275
Doran, Kathleen Brewer, 127, 157, 194, 198

Dornoff, Ronald J., 305, 306
Douglas, Susan P., 182, 183, 189, 191, 192, 193, 195, 197, 202, 203, 222, 225, 304, 306, 421
Dowd, Lawrence, 528
Dowling, G. R., 415
Droit, Michel, 390
Druckman, D., 507
Du Preez , J. P., 249
Dubé, Laurette, 285, 288
Dubini, Paola, 167
Dubinsky, Alan J., 469, 472
Dubois, Bernard, 86, 421
Dudley, James W., 430
Duerr, Edwin, 523
Dugan, Shaun, 55
Dun and Bradstreet Corp., 487
Duncan, Tom, 416
Dupuis, Marc, 342, 347
Dupuy, Francois, 301
Durden, Geoffrey R., 201
Durgee, Jeffrey F., 189
Durkheim, Emile, 15
Durr, Michael, 294
Durvasula, Srinivas, 182, 183, 412, 427
Dwyer, Johanna, T., 267
Dwyer, Robert F., 463, 496
Dyer, Barbara, 459

Easterby-Smith, Mark, 204
Eastman, Jacqueline K., 106
Eckhardt, Giana M., 137
Economist, 356
Eden, David, 232
Egan, Colin, 483
Eiteman, David K., 504, 517, 535
El Adraoui, Mostafa, 291
El Haddad, Awad B., 160
Eliade, Mircea, 8, 9
Eliasi, Jennifer R., 267
Eljabri, Jelloul, 289
El-Tigi, Jehan, 421
Emery, Charles, 355, 356
Engel, James F., 95
Enis, Ben M., 468, 471
Episcopo, Jo, 244
Erbil, Kurt, 431
Erevelles, Sunil, 189, 320
Ergin, Canan, 517
Erickson, Gary, 322
Erikki, Liikanen, 106, 113
Erikson, Erik, 17
Eroglu, Sevgin A., 291, 293, 305
Erramilli, M. Krishna, 414, 416, 423

Eshghi, Abdolezra, 122
Esposito, Odile, 165
Essad Bey, Mohammed, 67
Etchegoyen, Alain, 303
Ethnologue, 402
Ettenson, Richard, 135, 289, 291, 306
Etzel, Michael J., 305
Eurobarometer, 165
Euromonitor, 122, 349–50
European Communities, 167
Evans, Franklin B., 507
Evans, John, 163
Evening Standard, London, 150
Ewing, Michael T., 300

Fairhurst, Ann, 101, 322
Family Business, 150
Fan, Ying, 302
Fang, Tan Wai, 291
Farr, Robert M., 16
Farre, Maria Eugenia, 392
Fauld, David J., 321, 322
Faulk, Saskia., 112–15, 145–9, 150–4, 177–8, 241–4,
    272–7, 365–70, 400–4, 443–6, 451–6
Faure, Guy Oliver, 494
Fay, T., 186
Fei, X. T., 90
Feldman, Lawrence P., 42
Fernandez-Fanjul, Eufrasio, 178
Ferraro, Gary P., 27, 42, 45, 81–2, 381, 382, 394, 397
Finn, Adam, 350
Firat, A. Fuat, 125, 135–6, 136
Firoz, Nadeem M., 322
Fisher, Glen, 374, 394, 503, 514, 515, 540, 541
Flaherty, Theresa B., 356
Florenthal, Bella, 232
Ford, David, 348, 463, 464
Foreign Agricultural Service, 366
Forrester Research, 329
Forsythe, Sandra, 93, 95
Foster, Dean Allen, 494
Foster, G. M., 502
Fournier, Susan, 458
Fournis, Y., 165
Fox, Richard J., 123, 355
Foxman, Ellen R., 357, 359
Francis, June, 300, 414, 504, 509
Franke, George R., 415
Frazer Winsted, Kathryn, 257
Fredenberger, Bill, 106
Freedman, Michael, 275
Freivalds, John, 463

Frese-Weghöft, Gisela, 53
Freud, Sigmund, 60, 74
Friederes, Geroen, 139, 143
Friedland, Roger, 268
Frijda, N., 185, 203
Fritzsche, D. H., 481
Froot, Kenneth, 316
Fu, Marilyn Y., 417
Fuentes, Carlos, 509
Fukuyama, Francis, 496, 522
Fullgrabe, L., 353
Fuma Shapiro, Simona, 273, 277
Furrer, Olivier, 257

Gabrielsson, Mika, 350
Gaedeke, Ralph, 139, 306
Gaeth, Gary J., 135, 306, 322
Gahlot, Deepa, 244
Gallant, Katheryn, 479
Galtung, Frederick, 397, 475, 477
Galtung, Johan, 70, 549
Gambiez, Chantal, 357
Ganesh, Gopala, 291
Ganley, Elaine, 268
Gannet News Service, 445
Gannon, Martin J., 396
Gans, Herbert, 100–1
Garncarz, Joseph, 273, 274, 275
Garner-Earl, Bettina, 287
Garolera, Jordi, 132
Garreau, J., 235
Garten, Jeffrey E., 474
Gauthey, Franck, 389, 390, 391
Gaydos, Steven, 276
Geertz, Clifford, 78, 129, 183
Gehrt, Kenneth C., 232
Gelb, Betsy D., 423, 425
Gentleman, Amelia, 147
Gentry, James W., 431
George, Jennifer M., 514, 517
Gephart, Werner, 130
Ger, Güliz, 101, 105, 106, 120, 123, 133, 134, 135, 220,
    225, 289
German, Peter M., 484
Ghauri, Pervez N., 169, 415, 506
Gilbert, Alorie, 153
Gillan, Tamara, 64
Gillespie, Kate, 304, 475, 481
Gilligan, Gregory J., 153
Gilly, Mary C., 257, 420
Gilmore, James H., 228
Giordan, Alain Eric, 253, 299

Glazer, Herbert, 343
Glenn, E., 68
Glowacka, Aleksandra E., 289
Godiwalla, Yezdi M., 201
Gold, Sarah, 517
Goldman, Alan, 494, 502
Goldman, Arieh, 348
Gonzalez, Jorge A., 514, 517
Goodenough, Ward H., 5, 10, 28
Goodyear, Mary, 193, 195, 196
Gopalakrishna, Pradeep, 425
Gordon, Geoffrey L., 419
Gorn, Gerald J., xv
Gough, Neil, 327
Graby, Françoise, 139, 306
Graham, John L., 201, 257, 301, 467, 470, 482, 494, 498,
   499, 505, 506, 507, 508, 510, 512, 514, 516, 519, 521,
   535, 537, 538, 540, 541
Graham, Robert J., 28
Grainger, Richard, 389
Granzin, Kent L., 135
Graves, Roger, 355
Green, Paul E., 183, 204, 214
Green, Robert T., 87, 106, 183, 232, 328, 416
Gregerson, Hal B., 145
Gregory, Gary D., 423, 425
Greif, Avner, 523
Griffin, Mitch, 166, 170, 351
Griffith, David A., 348, 459
Griggs, Lewis, 264, 381
Grønhaug, Kjell, 201
Grover, Ron, 243
Groves, Don, 276
Grubbs Hoy, Mariea, 159
Grüber, Ursula, 417
Gruère, Jean-Pierre, 390, 540
Grunert, Klaus G., 92, 185
Grunert, Suzanne C., 185
Grunewald, Orlen, 321, 322
Gu, Quingliang, 93, 95
Guardian, 145
Gudykunst, William B., 105
Guetzkow, H., 506
Guider, Elizabeth, 272
Gupta, Susan Forquer, 87, 93
Gurevitch, A. J., 24
Gürhan-Canli, Zeynep, 292
Guyotat, Régis, 148

Ha, Louise, 428, 429
Habib, Mohsin, 480
Halborg, Al, 466

Haley, Eric, 159
Hall, Edward T., 22, 24, 25, 26, 28, 30, 34, 258, 260, 375,
   376, 380, 396, 397, 423, 468, 469, 508, 510, 513, 514,
   515, 519, 520
Hall, Mildred Peirce, 423
Hall, Patrick A.V., 403
Halliburton, Chris, 414, 418
Hampden-Turner, C., 64
Hampton, G., 139, 227, 306
Hamra, Wayne, 480
Han, C. Min, 294
Han, Jin K., 128, 135, 291, 292, 294, 299, 423
Hanna, Nessim, 419, 470
Hannerz, Ulf, 12
Hanson, David P., 467
Hanson, John H., 105
Hao, J., 197
Hardy, Tom, 106, 113
Harich, Katrin, 425
Harnett, Donald L., 504, 507, 508, 522
Harris, Philip R., 27, 381, 382, 507
Harris, Richard Jackson, 287
Harris, Shane, 444, 446
Harvey, Michael G., 432
Harzing, Anne-Wil, 195
Hatch, Denny, 152
Häubl, Gerald, 139, 143
Haugland, Sven, 503, 521
Hawking, Stephen W., 9
Hawrysh, Bryan Mark, 502, 509, 515, 517, 536
Hayashi, Shuji, 28, 29
Hayek, F. A., 156
He, Xiahong, 124, 232
Hedges, Pamela, 389
Heeler, Roger, 424
Hemingway, Ernest, 376
Hempel, Paul S., 467
Hensel, Paul J., 413
Heppner, Janet, 392
Herberger, Roy A. Jr, 508, 510, 537
Herbig, Paul A., 494
Herche, Joel, 293
Hernandez, S. L., 185, 193, 194, 196
Heslop, Louise A., 95, 134, 139, 288
Hester, Susan B., 294
Heuberger, Andres, 392
Hewett, Kelly, 231, 265
Heyman, S., 105
Hightower, Roscoe, 249, 250
Hilger, Marye Tharp, 312–5
Hill, Jim, 148
Hill, John S., 227, 231, 424, 433, 467, 470, 471, 483

Hills, Stephen M., 164
Hirschmann, Elisabeth C., 86, 199
Ho, Suk-Ching, 157, 436, 460
Hodges, Mark, 355
Hofstede, Geert, 12, 22–23, 27–28, 56–64, 73, 77, 121,
    123, 163, 171, 192, 204, 232, 348, 352, 415, 425, 468,
    469, 470, 503, 504, 539
Hofstee, Natascha, 420
Holden, Nigel, 384
Holland, Jonna, 431
Hollensen, Svend, 225
Holzmüller, Hartmut H., 201, 231
Homer, Pamela, 106
Honeycutt Jr, Earl D., 423
Hong, F. C., 300
Hooley, Graham J., 306
Hoon, Ang Swee, 294
Hoon-Halbauer, Sing Keow, 514
Hooper, John, 272
Hoover, Robert J., 416
Hopkins, Nic, 147
Hornik, Jacob, 42, 424
Houston, Michael J., 137
Howard, David, 386
Howard, J., 95
Howes, David, 135, 136
Hoyer, Wayne D., 418, 419
Hsee, Christopher, 185, 504
Hsieh, Ming H., 302
Hsieh, Y. W., 90
Hsu, F. L. K., 90
Hu, Michael Y., 459
Huang, Jen-Hung, 419
Huang, Yue Yuan, 419
Hugstad, Paul S., 294
Hui, Ang Kah, 291
Hui, Michael K., 459
Hulnick, Gail, 458
Hult, G. Thomas M., 12, 195, 221, 222, 249, 250
Hundley, Tom, 178
Hung, Kineta, 424
Huszagh, Sandra M., 122
Hutchings, Kate, 464
Huth, Sabine, 418
Hyman, Michael R., 423

Ibison, David, 329
Inagaki, Yoshihiko, 346
Inkeles, Alex, 13, 17
International Federation of Red Cross and Red Crescent
    Societies, 404
Ishibashi, Asako, 152
Ishida, Hideto, 344, 346

Ishihara, Shintaro, 39
Ivenko, Leonid I., 541

Jackson Jr., Donald W., 204
Jackson, Barbara B., 496
Jacobs, Laurence, 424
Jacobs, Lawrence W., 251, 265, 415
Jacoby, Jacob R., 24, 42, 320
Jaffé, Eugene D., 288, 290, 291, 294
Jahoda, G., 185, 203
Jain, Subhash C., 135
Jamal, Ahmad, 30, 34
James, Karen E., 413
James, William L., 231, 424
Januszewska, Renata, 235
Jarvis, Susan, 304
Jatania, Lynn, 244
Javalgi, Rajshekhar G., 255, 413, 414, 416, 420, 421,
    423, 425
Jefferey, Simon, 178
Jeon, Jung Ok, 413
Jeong, Insik, 248
Jha, Subhash K., 244
Joachimsthaler, Erich, 303
Jodelet, Denise, 16, 397
Johanson, J., 224
Johansson, Johny K., 159, 161, 198, 199, 204, 291, 305,
    306, 322, 326, 342, 343, 463
Johar, J., 102, 235
John, J., 235
Johnson, Denise, 321, 322, 412
Johnson, J. L., 204
Johnson, James P., 235, 291, 292, 356
Johnson, Lester W., 354
Johnson-Bailey, Juanita, 503
Johnstone, Harvey, 415
Jolibert, Alain, 139, 288, 293, 465, 505, 507, 508, 538
Jones, Gareth R., 514, 517
Jones, Marylin, 232
Jordan Times, 444
Jordt, Ingrid, 106, 126, 129
Joy, Annamma, 99
Jun-Chen, Hu, 516, 517
Ju-Pak, Kuen-Hee, 433

Kacen, Jacqueline J., 91
Kadima, K., 47
Kagame, Alexis, 47
Kahle, L. R., 106, 235, 419
Kale, Sudhir H., 232, 233, 352, 353, 425
Kalliath, Thomas J., 26
Kamakura, Wagner A., 232, 289
Kamamoto, Mitsuko, 259

Kamins, Michael A., 290, 301
Kang, Jikyeong, 101
Kang, Kyeong Soon, 403
Kanso, Ali, 433
Kanti, K., 221
Kapferer, Jean-Noel, 301, 303
Kapur, Shekhar, 274
Karakaya, Yunus, 516
Karande, Kiran, 420
Karg, Pamela J., 366
Karimalis, Grigorios, 145
Kariuki, John, 274
Karns, David, 290
Kashani, Kamran, 23, 357, 409, 472
Kasim, Sharifah, 356
Kassaye, W. Wossen, 428
Katsikeas, Constantine S., 353
Katz, Helen, 425
Kaufman, Carol Felker, 26, 28
Kaushal, Raj, 242
Kauth, Jr, Robert K., 145
Kaynak, Erdener, 98, 293, 415
Kearney, A. T., 134, 174
Kee, Youngwha, 503
Keegan, Warren J., 233, 324, 518
Keillor, Bruce D., 12, 195, 249, 250
Keller K. L., 195, 285
Kelley, Harold H., 498
Kemmelmeier, Markus, 105
Kennedy, Miranda, 267
Keown, Charles F., 265, 327, 415
Kerin, Roger A., 303
Kersten, Gregory E., 516, 523
Ketchen Jr, David J., 221, 222
Khanna, Sri Ram, 290
Khera, Inder, 290
Khuri, Fuad I., 318
Kibarian, Thomas M., 322
Kieser, A., 5
Kim, C. Y., 290
Kim, Chankon, 106
Kim, Daniel H., 76
Kim, Dong Han, 123
Kim, Donghoon, 377
Kim, G., 293
Kim, Jai-Ok, 93, 95
Kim, K., 105
Kim, Keysuk, 352
Kim, Michael, 316
Kim, M. S., 105
Kim, U., 100
Kim, Youn-Kyung, 101
Kirpalani, V. H. Manek, 350

Kish, Paulette, 303
Kishii, T., 414
Kitayama, Shinobu, 51, 90
Klein, Jill Gabrielle, 135, 289
Klein, Lisa R., 355
Klein, Naomi, 294–5, 443
Kluckhohn, Clyde, 4
Kluckhohn, Florence R., 5, 16, 20, 21, 22, 27, 75, 96
Knobel, Michele, 383
Koc, Erdogan, 233
Koh, Anthony C., 202
Kondo, Mari, 516, 517
Kopytoff, Igor, 120, 128, 129
Koranteng, Julia, 147, 148, 149
Kosaka, Hiroshi, 67, 95, 160
Koslow, Scott, 378
Kostecki, Michel Maciej, 255
Köszegi, Sabine, 516
Kotabe, Masaaki, 469, 472
Kotler, Philip, 86, 160, 294
Koudelova, Radka, 425
Kozan, M. Kamil, 517
Kraft, Frederick B., 290, 293
Kragh, Simon Ulrik, 103, 136, 137
Kreutzer, R. T., 233
Krieger, Nathalie, 306
Kripalani, Manjeet, 243
Krishna, Kishore, 304
Krishnakumar, Parameswar, 305
Kristensen, Kai, 92, 185
Kroeber, Alfred L., 4
Kroeber-Riel, Werner, 417, 424
Kropp, Fredric, 353, 419
Kujawa, D., 292
Kumar, Rajesh, 8, 66, 516, 517
Kumar, V., 202, 235
Kunita, Motoko, 414
Kuribayashi, S., 342, 344,
Kushner, Kenneth, 45–6, 82
Kushner, J. M., 46, 105, 195
Kwak, Hyokjin, 355
Kwak, R. S., 521
Kung-Il, Ghymn, 265, 415

La Porta, Rafael, 522
Lackman, Conway L., 467
Lafferty, Barbara A., 195
Lagaan, 243
Lagerlöf, Selma, 21, 42
Lai, Mengkuan, 89
Lam, Danny K. K., 343, 346, 347

Lam, Janet P. Y., 300
Lamb, Charles W. Jr, 38, 227, 289, 305
Lambin, Jean-Jacques, 301
Lampert, Shlomo I., 288, 290
Lanasa, John M., 467
Lane, Henry W., 353
Lane, Paul M., 26, 28
Lange, André, 273
Langeard, Eric, 183
Lankshear, Colin, 383
Laroche, Michel, 106, 235, 418
Larrick, Richard, 516, 517
Larsen, Trina, 353
Lascu, Dana-Nicoleta, 293
Latour, Michael S., 463
Lau, K. F., 419
Laughlin, Kirk, 106, 115
Laurent, André, 75, 76, 77, 136
Laurent, Clint R., 89, 105
Lazarde, Michelle M., 306
Lazer, William, 67, 95, 160
Le Clézio, J. M. G., 17
Leardi, M., 357, 360
Leclerc, France, 285, 288
Lee Manzer, L., 235
Lee, Angela, Y., 91
Lee, Byoung-Woo, 294
Lee, Chol, 87, 418, 419
Lee, Dongdae, 291, 425
Lee, Eun-Ju, 101
Lee, George, 528, 532–3
Lee, James A., 388, 509
Lee, Jangho, 76
Lee, Julie Anne, 87, 89, 91, 128
Lee, K. H., 87, 89, 481
Lee, Khai S., 327, 328, 329
Lee, Ming-Yeh, 503
Lee, Ruby, 93
Lee, Wei-Na, 425
Leeflang, Peter S. H., 121, 139, 166
Lefebvre, Victorina D., 541
Lehmann, Donald R., 258
Lehman-Wilzig, Sam, 388
Lelièvre, Hélène, 358
Lemmink, Jos, 257
Lemak, David J., 106
Lenartowicz, Tomasz, 12, 235
Leonard, Mark, 444
Leonidou, Leonidas C., 228, 248, 250
Lessem, Ronnie, 164
Leung, Kenneth, 182, 183
Leung, Kwok, 55, 494, 503, 508, 509, 516, 517
Leung, T., 105

Levine, Robert A., 389
Levine, Robert V., 384
Levinson, Daniel J., 13, 17
Levitt, Theodore, 86, 120, 124, 125, 137, 254
Levy-Bruhl, Lucien, 15
Lewis, Steven A., 479, 505
Li, Ji, 219
Li, Jianfeng, 516, 517
Li, S., 353
Li, Tiger, 123, 230
Lian, Brad, xviii
Liang, Kong, 424
Lieberthal, K., 123
Liefeld, John P., 95
Light, C. David, 428
Lilien, Gary, 322
Lillis, Charles M., 139
Lim, Chae Un, 469, 472
Lim, Guan H., 327, 328, 329
Lin, Carolyn A., 414, 415, 416
Lincke, Andreas, 516
Ling, Chew Pei, 291, 292
Ling, Lee Boon, 419
Linton, Ralph, 5, 13, 73
List, Friedrich, 120
Littler, Dale, 306
Littré, Emile, 4
Littrell, Mary A., 250
Lituin, Deborah R., xviii
Liu, Ben Shaw-Ching, 257
Liu, Raymond, 97, 106
Lloyd, John, 158
Loeffler, Michael, 285
Lohnes, Colleen, 139, 293
Longworth, John W., 262
Lopez-de-Silanes, Florencio, 522
Louis, Ernst A., 295
Louviere, Jordan J., 350
Lowe, Andy, 204
Lu, Caixia, 388
Lui, Tan Jee, 201, 202
Luk, Sherriff T. K., 185, 186, 190, 193, 353
Lumpkin, J. R., 293
Lumwanu, F., 47
Luna, David, 87, 93, 378, 418
Lundquist, Jay D., 26
Lundstrom, Martin, 106
Lundstrom, William J., 106
Luo, Jin-Lian, 516, 517
Luo, Yadong, 464, 535
Luostarinen, Reijo, 350
Luqmani, Mushtaq, 422
Lwin, May, 387

Lysonski, Steven, 64, 182, 302, 412, 427
Lytle, Anne E., 517

Maalouf, Amine, 36–37
MacFarquhar, Niel, 268
Machleit, K. A., 291, 293
MacLean Johns, Cort, 254, 347
MacLeod, Marcia, 378
Macneil, Ian R., 496
Macrae, Chris, 303
Madden, Normandy, 173
Madden, Thomas J., 265
Madsen, T. K., 232
Maheswaran, Durairaj, 292, 414
Majidi, Nassim, 178
Malcolm, Derek, 244
Malhotra, Naresh K., 87, 222, 232, 248, 413, 416,
    420, 421
Malinowski, Bronislaw, 6–7
Malliaris, P., 139
Manrai, Ajay K., 293
Manrai, Lalita A., 293
Marcel, Claude, 306
Marchetti, Renato, 187, 188
Margonelli, Lisa, 151, 152, 153
Mariet, François, 428, 431
Marks, Lawrence J., 477
Markus, Hazel Rose, 51, 90
Marn, Mike, 330
Maroto, Jésus, 401
Marques, Gabriel, Garcia, 52
Martenson, Rita, 414, 415, 424, 427
Martin, Ingrid M., 305
Martin, Gregg D., 26
Martinez-Zarzoso, I., 38
Maruyama, Magoroh, 196, 197–8
Mascarenhas, O. A. D., 292
Maslow, Abraham H., 88
Masten, Cheskin, 128
Mather, Anne, 245–6
Mathiot, Cedric, 267
Mathur, Anil, 172
Mathur, Arti, 243
Matsumoto, M., 502
Matsumoto, Y., 105
Matthyssens, Paul, 227
Mattsson, Jan, 257, 463
Mauviel, Maurice, 39, 40, 42
Mavondo, Felix T., 464
Maxwell, Sarah, 320
Mayer, C. S., 187
Mayo, Michel A., 477
Mazur, Jolanta, 353

McCall, J. B., 499
McCarthy, E. Jerome, 457
McCartney, Laton, 501, 502
McClure, Peter, 97
McCornell, J. D., 261
McCort, J. Daniel, 87
McCracken, Grant, 102, 126, 129
McCullough, Lynette S., 418
McCullough, Wayne R., 435
McFarland, Jeff, 106, 113
McGowan Kennedy, Karen, 322
McGowan, Karen M., 322
McGrory, Daniel, 178
McIntyre, Roger P., 352, 353
McKersie, Robert B., 505
McLeod, Douglas M., 414
McNaughton, Rod B., 348
McNulty, Brian, 266
McQuirk, Jim, 415
Mead, Margaret, 11, 14, 53, 537
Mehta, Rajiv, 353
Meindl, James R., 55
Meissner, Hans Günther, 505, 507, 508, 538
Melewar, T. C., 292, 296
Mendenhall, Mark, 88
Mendoza, Teresa M., 516, 517
Meng, Leong Siew, 294
Merriam, Sharan B., 503
Merrilees, Bill, 353
Merton, Robert, 26–27
Miao, Jiawen, 173
Michaels, R. E., 505
Michell, Paul, 421
Michon, Christian, 161
Mick, David Glen, 106, 458
Milhomme, Albert J., 147
Miller, Dale, 353
Miller, Fred, 351, 422
Miller, J. A., 97
Miller, Nancy J., 250
Minde, T., 100
Miniard, Paul W., 95
Mintu, Alma T., 494, 506
Mishima, Yukio, 379
Mitchell, V. W., 95
Modianos, Doan, 166, 351
Modood, Tariq, 268
Mok, D., 100
Money, R. Bruce, 257, 467, 470, 521
Montesquieu, Charles de, 13–14, 38, 66
Montgomery, David B., 342, 344, 347
Moon, Byeong Joon, 135
Moon, Sook Jae, 93, 95

Moore, Don A., 494, 498, 499, 506, 509, 514, 516, 521, 523
Moore, Elizabeth S., 89, 192
Moore, Marguerite, 322
Moran, Robert T., 27, 381, 382, 507
Moran, Sarah, 382
Morand, David A., 383
Morel, Pierre, 390, 540
Morello, G., 139
Morganosky, Michelle A., 306
Morris, Jon D., 191
Morris, Marlene D., 289
Morris, Michael, 102, 235, 516, 517
Morsbach, Helmut, 382
Moscovici, Serge, 15
Moscow Times, 150
Mosterd, Igor, 511
Mourier, Pascal, 430
Mowen, John C., 24
Mueller, Barbara, 413, 417, 421
Mueller, Rene, 292, 433
Muhamad, Mazanah, 503
Mühlbacher, Hans, 354
Mühlfeld, Katrin, 433
Mullen, Michael R., 190
Mullen, Thomas, 504, 537, 541
Muller, 235
Mummalaneni, Venkatapparao, 417, 420
Munch, James M., 423, 425
Murata, Shoji, 67, 95, 160
Murphy, Dan, 267
Murray, Georgina, 464
Murray, Noel M., 436
Murray, Sandra B., 436
Muslim Consumer Group, 267
Mussey, Dagmar, 179–80
Myers, Hayley, 348
Myers, Matthew B., 190, 204, 327
Myrdal, Gunnar, 171
Mytton, Graham, 183, 193, 195

Nagashima, Akira, 139, 290, 305
Nagpal, Anish, 235
Naidu, G. M., 221
Nakane, Chie, 345
Naor, Jacob, 168
Napier, Nancy K., 172
Napoléon-Biguma, Constantin, 48
Napoli, Julie, 300
Narayana, Chem L., 139
Narayandas, Das, 325
Naresh, K., 222
National Honey Board, 366, 367
Naumann, Earl, 204

Ndao, Cheikh Alioune, 479
Nebenzahl, Israel D., 288, 290, 291, 294
Neelankavil, James P., 172, 417, 420, 423
Nelson, Richard Alan, 433
Nes, Erik, 288
Netemeyer, Richard G., 182, 183
Neubauer, Fred, 164
Newman, David, 173
Newmann-Baudais, Susan, 273, 274
News Hour Media Unit, 444
Ng, Sharon, 184
Nicholls, J. A. F., 123
Nielsen, 402
Nijssen, Edwin J., 304
Nishida, T., 105
Nishina, Sadafumi, 287
Nonaka, Ikujiro, 160, 198, 199, 204, 306, 326, 343
Norenzayan, Ara, 384
Noronha, Sunil J., 516, 523
Novak, Thomas P. 232
Nowakowski, Marcin, 255
Nti, Kofi O., 517
Ntseane, Gabo, 503
Nueno, Jose Luis, 349

O'Brien, Tim, 149
O'Connor, Gina Colarelli, 189
O'Donnell, Sharon, 230, 248
O'Flynn, Kevin, 177
O'Grady, Shawna, 353
Oberg, Kalvero, 391
Odekerken-Schroder, Gaby, 420
Ofir, Chezy, 258
Ogram, Ernest W., 476
Oh, Chango, 352
Oh, Sejo, 463, 496
Oh, T. K., 536
Ohler, Jason, 38
Ohmae, Kenichi, 347, 497, 498
Ohye, Kazuko, 56
Okumura, Tetsushi, 494, 498, 506, 507, 509, 514, 515, 521
Oldfield, Brenda M., 251, 252, 264
Oliver, Elizabeth Goad, 62
Oliver, Lauren, 298
Ollivier, Alain, 134, 161, 338–9, 519
Olsen, Barbara, 105
Olsen, Svein Ottar, 202
Olson, Jerry C., 320
Oneal, John R., xviii
Onkvisit, Sak, 296, 423
Onzo, Naoto, 204, 301
Ooi, Can-Seng, 172

Orris, Michelle, 445, 446
Ortiz-Buonafina, Marta, 463
Orwell, George, 515
Ostergaard, Per, 101
Oswald, Laura R. 102
Ottosen, Rune, 78
Owens, Deborah, 195
Owens, Margaret, 327, 329
Oxenfeldt, A. R., 321
Oyserman, Daphna, 105
Ozsomer, Aysegul, 230, 231

Page Jr, Thomas J., 190, 204
Pahud de Mortanges, Charles, 254, 347
Painter, John J., 135
Palia, Aspy P., 327
Palmer, David K., 26
Pan, Yigang, 299, 300, 301, 377
Papadopoulos, Nicolas G., 134, 139, 288
Parameswaran, Ravi, 189
Park, Heung Soo, 377
Park, Seong-Yeon, 99
Parker, Philip M., 123, 126, 174, 322
Parvatiyar, Atul, 458
Passariello, Christina, 178
Pastore, Michael, 401
Pauwels, Pieter, 227
Paz, Octavio 540
Péan, Pierre, 475, 478
Pearson, Bryan, 243, 244
Pearson, Emil, 47–8
Pechmann, Cornelia, 426
Pecotich, Anthony, 300
Pedersen, Paul B., 19–20, 48–9, 81
Peebles, Dean M., 303, 433, 434, 435
Pells, Richard, 273
Penaloza, Lisa, 103
Penbera, Joseph J., 329
Peracchio, Laura A., 378, 418
Perdue, B. C., 505
Perlez, Jane, 444
Perlmutter, Howard, 222
Perrin, Michel, 306
Peterson, Blyth, 128
Peterson, Mark F., 55, 232, 423
Peterson, Robert A., 288
Petit, Karl, 42
Pettijohn, Charles, 195
Phillips, Leigh, 106, 113
Phillips, W. E., 416
Philpot, J. W., 204
Phua Cheay Thengh, Eleanor, 419
Picard, Jacques, 230

Pichene, B., 95
Pidluska, 475
Piercy, Nigel F., 353
Pike, K., 182
Pimblett, Carole, 229
Pine, B. Joseph II, 228
Pinsdorf, Marion K., 473
Pirog, Stephen F., 343, 346, 347
Pitt, Leyland F., 300
Pittula, Madan M., 507, 508, 509
Plasser, Fritz, 125
Pohl, Manfred, 171
Polonsky, Michael Jay., 412
Polsa, Pia, 353
Poortinga, Ype H., 15, 17, 38, 42, 183, 190, 203
Pornpitakpan, Chantikha, 414, 507, 521
Porter, Michael E., 218, 226, 330
Potter, Richard E., 516
Prahalad, C. K., 123
Pras, B., 190, 204
Prasad, V. Kanti, 221
Prendergast, Gerard, 419
Pruitt, Dean G., 505, 506
Prus, Robert C., 319
Pruyn, Ad, 165, 166
Public Broadcasting Service, 445
Pulley, Brett, 145, 146, 147
Punnett, Betty Jane, 88, 504, 537, 541
Pye, Lucian W., 509, 510, 512, 516, 517, 519, 534, 535

Qian, Gongming, 219
Qibla, Cola, 178
Queau, Philippe, 356
Quelch, John, 325, 355
Quester, Pascale, 426
Quichao, Liang, 35
Quraeshi, Zahir, 422

Radebaugh, Lee H., 476
Rajan, Mahesh N., 541
Ralston, David A., 172, 235
Ramachander, S., 289
Ramaprasad, Jyotika, 416
Ramaswamy, Venkatram, 289
Ramuz, Charles Ferdinand, 17
Rao, Akshay R., 184
Rao, Asha, 506
Rao, C. P., 292
Rao, S. R., 414
Ratz, David G., 432
Raveed, S., 415
Ravendran, Anuja, 356
Rawls, John, 482

Rawwas, Mohammed Y. A., 354, 478
Raymore, Leslie, 64
Redding, S. G., 89, 105, 470
Reed, Mary Lynn, 235
Reierson, Curtis, 139, 305
Reilly, Michael D., 102
Reinhard, K., 416
Reischauer, Edwin O., 35, 42
Renforth, William, 415, 421
Resnik, Alan J., 415
Reynolds, Nina L., 97, 194
Ribeiro, Gustavo Lins, 355
Ricardo, David, 119, 120
Rice, Marshall D., 424
Richins, M., 89, 97
Ricks, David A., 88
Riding, Alan, 273, 274, 275
Ridnour, Rick E., 419
Ries, Al, 178
Riesz, Peter C., 321
Rietbroek, Jan-Willem, 254, 347
Rim, Ik-Tae, 293
Rindfleisch, Aric, 197
Riskey, Dwight R., 303
Ritzer, George, 124, 133, 138
Ro, Kong-Kyun, 294
Robertson, Christopher J., 55, 257
Robertson, Kim R., 201, 296
Robinson, Chris, 93, 105
Robinson, Francis, 268
Robles, Fernando, 353
Rodgers, Waymond, 494, 506
Rodrigo, Elaine, 464
Rodrik, Dani, 133
Roeber, Carter A., 318
Roehl, Thomas W., 76
Rogers, E. M., 254
Rogoff, Kenneth, 316
Ronkainen, Illka A., 121, 296, 348, 349, 357, 423, 473
Rose, Gregory M., 89, 104, 192, 232, 353, 419
Rose, Steve, 241
Rosen, Barry-Nathan, 295
Rosenberg, Larry J., 347
Rosenbloom, Bert, 353
Rosenfield, James R., 354
Rosenshine, Allen, 443
Rosenthal, Walter, 347, 432
Roslow, Sychey, 123
Ross, Caroline, 466
Rotella, Mark, 517
Roth, Kendall, 12, 229, 248
Roth, Martin S., 265
Rotter, J. B., 63

Rowley, Jennifer, 258
Roy, Abhik, 185, 186, 189, 190, 193, 320
Royo, Marcelo, 415
Rubicam, Inc., 244
Rubin, J. Z., 494, 506
Rudich, Joe, 388
Rugman, Alan, 219
Russel, Miller R., 157
Rutte, Christel G., 511
Ryans Jr, John K., 411, 459, 477
Ryans, John K., 432, 434, 435

Saad, Gad, 106
Saegaert, Joel, 416
Saghafi, Massoud M., 290
Sahagun, Bernardino de, 17
Saito Duerr, Mitsuko, 337, 405–6
Sakade, Florence, 495
Sakai, John T., 364–5
Sakano, Tomoaki, 204, 301
Salk, Jane E., 521, 522, 523
Salles, Robert, 306
Saloner, Garth, 38
Salwen, Michael B., 415, 416
Samiee, Saeed, 139, 229, 248, 288, 291, 292
Samli, A. Coskun, 251
Saner, Raymond, 494
Sanford, M. T., 368
Sano, Yoshihiro, 499, 510, 512, 519
Sapir, Edward, 182, 383, 392, 397
Saporito, Bill, 226, 230
Sarathy, Ravi, 429, 430
Saskin, Rose, 355
Satloff, Robert, 443
Saunders, John A., 139, 296
Savishinsky, Joel, 36
Sawyer, J., 506
Scanzoni, J., 497
Schaefer, Anja, 292
Schein, Edgar H., 75
Scheucher, Christian, 125
Schiffman, Leon, 415
Schindler, Robert M., 322
Schlechter, Michael G., 120
Schlegelmilch, Bodo B., 249
Schlieper, Katrin, 306
Schmidt, Klaus D., 539
Schmidt, Richard W., 415
Schmidt, Stuart M., 507
Schmitt, Bernd H., 91, 285, 288, 299, 300, 301
Schneider, Peter A., 343, 346, 346
Schneider-Lenné, E., 393
Schooler, Robert D., 305

Schoorman, F. David, 26
Schroeder, Michael, 415
Schuh, Arnold, 229, 230, 254
Schultz, Don E., 160
Schultz, Clifford J., 300
Schurr, Paul H., 463, 496
Schuster, Camille P., 494
Schwartz, Shalom H., 12, 64
Schwarz Gehrke, Theodore, 510, 540
Schweiger, Günther, 139, 143
Schweitzer, John C., 424
Schwiercz, Paul M., 468
Sechrest, L., 186
Segall, Marshall H., 15, 17, 38, 42
Seiminski, Gregory C., 445
Sentell, G. D., 204
Sessions, David N., 417, 420
Sethi, S. Prakash, 125
Sethuraman, S., 173
Severin, Valerie, 350
Shadid, Anthony, 268
Shah, Deepa, 244
Shalofsky, Ivor, 302
Shamdasani, Prem, 378
Shapiro, Debra L., 517, 521
Sharif, Mohammed, 134
Sharma, Arun, 458
Sharma, Subash, 135, 292, 293
Shavitt, Sharon, 128, 423
Shaw, John J., 296, 432
Shehzad, Waseem, 267
Shenkar, Oded, 38, 227
Sherry, John F., 37, 134, 139, 417
Sheth, Jagdish N., 95, 122, 125, 219, 221, 458
Shih, Chuan-Fong, 426
Shim, Soyeon, 232
Shimaguchi, Mitsuaki, 342, 343, 344, 345, 347
Shimp, Terence A., 135, 292, 293, 295
Shin, J., 135, 292, 293, 295
Shipley, David, 306
Shleifer, Andrei, 522
Shoemaker, Robert, 197
Shoham, Aviv, 104, 232, 248, 250, 353
Sikora, Ed, 329
Silk, A. J., 189
Simintiras, Antonis C., 97, 194, 379
Simmonds, Kenneth, 349
Simon, Paul, 393
Sin, Leo Y. M., 93
Sin, Yat-ming, 436
Sinatra, Alexandro, 167
Singelis, T. M., 105
Singh, Jagdip, 190

Sissmann, P., 234, 235
Siu, Wai-Sum, 419
Sjolander, Richard, 322
Skelly, 101
Slack, Frances, 258
Slatter, Stuart St P., 460
Slavin, Terry, 154
Smith, Adam, 50, 482
Smith, Charles G., 164
Smith, David E., 122
Smith, Kenwin, 397
Smith, N., 289
Smith, Peter B., 55
Smith, Tasman, 328
Snyder, Leslie B., 425
Soehl, Robin, 230
Solberg, Carl Arthur, 423
Solgaard, Hans Stubbe, 122
Solomon, Michael R., 88, 101, 102, 111, 261, 312
Solomon, Norman, 444, 445
Somasundaram, T. N., 428
Sondergaard, Michael, 57
Song, Michael X., 459
Sood, James H., 123, 190
Sorokin, Piritim, 26–27
Souchon, Anne L., 201
Souiden, Nizar, 233
Soutar, Geoffrey N., 89, 389
Spar, Deborah L., 122
Sparkman Jr, Richard M., 415
Spears, Nancy, 24
Spiegelman, Paul, 458
Springborg, Robert, 266
Spotts, Harlan E., 415, 418
Sprick, Sara J., 287
Sproles, George B., 321
Sriram, Ven, 425
Srivastava, Tanuja, 470
St Petersburg Times, 150
Stalk, George Jr, 301, 331
Stanton, J. L., 185, 193, 194, 196
Steele, Murray, 136
Steenkamp, Jan-Benedict E. M., 12, 64, 93, 133, 183, 190, 197, 230, 232, 233, 254, 288, 289, 293, 302, 303, 431
Steidelmeier, P., 479
Stern, Bruce L., 415
Stern, Louis W., 505, 516
Sternquist, Brenda J., 322
Sternstein, Aliya, 243
Stevenson, Thomas H., 325
Stewart, Sally, 436
Still, Richard R., 227, 467, 470, 471
Stobaugh, Robert B., 228

Stöllnberger, Barbara, 231
Stottinger, Barbara, 325
Strandskov, Jesper, 528
Straughan, Robert, 93, 351
Straus, Karen, 102
Stripp, William, 538, 540
Strodtbeck, Frederick L., 5, 16, 21, 22, 27, 75, 96
Strube, Michal J., 26
Strutton, David, 354
Su, Chenting, 95
Sudharshan, D., 233, 257
Sugimoto, Naomi, 386
Suls, J., 418
Sumner, G. A., 388
Sunoo, D. H., 305
Surget, Véronique, 358
Sussman, Lyle, 397
Swanson, Lauren A., 424, 436
Swarz, Gordon, 325
Sweeney, Tim, 204
Swift, Jonathan B., 38, 227
Swinder, Janda, 292
Sylvester, Rachel, 443
Szpakowicz, S., 523
Szybillo, George J., 24, 42

Tai, Susan H. C., 233, 433
Taja, Waheed, 266
Takashi, S., 197
Tam, Jackie L. M., 233
Tam, Tammy, 101
Tamate, Mariko, 414, 419
Tambyah, Siok-Kuan, 420
Tan, Soo J., 327, 328, 329
Tan, Thomas Tsu Wee, 201, 202, 419
Tankersley, Clint B., 305, 306
Tanner, John F., 468, 470, 471
Tanouchi, Koichi, 103, 104
Tansey, Richard, 423
Tansuhaj, Patriya S., 106, 235, 357, 359, 360
Tarn, David D. C., 89
Tavassoli, Nader T., 299
Taylor, Charles R., 190, 204
Taylor, Humphrey, 194
Taylor, Ronald E., 159, 418
Teas, R. Kenneth, 123
Teinowitz, Ira, 443, 446
Telesio, Piero, 228
Tellis, Gerard J., 321, 322
Tenbrunsel, Ann E., 494, 498, 509, 514
Ter Hofstede, Frenkel, 93, 232, 233
Terpstra, Vern, 291
Thang, Nguyen Van, 172

Thengh, Eleanor Phua Cheay, 419
Theodosiou, Marios, 228, 248, 250
Theodoulou, Michael, 178
Thoenig, Jean-Claude, 301
Thomas, Edward G., 414
Thomas, M., 221
Thompson, Courtenay, 476
Thorelli, Hans B., 289, 291, 306, 463
Thorpe, Jim, 424
Thorpe, Richard, 204
Tian, Robert G., 355, 356
Tietz, B., 169
Ting-Toomey, S., 105
Tinsley, Catherine H., 507, 508, 509, 517, 521
Tiong, Tan Chin, 294
Tixier, Maud, 416, 465
Tjernlund, Anders, 419, 420
Toffoli, Roy, 418
Toften, Kjell, 202
Tomiuk, Marc-Alexandre, 235
Tongberg, R. C., 306
Touchstone, Ellen, 378
Traoré Sérié, Régina, 519
Treece, James B., 474
Triandis, Harry C., 22, 31, 51, 54, 68, 91, 130, 500
Trompenaars, Fons, 22, 64, 71, 260, 516
Tsalikis, John, 463
Tse, David K, 250, 424, 504
Tsurumi, Hiroki, 331
Tsurumi, Yoshi, 331
Tull, Donald S., 183, 204, 209–14
Tuncalp, Secil, 193, 194, 248, 426
Tung, Rosalie L., 172–3, 464, 509, 512, 519, 535, 537
Turcq, Dominique, 342, 351
Turpstra, Vern, 294
Tylor, Edward, 6

Ueda, Keiko, 377
Ulijn, Jan M., 516
UNAIDS, 451
Unger, Fritz, 418
Unger, Lynette S., 418
Usdin, S., 454
Usher, Rod, 253
Usunier, Jean-Claude, 25, 27, 48, 71, 112–15, 139, 145–9, 150–4, 155, 169, 177–9, 179, 187, 188, 200, 226, 234, 235, 241–4, 272–7, 288, 291, 293, 294, 306, 342, 351, 365–70, 400–4, 443–7, 447, 451–6, 481, 506, 513

Vahlne, J. E., 224
Valentine, Gill, 118, 139
Valette-Florence, Pierre, 27

Valla, Jean-Paul, 306
Valley, Kathleen L., 494, 499, 506, 509, 516, 521, 523
Van Birgelen, Marcel, 257
Van de Vijver, F. J. R., 182, 183, 190
Van de Vliert, Evert, 14
Van der Zee, Karen I., 38, 227
Van Doorn, Jenny, 433
Van Herk, Hester, 183, 197
Van Maanen, John, 136
Van Mesdag, Martin, 252
Van Oudenhoven, Jan Pieter, 38, 227
Van Raaij, W. F., 95, 121, 139, 160, 166, 185, 433
Van Tubergen, G. Norman, 421
Van Wijk, Jeroen, 328
Van Zandt, H. R., 506
Vandenbergh, Bruce, 298
Vargo, Stephen L., 320
Varvoglis, Fanis, 290
Veblen, Thorstein, 88
Veeck, Ann, 322
Vega, Tomas, 290
Venkatraman, N., 183
Verbeke, Vim, 235
Verhage, B., 97, 232
Verhallen, Theo M., 183, 197, 232
Verlegh, Peeter W. J., 288, 289, 293
Verna, Gérard, 334, 460, 481
Vernon, Raymond P., 224
Vertinsky, Ilan, 255, 424
Veryzer, Robert W., 189
Vetschera, Rudolf, 516
Viaene, Jacques, 235
Vignali, Claudio, 131
Vishny, Robert W., 522
Viswanathan, Madhubalan, 89, 192
Vitell, Scott J., 478
Vogl, Frank, 476
Von Glinow, M. A., 521
Von Stackelberg, H., 331
Vrontis, Demetris, 131, 248, 249
Vuursten, Karel, 204

Waarts, Eric, 165, 166
Wade-Benzoni, Kimberly A., 494, 498, 509, 514
Wafai, Mohamed, 421
Wagner, J., 135, 306
Walker, Bruce J., 305
Wall, Marjorie, 95
Walle, A. H., 424
Wallendorf, Mélanie, 102
Waller, David S., 412
Walls, Jan, 300, 504
Walsh, Len, 37

Walsh, Michael J., 328
Walter, Ingo, 475
Walters, Peter G. P., 185, 186, 190, 193
Waltner, Charles, 356
Walton, Richard E., 505
Wang, Chih-Kang, 289, 305, 306
Ward, James W., 415
Warnaby, Gary, 118
Warrington, M. B., 499
Watkins, Harry S., 105
Watson, John., 64
Watt, James, 425
Wattenberg, Ben, 275
Wattenberg, Daniel, 275
Watts, Alistair, 300
Wax, Emily, 267
Waxman, Sharon, 272
Weber, Elke U., 185, 504
Weber, Max, 323, 324
Webster, Cynthia, 196
Wedel, Michel, 93, 232, 233
Wee, Chow Hou, 387, 420
Weeks, William H., 19–20, 80
Weigand, Robert E., 326, 329, 344
Weinberger, Marc G., 415, 418
Weiser, Carl, 445
Weiss, Brad, 203
Weiss, Stephen E., 513, 517, 538, 540
Weitz, B., 38, 227, 507
Wells, Robert A., 445
Wentz, Laurel, 359
Werner, Cynthia, 475, 476, 479
Werner, O., 186, 188
Wesley, John, 323
West, Douglas C., 414, 419
Wetzels, Martin, 257
Wheatley, Malcolm, 150
White, 101
White, Carolyn T., 235
White, D. Steven, 106, 255
White, Gregory P., 305, 306
White, Phillip D., 306
Whitelock, Jeryl M., 229, 425
Whitlow, S. Scott, 421
Whorf, Benjamin Lee, 6–7, 383, 392, 396, 397
Wierenga, Berend, 165, 166
Wildt, A. R., 305
Wiles, Charles R., 419, 420
Wiles, Judith A., 419, 420
Wilk, Richard, 91
Wilke, Margaritha, 300
Wilkinson, Ian F., 225
Willenborg, Bartjan, 425

Williams, Katherine Y., 516, 517
Williams, Patti, 91, 413
Williams, Stephen C., 262
Wills, James R., 251, 411
Wilsher, Peter, 295
Wimalasiri, Jayantha, 89, 192
Wind, Yoram, 203, 222, 227
Winski, J. M., 433
Witkowski, Terrence H., 257, 292
Wolf, Martin, 164
Wolfe, William G., 204
Wolfinbarger, Mary F., 257
Wong, C., 38, 227
Wong, John K., 357, 359, 360
Wong, Nancy, 51, 53, 87, 91, 106, 128, 197
Wood, Van R., 201
Woods, Walter A., 123
Woodward, Nancy Hatch, 377, 378
World Trade Organization, 162, 226, 255
Woronoff, Jon, 342, 345, 348
Worthley, Reginald, 265
Wright, Len Tiu, 229

Xardel, Dominique, 354, 389
Xiaohua, Lin, 24
Xie, Jinhong, 459
Xu, Dean, 227

Ya-Fei, 201
Yamada, Y., 322
Yamaguchi, Yuzo, 474
Yamin, Mo, 95
Yan, Chen, 35
Yan, Leung Kwok, 419
Yang, Chung-Fang, 89, 90, 95, 105
Yang, M. C., 90
Yankelovitch, 101
Yaprak, Attila, 132, 189, 289
Yau, Oliver H. M., 95, 105
Yavas, Ugur, 232, 305, 422
Yeung, Kevin, 419
Yip, L. S. C., 189
Yong, Mahealani, 45–6, 82

Yoon, Gee Hong, 106, 113
Yoon, Eunsang, 322
Yoshida, Susumu, 390
Yoshimori, Masaru, 296, 301, 304
Yoshino, Michael Y., 346
Youssef, Fahti, 381
Yu, C. J., 38, 227
Yu, Julie H., 134
Yucelt, Ugar, 322
Yuen, Mary, 294
Yunker, John, 392

Zafiropoulos, Costas, 302
Zaharna, R. S., 391
Zaichkowsky, Judith L., 123, 502, 509, 510, 515, 517, 536
Zaidi, S. M., 186
Zaltman, Gerald, 190, 458
Zandpour, Fred, 414, 416, 424
Zartman, William, 494
Zawada, Craig, 330
Zax, M., 197
Zayed, Dahlia, 266
Zeithaml, Carl P., 458
Zeithaml, Valarie A., 312, 319, 322, 458
Zeldin, Theodore, 392, 514
Zeller, Eric, 345
Zhang, Shi, 299, 300
Zhang, Weijiong, 424
Zhang, Yong, 172, 423
Zhao, Xiaoyan, 232
Zhou, Dongsheng, 255, 424
Zhou, Kevin Zheng, 95
Zhou, Nan, 2, 424
Zia, Amir, 267
Ziamou, Paschalina, 302
Zietlow, D. S., 38, 227
Zinkhan, George M., 355, 423
Zotos, Yorgos, 302
Zou, Shaoming, 228
Zubaida, Sami, 268
Zugelder, Michael T., 356
Zurawicki, Leon, 480

Subject index

Act of God, 392
Acculturation, 101–2
Adaptation to climate, 252–3
Advertiser-agency relationships, 432, 483–6
Advertising, 409–435
  agencies, 431–2
  attitudes, 411–13
  execution, 417–25
  expenses per capita, 425–6
  global, 431–5
  legislation, 96, 411–12, 422–4
  strategy, 413–16
  standardization, 386–7, 423–4, 432–3
Affective cultures, 65, 71–2
Africa,
  advertising, 420
  consumer behaviour, 27
  culture, 4, 10, 32, 61, 129
  negotiation style, 520, 534, 539–40
Amae, 345
American way of life, 126
Anglo-Saxon, 73, 76, 165, 357, 382, 495
Anti-trust legislation, 473
Arabs, 27, 36, 61, 137, 248, 382, 410, 420, 507, 508
Arbitrage, 327, 518
Argentina, 61, 287
Armenians, 39, 536
ASEAN, 163
Asia, 27, 54, 55, 76, 89, 90, 93, 165, 171–3, 299, 382
Attitude towards action, 22, 64–9
Australia,
  advertising, 420
  brands, 128, 221, 251
  culture, 11, 24, 31, 52, 61, 93, 232, 376, 389–90, 393
  consumer behaviour, 36, 91
  made in, 135
  negotiation style, 464
Austria, 61, 122, 163, 376
Azerbaijan, 39

Back-translation, 186–7, 188
Baksheesh, 474
Bali, 11

Bantu (People), 27, 28, 191, 421
Bargaining, 317–19
Belgium, 39, 61, 77, 122, 163, 327, 412
Body gestures, 381–3
Bolivia, 193
Brand image, 286–8, 304
Brand loyalty, 93–5
Brand names, 286–8, 294–9
Brand, 286–304
  see also trademark
  linguistic connotations, 295–300
  functions, 301–2
  global, 294–8, 302–4
  international, 56, 294–8, 302–4
Brazil,
  advertising, 423, 427
  culture, 61
  consumer behaviour, 74, 157, 235
  made in, 287
Bribery, 474–82
Bulgaria, 157, 169, 381, 478
Buy National campaigns, 135
Buyer-seller relationships, 320, 465–7

Cameroon, 253
Canada,
  advertising, 414, 415, 418, 426, 427
  consumer behaviour, 125, 135, 418, 426, 427
  culture, 12, 61, 376
  made in, 289
  negotiation style, 506, 519
Cartesian logic, 161, 514
Cassis de Dijon ruling, 165, 255
Castes, 53–4
Catalogue sales, 91, 158
Catholic, 323–4
Chile, 61, 63
China,
  consumer behaviour, 35, 89, 90, 93, 95, 123, 126, 127, 135, 172, 173, 321
  culture, 8, 53, 90, 233, 235
  made in, 300
  management style, 77

China (*continued*)
  negotiation style, 464, 465, 509, 514, 516, 519, 534–5
  value survey, 27
Clan,
  see Group membership
Code law, 68, 163
Cognitive styles, 76, 87, 95
Collectivism, 51, 56–7, 58, 60–64, 87, 88, 89, 93, 94, 171, 172, 257, 352, 353, 469
Colloquial speech, 190, 416
Colombia, 61
Colonization, 35
Colours (cultural meaning of), 189, 423
Commerce, 457–60
Common Law, 68
Common sense, 69
Communication, and context, 375–80
  high context, 375, 377–8
  low context, 375, 376–7
Comparative advantage (law of), 119–20, 549
Comparative advertising, 412–13
Competencies (cultural relativity of), 13–14
Competition, 330, 349
  avoidance, 330–2
  globalization of, 225–7
Competitions (sales promotion), 358
Conceptual equivalence, 183–5
Confucian values, 8, 27, 56, 171, 502
Constructs, 97
Consumer behaviour, 84, 86–109, 121–38
  dissatisfaction, 97–8
  ethnocentrism, 87, 133
  involvement, 95
  loyalty, 93–5
  perceived risk, 95
Consumerism, 87, 96, 112, 156, 321–2, 411
Consumption, 120–30, 137–8
Contextual equivalence, 183, 195
Copts, 536
Copy strategy, 410, 413–24
Corn Laws, 120
Corporate culture, 75–6, 473–4
Corporate image, 432
Costa Rica, 61
Costs, 218–20, 250–1, 325–6, 349, 353
Cost-volume relationships, 219
Country of origin images, 221, 285, 286–94, 305, 306
Courtesy bias, 228
Credibility, of brands,
  collective, 501–2
  personal, 375, 460–3, 500–1
Creolization, 136
Cross-border cultures, 10–2
Cross-cultural equivalence, 23, 182–3

Cuba, 102, 500
Cultural affinity classes and zones, 232–235
Cultural assumptions, 21–9, 34, 50, 67, 72, 75–7, 258
Cultural borrowing, 35, 36, 159–62
Cultural codes and rituals, 72
Cultural competence, 13–14, 15
Cultural convergence, 87, 166–8, 173–4
Cultural hostility, 38–40
Cultural identification, 101, 231–2
Cultural identity, 4–16, 232
Cultural orientations, 51, 57, 65
Cultural resistance, 131–4
Cultural similarity, 38–9
Cultural sources, 10–11
Culture bound, 165–6
Culture and consumer behaviour, 86–105
  and nationality, 6, 9, 10
  and perceptions, 15, 28
  definitions of, 4–6, 21
  elements of, 6–9
Culture-free, 126–9
Culture shock, 391
Custom duties, 162
Cyprus, 163
Czech Republic, 134, 163, 169, 425

Data collection, 194
Decentring, 188
Decision-making process, 89, 94
Delivery dates, 223
Denmark, 61, 77, 78, 103, 105, 122, 185, 131, 136, 137, 163, 164, 185, 230, 412, 420
Direct marketing, 353–6
Distribution, channels, 158, 341–60
  choice of foreign distribution channels, 348–50
  exclusive distribution agreements, 320
  Internet, 355–6
  Japanese, 341–8
  role of, 350–3
Distributive orientation, 504–5, 553
DPPO (*Direction participative par objectifs*), 62
Dual concern model, 505
Dumping, 325

Eastern Europe, 168–70
Eating habits, 6, 91–3, 124, 126
Economicity of time, 25, 28
Economies of scale, 220
Economies of scope, 220
Ecuador, 61, 415
Educational practices, 14–15, 50, 100
Egypt, 62, 157, 519
El Salvador, 61
Emic, 87, 182

Emotion, 103–4
Empathy (international), 391–2
Equivalence,
    conceptual, 183–5
    data collection, 194–8
    functional, 185
    measure, 189–91
    sample, 192–4
    translation, 185–8
Eskimos, 387
Estonia, 163
Ethiopia, 62
Ethnic consumption, 86–8, 99, 100–1
Ethnocentrism, 135, 222, 263, 292, 324, 388–9, 392
Etic, 87, 182
Euro-brands, 56, 229
Europe,
    consumer, 165–6
    culture, 53, 61, 68, 98
    internal market, 163–8
    language, 166–8
    legal, 164–5
European consumer, 52, 97, 129, 165
European Union, 12, 118, 121, 162, 163–5, 168, 219, 226, 328, 412
Expatriates, 127–8, 252
Experience effects, 219–20, 224
Experiential equivalence, 183, 186
Extended family, 94, 183
Extrinsic rewards, 62, 471–2

Familism, 90
Fatalism, 66–7
FCPA (Foreign Corrupt Practices Act), 74, 475, 477, 479
Femininity, 57, 58–63, 103, 118, 352, 470–1
Fiji, 89, 192
Finland, 11, 61, 131, 163, 377, 418
Food and Drug Administration (FDA), 138, 251
Force majeure, 392, 397
France,
    advertising, 412, 415, 416, 417, 423, 424, 430
    business ethics, 484, 491–2
    consumer behaviour, 91, 92, 118, 122, 125, 126, 129, 131, 260, 351
    culture, 4, 9, 10, 11, 26, 31, 36, 42, 55, 59, 61, 68, 71, 73, 78, 165, 381, 390, 411
    management style, 62, 63, 77
    made in, 287, 291
    marketing management, 163, 169
    negotiation style, 506, 507, 511, 537, 538–9
    sales promotion, 358
Franchise, 364–5
Free-trade, 199–21, 163
Friendship, 52, 318, 380, 517, 534–6, 539

Functional equivalence, 185
Future orientation, 27, 28, 125

Gai-jin, 30, 344
GATT (General Agreement on Tariffs and Trade), 118, 155, 162, 291, 326, 341
Geocentrism, 222, 325
Germany, 377
    advertising, 412, 414, 415, 417, 418, 424, 426, 427, 430
    business ethics, 474–5, 481
    competition, 331
    consumer behaviour, 118, 122, 129, 130, 131, 166, 257
    culture, 4, 8, 10, 12, 36, 53, 62, 68, 69, 71, 73, 75, 78, 125, 165, 376, 383, 393
    made in, 289
    management style, 77
    marketing management, 62, 63, 163, 169
    negotiation style, 506, 521, 534, 539
    selling style, 466
Ghana, 62, 457
Gifts (promotional), 356–60
Global advertising campaigns, 433
Global consumer culture, 84–5, 86–8, 123–6
Global convergence, 121–3
Global marketing, 9, 120, 122, 218, 224, 227–31, 387, 431
Global markets, 120–1
Global media, 427–35
Global strategy, 123, 218–25, 227–31
Globalization of demand, 118
Greece, 61, 67, 118, 163, 165, 381, 412, 430, 520
Grey markets, 327–8
Group membership, 31–5, 51, 54–6, 57, 63–4
Guatemala, 61

Habits, 130–1
Hard sell approach, 465–7
Hierarchy, 58, 64, 386
Hierarchy of needs, 88–9
Hinduism, 54, 70, 88
Hiragana, 37–8, 103, 393
Hispanics, 101
Holland, 71, 97
Home country rule, 165
Hong Kong, 27, 61, 89, 99, 135, 233, 359
Hopi Indians, 385
Human nature, 52, 73
Hungary, 39, 134, 163, 169
Hypermarkets, 302

Icon, 261, 292
Ideologism, 65, 68, 69, 513
Idiomatic equivalence, 186
Implicit messages, 377–8, 525

Implicit salary, 475
Incentives, 468, 471
India, 416, 423, 425
  consumer behaviour, 35, 123, 412
  culture, 4, 8, 10, 61, 66, 235
  made in, 290
Indians (American), 9, 28, 88, 103
Individualism, 51, 56–7, 58, 60–4, 87, 88, 89, 94, 106, 125,
    171, 172, 257, 353, 469, 537
Individuals (acculturation of), 5
Indonesia, 11, 61, 157
Inflation, 332–3
Ingroup orientation
    See Group membership
Informative advertising, 413–16, 425–6
Insh'Allah, 45, 81
Institutions, 91, 158–9
Integrative orientation, 499, 504–5
Intercultural communication, 392–5
Intercultural marketing, 218–36
Intellectual styles, 65
International diffusion of innovations, 254
International trade, 394–5
Internet marketing, 173, 202, 221, 233, 329, 355–6, 378,
    392, 458, 465
Interpreters, 394–5
Interviews, 184, 195–6, 203
Intracultural setting, 498–9
Intrinsic rewards, 62
Involvement (consumer), 95
IQ tests, 15, 39
Iran, 61, 134, 139, 332
Iraq, 62, 10, 174
Ireland, 61, 163, 415
Islam, 36, 67, 172, 184, 536
Islamic law, 536–7
Israel, 61, 78, 134
Italy,
  advertising, 412
  consumer behaviour, 86, 122, 132, 135, 185, 263
  culture, 9, 10, 31, 36, 73
  made in, 189, 287
  management style, 77
  selling style, 466, 545–7
Ivory Coast, 32

Jamaica, 61
Japan bashing, 39
Japan,
  advertising, 414, 416, 417, 418, 419, 426
  competition, 224–5
  consumer behaviour, 26, 27, 34, 89, 95, 99, 104, 122,
    126, 127, 132, 135, 257, 263

culture, 11, 24, 28, 35, 36, 37, 39, 42, 56, 61, 69, 70, 71,
    75, 259, 381, 382, 393, 461–2
  distribution, 342–8
  language and communication, 37, 67, 376
  made in, 290, 291, 305
  management style, 77
  market research, 192, 198–9, 204
  marketing management, 76, 103, 160
  negotiation style, 461–3, 464, 467, 494, 501, 511, 518,
    519, 520, 521, 535–6
  sales promotion, 470
John Wayne Style, 508, 537
Joint ventures, 169

Kamei, 301
Kanban, 343
Kanji, 37, 376
Katakana, 37–8, 393
Kazakhstan, 475
Keiretsu, 104, 217, 224, 301, 341–8, 459
Kenya, 62, 382
Kikuyus, 382, 385
Korea, 76, 89, 99, 133, 172–3, 187, 225, 416, 425
Koran, 184
Kultur, 4
Kuwait, 81, 411

Language, 6, 11, 12, 37, 67, 128, 156, 166–8, 185–7, 296,
    374–88, 416–18
Latin America, 28, 63, 185, 191, 195, 290, 333, 374, 380,
    421, 463
Latin Europe, 163, 234, 359
Latins, 63, 76, 78, 118, 379, 540
Latvia, 163
Law of one price, 316
Learning, 220, 224, 542
Lebanon, 32, 62
Legal environment, 157–8
Legal systems, 68, 96, 164, 499, 527
Lexical equivalence, 186, 303
Libya, 62
Life insurance, 184
Lifestyles, 123, 232–3
Lithuania, 163
Litigation, 520
Logo, 296
Long-term orientation, 28, 60–3, 128, 467, 471, 496, 535,
    537, 541
Lotharingian Europe, 234
Lotteries, 96, 356
Loyalty, 31, 93–5
Luxembourg, 122, 163

MBO (management by objectives), 62
Made in label, 126, 286–8
Makimono time, 24, 27, 28–9, 346
Malaysia, 61, 91, 157, 233, 420
Malta, 163
Management of marketing communications, 58
Management theories, 60
Market research, 182–203
  cross-cultural, 198–203
Maronites, 536
Masculinity, 57, 58–9, 60–3, 64, 103, 470–1
Mastery over nature, 22, 65, 111, 468
Material productions, 6, 8–9
Mauritania, 195
Media availability, 425–31
Media planning, 410
Meiji era, 35, 56
Mercatique, 160
Metalanguage, 103
Metempsychosis, 66
Methodism, 323
Mexico, 9, 17, 61, 102, 416, 420, 466, 540–1
Middle East, 380, 518, 519, 536–7

Misunderstandings (cultural), 387–8, 495, 498, 513–17
MNCs (multinational companies), 76, 126
Modal personality, 13
Monochronism, 24–8, 513
Monopoly, 331–2
Monopsony, 332
Morocco, 193
Motivation, 58, 94, 99
Multidomestic, 218, 226
Muslims, 27, 36, 410, 420

NAFTA (North American Free Trade Agreement), 118, 162, 163
National character, 12, 13, 14, 58, 134
Nationality (and culture), 9–10, 11, 12, 13
Nation-state, 12
Navajo Indians, 129
Negotiation, 460, 494–522, 534–42
  agreements, 517–21
  styles, 504–22, 534–42
  rules, 544
Nepal, 35, 513
Nestorians, 536
Netherlands, 357, 420
  consumer behaviour, 97, 166, 234, 257
  culture, 42, 61
  management style, 77
Neutral cultures, 71–2
New Zealand, 61, 376, 412

Nigeria, 40, 62, 183, 540
Ningensei, 502, 506, 534
Non-tariff barriers, 162, 226
Non-verbal communication, 380–3, 395
Northern Europe, 133, 163, 323, 351, 359, 394
Norway, 59, 61, 78

Objectives of communication, 410
Oligopoly, 332, 496
Oneiric style of advertising, 413–14
Oral agreement, 517–18
Organization of international advertising, 433
Outgroup, 31–4, 388–9, 468, 535
  see Group membership
Over- and under-invoicing, 333–4
Overlapping of media, 430

Packaging, 263–4
Pakistan, 61
Palanca, 540
Panama, 61
Pan-European market segments, 232–3, 430
Paraguay, 475
Parallel imports, 327–9
Past orientation, 22–8, 163, 499
Perceived risk, 95, 185, 293
Perception, 15, 183, 189–90, 261
Personalization, 29
PERT (programme evaluation and review techniques) 25, 513
Peru, 61
Philippines, 61, 416, 425
Poetry, 67
Poland, 134, 163, 166, 169, 353, 360
Political environment, 157
Polycentrism, 222, 392
Polychronism, 24–7, 513
Portugal, 61, 119, 122, 135, 163, 166, 187
Potential reality, 69–70
Power distance, 57, 58–9, 60–3, 64, 72–3, 353, 503
Pragmatism, 65, 68, 69, 161
Present orientation, 22–8, 163
Price, 316–34
  declaring prices, 319
  evaluation, 319–24
  manipulating prices, 324–30
  signal, 316–17
Problem solving, 499, 505–9
Procedural traditional time, 28
Product adaptation, 165, 248–55
Product attributes, 250–5
Product liability, 253, 474
Product life cycle (international), 224

Product standardization policy, 249–50
Production flexibility, 227–9
Protestants, 323–4
Proxemics, 34, 382
Public relations, 472–4
Publiphobia, 411

Quality, 319–24
Québecois, 498–9, 506
Questionnaire, 188, 190

Racism, 38
Rationality, 499, 513–14
Record industry, 234, 327
Regiocentrism, 222
Regional convergence, 85, 162–8
Regional differences, 235–6
Relational exchange, 497
Relational marketing, 496–7
Reliability (of a research instrument), 185, 189, 202, 204
Religion, 11, 12, 26, 27, 36, 39, 66–7, 70, 323–4, 385, 421–3, 540
Representative communication, 506
Resale Price Maintenance, 328
Respondents, 192–8
Response style, 196–7
Riba, 536
Ringi, 463, 501
Rituals, 72–75
Romania, 169
Rules, 72–5
Russia, 17, 170, 291, 351, 389, 541–2

Saint-Simonism, 411
Sales force compensation systems, 468–72
Sales force management, 467–72
Sales objectives, 469
Sales promotion, 356–60, 467–8
Salespeople, 465–72
Salvador, 61
Sample, representativeness of, 193–4
Sampling equivalence, 182
Sampling unit, 183
Satellite television, 428–30
Saudi Arabia,
    advertising, 421, 422, 423, 426, 427
    business ethics, 475–6
    consumer behaviour, 290
    culture, 62, 78
    consumer behaviour, 290
    marketing management, 137, 536–7
Scale (psychometry), 190
Scale effects, 219
Scandinavia, 11, 127, 233

Schwartz values, 64
Secrecy bias, 194
Segmentation of markets, 12, 231–6, 430
Self-concept, 50–7, 89–91, 94, 391
Seller's status, 465
Selling styles, 465–7
Semantic differential, 190
Senegal, 479
Service attributes, 249, 255–61
    adaptation, 256–8
    standardization, 260–1
Sex cultures, 11, 53
Sex roles, 53, 94, 420
Sexual bias, 195
Sharia, 442
Shipping charges, 220–1
Sierra Leone, 62
Similarity hypothesis, 499
Singapore, 61, 89, 91, 233, 419, 420
Ski resorts, 221
Slogans, 416–17
Slovakia, 163, 166, 169
Slovenia, 163
Social representations, 15–16, 321, 411
Sociodemographic variables, 232–3
Soft sell approach, 466–7, 538
Sogo-shosha (general trading company), 461
South Africa, 39, 61
South America, 55
South Korea, 171
    consumer behaviour, 93, 97, 135, 351
    culture, 61, 171, 172, 197, 265, 522
    made in, 290, 291, 293
    marketing management, 312–13, 352, 464, 472, 506, 508
Soviet Union, 13, 504
Space (cultural language of), 22, 29–35, 397
Spain, 9, 10, 14, 61, 122, 132, 163, 165, 235, 516
SRC (Self Reference Criterion), 388–9
Sri Lanka, 10, 157
Standardized advertising, 124, 167
Standards, international, 255–6
    technical, 251–4, 255
Stereotypes, 289, 388, 389–90, 420
Sweden,
    advertising, 415, 419, 420, 424, 427
    culture, 11, 12, 59, 61, 76, 235, 257
    made in, 286
    management style, 77
    marketing management, 163, 181, 257, 322, 406–8, 470
Switzerland, 10, 179, 235, 472, 474, 476
    advertising, 409, 420, 430
    culture, 9, 10, 53, 61, 73, 376

Switzerland (*continued*)
  made in, 135
  management style, 77
  sales promotion, 358
  selling style, 466
Symbolic aspects of
  colours, 261–5
  money, 540
Symbolic attributes, 261–5
Symbolic meaning, 102–3, 104–5
Symbols, 6–9, 261–5, 424
  definition of, 261

Taiwan, 61, 91, 233, 290, 362, 423
Tamil, 10, 157
Tanzania, 62, 203
Temporal equivalence, 182, 191
Temporal orientations, 25, 27
Tender, 508
Territoriality, 7, 21, 32
Thailand, 61, 66, 78, 89, 291, 359, 470
Theory of climates, 12, 14
Third World consumer, 73, 134
Time (cultural patterns of), 22, 23–9, 163, 310–3, 385
Tokugawa era, 39, 42
Trademark, 299, 304
Trading company,
  see sogo-shosha
Translation, 167, 183, 185–8, 204, 385, 387–8
Transliteration, 296, 463
Transportability, 220
Treaty of Rome, 163, 164, 328
Triad, 222
Tribe, 7, 540
  see Group membership
Trust, 495–6, 517, 536
Tunisia, 173, 410
Turkey,
  advertising, 233, 415, 422
  consumer behaviour, 105, 134, 351
  culture, 10, 61
  made in, 135
Turnkey operations, 460, 476, 528–32
TV programmes, 167, 427, 428–30

Uncertainty avoidance, 57, 58–9, 60–3, 64, 163, 352, 415, 468–9, 499, 504, 539
United Arab Emirates, 61
United Kingdom,
  advertising, 414, 415, 423, 430
  consumer behaviour, 98, 103, 122, 135, 137, 139, 185, 229, 233
  culture, 10, 34, 42, 61, 68, 69, 71, 235, 378, 381
  made in, 134–5, 139, 289

  management style, 77
  marketing management, 143, 248, 349, 354
  negotiation style, 506, 538
  sales promotion, 357, 359
  selling style, 466
United States,
  advertising, 412, 415, 418, 419, 420, 423, 425, 426, 427
  brands, 128
  business ethics, 389, 473, 478
  consumer behaviour, 24, 26, 28, 86, 91, 93, 95, 96, 104, 121, 123, 127, 128, 129, 167, 174, 257, 351
  culture, 10, 11, 12, 17, 23, 31, 34, 52, 59, 61, 68, 69, 71, 75, 89, 101, 132, 185, 235, 376
  made in, 126, 160, 286, 290, 305
  management style, 62, 77
  market research, 191, 198–202, 204
  marketing management, 122, 128, 159–60, 227–31, 253, 254, 321–2, 332, 347–8, 353–6, 467–8, 470–1, 472
  negotiation style, 352–3, 467, 506, 507, 512, 516, 518, 520, 521, 537–8
  sales promotion, 468, 470, 472
  technical standards, 252–3
Uruguay, 61

Validity, 185, 204, 294
Values, 5, 64, 389, 414, 424, 467
Veblen effect, 88
Venezuela, 62, 423, 466
Vietnam, 172, 520, 537
Visual illusions, 15

Waiting, 258–60, 385
Walloon, 39, 431
Weltanschäuung, 374, 383
Whorfian hypothesis, 6, 166, 383, 387–8, 392–3, 397
Wishful thinking, 65, 70, 71, 78, 499
Word-of-mouth communication, 95–6, 123
World Intellectual Property Organization (WIPO), 304
World market share, 223–5
World production (growth of), 225–6
World Trade Organization (WTO), see GATT, 118, 155, 162, 218, 226, 341
Written agreement, 517–18, 520

Yea-saying, 196–7
Yemen, 53
Yugoslavia, 39, 62

Zaibatsus, 331
Zaire, 32, 477
Zambia, 62
Zapping, 427
Zulu, 39